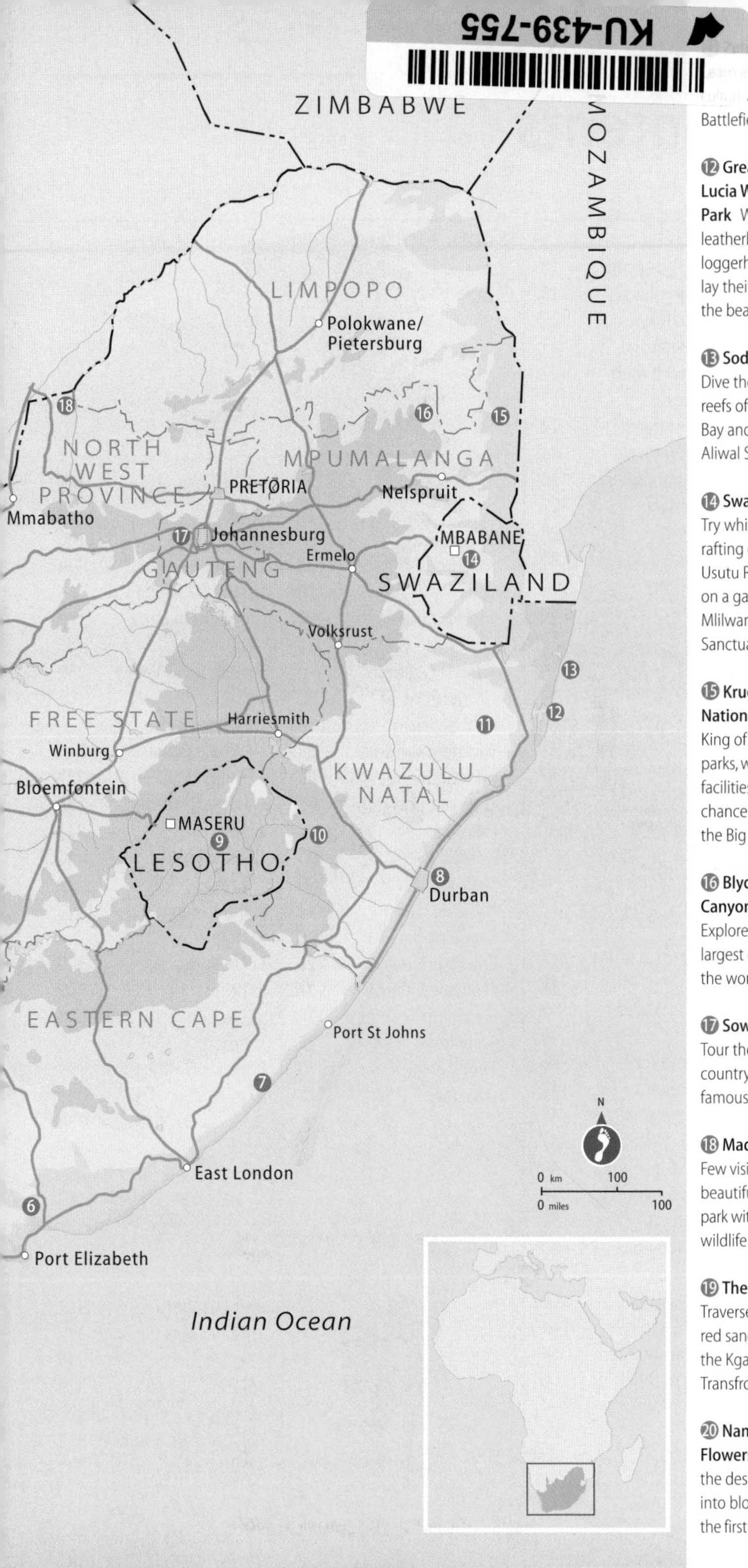

…land …bout Zulu … and tour the Battlefields Route

⑫ Greater St Lucia Wetland Park Watch leatherback and loggerhead turtles lay their eggs on the beach

⑬ Sodwana Bay Dive the tropical reefs off Sodwana Bay and Aliwal Shoal

⑭ Swaziland Try whitewater rafting on the Usutu River or go on a game walk in Mlilwane Wildlife Sanctuary

⑮ Kruger National Park King of the game parks, with top facilities and the chance of spotting the Big Five

⑯ Blyde River Canyon Explore the third largest canyon in the world

⑰ Soweto Tour the country's most famous township

⑱ Madikwe Few visitors see this beautiful game park with its superb wildlife

⑲ The Kalahari Traverse the rolling red sand dunes of the Kgalagadi Transfrontier Park

⑳ Namakwa Flowers Watch the desert explode into blossom after the first spring rains

Contents

KwaZulu Natal

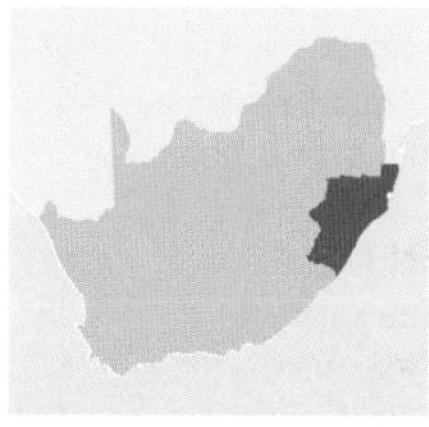

Gauteng

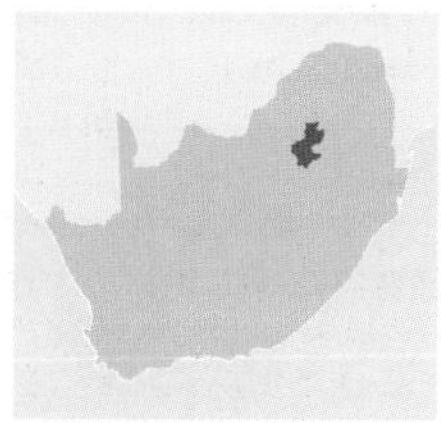

North West Province

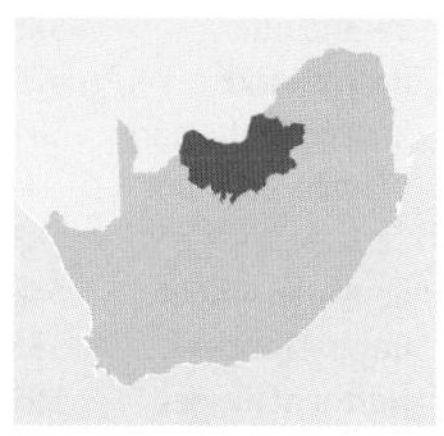

Mpumalanga

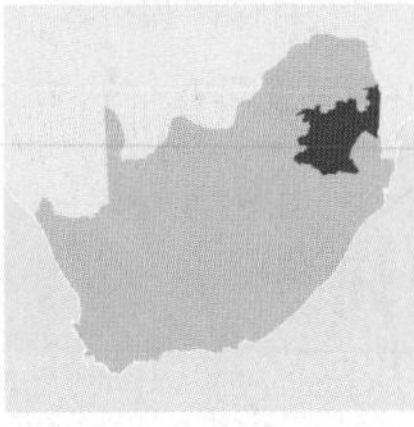

Limpopo

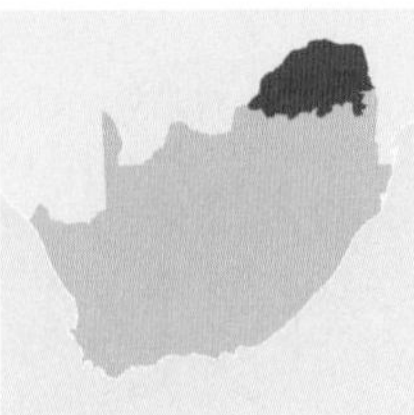

Free State

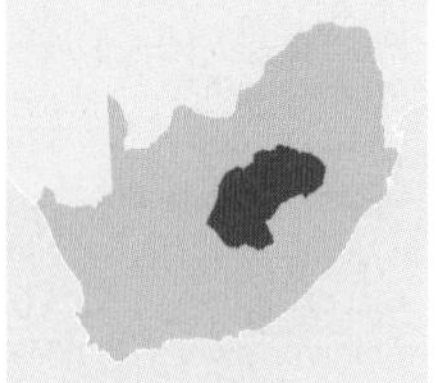

Northern Cape

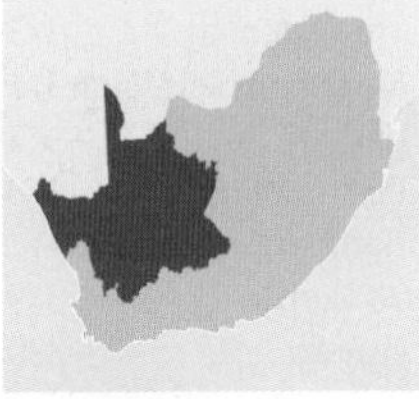

Background

Lesotho

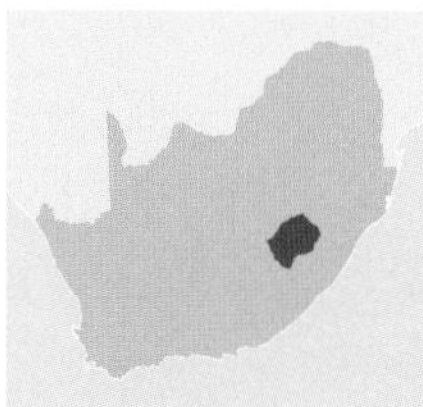

Swaziland

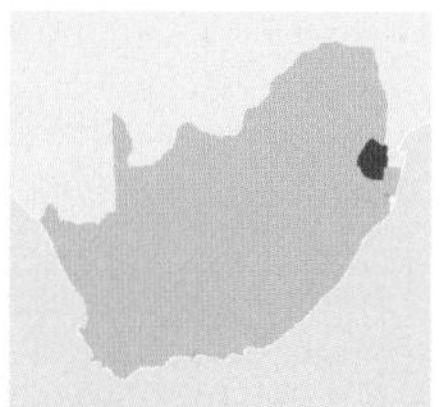

Footnotes

River deep, mountain high
The dramatic Blyde River cuts its way through the Drakensberg escarpment, forming the third largest canyon in the world.

A foot in the door

South Africa is celebrated, first and foremost, for its incredible natural beauty. It has some of the most varied and extreme environments in the world, from the tropical beaches of KwaZulu Natal to the sweeping emptiness of the Kalahari Desert. Yet it is the people, a fascinating mix of cultures, religions and ethnicities, who are the beating pulse of South Africa, and who give meaning to its nickname, 'Rainbow Nation'.

Many visitors come here to see the Big Five – the collective term for the big-bucks players of wildlife spotting: elephant, black rhino, buffalo, leopard and lion. While the choice of excellent game reserves virtually guarantees sightings, the country's vibrant cities are an equally compelling reason to visit. There's the fast-paced sophistication of Johannesburg and Pretoria, the steamy humidity and spicy Indian influence of Durban, or the spectacular setting and quirky beach-side hedonism of Cape Town.

One of the most appealing aspects of South Africa is its ongoing transformation. Although still struggling to recover from the hangover of Apartheid, the country has changed unimaginably in the last decade. That's not to say that racial boundaries have disappeared but, by straying just marginally from the tourist route, visitors can gain an insight into the country's myriad sides and a marvellous glimpse of how the Rainbow Nation got its name.

10 Contemporary South Africa

Since the grandfather of the nation, Nelson Mandela or Madiba as he is affectionately called, made his famous inauguration speech during South Africa's first democratic elections in 1994, the country has witnessed unprecedented positive change. Basic services like housing, education and access to electricity, previously denied to most black people during Apartheid, have considerably improved. Racial barriers have been demolished and the country now has a substantial black middle class. Today's blend of cultures – manifested by 11 official languages, numerous religions and countless ethnic groups – live in Africa's fastest-growing economy, founded on one of the world's most progressive, liberal constitutions.

Township fare

A street vendor prepares mealies the traditional way at the baragwanath taxi rank in Soweto.

The aftermath of Apartheid, however, is yet to dissipate completely. Problems such as unemployment and crime remain, and there are more people living with HIV/AIDS here than in any other nation. But progress is being made, and the country has a palpable sense of optimism – no more so than in those areas once marginalized by the government. Soweto, for example, was once an infamous township but today has developed into a city in its own right, and is currently planning one of the country's largest shopping malls, worth R1 billion – unthinkable a decade ago. And the fact that a number of Apartheid museums now document the country's turbulent history reflects that it is just that – history. Confidence is high and, as the country gears up to host the football World Cup in 2010, the future is looking very bright.

Rural homes
Traditional Xhosa villages can still be seen in the former Transkei region near Matatiele.

1
2
4
5
7
8
10
11

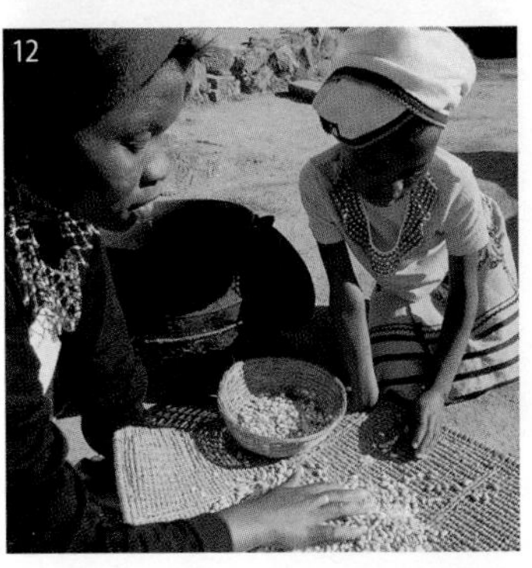

1 *Flowering aloes in the fertile valleys and peaceful countryside of the Little Karoo.* *▸▸ See page 300.*

2 *Local herbs add to the distinctive flavour of traditional Cape Malay cooking: sweet and spicy curries, and meat dishes cooked with dried fruit.* *▸▸ See page 45.*

3 *Bo-Kaap is one of Cape Town's most colourful areas with brightly painted buildings and cobbled streets.* *▸▸ See page 81.*

4 *Hermanus, on the Whale Coast, is famous for its land-based whale watching. The best time to see them is from July to November.* *▸▸ See page 217.*

5 *Beautiful Camps Bay is one of South Africa's most popular and most photographed beaches.* *▸▸ See page 90.*

6 *Hiring a canoe is a good way of exploring the remote Eastern Cape.* *▸▸ See page 371.*

7 *Adrenaline junkies can get their fix at Gourits River bridge in the Western Cape.* *▸▸ See page 243.*

8 *The Outdshoorn area has 97% of the world's ostriches and is a good place to visit one of the many farms.* *▸▸ See page 303.*

9 *Seafood is as fresh as it comes in the West Coast fishing villages.* *▸▸ See page 170.*

10 *Kamberg Nature Reserve, in the Drakensberg, has some fascinating San rock art, as well as fossilized dinosaur prints.* *▸▸ See page 455.*

11 *The flat top of Table Mountain is one of the world's best-known city backdrops and dominates the city skyline from all around.* *▸▸ See page 70.*

12 *The Xhosa are one of the largest tribal groups to be found in South Africa and maintain a traditional way of life.* *▸▸ See pages 374 and 740.*

The famous five

South Africa is an excellent place for first-time safaris, with a number of good-value game reserves that give visitors an excellent chance of spotting the Big Five. In addition to the king of game reserves, Kruger Park, South Africa also offers the most varied landscapes in Africa for wildlife viewing. In the Northern Cape is the spectacular Kgalagadi Transfrontier Park, defined by the rolling red sand dunes of the Kalahari; KwaZulu Natal has contrasting tropical swamps and forests, while Addo Elephant Park stretches through the rolling hills of the Eastern Cape.

City life

Cape Town, known as the 'Mother City', is South Africa's most attractive urban centre and one of the most beautiful cities in the world. Its setting, dominated by the soaring presence of Table Mountain and surrounded by the wild Atlantic, is unrivalled. Johannesburg and Pretoria, despite their bad press, are exciting and intriguing cities, in which cutting-edge jazz and Kwaito clubs contribute to vibrant nightlife and music scenes.

Easy does it

Away from the frenetic pace of the cities, South Africa has an appealingly slow pace of life, so kick back and take a few days to relax. In the east lie the magnificent Drakensberg mountains, offering the best hiking in the country,

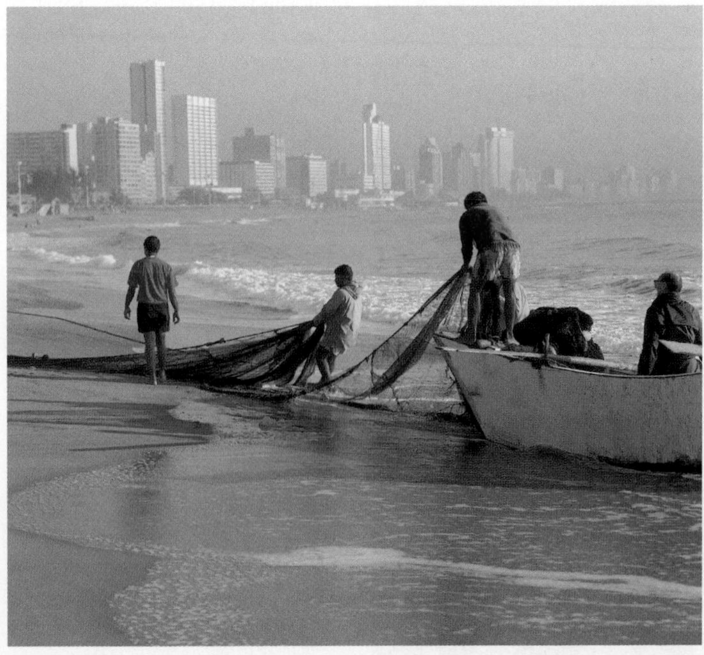

As the rest of Durban is just waking up, fishermen drag the early-morning catch up onto Addington Beach.

The Franschhoek Valley is one of the most pleasant wine regions in South Africa, surrounded by rolling vineyards and scattered with gourmet restaurants.

while the Tsitsikamma National Park is a lush forested area, fringed by the Indian Ocean. The Great Karoo, with its vast stretches of shimmering semi-desert, is perfect for experiencing the slow pace of small-town life, while the traditional Xhosa kraals of the Transkei offer a glimpse of rural Africa. Stunning beaches abound, from the wide, empty stretches of the Wild Coast to the popular seaside resorts of the Garden Route.

Having a vine time

South African wines are fast finding their feet in the international market, and the Western Cape winelands are a beautiful region in which to taste them. Within a few hours' drive of Cape Town are hundreds of estates that have opened up their cellars, providing tastings and meals in a classic Cape Dutch setting.

Highs and lows

South Africa has become a major playground for the fast and the furious, offering some of the wildest and best organized adrenaline sports in the world. It has varied environments to cater for a wide range of activities and the outdoor lifestyle of many South Africans has encouraged an ever-expanding market for sports fanatics. You can try just about anything here, from the world's highest bungee jump to cage-diving with great white sharks.

Out in bloom

Each spring, the barren, rocky countryside of Namakwa is transformed into a spectacular carpet of wild flowers.

Essentials

Footprint features

Planning your trip

South Africa has more to offer than you could ever see or do in one trip. The choice of worthwhile destinations within the country is expanding year by year and it's a very easy place to get around. South Africa's main attraction is its magnificent natural beauty, represented in a multitude of game reserves and national parks, which are home to a whole host of animals. Another major draw is its vibrant cities, characterized by the cosmopolitan populations you'd expect from the Rainbow Nation. Here there are numerous exciting urban attractions as well as the best eating and shopping opportunities on the African continent. South Africa's history, too, is compelling, from the Boer War to the more recent breakdown of Apartheid, reflected in its colonial architecture, lively townships, moving battlefields and contemporary museums. Being outdoors is also very much a way of life here and you can try hiking and surfing or one of the booming adrenaline sports such as bungee jumping or whitewater rafting. In short, the choice of destinations, activities and itineraries is virtually inexhaustible, so careful planning is needed to make best use of your time. Rather than cram in too much, try to arrange stops of two to four days in each location or region to fully appreciate what there is on offer; you can always return at some time in the future.

Where to go

South Africa's facilities, food and accommodation tend to be of a very high standard, and there's a wide range of travel options available. Independent travel is one of the most popular ways of seeing the country and South Africa's transport network is one of the best on the continent. Modern highways, a train network and comprehensive internal flights link the main urban centres, while buses connect the larger towns. The best way of getting around is to hire a car. This allows the freedom to explore more remote areas and also provides independent access to national parks. There are also ever- expanding choices of organized tours, taking in the national parks and historic sites, focusing on sports such as scuba diving, or tailored to specific interests such as history, or flora and fauna. None of the routes described below are a complete itinerary in itself, nor are they set in stone. Rather, they are regional suggestions for travellers wishing to explore a certain region, or for returning visitors to travel somewhere new. The absolute minimum time to spend in South Africa is two weeks. As arrival in the country will probably be either via Johannesburg or Cape Town, it's best to stick to the areas around these cities on a shorter holiday, and there are plenty of worthwhile attractions within striking distance of both Jozi and the Mother City as they are respectively affectionately known. If you have more time, venture further afield into the other provinces too. For information on activities and safaris, see pages 50 and 52.

Two weeks

From Cape Town A minimum of four or five days is needed in Cape Town to explore the sights and enjoy the fine shops and restaurants. The city is home to historic buildings, museums, beautiful beaches, the botanical gardens of Kirstenbosch, and the famous Constantia wine estates. Climbing to the top of Table Mountain, or riding in the cable car, is a Cape Town must-do; organized and thought-provoking tours to Robben Island and the townships on the Cape Flats offer a glimpse of South Africa's fragile past. Several day trips area available to the Cape of Good Hope and

Cape Point via the spectacular Cape Peninsula, or to the wine estates around Stellenbosch. From Cape Town you could explore the west coast for a few days via Langebaan and other typical west coast fishing communities. The West Coast National Park is an important bird sanctuary and a base from which to see wild flowers and look for whales along the coast. Another option from Cape Town is to follow the coast along the Garden Route, stopping off along the way at pretty towns such as Hermanus on the Whale Coast, Knysna or George, and the beautiful Tsitsikamma National Park. At the end of the Garden Route in the Eastern Cape Province is the quirky surfing town of Jeffrey's Bay, the excellent Greater Addo Elephant National Park, and Shamwari Game Reserve. This tour would take a minimum of six or seven days but you could cut this short by taking an internal flight from Port Elizabeth back to Cape Town or on to Johannesburg.

If you are flying through Johannesburg International Airport be sure to allow at least a couple of days to explore Johannesburg or Pretoria at the beginning or end of your trip.

From Johannesburg From both Johannesburg and Pretoria there are informative township and city tours and some interesting historic buildings and museums to visit, such as Pretoria's Voortrekker Monument or Johannesburg's excellent Apartheid Museum. Johannesburg in particular is also known for its chic shopping malls, trendy craft markets, varied restaurant districts and happening nightlife, and it regularly hosts some major sporting events. Sun City, the hedonistic casino and leisure resort next to the Pilanesberg National Park in the North West Province, can be visited on a very long day trip from Johannesburg or Pretoria, but to appreciate all there is on offer at least one overnight stay is recommended. From Gauteng one option is to head east into Mpumalanga to visit the Kruger National Park, South Africa's premier wildlife destination which warrants at least three or four days. The area around Kruger is commonly known as the Panorama Region because of its stunning mountain scenery. Game drives in the park can be combined with a visit to the Blyde River Canyon, one of the deepest canyons in the world, and an exploration of the pretty mountain towns such as Graskop and Sabie, surrounded by lush forests and rivers. Also in this region are the historic gold-mining towns of Pilgrim's Rest and Barberton. From here you could head south into Swaziland for a couple of days relaxation at the Mlilwane Wildlife Sanctuary or one of the lesser-known nature reserves and try some cycling, horse riding or hiking through the tranquil bush.

Four weeks or more

The south From Durban you could head north up the tropical coast road to the game reserves of Zululand and the lakes and beaches at St Lucia. Hluhluwe-Imfolozi National Park is home to one of the world's largest rhino populations and has been instrumental in saving this creature from extinction. Turning inland, go via the mountain reserve of Itala and on to Dundee, which is a suitable base for exploring the numerous battlefield sites relating to the Anglo-Boer and Anglo-Zulu wars. Head across the Natal Midlands towards the magnificent mountain chain which forms a natural border with Lesotho – the uKhahlamba-Drakensberg National Park. There are plenty of mountain resorts and country hotels to choose from and at least two or three days should be spent here to enjoy the wonderful scenery. Further south on the way back to Durban, spend at least a day in Pietermaritzburg, a British colonial town, or you can head back towards the coast via the small reserve at Oribi Gorge and explore the holiday towns along the coast south of Durban before reaching the Wild Coast in the Eastern Cape. There are a number of resorts on this dramatic coast which are ideal for family holidays, so at least a few days are needed to soak up the splendid scenery of this isolated area.

KwaZulu Natal has some principal nature reserves, historic sites and some of the best coastline in the country.

The north Starting in Johannesburg you could head due north into Limpopo Province and visit the Kruger National Park via the Phalaborwa Gate, which opens up possibilities of seeing less-frequently visited areas of the park. After Kruger head west and explore a bit of the Northwest: Sun City and the Magaliesberg Mountains, and then continue south towards the Eastern Highlands and the scenic Golden Gate National Park in Free State. From here you can cross the border into Lesotho and spend two or three days in a resort, hiking or pony trekking in the cool mountain kingdom. From Free State you can head further inland and visit the historic towns of Bloemfontein and Kimberley before crossing the northern desert region to Upington and Springbok in Northern Cape. The intrepid can venture further north and visit the Kgalagadi Transfrontier Park, a stunning Kalahari wilderness with a unique ecosystem, or the Ai-Ais Richtersveld Transfrontier Park where the Gariep (Orange) River winds its way towards the ocean between soaring granite cliffs. From the extreme north it's a day's drive south to Cape Town, though there are a number of distractions along the way such as the Namakwa flowers in season, the Cederberg Wilderness Area and the west coast.

The north is for travellers who want to see more unusual and isolated destinations, as well as the more popular tourist areas.

When to go

Generally the summers are hot and wet and winters are cool with clear sunny days. You will only come across truly tropical conditions in the northeast corner of KwaZulu Natal around Kosi Bay and the border with Mozambique. During summer it rarely gets hotter than 30°C, though Gauteng and KwaZulu Natal get very humid, and parts of the Northern Cape experience temperatures in the region of 45°C – too hot for most people. The coast around Cape Town and the Garden Route is at its best during the spring and summer months, though the best time for whale watching is in winter. During July and August, in the middle of winter, it can get cold at night in Cape Town and the interior mountains in the Drakensberg and Eastern Cape, with frosts and snowfalls. But winter is the best time to visit the northern desert areas around Upington and the Kalahari. Most of the rain falls in the summer months and, when it does rain, there are often very heavy storms. If driving in these conditions, slow down and pull over. Also be on the lookout for flash floods, especially if camping.

As a country in the southern hemisphere remember that mid-winter is June to July and mid-summer is December and January.

The best time of year for game viewing is during the winter months, when vegetation cover is at a minimum and a lack of water forces animals to congregate around rivers and waterholes. Winter is also the best time for hiking, avoiding the high temperatures and frequent thunderstorms of the summer months.

Despite being cooler, July and August are a popular time for visitors as they coincide with the European school holidays. December and January are by far the busiest months for South African tourism, as they coincide with the long summer holiday. Be sure to book your car hire and accommodation well in advance during these periods. One major disadvantage of visiting during the summer is that much of the accommodation is fully booked months in advance, and the coastal towns become horribly overcrowded.

There are a number of colourful festivals that are worth enjoying while you are in the country. While none are significant enough to base your entire trip around, should you be in the area at the time, they do provide an interesting insight into the ethnic heritage of this cosmopolitan country (see page 48). For further advice on when to go to South Africa, visit www.weathersa.co.za.

Tour operators

UK and Ireland

Abercrombie & Kent, T0845-0700611, www.abercrombiekent.co.uk.

Acacia Adventure Holidays, T020-7706 4700, www.acacia-africa.com.

African Odyssey, T01242-224482, www.africanodyssey.co.uk.

Africa Travel Centre, T0845-4501520, www.africatravel.co.uk.

Africa Travel Resource, T01306-880770, www.africatravelresource.com.

Cedarberg Travel, T020-8941 1717, www.cedarberg-travel.com.

Explore, T0870-3334002, www.explore.co.uk.

Global Village, T0870-999484, www.globalvillage-travel.com.

Rainbow Tours, T020-7226 1004, www.rainbowtours.co.uk.

Somak, T020-84233000, www.somak.co.uk

South African Affair, T020-7381 5222, www.southafricanaffair.com.

Steppes Africa, T01285-880980, www.steppesafrica.co.uk.

Sunvil Africa, T020-8232 9777, www.sunvil.co.uk/africa.

Tim Best Travel, T020-7591 0300, www.timbesttravel.com.

Wildlife Worldwide, T0845-1306982, www.wildlifeworldwide.com.

Rest of Europe

Iwanowski's Individuelles Reisen GmbH, T+49 (0)21-3326030, www.afrika.de.

Jambo Tours, T+49 (0)29-3579191, www.jambotours.de.

North America

Adventure Center, T1800-2288747, www.adventure-center.com.

Africa Adventure Company, T1800-8829453, T1954-4918877, www.africa-adventure.com.

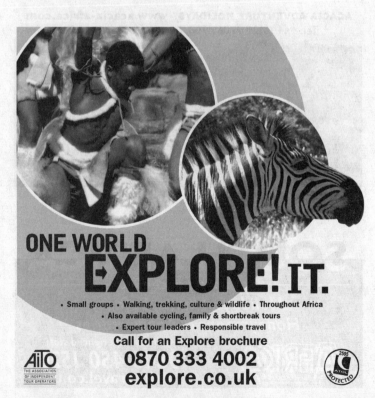

Backroads, T1800-4622848, www.backroads.com.
Big Five Tours and Expeditions, T1888-2443483, www.bigfive.com.
Bushtracks, T1800-9958689, www.bushtracks.com.
Cape Wineland Tours, T1610-3281531, www.capewinetours.com.
Maupintour, T1800-2554266, www.maupintour.com.

Australia and New Zealand
African Wildlife Safaris, T+61-(0)3-9696 2899, www.africanwildlifesafaris.com.au.
Africa Exclusive, T+61-(0)7-5474 8160, www.africaexclusive.com.
Classic Safari Company, T+61-(0)2-9327 0666, www.classicsafaricompany.com.au.
Peregrine Adventure, T+61-(0)3-8601 4444, www.peregrine.net.au.

Finding out more

The **South African Tourist Board** has a very useful website with information on special interest travel, maps, latest travel news, airlines, accommodation and national parks. The website is published in 13 languages and each version provides specific information for people coming from each individual country, T011-8953000, www.southafrica.net. The tourist board also has offices around the world (see below), which are useful for pre-travel information. Regional (see below) and local tourist boards are some of the best sources of information once in the country; even the smallest town will have a publicity bureau with details of local sights and accommodation. Local tourist offices are listed under individual towns.

Tourist offices overseas

Australia Level 1, 117 York St, Sydney, NSW 2000, T02-9261 5000, bangu@southafrica.net.
France 61 Rue La Boetie, 75008 Paris, T01-4561 0197, info.fr@southafrica.net.
Germany Friedensstr. 6-10, Frankfurt 60311, T069-9291250, info.de@southafrica.net.
India 44 Maker Chambers, Jamnalal Bajaj marg, Mumbai 400021, T022-2285 0409, india@southafrica.net.
Italy Via Mascheroni, 19 - 5th floor, 20145 Milano, T02-4391 1765, info.it@southafrica.net.
Japan Akasaka Lions Building, 1-1-2 Moto Akasaka, Minato-Ku, Tokyo 107-0051, T03-3478 7601, info@southafricantourism.or.jp.
Netherlands Jozef Isralskade 48 A, 1027 SB Amsterdam, T020-4713181, info.nl@southafrica.net.
UK 6 Alt Grove, London SW19 4DZ, T0870-1550044, info.uk@southafrica.net
USA 500 5th Av, 20th floor, Suite 2040, New York NY 10110, T1212-7302929, newyork@southafrica.net.

Regional tourist boards

Cape Town and Western Cape Tourism, www.tourismcapetown.co.za.
Eastern Cape Tourism, www.ectourism.co.za.
Gauteng Tourism Authority, www.gauteng.net.
Limpopo Province Tourism Board, www.limpopotourism.org.za.
Mpumalanga Tourism Authority, www.mpumalanga.com.
Northern Cape Tourism Authority, www.northerncape.org.za.
North West Province, www.tourismnorthwest.co.za.
Tourism KwaZulu Natal, www.zulu.org.za.

Other useful websites

There are thousands of websites about travel in South Africa in a number of languages, and these days even the tiniest dorps (villages) have their own website. These are listed in the relevant chapters.

www.africaguide.com Everything you need to know about African travel, also sells holidays and reviews guidebooks.
www.africanwildliferesources.org Research tool and resource centre promoting sustainable wildlife practices.
www.africaonline.com Comprehensive site covering news, sport and travel all over Africa.
www.fco.gov.uk UK Foreign Office, for the official advice on latest political situations.
www.gov.za South Africa's government website, up-to-date information about entry requirements.
www.gardenroute.co.za Wide-reaching website covering one of the most popular regions in South Africa.
www.go2africa.com Accommodation and holiday booking service, with useful practical information and links to overland companies.
www.southafrica.co.za General information and travel advice.
www.overlandafrica.com A variety of overland tours offered throughout Africa.
www.sanparks.org Full details of all the national parks, including online booking.

Language

There are 11 official languages in South Africa: English, Zulu, Xhosa, Afrikaans, Venda, Swazi, North Sotho, South Sotho, Tswana, Sindebele and Shangaan. Afrikaans is spoken by 60% of white South Africans and the majority of the Cape coloured population. In addition to this, there are six Asian languages spoken, mostly in KwaZulu Natal. English is widely spoken and understood, but it is always a good idea to learn at least a couple of basic phrases in the predominant language of the area that you're travelling in – a simple 'hello' in Xhosa or 'thank you' in Afrikaans can go a long way.

❢ *Lekker is an Afrikaans word for 'very good' or 'things are going well'.*

Specialist travel

Disabled travellers

Facilities for disabled travellers are developing quickly in South Africa and a number of accommodation establishments advertise wheelchair access. Many of the more modern hotels have specially adapted rooms and it is worth asking about these even in smaller or more remote places when enquiring about accommodation. Safaris should not pose too much of a problem either, given that most of the time is spent in the vehicle; wheelchair-bound travellers may want to consider a camping or tented safari which provides easy access to a tent at ground level. Some tourist attractions have been developed with disabled visitors in mind, such as the Braille Trail at Kirstenbosch Botanical Gardens, or the easily accessible cable car to the top of Table Mountain. The fact that South Africa is a very car-friendly country should make getting to the major sights no problem and most places have disabled parking right by the entrance.

Useful contacts

www.eco-access.org.za A useful website promoting access to nature for disabled people in South Africa.

Epic Enabled, T021-7829575, www.epic-enabled.com, offers an excellent range of tours for disabled travellers, using fully modified overland trucks, camp assistants and wheelchair-friendly accommodation.

Flamingo Tours, T021-5574496, www.flamingotours.co.za. Established Western Cape tour operator specializing in disabled travel; tailor-made tours are led by a registered guide and nurse (if necessary).

Rolling SA, T033-3304214, www.rollingsa.co.za. Organizes tours throughout South Africa specifically for wheelchair users.

Gay and lesbian travellers

The South African constitution is one of the most gay-friendly and progressive in the world and at the time of writing the government is legalizing same-sex marriages. Cape Town is the self-proclaimed Pink Capital of Africa and has a flourishing scene, with a yearly **Gay and Lesbian Pride** week usually held in February, www.capetownpride.co.za. Other annual events in Cape Town are the **Pink Loerie Mardi Gras** in May, www.pinkloerie.com (also held in Knysna); a popular annual gay and lesbian film festival in August known as **Out in Africa**, www.oia.co.za; and the annual **Mother City Queer Project**, a costume dance event in December, www.mcqp.co.za – a highlight on the city's social calendar that attracts local celebs and TV cameras. The *Pink Map* of the city, available at the tourist offices, lists gay friendly/oriented accommodation, restaurants and nightlife, tour operators, and even health spas and launderettes. Away from Cape Town, Johannesburg and Durban also have burgeoning gay scenes but, apart from these cities, South Africa remains deeply conservative. Overtly affectionate behaviour between gay and lesbian couples may elicit a disapproving response – from both black and white communities – particularly in more remote rural parts. It is wise for gay visitors to be discrete. By doing so you should encounter no problems.

Useful contacts

www.exit.co.za Leading gay and lesbian online newspaper.

www.galactic.co.za Association of gay-related businesses promoting gay commerce in Cape Town.

www.gaynetsa.co.za Lists clubs, bars and gay friendly accommodation around the country (and celebrity gossip).

www.mask.org.za A website dedicated to gay and lesbian affairs throughout Africa.

www.q.co.za South Africa's main gay and lesbian website with travel and entertainment news, chat rooms and a dating service.

Student travellers

Anyone in full-time education is entitled to an **International Student Identity Card** (ISIC). These are issued by student travel offices and travel agencies across the world and offer special rates on all forms of transport (including the Baz Bus) and other concessions and services. Visit www.isic.org for up-to-date information on cards and local contact details. For information on backpacker hostels visit www.hihostels.com and the **South African Youth Hostel Association**, www.hisa.org.za.

Travelling with children

South Africa is a popular family holiday destination; in December and January accommodation in the parks and along the coast is packed with South African families during the school holidays. In the main towns with supermarkets, you will find plentiful supplies of all you need to feed and look after your little ones. Hygiene throughout the country is of a good standard; stomach upsets are rare and the tap water everywhere is safe to drink. Be sure to protect your children from the sun's intense rays, and be aware of the potential dangers of wild animals, snakes and insects in the bush. Most of the accommodation options welcome families; many have either specific family rooms or adjoining rooms suitable for families, and there are plenty of family chalets or bungalows, especially in the parks. Children get significant discounts on accommodation and entry fees. South Africa has a great appeal to children: animals and safaris are very exciting for them (and their parents), especially when they catch their first glimpse of an elephant or lion. However, small children may get bored driving around a hot game reserve or national park all day if there is no animal activity. If you travel in a group, think about the long hours inside the vehicle sharing the small space with other people. Noisy and bickering children can annoy your travel mates and scare the animals away. Many travel agencies organize family safaris that are especially designed for couples travelling with children, and there is also the option of self-drive, which is ideal for families.

> ❢ *Inform the airline in advance that you are travelling with a baby or toddler and check out the facilities when booking as these vary with each aircraft. Also useful is www.babygoes2.com.*

Women travellers

Although South Africa has an unusually high incidence of rape, tourists are, as a rule, not targeted and South Africa is a relatively safe country for women to travel in. However, the usual rules of avoiding travelling alone after dark, never hitchhiking and avoiding quiet areas always apply. While women are not usually confronted with prejudice when checking into hotels or trying to be served, it is worth remembering that among most communities in South Africa there is a strong macho element. Women may experience some unwanted attention from men, but nothing that can't be dealt with assertively. It is often a good idea to cover up in more conservative or rural areas – avoiding tight, revealing tops and short skirts should help.

Working and volunteering in South Africa

There are no opportunities for travellers to obtain casual paid employment in South Africa and it is illegal for a foreigner to work without an official work permit. Most foreign workers in the country are employed through embassies, development or volunteer agencies or through foreign companies. For the most part these people will have been recruited in their countries of origin. A number of NGOs and voluntary organizations can arrange placements for volunteers, usually for periods ranging from six months to two years, visit www.volunteerafrica.org. **Amakhala Game Reserve,** www.amakhala.co.za, in the Eastern Cape, takes on gap-year students as volunteers in wildlife management, see page 340.

Before you travel

Visas and immigration

EU nationals and citizens from the USA, Canada, Australia and New Zealand don't need visas to enter South Africa. On arrival, visitors from these countries are granted temporary **visitor's permits**, lasting up to 90 days. You must have a valid return ticket to get a permit. It is possible to apply for an extension to the permit at one of the offices of the **Department of Home Affairs** ⓘ *Cape Town T021-4624970; Durban T031-3087930; Johannesburg T011-8363228; Pretoria T012-3148109; Port Elizabeth T041-4871026; www.home-affairs.gov.za*. This can take up to three weeks and costs around R550. You will need to produce documentation to show when you are leaving the country, such as a flight ticket or tour confirmation voucher, as well as proof of funds. Citizens of countries other than those listed above should consult the South African embassy or consulate in their country for information on visa requirements.

Note that going to Lesotho or Swaziland and returning to South Africa is not a valid way to extend your holiday visa or permit. On re-entering South Africa, immigration officials will scan your original South African entry stamp for its date of departure. If this date has passed while you are in Lesotho or Swaziland, South African immigration will extend your visa for two to four weeks, during which time you are expected either to leave the country or to extend your visa. ▸▸ *Details of immigration requirements for Lesotho and Swaziland are given on pages 757 and 800.*

South African embassies and consulates

Australia, Corner Rhodes Place and State Circle, Canberra, T02-62732424, www.sahc.org.au.

Austria, Sandgasse 33, 1190 Vienna, T320-6493, www.saembvie.at.

Belgium, Rue de la Loi 26, Wetstraat 26, Brussels T02-2854400, www.southafrica.be.

Canada, 15 Sussex Dr, Ottawa, T613-7440330, www.southafrica-canada.ca.

Denmark, Gammel Vartov VEJ, No 8, 2900 Hellerup, Copenhagen, T039-180155, www.southafrica.dk.

France, 59 Quai d'Orsay, Paris 75007, T01-5359 2323, www.afriquesud.net.

Germany, Tiergartenstr 18, 10785 Berlin, T030-220730, www.suedafrika.org.

Israel, Yakhin House, Top Tower, 50 Dizengoff St, Tel Aviv 64332, T03-5252566, www.safis.co.il.

Italy, Via Tanaro 14, Rome 00198, T06-8525 4262, www.sudafrica.it.

Japan, 414 Zenkyoren Bld, Hirakawa-cho, Chiyoda-ku 1020093, Tokoyo, T03-3265 3366, www.rsatk.com.

Netherlands, 40 Wassenaarseweg 2596 CJ, The Hague, T070-3105920, www.zuidafrika.nl.

Spain, Edificio Lista, Calle de Claudio Coello 91, 28006 Madrid, T91-4363780, www.sudafrica.com.

Sweden, Linngatan 76, 11523 Stockholm, T08-243950, www.southafricanemb.se.

Switzerland, Rue du Rhone 65, Geneva 1204, T022-8495454, www.missions.itu.int.

UK, South Africa House, Trafalgar Sq, London, WC2N 5DP, T020-7451 7299, www.southafricahouse.com.

USA, 3051 Massachusetts Av NW, Washington, DC 20008, T1202-2324400, www.saembassy.org; there are also consulates in Los Angeles and New York.

Customs and duty free

The official customs allowance for visitors over 18 years includes 200 cigarettes, 50 cigars, 250g of tobacco, two litres of wine, one litre of spirits, 50 ml of perfume and 250 ml of toilet water. Visitors are restricted to bringing in R5000 of South African rand from their home country. Tourists can reclaim the 14% VAT on purchases bought in South Africa exceeding the value of R250. You can do this when departing, at the VAT reclaim desks at airports or border posts. Refunds are given by cheque in South African rand, which can be paid into home bank accounts. Goods need to be shown to the refund officer as proof of purchase with VAT receipts, so be sure to ask for these when you buy something, and at the airport this needs to be done before you check in your luggage. The procedure is simple enough at the airports but allow plenty of time, especially if your flight is at night. At the border crossings such as Beitbridge (Zimbabwe) or Ramotswa (Botswana) the procedure is painstakingly slow, as there are few customs officials to check goods against receipts. Expect lengthy queues. Refunds only apply to items taken out of the country and not on services rendered, such as accommodation or goods consumed or used within the country. For example if you are buying clothes, keep the shop tags on them to prove that you haven't worn them in South Africa and you'll get the tax back. To save time at the airport or border, you can also go to one of the pre-processing offices, at the Clock Tower at Cape Town Waterfront, Sandton City shopping mall in Johannesburg, and the Riverside Mall in Nelspruit. At these offices you will be required to submit all the receipts to be checked off against goods you will be exporting from South Africa, as well as presenting your passport and air ticket. They will stamp your receipts for verification but cannot give out refunds. This still has to be done at the airport or border on departure. For more information visit www.taxrefunds.co.za.

Vaccinations

South Africa requires yellow fever vaccination certificates from visitors who have travelled through the yellow fever zones in Africa or South America. If you arrive from these areas without the certificate, you will be given the jab at the airport before being permitted entry. This currently costs around R400 at Johannesburg Airport, so it will be more than your arm that will feel the sting. The following other vaccinations are recommended: typhoid; poliomyelitis; tetanus; hepatitis A and B; BCG (against tuberculosis); rabies. Children should in addition be properly protected against diphtheria, whooping cough, mumps and measles. Teenage girls, if they have not had the disease, should be given a rubella (german measles) vaccination. It is worth remembering that if a vaccination needs renewing during your stay in South Africa, or your travel plans change, there are a number of vaccination clinics in Johannesburg, Cape Town and Durban, where malaria prophylaxis can also be purchased. » *For other pre-travel health advice, see Health, page 56.*

What to take

A good rule of thumb is to take half the clothes you think you'll need and double the money. A backpack or travelpack (a hybrid backpack/suitcase) rather than a rigid suitcase, covers most eventualities and survives the rigours of a variety of modes of travel well. A lock for your luggage is strongly advised – there are cases of pilfering by airport baggage handlers the world over. Light cotton clothing is best, with a fleece or woollen jumper for evenings. Hikers will need comfortable walking boots that have been worn in. Those going on camping safaris will need a sleeping bag, towel and torch. Everything you could possibly need on holiday is available to buy in South Africa so you don't have to fret about leaving anything at home.

Send yourself an email with details of traveller's cheques, passport, driving licence, credit cards and travel insurance numbers. Someone at home should also have access to important details.

Checklist

Air tickets, cash, mobile phone and charger, contact lens solution, contraceptives, credit cards, ear plugs, electric plug adaptor, first aid kit, insect repellent, passport, photocopies of main documents (keep separate), small torch plus batteries, sunglasses, sun protection cream, Swiss army knife or Leatherman, toiletries, traveller's cheques, water bottle.

Insurance

Before departure, it is vital to take out full travel insurance. There is a wide variety of policies to choose from, so shop around. At the very least, the policy should cover medical expenses, including the possibility of medical evacuation by air ambulance to your own country, and personal effects. Make sure that it also covers all activities that you might do while away, trekking or skydiving for example. There is no substitute for suitable precautions against petty crime, but if you do have something stolen whilst in South Africa, report the incident to the nearest police station and ensure you get a police report and case number. You will need these to make any claim from your insurance company.

Money

Currency

The South African currency is the **rand** (R) which is divided into 100 cents (c). Notes are in 200, 100, 50, 20 and 10 R, and coins are in 5, 2, 1 R and 50, 20, 10 and 5 c. You can carry your funds in several forms, including traveller's cheques, credit cards, rands, US dollars, euros or pounds sterling.

Visitors are restricted to bringing R5000 cash in person into the country and should change any surplus rand back into their own currency before leaving South Africa. This is most easily done at the airport; high street banks usually require proof of initial transactions. If you plan on visiting neighbouring countries, note that most of their currencies can only be purchased within South Africa and not before you leave home. However, rand can easily be exchanged in all South Africa's neighbouring countries and in some cases, such as Namibia and Mozambique, is used interchangeably alongside the local currency.

Useful websites include: www.visa.com, www.americaexpress.com and www.mastercard.com. For up-to-the-minute exchange rates, visit www.xe.com.

Changing money

Normal banking hours are Monday-Friday 0900-1530; Saturday 0900-1030/1100. All of the main high street banks offer foreign exchange services. You can also change money at branches of **Rennies Travel**, www.rennies.co.za, which acts as an agent for Thomas Cook. There are Rennies branches in all regional and tourist centres and most shopping malls. **American Express Foreign Exchange Service**, www.americanexpress.co.za, has offices in the larger cities and offers a poste restante service to card holders. Larger hotels offer exchange facilities, but these often charge exorbitant fees.

Credit and debit cards

You can get all the way around South Africa with a credit or debit card. Not only do they offer a convenient method of covering major expenses but they offer some of the most competitive exchange rates when withdrawing cash from ATMs. They are particularly useful when hiring a car – indeed, many companies will only hire a car to foreign visitors if they have a credit card. The chip and pin system is beginning to feature in the country and is likely to catch on fast. Note that credit cards are not accepted as payment for petrol, which can only be purchased with cash. ATMs are everywhere; Plus, Cirrus Visa, Mastercard, American Express and Diners' Club are all accepted. The amount you can withdraw varies between systems and cards, but you should be able to take out up to R1000 a day. Note that theft during or immediately after a withdrawal can be a problem, so never accept a stranger's help at an ATM, be aware of your surroundings and avoid using street-side ATMs. Instead, go into a bank or shopping mall, where guards are often on duty.

Lost or stolen cards: American Express, T011-3590200; Diners Club, T011-3588406; MasterCard, T0800-990418; Visa, T0800-990475.

Traveller's cheques

The major advantage of traveller's cheques is that if they are lost or stolen there is a relatively efficient system for replacement. Make sure you keep a full record of the cheques' numbers and value and always keep the receipts separate from the cheques. The drawback is that replacement cheques can usually only be collected from banks in major cities. The disadvantages of traveller's cheques are the time it takes to cash them and the commission charged, which ranges from 0.2% to 2%. The most widely accepted cheques are American Express, Thomas Cook and Visa. Thomas Cook issues South African rand travellers' cheques, which are sometimes accepted as payment in shops and hotels.

Cost of travelling

Prices in South Africa used to be especially cheap by European standards and offered excellent value for money for the tourist spending US dollars, pounds sterling or euros. This is not quite the case these days: over the last three or four years the South African rand has gone from strength to strength against these other currencies, and exchange rates are about half of what they were four years ago. If you are travelling independently and propose to hire a car, you will need to budget R200-300 per day, depending on the season, type of vehicle and equipment included – a considerable outlay, but for a family of four or group of friends, the cost per person is less. The cost of fuel is similar to that in the US, about two thirds of what Europeans are used to, but distances travelled can be considerable so be prepared for a hefty fuel bill too.

At the time of writing the exchange rates were:
GBP1 = R12
US$1 = R6.4
AUS$1 = R4.9
Euro1 = R8.2

Accommodation will represent your other principal daily expense. In first-rate luxury lodges, tented camps or guest farms expect to pay in excess of R1000 per night for a double, rising to R6000-7000 per person per night in the most exclusive establishments. For this you will get impeccable service, cuisine and decor in fantastic locations. If staying in simple B&Bs and hotels, budget R350-700 per couple per night. By camping or staying in dormitory accommodation in backpacker hostels, you can bring this down to R100-150 on average per person per night. Food and drink is still good value in southern Africa and an evening meal with wine in a reasonable restaurant will cost under R200 for two people, and you can be pretty assured of good food and large portions. For the budget traveller there are plenty of fast food outlets, and almost every supermarket has a superb deli counter serving hot and cold meals. Costs can be brought down by self-catering, either at campsites or in self-catering accommodation. Food in supermarkets is considerably cheaper than, say, in Europe, especially meat and fresh fruit and vegetables, and a bottle of wine and beer are an affordable R30 and R10 respectively. ▸▸ *For further information on accommodation and restaurant prices, see Sleeping and Eating, pages 42 and 45.*

Getting there

Air

The three main international airports are Johannesburg, Cape Town and Durban. Johannesburg is the regional hub with numerous daily flights to Europe, North America, Asia and Australia. Although most flights arrive in Johannesburg, a fair number of carriers fly directly to Cape Town. There is a huge choice of routes and flights, but for the best fares you need to book three or four months in advance, especially over Christmas.

From Europe

British Airways, Virgin and **South African Airways** are the main operators with daily flights between London Gatwick or Heathrow and Johannesburg or Cape Town. Flying time is 10½ hours to Johannesburg and 11 hours to Cape Town. During peak season, a direct return flight can cost as much as US$1800 but if you book several months in advance this can drop to below US$900. **Nationwide** is a regional carrier in southern Africa but also has one daily flight between Johannesburg and London Gatwick. Other European carriers include **Air France, Air Portugal, Alitalia, Austrian Airlines, Iberia, Lufthansa, KLM** and **Swiss International (LX)**. Indirect flights from other airlines can also be good value: **Kenya Airways** flies between London and Johannesburg, via Nairobi; **Air Namibia** flies between Frankfurt and London to Johannesburg and Cape Town via Windhoek; and **Emirates** flies daily to Johannesburg via Dubai from just about anywhere else in the world.

Jetlag is not an issue if flying from Europe to South Africa as there is only a minimal time difference.

From North America

South African Airways runs daily direct flights from Atlanta to Johannesburg, with connections to Cape Town. Flight time is around 17 hours, with prices hovering around the US$1600 mark. **American Airlines** has an agreement with **British Airways,** with flights to Johannesburg and Cape Town via London Heathrow. **Delta Airlines** has a more convenient code share agreement with **South African Airways.**

From Australia, New Zealand and Asia

Qantas code shares with **South African Airways,** and between them they run a direct daily flight to and from Perth and Johannesburg, flying time 10 hours, with connections from across Australia. Flights run approximately four times per week, with prices from around US$1400, although this can double in high season. **Singapore Airlines** offers regular flights between Sydney and Johannesburg via Singapore, and has a code sharing agreement with **Air New Zealand** (which means that flights from Wellington to Johannesburg have two stops). **Malaysia Airlines** has regular flights from Perth, Melbourne, Sydney and Darwin in Australia and Auckland in New Zealand to Kuala Lumpur, connecting with a flight to Johannesburg three times a week, which continues on to Cape Town and then Buenos Aires (Argentina). **Cathay Pacific** flies to/from Johannesburg from Hong Kong once a week.

From Africa

Johannesburg and, in some instances, Cape Town are served by a number of regional airlines that link all the major cities of Africa. These include **Air Botswana, Air Madagascar, Air Mauritius, Air Malawi, Air Namibia, Air Seychelles, Air Tanzania, Air Zimbabwe, Egypt Air, Ethiopian Airlines, Ghana Airways, Kenya Airways, Kulula.com** and **South African Airways** and its subsidiaries **SA Express** and **SA Airlink**.

Airlines

From the UK and Europe

Air Namibia, T020-7960 6016, www.airnamibia.com.na.

British Airways, T0870-8509850, www.britishairways.com.

Emirates, T0870-2432222, www.emirates.com.

Kenya Airways, T01784-888222, www.kenya-airways.com.

KLM, T0870-5074074, www.klm.com.

Lufthansa, T0870-8377747, www.lufthansa.com.

Nationwide, T0870-3000 767, www.flynationwide.co.za.

South African Airways, T0870-7471111, www.flysaa.com.

Virgin, T0870-5747747, www.virgin-atlantic.com.

From North America

Delta, T1800-2211212 (USA), www.delta.com.

United Airlines, T1800-5382929 (USA), www.united.com.

From Australia, New Zealand and Asia

Cathay Pacific, T+852-2747 1888 (Hong Kong), www.cathaypacific.com.

Qantas, T+2-9691 3636 (Australia), www.qantas.com.au.

Singapore Airlines, T+065-6223 8888, (Singapore), www.singaporeair.com.

Air Malaysia, T+603-7846 3000 (Malaysia), www.malaysia-airlines.com.

Air New Zealand, T0800-737000 (New Zealand), www.airnewzealand.com.

Discount flight agents

In the UK and Ireland

Flightbookers, T0870-814000, www.ebookers.com.

Flight Centre, T0800-5870058, www.flightcentre.co.uk.

STA Travel, T0870-1600599, www.statravel.co.uk.

Trailfinders, T0845-0585858, www.trailfinders.com.

Travelbag, T0800-0825000, www.travelbag.co.uk.

In North America

Air Brokers International, T1800-8833273, www.airbrokers.com.

Airtech, T1212-2197000, www.airtech.com.

Discount Airfares Worldwide On-Line, www.etn.nl/discount.htm.

STA Travel, T1800-7814040, www.statravel.com.

Travel CUTS, T1866-2469762 (Canada), www.travelcuts.com.

Worldtek, T1800-2421723, www.worldtek.com.

In Australia and New Zealand

Flight Centre, T133-133 (Australia), www.flightcentre.com.au.

Skylinks, T02-9223 4277, www.skylink.com.au.

STA Travel, T03-92075900 (Australia), T0508-782872 (New Zealand), www.statravel.com.au.

Sydney Travel, T02-9250 9320, www.sydneytravel.com.au.

Travel.com.au, T1300-130483, www.travel.com.au.

Rail

Trains run from Maputo (Mozambique) to Johannesburg via Komatipoort (where you will have to change trains) and Nelspruit, transporting huge numbers of migrant workers employed as miners around Gauteng. Luckily the lengthy customs and immigration formalities don't affect most tourists, who are dealt with separately. Visas for Mozambique are now available at the border. Train services also run (in theory) from Victoria Falls, Bulawayo and Harare in Zimbabwe to Johannesburg, although this service has been affected by fuel shortages in Zimbabwe in recent years. The South African national railway company is **Spoornet**, T0860-008888, www.spoornet.co.za.

Namibia's railway company, **Transnamib Starline Passenger Services**, T+264 (0)61-2982032, www.transnamib.com.na, runs a service between Upington in South Africa and Windhoek twice a week. However as Namibia's trains are primarily used for freight, it is slow going with a lot of stops. Despite this the passenger compartments are comfortable with airline-like seats, videos are shown and there are vending machines for drinks and snacks. Note that the Intercape bus takes 10 hours to do the same route as opposed to around 24 hours on the train.

Road

There are good road connections between South Africa and Namibia, Botswana, Mozambique, Lesotho (see page 758), Swaziland (see page 797) and Zimbabwe. In total South Africa shares 55 border crossings with neighbouring countries.

Botswana The main border crossings into South Africa are at Pioneer Gate, Ramatlabana and Tlokweng Gate. The crossing is usually swift and efficient. The R505 from Tlokweng connects with the R27 at Zeerust heading towards Johannesburg. From Ramatlabana there is a road leading to Mafeking, which connects with the R52 to Johannesburg.

The Department of Home Affairs in Pretoria can provide up-to-date details of border opening hours: T012-8108911, www.home-affairs.gov.za.

Lesotho From Lesotho, the main border crossings are Maseru Bridge, Maputsoe Bridge and Calendonspoort. There are several others, such as Sani Pass, that are open for limited periods and can only be crossed by 4WD, by horse or on foot.

Mozambique The journey between South Africa and Maputo has improved considerably since the completion of a toll road between Nelspruit and Maputo via the border at Komatipoort. Visas for Mozambique are available at the border for US$25.

Namibia The main crossing point is Vioolsdrift which is open 24 hours, with less frequently used borders at Ariamsvlei and Rietfontein. Cape Town is 714 km south of Vioolsdrift along the N7. However to Johannesburg and northern South Africa the most direct route from Namibia is via Botswana. You can enter Botswana at the Buitepos border post which is 120 km east of Gobabis on the road to Windhoek. Then the road crosses Botswana via Lobatse as the newly tarred Trans-Kalahari Highway. It crosses into South Africa at the Pioneer Gate border post and becomes the N4 that goes to Johannesburg and Pretoria via Zeerust. The journey from the Namibian border to Johannesburg is roughly 1070 km and fuel stations are infrequent so fill up when you see one. The longest stretch between petrol stations on this route is 350 km.

Swaziland Border crossings are possible at Ngwenya/ Oshoek, Lavumisa and Mahamba. The R38 heads from Oshoek to Johannesburg via Carolina and the N4.

Zimbabwe The only border crossing is at Beitbridge, a notoriously slow crossing during peak periods, with long queues and thorough searches.

Bus

The three main coach companies cover routes across South Africa's borders and some services go as far as Malawi. All bus tickets can be booked online. **Translux,** T011-774333, www.translux.co.za, runs services from Johannesburg to Blantyre, Buluwayo, Harare and Lusaka, and from Pretoria to Maputo. **Intercape,** T0861-287287 in South Africa, T012-3804400 from overseas, www.intercape.co.za, runs coaches from Johannesburg/Pretoria to Gaborone, Windhoek, and Maputo, and from Cape Town to Livingstone in Zambia (via Namibia). **Greyhound,** T012-3231154, www.greyhound.co.za, runs coaches from Pretoria to Maputo, Harare and Bulawayo.

Car

If crossing any international borders in a private car, you must have a registration document, insurance and a driving licence printed in English with a photograph. With the exception of Zimbabwe, you should be able to take a hire car into all the above-mentioned countries, though check with the rental company first. You will need a letter of permission to take a car across a border if it is not registered in your name, and a ZA sticker (available in South Africa from any AA shop). Botswana, Namibia and South Africa are all part of SADC's (Southern Africa Development Community) joint customs agreement, so if you are in your own car travelling on a carnet, you only have to produce this when crossing your first or last border to the SADC countries.

Trucks

Overland truck safaris are a popular way of exploring southern and East Africa by road. They demand a little more fortitude and adventurous spirit from the traveller, but the compensation is usually the camaraderie and lifelong friendships that result from what is invariably a real adventure, going to places the more luxurious travellers will never visit. The standard three-week overland route most commercial trucks take through southern Africa (in either direction) is from Cape Town up to Namibia, across to Botswana, finishing in either Victoria Falls in Zimbabwe or Livingstone in Zambia. This three-week trip can be combined with another three weeks to/from Nairobi via Zambia, Malawi, Tanzania and Zanzibar, and finishing in Kenya. Again the circuit continues with a two-week route into Uganda to see the mountain gorillas via some of the Kenya national parks. There are several overland companies with departures almost weekly from Cape Town, Livingstone/Victoria Falls and Nairobi throughout the year. You can also do this trip starting or ending in Johannesburg but will miss out on Namibia.

Overland truck safari operators

In the UK

Dragoman, T01728-861133, www.dragoman.co.uk.
Encounter, T01728-861133, www.encounter.co.uk.
Exodus Travels, T0208-7723822, www.exodus.co.uk.
Explore, T0870-3334002, www.explore.co.uk.
Kumuka Expeditions, T0207-9378855, www.kumuka.com.
Oasis Overland, T01963-363400, www.oasisoverland.co.uk.
Phoenix Expeditions, T01509-881341, www.phoenix-expeditions.co.uk.

In South Africa

Africa Travel Co, T021-5568590, www.africatravelco.com.
Wildlife Adventures, T021-7020643, www.wildlifeadventures.co.za.

Touching down

Airport information

Information on airport facilities and flight arrivals, T086-7277888, www.airports.co.za.

The three international airports in South Africa are at Cape Town, Durban and Johannesburg. Each is modern and efficient with food courts, shops, banks and ATMs, post offices, car and mobile phone rental desks, and shuttle services into the respective cities. Although there are some direct flights to Cape Town, the majority of international flights arrive in Johannesburg, and then connect on to Durban, Cape Town and the other cities. Johannesburg International Airport has undergone a major upgrade in the last few years and now has a brand new domestic terminal alongside the international terminal, which is a short walk away. Regardless of your eventual destination, immigration is done at Johannesburg, which usually means you have to pick up your luggage from the international terminal and check in again at the domestic terminal. Remember to put locks on your bags – there have been many incidents of things going missing from luggage en route through Johannesburg airport. »» *For further details, see Ins and outs, pages 66, 389 and 502, and Transport, pages 130, 405 and 523.*

Touching down

→ **Business hours**
Banks Mon-Fri 0900-1530, Sat 0830/0900-1030/1100. **Businesses** Mon-Fri 0830-1700, Sat 0830-1400. **Government offices** Mon-Fri 0830-1300, 1400-1630. **Post offices** Mon-Fri 0830-1600, Sat 0800-1200, minor branches have slightly shorter hours. **Shops and supermarkets** Mon-Fri 0800-1800, Sat 0800-1300, Sun 0900-1300.

→ **Country code** +27

→ **IDD code** 09

→ **Official language** English.

→ **Official time** Despite its size, South Africa only has one time zone: GMT +2 hours, 7 hours ahead of USA Standard Time, 1 hour ahead of Europe; 8 hours behind Australian Eastern Standard Time. There is no daylight saving.

→ **Voltage** 220/230 volts AC at 50 Hz, except for Pretoria, where it is 250 volts AC. Most plugs and appliances are 3-point round-pin (one 10 mm and two 8 mm prongs). Hotels usually have two round-pin sockets for razors.

→ **Weights and measures** The metric system is used.

Local laws and customs

Dress

Dress in South Africa tends to be casual and most people on holiday wear shorts, sandals and a T-shirt. If you intend to do any game viewing, clothes in dark green, muted browns and khaki colours are best. In general, bars and restaurants are casual, though some of the more upmarket establishments have dress codes where sandals, vest and shorts are not appreciated.

South African fashion is similar to Europe and the USA, and clothes cost about the same.

Tipping

Waiters, hotel porters, stewards, chambermaids and tour guides should be tipped 10-15%, according to the service. When leaving tips make sure it goes to the intended person, as there is no guarantee that money collected in a kitty will be distributed fairly to everyone. It is common practice to tip petrol pump attendants, depending on their service – up to R5 for a fill up, oil and water check and comprehensive windscreen clean. On safari it is also expected to tip guides, but remember excessive tipping can make it difficult for the next customer. If in any doubt, ask the company that you booked with for advice on how much to tip.

Prohibitions

Although marijuana, locally known as *dagga*, is grown in rural areas, such as the Wild Coast and Lesotho, and smoking it is relatively widespread, it is illegal and strict penalties apply. Traditionally, poor people have smoked a lethal cocktail of mandrax (*buttons*) and marijuana (*dagga*), which will almost instantly comatose inexperienced users. Another highly potent drug is Tik or methamphetamine, part of the amphetamine group of drugs, has also more recently become a major problem in urban areas, especially on the Cape Flats in Cape Town. Hard drugs such as cocaine and heroin, along with their associated problems, are also prevalent. Since independence there has been an alarming growth in drug-related crime and inner-city areas of Cape Town, Johannesburg and, more recently, Durban have become major transit points for drugs en route to Europe and America.

How big is your footprint?

- The point of a holiday is, of course, to have a good time, but if it's relatively guilt-free as well, that's even better. Perfect ecotourism would ensure a good living for local inhabitants, while not detracting from their traditional lifestyles, encroaching on their customs or spoiling their environment. Perfect ecotourism probably doesn't exist, but everyone can play their part. Here are a few points worth bearing in mind:
- Think about where your money goes, and be fair and realistic about how cheaply you travel. Try and put money into local people's hands; drink local beer or fruit juice rather than imported brands and stay in locally owned accommodation wherever possible.
- Haggle with humour and not aggressively. Remember that you are likely to be much wealthier than the person you're buying from.
- Think about what happens to your rubbish. Take biodegradable products and a water bottle filter. Be sensitive to limited resources like water, fuel and electricity.
- Help preserve local wildlife and habitats by respecting rules and regulations, such as sticking to footpaths, not standing on coral and not buying products made from endangered plants or animals.
- Don't treat people as part of the landscape; they may not want their picture taken. Ask first and respect their wishes.
- Learn the local language and be mindful of local customs and norms. It can enhance your travel experience and you'll earn respect and be more readily welcomed by local people.
- And finally, use your guidebook as a starting point, not the only source of information. Talk to local people, then discover your own adventure.

Drink-driving is a big problem in South Africa, and although it is illegal, the laws are routinely ignored by locals. Be especially wary on the roads over Christmas when the number of road deaths soars dramatically. Reputedly there are more deaths caused by road accidents in December in South Africa, than there are in a whole year in Australia!

Responsible tourism

Visit www.tourismconcern.org.uk, which works with communities in destination countries to reduce social and environmental problems connected to tourism.

Sustainable or ecotourism has been described as "ethical, considerate or informed tourism where visitors can enjoy the natural, historical and social heritage of an area without causing adverse environmental, socio-economic or cultural impacts that compromise the long-term ability of that area and its people to provide a recreational resource for future generations and an income for themselves". South Africa is a beautiful , dramatic and wild country but also a living, working landscape and a fragile, vulnerable place. By observing the guidelines outlined in the box above and behaving responsibly you can help to minimize your impact and protect the natural and cultural heritage of this wonderful country.

Environmental legislation, too, plays its part in protecting tourist destinations. **CITES** (Convention on International Trade in Endangered Species of Wild Fauna and Flora) aims to control the trade in live specimens of endangered plants and animals and also "recognisable parts or derivatives" of protected species. International trade in elephant ivory, sea turtle products and the skins of wild cats, such as the leopard, is illegal. Restrictions have also been imposed on trade in reptile skins, coral and certain plants and wild birds. If you feel the need to purchase souvenirs and trinkets derived from wildlife, it would be prudent to check whether they are protected. Importation of CITES-protected species can lead to heavy fines, confiscation of goods and even imprisonment.

Safety

South Africa has had more than its fair share of well-publicized crime problems. In the 1980s and '90s Johannesburg was frequently dubbed the most dangerous city in the world, although crime rates are declining there today. Despite the statistics, much of the serious, violent crime is gang-based and occurs in areas that tourists are unlikely to visit, such as Mitchells Plain in Cape Town's townships, or the inner-city ghettos such as Hillbrow in Johannesburg or Point Road in Durban. Dangers facing tourists are on the whole limited to traditional mugging or, on occasion, car jacking. Guns are widely available and you should be aware that your assailant may well be armed and any form of resistance could be fatal.

Bear in mind that safety is not just a matter of avoiding crime. South Africa has a severe HIV epidemic and travellers should always take precautions, see page 57.

Nevertheless, visitors need not worry about their safety outside the inner cities any more than they would in any foreign country. The most simple points to remember are to avoid altogether what are considered to be dangerous areas, not to walk about any urban centres at night and to avoid driving after dark. If you are going to be travelling alone in a car, it's a good idea to bring (or hire) a mobile phone; useful in any case if you break down. » *For specific advice for women travellers, see page 25.*

Problem areas

City centres Horror stories abound among travellers passing through Johannesburg. The city centre, Hillbrow, and Yoeville have the worst reputation and the crime rate remains high. There are few facilities or accommodation options in these areas, so it is feasible to avoid them altogether and visit the sights only on an organized tour. Travellers arriving at the Park City Transit Centre in Johannesburg should not walk into town. Instead, take a taxi directly to your hotel. The crime rate in Johannesburg's suburbs, where most of the hotels, hostels, nightlife, and shops are located, has improved greatly in recent years, due mainly to an increase in security measures, and you should experience few problems in these areas.

Footprint is a partner in the Foreign and Commonwealth Office's 'Know before you go' campaign, www.fco.gov.uk/travel

Apart from Johannesburg, city centres are generally safe during daylight hours, although listen to advice from locals about which areas to avoid. Crime rates in Durban city centre, for example, have increased in recent years (see page 390). Closed-circuit cameras and private security guards have made Cape Town city centre as safe as any European cities, but the likelihood of being mugged increases sharply after dark. The safest way to travel around cities at night is to take a taxi directly to and from your destination.

Townships While by no means out of bounds to tourists, it would not be wise to wander into a township by yourself. On the other hand, if you know a local or have friends living and working in South Africa who know their way around, a trip to a township market or nightclub can be an interesting and rewarding experience. Alternatively go on a township tour which will undoubtedly give you a different picture of the way a very large number of urban South Africans live.

Carjacking Carjacking remains a problem in South Africa's cities, although the number of incidents is constantly declining thanks to collaboration with neighbouring countries to crack down on stolen cars crossing borders. The favoured location for this crime is at red traffic lights on a junction. It is a good idea to travel with the windows closed and the doors locked. When faced with a suspicious situation at a junction, it is general practice to jump the lights and get away as fast as possible. Again, it is important to remember that carjackers are almost always armed and will use their weapons when faced with resistance. Note that the insurance on hire cars in South Africa is correspondingly high.

Getting around

South Africa has an efficient transport network linking its towns and cities. The road systems and flight networks are the best in Africa, making travelling the considerable distances a straightforward experience. Affordable domestic flights link the cities, a sophisticated army of private coaches criss-crosses the country, and the train system, although painfully slow, offers another way of getting from A to B. City transport, however, is a problem. South Africa's cities universally lack safe and reliable urban public transport, often making private transport the only option.

Air

There is a far-reaching and efficient domestic service and regular daily flights connect Johannesburg with other major towns, all of which can be reached within a couple of hours' flying time. On popular routes where there is some competition, such as Durban-Johannesburg or Johannesburg- Cape Town, the cost of a single ticket is usually only a little more expensive than a bus ticket.

By booking early online, good deals can be found with all the airlines.

Airlines

British Airways Comair, T011-9210222, www.britishairways.com, has several flights per day between the major cities as well as to Windhoek, Livingstone, Victoria Falls and Harare.

Kulula, T0861-585852, www.kulula.com, also owned by British Airways, is a hugely successful no-frills airline and fun to travel with (when you get off the plane the crew in their jeans and T-shirts tell you not to forget to take your husband and children with you). Daily services between Cape Town, Durban, Johannesburg, Port Elizabeth, Mpumalanga, East London and George. Also now flies to Windhoek and Harare on a code share agreement with BA.

Nationwide, T0861-737737, www.flynationwide.co.za. Flies daily between Johannesburg, Cape Town, Durban, Mpumalanga, Port Elizabeth, George and Livingstone in Zambia. Also worth checking out is their good-value flight from London Gatwick to Johannesburg.

One Time, T0861-345345, www.1time.co.za, is another budget carrier that flies between Johannesburg, Cape Town, Durban, George, Port Elizabeth and East London. They have rather stylish planes with spacious leather seats, bought from a bankrupt airline.

South African Airways, (SAA), central reservations T011-9781111, www.flysaa.com, cover most of the country as well as other southern African cities in conjunction with both **SA Airlink**, also T011-9781111, www.saairlink.co.za, and **SA Express**, T011-9785569, www.saexpress.co.za.

Rail

All of the major cities are linked by rail and while this is a comfortable and relaxing way to travel, it is very slow. The trains are run by **Shosholoza Meyl**, part of the national network **Spoornet**, T0860-008888, www.spoornet.co.za. Full timetables and fares can be found on the website. Shosholoza means 'to push forward' or 'to strive' and is the name of a popular traditional African song favoured particularly by hard-working men whose job it was to lay railway lines. All the trains travel overnight, the Cape Town-Durban service over two nights, so they arrive at some stations en route at inconvenient times. There are sleeping carriages, with coupés that sleep four or six people, with a wash basin, fold-away table and bunk beds. The 'sitter' carriages are not recommended for long journeys as there is only open coach seating. Always book well in advance for sleeping compartments, especially during local holidays. Refreshments are available from trolleys or dining cars, but these have been franchised to burger-type chains, so don't expect brilliant food. Note that all trains have a problem with security: if you leave your compartment, make sure a train official locks it after you. Accompanied children under four travel free; children between seven and 12 years pay half price.

Routes include: Johannesburg-East London (daily in both directions except Wed and Sat, 19 hrs); Johannesburg-Musina (daily in both directions except Sat, 14 hrs); Johannesburg-Komatipoort (daily in both directions except Sat, 13 hrs); Johannesburg-Bloemfontein (Wed, Fri, Sat in both directions, 12 hrs); Johannesburg-Durban (daily in both directions except Tue and Sat, 8 hrs); Durban-Cape Town (Wed), Cape Town-Durban (Mon, 38 hrs), Pretoria-Cape Town (daily in both directions, 29 hrs); Johannesburg-Port Elizabeth (daily in both directions except for Tue and Sat, 18 hrs).

Luxury trains

If the journey is more important than the destination, then experience a trip on either a steam train or an old-fashioned luxury train, which operate much like five-star hotels on wheels. The **Blue Train**, T021-3348459, www.bluetrain.co.za, is considered to be southern Africa's premier luxury train with 18 carriages that can accommodate 84 passengers. It runs scheduled services between Pretoria and Cape Town, one day and one night, and occasional trips further afield to Victoria Falls. At the time of writing one of the Blue Trains was involved in a head-on collision with another train in the Karoo, which resulted in a number of injuries and damage to most of the carriages. Then, to top it all, as the disabled train was being towed to Cape Town after the collision, at a speed of less than 15 kph, all the crystal, drapes, booze, china and other furnishings were stolen from the carriages. And this only a year after it was completely refitted to the tune of US$9 million after a fire in 2003. They are currently refitting the train and still offering services on a second train. Other luxury trains are the **Pride of Africa**, operated by Rovos Rail, T012-3158242, www.rovos.co.za, **Union Limited Steam Rail Tours**, T021-4494391, www.transnet heritagefoundation.co.za, and **Premier Classe**, T012-3348039 www.premier classe.co.za. Check out the websites for routes and prices.

Metro commuter trains

Many of the larger cities such as Pretoria, Johannesburg and Cape Town have a network of metro commuter services linking the suburbs to the business districts. These should generally be avoided as there have been many cases of robbery. Avoid the metro around Johannesburg and Pretoria at all costs. Some tourists use the Cape Town metro, www.metrorail.co.za, on selected routes; namely from the city to Simonstown on the Cape Peninsula, and experience no problems. If you do use it, stick to first class and travel only during rush hour (0600-0800, 1600-1800) and avoid it at weekends.

Road

Intercity coaches

Greyhound, T012-3231154, www.greyhound.co.za, **Intercape**, T086-1287287, www.intercape.co.za, and **Translux**, T011-7743333, www.translux.co.za, are the three major long-distance bus companies that run between towns and popular destinations, with a large number of buses on each route. All have online booking and seats can be reserved several months in advance. The coaches are air-conditioned and have a toilet; some sell refreshments and show videos. They will stop every four or five hours to change drivers and give the passengers a chance to stretch their legs. For long journeys, the prices are reasonable, but short routes are expensive for budget travellers. However, they are an efficient and a safe way of travelling and, on night routes, bear in mind that you will be saving the cost of a hotel room.

Baz Bus

The **Baz Bus**, T021-4392323, www.bazbus.com, is a hop-on, hop-off bus that offers a convenient and sociable alternative to the main bus services. It is specifically designed for backpackers visiting South Africa and remains one of the most popular ways of seeing the country on a budget. One of the best aspects of the service is that the bus collects and drops off passengers at their chosen backpacker hostel. There are a few exceptions such as Hermanus, Coffee Bay and Sani Pass, where the bus will drop you off at the closest point on the main road, and the hostels will then meet you for an extra charge, though you must arrange this in advance. The Baz Bus route is Cape Town-Durban along the coast, and Durban-Pretoria via either Swaziland or the Drakensberg. Visit the website for the full timetable.

Tickets are priced per segment, for example from Cape Town to Durban. You are allowed to hop off and on the bus as many times as you like in the given segment, but must not backtrack. This is where the savings are made, since other commercial buses, such as Translux and Greyhound, charge high prices for short journeys. However, note that for long distances without stops, the mainline buses are better value. YHA and ISIC card holders are entitled to a 5% discount on Baz Bus tickets.

The Baz Bus drivers are a great source of information, both about the places of interest along the route and what to expect at each hostel. The buses are fairly cramped Mercedes vehicles, although a trailer at the back has space for rucksacks, surf boards and other luggage.

Car hire

Hiring a car for part, or all, of your journey is undoubtedly the best way to see the country. The roads are generally in good condition and, away from the major urban centres, there is little traffic. South Africans are, however, notoriously bad drivers – speeding and drink-driving are common. Do not drive at night for safety reasons. The advantage of hiring a car is that you get to explore more isolated areas, as well as seeing the national parks and nature reserves at a more leisurely pace without being tied to a tour. For budget travellers, hiring a car is ideal for carrying camping equipment and costs come down considerably if you share with three or four people. Petrol, not a major expense, is available 24 hours a day along the national highways. Driving is on the left side of the road and speed limits range from 60 kph in built-up areas to 120 kph on the main highways. The police are cracking down on drink-driving and while many locals still disregard the laws, speed traps with on-the-spot fines are employed. Also remember that if you are caught by a speed camera, the fine will go to the hire car company who have every right to deduct the amount from your credit card.

Automobile Association of South Africa, emergency breakdown and traffic update information: T083-84322, www.aasa.co.za.

It is worth asking at hostels or hotels for recommended car hire companies, and be sure to shop around. Car hire companies have a range of vehicles, from basic hatchbacks and saloon cars, to camper vans and fully equipped 4WD vehicles. In general there are two types of deal on offer: a short weekend package including free mileage; or longer-term deals for a week or more. In the first case you can get very good rates for a Group A car, although you might want a larger vehicle for long journeys – bear in mind that during a two- to three-week holiday you're likely to clock up over 3000 km. The extra engine power and space of a Group B car will make for more comfortable and safe driving. Air conditioning is also well worth the extra but make sure it works before you sign.

Tourist offices usually recommend large international organizations such as Avis or Budget, but there are a number of reliable local companies, usually with a good fleet of cars and follow-up service. Backpacker hostels are often a useful source of information and can offer competitive rates.

If you are intending to visit more remote areas, such as Maputaland, the Kalahari and the Richtersveld, consider hiring a 4WD vehicle. There are specialist companies in Cape Town and Johannesburg that hire out fully equipped safari Land Rovers or pickups with all necessary camping equipment. Fully equipped camper vans or motorhomes represent excellent value for a group or a family as they can save on accommodation.

Make sure you have the correct documents from the rental company if you wish to take the car into Namibia, Botswana, Lesotho or Swaziland. Most companies will not allow you to take a car into Mozambique or Zimbabwe.

Car hire companies

See also the Transport sections under individual towns.
Avis, T0861-021111, www.avis.co.za.
Budget, T0861-016622, www.budget.co.za.
Europcar, T0800-011344, www.europcar.co.za.
Hertz, T0861-600136, www.hertz.co.za.
Imperial Car Rental, T0861-131000, www.imperialcarrental.co.za.

Buying your own car

If you plan to stay in the country for a while, or plan a grand tour of southern Africa, buying your own car may be a sensible option. Johannesburg or Cape Town are the best places to buy or sell. Check the local press for private sales, or visit a second-hand car dealership. Alternatively consider buying a car on a buy-back scheme. There are companies that will sell you a car with a buy-back guarantee once you have finished with it. Work out the costs, though, and compare them to long-term car hire. Sometimes the price difference is minimal and with the buy-back scheme you don't get the back up of a car hire company in the case of an emergency. The following websites are useful: www.drivesouthafrica.co.za, www.drivesouthernafrica.com, www.resqrentacar.co.za.

Cycling

Mountain bikes are available for hire at some backpacker hostels, family resorts and the occasional hotel close to a nature reserve. However, many of the best trails have no facilities nearby for hiring bikes, so enthusiasts should bring their own. When you buy your ticket to fly to South Africa, check the airline's policy on transporting bicycles. You will be expected to pack the bicycle in a cardboard box (available from cycling shops), take the pedals off and deflate the tyres. The weight will count towards your baggage allowance.

When cycling in South Africa, avoid the hottest part of the day, beware of dehydration and sunstroke, wear a hat and drink plenty of liquids.

There are a number of cycling events in South Africa that are open to foreign cyclists. The largest is the Cape Argus/Pick and Pay Cycle Tour in Cape Town in March, www.cycletour.co.za.

Hitchhiking

Hitchhiking is not common in South Africa and can be unsafe. Women should under no circumstances hitch alone or even in a group of two or more. If you do hitch, be very wary of who you are accepting a lift from; a car with a family or couple in may be fine, but avoid getting into a vehicle with a group of men. It is also a good idea to take public transport out of towns and then start hitching once you've passed the townships. Make sure you look as smart as possible – you're more likely to get a lift if you look clean-cut. In rural areas you may be expected to pay if a lorry or a pickup gives you a life.

Motorbike

Probably the only European bikers you will see in South Africa will be bearded, tanned, trans-Africa adventurers, but for the tourist with a motorbike licence it is possible to go on a guided tour of southern Africa. Both these companies also hire out bikes: **Ayres Adventures Motorcycle Tours,** T083-3778855, www.ronayres.com, and **Go-mad Enduro Motorbike Adventures,** T011-9074121, www.gomad.co.za.

Taxis

There are few taxi ranks in South African towns so it's generally a better idea to order a taxi in advance. Any hotel, hostel or restaurant will make a booking for you. Make sure you get an advance quote on your proposed journey. Travelling by taxi, especially at night, is one of the safest ways to cross city centres when visiting a restaurant or nightclub; don't walk just to save a few cents.

Minibus taxis

The majority of South Africa's population travel by minibus taxis and, in many areas, including inner cities, they are the only way of getting around. However, the accident rate of such vehicles is notoriously high, with speeding, overcrowding and lack of maintenance being the main causes. There is also the problem of possible robbery, especially at the taxi ranks, so many visitors and locals remain wary of using them.

Nevertheless, minibus taxis remain the cheapest and most extensive form of transport in the country. Many routes have experienced little or no crime, but you should exercise extreme caution and always ask people in the know before using them. In central Cape Town minibus taxis provide an efficient (and relatively safe) means of transport into the city centre from places such as Observatory, Camps Bay, Sea Point, Rondebosch and Claremont.

Maps

The best map and travel guide store in the UK is **Stanfords** ⓘ *12-14 Longacre, Covent Garden, London, WC2E 9LP, T020-7836 1321, www.stanfords.co.uk*, with branches in Manchester and Bristol. Within South Africa, the **Shell Road Atlas to Southern Africa,** available at all Shell service stations, is comprehensive and includes maps of major tourist areas, marking sights and some accommodation facilities, and detailed city maps. The **Automobile Association of South Africa,** www.aasa.co.za, has shops in all major cities selling national, regional and touring maps. The **Map Studio,** www.map studio.co.za, produces a wide range of maps covering much of Africa. South African bookshops such as **Exclusive Books** and **CNA** carry a full range of maps.

Accommodation price codes

Hotels and guesthouses

L	over R2000	AL	R1000-2000
A	R700-1000	B	R330-700
C	R170-330	D	R100-170
E	R70-100	F	under R70

Prices refer to the cost of a double room, not including service charge or meals unless otherwise stated. See page 29 for exchange rates.

Private game reserves

L4	over R5300	L3	R4300-5300
L2	R3300-4300	L1	R2500-3300

Prices are based on two people sharing accommodation and are inclusive of all meals, game walks and game drives.

Sleeping

South Africa offers a wide variety of accommodation from top-of-the-range game lodges and tented camps that charge R1000-6000 or more per couple per day, to mid-range safari lodges and coastal guesthouses with self-contained air-conditioned double rooms for R350-750, to dormitory beds or camping for around R100-150 a day. Generally, accommodation booked through agents in Europe will be more expensive than if you contact the hotel directly by email or book online. Make sure you keep a copy of all correspondence and reconfirm your bookings once you arrive in the country. Comprehensive accommodation information can be found on the **Where to stay** website, www.wheretostayonline.com, as well as on the regional tourism websites listed in each area.

Hotels

Every town has at least one hotel of two- or three-star standard but, where tourists are not expected, the service can be poor and dismissive. These hotels tend to be aimed at business travellers and may be characterless buildings with restaurants serving bland food. But there are lots of alternatives and there are some delightful family-run hotels, boutique hotels with stylish interiors and for those who enjoy the anonymity of a large hotel, chains such as **Holiday Inn** and **Protea**. In the main cities, hotels often remain a practical option, although note that Cape Town and Johannesburg suffer from a shortage of hotel beds, and you should always book well in advance.

Guesthouses

Guesthouses can offer some of the most characterful accommodation in South Africa, with interesting places springing up in both cities and small towns. Standards obviously vary enormously; much of what you'll get has to do with the character of the owners and the location of the homes. Some are simple practical overnight rooms, while at the more luxurious end, rooms may be in historic homes filled with antiques, and offering impeccable service. Breakfast is almost always included and, in some, evening meals can be prepared if you phone ahead. For further information contact

Lighthousing

A relatively new initiative by South Africa's National Ports Authority is the **SA Lighthouse Adventure Tour**, which since 2002 has seen more than 19,000 participants. The authority has opened up many of the country's 45 lighthouses as self-catering accommodation in what was once the light keepers' accommodation along the approximately 3700 km of South African coastline. These are found at Cape Columbine on the West Coast in the Saldanha Bay area, Danger Point near Gansbaai on the Atlantic side of Cape Agulhas, Cape St Blaize at Mossel Bay, Great Fish Point in Port Alfred and North Sand Bluff on the Hibiscus Coast near Port Edward. Owing to the success of this venture, more lighthouse venues are being investigated with the aim of converting them into self-catering accommodation in the future. Contact the central reservation office, T021-4492400, or visit the National Ports Authority website, www.npa.co.za.

the **Guest House Association of Southern Africa,** T021-7620880, www.ghasa.co.za, or the **Portfolio Collection,** T021-6894020, www.portfolio collection.com.

Bed and breakfast

B&B accommodation is hugely popular in South Africa; even the smallest town will usually have one private home that rents out rooms, and B&Bs in townships are catching on fast. Local tourist offices are the best source of information for finding B&Bs. Assuming you get on with your hosts, they can offer a valuable insight into local life. In rural areas, farmhouse B&Bs are often in beautiful settings where guests will have access to a garden and swimming pool as well as to hikes and horse riding. Increasingly, some establishments are providing TVs, air-conditioning or fans, and have separate entrances for those who want more privacy away from the owners. The breakfasts are almost always good and in large enough quantities to fill you up for the day. Full English breakfasts are usually served but it is increasingly common to have a choice of continental breakfast or even a traditional South African breakfast of boerewors, mince on toast and mealie porridge.

Backpacker hostels

Apart from camping, backpacker hostels are the cheapest form of accommodation, and a bed in a dormitory will cost as little as US$12 a night. Some also have budget double rooms with or without bathrooms, while others have space to pitch a tent in the garden.

While hostel standards can obviously vary, stiff competition means that most hostels are clean and have good facilities. You can usually expect a self-catering kitchen, hot showers, a TV/video room and internet access. Many hostels also have bars and offer meals or nightly braais, plus a garden and a swimming pool. Most hostels are a good source of travel information and many act as booking agents for bus companies, budget safari tours and car hire. On the whole, hostels are very safe and security is not a problem. Your fellow travellers remains the greatest threat, especially in dormitories in the busy city hostels. The **Baz Bus** (see page 39) caters for backpackers and links most hostels along the coast between Cape Town and Johannesburg, including Swaziland.

For information, visit **Backpacking South Africa**, www.btsa.co.za, or **Coast to Coast,** www.coastingafrica.com, which publishes a free annual backpackers' accommodation guide and is available in all the hostels.

Camping and caravan parks

Camping is the cheapest and most flexible way of seeing South Africa. Every town has a municipal campsite, many of which also have simple self-catering chalets. These vary in quality and facilities, from basic rondavels with bunks, to chalets with a couple of bedrooms and fully equipped kitchens. They can be excellent value and are often the only budget accommodation available in a town.

As camping is very popular with South Africans, sites tend to have very good facilities, although they may be fully booked months in advance, especially during the school holidays in the most popular game reserves and national parks. Even the most basic site will have a clean washblock with hot water, plus electric points and lighting. All sites have braai facilities, with charcoal, wood and firelighters available in campsite shops. Some sites also have kitchen blocks. At the most popular tourist spots, campsites are more like holiday resorts with shops, swimming pools and a restaurant – these can get very busy and are best avoided in peak season.

For most of the year, the weather is ideal for camping, although be prepared for frosts at night in some parts.

Camping equipment is widely available in South Africa and usually at lower prices than in the UK. If your time is limited, you should bring your own tent and sleeping bag, but if you're not on a tight schedule you may want to shop around once you've arrived. Lightweight tents, sleeping bags, ground mats, gas lights, stoves and cooking equipment can be bought at good prices in all the major cities.

Self-catering apartments

Self-catering apartments are particularly popular with South African holidaymakers and there is an enormous choice, especially along the coast. Prices vary with the seasons: Christmas is the most expensive time of year, but off season many resorts are virtually empty and discounts can be negotiated. If you are travelling in a group, a flat could cost as little as R100 per person per day and these are ideal for families on a budget.

National park accommodation

While the larger rest camps in Kruger have supermarkets, launderettes, post offices and banks, most camps are rather more basic. All have at least a small shop selling maps, basic food provisions and firewood. Most accommodation is self-catering, but larger camps may have restaurants. Petrol is usually available at camps and road conditions between them are usually good. Reception is usually located within the shop or office, where you can arrange guided walks and game drives. Both are highly recommended for learning about and spotting wildlife. Some parks also offer night drives where visitors have the chance of seeing unusual nocturnal animals. Most parks and reserves are under the jurisdiction of **South African National Parks** (SAN Parks), central reservations T012-4289111, www.san parks.org, which also has drop-in offices in Pretoria, T012-4289111, two offices in Cape Town, at the Clock Tower Centre and the V&A Waterfront, T021-4054500, or at the Cape Town tourist office on the corner of Burg and Castle streets T021-4264260, and at the Tourist Junction in Durban, T031-3044934. In the Western Cape, contact **Cape Nature Conservation**, T021-4260723, www.cape nature.org.za, and in KwaZulu Natal, contact **KZN Wildlife**, T033-8451000, www.kznwildlife.com.

It is quite possible to travel around South Africa and only ever stay in nature reserves and national parks.

The central reservations offices are a good source of advice and can help plan your trip in advance. In peak season, it's wise to book a month or two before you arrive. All bookings can be made over the telephone, by email or through the websites. Most international credit cards are accepted. If you are already staying in a park, the reception will often help make advance bookings for other parks.

Restaurant price codes

🍴🍴🍴 over R200
🍴🍴 R100-200
🍴 under R100

Prices refer to the cost of a two-course meal for one person including one drink and tax.

Luxury game lodges

The most famous luxury game lodges are on private game farms adjoining Kruger National Park, although there are others around the country. Their attraction is the chance to combine exclusive game viewing in prime wilderness areas, with top-class accommodation, cordon bleu meals, vintage wines and a spectacular natural setting.

The cost of staying in a luxury game lodge varies from R2000 to over R7000 per person per night. This includes all meals, drinks and game viewing trips. In order to get the most from the experience, guests tend to stay for at least two nights. The lodges are often isolated and not easily accessible by road so many reserves have their own airstrips where light aircraft can land. Charter flights save time and avoid long dusty journeys, and can be booked through the game lodge or from Johannesburg, Durban or Cape Town. ▸▸ *For details of the luxury reserves around Kruger National Park, see pages 594-603.*

Eating

Food

South African food tends to be fairly regional, although a ubiquitous love of meat unites the country. In and around Cape Town visitors will find many restaurants offering Cape Malay cuisine, a blend of sweet and spicy curries and meat dishes cooked with dried fruit. Seafood along the coast is excellent and usually very good value. KwaZulu Natal is famous for its Indian curries, especially the delicious bunny chow, served in a hollowed-out loaf of bread. Portuguese influences, thanks to neighbouring Mozambique, are strong – spicy peri-peri chicken or Mozambiquan prawns are widespread. Meat, however, is universal and South Africa offers plenty of opportunities to try an assortment of game, from popular ostrich or springbok to more acquired tastes such as crocodile or warthog. Two local meat products which travellers invariably come across are biltong and boerewors. Biltong is heavily salted and spiced sun-dried meat, usually made from beef but sometimes made from game such as ostrich, kudu or impala. Boerewors is a strongly seasoned beef sausage usually grilled on a braai. The staple diet for much of the black South African population is a stiff maize porridge known as pap, served with a stew. Pap tends to be rather bland, although the accompanying stews are often quite tasty.

Supermarkets (see page 50) tend to have a similar selection of groceries to that found in Europe. Meat is generally significantly cheaper than in Europe, but fruit and vegetables can be relatively expensive. South Africa is a great source of fresh fruit, and during the summer months you should be able to get a good range of exotic fruits from the better supermarkets (Woolworth's is always a good bet). Local produce such as apples in Ceres or pineapples along the Wild Coast will always be excellent.

Drink

South Africa is a major player in the international market and produces a wide range of excellent wines. The Winelands in the Western Cape has the best-known labels (see pages 136-165) but there are a number of other wine regions dotted around the country. South Africa also produces a range of good beer. Major names include Black Label, Castle and Amstel. Windhoek, from Namibia is also widely available and more popular than some of the South African beers. Home-brewed beer, made from sorghum or maize, is widely drunk by the African population. It has a thick head, is very potent and not very palatable to the uninitiated. Bitter is harder to come by, although a good local variety is brewed at Mitchell's Brewery in Knysna and Cape Town and can be found at outlets along the Garden Route.

No liquor may be sold on Sundays (and public holidays) except in licensed bars and restaurants. The standard shop selling alcohol is known as a bottle store, usually open Monday-Friday 0800-1800, Saturday 0830-1400 (some may stay open until 1600). Supermarkets do not sell beer or spirits, stop selling wine at 2000, and don't sell alcohol on Sundays. Note that despite drink-driving being a very serious offence, it remains a problem especially in rural areas.

Soft drinks

Tap water in South African towns is chemically treated and safe to drink. Bottled mineral water and a good range of fruit juices are available at most outlets including petrol stations – the Ceres and Liquifruit brands are the best. Another popular drink is Rooibos tea, literally red bush tea. This is a caffeine-free tea with a smoky flavour, usually served with sugar or honey. The main area producing Rooibos is around Clanwilliam by the Cederberg in the Western Cape.

Eating out

Restaurants and cafés vary widely in quality and service, depending largely on where you are. Small-town hotels tend to serve bland meals focusing on standard meat-and-two-veg dishes, while town restaurants are often part of a chain. The main cities, however, have an excellent variety of restaurants and South Africa is fast gaining a reputation as a culinary hotspot. Cape Town in particular has experienced a boom in top-class restaurants, from traditional Cape Malay cooking to cordon bleu seafood, all at incredibly good prices. Johannesburg and Pretoria also have a wide selection of smart restaurants in the more affluent suburbs. Some of the best restaurants in the country are found in the Winelands around the Western Cape, many of which are part of historic wine estates. Franschhoek has a particularly good reputation, with a number of excellent French restaurants, while the Garden Route offers fresh, good value seafood. Because of the Indian influence in KwaZulu Natal, the best curries are found in Durban and the authenticity of the dishes is better than you would expect in Europe. Meat is almost always of a high standard wherever you are, and a number of restaurants offer a variety of game such as springbok, ostrich and kudu.

Vegetarians, however, will find their choice rather limited. South Africa is a meat-loving country and menus rarely include anything but the most basic dishes for vegetarians. Away from the major cities, you'll have to make do with salads, pasta and chips. Cape Town, Pretoria and Johannesburg have a better range for vegetarians, with some trendy meat-free restaurants appearing on the scene in recent years. Self-catering is often a better option.

Eating out continues to be very good value, despite the strengthening Rand. Outside the major tourist centres, people eat early and many kitchens will close around

2100, except at the weekend. Private restaurants are often closed on Sunday evenings, when hotel dining rooms or fast food outlets may well be the only choices for eating out.

Braais

One of the first local terms you are likely to learn will be braai, which quite simply means barbecue. The braai is incredibly popular, part of the South African way of life, and every campsite, back garden and picnic spot has a braai pit. Given the excellent range of meat available, learning how to cook good food on a braai is an art that needs to be mastered quickly, especially if you are self-catering, and is part of the fun of eating in South Africa. Once you have established a core of heat using firelighters and wood or charcoal (charcoal is more eco-friendly and less smoky but wood makes for a wonderful fire), wrap up potatoes, sweet potatoes, squash, butternut, etc, in heavy-duty foil and cook them in the coals for an hour or so. Set beside a good piece of meat, with a sauce and a cold beer, and you will be living the South African dream.

To check whether your braai is the right heat to cook on, hold your hand over the braai grill and count to 10. If you have to pull your hand back before 10 it's too hot, any later than 10 then it's too cold.

Entertainment

Everyone in the cities eats out regularly, parties until late, catches a movie at the cinema, and goes to see shows or exhibitions. If you're a city person, you will love Johannesburg, Cape Town and Durban, which have all the modern entertainment options you would expect of a European city. The smaller towns and cities will have cinemas, restaurants and bars, sometimes bowling alleys and increasingly casinos, and these are often grouped together in one of the shopping malls. The word 'shoppertainment' is being coined to describe these malls where everything is under one roof. In the very small towns nightlife is restricted to a few hotel bars which only really get going at weekends and on the major holidays. On these evenings you'll mingle with beer-bellied farmers in their trademark khaki shorts and shirts and vellies (leather boots) speaking in English and Afrikaans.

Bars and clubs

South Africans go out a lot and, as usual, Saturday night is the big one, though unusually Wednesday follows a close second. As with anywhere, clubs and bars go in and out of fashion regularly, but their popularity is also affected by season. A nice homely pub with perhaps a crackling fire maybe popular in winter, but during summer a bar with an outside wooden deck with great views of the sunset or ocean will be the in place for bright young things. Most bars double up as restaurants and many have large- screen TVs, which are full to the brim if there is an especially important rugby or football match on.

'Jol' is a slang word derived from the Cape dialect, which can refer to anything from a nice picnic to an all-night rave.

Cinema

Every modern shopping mall has a cinema complex with several screens and a food court for popcorn and soft drinks. The malls open early and there are screenings throughout the day until late at night. Movie tickets are comparatively cheap, about R35, and one day a week tickets will be half price (usually Tuesdays). Hollywood movies are shown, but in the more Asian areas such as Durban, there are also Bollywood films. The main cinema chains are **Ster-Kinekor**, www.sterkinekor.com, **Nu Metro,** www.numetro.co.za, and **Cinema Nouveau**, also found at www.sterkin ekor.com. The latter tends to show less mainstream films and concentrates on grittier releases and foreign films. It also runs occasional film festivals. All schedules are on the websites and you can book tickets online. There are three IMAX movie theatres in South Africa, www.imax.com, with giant screens and digital sound, showing mostly wildlife or scenic movies, but occasionally the likes of the Matrix. These are in the Waterfront in Cape Town, Menlyn Park Shopping Mall in Pretoria and the Gateway Mall in Durban.

Theatre and the arts

All the cities have theatres, comedy clubs, art galleries and various performance venues offering everything from indigenous drama, music, dance, cabaret and satire to imported West End and Broadway hits, classical opera, and ballet. Johannesburg has a wealth of venues, and the newly rejuvenated Newtown area with the Market Theatre, Newtown Music Centre and Kippies Jazz Club is well worth a visit now the area has been made safe for visitors. In Cape Town the Spier Wine Estate makes a great outdoor venue, as does the Kirstenbosch Botanical Gardens, both of which hold a series of concerts over the summer. The annual National Festival of the Arts in Grahamstown, which in its 27 years has showcased the cream of the country's emerging talent and creativity in both the performing and graphic arts, has spawned a variety of smaller festivals all over the country, each with its very particular personality (see below). After years of isolation, South Africa has finally made it onto the world tour circuit of many international pop stars who pack out stadiums in Cape Town, Durban, Johannesburg and Pretoria. Check local press to find out what's on, or visit one of the Computicket, www.computicket.co.za, offices which are found in shopping malls.

Festivals and events

Festival calendar

January

Cape Town Carnival, Bo-Kaap district of Cape Town. A New Year's parade staged by the Cape coloured community in the Bo-Kaap district of Cape Town. There is a float procession, minstrel bands and dancers, culminating with a huge competition and carnival held in Green Point Stadium.

February

FNB Dance Umbrella, Johannesburg, www.at.artslink.co.za. A festival of contemporary choreography and dance from community-based dance troupes to international companies.

Prickly Pear Festival, Uitenhage, Eastern Cape, www.nmbt.co.za. A day of traditional food such as ginger beer, pancakes, potjiekos, homemade jam, a spit braai and fish braai, bunny chow and homemade puddings.

March

Cape Town Jazz Festival, Cape Town, www.capetownjazzfest.com. 2-day festival featuring some 40 international and African acts performing on 5 stages to an audience of 15,000.

Lambert's Bay Kreeffees, Lambert's Bay, West Coast, www.kreeffeeslambertsbaai.co.za. Crayfish festival and rock concerts by some of South Africa's best musicians, bungee jumping, aerial displays, a half-marathon, beer tents.

Sasol Scifest, Grahamstown, Eastern Cape, www.scifest.org.za. The 7-day festival features 600 events: game drives, laser shows, robotics competitions, science olympics and a film festival. Attendance now exceeds 35,000 visitors a year.

April

Splashy Fen, Underberg, KwaZulu Natal, www.splashyfen.co.za. A musical gathering on a farm close to Underberg. This is a mix of popular sounds and jazz bands from all walks of life, akin to the summer festivals held in Europe, with camping and fringe activities.

May

Pink Loerie Mardi Gras, Knysna and Cape Town, www.pinkloerie.com. A gay festival with parade and four days of non-stop entertainment for anyone who enjoys a party.

Prince Albert Olive, Food & Wine Festival, Prince Albert, Western Cape, www.pa tourism.co.za. 2-day festival with an art exhibition, beer tents, live music, wine and olive tastings, a cycle race, an olive pip-spitting competition, and live entertainment.

June

National Arts Festival, Grahamstown, Eastern Cape, www.nafest.co.za. South Africa's oldest, biggest and best-known arts festival. A 10-day event with hundreds of performances of theatre, music, song, dance and film. If there's one South African festival you have to attend, this is it.

July

Knysna Oyster Festival, Knysna, Western Cape, www.oysterfestival.co.za. Oyster braais, oyster tasting, oyster-eating competitions and other molluscular activities; there's live entertainment and lots of sporting events - cycling, running, canoeing, downhill racing and sailing.

August

Joy of Jazz, Johannesburg, www.joyof jazz.co.za. Jo'burg's biggest annual jazz festival with over 200 local and international performers at different venues across the city, particularly in Newtown.

Oppikoppi Bushveld Festival, Northam, North West, www.oppikoppi.co.za. Popular rock festival that has helped establish many South African musicians' careers. This is real bushveld: hot, dry and covered in red dust and thorn trees. Expect to shower a lot when you get home. (Oppikoppi also hosts an Easter Festival in Mar.)

September

Arts Alive, Johannesburg, www.artsalive.co.za. 4-day festival with over 600 performers in dance, visual art, poetry and music at venues in the Jo'burg inner city area; the main concert is held at the Johannesburg Stadium.

Awesome Africa Music Festival, Durban, www.awesomeafricafestival.co.za. 3 stages of non-stop music in Durban's Albert Park, with over 200 artists from more than 20 countries. The focus is on collaboration with musicians from Africa and beyond.

Hermanus Whale Festival, Hermanus, Western Cape, www.whalefestival.co.za. An entertainment-packed festival, with the best land-based whale watching in the world.

Macufe, Bloemfontein, Free State, www.pacofs.co.za. 10-day African cultural festival, featuring jazz, gospel, kwaito, hip-hop, R&B, rock and classical music, as well as dance, drama, musical theatre, poetry, fine art and traditional arts and crafts. Attracts a staggering 140,000 people.

Southern Cross Music Festival, Mooi River, KwaZulu Natal, www.southerncross music.co.za. 3-day event on the banks of the Mooi River: music, fishing, swimming, whitewater rafting, abseiling, mountain biking and 4WD courses. The farm caters for 6000 festival-goers.

Woodstock, Hartbeespoort Dam, North West, www.woodstock.co.za. 4-day youth-oriented music and lifestyle festival, with bands and a market of crafters and alternative lifestyle products.

December

Rustler's Valley, Fouriesburg, Free State, www.rustlers.co.za. South Africa's original music festival venue, Rustlers hosts some of its best trance/dance/drumming festivals in late Nov and Dec, including a New Year celebration – as well as the Spring Equinox Celebration in Sep.

Spier Summer Festival, Stellenbosch, www.spierarts.co.za. At the amphitheatre on the Spier Estate, four months of music, opera, dance, stand-up comedy and theatre from Dec to Mar.

Public holidays

When a public holiday falls on a Sun, the following Mon becomes a holiday. Most business will close but large supermarkets in city centres remain open.

New Year's Day, 1 Jan
Human Rights' Day, 21 Mar
Good Friday, Fri before Easter Sun
Family Day, Mon following Easter Sun
Freedom Day, 27 Apr
Workers' Day, 1 May
Youth Day, 16 Jun
National Women's Day, 9 Aug
Heritage Day, 24 Sep
Day of Reconciliation, 16 Dec
Christmas Day, 25 Dec
Day of Goodwill, 26 Dec

School holidays

Mid-Dec to mid-Jan; mid-Apr to early May; early Aug to early Sep. The website www.routes.co.za has exact dates for South African school holidays. While seemingly trivial, they can have a significant bearing on your visit. Not only are prices of accommodation often higher, but most of the popular destinations become fully booked.

Shopping

African art and **curios** are of widely varying quality but and be surprisingly expensive as many are imported from other African countries. With the current popularity of traditional African art, there is a multitude of shops in all the major cities and tourist spots, although markets ten to be better value and you can generally bring prices down with a bit of good-humoured bartering. Sculptures, baskets, ceramics and beadwork sold at the roadside can be extremely good value and make excellent souvenirs. In the major cities, wirework sculptures and keyrings are sold at junctions and make good presents, with the added bonus of being light to carry home.

Animal products made from ivory and reptile skins are on sale in some areas but if you take them back home you could well fall foul of CITES regulations (see page 35). A more popular and safe animal product is (empty) ostrich egg shells, which you can find in most curio shops. **Jewellery** and **clothes** are also good buys, with a number of local designers making it big both at home and abroad. Traditional African jewellery can be bought in most curio shops – bigger shops will stock interesting pieces from across Africa. Johannesburg, with its enormous shopping malls, is one of the best places to seek out designer bargains, as well as slightly cheaper versions of international brands, such as Levi's, Nike, Guess or Quiksilver.

The principal **supermarket** chains are Pick 'n' Pay, Woolworths, Shoprite, Checkers, Hyperama and OK Bazaars; larger branches are often open on Sunday 0900-1300. The **Gateway Shopping Mall**, just outside Durban, is the largest mall in the southern hemisphere and well worth a visit. For information on VAT refunds, see page 27.

Sport and activities

South Africa offers a huge range of adrenaline sports, from kitesurfing and kloofing to sandboarding or skydiving. Details of local operators are given in the Activities and tours sections of each chapter.

The free fall from the Bloukrans bungee jump lasts seven seconds, during which the jumper travels downwards at over 170 kph. The first rebound bounce is higher than the full 111 m descent at Victoria Falls.

Hiking in the bush

As experienced walkers will know, good preparation is the key to a successful and enjoyable hike. It is also important to remember that, however short or easy a walk may appear to be, walking in the bush is not like going for a stroll in the park – a few basic steps should be followed. Below is a short checklist of equipment and guidelines for hiking in the bush:

Day hikes Good walking boots or shoes; sunhat; minimum of 2 litres of water per person; first aid kit; penknife; trail snacks (peanuts, biltong, dried fruit); binoculars, camera and birdbook/gamebook; toilet paper; matches to burn paper.

Additional overnight gear Sleeping bag; fleece or equivalent top (even in summer); torch; lightweight camping stove (it is not always permitted to collect firewood); matches/lighter/firelighters; dehydrated food (pasta, instant soups etc.).

➔ Don't leave litter or throw away cigarette butts.

➔ Leave everything as you find it; don't pick plants or remove fossils or rocks.

➔ Stick to marked trails especially in the bush – it's easy to lose your way.

➔ Camp away from waterholes so as not to frighten game away.

➔ Never feed the animals.

➔ Remember , in the southern hemisphere the sun goes via the north not the south.

Birdwatching

With over 700 species of bird recorded in South Africa, birdwatching has become a popular pastime that is easily combined with game viewing. The country's incredibly diverse ecosystems, ranging from fynbos and semi-desert to rainforest, support a fascinating variety of birds, including rare species that are endemic to South Africa. For further information contact **Southern African Birding**, T031-2665948, www.sabirding.co.za. Birdwatching tours are offered by **Bird-Watch Cape,** T021-7625059, www.birdwatch.co.za, and **Safariwise,** T057-3882811, www.birdwatching.co.za.

Bungee jumping

The most popular location in the country is at the **Bloukrans River Bridge** between Plettenberg Bay and Tsitsikamma (see page 269). This also claims to be the highest jump in the world, with a drop of just over 200 m. Another popular jump is the 60-m leap from the **Gouritz River Bridge** on the Cape Town side of Mossel Bay (see page 243). **Face Adrenaline,** T042-2811255, www.faceadrenalin.com, operates both jumps.

Golf

South Africa has some excellent facilities and stunning golf courses, such as the championship course at **Milnerton** in Cape Town, the **Fancourt Country Club** in George, which was host to the 2004 President's Cup, or **Houghton** in Johannesburg, venue for the SA Open. Check out the **South African Golf Association** website, www.saga.co.za, or visit www.golfinginsouthafrica.co.za.

Hiking

South Africa has an enormous number of well-developed hiking trails, many passing through spectacular areas of natural beauty. These range from pleasant afternoon strolls through nature reserves to challenging hikes in wilderness areas. Hiking in South Africa does involve some forward planning and permits, but the rewards and the choice of trails are well worth the effort.

Hiking opportunities begin in Cape Town on **Table Mountain** and the coastal trails around **Cape Point**, with a number of longer trails along the **Garden Route**. Inland, the **Cederberg** is an excellent and isolated hiking area, but the most popular and best-known region is the **uKhahlamba-Drakensberg National Park** (see page 440), bordering Lesotho. This is a national park nearly 300 km long where a network of trails (some climbing to over 3000 m) offers hikers a vast mountain region with possibilities comparable to regions of the Himalayas.

For further information on trails and permits, contact the following organizations: **Cape Nature Conservation**, T021-4260723, www.capenature.org.za, **KZN Wildlife**, T033-8451000, www.kznwildlife.com, **South African National Parks (SAN Parks)**, T012-4289111, www.sanparks.org, or visit www.hiking-south-africa.info.

Horse riding

Horse riding is a popular activity amongst farming communities and in mountainous areas. The **Drakensberg** is a good place to try it, where hotels can organize anything from a short morning trot to a six-day mountain safari. Longer treks are very popular in **Lesotho**, where ponies are the main form of transport in rural areas. Western-style riding in the **Maluti Mountains** is organized by **Bokpoort Farm** outside Clarens in the Free State. On the **Garden Route** you can ride in the ancient forests close to Knysna and on the beaches in the Western Cape. For more information on specialist horse safari operators, contact the **African Horse Safari Association** (AHSA), www.africanhorse.com.

Mountain biking

Many nature reserves and wilderness areas have increased their accessibility for mountain bikes, with some excellent routes suitable for all levels of fitness. Some of the best organized regions include **De Hoop Nature Reserve** in the Overberg; the **Tulbagh Valley**, **Kamiesberg** in Namaqualand, **Goegap Nature Reserve** outside Springbok, and the mountains around **Citrusdal**. Check out **Mountain Bike South Africa**, www.mtbsa.co.za, for information on trails and events. Cape Town is also well equipped for mountain bikers; contact **Downhill Adventures**, T021-4220388, www.downhilladventures.com, who offer a number of day trips and rent out bikes.

Paragliding

South Africa has several world-renowned paragliding locations; leaping from **Lions Head** in Cape Town or floating above the **Kalahari** are two of the most popular options. Cape Town aside, most of the action is around **Kuruman** in the Northern Cape and **Barberton** in Mpumalanga. Climatic conditions in South Africa are ideal – good thermal activity allows gliders to climb between 6 and 8 m a second and the cloud base is usually at 5000 m. The best season is between November and February. For a full list of clubs offering courses and tandem glides, visit the website of the **South African Paragliding and Hang-gliding Association**, www.paragliding.co.za.

Safaris

No visit to South Africa is complete without at least one visit to a major game reserve. The best parks for seeing animals are **Kruger**, **Pilanesberg**, **Itala**, **Addo**, **Hluhluwe-Imfolozi** and **Kgalagadi Transfrontier**. The game reserves here are not as crowded as the East African game parks and offer visitors the chance of seeing splendid African landscapes and wildlife including the Big Five: elephant, buffalo, rhinoceros, lion and leopard. The optimum times to go viewing are early in the morning and late in the afternoon. The best season is during the winter months, from July to September, when dry weather forces animals to congregate around waterholes, and vegetation is lower and less dense, making it easier to spot wildlife. Summer weather, from November to January when rainfall is at its highest,

Game viewing rules and regulations

Keep on the well-marked roads and track; off-road driving is harmful because smoke, oil and destruction of the grass layer cause soil erosion. Do not drive through closed roads or park areas. It is mandatory to enter and exit the parks through the authorized gates. For your own safety, stay in your vehicle at all times. Your vehicle serves as a blind or hide since animals will not usually identify it with humans. In all the parks that are visited by car, it is forbidden to leave the vehicle except in designated places, such as picnic sites or walking trails. Stick to the parks' opening hours; it is usually forbidden to drive from dusk to dawn unless you are granted a special authorization. At night you are requested to stay at your lodge or campsite. Never harass the animals. Make as little noise as possible; do not flash lights or make sudden movements to scare them away; never try and attract the animals' attention by calling out or whistling. Never chase the animals and always give way to them, they always have right of way. Do not feed the animals; the food you provide might make them ill. Once animals such as elephants learn that food is available from humans they can become aggressive and dangerous when looking for more and will eventually have to be shot. If camping at night in the parks, ensure that the animals cannot gain access to any food you are carrying. Do not drop any litter, used matches and cigarette butts; this not only increases fire risk in the dry season, but also some animals will eat whatever they find. Do not disturb other visitors: they have the same right as you to enjoy nature. If you discover a stopped vehicle and want to check what they are looking at, never hinder their sight or stop within their photographic field. If there is no room for another car, wait patiently for your turn, the others will eventually leave and the animals will still be there. If there is a group of vehicles, drivers should take it in turns to occupy the prime viewing spot. Always turn the engine off when you are watching game at close range. Do not drive too fast; the speed limit is usually 40 kph. Speeding damages road surfaces, makes more noise and increase the risk of running over animals. Wild animals are dangerous; despite their beauty their reactions are unpredictable. Don't expose yourself to unnecessary risks; excessive confidence can lead to serious accidents.

also has its advantages as animals will be in good condition after feeding on the new shoots, and there are chances of seeing breeding displays and young animals. The landscape is green and lush, although the thick vegetation and the wide availability of water means that wildlife is far more widespread and difficult to spot. South Africa's wildlife parks are well-organized with good facilities for game viewing, including well- surfaced roads and hides overlooking waterholes. There are numerous safari companies operating out of Johannesburg, Durban and Cape Town, which can arrange accommodation and game viewing trips as part of a tour. The cost varies, with companies offering everything from bargain backpacker tours to expensive luxury safaris. Organized tours can often provide more game viewing opportunities – quite simply because a group means there are more pairs of eyes on the lookout. Experienced guides will also be adept at spotting well-camouflaged animals. Most of the national parks and hane reserves are

Buy a good pair of binoculars before you reach South Africa as they are imported here and tend to be quite expensive.

under the jurisdiction of the following organizations; **South African National Parks** (SAN Parks), T012-4289111, www.sanparks.org; **Cape Nature Conservation,** T021-4260723, www.capenature.org.za, and **KZN Wildlife,** T033- 8451000, www.kznwildlife.com. If you are travelling independently and planning to visit a number of parks that come under the jurisdiction of SAN Parks during your visit to South Africa, then it might be well worth in investing in a Wildcard, or the newly launched Wild Visitors Card, aimed at international visitors. You pay a set fee that lasts for a year, and in the case of the Wild Visitors Card, a set number of days, say seven or 21 days, which covers all entry fees into the national parks. There is a variety of cards on offer for specific regions or families, and these represent great savings, especially if you are spending a considerable amount of time in the parks. Work out the costs before you buy however, by studying your itinerary and assessing the costs of individual entry fees and comparing with the price of the card. All the details are on the SAN Parks website and the Wildcard website www.wildinafrica.com. » *For details and photographs of South African wildlife, see the central colour section.*

The occasional traffic jam at Kruger is the worst that most visitors experience of over-crowding in the parks.

Scuba diving

The convergence of two major ocean environments provides the South African coast with a particularly rich and diverse marine flora and fauna. The Agulhas current continually sweeps warm water down from the subtropical Indian Ocean and meets the cold nutrient-rich waters of the Atlantic. This mixing of water temperatures has created a marvellous selection of marine ecosystems, ranging from the tropical coral reefs of KwaZulu Natal to the temperate kelp forests around Cape Point. The best time of year to dive the east and southern coast is during the South African winter from April to October when the prevailing wind is from the west. Visibility is generally better and the waters calmer. Summertime, October to March, is when you can brave the icy waters of the Atlantic for some incredible wreck and kelp dives – visibility often exceeds 20 m. If you want to get away from the crowds avoid South African holidays whenever possible. Dive schools are listed in the relevant chapters.

In KwaZulu Natal **Sodwana Bay**, just south of the Mozambique border, is something of a mecca for South African divers due to its warm, clear waters, tropical reefs and rare but magical whalesharks. There are common sightings of turtles, reef sharks and stingrays, along with a huge variety of hard and soft corals and colourful reef fish. **Aliwal Shoal**, 5 km offshore, south of Umkomaas, is famous for its ragged tooth shark season, while **Protea Banks**, 8 km off Shelly Beach, is for experienced divers only and known for its hammerheads. In the Eastern Cape, despite low visibility, the sites around **Port Elizabeth** are magnificent and boast coral colours more vivid than tropical waters. It is not unusual to see huge pods of dolphins, African penguins and southern right whales in the bay. Along the Garden Route the **Underwater Trail** at Storms River Mouth camp, Tsitsikamma National Park, is reasonably protected and there are a number of wreck and lagoon dives around **Knysna**. The area is notorious area for great white sharks and dive briefings include rules for reducing the risk of inviting their attention. **Plettenberg Bay** is popular for its soft coral reefs and sheltered location. Home to dolphins and seals, the bay also acts as a nursery to the endangered southern right whales, which come to calve in winter and spring (July-December). From Cape Town, kelp diving is very popular: the sealife is prolific and the sighting of playful and inquisitive seals and shy sharks (dogfish) common. If the Cape waters are too cold, you can dive in the tanks at the aquarium, at the **V&A Waterfront**. The tank is surprisingly large, with inquisitive ragged tooth sharks, stingrays, turtles and large predator fish.

South Africa is a good place to take an Open Water (beginner) course from PADI or NAUI.

Great white shark cage diving

Dyer Island is located 10 km off Gansbaai on Walker Bay. Populated by seals, penguins, large gamefish and birds, the area is a natural hunting ground for the protected great white sharks. Shark cage diving raises many questions about teaching sharks to associate humans with food but, for many, cage diving is a chance to witness this magnificent animal in its natural habitat safely. For non divers there is the opportunity to snorkel at the top of the cage. » *For operators, see Gansbaai, page 235.*

Surfing

South Africa has quickly established itself as a major surfing hotspot and has some of the best waves in the world. There are, however, two drawbacks to surfing in South Africa. Firstly, the water is cold, especially around the Cape, and full-length wetsuits are generally essential. Second, there is a small risk of shark attack – but remember that attacks on surfers are very rare. Wherever you surf, be sure to listen to local advice, vital not just for safety but also for learning about the best surf spots.

Jeffrey's Bay on the south coast of the Eastern Cape is undoubtedly South Africa's surfing mecca, known for its consistently good surf and host to the annual Billabong surf championships in July. This is also a good place to learn to surf, with a number of courses available and areas of reliable, small breaks which are perfect for beginners. The whole southern coast is in fact dotted with good breaks, particularly around **Port Elizabeth** and **East London**. **Cape Town**, too, has an ever-expanding surfing community with some excellent, reliable breaks on the Atlantic and False Bay beaches. Surfing in the Indian Ocean at Durban and the KwaZulu Natal beaches is a far warmer experience than the cool oceans of the Cape, though it's only permitted at designated areas due to the unpredictable currents. The **Golden Mile** on Durban's beachfront has good surf, well-protected by lifeguards and the presence of shark nets. Floodlit night surfing is sometimes arranged in Durban, which is equally entertaining for spectators. The many backpackers hostels around the country are geared up for board rental, escorted surfaris and surfing lessons, and there are dedicated surf schools in Jeffrey's Bay, Durban and Cape Town. For more information visit www.wavescape.co.za, which has everything you need to know about surfing in South Africa including SMS numbers to get the low-down on local wave action. Spike, who runs the website, is also the author of the book *Where to Surf in South Africa*. Also check out Footprint's *Surfing the World* guide.

Whale watching

The **Whale Coast**, along Walker Bay near Cape Town, trumpets itself as the world's best land-based whale watching spot, and with good reason. Between July and November southern right and humpback whales congregate in impressive numbers in the bay to calve. Whales can also be seen in the sheltered bays from **Elands Bay** on the west coast all the way round to **Mossel Bay** and even **Ttsitsikamma** on the south coast. Contact the **Greater Hermanus Tourism Bureau**, T021-3122629, www.hermanus.co.za, for more details. Boat-based whale watching is also popular from points along the **KwaZulu Natal** coast, particularly from June to October, when southern right, mink and humpback whales travel from Mozambique to their breeding grounds at the Cape. Visit www.whaleroute.com for information about whales' migration routes throughout the world and explanations of breaching, blowing, lobtailing and spy hopping.

Whitewater rafting

There are several excellent rapids in South Africa: the **Umzimkulu River** in KwaZulu Natal; the **Gariep (Orange) River** by the Augrabies Falls or near Kimberley in the Northern Cape; the **Great Usutu River** in Swaziland and the **Sabie, Olifants** and **Blyde** rivers in Mpumalanga. Details of operators are listed in the relevant chapters.

Wild flowers

Between mid-August and mid-September the fynbos areas of the **West Coast** and the semi-desert of **Namaqualand** explode into blossom as wild flowers bloom after the first rains. This is one of the great natural sights in the country and well worth a detour. **Springbok** has developed much of its tourist industry around the flowers and the area gets very busy during the season. The protea is South Africa's national flower.

Wine tasting

The **Winelands**, near Cape Town, is South Africa's oldest and most beautiful wine-producing area and the most popular tourist destination in the province after Cape Town itself. There are several wine routes criss-crossing the valleys, visiting hundreds of wine estates, which open their doors for tastings, cellar tours and sales. There are also an increasing number of wine routes around the country, such as along the **Gariep (Orange) River**. For details of all the routes, visit www.wine.co.za.

Spectator sports

South Africans love watching sport, although racial divisions continue to play a part in who watches what. **Cricket** and **rugby** are largely the preserve of white South Africans, while **soccer** is hugely popular among the black population. Facilities are excellent, with first-class stadiums in all the major cities, and new ones being planned for the forthcoming 2010 Fifa World Cup. The national soccer team is known as **Bafana Bafana** (roughly meaning 'our boys'). The female side, **Banyana Banyana** ('our girls') is one of the most successful women's soccer teams in the world.

South Africa hosted the rugby World Cup in 1995. The national team, the **Springboks**, won the tournament and were memorably presented with the trophy by then-president Nelson Mandela, wearing a Springboks' jersey – traditionally regarded as a 'whites-only' piece of clothing. South Africa also hosted the cricket World Cup in 2003 and, most recently, was awarded the football World Cup for 2010 – the country will be the first African nation to host the event.

Health

Before you go

Ideally, you should see your GP/practice nurse or travel clinic at least six weeks before your departure for general advice on travel risks, malaria and recommended vaccinations. Your local pharmacist can also be a good source of readily accessible advice. Make sure you have travel insurance, get a dental check (especially if you are going to be away for more than a month), know your own blood group and if you suffer a long-term condition such as diabetes or epilepsy make sure someone knows or that you have a Medic Alert bracelet/necklace with this information on it.

Recommended vaccinations

The following vaccinations are commonly recommended for diphtheria; tetanus; poliomyelitis; hepatitis A. Vaccines sometimes advised: tuberculosis; hepatitis B; rabies; cholera; typhoid. Yellow fever certificate required if over 1 year old and entering from an infected area. The final decision, however, should be based on a consultation with your GP or travel clinic. See the www.fitfortravel.scots.nhs.us website for further details.

A-Z of health risks

AIDS

Southern Africa has one of the highest rates of HIV and AIDS in the world. Efforts to stem the rate of infection have had limited success, as many of the factors that need addressing such as social change, poverty and gender inequalities are long-term proesses. Visitors should be aware of the dangers of infection from unprotected sex and always use a condom. Do not inject non-prescribed drugs or share needles. Avoid having a tattoo or piercing, electrolysis or acupuncture unless you're sure the equipment is sterile. If you have to have medical treatment, ensure any equipment used is taken from a sealed pack or is freshly sterilized. It may even be worth taking your own sterlized needles as part of a first-aid kit. If you have to have a blood transfusion, ask for screened blood.

Altitude sickness

Acute mountain sickness can strike from about 3000 m upwards and in general is more likely to affect those who ascend rapidly (for example by plane) and those who over-exert themselves. Acute mountain sickness takes a few hours or days to come on and presents with heachache, lassitude, dizziness, loss of appetite, nausea and vomiting. Insomnia is common and often associated with a suffocating feeling when lying down in bed. You may notice that your breathing tends to wax and wane at night and your face is puffy in the mornings - this is all part of the syndrome. If the symptoms are mild, the treatment is rest and painkillers (preferably not aspirin-based) for the headaches. Should the symptoms be severe and prolonged it is best to descend to a lower altitude immediately and reascend, if necessary, slowly and in stages. The symptoms disappear very quickly - even after a few hundred metres of descent.

The best way of preventing acute mountain sickness is a relatively slow ascent. When trekking to high altitude, some time spent walking at medium altitude, getting fit and acclimatising is beneficial. When flying to places over 3000 m a few hours' rest and the avoidance of alcohol, cigarettes and heavy food will go a long way towards preventing acute mountain sickness.

Bites and stings

This is a very rare event indeed for travellers, but if you are unlucky (or careless) enough to be bitten by a venomous snake, spider, scorpion or sea creature, try to identify the culprit, without putting yourself in further danger (do not try to catch a live snake).

Snake bites in particular are very frightening, but in fact rarely poisonous - even venomous snakes bite without injecting venom. Victims should be taken to a hospital or a doctor without delay. It is not advised for travellers to carry snake bite antivenom as it can do more harm than good in inexperienced hands. Reassure and comfort the victim frequently. Immobilize the limb with a bandage or a splint and get the patient to lie still. Do not slash the bite area and try to suck out the poison. This also does more harm than good. You should apply a tourniquet in these circumstances, but only if you know how to. Do not attempt this if you are not experienced.

Certain tropical fish inject venom into bathers' feet when trodden on, which can be exceptionally painful. Wear plastic shoes if such creatures are reported. The pain can be relieved by immersing the foot in hot water (as hot as you can bear) for as long as the pain persists.

Dengue fever

This is a viral disease spread by mosquitoes that tend to bite during the day. The symptoms are fever and often intense joint pains, also some people develop a rash. Symptoms last about a week but it can take a few weeks to recover fully. Dengue can be difficult to distinguish from malaria as both diseases tend to occur in the same countries. There are no effective vaccines or antiviral drugs though, fortunately, travellers rarely develop the more severe forms of the disease (these can prove fatal). Rest, plenty of fluids and paracetamol (not aspirin) is the recommended treatment

Diarrhoea and intestinal upset

Diarrhoea can refer either to loose stools or an increased frequency of bowel movement, both of which can be a nuisance. Symptoms should be relatively short-lived but if they persist beyond two weeks specialist medical attention should be sought. Also seek medical help if there is blood in the stools and/or fever.

Adults can use an antidiarrhoeal medication such as loperamide to control the symptoms but only for up to 24 hours. In addition keep well hydrated by drinking plenty of fluids and eat bland foods. Oral rehydration sachets taken after each loose stool are a useful way to keep well hydrated. These should always be used when treating children and the elderly.

Bacterial traveller's diarrhoea is the most common form. Ciproxin (Ciprofloxacin) is a useful antibiotic and can be obtained by private prescription in the UK. You need to take one 500 mg tablet when the diarrhoea starts. If there are so signs of improvement after 24 hours the diarrhoea is likely to be viral and not bacterial. If it is due to other organisms such as those causing giardia or amoebic dysentery, different antibiotics will be required.

The standard advice to prevent problems is to be careful with water and ice for drinking. Ask yourself where the water came from. If you have any doubts then boil it or filter and treat it. There are many filter/treatment devices now available on the market. Food can also transmit disease. Be wary of salads (what were they washed in, who handled them), re-heated foods or food that has been left out in the sun having been cooked earlier in the day. There is a simple adage that says wash it, peel it, boil it or forget it. Also be wary of unpasteurized dairy products as these can transmit a range of diseases.

Hepatitis

Hepatitis means inflammation of the liver. Viral causes of the disease can be acquired anywhere in the world. The most obvious symptom is a yellowing of your skin or the whites of your eyes. However, prior to this all that you may notice is itching and tiredness. Pre-travel hepatitis A vaccine is the best bet. Hepatitis B (for which there is a vaccine) is spread through blood and unprotected sexual intercourse, both of which can be avoided.

Malaria

Malaria can cause death within 24 hours and can start as something just resembling an attack of flu. You may feel tired, lethargic, headachy, feverish; or more seriously, develop fits, followed by coma and then death. Have a low index of suspicion because it is very easy to write off vague symptoms, which may actually be malaria. If you have a temperature, visit a doctor as soon as you can and ask for a malaria test. On your return home, if you suffer any of these symptoms, have a test as soon as possible. Even if a previous test proved negative, this could save your life.

Treatment is with drugs and may be oral or into a vein depending on the seriousness of the infection. Remember ABCD: Awareness (of whether the disease is present in the area you are travelling in), Bite avoidance, Chemoprohylaxis, Diagnosis.

To prevent mosquito bites wear clothes that cover arms and legs, use effective insect repellents in areas with known risks of insect-spread disease and use a mosquito net treated with an insecticide. Repellents containing 30-50% DEET (Di-ethyltoluamide) are recommended when visiting malaria endemic areas; lemon eucalyptus (Mosiguard) is a reasonable alternative. The key advice is to guard against contracting malaria by taking the correct anti-malarials and finishing the recommended course. If you are popular target for insect bites or develop lumps quite soon after being bitten use antihistamine tablets and apply a cream such as hydrocortisone. Remember that it is risky to buy medicine, and in particular anti-malarials, in some developing countries. These may be sub-standard or part of a trade in counterfeit drugs.

There is a substantial malaria risk in the east of the country, for a map of malaria regions in South Africa – see http://www.sa-venues.com/malaria-risk-areas.htm

Rabies

Rabies is endemic throughout certain parts of the world so be aware of the dangers of the bite from any animal. Rabies vaccination before travel can be considered but if bitten always seek urgent medical attention – whether or not you have been previously vaccinated – after first cleaning the wound and treating with an iodine base disinfectant or alcohol.

Sun

Take good heed of advice regarding protecting yourself against the sun. Overexposure can lead to sunburn and, in the longer term, skin cancers and premature skin aging. The best advice is simply to avoid exposure to the sun by covering exposed skin, wearing a hat and staying out of the sun if possible, particularly between late morning and early afternoon. Apply a high factor sunscreen (greater than SPF15) and also make sure it screens against UVB. A further danger in tropical climates is heat exhaustion or more seriously heatstroke. This can be avoided by good hydration, which means drinking water past the point of simply quenching thirst. Also when first exposed to tropical heat take time to acclimatize by avoiding strenuous activity in the middle of the day. If you cannot avoid heavy exercise it is also a good idea to increase salt intake.

Tuberculosis

Tuberculosis is most commonly transmitted via droplet infection. Ensure that you have been immunized, especially those mixing closely with the local population and those at occupational risk, e.g. health care workers. Check with your doctor or nurse.

Underwater health

If you plan to dive make sure that you are fit do so. The **British Sub-Aqua Club** (BSAC), Telford's Quay, South Pier Road, Ellesmere Port, Cheshire CH65 4FL, UK, T01513-506200, www.bsac.com, can put you in touch with doctors who will carry out medical examinations. Check that any dive company you use are reputable and have appropriate certification from BSAC or **Professional Association of Diving Instructors** (PADI), Unit 7, St Philips Central, Albert Rd, St Philips, Bristol, BS2 0TD, T0117-3007234, www.padi.com.

Water

There are a number of ways of purifying water. Dirty water should first be strained through a filter bag and then boiled or treated. Bring water to a rolling boil for several minutes. There are sterilising methods that can be used and products generally contain chlorine (eg Puritabs) or iodine (eg Pota Aqua) compounds. There are a number of water sterilizers now on the market available in personal and expedition size. Make sure you take the spare parts or spare chemicals with you and do not believe everything the manufacturers say.

Other diseases and risks

There are a range of other insect borne diseases that are quite rare in travellers, but worth finding out about if going to particular destinations. Examples are sleeping sickness, river blindness and leishmaniasis. Fresh water can also be a source of diseases such as bilharzia and leptospirosis and it is worth investigating if these are a danger before bathing in lakes and streams. Also take heed of advice regarding protecting yourself against the sun (see above) and remember that unprotected sex always carries a risk and extra care is required when visiting some parts of the world.

Further information

Websites

Foreign and Commonwealth Office (FCO) (UK), www.fco.gov.uk
The National Travel Health Network and Centre (NaTHNaC) www.nathnac.org/
World Health Organisation, www.who.int
Fit for Travel (UK), www.fitfortravel.scot.nhs.uk This site from Scotland provides a quick A-Z of vaccine and travel health advice requirements for each country.

Books

Dawood R, editor, *Travellers' health* (3rd edition, Oxford University Press, 2002).
Warrell, D and **Anderson, S**, editors, *Expedition Medicine* (ISBN 1 86197 040-4, Royal Geographic Society).

Keeping in touch

Communications

Internet

South Africa is well served by the internet and most companies, hotels, tourist offices, guesthouses and individuals have email addresses and websites. There are plenty of internet cafés in all major urban centres and many hotels, guesthouses or backpacker hostels offer email access as a service. Wireless internet is available and many internet cafés offer stations to plug in your laptop as well as a service to download digital photographs onto disk. In the more remote regions you are unlikely to find somewhere to use the internet unless the town is served by a university or college. The Directory sections in each chapter give listings. Expect to pay around R10 per hour.

Post

The internal mail service is notoriously slow, but international post is generally reliable if you use airmail. If you are sending home souvenirs, surface mail to Europe is the cheapest method but will take at least six weeks. Letters to Europe and the United States should take no more than a few days, although over the busy Christmas season can take longer. There is a 'speed service', but this costs significantly more. Parcels have been known to disappear en route, so it's probably best to use registered mail for more valuable items so that you can track their progress. Courier services are useful for sending heavier objects such as wooden sculptures and furniture. Contact **DHL** T0860-345000, toll free, for the nearest branch, or visit www.dhl.co.za.

Telephone

The telephone service is very efficient. Card and coin phones are widespread and work well – even in remote national parks there are usually card phones from which one can dial direct to anywhere in the world. Note that hotels usually double the rates and even a short international call can become very expensive. There are a number of private companies that offer fax and mail services but these also tend to charge double the usual rate for calls. Phone boxes found in backpacker hostels, shops and bars are known as 'chatterboxes' and are usually set at a higher rate.

Blue call boxes are coin-operated telephones but these are becoming rare as green card phones take over. Phone cards are sold for R10, R20, R50 and R100. They are available in larger supermarkets, newsagents, some chemists and Telkom vending machines. A R50 card is sufficient to make an international call to Europe for a few minutes. Cheaper calls, known as 'Callmore Time' are available between 1900 and 0700 on weekdays and from 1900 on Friday until 0700 on Monday. Discounts only apply to national calls. You can usually speak for up to 50% longer for the same charge. **Worldcall** cards are increasingly available in shops, post offices and backpacker hostels. They cost R50 and offer slightly cheaper rates than regular phone cards. To use them, dial 10136, then enter the code on the back of the card, followed by the international number you require.

You must dial the full 3-digit regional code for every number in South Africa, even when you are calling from within that region.

Mobile phones

South Africa uses the GSM system for mobile phones and overseas visitors should be able to use their mobiles, as long as it has been arranged with their service provider prior to departure. Mobile numbers consist of 10 digits and start with 082, 083, 084 or 072 depending on the network. Mobile phones and SIM cards are available for hire at each of the three international airports – Cape Town, Durban and Johannesburg. For anyone travelling alone by car, especially women, it is essential to hire one for emergencies.

Country code +27; international dialling code 09; directory enquires T1023; international operator T0009; international enquires T1025.

Media

Magazines

There are a number of publications that travellers will find useful in South Africa. The annual *Eat Out* lists the best restaurants in the country, although it tends to concentrate on the more upmarket eateries. *Time Out Cape Town* is a useful annual magazine with good nightlife and culture listings. Similar content can be found in the monthly *Cape Etc*, which also has interesting articles on shopping, day trips, and eating out. The monthly *Getaway* is aimed at outdoorsy South Africans, but has excellent travel features and ideas, as well as reviews of accommodation alternatives and activities throughout southern Africa. *Africa Geographical* is a glossy monthly with high-quality photographs, which publishes regular articles on southern Africa's parks, reserves and wildlife. Its sister magazine, *Africa, Birds & Birding*, also monthly, is a must for anyone with an interest in birdwatching in South Africa. For inspiration before you leave home, pick up a copy of *Travel Africa*, www.travelafricamag.com.

Newspapers

The *Sunday Times* and *Sunday Independent* are weekly English-language papers with national coverage, although several editions are produced for different areas. The excellent weekly *Mail & Guardian* (with close links to the British *Guardian*) provides the most objective reporting on South African issues and has in-depth coverage of international news. Daily English-language newspapers include: *The Star* and *The Citizen* (Johannesburg); *The Daily News* and *The Natal Mercury* (Durban); *The Argus* and *The Cape Times* (Cape Town). *The Sowetan* provides a less white-oriented view of South African news and has the best coverage of international soccer. There are also a number of newspapers published in Afrikaans, Zulu and Xhosa.

Radio

Given South Africa's low literacy rate, radio is the most popular form of media in the country and even the most remote corners are reached by broadcasters. The **South African Broadcast Corporation** (SABC) has numerous national stations catering for the 11 official languages. The corporation has an agreement with the BBC, which means that listeners can hear BBC news and programmes at certain times of day. 5FM is the SABC national pop music station, while Metro FM offers R'n'B, hip-hop and Kwaito. There is also an abundance of local commercial and community radio stations, such as Good Hope FM in Cape Town or Radio Zulu in Johannesburg.

Television

The SABC – the state broadcaster – has significantly restructured its service in the last decade to accommodate all 11 official languages. The majority of programmes are in English, followed by Afrikaans, Zulu and Xhosa. There are now four free channels available, known as SABC 1, 2 and 3, and the newer e channel. The latter is the most popular and tends to have better news and entertainment programmes, although SABC 3 has a link with CNN, providing live CNN broadcasts on most afternoons. The paying channel, M-Net, is available in most hotels and backpacker hostels, and offers a range of sport, sitcoms and movies. It is available for free from 1700-1900, known as 'open time'. Many hotels also have satellite TV, known as DSTV, with a range of sports, movie and news channels.

Cape Town

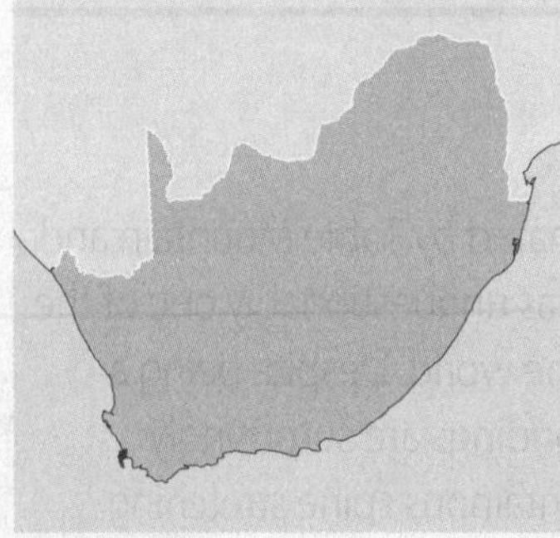

Footprint features

Introduction

South Africa's 'Mother City', dominated by Table Mountain and surrounded by the wild Atlantic, has unquestionably one of the most beautiful city backdrops in the world. Despite being a considerable urban hub, its surroundings are surprisingly untamed, characterized by a mountainous spine stretching between two seaboards and edged by rugged coast and dramatic beaches.

The city, even by South African standards, is uncommonly diverse, with grandiose colonial buildings and beautiful public gardens crammed in with 1960s eyesores. Atmospheric Victorian suburbs stretch around the lower slopes of the mountain, while further out lie the Cape Flats, their sprawling townships a lasting testimony of the Apartheid era.

To mirror these surroundings, Cape Town's population is the most cosmopolitan in the country, a unique mix of cultures, ethnicities and religions that drive the very pulse of the city. It has a comparatively small black African population – about a quarter of the total – while the distinctive 'Cape Coloured' community makes up over half of the population. These are descendants of slaves brought from the Far East and West Africa who interacted with European and local indigenous people. The remaining quarter is made up of white descendants of Dutch and British settlers. This mishmash results in a vibrant cultural scene – music, and particularly Cape Jazz, lies at the very core of city life.

It is this mixture of environments and communities that makes Cape Town such an instantly likeable and captivating place. Few places in the world can offer mountain hiking, lazing on a beach, tasting world-class wines and drinking beer in a township shebeen all in one day. Put simply, it is a city worth crossing the world for.

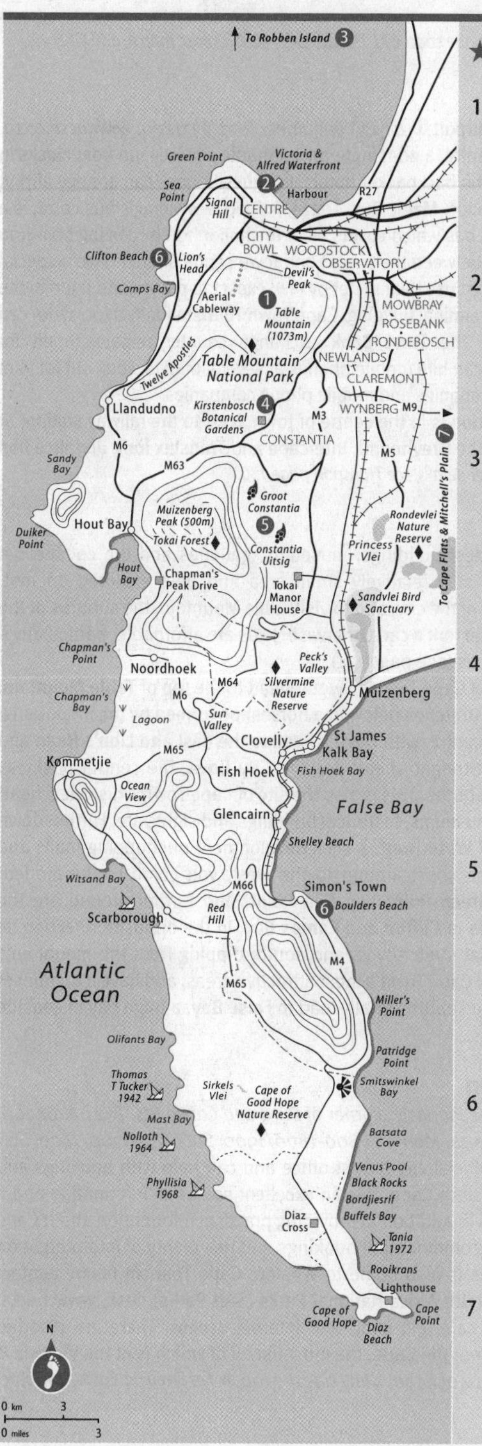

★ Don't miss...

1 Table Mountain Marvel at the views from the summit and watch dassies boulder-hop, page 70.

2 V & A Waterfront Watch the to-ing and fro-ing of boats and Cape fur seals in the harbour, page 82.

3 Robben Island Learn about the country's turbulent past on a tour of this notorious island prison, page 84.

4 Kirstenbosch Botanical Gardens Spread out a picnic and enjoy a Summer Sunset Concert on the lawns, page 87.

5 Constantia wine Try a glass of the famous Vin de Constance, among the historical estates and rolling vineyards, page 88.

6 Beaches Join the beautiful people at Clifton and swim with the penguins at Boulders Beach, pages 90 and 100.

7 Township shebeen tour Listen to live Cape Jazz and sample home-brewed beer, page 128.

Ins and outs ›› *Phone code: 021. Postal code: 8000. Colour map 4, grid C1 & 2.*

Getting there

Cape Town International Airport ⓘ *airport enquiries, T021-9371200, www.acsa.co.za,* is 22 km east of the city centre, a 20-minute drive. Shuttle services run from kiosks in the arrivals hall. Many of the backpacker hotels and guesthouses can arrange airport pick-ups at a reasonable price. **Magic Bus,** T021-5056300, www.magic bus.co.za, is a good-value shared shuttle bus which covers all of the major hotels, costing from R90 per person. Taxis running between the airport and town centre should have a special airport licence and they must use their meter by law; expect to pay around R300 to the centre of town. Within the terminal building, **Cape Town Tourism** (daily 0700-1700) can arrange accommodation. The **Trust Bank** exchange counter remains open for international arrivals. You can hire mobile phones at several outlets. Look out for joint deals between car hire companies and mobile phone companies.

The main **railway station** is in the centre of town. Next to the railway station, at Adderley Street, is where the **Greyhound, Intercape** and **Translux long distance bus** services arrive. ›› *For further details, see Transport page 130.*

Getting around

Most of Cape Town's oldest buildings, museums, galleries and the commercial centre are concentrated in a relatively small area and best explored on foot. However, to explore more of the city, and to visit Table Mountain, the suburbs or the beaches, it's a good idea to rent a car. Otherwise, taxis are affordable, particularly if you use **Rikki**'s shared taxis (see page 131).

To get the best idea of Cape Town's layout, head to the top of **Table Mountain**. From its summit, the city stretches below in a horseshoe formed by the mountains: Table Mountain is in the centre, with **Devil's Peak** to the east and **Lion's Head** and **Signal Hill** to the west. Straight ahead lies the **City Bowl**, the central business district backed by leafy suburbs. This is also the site of Cape Town's historical heart and where all the major museums, historical buildings and sights are. Further down is the **Victoria and Alfred Waterfront**, a slick development of shopping malls and restaurants. Following the coast around to the west, you come to the modern residential districts of **Green Point** and **Sea Point**, and further around are the beautiful Atlantic beaches of **Clifton** and **Camps Bay**. In the opposite direction lie the **southern suburbs** that stretch west and south, dipping from the mountain's slopes. These are some of Cape Town's most attractive areas, and have a number of interesting sights too. The suburbs finally lead to **False Bay**, a huge bay of seaside villages and long beaches.

Tourist information

Cape Town Tourism ⓘ *The Pinnacle, corner of Burg and Castle Sts, T021-4264260, www.tourismcapetown.co.za, Mon-Fri 0800-1800/1900, Sat 0830-1300/1400, Sun 0900-1300,* this is the official city tourist office and can help with bookings and tours throughout the Western Cape. It is an excellent source of information and a good first stop in the city. In addition to providing practical information about Cape Town, it can help with accommodation bookings and has plenty of information on nightlife and events. This is also home to **Western Cape Tourism** (same contact details) and there is a **South Africa National Parks (SAN Parks)** desk, www.parks-sa.co.za. There's also a café, gift shop and internet access. There are 18 other branches/desks throughout the Cape, the most useful of which is at the **Victoria & Alfred Waterfront** ⓘ *T021-4054500, daily 0900-2100.* ›› *For Sleeping, Eating and other listings, see pages 100-132.*

Background

First people

The first evidence of human inhabitants in the Cape has been dated back to nearly 30,000 years ago. Rock art found in the area was created by nomadic San people (also known as Bushmen), a hunter-gatherer group which roamed across much of Southern Africa. Some San groups continue to survive today, mostly in Namibia and Botswana, despite continuing persecution. The original San were replaced about two thousand years ago by Khoi groups, a semi-nomadic people who settled in the Cape with herds of sheep and cattle.

First landing

António de Saldanha, a Portuguese admiral who lost his way going east, landed in Table Bay in 1503. They called the bay Aguada da Saldanha (it was renamed Table Bay in 1601 by **Joris van Spilbergen**). Saldanha and a party of the crew went ashore in search of drinking water. They followed a stream to the base of Table Mountain and then proceeded to climb to the top. From here Saldanha was able to get a clear view of the surrounding coastline and the confusion caused by the peninsula. On their return they found the crew unsuccessfully trying to barter with local indigenous Khoi for livestock. The trade quickly developed into a row which ended in bloodshed. There was another battle between the Portuguese and the Khoi in March 1510. On this occasion the Khoi had struck back after children and cattle were stolen by the sailors. Seventy five Portuguese were killed, including **Dom Francisco de Almeida**, who had just finished five years as the first Portuguese Viceroy to India. Few Portuguese ships landed in Table Bay after this.

The Dutch and the VOC

By the end of the 16th century British and Dutch mariners had caught up with the Portuguese and they quickly came to appreciate the importance of the Cape as a base for restocking ships with drinking water and fresh supplies as they made their long journeys to the east. Indeed, seafarers found that they were able to exchange scraps of metal for provisions to supply a whole fleet.

The first moves to settle in the Cape were made by the Dutch, and on the 6th April 1652 **Jan Van Riebeeck** landed in Table Bay. His ships carried wood for building and some small cannons, the first building to be erected being a small fort at the mouth of the Fresh River. The site of the original fort is where Grand Parade in the centre of Cape Town is today. Van Riebeeck was in charge of the supply station that belonged to the Dutch East India Company (Vereenigde Oost-Indische Compagnie or VOC). After the fort was built, gardens for fruit and vegetables were laid out and pastures for cattle acquired. As the settlement slowly grew, the Khoi people were driven back into the interior. Surprisingly, the early settlers were forbidden from enslaving the Khoi; instead, slaves were imported by the VOC from Indonesia and West Africa. Although many died, these slaves were the origin of the Cape Malay community.

In 1662 Jan van Riebeeck was transferred to India. Because of rivalries in Europe, the VOC was worried about enemy ships visiting the Cape, so work started on a new stone fort in 1666. Over the next 13 years several Governors came and went. During this time the French and British went to war with Holland, but the British and the Dutch East India companies joined in a treaty of friendship in March 1674, and then in July 1674 a ship arrived with the news that the British and Dutch had made peace. In October 1679 one of the most energetic Governors arrived in the Cape, **Simon van der Stel**. For the next 20 years van der Stel devoted his energies to creating a new Holland in southern Africa. During his period as Governor, van der Stel paid particular attention to the growth and development of Cape Town and the surrounding farmlands. The company garden was replanted, nursery plots were created and new experimental plants were collected from around the world. North of the gardens he built a large hospital and a lodge to house VOC slaves. New streets were laid out which were straight and wide with plenty of shade. New buildings in the town were covered in white limewash, producing a smart and prosperous appearance. In 1685, in appreciation for his work, he was granted an estate by the VOC, which he named **Constantia**. During his life he used the estate as an experimental agricultural farm and to grow oak trees which were then planted throughout the Cape.

One of his more significant contributions was the founding of the settlement at Stellenbosch. He directed the design and construction of many of the town's public buildings, and then introduced a number of the crops to be grown on the new farms. For many years he experimented with vines in an effort to produce wines as good as those in Europe. He was particularly pleased when in 1688 French Protestant Huguenot refugees arrived in the Cape. He saw to it that they were all settled on excellent farmlands in what became to be known as **Franschhoek** (French glen), the upper valley of the Berg River. In 1693 he had the foresight to appoint the town's first engineer to tackle problems of a clean water supply, and the removal of rubbish. Van der Stel died in June 1712 at Constantia.

Under the British

The next period of Cape Town's history was closely related to events in Europe, particularly the French Revolution. The ideas put forward by the revolution of liberty, fraternity and equality were not welcome in colonies such as the Cape. The Dutch East India Company was seen to be a corrupt organization and a supporter of the aristocracy. When the French invaded Holland, the British decided to seize the Cape to stop it from falling into French hands. After the Battle of Muizenberg in 1795, Britain took over the Cape from the representatives of the Dutch East India Company, which was bankrupt. In the Treaty of Amiens (1803) the Cape was restored to the Batavian Republic of the Netherlands. In 1806 the British took control again at the resumption of the Anglo-French wars.

When the British took over power it was inevitable that they inherited many of the problems associated with the colony. The principal issue was how to manage European settlement. The Dutch East India Company had only encouraged settlement as a cheap and efficient means of supplying their base in Cape Town. Thereafter they were only interested in controlling the Indian Ocean and supplying ships. By the time the British arrived, the Dutch settler farmers (the Boer) had become so successful that they were producing a surplus. The only problem was high production costs due to a shortage of labour. To alleviate the situation, a policy of importing slaves was implemented. This in turn led to decreased work opportunities for the settler families. Gradually the mood changed and the Boer looked to the interior for land and work. They were not impressed by the British administration and in 1836 the Great Trek was under way.

The growth of the city and the port

Industrialization in Europe brought great change, especially when the first steamship, the *Enterprise*, arrived in Table Bay in October 1825. After considerable delay and continual loss of life and cargoes, work began on two basins and two breakwater piers. The first truckload of construction rocks was tipped by Prince Alfred, the 16-year-old son of Queen Victoria, on 17 September 1860. The Alfred Basin was completed in 1870 and a dry dock was added in 1881.

No sooner had the first basin been completed than diamonds and gold were discovered in South Africa. Over the next 40 years Cape Town and the docks were to change beyond recognition. In 1900 work began on a new breakwater which would protect an area of 27 km. After five years' work the **Victoria Basin** was opened. This new basin was able to shelter the new generation of ships using Table Bay but was unable to cope with the increase in numbers during the **Anglo-Boer War**. A third basin was created to the east of Victoria Basin in 1932 and for a while this seemed to have solved the problem, but fate was against Cape Town. In January 1936 the largest ship to visit South Africa docked with ease at B berth in the new basin. The boat, which was being used to help promote tourism in South Africa, was filled with wealthy and famous visitors. The morning on which she was due to sail, a strong southeasterly wind blew up and pressed the liner so firmly against the quay that she couldn't sail. In one morning all of the new basin's weaknesses had been exposed.

The next phase of growth was an ambitious one, and it was only completed in 1945. The project involved the dredging of Table Bay and the reclaiming of land. The spoil from the dredging provided 140 km of landfill, known as Foreshore. This new land extends from the present day railway station to **Duncan Dock**. As you walk or drive around Cape Town today, remember that just over 50 years ago the sea came up to the main railway station.

For the best record of the vibrant community that once thrived here, visit the excellent District Six Museum (see page 78).

Impact of the Apartheid years

The descendants of the large and diverse slave population have given Cape Town a particularly cosmopolitan atmosphere. Unfortunately Apartheid urban planning meant that many of the more vibrant areas of the city in the earlier part of this century were destroyed. The most notorious case is that of District Six, a racially mixed, low income housing area on the edge of the City Bowl. The Apartheid government could not tolerate such an area, especially so close to the centre of the city, and the residents, most of whom were classified as 'Coloured', were moved out to the soulless townships of the Cape Flats, such as Mitchell's Plain. The area was bulldozed but few new developments have taken place on the site: this accounts for the large areas of open ground in the area between the City Bowl and the suburb of Woodstock. Happily, the government recently handed over the first pocket of re-developed land to a small group of ex-residents of District Six and their descendants. What the area will become remains to be seen – the issue remains controversial as many ex-residents feel the open, barren land should remain as a poignant testimony to the forced removals.

Other reminders of the cosmopolitan history of Cape Town can be experienced in the area to the west of Buitengracht Street. This district, known as **Bo-Kaap**, is still home to a small Islamic (Cape Malay) community that somehow managed to survive the onslaught of Apartheid urban planning. The coloured population of Cape Town has historically outweighed both the white and African populations, hence the widespread use of Afrikaans in the city. This balance was maintained by Apartheid policies that prevented Africans from migrating into the Western Cape from the Eastern Cape and elsewhere. This policy was not, however, able to withstand the pressure of the poor rural African's desire to find opportunities in the urban economy. Over the past couple of decades there has been an enormous growth in the African population of Cape Town. Many of these new migrants have been forced to settle in squatter areas, such as the notorious Crossroads Camp next to the N2 highway. During the Apartheid era these squatter camps were frequently bulldozed and the residents evicted but as soon as they were cleared they sprang up again. Crossroads was a hotbed of resistance to the Apartheid state and much of the Cape Flats area existed in a state of near civil war throughout much of the 1980s.

Today, Cape Town remains the most cosmopolitan city in South Africa. The official colour barriers have long since disappeared and residential boundaries are shifting. The economic balance, too, is beginning to change: a black middle class has emerged in recent years, and the coloured middle class is strengthening.

Sights

Table Mountain National Park

Cape Town is defined, first and foremost, by Table Mountain. Rising a sheer 1073 m from the coastal plain, it dominates almost every view of the city, its sharp slopes and level top making it one of the world's best-known city backdrops. For centuries, it was the first sight of Cape Town afforded to seafarers, it's looming presence visible for hundreds of kilometres. Certainly, its size continues to astonish visitors today, but it is the mountain's wilderness, bang in the middle of a bustling conurbation, that makes the biggest impression. Table Mountain sustains over 1400 species of flora, as well as baboons, dassies (large rodents) and countless birds. It was recently designated the **Table Mountain National Park**, www.tmnp.co.za, which encompasses the entire peninsula stretching from here to Cape Point. Between September and March you have the additional pleasure of seeing the mountain covered in wild flowers. The most common vegetation is fynbos, of which there is an extraordinary variety, but you'll also see proteas plus the rare silver tree, *Leucadendron argenteum*.

Aerial Cableway

ⓘ *Bookings T021-4248181, www.tablemountain.net, 0830-2000/2200 (last car down 1900 in winter), R115 return.*

The dizzying trip to the top in the Aerial Cableway is one of Cape Town's highlights. There are two cars, each carrying up to 65 passengers, and as you ride up the floor rotates, allowing a full 360° view. Journey time is just three minutes. There is a bistro restaurant and souvenir shop at the top station, as well as a self-service café that gets busy when the cableway queues are long. An extensive network of paths have been laid out from the top station, allowing walks of various lengths, leading to different look-out points. There are also free guided walks daily at 1200 and 1400. A shuttle bus service is run by the tourist office, which leaves every half hour from the main office on Burg Street, R40 one-way.

Mountain Rescue: T021-9489900. Latest mountain weather reports: T021-4245148.

Activities

The entire area is a nature reserve, and the mountain itself is protected as a national monument. There are numerous paths climbing to the top of the mountain. The most popular route starts from Kirstenbosch Botanical Gardens and takes about three hours to the top. However, even busy routes should not be taken lightly. Given Table Mountain's size and location, conditions can change alarmingly quickly. The weather may seem clear and calm when you set out, but fog (the famous 'Table Cloth' which flows from the top) and rain can descend without warning. Numerous people have been caught out and the mountain has claimed its fair share of lives.

Before venturing out, make sure you have suitable clothing, food and water. Take warm clothes, a windbreaker, a waterproof jacket, a hat, sunscreen, sunglasses, plenty of water (2 litres per person) and energy foods. Never climb alone and inform someone of which route you're taking and what time you should be back. A detailed map is essential – these can be purchased at the tourist office. For those wanting to spend more time on the mountain, an overnight trail – the **Hoerikwagga Trail** – was introduced in 2005. The four-day trek involves sleeping in renovated forester houses dotted along the top of the mountain. For full details, contact the tourist office. If you're interested in learning about the mountain's flora and fauna, take a guide or a tour (see Hiking on page 125).

There are also several mountain biking trails set out across the mountain. There have been reports of increased crime along these trails, but the local police force has reacted by increasing the police presence.

Signal Hill

Signal Hill's summit offers spectacular views of the city, the Twelve Apostles (the mountainous spine stretching south from Table Mountain) and the ocean. It is possible to drive to the 350 m summit, which means that it can get pretty busy with tour groups around sunset. Nevertheless, watching the sun dip into the Atlantic from this viewpoint with a cold sundowner in hand is a highlight of a visit to Cape Town. Avoid being there after dark, as there have been reports of muggings. From the town centre, follow signs for the Lower Cableway station and take a right opposite the turning for the cableway station. The hill is home to the Noon Gun which is fired electronically at noon every day, except Sunday. There is also a *karamat* (Islamic tomb) on the hill.

Lion's Head

Halfway along the road up Signal Hill you pass Lion's Head, a popular hiking spot. The climb to the peak is fairly easy going, and takes about two hours, and the 360° views from the top are incredible. There are two routes to the top: the easier of the two winds around the mountain; the quicker one involves climbing up a couple of drops with the aid of chains. Both are signposted. Hiking to Lion's Head is especially popular at full moon, when Capetonians watch the sunset from the peak and then descend by the light of the moon. Take plenty of water and a torch, and always climb in a group.

City Bowl

» pp100-132.

From the Lower Cableway Station, you look out over the central residential suburbs of Tamboerskloof (Drummers' Ravine), Gardens, Oranjezicht (Orange View), and Vredehoek (Peaceful Corner), and beyond here lie the high-rise blocks of the business district. Together these form the City Bowl, a term inspired by the surrounding mountains. Closest to the mountain is **Oranjezicht**, a quiet district with a good selection of guesthouses and B&B accommodation. Up until 1900 the area was a farm of the same name. On the boundary with Gardens is the **De Waal Park** and **Molteno Reservoir**. Originally built as a main storage facility for the city in 1881, the reservoir now provides a peaceful wooded spot from where you can enjoy a view of the city. Close by, on the corner of Prince Street and Sir George Grey Street, is an **old iron pump**. Such pumps were once dotted about the city for people to draw water for domestic use.

There is nothing peaceful about **Vredehoek** today, as the De Waal Drive (M3) brings rush hour traffic into the top end of town from the southern suburbs and beyond. Most of the area has been given over to ugly high-rise apartments, though the residents benefit from some excellent views. This was the area in which many Jewish immigrants from eastern Europe settled, and have to a large part remained.

Gardens is a lively neighbourhood with a choice of quality restaurants and comfortable guesthouses. Cape Town's best-known hotel, the **Mount Nelson**, is situated here in its own landscaped gardens. The grand gateway to the hotel was built in 1924 to welcome the Prince of Wales. From here the land slopes gently towards the Waterfront, with the commercial heart of the city laid out in between. This was the area where the Dutch East India Company first created fruit and vegetable gardens to supply the ships' crews who suffered greatly from scurvy. Across Orange Street from the entrance to the Mount Nelson Hotel is the top end of **Government Avenue**, a delightful pedestrian route past Company's Garden and many of the city's main museums. Originally sheltered by lemon trees, it is now lined with oaks and myrtle hedges, and is one of Cape Town's most popular walks. It was declared a national monument in 1937.

Cape Town centre

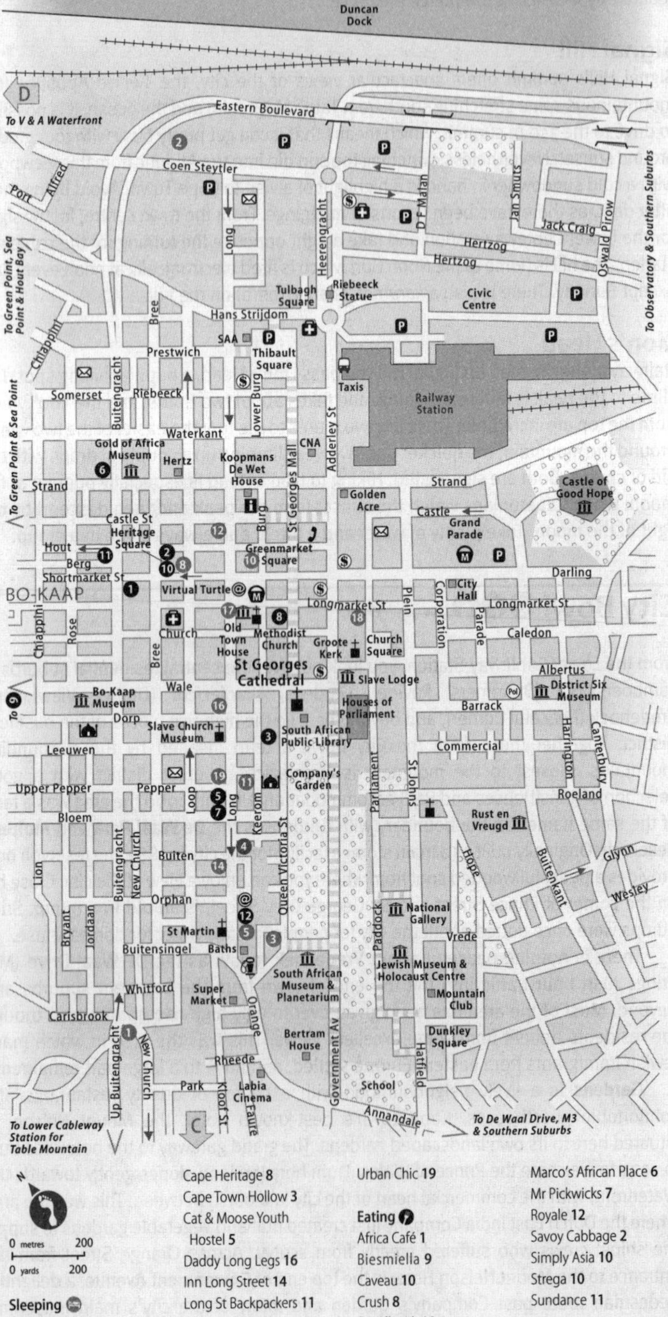

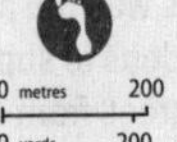

Sleeping
- Arabella Sheraton 2
- Backpack 1
- Cape Diamond 18
- Cape Heritage 8
- Cape Town Hollow 3
- Cat & Moose Youth Hostel 5
- Daddy Long Legs 16
- Inn Long Street 14
- Long St Backpackers 11
- Metropole 12
- Park Inn 10
- Tudor 17
- Urban Chic 19

Eating
- Africa Café 1
- Biesmiella 9
- Caveau 10
- Crush 8
- Fat Albert's 10
- Five Flies 3
- Mama Africa 5
- Marco's African Place 6
- Mr Pickwicks 7
- Royale 12
- Savoy Cabbage 2
- Simply Asia 10
- Strega 10
- Sundance 11

Bars & clubs
- Kennedy's Cigar Bar 4

South Africa Museum and Planetarium

ⓘ *25 Queen Victoria St, at the top end of Company's Garden, T021-4813800, daily 1000-1700, R10, free on Sat. There's a shop and café in the museum.*

This is the city's most established museum, specializing in natural history, ethnography and archaeology, and it is a good place to take children. There are extensive displays of the flora and fauna of southern Africa, including the popular Whale Well and interactive Shark World area, but the highlight is the 'IQe – the Power of Rock Art' exhibition. The displays of ancient San rock art have been in the museum for almost a hundred years, but following a process of consultation and dialogue with Khoi-San communities, they have been re-interpreted in a far more sensitive and illuminating manner. The exhibits focus on the significance and symbolism of San rock art, with some fascinating examples including the beautifully preserved Linton panel, which depicts the trance experiences of shamans. Other themes explored include rainmaking and the significance of animal imagery; the eland, for example, appears more often than any other animal in San rock art, and it holds a central role in all major rituals, from teenage initiation to marriage and rainmaking. The whole exhibition, although short, is beautifully arranged and accompanied by the sound of San singing, a disjointed and haunting sound.

Nearby are the ethnographic galleries, offering interesting displays on the San, Khoi and Xhosa, among others, as well as the original Lydenburg Heads (see page 606). There is also a small display of pieces recovered from Great Zimbabwe that illustrate its importance as a trade centre – there are beads from Cambay, India, Chinese Celadon ware, 13th-century Persian pottery and Syrian glass from the 14th century. A recent addition to the museum is Stone Bones, en exhibition about the fossilized skeletons found in the Karoo, which date back 250 million years – predating dinosaurs. There are life-sized reproductions of the reptile-like creatures, including walk-around dioramas and examples of the actual fossils.

Next door, at the **Planetarium** ⓘ *T021-4813900, show times Mon-Fri 1400, Sat and Sun, 1300, 1430, late showing on Tue 2000, R20*, presentations change every few months, but a view of the current night sky is shown on the first weekend of each month. Shows last an hour and are fascinating.

Bertram House

ⓘ *Corner of Government Av and Orange St, T021-4249381, Tue-Thu 1000-1630, R5.*

This early 19th-century red brick Georgian House has a distinctly English feel to it. The building houses a collection of porcelain, jewellery, silver and English furniture, the majority of which was bequeathed by Ann Lidderdale. Winifred Ann Lidderdale was an important civic figure in Cape Town in the 1950s. After her marriage to Henry Maxwell Lidderdale, she lived in England and the USA, but in 1951 the couple returned to Cape Town for their retirement. It was her desire to establish a house museum to commemorate the British contribution to life at the Cape. Downstairs the two drawing rooms contain all the trappings of a bygone elegant age – card tables, a Hepplewhite settee, a square piano and a fine harp. Three rooms have wallpaper from London, a very expensive luxury for the period.

Jewish Museum

ⓘ *88 Hatfield St, T021-4651546, www.sajewishmuseum.co.za, Sun-Thu 1000-1700, Fri 1000-1400, closed on Jewish and public holidays, R50.*

Inside this excellent, contemporary museum is a rich and rare collection of items depicting the history of the Cape Town Hebrew Congregation and other congregations in the Cape Province. The history of the community is interesting in itself: in 1841 a congregation of 17 men assembled for the first time in Cape Town to celebrate Yom Kippur. At the meeting they set about the task of raising funds to build a synagogue, and in 1862 the foundation stone was laid for the first synagogue in Southern Africa.

 The following year the building was completed and furnished – quite a feat for such a small community at the time. On display upstairs are bronze Sabbath oil lamps, *Chanukkah* lamps, *Bessamin* spice containers, *Torah* scrolls, *Kiddush* cups and candlesticks. There is a beautiful stained-glass window depicting the Ten Commandments in Hebrew. From here a glass corridor leads you to a newer section of the museum that is devoted to the history of Jewish immigration to the Cape, mainly from Lithuania. A lot of thought has been put into the displays, which include photographs, immigration certificates, videos and a full reconstruction of a Lithuanian *shtetl*, or village. There are special displays outlining the stories of famous Jewish South Africans, including Helen Suzman and Isie Maisels. The museum complex also houses a library, café and bookshop.

Holocaust Centre

ⓘ *88 Hatfield St, T021-4625553, www.ctholocaust.co.za, Sun-Thu 1000-1700, Fri 1000-1300, entry by donation.*

An intelligent and shocking examination of the Holocaust can be found next door at this modern museum. Exhibits follow a historical route, starting with a look at anti-Semitism in Europe in previous centuries, and then leading to the rise of Nazism in Germany, the creation of ghettos, death camps and the Final Solution, and liberation at the end of the war. Video footage, photography, examples of Nazi propaganda and personal accounts of the Holocaust produce a vividly haunting and shocking display. The exhibits cleverly acknowledge South Africa's recent emergence from Apartheid and draw parallels between both injustices, as well as looking at the link between South Africa's Greyshirts (who were later assimilated into the National Party) and the Nazis. The local context is highlighted further at the end of the exhibition, with video accounts of Jews who survived the Holocaust and moved to Cape Town.

National Gallery

ⓘ *Government Av, T021-4674660, Tue-Sun 1000-1700, R10.*

The National Gallery is one of the city's finest museums, housing a permanent collection but also host to some excellent temporary exhibitions that include the best of the country's contemporary art. The original collection was bequeathed to the nation in 1871 by Thomas Butterworth Bailey, and features a collection of 18th- and 19th-century British sporting scenes, portraits and Dutch paintings. Far more interesting are the changing exhibitions of contemporary South African art. These have recently included 'Revisions – A narrative of South African Art', a brilliant private collection, with four rooms covering five decades of the country's contemporary art, including pieces by Irma Stern, fascinating lino prints by Vuminkosi Zulu and violent and humorous charcoal drawings by Dumile Feni. Snacks and light lunches are available at the **Gallery Café** and there's a good souvenir shop on site.

Rust en Vreugd

ⓘ *78 Buitenkant St, T021-4643280, Tue-Thu 0830-1630, R5.*

A few hundred metres east of the National Gallery, hidden behind a high whitewashed wall, is this 18th-century mansion. It was declared a historical monument in 1940, and subsequently restored to its best period. Today it houses six galleries displaying a unique collection of watercolours, engravings and lithographs depicting the history of the Cape. Of particular note are Schouten's watercolour of Van Riebeeck's earth fort (1658), watercolours by Thomas Baines (a British artist who travelled extensively in South Africa and Australia) of climbing Table Mountain, lithographs by Angas of Khoi and Zulus and a collection of cartoons by Cruikshank depicting the first British settlers arriving in the Cape. These are all part of the William Fehr collection. Commercial exhibitions are held in the galleries upstairs.

Company's Garden

ⓘ *Daily 0700-1900.*

Running alongside Government Avenue is the peaceful Company's Garden, situated on the site of Jan van Riebeeck's original vegetable garden, which was created in 1652 to grow produce for settlers and ships bound for the East. It is now a small botanical garden, with lawns, a variety of labelled trees, ponds filled with Japanese Koi and small aviary, although it is not as peaceful as it might be thanks to groups of snoozing men who seem to spend their days lounging around on the lawns. The grey squirrels living amongst the oak trees were introduced by Cecil Rhodes from America. There are also a couple of statues here: opposite the South African Public Library at the lower end of the garden, is the oldest statue in Cape Town, that of Sir George Grey, governor of the Cape from 1854 to 1862. Close by is a statue of Cecil Rhodes, pointing northwards in a rather unfortunate flat-handed gesture, with an inscription reading, "Your hinterland is there," a reminder of his ambition to paint the map pink from the Cape to Cairo. There is a café in the garden, serving drinks and snacks beneath the trees, and a small **information centre** ⓘ *T021-4225946, Mon-Fri 1000-1800, Sat 1000-1600*, which helps organize a monthly craft market in summer, held on a Wednesday usually at the end of the month.

South African Public Library

ⓘ *Queen Victoria St, behind St Georges Cathedral, T021-4246320, www.ulsa.ac.za, Mon-Fri 0900-1700, Wed from 1000.*

Adjoining the gardens is the South African Public Library, which opened in 1818. It is the country's oldest national reference library and was one of the first free libraries in the world. Today it houses an important collection of books covering South Africa's history. The building also has a bookshop and an internet café.

Houses of Parliament

ⓘ *T021-4032537, phone ahead for tours of the chambers and Constitutional Assembly.*

On the other side of the avenue are the Houses of Parliament. The building was completed in 1885, and when the Union was formed in 1910 it became the seat for the national parliament. In front of the building is a marble statue of Queen Victoria, erected by public subscription in honour of her Golden Jubilee. It was unveiled in 1890.

St George's Cathedral

The last building on Government Avenue is St George's Cathedral, best known for being Archbishop Desmond Tutu's territory from 1986 until 1996 (see page 76). It is from here that he led over 30,000 people to City Hall to mark the end of Apartheid, and where he coined the now universal phrase 'Rainbow Nation'. The building was designed by Sir Herbert Baker in the early 20th century. Inside, some of the early memorial tablets have been preserved, while over the top of the stairs leading to the crypt is a memorial to Lady D'Urban, wife of Sir Benjamin D'Urban, the Governor of the Cape from 1834 to 1838. Under the archway between the choir and St John's Chapel is a bronze recumbent statue of Archbishop West Jones, the second Archbishop of Cape Town (1874-1908). The Great North window is a fine piece of stained glass depicting the pioneers of the Anglican church. There is a small café, **The Crypt**, open during the day for light snacks and breakfasts.

Slave Lodge

ⓘ *T021-4608240, Mon-Fri 0830-1630, Sat 0830-1300, R10.*

On the corner of Adderley and Wale streets is Slave Lodge, the second oldest building in Cape Town. The building has had a varied history, but its most significant role was as a slave lodge for the VOC (see page 67) – between 1679 and 1811 the building housed up to 1000 slaves. Local indigenous groups were protected by the VOC from being enslaved; most slaves were consequently imported from Madagascar, India

Desmond Tutu

Like Nelson Mandela, Desmond Tutu is accepted as an influential and respected figure far beyond the borders of South Africa. His powerful oration and his simple but brave defiance of the Apartheid state has impressed the world. Tutu first caught the international headlines as an outspoken secretary general of the South African Council of Churches in the late 1970s, especially with his call for the international community to stop buying South African goods. But it was the award of the Nobel Peace Prize in 1984 that really established him as an international figure.

Desmond Tutu was born on 7 October 1931 in Klerksdrop and was educated in local mission schools and the Johannesburg Bantu High School in the Western Native township. After obtaining a BA and teaching diploma he taught at a high school in Krugersdorp before going to St Peter's Theological College to train as an Anglican priest. After being ordained he moved to London with his wife and young family, living in Golders Green, while he studied for both a BA and an MA in Theology. In 1966 he returned to South Africa.

After a spell teaching in the Eastern Cape Tutu became a lecturer at the National University of Lesotho. He was in England again for three years in the early 1970s, before taking an appointment as the Anglican Dean of Johannesburg, but then quickly moved back to Lesotho to become Bishop. In 1978 he moved to Johannesburg once again, now as the secretary general of the South African Council of Churches. It was at about this time that the press began to take notice of Tutu's forceful anti-Apartheid statements.

In response to Tutu's comments about Apartheid the South African government took away his passport to prevent him speaking at international conferences, though he was occasionally allowed temporary travel documents and was able to address some important meetings and hold discussions with other religious leaders. Tutu made it clear that he believed that economic sanctions on South Africa were essential to make the Apartheid state introduce reforms at a faster pace. These comments obviously annoyed the South African government and

and Indonesia, creating the most culturally varied slave society in the world. Conditions at the lodge were appalling and up to 20% of the slaves died every year.

Finally, after several years of hand-wringing and coffer-digging, this history is being made visible at the museum. At the time of writing, the ground floor was being developed into a museum chartering the history of the building and slavery in South Africa. At the entrance to the exhibition is at present a slick cinema room, with two flat-screen TVs showing a 15-minute film on the history of slavery in the Cape, highlighting the rules under which slaves lived, the conditions in which they were imported and sold, and the fundamental role slavery played in the success of Cape Town. Beyond here, the museum is planning a series of displays, including a model of a slave ship, images and sounds of what life was like in the lodge, and a 'Wheel of Names', which will display 1000 names of slaves from the 17th and 18th centuries. The other wing of the museum holds excellent temporary exhibitions, such as the 'Hands that Shaped Humanity' exhibition, run by the Desmond Tutu Peace Trust (the trust is planning on building a walk-in centre at the Foreshore, due to be completed in 2008). The top floor houses a muddle of British and VOC weapons, household goods, furniture and money, as well as relics from Japan and ancient Rome, Greece and Egypt.

they regarded Tutu as a dangerous opponent. They were, however, always wary of treating him as cruelly as they treated many of their other opponents. They were aware that any mistreatment would lead to an enormous international outcry. This was especially so after 1984, when he was awarded the Nobel Peace Prize.

In February 1985 Tutu was made Bishop of Johannesburg and finally in April 1986 he was elected Anglican Archbishop of Cape Town. His election was not popular with many white rank and file members of the Anglican Church who believed his calls for economic sanctions were harming their economic interests. The Anglican Church's white congregation have tended to come from the English-speaking sections of the community who regard themselves as more liberal than the Afrikaners. They did not want to be seen to oppose Tutu on grounds of race. Furthermore, it would have appeared unchristian to complain too vocally about how their privileged pockets had been affected by his stance on sanctions. Opposition was, therefore, most commonly expressed through the criticism that he was mixing religion with politics. This claim was not easy to sustain, however, as Tutu always brought a strictly moral and Christian approach to all his 'political' interventions. He often headed protest marches dressed in his Archbishop's robes, though this did not stop him being arrested on a couple of occasions and even teargassed.

Since the arrival of democracy in South Africa Tutu has continued to play a prominent though not quite as central a public role. During 1996 he chaired the hearings of the Truth and Reconciliation Committee and argued forcibly that the policy of granting amnesty to all who admitted their crimes was an important step in healing the nation's scars. His continued espousal of a Christian philosophy of forgiveness has at times angered some of the families of the victims of Apartheid, who emphasize instead the need for justice, but few could deny the sincerity of Tutu's belief in what he sees as a healing process.

Groote Kerk

ⓘ *Mon-Fri 1000-1400, free guided tours available on request.*

Nearby is one of Cape Town's older corners, **Church Square**, site of the Groote Kerk. Up until 1834 the square was used as a venue for the auctioning of slaves from the Slave Lodge, which faced onto the square. All transactions took place under a tree – a concrete plaque marks the old tree's position.

The Groote Kerk was the first church of the Dutch Reformed faith to be built in South Africa (building started in 1678 and it was consecrated in 1704). The present church, built between 1836 and 1841, is a somewhat dull, grey building designed and constructed by Hermann Schutte after a fire had destroyed most of the original. Many of the old gravestones were built into the base of the church walls, the most elaborate of which is the tombstone of Baron van Rheede van Oudtshoorn. Inside, more early tombstones and family vaults are set into the floor, while on the walls are the coats of arms of early Cape families. Note the locked pews, which were rented out by wealthy families in the 19th century. Two of the Cape's early governors are buried here – Simon van der Stel (1679-1699) and Ryk Tulbagh (1751-1771).

District Six Museum

ⓘ *25A Buitenkant St, T021-4667200, www.districtsix.co.za, Mon 0900-1500, Tue-Sat 0900-1600, entry by donation. There is a small café and a bookshop in the museum.*

This small museum, housed in the Methodist Church, is one of Cape Town's most powerful exhibitions and gives a fascinating glimpse of the inanity of Apartheid. District Six was once the vibrant, cosmopolitan heart of Cape Town, a largely coloured inner city suburb renowned for its jazz scene. In February 1966, P W Botha, then Minister of Community Development, formally proclaimed District Six a 'white' group area. Over the next 15 years, an estimated 60,000 people were given notice to give up their homes and moved to the new townships on the Cape Flats. The area was razed, and to this day remains largely undeveloped, although there are now plans to relocate some of those who were originally displaced to new housing in the area.

The museum contains a lively collection of photographs, articles and personal accounts depicting life before and after the removals. There are usually a couple of musicians at the back, tinkering away at their guitars and tin pipes and adding immeasurably to the atmosphere of the place. Highlights include a large map covering most of the ground floor on which ex-residents have been encouraged to mark their homes and local sights. The **Namecloth** is particularly poignant: a 1.5-m-wide length of cloth has been provided for ex-residents to write down their comments, part of which hangs by the entrance. It has grown to over 1 km, and features some moving thoughts. A display in the back room looks at the forced removals from the Kirstenbosch area.

City Hall and Grand Parade

From Adderley Street, a short walk down Darling Street will take you to the City Hall and the Grand Parade. The latter is the largest open space in Cape Town and was originally used for garrison parades before the castle was completed. In 1994, Nelson Mandela made his first speech from City Hall after his release from prison, to over 100,000 people. Today the oak-lined parade is used as a car park and twice a week it is taken over by a colourful market (see page 125). The neoclassical City Hall, built to celebrate Queen Victoria's golden jubilee, overlooks the parade. Its clock tower is a half size replica of Big Ben in London. In 1979 the municipal government moved to a new Civic Centre on the Foreshore, a dominant tower block which straddles Hertzog Boulevard. The hall is now headquarters of the Cape Town Symphony Orchestra and houses the **City Library**.

Castle of Good Hope

ⓘ *Entry from the Grand Parade side, T021-7871082, www.castleofgoodhope.co.za, 0900-1600, R20. Expect to have any bags checked since the castle is still used as the regional offices for the National Defence Force.*

Beyond the Grand Parade, on Darling Street, is the main entrance of South Africa's oldest colonial building, the Castle of Good Hope. Work was started in 1666 by Commander Zacharias Wagenaer and completed in 1679. Its original purpose was for the Dutch East India Company to defend the Cape from rival European powers, and today it is an imposing sight, albeit a rather gloomy one. Under the British, the castle served as government headquarters and since 1917 it has been the headquarters of the South African Defence Force, Western Cape.

Today the castle is home to three museums. The **William Fehr Collection** is one of South Africa's finest displays of furnishings reflecting the social and political history of the Cape. There are landscapes by John Thomas Baines and William Huggins, 17th-century Japanese porcelain and 18th-century Indonesian furniture. Upstairs is an absurdly huge dining table which seats 104, in a room still used for state dinners.

To the left of the Fehr Collection is the **Secunde's House**. The Secunde was second in charge of the settlement at the Cape, responsible for administrative duties for the Dutch East India Company. None of the three rooms contain original furniture from the Castle, but they do recreate the conditions under which an official for the Dutch East

India Company would have lived in the 17th, 18th and early 19th centuries. The third museum is the **Military Museum**, a rather indifferent collection depicting the conflicts of early settlers. More absorbing are the regimental displays of uniforms and medals.

There are free guided tours at 1100, 1200 and 1400. These are informative and fun, although a little short. Tour highlights include the torture chambers, cells, views from the battlements and Dolphin Court, where Lady Anne Barnard was supposedly seen bathing in the nude by the sentries. While waiting for a tour you can enjoy coffee and cakes at a small café, or explore van der Stel's restored wine cellars, where you can taste and buy wines. There is full ceremonial changing of the guard at noon.

Adderley Street and Heerengracht

Adderley Street is one of the city's busiest shopping areas, and is sadly marred by a number of 1960s and 1970s eyesores, but it does still boast some impressive bank buildings. On the corner of Darling Street is the **Standard Bank Building** (1880), a grand structure built shortly after the diamond wealth from Kimberley began to reach Cape Town. Diagonally across is the equally impressive **Barclays Bank Building** (1933), a fine Ceres sandstone building which was the last major work by Sir Herbert Baker in South Africa. At the corner of Adderley Street and Strand Street stands a modern shopping mall complex, the **Golden Acre**. On the lower level of the complex the remains of an aqueduct and a reservoir dating from 1663 can be viewed. The line of black floor tiles close to the escalator which links the centre with the railway station mark the position of the original shoreline before any reclamation work began in Table Bay. Continuing down towards the docks, Adderley Street passes Cape Town Railway Station. At the junction with Hans Strijdom Street is a large roundabout with a central fountain and a bronze statue of **Jan van Riebeeck**, given to the city by Cecil Rhodes in 1899. At the bottom end of Adderley Street on the foreshore are statues of Bartholomew Dias and Maria van Riebeeck, donated respectively by the Portuguese and Dutch Governments in 1952 for Cape Town's tercentenary celebrations.

In front of the Medical Centre on Heerengracht is the **Scott Memorial**. What is on show is in fact a bronze replica; the original, a stone argosy, was smashed by vandals. Its location has barely changed, but when it was unveiled in 1916 it was on the approach to a pier at the foot of Adderley Street, a further indication of how much additional land has been reclaimed from Table Bay over the years. The palm trees once graced a marine promenade in this area. Up until the 1850s there was a canal running the full length of Heerengracht and Adderley streets. This was covered over as the city prospered and traffic congestion became a problem.

Koopmans-De Wet House

ⓘ *Strand St, T021-4813935, Tue-Thu 0900-1630, R5.*

Just off St George's Mall, a pedestrianized road lined with shops and cafés, is the delightfully peaceful Koopmans-De Wet House. The house is named in memory of Marie Koopmans-De Wet, a prominent figure in cultured Cape Society who lived here between 1834 and 1906. The inside has been restored to reflect the period of her grandparents who lived here in the late 18th century. All of the pieces are numbered and a small catalogue gives a brief description. Though not too cluttered, there is a fascinating collection of furnishings which gives the house a special tranquil feel. Look out for the early map of the Cape coastline at the head of the stairs, dating from 1730 – Saldanha Bay and Cape Agulhas are clearly visible. At the back of the house is a shaded courtyard and the original stables with the slave quarters above.

Gold of Africa Museum

ⓘ *96 Strand St, T021-4051540, www.goldofafrica.com, Mon-Sat 1000-1700, R20.*

A few blocks west of Koopman's-De Wit House is the Lutheran Church, and next door is the Martin Melck House, now home to the Gold of Africa Museum. Originally the house served as a clandestine Lutheran church, as in the 18th century the Dutch authorities refused to tolerate any churches other than those belonging to the Dutch Reformed Church. The present museum is a slick presentation of the history of gold mining, outlining the first mining by Egyptians in 2400 BC and the subsequent development of trade networks across Africa. There are comprehensive displays of 19th- and 20th-century gold artworks from Mali, Ghana and Senegal, including jewellery, masks, hair ornaments and statuettes. It's a reasonably diverting collection, but you need a real interest in precious metals to stay for long. Downstairs there's a café and workshop where you can watch goldsmiths at work.

Greenmarket Square

A couple of blocks south of the junction of Strand Street and St George's Mall is Greenmarket Square, the old heart of Cape Town and the second oldest square in the city. It has long been a meeting place, and during the 19th century it became a vegetable market. In 1834 it took on the significant role of being the site where the declaration of the freeing of all slaves was made. Today it remains a popular meeting place, with a busy daily market selling African crafts, jewellery and clothes.

Most of the buildings around the square reflect the city's history. Dominating one side is a **Park Inn** hotel, housed in what was once the headquarters of Shell Oil – note the shell motifs on its exterior. Diagonally opposite is the **Old Town House** (1751) ⓘ *Mon-Fri 1000-1700, Sat 1000-1600*, originally built to house the town guard. It became the first town hall in 1840 when Cape Town became a municipality. Much of the exterior remains unchanged, and with its decorative plaster mouldings and fine curved fanlights is one of the best preserved Cape baroque exteriors in the city. The first electric light in Cape Town was switched on in the Old House on 13 April 1895. Today the white double-storeyed building houses the Michaelis collection of Flemish and Dutch paintings, as well as the **Courtyard Café** which serves snacks. At the entrance to the house is a circle set into the floor which marks the spot from which all distances to and from Cape Town are measured. Next to the **Tudor Hotel** is the second oldest building in the square – the **Metropolitan Methodist Church** (1876). This is the only high Victorian church in Cape Town and has a tall spire with a unique series of miniature grotesques decorating its exterior. The church was designed by Charles Freeman and is regarded as one of the finest in the country.

For antiques, walk out of the square past the Methodist church to Church St. The area between Burg and Long streets is the venue for a daily antiques market.

Long Street

This is one of the trendiest stretches in Cape Town, and gets particularly lively at night. Lined with street cafés, fashionable shops, bars, clubs and backpacker hostels, it has a distinctly youthful feel about it, although a clutch of new boutique hotels, posh apartment complexes and upmarket restaurants is injecting the area with a new sophisticated edge. Long Street is also home to some fine old city buildings. One of Cape Town's late Victorian gems is at number 117, now an antiques shop. On the outside is an unusual cylindrical turret with curved windows; inside is a fine castiron spiral staircase leading to a balustraded gallery.

The **Slave Church Museum** ⓘ *No 40, T021-4236755, Mon-Fri 0900-1600, free*, is the oldest mission church in South Africa, built between 1802 and 1804 as the mother church for missionary work carried out in rural areas. Fortunately the building was saved from demolition in 1977 and restored to its present fine form. Though utilized by directors and members of the South African Missionary Society, it was more commonly used for religious and literacy instruction of slaves in Cape Town; by 1960 most of its congregation had been moved to the Cape Flats. Inside are displays of missionary work throughout the Cape, and behind the pulpit are displays showing early cash accounts and receipts for transactions such as the transfer of slaves.

Karamats

Karamats are the tombs of Imams who lived and worked with the Muslim community of Cape Town. They are dotted around Cape Town in a circle that is believed to provide the city with a protective spiritual boundary, preventing natural disasters. Surprisingly little is made of the *Karamats* in tourist literature, but for devout Cape Muslims they are very important. For an overseas visitor they are worth visiting for their pleasing architecture and peaceful locations. Before embarking upon haj a local muslim will visit each *Karamat* in turn. Sheik Yussuf's *Karamat* is the first and most important. The memorial was only built in 1925 by Hadji Sullaiman Shah. It is situated on a hillock close to the Eerste River, Macassar. Take the Firgrove turning off the N2 just before Somerset West. Five other *Karamats* complete the magic circle – off the road to the Signal Hill viewpoint, Sayed Muhammad Hassan Gaibi Shah is buried here; at the top end of Strand Street, on the slopes of Signal Hill, the bodies of four holy men entombed here including that of Tuan Guru, the first Imam in the Cape, and founder of the first mosque; on Robben Island, the tomb of Sayed Abdurahman Matura, Prince of Ternate; Oudekraal, off the Victoria Road, near Bakoven Beach, a concrete stairway leads up to the tomb hidden in the trees, Nureel Mobeen buried here; and Constantia Valley, on the slopes of Islam Hill, is the tomb of Abdumaah Shah, by the gate to the farm Klein Constantia.

Special tours are organized by Sulayman Habib, a registered guide, T021-235579.

Heritage Square

A few blocks north of Long Street is this renovated block of 17th- and 18th-century townhouses, which include one of the city's oldest blacksmiths, but is better known for its excellent restaurants and the **Cape Heritage Hotel** (see Sleeping, page 101). In the centre is a cobbled courtyard holding the Cape's oldest living grape vine, which was planted in 1781.

Bo-Kaap and the Bo-Kaap Museum

About 600 m west along Wale Street is the Bo-Kaap, Cape Town's historical Islamic quarter and one of the city's most interesting residential areas. The area was developed in the 1760s and today feels a world away from the nearby CDB. Here the streets are cobbled and tightly woven across the slopes of Signal Hill, and the closely packed houses are painted in bright hues of lime, pink and blue. To the west, the Bo-Kaap blends into the trendy new gay area of De Waterkant.

The **Bo-Kaap Museum** ⓘ *Wale St, T021-4813939, Mon-Sat 0900-1600, R5*, housed in an attractive 18th-century house, is dedicated to the Cape's Muslim community and contains the furnishings of a wealthy 19th-century Muslim family. There are antique furnishings and Islamic heirloom such as an old Koran and *tasbeh* beads set in front of the mihrab alcove, while the back room has displays dedicated to the input that slaves has in the economy and development of Cape Town. The photos are the most interesting articles, giving a fascinating glimpse of life in the Bo-Kaap in the early 20th century. At the back is a community centre, with temporary photographic exhibitions. The house itself is one of the oldest buildings in Cape Town surviving in its original form. It was built by Jan de Waal for artisans in 1763 and it was here that Abu Bakr Effendi started the first Arabic school and wrote important articles on Islamic Law. He originally came to Cape Town as a guest of the British government to try and settle religious differences amongst the Cape Muslims.

Victoria and Alfred Waterfront

» pp100-132.

The Victoria and Alfred Waterfront, Cape Town's original Victorian harbour, is the city's most popular attraction. The whole area was completely restored in the early 1990s, and today it is a lively district packed with restaurants, bars and shops. Original buildings stand shoulder to shoulder with mock-Victorian shopping malls, museums and cinemas, all crowding along a waterside walkway with Table Mountain towering beyond. Prices are a little higher in restaurants and bars here and many have argued that the area is over-sanitized and artificial. But despite being geared towards tourists it remains a working harbour, which provides much of the area's real charm. Even if it's not to your taste, the choice of shops, restaurants and entertainment is unrivalled.

Ins and outs

There is a **tourist information office** ⓘ *T021-4054500, www.tourismcapetown.co.za, daily 0900-2100*, in the Clock Tower Centre across the swing bridge from the main development. They stock a good selection of maps and guides for the whole country; there are also desks for car hire and safari companies, and a **SAN Parks** booking desk.

Background

The Victoria and Alfred Waterfront derives its name from the two harbour basins around which it is developed. Construction began in 1860, when Prince Alfred, Queen Victoria's second son, tipped the first load of stone to start the building of the breakwater for Cape Town's harbour. Alfred Basin could not handle the increased shipping volumes and subsequently a larger basin, the Victoria Basin, was built. A number of original buildings remain around the basins and are an interesting diversion from the razzmatazz of the shops and restaurants.

Clock Tower

At the narrow entrance to the Alfred Basin, on the Berties Landing side, is the original Clock Tower, built in 1882 to house the port captain's office. This is in the form of a red octagonal Gothic-style tower and stands just in front of the **Clock Tower Centre**, a modern mall with a collection of shops, offices and restaurants. The Clock Tower Centre houses the Nelson Mandela Gateway to Robben Island, from where you catch the main ferry to the island. This side of the Waterfront is connected the bulk of the area by a swing bridge, which swings open every 10 minutes to allow boats to pass underneath.

Union Castle Building

Walking across the swing bridge (look out for the Cape fur seals as you cross), you come to the stocky square building known as **Union Castle Building** (1919), designed by the firm of architects owned by Sir Herbert Baker. The Union Steamship Company and the Castle Line both ran monthly mail ships between Britain and South Africa in the late 19th century. In 1900 they amalgamated and from then on mail was delivered every week. The last Union Castle ship to sail to England with the mail was the *Windsor Castle* in 1977.

Opposite the Union Castle Building is the **Victoria and Alfred Hotel.** Now a luxury four-star hotel, the building was originally a coal store before being converted into Union Castle's warehouse and customs baggage store. It originally had a third floor but this was destroyed in a fire in 1939. This was the first hotel to be opened at the Waterfront and it is an important part of the success of the whole venture.

Time Ball Tower

Heading west from there, on the other side of Dock Road above the car park, is the Time Ball Tower. This dates from 1894; its purpose was to act as an accurate reference for ships' navigators to set their clocks as the ball on the roof fell. Correct time was vital for the navigator to be able to determine precise longitude before the development of more modern equipment. Beside the tower is a 100-year-old dragon tree, *Dracaeno draco*, from the Canary Islands, and next to the tree is the original **harbour master's residence** (1860).

Two Oceans Aquarium

ⓘ *Entrance is on Dock Rd next to the Maritime Museum, by the Waterfront Craft Market, T021-4183823, www.aquarium.co.za, daily 0930-1800, R65.*

The top attraction on the Waterfront is this aquarium focusing on the unique Cape marine environment created by the merging of the Atlantic and Indian Ocean. The display begins with a walk through the Indian Ocean, where visitors follow a route past tanks filled with a multitude of colourful fish, turtles, seahorses and octopuses.

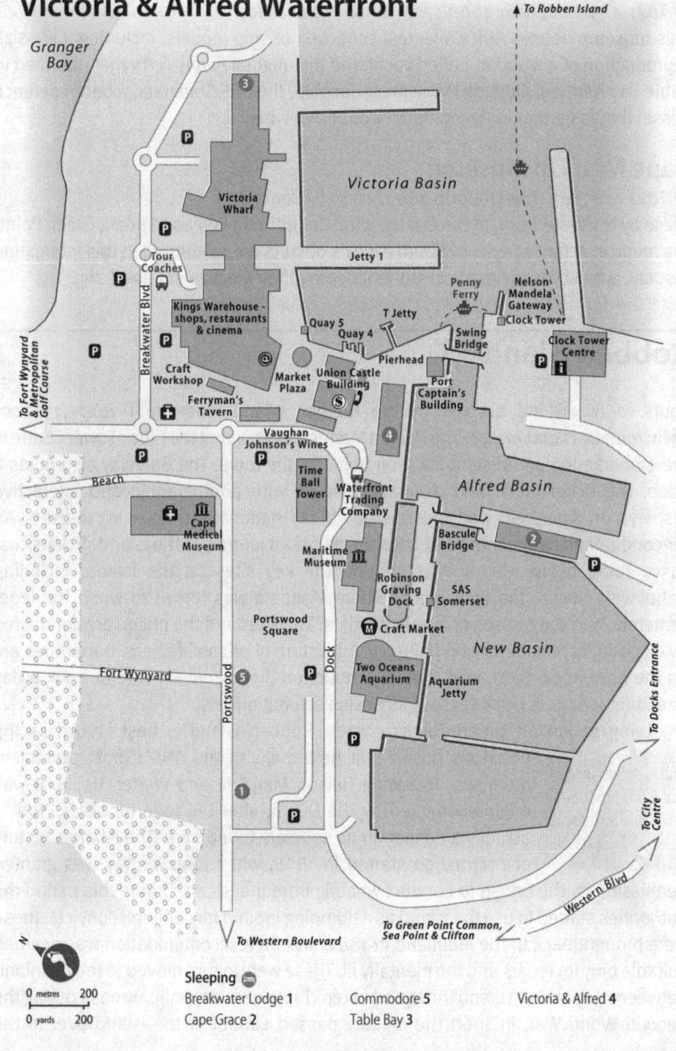

Highlights here include giant spider crabs and phosphorescent jellyfish, floating in a mesmerizing circular current. From here you walk past touch pools, where children can pick up spiky starfish and slimy sea slugs. The basement holds the Alpha Activity Centre, where free puppet shows and face painting keep children busy. The main wall here is part of the Diving Animals Pool, where you can watch Cape fur seals dart and dive before the glass. Upstairs is a vast tank holding the Kelp Forest, an extraordinary tangle of giant kelp that sways drunkenly in the artificial tides. The highlight is the Predators exhibit, a circular tank complete with glass tunnel, holding ragged-tooth sharks, eagle rays, turtles, and some impressively large hunting fish. There are daily feeds at 1530, and those with an Open Water diving certificate can arrange to dive with the sharks (booking ahead essential). The aquarium also has a new conservation programme, where it releases ragged tooth sharks back into the sea; the sharks are tagged, providing valuable data on their movements.

Maritime Museum

ⓘ *T021-4052880, daily 1000-1700, small entrance fee.*
This museum houses Africa's largest collection of ship models, including a life-size reproduction of a wooden-hulled yacht and the original *Penny Ferry* that operated in Table Bay harbour. Outside is the museum ship, the *SAS Somerset*, a boom defence vessel that is permanently moored for public viewing.

Cape Medical Museum

ⓘ *T021-4185663, Tue-Fri 0900-1600, entry by donation.*
Close by the Waterfront, at the City Hospital Complex on Portwood Road, Green Point, the medical achievements of South Africa's doctors are celebrated in this interesting display, a must for any medical students doing their elective in Cape Town.

Robben Island

Tours to the island are run by the **Robben Island Museum** ⓘ *T021-4134200, www.robben-island.org.za*. The Nelson Mandela Gateway at the Clock Tower Centre is the embarkation and disembarkation point for the tours. The Gateway also holds a shop, the ticket office and a small museum with photographic and interactive displays on Apartheid and the rise of African nationalism, open 0730-2100. An air-conditioned catamaran completes the half-hour journey to the island. Tickets cost R150. Tours begin with a drive around the key sites on the island, including Sobukwe's house, the lime quarry where Mandela was forced to work, the leper cemetery, and the houses of former warders. Tours around the prison are conducted by ex-political prisoners, who paint a vivid picture of prison life here. Departures are on the hour 0900-1500, and allow 2½ hours on the island. Be sure to book a day ahead (or 3 days in peak season) as tickets sell out quickly.

You must remain with your guide during the tour. Do not drink any tap water on the island.

Lying 12 km off Green Point's shores, Robben Island is best known as the notorious prison that held many of the ANC's most prominent members, including Nelson Mandela and Walter Sisulu. It was originally named by the Dutch, after the term for seals, 'rob' – actually a misnomer as none are found here. The island's history of occupation started in 1806, when John Murray was granted permission by the British to conduct whaling from the island. During this period the authorities started to use the island as a dumping ground for common convicts; these were brought back to the mainland in 1843, and their accommodation was deemed suitable only for lepers and the mentally ill. These were in turn moved to the mainland between 1913 and 1931, and the island entered a new era as a military base during the Second World War. In 1960 the military passed control of the island over to the

Department of Prisons, and it remained a prison until 1996. On 1 December 1999 the island was declared a World Heritage Site by UNESCO.

Robben Island's effectiveness as a prison did not rest simply with the fact that escape was virtually impossible. The authorities anticipated that the idea of "out of sight, out of mind" would be particularly applicable here, and to a certain extent they were correct. Certainly, its isolation did much to break the spirit of political prisoners, not least Robert Sobukwe's. Sobukwe was the leader of the Pan African Congress, and was kept in solitary confinement for nine years. Other political prisoners were spared that at least, although in 1971 they were separated from common law prisoners, as they were deemed a 'bad' influence. Conditions were harsh, with forced hard labour and routine beatings. Much of the daily running of the maximum security prison was designed to reinforce racial divisions: all the wardens, and none of the prisoners, were white; black prisoners, unlike those deemed coloured, had to wear short trousers and were given smaller food rations. Contact with the outside world was virtually non-existent – visitors had to apply for permission six months in advance and were allowed to stay for just half an hour. Newspapers were banned and letters were limited to one every six months.

Yet despite these measures, the B-Section, which housed Mandela and other major political prisoners, became the international focus of the fight against Apartheid. The last political prisoners left the island in 1991.

It is also possible to view wildlife on the island – as a prison, the area was strictly protected allowing the fish and bird populations to flourish. There are over 100 species of bird on the island, and it is an important breeding site for African penguins.

Southern suburbs » *pp100-132.*

Primarily encompassing the more affluent residential areas of Cape Town, the suburbs, stretching southeast from the city centre, are an interesting diversion to the usual tourist spots. Although a car is the best way to visit them, it is possible to reach all by train – the metro service between the city centre and Simon's Town runs through all the suburbs, although safety can be an issue. It's best to avoid the trains when it's not busy. » *For further details, see Transport, page 130.*

Woodstock and Observatory

The first suburb, **Woodstock**, is a mixed commercial and residential area, historically a working class coloured district. Today it is somewhat run down and depressing, although the back streets are an attractive mesh of Victorian bungalows, some of which have been taken over by fashionable bars and restaurants.

Observatory is an appealing area of tightly packed houses, narrow streets and student hangouts. Being close to the university, there is a good range of trendy bars, cafés and restaurants catering for a mixed scene of students, bohemian types and backpackers. This is a good area to stay in and has an enjoyably liberal atmosphere not so easily found in some of the other suburbs. The observatory after which the suburb is named is where Station Road intersects Liesbeeck Parkway. The first Astronomer Royal to work at the Royal Observatory was also a clergyman, the Reverand Fearon Fellowes. Aside from making astronomical observations the observatory was responsible for accurate standard time in South Africa. It has also been an important meteorological centre and has a seismograph which records earthquakes around the world. Observatory is also where you'll find the **Groot Schuur Hospital** on Main Road, the site of the world's first heart transplant. A small **museum** ⓘ *T021-4045232, Mon-Fri 0900-1400, R5*, in the hospital commemorates this, with a restored theatre built to look as it did when the transplant took place.

Mowbray, Rosebank and Rondebosch

The next suburbs of Mowbray, Rosebank and Rondebosch lie just below the **University of Cape Town**. Again, they are popular with students and have a good selection of restaurants and shops. **Mowbray** was originally known as Driekoppen, or three heads, after the murder by three slaves of a European foreman and his wife in 1724. On their capture they were beheaded and their heads impaled on stakes at the farm entrance to act as a deterrent. **Rondebosch**, conversely, has for some time been associated with education. Aside from the university, several important schools were founded in the district. The area was also important from a practical point of view: in 1656 Van Riebeeck realized that Company's Garden was exposed to a damaging southeast wind. His first choice of a more sheltered spot was Rondebosch. This proved a success and a grain storage barn was built. Early written accounts describe the area as wild country, with the farmers frequently losing livestock to hyenas, lion and leopards – an image that is hard to imagine as you sit in the evening rush hour on Rhodes Drive. Also in Rondebosch is **Groot Schuur**, the Prime Minister's official residence; **Westbrooke**, home of the State President; and the original residence of the Cape Governor over 200 years ago, **Rustenburg**.

Irma Stern Museum

ⓘ *Cecil Rd, Rosebank, T021-6855686, Tue-Sat 1000-1700, www.irmastern.co.za, R8.*

A lesser-known but fascinating attraction in the area is this museum. Irma Stern was one of South Africa's pioneering artists and her lovely house displays a mixture of her own works, a collection of artefacts from across Africa, and some fine pieces of antique furniture from overseas, including 17th-century Spanish chairs, 19th-century German oak furniture and Swiss *mardi gras* masks. Her portraits are particularly poignant and those of her close friends are superb, while her religious art is rather more disturbing. Stern's studio, complete with paint brushes and palettes, has been left as it was when she died. The most important African items were collected in the Congo and Zanzibar. Of particular note is the Buli Stool, one of only 20 known carvings by a master carver from southeast Zaire. The kitchen houses a collection of Chinese ceramics including two fine Ming celadon dishes.

Rhodes Memorial

ⓘ *T021-6899151, Nov-Apr 0700-1900, May-Oct 0800-1800.*

The best-known attraction in the area is the Rhodes Memorial, off Rhodes Drive, by the Rondesbosch turning. The imposing granite memorial to Cecil John Rhodes (Cape Prime Minister from 1890 to 1896) was designed by Francis Masey and Sir Herbert Baker. Four bronze lions flank a wide flight of steps which lead up to a Greek Temple. The temple houses an immense bronze head of Rhodes, wrought by JM Swan. Above the head are the words "slave to the spirit and life work of Cecil John Rhodes who loved and served South Africa". At the base of the steps is an immense bronze mounted figure of *Physical Energy* given to South Africa by GF Watts, a well regarded sculptor of the time; the original stands in Hyde Park, London. Other than the memorial, the great attraction here is the magnificent view of the Cape Flats and the southern suburbs. Behind the memorial are a number of popular trails leading up the slopes of Devil's Peak. Also tucked away here is an excellent little tea house set in a garden of blue hydrangeas that serves good cheesecake, sandwiches and cream teas.

South of Rondesbosch

By this point the southern suburbs have reached right around Devil's Peak and the shadowy mountains now dominating the views represent an unfamiliar view of Table Mountain. The suburb of **Newlands** backs right up to the slopes of the mountain and is probably best known for being the home to Western Province Rugby Union and the beautiful Newlands cricket Test ground. Sports fans shouldn't miss the chance of seeing a game here. There are several good hotels and guesthouses in the area. On Boundary Road in Newlands is the **Rugby Museum** ① *T021-6596700, Mon-Fri 0830-1700, free*, housed in the Sports Medical Research Institute Building. The somewhat chaotic collection commemorates the history of the sport in the country and is also home to the Currie Cup, the premier domestic competition trophy.

Also on Boundary Road is **Josephine Mill** ① *T021-6864939, Mon-Fri 1000-1600, small entrance fee*, the only surviving watermill in Cape Town, which has been restored as a working flour mill. Of particular note is the massive waterwheel (1840). The building is in the style of a Cornish red-brick mill, built by a Swede, Jacob Letterstedt, and named in honour of his Crown Princess, Josephine. The mill is tucked away near the Newlands Rugby Stadium and has a brewery and a peaceful tea garden. During the summer months, concerts are held on Sundays on the banks of the tree-fringed Liesbeek River, as part of the **Nedbank Summer Concert** season (see page 123).

Claremont offers little of interest. On the main road is the upmarket **Cavendish Square Complex**, another shopping mall. There are two good cinema complexes here – the Ster-Kinekor Commercial, on the second floor, shows big releases, while the Ster-Kinekor Nouveau specializes in alternative and foreign-language films.

Nearby are **Ardene Gardens** ① *0800-sunset*, a Victorian park first planted in 1845 by Ralph Arderne, who was so charmed by the Cape while en route for Australia that he decided to settle here instead. He succeeded in creating a garden that would represent the flora of the world. When his son died the estate was split up but fortunately in 1927 the Cape Town Municipality bought 11 acres of the garden. Today the arboretum with specimens from all over the world is probably the best collection of trees in South Africa. There is an obelisk that marks the site from which the famous astronomer, Sir John Herschel, carried out his research from 1834 to 1838.

A little further along the main road takes you to **Wynberg**. Apart from a few curio shops, the main attraction here is the district known as **Little Chelsea**. This is a group of well-preserved 19th-century homes. South of Wynberg the countryside opens up. To the west lie the fertile and prosperous valleys of Constantia and Tokai; due south the road quickly brings False Bay (see page 94) into view and the coastal resort of Muizenberg. To the east lie the exposed high density suburbs on the Cape Flats – Crossroads, Guguletu, Khayelitsha, Langa and Mitchells Plain.

Kirstenbosch Botanical Gardens

① *T021-7998899, www.nbi.ac.za, Sep-Mar 0800-1900, Apr-Aug 0800-1800, R25. By far the easiest way of getting here is by hire car. Otherwise there are trains to the nearest station at Mowbray, 10 mins from the city centre. From here there is an erratic bus service or a very long walk. Alternatively, take a Rikki taxi – they will pick up and drop off at any time other than rush hour. Most of the organized city tours also include the gardens on their itinerary.*

Five kilometres south of Rondesbosch is Kirstenbosch, South Africa's oldest, largest and most exquisite botanical garden. It is one of the finest in the world, and its setting alone is incomparable. The gardens stretch up the eastern slopes of Table Mountain, merging seamlessly with the fynbos of the steep slopes above. Cecil Rhodes bought Kirstenbosch farm in 1895 and promptly presented the site to the people of South Africa with the intention that it become a botanical garden. It was not until 1913 that Kirstenbosch was proclaimed a National Botanical Garden – the Anglo-Boer War had caused the delay. The first director of the gardens was Professor Harold Pearson, who sadly only lived for a further three years after the garden's creation. A granite Celtic Cross marks his grave in the Cycad garden. There is a fitting epitaph on the grave: "If ye seek his monument, look around you." The real development of the gardens was under Professor RH Compton, who cared for the gardens for 34 years. The herbarium is named after Compton – it houses over 250,000 specimens, including many rare plants.

A great deal of time and effort has been made to make the gardens accessible to the general public, making them a pleasure for both serious botanists and families enjoying a day out on the slopes of Table Mountain.

The **Fragrance Garden** features herbs and flowers set out to make appreciating their scents effortless. On a warm day, when the volatile oils are released by the plants, there are some rather overpowering aromas; the plaques are also in Braille. The **Dell** follows a beautifully shaded path snaking beneath ferns and along a stream. Indigenous South African herbs can be inspected in the **Medicinal Plants Garden**, each one identified and used by the Khoi and San peoples in the treatment of a variety of ailments. The plants' uses are identified on plaques, and it seems that most ailments are covered – kidney trouble, rheumatics, coughs, cancer, piles and bronchitis. For a sense of the past, it is worth visiting what is known as **Van Riebeeck's Hedge**. Back in 1660 a hedge of wild almond trees (*Brabejum stellatifolium*) was planted by Van Riebeeck as part of a physical boundary to try and prevent cattle rustling. Segments still remain today within the garden.

The **Skeleton Path** can be followed all the way to the summit of Table Mountain. It starts off as a stepped path, but becomes fairly steep near the top. It involves a climb up a rocky waterfall – take special care in the wet season.

Perhaps the most enjoyable way of experiencing the gardens is at one of the Sunday sunset concerts held throughout summer (see Music, page 122). Also available for a small fee are eco-adventure tours, and tours by motorized golf cart. Just beyond the entrance concourse is an excellent shop and a café on the courtyard terrace. The shop has the usual collection of curios, along with a good choice of books on South Africa and a selection of indigenous plants for your garden. The café serves over-priced sandwiches and cakes; better value and with far nicer views is the **Silver Tree** restaurant inside the gardens, just around the corner from the entrance, which serves good meals and is open until 2200. It also offers picnic hamper service. For a reasonable price you can have a ready-made picnic with wine and join the Capetonians for a picnic lunch on the lush lawns.

Constantia

South of the Botanical Gardens lies Cape Town's most elegant suburb, the verdant area of Constantia and its winelands. This historical district was the first site of wine-making in South Africa and today it is an attractive introduction to the country's wines as well as offering some fine examples of Cape Dutch architecture. There are five estates here, of which Groot Constantia (see below) is the best known and definitely worth a visit. **Buitenverwachting** ⓘ *T021-7945190, www.buitenverwachting.co.za*, is a working estate with an excellent restaurant (see page 115). **Klein Constantia** ⓘ *T021-7945188, www.kleinconstantia.com*, is a beautiful hilly estate with a great tasting centre, and famed for its dessert wine, Vin de Constance, allegedly Napoleon's favourite wine. **Constantia Uitsig** ⓘ *T021-7941810, www.constantia uitsig.co.za*, has excellent wines, luxury accommodation and three restaurants (see page 106). **Steenberg** ⓘ *T021-7132222, www.steenberghotel.com*, offers superb wines as well as having luxurious lodgings, a good restaurant and a golf course (see page 106).

Groot Constantia

ⓘ *T021-7945128, www.grootconstantia.co.za, 0900-1700/1800, free entrance to the main estate, museum R10. 2 restaurants: Jonkershuis has traditional Cape food; Simon's serves burgers, salads and seafood. Wine tastings take place at the sales centre, R25 for 5 wines; cheese platters available. Cellar tours every hour on the hour.*

This old wine estate has some of the finest Cape Dutch architecture in South Africa, and with its rolling, vineyard setting and wine-tasting centre is a delightful place to spend a few hours – although it does get swamped with tour buses in high season.

The main house was originally home to Cape Governor Simon van der Stel between 1699 and 1712. He named the estate after Constantia, the daughter of the company official who had granted the land to him. Before his death, van der Stel planted most of the vines, but it was not until 1778 that the estate became famous for its wines. During this period the estate was unable to meet the demands from Europe, especially France. The magnificent wine cellar behind the main house was designed by the renowned French architect, Louis Thibault.

The main house is now a museum full of period furniture. A booklet is available giving a brief description of the objects on show. Behind the house is a shady garden and pool overlooked by the wine cellar, with displays on brandy and wine making. There are two impressive giant oak vats each with a capacity of over 4000 litres.

Rondevlei Nature Reserve

Despite being surrounded by suburban sprawl the reserve is one of the best birdwatching spots around Cape Town.

ⓘ *From Cape Town take the M5, Prince George Dr, turn left into Victoria Rd in Grassy Pk, and then right into Fisherman's Walk, 17 km from the town centre, 6 km from Muizenberg, T021-7062404, www.rondevlei.co.za, 0730-1700/1900, R5.*

This 220-ha reserve was originally established to protect the birdlife and the coastal fynbos vegetation. Today it is an important environmental education centre for local schools. Only the northern shore of the lake is open to the public. A path follows the vlei's edge, along which there are two lookout towers equipped with telescopes. There are several hides along the water's edge, and cuts within the reeds allow views across the water. The best time to visit the reserve is from January to March when many European migrants can be seen. Over 200 bird species have been recorded; on a good day visitors should be able to see more than 65 species. There are a few small, shy mammals in the reserve, plus a small population of hippos. Inside the reserve is a small **aquarium** showing the fresh water fish that inhabit the area.

Tokai Forest

ⓘ *Take the M3 out of town towards the southern suburbs. Just before Muizenberg, turn right into Tokai St and follow the signs for Tokai Manor House, T021-7127471, daily during daylight hours, entry by donation.*

Tokai was set up as a forest nursery in 1883 to try to stem the destruction of forest reserves, and start a programme of conservation and reforestation. Today, the forest is part of Table Mountain National Park. This is one of the few areas where the region's indigenous forest and some wildlife have been fully protected and preserved. The arboretum contains 40 tree species – there are two walking trails, and horse riding and mountain biking are possible in the low-lying section (permits from the main gate).

Atlantic seaboard » pp100-132.

The Atlantic seaboard, stretching from Green Point to the Cape of Good Hope, is the area's most spectacular coastline, at times clinging dramatically to the Twelve Apostles, the spine of mountains stretching south. This is where the most immediately attractive beaches are, although the water on this side of the peninsula is far colder that on the False Bay side – swimming is often not an option. Nevertheless, the area is hugely popular with day-trippers and domestic tourists. Although Green Point is close to the Waterfront, the rest of the coast is a drive away.

Ins and outs

Public transport is limited to a regular bus that departs from in front of **OK Bazaars** on Adderley Street and runs along the Atlantic coast road as far as Hout Bay. Minibus taxis plough this route; alternatively, take a **Rikki** taxi.

De Waterkant, Green Point and Sea Point

These suburbs are the closest seaside residential areas to the city, and are undergoing rapid transformation. De Waterkant – until fairly recently a run-down area of flaking bungalows – is now Cape Town's most fashionable district, with beautifully restored Victorian homes painted in bright hues crammed into a tight cobbled grid of streets, climbing up towards Signal Hill. This, with Green Point, is the city's main gay area, with excellent nightlife and a wide choice of super-trendy restaurants and bars. Moving towards Sea Point, the buildings become taller and develop into a series of high-rise apartment blocks running along the coast. The beach is unsafe for swimming, although there are a couple of rock pools, including Graaf's Pool (men only) and Milton's Pool. Although Sea Point has a bit of a scruffy reputation, new developments are giving it a facelift and bringing in a number of upmarket shops and restaurants.

Clifton Beach

Cape Town's best-known beaches stretch along Clifton, and are renowned as the playground of the young and wealthy – this is the place to see and be seen. Other than being hotpots of high society, Clifton's four sheltered beaches are stunning, perfect arches of powder-soft white sand sloping gently into turquoise water. The beaches, reached be a series of winding footpaths, are divided by rocky outcrops and are imaginatively named First, Second, Third and Fourth. Each has a distinct character – if you're bronzed and beautiful, head to First beach. More demure visitors may feel more comfortable on Fourth, which is popular with families and was awarded a Blue Flag in 2004. The sunbathing and swimming are good on all the beaches, but note that the water is very cold – usually around 12°. Most of the relatively small-scale, high-luxury development has been behind the beaches (some impressive houses can be glimpsed from the winding steps leading down). Be warned that there is limited parking in high season, so get here early.

Camps Bay

Following the coast south, you soon skirt around a hill and come out over Camps Bay, a long arch of sand backed by the Twelve Apostles. This is one of the most beautiful (and most photographed) beaches in the world, but the calm cobalt water belies its chilliness. The sand is also less sheltered than at Clifton, and sunbathing here on a windy day can be painful. But there are other distractions; the beachfront is lined with excellent seafood restaurants, and having a sundowner followed by a superb meal is quite the perfect ending to a day in Cape Town.

The drive between Camps Bay and Hout Bay runs along the slopes of the Twelve Apostles and is beautiful. Apart from the turning to Llandudno, there is no easy access to the coast until you reach Hout Bay. **Llandudno** itself is a small, exclusive settlement with a fine beach and excellent surf.

Hout Bay

Hout Bay, a historical fishing harbour with an attractive beach, attracts swarms of South African families during peak season. Most come for the seafood restaurants and boat trips, but the best reason for heading here is for spectacular Chapman's Peak Drive (see below), which begins just outside town. As the sun sets in the summer months every pullover along the road is filled with spectators, drink in hand.

Hout Bay itself is fairly attractive, with a busy fishing harbour at the western end of the bay; at the other end is a collection of shops and popular restaurants. By the harbour is a commercial complex known as **Mariners Wharf**, the first of its kind in South Africa and a popular attraction, although looking a little wind-worn these days. It is based upon Fisherman's Wharf in San Francisco, with a whole string of fish 'n' chips restaurants, souvenir shops, boats for hire and a fish market known as **Snoekies Fresh Fish Market**, close to the harbour gates. Even if you're not intending to buy anything it is worth a quick look to see the huge variety of fish that are caught off this coast. Boats run from here to see the seals on **Duiker Island** (see Boat tours, page 129).

Back in the town, next to the **tourist office** ⓘ *T021-7901264, www.tourismcapetown.co.za*, is the **Hout Bay Museum** ⓘ *4 Andrews Rd, T021-7903270, Tue-Sat 1000-1630, R5*, with displays on the history of the area, aimed at visiting school groups. More popular with families is **The World of Birds** ⓘ *Valley Rd, T021-7902730, www.worldofbirds.org.za, daily 0900-1700*, with over 400 species of birds housed in impressive walk-through aviaries. There's also the Monkey Jungle, populated with squirrel monkeys.

Chapman's Peak Drive

It is worth hiring a car for a day just to drive along Chapman's Peak Drive, a breathtaking 15-km route carved into the cliffs 600 m above the sea. The route was re-opened a couple of years ago, following extensive repairs and the rigging of giant nets to catch falling rocks. It's now a toll road, costing R22 per car. Although the road up to the toll gates is fairly busy with groups pulled over in view points, the Drive itself is remarkably quiet, allowing outstanding and uninhibited views of the craggy coastline and thrashing ocean. The best time to drive along here is close to sunset in the summer, but the views of the crescent of white sand at Hout Bay on one side, and the vast stretch of Noordhoek on the other, are recommended at any time.

Noordhoek

The greatest attraction here is the 8-km-long deserted beach, backed by a couple of tidal lagoons which offer excellent birdwatching. There's very little to the village itself, but the **Noordhoek Farm Village** on Beach Road is a pleasant spot for a coffee or light lunch, with two family restaurants and a couple of shops selling antiques, crafts and organic produce. The beach also offers the Cape's finest setting for horse riding along the shore. Contact the **Imhoff Equestrian Centre**, T082-7741191 (mob), www.horseriding.co.za, or **Sleepy Hollow Horse Riding**, T021-7892341.

Kommetjie → *Colour map 8, grid A2.*

Driving along the Atlantic side of the peninsula, you could miss Kommetjie altogether. Kommetjie means 'little basin', a reference to the natural inlet in the rocks which has been developed into a tidal pool. The settlement is small with a pub, restaurant, caravan park and little else. It is, however, a major surfing spot and Long Beach to the north is always busy with surfers, even in winter. There is also an interesting walk along Long Beach to the wreck of the *Kakapo*, offering a rare opportunity to examine a wreck at close quarters without having to don full scuba equipment. The *Kakapo* is a steamship which was beached here in May 1900 on her maiden voyage when the captain apparently mistook Chapman's Peak for Cape Point during a storm. The boiler and shell are still intact about 100 m above the high tide mark.

Scarborough

Scarborough consists of a scattering of weekend and holiday homes on the hillside overlooking the Atlantic. The beach is broad and long but swimming is not a good idea as the water is cold and there are strong currents. Just outside Scarborough, close to the entrance to Cape of Good Hope Nature Reserve, is the **Cape Point Ostrich Farm** ⓘ *T021-7809294, www.capepointostrichfarm.com, daily 0930-1730*, worth a visiting for its in-depth tours, describing the lifecycle of the ostrich; during breeding season you can watch eggs hatching. There's a pleasant tea garden on site.

Cape of Good Hope

» *Colour map 8, grid A2.*

ⓘ *To21-7018692, www.cpnp.co.za, Oct-Mar 0700-1800, Apr-Sep 0700-1700, R45.* The Cape of Good Hope Nature Reserve, now part of Table Mountain National Park, was established to protect the unique flora and fauna of this stretch of coast. In 1928 the area came under threat from developers who were looking to build more seaside resorts. Those in favour of a reserve persuaded local families to sell their land, and in 1939 the reserve came into existence. Some game animals were introduced and the land has since been left to its own devices. Today, it is a dramatically wild area of towering cliffs, stupendous ocean views, excellent hiking and beautiful, deserted beaches.

Ins and outs

Getting there Given its location at the southern tip of the peninsula, you can approach the reserve from two directions: along the False Bay shoreline via Muizenberg and Simon's Town; or by the quieter M65 via Kommetjie and Scarborough. It is about 70 km from Cape Town centre to the reserve gates. There is no public transport to the reserve, although you can take a **Rikki** taxi from Simon's Town (accessible by train). Ask on your outward journey about arrangements for the return leg.

Getting away From the entrance to the reserve take a left and follow the M65 along the edge of the reserve. After 8 km the road divides; the right turn winds over the Swartkopberge to Long Beach and Simon's Town. Known as Red Hill (M66), this is a quicker route back to Cape Town if your time is short. There are two picnic spots with braai facilities along here. The road to the left leads down to Scarborough, and then along the coast to Kommetjie, 18 km from the reserve gates. There is a craft centre just after the junction, on the right.

Getting around We strongly recommend you come with your own transport to see the reserve; alternatively, there are several companies that organize good day trips from the city. A **funicular railway** ⓘ *0800-1700; R32 return, R24 single*, takes visitors up from the main car park to the original lighthouse where there are a series of paved footpaths and viewpoints. The walk is fairly steep and takes about 20 minutes, depending on how fit you are. Next to the car park is the **Two Oceans Restaurant** ⓘ *To21-7809200, www.destinationrestaurants.co.za, 0930-1700*, specializing in seafood but also serving steak, chicken dishes and salads. Between December and March it is advisable to book a table. There is also a takeaway cafeteria which sells hamburgers, sandwiches, cold drinks, tea and coffee, as well as an information centre, curio shop, toilets and telephones (card and coins).

Around the reserve

The Cape of Good Hope is an integral part of the Cape Floristic Kingdom, the smallest but richest of the world's six floral kingdoms. A frequently quoted statistic is that within the 7750 ha of the reserve there are as many different plant species as there are in the whole of the British Isles. In addition to all this there are several different species of antelope: eland, bontebok, springbok, cape grysbok, red hartebeest and grey rhebok, as well as the elusive cape mountain zebra, snakes, tortoises and pesky baboons.

Although the strong winds and the low-lying vegetation are not ideal for birds, over 250 species have been recorded here, of which about 100 are known to breed within the reserve. There are plenty of vantage points where you can watch open sea birds – you can expect to see the Cape gannet, shy albatross, sooty shearwater, white-chinned petrel, Sabine's gull and Cory's shearwater. In the Strandveld vegetation along the coast you can expect to see many fruit eating birds such as the southern boubou, Cape robin and bully canary. Around Sirkels Vlei you will find some freshwater birds. Finally there are a couple of rarities: the white-rumped sandpiper from South America, macaroni penguins from Antarctica, and the purple gallinule from the US have all been seen within the reserve. The **Vlei Museum** issues a checklist of 100 birds. Alongside each name is a code telling you the typical habitat and the bird's resident status.

Cape Point

Cape Point Lighthouse is nothing special in itself, but the climb is well worth it for spectacular views of the peninsula. On a clear day the ocean views stretching all around are incredible – as is the wind, so be sure to hold on to hats and sunglasses. You can take the funicular to the top, but the 20-minute walk allows better views of the coast. There are plenty of viewpoints, linked by a jumble of footpaths.

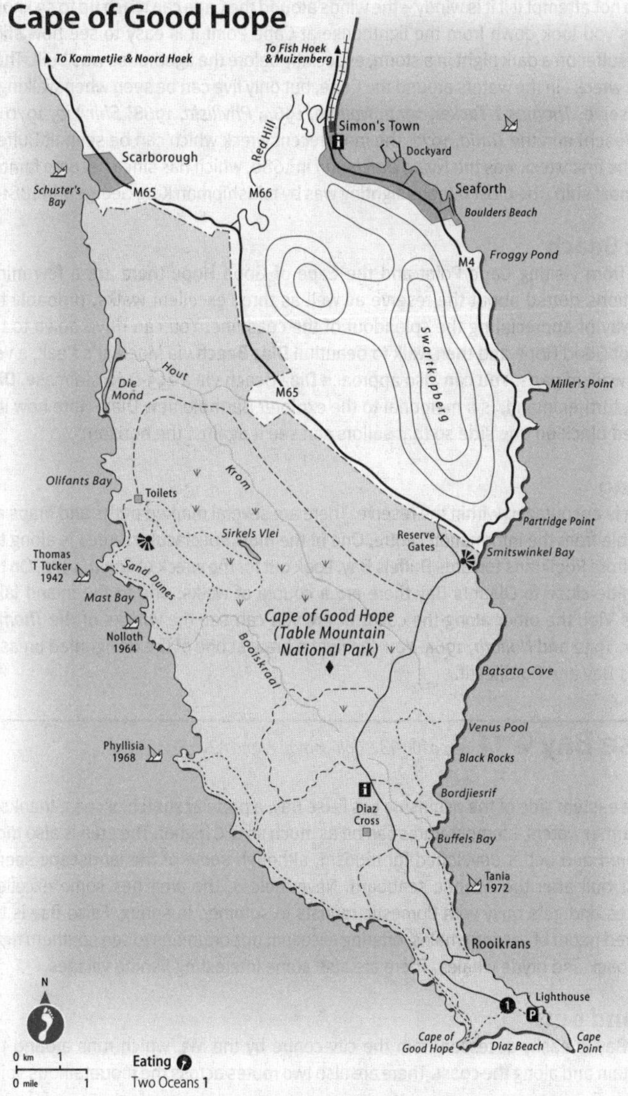

The first lighthouse came into service in May 1860, but it quickly became apparent that the most prominent point on a clear day was far from ideal in poor weather. It was quite often shrouded in cloud while at sea level all was clear. In 1872 the Lighthouse Commission decided on a lower site, but it was only after the Portuguese ship, the *Lusitania*, struck Bellows Rock in April 1911, that work started on a new lighthouse. This was built just 87 m above sea level, close to Diaz Rock and remains the Cape's most important lighthouse today. The current beam can be seen up to 63 km out to sea, and 18 km out there is a red lamp that warns ships that they are in the danger zone.

From the top point of the railway there are still approximately 120 steps to the old lighthouse where you get some of the finest views. If you are reasonably fit and have a good head for heights, there is a spectacular walk to the modern lighthouse at Diaz Point. From the renovated old lighthouse you can see the path running along the left side of the narrow cliff that makes up the point. The round trip takes about 30 minutes, but do not attempt it if it is windy – the winds around the Cape can reach up to 55 knots.

As you look down from the lighthouse at Cape Point it is easy to see how ships could suffer on a dark night in a storm, especially before the lighthouse was built. There are 23 wrecks in the waters around the Cape, but only five can be seen when walking in the reserve: *Thomas T Tucker*, 1942; *Nolloth*, 1964; *Phyllisia*, 1968; *Shir Yib*, 1970 (at Diaz Beach) and the *Tania*, 1972, the most recent wreck which can be seen at Buffel's Bay. The first wreck was the *Flying Dutchman* in 1680, which has since become famous as a ghost ship. The most famous sighting was by midshipman King George V in 1881.

Diaz Beach

Apart from visiting Cape Point and the Cape of Good Hope there are a few minor attractions dotted about the reserve as well as three excellent walks, probably the best way of appreciating the splendour of the coastline. You can drive down to the Cape of Good Hope and then walk to beautiful **Diaz Beach** via Maclear's Peak, a very steep walk in parts. You can also approach Diaz Beach via a 253-step staircase. **Diaz Cross**, further inland, is a memorial to the explorer Bartholomew Diaz. Note how it is painted black on one side so that sailors can see it against the horizon.

Hiking

Hiking is encouraged within the reserve. There are several marked paths and maps are available from the information centre. One of the most spectacular routes is along the coast from Rooikrans towards Buffels Bay. Look out for the wreck of *Tania*, 1972. On the west side close to Olifants Bay there are a couple of walks; one to the inland lake, Sirkels Vlei, the other along the coast where you can see the wrecks of the *Thomas Tucker*, 1942 and *Nolloth*, 1964. You can light a braai at one of the designated areas at Buffels Bay and Bordjiesrif.

False Bay

» *pp100-132. Colour map 8, grid A2.*

On the eastern side of the peninsula lies False Bay, a popular stretch of coast thanks to the warmer waters – temperatures can be as much as 8°C higher. The area is also more sheltered and better developed for tourism, although some of the landscape seems almost dull after the Atlantic seaboard. Nevertheless, the area has some excellent beaches and gets busy with domestic tourists in summer. In spring, False Bay is the favoured haunt of calving whales, offering excellent opportunities to see southern right, humpback and bryde whales. There are also some interesting fishing villages.

Ins and outs

False Bay is easily accessed from the city centre by the M3, which runs around the mountain and along the coast. There are also two routes across the mountainous spine linking the roads that hug the coast around the peninsula: you can cross from Noordhoek to Fish Hoek via the M65 and Sun Valley, or further south take the Red Hill road from Scarborough to Simon's Town. Each route is convenient if your time is short, but the most scenic route is to follow the M65 along the coast from the Atlantic seaboard to False Bay. It is impossible to get lost as there is only one road along the shoreline.

Alternatively, the metro (for up-to-date times: T0800-656463, www.mti.co.za) continues through the southern suburbs to Simon's Town – the stretch following False Bay is spectacular. Trains go as far as Simon's Town and leave every 30 minutes, with the last trains leaving Simon's Town at around 2000. There have been some reports of crime on the trains, so it's best to avoid them at quieter times and in the evening.

Muizenberg

Travelling out from the city centre, Muizenberg is the first settlement you reach on False Bay and as such has long been a popular local bathing spot. The settlement was first propelled to the forefront of popularity when Cecil Rhodes bought a cottage here in 1899. Many other wealthy people followed, building some fine Victorian and Edwardian cottages along the back streets and attracting the likes of Agatha Christie and Rudyard Kipling to its shores. Although the resort decayed significantly in the last decade, various recent regeneration projects mean that the area is starting to look like its old cheerful self again. The beach certainly remains beautiful: a vast stretch of powdery white sand sloping gently to the water. It is safe for swimming as there is no backwash, and it is very popular with surfers who head out to the bigger breakers. At low tide you can walk into the shallow sea for more than 300 m without having to swim.

The walk along the main street towards St James is known locally as the **Historic Mile** and will take you past a number of interesting old buildings. Some of these are national monuments, but most are closed to the public. The first of note is the **Station building**, a fine example of art-deco architecture built in 1912. Further along on the right is **Het Post Huijs** ⓘ *T021-7887972, daily 1000-1600, entry by donation*, thought to be the oldest building in False Bay, dating back to 1673. The building itself is a picturesquely squat stone house, with thick whitewashed walls and a thatched roof. Inside are exhibits on the history of Muizenburg, with photos of the resort in its heyday and displays on the Battle of Muizenburg of 1795. There are original English canonballs which the cheery curator will happily let you lift.

A few doors down is the grand Italian mansion that until recently held the **Natale Labia Museum**. This was part of the National Gallery but was closed at time of writing and looks unlikely to reopen. The house was built in 1929 as the official residence for Italy's diplomatic representative to South Africa, Prince Natale Labia. Designed in a Venetian style, the fittings were all imported from Venice.

Rhodes Cottage ⓘ *T021-7881816, Mon-Sat 0930-1630, Sun 1030-1630, entry by donation*, at number 246, is surprisingly small and austere for someone as wealthy as Cecil Rhodes. It has been restored and now contains many of his personal items and displays on his life and achievements. It's a pleasant place to wander around, with a lovely garden around the side. This is where he died on 26 March 1902, and his body was transported with great ceremony to the Matobo Hills outside Bulawayo in Zimbabwe, where he was buried in a giant rock outcrop. The volunteers that keep the place open make for charismatic and enthusiastic guides.

Graceland, further along Main Road, is one of the largest and most impressive mansions along the coast. It was the home of John Garlick, a well-known merchant at the turn of the 20th century. The house has a Spanish feel to it, with arched balconies and glazed clay roof tiles. Unfortunately the house is not open to the public. Just before you reach St James you pass another grand house, with palm trees in the garden, known as **Stonehenge**. Built in the style of an Italian villa this house once belonged to HP Rudd of De Beers Consolidated Mines.

St James

Just beyond Muizenberg lies the more upmarket resort of St James, an appealing village with characteristic brightly coloured bathing huts lining the tidal pool. The village is named after a Roman Catholic church which was built here in 1854 to save Catholics having to travel as far as Simon's Town to attend services – interestingly, some of the early settlers were Catholic Filipino fishermen. There is a small sheltered beach and reasonable surf off **Danger Beach**. Several readers have recommended the tidal pool as a safe place for a swim. During the week all is quiet, but at the weekend this is a popular spot and you'll have trouble finding a parking space; take the metro instead.

St James is also a suitable starting point for a hike in the excellent Silvermine section of the Table Mountain National Park. A path starts on Boyes Drive and climbs up through the Spes Bona Forest to Tartarus Cave. The views alone are worth the hike (see page 97 for further details of hiking in the reserve).

Kalk Bay

Kalk Bay is one of the most attractive settlements on False Bay, with a bustling fishing harbour and a bohemian vibe making it a great spot to relax for a day or two. The town is named after the lime kilns that produced kalk from shells in the 17th century. An important local product, the lime created the white-walled appearance of many houses in the Cape, especially amongst the Bo-Kaap community. Until the arrival of the railway in 1883, the local fishermen hunted whales, seals and small fish. Today it remains a fishing harbour, worked mainly by a coloured community which somehow escaped the Group Areas Act under Apartheid. It is one of the few remaining coloured settlements on the peninsula.

Main Road is an appealing spot, lined with bric-a-brac and antiques shops and a handful of arty cafés, and the beach is sandy and safe for swimming, with a couple of tidal pools for children to explore. Between June and July the harbour is busy with the season for snoek, one of the most plentiful local fish harvests. Look out for the returning deep-sea fishing boats around the middle of the day, as there's a daily impromptu quayside auction. You can buy a variety of fresh fish at the counters and for an extra R3 get them to gut them for you too. Another attraction is **Seal Island**, an important breeding ground for birds and seals, the latter attracting hungry great white sharks. Cruises run from Simon's Town (see page 98).

You should also look out for the **Holy Trinity Church** on Main Road. It has a thatched roof, but its appeal is its windows, considered to be some of the finest in the Cape. On Quarterdeck Road is a tiny mosque built in the 1800s. If you fancy browsing for local art and antiques, take your pick from Main Road, where a dozen shops vie for custom – **Kalk Bay Gallery, Cape to Cairo** and **Curiosity** have the most intriguing offerings. On the other side of the road is the entrance to Kalk Bay's most popular attraction, the **Brass Bell**, a simple seafood restaurant and pub wedged between the railway tracks and the water (see Eating page 117).

High up behind the town is **Boyes Drive**, a scenic route connecting the bay with Muizenburg. It's a spectacular route offering sweeping views of False Bay and the Atlantic, and takes just 10 minutes to complete – look out for the signs from Main Road as you head out of Kalk Bay towards Simon's Town.

Clovelly

Continuing along the main road, the next settlement you reach is Clovelly, tucked between the waters of False Bay and the mountains of the Silvermine reserve. Along the main street are several shops and places to have a snack. Anyone visiting from the west country in Britain will be interested to know that this community is named after the village in Devon. Golf enthusiasts should head a little way inland for the **Clovelly Country Club**.

Silvermine

This is a popular local reserve, now part of the Table Mountain National Park, but not often visited by overseas visitors. Table Mountain and Cape Point tend to dominate the open-air attractions, and rightly so, but this reserve is well worth a visit if you enjoy hiking, plus there are great views across False Bay and the Atlantic Ocean.

The reserve encompasses, like much of the Cape, one of the oldest floral kingdoms in the world. Over 900 species of rare and endangered species have been recorded in the mountains, including many types of proteas, ericas, and reeds. In addition to the plants there are a couple of patches of indigenous forest in the Spes Bona and Echo valleys. Ornithologists should look out for black eagles, ground woodpeckers, orange-breasted sunbirds and rock kestrels. If you're extremely lucky, you may also come across small shy mammals such as lynx, porcupine and various species of mongoose.

Ins and outs The reserve is split into two sections by the Ou Kaapseweg Road as it crosses the Kalk Bay Mountains – the eastern sector and western sector. There is no public transport along this road. By car you can approach either from the Cape Town side or from Noordhoek and Fish Hoek. Driving out from Cape Town, follow the M3 from Newlands to its very end and then take a right. After 2 km turn left into Ou Kaapseweg Road, M64. Note that this road has one of Cape Town's highest accident rates, so take care when driving.

A variety of footpaths from Muizenberg, St James, Kalk Bay and Chapman's Peak Drive lead into the reserve and make a pleasant day trip from Cape Town. Access into the reserve is allowed between sunrise and sunset. Toilet facilities are found at Silvermine Reservoir, Hennies Pool, Bokkop Peak, and at the car park near Maiden Peak in the eastern sector of the reserve. Braais are only permitted within the Hennies Pool, Silvermine Reservoir and Bokkop picnic areas.

Around the reserve A tarred road leads from the western sector gates to the Silvermine Reservoir built in 1898 to supply Kalk Bay and Muizenberg with water until 1912. There is a shady picnic site under some pine trees close to the dam. One of the more popular walks from here is to **Noordhoek Peak** (754 m), a circuit of about 7 km from the dam. The path is marked by stone cairns. At the summit there are spectacular views of the Sentinel and Hout Bay. Another interesting walk is from the car park to **Elephant's Eye Cave** covered with ferns and hanging plants. En route you pass the **Prinz Kasteel waterfall**. Allow about three hours for the round trip. The cave can also be reached from Tokai Manor through the Tokai Forest.

The eastern sector of the reserve has plenty of sandstone caves to explore, while the views from the peaks here are across False Bay. One of the popular trails is to **Steenberg Peak** (537 m) via the Wolfkop picnic site. If you have made your way to the top without a car, try an interesting walk which drops down to Muizenberg or St James via the **Spes Bona Valley**. Be careful if exploring any of the caves as there are dangerous deep drops. The Speleological Association in Cape Town regularly organizes trips to the Kalk Bay Mountains.

Fish Hoek

Fish Hoek is one of the most conservative settlements on the coast, not least because the sale of alcohol is prohibited here. It does, however, have a fine beach – perhaps the best for swimming after Muizenberg – which stretches right across the Fish Hoek valley. Swimming is safe at the southern end of the bay, but avoid the northern end where a small river enters the sea, as there is the danger of quicksand. From mid-August to October, there is a good chance of catching a glimpse of whales from here. The valley which stretches behind the town

An elderly female was killed by a great white shark about 20 m off the coast at Fish Hoek in 2004; however, South Africa has had less than 10 shark attack fatalities in the last couple of decades.

joins with Noordhoek beach on the Atlantic coast. In recent geological times this was flooded and all the lands towards Cape Point were in fact an island.

Peers Cave, inland from the country club, is a well-known rock shelter where six fossilized human skeletons were discovered in 1927, dated at over 10,000 years old. One of the skulls is on display in the South Africa Museum in Cape Town. There are also some paintings on the walls, and it is now a national monument. The shortest route to the cave is to approach along Kommetjie Road from Fish Hoek, turning down 20th Avenue to the police station. From here it is a 45-minute walk, crossing ancient sand dunes, further evidence of the change in sea level. For more information call T021-7821752.

Glencairn

It is easy to drive through this coastal resort without realizing you've actually been here, although it does have one of the best mid-range hotels in False Bay (see Sleeping page 111). There is a small beach by the railway station but it is exposed to the southeast winds. Be wary of the cross currents close to the inlet where a small river enters the sea. At low tide you can occasionally see the remains of a steamship, the *Clan Stuart*. She was blown aground on 20 November 1914 while the crew drank in the local hotel.

Simon's Town

This is the most popular town on False Bay, with a pleasant atmosphere and numerous Victorian buildings lining Main Street. If you want a break from Cape Town, this makes for a good alternative base from which to explore the southern peninsula. For information, contact the helpful **tourist office** ⓘ *T021-7865798, www.tourismcapetown.co.za.*

The town is fairly quiet for most of the year but becomes very busy with families during the summer school holidays. Whenever you visit, take some time to wander up the hill away from the main road – the quiet, bougainvillea-bedecked houses and cobbled streets with their sea views are a lovely retreat from the bustling beaches. The main swimming spot is **Seaforth Beach,** not far from Boulders. To get there, turn off St George's Road into Seaforth Road after passing the navy block to the left. The

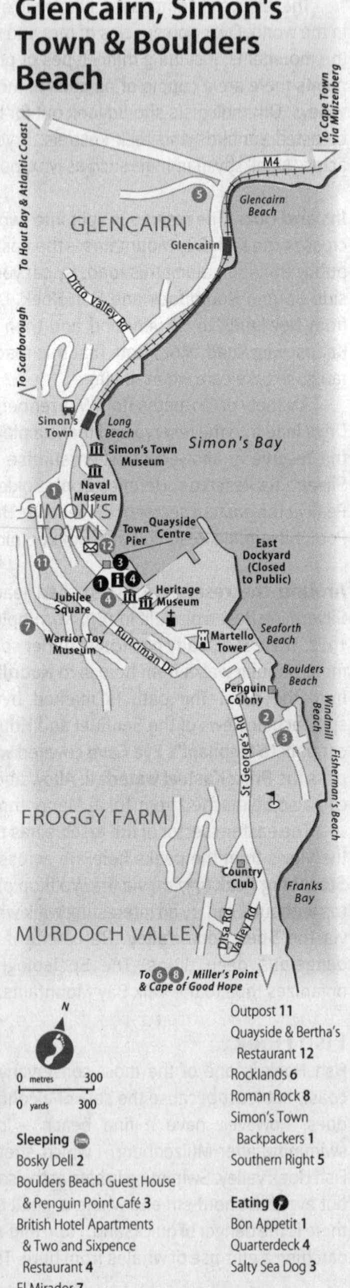

beach is the second on the right, on Kleintuin Road. A little further towards Cape Point are two other popular bathing beaches, **Windmill** and **Fisherman's**. Seaforth Beach has changing and toilet facilities, snack bars, restaurants and a clean stretch of shady lawn bordering the beach with some picnic spots and bench seats. The swimming is safe, but there is no surf due to offshore rocks which protect the beach. For children there is a water slide and a wooden raft in the water. Look out for some giant pots, a legacy from whaling days, when they were used for melting whale blubber.

Simon's Town is named after Simon van der Stel, who decided that an alternative bay was needed for securing ships in the winter months as Table Bay suffered from the prevailing northwesterly. However, because of the difficult overland access, the bay was little used in the early years. It was not until 1743 that the Dutch East India Company finally built a wooden pier and some barracks here. In 1768 the town transferred into British hands, and following the end of the Napoleonic Wars in Europe, the British decided to turn Simon's Town into a naval base. It remained as such until 1957.

Just before you hit the centre of town is the **Simon's Town Museum** ⓘ *Old Residency, Court Rd, T021-7863046, Mon-Fri 1000-1600, Sat 1000-1300, Sun 1100-1300, entry by donation, guided walks along the 'Historical Mile' on request, R15*, with displays related to the town's history as a naval base for the British and South African navies. Several displays are dedicated to Just Nuisance, a great dane who became something of a local hero in the 1930s. He was officially registered as personnel aboard *HMS Afriander* and is the only dog in history to have been given a full military burial on his death. His image has become Simon's Town's unofficial mascot, and there is a bronze statue of him on Jubilee Square. Also of interest is the Peoples of Simon's Town exhibit, a collection referring to the forcible removal of coloured families from the area in the 1960s and 1970s, photos, family trees and household goods.

Nearby, the **South Africa Naval Museum** ⓘ *Court Rd, T021-7874635, daily 1000-1600, entry by donation*, includes a collection of model ships, gunnery displays, information on mine-sweeping, a modern submarine control room plus relics from the Martello Tower.

In the centre of town, the **Quayside Centre** is a smart development on Wharf Street, next to Jubilee Square in the centre of town, which has greatly enhanced the seafront. Above the shops and restaurants is a comfortable new hotel, the **Quayside Lodge**. Cruises to Cape Point can be booked here.

A recommended guide is 'A Walking Guide for the Hout Bay to Simon's Town Mountains', by Shirley Brossy. The trails are well described and the illustrations clear enough to use as a map.

Just round the corner from Jubilee Square, and worth a quick peek, is the **Warrior Toy Museum** ⓘ *St George's St, T021-7861395, daily 1000-1600, entry by donation*, a tiny museum with an impressive collection of model cars, trains, dolls and toy soldiers. This is a great little place and definitely worth a stop – nostalgic for adults and fun for kids. New and old model cars are also for sale.

The nearby **Heritage Museum** ⓘ *Amlay House, King George Way, T021-7862302, Tue-Fri 1100-1600, entry by donation*, faithfully charts the history of the Muslim community in Simon's Town. The town was designated a 'white' area during the Group Area Act and over 7000 people classified as coloured were relocated. The Amlay family were the last to be forcibly removed from Simon's Town – today the Muslim community has all but disappeared here, although there is still an attractive working mosque up behind Main Road. The exhibition consists mainly of pictures and artefacts dating back to the turn of the century. There is a traditional bridal chamber, with wedding clothes and a display in the Hadj room. Zainab Davidson is the co-founder of the Nourul Islam Historical Society and began the museum.

Mineral World ⓘ *T021-7862020, Mon-Fri 0830-1645, Sat and Sun 0900-1730*, on Dido Valley Road, is an important gemstone factory where you can watch the different stages of polishing and buy the finished product. There is also the 'Scratch Patch', a large landscaped yard covered with a deep layer of polished stones.

Boulders Beach

About 2 km south of Simon's Town is a lovely series of little sandy coves surrounded by huge boulders (hence the name). It is a peaceful spot, safe for swimming and gently shelving, making it good for children.

The real attraction here, however, is the colony of African penguins that live and nest between the boulders. **Boulders Coastal Park** ⓘ *T021-7862329, boulders@parks-sa.co.za, R20, 0800-1700*, has been created to protect the little creatures, and their numbers have flourished. Bizarrely, they take little notice of their sunbathing neighbours and happily go about their business of swimming, waddling and braying (their characteristic braying was the reason they were, until recently, known as Jackass penguins). This is one of two colonies on mainland Africa, the other being in Lambert's Bay (see page 172). The best time to see large numbers of penguins is just before sunset, when they return from a day's feeding at sea. The beach is a protected area, and the admission charge is well worth it to get close to the penguins – but be sure to avoid the nesting areas. Note that the first cove gets very busy with families at weekends and during school holidays. Walk along the boardwalk or crawl under the rocks on one side of the beach to get to a more peaceful spot.

Miller's Point

This is the last easy access to the sea on this side of the peninsula. Beyond **Partridge Point** the main road cuts into the hillside, and access to the beach is via steep footpaths. Miller's Point is one of the few remaining beaches to levy a small entrance fee. Gates close at 2000. There is a large caravan site here plus a picnic area and a restaurant. The road climbs above the sea before rounding the mountains by **Smitswinkel Bay**. On a clear day you can look back to a perfect view of the cliffs plunging into the sea. A short distance from the shore is the Cape of Good Hope nature reserve entrance (see page 92).

A number of **boat trips** to the Cape of Good Hope originate from Simon's Town harbour. Taking a trip from here allows views of the spectacular coastline and its hinterland from a different angle. In addition to straightforward sightseeing tours, there are several options for viewing bird life, seals and whales during the right season. For operators, see page 129.

Sleeping

If visiting Dec-Jan, it's worth booking a month or so in advance as hotels get booked up quickly. Secure parking has been mentioned in the listings wherever available.

Several agencies specialize in medium and long-term holiday lets of private homes, self-catering flats or home swaps. These are good value for families or groups; bring reliable references with you.

Apartments and Homes, 154 Main Rd, Sea Point, T021-4394126, www.capeholidays.co.za. Apartments, family homes, furnished or unfurnished.

Cape Holiday Homes, T21-6869759, www.capehomes.co.za. Comprehensive website listing private homes in the Peninsula and coastal area.

Holiday Booking Service, T021-4343930, www.capeholiday.com. Choice of 250 properties around Cape Town.

International Home Exchange, T021-7943433, www.homelinksouthafrica.org. Affiliated to HomeLink International in the UK. A homeswap directory in over 40 countries.

City Bowl *p71, map p72*

AL Arabella Sheraton, Convention Sq, Lower Long St, T021-4129999, www.arabellasheraton.com. Fairly new addition to the city's ultra-smart business hotels. Huge grey-glass structure overlooking the convention centre with 483 rooms, modern and minimalist style, huge beds, floor-to-ceiling windows, dark red theme, stone bathrooms, satellite TV, internet access, fax machines. Popular spa, gym, 5 restaurants and bars, swift, efficient and impressively modern service.

AL **Cape Heritage Hotel**, 90 Bree St, Heritage Sq, T021-4244646, www.capeheritage.co.za. Charming hotel set in a rambling renovated town house dating from the late 17th century. 15 huge rooms, each individually styled, with muted coloured walls (avocado, rust-red, eggshell blue), some with 4-poster beds. All have large windows and sound-proofing to protect from busy Bree St, plus newly renovated bathrooms, minibar, a/c, M-Net TV. Breakfast served under historical vine in the courtyard, or in airy black-and-white breakfast room. Good location on Heritage Sq, close to Long St. Friendly management, recommended.

AL **Metropole**, 38 Long St, T021-4247274, www.metropolehotel.co.za. Long St's first boutique hotel. 45 double rooms with understated decor, huge beds, attractive dark-wood furniture and abstract prints on the walls, some rooms rather small though. Beautiful stone bathrooms with bath and shower. Rooftop pool, with mountain views. The M Bar & Lounge has become a trendy after-work drinks place, and with its red ostrich-leather chairs and subdued lighting feels more like Manhattan than South Africa. Elegant restaurant on 1st floor serves a mix of Italian and modern South African cuisine. Excellent and friendly service. Recommended.

AL **Urban Chic**, corner of Long and Pepper Sts, T021-4266119, www.urbanchic.co.za. Italian-owned newcomer in a trendy newly-built corner block. 20 rooms spread over several floors (prices rise the higher you go, as the views of the mountain improve). Beautiful, airy decor, with pale colours, modern art on the walls, large stone-clad bathrooms, some with sliding partition walls to the bedroom. Stylish bar attached, and on the 1st floor is the Gallery Café with a large fusion menu and for-sale art on the walls, and understated, spacious seating, including in a covered balcony over Long St.

A **Cape Town Hollow**, 88 Queen Victoria St, T021-4231260, www.capetownhollow.co.za. Pleasant newish hotel overlooking Company's Garden. 56 rooms with fairly bland but comfortable furnishings, spotless bathrooms, fantastic views of the mountain from front-facing rooms. Small, sunny pool deck on 1st floor, some gym equipment, conference centre. Spa and rooftop cocktail bar soon to open. Smart Italian restaurant on the ground floor with adjoining bar. Pleasant all-rounder, but shame about the piped muzak in the public areas.

B **Cape Diamond**, corner of Longmarket and Parliament Sts, T021-4612519, www.capediamondhotel.co.za. New addition to the city's hotels, in a great location just round the corner from Government Av and a short walk from Long St. 60 double rooms, with contemporary decor, understated colours with the occasional splash of bright, en suite. Rooftop jacuzzi, bar, Patat restaurant specializing in Cape cuisine. Owner-run, good value.

B **Daddy Long Legs**, 134 Long St, T021-4223074, www.daddylonglegs.co.za. 13 rooms spread across a town house, offering funky, artistic rooms – each is individually designed, with walls covered in art works. Rooms are small, but the stylish, original decor makes up for it. Breakfast is offered for R25 in the café downstairs. Good value and refreshingly different. Also offers self-catering apartments on Long St, with exposed brick walls and polished wood floors.

B **Park Inn**, 10 Greenmarket Sq, T021-4232050, www.parkinn.com. City centre hotel set in the historical Shell building right on bustling Greenmarket Sq. 166 fairly recently-renovated rooms with pleasant neutral decor and functional, attractive bathrooms (shower only). Small pool deck with sauna and gym with view of Table Mountain. Decent steak restaurant – The Famous Butcher's Grill – on ground floor with tables overlooking the market, plus pleasant, if dark, cigar bar. Excellent service, good central location and secure parking. A practical and comfortable choice.

B **Tudor Hotel**, Green Market Sq, T021-4241335, www.tudorhotel.co.za. Recently refurbished hotel in historic building right on bustling Greenmarket Sq. 26 en suite rooms, choice of doubles and family rooms, all en suite with TV, some a/c, modern but fairly bland decor, trendy bathrooms with shower. Breakfast served in stylish downstairs café, off-street parking R45 per day. Great location, friendly staff.

Backpacker hostels

There is good choice of hostels in the centre and around; all are of a similar price and most are a good source of information. Many people travelling overland from Nairobi end their journey here, so the hostels are often good places to meet people and swap travelling information. A lot of hostels also offer non-dormitory rooms at reasonable rates – usually around R180 for a double. Dorms are about R80 per person in the peak season, although if you are looking for a long-term room or bed you should be able to negotiate a discount. During peak periods, be sure to call in advance to check availability, especially around Christmas and the New Year.

C-D **Cat & Moose Youth Hostel**, 305 Long St, T021-4237638, www.catandmoose.co.za. Bright set-up and central location in an atmospheric old town house. Dorms and doubles are nicely furnished but a bit dark, those at front can be noisy, some have balconies overlooking Long St, lovely courtyard with sun deck and braai, good bar, small travel centre, TV/video lounge, breakfast available, laundry room. Laid-back, friendly atmosphere.

C-D **Inn Long Street**, 230 Long St, T021-4241660, innlongstreet@ataris.co.za. Run by young, friendly South Africans, this recently renovated hostel has a great location on Long St, with a wide wrap-around balcony overlooking the goings on. 3 dorms with 6 beds, and 7 private rooms (sleeping 2-4), all with polished wooden floors, simple decor. Pleasant, airy TV lounge and bar. Self-catering kitchen and laundry room. Some rooms have views of Table Mountain. One of the friendliest on Long St.

C-D **Long St Backpackers**, 209 Long St, T021-4230615, www.longstreetback packers.co.za. Sociable, vaguely pretentious hostel spread around leafy courtyard, 80 beds in small dorms and doubles which feel cramped, fully equipped kitchen, TV/video lounge, pool room, internet access, travel centre, free pickup. Great mosaics in some of the bathrooms. Good security with 24-hr police camera opposite. Lively atmosphere, occasional parties organized and weekly communal braais, can be noisy.

Oranjezicht, Gardens and Tamboerskloof *p71, map p103*

L **Mount Nelson**, 76 Orange St, Gardens, T021-4831000, www.mountnelsonhotel.orient-express.com. Cape Town's famous colonial hotel with 131 luxurious rooms, 31 recently-redesigned 'Oasis' garden suites. Emphasis on traditional decor – lots of floral fabrics, antique-style furniture, heavy curtains, but all in bright, airy colours. Set in beautiful landscaped parkland with heated swimming pool, tennis courts, squash court and beauty centre. Celebrated **Cape Colony** restaurant serves Cape specialities and contemporary fare to live jazz. Also has the **Oasis Restaurant** (well worth visiting for the daily cream teas on the veranda) and the trendy new **Planet Champagne Bar**.

AL **Cape Cadogan**, 5 Upper Union St, T021-4808080, www.capecadogan.com. Ultra-elegant 2-storey mansion with 12 rooms, spacious with grass mat flooring, private terraces, subtle lighting and décor, large 4-poster beds, interesting touches like driftwood chandeliers, fabulous bathrooms, some with enormous stone walk-in showers for 2. Shady courtyard with small pool, all-white dining room with pleasant breezes. Also has four self-catering mews houses.

A **Alta Bay**, 12 Invermark Cres, Higgovale, T021-4878800, www.altabay.com. Quiet, secluded choice in fashionable Higgovale, nestled on leafy slopes just below Table Mountain. Beautifully-designed rooms use a pale palette, beige and cream fabrics, and warm wood furniture. Each room has its own private terrace, flat-screen TVs, large stone bathrooms. Plunge pool with peaceful sun deck, huge healthy buffet breakfast served in airy room or overlooking pool. Free bar and high-ceilinged lounge area. Recommended.

A **Cape Milner**, 2a Milner Rd, Tamboerskloof, T021-4261101, www.threecities.co.za. Fashionable business-oriented hotel, popular with media types. 57 rooms spread through a modern building on a busy road, all have neutral pale grey decor and slick dark wood furniture, plus tiled bathrooms (bath and shower), and M-Net TV. Lovely pool area, with sun deck, small infinity pool and bar, popular local meeting place, and decent

For an explanation of the sleeping and eating price codes used in this guide, see inside the front cover. Other relevant information is found in Essentials pages 42-47.

restaurant serving good Capetonian cuisine. Laid-back, media-savvy choice.

A Kensington Place, 38 Kensington Gardens, Higgovale, T021-4244744, www.kensingtonplace.co.za. Cape Town's original boutique hotel in a quiet, leafy area. Small and well-run with excellent and friendly service. 8 beautiful and good-sized rooms, each individually styled with a Afro-chic furnishings, big bathrooms, lots of light from the large windows, great views over the city, bar, small pool and tropical gardens, breakfast served on a leafy veranda, excellent restaurant.

B Parker Cottage, 3 Carstens St, Tamboerskloof, T021-4246445, www.parkercottage.co.za. Award-winning B&B, stylish and atmospheric set in a restored Victorian bungalow, 8 bedrooms, en suite bathrooms with claw-foot baths, polished wood floors, lots of antiques, flamboyant colours with a Victorian touch, good breakfasts, friendly service, gay-friendly. Recommended.

Oranjezicht, Gardens & Tamboerskloof

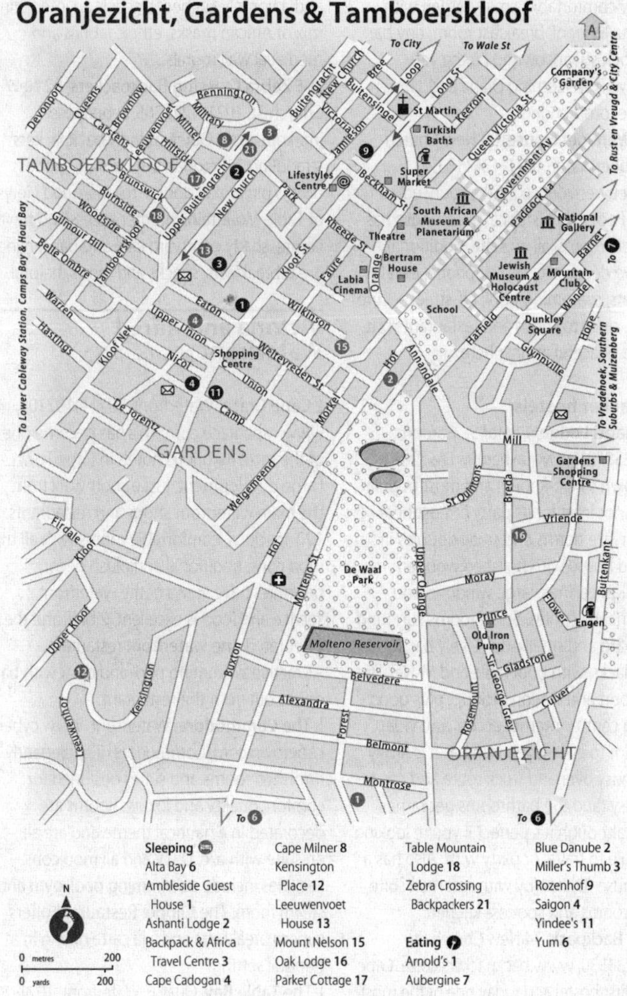

B Ambleside Guest House, 11 Forest Rd, Oranjezicht, T021-4652503. Quiet house set on a leafy road with 4 bright, comfortable rooms, some with views of Table Mountain, pleasant solid wood furniture and neutral decor. Family rooms available. Breakfast served in your room. Friendly service.

B Table Mountain Lodge, 10a Tamboerskloof Rd, T021-4230042, www.tablemountainlodge.co.za. Characterful house with 7 beautifully decorated rooms, stripped wooden floors, white linen, large spotless bathrooms, breezy and very comfortable, small garden with even smaller pool, breakfast room, tiny bar called **Jock's Trap**, owned by the very friendly and welcoming Diana and Janne Dagh. Recommended.

C Leeuwenvoet House, 93 New Church St, Tamboerskloof, T021-4241133, www.leeuwenvoet.co.za. Pronounced Loo-en-Foot, this historical guesthouse has 12 double rooms, all en suite, traditional, attractive décor, a/c, TV, telephone, excellent breakfasts, swimming pool, off-street secure parking, close to shops and restaurants but retains a peaceful atmosphere.

Backpacker hostels

C-E Ashanti Lodge, 11 Hof St, Gardens, T021-4238721, www.ashanti.co.za. One of Cape Town's best-known and most popular hostels, not least for its party atmosphere. Medium-size dorms and small doubles in huge old house with polished wooden floors, high ceilings, large windows and communal balconies. Some rooms surround a courtyard and small pool. Lively bar serving good snacks, with pool table and M-Net TV. Free airport and station pick-up, plus good booking centre, internet access and video room. Not to everyone's liking as it is firmly on the busy overland truck route and can be very noisy (and the bathrooms get rather messy), although it's perfect if you're looking for people to travel or party with. Also has a guesthouse (**D**) nearby with smart en suite double rooms and spotless kitchen.

C-E The Backpack, 74 New Church St, T021-4234530, www.backpackers.co.za. Cape Town's first hostel and today one of the most comfortable and best run in town. Set across several houses with spotless dorms, doubles and en suite doubles and singles. Polished wood floors, upmarket decor, tiled courtyard and linked gardens with pool, lovely bar with TV, meals and snacks served throughout the day, one of the best backpacker travel centres around. Recommended.

D-E Oak Lodge, 21 Breda St, T021-4656182. Beautiful Victorian house which started out as a commune and was developed into a hostel several years ago. The hippie vibe continues throughout. Large, attractive dorms, comfortable doubles (some in apartments next door), great showers, relaxed bar, chill-out room, 2 video rooms and a homely kitchen. Decor is an interesting mix of African masks, ethnic fabrics and medieval wall murals.

D-E Zebra Crossing Backpackers, 82 New Church St, T021-4221265, zebracross@intekom.co.za. Quiet, friendly backpackers straddling 2 Victorian bungalows, spotless dorms plus small double rooms, good views of Table Mountain, internet access and travel centre, shady courtyard café and bar serving great breakfasts, snacks and meals, helpful.

Victoria and Alfred Waterfront *p82, map p83*

L Cape Grace, Waterfront, T021-4107100, www.capegrace.com. This has become one of the most luxurious hotels in Cape Town. Large development, just a short walk from the main waterfront shops and restaurants. 122 spacious, comfortable rooms with all the mod cons, traditional and plush decor, balconies have views of the waterfront, service and food is excellent, 2 bars and the celebrated **one.waterfront** restaurant. Attractive swimming pool and deck with bar opens out from the restaurant.

L The Commodore, Waterfront, www.cybercapetown.com/Commodore. 236 elegantly furnished rooms and suites designed for comfort, quality and luxury. Rooms are decorated in a nautical theme and are all en suite with a/c, DSTV and all mod cons. Facilities include a swimming pool, gym and steam room. The **Clipper Restaurant** offers superb breakfasts and à la carte dining in a tranquil setting.

L The Table Bay, Quay 6, Waterfront, T021-7807878, www.suninternational.co.za. Enormous luxury offering from the Sun International Group, 329 top-notch rooms, what they lack in character they make up for in facilities and comfort. Large pool and sun deck, health club and spa, bar and good restaurant. Expensive by Cape Town standards, efficient service but feels ostentatious (note the sculpture by the main entrance commemorating the stays of celebrities and politicians).

A **Victoria & Alfred**, Pierhead, Waterfront, T021-4196677, www.vahotel.co.za. Stylishly converted warehouse with 96 rooms, spacious with cool and comfortable furnishings, recently-refurbished, king-size beds, a/c, TV with DVD player, minibar, dramatic mountain views, large marble and stone bathrooms with separate WC. Excellent restaurant serving seafood and steaks, fashionable, airy bar attached. Friendly and efficient service. Recommended.

B-C **Breakwater Lodge**, Portswood Rd, Waterfront, T021-4061911, www.break waterlodge.co.za. This hotel, owned by the **Protea** group, fills what was once the notorious Breakwater Prison (1859) and is today aimed at the business market. The 268 rooms are fairly small but comfortable, with functional corporate-style decor. 2 restaurants, bar, conference centre, good setting close to the Waterfront.

Southern suburbs *p85*

These suburbs extend east of the city, along the Eastern Blvd and around Devil's Peak towards Constantia, in the following order: Woodstock, Observatory, Mowbray, Rosebank, Rondebosch, Newlands, Claremont, Kenilworth and Wynberg. All suburbs are a short drive or train journey from the city centre. Each district has its own character and plenty of shops and restaurants close by.

AL **Andros**, 6 Paradise View Rd, Upper Claremont, T021-7979777, www.andros.co.za. Grand old Cape Dutch house set in neat parkland, elegant and homely ambience. 10 well-appointed rooms with TV, en suite bathrooms, under-floor heating, white and cream decor, smart breakfast room, terrace and swimming pool set in gardens. Picnic hampers and meals arranged on request. Swiss-owned so several languages spoken.

AL **The Vineyard Hotel**, Protea Rd, Newlands, T021-6574500, www.vineyard.co.za. 155 a/c rooms set around an 18th-century house; the decor is a mix of Cape Dutch with yellow-wood furniture and modern. The oldest part was originally built as a country house for Lady Anne Barnard in 1799. 2 restaurants, 2 cafés, spa and gym.

A **Harfield Guest Villa** , 26 1st Av, Claremont, T021-6837376, www.harfield.co.za. Award-winning, elegant B&B with individually designed rooms. All are spacious, en suite, with TV, minibar and views of Table Mountain. Lounge/bar, sun deck and swimming pool, bicycle hire, secure off-street parking. Relaxing ambience during the winter months when log fires keep guests warm. Recommended.

C **Koornhoop Manor House**, 24 London Rd, Observatory, T021-4480595, www.geo cities.com/koornhoop. Converted Victorian home in a large, peaceful garden, with 8 rooms, all en suite, TV, floral and homely decor, lounge and breakfast room, off-street parking. Also has 2 huge and extremely good value self-catering apartments with 3 bedrooms, open-plan kitchens, TV lounges, private entrance and access to garden. Run by friendly English couple Vic and Trish.

Backpacker hostels

D-E **The Green Elephant**, 57 Milton Rd, Observatory, T021-4486359, www.hostels.co.za. A full-on backpacker joint set in an old Observatory mansion, plenty going on in the area away from the city centre, dorms plus 5 double rooms, some en suite, with rustic 4-poster beds in a separate house, also a long-stay house, garden with pool and jacuzzi, small bar, pool table, TV room, laundry facilities. Happy to organize trips to the regional sights, free collection.

E **SA's The Alternative Place**, 64 St Michaels Rd, Claremont, T021-6742396, www.alternativeplace.co.za. Clean dorms sleeping 4, 2 double rooms, kitchen, garden with pool, bar and braai. A small homely set-up run by Susan and Alun who have excellent southern and east African travel experience. A bit far from the town centre, but worth checking out. Free airport pick-up.

Constantia *p88*

The original Cape Dutch homestead and vineyard that gave the area its name is today surrounded by one of Cape Town's most exclusive suburbs, dotted with luxury hotels.

L The Cellars-Hohenhort Hotel, 93 Brommersulei Rd, 15 mins from Cape Town city centre, T021-7942137, www.cellars-hohenort.com. Part of the **Relais & Chateaux** group. One of the most luxurious hotels in Cape Town, set in 2 converted manor houses on a wine estate, with 13 spacious suites and 33 individually decorated double rooms, plus the Madiba Presidential Suite, a 2-storey house with private pool, and the Dove Cote suite overlooking the golf green. 2 excellent restaurants (see Eating page 115). 2 swimming pools, tennis court, golf course, set in 3 ½ ha of mature gardens which overlook False Bay, impeccable service.

L Constantia Uitsig, Spaanschemat, River Rd, T021-7946500, www.constantia uitsig.co.za. Set on the well-known wine estate, with 16 luxurious and spacious cottages set in neat gardens with views across vineyards to the mountain. Plush furnishings, private verandas, activities include horse riding and vineyard walks. 2 excellent restaurants.

L Steenberg Country Hotel, 20 km from Cape Town in the Constantia Valley, T021-7132222, www.steenberghotel.com. Luxurious country hotel with 30 elegant, traditional rooms furnished with beautiful antiques, in converted farm buildings overlooking manicured gardens and working vineyards. Swimming pool, gym, steam room, horse riding and 18-hole golf course. **Catharina Restaurant** has excellent reputation. Relaxed and friendly atmosphere.

AL Alphen Hotel, Alphen Dr, 20 mins' drive from the city centre, located at the head of Constantia Valley, T021-7945011, www.alphen.co.za. 21 spacious rooms on elegant 18th-century Cape Dutch estate. Suites and rooms decorated with fine antiques, polished floors and log fires. Lunches in the pub or in the gardens during the summer, popular restaurant in the manor house. Swimming pool and free use of a nearby sports centre.

Atlantic seaboard *p89, map p108*

De Waterkant and Green Point

p90, map p108

AL-D De Waterkant Village, 1 Loader St, De Waterkant, T021-4304444, www.village andlife.com. Village and Life own over 50 historical Bo-Kaap style houses and apartments in the trendy Waterkant area, each stylishly and individually decorated, sleeping 1-6. Also has **Waterkant House**, a guesthouse with 9 chic rooms with all mod cons, a splash pool, beautiful lounge and terrace. Other main property is **House of the Traveller**, a 'luxury' backpackers with double rooms and shared bathroom and kitchen, usually occupied by long-term residents. Also has a range of properties available across Cape Town. A fantastic range, offering convenient accommodation in stylish and historical buildings. Recommended.

A The Village Lodge, 49 Napier St, De Waterkant, T021-4211106, www.the villagelodge.com. Relative newcomer to the area, offering 14 double rooms spread across two converted houses. Decor is trendy greys and white, with shimmery black stone bathrooms (shower only), some with a/c, all M-Net TV, but they feel a little cramped. Attractive restaurant attached, **Soho**, serving Thai food in slick black surrounds. Also has a choice of cottages and apartments in the area. Good location, but overpriced.

B Cape Victoria, 13 Torbay Rd, Green Point, T021-4397721, www.capevictoria.co.za. A mix of exclusive hotel service and the privacy of a guesthouse. 10 tastefully furnished rooms with antiques, en suite bathrooms, TV, minibar and views of the sea or Table Mountain, swimming pool, booking essential. Run by the affable Lilly.

B Hotel Graeme, 107 Main Rd, Green Point, T021-4349282, www.hotelgraeme.co.za. Smart hotel set on the busy Main Rd, a few min's walk to the Waterfront. 31 en suite double rooms and 5 self-catering suites sleeping 2-6, all with TV, phone, DVD, small pool deck at back, secure off-street parking, laundry, internet access, business centre. Breakfast served in a glazed courtyard; also has pub and café facing onto the street.

C 40 Winks Guest House, 2 Ravenscraig Rd, Green Point, T021-4347936, www.40winks guesthouse.co.za. Comfortable set-up in a brightly painted family house set on a quiet street above Green Point. 7 en suite rooms plus 1 self-catering cottage next door sleeping 4-6, garden with pool, pleasant dining room where cooked breakfasts are served, off-street parking, friendly management.

C Atlantic Villa, 5 Norman Rd, Green Point, T021-4343222, www.atlanticvilla.co.za. Comfortable accommodation in Victorian-style terraced house, high ceilings, airy room, all en suite, recently renovated with beach-house feel, TV, mini-bar, good breakfasts served. Friendly and good value.

C Brenwin Guest House, 1 Thornhill Rd, Green Point, T021-4340220, www.brenwin.co.za. Recently renovated guesthouse with 15 large, well-appointed rooms with en suite bathrooms, wooden floors, simple, airy decor, shady patio overlooking tidy tropical garden with swimming pool, within easy walking distance of the Waterfront.

Backpacker hostels

D-E Big Blue, 7 Vesperdene Rd, Green Point, T021-4390807. Spotless and airy backpackers set in a gorgeous mansion dating from 1885. 86 beds, with spacious dorms with bunks, single and double rooms (en suite or sharing bathrooms), all with polished yellowwood floors, high ceilings, ceiling fans, yellow walls and framed pictures. The doubles have great extras such as complimentary toiletries, and some have coffee-making facilities and free chocolates. Pleasant breakfast room, bar with outdoor section leading onto small pool, internet café, travel centre, TV room, spotless kitchen. Friendly and helpful staff, refreshingly un-cliquey. Recommended.

D-E Sunflower Stop, 179 Main Rd, T021-4346535, www.sunflowerstop.co.za. Dorms with a bit more room than most, smallish doubles, clean place with a huge kitchen. Pleasant garden with swimming pool, bar, satellite TV, tours and travel advice. Good location close to restaurants and bars. Free airport and city pick-up.

Sea Point *p90, map p110*

This area has a holiday resort feel but has far less character than other areas in town. It does have an excellent range of accommodation though, and there is some good nightlife towards Green Point.

L Le Vendôme, 20 London Rd, T021-4301200, www.le-vendome.co.za. Large, well-designed luxury hotel with a French theme. Traditional and very comfortable rooms and suites with a/c, TV and internet facilities. Attractive courtyard with pool, 1 restaurant overlooks the pool and serves snacks and lunch, the other is for fine dining. Secure parking.

A The Clarendon, 67 Kloof Rd, T021-4393224, www.clarendon.co.za. Luxurious Italian-style guesthouse with 10 spacious rooms spread across main house and garden suites, plus extra house further up the street. Rooms are large and grandly furnished with posh bathrooms, some with great views of Lion's Head. Attractive garden with large pool shaded by banana trees, breakfast served on terrace, beautiful lounge, off-street parking. Also has guesthouse in Camps Bay at 158 Kloof St.

A The Glen, 3 The Glen, T021-4390086, www.glenhotel.co.za. Gay boutique hotel in an Italian-style villa with views of Signal Hill. Classy decor and super-trendy stone bathrooms some of which have double showers. Tropical garden with palm trees and pool, Moroccan-themed steam room with splash pool. Secure parking.

A Winchester Mansions, 221 Beach Rd, T021-4342351, www.winchester.co.za. A well-run family hotel. 76 recently refurbished with TV, en suite bathroom with separate shower, some with views of the Altantic. Pleasant pool deck and new **Ginkgo Spa**. All rooms overlook a large courtyard where meals are served beneath the palms. Also has **Harvey's** restaurant, offering fusion cuisine and Sun jazz brunches.

B Blackheath Lodge, 6 Blackheath Rd, T021-4392541, www.blackheathlodge.co.za. 7 smart doubles in a Victorian mansion. Large rooms with TV and minibar, attractive decor with muted colours, off- street parking, palm-fringed patio, good size swimming pool, no children. Good for couples.

B Huijs Haerlem, 25 Main Drive, T021-4346434, www.huijshaerlem.co.za. 2 beautifully converted neighbouring houses with 4 rooms in each, connected by well-tended gardens. All rooms are en suite and extremely comfortable, with solid antique furniture, brass beds (some 4-poster), big bathrooms, fabulous sea views. Solar-heated saltwater swimming pool. Both houses have breakfast rooms and lounge. Very friendly Dutch owners. Recommended.

B Villa Rosa, 277 High Level Rd, T021-4342768, www.villa-rosa.com. Rose-coloured Victorian villa with 8 bright and comfortable rooms, traditional, appealing furnishings, original fireplaces, new stone-tiled bathrooms, all rooms en suite with TV, some with fridges, 1 family room and 1 'flatlet'. Brilliant breakfasts served with homemade breads and jams. Off-street parking, pleasant veranda with sea views. Friendly, welcoming and relaxed place to stay. Recommended.

C **Olaf's**, 24 Wisbeach Rd, T021-4398943, www.olafs.co.za. Relaxed guesthouse with 8 individually decorated rooms with en suite shower, telephone, a/c and M-Net TV, mix of antiques and animal prints, breezy communal areas, breakfast served on sunny patio, small pool. Well run and friendly. German spoken.

D **Ashby Manor**, 242 High Level Rd, T021-4341879, www.ashbyaccommodation.co.za. 10 self-catering apartments in a medium-sized rambling Victorian house. Secure and clean rooms with kitchen facilities, some with shared bathrooms and balconies, large communal lounge and dining area, limited off-road parking, 5-min walk from Sea Point.

D **Bellevue Manor**, 5 Bellevue Rd, T021-4340375, www.bellevuemanor.co.za. Beautiful Victorian town house with double rooms, and self-catering rooms on a quiet side street. wrought-iron balconies and fine palm trees, all rooms have en suite bathrooms, homely decor, TV and laundry.

Backpacker hostels

C-E **Aardvark Backpackers**, 319, Main Rd, Sea Point, T021-4344172, www.lions-head-lodge.co.za/aardvark.htm. Upmarket backpackers centrally located on Main Rd close to restaurants and shops, also known as **Lions Head Lodge**. The lodge side has 37 comfortable en suite hotel rooms with TV. Dorms located in former self-catering flats so each 6- to 12-bed dorm has its own kitchen and bathroom. Restaurant, lodge bar, beer garden, backpackers' bar, TV lounge, library, pool, informative travel centre, internet café. Friendly set-up.

Green Point, De Waterkant & Waterfront

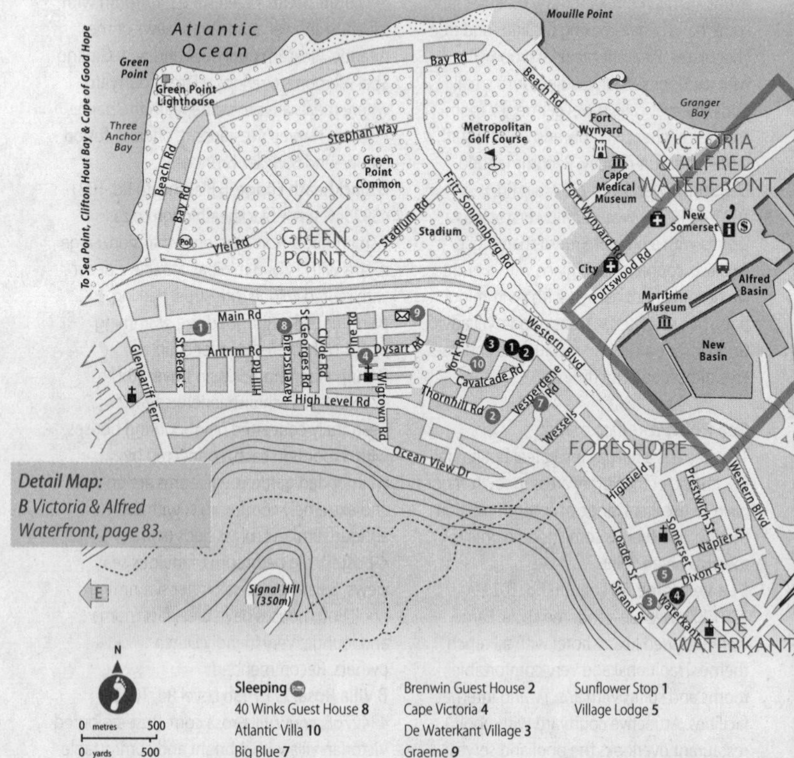

Camps Bay p90

AL The Bay, Victoria Rd, T021-4304444, www.thebay.co.za. Set just across the road from the beach, member of the Small Luxury Hotels of the World, with 70 modern de luxe a/c rooms all with views across the bay, pleasant contemporary feel, large pool with deck and beach-facing restaurant with a good reputation. Excellent service, a well known place for the rich and famous.

C Bay Atlantic, 3 Berkley Rd, T021-4384341, www.thebayatlantic.com. Family-run guesthouse with some of the best views in Cape Town. 6 en suite rooms, TV, light and airy with terracotta tiles and white linen, some with private balcony. Also has 2 self-catering apartments next door. Quiet garden with good-sized pool, breakfast served on balcony overlooking the bay, relaxed atmosphere. Run by welcoming Smith family. Great value, recommended.

C Whale Cottage Guesthouse, 57 Camps Bay Dr, T021-4383840, www.whalecottage.com. Small tasteful place with marine decor, 4 sunny double rooms with en suite bathrooms, breakfast deck overlooking the beach, good views of the Twelve Apostles, satellite TV and internet access, 5 mins' walk to the shops and beach. Also has another property in nearby Bakoven and Hermanus on the Whale Coast.

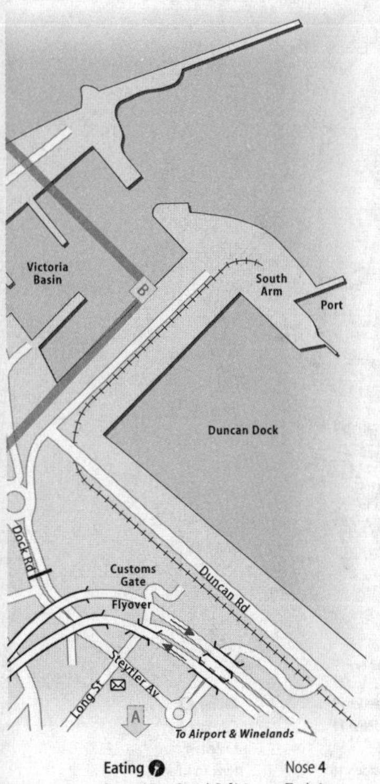

Hout Bay p90

B Chapmans Peak Hotel, Main Rd, T021-7901036, www.chapmanspeak hotel.co.za. This raditional hotel offers 11 double rooms, all but one are en suite, with simple, contemporary decor, beige fabrics, large windows, some with sea views. Good restaurant and popular bar with seating on veranda, great location just across the from beach and close to Chapman's Peak Drive.

B Froggs Leap, 15 Baviaanskloof Rd, T021-7902590, www.froggsleap.co.za. Converted 'plantation' house with stunning veranda overlooking the bay. 3 double rooms with en suite bathroom, TV, minibars and airy decor with a seaside feel, wicker furniture. Good breakfasts served on veranda. Also arranges trips on their catamaran.

B Sorgh Vliet Lodge, 3060 Valley Rd, T021-7902767, www.sorghvlietlodge.com. 2 self-catering cottages and 1 B&B cottage set in peaceful gardens with mountain views. Bright and comfortable with wooden floors, cane furniture, open-plan kitchens, access to gardens, patio and pool, small terraces at back. Breakfast on request. Run by the friendly Mike and Lindy.

Noordhoek p91

B Monkey Valley, Mountain Rd, T021-7891391, www.monkeyvalleyresort.com. Luxurious resort with self-catering thatched log cottages set in woodland overlooking Noordhoek Bay. Each sleeps 4-8, with 2 or 3 bedrooms, kitchen, lounge and bathroom, plus secluded veranda with superb views.

C Goose Green Lodge, Briony Close, T021-7892933, www.goosegreen.co.za. B&B accommodation in main house, also has 5 self-catering cottages in converted family homes dotted around pretty gardens, sleeping up to 6, very comfortably furnished, close to Chapman's Peak and the beach.

E-F Chapman's Peak Caravan Farm, Dassenheuwel, T021-7891225. 5 caravans with hot water and power points, space for tents, swimming pool, peaceful rural setting overlooking the beach at the end of Chapman's Peak Drive.

Kommetjie *p91*

E-F Imhoff Caravan Park, Wireless Rd, T021-7831634, www.imhoff.co.za. Large site with self-catering chalets, all grass, electric points, well lit, laundry, games room, TV lounge, 500 m from beach. An ordered upmarket aimed at domestic families.

False Bay *p94*

Muizenburg *p95*

B Sonstraal Guest House, 4 Axminster Rd, T021-7881611, www.sonstraalguesthouse.com. Pleasant, old-fashioned guesthouse a short walk from the beach and seafront. 7 en suite rooms in the main house, plus self-catering cottages sleeping 4-6 and studios sleeping 2. Simple decor, spotless rooms and bathrooms, sunny breakfast room, plant-filled courtyard, pool.

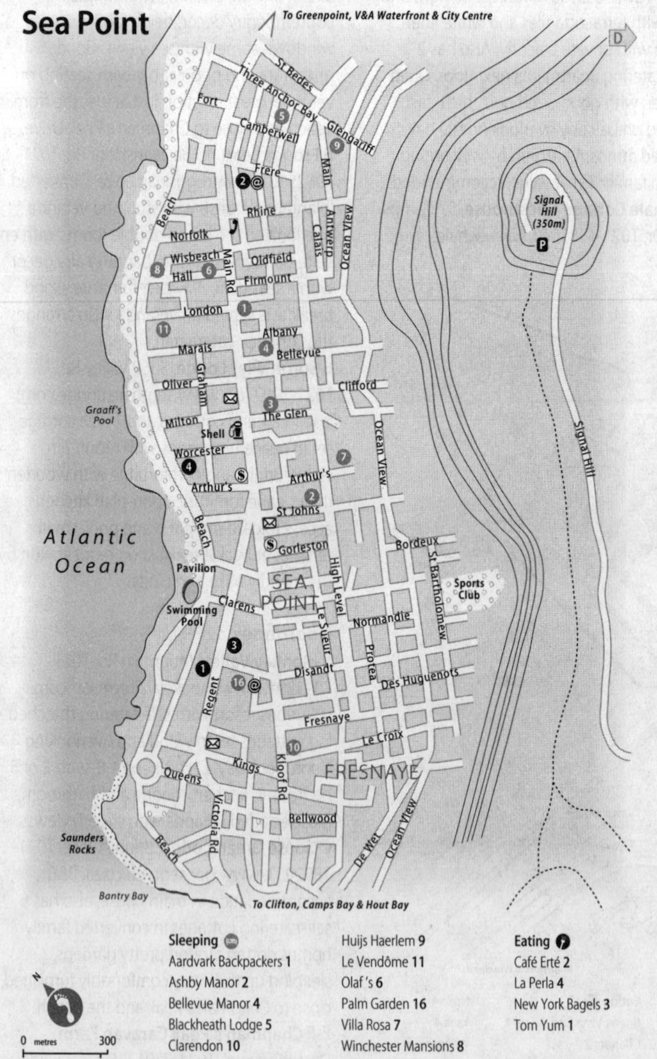

Sleeping
Aardvark Backpackers 1
Ashby Manor 2
Bellevue Manor 4
Blackheath Lodge 5
Clarendon 10
Glen 3
Huijs Haerlem 9
Le Vendôme 11
Olaf's 6
Palm Garden 16
Villa Rosa 7
Winchester Mansions 8

Eating
Café Erté 2
La Perla 4
New York Bagels 3
Tom Yum 1

Kalk Bay *p96*

A The Inn at Castle Hill, 37 Gatesville Rd, T021-7882554, www.castlehill.co.za. Elegant restored Edwardian house with wrought-iron balconies and veranda offering fine sea views. 5 comfortable en suite rooms with white linen and fresh flowers, guest lounge and breakfast room, veranda is the most pleasant part of the house and perfect for whale watching during the season. Secure parking, clean, well run.

Fish Hoek *p97*

A-B Tudor House by the Sea, 43 Simon's Town Rd, T021-7826238, www.tudorhouse.co.za. 6 luxury self-catering apartments with 1-3 bedrooms, friendly and very reasonably priced. Apartments have all mod cons, serviced daily, secure parking, secluded gardens, ideal for a longer break for those wishing to explore the area, very popular in season, advance reservations necessary.

B Sunny Cove Manor, T021-7822274, www.sunnycovemanor.com. Friendly, family-run B&B in a solid old manor house overlooking False Bay. 5 en suite rooms, comfortably furnished in green and white or floral fabrics, some have wide ocean views, breakfast room and lounge. Well run and welcoming. Recommended for families.

Glencairn *p98, map p98*

B Southern Right, 12-14 Glen Rd, T021-7820314, www.southernright.info. Delightful hotel in turn-of-the-century building set a short walk from the sea. Double and twin en suite rooms with high ceilings, dark polished wood floors, subtle decor, some with 4-poster beds and baths only, others with shower and bath. Stylish bar and restaurant serving pub meals, seafood and grills. Fashionable place but family friendly. Recommended.

Simon's Town *p98, map p98*

A Bosky Dell, 5 Grant Av, near Boulders Beach, T021-7863906. Peaceful cluster of converted houses overlooking Boulders Beach, choice of self-contained self-catering units with 1-3 bedrooms. Clean and tidy, each with TV, private garden and braai area, serviced daily, secure parking and direct access down to beach. Advance booking essential during local holidays.

A Quayside Hotel, Quayside Centre, Wharf St, on the seafront, T021-7863838, www.quayside.co.za. A smart, modern development in a great central location overlooking the harbour. 26 double rooms, comfortable marine decor, bright and sunny with good views but rather overpriced. Book well in advance for visits during local holidays. Good restaurant attached.

A-B Boulders Beach Guest House, 4 Boulders Place, T021-7861758, www.bouldersbeach.co.za. One of the most relaxing places you could stay in the area. This friendly, well-run beachside guesthouse is a firm favourite. 12 double rooms with en suite bathrooms, most arranged around a paved yard without sea view, good size beds and baths, simple refreshing design. Also has 2 self-catering apartments. At night you're likely to see penguins exploring the grounds after everyone has gone home. Good restaurant. Recommended.

A-B British Hotel Apartments, 90 St George St, T021-7862214, www.britishhotelapartments.co.za. Despite the unpromising name, this is one of the best places to stay in False Bay. Converted characterful Victorian hotel with 4 elegant self-catering apartments. Each apartment is enormous, stretching over 2 open-plan floors, with 3 bedrooms, all en suite with delightful Victorian bathrooms. Polished wood floors throughout, attractive mix of maritime antiques, art deco and stylish modern furnishings, open-plan kitchen and lounge, separate TV room, great views of the bay from magnificent balconies, breakfasts available on request. Highly recommended.

B The Outpost, 28 Nelson Way, T021-7865594, dulci@mweb.co.za. Lovely B&B set high above Simon's Town, 2 en suite rooms on ground floor, family room covers entire top floor with 2 double rooms, all with attractive, clean decor and great views of False Bay, quiet and relaxing place. Book ahead.

C El Mirador, 15 Victory Way, T021-7861066, dennisla@iafrica.com. Self-catering apartment set high above the town with spectacular views of False Bay. Sleeps up to 5 in 2 bedrooms (1 double, 1 twin), both en suite, small open-plan kitchen and eating area, lounge, pleasant decor with terracotta floors, great private terrace overlooking the sea, friendly owner. Good value.

C Rocklands, 25 Rocklands Rd, Murdoch Valley South, T021-7863158, simonstown@ mweb.co.za. Cool and comfortable B&B, airy tiled rooms with balconies overlooking the sea, simple furnishings, short walk to the beach. Also offer self-catering apartments and holiday homes.

C-D Roman Rock, 432 Main Rd, past Simon's Town on way to Cape Point, T021-7863431, rrock@iafrica.com. Comfortable and modern self-catering apartments sleeping 4-6, in a secluded setting overlooking the beach and sea, cool tiled interiors, large balconies, braai facilities, 3 mins' walk to beach, parking.

C-D Simon's Town Backpackers, 66 St George's Mall, T021-7861964, www.capepax.co.za. 38-bed backpacker joint spread across cramped dorms and fairly pleasant doubles, brightly painted walls and bush-camp-style furniture, small kitchen, honesty bar, braai on balcony overlooking the main street and harbour, bikes for hire.

Eating

Capetonians likes to eat out, a fact which is reflected in its multitude of restaurants – and the extent to which they get packed out. Booking ahead is often a good idea. A great starting point for choosing a restaurant is buying the latest edition of *Eat Out*, a magazine guide edited by Lannice Synman, which features South Africa's best choice of restaurants. The magazine costs R39.95 and is available in newsagents and tourist offices.

City Bowl *p71, map p72*

TTT Savoy Cabbage, 101 Hout St, T021-4242626, Mon-Fri 1200-1430, 1900-2230, Sat 1900-1030, closed Sun. Widely regarded as the best restaurant in Cape Town, producing its own best-selling cookbook, the Savoy Cabbage serves beautifully prepared contemporary South African cuisine. The menu changes daily, and includes dishes such as gemsbok carpaccio, free-range duck breast and a gorgeous soft-centred chocolate pudding. Good winelist too, especially on reds. Bookings essential.

TT The Africa Café, Heritage Sq, 108 Shortmarket St, T021-4220221, www.africa cafe.co.uk, 1830-2300. African-themed restaurant geared at tour troups, offering an excellent introduction to the continent's cuisines. The menu is a set 'feast' and includes 10 dishes from around Africa, such as Egyptian-smoked fish, Kenyan patties, Cape Malay mango chicken curry and springbok stew. The price includes as many dishes you like, as well as coffee and dessert. Excellent service, but it's pricey and very touristy.

TT Five Flies, 14 Keerom St, T021-4244442, www.fiveflies.co.za, 1100-2400. A long-standing local favourite a historic setting. Lovely string of dining rooms, excellent menu of traditional food with a modern slant. The preferred haunt of lawyers and judges but also attracting well-heeled media types; its recent restyling has made it even more popular.

TT Mama Africa, 178 Long St, T021-4248634, Mon-Sat 1900-late. Popular restaurant and bar serving 'traditional' African dishes often with great live music. Looking a little faded around the edges, but remains popular with tourists, tasty food if overpriced and notoriously slow service. Centrepiece is a bright green carved Mamba-shaped bar. Somewhat tacky but a fun place nevertheless.

TT Strega, Heritage Sq, T021-4221300, closed Sun. Large, open-plan Italian restaurant with tables set around an indoor courtyard. High- quality Italian cuisines, ranging from pizza and pasta to modern seafood dishes. Good service, but the crowd verges on pretentious. Bookings recommended.

T Biesmiellah, 2 Upper Wale St, T021-4230850, Mon-Sat 1200-1500, 1800-2200. One of the better-known and well-established Malay restaurants, serving a delicious selection of Cape Malay dishes. This is the place to come for sweet lamb and chicken curries and sticky malva pudding. A treat for any fan of spicy food. No alcohol.

T Caveau, 92 Bree St, Heritage Sq, T021-4221367, 0800-late, closed Sun. Laid-back, stylish deli and restaurant with stone-clad walls, comfy banquettes and tables overlooking Bree St. Menu changes daily, but includes tapas, excellent cheese and meat platters, salads and adventurous mains.

Fat Albert's, Heritage Sq, T021-4244206, closed Sun. Huge range of gourmet burgers on offer in this trendy establishment, including some brilliantly inventive ones – try the ostrich burger, or the crab and shrimp burger – all served in a choice of buns and with various types of fries.

Marco's African Place, 15 Rose St, T021-4235412, www.marcosafricanplace.co.za, 1200-late. Good value 'African' menu covering everything from slow-roasted Karoo lamb to samp and beans, plus popular Pan-African platter with assortment of grilled game. Huge place with a friendly atmosphere, tasty starters but main courses can be disappointing. Daily live music.

Royale, 273 Long St, T021-4224536, 1200-late. Ultra-trendy eatery specializing in gourmet burgers – try the 'Miss Piggy' with bacon and guacamole, served with sweet potato fries. Attractive decor with booths and tables spiling onto the pavement. Friendly service, popular place, expect to queue (no bookings). The **Royale Kitchen**, just around the corner, has the same menu and does take bookings.

Simply Asia, Heritage Sq, T021-4263363. Outlet of a popular noodle chain, with a long list of freshly-prepared stir-fries, Thai curries, noodles and sweet and spicy soups. Tables spill outside in summer, overlooking Shortmarket St.

Cafés

Crush, 100 St Georges Mall, T021-4225533, 0900-1700. Lunch spot spilling onto St Georges Mall serving delicious and healthy wraps, salads, soups and freshly squeezed juices. Airy, cushion-filled interior if it's colder.

Mr Pickwicks, 158 Long St, T021-4233710, Mon-Sat 0830-late. Trendy spot, a favourite with pierced and tattooed Long St locals, serving the best milkshakes in town. Excellent baguettes, toasties, quiche of the day, healthy salads, large pasta portions. Pumps out loud funk and dance tunes, licensed, gets very busy with an after-work crowd, open late. Also sells tickets to Cape Town's major club nights and gigs.

Rcaffé , 138 Long St, T021-4241124, Mon-Sat 0830-1700. Airy, high-ceilinged café serving great Italian coffees and a delicious range of cakes and pastries – the double-chocolate muffins are to die for. Also serves light lunches, such as butternut quiche and feta salads. Friendly service.

Sundance, 59 Buitengracht St, T021-4241461. Bare brick walls, an airy mezzanine and brisk service make this a popular choice for stylish Capetonians after a quick caffeine fix. Great choice of coffees, and excellent sandwiches on a variety of interesting breads.

Oranjezicht, Gardens and Tamboerskloof *p71, map p103*

Aubergine, 39 Barnet St, Gardens, T021-4654909, www.aubergine.co.za, Mon-Sat 1800-2200. Sophisticated and award-winning menu, modern slants on classical European dishes, excellent wine list. One of the best in town. Stylish shaded courtyard, lounge/bar, good service.

Blue Danube, 102 New Church St, Tamboerskloof, T021-4233624, www.blue danube.co.za, Tue-Fri 1200-1430, daily 1830-2300. Chef Thomas Sinn combines traditional Austrian dishes with an international fusion menu, served in a fine old building with attractive, blue-themed spacious rooms and mountain views. Recommended.

Cape Colony, Mount Nelson Hotel, 76 Orange St, T021-4831000, 1800-2200. One of Cape Town's finest restaurants in the impressive setting of the Mount Nelson. Dishes are a mix of traditional British (think sensible roasts) and Cape classics, such as Bo-Kaap chicken and prawn curry, plus lots of game. Impeccable service, live jazz most evenings. Also has the **Oasis**, where fabulous cream teas are served every afternoon.

Rozenhof, 18 Kloof St, T021-4241968, Mon-Sat 1200-1500, 1800-2200, closed for lunch on Sat. Smart restaurant set in an attractive 18th-century town house, decorated with local artwork and chandeliers, with cool wooden floors, food to match the surrounds, look out for seasonal dishes such as asparagus and springbok, good choice for vegetarians.

Saigon, corner of Camp and Kloof Sts, T021-4247670, 1200-1430, 1800-2230. Superb Vietnamese cuisine, very popular place set on a corner overlooking busy Kloof St, brilliant crystal spring rolls, barbecued duck and caramelized pork with black pepper. Book ahead. Recommended.

ǂǂ Yindee's, 22 Camp St, Tamboerskloof, T021-4221012, yindees@mweb.co.za, Mon-Sat 1230-1430, 1830-2200. An excellent Thai restaurant serving authentic spicy curries, stir-fries and soups. Served in a sprawling Victorian house with traditional low tables. Service can be very slow, but the place is always popular, so book ahead.

ǂ Arnold's, 60 Kloof St, Gardens, T021-4244344, www.arnolds.co.za, 0900-2300. Good value lunch spot on busy Kloof St, good salads, pasta and more substantial meals like ostrich steak. Fast, friendly service. Happy hour 1630-1830.

ǂ Miller's Thumb, 10b Kloof Nek Rd, T021-4243838, Mon-Sat 1230-1400, 1830-2230, no lunch Mon or Sat. Beloved by locals, this place serves delicious and good value seafood, plus steaks and some veggie choices, lots of spices and a Creole twist on some dishes. Friendly, laid-back place, plenty of regulars.

ǂ Yum, 2 Deer Park Dr, Vredehoek, T021-4617607. Stylish deli and restaurant serving excellent sandwiches, salads and original pasta dishes, such as roast lamb tortellini or goat's cheese and roasted pepper lasagne. Good service, relaxed young crowd, delicious pickles and chutneys on sale. Arrive early if you want to try their legendary weekend brunches. Recommended.

Cafés

Vida e caffe, 34 Kloof St, T021-4260627, Gardens, T021-6837288. The original of what has become the city's most successful coffee chain. Retains its quirky atmosphere, serving excellent coffees and a choice of muffins and melting hot paninis. The minimalist interior is packed throughout the day.

Victoria and Alfred Waterfront *p82, map p83*

The Waterfront is one of the most popular districts in Cape Town for eating out and gets very busy. There is a wide range of places to eat but prices are steeper than elsewhere.

ǂǂǂ Baia, top floor, Victoria Wharf, T021-4210935, 1200-1500, 1900-2300. Fine seafood restaurant spread over 4 terraces with moody, stylish decor and lighting. Very smart (and expensive) venue, delicious seafood dishes following a Mozambique theme – try the spicy beer baked prawns. Very stylish with views of Table Mountain, slightly erratic service. Book ahead.

ǂǂǂ Emily's, Clock Tower Centre, T021-4211133, Mon-Sat 1200-1500, 1800-2200. Very smart restaurant serving excellent French-style cuisine, superb wine list, has won several awards, great views from balcony overlooking the Waterfront, polite service, slightly fussy but popular.

ǂǂ Balducci's, Victoria Wharf, T021-4216002, www.balduccis.co.za, 0900-2230. Popular, elegant Italian restaurant with seats overlooking the harbour. Good choice of pasta dishes and mains ranging from ostrich steak and luxury lamb burgers, to confit de canard and blackened kingklip. Also has a very popular sushi bar.

ǂǂ Belthazar, Victoria Wharf, T021-4213753, www.belthazar.co.za. Top-of-the-range steak house with tables overlooking the harbour. Excellent Karan dry- and wet-cured steaks, plus range of seafood and with a staggering 600 South African wines to choose from, including 100 wines by the glass – this claims to be the world's largest wine bar.

ǂǂ Cape Town Fish Market, ground floor, Victoria Wharf, T021-4135977,1100-2300. Fish restaurant, but the reason to come here is the revolving sushi bar, serving excellent sushi and sashimi. Dishes are limited but very fresh and good value.

ǂǂ Den Anker, Pierhead, T021-4190249, www.denanker.co.za, daily 0900-2300. Popular Belgian restaurant and bar with a continental feel, high ceiling flying the various duchy flags, airy bar, views across Alfred Basin of Table Mountain, civilized atmosphere. Good menu serving French and Belgian dishes, lots of seafood and an impressive selection of imported bottle beers.

ǂǂ Hildebrand, Pierhead, T021-4253385, www.hildebrand.co.za, 1100-2300. Well-established Italian seafood place right on the harbour's edge , superb hand-made pasta and good antipasto platters, plus traditional Italian deserts. Good reputation, but touristy given the location.

ǂǂ Quay Four, T021-4192008, 1800-2230. Popular bistro above the more relaxed pub downstairs (open all day and evening). Great views over the Waterfront, seafood is the focus but also has grills and vegetarian options.

Cafés

Mugg & Bean, Victoria Wharf, T021-4196451, 0830-2330, also branches in Cavendish Sq, Claremont, and the Lifestyles centre on Kloof St. Café serving mouth-watering muffins, cakes and sandwiches and good coffee. Service can be slow.

Southern suburbs *p85*

ƬƬƬ Au Jardin, Vineyard Hotel, Colinton Rd, Newlands, T021-6574500, www.vineyard.co.za, Mon-Sat 1900-2200. A very smart hotel restaurant with a great French menu. 6 course meals or a quick plat du jour served in a stylish setting with views of the mountain. Polite service, excellent presentation. Booking always advised.

ƬƬ Barristers Grill, corner of Kildare and Main Sts, Newlands, T021-6717907, Mon-Sat 0800-2300, Sun 1700-2300. A popular steakhouse that has expanded into a trendy bistro/café during the day with plenty of alfresco tables. Great steaks and ribs, plus veggie choices. Still retains the mock-Tudor timber decor of the steakhouse.

Ƭ Don Pedro's, 113 Roodebloem Rd, Woodstock, T021-4470482, info@donpedro.co.za. Informal, bustling restaurant serving huge portions of South African food, pasta and pizza at cheap prices. Very popular, focal point of the community, great mixed crowd, book ahead.

Ƭ Pancho's, Lower Main Rd, Observatory, T021-4474854, 1200-late. Mexican dishes in a lively atmosphere, all the usual tacos and fajitas, good home made nachos, big portions, nothing fancy but a fun place. Tasty cocktails – try the strawberry margarita.

Cafés

Obz Café, 115 Lower Main Rd, Observatory, T021-4485555, 0730-late. Popular place open all day for light meals, coffee or cocktails, great salads and sandwiches, also has main meals in the evenings and occasional live music.

Constantia *p88*

ƬƬƬ Buitenverwachting, Klein Constantia Rd, T021-7945190, www.buitenverwachting.co.za, Mon-Sat 1200-1330, 1900-2100. The main restaurant serves a cosmopolitan menu with flawless Italian, French and South African dishes. Good service, upmarket, prices reflect the quality of the food.

ƬƬƬ Catharina's, Steenberg Country Hotel, Spaanschemat River Rd, T021-7132222, 0700-2130. The principal restaurant in a 5-star hotel (see Sleeping page 100). Breakfast is served in the conservatory, lunch and dinner under the oaks or at tables set in cosy alcoves created from old wine vats. Elegant hotel restaurant serving excellent South African fare such as West Coast mussels, Knynsa oysters and springbok loin on polenta. Fine wine list.

ƬƬƬ The Greenhouse, The Cellars-Hohenort Hotel, 93 Brommersvlei Rd, T021-7942137, www.cellars-hohenort.com, 0730-2200. One of 2 highly-rated restaurants at this 5-star hotel (see Sleeping page 106), set in a pretty conservatory with white wicker furniture. The Michelin-trained chef produces top-quality fare – mostly modern South African, so expect fresh fish and game, and divine deserts. Excellent wine list to match. One of the finest restaurants in the area.

ƬƬƬ La Colombe, Constantia Uitsig, T021-7942390, www.constantiauitsig.co.za, 1200-1500, 1830-2200, closed Jul and Aug. Regarded as one of the finest restaurants in the Cape. Excellent French menu with strong Provençal flavours. Delicious fresh fish and a range of meat and duck dishes, with an emphasis on rich sauces. In fine weather you can sit outside and look over the gardens and a pool. Also here is the **Constantia Uitsig Restaurant** and the **River Café**.

ƬƬ Silver Tree, Kirstenbosch Botanical Gardens, T021-7629585. Lovely terrace with views of the gardens and mountain looming behind. Decent Cape menu, including a great sweet and spicy bobotie, butternut ravioli, ostrich burgers, plus sandwiches and salads. Also offers a picnic hamper service.

Atlantic seaboard *p89, map p108*

De Waterkant and Green Point *p90, map p108*

ƬƬƬ Tank, T021-4190007, www.the-tank.co.za, Cape Quater, Dixon St, 1100-late. Airy, super-fashionable seafood restaurant with attractive tables spilling out onto the piazza. Inside, tables are dotted around 2 rooms, with a huge central aquarium. Good menu with daily specials, but slightly overbearing clientele.

Ƴƴ **Buena Vista Social Café**, Main Rd, T021-4330611, 1200-0200. Cuban-themed bar and restaurant in a great location with balconies overlooking Main Rd. Fashionable crowd tuck into a mix of Cuban and Tex-Mex-style dishes washed down with mojitos. Live Latin music at weekend, good but pricey.

Ƴƴ **The Nose**, Cape Quater, Dixon St, T021-4252200, www.thenose.co.za, Mon-Sat 1000-2300, Sun 1700-2200. Wine bar with tables leading onto the Waterkant piazza, serving a wide range of wines accompanied by excellent seafood (the mussels in white wine and cream are especially good), steaks and burgers. Cosy interior, dishes can be ordered in large or small portions.

Ƴ **Chariots**, 107 Main Rd, T021-4345427, 0800-2130, Sun closes at 1700. Excellent local Italian restaurant serving traditional and innovative pasta dishes (try the curried butternut ravioli), superb risotto, salads and meat dishes. Low-key and relaxed, good service, tables overlooking Main Rd, popular with young professionals. Excellent value for money. Recommended.

Ƴ **Wangthai**, 105 Paramount Pl, T021-4396164, Sun-Fri 1200-1430, 1800-2300, Sat 1800-2300. Great Thai restaurant serving mouth-watering stir-fries, well known for its spicy curries with coconut milk and lemon grass. Reservations advised.

Cafés

News Café, corner of Main and Ashtead Rds, T021-4346196, 0700-2300. Popular café and bar serving sandwiches, salads, pub meals, stylish decor, gets busy in the evenings.

Sea Point *p90, map p 110*

Ƴƴ **La Perla**, corner Church and Beach Rds, Sea Point, T021-4342471. A long-term Sea Point favourite. Extensive Italian menu specializing in seafood. Excellent anitpasto, plenty of vegetarian options, wonderful desserts. Indifferent service, though.

Ƴ **New York Bagels**, 51 Regent Rd, Sea Point, T021-4397523, 0700-2230 (deli closes at 2130). Cafeteria-style deli serving a good range of food, from hearty American breakfasts and smoked salmon bagels to salads, hot dogs and fish and chips. Attached deli shop next door sells bagels and other Jewish tit-bits to take away.

Ƴ **Tom Yum**, 72 Regent Rd, T021-4348139, 1200-1430, 1800-2230. Simple, popular Thai restaurant serving delicious noodle and rice dishes including great seafood and ostrich stir-fries, very spicy, great tom yum soup.

Cafés

Café Erté, 265 Main Rd, Sea Point, T021-4346624, 1000-0400. Trendy café playing loud trance and techno, good breakfasts and snacks, internet access.

Clifton *p90*

Ƴ **Clifton Beach House**, 4th Beach, T021-4381955, 1030-2200. Breakfast, lunch and dinner overlooking Clifton's beautiful beach, good seafood plus some Thai dishes, relaxed during the day but smarter in the evening. Pleasant, bustling atmosphere, good cocktails.

Camps Bay *p90*

ƳƳƳ **Blues**, Victoria Rd, T021-4382040, www.blues.co.za, 1200-late. Popular and well-known seafood place with superb views, Californian-style seafood menu served to a beautiful crowd. Good, stylish food, famous seafood and oyster platters, but you pay for the restaurant's reputation.

Ƴƴ **The Codfather**, corner of Geneva Dr and The Drive, T021-4380782, 1200-1700, 1800-2300. One of the best seafood restaurants in Cape Town, stylish laid-back place offering a range of superbly fresh seafood. No menu – the waiter takes you to a counter and you pick and choose whatever you like the look of. Also has an excellent sushi bar. Highly recommended.

Ƴƴ **Ocean Blue**, Victoria Rd, T021-4389838, blufish@mweb.co.za. Friendly seafood restaurant on road overlooking the beach. Good fresh seafood, especially daily specials, superb grilled prawns and butterfish kebabs. Less pretentious than many of the restaurants in the area. Recommended.

Ƴƴ **Tuscany Beach**, 41 Victoria Rd, T021-4381213, www.tuscanybeachrestaurant.com, 1000-late. Italian seafood place overlooking the beach. Delicious seafood specials – don't miss the kingclip kebabs served on a dangling sword. Also serves wood-fired pizzas, salads, burgers and steaks. Trendy place, gets very busy for sundowners.

Cafés

Marc's Deli Bar, Shop 16, The Promenade, Camps Bay, T021-4382322, 0800-2100. Smart first-floor deli and café overlooking Camps Bay beach, serving pastries, muffins and cakes as well a fine selection of breads and cheeses. Great for setting up a picnic.

Hout Bay *p90 and p91*

ΨΨ Dunes, Hout Bay Beach, T021-7901876, 0900-late. Sprawling restaurant overlooking the dunes behind the beach, very popular with families, large menu, quick service but the food can disappoint – stick to the tasty fish and chips. Book ahead at weekends or you'll be stuck in the hot courtyard instead of the breezy balcony tables.

Ψ Chapman's Restaurant, Chapman's Peak Hotel, T021-7901036, 1100-2200. A lively restaurant and bar with wood panelled interior, serving good seafood dishes in frying pans, also grills and pub fare. The outside terrace gets packed in summer. Be sure to book ahead.

Ψ Fish on the Rocks, Harbour Rd (beyond Snoekies Market), T021-790001, 1000-2100. Simple and delicious fresh fish and chips, deep-fried calamari and prawns, overlooking harbour. No frills, and getting popular with big tour groups.

False Bay *p94*

Muizenburg *p95*

Ψ Balmoral On Beach , Beach Rd, T021-7886441, 0900-1700, closed Tue. Despite the grand name, this is little more than a stylish little café serving healthy breakfasts and surfer-friendly fry-ups as well as light lunches such as butternut risotto cakes.

Ψ Empire Café, 11 York Rd, T021-7881250, Tue-Sun 0700-1600, Fri and Sat until 2100. Hip eatery serving eclectic breakfasts and lunchtime fare, including interesting salads and omelettes (try the famous bacon, banana and honey) and some seafood specials. Popular with local surfers and trendy day-trippers.

Ψ Gaylords, 65 Main Rd, T021-7885470, Wed-Sun 1200-1500, 1700-2100, also Mon 1700-2100. Unpretentious, bustling Indian restaurant set in an old Victorian cottage with suitably tacky decorations and good value, highly rated north and south Indians curries, recommended for vegetarian dishes.

Kalk Bay *p96*

ΨΨ Cape to Cuba, Main Rd, T021-7881566, 1130-1600, 1800-1030. Atmospheric Cuban restaurant and cocktail bar serving good-value seafood with Caribbean flavours. Great setting on water's edge with tables overlooking the harbour, funky decor, Cuban music, good cocktails and cigars for sale. Bar open till 0200.

Ψ Brass Bell, by the railway station, T021-7885455, Mon-Fri 1200-1600, 1800-2300, Sat-Sun also 0800-1100, pub open throughout the day. A well-known and very popular pub and restaurant in a great location. Simple set-up serving pub meals and good pizzas and fish and chips. Downstairs gets packed with a young crowd, gets very busy around sunset, great for a cool beer outside close to the waves. More expensive restaurant upstairs serving fresh fish and steak.

Ψ Olympia Café, 134 Main Rd, T021-7886396, olympia@my.co.za, 0700-2100. Another Kalk Bay institution, this laid-back café serves some of the freshest bread on the peninsula, plus light lunches, fabulous cakes and fresh daily specials. Great atmosphere and good service, but expect to queue at weekends. The bakery at the back turns into a restaurant and tiny theatre at night.

Ψ Sirocco, 82 Main Rd, T021-7881881. Stylish new restaurant set right on the main road, with blue and white tables in a shady terrace area. Seafood, steaks, good spot for coffee.

Ψ The Timeless Way, 106 Main Rd, T021-7885619, 1200-1600, 1800-2230, Sat and Sun from 0900. An excellent, old-fashioned restaurant serving Cape cuisine, steaks and seafood. The bobotie is good, as is the pasta.

Simon's Town *p98, map p98*

ΨΨΨ Bon Appetit, 90 St George's St, T021-7862412, Tue-Sat 1200-1400, 1830-2200. One of the finest restaurants on the peninsula specializing in top-notch French cuisine – the chef is Michelin-trained. Excellent set menus and imaginative main meals such as ravioli of rabbit plus French staples like confit de canard. Popular and quite small. Be sure to book ahead.

ΨΨ Bertha's, Quayside Centre, Wharf Rd, T021-7862138. A seafood grill in the centre of town in a prime location overlooking the yacht harbour. During the day the outside terrace is a good place to enjoy good fresh seafood and watch the goings on in the harbour. Inside is a dining area perfect for large family meals. Great selection of fresh seafood dishes, good value.

ƒƒ **Black Marlin**, Miller's Point, 2 km from Simon's Town, T021-7861621, www.blackmarlin.co.za, 1200-1600, 1800-2000 (lunch only on Sun). Set in an old whaling station, this place is well known for its excellent seafood and is a good point to stop for lunch on the way to Cape Point. Fabulous sea views and wide range of fresh seafood, delicious crayfish and kingclip skewers, also good value evening menu. Great wine list. Recommended, although it can get busy with tour buses in summer.

ƒƒ **Penguin Point Café**, Boulders Bay Guest House, T021-7861758, www.bouldersbeach.co.za. Great family restaurant with bar and sun deck which gets busy with day-trippers. Good English breakfasts, cocktails (including the popular Pickled Penguins), delicious seafood platters and daily specials, plus salads for a light meal.

ƒ **Quarterdeck**, Jubilee Sq, T021-7863825, 0800-1900, Fri till 2300. Simple café with great views over the harbour, serving sandwiches, burgers and interesting salads like avocado with smoked chicken and biltong. Also has a Cape Malay buffet on Fri evenings.

ƒ **Salty Sea Dog**, next to Quayside Centre, T021-7861918, Mon-Sat 1000-2100, Sun 1000-1630. Cheap and cheerful place serving fresh fish and chips with seats overlooking the harbour. Good value, friendly and swift service. Popular with groups.

ƒ **The Two and Sixpence**, St George's St, next to the **British Hotel**, T021-7861371, 1000-2400. Local pub serving standard bar food such as burgers and bangers and mash, plus Yorkshire pudding specials, Sun roasts and curry nights. Also has pool tables and occasional live music.

Bars and clubs

City Bowl *p71, map p72*

The *Cape Times* and *Argus* newspapers have good listings sections, as does *Cape etc* magazine, out twice a month, R19.95. See also Gay and lesbian Cape Town, page 120.

169, 169 Long St, T021-4261107. R&B club with a glamorous, mixed crowd – dress up if you want to get. Gets packed on Fri. Great balcony overlooking Long St.

Black Sheep, 4 Buiten St, T021-4240681. corner of Longmarket and Long Sts, T021-4224832, doors open 0900. One of Cape Town's newest clubs, aimed firmly at the serious dance crowd. Mostly house music, played in a series of interlinked rooms. Good drum 'n' bass night on Tue.

Deluxe, corner of Longmarket and Long Sts, T021-4224832, Wed, Fri and Sat 2200-0400. Popular nightclub in the centre of town, minimalist style with cosy seating areas, large dance floor, deep house, VIP room with furry walls.

Jo'burg, 218 Long St, T021-4220142, 1500-late. Trendy bar serving pints and cocktails to a mixed crowd, gay-friendly, relaxed during the week but gets very busy at weekends when DJs spin funky house and drum 'n' bass. Recommended.

Kennedy's Cigar Bar, 251 Long St, T021-4241212, 1200-late. Upmarket, old-fashioned cigar and cocktail lounge with daily live jazz and smart restaurant upstairs. Noticeably older crowd than elsewhere along Long St. Lunch buffet served during the week.

Mama Africa, 178 Long St, T021-4248634, Mon-Sat 1900-late. Great live music played by the large green mamba snake bar every night, usually marimba, but more popular with tourists than locals.

Marvel, 236 Long St. Another fashionable watering hole, less busy than Jo'Burg, with vinyl booths, a dimly-lit bar and chilled out tunes. The pace picks up in the evenings, when überkool kids arrive to hang out on the pavement outside.

Poo Na Na Souk Bar, Heritage Sq, 100 Shortmarket St, T021-4234889, Mon-Fri 1100-0130, Sat and Sun 1800-0130. Ultra-trendy bar decked out in Moroccan lanterns and expensive fabrics, lovely balconies overlooking the even trendier Strega restaurant, usually relaxed atmosphere but sometimes host to big-name international DJs.

Sutra, 86 Loop St, T021-4244218, www.sutragroovebar.co.za. Wed-Sat 2100-0400. 'Retro-East' styled bar and club, 2 floors, dancefloor on first floor, cocktail waitresses do the rounds downstairs, mix of hip-hop, deep house and Afro-Caribbean music. Free entry before 2300.

Zula, 194 Long St. T021-4247636, www.zulabar.com. Wed, Fri and Sat 2100-0200. Fashionable bar, club and restaurant with several small rooms, big sofas, hip-hop on most nights, great balcony overlooking Long St. Closes at 0200, but don't bother turning up before 2400.

Oranjezicht, Gardens and Tamboerskloof *p71, map p103*

Drum Café, T021-4611305, www.thedrumcafe.com. Live drumming outfit where customers grab a drum and join in; the venue was moving at time of writing, so check the website for updates.

Mercury Live & Lounge, 43 de Villiers St, T021-4652106, www.mercuryl.co.za, Mon, Wed-Fri 2100-late. Live music venue and club nights, rock and hip-hop acts play regularly, also holds weekly hip-hop parties and 'nostalgia' alternative rock nights. Cape Town's leading live music venue, lively, young crowd.

Rafiki's, 13 Kloof Nek Rd, T021-4264731. Popular bar overlooking Kloof Nek with a huge wrap-around balcony perfect for a sundowner. Relaxed atmosphere, friendly crowd. Occasional live music and braai evenings, and seafood specials on offer during the summer.

Rhodes House, 60 Queen Victoria St, Gardens, T021-4248844, www.rhodehouse.com, Thu-Sat 2100-late. Rated as one of the best nightclubs in the city. Swanky lounge with dancefloor and alfresco courtyard, super-trendy decor, frequented by models and celebs (including a recent visit from Prince Harry). Good music, fantastic but pricey cocktails.

Victoria and Alfred Waterfront *p82, map p83*

Cantina Tequila, Quay 5, Victoria Wharf, T021-4190207, www.cantinatequila.com. This Mexican restaurant transforms into a packed nightclub after about 2300, mostly chart music, popular with tourists.

Den Anker, Victoria and Alfred Pierhead, T021-4190249, www.denanker.co.za, daily 0900-2300. Belgian restaurant and bar specializing in a range of Belgian draught and bottled beers.

Ferryman's Tavern, Waterfront, T021-4197748, 1100-2300. A popular haunt with restaurant upstairs, huge outside seating area, TV continually showing sports action, the olives and feta go well with the Mitchell's Beer brewed on site, a lively mixed crowd.

Quay Four, T021-4192008, 1100-2400. Large shady deck overlooking the water, popular with well-heeled locals and tourists, good meals and great draught beer, one of the more pleasant pubs on the Waterfront.

Sports Café, Victoria Wharf, T021-4195558, 2200-late. Large sports bar showing matches on big screens, can get rowdy, serves American-style snacks and meals.

Southern suburbs *p85*

Observatory is the city's alternative nightlife centre and the place to head for laid-back bars and clubs with a bohemian feel, while Rondebosch and Claremont have plenty of sports bars popular with sporty types.

A Touch of Madness, Pepper Tree Sq, Nuttal Rd, Observatory, T021-4482266, 1500-late. Flamboyant bar with series of rooms decked out with tongue-in-cheek opulence, eccentric regulars, great atmosphere, good light meals.

Café Ganesh, 46 Trill Rd, T021-4483435, Observatory, 1200-0100. Lively little café and bar serving hearty Cape dishes and ice-cold beers in a leafy courtyard leading to a characterful interior. Very friendly, great place to meet local characters.

Carte Blanche, 42 Trill Rd, T021-4478717, Observatory. Tiny bar and café set in a narrow 2-storey Victorian house, filled with little nooks and crannies which get taken over by young groups of friends early in the evening. Serves meals, popular for after-dinner drinks in ramshackle surroundings.

Forester's Arms, Newlands Av, T021-6895949, 1100-late. Old fashioned English-style pub, popular with weird mix of suited types on their back from work and studenty sports jocks. A fun-loving, boozy scene.

Gay and lesbian Cape Town

Cape Town is rated, along with Sydney and San Francisco, as one of the 'gay capitals' of the world. Certainly, it is the most gay- and lesbian-friendly city in Africa and is drawing increasing numbers of gay travellers from across the country and continent. The scene is vibrant, with plenty of bars, clubs and events aimed at a gay crowd. These venues tend to be the trendiest in town, so nights are generally very popular and more mixed than you might expect. The area around Green Point and De Waterkant is the focus of Cape Town's gay and lesbian scene, and all the main bars and clubs are found along Somerset and Main Road. The main gay event and one of the best parties of the year is the **Mother City Queer Project**, www.mcqp.co.za, a fantastically extravagant costume party and rave – not to be missed if you're in town in December. There is also the annual **Cape Town Pride Festival**, www.capetownpride.co.za, which takes place in February, with a parade touring the city centre and a street party going on until the early hours around Green Point.

Information
An excellent guide to the gay scene is the free *Pink Map*, available at tourist offices and a number of trendy shops and bars. It has useful listings and up-to-date details of everything from accommodation and shops to steam baths. The tourist office also has copies of the *Cape Gay Guide*, an annual booklet with information on nightlife and accommodation.
Friends of Dorothy Tours, T021-4651871, www.friendsofdorothytours.co.za. Gay tour company organizing day trip to Cape Point,

Independent Armchair Theatre, 135 Lower Main Rd, Observatory, T021-4471514, 2000-late. Dark, vibey venue with huge sofas to lounge in, featuring films on Mon, jazz on Thu, live bands most nights, stand-up comedy from the Cape Comedy Collective on Sun. Excellent venue, with something going on every night. Recommended.
Oblivion, corner 3rd Av and Chichester Rd, Harfied Village, T021-6718522, www.oblivion.co.za, daily 1130-0200. Wine bar and restaurant. Laid-back bar, which turns into a raucous dance venue later on. Good food and an impressive wine list.

Atlantic seaboard *p89, map p108*

Green Point *p90, map p108*
The area around De Waterkant and Green Point is the focus of Cape Town's gay and lesbian scene, with a number of trendy bars and clubs with mixed crowds.
Bossa Nova, 43 Somerset Rd, T021-4250295, Tue-Sat 2000-0200. Large Latin bar over-looking the street, 2 bars, dance floor, salsa and house music, looking a bit run down these days, popular with a young crowd.
Bronx, 35 Somerset Rd corner Napier St, www.bronx.co.za, 2000-late. Probably Cape Town's best known and most popular gay bar and club, gets packed out at weekends, mostly men but women welcome, live DJs spin out thumping techno every night.
Buena Vista Social Café, Main Rd, T021-4330611, www.buenavista.co.za, Mon-Fri 1200-0200, Sat and Sun 1700-0200. Cuban-themed bar and restaurant catering to a well-heeled crowd. Latin music, live bands at weekend, tasteful decor and a relaxed atmosphere, nice balcony overlooking Main Rd, great spot for sophisticated cocktails on a hot evening.
Opium, 6 Dixon St, T021-4254010, www.opium.co.za, Wed- Sun 2100-late. Great mix of stylish lounge areas and decent dance music. The main bar area is huge and long, lit by pink and red lighting and with cosy booths and sofas. Gorgeous stone courtyard, overlooked by balconies. Also has

the Winelands, whale-watching tours, private or small groups.
Gay & Lesbian Helpline, T021-4222500, daily 1300-2100.
Life Line Aids, T0800-012322, 24 hours.
Out in Africa, T021-4614027/4614063, www.oia.co.za. Organizes annual gay film festival, Feb-Mar.
Q-online, www.q.co.za. South Africa's main gay and lesbian website with email access, chat rooms and a dating service.
Triangle Project, T021-4483812/3. HIV testing, counselling and a library.
Wanderwomen, T021-7889988, www.wanderwomen.co.za. Professional tours run by and for lesbians, around Cape Town and along the Garden Route.

Bars and clubs
The area around Green Point and De Waterkant is filled with gay-friendly bars. Some long-standing clubbing institutions include:
Bar Code, 18 Cobern St, T021-4215305, www.leatherbar.co.za, 2200-0200. Full-on leather bar, the only one of its kind in town.
Bronx, 35 Somerset Rd, corner of Napier St, Green Point, www.bronx.co.za, 2000-late. Probably Cape Town's best-known and most popular gay bar and club, gets packed out at weekends, mostly men but women welcome, live DJs spin out thumping techno every night, karaoke on Monday.
Evita se Perron, Darling Station, Darling, 55 mins from Cape Town, T022-4922831, www.evita.co.za. Evita is a gay institution, a sort of Afrikaans Dame Edna, hosting lively events at her café-theatre, including Bambi's Berlin Bar, a shop, restaurant and gallery.

regular live music. Currently the most popular club in town; expect to queue.
Sliver, 27 Somerset Rd, T021-4215798. Trendy lounge bar, mostly gay clientele but also very popular with a trendy, mixed crowd. Relaxed atmosphere, heats up later at night.
Tank, Cape Quater, Dixon St, T021-4190007, www.the-tank.co.za, 1100-late. Pretentious but hugely popular bar and restaurant, white cube seats surround low tables, large tropical fish tank is the centerpiece. Hair-flicking models and body-builders will feel at home.

Camps Bay *p90*
Café Caprice, Victoria Rd, T021-4388315, 0900-late. Popular café and bar with outdoor seats, great fresh-fruit cocktails get packed and very noisy around sunset, loud house music played 'till late.
Dizzy Jazz Café, 41 The Drive, T021-4382686. Busy bar and live music venue, popular at the weekend, mostly jazz but has everything from funk to rock music.
Eclipse, Victoria Rd, T021-4380882, 1730-late. London-owned lounge bar overlooking the beach, minimalist interior, fashionable place to seen at sunset, great but relatively pricey cocktails.
Sandbar, Victoria Rd, T021-4388336. Popular for sundowners at one of the shady tables looking onto the beach. Small place so get here early if you want to secure a table.
Tuscany Beach, 41 Victoria Rd, T021-4381213. Restaurant and bar with beach views, gets packed at sunset with cocktail-quaffing locals.

Clifton *p90*
La Med, Glen Country Club, Victoria Rd, T021-4385600, www.lamed.co.za, 1100-late. Something of a Cape Town institution, hugely popular meeting place for locals, busy bar overlooking the sea, good pub food, great for a sundowner when you'll be hard pressed to find a seat, turns into a raucous club later on.

Entertainment

Cinema

The 2 major cinema groups are **Nu Metro**, www.numetro.co.za, and **Ster-Kinekor**, www.sterkinekor.com. New films are released on Fri. Evening shows are very popular, booking advised especially at weekends (this is not possible over the phone with an international credit card – you'll have to go to the cinema in person). Daily newspapers and the bi-monthly *Cape etc* have full listings. There are multi-screen cinemas at Century City, the V&A Waterfront and Cavendish Sq. The latter 2 also have a seperate Cinema Nouveau, which screens international and art-house films. Every February, Cape Town hosts the **Cape Town World Cinema Festival**, www.sithengi.co.za with films screened at Cinema Nouveau. There is an annual gay and lesbian film festival, known as the **Out in Africa** festival, www.oia.co.za, held every year in Mar-Apr, with screenings at Labia.

Imax, T021-4197365, www.imax.co.za, in the BMW Pavilion at the V&A Waterfront shows special format films on a giant screen with 'six-channel wrap-around digital sound'. Check the papers for listings. Tickets cost approximately R70 and each film lasts 1 hr.

Labia, 68 Orange St, Gardens, T021-4245927, www.labia.co.za. Perhaps Cape Town's most enjoyable cinema, showing independent international films and with a café serving good pre-movie snacks. It is licensed, so you can take your glass of wine into the movie.

Labia on Kloof, Lifestyle Centre, Kloof St, T021-4245927. The mainstream version, with two screen showing Hollywood releases.

Music

See Bars and clubs, page 118, for live music venues. such as **Dizzy Jazz Café**, **Drum Café**, Independent Armchair Theatre, **Kennedy's Cigar Bar**, **Mama Africa** and **Mercury Live & Lounge**.

Green Dolphin, V&A Waterfront, T021-4217471, www.greendolphin.co.za. Restaurant and jazz venue featuring top local jazz groups that play while you eat.

Kirstenbosch Summer Concerts, www.nbi.ac.za, every Sun at 1700 Nov-Mar. Idyllic setting, picnics on the lawns, concerts varying from folk and jazz to classical and opera. Recommended.

V & A Waterfront Amphitheatre, outdoor venue on the Waterfront with daily concerts and live performances, mainly jazz.

Theatre

All tickets can be purchased from **Computicket**, T083-9158000 (mob), www.computicket.co.za. No foreign credit cards accepted over the phone or online, but there are kiosks which do accept cards at the V&A Waterfront and Cavendish Sq.

Artscape, DF Malan St, Foreshore, T021-4217839, www.artscape.co.za. Major complex offering opera, theatre and music.

Baxter, Main Rd, Rondebosch, T021-6857880, www.baxter.co.za. Long- established involvement in black theatre, good reputation for supporting community theatre, international productions and musicals.

Theatre on the Bay, Link St, Camp's Bay, T021-4833301, www.theatreonthebay.co.za. Slightly alternative shows, licensed, interesting mix of plays, comedy and musicals.

V&A Amphitheater, V&A Waterfront, T021-40876000. Occasional one-man shows, musicals and small plays held here.

Festivals and events

Celebrations are a serious business in Cape Town, and during the summer months you'll be hard pressed to find a free weekend. Street carnivals and festivals compete with cultural and sporting events, although publicity is often limited. See *The Cape Times* or www.capetownevents.co.za, for more listings.

January

Karnaval, 2nd Jan, begins in the Bo-Kaap district and ends up in the Green Point Stadium, this is city's most popular festival, includes procession of competing minstrel bands, complete with painted faces, straw boaters and bright satin suits.
Cape to Rio yacht race, every 2 years, next race is in 2008, starts first weekend Jan.
J&B Metropolitan Handicap, last Sat in Jan, www.jbmet.co.za, South Africa's major horse-racing meet at Kenilworth Race Course.

February

Cape Town Price, www.capetownpride.co.za. The biggest gay event in town, floats and a parade around Green Point culminating in a street party.

March

Cape Town Festival, www.capetown festival.co.za. Week-long arts and cultural festival held at the end of the month, various venues.
Cape Town International Jazz Festival, International Convention Centre, www.capetownjazzfest.com. 5 stages with huge array of local and international jazz artists, used to be known as the North Sea Jazz Festival, last weekend in Mar.
Cape Argus Pick 'n' Pay Cycle Tour, www.cycletour.co.za. World's largest timed cycling event taking an impressive route around Table Mountain and along the shores of the peninsula.
Two Oceans Marathon, www.twooceans marathon.org.za. 56 km race with over 9000 competitors, last weekend in Mar.

April

Start of **Rugby season** at Newlands and the **Film festival**, see cinema, page 122.

June

Red Bull Big Wave, Hout Bat, www.redbullbwa.com. Surf festival where professionals only surf waves that are 5 m high or higher.
Cape Times Wine Festival, V&A Waterfront, taste 300 wines from 85 estates, plus cheese hall, last weekend in Aug.

September

Hermanus Whale Festival, www.whale festival.co.za. Marks beginning of calving season of southern right whales, excellent viewing, last week in Sep.

October

Cape TimesNB Big Walk, www.bigwalk.co.za. World's largest timed walk started in 1903.
Cape Town Comedy Festival, Baxter Theatre, week-long festival featuring local and international talent.

November

Nedbank Summer Concerts, musical performances, classical, jazz, folk, swing and choral, held at the Josephine Mill, Newlands, every Sun through to Feb.
Cape Town World Cinema Festival, www.sithengi.co.za. Screenings of international films with focus on promoting South African film.

December

Obz Festival, Observatory, huge street party with stalls, live music and all-nights parties.
Long Street Carnival, street party with several stages of live music and comedy, plus stalls and fairground rides.
Clifton Challenge, Clifton Beach 4. Fitness challenge between Springbok rugby team and Clifton lifesavers, the event for beautiful people.
Kirstenbosch Summer Concerts, www.nbi.ac.za, every Sun until Mar. Picnics on the lawns, concerts varying from folk and jazz to classical and opera.

Shopping

Arts, crafts and curios

African Image, 52 Burg St, T021-4238385, www.african-image.co.za. Excellent alternative to the tired souvenir shops, this gallery sells contemporary African art, such as bags made from traditional weavings, beautiful baskets, old township signs, photography, plus quirky souvenirs like coke-bottle-top bags and chickens made from colourful plastic bags. Also has an outlet in Victoria Wharf, V&A Waterfront.

City Living, 8 Kloof St, T021-4249424. Large furniture and crafts store, selling hand-made furnishings and kitchen accessories.

Greenmarket Square Market, lively market selling crafts, textiles and clothes from across the continent. Be prepared to take part in some cheerful haggling.

Monkeybiz, Rose St, T082-5531015 (mob). Something of a local sensation, Monekybiz creates employment for women (many of them HIV Positive) in the townships of Mandela Park and Khayelitsha. The women create beautiful and quirky one-off bead works, including figures, animals and accessories. Sold at the tourist office.

Out of This World, V&A Waterfront, T021-4213507. One of many African arts and crafts shops at the Waterfront, better value and more tasteful selection than many.

The Pan African Market, Long St, T021-4264478, www.panafrican.co.za. 2-storey centre set in a converted Victorian house, selling crafts from across the continent, good local crafts made from recycled material, beadwork, ceramics. Café specializing in African food, plus a book shop and holistic healing area.

Red Shed, part of Victoria Wharf shopping centre. Handful of local craftsmen, glass blowers, goods are of suspect taste.

Streetwires, 77 Shortmarket St, T021-4262475, www.streetwires.co.za. Building housing a wire sculpture cooperative, useful place to browse these interesting South African craft works without feeling under pressure from the usual street vendors.

Books and maps

Bell-Roberts, 199 Loop St, T021-4221100. Gallery, café and publishing house specializing in art books.

Clarke's Bookshop, 211 Long St, T021-4235739, www.clarkesbooks.co.za. A mass of antiquarian, 2nd-hand and new books in a muddled old shop, a must for any book lover.

CNA (Central News Agencies), city-wide chain of shops carrying a reasonable stock of guide books, glossy coffee table publications, some colourful maps, foreign newspapers and magazines.

Exclusive Books is a more upmarket chain with branches at the Waterfront and Cavendish Square mall. Good for travel and coffee table books.

The Map Studio, T021-5104311, www.mapstudio.co.za. Tourist maps of towns and regions as well as official survey maps.

Select Books, 232 Long St, T021-4246955. Something of a local institution, with a pleasantly ordered interior and vast range of books on the country and Southern Africa, including great contemporary choices.

Wordsworth Books, Gardens Centre, T021-4618464. Knowledgeable staff help assist in this comprehensive bookstore.

Clothes

Long St and Kloof St in the City Bowl have become the powerhouse of Cape Town's fashion scene, and have a good choice of kooky boutiques selling one-offs and locally-designed clothes and accessories. For better-known clothes chains and upmarket boutiques, head to the shopping malls. Particularly popular with the young and well-heeled are the units in Victoria Wharf, at the Waterfront, T021-4182369, and Cavendish Square, in Claremont, T021-6743050. Prices here are only marginally cheaper than in Europe.

Aguila, 217 The Chambers, Long St, T021-4223464. Airy shops selling suitably floaty and wearable clothes, including gorgeous sandals. Great for summery wardrobes.

Carnival, 110 Long St, T021-4265007. One of the few clothes shops along Long St catering to men and women. 2 floors filled with expensive designer label gear, including top-of-the-range jeans, Playboy t-shirts and fashionable sunglasses. Intimidating staff.

India Jane, Station Rd, Kalk Bay, T021-6837607. One of several outlets selling expensive designer items, including African-inspired designs and lots of one-off pieces.

Milk, 285 Long St, T082-5865850. Local designer-owned store, with stylish women's clothes, including cocktail dresses made from vintage material and colourful baggy tops. Chunky accessories and bright belts.

Misfit, 287 Long St, T021-4225646. Has the latest designs for well-heeled 20-somethings, including groovy strapless dresses, plus trendy shoes and sandals.

Nylon, 24 Kloof St, T0728527187. Interesting African-inspired designs, small selection including skirts made from traditional east African prints. Also has trendy second-hand furniture and accessories in the back.

Scar, 22 Kloof St, T021-4225085. Is one of the best known of this area's quirky shops, although the clothes line has diminished as the business has moved towards hair styling. Still has a few one-offs though.

Yaa-Ba Collection, 301 Long St, T021-4247519. Local designers outlet spread over one floor and mezzanine, with elegant dresses and outfits, plus interesting accessories and jewellery. Shame about the frosty owners, though.

Markets

Church St Antiques Market, on Church St, between Long and Burg Sts, Mon-Sat 0900-1400. Offbeat antiques, most interesting pieces shown on Fri and Sat.

Grand Parade Market, Mon-Sat 0800-1400. General market at the large parade ground in front of the old City Hall, selling clothes, fabrics and flowers.

Greenmarket Square, Mon-Sat 0900-1600. A lively arts and crafts market on a picturesque cobbled square, goods from across Africa, formerly a fruit and vegetable market, flanked by several terrace cafés.

Green Point Market, beside Green Point stadium, 0800-1700 Sun only. Good mixture of curios, plenty of buskers.

The Red Shed, V&A Waterfront, 0900-2100. Mix of arts and crafts.

Music

Musica is the biggest music shop chain, selling all the latest CDs, videos and DVDs, and can be found in every shopping centre and along high streets.

The African Music Store, 90a Long St, T021-4260857, africanmusic@sybaweb.co.za, Mon-Fri 0900-1800, Sat 1000-1600. Stocks an excellent choice of albums by major Southern African artists as well as compilations and reggae. The staff are incredibly helpful and are happy to let you listen to any number of CDs before purchasing.

Loud on Long, 43 Long St, T021-4223801. Relative newcomer selling a small but well thought-out selection of South African CDs, plus some good quality artefacts.

Supermarkets

Each of the suburbs has its own shopping complex with a branch of one of the major supermarket chains – **Pick 'n' Pay, Chequers, Shoprite, OK Bazaar** and **Spar**. For high-quality groceries head to **Woolworths** which is much the same as Marks & Spencer in Britain, with the equivalent price premium.

Activities and tours

With its equitable climate and outdoor lifestyle, Cape Town's adventure sports scene has boomed in recent years. Most of the backpacker hostels promote a huge choice of activities, particularly the more strenuous and action-packed such as kloofing, abseiling, paragliding and the ubiquitous bungee.

Abseiling

Abseil Africa, T021-4244760, www.abseil africa.co.za. Operates one of the world's highest and longest commercial abseil – 112 m down Table Mountain. Also runs day trips to other abseil points around the Cape.

Cricket

In the southern suburb of Newlands is the famous Cape Town Test match ground named after the suburb. Despite considerable redevelopment, a few of the famous old oak trees remain and it is still possible to watch a game from a grassy bank with Table Mountain as a backdrop. Some of the public seats are very exposed – wear a hat and have plenty of suncream to hand.

Newlands, PO Box 23401, Claremont 7735, 161 Camp Ground Rd, Newlands. Tickets: T021-6572003, wendyp@cricket.co.za.

Fishing

The most common catches are mako shark, long fin tuna and yellowtail, but there are strict rules governing all types of fishing. The simplest way of dealing with permits and regulations is through a charter company.

Hooked on Africa, T021-7905332, www.hookedonafrica.co.za. Deep sea tuna trips, in-shore light tackle and fly fishing and crayfish charters. Leaves from Hout Bay. 4 boats to choose from, all gear supplied.

Nauticat Charters, T021-7907278, www.nauticatcharters.co.za. Game fishing and boat charters.

Golf

For further details contact the **Western Province Golf Union**, T021-6861668, www.wpgu.co.za. Expect to pay green fees of around R200 for 18 holes. The following golf clubs are open to overseas visitors.

Milnerton Golf Club, Bridge Rd, Milnerton, T021-5521047, www.milnertongolf club.co.za. 6,011 m, par 72. Green fees about R150. This is a true links course in the shadow of Table Mountain, watch your par when the wind blows. A popular course set between the Atlantic Ocean and a river.

Mowbray Golf Club, Ratenberg Rd, Mowbray, T021-6853018, www.mowbraygolfclub.co.za. One of the oldest clubs, hosts national championships, a par-74 course with plenty of trees, bunkers and water holes.

Rondebosch Golf Club, Klipfontein, Rondebosch, T021-6894177, www.ronde bosch-golf-club.co.za. A tidy course with the Black River flowing through it.

Royal Cape Golf Club, 174 Ottery Rd, Wynberg, T021-7616551, www.royal capegolf.co.za. Length: 6,174 m, par 74. Expect to pay about R250 for green fees. An old course that has been the venue for major professional tournaments.

Simon's Town Country Club, T021-7861233, is a 9-hole, 18 tee, links course on the seafront, just by the turning for Boulders Beach. This is a narrow course and is a real test for anyone not used to playing in very windy conditions.

Hiking

Active Africa, T021-7886083, www.active-africa.com. Leading operator organizing walking tours on Table Mountain and Cape Point, plus hiking trips to the Winelands and the Garden Route. Also has guided climbs on Table Mountain; all transport, food and guides included in price.

Due South, T083-2584824 (mob), www.hikesandtours.co.za. Organizes half- and full-day walking trips up Table Mountain. Rates include transport to the start point for your hike, snacks and water, and a packed lunch on full-day hikes.

Horse riding

There are plenty of interesting riding trails around the city, and Nordhoek Beach is especially popular at sundown.

Nordhoek Beach Horse Rides, T082-7741191 (mob), www.horseriding.co.za.

Sleepy Hollow Horse Riding, T021-7892341.

Kitesurfing

The Cape's strong winds have made it a very popular site for kitesurfing. The best spot is Dolphin Beach at Table View, north of the city centre where winds are strong and waves perfect for jumping.

Windsports, Table View, T021-5562765, capetown@ windsports.co.za. A good place to start if you're new to the sport, tuition starts at R380 for 1 hr.

Kloofing

Kloofing (canyoning) involves hiking, boulder-hopping and swimming along mountain rivers. It is very popular on and around Table Mountain; many of the tour operators listed (page 128) organize daily excursions.

Mountain biking

Downhill Adventures, T021-4220388, www.downhilladventures.com. Organizes a range of mountain biking excursions, including the popular Table Mountain double descent (90% downhill), rides around Cape Point and the Winelands Meander. Also offers bike rentals.

Homeland, Long St, T021-4260294, www.homeland.co.za. Mountain bike rentals cost R80 for 24 hrs; cheaper rates the longer you hire.

Mountain climbing

Active Africa, T021-7888750, www.active-africa.com. Climbs on Table Mountain.

Mountain Club of South Africa, 97 Hatfield St (close to the Jewish museum), T021-4653412, www.mcsa.org.za. Good source of information for the whole of the country.

Paragliding

Paragliding from Lion's Head is very popular, with gliders landing by the sea between Clifton and Camps Bay. For tandem paragliding sessions contact **Para-Pax**, T082-8814724 (mob), www.parapax.com. All flights include pick-up and drop-off, drinks and refreshments.

Rugby

International games are played at the **Western Province Rugby Football Union** ground, Boundary Rd, Newlands, T021-6894921. Tickets for major games can be bought through **Computicket**, T083-9158000, www.computicket.co.za.

Sailing

Regattas are regularly held in Table Bay.

Royal Cape Yacht Club, T021-4211354, The club is for members only, but accommodates visitors if they are a member of an affiliated international club. For charters and day-trips, see Boat tours, page 129.

Sandboarding

Try the latest addition to board sports on sand dunes. It is not a very fast sport and can be frustrating if you're used to snow, but it can be a fun day out.

Downhill Adventures, T021-4220388, www.downhilladventures.com. Organizes day trips to dunes about 1 hr from Cape Town.

Scuba diving

The Cape waters are cold but are often very clear and good for wreck and reef diving. The best season for diving is during the winter months when the weather ensures the sea is flat as the prevailing winds blow offshore. Water temperatures are between 12°C-18°C; visibility is usually between 5-10 m. When the winds change direction in the summer months visibility can be reduced to almost zero. There are a number of interesting wreck dives along the coast and most sites can be reached direct from the shore. A number of dive companies also specialize in great white shark cage dives.

Dive Action, T021-5110800, www.dive action.co.za, Table Bay. Full dive shop and training centre offering a range of wreck, shore and coral dives around the Cape.

Great White Ecoventures, T021-5300470, www.white-shark-diving.com. Runs cage diving trips to see great white sharks in Gansbaai, a two-hour drive away. Can arrange transfers from Cape Town.

Scuba Shack, 289 Long St, T021-4249368, www.scuba-shack.co.za; also in Glencairne, False Bay, T021-7827358. Well-run local scuba diving school. Full range of PADI-recognized instruction and equipment hire, as well as organized tours to the best dive sites and great white shark cage dives.

Table Bay Diving, V & A Waterfront, T021-4191780, boatrips@iafrica.com. Dive charters and full range of PADI courses, and sells scuba and snorkelling gear.

Skydiving

Skydive Cape Town, T092-8006290 (mob), www.skydivecapetown.za.net. Offers tandem jumps and static-line courses on the West Coast.

Snooker and pool

Rolling Stones, popular pool bar chain with branches on Long St, and in Observatory and Claremont. Plenty of tables, loud music, good atmosphere, open till late.

Surfing

Surfing is a serious business in Cape Town, and there are excellent breaks catering for learners right through to experienced surf rats. Some of the best breaks are on **Long Beach, Kommetjie, Noordhoek, Llandudno, Kalk Bay, Muizenberg** and **Bloubergstrand.** Daily surf report: T021-7881350.
Downhill Adventures, T021-4220388, www.downhilladventures.com. Organizes day and multi-day courses as well as 'Secret Surf Spots' tours.

Swimming

The beaches on the Atlantic seaboard are almost always too cold to swim in – even during the hottest months, the water temperatures rarely creep above 16°C. **Camps Bay** has a tidal pool and shady, grassy areas, see page 90. **Nordhoek** is too rough for swimming, but is a great place for kite-flying or a horse ride, see page 91. False Bay is always a good 5°C warmer, and is perfectly pleasant for a dip during summer. **Boulders Beach** is one of the most attractive beaches on the False Bay seaboard and is also the best place for spotting African penguins, see page 100. **Fish Hoek** has a pleasant beach with small waves and a playground, see page 97. Additionally, a number of beaches have artificial rock pools built by the water, which although rather murky can be perfect for paddling children. There are some very good municipal swimming pools in Cape Town, in Newlands, Sea Point and Woodstock. All are open air and with views of the mountain.

Whale watching

The whale-watching season starts in Oct. Rules surrounding trips to the see the whales are very stringent, and only one boat a year is given a permit to run whale-watching cruises. These change every year, check with the helpful tourist office in Simonstown, T021-7865798, www.tourismcapetown.co.za.

Windsurfing

Langebaan has the best reputation for surfable winds on the Cape; the south-easterly roars between Sep and Apr. In Mar there is a **Boardsailing Marathon** in False Bay, while **Big Bay** at Blouberg is a good spot for wave-jumping. Daily windsurf report: T082-2346324 (mob).
Windsports, T021-5562765, capetown@windsports.co.za, Table View. Equipment and tuition.

Tour operators

City centre tours

Cape Town's layout can be quite confusing, especially if you're staying in the suburbs or along one of the seaboards. When you first arrive, it's a good idea to join a city tour in an open-top bus to get a feel for the city's layout and what each district has to offer.
Explorer Bus, owned by **Cape Town Tourism**, T021- 4264260, www.tourism capetown.co.za, is a double-decker topless bus that follows a 2-hr route around the city. Contact the main tourist office for details.
Hylton Ross, T021-5111784, offers 2-hr 'Topless' city tours.

Cultural tours

Cape Capers, T083-3580183 (mob), tourcape@mweb.co.za. Cultural tours led by Faisal Gangat who won the 'Tourist Guide of the Year' award in 2003. Range of trips, from half-day tours looking at Cape Town's slave history, District Six and Bo-Kaap tours, and the Urban Trail of Two Cities. Recommended.
Grassroute Tours, T021-7061006, www.grassroutetours.co.za. Specializes in township tours beginning in District Six and continuing to Langa and Khayelitsha, also History of Cape Muslims tour. This company works with the communities it visits, putting back some of the proceeds, and has been strongly recommended by readers. Half-day tours cost around R300.
Tana-Baru Tours, T021-4240719, www.tana barutours.co.za. Specialist tours of the Bo-Kaap lasting 2 hrs, interesting and good value, around R200 per person, including

Cape Malay tea in a private home. Township tours last 3 hrs and cost from R300.
Trail of Two Cities, organized by the tourist office, T021-4264260, www.tourismcapetown.co.za, showcases projects where local people are caring for the environment and community, such as the Oude Molen Village, Joe Slovo township, and the Tsoga Environmental Centre.

Boat tours

Also see page 84 for Robben Island Tours.
Nauticat, T021-7907278, www.nauticatcharters.co.za. Daily cruises around Hout Bay and to see the seals at Duiker Island.
Spirit of Just Nuisance, Simonstown T082-7375263 (mob), dhurwitz@iafrica.com. Short tours around the harbour area which include a special visit to the naval dockyard. Also organizes longer trips to Seal Island and Cape Point, and can be chartered for private cruises. Regular departures from the main pier.
Tigger Too, T021-7905256, www.tiggertoo.co.za. Upmarket outfit with daily departures from the Waterfront, sunset cruises and day trips, fishing can be organized, booking advised during peak periods.
Waterfront Boat Company, Quay 5, V&A Waterfront, T021-4185806, www.waterfrontboats.co.za. 6 boats to choose from including large catamaran and stylish yacht, range of boat tours including around Robben Island, whale watching, sunset and dinner cruises. Prices from R120 for 1½-hr sunset cruise, adventure sailing from R70.

Coach tours

Day Trippers, T021-5114766, www.daytrippers.co.za. Small-scale bus tours, day-trips to Cape Point, the Winelands, Township tours or the Whale Coast. Good value and fun, popular with backpackers.
Hylton Ross, T021-5111784, www.hyltonross.co.za. The best-known coach tour operator, with an excellent range of trips such as city tours, Winelands trips, Cape Point, False Bay and Hermanus. 10% of fees go towards the Tourism Community Development Trust, www.tcdtrust.org.za.

Other tour operators

See also tour operators listed in the Gay and lesbian box page 120.
Adventure World, Long St, T021-4224905, www.adventureworld.co.za. Range of adventure tours in and around Cape Town.
Day Trippers, 8 Pineway, Pinelands, T021-5114766, www.daytrippers.co.za. Active tours popular with backpackers, good value day trips as well as longer tours to the Cederberg and the Karoo. Also leads bike tours, horseback safaris, quad biking and kloofing. Recommended.
Downhill Adventures, T021-4220388, www.downhilladventures.com. Rents out bikes and organizes adventure tours on Table Mountain, Cape Point Nature Reserve, along the coast and in the Winelands.
The Eco-Ist, T082-4799688 (mob), www.eco-tourisminvestments.co.za. Special interest tours with a focus on environment, flora and fauna. Trips go to Table Mountain, Kirstenbosch and the West Coast. No more than 6 people per trip.
Friends of Dorothy, T021-4651871, www.friendsofdorothytours.co.za. Gay-friendly tours, including a gardens tour, Four Passes tour, Cape Winelands and whale-watching trips.
Greencape Tours, T021-7970166, infor@greencape.com. Specialist natural history trips run by Bruce Terlien who has a keen interest in the flora and fauna of the Cape, maximum group size is 7.
Homeland, Long St, T021-4260294, www.homeland.co.za. Cape Point Classic tour, full day taking in Cape Point, including biking, a braai lunch and all transport. R350 per person. Also arranges airport shuttles from R47 per person.
Legend Tours, T021-6974056, www.legendtourism.co.za. Usual selection of trips around Cape Town – Winelands, Cape Flats, Peninsula, Table Mountain, Cape Point and Waterfront, free collection from your accommodation.
Namibian Tourist Office, The Pinnacle, corner of Burg and Castle Sts, underneath Cape Town Tourism, T021-4223298, www.namibiatourism.com.na, Mon-Fri 0800-1700. If you are planning a trip to Namibia it is well worth picking up a copy of the government guide to hotels and national parks accommodation. (See Footprint's Namibia Handbook).
Vineyard Ventures, 5 Hanover Rd, Fresnaye, T021-4348888, www.vineyardventures.co.za.

Transport

Air

See also Ins and outs, page 66, for details of getting to/from the airport. Departure tax is normally included in the ticket price.
South African Airways, (SAA), central reservations, T011-9781111, www.flysaa.com, and its subsidiaries have numerous flights every day to every city in South Africa. British Airways Comair, T011-9210222, www.comair.co.za, has several flights/day to **Johannesburg**. Kulula, T0861-585852, www.kulula.com, flies to **Durban** and **Johannesburg**. Nationwide, T0861-737737, www.flynationwide.co.za, has daily flights to **Johannesburg**.

Bus

Greyhound, Intercape and Translux all depart/arrive from Adderley St, next to Cape Town railway station. Booking offices are also here. Buses tend to be good value and reliable over long distances, although they do often have many stop-off points.

Greyhound, T021-5056363, www.greyhound.co.za, has regular departures to **Bloemfontein , Durban, East London, George, Johannesburg** and **Pretoria, Kimberley, Knysna** and **Port Elizabeth**.

Intercape, T086-1287287, www.intercape.co.za, (reservations must be made 72 hrs before departure), has regular departures to **Bloemfontein, Johannesburg** and **Pretoria, Port Elizabeth** stopping at most Garden Route towns, and to **Upington, Windhoek** stopping at a number of west coast towns.

Translux, T0861-287287, www.translux.co.za, has regular departures to **Beaufort West, Bloemfontein, Durban, East London, Johannesburg** and **Pretoria, Kimberley, Knysna, Port Elizabeth** via the **Garden Route**.

Budget buses

The Baz Bus, T021-4392323, www.bazbus.com, has a daily service from Cape Town to **Port Elizabeth**. The service continues from Port Elizabeth to **Lesotho, Durban, Swaziland, Johannesburg** and **Pretoria**. See page 39 for more details.

Car

Car hire

Cape Town and the surrounding Winelands are best explored in a hired car. The cheapest local car hire companies change frequently – it's a good idea to check at backpacker hostels to see which ones they recommend. All of the large firms now have toll free phone numbers which can be dialled from anywhere within South Africa, and most of them have kiosks at Cape Town International Airport – but be sure to book in advance as they often get booked up weeks ahead in the high season. See page 39 for further advice on car hire and driving.

Atlantic Car Hire, T021-9344600, www.atlanticcarhire.co.za.
Avis, T021-4241177, www.avis.co.za
Budget, T021-3803140, www.budget.co.za.
Camper King, T021-5582203, www.camperking.co.za. Campers and motor homes.
Cape Car Hire, T021-3830445, www.capecarhire.co.za.
Europcar, T021-9342264, www.europcar.co.za.
Hertz, T021-9354800, www.hertz.co.za.
National Alamo, T021-9347499, www.nationalcar.co.za.

Metro

The suburban train service, **Metrorail**, T0800-656463, www.mti.co.za, serves the suburbs. Services run as far as Simon's Town, but also go out as far as Worcester. These trains are fine to use in rush hour (0700-0800 and 1600-1800), but are best avoided at quieter times due to safety issues. It's always a good idea to travel 1st class only; each station has signs as to where the 1st class carriage will be when the train comes in. Tickets cost about R20 for a single.

Taxi

There are several ranks dotted around town – the most useful ones are outside the train station at Adderley St, by the **Holiday Inn** on Greenmarket Sq, and on Long St. You can also flag down any that you see cruising around. If you are outside the city centre, you will have to call one in advance. Be sure to get a quote as prices can vary a lot. Companies change regularly, so either ask your hotel or restaurant to call one for you, or ask at the tourist office for reliable numbers, T021-4264260.

Rikki Taxis, T021-4234888, are small, shared people-carriers and a cheaper alternative to getting around the city. You need to call one, but they pick up several people along the route, bringing down costs.

Minibus taxis

These serve all areas of the city on fixed routes, and leave from the minibus terminal accessed from the top floor of the **Sanlam Golden Acre** shopping centre on Adderley St. They can also be flagged down from the street. Minibuses to the Atlantic coast usually leave from outside **OK Bazaar's** on Adderely St. Most trips cost around R5. Buses stop running at 1900. These are generally safe to use, although you'd be advised to do your best not to look like a tourist and leave all valuables at home. Avoid taking them on the highways, too, as the buses have high accident rates.

Train

Cape Town has one main railway station in the centre of town. Both long distance and suburban services leave from here. Leaflets with train times and fare structure are available in the concourse. The rail network is run by **Spoornet**, www.spoornet.co.za. For more details of train travel, see page 38.

The **Blue Train**, T021-3348459, www.bluetrain.co.za, is South Africa's premier luxury train, which departs from Cape Town, see page 38 for details. **Rovos**, T021- 3158242, www.rovos.co.za. Also has luxury trains that travel between Cape Town and **Pretoria**.

Directory

Banks

Only change money in hotels as a last resort: their exchange rates are unbelievably poor. There are plenty of 24-hr cash machines (ATMs) throughout the city, making it easy to remain cash rich. There are also a number of banks where you can cash traveller's cheques. All the main branches are open weekdays 0830-1530 and Sat 0800-1100. The following telephone numbers are for the principal branches in Cape Town city centre (Adderley St). **ABSA**, T021-4801911. **First National Bank**, T021-4232202. **Standard Bank**, T021-4017500.

There are 2 main bureaux de change: **Amex**, T021-4193917, Alfred Mall, V&A Waterfront, open Mon-Sat 0900-1700, who will receive and hold mail for card holders. **Rennies Travel** (Thomas Cook representatives), also have a branch at the Waterfront, on the upper level of Victoria Wharf, T021-4183744. **Rennies Travel** also provides all the usual services of a travel agent.

Embassies and consulates

Most foreign representatives have their head offices in either Pretoria or Johannesburg, but many countries also have representatives in Cape Town and Port Elizabeth. **Australia**, 14th floor, BP Centre, Thibault Sq, T021-4195425. **Belgium**, Vogue House, Thibault Sq, T021-4194690. **Canada**, Reserve Bank Building, 30 Hout St, T021-4235240. **Denmark**, 5 Toaki Rd, Tokai, T021-4196936. **Finland**, Lincoln Rd, Oranjezicht, T021-4614732. **France**, 2 Dean St, Gardens, T021-4231575. **Germany**, 825 St Martini, Gardens, Queen Victoria St, T021-4053000. **India**, The Terraces, 34 Bree St, T021-4198110. **Italy**, 2 Greys Pass, Gardens, T021-4873900. **Japan**, Main Tower, Standard Bank Centre, Heerenracht, T021-4251695. **Mozambique**, 45 Castle St, T021-4262944, visas issued within 24 hrs. **Netherlands**, 100 Strand St, T021-4215660. **Portugal**, Standard Bank Centre, Herzog Blvd, T021-4180080. **Russian Federation**, Southern Life Centre, Hertzog Blvd, T021-4183656. **Spain**, 37 Short Market St,

T021-4222415. **Sweden**, 10th floor, Southern Life Centre, 8 Riebeeck St, T021-4181276. **Switzerland**, 26th floor, 1 Thibault Sq, T021-4183665. **UK**, Southern Life Centre, 8 Riebeeck St, T021-4052400. **USA**, 2 Reddam Ave, Westlake T021-7027300.

Hospitals

Casualty facilities available at **Groote Schuur**, Observatory, T021-4049111, 24 hrs; **Red Cross Children's Hospital**, Mowbray, T021-6895277. **Travel Clinic**, V&A Waterfront, T021-4054500

Internet

Access is available at backpacker hostels, **Postnet** branches (see Telephone, below) and at the main tourist office. **Virtual Turtle** is a 24-hr internet café on the 1st floor of the Purple Turtle building, Short Market St, T021-4241037. **m@in internet café**, Lifestyle Centre, 50 Kloof St, T021-4223431, and outlet at 37 Roeland St, T021-4623248. Broadband internet access costing around R10 for 15 minutes, prices go down the longer you stay. Also has wi-fi for lap-top users. **Catwalk**, 16 Burg St, T021-4248899. Huge internet café with dozens of screens, excellent value at R10 for an hour, open 24 hours and serves range of sandwiches and burgers.
There are also internet cafés in all the shopping centres, including Victoria Wharf at the Waterfront, and in the main tourist office on Burg St.

Newspapers

Cape Town has an English morning paper, the *Cape Times*, and an evening paper, the *Argus*. Both are good sources of what's going on in the city, with daily listings and entertainment sections. There is also a daily paper in Afrikaans, *Die Burger* and *Xhosa*.

Post office

The **General Post Office** is between Parliament and Plein Sts by the Golden Acre shopping centre. **Post restante** is in the main hall, Mon-Fri 0800-1630, Sat 0800-1200. There is a separate entrance for parcels in Plein St. Post offices are found in the suburbs close to the principal shopping centres.

Radio

Radio KFM: 94.5 FM, contemporary music, mix of old classics and new hits. **Radio Good Hope FM**: 94-97 FM, teenage pop music, current hits. **Radio Lotus**: 97.8 FM, general Indian affairs and music.

Telephone

International enquiries: T0903. Local enquiries: T1023. **Postnet** is a useful chain found throughout the city, usually in shopping malls. The main branch is in the Union Castle Building, 6 Hout St, T021-4260179, www.postnet.co.za, open Mon-Fri 0830-1700, Sat 0830-1300. Services include sending parcels, internet access, fax sending and receiving, phonecards, passport photos.

Useful addresses and telephone numbers

Ambulance: T10177. **Cape Nature Conservation**: T021-4260723, www.capenature.org.za. **Computicket**: T0839158000, www.computicket.co.za, for nationwide theatre, concerts and sport events. **Fire**: T021-5351100. **Mountain rescue**: T021-9489900. **Mountain weather reports**: T021-4245148. **Police**: T10111. **Sea rescue**: T021-4053500. **South African National Parks (SAN Parks)**: www.parks-sa.co.za, has a desk at the main tourist office.

Western Cape

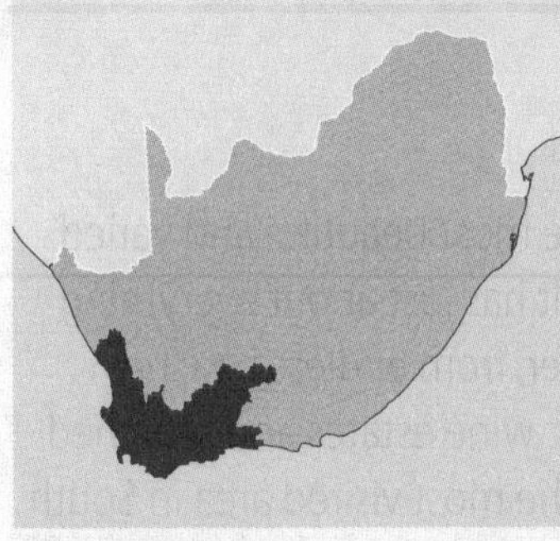

Footprint features

Introduction

The Western Cape is arguably the most beautiful and varied of South Africa's nine provinces. It has just about everything that the entire country has to offer, from endless beaches and indigenous forests to historic wine estates and scorched semi-desert. Consequently, it is the most visited area in South Africa, with a well-developed tourist infrastructure and the inevitable seasonal overcrowding.

The first port of call for most visitors to the Cape is the beautiful Winelands region, with the historic towns of Stellenbosch, Franschhoek and Paarl stretching across a range of mountains and surrounded by old wine estates. The Breede River Valley is better known for its farming, with isolated settlements tucked away along the banks of its river. Further east lie the parched plains of the Karoo, their endless shimmering horizons peppered with craggy mountains and lonely farmsteads. The southern coast begins with Walker Bay, which claims to have the best land-based whale watching in the world. Further east stretches the celebrated (and somewhat overrated) Garden Route, an area with long stretches of sand, nature reserves, lush forests and tourist-friendly seaside towns.

Far less visited is the west coast, north of Cape Town, a wild area of fynbos-covered sand dunes, sun-bleached beaches and remote fishing villages. Inland lie the Cederberg Mountains, a rugged range with ancient San rock art and some of the best hiking in the country.

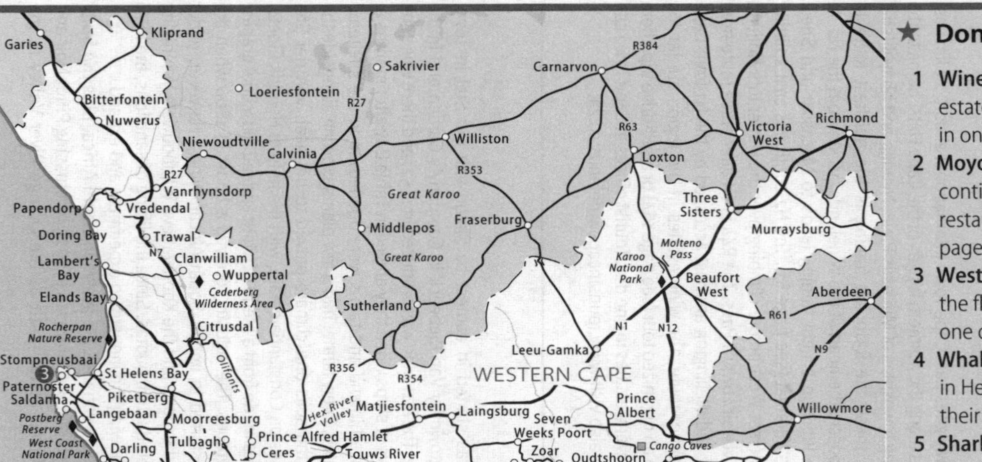

★ Don't miss...

1 **Winelands** Spend a day wine tasting at the beautiful estates around Stellenbosch and Paarl, and enjoy a meal in one of Franschhoek's fine restaurants, page 136.

2 **Moyo at Spier** Eat great food from all over the African continent in a tree house at this fantastically decorated restaurant, where singers will entertainyou at your table, page 160.

3 **West Coast** Head up to the fishing villages to catch the flowers in season and a long lazy seafood lunch at one of the outdoor restaurants, page 166.

4 **Whale watching** Spend a morning sitting on a cliff top in Hermanus watching southern right whales flipping their magnificent tails, page 217.

5 **Shark spotting** Have an exhilarating close encounter with a great white shark from a cage in the ocean near Gansbaai, page 235.

5 **Knysna Lagoon** Slurp down half a dozen Knysna oysters before exploring the wide protected lagoon by boat, page 260.

6 **Tsitsikamma National Park** Fly through the giant trees on a canopy tour, or hike along some beautifully rugged coastline, page 269.

The Winelands

The Winelands is South Africa's oldest and most beautiful wine-producing area, a fertile series of valleys quite unlike the rest of the Western Cape. It is the Cape's biggest attraction after Cape Town, and its appeal is simple: it offers the chance to sample several hundred different wines in a historical and wonderfully scenic setting.

This was the first region after Cape Town to be settled, and the towns of Stellenbosch, Paarl and Franschhoek are some of the oldest in South Africa. Today, their streets are lined with beautiful Cape Dutch and Georgian houses, although the real architectural gems are the manor houses on the wine estates. While the wine industry flourished during the 18th and 19th centuries, the farmers built grand homesteads with cool wine cellars next to their vines. Most of these have been lovingly restored and today can be visited as part of a winelands tour – a few have even been converted into gourmet restaurants or luxury hotels. » *For Sleeping, Eating and other listings, see pages 154-165.*

Ins and outs

Getting there The N2 highway goes past Cape Town International airport, 22 km east of the city, and then continues along the northern fringes of the Cape Flats, home to the sprawling townships of Mitchells Plain, Nyanga and Khayelitsha. Beyond these the R310 left turning is the quickest route to Stellenbosch, the heart of the Winelands, 16 km from the N2. At Firgrove junction a right turning leads to Macassar and Sheik Yussuf's Karamat (see page 81). The N2 continues east splitting the towns of Strand and Somerset West before climbing over the Hottentots Holland Mountains into the Overberg via Sir Lowry's Pass. The R44 is an alternative route from Strand to Stellenbosch. Paarl and Wellington are best accessed by the N1 from Cape Town, and Franschhoek by either route. The wine estates in the region are far too numerous to list in full, but on an organized tour (see page 164) or a self-drive trip, there is ample opportunity to visit several estates in one day. Tourist offices in Cape Town can provide brochures and maps; also visit www.tourismcapewinelands.co.za.

Wine estates charge a small tasting fee of about R5-20, which often includes a free wine glass.

Background

The Cape's wine industry was started in earnest by Simon van der Stel in 1679. Previously, vines had been grown by Van Riebeeck in Company's Garden and in the area known today as Wynberg. The first wine was produced in 1652, and there was soon a great demand from the crews of ships when they arrived in Table Bay after months at sea. As the early settlers moved inland and farms were opened up in the sheltered valleys, more vines were planted. Every farmer had a few plants growing alongside the homestead, and by chance the soils and climate proved to be ideal. Van der Stel produced the first quality wines on Constantia estate, with the help of Hendrik Cloete. These were mostly sweet wines made from a blend of white and red Muscadel grapes, known locally as *Hanepoot* grapes. The industry received a boost in 1806 when the English, at war with France, started to import South African wines. However, under Apartheid, sanctions hindered exports and the Kooperatieve Wijnbouwers Vereniging (KWV) controlled prices and production quotas. Since the lifting of sanctions, the KWV has lost much of its power, allowing the industry to experiment and expand.

Today, all major wine grape varieties are grown in South Africa, plus the fruity red Pinotage, a variety produced in Stellenbosch in 1925 by crossing Pinot Noir and Cinsault. Wine is now produced as far north as the Orange River Valley in the Northern Cape.

Strand and around

» pp154-165. Colour map 8, grid A2.

Although principally an industrial area, Strand is a popular seaside resort and commuter town with an excellent 5-km white sand beach. It mainly caters for domestic tourists and despite its proximity to Cape Town, the Winelands and the Whale Coast, it holds little appeal. Further inland, **Somerset West** is a prosperous town and again a major commuter centre. It has a beautiful location on the slopes of the Helderberg Mountains, with unimpeded views of False Bay and, occasionally, Cape Point.

Vergelegen Estate

ⓘ *From Somerset West take the R44, turn right at the traffic lights and after 1 km turn left into Lourensford Rd; the estate is 4 km on the right. T021-8471334, www.vergelegen.co.za, daily 0930-1600. There is a shop, displays on the history of the estate, a smart wine-tasting room and 2 restaurants: Lady Phillips Restaurant is à la carte, 1200-1430, booking essential T021-8471346; the Rose Terrace is an open-air lunch spot, Nov-Apr 1000-1600. There is also a picnic hamper service.*

This is one of the Cape's finest estates and the highlight is a visit to the magnificent manor house filled with beautiful period furniture and historical paintings, similar to

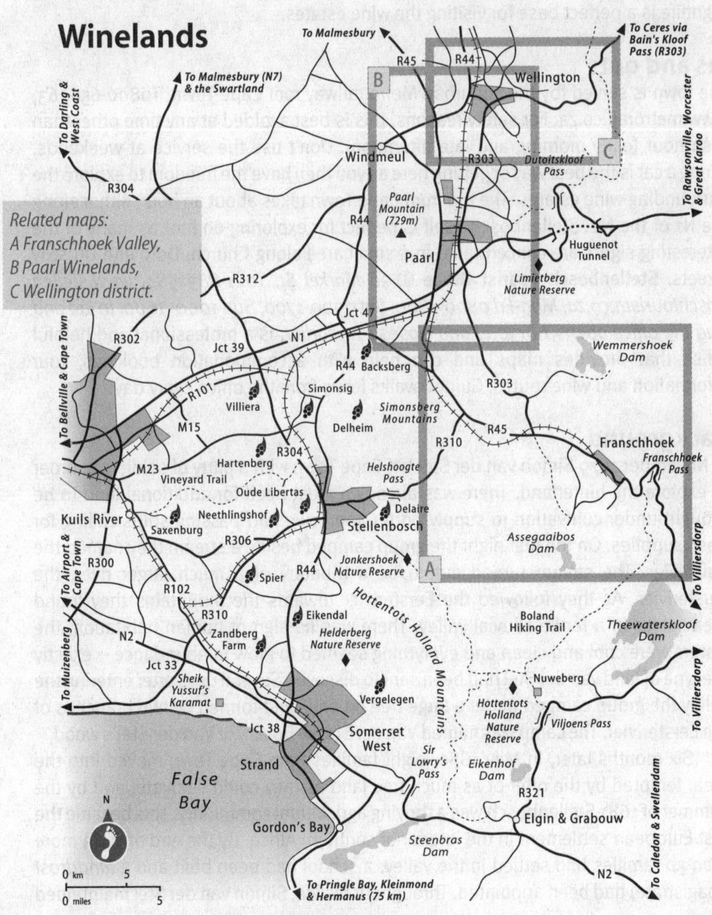

the collection at Groot Constantia. At the front of the house are five **Chinese camphor trees** that were planted by Willem van der Stel between 1700 and 1706. They are the oldest living documented trees in South Africa and are now a national monument. Behind the house is a walled octagonal garden – many of the plants were planted here by Lady Phillips (wife of Sir Lionel Phillips, owner for 25 years from 1917), who wished to recreate a typical English garden, complete with herbaceous border. Look out for the collection of roses next to the main house. The surrounding parkland, much of it similar to an English country estate, is also open for exploration.

Stellenbosch » pp154-165.

Colour map 8, grid A2.

Stellenbosch

Stellenbosch, the centre of the Winelands, is the oldest and most attractive town in the region, with a large university giving it a liveliness which is lacking in nearby towns. The centre has a pleasing mix of architectural styles: Cape Dutch, Georgian, Regency and Victorian houses line broad streets, dappled with shade from centuries-old oak trees, and furrowed with water ditches which still carry water to the gardens. It's a fairly large place, but with its handful of good museums and fun nightlife is a perfect base for visiting the wine estates.

Ins and outs

The town is served fby the suburban Metro railway rom Cape Town, T0800-656463, www.metrorail.co.za. For safety reasons, this is best avoided at any time other than rush hour (early morning and late afternoon). Don't use the service at weekends. Hiring a car is the best way of getting here as you then have the freedom to explore the surrounding wine estates. The trip from Cape Town takes about an hour, either along the N1 or the N2. Stellenbosch itself is perfect for exploring on foot as many of the interesting sights are concentrated in a small area along Church, Dorp and Drostdy streets. **Stellenbosch Tourist Office** ⓘ *36 Market St, T021-8833584, www.stellen boschtourism.co.za, Mon-Fri 0800-1800, Sat 0900-1700, Sun 1000- 1600, in Jun and Aug the office opens 1 hr later and closes 1 hr earlier*, is a professional and helpful office that provides maps and can help with accommodation bookings, tour information and wine routes. Guided walks leave from the office every day.

Background

In November 1679 Simon van der Stel left Cape Town with a party of soldiers in order to explore the hinterland. There was already a great need for additional land to be brought under cultivation to supply both Cape Town and passing ships calling for fresh supplies. On the first night the group camped beside a stream they named the Kuilsrivier. The stream turned out to be a tributary of a much larger river, the Eersterivier. As they followed the Eersterivier towards the mountains they found themselves in a fertile alluvial valley. There was no sign of human habitation, the waters were cool and clean and everything seemed to grow in abundance – exactly the type of land van der Stel had been sent to discover. Several days after entering the valley the group camped under a large tree on an island formed by two branches of the Eersterivier. The camp was named Van der Stel se Bosch, or Van der Stel's wood.

Six months later, in May 1680, eight families from Cape Town moved into the area, tempted by the offer of as much free land as they could cultivate, and by the summer of 1681 Stellenbosch was a thriving agricultural community. This became the first European settlement in the interior of southern Africa. By the end of 1683 more than 30 families had settled in the valley, a school had been built and a *landdrost* (magistrate) had been appointed. Throughout his life, Simon van der Stel maintained

Willem van der Stel

Two of the farms on the banks of the Lourens River, Parelvallei and Vergelegen, belonged to two sons of Governor Simon van der Stel. When Simon van der Stel retired as governor of the Cape he went to live on his estate of Constantia. The directors of the Dutch East India Company honoured his works in the Cape by appointing his son, Willem Adriaan, as his successor to the governorship. This proved to be a disaster since Willem principally devoted his energies to building up his estate, Vergelegen. Over the next six years he acquired most of the land in the valley and used the Cape's resources to improve the estate. He was not unskilled at farming and, before he was found out, Vergelegen was regarded as one of the most gracious and successful country estates in the Cape.

However, in 1707 the Dutch East India Company was made aware of the corrupt nature of Willem's dealings and he was recalled to the Netherlands. Vergelegen was confiscated, divided into four farms and sold. Since Simon van der Stel died at Constantia on 24 June 1712 there have been no Van der Stels in the Cape, a sad fact considering what an important role the family had in the foundation of the colony.

a close interest in the development of the town. One of his greatest legacies was to order the planting of oak trees along the sides of every street. Canals were also built to bring water to the town gardens. Today, a number of the original oaks are still standing and some have been proclaimed national monuments.

It is difficult to picture it today, but at the end of the 17th century this new settlement was a frontier town. For the next 100 years the magistracy had dealings with the explorers, hunters, adventurers and nomadic peoples who lived beyond the Cape, and the authority extended over 250,000 sq km. In the meantime, the town prospered as an agricultural centre and also emerged as a place of learning. In 1859 the Dutch Reformed Church started a Seminary which in 1866 became the Stellenbosch Gymnasium, renamed Victoria College in 1887. After the creation of the Union of South Africa in 1910, there was pressure on the new government to establish a single national university. By this stage Victoria College had emerged as a respected Afrikaner school, and Stellenbosch itself was regarded as an important centre of Afrikaner culture. In 1915 a local farmer, Johannes Marais died and left £100,000 towards higher education in Stellenbosch. This bequest finally persuaded the government to yield to public pressure and in April 1918 the Victoria College became the University of Stellenbosch.

Sights

Stellenbosch offers two approaches to sightseeing: walking around the town centre viewing public buildings, oak-lined streets and stately homes; or going on a wine tour, visiting any number of the roughly 100 wineries and private cellars. Spend a couple of days in Stellenbosch and you'll get to do both.

No other town in South Africa has such an impressive concentration of early Cape architecture. However, like Swellendam (see page 238), many of the earliest buildings were lost to fires in the 18th and 19th centuries; what you see today is a collection of perfectly restored buildings. Following each fire, the destroyed buildings were recreated with the help of photographs, original plans and sketches, although the technology and materials of the day were used. This is perhaps why they appear to have survived in such good condition. This restoration process is not unusual: the town of Tulbagh in the Breede River Valley was completely destroyed by an earthquake in 1969, but today it has the look and feel of an unspoilt quaint Victorian village.

Dorp Street, which runs east-west in the southern part of town, has all the classic features – an avenue of oak trees, running water in open furrows and carefully restored white-walled buildings. A walk from the **Libertas Parva** building to the Theological College takes you through the oldest parts of town and past some of the best-preserved old buildings. Libertas Parva is a beautifully restored classic H-shaped manor house built in 1783. Today it serves as an **art gallery** ⓘ *Mon-Fri 0900-1245, 1400-1700, Sat 1000-1300, 1400-1700*, with pictures of Cape Town. The cellar behind the house has a small wine and cork museum. Continue east along Dorp Street, where you'll pass the famous **Oom Samie se Winkel** at number 82, a Victorian-style general store that is still functioning as a shop today. Of particular note are the town houses just past the junction with Helderberg Street. Numbers 153, **Hauptfleisch House**, 155, **Bakker House**, 157, **Loubser House**, and 159, **Saxenhof**, are regarded as the best-preserved street façades in old Stellenbosch.

Branching off from Dorp Street is Drostdy Street, dominated by a building with a tall tower. Also in this street is the town church, the **Moederkerk**; its current steeple church was designed by Carl Otto Hagen and built in 1862. Inside, it is worth admiring the pulpit and the unusually thick stained-glass windows.

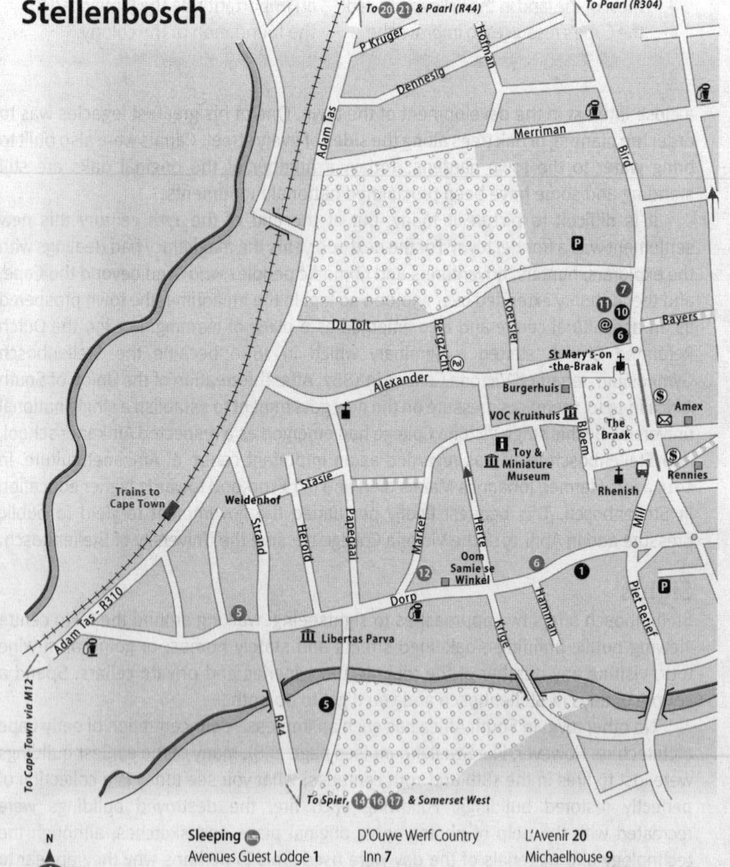

Turn right at the top of Drostdy Street into Van Riebeeck Street, then turn left into Neethling Street to reach the **Botanical Gardens** ⓘ *Mon-Fri 0900-1630, Sat 0900-1100*. These are part of the University of Stellenbosch, with a fine collection of ferns, orchids and bonsai trees. One of the more unusual plants to look out for is the *Welwitschis* from the Namib Desert.

Heading west back along Van Riebeeck Street brings you to Ryneveld Street, where you'll find the entrance to the engaging **Village Museum** ⓘ *T021-8872902, www.museums.org.za/stellmus, Mon-Sat 0930-1700, Sun 1400-1700, R20*. The complex currently spreads over two blocks in the oldest part of town. If you follow the guide numbers you will be taken through four houses, each representing a different period of the town's history. The oldest of these is **Schreuderhuis** (1709), one of the earliest houses to be built in Stellenbosch. The simple furniture and collection of household objects are all of the same period. The house was built by Sebastian Schreuder, a German. **Blettermanhuis** (1789) is a perfect example of what has come to be regarded as a typical H-shaped Cape Dutch home. The furnishings are those of a wealthy household between 1750 and 1780. The house was built by Hendrik Lodewyk Bletterman, the last *landdrost* to be appointed by the Dutch East India Company.

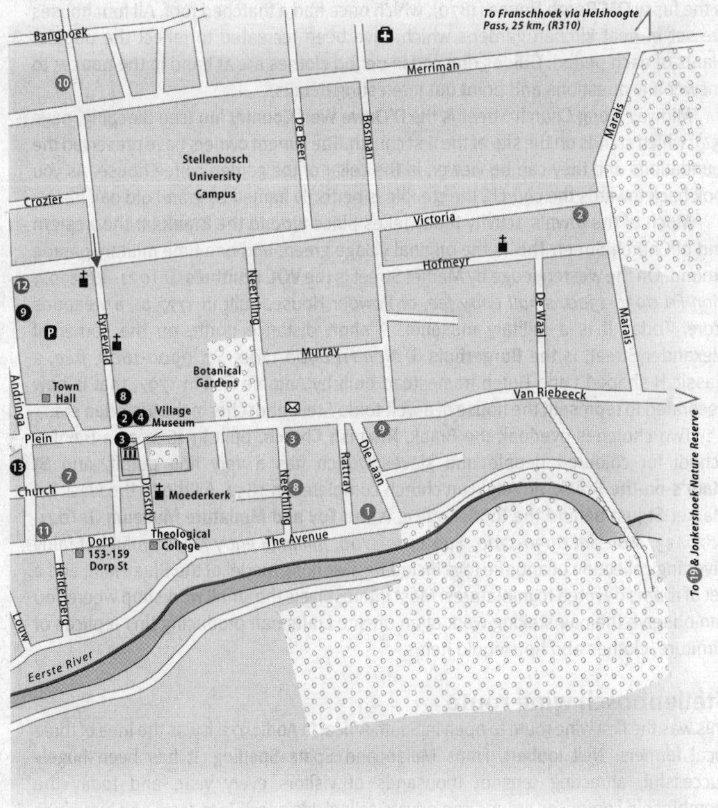

Stumble Inn 12
Wilfra Court 21

Eating
Blue Orange 1
Café Nouveau 2
Coachman 3
Decameron 4
Dros 6
Fishmonger 8
Mexican Kitchen 10
Naked Truth 9
Volkskombuis 5
Wijnhuis 13

Bars & clubs
Bohemia Pub 12
Fandango 7
Tollie's 11

Vineyard Trail

An energetic way to get a feel for the Winelands is to walk along part or all of the Vineyard Trail. The full hike which runs between Stellenbosch and Kuils River is 24 km long. The trail passes through vineyards, olive groves, and a few patches of indigenous vegetation. There are two shorter options but these are still 12 km and 16 km long. The tourist bureau issues an excellent map showing all the alternative trails. All the trails start at the Oude Libertas Amphitheatre complex of Stellenbosch Farmers' Winery, close to the old cemetery.

Notice the contrast in furnishings between Schreuder the messenger and Bletterman the magistrate. The third building in the museum to have been restored is **Grosvenor House** (1803), in Drostdy Street. This is an excellent example of the two-storeyed town houses that once dominated the streets of Cape Town. The home was built by Christian Ludolph Neethling, a successful farmer, in 1782. The fourth and final house is the fussy **OM Bergh House** (1870), which once had a thatched roof. All four houses are set in neat kitchen gardens which have been recreated to reflect the popular plants of each period. Guides dressed in period clothes are at hand in the houses to answer any questions and point out interesting details.

Midway along Church Street is the **D'Ouwe Werf Country Inn** (see Sleeping, page 154), which stands on the site of the first church. The current owners have preserved the foundations and they can be viewed in the cellar of the garden coffee house. As you look back towards the church, the steeple is perfectly framed by grand old oak trees.

Much of the town's activity today takes place around the **Braak**, at the western end of Church Street. This is the original village green, and one-time military parade ground. On the western edge by Market Street is the **VOC Kruithuis** ⓘ *T021-8872902, Mon-Fri 0930-1300, small entry fee*, or Powder House, built in 1777 as a weapons store. Today it is a military museum. A short distance north, on the corner of Alexander Street, is the **Burgerhuis** ⓘ *Mon-Fri 0900-1700, Sat 0900-1600, free*, a classic H-shaped Cape Dutch homestead built by Antonie Fick in 1797, that is now decorated to represent the house of a well-to-do Stellenboscher in the Victorian era.

Two churches overlook the Braak, **Rhenish Church**, built in 1832 as a training school for coloured people and slaves, which has a very fine pulpit, and **St Mary's-on-the-Braak**, an Anglican church completed in 1852. A little to the west, on Market St just behind the tourist office, is the **Toy and Miniature Museum** ⓘ *T021-8879433, Mon-Sat 0930-1700, Sun 1400-1700, minimal entry fee*, a small but fairly diverting collection of antique toys including a working model of the Blue Train, and a set of rooms devoted to miniatures. Most interesting is the small workshop where you can observe the painstaking work of an on-site craftsman producing tiny replicas of furniture, clothes and household items.

Stellenbosch wine route

This was the first wine route to open in South Africa, in April 1971. It was the idea of three local farmers: Neil Joubert, Frans Malan and Spatz Sperling. It has been hugely successful, attracting tens of thousands of visitors every year, and today the membership comprises around 100 private cellars. It's possible to taste and buy wines at all of them, and the cellars can arrange for wine to be delivered internationally. Many of the estates have excellent restaurants as well as providing very popular picnic lunches – at weekends it is advisable to book in advance. Maps and brochures on the wine route can be picked up at the tourist offices in Stellenbosch and Cape Town.

Brandy Route

South Africans consume over 45 million litres of brandy each year. For more information on the Brandy Route, visit www.sabrandy.co.za.

The Brandy Route starts at the **Van Ryn Brandy Cellar**, T021-8813875, www.vanryn.co.za, at Vlottenburg, 8 km from Stellenbosch. This is the oldest working cellar in the Cape. You not only view the distillation process but the tour includes a visit to the workshop where the coopers make the maturation barrels from French oak. During the peak season (Dec and Jan), tours start Mon-Fri 1000, 1130, 1500; Sat 1000, 1130. For the rest of the year there is one morning tour and one afternoon tour, Mon-Fri only.

The route continues to the **Oude Molen Brandy Museum** in Stellenbosch, visits by appointment only, T021-8086911. This is where the Frenchman, Rene Santhagens, the "saint of brandy in South Africa", established the first pot stall at the beginning of the 20th century.

Next is **Backsberg**, T021-8755141, www.backsberg.co.za, a well-known wine estate between Simondium and Klapmuts. Mon-Fri 0830-1700, Sat 0800-1300, Sun 1100-1500.

The route continues into Paarl to the **Paarl Rock Brandy Cellar**, T021-8626159, founded by the De Villiers family in 1856. Visitors are offered a taste of the only Hanepoot brandy in the world. Mon-Fri only.

From Paarl you can either visit a cellar in Franschhoek or continue along the N1 to Rawsonville and Worcester where the route ends at the **KWV Brandy Cellar**, T023-3420255, www.kwv-international.com. This is the largest brandy cellar in the world – there are 120 copper pot stills in use. Tours are conducted in English (1400) and Afrikaans (1430). Book in advance for tours in French, Portuguese, Spanish, Italian and German.

The **Oolf Bergh Brandy Cellar**, T023-3493600, in Rawsonville is unusual in that it is the only one in South Africa which employs the solera method of maturation. The cellar opened to the public for the first time late in 1997.

Delaire ⓘ *T021-8851756, www.delairewinery.co.za, sales and tastings: Mon-Fri 0900-1700, Sat 1000-1700, Sun 1000-1600*. This small estate has some of the best views in the valley, and has produced some very high-standard wines. Their flagship Merlot is very popular, while the Chardonnay remains a favourite export label. The **Green Door** restaurant serves lunch Tuesday to Sunday; picnic hampers are available. On a clear day visitors are rewarded with views of the Simonsberg Mountains.

Delheim ⓘ *T021-8884600, www.delheim.com, sales and tastings: Mon-Fri 0900-1700, Sat 0900-1530, Sun 1030-1530 (Oct-Apr only), cellar tours: Mon-Fri 1030 and 1430, Sat 1030, restaurant: Mon-Sat 1230-1500, Sun 1230-1500 (Oct-Apr only)*. This is one of the more commercially oriented estates and may seem a little too impersonal. However, the restaurant has a beautiful setting with views towards Cape Town and Table Mountain. Tastings are conducted in a cool downstairs cellar.

Remember the drink-drive laws in South Africa. When wine tasting, you may be offered up to 15 different wines to sample at each estate, so make sure one of you stays sober.

Eikendal ⓘ *T021-8551422, www.eikendal.com, sales and tastings: Mon-Fri 0900-1630, Sat-Sun 1030-1500 (closed Jun-Sep), cellar tours: 1000 and 1500*. The microclimate on the western slopes of the mountain is ideal for viticulture, and there is a wide selection of both whites and reds. Lunch is served in the wine-tasting room or the gardens; Swiss cheese fondues are sometimes served in the evenings.

Hartenberg ⓘ *T021-8652541, www.hartenbergestate.com, sales and tastings: Mon-Fri 0900-1700, Sat 0900-1500, lunches: 1200-1400*. This privately owned old

The Huguenots

The Huguenots were French Calvinists who, during the 16th century, became an influential force under the leadership of the Prince de Condé, Gaspard de Coligny and Prince Henry of Navarre. After the death of King Henry IV, the Catholics at the royal court started to pursue a policy of persecution. In 1685 the rights of all Protestants were revoked in the Edict of Nantes. Soon afterwards thousands were forced to flee France to Britain, Germany and the Netherlands. This coincided with the Dutch looking for additional settlers in their new Cape colony to help provide sufficient supplies for passing ships. Between 1688 and 1720 about 270 Huguenots settled at the Cape. Within two generations the only reminder of their French past was their family and farm names. From the outset Governor Simon van der Stel had forced the use of Dutch in schools and at church.

estate, founded in 1692, is off the Bottelary Road, 10 km north of Stellenbosch. During the summer, lunches are served in the shade and peace of the gardens; come winter the tasting room doubles up as a restaurant with warming log fires. A number of red and white wines are produced, but their reds seem the most successful – recent award winners include their 2000 Shiraz and the 2001 Merlot.

Neethlingshof ⓘ *T021-8838988, www.neethlingshof.co.za, sales and tastings: Mon-Fri 0900-1700, Sat-Sun 1000-1600, cellar and vineyard tours: by appointment, meals are served in 2 restaurants, Lord Neethling and Palm Terrace, 0900-2100.* With its fine restaurants, Cape Dutch buildings and grand pine avenue (which now features on the labels of the estate wines), this estate is a very pleasant one to visit. The first vines were planted here in 1692 by a German, Barend Lubbe, and the manor house was built in 1814 in traditional Cape Dutch H-style. Today this has been converted into the Lord Neethling restaurant renowned for its venison and veal. Neethlingshof has won a clutch of awards – the Lord Neethling Pinotage '98 has won trophies.

Saxenburg ⓘ *T021-9036113, www.saxenburg.co.za, sales and tastings: Mon-Fri 0900-1700, Sat 0900-1600, Sun 1000-1600 (Sep-May only). The Guinea Fowl restaurant is open daily for lunch and Wed-Sat for dinner.* Saxenberg has a long history, starting in 1693 when Simon van der Stel granted land to a freeburgher, Jochem Sax. Sax planted the first vines and built the manor house in 1701, and the estate has been producing ever since. It produces a small number of cases each year; its Private Collection of red wines is very good. The restaurant attracts most of the visitors.

Spier ⓘ *Welcome Centre, T021-8091100, www.spier.co.za, sales and tastings: daily 1000-1630. Meals are available throughout the day and evening at 4 on-site restaurants (book several days ahead); picnics and a deli are also available. Accommodation is in The Village at Spier (see Sleeping, page 154).* This is the Winelands' most commercial wine estate, offering a vast array of activities and wine tastings – of both Spier's own wines and those of other Stellenbosch estates. Spier wines are well regarded, and their Private Collection Chenin Blanc '01 is especially good. As well as wine tasting, there is a cheetah outreach programme (although the creatures seem rather lacklustre) and a birds of prey area, plus horse riding, fishing, an 18-hole golf course and the Camelot spa. There are four superb restaurants on site including a riverside pub, the outdoor 'African' Moyo BBQ, and the **Jonkershuis,** which has superb (if expensive) Cape Malay buffets. These are hugely popular with tourists and are listed separately under eating. An annual music and arts festival is held at the open-air amphitheatre during the summer months.

Simonsig ⓘ *T021-8884900, www.simonsig.co.za, sales and tastings: Mon-Fri 0830-1700, Sat 0830-1600, cellar tours: Mon-Fri 1000 and 1500, Sat 1000.* This large estate has been in the Malan family for ten generations, and in recent years has produced some exceptionally fine wines. There is an attractive outdoor tasting area with beautiful views out over the mountains. One wine worth looking out for is the Kaapse Vonkel, a sparkling white considered the best of its kind in South Africa. Their Chardonnay is consistently very good, and good value too.

Villiera ⓘ *T021-8652002, www.villiera.co.za, sales and tastings: Mon-Fri 0830-1700, Sat 0830-1300.* Villiera is highly regarded and produces some of the best wines in the Cape. There are plenty of classic wines to choose from, including the Cru Monro, the Merlot 2001 and their Sauvignon Blanc. They no longer conduct cellar tours, but allow self-guided tours.

Franschhoek Valley

» *pp154-165. Colour map 8, grid B2.*

Franschhoek

> *You'll need to book ahead to get a table at Franschhoek's restaurants, especially at weekends.*

This is the most pleasant of the Wineland villages, with a compact centre of Victorian whitewashed houses backed by rolling vineyards and the soaring slopes of the Franschhoek Mountains. It does, however, have an artificial feel to it as most of the attractions here have been created to serve the tourist industry. The outlying wine estates all have their individual appeal, but the village itself is made up of restaurants and touristy craft shops. Nevertheless, Franschhoek is famed for its cuisine and dubs itself as the gastronomical capital of the Western Cape, so a visit here should guarantee an excellent meal accompanied by a fine glass of wine.

Ins and outs Franschhoek is 71 km from Cape Town (via the N1), 26 km from Paarl and 31 km from Stellenbosch. There is no regular public transport so you will need a car. Most of the tour operators offering Winelands tours don't usually include Franschhoek. The **tourist office** ⓘ *29a Huguenot Rd, T021-8763603, www.franschhoek.org.za, Mon-Fri 0900-1800, Sat 1000-1700, Sun 1000-1600,* has helpful staff with a good

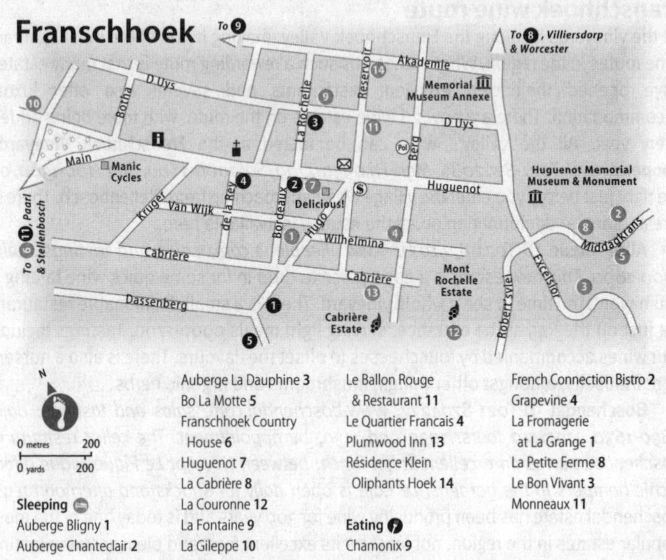

 knowledge of accommodation and restaurants. The office also has a wine estates desk and a wine and cheese tasting area, and there's a plant nursery at the back.

Background Although the first Huguenots arrived at the Cape in 1688, the village of Franschhoek only took shape in 1837 after the church and the manse had been built. The first immigrants settled on farms granted to them by Simon van der Stel along the Drakenstein Valley at Oliphantshoek in 1694. Franschhoek is built on parts of **La Motte** and **Cabrière** farms. The village became the focal point of the valley but the oldest and most interesting buildings are to be found on the original Huguenot farms and estates.

Sights The **Huguenot Memorial Museum and Monument collection** ⓘ *T021-8762532, Mon-Fri 0900-1700, Sat 0900-1300, 1400-1700, Sun 1400-1700, R5*, is housed in two buildings either side of Lambrecht Street. The main building, to the left of the Huguenot Monument, is modelled on a house designed by the French architect, Louis Michel Thibault, built in 1791 at Kloof Street, Cape Town. The displays inside trace the history of the Huguenots in South Africa. There are some fine collections of furniture, silverware and family bibles, but the most interesting displays are the family trees providing a record of families over the past 250 years. One of the roles of the museum today is to maintain an up-to-date register of families, so that future generations will be able to trace their ancestors.

Next door to the museum is the rather stark and unattractive **Huguenot Monument**, a highly symbolic memorial built to mark 250 years since the first Huguenots settled in the Cape. It is set in a peaceful rose garden with the rugged Franschhoek Mountains providing a contrasting background. The three arches represent the Trinity, and the golden sun and cross on top are the Sun of Righteousness and the Cross of Christian Faith. In front of the arches is a statue of a woman with a bible in her right hand and a broken chain in her left, symbolizing freedom from religious oppression. If you look closely at the globe you can see several objects carved into the southern tip of Africa: a bible, a harp, a spinning wheel and a sheaf of corn and a vine. These represent different aspects of the Huguenots' life, respectively their faith, their art and culture, their industry and their agriculture. The final piece of the memorial, the curved colonnade, represents tranquillity and spiritual peace after the problems they had faced in France.

Franschhoek wine route

All the vineyards lie along the Franschhoek Valley, making it one of the most compact wine routes in the region. What makes this such a rewarding route is that many estates have opened their own excellent restaurants and several also offer luxury accommodation. There are now 26 wine estates on the route, with more being added every year. All the valley's wine can be tasted at the **Franschhoek Vineyards Cooperative** ⓘ *T021-8762086, Mon-Fri 0930-1700, Sat 1000-1600, Sun 1100-1500*, on the right just before you enter the village when approaching from Stellenbosch. There is a restaurant, and information on all the estates is available here.

Allée Bleue ⓘ *T021-8741021, www.alleebleue.com, sales and tastings: daily 1000-1600*. This new estate is a good place to drop in for some quick wine tasting if you haven't the time to see a whole vineyard. There is a small, fashionable restaurant set just off the R45 at the entrance, serving light meals 0900-1700. Tastings include four wines accompanied by four cheeses to offset the flavours. There is also a nursery here that sells, amongst other things, mushrooms and organic herbs.

Boschendal ⓘ *T021-8704272, www.boschendal.com, sales and tastings: daily 0830-1630, vineyard tours: 1030 and 1130, by appointment. The cellar restaurant, Boschendal, serves an excellent buffet lunch; between Nov-Apr Le Pique Nique offers picnic hampers in the gardens. Le Café is open daily for snacks and afternoon teas.* Boschendal estate has been producing wine for 300 years and is today one of the most popular estates in the region, not least for its excellent food and pleasant wine-tasting area underneath a giant oak. The estate started life as two farms in 1687, and was bought in 1715 by Abraham de Villiers. The restored H-shaped manor house (1812) is one of the finest in South Africa, and is open as a museum to the public. Interestingly, a third of the estate is now owned by a black empowerment consortium. Most of the wine produced on the estate is white; their sparkling wines are highly regarded. In 2004 Boschendal was named South African Wine Producer of the Year.

Cape Chamonix ⓘ *T021-8762494, www.chamonix.co.za, sales and tastings: daily 0930-1630, cellar tours: by appointment.* This is one of the largest farms in the valley, with an underground cellar providing pleasantly cool tours at the height of summer. Wine tastings are held in the Blacksmith's Cottage; you can also try their fruit schnapps or the Chamonix mineral water. The **Chamonix** restaurant (see Eating, page 160) is family-friendly and highly rated.

Mont Rochelle ⓘ *T021-8763000, www.montrochelle.co.za, sales and tastings: daily 1000-1800, cellar tours: Mon-Fri 1100, 1230, 1500.* This estate has one of the most attractive settings in the region with beautiful views of the valley. Owner Miko Rwayitare has doubled the area under vines in the last few years and completely redeveloped the estate, now offering three white and four red wines. Tastings are informal and friendly.

La Motte ⓘ *T021-8763119, www.la-motte.co.za, sales and tastings: Mon-Fri 0900-1630, Sat 1000-1500, cellar tours: by appointment, light lunches served in summer.* The original manor house was built in 1752 and the grand old cellars, worth a visit in themselves, are now used as a classical concert venue in the evenings. Wine tasting takes place in a smart tasting centre overlooking the cellars. As a relatively small

Franschhoek Valley

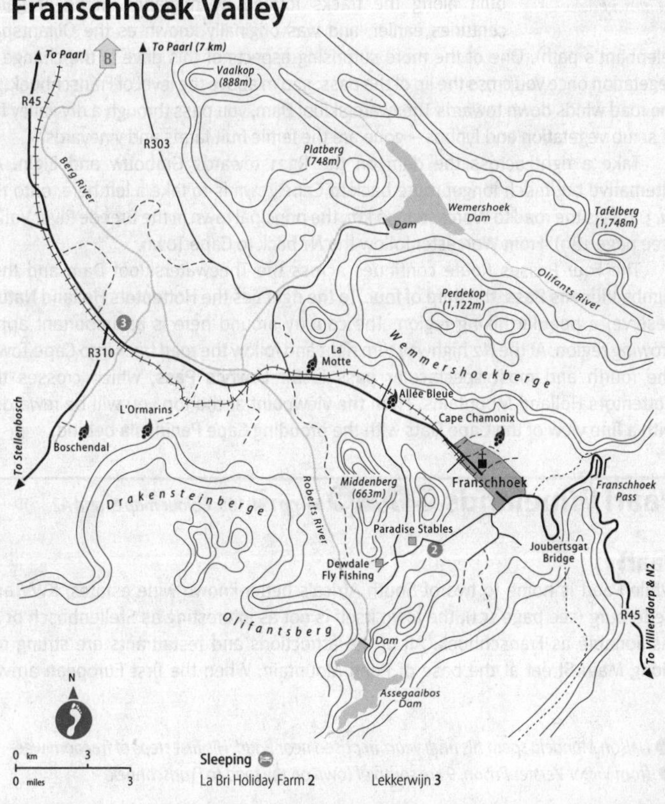

 producer, only 15,000 cases a year, the estate has managed to create some excellent wines. The La Motte Millennium Claret blend remains their most popular wine.

L'Ormarins ① *To21-8741026, www.lormarins.co.za, sales and tastings: Mon-Fri 0900-1630, Sat 1000-1500, cellar tours: by appointment.* This vineyard has a beautiful setting on the slopes of the Drakensteinberge, above the Bellingham estate (excellent, but no longer open to visitors). The original land was granted to the Huguenot, Jean Roi, in 1694, who named the farm after his village in the South of France. The present homestead was built in 1811 – from its grand marble halls and staircases you look out across an ornamental pond and neat gardens. The other notable attraction is the original wine cellar; this has been carefully restored and now houses a set of giant wine vats. On offer is the classic range of wines, plus the Italian varietal range, Terra del Capo. Cheeseboards available during summer.

Four Passes route

One of the popular recommended day drives from Cape Town is known as the Four Passes route. This takes you through the heart of the Winelands, and, as the name suggests, over four mountain passes. The first stop on the drive is Stellenbosch. From here you take the R310 towards Franschhoek. Driving up out of Stellenbosch you cross the first pass – **Helshoogte Pass.** After 17 km you reach a T-junction with the R45: a left turn would take you to Paarl, 12 km, but the route continues to the right. This is a pleasant drive up into the Franschhoek Valley. The road follows a railway line and part of the Berg River. After passing through Franschhoek, take a left in front of the Huguenot Monument and climb out of the valley via the **Franschhoek Pass**. This pass was built along the tracks formed by migrating herds of game centuries earlier, and was originally known as the Olifantspad (elephant's path). One of the more surprising aspects of this drive is the change in vegetation once you cross the lip of the pass, 520 m above the level of Franschhoek. As the road winds down towards Theewaterskloof Dam, you pass through a dry valley full of scrub vegetation and fynbos – gone are the fertile fruit farms and vineyards.

This is a wonderful day out from Cape Town, especially if combined with fine wine and gourmet food in Franschhoek.

Take a right across the dam on the R321 towards Grabouw and Elgin. An alternative but much longer route back to Cape Town is to take a left here, onto the R43. This is the road to Worcester, 50 km, the principal town in the Breede River Valley (see page 189). From Worcester follow the N1 back to Cape Town.

The Four Passes Route continues across the Theewaterskloof Dam and then climbs **Viljoens Pass**, the third of four. To the right lies the Hottentots Holland Nature Reserve, a popular hiking region. The country around here is an important apple growing region. At the N2 highway turn right and follow the road back into Cape Town. The fourth and most spectacular pass is **Sir Lowry's Pass**, which crosses the Hottentots Holland Mountains. From the viewpoint at the top you will be rewarded with a fine view of the Cape Flats with the brooding Cape Peninsula behind.

Paarl Winelands

» *pp154-165. Colour map 8, grid A2.*

Paarl

While Paarl is home to two of South Africa's better-known wine estates, KWV and Nederburg (see page 151), the town itself is not as interesting as Stellenbosch or as fashionable as Franschhoek. All of the attractions and restaurants are strung out along Main Street at the base of Paarl Mountain. When the first European arrival,

Nelson Mandela spent his final years in prison near Paarl. His first steps of freedom were from Victor Verster Prison, 9 km south of town on the road to Franschhoek.

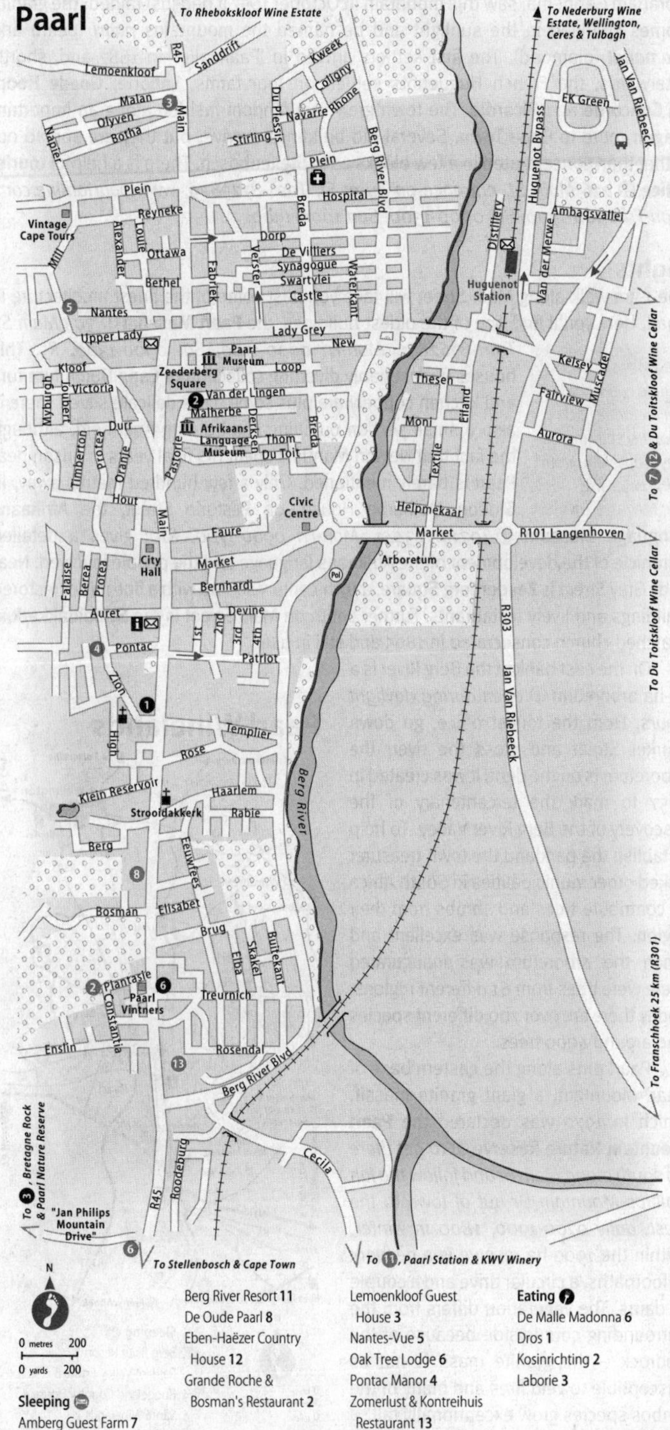

Paarl
To Rheboksfloof Wine Estate
To Nederburg Wine Estate, Wellington, Ceres & Tulbagh
Lemoenkloof
R45
Sanddrift
Kweek
Coligny
Malan
Olyven
Botha
Napier
Main
Du Plessis
Navarre
Rhone
Stirling
Berg River Blvd
Plein
Hospital
EK Green
Jan Van Riebeeck
Huguenot Bypass
Reyneke
Vintage Cape Tours
Alexander
Louw
Ottawa
Breda
Dorp
De Villiers
Synagogue
Swartvlei
Castle
Verster
Fabriek
Waterkant
Distillery
Ambagsvallei
Van der Merwe
Huguenot Station
Mill
Bethel
Nantes
Upper Lady
Lady Grey
New
Paarl Museum
Loop
Zeederberg Square
Van der Lingen
Malherbe
Afrikaans Language Museum
Derksen
Thom
Du Toit
Kloof
Victoria
Myburgh
Joubert
Durr
Timberton
Protea
Oranje
Pastorie
Thesen
Moni
Eiland
Textile
Kelsey
Muscadel
Fairview
Aurora
To 7 12 & Du Toitskloof Wine Cellar
Hout
Civic Centre
Helpmekaar
Faure
Market
R101 Langenhoven
City Hall
Arboretum
Falaise
Berea
Bernhardi
Auret
Devine
1st
2nd
3rd
4th
Pontac
Patriot
R303
Jan Van Riebeeck
To Du Toitskloof Wine Cellar
Zion
High
Templier
Rose
Berg River
Klein Reservoir
Haarlem
Strooidakkerk
Rabie
Berg
Leeuwfees
Bosman
Elisabet
Brug
Elba
Skakel
Buitekant
Plantasie
Paarl Vintners
Constantia
Treurnich
Enslin
Rosendal
Berg River Blvd
To Franschhoek 25 km (R301)
Roodeburg
Cecilia
To 3, Bretagne Rock & Paarl Nature Reserve
"Jan Philips Mountain Drive"
To Stellenbosch & Cape Town
To 11, Paarl Station & KWV Winery
N
0 metres 200
0 yards 200
Sleeping
Amberg Guest Farm 7
Berg River Resort 11
De Oude Paarl 8
Eben-Haëzer Country House 12
Grande Roche & Bosman's Restaurant 2
Lemoenkloof Guest House 3
Nantes-Vue 5
Oak Tree Lodge 6
Pontac Manor 4
Zomerlust & Kontreihuis Restaurant 13
Eating
De Malle Madonna 6
Dros 1
Kosinrichting 2
Laborie 3

 Abraham Gabbema, saw this mountain in October 1657 it had just rained; the granite domes sparkled in the sunlight and he named the mountains *paarl* (pearl) and *diamandt* (diamond). The first settlers arrived in 'Paarlvallei' in 1687 and, shortly afterwards, the French Huguenots settled on four farms, **Laborie**, **Goede Hoop**, **La Concorde** and **Picardie**. The town grew in a random fashion along an important wagon route to Cape Town. Several old buildings survive, but they are spread out rather than concentrated in a few blocks as in Stellenbosch. There is a helpful **tourist office** ⓘ *216 Main St, entrance on Auret St, T021-8723829, www.paarlonline.com, Mon-Fri 0900-1700, Sat 0900-1300, Sun 1000-1300.*

Sights

The 1-km walk along Main Street will take you past some of the finest architecture in Paarl. Here you'll find one of the oldest buildings, the **Paarl Museum** ⓘ *303 Main St, T021-8762651, Mon-Fri 0900-1700, Sat 0900-1300, R5*. This houses a reasonably diverting collection of Cape Dutch furniture and kitchen copperware plus some more delicate silver. There is also a small section outlining Paarl during Apartheid, although the fact that Nelson Mandela spent his final years in prison near Paarl is barely mentioned. Only a few hundred metres away, in Gideon Malherbe House, on Pastorie Street, the **Afrikaans Language Museum** ⓘ *T021-8723441, Mon-Fri 0900-1700, R10*, gives a detailed chronicle of the development of the Afrikaans language and the people involved. Near Lady Grey Street is **Zeederberg Square**, a 19th-century square with a fine mix of restored buildings and lively restaurants. Further south on Main Street is the **Strooidakkerk**, a thatched church consecrated in 1805 and still in use.

The best views of the surrounding countryside are from Bretagne Rock; on a clear day you can see False Bay, Table Mountain and all the vineyards.

On the east bank of the Berg River is a 31-ha **arboretum** ⓘ *open during daylight hours*. From the tourist office, go down Market Street and cross the river; the arboretum is on the right. It was created in 1957 to mark the tercentenary of the discovery of the Berg River Valley. To help establish the parkland the town treasurer asked other municipalities in South Africa to contribute trees and shrubs from their region. The response was excellent and when the arboretum was inaugurated there were trees from 61 different regions. Today there are over 700 different species and around 4000 trees.

Paarl runs along the eastern base of Paarl Mountain, a giant granite massif, which in 1970 was declared the **Paarl Mountain Nature Reserve** ⓘ *to get there go south along Main St and follow the Jan Phillips Mountain Dr out of town to the west, daily 0700-1900, 1800 in winter*. Within the 1900-ha reserve is a network of footpaths, a circular drive and a couple of dams. The vegetation differs from the surrounding countryside because of the bedrock – the granite mass is not as susceptible to veld fires and many of the fynbos species grow exceptionally tall.

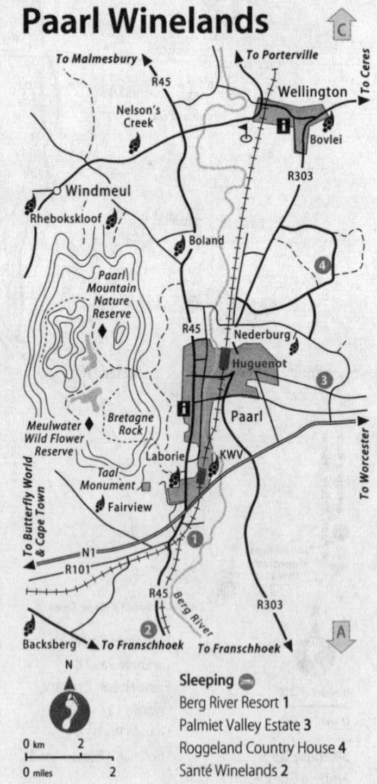

The domed summit is easy to climb, and near the top is an old cannon dating from the early days of the Cape Colony. On the summit are three giant granite rocks. The highest point is 729 m and there is a chain to help you up the last steep incline. Nearby is **Gordon's Rock**, named after Colonel Robert Jacob Gordon who commanded the British troops at the Cape from 1780 to 1795. This rock is dangerous and should only be tackled by experienced climbers. The third rock is known as **Paarl Rock**. Just below the summit a mountain stream flows through the **Meulwater Wild Flower Reserve**. This garden was created in 1931, and contains specimens of the majority of flowers found around Paarl Mountain.

There is a small entrance fee to the reserve, but you do not need to obtain further permits for hiking. The tourist office should be able to give you a clear colour map which has details of access roads and footpaths. There are several car parks with toilets and braai spots. If you wish to fish in one of the dams you need to go to the municipality for a permit.

Set high on the slopes of Paarl Mountain amongst granite boulders and indigenous trees stands the controversial **Taal Monument** ⓘ *daily 0800-1700*, three concrete columns linked by a low curved wall. This is the Afrikaans language monument, inaugurated in October 1975 and designed by Jan van Wijk. Each column represents different influences in the language. The relative heights of each column and the negative connotations associated with them have been the subject of criticism in recent years. There is a **coffee shop** ⓘ *Mon 0830-1700, Tue-Sun 0830-2200*, with excellent views across the Berg River Valley.

Those with children in tow may wish to visit **Butterfly World** ⓘ *Klapmuts, T021-8755628, daily, 0900-1700, R30, children R12*, the largest such park in South Africa, with butterflies flying freely in colourful landscaped gardens. There is a craft shop and tea garden on site.

Paarl wine route

ⓘ *The wine route information office can be found at Paarl Vintners at 86 Main Road, , T021-8634886, www.paarlwine.co.za.*

The route was set up in 1984 by local producers to help promote their wines and attract tourists into the area. The programme has been a great success and some of the estates have opened their own restaurants. All of the estates have tastings and wine sales on a daily basis. Today there are 26 members, but only the largest estates conduct regular cellar tours. Below is a short selection.

Boland ⓘ *T021-8626190, www.bolandwines.co.za, sales and tastings: Mon-Fri 0800-1700, Sat 0840-1300, cellar tours: by appointment.* The estate has an excellent wine cellar, and offers one of the most interesting cellar tours. One of their best wines is the 2002 Chardonnay, which has won awards. Picnics and cheese platters on offer.

Fairview ⓘ *T021-8632450, www.fairview.co.za, wine and cheese sales and tastings: Mon-Fri 0830-1700, Sat 0830-1300.* This popular estate has a rather unusual attraction in the form of a goat tower, a spiral structure which is home to two pairs of goats. In addition to a variety of good wines (look out for the popular Goats do Roam blend) visitors can taste delicious and award-winning goat and Jersey milk cheeses. The goats are milked each afternoon from 1530.

The Laborie ⓘ *T021-8073390, www.kwv-international.com, sales and tastings: daily 0900-1700, closed Sun from May-Sep, cellar tours: by appointment.* Part of KWV (see below), this is a beautifully restored original Cape Dutch homestead – in many ways the archetypal wine estate, and developed with tourism firmly in mind. It's an attractive spot, with a tasting area overlooking rolling lawns and vineyards, and a highly rated restaurant.

KWV ⓘ *T021-8073007, www.kwv-international.com, sales and tastings: Mon-Sat 0900-1630, open Sun December only, cellar tours: Mon-Sat 1000, 1015 (in German), 1030, 1415.* A short distance from the Laborie estate is the famous KWV

Bain's Kloof Pass

No matter which direction you take when leaving the Cape by road you will at some stage have to cross the mountains via a spectacular pass. Bain's Kloof is regarded as one of the greatest passes; as you drive through, enjoy the views but also take note of its construction history. The pass was a tremendous feat of engineering and the route has not changed since the it was built; the only change made in 144 years of use was to tar the road in 1934.

In 1846 Andrew Geddes Bain, the inspector of roads, noticed a gap in the mountain range in the direction of Wellington while working in the Breede River Valley. A few months later, he traversed the mountains via the 'gap' and put forward a proposal for a new pass. John Montagu, the colonial secretary, gave his full backing to the project, but work did not start until 1849.

This was the greatest period of road building in the Cape, but these ambitious projects could only be afforded by using convict labour. On his arrival in the Cape, John Montagu had been shocked by the conditions on Robben Island, where convicts were incarcerated. In 1847, Ordinance 7 was promulgated, for the "discipline and safe custody of convicts employed on public roads". This was Montagu's plan to reform prison conditions and ways of punishment. The first pass to be constructed under the new system was Mitchell's Pass in 1846. From then until 1888 all the major roads and passes were built using the convict system. It was considered a great success, but the labour was hard and the prisoners wore chains. The only tools available were picks, shovels, sledgehammers, rock drills and gunpowder.

Before work could start at Bain's Kloof neat stone barracks were built to house over 200 convicts. Conditions were better than in prison and local farmers were contracted to supply fresh straw for palliasses on a weekly basis. The total cost of Bain's Kloof Pass was £50,000; the convicts were paid 60 pence per month, but the cost of their daily rations, seven pence, was deducted from this; Bains was paid an annual salary of £300; the head warders and chaplains were paid £100 per annum, while the ordinary warders received £12 per annum plus rations. The cost of gunpowder used was £1223 – over 10 km of rock had to be blasted out.

The pass took 1608 days to complete, a considerable achievement considering the terrain and the tools available. Most of the labour was unskilled (at the outset) and yet retaining walls, culverts, aqueducts and drains were built – all using drystone masonry techniques. What's more, all these features are still in place and in use today. The pass was opened by Petrus Borchardus Borcherds, chairman of the Central Roads Board, Cape Town, on 14 September 1853, amidst great celebrations. The new route between Cape Town and Worcester was 57 km shorter and it saved two days' travel.

Cellar Complex which contains the five largest vats in the world. The Ko-operative Wijnbouwers Vereniging van Zuid-Afrika (Cooperative Wine Growers' Association) was established in Paarl in 1918 and is responsible for exporting many of South Africa's best-known wines. They are also well known for their brandy.

Nederburg ⓘ *T021-8623104, www.nederburg.co.za, sales and tastings: Mon-Fri 0830-1700, Sat 1000-1600, Sun 1100-1600, cellar tours: available in English, German and French but must be booked in advance. From the centre of Paarl, cross the Berg River and take the R303 towards Wellington as you leave town, the estate is signposted* *to the right. Picnic lunches are available for R80 per person (vegetarian and children's menu available)*. This is one of the largest and best-known estates in South Africa. Their annual production is in excess of 650,000 cases. As such a large concern they are involved in much of the research in South Africa to improve the quality of the grape and vine. Every April the annual Nederburg Auction attracts buyers from all over the world and is considered one of the top five wine auctions in the world. The homestead was built in 1800, but throughout the 19th century the wines were not considered to be anything special. This all changed in 1937 when Johann George Graue bought the estate. Riesling and Cabernet Sauvignon vines were planted, and the cellars completely modernized. Today their wines win countless annual awards.

Nelson's Creek ① *T021-8698453, www.nelsonscreek.co.za, sales and tastings: Mon-Fri 0800-1800, Sat 0900-1400, restaurant is open during the summer months, picnic baskets also available for lunches on the estate.* This is a very pleasant estate to spend the afternoon exploring. Its most recent owner, Alan Nelson, has been successfully producing wines since 1987. In 1996, he donated part of his estate to his farm labourers, who now produce wines under the 'New Beginnings' label. Their 2002 Sauvignon Blanc has won several national awards.

Rhebokskloof ① *T021-8698386, www.rhebokskloof.co.za, sales and tastings: daily 0900-1700, cellar tours: by appointment, 2 restaurants on site: Victorian Restaurant, and Cape Dutch Restaurant.* This old estate is now a thoroughly modern outfit. The Cape Dutch Restaurant serves an excellent Sunday lunch, though booking is advised during local holidays. The terrace café is popular with tour groups. One of their best wines is the 2001 Chardonnay Grand Reserve.

Wellington district

» *pp154-165. Colour map 8, grid A1.*

Wellington

Wellington, like the other Winelands towns, is surrounded by beautiful countryside and has a number of fine historic buildings, with the added bonus of far fewer tourists thronging the streets. Nevertheless, there is little in the town to keep visitors for long – there are a few wine estates in the surrounding area, but the town is best known for its

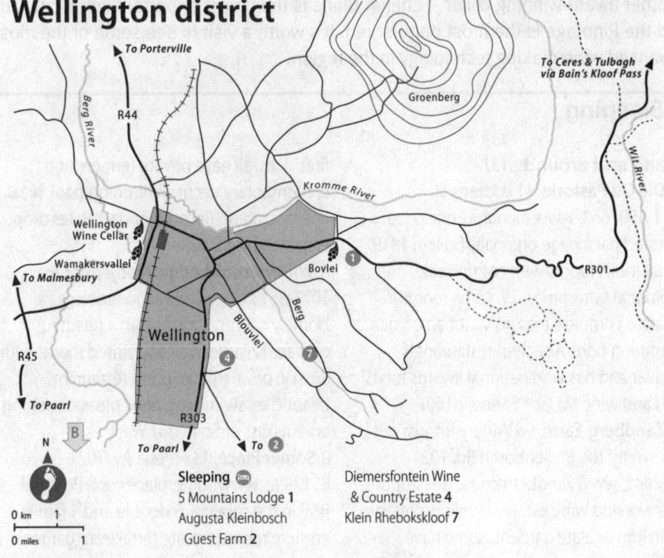

dried fruit. (The other important fruit centres, Ceres and Tulbagh, are on the eastern side of the Limietberg. They can be visited via the magnificent Bain's Kloof Pass, see page 152) To the north, the countryside opens up into the rolling Swartland, an important wheat region. A short drive to the south reveals steep hills where all the farmland is given over to vines. **Wellington Tourism Bureau** ⓘ *104 Main St, housed in the Old Market Building next to the Dutch Reformed Church, T021-8734604, www.wellington.co.za, Mon-Fri 0800-1700, Sat and Sun 0800-1300*. The staff are helpful and well organized and there is a good selection of local wines on sale.

Sights The Murray Jubilee Hall and Samuel House were once an institute for training Dutch Reformed Church missionaries; they are now part of **Huguenot College**. The shady **Victoria Park** in Church Street is notable for its roses. Look out for the archway which was built to commemorate the coronation of King Edward VII in 1902. The fountain in **Joubert Square** was unveiled in 1939 as a memorial to the Huguenot settlers in the valley. The **Wellington Museum** ⓘ *T021-8734710, Mon-Fri 0900-1700, also Sat 0900-1300 from Oct-May, free*, on Church Street has a small collection on the history of the town and the Huguenot farms in the district. The archives of the Huguenot Seminary are kept here.

Wellington wine route

This is one of the smallest routes in the area, with only 13 members. Much of the farmland in the district is devoted to the production of wheat, and grapes used for dried fruit. The following is a selection of winemakers who open their doors to the public.

Bovlei ⓘ *T021-8731567, www.bovlei.co.za, sales and tasting Mon-Fri 0830-1300, 1400-1700, Sat 0830-1230, out of town on the R301 towards Bain's Kloof Pass*, was established in 1907 and has a completely modernized cellar. They produce mainly white wines and the Chenin Blanc won a gold award in 2004.

Wamakersvallei ⓘ *T021-8731582, www.wamakersvallei.co.za, sales and tasting Mon-Fri 0800-1700, Sat 0830-1230, north of town on the R44*, is one of the largest wine producers on the Wellington route. It has won several awards in recent years, for its Cabernet Sauvignon and Pinotage varieties amongst others.

Wellington ⓘ *T021-8731163, www.wellingtoncellar.co.za, sales and tasting Mon-Fri 0800-1300, 1400-1700, cellar tours by appointment, close to the railway station*, is another award-winning cellar – Chenin Blanc is their most important white cultivar, and the Pinotage is the most popular red. It's worth a visit to see some of the most advanced wine-making technology in the region.

Sleeping

Strand and around *p137*

AL Die Ou Pastorie, 41 Lourens St, T021-8501660, www.dieoupastorie.co.za. Restored parsonage originally built in 1819. 16 luxurious rooms with comfortable, traditional furnishings, TV, some rooms in separate complex, mature Victorian gardens, swimming pool. Attached restaurant is popular and has won national awards for its food and wine list (see Eating, p160).

AL Zandberg Farm, 96 Winery Rd, just out of town off the Stellenbosch Rd, T021-8422945, www.zandberg.co.za. Guesthouse on a working wine estate, 11 luxury cottages set in immaculate gardens, some have fireplaces, all have private terraces and contemporary decor. Swimming pool, braai, fine restaurant. Recommended. Rates drop considerably in winter.

A Willowbrook Lodge, Morgenster Av, T021-8513759, www.willowbrook.co.za. Homely country lodge set in a beautiful garden, 12 large, well-appointed rooms with a/c, TV, private patio, good restaurant, beautician, swimming pool, pleasant setting on outskirts of Somerset West.

B Somer Place, 14 Freesia Av, T021-8517992, www.somerplace.com. Peaceful B&B in the suburbs, 5 double and 1 family en suite rooms, private terraces or gardens,

TV, attractive pool and garden, meals on request, homely atmosphere in a modern bungalow.

Stellenbosch *p138, map p140*

The Winelands has a fine selection of accommodation, much of it in historic buildings furnished with antiques, but room rates are very high. However Stellenbosch has an excellent backpacker hostel, which enables budget travellers to explore this region on an overnight stay.

Central

AL-A **D'Ouwe Werf Country Inn**, 30 Church St, T021-8874608, www.ouwewerf.com. Converted Georgian house with 31 recently renovated a/c rooms, all individually decorated with antique furnishings and polished floors. Off-street parking, good sized pool, beauty salon and vine-shaded terrace where breakfast and lunch are served. Restaurant **1802** offers traditional Cape cooking in smart surroundings, and has had good reports. Recommended as a treat.

A **Dorpshuis**, 22 Dorp St, T021-8839881, www.dorpshuis.co.za. A very smart Victorian townhouse with 22 a/c rooms, some of which are suites, all have TV, marble-clad bathrooms, heavy fabrics and dark furniture, private patios, antiques, large breakfasts with plenty of choice, neat gardens, swimming pool.

A **Stellenbosch Hotel**, 162 Dorp St, T021-8873644, www.stellenbosch.co.za/hotel. Central hotel with 27 a/c rooms and 2 apartments in a national monument building. Each room has TV, minibar and pleasant bathroom, although the decor could do with an update. Friendly bar popular with locals, bright dining room with tables on terrace overlooking the street, serving game and seafood (see Eating page 160).

A-B **Fynbos Villa**, 14 Neethling St, T021-8838670, www.fynbosguesthouse.co.za. Converted family home with garden extension. 13 a/c rooms, all with TV, en suite bathroom and kettle. 1 self-catering cottage sleeping up to 4. Large courtyard, pool, private parking, friendly, homely feel. Short walk to town centre. German spoken.

A-B **Labri Manor**, 71 Victoria St, T021-8865652, www.getaway-gateway.com. 10 luxury rooms with beautiful decor, polished wooden floors, huge 4-poster beds, subtle yellow walls and dark wood antiques. Spacious Victorian-style en suite bathrooms, TV lounge, cobbled courtyard, dinner and picnic baskets on request, extras include fresh flowers and a glass of port, a fine Victorian house. Recommended.

A-B **Michaelhouse**, 29 van Riebeeck St, T021-8866343, www.michael housegh.com. Stylishly converted corner house with 4 attractive a/c double rooms, individually decorated, some with 4-poster beds, big sofas, antiques, burnt-orange walls, stripy bathrooms with free-standing baths, TV, lovely sunny courtyard. Close to botanical gardens and town centre. Welcoming and stylish place to stay. Recommended.

B **Avenues Guest Lodge**, 32 The Avenue, T021-8871843, www.theavenues.co.za. 8 rooms, some non-smoking, with double or twin beds, all with en suite bathrooms, wooden floors and bright, simple furnishings. The garden-facing room (No 5) is the nicest, with original fittings in the bathroom. TV lounge, small pool, secluded gardens (can be noisy from traffic), huge breakfasts served. Recommended.

B **Bonne Esperance**, 17 Van Riebeeck St, T021-8870225, www.bonneesperance.com. Appealingly rambling Victorian townhouse with wrap-around veranda, opposite the botanical gardens. 15 comfortable en suite rooms with high ceilings and an English feel to the decor, sunny and spacious dining room, lovely garden with small swimming pool.

B **De Goue Druif**, 110 Dorp St, T021-8833555, www.gouedruif.hypemart.net. Small guesthouse in a national monument building. 4 well-appointed if somewhat old-fashioned rooms (lots of ruffs and heavy curtains), spacious spotless bathrooms, lush garden, small pool and shady terrace, tiny gym, sauna and steambath. Secure off-street parking. Friendly service, several European languages spoken, ideal location for exploring town on foot.

B **Ryneveld Country Lodge**, 67 Ryneveld St, T021-8874469, www.ryneveldlodge.co.za. B&B in a smart Victorian house with 15 a/c rooms (some in more expensive cottages). Beautiful house full of antiques with breakfast room, shady terrace, small pool, secure parking, but overpriced.

C-D Helen's, 97 Buitekring Av, T021-8833942, helens@absamail.co.za. 2 en suite rooms with separate entrances, off-street parking, use of gardens and pool, breakfast is extra but still one of the cheaper options in town.

C-D Stumble Inn, 12 Market St, T021-8874049, www.jump.to/stumble. Popular hostel in 2 separate Victorian bungalows. Spacious double rooms and cramped dorms. Original house has attractive garden, bar, TV room, kitchen, hammocks, shady cushion banks; other house has small pool, kitchen. Very relaxed and friendly place. Excellent value **Easy Rider** wine tours (see page 164), bicycles to hire, remains by far the best budget option in town.

Out of town

L Lanzerac Manor, 2 km from town centre towards Jonkershoek Reserve, Jonkershoek Rd, T021-8871132, www.lanzerac.co.za. Very expensive but fittingly luxurious hotel set around an 18th- century Cape Dutch manor house on a wine estate, tastings and cellar tours on offer. 48 suites, some around a patio and swimming pool, spacious and plush with all mod cons. 2 restaurants: the formal **Governor's Hall**, which is rather fussy with slow service; and the relaxed and more enjoyable **Lanzerac Terrace** for al fresco dining during summer. New addition is an extensive wellbeing centre and beauty spa.

L The Village at Spier, Spier Wine Estate on the R44, T021-8091100, www.spier.co.za. Probably the Winelands' most commercial wine estate, but a thoroughly enjoyable place to stay. Accommodation is in condo-style buildings set around courtyards with private pools for each section. The 155 rooms are enormous and very comfortable, with neutral, stylish decor, trendy polished concrete floors, huge beds, lots of windows, TV, minibar, beautiful bathrooms stocked with aromatherapy products. 4 restaurants on site. See page 160 for details on the wines and all the activities on offer. Recommended if you only have a day in the Winelands.

AL Wedgeview Country House and Spa, The Bonniemile, 5 km south of town, T021-8813525, www.wedgeview.co.za. Attractive thatched farmhouse, converted family home with 11 garden-based thatched suites and 1 family cottage, main house has snooker room, bar, drawing room, dining room, all set in 4 acres of attractive gardens surrounded by vineyards, 2 swimming pools, jacuzzi and treats on offer such as massages.

A Bellevue Manor, 5 km south of Stellenbosch on Strand Rd (R44), T021-8801086, www.bellevuestellenbosch.co.za. Purpose-built a/c cottages in Cape Dutch style with thatched roofs, pleasant country-style furnishings, TV, fireplace, bathroom, honesty bar fridge, private terrace, good-sized pool with braai area, close to 2 golf courses.

B L'Avenir, 5 km north of Stellenbosch off the R44 towards the N1 and Paarl, T021-8895001, www.lavenir.co.za. A peaceful setting on a smart wine farm with 9 elegant en suite bedrooms, 5 in the main house and 4 luxury pool-side rooms. Price includes breakfast and wine tasting, meals arranged on request. Substantial discounts are available off season. Well-run, peaceful and elegant place to experience the Winelands. Recommended.

C Wilfra Court, 16 Hine St, approximately 3 km from town centre, turn left off the R44 road to Paarl at the Welgevonden Estate, T021-8896091, wilfra@tiscali.co.za. 2 double rooms with shared bathroom, spotless and comfortable, choice of continental or English breakfast, secure parking. Run by William and Frances, a very friendly couple. Anyone with an interest in South African political affairs should stay here, as this was the first guesthouse in the region run by coloured people. William was an MP for more than 30 years. Strongly recommended.

C-E Mountain Breeze, 6 km south of town on R44, T/F021-8800200, rpv@adept.co.za. Caravan and camping site in forest setting, 3 fully equipped self-catering chalets, hot water, electric points, swimming pool. Popular with South African family groups.

Franschhoek *p145, map p145*

L Franschhoek Country House, Main Rd, T021-8763386, www.fch.co.za. Very elegant boutique hotel with 14 rooms and 12 suites, some with fireplace, underfloor heating, private verandas, the new suites are 100 sq m and very luxurious, French style furniture, dramatic drapes and candelabra, 2 swimming pools, lovely fountains in the grounds, excellent restaurant.

L La Couronne, Dassenberg Rd, T021-8762770, www.lacouronnehotel.co.za. 24 luxury suites and rooms set in the main manor house or in garden units, elegantly decorated with enormous bathrooms, superb award winning restaurant (see Eating, p161) cigar bar, swimming pool, gym and sauna, attentive service, good mountain views and pleasant rolling gardens. Rates vary considerably depending on room and season.

L Le Quartier Français, corner of Wilhelmina and Berg Sts, T021-8762151, www.lequartier.co.za. An elegant country house with 17 enormous en suite rooms all with fireplaces, beautiful bathrooms, plush furnishings and views over the gardens. Small central swimming pool and peaceful, shady courtyard. The attached restaurant (see Eating page 160) is rated as one of the best in the Western Cape. A superb hotel with impeccable service, child-friendly, winner of 'Best small hotel in the world' by UK's *Tatler* magazine in 2005. Recommended.

AL-A Auberge Chanteclair, 500 m behind the Huguenot Monument on Middagkrans Rd, T021-8763685, www.chanteclair.co.za. 5 beautiful, spacious rooms with en suite bathrooms and old-fashioned decor, in a Victorian farmhouse. Comfortable lounge, swimming pool, secluded gardens set among 30 ha of orchards and vineyards. A superior B&B with attentive service to match. Recommended.

A La Cabrière, Middagkrans Rd, T021-8764780, www.lacabriere.co.za. Small luxurious and stylish guesthouse set just outside town in formal lavender and herb gardens. 5 a/c rooms with Provençal decor, limed wood furniture, grass matting floors and large stone en suite bathrooms, some rooms have fireplaces and views of vineyards and mountains, swimming pool.

A La Fontaine, 21 Dirkie Uys St, T021-8762112, www.lafontainefranschhoek.co.za. One of the finest guesthouses in Franschhoek, with 12 rooms set in a Victorian house near the village centre, elegant decor with antiques and fine wooden floors, some rooms set in garden around pool with tasteful ethnic decor. Friendly, efficient and a beautiful place to stay. Highly recommended.

A Plumwood Inn, 11 Cabrière St, T021-8763883, www.plumwoodinn.com. 8 individually-styled en suite bedrooms, each with private entrance, TV, country-style furniture and brightly painted walls, breakfast served in the well-kept garden by a small swimming pool, dinner available on request. No children.

A Résidence Klein Oliphants Hoek, 14 Akademie St, T021-8762566, www.kleinoliphantshoek.com. A very fine guesthouse close to the centre of Franschhoek which was built originally as a missionary hall in 1888. 7 comfortable and old-fashioned en suite a/c double rooms with TV (M-Net). The vast, high-ceilinged lounge, once the original meeting hall, is filled with antiques, big sofas and has a fireplace. Good sized pool. Very smart dining room with a daily changing set menu serving excellent French cuisine. Recommended.

A-B Auberge Bligny, 28 Van Wijk St, T021-8763767, www.blignyco.za. A beautifully restored house dating from 1861, with 8 en suite double rooms, including a special honeymoon suite which opens onto a shaded veranda, and 1 wheelchair-friendly room. TV, lounge with a small library and open fire in winter, neat gardens, swimming pool, friendly management, German spoken.

B Auberge La Dauphine, at La Dauphine Wine Estate off Excelsior Rd, T021-8762606, www.ladauphine.co.za. One of the most peaceful locations in the valley. 5 luxury en suite, a/c rooms each with a spacious lounge and patio in a carefully restored and converted wine store, surrounded by beautiful gardens and vineyards. There is a large swimming pool, guided tours of the farm available, plus mountain bike trails and horse riding in the nearby mountains.

B Bo La Motte, Middagkrans Rd, T021-8763067, www.bolamotte.com. 4 fully equipped cottages with fireplaces, braais, shared pool, great views of the mountains. English-run. Peaceful spot on a working farm just outside the village. Fly-fishing also available on the farm's dams.

B Le Ballon Rouge, 7 Reservoir St, T021-8762651, www.ballon-rouge.co.za. 7 double rooms set in a converted Victorian bungalow with wrap-around shady veranda offering private entrances to the rooms, which are small but nicely and individually decorated, swimming pool, bright dining room which is a very popular restaurant for lunch and dinner (see Eating page 160).

B La Gileppe, 47 Huguenot Rd, T021-8762146, www.lagileppe.co.za. Beautifully restored Victorian town house with braai spots dotted about the neat garden, and plunge pool. 4 spacious double rooms with en suite bathrooms, tiled floors, neutral decor, honeymoon suite. Set on main road just a brief walk from the shops and restaurants.

B Lekkerwijn, T021-8741122, www.lekkerwijn.co.za. 10 mins' drive from the centre of Franschhoek, heading towards Paarl, just before the junction with the R310 to Stellenbosch. A fine B&B in an old Cape Dutch homestead close to Boschendal wine estate. 3 double rooms and 1 single, plus a cottage suitable for a family of 4. The bedroom wing was designed by Herbert Baker and is arranged around a private pillared courtyard, tastefully furnished lounge and swimming pool.

B-C Huguenot, 34 Huguenot Rd, T021-8762092, atielouw@mweb.co.za. 8 spacious self-catering apartments set on the main road, sleeping 2-3. Simple bedrooms, lounge and kitchen, en suite bathrooms, some rooms have mountain views. Excellent location right in the village centre.

C-D La Bri Holiday Farm, Robertsvlei Rd, T021-8763133. Choice of self-catering cottages, which can sleep up to 6, or dorms. Peaceful rural location, braais, child-friendly, swim in the farm dam, must have your own transport to get here.

Paarl Winelands *p148, map p149*

L Grande Roche, Plantasie St, T021-8632727, www.granderoche.co.za. An 18th-century manor which has established itself as one of the top hotels in South Africa. The 34 luxury a/c suites, non-smoking rooms, are set in a collection of restored farm buildings that stand in peaceful gardens, surrounded by vineyards, 2 floodlit tennis courts, 2 swimming pools, gym. Bosman's restaurant is regarded as one of the best in the country (see Eating page 162). Will collect from Cape Town airport.

L Pontac Manor Hotel, 16 Zion St, T021-8720445, www.pontac.com. Elegant fully restored Victorian manor house with manicured gardens full of oak trees that are home to an army of squirrels. 22 spacious individually decorated rooms, TV and a/c, a mix of African and antique decor, the 5 rooms in the pool annexe also have microwave and fridge and there's a 5-bed cottage with kitchenette. Smart bar, lounges with fat armchairs and very good restaurant (see Eating page 162).

L Santé Winelands, Klapmuts, T021-8758100, www.santewellness.co.za. Working wine estate with new luxury 'Wellness' centre spa and hotel. 90 luxuriously appointed non-smoking rooms set across the estate, all with impeccable decor, huge bathrooms, TV and minibar. Huge range of 'vinotherapy' treatments available, which are basically massages and facial with a wine theme, such as the humorously named 'Chardonnay Cocoon Wrap'. Also has 3 restaurants, bar, several pools, lots of sporting activities, a yoga pavilion and an army of on-site masseurs. Finally there are 3 'multi-experience showers' where you can choose water pressure from tropical rain to mountain mist. Day visitors are permitted for R300 plus cost of treatments.

AL Roggeland Country House, Roggeland Rd, Dal Josafat, T021-8682501, www.roggeland.co.za. A fine Cape Dutch farmhouse (declared a national monument) with 10 spacious luxury rooms, large en suite bathroom, Cape-style furnishings, mature gardens, swimming pool. Highlight of a stay here is the excellent cuisine: lodging prices include dinner, bed and breakfast.

AL-A Palmiet Valley Estate, T021-8627741, www.palmiet.co.za. A restored 1642 historic Cape Dutch homestead located on a wine estate to the east of the town centre, surrounded by vines and giant oak trees. 10 spacious en suite doubles and 1 honeymoon suite with TV, CD player, each decorated with antiques, private balconies or terraces, neat garden, swimming pool, very good food served in the dining room or terrace. Very popular wedding venue.

A De Oude Paarl, 132 Main St, T021-8721002, www.deoudepaarl.com. Swanky hotel in a set of national monument buildings dating back to 1700 on the main road, with 26 individually designed rooms, rather dark but comfortable with a nod at 'boutique' hotel style, fine stone bathrooms. Excellent restaurant (see Eating page 162), wine boutique and bar, Belgian chocolate deli, friendly and efficient service.

A **Lemoenkloof Guest House**, 396a Main St, T021-8723782, www.lemkloof.co.za. Luxurious converted country house on northern edge of town. 25 a/c rooms and a family unit grouped in several buildings set around gardens and palm-shaded pool. Each room has TV, minibar, floral fabrics, fresh flowers in vases, black-and-white tiled bathrooms, separate entrance. Large breakfasts, evening meals on request for large groups, friendly owners. Recommended.

A **Zomerlust**, 193 Main St, T021-8722117, www.zomerlust.co.za. 14 rooms in a restored historic country house in the centre of town. All rooms are en suite, with TV, fireplaces and decked out in antiques. Some rooms are in converted stables. Courtyard, terrace, swimming pool, library, cellar pub and popular attached **Kontreihuis** restaurant. Check for winter discounts. Recommended.

B **Eben-Haëzer Country House**, Sonstraal Rd, T021-8627420, www.eben-haezer.co.za. Original Cape Dutch homestead, 6 large and very comfortable double rooms, individually decorated with antiques and with Victorian-style bathrooms, 1 self-catering cottage, swimming pool, breakfast served under oak trees in the tea garden or in the 18th-century dining room, restaurant open to all Mon-Fri 0830-1700, best known for its Dutch pancakes. Friendly management, also offers fishing in the dam.

B **Nantes-Vue**, 56 Mill St, T021-8727311, www.nantes-paarl.co.za. Elegant B&B set in a Victorian house in the centre of town. 4 double rooms and 1-bedroom cottage in garden, all with high ceilings and TV, understated decor, iron bedheads, enormous showers and free-standing baths, breakfast room has country farm feel to it, splash pool. Good value. Recommended.

B **Oak Tree Lodge**, 32 Main St, T021-8632631, www.oaktreelodge.co.za. 18 modern en suite rooms with TV, set in a large family home, underfloor heating, children well catered for, rather twee decorations, sunny breakfast room, garden, pool, secure parking, central location.

C **Amberg Guest Farm**, Klein Drakenstein, T021-8620982, amberg@mweb.co.za. Good budget option on farm with spectacular setting. 2 self-catering cottages sleeping 2, plus 1 apartment sleeping 4-6. Gardens, large pool, braai facilities, friendly Swiss owners (German and French spoken).

C-E **Berg River Resort**, 5 km out of town towards Franschhoek (R45), south side of the N1, T021-8631650. Self-catering chalets of varying comfort sleeping 2-6, caravan and camping space available (first come, first served basis), hot water, electric points, swimming pool, mini-golf, kiosk, nice spot next to the river but lock everything up as theft has been a problem here in the past.

Wellington district *p153, map p153*

A **5 Mountains Lodge**, east of town on the R301 towards Bain's Kloof, T021-8643409, www.5mountainslodge.com. Mix of luxurious garden cottages and suites in original homestead, stylish bedrooms with 4-poster beds, en suite bathrooms, private deck with beautiful views, breakfast served by the pool or in an attractive dining room, meals on request. Very friendly, family-run, excellent choice for a relaxing night. Recommended.

A-B **Augusta Kleinbosch Guest Farm**, south of the town off the R303 (close to Paarl), T021-8682481, www.kleinbosch.de. German-run guesthouse in a fine Cape Dutch homestead and converted Afrikaans school set among orchards on a working wine and guava farm. 9 en suite rooms, spacious and elegant, with mini-fridges, CD players, some with TV, 4-poster beds, à la carte restaurant, swimming pool, walks around the vineyards possible.

A-B **Diemersfontein Wine and Country Estate**, Van Riebeck Dr, off the R303, T021-8645050, www.diemersfontein.co.za. A classic luxury country house set in beautifully tended gardens on a wine estate. 17 rooms, either in the main house or in garden annexe, traditional, plush furnishings, elegant teak-panelled lounge, grand veranda, swimming pool, restaurant and horse riding. Wine tasting daily 1000-1700.

B **Klein Rhebokskloof**, 4 km out of town, off Berg St, T021-8734115, www.wine-estate-hildenbrand.co.za. Old country guesthouse set on an olive and wine farm. 4 double rooms, simple and comfortable with TV, ceiling fans, private terrace, plus 2 self-catering apartments, shared lounge, restaurant, swimming pool with sun deck and beautiful garden.

C **Soete Huys**, 1 Stadsig, T021-8643442, www.soetehuys.com. Beautiful converted family house, 4 en suite double rooms, pleasant furnishings with wrought iron beds, terracotta tiled floors, good breakfasts served, garden and pool, quiet location on the outskirts of town.

Eating

Strand and around *p137*

TTT **Die Ou Pastorie**, 41 Lourens St, T021-8522120, www.dieoupastorie.co.za, 1200-1400, 1900-2130, no lunch on Mon or Sat. Award-winning French restaurant set in a luxury lodge in a gracious Victorian parsonage. Changing menu of traditional French cuisine, also has good vegetarian options and makes good use of game. Silver service, award winning wine list. Booking advised.

TT **Zandberg Wine Estate**, 96 Winery Rd, T021-8422945, www.zandberg.co.za, www.96wineryroad.co.za. An excellent award winning restaurant in an informal farmhouse setting. Very good grills, and some fish such as Norwegian salmon, popular braai on a Sun eve. Also has luxury overnight cottages on the estate (see Sleeping page 154). Recommended.

Stellenbosch *p138, map p140*

As well as restaurants in town, most of the wine estates on the Stellenbosch wine route also have restaurants that are especially nice for lazy lunches in a picturesque setting. Recommended for the overseas visitor are the restaurants at **Spier Estate**, which are a very special dining experience. You may even want to consider making a reservation before your arrival in South Africa.

TTT **Jonkershuis**, Spier Estate, on the R44, T021-8091172, 1230-1530, 1830-2230. Atmospheric Cape Malay restaurant set in restored farmhouse decorated with fine antiques, outside tables in the shade of oak trees, spicy bredies, curries, seafood, homemade breads and soups, baked puddings and biscuits, huge variety of food buffet style – a good opportunity to try all of South Africa's unique recipes. Recommended but book well in advance.

TTT **Moyo**, Spier Estate, on the R44, T021-8091133, www.moyo.co.za, 1200-1600, 1800-2300. Consistently fully booked so make a reservation at least a week ahead. Superb restaurant in a beautiful location and a highlight of a trip to South Africa. Arranged in Bedouin tents with outside tables in delightful tree houses or wrought-iron gazebos lit by candles. The vast buffet has just about everything imaginable from hot mussels to fine cheese and pan-African food. As well as wine and food, each table is entertained by women who decorate your face with traditional Xhosa white paint, Zimbabwean musicians, jazz bands and township opera singers. Touristy yes, but the atmosphere is unbeatable. A magical experience and highly recommended. Other branches in Johannesburg.

TTT **Stellenbosch Hotel**, 162 Dorp St, T021-8873644, 0700-2200. Part of the hotel and well known for its game dishes. Just about everything from the African bush is served up, from crocodile kebabs to kudu steaks. Also has specials like ostrich cottage pie or warthog ribs, plus some seafood including excellent fresh crayfish. Cheaper pub lunches available.

TT **The Coachman**, Ryneveld St next to the Village Museum, T021-8832230, 1200-2400. Cobbled courtyard with a beer garden feel, serving light meals and Cape specialities such as bobotie, springbok stew and lamb chops. Convenient location but can get very busy with tour groups.

TT **Decameron**, 50 Plein St, T021-8833331, 1200-1430, 1800-2200. Long-standing Italian favourite with a popular beer garden shaded by vines. The wood-fired pizzas and fresh pasta are delicious, but there's also a choice of reliable, traditional Italian mains.

TT **Dros**, corner of Bird and Alexander Sts, T021-8864856, 0800-2400. A large bar-cum-restaurant with outdoor seating in a lively square. Popular chain serving standard pub fare such as burgers, steaks, ribs, pizza. Good value, but portions are on the small side.

TT **Fishmonger**, corner of Plein and Ryneveld Sts, T021-8877835, www.fishmonger.co.za, 1200-2230. Portuguese-style seafood restaurant serving a great choice of fresh Cape seafood – kingclip, calamari, tiger prawns, oysters and the like – including taster platters for those who can't decide.

Also has a sushi chef, and a choice of vegetarian dishes. Good service, booking essential. Recommended.

🍴🍴 **Mexican Kitchen**, 25 Bird St, T021-8829997, www.mexicankitchen.co.za, 1100-2400. Lively cantina-style restaurant serving huge portions of nachos, bean soup, fajitas, tacos and steaks. Relaxed setting with inventive decor – some of the seats are swings. Also hosts salsa sessions and serves good shooters and cocktails including excellent margaritas. Recommended.

🍴🍴 **Volkskombuis**, Aan de Wagen Rd, T021-8872121, www.volkskombuis.co.za, 1200-2100. High standards of food and service, with a focus on traditional Cape cooking. Try the homemade oxtail or springbok pies. Housed in a characterful building – a restored Herbert Baker Cape Dutch homestead, with views across the Eerste River. A sensibly priced treat.

🍴🍴 **Wijnhuis**, Andringa St, T021-8875844, 0800-late. Bustling wine bar and wine shop, pretty outside eating in a courtyard, full menu of steak, some seafood, and venison, delicately presented, over 20 wines available by the glass.

🍴 **Blue Orange**, 77-79 Dorp St, T021-8872052, Mon-Sat 0800-1800, Sun 0830-1700. Delicious range of breakfasts, good-value snacks and sandwiches plus light lunches such as quiche and pasta. Interesting mix of students, well-coiffed locals and backpackers. Also has an attached deli selling local produce such as jams, bread, fruit and veg.

🍴 **Café Nouveau**, corner of Plein and Ryneveld Sts, T021-8875627, Mon-Fri 0700-2200, Sat 0730-2200, Sun 0830-2200. Lovely old-fashioned café with gilt mirrors and tightly packed tables serving sandwiches, coffee and cakes, as well as robust German dishes like bratwurst with fried potatoes.

🍴 **The Naked Truth**, 62 Andringa St, T021-8829672, 0800-late. Friendly, informal coffee shop serving good wholesome filled ciabattas, wraps and soup, also does affordable evening meals, checked tablecloths and outside seating in the courtyard.

Franschhoek *p145, map p145*

Franschhoek is dubbed 'gourmet capital of South Africa', and for good reason. There are some superb restaurants here. Booking ahead, especially at the weekends, is advised.

🍴🍴🍴 **Ici at Le Quartier Français**, 16 Huguenot Rd, T021-8762151, www.lequartier.co.za, 1200-2200. Rated as one of the best restaurants in the Western Cape with a chef trained in New York. French and South African dishes, and some world food such as Thai fishcakes. Nice decor with bright orange walls, expensive but a place for a treat.

🍴🍴🍴 **La Couronne**, Dassenberg Rd, T021-8762770, www.lacouronnehotel.co.za, 0700-1100, 1200-1430, 1830-2130. Small, formal restaurant based at the ultra-smart **Couronne Hotel** and wine estate. Perfect setting overlooking the vineyards, excellent gourmet menu with separate vegetarian section, light lunches are proving popular, also arranges picnics and offers 5-course dinners, long wine list. Voted in *Condé Nast Traveller* magazine's top 50 most exciting dining venues in the world.

🍴🍴🍴 **Le Ballon Rouge**, 7 Reservoir St, T021-8762651, www.ballon-rouge.co.za, 0815-2200. Part of the guesthouse. Well-known restaurant set in bright dining room and shady courtyard serving unusual and eccentric French dishes. Examples include fried 4-cheese cannelloni or frozen chicken liver pâté with beetroot cream, and roast springbok topped with sweet potato ice cream. Be prepared for strange mixes of sweet and savoury, cold and hot. Also has award-winning wine list.

🍴🍴🍴 **Monneaux**, Franschhoek Country House, Main Rd, T021-8763386, www.fch.co.za, 0800-late. Highly rated restaurant serving contemporary fusion cuisine, more up-to-date than many restaurants in Franschhoek, attractive outdoor terrace and cosy dining room. Lots of game and fish with strong spicing; to whet your appetite consider grilled linefish in a lemongrass emulsion topped with a macadamia nut crush. Good local wine list.

🍴🍴 **Chamonix**, 1 Uitkyk St, T021-8762393, www.chamonix-restaurant.co.za, lunch daily 1200-1600, dinner Fri only from 1830. Highly rated upmarket country-style restaurant set on a wine estate (see page 147). Ideal for a long lazy lunch with a fine selection of South African and international dishes including a vegetarian menu. Better equipped than most to take families, with an on-site jungle gym and children's menu.

The French Connection Bistro, corner of Bordeaux and Huguenot Rds, T021-8764056, 1200-1530, 1830-2130. French bistro serving refreshingly unfussy food such as steamed mussels, steak-frîtes or Toulouse sausages and mash. Children have their own menu. Pleasant bustling atmosphere and you can watch the chef at work in the kitchen behind glass.

The Grapevine, Huguenot Rd, T021-8762520, 0800-2100. Family restaurant serving big breakfasts, light lunches (try the tasty butternut soup) and game braais in the evening. Also some good Cape Malay dishes like the ever-popular bobotie.

La Fromagerie at La Grange, 13 Daniel Hugo St, T021-8762155, Mon-Fri 0900-1700, Sat and Sun, 1000-1700. Excellent deli specializing in cheese with 40 varieties for sale, set up in a 200-year-old barn, salads and quiches, soups and all things cheesy such as soufflé and pasta, recommended is the Camembert with caramelized pears. The owner is a jazz pianist who plays here occasionally.

La Petite Ferme, on Franschhoek Pass Rd, T021-8763016, 1200-1600. Spectacular views over the Franschhoek Valley from this smart country hotel and 'boutique' winery. The restaurant is well known for its wholesome country fare as well as delicate fusion dishes like smoked salmon on sweet potato and coconut mash, or hearty French cassoulet. Good desserts and wine list, too.

Le Bon Vivant, 22 Dirkie Uys St, T021-8762717, lebonvivant@mweb.co.za, 0800-2100. Small garden restaurant with tables set in dappled shade, serving delicious light lunches (don't miss the local smoked trout sandwich) and a 5-course dinner which has had excellent reports. Good value, friendly service. Recommended.

Paarl Winelands *p148, map p149*

Bosman's, **Grande Roche Hotel**, Plantasie St, T021-8632727, 0700-1030, 1200-1400, 1900-2100, closed mid-May to 31 July. Award-winning international cuisine of the highest standard in a grand vineyard-fringed setting. Popular 3-course set lunch, but the real treat is the celebrated 5-course 'Flavours of the Cape' menu (R400), offering superbly created examples of Cape cuisine. Good choice of vegetarian dishes, award-winning wine list. Regarded as one of the finest restaurants in South Africa.

De Oude Paarl (see Sleeping page 158), 132 Main St, T021-8721002, www.deoudepaarl.com, Mon-Sat 0700-1000, 1200-2200, Sun evenings in high season. Fashionable, moodily-lit restaurant, light lunches served in the courtyard, or formal suppers indoors. Lots of modern twists on traditional dishes, such as springbok loin coated in biltong dust, or duck served with pawpaw salsa. Good wine list.

De Malle Madonna , 127 Main Rd, T021-8633925, Wed and Sun 0830-1000, Thu-Sat 0830-1730. Cool and kooky café serving creamy quiches, huge sandwiches, burgers and wraps, plus towering cakes and muffins in the afternoon. Refreshingly modern spot for a snack.

Dros, Main Rd, T021-8630350, 0900-late. Outlet of pub-style chain serving steaks, ribs and pasta dishes in a cellar atmosphere. Also has a good choice of beers at the bar.

Kontreihuis, Zomerlust Guesthouse, 193 Main St, T021-8722808. Traditional Cape meals served alfresco in an attractive rose and herb garden, or dine inside the wine cellar. Try lamb sosaties (kebabs) with dried fruit, Malay pickled fish, or local smoked trout. Also serves lighter meals such as sandwiches and filled pancakes.

Laborie, Taillefer St, T021-8073095, 1000-1600. Lunchtime restaurant on wine estate with pleasant seating under giant oak trees. Delicious Cape and Mediterranean dishes, lots of contemporary choices such as kudu fillet in bacon-wrapped figs, as well as Cape specialities like bobotie and some vegetarian options. Smart but relaxed atmosphere, good service. Recommended.

Pontac, **Pontac Manor Hotel**, 16 Zion St, T021-8720445, www.pontac.com, 1200-2100. Informal and friendly restaurant in a cosy setting in a 17th-century manor house, serving traditional dishes (lots of game), weekly specials and imaginative vegetarian options, everything on the menu is available in full or half portions. Good service.

Rhebokskloof, Rhebokskloof Estate, T021-8698606, www.rheboksskloof.co.za, 0800-1700, also open for dinner Thu-Mon. Wonderful views from the terrace, where light lunches are served. Old-fashioned interior is the setting for a heavier international evening menu. The club sandwiches and salads are good, as is the Sun starter buffet.

Wilderer's, Wilderer's distillery, 3 km outside Paarl on R45, T021-8633555, Tue-Sun 1100-1700. Relaxed French restaurant in a schnapps distillery, speciality is *lammkuchen*, a type of pizza from Strasbourg. Finish off with a shot of their pear or fynbos schnapps. Live jazz on the first Sun of the month.

Kosinrichting, 19 Pastorie Av, T021-8711353, Mon-Fri 0800-1600, Sat 0900-1400. Coffee shop serving light meals, sandwiches and coffee and cakes, pancakes with sweet and savoury fillings, tables outside on the veranda are in the dappled shade of oak trees.

Wellington district *p153, map p153*

D'Olives Restaurant and Tea Garden, 41 Kerk St, T021-8643762, Mon-Sat 0800-2200, Sun 0900-1500. Pleasant restaurant with cool terracotta tiled floor and wrought iron furniture, olive themed menu, from salads to pasta, also good grills and fish, try their signature dish of sirloin strips with tomatoes and olives.

Oude Wellington, Bain's Kloof Rd, 5 km south of town, T021-8731008, 1230-1500, 1830-2100, closed Mon. Lovely spot in an old whitewashed farmstead, with dogs, peacocks and ostriches roaming around, good country-style cooking, homemade bread, pasta and ice cream, also a wine estate.

The Oasis, Bain's Kloof Rd, T021-8734231, Tue-Sun 0830-1800. Well-placed tea garden serving light lunches, homemade cakes and a popular carvery on Sun, good home cooking, refresh here after a hike.

Bars and clubs

Stellenbosch *p138, map p140*

Bohemia Pub, corner of Andringa and Victoria Sts, T021-8828375, www.bohemia.co.za, 1000-late. One of the main student haunts with an eccentric brightly coloured interior and attractive wrap-around veranda. One of the most popular bars in town. Gets very busy with a young clientele who come for the cold beers, relaxed atmosphere and occasional live music.

Dros, corner of Bird and Alexander Sts, T021-8864856, 0800-2400. The restaurant turns into a noisy bar later at night. Tables spill out onto the square and get crowded with backpackers and students.

Fandango, Shop 11, Drostdy Centre, T021-8877506, www.fandango.co.za, 0900-0100. Café and bar offering internet access with tables outside on the square, popular for after-work cocktails, occasional live music.

Mexican Kitchen, 25 Bird St, T021-8829997, www.mexicankitchen.co.za, 1100-2400. Lively Mexican cantina with weekly salsa sessions, gaudy cocktail and shooter specials. Women get a free cocktail on Tue nights.

Tollie's, Drostdy Centre, Bird St, T021-8865497, 2100-late. Popular nightclub, packed with students on weekend nights, dance and pop music, occasional live bands.

Entertainment

Stellenbosch *p138, map p140*

Theatre

Dorp Street Theatre, T021-8866107, www.dorpstraat.co.za. Local productions, plays in Afrikaans, and jazz on Sun.

Endler Hall, at the university, T021-8082340, www.sun.ac.za/music. Classical music concerts and university productions.

Oude Libertas Amphitheatre, on a wine estate just to the west of the centre off the R306, T021-8087473, www.oudelibertas.co.za. Outdoor events from Nov-Mar.

Spier Amphitheatre, T021-8091100, www.spier.co.za. Open-air summer concerts, jazz events, plays and comedy on the wine estate. The open-air amphitheatre here is a great venue.

Festivals and events

Stellenbosch *p138, map p140*

Sep The Stellenbosch Festival is a 3-day music and arts event concentrating on chamber music and art exhibitions, www.stellenboschfestival.co.za.

Oct The Stellenbosch Wine Festival, in the last week of Oct, is an annual event to promote local award-winning wines along with traditional rural cuisine, www.wineroute.co.za.

Shopping

Stellenbosch *p138, map p140*
Oom Samie se Winkel (Uncle Sammy's Shop), 84 Dorp St. Has been trading since 1791. The first owner, Pieter Gerhard Wium, traded in meat, but the shop became famous between 1904 and 1944 when the store was owned and run by Samuel Johannes Volsteedt. He stocked virtually everything you could need, and was known throughout the town. Today the shop still sells a wide range of goods and it has retained its pre-war character with items hanging from all corners, and old cabinets full of bits and pieces. It has all the makings of a tourist trap, but unlike many others it is genuine.

Franschhoek *p145, map p145*
Bordeaux Street Gallery, Huguenot Rd, T021-8762960, bordeauxgallery@saol.com. Series of rooms selling local arts and crafts, including antique furniture, Massai jewellery, woven baskets, fabrics and batiks.
Delicious!, Huguenot Rd, T021-8764004. Deli selling fresh produce from 2 well-known local restaurants. Ideal place to pick up ingredients for a picnic.

Activities and tours

Stellenbosch *p138, map p140*

Bicycle hire

Adventure Centre, next to the tourist office, T021-8828112, www.adventureshop.co.za.
Stumble Inn, 12 Mark St, T021-8874049, www.jump.to/stumble, good advice.

Horse riding

Spier Horse Trails, T021-8813683. Expect to pay R160 per hr. The horses are well trained and can take complete novices. Morning rides include breakfast in **Spier's** deli, sunset rides are followed by cocktails at the **Moyo** restaurant. Pony rides for children and carriage rides for non-riders also on offer.

Wine tours

As well as those listed below, many Cape Town tour operators organize day trips to the Winelands starting, see page 128.
Easy Rider Wine Tours, T021-8864651, stumble@iafrica.com. Hugely popular day-long wine tour aimed at backpackers organized by the **Stumble Inn** (see Sleeping, page 154). Tours take in 4 estates, with several tastings in each, restaurant, lunch and cheese tasting included, good value (R260 all inclusive) although they seem to take too many people, making it rather chaotic.
Vine Hopper, T021-8828112, or book through the Adventure Centre (above). A useful hop-on, hop-off bus that tours between 6 estates and the tourist office in town, costing R135 per person. Farms on the route are Vredenheim, Van Ryn Brandy Cellar, Spier, Dombeya, Bilton and Kleine Zalze.
Wine Walks , T021-8512785. Organizes full-day walking tours including picnic lunch and wine tasting. Alternatively, there are a number of private registered tour guides – enquire at the tourist office.

Franschhoek *p145, map p145*

Bike hire

Manic Cycles, Huguenot St, T021-8764956. Mountain bike hire.

Fly-fishing

Dewdale Fly Fishing, off the Robertsvlei Rd, 7 km from Franschhoek, T021-8762755, www.dewdale.com. Specializes in rainbow and brown trout, and American steelhead trout, lovely setting in the mountains. Rods can be hired and tuition can be arranged.

Horse riding

Mont Rochelle Stables, T083-3004368 (mob). 1- to 3-hr tours around the region including wine-tasting rides.
Paradise Stables, outside of the village on the Robertsvlei Rd, T021-8762160, www.paradisestables.co.za. Guided trails throughout the vineyards, wine-tasting tours with lunch, no rides on Sun.

Tour operators

The Franschhoek Experience, T083-2344038 (mob), www.franschhoek-experience.co.za. Daily scheduled food and wine tours.

Paarl Winelands *p148, map p149*

Bike hire

Bike Point, T021-8633901, www.bikepoint.org. Organizes fun rides in the regions, as well as renting out bikes and providing route maps.

Tour operators

Vintage Cape Tours, 94 Mill St, T021-8729252, www.vintagecape.co.za. Specialist wine tours, historical walking tours and hiking. More suited to the older client.

Transport

Strand and around *p137*

Metro

There is a daily commuter service between Somerset West and **Cape Town** on the metro train, www.metrorail.co.za, but only use this during rush hour (0600-0800, 1600-1800) when there are plenty of people around, as this runs through the townships; 31 km from Cape Town International Airport.

Stellenbosch *p138, map p140*

Metro

Again the town is served from **Cape Town** by the suburban Metro railway, www.metrorail.co.za. For safety reasons, this is best avoided at any time other than rush hour.

Taxi

Solomon Taxis, T021-8813497.

Paarl Winelands *p148, map p149*

Metro

Cape Town, platform 1. There are a number of daily trains between Paarl and Cape Town, but other than during rush hour when commuters are travelling, it's best to avoid it.

Taxi

Paarl Radio Taxis, T021-8725671.

Train

There are 2 train stations in town: Paarl station is at the southern outskirts whilst Huguenot station is across the river from Lady Grey St. Huguenot is on the Cape Town- Pretoria via Bloemfontein and the Cape Town-Durban via Bloemfontein routes. **Spoornet**, T0860-008888, www.spoornet.co.za.

Wellington district *p153, map p153*

72 km to **Cape Town**, 131 km to **Saldanha**, 49 km to **Stellenbosch**. To return to **Cape Town** take the R44 around Paarl Mountain, and turn right after 20 km onto the N1. The R45 to Malmesbury continues west towards Saldanha Bay and the Atlantic. Alternatively, travel north on the R44 to Porterville and join with the N7 before it starts to climb Grey's Pass. From the top of the pass you descend into the Olifants River Valley.

Bus

Connections are poor. You'll have to make your own way to Paarl if you intend to travel by the long distance coach services. Neither Translux nor **Greyhound** stop in Wellington.

Train

The daily service between **Cape Town** and **Durban** stops in Wellington. This is the best option for travel to Cape Town. Departs Wellington 1350 for **Cape Town** (80 mins), and departs Cape Town at 1000. See www.spoornet.co.za for timetables.

Directory

Stellenbosch *p138, map p140*

Banks All the main South African banks are found here, all with ATMs. The following **Bureaux de Change** are open Mon-Fri 0830-1700, Sat 0900-1200: **Rennies Foreign Exchange** (local representatives of Thomas Cook), Mill St, T021-8865259; **American Express**, 4 Plein St, T021-8870818. **Internet** Fandango, Shop 11, Drostdy Centre, T021-8877506, www.fandango.co.za, 0900-0100, café and bar offering internet access; you can also check your email at the tourist office on Market St. **Medical services** Hospital, T021-8870310. 24-hr Private Medi-Clinic, T021-8509000. **Post office** Main post office, Plein St, a post restante service is available. **Useful telephone numbers** Ambulance, T10177; Police, T10111.

West Coast

The West Coast is vastly different from the more visited Garden Route – a wild, bleak stretch lashed by the icy Atlantic and backed by rolling dunes covered in coastal fynbos, far removed from the lush green landscape full of rivers and waterfalls found in the south. It has only recently become a standard fixture for tourists, who are attracted by both the sun-bleached coast and the spectacular flowers that blanket the area in spring. The cold Benguella of the Atlantic also brings with it some of the most nutrient- rich waters found on the planet. This fertile sea supports an enormous wealth of marine life; the fishing is superb, and the coast is famous for its excellent seafood. Inland lies a fertile farming region, the Swartland, known for its grain and wine. Further north, the N7 highway passes along the magnificent Cederberg, a wilderness area with some of the best hiking in South Africa. ▸▸ *For Sleeping, Eating and other listings, see pages 174-178.*

Ins and outs

Getting there Driving out of Cape Town, follow the N1 through Durbanville and the northern suburbs for the West Coast. If time is not an issue, turn off the N1 at the Maitland junction, signposted Milnerton M5, and follow the signs for the R27. This is the old coast road which runs all the way north to Velddrif, north of the West Coast National Park. If you are pressed for time, take a left at Acacia Park and follow signs for the N7. This is the main highway from Cape Town to Namibia, which runs up the west coast through the Northern Cape Province.

Tourist information and climate For information on the West Coast visit www.capewestcoast.org. While the sea may be too cold for swimming, the region's climate is very favourable. As you travel north from Cape Town the summer temperatures are higher, and the rainfall is less. The air is dry and, even in winter, providing the winds aren't blowing, it can be very warm. Most of the rain falls between June and September.

Cape Town to Vanrhynsdorp via the coast

▸▸ *pp174-178.*

Darling → *Colour map 8, grid A1.*

Less than an hour's drive north of Cape town, fthe irst settlement of note is Darling, a small, thriving town, named after a Lieutenant Governor of the Cape, Sir Charles Henry Darling. Reflecting the prosperity of the surrounding area, it is in typical **Swartland** country, surrounded by vast expanses of wheat fields and lush irrigated pastures for dairy herds. Few visitors will spend much time here, except during the spring months of August and September, when the wild flowers on the veld are blooming - a **Wild Flower Show** has been held here during the third weekend of September since 1917. The most common flowers found in the area include daisies, nemesias, vygies and lilies. There are four vineyards in the Darling region which are all open for tastings and sales. The **tourist information office** ⓘ *in the museum on Pastorie St, T022-4923361, www.darlingtourism.co.za, or www.tourismdarling.co.za*, is a good source of local information especially when the wild flowers are in bloom.

More recently, Darling has become well known as the home of Evita Bezuidenhout, a sort of Afrikaans Dame Edna created by comedian Pieter Dirk-Uys. Evita is something of a South African gay institution, and hosts lively cabaret shows at her **Evita se Perron** café-theatre in the tiny old railway station (see Eating page 176).

In the old City Hall, Pastorie Street, is a **museum** ⓘ *Mon-Sat 0900-1200, T022-4923361*, with a typical small town collection devoted to depicting the region's history. The slightly unusual display traces the history of the butter industry in Darling. Staff at the museum will direct you to local private farms which are open for viewing wild flowers during the spring. It is not unusual to see a gaggle of geese waddle down the streets of Darling.

At Kraalbosdam farm, 6 km to the north, stands the **Hildebrand Memorial**. This commemorates the southernmost confrontation of the Anglo-Boer War (1899-1902). There is a memorial and the gravestone of Hildebrand, a Boer Commando who was killed here. The local farm, Oudepost, is famous for its orchid nursery, the largest in South Africa. These amazing blooms are available locally, but the majority are for the export market.

Whales along the West Coast start arriving around May, where the mating pairs and family pods remain until December.

Yzerfontein → *Colour map 8, grid A1.*

Driving north from Cape Town (85 km) on the R27, Yzerfontein is the first settlement of any size along the West Coast, still with distant views of Table Mountain in clear weather. It is named after a local spring rising from an ironstone formation. The village sits on the edge of an exposed rocky headland which in turn forms a sheltered bay. The harbour has a slipway suitable for the launching of small fishing boats, popular for the abundant shoaling snoek found off the coast. At times it may be possible to see whales sheltering in the bay, although there are better spots along this coast for whale watching. To the south of the village is an excellent sandy beach which is safe for swimming, although the water is always cold. A further attraction is the strong swell in the bay which makes it great for surfing. For information, contact the Yzerfontein **Tourism Bureau** ⓘ *46 Main Rd, T022-4512366, www.tourismyzerfontein.co.za, Mon-Fri 0730-1230, 1300-1500, weekends in season 1000-1400.* Many of the local holiday homes stand empty and the town can be very quiet out of season. Most of the local amenities are concentrated around the petrol station.

If you have access to a boat, **Dassen Island**, 9 km to the southwest, makes for an interesting day trip. The island, the largest along the west coast, is the peak of an underwater mountain. When Jan van Riebeeck first visited here in 1654, the island was home to hundreds of seals. These have long since been hunted out, but there remain large cormorant and African penguin breeding populations. A caretaker lives on the island to monitor and protect the only breeding ground in the Cape for the great white pelican. Closer to the shore is a smaller island, **Meeurots**, which has become home for cormorants and gulls.

Langebaan » *pp174-178. Colour map 6, grid B4.*

A little more than an hour by road from Cape Town (125 km), this is a very popular family resort which has been all but spoilt by heavy development. Situated on the sheltered waters of the beautiful **Langebaan Lagoon**, it is an ideal centre for watersports – sailing conditions are reputedly the best along the Western Cape coastline. The beach is also good and sheltered so it's not too cold for swimming. The **Langebaan Tourism Bureau** ⓘ *is in the municipality, corner of Breë and Oostewal Sts, T022-7721515, www.langebaaninfo.com, Mon-Fri 0900-1700, Sat 0900-1300.*

Today it is impossible to picture the town's origins as a small fishing village in the 1880s. The hillside is a mosaic of new houses and vacant plots waiting for the next building to obstruct the view of an earlier speculator. The town is dominated by the hideous-looking *Club Mykonos* timeshare complex and hotel, a collection of elaborate pastel-coloured town houses built to look like so-called Greek tavernas where holidaymakers from Cape Town spend their allotted two weeks of time share, parking their ski boats in the little harbour, and gambling in the on-site 24-hour casino.

The first Europeans to visit the region were French whales and seal hunters in the 17th century who stored their booty – whale oil and seal skins - on an island in the lagoon known as Isle la Biche. This was renamed by the first Dutch settlers as **Schaapen Island**. It was not until 1870 that a village began to take shape. Prior to this, Langebaan was put on the map by Lord Charles Somerset, Governor of the Cape in the 1820s, who built a hunting lodge on a private farm overlooking the lagoon. The growth of the village was slow due to a shortage of fresh water, a problem which was only solved after the Second World War when a pipeline was built to bring water from the Berg River to the northeast.

The lagoon is an important feature of the region. The northern part, opening onto the Atlantic Ocean, is known as **Saldanha Bay** and is the deepest and safest natural harbour in South Africa. Not surprisingly, it has been fully utilized by the South African navy. More recently, mining interests have built a large iron-ore wharf and steel mill on the bay, a real eyesore which is visible from all angles. In contrast, the southern shores and waters are part of the fascinating **West Coast National Park** (see page 168) – a rather precarious situation, as heavy ore carriers and naval boats frequenting the lagoon threaten the fragile marine environment.

West Coast National Park

» *pp174-178. Colour map 8, grid A1.*

ⓘ *Apr-Sep 0700-1930, Oct-Mar 0600-2000, R60 in flower season, R20 otherwise.* Although it may not seem very remarkable at first sight, this park remains unmatched in South Africa. Covering 30,000 ha, it was established in 1985 to protect the rich marine life in the lagoon and the rare coastal wetlands. It extends from just north of Yzerfontein to Saldanha Bay, and includes the Postberg Nature Reserve, Langebaan Lagoon and the islands – Malgas, Jutten, Marcus and Schaapen. The diversity of species here is impressive, but the main attraction is the excellent variety of birdlife.

Ins and outs

Getting there You can enter the park from two directions: from the south (look out for the signs along the R27); or by driving south out of Langebaan town. If you don't mind paying the small entrance fee, it is a pleasant alternative to drive through the park when travelling between Langebaan and Cape Town. All the roads are surfaced.

Tourist Information SAN Parks ⓘ *T022-7722144, www.sanparks.org*. The main information centre is just before the entrance to the park (follow the signs from Langebaan centre) and has maps and information on the area. Within the park, a beautiful farmstead dating from 1860 has been fully restored and turned into an environmental centre and tea rooms. This is found at the southern end of the lagoon and is known as the **Geelbek Homestead.** Most visitors, including tour groups, stop here. Apart from the attraction of a pot of tea or toasted sandwich, there are some interesting displays on the different ecosystems found in the park. Several walks start from here, leading to simple hides in amongst the reed beds and the mud flats.

Postberg Nature Reserve

Apart from the prolific birdlife in the park the other major attraction is its wild flowers which bloom after the first spring rains. Because of the variety of soil types, you can see many different flowers within a small area. The most colourful spreads are frequently found in Postberg Nature Reserve. Since 1987, this private nature reserve has been administered by the national park, while the actual lands remain the property of farmers. Three farms make up the reserve: Nieuwland, Kreeftebaai and Oude Post. Between 1838 and 1966 the land was used as winter grazing for cattle. In 1969 it was declared a private nature reserve which would be open during the flower season. It is found at the tip of the peninsula that forms the western shore of the lagoon. It is still only open from August to September, but during the spring it is one of the best places to see wild flowers. The land has also been stocked with eland, zebra, hartebeest, kudu and wildebeest. There are three picnic sites with toilets. Allow sufficient time to exit the park at the end of the day as it is a long drive all the way round the lagoon.

Langebaan Lagoon

The beautiful lagoon, a wide expanse of sparkling turquoise water, is an important and integral part of the park. It is rich in nutrients – twice a day the tides replenish the lagoon with cold plankton-rich water – and home to thousands of birds. Looking down from a high vantage point helps one appreciate how exceptionally clear the waters are. This has been attributed to colonies of mussels which filter the microscopic particles brought in by the tide.

Every year 50,000-70,000 birds fly more than 15,000 km from northern Russia to spend the summer feeding on Lagebaan lagoon.

Saldanha

→ *Colour map 8, grid B1.*

At the northern end of Langebaan Lagoon, Saldanha is the largest town in the area and is certainly the less appealing part of the lagoon. Large numbers of fishing vessels offload their harvests here to be processed in one of three factories. The

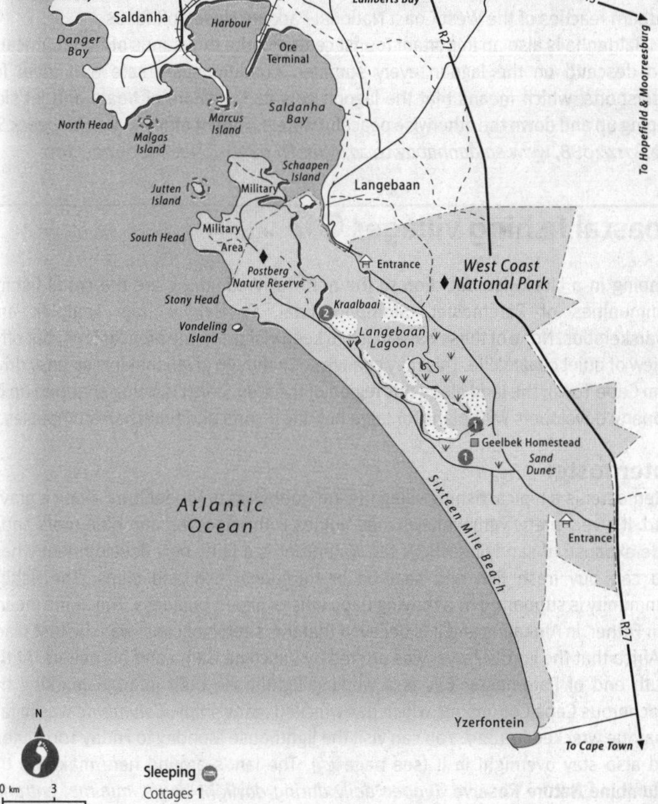

Sishen-Saldanha Railway

Anyone driving north from Saldanha Bay is likely to follow a route close to the Sishen-Saldanha railway. This was purpose-built between 1973 and 1976 to transport high-grade iron ore from the Northern Cape to a new deep-water harbour in Saldanha Bay. The line is 861 km long and only has three bends. It has earned a place in the Guinness Book of Records. In 1989 a world record was set when the longest and heaviest train covered the route. The train was 7.3 km long, there were 660 loaded trucks weighing 71,210 metric tonnes and it was pulled by 16 locomotives. You can see long segments of a train in the marshalling yards just outside the harbour. When there is a waiting train the road to Langebaan is diverted.

greatest blight on the area, however, is the massive steel mill, the long iron ore jetty and the bulk ships which sit complacently in the bay waiting to transport the ore. Aquaculture in the lagoon has grown into a very important local industry. The first harvest was in 1984, and the quality was exceptional – surprising perhaps, considering the vicinity of the jetty. The main crop is the Mediterranean blue mussel, along with Japanese oysters and local clams. Saldanha is also the location of a South African naval base and is home to the South African Military Academy. Some of the northern reaches of the West Coast National Park are closed off for use.

Saldanha is also an important tourist centre for the thousands of South Africans who descend on the lagoon every summer. Conditions are safe and ideal for watersports, which means that the lagoon gets its fair share of boats and jet skis zipping up and down the otherwise peaceful waters. **Tourist office** ⓘ *Van Riebeeck St, T022-7142088, www.saldanhabay.co.za, Mon-Fri 0830-1630, Sat 0900-1200.*

Coastal fishing villages

» *pp174-178. Colour map 6, grid B4.*

Running in a clockwise direction to the north of Vredenburg are the small fishing communities of Paternoster, Stompneusbaai, St Helena Bay, Laaiplek and Dwarskersbos. None of these have much to keep visitors in the area for long, but offer a view of quiet coastal life. This may change soon though given that it is an easy drive from Cape Town; the land along this region of the West Coast is being snapped up by property developers with plans for large holiday resorts and timeshare complexes.

Paternoster

Paternoster is a typical fishing village 15 km northwest of Vredenburg along a gravel road. It's very pretty with whitewashed homes with bright red and blue roofs and a wide expanse of sandy beach. At the waterfront is a fairly new development where you can buy fresh fish and seafood or traditional fish and chips. The fishing community is supported by a thriving Cape lobster export business. The name means 'Our Father' in Afrikaans and it is believed that this stretch of coast was the first place in Africa that the Lord's Prayer was uttered by Vasco de Gama and his sailors. At the south end of Paternoster Bay is a working lighthouse built in 1936 marking the treacherous Cape Columbine, which has wrecked many ships. *Columbine* was in fact a barque wrecked in 1829. You can visit the lighthouse Monday to Friday 1000-1500, and also stay overnight in it (see page 43). The lands around here make up the **Columbine Nature Reserve** ⓘ *open daily during daylight hours, minimal entrance charge, T022-7522718.* This area of protected coastline has a rich mix of wild flowers

West Coast National Park birdwatching

The main attraction in the park is the varied and impressive birdlife, and there are a number of hides allowing good viewing. Almost 250 species of bird have been recorded here, and the variety is quite remarkable: flamingos from the Etosha Pan in Namibia are found here; an estimated 50% of the world's population of swift terns live here during season; 25% of the world's Cape gannets are also found here, as are a sizeable number of rare African black oystercatchers. Other rare birds to look out for are the black harrier, great crested grebe and the silver gull. Each year over 65,000 waders visit the lagoon – many of these birds started life in the Siberian marshlands. The greatest influx of birds occurs between September and April. It takes the birds about six weeks to complete the 15,000 km journey from Siberia to Langebaan. Without the protected environment of the lagoon, it is uncertain where these birds could or would migrate to. For this reason alone it is vital that the habitat is protected as far as possible.

in the spring, also Karoo succulents and nesting seabirds, and there is a simple beach camp here (see Sleeping, page 175).

Stompneusbaai

Stompneusbaai is a similar coastal village. The presence of a fish-processing factory detracts somewhat from the attractive local fishermen's cottages, but it is an important source of income for the village. This is also the area where Vasco da Gama landed in 1497 after three months at sea, the first voyage he had made this far south. The modern monument commemorating this is hardly worthy of his feat.

St Helena Bay

A surfaced road links Stompneusbaai with St Helena Bay, an important centre of South Africa's commercial fishing industry, especially for lobster. Remember it is illegal to buy lobster directly from the fishermen. The bay was named by Vasco da Gama who anchored here with four vessels on 7 November 1497, St Helena Day. Fortunately for the crews they found plenty of fresh spring water. A granite monument commemorating this event stands on the shore near Sandy Point.

Rocherpan Nature Reserve → *Colour map 6, grid A4.*

ⓘ *Daily, Sep-Apr 0700-1800, May-Aug 0800-1700, T022-9521727, www.capenature.org.za. There are no staff at the small interpretive centre next to the gate, but visitors should sign in and drop their fee (R20) into the honesty box. You can also pick up an excellent bird checklist with map from here. The reserve office is another 100 m into the reserve. There are 2 sturdy bird hides beside the freshwater lake. Behind the car park a footpath leads across the dunes to the desolate beach.*

This important and rarely visited bird sanctuary is 12km beyond Dwarskersbos. More often than not, you'll have the reserve to yourself with only the sound of thousands of birds feeding and an endless beach to stroll along. This 914-ha reserve was established in 1967 around a seasonal *vlei*. In 1988 the boundaries were extended to include all the area up to the shore of the Atlantic Ocean. When fully flooded the *vlei*, fed by the Papkuils River, is nearly 3 km long, although it is unable to drain into the sea because of the sand dunes. This mix of protected habitats provides excellent breeding and feeding conditions for over 180 bird species. Nearly 70 different varieties of waterbirds have been recorded here, including some endangered species. If you are lucky you might spot the African black oystercatcher, one of the rarest endemic breeding coastal birds in South Africa. During its breeding season, between November and March, listen out for its high-pitched call, designed to startle intruders. It usually feeds at low tide, looking for mussels and limpets. White pelicans, Cape shovellers and flamingos are often seen here. There is also the chance of spotting a few of the resident small mammals such as steenbok, duiker and the water mongoose, as well as the shy African wild cat.

Elands Bay → *Colour map 6, grid A4.*

There are three very good reasons for visiting this small and isolated coastal community, which makes it all the more surprising to find that tourism has barely made its mark. First, the bay is a good location for whale watching – this is about the furthest north that southern right and humpback whales can be seen from the shore. Second, the bay is well known for its good surfing conditions. Finally, it lies at the mouth of **Verlorenvlei**, a stream with marshlands that support a large and varied aquatic bird population. Over 240 bird species have been recorded in the area. There is also an interesting walk out to Baboon Point with good views of the bay. Ask for directions to the cave which has some San paintings. All activities are concentrated around an open square by the **Eland Hotel**. There is a post office, bottle shop, supermarket and a cheap café. The **Eland Hotel** also acts as the local **tourist information office**, T022-9721640.

Wadrif Salt Pan

Nearby, on the way to Lambert's Bay, is Wadrif Salt Pan. After rains there are a couple of shallow ponds here, providing an excellent chance of seeing flamingos. Take a left by the railway bridge and follow the railway line to **Lambert's Bay**. One short stretch belongs to the railways and you may have to pay a small toll fee. Wadrif Salt Pan is by the railway line.

Lambert's Bay » *pp174-178. Colour map 6, grid A4.*

Once just a small fishing village, Lambert's Bay has become a popular holiday town and gets very busy during summer. The excellent **Muisbosskerm** restaurant (see Eating page 177) played an important role in drawing visitors to the region, but the bay has in fact appeared on maps for many years – this was the last point at which Bartholomeu Dias went ashore, before sailing around the Cape for the first time in 1487. The village is named after the British admiral, Sir Robert Lambert, who produced detailed charts of this coastline between 1826-1840. In 1918 Axel Lindstrom established the **Lambert's Bay Canning Co** and the future of the small fishing community was assured. **Lambert's Bay Tourism Bureau** ⓘ *Main St, T027-4321000, www.lambertsbay.info, Mon-Fri 0900-1300, 1400-1700, Sat 0900-1230. Also open Sun during the flower season.*

Between July and November you have a good chance of seeing the southern right whale migrating north.

The town itself is modern and rather unattractive, although it has one absorbing, if pungent, attraction – **Bird Island**. No longer an island, this 3-ha rock outcrop is now joined to the land by a concrete jetty. It is an important breeding ground for African penguins, Cape gannets and cormorants, and it attracts Cape fur seals. Most of the island is fenced off, but there is a rather dilapidated viewing tower. Early morning and evening are the best time to see the birds, as during the day they are at sea looking for food. Although the birds make for interesting viewing, their cantankerous screeching and overpowering smell leaves a rather longer-lasting impression. If you have the time, walk to the end of the jetty where there are good views of the fishing fleet and more sea birds. Note that around high tide, breakers crash across the jetty as you walk out to the island. Wear shoes with grip, as the surface is very slippery and uneven. The **Bird Island**

Jackass penguins

This flightless sea bird is only found on the coast of southern Africa. Once they nested in guano burrows, today on Bird Island concrete piping provide the necessary shelter. In the 1930s estimates put their population at over one million birds, today less than 110,000 penguins are left. This considerable decline in the population has been put down to commercial fishing competing with their food stocks and the collection of their eggs for food. They eat sardines, maasbanker, anchovy and squid. Along with Boulders Beach just outside Simon's Town in the Cape Peninsula, this is the only place where they can be seen nesting on the mainland. These are some of the smaller penguins, but you won't get a better view unless you go to Antarctica or the Falkland Islands.

Interpretation Centre ⓘ *T022-9312900, daily 0700-1700*, has exhibits on the birds and a feature on the history of collecting guano, traditionally used as fertilizer, plus a mini aquarium, and a rather sad-looking penguin pool.

Lambert's Bay to Vredendal

Doring Bay is a small fishing village based around a crayfish factory. The rocky coastline and deep coastal waters make this an ideal spot for crayfish to live in. Diamond boats can sometimes be seen around the jetty. There is a good restaurant here, the **Cabin**, on the seafront which is, worth a visit (see Eating, page 178).

About 8 km further on is the northernmost village on the coast, **Strandfontein**. This is a delightful settlement built on the slopes of a small basin. The coastline is quite rocky and mountainous along here with a clean white sand beach with excellent surfing conditions. Although usually quiet, the village is very popular during the school holidays when there are full-time lifeguards present on the beach. There are strong cross currents so only swim in front of the town where there is a tidal pool for children.

Papendorp, close to the estuary of the Olifants River, is more of a cluster of fisherman's cottages than a village. There is a small island in the middle of the river mouth, and at low tide there are thousands of waterbirds on the mud flats. As an important wetland reserve, it is being considered as a future world RAMSAR site. From this point the road turns inland towards Lutzville (20 km from Strandfontein), a small farming village, and on to Vredendal.

Vredendal → *Colour map 6, grid A4.*

Despite the fact that it is some distance west of the main N7, Vredendal is the principal commercial centre in the northwestern Cape. It is a modern town which owes its existence entirely to the Olifants River irrigation scheme. The first settlers came to the region as early as 1732 when the Dutch East India Company granted a farm to Pieter van Zyl, but it was only when the Bulshoek Dam was built that new farmers were attracted to the area. In 1925 a bridge was built across the Olifants River and the town grew rapidly into its present form. There are few sights, although one of the more unusual local industries open to the public is a seaweed-drying factory just outside the town. (It's used as a binding agent in ice cream, to make jelly sweets and as pet food.) The region is also home to several quarries which extract dolomite and limestone. For tourist information contact the **Vredendal Information Office** ⓘ *11 Church St, T027-2013376, www.tourismvredendal.co.za, Mon-Fri 0800-1300, 1400-1700, Sat 0830-1300.*

Darling *p166*

C **Darling Lodge**, 22 Pastorie St, T022-4923062, darling@mweb.co.za. A comfortable, restored 19th-century town house with a stream running through the garden. 5 en suite double rooms with shared lounge with TV and fridge. Recommended.

C **Trinity Guest Lodge**, 19 Long St, T022-4923430, mclaughlin@worldonline.co.za. Beautifully converted family home, with 4 stylish, understated bedrooms, each with their own entrance, old-fashioned bathrooms, lovely bright restaurant also open to non-guests, friendly owners Shaun and Debbie. Recommended.

Yzerfontein *p167*

B **Emmaus on Sea**, 30 Versveld St, T022-4512650, www.emmaus.co.za. B&B or self-catering, upstairs family unit with 2 double rooms and 1 bathroom, downstairs 3 double rooms, 2 en suite, 1 with private bathroom, enclosed terrace and pub offers sea views without the wind.

B **Kaijaiki Guest House and Restaurant**, 36 Park Rd, T022-4512858, www.kaijaiki.co.za. Comfortable, homely guesthouse. Each of the 5 en suite rooms has its own fireplace and separate entrance, decorated with old photos and antiques, good restaurant attached serving West Coast traditional food. German, Dutch and French spoken. Recommended.

D **Caravan Park**, Park St, T022-4512211. Good facilities, next to the dunes on the main beach, bungalows and caravans for hire, but camping not allowed.

Langebaan *p167*

There are plenty of options, given the town's popularity on the domestic holiday front, but many of these choices are for a minimum period of a week and close in the winter. Nevertheless, visitors have considerable bargaining power in the winter months. As with all South African coastal resorts advance booking is necessary during the school holidays, especially Dec and Jan.

A **Falcon's Rest**, 21a Zeeland St, T022-7721112, www.falconrest.co.za. Large converted family home with 12 en suite double rooms with TV, several lounges, panoramic views from the garden, pool, sun deck. Attentive service.

A **The Farmhouse**, 5 Egret St, T022-7722062, www.thefarmhouselangebaan.co.za. A smart and cosy converted Cape Dutch farmhouse. 18 rooms, some with fireplace, en suite bathroom or shower, TV, good restaurant with pine furnishings open to non-guests, swimming pool, overlooks Langebaan Lagoon, library, no young children. Recommended.

A-B **Club Mykonos**, T0800-226770, www.clubmykonos.co.za. Dominating the whole village, this is an enormous Greek-style resort with over 330 *kalivas* – 1- to 3-bedroom villas, most self catering, arranged in a village with views of the ocean or the lagoon. Facilities include several swimming pools, casino and restaurant complex, and watersports can be arranged. A lot of the units are timeshare and, whilst comfortable, the resort has a very impersonal feel about it.

B **Langebaan Beach House**, 44 Beach Rd, T022-7722625, www.langebaanbeachhouse.com. Small guesthouse in idyllic setting right on beach overlooking the lagoon. 4 tastefully furnished rooms, understated with terracotta-tiled floors, white linen, en suite, TV, private lounge or veranda overlooking beach, cooked breakfasts served on terrace, neat gardens and pool. Recommended.

C-E **Oliphantskop Farm Inn**, opposite turning for Club Mykonos, T022-7722326. Set in converted farm buildings, 17 en suite rooms plus some self-contained chalets, though poor reports recently about rooms becoming run down. In the low season backpackers are put in main rooms for budget rates, making it extraordinarily good value. Stables on the farm specialize in horse trails. Candlelit restaurant set in long barn with log fires, choice of good-value seafood and steaks, beer garden.

West Coast National Park *p168, map p169*

Until recently there was no accommodation in the park, but SAN Parks have introduced a couple of options within the park's boundaries. Reservations through SAN Parks Pretoria office, T012-4289111, www.sanparks.org. Bookings can also be made in person at the offices in Cape Town and Durban (see page 44). For cancellations or reservations under 72 hrs contact the park directly, T022-7722144.

A Cottages 2 6-bed fully equipped self-catering cottages, 1 near the Geelbek Centre with electricity, 1 near the lagoon with gas appliances. Linen, towels and all cooking equipment provided, you just need to bring food.

A Houseboat Permanently moored in the lagoon, can accommodate 4 adults and 2 small children, with gas-operated kitchen, shower, flush toilet, braai and parking. There's also a larger houseboat that sleeps 22 but this is more suited to corporate groups than holidaymakers. These have their own website, www.houseboating.co.za.

C Rustic Cottage 10 km from the main entrance gate, also sleeps 6 with gas appliances but here you need to bring your own bedding as well.

Saldanha *p169, map p169*

A-B Blouwaterbaai (Bluewater Bay) Hotel and Resort, Henry Wicht Av, T022-7141177, www.blouwaterbaai.com. 20 1- to 3-bed fully equipped, self-catering cottages with TV, simple furnishings but big views from the large windows, patio and lawn in front leading to the beach, 16 more luxurious rooms in the whitewashed hotel, swimming pool, tennis, windsurfing, full range of beauty treatments on offer, restaurant and bar overlooking Saldanha Lagoon.

B Protea Hotel Saldanha Bay, 51 Main Rd, T022-7141264, www.proteahotels.co.za. Standard chain hotel in centre of town, 58 rooms, some non-smoking, TV, restaurant, swimming pool, secure parking. One of the less characterful Proteas but reasonable value.

B-C Jane's Guest House and Coffee Shop, 8 Beach Rd, T022-7143605, www.janes.co.za. A selection of luxury en suite rooms, self-catering units or a family town house all overlooking the beach. Decorated to a very high standard with either private veranda or balcony, B&B available. Coffee shop serves light meals all day on a terrace overlooking the ocean.

C Oranjevlei Guest Farm, T022-7142261, oranje@mweb.co.za. 9 rooms in converted historic farm buildings, hiking trails on a working wheat and cattle farm, pub lunches, swimming pool, tennis courts, a well-run rural set-up.

E Saldanha Holiday Resort, Camp St, T022-7142247. Large, grassy camping and caravan site close to the beach, gets very busy over Christmas with families.

Paternoster *p170*

There are a number of holiday cottages in the village, contact **Paternoster Properties**, T022-7522087, www.paternosterprop.co.za.

B Paternoster Hotel, St Augustine St, T022-7522703, www.paternosterhotel.co.za. 10 spacious en suite rooms, with 1 double and 1 single bed, DSTV, 4 have balconies with sea view, great pub with crackling fire, restaurant open to all serving good range of seafood including crayfish. Also lets out a number of self-catering cottages in the village, which are good for families.

D Beach Camp, Cape Columbine Nature Reserve, T082-9262267, www.ratrace.co.za. A-frame huts and tents with beds, you'll need to bring your own sleeping bag, lovely setting in the nature reserve, hot communal showers, self-catering facilities, *lapa* area, also serves seafood dinners and can arrange sea kayaking and boat trips. Excellent budget option, ask about transfers from Cape Town.

St Helena Bay *p171*

B-D St Helena Hotel, Main Rd, T022-7361560. Has a mix of 20 en suite double rooms, 10 cottages, 4 self-catering chalets and a caravan park. There is a restaurant that serves crayfish, bar with karaoke, TV lounge, swimming pool, curio shop and a conference centre. All the rooms have panoramic views of the bay. Good base for exploring the region.

E Laingville Caravan Park, Strand St, T022-7361684. Standard park with basic sites and ablution block. Quiet until the school holidays, when it gets far too crowded.

Elands Bay *p172*

B Eland Hotel, Beachfront, T/F022-9721640. Comfortable en suite rooms with sea views, large and airy seafood restaurant, TV lounge, braai facilities, the principal building in the village, cheaper rooms in annexe, prices are for full board.

E **Elands Bay Caravan Park**, T022-9721736. Small municipal site right on beachfront in the village centre, windy but low thick hedges provide some shelter, ideal for surfing, short walk from shops and **Eland Hotel**.

Lambert's Bay *p172*

B **Lambert's Bay Hotel**, Voortrekker St, T027-4321126, www.lambertsbayhotel.co.za. 47 large rooms with marine decor, front upstairs rooms have a mixed view of the scenic harbour and ugly fish-processing factory - do NOT open your windows when the factory is working. Popular **Waves** restaurant specializes in fresh, quality seafood, lively bar, within walking distance of shops plus Bird Island, ask about whale-watching boat trips.

E-F **Lambert's Bay Caravan Park**, T027-4322238. Overlooks the main beach, a bit exposed, very busy in peak season.

Lambert's Bay to Vredendal *p173*

C **Die Anker**, Doring Bay, T027-2151016, www.doringbaai.com. Main local hotel, mix of accommodation including B&B rooms in the main house, self-catering units and some camping space, all with sea views, walking distance to beach, fully licensed restaurant.

C-E **Strandfontein Resort**, Kreef Rd, Strandfontein, T027-2151169. A well-equipped park which is a bit hectic when all 150 stands are occupied during the holidays. At quieter times, this is a relaxing spot to have a break. It is situated next to the beach, with 4- and 6-bed self-catering chalets, power points, tidal swimming pool, café open all year plus a small kiosk (open in peak season).

Vredendal *p173*

B **Tharrakamma Guesthouse**, 18 Tuin St, T027-2135709, www.tharrakamma.co.za. 3 double rooms, 2 family self-catering chalets, a/c, TV, non-smoking available, lovely wooden African furniture, beautiful house with wide verandas, pretty garden full of palms, award winning guesthouse. Recommended.

C **Vredendal Hotel**, 11 Voortrekker St, T027-2131064, www.vredendalhotel.co.za. Main hotel in town, 2-storey brick building with 51 a/c rooms with TV, **Saddles Steak Ranch** restaurant, bar with pool table, swimming pool.

Eating

Darling *p166*

TT **Evita se Perron**, in the old railway station, T022-4922831, www.evita.co.za. Open for breakfast and lunch, Tue-Sun, 0900-1700 and dinner when performances are on – check out the website. A range of entertainments set in the old railway building, including a restaurant, coffee shop and famous cabaret shows performed by Evita Bezuidenhout. Good food and excellent entertainment.

TT **Trinity**, at the **Trinity Guest Lodge** (see Sleeping page 174), dinner by arrangement only. A Victorian building with outside tables next to the pool, home cooked food using produce from their own garden, variable and innovative menu depending what's in season, Debbie the chef is especially well known for her pear and chocolate tart. Occasional wine tasting evenings are held.

Yzerfontein *p167*

TT **Beaches**, T022-4512200. 1200-1500, 1800-2100, open only for lunch in low season and closed mid-Jul to mid-Aug. À la carte restaurant specializing in seafood, also serves steaks and some vegetarian dishes, both the seafood curry and seafood potjie are worth a try, also has lite bites and pizzas in the bar, all with ocean views.

TT **Die Strandkombuis**, T082-5759683. Closed Jun-Aug, otherwise open for lunch daily at 1300, and dinner by arrangement only, also weather dependent so phone first. Open-air seafood braai, one of many beach seafood set-ups popular on the west coast. Start with seafood soup, and move on to smoked snoek, mussels and crayfish all cooked over hot coals. If it's a little chilly you can hire heaters.

Langebaan *p167*

TTT **Strandloper**, T022-7722490, www.strandloper.co.za, daily Oct-May, open Wed, Sat and Sun for lunch only 1 May-1 Oct. Follow signs for **Club Mykonos**, on the beach, casual, romantic surroundings with wooden tables under sunshades, cooking is done in a central fire pit. Excellent seafood buffet, award winning, booking advised at weekends, light guitar music in the evenings. Lunch begins at noon and dinner at 1800. Mussels are served for starters, then the empty mussel shells are used as cutlery for about 10 courses of fish served in the West Coast tradition with homemade bread and apricot jam. The final course is half a crayfish. Expect to pay approximately R150 per head for an all-you-can-eat meal. Discounts for children. Charming, one of the best eating experiences in South Africa, highly recommended.

🍴🍴 **The Farmhouse**, in the guesthouse (see Sleeping page 174), 5 Egret St, T022-7722062. 0700-late. Good lamb steaks, fresh seafood, quality food, vegetarian menu, Sunday roasts, views across the bay from an 1860s farmstead. The pub has a cheaper menu of sandwiches, fish and chips and lasagne.

🍴🍴 **La Taverna**, 1 Breë St, T022-7722870. Closed Mon and Tue out of season. Good-value seafood, pizza and pasta, and a menu with Austrian overtones, sauerkraut and eisbein, very popular during holiday season.

🍴🍴 **Pearly's** and **Driftwood Restaurant**, 46 Beach Rd, T022-7722734, 0900-late. Sister restaurants right next to the beach, fresh seafood and spare ribs, very popular, be prepared to wait during busy periods since all the dishes are freshly prepared, relaxing views across the lagoon. Recommended.

🍴 **Lagoon Fisheries**, Breë St. Fast-food joint dishing out tasty fish and chips.

Saldanha *p169, map p169*

🍴🍴 **Blouwaterbaai**, restaurant in the holiday resort (see Sleeping page 175), T022-7141177, 0700-2200. Stylish dining room serving up some surprising dishes for such a remote location, Moroccan lamb with chorizo sausage, truffles, and duck, very popular with people from Cape Town, booking essential.

🍴🍴 **Mussel Cracker**, 51 Main Rd, T022-7141264, 0630-1030, 1230-1430, 1900-2200. Part of **Protea Hotel**, smart seafood restaurant with views across bay, good fresh fish, crayfish and mussels, also steak combos such as rump with calamari. On Sat night is a good seafood buffet and there's a carvery on Sun lunchtime.

🍴🍴 **Slipway**, Main Harbour, T022-7144235, 0900-2100, closes at 1630 in the winter. Seafood, vegetarian and pasta dishes, steak and seafood combos are recommended, as are the unusual mussels in coconut cream, all overlooking the yachts at the jetty.

St Helena Bay *p171*

🍴🍴 **Cattle Baron Oystercatcher**, First Av, T022-7421042. 1100-1500, 1800-2300. In low season closed Sun evening and all day Mon. Great views and the restaurant is perched right on the rocks, lots of choice of steaks and sauces, the brandy sauce is especially good with a melt-in-your-mouth fillet, also a full range of seafood.

Lambert's Bay *p172*

🍴🍴🍴 **Die Kreef Huis**, T027-4322235, closed Sun. An excellent seafood restaurant opposite the entrance to Bird Island. Quality shellfish - you can select your own crayfish from the tank. Good selection of wines, light easy-going atmosphere, high standard of service, a must if you are in the area, booking advised during peak periods. Acts as a coffee shop in the mornings and after lunch when homemade cakes and breads are served. Very limited for vegetarians though.

🍴🍴 **Boesmanland Plaaskombuis**, 9 km south of town on Steenbokfontein Farm, T027-4322720. A traditional Sandveld farm menu with plenty of fresh produce straight off the farm. Large meals which should not be rushed. Try the homemade sausages plus the pot roast lamb. Breakfast is also recommended. For all meals reservations must be made in advance but you can drop in unannounced for tea from 1000-1630. Recommended.

🍴🍴 **Bosduifklip**, 4 km out of town towards Clanwilliam, T027-4322735. Open depending on weather and number of customers; call in advance to check. Set outside amongst some rock formations on Albina farm. A popular open-air restaurant serving buffet meals in West Coast style, bar or bring your own drink, booking essential at weekends and in holidays. Enjoy a tasty selection of seafood dishes including mussels, crayfish, smoked snoek and pickled fish, and farm cuisine such as lamb on the spit and venison stew. The salads are slightly unusual, but go well with the homemade breads and butter.

🍴🍴 **Muisbosskerm**, 5 km towards Elands Bay, T027-4321017, summer, lunch 1300, dinner 1900, winter open at weekends depending on weather. Several years ago a new style of restaurant evolved on the outskirts of Lambert's Bay – an open-air, no-frills seafood braai. Today there are several such places along the coast, but the first was the Muisbosskerm. When it began the only evidence of its existence was a thorn hedge to shield guests from the wind, and lines of parked cars plus the occasional helicopter. Extremely successful and popular restaurant. For a fixed price (approximately R150) you have a wide choice of seafood dishes cooked over a braai, baked and smoked, eat as much as you like, meals last about 3 hrs, bring your own drink, small corkage fee, book even out of season. During peak periods there can be more than 150 people eating here - it can become a bit of a scrum around the braais.

Lambert's Bay to Vredendal *p173*

The Cabin, on the edge of Doring Bay village, T027-2151016, 1200-1300, 1800-2100, run by a family team, the outside tables are on a mock-up of a boat hull, and inside you can sip sherry by a roaring fire. Well known for its fish soup and calamari.

Shopping

Langebaan *p167*

Freeport is a large shopping and accommodation development with a supermarket, bakery, bottle shop and café. All other shops and restaurants are in Breë St, close to the town hall. Here you will find a bookshop, launderette, Standard Bank and curio shops.

Activities and tours

Langebaan *p167*

Golf and tennis

Langebaan Country Club, T022-7722112.

Mountain bikes

Cape Sports, on the beach on the northern reaches of town, T022-7721114, www.capesport.co.za. Bikes available for hire. Also organizes windsurfing, kitesurfing and watersports with full instruction per hr or per day.

Lambert's Bay *p172*

Fishing

Game fishing is very popular along this stretch of coast, as is collecting crayfish. Crayfish permits are issued by the Department of Sea Fisheries in the harbour area, T027-4321631, or by the post office.

Golf

There is a 9-hole golf course among the old dunes, T027-4321167.

Tour operators

Lambert's Bay Boat Charters, Waterfront, T082-9224334 (mob). A strongly recommended boat trip to see dolphins, seals, whales (and sharks if you're lucky), and excellent for bird watchers, expect to pay R330-350 per person.

Directory

Langebaan *p167*

Medical services West Coast Private Hospital, T022-7191030. **Useful telephone numbers** Police T022-7722111; Sea rescue, T082-9905966.

Lambert's Bay *p172*

Banks Standard Bank in Church St is the best place to change money, with an ATM. **Useful telephone numbers** Police, T027-4321122.

Up the N7 to the Northern Cape

If your time is short or you want to get to the Northern Cape, the quickest way out of Cape Town is to take the N7 highway. The first part of the route passes through rolling wheat country known as the Swartland, or 'Black Country', named after the dark hue of rhinoceros bush which once covered the area. Most of the towns in the region are small, prosperous farming communities, with little in terms of sights, despite their long history. The principal centres of the wheat industry are Malmesbury and Moorreesburg. The eastern boundary of the Olifants River valley is made up of the spectacular Cederberg Mountains, a striking wilderness area offering some of the best hiking in South Africa. Both Citrusdal and Clanwilliam are a two- to three-hour drive from Cape Town and make good bases for exploring the area, their irrigated valleys providing a powerful contrast to the seemingly barren Cederberg. *▸▸ For Sleeping, Eating and other listings, see pages 185-188.*

Malmesbury → *Colour map 8, grid A1.*

About 50 km north of Cape Town the N7 passes Malmesbury, the centre of the surrounding wheat industry and the principal settlement in the Swartland. The sleepy town lies in a shallow valley close to the Diep River. For information visit the **Malmesbury Tourism Bureau** ⓘ *De Bron Centre, Voortrekker Rd, T022-4871133, www.tourismswartland.co.za. Daily 0900-1600.*

The town was given its current name in 1829 when the British Governor, Sir Lowry Cole, visited and renamed it in honour of his father-in-law, the Earl of Malmesbury. Today the skyline is dominated by the unsightly grain silos and huge flour mills. **Swartland Cellars**, 4 km outside town, produces a full-bodied red wine and the famous Hanepoot, with its strong honey flavour, is popular as a dessert wine. The winery has won a number of awards, despite the fact that experts claim local climatic conditions are far from ideal. One of the grandest buildings in town is the **Dutch Reformed Church** on Church Street, opposite the city hall. Although the original building was completed in 1751, the present form dates from around 1899 when the church was enlarged by building the existing transepts.

Moorreesburg → *Colour map 8, grid A1.*

Further north on the main N7, 102 km north of Cape Town, is this important farming and railway centre in the heart of the Swartland. Like Malmesbury, the surrounding area is devoted to wheat fields and sheep farming. Close to the railway are enormous grain silos and flour mills – wheat has been grown in the area since 1752. The settlement was founded in 1879 as a church centre, on a farm called **Hooikraal**. The town was named after the Reverend HA Moorrees. For information contact the **tourist office** ⓘ *Municipality building, corner of Plein and Retief Sts, T022-4331072, www.tourismmoorreesburg.co.za. Mon-Fri, 0830-1630*, or **West Coast Tourism** ⓘ *58 Long St, T022-4332380, www.capewestcoast.org.*

The **Wheat Industry Museum** ⓘ *Main Rd, T022-4331093, Mon-Thu 0900-1700, Fri 0800-1600, small entrance fee,* proudly proclaims that it is one of only three in the world and has a fairly diverting collection that traces the history of the crop. Before the cultivation of the area, the dominant vegetation was rhinoceros bush, a dark shrub found throughout the Swartland, which first gave it its name. Some of the early harvesting and threshing machines are well worth a look; they remind one of kit models, which in many ways is what they are, having been shipped out from England in pieces.

The magnificent heavy church bell isn't rung for fear of the vibrations damaging the structure – instead, a recording is played at services.

Piketberg → *Colour map 6, grid B5.*

After 31 km the N7 passes the turning for Velddrif and the small town of Piketberg. The Piketberg hills rise as a large massif to the east as the road heads across the plains to the Olifants River Mountains. Before the road starts to climb, you pass the turning on the right for Porterville. This is the R44 and takes you back towards Paarl and Cape Town. Piketberg is another typical agricultural town, with a few old buildings and churches in the centre surrounded by modern suburbs, which in turn give way to rolling wheat fields. Look out for an old cannon in the grounds of the high school. There was once a series of cannons along the mountain slopes all the way to Cape Town, which were fired to let farmers know when a new ship was arriving in Table Bay to take on board fresh supplies. The cannon was also used to warn of the approach of Khoi-San people. The name of the town dates back to 1792 when a lookout post was set up on Honigberg Farm to protect the local farmers from looting by the Khoi-San. The actual word is derived from the French word *picquet*, referring to a small group of soldiers on the lookout. For information, contact the local **tourist office** ⓘ *Kerk St, T022-9132063, www.piketberg.com, Mon-Fri 0830-1630.*

Like most of the small towns in the region, the dominant building is the **Dutch Reformed Church**, built 1880-1882. It is a striking building, neo-Gothic in style with plenty of turrets and plastered panels. There is an obelisk in its grounds commemorating the 1838 Great Trek. In 1938 the building was declared a national monument. There is a small museum housing antiquities donated by the community.

Olifants River Valley » *pp185-188.*

As you drop down from the Piekenierskloof Pass, the scenery changes significantly with the arrival of the Olifants River. Although not one of South Africa's largest rivers, it is of vital importance to the region, irrigating over 12,000 ha of farmland. This is most immediately obvious in the brilliant green citrus farms interspersed with vineyards. Marking the east of the valley are the stark and magnificent Cederberg Mountains.

Citrusdal → *Colour map 6, grid A5.*

As the name implies, this modern rural town is the centre of the local citrus industry, nestling in a valley filled with citrus farms. During spring, the air is heavy with the scent of orange blossom, and from May hundreds of thousands of oranges are packed up and exported. Even more striking is the town's setting at the southern edge of the Cederberg Mountains. Along with Clanwilliam, Citrusdal makes an ideal base for exploring the wilderness of the mountains, though there are no roads from Citrusdal into the Cederberg; from here you will have to continue along the N7 to the turning to Algeria. The **tourist office** ⓘ *39 Voortrekker St, T022-9213210, www.citrusdal.info*, is housed in a recently built example of a typical Sandveld dwelling.

Many of the surrounding farms are now growing grapes, and the region is known for its excellent Goue Valley wines. There is a **Goue Valley shop** ⓘ *Voortrekker St, near the tourist office, with sales and tastings, T022-9212233, www.gouevallei.co.za, Mon-Fri 0900-1700, Sat 0900-1230*, and tours can be arranged to the **Goede Hoop Citrus Co-op** ⓘ *T022-9212211, www.ghcitrus.com*, to see the packing of fruit.

Just out of town, by the turning for **The Baths** (see Sleeping, page 186), is **Craig Royston**, a historic building and one of the first in the area. It houses a small country **museum** ⓘ *T082-7349467, Mon-Fri 0900-1300, 1400-1630*, outlining local history, but its main appeal is as a farm stall offering good light meals and wine tasting.

The area was once home to huge elephant herds, giving the river its name, but these are sadly long gone.

Clanwilliam

» pp185-188. Colour map 6, grid A5.

Clanwilliam, lying at the northern edges of the Cederberg, is a peaceful agricultural centre and one of the oldest towns in South Africa. During the spring, the profusion of wild flowers that blanket the area attract a large number of visitors, many of whom travel up from Cape Town (240 km). Just off the N7, Clanwilliam is a good base for exploring the Cederberg, and more peaceful and picturesque than Citrusdal. **Clanwilliam Tourism Bureau** ⓘ *Main Rd, just to the left of the Old Jail, T027-4822024, www.clanwilliam.info, Mon-Fri 0830-1700, Sat 0830-1230 (longer hrs during flower season)*, is a very helpful and friendly office. Worth a visit, although for more detailed advice on hiking in the area, you'll have to go to the office in Algeria in the Cederberg Wilderness Area (see page 183).

Background

The entire area of the Cederberg was populated by nomadic San people for over 20,000 years, and a profusion of rock art bears testament to their presence and displacement from the area. The land was first settled by white farmers in 1726; Jan Dissels started one of the first farms here, building a homestead close to the wagon track route from Table Bay. At the time, this spot was referred to as *Aan de Renoster Hoek*, literally, 'By the Rhinoceros Corner'. Similar names in the region refer to *olifants* and *seekoei*, elephant and hippopotamus, providing further evidence of the wildlife that once roamed the area.

In 1808 a garrison was constructed to try to deal with the problem of cattle rustling by Khoi people. The hot and arid farming conditions further dissuaded families from settling here, and the first British settlers were in fact brought here by the British government to create a human buffer in a grand scheme to stabilize the border from further tribal incursions. Only six families remained and, when the village was renamed in 1814, there were only 16 families living in the area. The new name was given by Sir John Cradock, the Governor of the Cape, in honour of his father-in-law, the Earl of Clanwilliam. Despite being a strong Afrikaner region, the name has stuck.

Sights

The majority of South Africans come to Clanwilliam to make use of the sporting facilities on and around the beautifully situated **Clanwilliam Dam**, though there are a couple of sights worth seeing in town. The **Old Jail** ⓘ *Mon-Fri 0800-1300*, built in 1808, is a stocky white fort-like building overlooking the main street. The first part of the museum is devoted to the works of Clanwilliam's two famous residents: Dr P le Fras Nortier, who worked on citrus and the rooibos bush; and Louis Leipoldt, a well-known nature poet. There are also some displays on the rooibos (red bush) and cedar industries. At the back of the museum is an incredible giant threshing machine which was shipped out to South Africa in parts from Ipswich, England.

The road to the right of the old jail leads to the **Rooibos Tea Factory** ⓘ *T027-4822155*. The industry originally flourished during the Second World War when teas from the Far East were difficult to obtain in Europe. After the war the market collapsed, but in recent times it has grown in popularity since it is caffeine-free and low in tannin. Today it is the biggest industry in the area and the tea is a refreshing, if acquired, taste. For a cup of tea and a video show contact the factory. Further along the same road is the **Clanwilliam Dam Resort**, part of which is the **Ramskop Nature Reserve** ⓘ *T027-4822133, mid-Jul to Oct*, worth visiting in season to view its magnificent wild flowers in bloom, of which there are over 400 species.

Cederberg Wilderness Area

» pp185-188. Colour map 6, grid A5.

The Cederberg is famous for its rugged scenery, stunning rock formations and ancient rock art, all of which make it fantastic walking country. There are over 250 km of paths in the mountains, passing streams and waterfalls and bizarre mountain flora. The highest peaks are Snow Peak (2028 m) and Table Peak (1969 m), while the most notable sandstone features include the **Wolfberg Arch**, the **Maltese Cross**, the **Wolfberg Cracks**, **Lot's Wife**, the **Town Hall** and the **Valley of the Red Gods**.

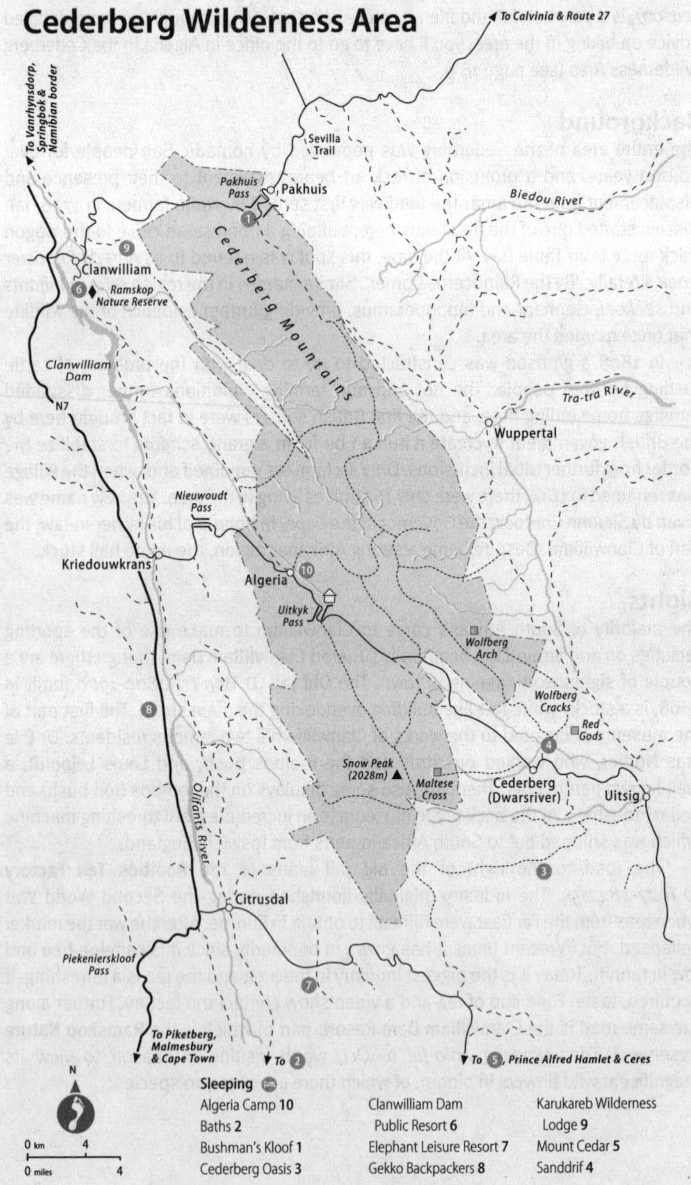

Ins and outs

Getting there and around All of the roads into the Cederberg Mountains are gravel, with steep and twisting sections, although some of the steeper parts have been covered with tarmac. The principal administrative centre for the wilderness is Algeria. Approaching from Citrusdal, the quickest route to Algeria is north along the N7; after 27 km take a right, signposted Kriedouwkrans and Algeria. You will cross the Olifants River via a low-level bridge and then descend into Algeria via Nieuwoudt Pass.

Best time to visit Climate is an important factor to bear in mind when planning a hike. During the summer months daytime temperatures are high, most streams and pools are dry, and you will need to carry plenty of water. Conversely, in the winter there can be heavy snowfalls, so you must carry the appropriate equipment. The best months for hiking are March to April and September to December. January and February are very hot and few people walk during these months; between June and August you can expect to encounter snow on the high ground.

Tourist information Cape Nature Conservation office ⓘ *Algeria, T027-4822812, www.capenature.org.za,* is the best source of information and issues hiking permits and maps. The region is divided into three areas and 50 people are allowed in each area per day, but you shouldn't have to book permits in advance, even in peak season.

Hiking

Beware of baboons stealing food at night from your camp.

As an officially declared wilderness, you are allowed to walk and camp anywhere in the mountains. There are, however, important rules to observe. No fires are allowed, so gas or paraffin stoves must be carried on overnight hikes. All waste material must be taken away – if you come across other people's rubbish, don't ignore it but carry it with you. Finally, while you are allowed to swim in the streams and pools, **do not wash with any form of soap** in the waters. The idea behind a wilderness is that the entire watershed is left to its own devices with minimal interference from man. There are few areas, even in South Africa, where you can wander so freely, so enjoy it and respect the rules. While there are recognized trails, these are not always easy to follow. Anyone planning a hike of more than one day should buy the excellent Cederberg map available at the Cape Nature Conservation office, and always carry a compass.

Warning There are 16 species of snake found in the mountains. Hikers may encounter a snake sunning itself on a path and although they are not aggressive it's best to wear strong hiking boots; also check your camp at night. The most harmful species are the puff adder and berg adder, both of which can be sluggish but are highly venomous.

Vegetation and wildlife

Although once covered in cedar trees, the vegetation that remains is predominantly mountain fynbos. There are few trees found along the major hikes – shade and shelter is usually provided by rock overhangs. In the wetter gullies and valleys you will find yellowwoods, hard pears and the Cape beech. The rare endemic snow protea, *Protea cryophila*, grows above the snowline. It is only found in a few locations but these are kept a secret. There are some photos of the flowers in the Clanwilliam museum.

The most common antelope found here include klipspringers, duiker and grey rhebok, but it is unlikely that you'll see any of these during a hike. Since 1988 there has been a programme to protect the leopard population, and apparently there are plenty in the mountains, although it is virtually impossible to see them. Due to the lack of vegetation at higher altitudes, the birdlife is not very varied, but look out for grey-wing francolin, Cape siskin, Cape sugarbird and victorin's warbler.

Cedar trees – long term conservation

The Cederberg mountains owe their name to the large stands of cedar trees that once covered the slopes. In a very short time this magnificent tree, *Widdringtonia cedarbergeensis*, has almost completely disappeared. These slow-growing trees were ruthlessly felled for telegraph poles and beams in houses. Records show that 7200 young trees were felled between Piketberg and Calvinia. In 1967 the removal of dead trees was halted, and other forms of exploitation ended in 1973. This is despite the fact that the first forester to oversee the region was appointed in 1876. Sadly, it seems the lessons have been learnt too late.

These days the area is an important target for conservationists. It will be difficult to restore the hills to their former forested glory as this slow-growing tree can live for over 800 years. The few cedar trees that remain are found above 1000 m, against cliffs and overhangs. Despite conservation efforts their numbers are still in decline. Unfortunately nature's way in the mountains results in fires, which now cause more damage than good, given the limited number of trees. Currently there is a programme of planting young trees in suitable places within the reserve, but it will take years before the success of such a project can be measured .

Rock art

The Cederberg is literally riddled with ancient San rock art, and peeking underneath a rocky ledge or in a cave will often reveal the faint markings of worn away images. Some of the better-preserved sites have become major tourist attractions, and seeing these ancient paintings in such a stunning setting is a real highlight.

One of the best ways of seeing a good selection of San art is by walking the **Sevilla Trail**, an 8-km hike on private land. The walk is fairly easy going and crosses a rocky plain, passing along a 4-km stretch of rocky overhangs, outcrops and caves. There are 10 sites in total, ranging from simple hand prints to extraordinary images of hunters, processions of women, running antelope and elephants. The highlight of the hike is Site Five, a rocky overhang covered with images in various stages of erosion, with a beautifully clear hunter carrying a bow, and a painting of a zebra foal, perfectly embodying its first uncertain steps. Even those with just a passing interest in San art will find this walk thoroughly absorbing. The stunning rock formations, silent bush and shimmering mountains add to the atmosphere. The trail begins at **Traveller's Rest Farm** ⓘ *34 km from Clanwilliam on Wupperthal Rd, over the Pakhuis Pass, T027-4821824, www.travellersrest.co.za*. Permits are issued at the farm and there are also two self-catering cottages. If your interest in rock art isn't satiated and you've got plenty of cash, spend a day or two at **Bushman's Kloof** (see Sleeping, page 186).

North of Cederberg » *pp185-188.*

Calvinia → *Colour map 6, grid A5.*

Although Calvinia is actually in the Northern Cape, it is relatively far from most sights in the north, and therefore usually visited as part of the Western Cape. It is a typical hot, sleepy Karoo town that most people just pass through, perhaps stopping for petrol and a cool drink. It has a beautiful setting though, at the foot of the Hantams Mountains. It's also an important sheep farming centre though, given the vast size of the farms, chances are you won't see any sheep. It also has clear star-filled skies at night 80% of the time, and attracts many South African astronomers.

Your first port of call should be Church Street where you'll find the **tourist office** ⓘ *T027-3418128, www.calvinia.co.za*, and the **Calvinia Museum** ⓘ *T027-3418500, Mon-Fri 0800-1300, 1400-1700, Sat 0800-1200*. The museum building was once a synagogue dating from 1920. As in many rural towns, the Jewish community has almost disappeared as Jewish families have moved to urban centres. The collection in the museum relates to the early history of the region, made up of photographs and farming implements. In the garden is a Class 24 steam locomotive from England and a horsemill. These are still in use on farms in the depths of the Karoo. Also in town is **Hantem House**, the oldest surviving building in town, which started life as a homestead in 1854 and today is a smart café and gift shop.

Vanrhynsdorp → *Colour map 6, grid A4.*

This town is known as the gateway to arid Namakwa region (see the Northern Cape chapter). North from here the countryside seems a thousand miles from the fertile Cape. The town is named after Petrus Benjamin van Rhyn, the first representative for Namaqualand to sit in the old Cape Legislative Council. Although the region was first visited by Pieter Crythoff in 1662 it was only settled in the 1740s. The town itself first took shape in 1887 with the building of a church. The **tourist office** ⓘ *T027-2191552, www.tourismvanrhynsdorp.co.za, Mon-Fri 0800-1230, 1500-1600, sometimes Sat in flower season*, is in the museum on Van Riebeeck Street, near the old jail.

The green-fingered may want to visit the **Kokerboom Succulent Nursery** ⓘ *74 Voortrekker St, T027-2191062, Mon-Fri 0800-1700, small entrance charge*, on the outskirts of town. Gardeners come here from afar, and it's worth a visit if you're here out of the flower season. It claims to be the largest such nursery for the distinct kokerboom (aloe) trees in South Africa. **Latsky Radio Museum** ⓘ *T027-2091032, Mon-Sat 0900-1200, 1400-1700*, is a private collection of over 200 domestic radios covering the period 1915-1965, close to the post office on Church Street.

Sleeping

Malmesbury *p179*

C Bergzicht, T022-4824274. B&B with 3 double rooms and 3 flats sleeping 2-4. Swimming pool, big farm breakfasts.

C-E Caravan & Chalet Park, Piketberg Rd, T022-4873266. Chalets sleeping 4-6 and shady caravan stands, laundry, telephone, swimming pool, a small, well-run site.

Moorreesburg *p179*

C Kolskoot Guest House, 10 km from the town centre, T022-4332528, www.kolskoot.com. This building was constructed during the Second World War by Italian POWs as a chicken coop. Today it has 6 en suite doubles, a family room, each decorated with rustic furniture and paintings by a local artist. Activities include mountain biking, horse riding and clay-pigeon shooting. Also has good-value backpacker accommodation. Recommended. Booking is essential.

C Samoa Hotel, Royal St, T022-4331201. Friendly rural hotel with comfortable a/c rooms, popular **De Kraal** restaurant with a good range of meals for a small town including blackboard specials and pizza oven, bar, swimming pool, secure parking.

Piketberg *p180*

B-C Dunn's Castle, T022-9132470, www.dunnscastle.co.za. Dunn's Castle was built in the 1890s for George Dunn and was designed by Sir Herbert Baker. 5 pretty double rooms in the castle with Victorian finishes, country decor, fireplaces and free standing bathtubs; self- catering cottages in the grounds, swimming pool, restaurant and bar.

Citrusdal *p180*

Plenty of farms in the region provide accommodation, convenient for hiking. Full lists are available from the tourist office.

B Elephant Leisure Resort, 7 km from Citrusdal in the shadow of the Cederberg Mountains, T021-9212884, www.elephantleisure.co.za. 10 well-equipped cottages on a private nature reserve with views of the valley and nearby dam. Each cottage sleeps

4, a/c, TV, fridge, cooking facilities including microwave, fireplace, braai area and veranda. Rather unusually each has a 4-seater jacuzzi and there's a swimming pool.

B-C Cederberg Lodge, 67 Voortrekker St, T022-9212221, www.cederberglodge.co.za. Family-run town hotel with 26 a/c rooms, TV with M-Net, swimming pool, full-size billiard table, gardens and gym. **Tangelo's** restaurant has a good reputation, mix of usual steaks with country cooking, pub with big-screen TV showing sports.

B-E The Baths, 18 km to the south of Citrusdal, the well-signposted turning is between the N7 and the town, T022-9218026, www.thebaths.co.za. A popular and long-established site at a natural hot water spring surrounded by citrus groves, the first resort was established here in 1739 and the main Victorian stone buildings survive. 16 well-equipped chalets, 12 flats and 15 camping pitches, all self-catering, shop on site but buy fresh groceries in Citrusdal, restaurant and bar, hot and cold swimming pools, tennis courts, mountain biking, hiking trails, individual spa baths/jacuzzis, all set in a tract of indigenous woodland. A lovely spot, recommended.

D-E Gekko Backpackers, 20 km north of Citrusdal on the N7, turning to left is signposted, T022-9213721, vism@mweb.co.za. Excellent backpacker lodge on a citrus farm. Double rooms, dorms, camping, brightly painted bathrooms, large kitchen, bar, meals on request, table-tennis room, small lounge, hammocks strung underneath trees for relaxing on the lawns. Access to swimming holes in river and added bonus of San rock art on the farm. Popular with overlanders, so can be lively, but usually very peaceful. Will pick up from the Intercape bus in Citrusdal by prior arrangement. Highly recommended.

Clanwilliam *p181*

A Karukareb Wilderness Lodge, 13 km from Clanwilliam in the Cederberg, T027-4821675, www.karukareb.co.za. 5 colonial-style rooms, very stylish with a/c, wooden floors, lovely restaurant and bar in a thatched *lapa*, swimming pool, lots of activities from hiking trails, horse riding and mountain biking. An excellent base to explore the Cederberg, but no children permitted.

B Strassberger's Hotel, Main St, T027-4821101, strassberger@lando.co.za. Friendly and homely family-run hotel, excellent as a base. Large comfortable rooms, en suite, a/c, TV, good restaurant and tea room, swimming pool, sauna, good value and excellent service. Recommended. The hotel has been owned by the same family for 50 years.

C Blommenberg, 1 Graafwater Rd, T027-4821851, blommenberg@clanwilliam.co.za. Comfortable set of 13 units, en suite, M-Net TV, breakfasts served, lovely gardens, braai areas, pool, hard to miss on the right-hand side just before town.

D-F Clanwilliam Dam Public Resort, 1 km out of town beside the dam, T027-4828000. Huge resort with 180 grassy caravan and tent stands on tiers up the hillside, modern but plain self-catering chalets, plenty of trees offering shade, electric and gas points, gets very busy and noisy in season when you should watch security. Out of season you should be able to turn up on the day and find space. No restaurant, bar or shop.

Cederberg Wilderness Area

p182, map p182

Outside Citrusdal and Clanwilliam are a host of private farms. The list includes those closest to the mountains. If you are self-catering, stock up in advance. Basic groceries can be bought at a shop just before Algeria.

L2 Bushman's Kloof, Wupperthal Rd over the Pakhuis Pass, central reservations, T021-6852598 (Cape Town), www.bushmanskloof.co.za. This private reserve claims to have the 'world's largest open-air art gallery', and it certainly is one of the best places to see San art in South Africa with over 130 sites, dating back as far as 10,000 years. Other activities include 4WD game drives, mountain biking and abseiling. Accommodation is in luxurious cottages and in the main building. All rooms are a/c, with en suite bathrooms, 4-poster beds, tasteful decor, log fires and wooden decks overlooking a lake. There are 4 swimming pools, sauna, beauty spa treatments, excellent restaurant with outdoor *boma*, gift shop, library, billiards room, and wine cellar. An overnight itinerary begins with check-in at 1400, followed by afternoon tea, an evening game drive and dinner; the next morning is an excursion to the rock art followed by lunch and check out at 1200.

Prices include all meals, game drives and tours but at almost R4000 per night for 2 people the experience does not come cheap; ask about specials Apr-Jun. Air and road transfers can be arranged from Cape Town.

A Mount Cedar, off the R303 halfway between Citrusdal and Ceres, better approached via Ceres, T023-3170113, www.mountcedar.co.za. 9 luxury self-catering cottages sleeping 4, with M-Net TV, ceiling fans, nicely decorated, carports, braai areas, wheelchair friendly. All next to a picturesque stream with good mountain views, B&B rates available, dinner extra, fishing and swimming in the farm river.

B-D Algeria Camp, run by **Cape Nature Conservation**, reservations through their Porterville office, T022-9312088, www.cape nature.org.za. Take the N7 27 km north of Citrusdal, turn right on Algeria Rd; it is 18 km to the camp on a dirt road. The camp is in a beautiful setting on the edge of a pine forest by a mountain stream and swimming hole. It is exceptionally clean, well run and very popular; book in advance especially for school holidays. Self-catering stone cottages sleep 4-8, all fully equipped, plus 48 shady camping spots, some with electric points.

5 km to the south of Algeria are 2 more cottages at the foot of Uitkyk Pass, sleeping 4-6. These are very basic, with solar electricity, although there is a gas-run fridge and stove, and hot water. You'll need to bring bedding, towels and extra candles with you. The helpful information office and camp reception is open 0730-1600; you must arrive before 1600 to collect keys for accommodation. It also issues hiking permits and maps for some of the longer trails in the Cederberg Mountains starting from the camp. There is a card and coin phone next to reception and firewood is available. Guests can swim in the nearby river. Note that accommodation is more expensive at the weekend and on public holidays.

B-D Sanddrif, 25 km south of Algeria, T027-4822827, info@cederbergwine.com. 15 chalets, a choice of standard self-catering chalets, luxury chalets or a grassy and shady campsite. The standard chalets have no shade but views of the mountains, and all are close to the river. 20 mins' walk downstream is Maalgat, an 8-m-deep pool popular with divers. There are power points at the campsite, and campers can use the deep freeze in the office at Dwarsriver. The farm sells fresh milk, butter and their own wine. The advantage of staying here is that you can easily visit the Maltese Cross, Wolfberg Cracks and the Wolfberg Arch on a day's walk from the camp without having to drive anywhere, and hiking permits are available from the office. Recommended.

D-E Cederberg Oasis 30 km south of Algeria, T027-4822819, www.cederberg oasis.co.za. A well-placed backpacker hostel for many of the major hikes, and is part of the Cederberg conservancy. Good value cottages, some with dorms, self-catering, camping, restaurant, bar, swimming pool and internet access. Maps and information available. A good friendly set-up.

Calvinia *p184*

B Hantem House, 44 Hoop St,T027-3411606, www.calvinia.co.za. Several converted Victorian houses in the village, with luxury en suite rooms, wooden floors, antique furniture, cosy traditional kitchens, full of old world charm and no TVs, the only modern amenities are the electric blankets on the beds. Overall very smart and of a high standard. Light meals can be arranged in the house kitchens or eat at the main restaurant at Hantem House (🍴). Restored 19th-century homestead, the best place to try traditional Karoo cuisine, excellent breakfasts. Recommended.

B-C Hantam Hotel, Kerk St, T027-3411512. A large solid building with great shady verandas, 16 en suite rooms with a/c or fans, **Busibee** restaurant serving predominantly steaks, bar popular with local farmers, the principal town hotel but with far less character than the Victorian houses above.

Vanrhynsdorp *p185*

B-C Namaqualand Country Lodge, Voortrekker St, T027-2191633, www.namaqua lodge.co.za. Some old rooms plus new rooms in block at back, comfortable TV lounge and open central courtyard decorated with wood carvings, used by tour groups, set menu in restaurant, small bar, swimming pool, smart external appearance let down by rooms.

C Lombards Guest House, 15 Commercial St, T027-2191424. 3 double rooms, 2 family rooms, all with en suite bathrooms, TV, non-smoking room available, lunch and dinner also available or self-catering is an option, nice old house, comfortable gardens, central. Recommended.

C **Vanrhyn Guest House**, Van Riebeeck St, T027-2191429, virons@marques.co.za. 11 comfortable en suite rooms, non-smoking, in a pleasant old Victorian 1-storey house in gardens full of trees.

Eating

Malmesbury *p179*

Die Herehuis, 1 Loedolf St, T022-4871771, 0730-1400, 1800-2100, closed Sun evening. Enormous choice on the à la carte menu, 4-course set menu at Sun lunchtime includes a local roast with fresh vegetables. Friendly service, garden setting, oil lamps and roaring fires in winter. Recommended.

Moorreesburg *p179*

De Kraal, Samoa Hotel, Royal St, T022-4331201. 1000-2200. Good-value country fare, with an extensive menu of steaks, pasta and pizza. Sun roasts are a grand affair, popular with the townsfolk after church.

Citrusdal *p180*

Hebron, on Piekenierskloof Pass, before you descend into the Citrusdal Valley, T022-9212595. Lovely terrace setting and good gourmet food for this remote location. Freshly ground coffee, homemade bread and rolls, fresh vegetables, chickpea stew or beef with couscous, and lots of sticky puddings.

Patrick's, 75 Voortrekker St, T022-9213062, 1230-1500, 1830-2200, closed Sun, and Mon lunch. Friendly restaurant with an Irish theme, excellent ostrich steak, also good grilled line fish and wide range of steaks, good value.

Clanwilliam *p181*

Olifantshuis Pizzeria, Main St, T027-9822301, closed Sun. Popular and informal pub serving steaks and good pizzas. Garden tables and friendly atmosphere.

Reinhold's, T027-4821101, Tue-Sat 1900-2100, smart à la carte opposite Strassberger's Hotel, dinner only, small bar and cosy atmosphere, good range of steaks, fish and pasta, the best option in the area.

Nancy's Tearoom, Main St, T027-4821101, daily 0900-1600. Coffee shop set in beautiful gardens. Good sandwiches and cakes.

Activities and tours

Citrusdal *p180*

Mountain biking

Goede Hoop Cooperative has plotted 11 trails in the district from 6-60 km; you will need your own bike. Some have very steep climbs while others are all downhill. Collect a leaflet from the tourist office. There is an annual Citrus festival mountain-bike rally each Sep. Respect the conditions laid down by the owners who have agreed to allow cycling on their farms.

Sky diving

Skydive Citrusdal, T021-4625666, www.skydive.co.za. Offers tandem jumps from 10,000 ft with a 35-second freefall for R1100, from a nearby farm.

Clanwilliam *p181*

Tour operators

Blue Yonder, T027-4821546, www.blueyonder.co.za. Adventure trips using 4WD and 'Xumbugs', small 4WD go-carts, into the Cederberg mountains.

Cederberg Travel, T027-4822444, info@cederberg.co.za. Day tours in the mountains, adventure trips, hikes, also organize trips from Cape Town.

Transport

Bus

Intercape, T0861-287287, www.intercape.co.za. There is a daily service in both directions between **Cape Town** and **Namibia** along the length of the N7. The bus stops in **Malmesbury** outside Malmesbury Motors, **Moorreesburg** outside Swartland Motors, **Citrusdal** outside Sonop Motors, **Clanwilliam** outide Cedar Inn, **Vanrhynsdorp** outside Turck's Garage at the junction with the N7, and then on to **Springbok** and **Windhoek**. There is another service between **Cape Town** and **Upington** – the bus turns off the N7 at **Calvinia** where it arrives and departs in the middle of the night.

Directory

Calvinia *p184*

Banks Standard, 21 Hoop St; ABSA, 25 Hoop St.

Breede River Valley

Only 310 km long, the Breede River (also known as the Breë, meaning 'broad') is one of the most important rivers in the Cape, and its valley is a beautiful boundary zone. Fed by streams from the mountains, the river is a major source of water for a large number of orchards and vineyards. Leaving the mountains behind at Ceres, the river passes through the Bontebok National Park and then flows across an undulating coastal terrace, meandering through the wheat fields of the Overberg before entering the Indian Ocean at St Sebastian Bay.

Worcester is the principal town of the region. Along the broad valley are important farming centres such as Ceres, Prince Alfred Hamlet, Ashton and Bonnievale and the picturesque villages of Tulbagh, McGregor and Montagu. These old settlements are surrounded by vineyards and fruit farms that undergo beautiful colour changes through the seasons. Behind the farms are mountains rising to 2000 m with challenging hiking trails and hidden valleys, their peaks capped with snow in the winter. The valley acts very much as the dividing line between two contrasting regions of South Africa. To the southwest are the verdant Winelands and populous Cape Town, both very fertile and prosperous districts. To the northeast is the start of the Karoo, a vast expanse of semi-desert, dotted with the odd sheep farm or isolated Victorian town. ▸▸ *For Sleeping, Eating and other listings, see pages 205-214.*

Ins and outs

Since the opening of the Huguenot Toll Tunnel in 1988 it has been possible to drive to Worcester from Cape Town in less than an hour. Worcester lies just to the south of the N1, and is the largest town in the Breede Valley. From here you can continue your journey in three different directions. Firstly, the main N1 highway continues for another 1300 km to Johannesburg. Locals regard this road as dull and something to be got over with as quickly as possible. The road passes through the southern margin of the Great Karoo, known as the Koup. While most people only pause here to refuel or stay overnight, this is a wonderful region to explore with a couple of beautiful Victorian towns as well as the superb Karoo National Park outside Beaufort West.

Heading north from Worcester along the R43, you quickly reach the N7 highway. The N7 is the main road between Cape Town and Namibia, running up the West Coast. This route will take you to the upper reaches of the Breede River Valley and the agricultural centres of Tulbagh and Ceres.

The final direction you could take when leaving Worcester is to follow the R60 along the Breede River Valley as far as Swellendam in the Overberg and then head east along the N2 highway to the Garden Route and Port Elizabeth.

The 3.9-km-long Huguenot tunnel reduces the journey through the mountains by 11 km. As you emerge on the Cape Town side, the road is perched high on a viaduct with superb views of Paarl Mountain, its hillsides covered with ordered vineyards – a sharp contrast to the countryside at the other end of the tunnel.

Worcester and around

▸▸ *pp205-214.*

Colour map 8, grid B1.

This medium-size farming centre is the capital of the Breede River Valley, a prosperous town with many interesting historic buildings and a fine collection of museums. The excellent Karoo National Botanical Garden is well worth visiting, particularly during the flowering months of August to October, and there's a wine route to explore.

Ins and outs

Tourist information Worcester Wine and Tourism ⓘ *23 Baring St, T023-3428710, www.worcestertourism.com, Mon-Fri 0800-1700, Sat 0830-1230*, provides a walking-tour booklet that can also be downloaded from the website.

Background

The first Europeans to settle in the region were farmers, and when it became necessary to build a settlement, their land had to be acquired. The streets were laid out and the first plots were sold in 1820; the new settlement was named after the Marquess of Worcester, the eldest brother of the Governor of the Cape, Lord Charles Somerset. One of the first buildings to emerge was the local *drostdy* (magistracy), which was one of the finest Cape buildings in South Africa. Today it is part of the Drostdy Technical High School. The wealth in the region is almost entirely derived from agriculture, a fact that is easy to appreciate while travelling past the numerous vineyards and orchards of the valley. Many of the neat farms visible from the roadside depend upon irrigated waters. The highly fertile neighbouring Hex River Valley is in effect the last of the productive Cape farmlands. In contrast, driving east from the valley one quickly comes to the dry and arid Karoo.

Sights

If time permits, a short walk around the centre is very pleasant. The main sights are central and close together, and the grid street pattern makes it easy to find your way about. There are some fine Victorian town buildings, although the main road is made up of mostly modern shops and fast food outlets. Many of the old buildings are along **Church Street**, most of which were built between 1840 and 1855. Also in Church Street is the **Congregational Church**, housing some fine original examples of wooden church furnishings and standing in a well-kept garden. The **Dutch Reformed Church** dates from 1832, a Gothic-style building which dominates the town skyline. Its spire has an interesting history: the original was considered to be too squat and was

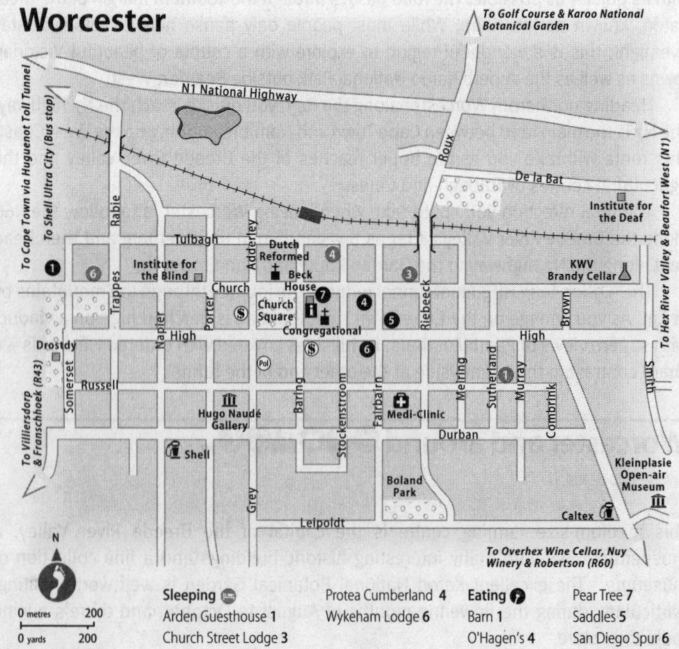

replaced by a cheap tin version in 1899. The current spire was built in 1927 after the tin one had twice been blown down by the summer gales from the southeast.

Next to Church Square is a **Garden of Remembrance** which contains some monuments commemorating local residents. It was designed by one of the town's more famous citizens, the artist Hugo Naudé. Each Saturday morning a **Flea Market** is held on Church Square. An interesting **Arts and Crafts Market** is also held once a month at 43 Russell Street, with some more unusual items on sale.

Worcester is well-known throughout South Africa as being the home of two important institutes for the disabled set up by the Dutch Reformed church. In 1881 an **Institute for the Blind** was opened, and a few years later an **Institute for the Deaf** was founded in De la Bat Street. Each institute has opened a shop in the town centre selling crafts made by members (see Shopping, page 213). The institutes are also open to visitors who wish to learn more about the pioneering work undertaken with blind and deaf people. Unlike most South African towns, the pedestrian crossings in Worcester emit sounds for the blind.

On the corner of Baring and Church streets is **Beck House** ⓘ *T023-3420936, Mon-Fri 0800-1230, 1400-1630, small entrance fee*, built in 1841 in typical Cape Dutch style. It has an interesting display depicting the town life of an important Worcester citizen, Cornelius Beck. There are some excellent examples of late 19th-century furnishings – the quality of the yellowwood and stinkwood furniture is regarded as some of the best in South Africa. Look out for the bath house, the delightful herb garden and the Cape cart in the old coach house. Today it is home to the **Pear Tree** restaurant and gift shop.

Another interesting house found nearby, at 23 Baring Street, is **Stofberg House,** now housing the tourist office. It is a slightly newer town house dating from 1920, with a full length veranda at the front. For many years this was the practice and home of a popular town dentist, Dr Stofberg.

The interesting **Hugo Naudé Gallery** ⓘ *113 Russell St, T023-3425802, Mon-Fri 0830-1630, Sat 0900-1200*, is home to a mixed collection of works by prominent South African artists. The first collection is of sculptures by Bill Davis, displayed in the garden. Inside are paintings by Jean Welz, Paul de Toit and Hugo Naudé. Hugo Naudé was a pioneer painter who also designed this large two-storey building and had it built as his home in 1904. He lived and worked here until his death in 1941.

The giant **KWV Brandy Cellar** ⓘ *T023-3420255, www.kwv-international.com, Mon-Fri 0800-1630 for tastings, guided tours of the distillery in English Mon-Fri at 1000 and 1400, tours in other languages organized on request*, on Church Street is the largest in the world under a single roof. There are 120 copper pot stills producing 10- and 20-year-old brandies.

There are 18 cooperative wine cellars, three wine estates, and several brandy distilleries in the Worcester region. KWV is the largest of its kind in the world.

Kleinplasie Open-air Museum

ⓘ *Robertson Rd, T023-3422225, www.kleinplasie.co.za, museum Mon-Sat 0900-1630, restaurant Mon-Sat 0900-1630, small entry fee.*

Kleinplasie is an open-air museum depicting the lifestyle of the early pioneer farmers. The collection is a series of old farm buildings, many with traditional skills on show such as tobacco rolling. There is also an indoor collection of smaller tools and implements as well as an excellent restaurant. Kleinplasie is also the home of **Worcester Winelands** ⓘ *T023-3428710, www.worcesterwinelands.co.za*, which is very helpful in giving information on the surrounding winelands, as well as offering tastings and sales of local wines. Allow at least two hours to look around all the exhibits. The first part of the display comprises 26 buildings which have been furnished or equipped in the styles of the period 1690-1900. Only the tobacco shed is an original structure,

Look out for the Braille labels on some of the local wine – these are the only Braille wine labels in the world.

dating from 1900; all the other buildings are reconstructions, but good ones. Several rural skills are demonstrated using traditional methods and tools. You can watch an ironmonger at work, or view the grinding of flour and baking of bread, plus cheese- and candle-making. Walking around the buildings gives one the feel of being on an old working farm: there are horses, cattle, pigs and geese in pens, not to mention all the farmyard smells and sounds. The second part of the collection is indoors and equally interesting. Most of the displays are of old farm implements and home industry pieces. All are clearly displayed and well labelled. A couple of items worth a closer look include the early example of a fruit grader, and a mean-looking self raker from the 1860s which was used in the wheat industry. The painted Voortrekker wagon near the entrance illustrates what the living conditions were like.

Beyond the outdoor section is a collection of buildings that can be viewed from a toy train which starts from close to the dipping kraal. Most of these buildings are from a rural village, including a post office, a general dealer and a cartwright's shop.

There is a craft shop at the entrance with a small selection of books. Just before the main entrance on the right is the **Kleinplasie Restaurant**. It is excellent value, serving fresh healthy meals. This is also a good place to sample local wines. There is a cheaper cafeteria inside the main building where snacks and cool drinks are sold. Behind the farm buildings is a picnic site.

Karoo National Botanical Garden

ⓘ *Off Roux St beyond the golf club on the north side of the N1, T023-3470785, www.nbi.ac.za, daily 0700-1800, small entry fee. Plant shop and tea garden.*

This garden, hidden away from the commercial centre of town, combines 144 ha of natural semi-desert plants and 10 ha of landscaped gardens filled with plants from similar arid regions within South Africa. The collection was originally started at Whitehill near Matjiesfontein in 1921, but moved to Worcester in 1946 to make the gardens more accessible to visitors from Cape Town.

Visiting during a time of year when many of the species are in flower allows you to appreciate how colourful deserts can be when it rains. August, September and October are good months to go, assuming the rains have been good. Stapelias bloom from the New Year through to mid-March, and June is the ideal period to see the exotic aloes in flower. In the formal gardens there are a few greenhouses which display a collection, world-famous among botanists, of stone plants, *conophytum*. Two common plants of the region to look out for are the Namibian wild grape, *Cyphostemma juttae*, and the Karoo bush, *Pteronia paniculata*. Given that the collection comprises over 400 species of flowering plants (*aloes, lampranthus, lithops, conophytum*) it is not surprising to find that the local birdlife is exceptionally rich. Over 70 species have been recorded in the gardens. There are also several short trails, including an excellent 1-km-long Braille Trail. Children will especially enjoy the porkwood plant maze.

Worcester wine route

There are 21 estates listed as part of the Worcester Wine Route. All are fairly local, and some of them offer tastings, tours and sales to visitors. Unlike many of the more visited wineries around Stellenbosch, most of the cellars here were founded in the 1940s – the farm buildings therefore lack much of the history and beauty found elsewhere. Furthermore, the countryside is not as dramatic as that around Paarl, and none of the cellars yet offers the excellent meals available on the Franschhoek Valley estates. That's not to say that the route is not worth visiting – one major advantage it has is that it is far less commercial than the Winelands and, by comparison, relatively tourist-free.

Listed below are some of the more interesting cellars. The **Worcester Winelands office** ⓘ *T023-3428710, www.worcesterwinelands.co.za*, is in the Kleinplasie Museum and is a good starting point. They can provide you with additional information on other members of the wine route and also offer tastings and sales of the area's best wines.

Botha Wine Cellar ⓘ *T023-3551740, sales and tastings: Mon-Fri 0730-1730, Sat 0900-1300, cellar tours: by prior arrangement, 20 km along the R43 towards Ceres.* This is a pleasant cooperative with a neat tasting centre beside a colourful rose garden. The cellar is known for its chardonnay, Hanepoort jerepiko and port. Several varieties are on sale including some dessert wines and very good grape juice.

Bergsig Estate ⓘ *T023-3551603, www.bergsig.co.za, sales and tastings: Mon-Fri 0800-1700, Sat 0900-1700, cellar tours and lunches: by prior arrangement, 40 km along the R43 towards Ceres.* This is the oldest estate in the region and Bergsig has belonged to the Lategan family for six generations – the first vine was planted in 1843. It is a friendly estate with some good off-dry and semi-sweet whites.

De Wet Kelder Wine Estate ⓘ *8 km north from Worcester along the N1 towards the Hex River Valley, T023-3412710, sales and tastings: Mon-Fri 0800-1700, Sat 0900-1200, cellar tours: Wed and Fri during the harvesting season, and by appointment only.* This is the one of oldest wine cellars in the Worcester region, founded in April 1946. Recently modernized, the cellar has produced the local champion wine for the past few years. They also produce a 'Heart Mark' wine, which is low in alcohol and calories. Most of their production is sent to wholesalers, but some of their semi-sweet whites, sweet muscadets and Hanepoort wines are available from the cellar.

Du Toitskloof Wine Cellar ⓘ *20 km from Worcester along the N1 towards Cape Town, T023-3491601, www.dutoitskloof.com, sales and tastings: Mon-Fri 0900-1800, Sat 0900-1700, cellar tours: Mon-Fri by appointment.* Some of the best award-winning local wines are produced here, on one of the most progressive estates in the country. It has a mixture of red wines, semi-sweet whites, dessert wines and grape juices.

Merwida Wine Cellar ⓘ *T023-3491144, www.merwida.com, sales and tastings: Mon-Fri 0830-1200, 1330-1730, cellar tours: by appointment, 10 km from Worcester off the road to Rawsonville.* Despite being a small and relatively young cellar, Merwida produces some excellent wines, including an award-winning ruby cabernet and an excellent white. Also has a luxurious guesthouse (see Sleeping page 206).

Nuy Winery ⓘ *T023-3470272, sales and tastings: Mon-Fri 0830-1630, Sat 0830-1230, no cellar tours, 22 km from Worcester along the R60 towards Robertson.* This excellent small cellar is well known for its award-winning dessert wines and is

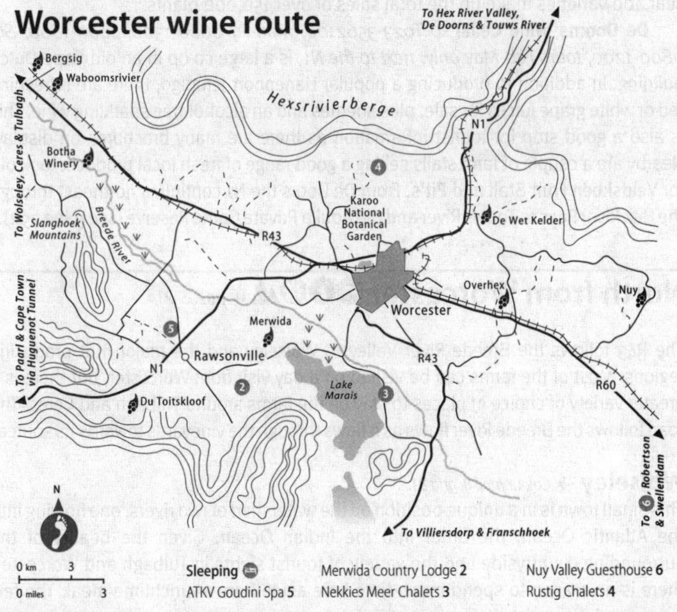

situated in the lee of the Langeberg Mountains. The office and shop are welcoming and there is a restaurant and guesthouse (see Sleeping page 206).

Overhex Wine Cellar ⓘ *T023-3475012, www.overhex.com, sales and tastings: Mon-Fri 0800-1700, cellar tours: by appointment, 6 km from Worcester along the Robertson Rd.* A smart, modern cellar, Overhex offers a range of wines from muscadets to sparkling whites plus some sweet grape juices.

Waboomsrivier Wine Cellar ⓘ *T023-3551730, sales and tastings: Mon-Fri 0800-1700, Sat 0800-1000, cellar tours: Mon-Fri, only by appointment, 25 km from Worcester on the Ceres road.* This cellar has a good tradition of wine makers. There are 47 members who farm from the banks of the Breede River to the slopes of the Mostertskop. Their whites include a chenin blanc, riesling, and Perlé. The reds on sale are a ruby cabernet, pinotage and cinsaut.

Hex River Valley → *Colour map 8, grid B1.*

No matter the time of year you visit, this is one of the most beautiful valleys in South Africa. Approaching from the arid landscapes of the east, this is the first glimpse one gets of the fertility and splendour of the Cape. The soils are naturally productive and this has for a long time been an important grape-growing region. Over 60 of the table wines grown for export originate from here, and there are an estimated eight million vines growing in the valley and on the mountain slopes. This multitude of vines provides a colourful backdrop: verdant green in summer, rich bronzes and reds in autumn, beautiful snow-capped peaks against the leafless plants in winter.

De Doorns → *Colour map 8, grid B1.*

Heading towards the interior, 32 km along the N1 from Worcester, is this small settlement lying in the centre of a major grape-producing region. The name is derived from a local thorn bush. Information is available from the **tourist office** ⓘ *Voortrekker St, T023-3562041, www.tourismdedoorns.co.za.*

Sonskyn Rose Garden ⓘ *T023-3568632*, essentially a nursery, is nonetheless a beautiful garden worth looking around and marvelling at for the variety of rose trees it holds, especially between October and May when the blooms are at their best. Every year 400 varieties make up the total sales of over 150,000 plants.

De Doorns Wine Cellar ⓘ *T023-3562100, Mon-Fri 0800-1300, 1400-1800, Sat 0800-1200, tours Feb-May only, next to the N1*, is a large co-op in an old Cape Dutch building. In addition to producing a popular Hanepoort Jerepigo, there are refreshing red or white grape juices for sale, plus sherries and an alcohol-free sparkling wine. This is also a good stop for tourist information as there are many brochures on display. Nearby are a couple of farm stalls selling a good range of fresh local produce; look out for **Veldskoen Fruit Stall** and **Pit's**. From De Doors the N1 continues northeast through the Hex River Pass to Touws River and the Aquila Private Game Reserve (see page 292).

North from Worcester » *pp205-214.*

The R43 follows the Breede River Valley to Wolseley and the major fruit producing regions. Most of the farms can be visited on a day visit from Worcester, but there is a greater variety of choice in places to stay on the farms around Tulbagh and Ceres. The road follows the Breede River flows as it flows through the vineyards towards its source.

Wolseley → *Colour map 8, grid B1.*

This small town is in a unique position on the watershed of two rivers, one flowing into the Atlantic Ocean, the other into the Indian Ocean. Given the beauty of the surrounding countryside and the variety of tourist sights in Tulbagh and Worcester, there is no reason to spend much time here aside from a lunchtime meal. The few interesting old buildings that had survived through time were destroyed in the same earthquake that caused much of the damage in Tulbagh in 1969. Local information can be found at www.wolseley.org.za.

Tulbagh

→ *Colour map 8, grid A/B1.*

Tucked away in the Tulbagh Valley, surrounded by the Winterhoekberg, Witsenberg and Saronsberg Mountains, is this small village with a beautifully preserved centre of traditional Cape buildings. Along with Swellendam in the Overberg, it rates as one of the best examples of a rural Victorian settlement in South Africa. Like Swellendam, however, the state of the buildings is somewhat artificial because much of the settlement was destroyed by a sudden earthquake on 29 September 1969. This was a significant local tragedy: nine people died and considerable damage was done to property. However, the earthquake gave way to the largest restoration project in South Africa's history. Many of the old buildings had been in a bad state of repair and some were practically derelict, but the village underwent heavy restoration and became the fine settlement you see today.

The original name of the valley was Land van Waveren, an outpost of the Dutch East India Company dating from 1699. In the early days of Dutch rule the western hinterland, stretching as far north as present day Piketberg and Porterville, was known as Waveren. The first settlers arrived in the valley on 31 July 1700 but it was another 40 years before permanent structures appeared and a village took shape. As with many settlements in the Cape, Tulbagh is named after a former Governor of the Cape (1751-1771), Ryk Tulbagh. Present day Tulbagh is a prosperous and peaceful settlement, isolated from Cape Town by several intervening mountain ranges. North of the town, the upper valley of the Little Berg River is a centre for some small wine estates and fruit farms. Sheep and wheat farming are also important to the local economy.

The **tourist office** ⓘ *4 Church St, T023-2301348, Mon-Fri 0900-1700, Sat 1000-1600, Sun 1100-1600*, is enthusiastic and friendly, with some interesting and useful leaflets covering the area. There is an attached restaurant and coffee shop with outdoor seating overlooking beautiful Church Street. The office is in one of the houses which is part of the museum; tickets for all the museum buildings are sold here.

Sights in the town The main attraction is the delightful tree-lined **Church Street**; 32 of its original buildings were restored after the earthquake, and the whole street feels like a living museum. The majority of the buildings are in private ownership, but three are part of the town museum (see below) and a couple have been converted into B&Bs. The old slave lodge is now the **Paddagang** ('frog passage') **Restaurant**, overlooking lush lawns. In complete contrast, the main commercial centre, Van der Stel Street, is a straight line of dull modern buildings saved by a colourful municipal garden.

If your time is short, the one place to visit in Tulbagh is the **Oude Kerk Volksmuseum** ⓘ *2 Church St, T023-2301041, Mon-Fri 0900-1700, Sat 0900-1600, Sun 1100-1600, small entrance charge*, which has one of the most interesting collections of Victorian furniture and objects in the Cape. The high ceiling and good light of the church makes it an ideal display case and it's a popular venue for weddings. There is also interesting information about the 1969 earthquake.

The **Town Museum** ⓘ *Mon-Fri 0900-1300, 1400-1700, Sat during the school holidays*, is housed in three different buildings in Church Street – numbers 4, 14 and 22. All are within walking distance of each other. At No 4 is an excellent photo display tracing the history of the houses in Tulbagh. There are pictures showing buildings before restoration and the earthquake damage, and the accompanying text lists the different families who lived there. Number 22 has been furnished with 19th-century items, while number 14 is now a guesthouse, restaurant and museum shop.

 Sights outside the town The **Old Drostdy Museum** ⓘ *T023-2300203, Mon-Sat 1000-1230, 1400-1630, Sun 1430-1630, small entrance charge*, is built on one of the early settler farms, Rietvlei, 4 km out of town. Designed by Louis Thibault, it has been restored and now houses a fine collection of sherry vats in the cellars, plus a museum devoted to antique furniture upstairs. Nearby are the Drostdy wine cellars where local wines and sherries are made (see below). The old Drostdy building appears on their wine labels. Their sherries can be tasted in the atmospheric, candle-lit cellars.

Wine route

This area is in fact better known for its fruit production – Ceres, the centre of the fruit industry, is only 35 km away. **Drostdy Wine Cellar** ⓘ *T023-2301086, sales and tastings: Mon-Fri 0830-1200, 1315-1700, Sat 0830-1200, cellar tours: Mon-Fri 1100 and 1500* (see above), is due north of the village, beyond the signs for Kliprivier Park. North of Tulbagh is **Theuniskraal Estate** ⓘ *T023-2300687, sales and tastings: Mon-Fri 0900-1700, Sat 1000-1200, tours by appointment only*, which has been in the hands of the Jordaan family since 1927. Their white wines have won several awards. Their Riesling, with John Platter's seal of approval, is highly acclaimed. **Twee Jonge Gezellen** ⓘ *take a left turn at the north end of Church St, T023-2300680, sales and tastings: Mon-Fri 0900-1600, Sat 1000-1400, cellar tours: Mon-Fri 1100 and*

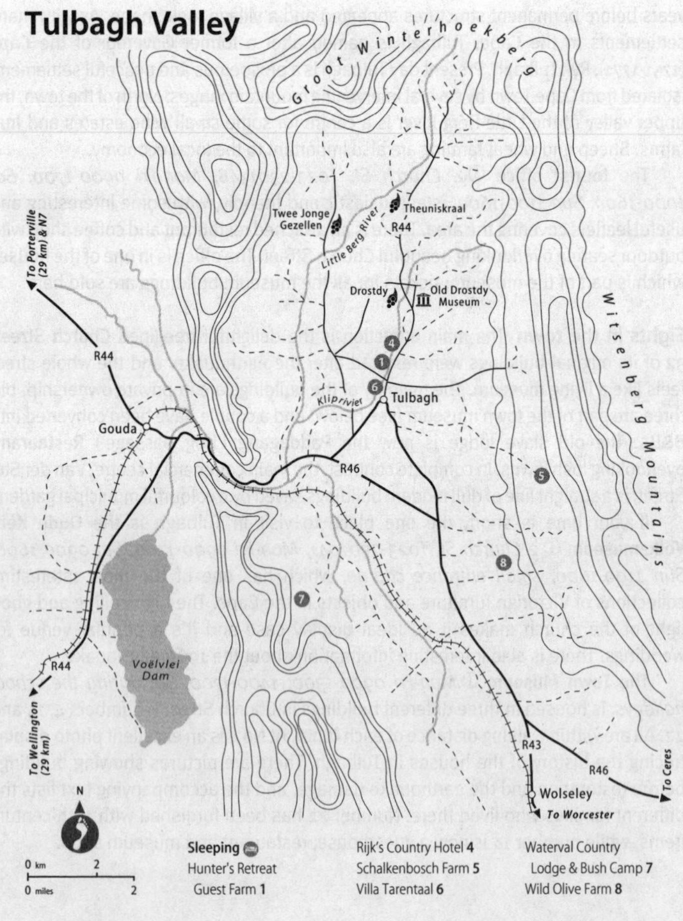

1500, Sat 1100, has the only underground champagne cellar in South Africa and there's a restaurant open during peak season. The tourist office can provide all the details of other estates in the valley.

Ceres → *Colour map 8, grid B1.*

Anyone travelling for some time in South Africa will undoubtedly try one of two brands of fruit juice – **Liquifruit** or **Ceres,** both of which are packed in Ceres. This is the most important fruit-growing centre in the country, and all types of soft fruits are grown and processed in the valley. Surrounded by the harsh and rugged Skurweberg Mountains, this attractive farming centre was founded in 1854 and aptly named after the Roman goddess of agriculture. During the winter months there can be heavy snowfalls in the mountains, enough at times for some limited winter sports. Snow is such a novelty in South Africa that when there is snow on the ground, curious Capetonians visit here in droves: cars line the country roads and the local farmers' fields are trampled by thousands of people. When the snows melt, the Dwars, Koekedouw and Titus rivers become the perfect environment for trout fishing. For information visit **Ceres Tourism** ⓘ *Owen St, T023-3161287, www.ceres.org.za* in the town library. They can arrange tours to fruit juice factories and working fruit farms.

One of the town's first magistrates, JA Munnik, was responsible for planting numerous trees around the town to provide shade. Fortunately, this tradition has been maintained and, as a result, there are plenty of mature trees lining the roads and the banks of the Dwars River, which flows through the town centre and the gardens of the **Belmont Hotel.**

Togryers' Museum (Transport Museum) ⓘ *8 Oranje St, T023-3122045, Mon-Fri 0830-1700, small entrance charge*, houses a fine collection of horse-drawn vehicles. All types of wagons and carriages are on show, celebrating the town's past importance as a centre for making these vehicles. Before the railways arrived, the fruit produced here had to be transported to the Cape in such wagons. Some excellent photographs capture the spirit of the time.

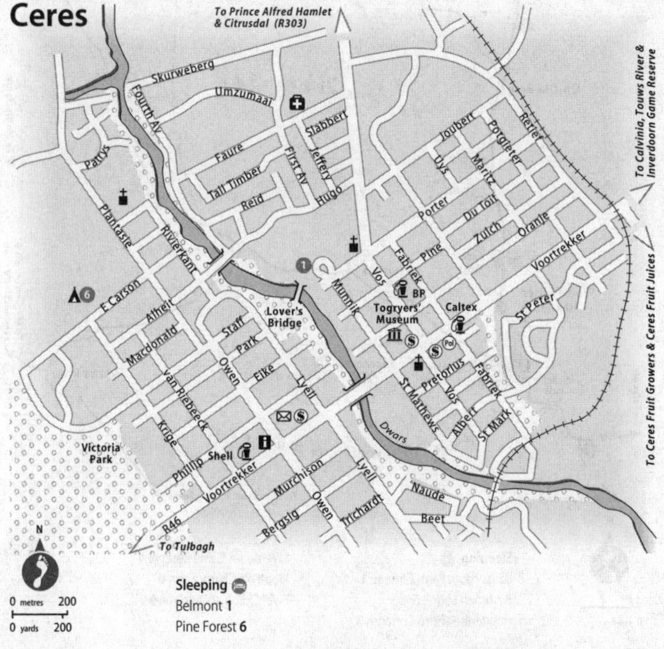

The following fruit packhouses and factories allow visitors to look around on tours – a sort of 'fruit route', if you like. It is surprisingly interesting to see how life starts for a peach or a potato that is going to end up on a local or even international supermarket shelf. Note that most of the factories insist on visitors wearing closed shoes and long trousers for hygiene purposes. **Ceres Fruit Growers (CFG)** is worth visiting to see its vast cold-storage facilities. This is one of the larger cooperatives specializing in deciduous fruits. **Ceres Fruit Juices (CFJ)** is home to the award-winning juices found on supermarket shelves around South Africa. **Ceres Potatoes** is a similar operation but with a crop of onions and potatoes. Tours run twice a week depending on demand but they must be booked in advance through **Ceres Tourism** (see page 197); two-hour tours cost R60 per person. During the fruit season, December to March, they can also organize tours to working fruit farms or drying yards in the Ceres region.

Prince Alfred Hamlet → *Colour map 8, grid B1.*

This small village is the second most important farming centre in the Warm Bokkeveld Valley. It was named after the second son of Queen Victoria, who was the first member of the British royal family to visit South Africa. In 1865 he went on a hunting expedition in this region. North from here the road skirts along the western fringes of the arid Karoo for over 100 km, without passing through any settlements of note. The farmlands in this area are very productive, so much so that a rail link was specially built from Ceres to transport fruits and vegetables. Apples, peaches, plums, nectarines and pears are grown in the valley, and the short drive north from Ceres

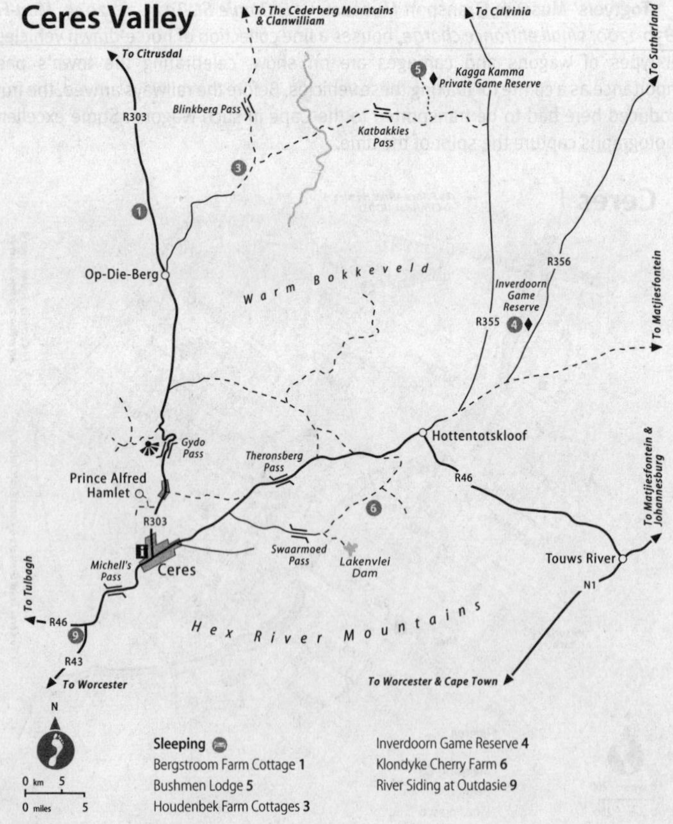

(R303) is particularly enjoyable during the spring when the orchards are in full blossom. Popular activities include fruit tours and trout fishing. Continuing north towards the Cederberg Mountains and Citrusdal, the road leaves the valley through **Gydo Pass**, R303. This is yet another pass built by Andrew Bain, this time while he was also working on the more important Michell's Pass. It was completed in 1848, and remained as a gravel road until the 1950s. The settlement is also the junction to the **Swartberg Pass** or R328 to 'The Hell', Oudtshoorn and the Cango Caves (see page 304). This is a good place to stop for a cool drink before climbing the scenic mountain pass. For local tourist information you're best off contacting the Ceres office, as Prince Alfred falls under their control.

Kagga Kamma Private Game Reserve

ⓘ *Off the R303 north of Prince Alfred Hamlet, T021-8724343, www.kaggakamma.co.za.*

Kagga Kamma Private Game Reserve is 90 minutes' drive from Ceres, on the fringe of the Cederberg Mountains. It is a nature reserve devoted to the history of the San people who lived here, the remarkable rocky landscape dotted with their ancient rock art. The reserve did have a resident San village within its boundaries, but the villagers have moved back to their ancestral lands in the Kalahari. They drop in periodically to sell traditional wares. The area is one of outstanding natural beauty and the best way of exploring it is on foot. Resident anthropologists accompany visitors to rock art sites to explain their meaning, and are also very knowledgeable about the traditions, lifestyle and beliefs of the San.

It is possible to go on game drives in the reserve, which has a good variety of antelope including eland, gemsbok, bontebok, springbok, and kudu. There are also lynx, caracal and leopard, but these are very elusive. If you're in a hurry and have money to burn, you can fly the 260 km from Cape Town in just 40 minutes. Access to the reserve is by overnight stays at the lodge (see Sleeping, page 208) or day trips can be arranged for R650. Visit the website for package deals.

Inverdoorn Game Reserve

ⓘ *T023-3161264, www.inverdoorn.com.*

Inverdoorn Game Reserve is 55 km from Ceres. Follow the R46 for Touws River and the N1. Take the R355 turning for Calvinia and almost immediately after join the R356 for Sutherland. The entrance is on the left. This is a private 3500-ha game reserve specializing in 4WD game safaris to view its range of wildlife, which includes rhino, buffalo, giraffe, zebra, wildebeest, eland, kudu and impala. A pair of lions and seven cheetahs have recently been introduced. The area is a typical Karoo landscape and quite beautiful to drive around. Other activities on offer include hikes to San rock art, birdwatching, fishing and mountain biking. There are a few options here: the first is a fully guided game drive for R330 per person, R460 with lunch. Alternatively, the overnight stays at the lodge also include one or two game drives (see page 208), or again, check out the website for packages.

South from Worcester » pp205-214.

As the Breede River meanders south from Worcester, the valley starts to broaden out and the level lands are given over to agriculture. As you drive along the R60 towards Robertson, the Langeberg mountains run parallel to the north. When the crops are maturing this is a beautiful drive through landscapes of contrasting colours. Along the roadside are farm shops selling fresh produce and several of the wine estates are open for wine tastings and sales. Both Worcester and Robertson have their own organized wine routes. After Robertson the R60 divides; the R317 runs close to the river as far as Bonnievale, while the R60 continues towards Ashton, Montagu and Swellendam.

Robertson → *Colour map 8, grid B2.*

This small, prosperous town has a vaguely time-warped feel to it, with tidy jacaranda-lined streets, orderly church squares and neat rose gardens. It is the centre of the largest area of irrigated vineyards in the Cape with over 20 wineries, many of which have won awards. The high quality dessert wines and liqueurs produced here have ensured the town's continued prosperity, as has the large brandy distillery. The town itself was founded in 1852 as a new parish to cope with the growing population of Swellendam further down the Breede River Valley. Conditions are ideal for agriculture as there is an abundant water supply from the Langeberg Mountains to the north and the Riviersonderend hills to the south. The lime-rich soil here provides good grazing for horses and there are a number of stud farms in the region. While there isn't a great deal to see in town, it is a pleasant place to spend a day exploring the sleepy centre and nearby vineyards. **Robertson Tourism Bureau** ⓘ *T023-6264437, www.robertsonr62.com, Mon-Fri 0900-1700, Sat and Sun 0900-1400*, is on the corner of Reitz and Voortrekker streets.

Ask about the Food and Wine festival held every Oct, worth stopping in for and an excellent chance to sample the region's varied fresh produce.

Robertson Museum ⓘ *50 Paul Kruger St, T023-6263681, Mon-Sat 0900-1200, free*, or 'Druids Lodge', remained in the hands of the same family for nearly 100 years. The original house was built circa 1860, only a few years after the grid pattern for the town had been first laid out. In 1883 the resident magistrate, Mr WHD English, bought the house and it remained the property of the family until 1976, when the last living member, Miss Violet English, died. The municipality bought the house and set up a museum. Most of the collection is devoted to the lives of William Henry Dutton English and his offspring, as well as the history of Robertson and the area. Of particular note is a beautiful collection of lace. Here you can pick up a useful guide for a historical walk around the village that takes in the villas built during the ostrich feather boom.

Robertson Valley wine route

ⓘ *Appointments are necessary for all cellar tours. None of the cooperatives are open for tastings or sales on Sun.*

This wine route follows the Breede River Valley and embraces the districts of Robertson, McGregor, Bonnievale and Ashton. In total there are 32 cooperatives and estates open

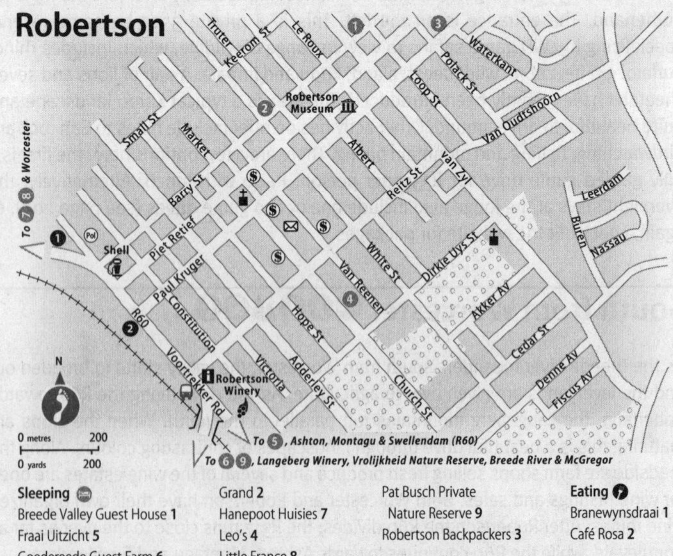

to the public. The greatest concentration of vineyards is found along the R317 as it follows the Breede River between Robertson and Bonnievale.

The region produces an excellent chardonnay and several good muscadets. Unlike the Stellenbosch and Franschhoek wine routes only a couple of the cellars have restaurants: **Fraai Uitzicht** in Klaasvoods East, and **Weltevrede Wine Estate**, off the R317 near Bonnievale. The former also happens to be the only estate that offers accommodation (see Sleeping page 209). Further details about the purchase of wines can be obtained from the **Robertson Valley Wine Route** ⓘ *T023-6263167, www.robertsonwinevalley.co.za.*

The Robertson Valley is home to 10% of South Africa's vineyards.

One of the most welcoming estates along the wine route is **Van Loveren** ⓘ *T023-6151505, www.vanloveren.co.za, Mon-Fri 0830-1700, Sat 0930-1500*. Try their Blanc de Noir wines. Tastings are conducted in a restored rondavel set in the middle of a colourful garden. Guests are allowed to taste the full range and someone is always close at hand to assist with any queries.

There are also some wine cellars closer to Robertson. **Langeberg** ⓘ *T023-6262212, Mon-Fri 0830-1800, Sat 0830-1300*, is a neat complex surrounded by vineyards with a few large shady trees between Robertson and the bridge over the Breede River on the McGregor road. This cellar is worth visiting if you are interested in tasting some local port and sherry. **Robertson** ⓘ *T023-6268017, www.robertsonwine.co.za, Mon-Thu 0800-1700, Fri 0800-1630, Sat 0900-1300*, is the oldest winery in the area. The shop and processing plant are located on Voortrekker Road. During the harvest time you can see tractor loads of grapes being delivered to the town.

Pat Busch Private Nature Reserve

ⓘ *15 km east of Robertson off the R60, T023-6262033, www.patbusch.co.za,*
This reserve encompasses 2000 ha of spectacular scenery in the foothills of the Langeberg Mountains. There is a 40-km network of circular walks which follow the kloofs between the hills. The highest point is Tafelberg at 742 m; a 2-km path leads to the summit. The vegetation consists of a mix of proteas and ericas, with lilies and ferns along the streams. This is an excellent spot for birdwatching. A few small antelope have been introduced, and 4WD trails are available for game watching.

McGregor → *Colour map 8, grid B2.*

This picturesque village lies off the beaten track in the lee of the Riviersonderend Mountains. The village is made up of a collection of perfectly preserved, whitewashed thatched cottages which radiate out from a **Dutch Reformed Church** which is in turn surrounded by a neat, colourful garden. Originally, McGregor was known as Lady Grey, after the wife of Sir George Grey, a former governor of the Cape Colony. In 1903 it was renamed, as there was another town in the province with the same name. The new name came from the Rev Andrew McGregor, a Scottish minister who had worked hard in the district during the formative years of the village.

The 25-km road from Robertson to McGregor has been surfaced for several years, which has encouraged more and more visitors. Today the village has a good choice of accommodation, as well as a range of shops and a couple of restaurants. In recent years, McGregor has attracted a creative population and there are a number of artists, potters and craftsmen living in the small cottages. The village surrounded by olive groves and vineyards remains far from spoilt, however, and is a beautiful, peaceful spot from which to explore the Breede River Valley. The **McGregor Tourism Bureau** ⓘ *T023-6251954, www.mcgregor.org.za, Mon-Fri 0900-1630, Sat 0900- 1300*, is housed between the municipal offices and the **Overdraught** pub on Voortrekker Street.

Dr Mary Cooke, a local historian, described McGregor as "easily the best-preserved and most complete example of mid-19th-century townscape in the Cape Province".

Boesmanskloof Trail

ⓘ *To23-625 1621. There is no official accommodation along the trail, and camping is not allowed. Follow the yellow footprints.*

This 16-km trail links McGregor with the village of **Greyton** on the northern side of the Riviersonderend Mountains. The path requires a reasonable level of fitness. In summer it's hot and you should carry drinking water. In winter, conditions are cold and wet. The trail follows forested valleys rich in protea and erica species. Antelope can sometimes be seen. In the spring this area is covered with a beautiful display of wild flowers.

Each direction can easily be completed in a day – the problem lies with transport. There is no easy way to travel quickly between the two towns. As hiking permits are only available from the **McGregor Tourism Office**, the logical option is to hike from McGregor to Greyton, stay overnight, and then hike back the next day. This is a popular trail and numbers are restricted to 50 people per day. It is advisable to book in advance during the local holidays. Rangers do patrol and check for permits.

Vorlijkheid Nature Reserve.

ⓘ *To23-6251621, www.capenature.org.za.*

Vorlijkheid Nature Reserve lies 15 km south of Robertson on the McGregor road. The landscape is rugged and strikingly scenic, with sandstone and underlying shale formations. Small mammals such as klipspringer, grysbok and springbok are fairly common, and if you are very lucky you may see a caracal, a type of wildcat. The terrain lends itself to raptors and there are often buzzards or goshawks circling the arid landscape during the summer months. Despite the fact that the reserve lies in an area a good distance to the west of the Karoo, many of the plants and trees are identical to those growing there. Grasses are scarce on the rocky lands, but there are plenty of succulents, and during September the land is covered with a colourful blanket of wild flowers, assuming the spring rains have been good enough.

Two hiking trails have been clearly marked out, known as the **Heron Trail** and the **Rooikat Trail**. The Heron trail is a simple 3-km walk to a couple of dams where there are some bird hides. Waterbirds can always be seen on the lakes. A rare attraction for enthusiastic herpetologists is the Robertson dwarf chameleon. The office at the gate has species lists and can help you with suggestions of what to look out for, and where. The Rooikat Trail is a much more strenuous 19 km and requires you to carry at least two litres of water per person (none is available en route). The terrain is rocky in parts and proper hiking boots should be worn. This is a circular walk through the Elandsberg Mountains, taking in a few peaks of over 500 m with views of the Langeberg and Riviersonderend Mountains. Allow at least eight hours. From November to March temperatures are high and precautions should be taken against sunstroke. Wear a hat and drink plenty of fluids before and during the walk. A pamphlet available at the gate contains a good scale map with contours shown, which will help you plan your day.

Bonnievale → *Colour map 8, grid B2.*

This small town is known for its wines and cheese, and is the site of the main Parmalat dairy factory, a brand that becomes very familiar to visitors in South Africa. The settlement was founded by one of the first farmers fully to appreciate the agricultural potential of the area, Christopher Rigg, who arrived in the valley and immediately set about building an ingenious system of canals to irrigate it. Most of the land is devoted to grape and wine production today, but you will also find several fruit orchards, including peaches, navel oranges, clementines and apricots. The **Bonnievale Tourism Office** ⓘ *Main St, To23-6163753, www.bonnievale.co.za, Mon-Fri 0800-1700*, is a well-organized and helpful office covering the whole Breede River region.

In the town itself the only real tourist attraction is the **Myrtle Rigg Memorial Church**, which is kept locked but keys can be obtained from the tourist office during working hours. This church has a rather sad story behind it. Two of the Rigg's children died when they were still very young, and their third child, Myrtle, died at the age of seven, in 1911. Before her untimely death, Myrtle asked that her parents build a small church to remember her by. This little Gothic-style building was constructed using the finest materials from around the world, including roof tiles from Italy, and a fine carved door from Zanzibar. It was consecrated in 1921, but fell quickly into disrepair after the Riggs' deaths. Fortunately the municipality saw fit to restore it in 1977, and today it is a museum. The **Parmalat cheese factory** ⓘ *T023- 6162100, factory tours hourly on the hour, Mon-Fri only*, is another legacy of Mr Rigg and today many Parmalat dairy products are found on South African supermarket shelves

The Parmalat cheese factory produces 40 tonnes of gouda and cheddar each day.

Bonnievale wine cellars

The following is a small selection of wine estates close to Bonnievale, open for tastings and purchases. They are all members of the Robertson Valley wine route (see page 200 for further details).

De Wetshof ⓘ *T023-6151853, www.dewetshof.co.za, Mon-Fri 0830-1630, cellar tours by prior arrangement*, a well-known export label, is a short drive from the town on the far side of the Breede River. This was the first registered wine estate in the region and is known for its excellent white wines, especially its award-winning chardonnay. **Langverwacht** ⓘ *T023-6162815, Mon-Fri 0800-1230, 1330-1700*, has good riesling and colombard. **Viljoensdrift** ⓘ *T023-6151901, Mon-Fri 1000-1700, Sat and Sun 1000- 1400*, is a relatively new member of the wine route which resumed producing wine after a 30-year gap. In addition to wine tastings you can enjoy a one-hour cruise on the raft *Uncle Ben*. **Weltevrede Estate** ⓘ *T023-6162141, Mon-Fri 0830-1700, Sat 0900-1530*, has a restaurant and self-catering cottages (see Sleeping and Eating pages 210 and 212)

Ashton and around → *Colour map 8, grid B2.*

The small settlement of Ashton is rather an odd place, dominated as it is by two major canning factories. Pass through here on a weekday, and it seems that the entire population of the town is dressed in either green or blue uniforms, depending upon which factory they work in. There is little of interest in town, although there are a couple of wine cooperatives. The **Tourism Bureau** ⓘ *Main Rd, T023-6142471, www.montagu-ashton.info, Mon-Fri 0800-1700*, is next door to a finely preserved steam locomotive built in 1919.

A large proportion of local wine production is handled by the **Ashton Wine Cooperative Wine Cellar** ⓘ *T023-6151135, sales and tastings: Mon-Fri 0800-1230, 1330-1700, Sat 0900-1300, guided tours by prior arrangement*, who are also well known for their excellent grape juice. If you are keen on your wines, the pleasant **Zandvleit Estate** ⓘ *T023-6151146, Mon-Fri 0900-1700, Sat 0930-1300*, on the banks of Cogmans River, is well worth a visit. Although the cellar's first wine, a shiraz, was initially produced as recently as 1975 it has won many prizes and is highly regarded in wine-producing circles. The estate has invested heavily in the latest techniques to help grow and produce quality wines. The estate house is a fine example of a traditional thatched Cape Dutch homestead.

The Montagu Market for crafts, food and collectables takes place on Saturday 0900-1300 on Bath Street, opposite the tourist office.

If you have taken the main road, the R60, between Robertson and Ashton you will pass **Sheilam Cactus Farm/Nursery** ⓘ *T083-6264133, www.sheilamnursery.com, small entry fee*, or 'Little Mexico', as it is now known, where you can admire some of the 3000 cactus plants and succulents. It rates itself as the biggest cactus nursery in the southern hemisphere. Plants and seeds can be bought here and sent back home.

Montagu and around → *Colour map 8, grid B2.*

Although Montagu is very much a Karoo town, it is usually visited by people exploring the Breede River Valley. It is 245 km from Oudtshoorn, the administrative centre for the Little Karoo, and only 15 minutes' drive from Ashton and the Breede River. It is a delightful place in a stunning setting, its long streets lined with oak trees and whitewashed Cape Dutch houses, sitting humbly beneath jagged mountain peaks. Founded in 1851, the settlement was named after John Montagu who, as the colonial secretary from 1843 to 1853, had been responsible for the first major road-building programme in the Cape. The greatly improved road network enabled previously remote settlements such as Montagu to thrive and grow. From its early days the region was recognized as ideal for fruit and wine production. The valley was fertile and the climate ideal for vines. In 1940 the Langeberg Co-op was formed, which proved to be the necessary boost for the local economy. Within 10 years, local production of apples and pears had doubled, while over a period of 16 years the wine produced increased by fivefold.

The exceptionally helpful and enthusiastic **Montagu Tourism Bureau** ⓘ *24 Bath St, T023-6142471, www.montagu-ashton.info, www.tourismmontagu.co.za, Mon-Fri 0800-1800, Sat 0900-1700, Sun 0930-1230, 1500-1700*, has several useful leaflets including one about the historic homes in the area (R10).

Joubert House ⓘ *25 Long St, T023-6141774, museum: Mon-Fri 0900-1300, 1400-1630, Sat 1030-1230, garden: Mon-Fri 0900-1300, 1400-1700, small entrance fee*, the oldest building in the town, is now part of the museum (housed further along Long Street). The house has a collection of late 19th-century furnishings and ornaments and part of the garden has been turned into an indigenous medicinal plant collection.

Long Street is a popular attraction, with 14 national monuments along its length. With so many well-preserved buildings, it is easy to get a vivid impression of how the settlement would have looked in its early days.

The **Centenary Nature Garden** ⓘ *Van Riebeeck St, T023-6142304, daily, small entrance fee, teas served on Tue and the first Sat of the month, May-Nov, the best time*

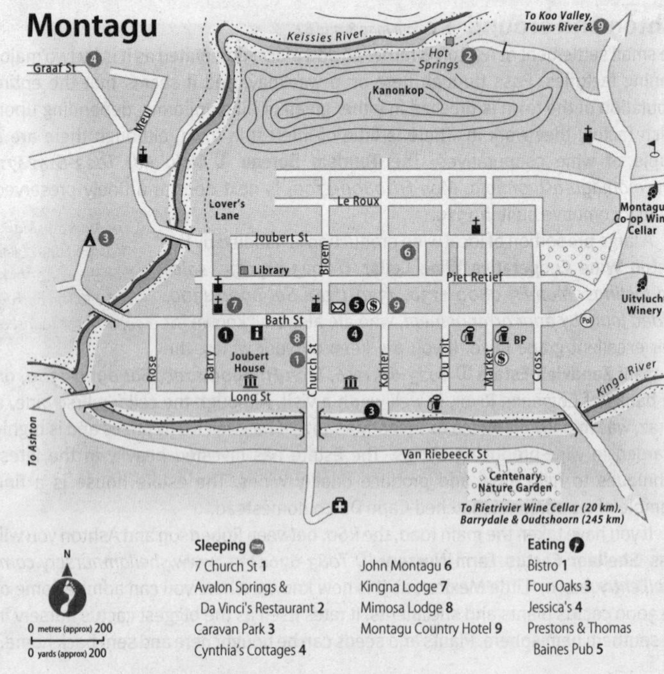

to visit is spring (Aug-Oct), on the south side of the Kinga River off Van Riebeeck Street, has the largest collection of *mesembryanthemums* in the country.

Just 3 km from the town centre are the hot mineral springs at the **Avalon Springs Resort**ⓘ *T023-6141150, R25, R18 child, see Sleeping page 211, for resort details*, which have been used for over 200 years for their healing powers. There are two indoor pools and five outdoor pools, all at different temperatures. At the weekends and holidays it gets very busy so try to go early in the morning or in the evening when it's cooler. The waters are radioactive and have a steady temperature of 43°C. In 1980 Montagu suffered a tragic setback when continued heavy rains in the Langeberg resulted in a flash flood down the Keisie River. It was a local catastrophe and 13 people were killed. The hotel was filled with several metres of sand and debris and the hot springs were covered with mud, but the town itself was barely touched.

Tractor ridesⓘ *contact the tourist office for reservations, T023-6142471, R50, R25 child, trips usually go Wed 1000 and Sat 0930 and 1400, wear warm clothes, to get there from Montagu, take the R318 towards Matroosberg, after 30 km the road descends the Burger Pass into the Koo Valley*, to the top of the Langeberg mountains are on offer from Neil Burger, a local farmer; the trip leaves from his farm in the **Koo Valley**. There are impressive views across the Karoo and down into the Breede River Valley from the summit. For an extra R50 you get an excellent meal of potjie, home-baked bread and a drink. Note that the tractor does not operate in October. It is also possible to do a 4WD trip around the farm and stay in their C-D self-catering cottages, T023-6143012, ideal for hikers.

Montagu wine route

The Montagu cellars are best-known for producing white wines with the muscadel grape, and tend to be fairly sweet, fortified dessert wines. There are several wineries in the district which can be visited for tastings and sales. Cellar tours are by appointment only. For further information visit www.kleinkaroowines.co.za.

Montagu Co-op Wine Cellarⓘ *T023-6141125, sales: Mon-Fri 0800-1230, 1330-1700, Sat 0900-1200*, is next to the golf course, heading out of town via Bath Street. **Rietrivier Wine Cellar**ⓘ *T023-6141705, sales: Mon-Thu 0800-1700, Fri 0800-1500*, is 20 km east of Montagu on the Barrydale road. **Uitvlucht Winery**ⓘ *T023-6141340, sales: Mon-Fri 0830-1730, Sat 0830-1330*, is just off the main road not far from the police station.

Sleeping

Worcester and around *p189, maps p190 and p193*

There are few hotels in the town itself; most of the private accommodation is on farms in the surrounding valleys. These are all very pleasant and in most cases good value.

Town centre

A-B **Protea Hotel Cumberland**, 2 Stockenstroom St, T023-3472641, www.cumberland.co.za. 55 comfortable a/c rooms, breakfast extra, smart à la carte **Gallery** restaurant, plus a daytime coffee shop and poolside cocktail bar, immaculate swimming pool, health complex including a gym, sauna, spa bath, squash courts and a tennis court. Check for special offers.

B **Church Street Lodge**, 36 Church St, T023-3425194, www.churchst.co.za. A modern guesthouse with 21 en suite bedrooms with extras such as coffee facilities, fridge and satellite TV. Swimming pool set in peaceful grounds with fountains.

C **Arden Guesthouse**, 57 Sutherland St, T023-3477899, ardenguesthouse@mweb.co.za. Pleasant family home with 4 comfortable rooms, English breakfasts served, meals on request, short walk to town.

C **Wykeham Lodge**, 168 Church St, T023-3473467, www.theguesthouse.ch. A pleasant B&B set in a lovely thatched 1835 homestead at the quieter end of Church St on the edge of town overlooking open parkland. 6 double rooms with en suite bathroom, TV, private balconies, secure off-street parking, restaurant, pretty gardens.

Out of town

A Merwida Country Lodge, 3 km from Rawsonville, 13 km from Worcester, T023-3491435, merwidalodge@worldonline.co.za. An elegant luxury lodge built in the style of an American colonial mansion, set on a wine estate. The façade is dominated by tall columns and a balcony. Inside, the reception hall contains a giant marble staircase that leads up to the bedrooms. Some suites have private balconies overlooking the mountains. Downstairs are 2 spacious lounges with open log fireplaces, a billiard room, restaurant, breakfast room and a pub. The back of the house opens onto a shaded terrace and crystal-clear swimming pool. The grounds are surrounded by vineyards and mountains. Booking essential. Recommended.

B-C Nekkies Meer Chalets, 4.5 km from Worcester on Lake Marais, T023-3432909. 14 self-catering log chalets built on stilts overlooking the lake, with 2 bedrooms and 2 bathrooms, fully equipped kitchen, balcony and fireplace, good for families.

B-D Nuy Valley Guest House, 19 km from town off the R60 towards Robertson, T023-3421258, www.nuyvallei.co.za. A large, well-kept guesthouse in an 1871 Cape Dutch building close to the river on a wine estate in the countryside. 27 en suite rooms, à la carte restaurant, self-catering kitchen, swimming pool, neat gardens with rose trees and ornamental ponds. A walk will take you to a refreshing waterfall. Call ahead to check if a wedding or conference is on. The wine cellar is nearby, with cheaper rooms for backpackers with shared bathrooms that work out very good value.

B-E ATKV Goudini Spa, 22 km from the town centre just off the N1 at Rawsonville, T023-3443013, www.atkv.org.za. A very popular family resort and warm mineral water spa. It has 154 fully equipped self-catering rondavels and duplex flats with 2-8 beds, 53 camping and caravan pitches, plus excellent facilities, outdoor pools, tennis courts, mini golf and jacuzzis, in beautiful setting in the lee of Slanghoek Mountains, surrounded by vineyards.

C-D Rustig Chalets, off the N1 close to the Brandwacht Mountains, T/F023-3427245. Good-value accommodation in 15 self-catering chalets in 3 categories with shaded timber balconies, self-catering lodge with 10 en suite rooms and TV lounge, camping and caravan sites with braai area and water, some electric points, laundry, swimming pool, shop and café.

Hex River Valley *p194*

Given the excellent choice of places to stay in the valley, De Doorns is usually only visited when driving through.

B-C De Vlei Country Inn, 5 km out of town on Voortrekker Rd, T023-3563281, devleicountryinn@telkomsa.net. A well-restored Cape Dutch coach house, peaceful location, 5 well-appointed double chalets with under-floor heating in pretty gardens surrounded by vines, good restaurant and bar, worth stopping for a meal here, French spoken.

C Arbeid Adelt Guest House, Voortrekker Rd, T023-3562204, arbeidadeltguest@telkomsa.net. Late 18th-century Victorian house on a grape farm, 7 double rooms, 3 en suite, B&B, dinner on request, tea garden with lawns and ornamental fountain, pretty veranda to take in the mountain views.

Wolseley *p194*

C Mill & Oaks, 7 km from Tulbagh, take the R46 and turn right onto the R43, T023-2310860, mill-oaks@lando.co.za. Double rooms with bathrooms and fireplaces, a peaceful country inn, best known for its restaurant that serves some beautifully presented food on a patio with mountain views, try the crème brûlée. A good lunch stop. Restaurant closed Mon.

Tulbagh *p195, map p196*

B De Oude Herberg, 6 Church St, T023-2300260, www.deoudeherberg.co.za. 4 en suite rooms with French windows onto the pretty veranda in a national monument Cape Dutch building, TV, ideal for walking to main town attractions, restaurant (closed

For an explanation of the sleeping and eating price codes used in this guide, see inside the front cover. Other relevant information is found in Essentials pages 42-47.

Mon), sheltered sunny courtyard, swimming pool, laundry service, can arrange sundowner trips to the mountains.

B **Tulbagh Country House**, 24 Church St, T023-2301171, www.tulbaghguesthouse.co.za. Delightful renovated 1809 Cape Dutch house, complete with thatched roof and neat flower garden. 5 attractive, comfortable en suite rooms with polished wood floors and antique furnishings, huge breakfasts are served up in an appealing dining room. Also acts as an art gallery. Perfect for a night in a historic Tulbagh home. Recommended.

C-E **Klipriver Park Holiday Resort**, Van der Stel St, T023-2300506. Large caravan park with excellent amenities, one of the prettiest in the Cape, also has 10 self-catering chalets with 2 bedrooms, hot water, electric points, shop, restaurant, swimming pool, set among trees close to river dam with fine mountain views, chalet prices lower out of season.

Out of town

Some of the rates are per cottage – if there are 4 or more of you staying, they are good value.

A-B **Rijk's Country Hotel**, Tulbagh, T023-2301006, www.rijks.co.za. Luxury development on a wine estate on the outskirts of town. 12 suites in a stunning thatched Cape-style house, 3 self-catering cottages, overlooking vineyards and a dam. Swimming pool, excellent restaurant, bar, extensive gardens, wine tasting and cellar tours. Recommended.

A-B **Schalkenbosch Farm**, 8 km east of Tulbagh in the lee of the Witsenberg Mountains, T023-2300654, www.schalkenbosch.co.za. Historic manor house (1792) on a wine farm, declared a national monument, 3 B&B rooms and 3 luxury self-catering cottages, swimming pool, billiard room, views across Tulbagh Valley, no young children.

B **Hunter's Retreat Guest Farm**, 2 km from Tulbagh, T023-2300582, esther@lando.co.za. On Ruimte farm, 4 en suite double rooms in an original labourer's cottage, shared lounge, plus 2 luxury suites with Victorian bathrooms, B&B, swimming pool surrounded by lawns and gardens. Ask about the aromatherapy, sauna and steam room.

B-C **Waterval Country Lodge & Bush Camp**, 8 km from Tulbagh, follow the R46 towards Wellington. A restored homestead on the edge of the Watervalsberg Hills, T023-2300807, www.waterval.co.za. There are a number of accommodation options here; 7 smart doubles with en suite bathrooms, communal lounge with a cosy log fire during winter months; 6 self-catering log cabins, or the bush camp has luxury tents of the highest standard, each with tiled floors, immaculate bathrooms, self-catering option or take your meals at the lodge, unimpeded views of Witsenberg Mountains, an exciting change from your average hotel room or guesthouse. Spring-fed swimming pool, dinner on request, peaceful location, no children, walk in the gardens and forested hills behind the house, a high-standard set-up. Recommended.

B-E **Wild Olive Farm**, 7 km south of Tulbagh turn-off on the R46, T023-2301160, www.wildolivefarm.com. 6 self-contained cottages, each with a different configuration, ranging from a basic room with hot plate to 2-bedroom cottage with kitchen, lounge, TV and fireplace. Also 10 caravan sites and 15 camping pitches with shared ablution block. The whole set-up is on a working farm with lovely mountain views. Firewood, fresh milk and eggs are provided, breakfast hampers can be ordered.

C **Villa Tarentaal**, 1 km from town, T023-2300868, mhunter@intekom.co.za. 2 attractive self-contained 2-bedroom cottages set on farm, open-plan kitchen, lounge, bathroom, veranda with beautiful mountain views, braai area. Professional beautician Christine offers aromatherapy massages, reflexology and facial treatments.

Ceres *p197, maps p197 and p198*

There is a surprisingly small choice of accommodation or restaurants within the town, but there are several excellent places in the surrounding countryside.

Town centre

B-C **Belmont Hotel**, Porter St, T023-3121150, www.belmonthotel.co.za. The main hotel in the district, old-fashioned and set in large grounds, characterful during season but distinctly spooky when quiet. 40 a/c rooms plus individual rondavels with 2 bedrooms and bathrooms. Neat, mature gardens, large outdoor pool, indoor pool with jacuzzi, tennis court, bar. 2 restaurants; **La Scala** with a full range of South African dishes and vegetarian menu, and **Pizza Nostra**, pasta and pizza, closed Sun and Mon evening.

D-E Pine Forest, Carson St, 1 km from town centre, T023-3161882, pineforest@ceres.co.za. Large caravan park with some self-catering rondavels, camping permitted on request. A well-organized municipal site in a great setting beneath towering pine trees, swimming pool, squash courts, mini golf, table tennis and pool table, boats can be hired on nearby dam, trout fishing. Book ahead during the school holidays.

Around Ceres

C Houdenbek Farm Cottages, 55 km from Ceres, follow the R303 towards Citrusdal up the Gydo Pass, take a right turn in the village of Op-Die-Berg (the road is surfaced as far as Sand River, but the last few kilometres are gravel), T023-3170748, sonja@morester.co.za. 2 fully equipped self-catering cottages sleeping 4, or B&B and evening meals available on week days. A beautiful and remote spot on the Môrester Estate, a working fruit and vegetable farm. Worth spending a few days here walking in the mountains, can also organize trout fishing and canoeing.

C Klondyke Cherry Farm, T023-3121521. 2 homely self-catering cottages sleeping 2 and 4 on farm with superb views of the mountains, camping also possible. Ideal for keen walkers, bass fishing in the farm dams, cherry picking mid-Nov to early Jan.

C-D River Siding at Outdasie, 9 km from Ceres on the R46 towards Tulbagh, T023-2310726, lidiag@mweb.co.za. Self-catering rondavel and cottage in beautiful setting right on the bank of the Breede River, both sleep 4, kitchen, bedding and towels provided, fireplace, 2 campsites. Recommended.

D Bergstroom Farm Cottage, 60 km from Ceres, off the Citrusdal Rd (R303), T023-3170628, jooschristae@lantic.net. Pleasant self-catering cottage in the mountains of the Koue Bokkeveld. Sleeps 6, kitchen, lounge, large fireplace. Good base for hiking trails, also possible to waterski in summer. Be prepared for snow in winter.

Prince Alfred Hamlet *p198*

There is only 1 hotel here, but there are several farms between here and Ceres that offer accommodation. See above for details.

C Hamlet Hotel, Voortrekker St, T023-3133070. Typical old town hotel, 6 spacious old-fashioned rooms, some with a/c or fans and coffee-making machines, bar and **Taylor's Grill** restaurant, permits and gate keys issued from the hotel to those wishing to go trout fishing on Lakenvlei Dam.

Kagga Kamma Private Game Reserve *p199*

L Bushmen Lodge, T021-8724343, (Cape Town), www.kaggakamma.co.za. 18 chalets built into caves in the rock, or free-standing. Voted one of the world's best honeymoon lodges, with stunning views over the landscape, a pool, open-air boma restaurant and bar, rates include all meals, game drives, a visit to the rock art, and sundowners at a 500-m-deep canyon.

Inverdoorn Game Reserve *p199*

L Luxury chalets, T023-3161264, www.inverdoorn.com. 5 a/c chalets with fireplace, plus 4 a/c luxury guest rooms, and a 100-year-old farmhouse with 2 bedrooms for families, all sumptuously decorated. Excellent restaurant on site serving French cuisine, several lounges, pool and deck, library, mini-gym, curio shop, all rates include meals and game drives, and there is a landing strip and helipad for those who want to arrive in style.

Robertson *p200, map p200*

Town centre

B-C The Grand, 68 Barry St, T023-6263272, www.grandhotel.co.za. Reasonable Victorian old-style town hotel on a corner of leafy White St. 9 double rooms with en suite bathrooms and TV. Good restaurant, bar, swimming pool, helpful staff. 4 cheaper rooms in the house next door.

C Breede Valley Guest House, 29 Loop St, T023-6265656, solomonv@lantic.net. A peaceful, restored Edwardian home with 6 double rooms with en suite bathrooms, TV, minibar, evening meals available on request. The rooms all have balconies with mountain views. Recommended.

C Leo's, 8 Church St, T023-6263911, leo@ripplesoft.co.za. Friendly guesthouse with 4 en suite rooms with TV, traditional furnishings, brass beds, big old-style baths, polished

wooden floors, TV, kettle, good breakfasts served, swimming pool, street can be noisy but it is a good location for the town's sights.
D-E Robertson Backpackers, 4 Dordrecht St, T023-6261280, www.robertsonbackpackers.co.za. Fairly new backpacker hostel in an old 1880s Victorian house, with pretty garden full of chill-out hammocks to enjoy the mountain views. Dorms and doubles with huge duvets or camping on the lawn. 3 meals a day or self-catering in the kitchen, can organize local activities including wine tours and boat trips on the Breede River. Will pick up from buses in town.

Out of town

L Fraai Uitzicht, 13 km from Robertson on the Ashton road, T023-6266156, www.fraaiuitzicht.com. Restored farm cottages on a wine estate, luxurious decor but rooms on the small side, decorated with embroidered linen and nice works of art, beautiful spot surrounded by orchards and vines, excellent award-winning restaurant (see Eating, page 212) that occasionally hosts live music. Several languages spoken.
C Hanepoot Huisies, 9 km from Robertson off the Worcester road, T023-6264139, www.hanepoothuisies.co.za. 3 restored old farm cottages set on a 190-ha farm, hidden away among vines and fruit trees. Each is self-catering and sleeps up to 5. Plenty of activities can be organized including boat trips and fishing. Recommended.
C Little France, 5 km from Robertson on the Worcester Rd, T023-6264174, ida@intekom.co.za. Attractive modern building with stylish furnishings, 5 en suite rooms, tasteful and comfortable with polished wooden floors, brass beds with bright white linen. Dining room, lounge, large pool and deck, good breakfasts served by pool or log fire in dining room, dinner on request. Recommended.
C Pat Busch Private Nature Reserve, 15 km from Robertson, off the R60 heading towards Ashton (see p201), T023-6262033, www.patbusch.co.za. Self-catering accommodation in 3 cottages, Peach, Fig and Oak, plus 2 simple farm houses located in the foothills of the Langeberg Mountains. There's a 40-km network of hiking trails to explore the streams and forested mountains, a peaceful spot to really get away from it all.
C-D Goedereede Guest Farm, T023-6264173, karlp@intekom.co.za. Converted farm buildings just out of town on a fruit farm through which the Breede River flows, 3 cottages with 2, 4, or 6 beds overlooking a picturesque dam, good farm breakfasts, TV lounge, self-catering, swimming, hiking.

McGregor *p201*

B Old Mill Lodge, Mill St, T023-6251841, www.oldmilllodge.co.za. This beautifully restored 1860s lodge is at the far end of the village among vineyards and fruit orchards. Accommodation in 4 cottages, each with 2 bedrooms and en suite bathrooms. The central building has a comfortable lounge with an open fireplace, much needed during the winter, and a bar and dining room looking out over the vineyard. Tucked away is a swimming pool and beauty treatments are on offer. Full board is excellent value given the quality of the evening meals that take on a French twist. There's an old watermill in the grounds. Recommended.
B-C Green Gables Country Inn, Voortrekker Rd, T023-6251626, grgables@telkomsa.net. A delightful old town house that was once a trading store. 8 en suite double rooms in the garden with separate entrances, B&B. Also has a splash pool, small lounge and good restaurant (see Eating page 212). Recommended.
C McGregor Country Cottages, Voortrekker St, T023-6251816, mcgregorcottages@mcgregor.org.za. 7 restored self-catering thatched cottages, communal lounge with TV, swimming pool, offers aromatherapy massages. Set in a mature garden with lush lawns and shady trees on edge of a 500-tree apricot orchard, just to the right as you enter the village.
C McGregor Country House, Voortrekker St, T023-6251656, mcgcountry@telkomsa.net. 3 double rooms and 1 family room with en suite facilities, shared TV lounge, swimming pool, decorated in a Georgian theme, good value. Located in the same building as the local pub, **The Overdraught**.
C Whipstock Guest Farm, T023-6251733, whipstock@netactive.co.za. 8 km from the village on the far side from the Robertson Rd. Choice of 4 cottages, each with a different style. Rietvlei cottage is the oldest building, sleeping 6. There is no electricity, but oil

lamps and candles help create a peaceful atmosphere in the evenings. Hot water for the bathroom comes from a gas geyser. Longlands is a Cape Georgian house tastefully furnished with rural antiques, sleeping 8. The Barn sleeps 6, and Winterfield Cottage can sleep 6, with en suite bathrooms. Excellent wholesome meals are available on request – don't miss the homemade bread. A good place to bring children as this is a working farm with plenty to see and do each day.

E **McGregor Camp Ground**, far end of Kerk St, T023-6251754. The old school building has been converted into a dorms aimed at school groups, but also open to backpackers. Also space for camping around the building. Enquire at the information office for details of further budget accommodation in the area. There is a selection of hikers' huts along the designated trails.

Bonnievale *p202*

There are several places to stay within the town centre, although staying on one of the many farms along the banks of the Breede River is more enjoyable. On most farms the river flows through the land, and there are often boats available for hire to explore this beautiful stretch as it winds its way through vineyards, orchards and stud farms.

A-C **Toy Cottages**, 6 km from town centre off R60, T023-6162735, www.toycottages.co.za. 3 a/c self-catering cottages with modern interiors, each can sleep up to 6 people so large price range depending on size of group, TV, fishing, canoe hire, set among vineyards right on the banks of the Breede River. A tranquil spot.

B **Kingfisher Cottages**, T/F023-6162636, kingfisher@lando.co.za. Choice of 3 self-contained cottages on the banks of the Breede River. Each cottage has its own private garden, a jetty and the free use of a boat, and the honeymoon cottage has a 4-poster bed. Lisa and Glenys provide a free bottle of wine on arrival. All meals available on request. Good value and a romantic retreat for couples. Recommended.

B-C **Bonnies B&B**, Van Zyl St, T023-6162251, www.bonniesb-b.co.za. 3 rooms with en suite bathrooms, M-Net TV, 2 of the rooms have patios leading into the garden. Evening meals available on request, healthy breakfasts served with freshly baked bread. Bicycles for hire, braai facilities. Good value. Run by Piet and Irena.

B-C **Weltevrede Wine Estate**, T023-6262073, www.weltevredegf.com. A beautiful and peaceful location on the wine estate 5 km to the east of the town; follow signs to Robertson. 6 self-catering cottages between the vines, fully equipped, sleeps 4, swimming pool, rose gardens, small art gallery selling work by local artists, estate restaurant open for lunch Mon-Fri, excellent value, evening meals on request.

C **Merwenstein Guest Farm**, 6 km from town centre off the Swellendam Rd, T028-6162806, www.merwenstein.co.za. An old fruit and vegetable farm with the Breede River running through, offering hearty homemade meals. 3 double rooms with en suite bathrooms, smart restaurant, swimming pool, birdwatching trips on the river. German spoken. Recommended.

D **Bonnievale Country Inn**, Main Rd, T023-6162155, bci@sdm.dorea.co.za. 5 very basic double rooms with en suite bathroom, 7 simple double rooms with shared bathroom, in a very tired motel-style concrete block, but the cheapest accommodation option in town. On the plus side huge breakfasts are served, and there's a reasonable steak restaurant attached and a swimming pool.

Montagu and around *p204, map p204*

Ask at the tourist office for details of budget accommodation suitable for hikers on surrounding farms.

A **Mimosa Lodge**, Church St, T023-6142351, www.mimosa.co.za. Excellent local hotel owned by a Swiss-German chef with 9 rooms (those upstairs have balconies), 3 suites, 3 guest lounges, library, very stylish decor, neat gardens, restaurant, bar, swimming pool. The restaurant menu reflects the wide variety of locally grown fresh produce, rates are half board. Recommended.

A-B **7 Church St**, T023-6141186, www.7churchstreet.co.za. Beautiful views from this stylish, friendly guesthouse, 1 large en suite family room and 3 garden suites with TV and extras such as embroidered linen and fresh flowers, exceptional views, large lounge, good English breakfast, rose and herb garden, off-road parking, swimming pool. Recommended.

A-B Avalon Springs, 3 km from town centre, Uitvlucht St, T023-6141150, www.avalonsprings.co.za. A well-developed resort centred on the hot springs including 30 self-catering apartments and 14 en suite hotel rooms, conference facilities and a health spa, 3 restaurants – **Da Vinci's** serves good pasta – bar, shops, several hot and cold swimming pools, jacuzzis and spa baths, gym and sauna, tennis courts. Comfortable and in a peaceful spot, but inconvenient for those wishing to explore the town. Check their website for out-of-season special rates.

A-B Kingna Lodge, 11 Bath St, T023-6141066, www.kingnalodge.co.za. 7 rooms in an 1898 Victorian house, some with private patio, TV, non-smoking lounge with collection of art and books, 5-course dinners on request served in an elegant black and gold dining room, swimming pool and jacuzzi in private gardens. Presidents Mandela and de Klerk both once stayed here. Recommended for its service and food.

A-B Montagu Country Hotel, 27 Bath St, T023-6143125, www.montagucountryhotel.co.za. A well-established central hotel in a 1920s art deco building, with 22 large rooms, a/c, TV, 4 suites, a smart dining room with open log fires during the winter, swimming pool, heated mineral pool, beauty treatments, secure parking. Recommended.

B The John Montagu, 30 Joubert St, T023-6141331, www.johnmontagu.co.za. 5 tastefully decorated rooms, antique furnishings, small pool and bar in the gardens at the back, off-street parking. The perfect place to relax after exploring the area. Recommended.

B-C Cynthia's Cottages, 3 Krom St, T023-6142760, www.cynthias-cottages.co.za. Delightful restored country cottages with thatched roofs. Brass beds add to the homely atmosphere. Suitable for 2-6 people, self-catering. Each with own garden and braai, some have fireplaces and outdoor spa.

D-E Caravan Park, west end of Bath St, across the Keissies River, T023-6143034. Camping and caravan sites, budget 4-bed log cabins with fridge and oven but shared ablution blocks, swimming pool, boating and fishing on the dam. Short walk into the town centre.

Eating

Worcester and around *p189, maps p190 and p193*

Surprisingly for a town with a reasonable population, Worcester has few restaurants, apart from the usual takeaways and family steakhouses; both **¥ Saddles**, T023-3427779, and the **¥ San Diego Spur**, T023-3423540, are on High St.

¥¥¥ The Pear Tree, 75 Church St, T023-3420947, Mon-Sat 0830-2300, Sun 0900-1600. A fairly new restaurant in the historic Beck House, fine dining and an excellent selection of Breede River wines. French country cooking and excellent service, intimate dining rooms with fireplaces or eat outside under the vines; very unusual dishes on the menu for a small South African town such as blue cheese, biltong and grilled pear salad. Recommended for a treat.

¥¥ The Barn, 170 Church St, T023-3428136. Sun and Mon 0900-1700, Tue-Fri 0900-late, Sat 0900-1400, 1830-late. There is an interesting collection of hand-blown glass objects here, with demonstrations by the master glass-blower, David Reede. The shop and restaurant are situated in a renovated wine cellar, unusual and delicious menu, such as mushroom filo parcels or butternut risotto, and lots of dishes using fresh herbs. A lighter and cheaper menu during the day.

¥¥ O'Hagen's, Church St, T023-3471698. An Irish-themed pub chain serving generous meals, steaks, pasta and hot stews, a meal here will fill you up for the day.

Wolseley *p194*

¥ Traders is an old-fashioned general store and coffee shop on the main road 1 km from Wolseley towards Worcester, selling local crafts and produce and serving good home-cooked meals. Try the refreshing homemade ginger beer.

Tulbagh *p288, map p196*

¥¥ Ballotina, 43 Church St, T023-2310427, dinner Tue-Sat summer, Fri-Sat winter, lunch Sun. Set in an 1817 building with red and white checked tablecloths this has an Italian edge where pasta lovers and vegetarians are well looked after. The Sun lunch is very popular; antipasti followed by a traditional carvery. The owner/chef is also an opera singer so be ready for some impromptu entertainment.

ΨΨ **Paddagang**, 23 Church St, T023-2300242, daily 0900-1630, Wed and Fri for dinner 1900. Good for late breakfasts, quality fresh Cape cuisine, the chocolate cake is to die for, selection of Tulbagh wines, set in well-kept tranquil gardens, very popular, well worth a visit, also conducts wine tastings of all the local wines. Recommended.

ΨΨ **Readers**, 12 Church St, T023-2300087, 1230-1500, 1900-2130, closed Tue. Quality home cooking in a pleasant old dining room in the oldest house in Tulbagh, decorated with colourful exhibits from the local art school. Varied and interesting menu with lots of tempting specials on the blackboard.

ΨΨ **Rijk's**, north of town at **Rijk's Country Hotel**, T023-2301006, 0730-1000, 1200-1400, 1900-2200. Very smart country hotel set on wine estate, excellent restaurant and wine cellar, the usual steaks, salads and pasta and more unusual offerings such as chicken stuffed with Camembert and pavlova, delicious food in a stylish environment, in summer you can pre-order picnics to enjoy on the lawns. Recommended.

Ψ **Shamrock & Thistle**, 22 Van der Stel St, T023-2300071. Daily 1100-late. Jovial traditional Irish pub and restaurant set in an old hotel, good home-cooked meals, popular local drinking hole with crackling fire, large range of malt whiskies.

Robertson *p200, map p200*

The town lacks a good choice of restaurants – only a handful are worth trying:

ΨΨΨ **Fraai Uitzicht**, Klaasvoods East, on the Ashton road, T023-6266156, 1200-late, closed Jun and Jul. Award-winning restaurant set on the historic wine estate in beautiful herb, bamboo and rose gardens. Very good food, choose the 6-course set menu with accompanying wines, or individual dishes such as salmon in champagne or desserts made from Belgian chocolate, good service.

ΨΨ **Branewynsdraai**, 1 Kromhout St, T023-6263202, Mon-Sat 1000-1600, Sun 1130-1530. Light meals at lunchtime with a good choice of wine, during summer you can sit outside in the neat gardens as long as the traffic is not too heavy – the restaurant is right next to the main road. In winter a blazing log fire greatly adds to the atmosphere.

ΨΨ **Grand Hotel**, 68 Barry St, T023-6263272. Exceptionally good food, popular carvery on Sun when all the townsfolk seem to eat out after church, good-value set-menu lunches, one of the best choices in town.

Ψ **Café Rosa**, Robertson Nursery, 9 Voortrekker Rd, T023-6262584, 0800-1730, closed Sun. Nice setting among the plants in the nursery, serving tea, coffee, wine, light lunches and homemade cakes, friendly service.

McGregor *p201*

The popularity of the village as a day-trip destination is reflected in the choice of a few good places to grab a meal or have afternoon teas in. Most overnight guests will take their evening meal at their guesthouse or self-cater.

ΨΨ **Green Gables**, at **Green Gables Country Inn**, Voortrekker St, T023-6251626, 0900-late. Popular family-run local restaurant serving light lunches and teas and good country fare such as roast dinners or cottage pie in the evenings. Eat in the cosy pub or on the candle-lit garden terrace. Recommended.

Ψ **Café Temenos**, corner of Bree and Voortrekker Sts, T023-6251115, Tue-Sun 0900-1630, for lunches and afternoon tea. Espresso, ciabatta, bruschetta, pasta, all things Italian, in a lovely garden setting with duck pond.

Ψ **Villagers**, corner of Tindall and Voortrekker Sts, T023-6251951, daily 0930-1700 except Sun. A typical all-purpose village shop selling curios and local crafts, as well as serving homemade food, fresh fruit juices including prune, pear and plum, and good cups of coffee in the garden or on the terrace.

Bonnievale *p202*

ΨΨ **Bonnievale Country Inn**, at the hotel, T023-6162155, 0700-0900, 1230-1400, 1830-2000. One of the most popular restaurants in the area, steakhouse and à la carte, plus a pub serving big English breakfasts and hearty lunches. Set menu in the evenings.

ΨΨ **Under the Vines**, at the **Weltevrede Wine Estate** on the R317, T023-6262073, www.weltevredegf.com. Tue-Sat 0900-1500. Pleasant country setting, wine available, daily blackboard specials, game pies, thick soups, salads and cheese platters.

Montagu and around *p204, map p204*
Montagu has a surprisingly large number of good restaurants, with a fine variation of cuisines – not just the usual steaks and pizzas. Opinions are divided over whether Jessica's or Prestons is the best place to eat. Both are excellent value.

ΨΨ **Four Oaks**, 46 Long St, T023-6142778, Tue-Fri 0830-1700, Sat-Sun 0900-1400. Good local cuisine and Mediterranean deli items in the historic setting of an 1855 farmhouse, lovely garden, 4 rooms next door (**C**).

ΨΨ **Jessica's**, 47 Bath St, T023-6141805, 1830-late, closed Sun during winter. A slightly off-beat place with bright pink walls and decorated with loads of pictures and ceramic statues of dogs. A good opportunity to sample the best of South African ingredients washed down with good local wines. Known for their rich creamy sauces, try ostrich with Amarula sauce and gooseberries. Recommended.

ΨΨ **Prestons & Thomas Baines Pub**, 17 Bath St, T023-6143013, daily 1030-1430, 1730-2200. Popular à la carte menu, tasteful decor with a small outside courtyard, friendly hosts. Try the Prestons Platter or the Karoo lamb, all served with excellent salads. The pub has a cosy wood bar and tables and outside terrace for warm days, stays open after the kitchen closes. Recommended.

ΨΨ **Wild Apricot**, at the **Montagu Country Hotel**, 27 Bath St, T023-6143125, 0730-2200. Excellent Sun lunch of roast meat and veg, traditional South African bobotie, cheeses and desserts. A la carte menu of local dishes such as tomato bredie and Karoo lamb chops, all set in the bright pink art deco hotel.

Ψ **The Bistro**, 20 Bath St, T023-6143108, 0900-1800, closed Tue. New daytime bistro and café, serving good snacks, sandwiches and salads. Internet access.

Bars and clubs

McGregor *p201*
Overdraught Pub, Voortrekker St, T023-6251656. A tiny, old-fashioned bar with an English pub feel that can only accommodate about a dozen people. Serves a selection of draught beers including Guinness and Caffery's imported from Ireland and a number of British bitters, but no food.

Festivals and events

Tulbagh *p195, map p196*
Sep The local **Agricultural Show** is held on the banks of the Kliprivier. This is the oldest of its kind in South Africa.
Oct The **Visual Arts Show** sees many of the historic houses on Church St open up as art and craft galleries.

Shopping

Worcester and around *p189, maps p190 and p193*
Curios
Blind Shop, 126 Church St. Furniture, woodwork and woven products made by the visually impaired and sold from this outlet. Visits to the workshop are possible.
Deaf Shop, De la Bat St. Handicrafts such as ceramics, cane work and art curios – some excellent pieces at very reasonable prices. Again it is possible to visit the workshop.

Activities and tours

Worcester *p189, map p190*
Canoeing
African Water Wanderers, based in nearby Rawsonville, T023-3491185, africanww@webmail.co.za. Full-day river rafting trips on the Breede River (Oct-Mar).

Golf
Worcester Golf Club, 3 km north of town across the N1, T023-3427482, www.worcestergolfclub.co.za. The club was founded in 1895. The present 18-hole course designed by the Gary Player Group is over 10 years old and has some large greens of tournament standard. The mountains are a perfect backdrop. The large modern club-house has good restaurant facilities.

Swimming
The **Cumberland Hotel** has a pool open to non-residents. The **municipal baths** are Olympic size.

Tulbagh *p195, map p196*
Horse riding
Vrolijkheid Farm, 8 km from the centre of Tulbagh, turn right off the Winterhoek Rd, T023-2300615, hauptfleisch@lando.co.za.

Horse trails must be booked in advance, outings last from 1 hr to 2 days; moonlight and sunset rides when conditions are right.

Mountain bike hire
Tulbagh Country House, T023-2301171, www.tulbaghguesthouse.co.za. Rents out mountain bikes and organizes trails on farms.

Robertson *p200, map p200*
Viljoensdrift, T023-6151901, www.viljoensdrift.co.za. Wine estate 12 km from Robertson on the Bonnievale road on the banks of the Breede River. Relaxed cruises on *Uncle Ben*, their river boat. You can pick up a picnic basket and a bottle of wine from their shop.

Bonnievale *p202*
Boat trips
The *Breede River Goose* a 2-storey pontoon with a tender boat for fishing, runs daily trips on the river, T023-6162175.

Montagu and around *p204, map p204*
Golf
Out of town, just before turning for the hot springs, 9 holes, T023-6141860. Need to take out temporary membership.

Mountain biking
Dusty Sprocket, Cottage Coffee Shop, 78 Bath St, T023-6141932. Bikes for hire and will direct you to 11 trails in the region.

Transport

Worcester and around *p189, map p190*
Worcester is 112 km from **Cape Town**, 60 km from **Ceres**, 50 km from **Paarl**, and 117 km from **Swellendam**.

Bus
All services arrive/depart from the Breede Valley Shell Ultra City on the N1 and the railway station. Each of the major long distance luxury bus services stop here as they head inland from the Cape to **Bloemfontein** (11 hrs), **Johannesburg** and **Pretoria** (16 hrs), but they do not offer good value for the 2-hr journey to/from **Cape Town**.

Greyhound, T012-3231154, www.greyhound.co.za. **Intercape**, T0861-287287, www.intercape.co.za. **Translux**, T021-7743333, www.translux.co.za.

Train
The station is off Tulbagh St to the north of the centre. Central reservations, T0860-008888, www.spoornet.co.za, timetables and fares are published on the website. To **Cape Town** (3 hrs) daily; to **Durban** (33 hrs) via **Bloemfontein** (20 hrs) and **Harrismith** (25 hrs); to **Pretoria** (24 hrs) daily via **Kimberley** (15 hrs) and **Johannesburg** (22 hrs).

Robertson *p200, map p200*
Robertson has surprisingly poor transport connections and at the time of writing was only accessible by Translux bus. 48 km to **Worcester**, 67 km to **Swellendam**.

Bus
Translux, T0861-5988282, www.translux.co.za. **Cape Town** (2 ½ hrs): daily, via **Worcester** (45 mins). **Port Elizabeth** (9 hrs) daily via **Swellendam** and the **Garden Route**.

Montagu and around *p204, map p204*
Bus
Translux buses stop here for an extended refreshment break at the Total Service Station on the R60, T0861-5988282, www.translux.co.za. **Cape Town** (3 hrs) daily via **Worcester** (1 hr). **Port Elizabeth** (9 hrs) daily via **Swellendam** and the **Garden Route**.

Directory

Worcester *p189, map p190*
Medical services Medi-Clinic, Russell St, T023- 3481500. **Useful telephone numbers** Ambulance, T10177; Police, T023-3471444.

Montagu and around *p204, map p204*
Banks Standard is on Market St and ABSA is on Bath St, both with ATMs. **Medical services** Hospital, Church St, T023-6141133.

Overberg and the Whale Coast

The evocatively named Whale Coast lives up to its title from July to November, when large numbers of whales seek out the sheltered bays along the coast for breeding. Whales can be seen close to the shore from False Bay all the way east to Mossel Bay, but by far the best place for whale spotting is Hermanus as the whales favour the sheltered Walker Bay, where daily sightings are guaranteed in August and September. Elsewhere along the coast there are opportunities to see the fearsome great white shark. There are seaside towns with miles of sandy beaches and rock pools, plus the southernmost point in South Africa, Cape Agulhas.

The most beautiful and exhilarating stretch of the coast is between Gordon's Bay and Hermanus, where the mountains plunge into the ocean forming a coastline of steep cliffs, sandy coves, dangerous headlands and natural harbours. This is an area of much beauty and also botanical significance and in 1998 it was the first UNESCO-declared Biosphere Reserve in southern Africa and is now known as the Kogelberg Nature Reserve. This route is often compared to the spectacular Chapman's Peak Drive on the Cape Peninsula, and rightly so. More than 120 ships have been wrecked along this coast (the first recorded wreck dates from 1673) – there are hazardous reefs, headlands and rocks all the way to Cape Infanta and the Breede River estuary. A museum in Bredasdorp traces the misfortunes of the wrecked ships. In addition to whale watching, this coast offers some of the best fishing in South Africa and an opportunity to dive historic shipwrecks. » *For Sleeping, Eating and other listings, see pages 227-235.*

Gordon's Bay to Hermanus » *pp227-235.*

Gordon's Bay, Rooiels and Pringle Bay → *Colour map 8, grid A2-B3.*

Set in the lee of the Hottentots Holland Mountains at the eastern end of False Bay, away from the more glamorous beaches of Cape Town, is the popular family seaside resort of Gordon's Bay. There are two sandy beaches, **Bikini** and **Main**, both of which

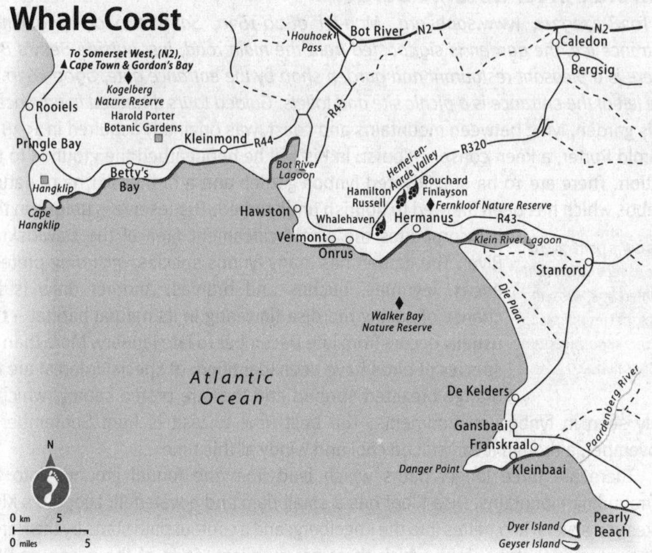

are safe for swimmers. The rocky shoreline, a short walk from the seafront, is popular for fishing. The most likely catch includes mackerel, steenbras and kabeljou. The beach road is lined with a number of seafood restaurants and this is a popular lunch spot at the weekends for people from Cape Town.

Following the R44 south, the first small coastal resort after Gordon's Bay is **Rooiels** (19 km), a cluster of holiday homes at the mouth of a small river. The beach has a strong backwash, so be wary if children are swimming. Continuing towards Hermanus, the road leaves its precipitous course and climbs the hills inland. After 5 km turn right to **Pringle Bay**, which is dominated by a large rock outcrop known as the Hangklip, 454 m. This is the rock you see when standing by the lighthouse at Cape Point looking across False Bay. The gravel loop road around **Cape Hangklip** is a scenic distraction; another track leads to Hangklip. The road rejoins the R44 just before Silver Sands.

Betty's Bay → *Colour map 8, grid A3.*

This small holiday village, midway between Strand and Hermanus, is known for its penguin colony and botanical garden. The community was named after Betty Youlden, the daughter of a local businessman who had plans to develop the Cape Hangklip area in the 1930s. Fortunately little came of the idea and today the village remains an untidy collection of holiday homes in a beautiful location. At Stoney Point there is a **reserve** ⓘ *R5, 0900-1700*, to protect a small breeding colony of African jackass penguins, one of the few places where you are guaranteed to see these birds breeding on the mainland. A boardwalk has recently been constructed to allow visitors good views of the penguins without disturbing them. Also here are the remains of a whaling station plus the hulk of a whaler, the *Balena*. The village has recently been given a grant to turn the station into an information centre about the penguins. Behind the village are the well-known **Harold Porter Botanic Gardens**, worth a visit if time permits. Along the main beach is another area of protected land, the **HF Verwoerd Coastal Reserve**. There is safe swimming close to the kelp beds, and the dunes above Silver Sands are a popular spot for sandboarding. For sandboarding operators, see Cape Town chapter, page 127.

Jackass penguins mate for life and return to t he same nest each year to breed.

Harold Porter Botanic Gardens

ⓘ *T028-2729311, www.sanbi.org, Mon-Fri 0800-1630, Sat-Sun 0800-1700, small entrance fee, the garden is signposted from the main road, just outside Betty's Bay. There is a pleasant restaurant and garden shop by the entrance gate, 0900-1630. To the left of the entrance is a picnic site and toilets. Guided tours arranged in advance.*

This garden, lying between mountains and coast, was originally acquired in 1938 by Harold Porter, a keen conservationist. In his will he bequeathed the grounds to the nation. There are 10 ha of cultivated fynbos garden and a further 191 ha of natural fynbos which has been allowed to flourish undisturbed. The reserve is unique in that it incorporates the whole catchment area of the Dawidskraal River. The garden has many fynbos species, including proteas, ericas, legumes, buchus and brunias. Another draw is the chance of seeing red disa flowering in its natural habitat – this usually occurs from late December to late January. More than 88 species of birds have been identified; of special interest are the orange breasted sunbird and the rare protea canary, which is only seen in fynbos environments. The best time to visit is from September to November, although it can still be cool and windy at this time

Fynbos is the term given to a type of vegetation that is dominated by shrubs and comprises species unique to South Africa's southwestern and southern Cape.

There are three longer paths which lead from the formal grounds into the surrounding mountains. Disa Kloof has a small dam and a waterfall; Leopard's Kloof takes you several kilometres into the Kogelberg; and a contour path starts by the Harold Porter memorial stone, from which there are excellent views of the ocean and the gardens. Fire prevention is an important issue, especially from January to March when the terrain is dry and the wind prevails from the southeast. Fynbos contains resin and oils which are highly flammable.

Kleinmond, Vermont and Onrus → *Colour map 8, grid A/B3.*

Kleinmond is a popular summer resort in Sandown Bay that has been frequented by the wheat farmers of the interior since 1861 and is today a sizeable resort. The name Kleinmond refers to the 'small mouth' of the Bot River lagoon. The settlement is overlooked by the magnificent Kogelberg Mountains which in the spring are full of flowering proteas. Information is available from the helpful **Hangklip-Kleinmond Bureau** ⓘ *signposted, just off the R44, T028-2715657, www.ecoscape.org.za, Mon-Fri 0800-1700, Sat 0800-1300.* The recently developed Harbour Road area has an intriguing collection of shops. To the east of the town is the Bot River Lagoon, a popular sailing and canoeing area. Where the Bot River meets the sea is a large marsh which is home to thousands of waterfowl. This is a birdwatchers' paradise, especially at low tide. The more common species are spoonbills, herons, pelicans, gulls, terns, kingfishers and geese. There is also a small herd of wild horses that roam the marshlands; after several attempts to cull them in the 1950s they are now protected.

After Kleinmond the R44 joins the R43, which then continues along the coast to the next sizeable settlements of **Vermont** and **Onrus**, these days more or less suburbs of Hermanus, before arriving in Hermanus proper. Vermont, named after the American state, was founded by CJ Krige who became the first speaker of the South African parliament. The beach here is sheltered by high dunes and is safe for children. Onrus, meaning 'restless', lying on the east bank of the mouth of the Onrus River, was named by the first European settlers because of the perpetual noise made by the waves along the rocky coastline. The Onrus River forms a small lagoon with a short sandy beach which is safe for children to swim from. The beach is also popular with surfers.

Exercise caution when swimming at Kleinmond as the sandy beach is steep; children should be watched at all times.

Hermanus and around » pp227-235.

Colour map 8, grid B3.

Hermanus has grown from a rustic fishing village to a much-visited tourist resort famed for its superb whale watching. It is the self-proclaimed world's best land-based whale watching site, and indeed Walker Bay is host to impressive numbers during the calving season (July to November). However, don't expect any private viewings – Hermanus is very popular and has a steady flow of binocular-clutching visitors throughout the year. While this means it can get very busy, there is also a good range of accommodation and restaurants, making it a great base for exploring the quieter reaches of the Overberg and, while you may find it far too crowded at Christmas, at other times it reverts to its small-town calm. Alternatively, Hermanus is only a few hours from Cape Town, making it an easy day trip from the city. The **Greater Hermanus Tourism Bureau** ⓘ *Old Station Building, Mitchell St, T028-3122629, www.hermanus.co.za, Mon-Fri 0800-1800, Sat 0900-1700, Sun 0900-1500 (shorter hours in winter)*, is extremely helpful and has lots of information on the surrounding area, plus an accommodation booking service.

Background

The town is named after Hermanus Pieters, an old soldier who set up camp in the bay while looking for better pastures for his animals during the hot summer months. The presence of a freshwater spring persuaded him to spend the whole summer here. Soon other farmers arrived with their families from the interior. Almost by accident it became a holiday destination – the herds required little attention, so the men turned their attention to fishing while the women and children set about enjoying themselves on the sandy beaches. When the farmers returned inland to the winter pastures, it was the fishermen who remained and settled here.

In the 1920s the town gained a reputation as an excellent location for convalescing, and even doctors from Harley Street in London were recommending the 'champagne air' of Hermanus. As it became popular with the gentry, so suitably smart hotels were built to accommodate them. After the Second World War the construction of a new harbour stimulated the expansion of the fishing industry and there are now three canning factories in Walker Bay.

Sights

The **Old Harbour** is a national monument and a focal point for tourist activities. A ramp leads down the cliff to the attractive old jetty and a group of restored fishermen's cottages, including the **museum** ⓘ *T028-3121475, Mon-Sat 0900-1300, 1400-1700, small entry fee.* The displays are based on the local fishing industry and include models of fish, a whale skeleton, some shark jaws, fish tanks and early fishing equipment. One of the most interesting features is the recordings of calls between whales. There is also a telescope to watch the whales further out. An information plaque helps identify what you see. Outside the museum on the harbour ramp is a collection of small restored fishing boats, the earliest dating from 1855. Also on show are the drying racks for small fish and cement tables which were once used for gutting fish.

The **De Wet's Huis Photo Museum** ⓘ *Market Sq, T028-3122629, Mon-Fri 0900-1300, 1400-1700, Sat 0800-1300, 1400-1600, R3*, houses an interesting collection of photography depicting the historical development of Hermanus.

Outside the old harbour is a memorial to those who died in the First World War. Set in the stonework is a barometer and the words "to help to protect the lives of present and future fishermen". Either side of the beehive-shaped monument are two ship's cannon. The new harbour, to the west of the old harbour in Westcliff, is still a

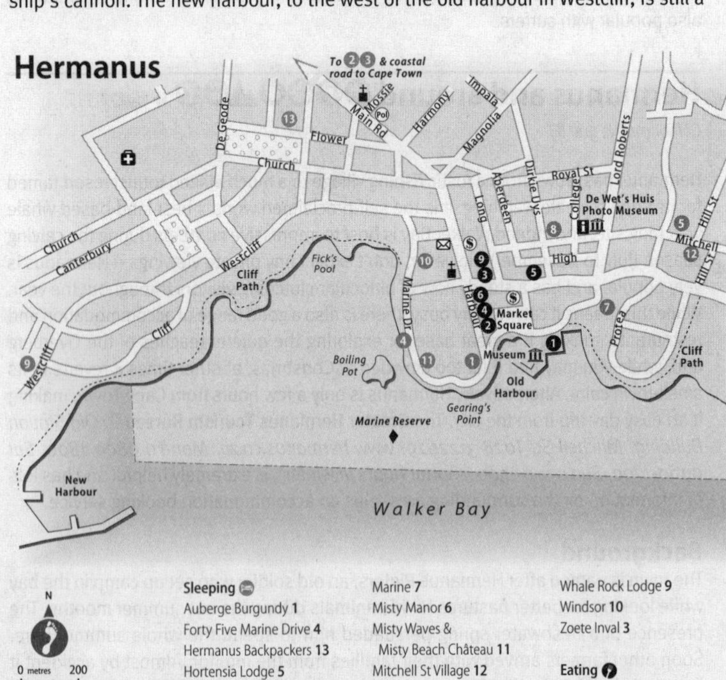

busy fishing port. It's a great idea to head down to the dockside to buy fresh crayfish, mussels or linefish from the fish shop. The staff will be happy to advise you on how best to cook your selection.

Walks around Hermanus

The excellent **Cliff Path** starts at the new harbour in Westcliff and follows the shore all the way round Walker Bay to Grotto Beach, a distance of just over 15 km. Between cliffs the path goes through stands of milkwood trees and takes you around the sandy beaches. The most popular viewpoints are Dreunkrans, Fick's Pool, Gearing's Point, the Old Harbour, Die Gang, Siever's Punt, Kwaaiwater and Platbank. On an ideal day allow at least a morning for the walk. Bench seats are provided at the prime viewpoints, which make them good spots for a picnic.

Beaches

There are some good beaches a short distance in either direction from the town centre. The best beaches to the west are found at Onrus and Vermont (see page 217). Heading east towards Stanford and Gansbaai, there are long, open beaches or secluded coves with patches of sand and rock pools. **Grotto Beach** is the largest, best developed and most popular for swimming and is one of just three Blue Flag beaches in South Africa. The fine white sands stretch beyond the Klein River Lagoon, and there are changing facilities, a restaurant and a beach shop. Slightly closer to the town centre is **Voëlklip Beach**, a little run down, but with well-kept lawns behind the sand. Conditions are good for swimming and surfing. The most popular spot for surfers is **Kammabaai** next door to Voëlklip beach. There are braai facilities under the shade of some milkwood trees, an ideal setting for beach parties.

Fernkloof Nature Reserve

ⓘ *T028-3138100, www.fernkloof.com, open 24 hrs, free. Reservation for the 4-berth overnight hut from Judy George, T028-3141562. The visitors' centre, 500 m from the entrance, has a display of the most common plants you are likely to see when walking in the reserve. All the hiking trails start from here.*

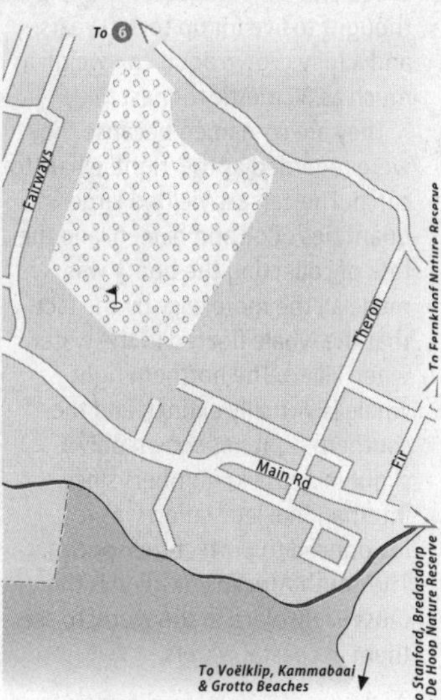

Set in the hills behind Hermanus, the reserve has 50 km of walks through an area rich in protea and coastal fynbos, with three colour-coded self-guided trails, plus a mountain biking route. Access is from the east end of Hermanus – just before the Main Road crosses Mossel River, turn up Fir Street. The reserve gates are just beyond the botanical society buildings. The diversity of plants in the reserve is due to the long period it has been under protection, plus its range of elevation from 60 to 850 m. With such a diverse plant population, there is also a wide range of bird and animal species. Higher up in the mountains, look out for breeding black eagles. Small patches of indigenous forest remain in some of the moist ravines.

To 6
Fairways
Theron
Main Rd
Fir
To Fernkloof Nature Reserve
To Voëlklip, Kammabaai & Grotto Beaches
To Stanford, Bredasdorp & De Hoop Nature Reserve

Bientang's Cave **1**
Burgundy **2**
Fisherman's Cottage **4**
Marimba Café **5**
Prince of Whales **9**
Zebra Crossing **3**

Whale watching

The World Wildlife Foundation acknowledges Hermanus as one of the 12 best places in the world to view whales. It is the ideal destination if you wish to see whales without bobbing around in a boat. The town promotes itself as the 'heart of the Whale Coast', and during the season most visitors should not be disappointed. The town's advantage is that whales can come very close to the shore. The combination of low cliffs and deep water at the base of the cliffs means that you are able to look down from above into clear water and see the outlines of whales from as close as 10 m. A whale-watching hotline, T028-3122629, provides visitors with the most recent information on their location. This covers the coastline from Betty's Bay to Gansbaai. There is also a special number for reporting any strandings, T0800-228222, which applies to dolphins as well as whales.

To add to the excitement there is a whale crier who between 1000-1600 during September and October strolls around the town centre blowing a kelp horn to announce the arrival of each whale in Walker Bay. The whale crier is easily identified by his appearance. He wears a giant Bavarian-style hat and carries a sandwich board which records the daily sightings of whales from different vantage points around Walker Bay.

The best months are September and October when daily sightings are guaranteed. You would be unlucky not to see some sign of a whale during this period, though of course they are just as likely to be in the middle of the bay as up close to one of the vantage points along the cliff path. The first southern right whales start to appear in Walker Bay from June onwards. By the end of December most have returned to the southern oceans. The whales migrate north to escape heavy winter storms in the oceans around Antarctica. In August and September most of the calves are born in the calm sheltered bays, where the cows then stay with their young for a further two months. Out of an estimated world population of only 6000 southern right whales, up to 80 have been recorded mating and calving in Walker Bay.

The southern right whale is distinguished from other whales by its V-shaped 'blow', produced by a pair of blowholes, and callosities which appear randomly on and around the oval head. The callosities are growths of tough skin which grow in unique patterns helping to identify individuals. Southern right whales are basically black with occasional streaks of grey or white on the back. Their flippers are short, broad and almost square. They are thought to live for up to 100 years, and a fully grown adult can weigh as much as 80 metric tonnes.

They are so-named because they were regarded as the 'right' whale to catch. The carcass yielded large quantities of oil and baleen, and the task of collecting the booty was made all the more easy by the fact that the whale floated in the water when killed. The northern right whale is virtually extinct, and the southern right has shown only a slight increase in numbers since international legislation was introduced to protect the species. The South African coastline is the most likely place in the world to see them in coastal waters.

Hermanus wine route

Hidden away in the **Hemel-en-Aarde Valley** behind Hermanus are a few vineyards producing some surprisingly good wines, mostly Burgundy varieties based around

Pinot Noir and Chardonnay grapes. Rarely crowded, three vineyards are open to the public and have tastings in their cellars. **Hamilton Russell Vineyards** ⓘ *T028-3123595, tastings: Mon-Fri, 0900-1700, Sat 0900-1300, closed Sun*, is one of the more picturesque estates. The cellar and tasting room are set beside a small trout lake. Follow the R43 out of Hermanus towards Cape Town, after 2 km take a right turn marked Caledon, R320; there is a signpost and right turn 5 km along this gravel road.

Whalehaven Wines ⓘ *T028-3161633, www.whalehavenwines.co.za, tastings: Mon-Fri 0930-1700, Sat 1030-1400, closed Sun*, is one of the newest vineyards in the valley, so all their wines are quite young – the Pinot Noir is their flagship wine. The cellars and production rooms are open to visitors. Take the R320 turning for Caledon, as above. The winery is almost immediately on the right after turning off the R43.

Bouchard Finlayson Wines ⓘ *T028-3123515, www.bouchardfinlayson.co.za, tastings: Mon-Fri 0900-1700, Sat 1030-1230, closed Sun*, on the Caledon road 1 km beyond the Hamilton Russell Vineyard, has won several awards.

Stanford and around

» *pp227-235. Colour map 8, grid B3.*

Stanford, the next town along the R43 17 km east of Hermanus, is a peaceful Victorian village set inland from the Atlantic, which in recent years has become a popular centre for artists and craftsmen. It is an attractive spot, with some well-restored Victorian thatched cottages and a beautiful setting on the Klein River. This is also the nearest village to the small **Salmonsdam Nature Reserve**. The **Stanford Tourism Bureau** ⓘ*T028-3410340, www.stanfordinfo.co.za*, is next to the library on Queen Victoria Street. Information can also be found at www.stanfordvillage.co.za.

Sights

The **Birkenhead Micro-Brewery** ⓘ *T028-3410183, www.birkenhead.co.za, 1100-1600*, is just out of the village off the R326 towards Caledon and is the most popular sight in the area. Five beers are brewed and sold, of which the Birkenhead Premium Lager is the tastiest, a slow-brewed beer using rich malted two-rowed barley and aromatic Hallertau and Saaz hop cones. Many of the ingredients are grown on the site and you can take a tour of the hops garden before going inside the modern buildings. Wine is also on sale and can be tasted. The restaurant and pub on the site is open for lunch daily and dinner at the weekends in high season.

Stanford's Blom & Blitz Festival, held in November, consists of a triathalon, arts, crafts, food, and witblits – a potent home-distilled brandy.

Another popular place to stop is **Klein River Cheese** ⓘ *T028-3410693, kleinriver@telkomsa.net, Mon-Fri 0900-1700, Sat 0900-1300, from the R43 take the left turn onto the R326 opposite the turning to Stanford and follow the signposts*, a factory specializing in Gruyère and other cheeses using Jersey and Friesland milk. Visitors can watch cheese being made, taste the produce in the shop, or enjoy a delicious picnic lunch on the banks of the Klein River. Baskets are filled with homemade breads, crackers, pâtés, pickles, cold meats, salads and a selection of cheese.

Walker Bay Nature Reserve

ⓘ *T028-3140062, www.capenature.org.za, open to day visitors 0800-1800.*

Driving out of Hermanus to the east you pass through the suburb known as **Voëlklip**. If you are planning to visit the Walker Bay Nature Reserve you must collect your entry permit from the **office** ⓘ *corner of 7th St and 17th Av, Voëlklip, Mon-Fri 0800-1600.* The reserve stretches from the Klein River estuary to De Kelders just before Gansbaai and covers about 1000 ha with a coastline of 17 km. It features a long beach, known as Die Plaat, with white sands and rocky limestone outcrops to the east. Most of the mammals occurring in the reserve are shy, but the tracks of Cape clawless otter,

The crucial whale lexicon

A couple of days along the cliffs of Hermanus is enough to persuade anyone to help save the whale. Here are some useful words to help you convince people of your dedication to the cause.

Breaching Probably the most spectacular sight, this is when whales lift their entire body out of the water in an effortless arc, creating a huge splash as they fall back into the sea. Not an isolated event, a whale will often leap several times so keep your binoculars trained. The experts have yet to agree on why the whale does this, and the whales aren't giving much away.

Blowing This is the sight we are all familiar with, the spout of water vapour accompanied by an echoing sound as air is expelled from its lungs through the blowhole. The seasoned whale watcher will be able to identify the species from the shape of the spout. The vapour is created by condensation when the warm breath comes in contact with the cooler outside air.

Grunting Just a loud grunting sound which carries a long way over water, a moving noise when heard on a calm moonlit night. No translations yet available.

Lobtailing The action of the whale slapping the surface with its tail producing a loud clap. This can be seen repeatedly over a long period. Interpreted as some form of warning or social communication.

Sailing The whale lifts its tail clear of the water for long periods. There are several theories about this action: to use the wind to 'sail' through the water (dubious), to feed on the sea-floor, or as a means of temperature control. The diehard watchers reckon the whales are just showing off.

Spyhopping When the whale lifts its head and part of its body above the water vertically. This gives the whale a 360° view of the sea.

bushbuck, duiker, grysbok and steenbok are occasionally seen. Offshore, whales can be spotted in season and the reserve is home to numerous species of seabirds, including the striking African black oystercatcher. Visitors can explore the coast on hikes though swimming is not recommended as the sea can be rough. There is no overnight accommodation in the reserve. There are two entrances; one to the west of Stanford on a back road, and one further south off the R43 just north of De Kelders.

Salmonsdam Nature Reserve

ⓘ *T028-3140062, www.capenature.co.za, open to day visitors 0700-1800. There are 3 basic cabins and a campsite (see Sleeping, page 230). The reserve is 33 km from Hermanus and 16 km from Stanford. It can easily be visited as a day trip from either of these towns. On reaching Stanford, turn right on to the R326. A few kilometres up this road turn right onto a gravel road. The reserve is clearly signposted.*

This small reserve was established in 1962 and covers 834 ha of the mountains which form part of the catchment area for the Paardenberg River. The main attraction here is the opportunity to view how the Overberg region would have appeared before much of it was cleared by farmers. As you either drive or walk up to the main viewpoint, Ravenshill, you pass by several deep, lush valleys which retain a number of indigenous trees. An added attraction is several waterfalls, best viewed after the rains. There are three distinct vegetation zones to look out for, each of which hosts different bird species. The high areas are covered with mountain fynbos – disas, waboom and ground proteas. Around the campsite and in the low-lying, flooded vleis are reeds, water heath and fountain bush. Between the high and low areas, stands of lush indigenous forest fill the kloofs formed by streams running off the mountains. These forested areas are the most rewarding parts to walk in – three short trails start behind the camping area. Look out for small antelope such as steenbok, grey duiker, grey rhebuck, klipspringer and bontebok.

Gansbaai and around » pp227-235. Colour map 8, grid B3.

The R43 reaches Gansbaai 22 km south of Stanford. The history of this popular fishing centre dates back over a century to when a local youth from Hermanus decided to make his home here. The story goes that in 1881 Johannes Cornelis Wessels walked across the sand dunes between Stanford and Gansgat. He found the fishing to be very good and the natural cove provided a safe and sheltered landing spot for the small fishing vessels in use at the time.

The bay was named by fishermen who used it for protection against large storms. The name *gansgat* refers to the colony of Egyptian geese, *kolganse*, which used to nest in the reeds that surrounded a natural spring in the bay. These days the village is a prosperous fishing harbour with a modern deep water wharf and several fish-canning factories. It has, however, managed to retain the character of a small community and busy fishing harbour, albeit with strong ties to the tourist industry. A number of Capetonians have second houses along this coast.

Ask at **Gansbaai Tourism Bureau** ⓘ *corner of Berg and Main Sts, To28-3841439, www.gansbaaiinfo.com*, for details of the best operators for shark diving. The office also produces some good maps of the coastline showing the area's walking routes.

Sights

Like Hermanus at the other end of Walker Bay, there are some excellent vantage points for whale watching. The southern right whales come close inshore to the sheltered deep waters to calve between June and November each year. A couple of kilometres up the coast at **De Kelders** are tall cliffs which quickly give way to a large white sand beach. The local lighthouse is 9 km away at **Danger Point**. On weekdays from 1000 to 1500, the lighthouse keeper will give you a tour. In May 1852 the *HMS Birkenhead* sunk here with a loss of 445 lives, though every woman and child on the ship escaped unharmed in the lifeboats. It took the sinking of a further 20 ships before a lighthouse came into operation in 1895.

Dyer Island is named after Samson Dyer, a black American who lived on the island collecting guano around 1806. Today the island is an important breeding spot for African penguins. On nearby **Geyser Island** there is a breeding seal population. Both can be visited on boat tours (see Activities and tours, page 235) The area between the two islands is known as Shark Alley, as great white sharks are attracted to the breeding seals. For details of great white shark cage diving see page 235.

South from Gansbaai

From Gansbaai the R43 continues southeast along the coast, passing through the small resorts of Kleinbaai, Franskraal, Pearly Beach and on to Die Dam at Sandbaai. Few visitors venture this far into the Overberg, although it is the area's relative isolation that is much of its appeal. From Sandbaai, the road turns inland and cuts across wild countryside that remains virtually untouched. During the spring the fields are full of wild flowers, and throughout the year the area is rich in varieties of fynbos. Follow signs for Wolvengat, formerly known as Viljoenshof, and continue on to Elim.

Elim → *Colour map 8, grid B3.*

Founded by German missionaries in 1824, this is one of the best-known Moravian mission stations in South Africa. The settlement is named from Exodus 15:27, after the spot where the Israelites rested after crossing the Red Sea. To live here you must be a member of the local Moravian church and your livelihood must come from the earth. A new industry has emerged in recent years, based upon two long-lasting species of wild flower – helipterum and helichrysum – which are now successful export crops. Once dried, they are very popular for wreaths in Germany, keeping the historical connections alive today.

The whole village has been declared a national monument, so it is not surprising that there is a variety of quaint old buildings still standing and in use. One attraction is a restored **watermill** dating from 1833. It has a huge Burmese-teak wheel, which replaced the original stone wheels. The mill was reopened in 1990 to produce wholewheat flour. Two other old buildings worth looking out for are the **parsonage**, and the original **mission church**, which has a thatched roof. Although Elim is an important centre, it has not been developed as a tourist destination, and some visitors are disappointed after their steady drive along empty gravel roads. But at the time of writing the contract had been awarded to tar the road to both Gansbaai and Bredasdorp so this should open up the region a little more.

Bredasdorp and around

» *pp227-235. Colour map 8, grid B3.*

This is South Africa's first *dorp*, founded in 1837 by Michiel van Breda, an important local figure. From his farm, Zoetendalsvlei, he played an active role in the development of the Merino sheep industry throughout South Africa and was the first mayor of Cape Town in 1840. The old farmstead can be visited by prior arrangement. For tourist information, head to the regional **Cape Agulhas Tourism Bureau** ⓘ *Dowling Building, Long St, T028-4242584, www.capeagulhas.info, Mon-Fri 0800-1700, Sat 0900-1300.*

Sights

Despite its age, there is little to keep you in town for long. Worth a peek is the **Shipwreck Museum** ⓘ *T028-4241240, Mon-Fri 0900-1645, Sat 0900-1300, 1400-1645, Sun 1100-1230, small entry fee*, on Independent Street. It houses a collection of odd bits and pieces salvaged from along the coast, 24 km away. The whole display is greatly enhanced by the sound effects. In the Shipwreck Hall you hear the distinct shrieks of seagulls and the thunderous sound of waves on a stormy night. Four wrecks are featured: the *Queen of the Thames*, *HMS Birkenhead*, the *Oriental Pioneer* and HMS *Arniston*. In the coach house is a collection of items relating to the sea, including some unusual pieces of ships' furniture.

South from Bredasdorp

Driving south on the R319 for a further 36 km takes you to **Cape Agulhas**. Before reaching the coast, the road runs close to some large *vleis* (marshes): Karsrivier and Soetendals. These are important breeding grounds for aquatic birds, and there is a good chance of seeing flamingos. At the coast the road passes through **Struisbaai** before ending at a lighthouse and some retirement homes. A second road going south from Bredasdorp, the R316, ends at Waenhuiskrans.

Malgas

This small settlement on the banks of the Breede River was a vital point in the transport route in the mid-19th century of the famous Overberg tycoon, Joseph Barry. Until the roads east from Cape Town were improved and the many mountain passes negotiated, the majority of goods were brought into the Overberg region through Malgas. The Barry family had a 158-ton vessel, *Kadie*, especially built to transfer goods from Cape Town to Port Beaufort. From here the cargo was transferred to river boats and taken upstream as far as Malgas, before the final stage of transportation was completed by ox wagon. Today the settlement is famous for having the last manually operated pontoon in South Africa. Cars are carried across the river during daylight hours.

Allow a few extra minutes to look around the fine church on the west bank built in 1856 by the Barry family.

Struisbaai and L'Agulhas

This attractive fishing village has good spear-fishing, safe swimming in the bay, and a 14-km white sand beach. L'Agulhas just to the south and at the end of the road is a rather wind-blown settlement of a few houses and shops. The principal attraction in this region is nearby **Cape Agulhas**. This is the southernmost point in Africa, but it is rather disappointing and lacks the grandeur one might hope for. Aside from the lighthouse, the surroundings are rather dull, although a paved road is being built and may attract some much-needed investment. The beach is very rocky, but excellent for fishing. This is where the warm waters of the Indian Ocean meet the cooler waters of the Atlantic Ocean, although most visitors seem to think they meet at Cape Point. The warm waters of the Indian Ocean do however reach as far west as False Bay.

The **Cape Agulhas Lighthouse** ⓘ *T028-4357506*, was built in 1848 and lies 1 km east of the tip of Africa. It was modelled on the Egyptian pharaohs' light in Alexandria and now houses a pleasant restaurant, decorated with antiques and museum pieces, (open 0800-2200), which serves breakfast, light lunches and dinners of steak and seafood. If you climb up the stairs there are good views over the unforgiving ocean that has claimed many ships and lives.

Agulhas National Park

ⓘ *For information contact T028-4356078, www.sanparks.org.*

The park encompasses a large area of coastland centred around Cape Agulhas, and it was created to help protect the rugged coastline and the immediate hinterland, known as the Agulhas Plain, which forms the southernmost area of Africa. The Agulhas Plain is home to almost 2000 species of indigenous plants, of which 100 are endemic to the area. A large part of the area is taken up by a variety of wetlands which attract more than 21,000 migrant and resident birds annually. The park also protects a couple of islands found just offshore which are home to seals and seabirds, as well as the whales which frequent this part of the coastline in spring and early summer. Finally, the area is regarded important in archaeological terms, with several ancient habitation sites already having been discovered. At present, there are limited tourist facilities in the park (a couple of toilets and little else), but there are ongoing plans to build a museum and lay out nature trails along the coastline. The quickest route from Cape Town (230 km) is to take the N2 highway as far as Caledon and then turn onto the R406 for Bredasdorp. From Bredasdorp follow the signs for either Struisbaai or L'Agulhas. At present these are the two closest settlements to the park with accommodation facilities.

Arniston (Waenhuiskrans)

This tranquil fishing village, which is known by its Afrikaans name, Waenhuiskrans, to locals (wagon house cliff), is made up of a jumble of whitewashed, thatched cottages. What were once the homes of poor fishermen are today smart, renovated holiday homes. The appeal of the place is its beaches – the water is noticeably warm and turquoise here on the Indian Ocean side, and is backed by bone-white dunes making the effect all the more startling. Just to the west of the village is **Waenhuiskrans Cave**, a huge cavern overlooking the sea, which can be explored at low tide. The cavern goes back into the cliffs and is named after the ox wagons which it once held.

The town's other name is derived from the wreck of the *Arniston* (1815), which lies about 1 km from the slipway. Items salvaged from the wreck are on display in the **Bredasdorp Shipwreck Museum**. The wreck can be dived, but there is a heavy swell. There is a monument to the deceased near the beach; only six of the 378 passengers survived. There are two beaches, **Slipway** in front of the **Arniston Hotel**, and **Bikini Beach**. The waters are warm and bright blue, with some good snorkelling. At low tide a couple of rock pools are exposed on Bikini Beach, fun for children to explore. A few shops in the village stock the basics for self-catering. You can only reach here in your own vehicle or by hitching; there is no public transport.

De Mond Nature Reserve

ⓘ *The gates are open daily from 0700 to 1600. Vehicles are not allowed in the reserve. There is a car park next to the office by the main gate from where the Sterna Trail begins. There is no accommodation within the reserve. Further information: T028-4242170, www.capenature.org.za. The best time to visit is Oct-Mar.*

This pleasant small reserve is centred around the mouth of the Heuningnes River, 26 km south of Bredasdorp. Two former farms were designated as a nature reserve in 1986. About 10 km of the shoreline is also protected, although most of the land remains inaccessible to the public. A 6.7 km hike known as the **Sterna Trail** starts from the office, following the beach for several kilometres. This is an easy path and winds through a range of different coastal habitats, including dune forest, stabilized dunes, riverine vegetation and some salt marshes.

De Hoop Nature Reserve

» pp227-235. Colour map 8, grid C3.

ⓘ *The reserve gates are open Mon-Thu 0700-1800, Fri 0700-2100, Sat and Sun 0800-1100. Overnight visitors must check in at the De Hoop office before it closes at 1600. There is a small entrance fee per person/vehicle. An additional cycling fee per person/day applies if you intend to use the mountain-bike trail in the eastern sector. Information and reservations for accommodation in the reserve (see Sleeping page 231) T028-4255020, www.capenature.org.za.*

This is an important coastal reserve which extends 5 km out to sea, protecting the shoreline and marine life. It is divided into two sectors. The **western region** is for hiking, game viewing and birdwatching while the **eastern section** is for mountain biking.

The reserve covers an exceptionally varied and rich environment – seven different ecosystems are found within the 34,000-ha reserve. De Hoop is a large freshwater *vlei* surrounded by marshlands which stretch for 15 km. The coastline is a mix of sandy beaches, rocky headlands and cliffs with wave-cut platforms. Further inland are giant sand dunes, some as high as 90 m, and behind these are limestone hills and the Potberg Mountains. The higher ground is clearly divided by kloofs covered with indigenous vegetation. It has been estimated that over 1500 plant species grow here, of which 34 are endemic to the reserve, including rare lowland fynbos species. Details of the rarer plants are displayed at the environmental education centres and the reserve offices at De Hoop and Potberg.

The region enjoys a Mediterranean climate with mild winters and warm summers. August is the wettest month, with some morning fogs. The sea has strong currents and is dangerous for swimming. Consult the reserve office for advice on safer spots.

Ins and outs

Getting there Coming from Bredasdorp, follow the R319 towards Swellendam. After 8 km is a signposted right turn onto a gravel road. After 40 km you reach Ouplaas – take a right for the western section or continue straight on for another 10 km for the entrance to the eastern section. The office and car park are at Potberg. Approaching from the N2, the quickest route is to take the Witsand (see also page 242) turning 12 km east of Swellendam. After 23 km turn right for Malgas and then follow the signs. Both entrances are about 20 km from Malgas.

Tourist information Cycling on the service tracks within the western sector is free. In the eastern sector cars are left at the Potberg Environmental Education Centre. It is 11 km from here to the accommodation at Cupidoskraal. Allow about one hour with a loaded bike. There are information displays at De Hoop and Potberg offices introducing the visitor to the environment and the diversity of species to be found in the reserve. The closest shops and petrol are in Ouplaas, 15 km from the De Hoop office.

Wildlife

With such a variety of terrain in a relatively small area, the region supports a diverse range of wildlife. Over 250 species of birds have been recorded here, while elusive leopard, bontebok and Cape mountain zebra roam around, along with the more common eland, grey rhebok, baboon and klipspringer. The last known breeding colony of the Cape vulture in the southwestern Cape is close to Potberg, and you may glimpse them circling high in the skies. The **Windhoek Cave** is home to a large colony of bats which have attracted their fair share of research interest. Other rare species that you might see include black oystercatchers, which forage amongst the dunes. Finally, there is a chance of seeing southern right whales, which calve in the shallow waters and can be seen between July and December (see page 220). Although the whales found here are often in larger concentrations than elsewhere, they are difficult to see as they remain beyond the breakers.

Hiking and mountain biking

The reserve is traversed by a number of self-guided hiking trails, as well as a popular mountain-biking route. There is also a 20 km circular drive for vehicles. Driving gives you the opportunity to appreciate quickly the diversity of the landscape and explore all corners, although it can detract from viewing wildlife – a quieter approach on foot is more rewarding.

Hiking Trails have been designed for all levels of fitness and with different interests in mind. There are four one-day walks close to the camps and car parks and a much longer five-day circuit along the coast. Simple overnight huts are found at suitable intervals. This trail needs to be booked at the office. The **Vlei Trail** follows the banks of the De Hoop Vlei where you'll find masses of waterbirds. A new five-day **Whale Trail** is soon to open, taking a winding route along the coast.

Mountain biking Cyclists are permitted to use any of the management roads in the western sector of the reserve. There is also the **De Hoop Mountain Bike Trail** laid out in the eastern sector (bookings essential). A hut at Cupidoskraal is used as an overnight base for cyclists on the trail. The trail varies in difficulty and cyclists will need to allow two to three days to complete it. Numbers are limited to 12 cyclists per day. The hut provides comfortable overnight accommodation for 12 people, with storage space for bicycles, gas, fireplace, no bedding. The only drinking water available is by the overnight hut, so make sure you carry enough for each day. Beware of dehydration and cramp when cycling in the heat. Always carry a rudimentary first aid kit; you will quickly appreciate how isolated you are in the reserve.

Sleeping

Gordon's Bay *p215*

A Eagles Place, 131 Beach Rd, T021-8561631, www.eaglesplace.co.za. Stylish and intimate guesthouse in 2 whitewashed houses with wooden floors, 11 rooms and 1 penthouse with white furnishings and bedding, terrace, splash pool, bar, within walking distance of restaurants, beauty treatments on offer.

B Van Riebeeck, Main Beach, T021-8561441, www.vrh.co.za. Functional hotel overlooking the main beach, some of the 66 en suite rooms are sea-facing with great balconies, all have TV. Restaurant and bar offer a sheltered view of the sea, pleasant deck, conference facilities, good value.

Pringle Bay *p215*

A **Moonstruck on Pringle Bay**, 264 Hangklip Rd, T028-2738162, www.moonstruck.co.za. Intimate guesthouse with large picture windows overlooking the ocean and mountains, 4 spacious rooms, stylish modern decor, balconies and fireplaces, sparkling pool with wooden deck, 100 m from the beach.

Betty's Bay *p216*

B **Buçaco Sud**, Clarence Drive, T028-2729628, www.bucacosud.co.za. Spanish-style villa with 6 tastefully decorated en suite rooms, terracotta tiles, fireplaces in public areas, all rooms have either mountain or coastal views, breakfast served in attractive courtyard with pool, no children under 12.

B-C **Peter's Place**, 4400 Wallers Way, T028-2729527, www.petersplace.co.za. 2 units each with 2 bedrooms and 1 bathroom, self-catering possible in one of the units, good breakfasts served, a quiet B&B well situated for hiking or the beach, good location close to the sea, homely, old-fashioned place, other meals on request.

Kleinmond *p217*

AL-A **The Beach House**, 13 Beach Rd, Sandown Bay, T028-2713130, www.relaishotels.co.za. Luxurious guesthouse right by the sea, comfortable en suite rooms, all with either ocean or mountain views, **Tides** seafood restaurant, peaceful location on the beach and great position for whale watching, swimming pool, part of the Relais Hotels group.

Vermont and Onrus *p217*

A-B **Windswael Whale Inn**, 36 Marine Dr, Vermont, T028-3163491, www.windswael.co.za. Smart seafront B&B with sea views, 4 luxurious en suite rooms, each with private entrance and patio, meals on request, stylish lounge, braai area, splash pool. Rather delightfully breakfast here is served on the rocks overlooking the ocean, and the inn was voted one of the top ten places to have breakfast in southern Africa by South Africa's Getaway magazine.

B **Flick's Places**, 8 Beach Rd and 69 Atlantic Dr, Onrus, T028-3162998, www.flicksplace.co.za. This is actually 2 B&Bs, owned by a well-known local caterer. 1 property is based right on the beach, the other a few mins' walk away. Both have comfortable en suite double rooms, private entrances, satellite TV. Also self-catering units. Delicious meals on request, excellent breakfasts.

C-D **Paradise Park**, Vermont, off the R43, T028-3163402. A small site with 16 self-catering chalets and camping, plenty of grass and shade, electric points, swimming pool, mini golf, shops nearby, snack shop open during holiday season.

Hermanus *p217, map p218*

There are hundreds of accommodation options in Hermanus, and we only have room to list a few examples. For a full listing visit www.hermanus.co.za or visit the tourist office on arrival. Be sure to book well ahead during whale season and school holidays.

L **The Marine**, Marine Dr, T028-3131000, www.marine-hermanus.co.za. Part of the Relais & Chateaux group, a historic hotel and one of the finest in the country. 42 luxurious rooms, some with stunning ocean views, all with exceptionally fine furnishings – silk curtains, plush carpets, pale suede armchairs and marble bathrooms. A/c, satellite TV, fresh flowers, 4-poster beds, some have his 'n' hers bathrooms. Also has a spa, heated swimming pool, shop, internet and 2 restaurants; the seafood restaurant has won many awards (see Eating page 232). Impeccable service. Highly recommended for a treat.

AL **Auberge Burgundy**, 16 Harbour Rd, T028-3131201, www.auberge.co.za. Provençal-style villa in the heart of Hermanus, 17 rooms, a mix of luxury doubles and suites, the penthouse can sleep 6, all set around a luxurious inner courtyard with a swimming pool, private terraces or balconies, some with fine views across Walker Bay. Also owns the **Burgundy** restaurant, opposite (see Eating p232). Good reports from some readers.

A **Misty Waves**, T028-3138460, www.hermanusmistybeach.co.za. A collection of luxurious accommodation: the **Misty Waves Boutique Hotel** and **Misty Beach Château** are on Marine Dr; the **Misty Manor Guest House** is on Fernkloof Dr. The hotel is a spacious modern building on 2 levels with ample decks and roof terraces, suites have ocean views, spa baths, swimming pool, restaurant, whilst the château and manor offer elegant B&B accommodation in smart white blocks, in rooms that have all the mod cons.

A Mitchell St Village, 56-60 Mitchell St, T028-3124560, www.56.co.za. 12 rooms, all very differently designed thanks to the owner being an interior decorator, some have private courtyards or balconies and fireplaces, 2 swimming pools, attractive lounge and breakfast rooms, no children under 12.

A-B Windsor Hotel, 49 Marine Dr, T028-3123727, www.windsor-hotel.com. Large and popular hotel set on cliffs overlooking the ocean. 60 en suite rooms with TV, some have sea views. Excellent views across Walker Bay from the glazed lounge. Slightly plain restaurant. Frequently used by tour groups, small boat hire service.

B Hortensia Lodge, 66 Mitchell St, T028-3124358, www.hortensialodge.co.za. Small comfortable guesthouse set in neat gardens with swimming pool. 5 rooms, en suite with TV and views of the garden, simple decor. German, French (and Hungarian) spoken, no children under 14.

B Livesey Lodge, 13 Main Rd, T028- 3130026, www.liveseylodge.co.za. Friendly guesthouse with 6 en suite double rooms set around garden with good-sized pool. Spacious and bright, all have separate entrances, individual decor, TV, mini-fridge, huge beds, nice touches like books in all the rooms. Off-street parking. Location a little outside town is a drawback, but otherwise a good value, attractive and well-run place. Recommended.

B Whale Rock Lodge, 26 Springfield Rd, T028-3130014, www.whalerock.co.za. Well-appointed B&B with 11 double rooms, en suite, TV, set in a thatched building decorated with antiques and oil paintings, close to the new harbour and a short walk from the cliff path. Garden with pool, lounge, no children under 10.

B-C Forty Five Marine Drive, 45 Marine Dr, T028-3123610, www.45marinehermanus.com. Large white block in a commanding position above the rocks and waves, 2-3 bedroomed fully equipped apartments with kitchen and lounge, underfloor heating, TV, lock-up garages, not very stylish but modern and functional with great views and good value for families.

C-D Hermanus Backpackers, 26 Flower St, T028-3124293, www.hermanusbackpackers.co.za. Well positioned behind Main Rd, dorms, doubles/twins with or without bathrooms, vibey atmosphere, bar with pool table, TV lounge with DVD library, pick-up from Baz Bus for a small fee, will book all activities and give out maps of the area.

C-D Moby's, 9 Mitchell St, T028-3132361, www.mobys.co.za. Backpackers' joint offering a good range of rooms: doubles, dorms sleeping 6-8, family rooms, all are en suite. Pub with DSTV, large garden with pool, daily braais, internet access, TV lounge, fully equipped kitchen. Friendly and laid-back place, does Baz Bus pick-ups for small fee. Also organizes cheap shark dives, wine tasting, sandboarding and the usual excursions.

D-E Zoete Inval, 23 Main Rd, T028-3121242, www.zoeteinval.co.za. Excellent budget choice with 3 double rooms, 2 family rooms (with toys) and a converted loft with 2 dorms. Pleasant TV lounge, self-catering kitchen, laundry, sunny deck, internet access, secure parking. Will meet the Baz Bus at Bot River Hotel for small fee. Friendly and good value.

Stanford and around *p221*

A-B Galashiels, 10 King St, T028-3410181, www.galashielshermanus.com. A family-run guesthouse with 4 en suite double rooms and 2 suites, traditional and plush furnishings, vague Scottish theme, cosy lounge with log fire, bar, evening meals on request, peaceful mature garden.

B Fairhill, off the R43 to Gansbaai, T028-3410230, www.fairhill.co.za. A private country house converted into a fine guesthouse set on a private nature reserve. 5 double rooms, en suite, private verandas, beautiful mountain and ocean views, pool, communal lounge, meals available. Bookings need to be made in advance.

B-C Springfontein, T028-3410651, www.springfontein.co.za. 4 comfortable self-catering cottages on a working farm 3 km from Stanford. Attractive thatched houses sleeping 2-6, excellent value for families. Also has an apartment sleeping 2. Spacious and comfortable, breakfast available, pool, gardens, beautiful setting surrounded by farmland and a small vineyard.

C **De Kleine Rivers Valley House**, 14 Church St, T028-3410048. Beautiful B&B set in one of the oldest houses in Stanford, dating from 1785. 2 doubles and 1 single en suite room, decked out with English furnishings and antiques, huge Victorian bathrooms, terracotta floors, excellent value, run by affable British couple. Recommended.

C-D **Stanford Inn**, Queen Victoria St, T028-3410900, www.stanfordvillage.co.za. Attractive historic country inn set in the heart of Stanford. Recently renovated, with 6 rooms of varying sizes, all en suite with wooden floors, wicker furniture, brass beds, simple and comfortable. Popular pub attached serving evening meals Wed and Thu and braais at weekends. Good value, recommended.

Salmonsdam Nature Reserve *p222*

C-D **Salmonsdam Cabins**, T028-4255020, www.capenature.org.za. 3 basic overnight cabins, 1 sleeps 8 with 3 rooms, living area, kitchen and bathroom, the other 2 sleep 4 in bunk beds, shared ablution block, suitable for hikers, no electricity but gas fridge and stove, cooking and eating utensils on request, small cement swimming pool.

Gansbaai and around *p223*

AL **Klein Paradijs Guest Farm**, T028-3819760, www.kleinparadijs.co.za, follow the main road south out of Gansbaai, direction Pearly Beach, 21 km. A pleasant farm just inland from the beautiful white sand beach. 5 individually decorated rooms, newly refurbished, with thatched ceilings, elegant table d'hôte dining room, superb food from a Swiss-trained chef. Also has 5 much cheaper self-catering cottages dotted about the farm (C) and guests can still eat in the restaurant. Recommended.

A **Casablanca**, 9 Slabber Rd, Klipfontein, just south of Gansbaai, T021-4341385, www.casablanca.co.za. Lovely 2-storey guesthouse with wrap-around balconies, great views and completely surrounded by fynbos, very stylish interiors, everything is bright white with some interesting African art and scented candles, 6 rooms, candlelit baths have sea views, dinner on request, usually seafood or fish braais.

B **De Kelders**, De Kelders, T028-3840045, www.dekelders.co.za, 3 km along Walker Bay towards Hermanus from Gansbaai. Smart and comfortable B&B with 3 en suite rooms, shared lounge with satellite TV, breakfast served on large deck overlooking the sea, private garden leads down to the water. Stunning location perched high up on the cliff, the perfect location for whale watching in the bay between Jun and Nov.

C **The Great White House**, 5 Geelbek St, T028-3843273, www.white-house.co.za. Popular thatched house with 3 'fishermen's cottages' with fireplaces, wood floors, en suite, pleasant African-themed decor, range of activities including whale watching and shark diving arranged, large restaurant popular with divers, good location close to the harbour.

E-F **Uilenkraalsmond Caravan Park**, T028-3880200, 5 km along the coast, south towards Pearly Beach. A vast modern campsite with 40 self-catering family chalets, wash blocks, grassy, limited shade, sea breeze can be a problem at times. Plenty of facilities for children, supertube, trampoline, crazy golf, swimming in the lagoon. Very busy during local school holidays, but for the rest of the year it is quiet.

Bredasdorp *p224*

B **Earl of Clarendon**, corner of Dirkie Uys and Clarendon Sts, T028-4251420. Historic building with 4 elegant rooms, all with wood floors, en suite with Victorian baths, 4-poster beds, antiques, crisp white linen. Restaurant, bistro and curio shop on site. Recommended.

C **Firlane Guesthouse**, 5 Fir Lane, T028-4251192, zondagh@dorea.co.za. Historic 1926 mansion with gleaming wooden floors and high ceilings with scrolled cornices, 3 double rooms, all en suite, individually decorated, spacious and luxurious bathrooms, breakfast served in smart dining room or in garden.

D-E **Suikerbossie Caravan Park**, T028-4251919. Camping ground with good-value but very simple self-catering chalets sleeping 4-5, bedding is extra.

For an explanation of the sleeping and eating price codes used in this guide, see inside the front cover. Other relevant information is found in Essentials pages 42-47.

Struisbaai *p225*

B **Harbour Lights**, 5 Kusweg, T028-4356053, harbour@isat.co.za. Smart bright-yellow B&B with 5 comfortable rooms with fans, TV, fridge and electric blankets, bar, evening meals available, no children under 12.

C **Struisbaai Hotel**, 4 Minnetoka, T028-4356625, struisbaaihotel@isat.co.za. Comfortable small 2-star hotel with 21 rondavels set just across from the beach. Also has popular restaurant and bar with big-screen TV for watching sports.

D-E **Struisbaai Caravan Park**, Main Rd, T028-4356820. 16 self-catering chalets and camping, good shade, laundry, shop and café in walking distance, overlooks the sea, short walk to lighthouse. All ablution facilities were modernized recently.

L'Agulhas *p225*

AL **Agulhas Country Lodge**, Main Rd, T028-4357650, www.agulhascountrylodge.com. An unusual building made of limestone set amongst the rocks with broad ocean views, 8 rooms with balconies and complimentary sherry, some with jacuzzis, restaurant, bar with nautical and aviation theme, cigar bar.

B **Villa@Cape Agulhas**, 17 Golf St, T028-4356917, www.villacapeagulhas.co.za. Very, very stylish upmarket B&B with views of the lighthouse, the walls in the communal areas are painted in bright orange, pink and lime green, funky furniture, fireplaces, rooms have TV, sea views and fridge. Jacuzzi, no smoking or credit cards.

Arniston *p225*

AL **Arniston**, Beach Rd, T028-4459000, www.arnistonhotel.co.za. An elegant seaside hotel, 40 rooms, thoughtfully decorated, small bathrooms, TV, sea-facing rooms have private balconies but are more expensive than the pool/courtyard facing rooms, restful reception rooms with fireplaces. Good restaurant, swimming pool, sheltered garden.

B-C **Arniston Seaside Cottages**, Huxham St, T028-4459772, www.arniston-online.co.za. Compact luxury development set among the dunes with 20 whitewashed thatched cottages, self-catering, log fireplaces, reed ceilings, pine furnishings, most with sea views from private balcony, cottages are serviced every day, all facilities close by, fresh fish from the boats as they land. Recommended.

C **Arniston Lodge**, 23 Main Rd, T028-4459175, www.arniston.co.za. An appealing thatched cottage which blends in well with the traditional fishermen's cottages. 4 double rooms, characterful upstairs rooms have thatch ceiling and views across the beach, sheltered swimming pool, lounge with log fireplace, evening meals can be arranged, a welcome peaceful retreat, German spoken.

C **South of Africa Backpackers Resort**, T028-4459240, www.southofafrica.co.za. A smart backpacker hostel, set in the wing of **Die Herberg Hotel**. More expensive than most hostels, but correspondingly more comfortable. No dorms – singles, doubles and triples, some with TV, kitchen, chill-out room, TV room, breakfasts served in hotel restaurant and included in price, full access to hotel's facilities including indoor pool, gym and squash courts.

De Hoop Nature Reserve *p226*

A variety of accommodation is within the reserve; below is a selection. All are managed by Cape Nature Conservation, T028-4255020, www.capenature.org.za.

C **Lekkerwater**, is a farmhouse situated right by the beach with wonderful ocean views, it sleeps 10 people in 5 rooms, gas powered stove, fridge and geysers but no electricity, lighting is by paraffin lights and candles, fully equipped kitchen.

C-E **Cottages and camping**, 10 self-catering cottages with fridge and stove. Some have bedding, but it's a good idea to bring your own, as well as kitchen utensils. The setting is perfect, right on the edge of the vlei. The campsite has basic facilities, with views over the vlei and set under milkwood trees. There are no electric points. Firewood is available from the De Hoop office. The Vlei Trail starts in the camp and 2 paths follow a route around the freshwater lake.

E **Cupidoskraal**, is a restored farmhouse now acting as the trail hut. 12 beds, storage space for bikes, gas stove, electric light, fireplace, pots and pans provided, but bring food and bedding. Firewood is available. Drinking water is collected in rain tanks.

Eating

Gordon's Bay *p215*

Bertie's Moorings, Harbour Island, T021-8563343, 1000-2400. Lively pub serving light meals and good seafood on the waterfront. Also venue for stand-up comedy and live bands at the weekends.

Harbour Lights, Gordon's Bay Harbour, T021-8561830, Tue-Sat 1200-1400, 1900-2200, Sun 1900-2200. Excellent seafood and good views of the yacht basin at night. Popular place, especially with families in the holidays, serving daily specials, linefish and seafood platters.

Indigo, Beach Rd, T021-8562460. Daily 1000-2200. Pleasant spot with outside wooden deck with umbrellas, overlooking the beach, light snacks and well-priced seafood including a generous platter for only R60. Next door in the blue building is Trawlers for takeaway seafood.

Pringle Bay *p215*

Miems, Hangklip Rd, T028-2738764. Wed-Sun 1130-1500, Tue-Sat 1800-2100. Cosy village pub serving good-value seafood and pub grub, hearty portions, a good place to hole up on a cold day.

Kleinmond *p217*

Europa and Café Atlantic, Harbour Rd, T028-2715872. 0800-2100. Large seafront restaurant and coffee shop, good views from the deck, seafood, spare ribs and steaks, long wine and spirit menu.

Potters Garden, Harbour Rd, T028-2715505. 0800-1700. Look out for the giant blue teapot in front. Light meals, coffees and snacks, big breakfast served throughout the day, Sun lunch popular with the local people.

Vermont and Onrus *p217*

Milkwood, Beach Rd, Onrus Beach, T028-3161516, 0900-2100. Standard breakfast and lunch menu, more upmarket dinners, good seafood including fresh grilled calamari and linefish plus venison and steaks, good views of the beach. R50 minimum charge on Sun.

What the Dickens, Onrus Trading Post, Main St, T028-3163946, 1000-late. Well-known and good-value pub lunches with a full menu in the evenings.

Hermanus and around *p217, map p218*

The tourist trade in Hermanus supports an enormous number of restaurants and cafés, far too many to list. It's just a case of wandering around town until you find something that takes your fancy, though it's advisable to book ahead in season.

Seafood at the Marine, The Marine, Marine Dr, T028-3131000, www.marine-hermanus.co.za, 1200-1400, 1900-2100. Voted the best seafood restaurant in South Africa in 2004, this superb establishment serves the freshest seafood in stylish surrounds. The menu is refreshingly unfussy, and includes a crayfish platter, seafood bunny chow, 'Rich man's' fish and chips and gorgeous prawn and leek ravioli with lobster bisque. The wine list is excellent and the service friendly and fast. Highly recommended. There is also the slightly cheaper **Seafood Express** in the hotel that is open for lunch only.

Annie se Kombuis, Warrington Arcade, Harbour Rd, T028-3131350. Tue-Sun 1000-late. Unusual menu of South African dishes such as waterblommetjies, babotie, oxtail, chicken pie, ostrich, venison and seafood, served up in a homely atmosphere.

Bientang's Cave, T028-3123454, www.bientangscave.com, 1130-1600, Fri and Sat 1900-2100. The name doesn't lie – the venue is an actual cave with an extended deck overlooking the waves. Superb spot for whale watching during season. Excellent seafood buffets and famous bouillabaisse soup, simple wood benches and long tables, very popular, book ahead. Access is via steps from the car park on Marine Drive between the village square and Marine Hotel – look out for the Bientang Seaworld sign.

The Burgundy, Market Sq, Marine Dr, T028-3122800, 0830-1700, 1900-2130, closed for dinner in winter. Restored rural cottage set back from the old harbour. One of the top restaurants in town but relaxed and good value, with tables spilling onto a shady terrace outside. Excellent seafood including superb grilled crayfish. Recommended.

Fisherman's Cottage, Old Harbour, T028-3123642, 1100-1500, 1800-2200. Tiny place set in an old thatched cottage serving excellent seafood, simple dishes such as seafood potjie, half and full portions available, charming setting. Choose a veranda table in good weather. Known as the smallest pub in town. No credit cards.

¶¶ **Mogg's Country Cookhouse**, Hemel-en-Aarde Valley, 12 km from Hermanus centre, take R43 out of town for Cape Town, after 2 km turn onto the R320 for Caledon, T028-3124321, Wed-Sun 1100-1600, Sat 1800-2100. Farm restaurant with a seasonal menu. Every dish is freshly prepared and served in a lovely rustic setting. Recommended.

¶ **Marimba Café**, 9 Royal Lane, off Main Rd, T028-3122148, 1100-late, closed Sun out of season. Fun 'African' restaurant with dishes from across the continent, including good seafood gumbo, Moroccan lamb shanks and Cape Malay curries. Also has daily specials and occasional live music.

¶ **Prince of Whales**, Astoria Village, T028-3130725, Mon-Fri 0815-1700, Sat 0815-1330. Excellent breakfasts, filled pancakes, sandwiches, cakes and fresh croissants.

¶ **Zebra Crossing**, corner of Long St and Main Rd, T028-3123906, Mon-Sat 0900-0200, Sun 1000-0200. Lively pub with zebra-print theme, serving burgers, steaks, salads and ploughman's lunches. Turns into a popular drinking haunt later at night.

Stanford and around *p221*

¶¶ **Blue Gum Estate**, on R326, T028-3410116, www.bluegum.co.za, 1200-1500, also Fri and Sat 1900-2200. Smart restaurant set on a luxurious country estate, stylish dining room and beautiful terrace, delicious local cuisine and good wine list.

¶¶ **Havercrofts**, 1 km from Stanford off the Hermanus road, T028-3410603. Lunch Sat and Sun, dinner Thu-Sat. No credit cards. Lovely setting with terrace overlooking the mountains, or inside next to a roaring fire, simple country menu, changes according to what is seasonally available, full wine list.

¶¶ **Mariana's Home Deli and Bistro**, 12 Du Toit St, T028-3410272, Fri-Sun, 0900-1600. Deli stocked with local products, cheeses, stuffed olives and chutneys. Also serves bistro-style meals on the vine-shaded terrace. The mussels are particularly good.

¶ **Stanhope Pub**, Matilda May St, follow the R43 towards Gansbaai, T028-3410536, 1200-1700. Worth a visit to sample the locally brewed Birkenhead beer in the surroundings of a proper pub. Pub lunches and a takeaway menu are available.

Gansbaai *p223*

¶¶ **The Great White House**, 5 Geelbek St, T028-3843273, www.white-house.co.za. At the lodge of the same name, see under Sleeping, 0730-1800. Daytime restaurant serving filling breakfasts, light lunches and snacks. The pan-fried calamari is very good, at Sun lunch the menu expands to include steaks. Can organize a 'catch and cook' outing – you go out in the fishing boat and catch your own fish, and they will cook it for you on your return.

¶ **Ciro's**, Franken St, T028-3841106, Tue-Sat 1100-late, Sun 1100-1600. Popular pub in a historic cottage, tiny interior or shady terrace outside, great seafood and steaks.

Bredasdorp *p224*

¶¶ **Blue Parrot**, Dirkie Uys St, T028-4251023, Mon-Fri 1130-1400, 1830-late, Sat 1830-late. Popular family restaurant, cosy candlelit tables, reliable food with standard steaks, pasta and salads, and local wine list.

¶¶ **Julian's**, 22 All Saints St, T028-4251201, 0900-late, closed Sun. Unusual purple and orange building next door to a ceramics factory that is worth a browse, the crockery is used and sold in the restaurant. Grills and seafood, sandwiches, pancakes and burgers, plenty of choice for vegetarians.

Struisbaai and L'Agulhas *p225*

¶¶¶ **Agulhas Country Lodge**, Main Rd, T028-4357650, www.agulhascountrylodge.com. Elegant restaurant set in a guesthouse which serves excellent fresh seafood – crayfish is a speciality. Also well known for its local lamb.

Festivals and events

Hermanus and around *p217, map p218*

Aug Hermanus Food and Wine Festival.

Sep Whale Festival, T028-3130928, www.whalefestival.co.za, is primarily an arts festival which attracts theatre and singing acts along with children's events and a craft market. A **Wild Flower Festival** is also held in Sep in Fernkloof Nature Reserve

Shopping

Hermanus and around *p217, map p218*

As befits a popular tourist town there are plenty of curio shops and speciality boutiques.

Market Sq has a small craft, curio and clothes market held daily. A popular shopping mall is the **Village Square**. To the west of the town centre is the larger **Gateway Centre**. This has all the high-street shops as well as restaurants and amusements for children.

Photography

Foto First, 102 Main Rd, T028-3130311, also at Gateway Centre inside the Spar supermarket T028-3130228. 1-hr processing.

Wine

Wine Village, at the entrance to the Hemel-en-Aarde Valley, corner of the R43 and the R320 on the way into town, T028-3163988, www.wine-village.co.za. Mon-Fri 0900-1800, Sat 0900-1700, Sun 1000-1500. This advertises itself as the biggest wine shop in South Africa and sells wine from over 380 estates. Can also organize international shipping.

Activities and tours

Hermanus and around *p217, map p218*

Diving

Scuba Africa, New Harbour, T028-3162362, www.scubaafrica.com. Equipment hire, dive courses (NAUI) and daily organized dives. In addition to coral reef and kelp forest dives, there are 3 stimulating wreck dives between here and Arniston. In Walker Bay, the most rewarding dives close to the shore are at Tamatiebank, which has been recommended for snorkelling, and The Haksteen, a pinnacle with steep drop-offs, 26 m. A short boat trip from the new harbour is Whale Rock, or Table Top. Conditions are quite calm, maximum depth is 40 m. Expect to see seafans and corals. From the high-tide mark to 500 m out to sea is a marine reserve. No marine animals may be collected or disturbed. **Warning** Do not attempt to dive when whales are in the bay. If you come within 300 m of a whale, either in a boat or the water, there are heavy fines, and visitors will be deported. Enjoy them from the cliff vantage points instead. For shark cage diving see under Gansbaai.

Fishing

For many local visitors the principal reason for coming to Hermanus is the excellent sea fishing. There are strict regulations concerning what you can catch, the bait you use and the actual season. Permits are available from any post office for R50. Most of the coastline in front of the town centre is a marine reserve so, although angling is allowed, nothing else may be removed from the sea in this area. Chartered fishing trips start from the new harbour; check with the tourist office for which charters are operating. Rock angling is popular with local fishermen, with steenbras, cob, red roman, silver fish, red stumpnose and John Brown often being caught. Deep-sea angling is more popular with foreign tourists, who hope to catch tuna, the local snoek and Cape salmon. Crayfish and perlemoen are a big draw for divers, but are subject to stringent regulations due to a problem with poaching.

Golf

Hermanus Golf Club, Main Rd, T028-3121954, www.hgc.co.za. This is a beautiful par-73 course in the lee of the mountains with heather-lined fairways, some holes have sea views, visitors welcome.

Hiking

There is a 10-km cliff path marked around Walker Bay, with plenty of potential whale-viewing spots.

Swimming

On a calm summer day Walker Bay looks cool and inviting from the cliff paths, but it has its dangers. There are strong undercurrents, so look out for warnings and advice, especially at spring tides. During the holidays all the popular swimming beaches have lifeguards on duty. Don't swim alone in isolated coves. There are several tidal pools which offer safe bathing for children and a fun place to snorkel for the first time. Below the Marine Hotel is the **Marine Tidal Pool** (*Bietang se Baaigat*), which always has plenty of sealife and fish. Along Westcliff Rd is a smaller pool known as **Fick's Pool**. This is a sheltered spot and has the bonus of a sandy bottom. There are toilets and changing rooms close by. Out of town there is a tidal pool at the Onrus River campsite which is open to day visitors.

Tour operators

Hermanus Whale Cruises, office in the New Harbour, T028-3132722, www.hermanus-

whale-cruises.co.za. Daily whale-watching cruises in season.
Southern Right Charters, office in the New Harbour, T082-3530550 (mob), seascapes@hermanus.co.za. Boat-based whale watching with a hydrophone on board allowing you to listen to the whales too.
Walker Bay Adventures, just out of town towards Gansbaai at Prawn Flats, T028-3140925, wbadventures@hermanus.co.za. All types of boats for hire, canoes, rowing boats, pedalos, plus fishing equipment. Daily cruises on the lagoon, weather permitting, for larger groups. The ever- popular sundowner cruise is also on offer.

Stanford and around *p221*
Boat cruises up the Klein River are a great way of enjoying the birdlife on the banks – there are around 130 species.
Klein River Cruises, T028-3410900, www.stanfordvillage.co.za.

Gansbaai *p223*
Great white shark cage diving
One of the most popular activities here is cage diving to see great white sharks. Several companies offer trips to view the sharks, and people with a diving certificate can see them from an underwater cage. Non-divers can snorkel at the top of the cage. The boats used are motorized catamarans and trips last 3-7 hrs. Alternatively you can go on a long shark diving day trip from Cape Town. This has become one of South Africa's booming tourist industries and viewing a great white at such close quarters is certainly an amazing experience. However, conservationists argue that these trips can be harmful to the sharks as they interfere with their natural eating patterns, and can encourage them to equate humans with food (contrary to popular belief, we do not feature on their standard menu). The companies beg to differ however, but if you are considering viewing the sharks off Dyer Island, check with the tourist offices in Cape Town or locally to find out which is currently the best company running trips, and try to choose one which is taking part in conservation and research into the species.
Shark Diving Unlimited, Gansbaai, T028-3842787, www.sharkdivingunlimited.co.za.
Shark Lady, Kleinbaai, T028-3123287, www.sharklady.co.za.
White Shark Adventures, 13 Main Rd, Gansbaai, T028-3841380, www.whitesharkdiving.com.
White Shark Diving Co., Kleinbaai, T028-3840782.

Tour operators
Dyer Island Cruises, T028-3840406, www.dyer-island-cruises.co.za. Boat trips to Dyer Island to see penguins and seals. All cruises depart from Kleinbaai harbour near Gansbaai and, during the season, whales and sharks may be spotted too.

L'Agulhas *p225*
Eco Quad, 612 Main Rd, T082-8545078, www.ecoquad.co.za. Guided nature trails on quad bikes in the Agulhas National Park.

Transport

Hermanus *p217, map p218*
Bus
Hermanus is 120 km from Cape Town (via N2). Despite being a popular destination, none of the 3 major coach companies runs a service via Hermanus. One of the easiest ways to visit, if you don't have a car, is to travel on the Baz Bus from **Cape Town** to **Bot Rivier** on the N2, which is 23 km from Hermanus. From here you can arrange to be collected by your hosts for a small fee, but this must be arranged in advance. **Splash Shuttle and Tours**, T028-3164004, splash@hermanus.co.za, can arrange a car shuttle service to and from **Cape Town**.

Directory

Hermanus *p217, map p218*
Banks Standard Bank, 99 Main Rd; ABSA, 67 Main Rd; there are also ATMs in all the shopping centres and arcades. **Internet** Great White Internet Shop, 2 Harbour Rd, T028-3130215. **Useful telephone numbers** Private Hospital, T028-3130168; Police, T10111.

Overberg interior

While most South Africans can tell you where the Overberg is, they might have difficulty defining its limits. It is a vague term which generally refers to the area to the east of the Hottentots Holland Mountains extending as far as Mossel Bay. To the north are the Langeberg Mountains and to the south the ocean.

Having climbed the spectacular Sir Lowry's Pass from Somerset West, the N2 highway cuts east across the interior of the Overberg towards Mossel Bay and George. The landscape is immediately very different on this side of the mountains – the road passes through serene forested hills before opening onto the endless dry, orange plains of the Overberg. To the north lie the Langeberg Mountains, their smooth foothills and sharp peaks providing a serene backdrop to the route. Most of the towns en route are quiet farming centres, and were some of the first areas settled by white farmers as they ventured east of Cape Town in search of new farmlands.

Most visitors choose to stick to the main road, and it is easy to pass quickly through the region without taking much in. If you are keen to get to the Garden Route, George can be reached in three hours, but there are several sights worth lingering over on the way. One centre that deserves a stopover is Swellendam, the third oldest town in the Cape. Nearby are a couple of nature reserves, and the town has some well-preserved examples of early Cape architecture.

In February 2006 there was the biggest fire in the Overberg in more than a century. During five long days the fire burnt an 80-km-long trail from Elim all the way to the fringes of Stanford (see pages 223 and 221), swallowing over 40,000 ha of farmland, natural and fynbos-fields and forestry plantation. It is expected to take many years for the vegetation to recover. Tragically, the Forest Lodge at Grootbos Private Nature Reserve was razed to the ground. ▸▸ *For Sleeping, Eating and other listings, see pages 243-247.*

East to Caledon on the N2

Ten kilometres from Sir Lowry's Pass is a turning signposted Villiersdorp, R321. This takes you back into the heart of the Winelands, or north to the Breede River Valley. A short loop takes you to the undistinguished twin towns of **Grabouw** and **Elgin**. Grabouw is presently enjoying fame all over South Africa as it is home to the country's hugely successful pop idol, Karin. She comes from an impoverished background and used to pack apples in a factory. So impressed was former president Nelson Mandela with her success in winning the popular competition, he asked to meet her and has used her as an example to all young South Africans of aspiration and achievement. Regional information is available from **Elgin Valley Tourism** ⓘ *T021-8591398, www.tourismelginvalley.co.za, Tue-Fri 1000- 1700, Sat and Sun 1000-1400*, on the main road. Continuing east, the N2 crosses the Houhoek Pass where there is a famous watering hole, the **Houw Hoek Inn**, always worth a stop (see Sleeping page 243). Also a short distance from Grabouw is a small flower park known as the **Kathleen Murray Reserve**. At Bot River is the turning for Hermanus. It is a further 23 km to the regional capital of the Overberg, Caledon.

Grabouw is the centre of South Africa's apple industry and is where the popular fizzy drink Appletizer is made.

Hottentots Holland Nature Reserve

ⓘ *The entrance to the reserve is at Nuweberg, high in Viljoen's Pass between Grabouw and Villiersdorp. To get there turn left at Elgin, on to the R321. After about 10 km, at the bottom of Viljoens Pass past Nuweberg Dam, turn left to the Nuweberg Forest Station and reserve office. Reserve information: www.capenature.org.za, enquiries: T021-8514060. There is an information centre, gift shop, nursery and restaurant open for breakfast, lunch and afternoon tea, which is an excellent spot for viewing the birdlife.*

The Hottentots Holland Mountains are the southern end of a continuous mountainous chain which extends inland as far as Ceres and beyond, effectively cutting the Cape off from the rest of South Africa, and overlooking False Bay. The 42,000-ha reserve stretches from Elgin in the south to beyond Villiersdorp in the north, and from the Stellenbosch Mountains in the west, eastwards to the Groenland Mountains. It's an important conservation area for mountain fynbos: over 1300 species have been recorded here, including some rare and endemic plants. There are also small populations of rhebuck, klipspringer, duiker and grysbok.

Being so close to Cape Town makes this an important and popular hiking region. Various restrictions are in force to help protect the flora and fauna as well as the physical landscape. The main trail in the reserve is the **Boland Hiking Trail**. The full circuit is 50 km and takes three days to cover. The shorter hikes are known as the **Nuweberg Circuit** and the **Riviersonderend Canyon**. Due to flooding, all hiking trails are closed from July to the end of August.

Caledon and around

» *pp243-247. Colour map 8, grid B2.*

The regional capital of the Overberg, 120 km from Cape Town, lies just off the N2 at the foot of the Swartberg Mountains. It is a typical rural town – small and quiet, with a couple of sights, but only really worth an hour or two; it's best to press on to Swellendam for an overnight stay. The town is famous for its six naturally occurring hot springs, which produce over 800,000 litres per day. The water has a high ferrous carbonate content. Not surprisingly the first European settler, Ferdinandus Appel, sought to develop the springs. He was granted an 18-ha freehold, on the condition that he built baths and accommodation. Word of the water's healing powers spread quickly, and distinguished guests from the Dutch East India Company frequented the springs. At the turn of the century the Caledon Mineral Baths and Sanatorium was built to cash in fully on their popularity. For 40 years they continued to be an attraction until a fire destroyed the complex in 1946. It was only in 1990 that a new hotel, **The Caledon** (see Sleeping page 243), was built. Day visitors can use the spa's facilities which includes a waterfall and a series of pools. The one at the top is the hottest with water temperatures averaging 40°C. There are additional saunas, gym, cold pool, steam room, and treatments available such as massages and facials.

75% of South Africa's blue cranes, the national bird, are found in the Overberg.

Today the prosperity of the town and the region is based on agriculture. Caledon was the centre of a major development in wool production with a new breed of sheep, the merino. For information visit **Caledon Tourist Bureau** ⓘ *22 Plein St, T028-2121511, calmuse@intekom.co.za, Mon-Fri 0800-1300, 1400-1630, Sat 0900-1300*; or **Cape Overberg Tourism Association** ⓘ *Church St, T028-2141466, www.capeoverberg.org, Mon-Fri 0800-1630.*

The **Caledon House Museum** ⓘ *11 Constitution St, T028-2121511, Mon-Fri 0800-1700, Sat 0800-1230, small entrance fee*, is based in a Victorian house that was originally the Freemasons' Lodge. It has displays on local history, domestic items and crafts. There is a working kitchen where bread is baked every few days. For a small fee the curator will show you around and make the items on display a bit more interesting. The museum shop in Donkin Square is full of local farm produce and curios. Mill Street has a collection of historic buildings which have been declared national monuments. The Holy Trinity Church on Prince Alfred Drive is a small, neat church dating from 1855. Outings to local wetlands and the nearby nature reserves

In the early days of settlement, people would refer to the area beyond the Hottentots Holland as 'over the berg'. It was not until the construction of Sir Lowry's Pass that the region began to be cultivated.

can be arranged for bird enthusiasts; contact the tourist office for details. Look out for the endangered blue crane which is found in the area on open farmland. Due to their vulnerable status, an Overberg Crane Group was created in 1991 by Cape Nature Conservation to devise a protection programme.

Caledon Nature Reserve

This small reserve, 214 ha, is just on the edge of town. Since 1892 the annual wild flower show has been held in the grounds, usually in September. Part of the reserve was turned into the **Victoria Wild Flower Garden** ⓘ *0700-1700*, by Cecil Young and CW Meiring in 1927, local enthusiasts who had the foresight to protect the amazingly rich local flora. Of the 630 known species of *erica* in the world, over 200 grow in the Caledon district. This may not be everyone's cup of tea (56 ha of the reserve were converted into formal gardens with ponds, shaded paths and picnic spots) but for the botanist it is a unique attraction. Within the reserve there is a 10-km walk, the **Meiring Trail**, a good chance to appreciate the many species of fynbos and birds of the area. There is no shelter and hikers must bring all their drinking water. Allow up to five hours for the full circuit. A leaflet from the tourist office has a simple map of the hiking trail.

Greyton → *Colour map 8, grid B2.*

Just a short drive north of the main N2 highway, the quiet village of Greyton is a popular place to retire and attracts many artists. The mixture of restored old buildings and streets, lined with oaks, have helped create a low-key and peaceful atmosphere. When the first streets were laid out in 1854, the settlement was named after Sir George Grey, who had served two periods as governor of the Cape Colony. To the north lie the **Riviersonderend Mountains**, which in winter often have snow on their peaks – Kanonberg (1466 m) is the tallest peak overlooking the village. The **Greyton Nature Reserve** is at the edge of town on the southern slopes of the Sonderend Mountains. The best time to visit is from September to November. There is a short 20 minutes' walk to the **Noupoort Gorge**, which can be followed close to the Kanonberg summit. There are a number of streams running off the hills through forested valleys, with the occasional waterfall which can be reached by paths. Greyton is at the end of the well-known **Boesmankloof Hiking Trail**. This 16-km trail links Greyton with the village of **McGregor** on the northern side of the Riviersonderend Mountains (see page 201 for further details). For tourist information, contact **Greyton Tourism** ⓘ *Library Building, Main St, T028-2549414, www.greyton.net, Tue-Fri 1000-1630, Sat 1000-1600.*

Swellendam and around

▸▸ *pp243-247. Colour map 8, grid C2.*

Founded in 1745, Swellendam is the third oldest European town in South Africa, and it is also one of its most picturesque. The main centre bears witness to its age with an avenue of mature oak trees and whitewashed Cape Dutch homesteads. Unfortunately, before the town fully appreciated their inherent charm and tourist potential, many of the trees and older buildings were knocked down in 1974 to widen the main street. Nevertheless, the town is very pretty and has an appealing, quiet atmosphere, which combined with the rural setting and beautiful views makes it a very pleasant spot to spend a day or two. Swellendam also acts as an important base for exploring the region, with the Breede River Valley, the Little Karoo and the coast all within easy reach, and it is roughly halfway between Cape Town and the Garden Route.

Tourist information is available at **Swellendam Tourism** ⓘ *Oefeningshuis, Voortrek St, T028-5142770, www.swellendamtourism.co.za, Mon-Fri 0900-1300, 1400-1700, Sat 0900-1200*. This office produces a leaflet called *Swellendam Treasures* which outlines the interesting Cape Dutch buildings still standing today.

Background

Swellendam started as a trading outpost for the Dutch East India Company. The new settlement was named after Governor Hendrik Swellengrebel and his wife, Ten Damme. Once established, all sorts of characters passed through looking for their fortunes or more land. One of the most successful was Joseph Barry who, in the 1800s, had a virtual monopoly on all trade between Cape Town and the new settlements in the Overberg and Little Karoo.

In 1795 a particularly strange event took place. Just at the point when British soldiers were bringing an end to Dutch rule in the Cape, the burghers of Swellendam declared themselves to be an independent republic, in a reaction to the maladministration and corruption of the Dutch East India Company. Hermanus Steyn was president from 17 June to 4 November 1795 – once the British had set up a new regime in Cape Town, the republic was quietly forgotten about. During the 19th century the town prospered and grew as the agricultural sector gradually expanded. This came to an abrupt halt in May 1865, when a fire that started in a baker's destroyed 40 of the town's finest old buildings. Even greater harm was caused by a prolonged drought, and when in 1866 the influential Barry Empire was declared bankrupt the whole region's fortunes declined. Today the town is a prosperous community, and many of the old buildings are still standing, or have been restored.

Sights

Drostdy Museum ⓘ *Swellengrebel St, T028-5141138, www.drostdymuseum.com, Mon-Fri 0900-1645, Sat and Sun 1000-1545, R10*. Of all the old Cape buildings in town, this museum is the most impressive and is often described as one of the country's great architectural treasures. The main building dates from 1747, built as the official residence and seat for the local magistrate or *landdrost*. Originally built in the shape of a T, the addition of two wings changed the form to an H. Inside, some of the floors have been preserved; what was the lounge has a lime-sand floor, while the kitchen floor is made from cow dung, which helps keep the room cool. The museum concentrates on local history, with a well-preserved collection of 18th- and 19th-century furniture. Within the grounds is a restored Victorian cottage, **Mayville**, which has an antique rose garden plus the original gazebo and is today home to a coffee shop.

Close by is an open-air display, on the Crafts Green, of many of the early farm tools, charcoal burners, wagons and a horse-driven mill complete with threshing floor. Opposite the museum is the **Old Gaol building**, T028-5143847, which housed both prisoners and local government officials, including the jailer who was also the postmaster. In the middle of all the cells was one without windows, known as the 'black hole'. Today, this is a local arts and crafts centre, with a good café (see Eating, page 246).

Not far from the town centre are more restored buildings from the town's early days. The **Oefeningshuis** (1838) first served as a place for the religious instruction of freed slaves; it now houses the tourist office. Note the painted plaster clock face, which reads 1215, set above a working clock. This was designed for illiterate church goers – if the painted face was the same as the clock's, it was time for service. Worth a look is the fine, domineering **Dutch Reformed Church**. This large whitewashed building has a tall central clock tower and a mix of architectural styles. Just next to the church, on **Church Square**, are some fine examples of early two-storey town houses built by wealthy farmers who used to visit the town for holy communion. The square had to be large enough to hold their ox wagons. Another grand town house is the **Auld House** dating from 1802 which for many years was the family home for the Overberg trader, Joseph Barry. Inside is some furniture, originally fitted on a steamer which used to sail between Cape Town and Port Beaufort. Also worth a visit is the small **church of St Luke** built in 1865. Finally, look out for the shop **Buirski & Co**, built in 1880. It has one of the finest examples of Victorian wrought-iron balconies and fittings in the town.

Swellendam is an ideal base for exploring this part of the Overberg. Close by is the small Bontebok National Park, and the larger Marloth Nature Reserve. They have only simple accommodation and both can easily be visited on a day trip. **Suurbraak**, 25 km towards Tradouw Pass, is a small village established by the London Missionary Society in 1812. Many of the buildings have been restored to their original forms, and it is very much a living museum. The village is well known for its hand-made wooden chairs.

Bontebok National Park → *Colour map 8, grid C2.*

Although this is one of South Africa's 17 national parks, it has less of interest than other parks. Nevertheless, this is a good place to spot several species of antelope, and has a pleasant riverside setting. Most of the park is accessible by car, and there are two 2-km self-guided nature trails which you can walk at any time without a permit or booking. Guided walks are organized when there is sufficient demand. Swimming and fishing are both possible in the Breede River, but only within the confines of the campsite. An angling licence must be shown.

Ins and outs The park is 238 km from Cape Town and 6 km from Swellendam. The turning off the N2 is clearly signposted, on the George side of Swellendam. There is a 5-km gravel road from the highway to the entrance. Information is available at the **office** ⓘ *T028-5142735, www.sanparks.org, Oct-Apr 0800-1900, May-Sep 0800-1800, R20.*

Background At the beginning of the 20th century the bontebok was the rarest species of antelope in Africa. It had been hunted and driven off its natural habitat by the settler farmers in the Overberg. Fortunately, something even scarcer came to their rescue – a group of local conservation-minded farmers, who recognized the need to set up a protected area to save the remaining animals. In 1931 the first reserve was established, but it was not until the herd was moved to a more suitable environment beside the Breede River in 1960 that the numbers started to recover significantly. This has proved to be a success, but although no longer endangered there are still not many places where the bontebok can be seen in the wild. Today, other antelope indigenous to the Overberg have been introduced to the reserve including red hartebeest, steenbok and duiker plus the rare Cape mountain zebra.

Marloth Nature Reserve → *Colour map 8, grid C2.*

This mountain reserve encompasses a number of the peaks and forested valleys of the Langeberg Mountains. Looking at the peaks from the centre of Swellendam, locals claim to be able to tell the time between 0700 and 1300 by the shadows cast by seven of the **Clock Peaks**. There is a variety of hiking trails, including a rewarding six-day route. Small stands of indigenous forest have been preserved. These are very important when you consider that the mountains were once forested all the way along this coast from Cape Town to Port Elizabeth and beyond. Today, only a few small pockets of forest remain. Some of the more common indigenous trees which can be seen in the reserve include yellowwood, red alder, hard pear, spoon wood, Cape beech and cherrywood. The wildlife is confined to mountain species – look out for klipspringer standing on rock outcrops, and if you're lucky you may glimpse bushbuck in the cooler, darker patches of forest. The colourful Cape sugarbird is a common sight on flowering aloes and ericas.

Ins and outs

Follow the signs to the forest station, 3 km to the north of Swellendam. The ideal time to visit is in the spring (September and October) when the flowers are at their best. The wettest months are March and October. Permits for the six-day walk or climbing the peaks are issued from the **office** ⓘ *T028-5141410, www.capenature.org.za, Mon-Fri 0800-1600.* Check availability at weekends, as numbers are limited. The only accommodation within the reserve is in basic huts (see Sleeping, page 245).

Hiking The **Swellendam Trail** is the principal hiking trail in and around Marloth Reserve. The complete circular route is 74 km long and hikers are advised to allow six days for the full circuit. This was the first trail designed in the Cape to return hikers back to their starting point without having to backtrack. Hiking conditions require a medium level of fitness, as there are strenuous segments when the trail goes around several peaks. Each day's walking passes through montane forest as well as open fynbos terrain. Be wary of the sun and carry plenty of water. The six overnight huts are fitted out with bunks, toilets and drinking water. Do not walk in heavy rain or misty conditions.

Shorter day walks are possible in the vicinity of the entrance gate by the forest station. Six trails have been defined, ranging from an easy stroll to the picnic site in a sheltered valley known as the Hermitage, to an all-day trail taking in two of the peaks closest to Swellendam. The most difficult day walk climbs from the car park to the Tienuurkop peak (1195 m), along a ridge to Twaalfuurkop (1428 m), and then zigzags back down to the entrance. The walk is 9 km and takes at least eight hours. The other day walks are on the lower slopes and most can be completed in less than three hours. Day walks do not require permits or pre-booking.

Heidelberg to Albertina

» *pp243-247. Colour map 8, grid C2.*

Continuing east from Swellendam along the N2 highway, the road bypasses several small agricultural towns which have little of interest to detain most tourists. One of these settlements is Heidelberg, which is dominated by its Dutch Reformed church on the banks of the Duivenhoks River. The first settlers arrived in the valley in 1725, and in 1855 it was named Heidelberg after the city in Germany. To the north in the Langeberg Mountains is the Grootvadersbosch Nature Reserve (see below). The Anglican church, St Barnabas, has some wood sculptures of note and particularly fine rose windows. **Tourist information** ⓘ *3 Eksteen St, T028-7222700, www.heidelberginfo.co.za.*

Grootvadersbosch Nature Reserve

→ *Colour map 8, C2.*

ⓘ *All advance details and reservations are made through the manager, T028-4255020, or www.capenature.org.za. Permits are available in the reserve on arrival, but note that the trails have a limit of 12 people so it is a good idea to pre-book.* One of the places worth visiting around here is the Grootvadersbosch Nature Reserve outside Heidelberg. The 250 ha of preserved forest is the finest remaining cover of indigenous forest in the southwestern Cape. There is an excellent hiking trail (see below) and paths which provide easy access to the forest. The early settlers in the Overberg managed to satisfy the huge demand for hardwoods at the turn of the 19th/20th century throughout South Africa, but in doing so almost totally destroyed the unique forests in the Cape. Grootvadersbosch was established to preserve the area and restore it to its former beauty. Between 1896 and 1913 alien trees such as ash, bluegum, Californian redwood, Australian blackwood and camphor were planted on the slopes, cleared of indigenous forest. Efforts are now being made to reclaim these areas. The wilderness areas remain untouched and this is reflected in the richness of wildlife and birdlife one encounters while walking here. There is a good chance of seeing the shy bushbuck in the forest.

Ins and outs The reserve is 22 km northwest of Heidelberg on the R322 towards Tradouw Pass. Coming from Swellendam, take the R324 turning for Suurbraak then keep heading in the direction of Heidelberg – the left turning for the reserve is 27 km further on. There is a simple campsite by the entrance gates with 10 camping pitches and two cottages, communal ablution block and thatched braai area with fridge. Look out for a bird hide 500 m into the reserve. The nearest comfortable accommodation is in Swellendam, 40 km away.

 Hiking The **Bushbuck Trail** is a series of paths allowing you to choose a route between 2 km and 10 km without having to backtrack too often. The paths weave between the moist and dry forest of the slopes of the Langeberg Mountains. The best periods for walking are May to July and December to January.

Witsand → *Colour map 8, grid C2.*

Just outside Swellendam is the R324 turning to Witsand, a quiet, picturesque seaside town at the mouth of the Breede River. The area is best known for its land-based whale watching and its excellent fishing, but there is little other reason to come here. The town is small and peaceful and as such attracts mainly older couples wanting to escape the bustle of larger resorts. From June to November southern right whales come to the bay to calve and rear their young and the town is frequently dubbed the 'whale nursery' by the regional tourist boards. In 2005 a count by helicopter recorded 94 whales including 43 calves in the bay on one day during the season. In town, one building of note is the wool store built for the Barry family business. The neighbouring settlement of **Port Beaufort** was built by Joseph Barry, a businessman from Swellendam who for a period dominated all forms of trade in the Overberg (see page 239). Large boats from Cape Town unloaded their cargo here, which was then transferred to river boats and taken upstream as far as Malgas. The Barry family built a church in the village in 1859, which is now a national monument. For tourist information contact the **Witsand Tourism Bureau** ⓘ *T028-5371010, www.witsandtourism.co.za, on the main street.*

Riversdale → *Colour map 8, grid C2.*

Riversdale is a small farming centre based around wheat, wool and potatoes. There is little in town for visitors other than fuel and food, although there is the small **Julius Gordon Africana Museum** ⓘ *Mon-Fri 0800-1300*, on Long Street, which outlines the lives of several local characters and is home to some paintings by Thomas Baines and Peter Wenning. Around the town are no fewer than 15 stone churches, the oldest being the St Matthew's Anglican Church, built in 1856. The district is well known for the growing of Agathosma shrubs which emit a very strong aroma. For anyone with an interest in wild flowers the **Van Riebeeck Garden** has a superb collection of aloes and vygies. The best time to visit is in May and June when the flowers are in full bloom. The **Werner Frehse Nature Reserve** outside the town has a few small antelope. The road to Ladismith in the north crosses the spectacular Garcia Pass before entering the Little Karoo. The **tourist office** ⓘ *corner of Mitchell and Hudson Sts, T028-7131996, www.tourismriversdale.co.za*, is not very used to drop-in visitors.

Still Bay → *Colour map 8, grid C3.*

This small fishing village is in a beautiful spot straddling both sides of the Kafferkuils River. On the west bank is a fishing harbour, while the east bank holds a cluster of holiday cottages and shops. The beach is sandy and safe for swimmers. Surfers speak of good waves here, while the river is ideal for small pleasure boats. The bridge joining the two settlements was opened in 1955, replacing a pontoon that had been in use since 1930. Like many South African seaside towns, Still Bay remains eerily quiet for much of the year, but during the school summer holidays the place comes alive with families. Next to the **tourist office** ⓘ *on the east bank, T028-7542602, www.stilbaaitourism.com*, eels are fed Monday to Saturday at 1100.

Albertina → *Colour map 8, grid C2.*

Being only a few hours from Cape Town and tantalizingly close to the Garden Route, few people stop here, though it does have its own **tourist office** ⓘ *at the Engen petrol station, T028-7351000, www.albertina.co.za*. The predominant business is still wheat and sheep farming, although the local economy was able to diversify following the discovery in the 1920s of large ochre deposits. Another unusual product collected around Albertina is the juice from aloe plants, *Aloe ferox*, which is an important ingredient in medicine and cosmetics. You can visit the **Alcare Aloe Factory** ⓘ *T028-7351454, www.alcare.co.za*, just outside town. They conduct free daily tours and sell a variety of aloe skincare products and there's a coffee shop.

Garden Route Game Lodge ⓘ *7 km east of Albertina off the N2, transfers from Cape Town can be arranged, T028-7351200, www.grgamelodge.co.za*, is a private game lodge that has been stocked with a number of species of large game including giraffe, white rhino, lion, elephant, kudu, zebra, wildebeest and buffalo. It's a popular overnight stay from Cape Town and one of the nearest places to the city for wildlife viewing. There is luxurious accommodation at the lodge but day visitors are also welcome for game drives and lunch, which must be pre-booked. As well as morning and evening game drives, tours of the reptile centre are on offer where the resident herpetologist (reptile man) will share his knowledge of snakes, crocodiles and other cold-blooded creatures. You can also visit the recently established cheetah breeding centre and there is a variety of programmes for children including bush survival skills, children's game drives and guided bush and insect walks. Also see Sleeping, page 245.

On the N2 10 km out of Albertina and 40 km before Mossel Bay you'll see a crowd of people gathered at the Gouritz River bridge. This is a popular **bungee jump** ⓘ *daily 0900-1700, T044-6977001, www.faceadrenaline.com, booking isn't necessary, just pitch up and jump, bungee R180, bridge swing R170 single, R240 tandem*, from the road bridge into the 65-m-deep river gorge. There's also a bridge swing, similar to a bungee but with an outward swing as opposed to a straight up and down jump. Both are fun but at only around 60 m, pale in comparison to the 216-m Bloukrans Bridge Bungee further up the Garden Route, which is the highest in the world.

Sleeping

East to Caledon on the N2 *p236*

L **Villa Exner**, 11 Essenhout Av, Grabouw, T021-8593596, www.villaexner.com. Country retreat with 4 suites in the main whitewashed manor house and 2 garden units, elegantly furnished with art and designer pieces, 2 lounges with fireplaces, library and dining rooms, swimming pool in rolling lawns, close to the Hottentots Holland Nature Reserve.

B **Houw Hoek Inn**, off N2 12 km past Grabouw, T021-2849646, www.houwhoekinn.co.za. The oldest licensed hotel in South Africa. 33 a/c rooms in an elegant country hotel, the oldest section dates from 1779, the upstairs was built in 1860. All the rooms have en suite bathrooms, the dining room is in a converted farm building, it is very popular at weekends when dinner dances are held. The gardens are dominated by large old oak and blue gum trees, swimming pool.

B **Wildekrans Country House**, Houw Hoek Farm, turn left at the Houw Hoek Inn sign, follow road round to left, the farm is on your right, T021-2849827, wildekrans@kingsley.co.za. 6 rooms, 1 apartment, TV, non-smoking room, restaurant, swimming pool, wild farm gardens with lots of rose bushes, national monument, quiet setting on a working farm.

Hottentots Holland Nature Reserve *p236*

There are 2 overnight huts in the reserve: F **Keurkieboom Chalet**, sleeping 2, and **Rusbos** which sleeps up to 6. There is no accommodation at the reserve entrance, Nuweberg, but there are some toilets and shower facilities. Each hut is equipped with bunks, mattresses, basic cooking facilities and water. Keurkieboom has solar panels to provide electricity. Fires are only allowed at braai sites as there is a high risk of veld fires.

Caledon and around *p237*

AL-A **The Caledon Hotel & Spa**, 1 Nerina Av, T028-2145100, www.thecaledon.co.za, 1 km out of town just off the N2. Unattractive modern complex based at the historic springs, with a flashy casino, 95 a/c rooms and a couple of restaurants, including **Ouma's Country Kitchen** restaurant and **Wheatlands** garden terrace for light meals, rates are half board. There is a pub with log fires, extensive gardens, a number of hot and cold pools, a beauty clinic, mountain bikes for hire, full-size snooker tables, 18-hole putting golf and the excellent Victorian hot-spring baths enclosed by a pavilion. Most people come here for the brash casino.

Greyton *p238*

B **Greyton Lodge**, 46 Main Rd, T028-2549876, www.greytonlodge.com. 12 en suite rooms, some with 4-poster beds, in a renovated 1882 trading store that has also served as a police station, excellent restaurant open to non-guests for dinner from 1900, swimming pool, gardens, comfortable country lodge feel, a neat whitewashed building with a corrugated-iron roof and small veranda.

B **The Post House**, 42 Main Rd, T028-2549995, www.posthouse.co.za. A high-quality country guesthouse, 13 rooms with a Beatrix Potter theme, the honeymoon suite is called Two Bad Mice. Each room has an open fire and a private veranda. The oldest parts of the building, which was once a post office, date back to 1860. Good food and service, picnic baskets prepared to order, colourful gardens, swimming pool, quiet setting, easy access to the village. Recommended.

C **Blue Crane Guest House**, 58 Main Rd, T/F028-2549839, robertsonc@mweb.co.za. 5 double rooms with en suite bathroom, each has a spectacular view of the mountains. Comfortable lounge and TV room with open log fire, ideal hideaway during a wet winter's day, swimming pool.

E **Municipal Campsite**, Krige Rd, T028-2549620, 2 km from village centre. Basic with clean washblocks and swimming downstream in the Riviersonderend River.

Swellendam and around *p238*

AL-A **Klippe Rivier Country House**, from the N2 take the R60, left at crossroads, 2 km, T028-5143341, www.klipperivier.com. 6 double rooms in and around a restored Cape Dutch homestead (1820), declared a national monument. Large rooms with brass beds, gleaming wooden floors, some with cosy fireplaces and under thatch, private balconies, superb restaurant (see Eating, page), swimming pool, a peaceful and superior location, look out for owls in the oak trees, family owned and managed. Recommended.

A **De Kloof**, 8 Weltevreden St, T028-5141303, www.dekloof.co.za. Elegant thatched house set in a neat garden, 6 double rooms with en suite bathroom, TV lounge, library and cigar bar, gym with mountain views, garden, swimming pool, evening meals available, very friendly. Recommended.

B **Adin & Sharon's Hideaway**, 10 Hermanus Steyn St, T028-5143316, www.adinbb.co.za. Award-winning B&B in the centre of town. 3 spacious, comfortable en suite rooms with a/c, in a Victorian cottage, overlooking a neat, shady garden with 600 rose bushes and a splash pool. Excellent breakfasts, very friendly hosts. Recommended.

B **Coachman Guesthouse**, 14 Drostdy St, T028-5142294, www.coachman.co.za. Lovely whitewashed converted historic homestead with 3 en suite double rooms with separate entrances, plus 2 thatched garden-cottages with log fires. TV lounge, laundry, evening meals available, swimming pool.

B **Moolmanshof**, 217 Voortrek St, T028-5143258, www.moolmanshof.homestead.com. A homestead built in 1798 and full of character with 3 en suite rooms, furnished with antiques, guest lounge with TV, swimming pool, mature gardens, ask for John or Allison. Recommended.

B **Old Mill Guest House & Restaurant**, 241 & 243 Voortrek St, T028-5142790, www.oldmill.co.za. En suite rooms in a beautiful listed building set in a spacious garden with a stream flowing through, superb meals served in the restaurant which is well known for its Belgian pancakes and waffles. Slightly overpriced, but still recommended.

B **Swellengrebel**, 91 Voortrek St, T028-5141144, swellengrebel@worldonline.co.za. Large, bland and modern hotel set on the main road, with 48 rooms, some with mountain views, restaurant with good food, swimming pool, pool room, jacuzzi, sauna and gym, noisy public bar. Comfortable, but seems a shame to stay somewhere so characterless compared to most of the B&Bs in town. Ask about weekend discounts.

B **Woodpecker Cottage**, 270 Voortrekker St, T028-5142924, www.woodpecker.co.za. Restored historic thatched cottage, 2 twin rooms with bathrooms, pleasant decor with some antiques, also 1 spacious garden cottage with veranda, swimming pool, and craft shop in the garden. The owner is an ex-tour guide and speaks several languages.

B-C **Klein Drostdy**, 12 Drostdy St, T028-5141542. 6 rooms with en suite bathroom in an old home full of beautiful antiques. Good breakfasts, swimming pool, billiard room, large leafy gardens, near the museum.

C-E **Swellendam Caravan Park**, Glen Barry Rd, T028-5142705, info@swellenmun.co.za. 20 fully equipped thatched chalets, 4 beds, bring own linen, 100 well-grassed and shady tent and caravan stands. A beautiful and peaceful setting with good mountain views within walking distance of town centre, popular during school holidays.

D-E **Swellendam Backpackers**, 5 Lichtenstein St, T028-5142648, www.swellendamback packers.co.za. An excellent hostel with a small dorm in the main house, plus individual Wendy houses (no electricity) in secluded corners around the garden, lots of camping space, internet, well-organized kitchen, home-cooked breakfasts and dinners. Can arrange local tours, hiking in the mountains and visits to the nearby Bontebok National Park. The Baz Bus calls here twice a day.

Bontebok National Park *p240*

Always check availability in advance if you plan to stay in the park. There is a small shop in the office selling basic groceries, meat, wine and beer; all other supplies can be bought 6 km away in Swellendam. Petrol is available in the park. Electricity is generated in the park and goes off at 2130.

Reservations through SAN Parks Pretoria office, T012-4289111, www.sanparks.org. Bookings can also be made in person at the offices in Cape Town and Durban (see p44). Direct number T028-5142735.

C Chalavans An unappealing option in a 6-berth caravan with a prefab structure on one side which provides more space and headroom. The caravans are a bit run down.

D Camping 21 pitches, no electric points, lanterns used, shower blocks. The location on the Breede River where you can swim makes up for the tired facilities. Given the park's proximity to Swellendam, many visitors choose to stay in town.

Marloth Nature Reserve *p240*

For reservations contact T028-4255020, www.capenature.org.za.

C Cottages 2 basic self-catering cottages, one sleeping 8, the other 5, good value for families or groups, fully equipped kitchens with microwave, stove, fridge and all utensils, bedding provided, comfortable option especially for the night before tackling the Swellendam Hiking Trail.

E Hiking huts 6 basic huts equipped with bunks, bush toilets and drinking water, which can accommodate 22 hikers. If you stay in these huts bring all your provisions, they only provide a roof and a mattress. Firewood is only provided at 2 of the huts, Koloniesbos and Wolfkloof, but you are not permitted to light fires elsewhere in the reserve. Bring a gas stove for cooking.

Witsand *p242*

A-B **Breede River Lodge**, T028-5371631, www.breederiverlodge.co.za. Comfortable en suite lodges and hotel cabins overlooking the river, well furnished, some with dining area and kitchenette, great views, restaurant serves fresh seafood. Bar, boats and fishing tackle for hire for trips up the river.

C **Big Cob Chalets**, 104 Main Rd, T028-5371942, bigcob@telkomsa.net. 4 self-catering chalets with 3 rooms, thatched roof, neat gardens, each room has twin beds, fully equipped, braai area, secure parking.

Riversdale *p242*

C **Sleeping Beauty**, 3 Long St, T028-7131651, sleepingbeauty@iafrica.com. A Victorian guesthouse with 5 double rooms, 1 family room, homemade breads for breakfast, lush gardens and double-storey veranda.

Still Bay *p242*

C **Papillon**, corner of Perlemoen and Seebreis St, T028-7542227, papillon@telkomsa.net. Beachfront cottage with 2 double rooms, 1 single, and a separate flat that sleeps 2. Fully-equipped kitchen, laundry, gardens rolling down to beach, views of the bay, braai area, TV and video, internet, wheelchair friendly.

Albertina *p242*

AL **Garden Route Game Lodge**, 7 km east of Albertina off the N2, transfers from Cape Town can be arranged, T028-7351200, www.grgamelodge.co.za. Accommodation in main lodge or in secluded thatched chalets, decorated with an African theme, superb restaurant serving local dishes, comfortable bar, swimming pool, rates include game drives and meals, special activities for children, horse riding and quad-biking also on offer.

C **Albertina Country Hotel**, Main St, T028-7351030, albertina-hotel@rvd.dorea.co.za. Comfortable town hotel with friendly service, 16 en suite rooms with TV, good traditional restaurant, rates are for B&B. If you are not staying the pub lunches are recommended on your way through.

Eating

East to Caledon on the N2 *p236*

ᛘ **Houw Hoek Farm Stall**, by the Houw Hoek Inn, see Sleeping page 243. Light lunches, coffee and picnic hampers, and it's open on Fri nights for dinner. Several local farms have small stalls selling a variety of fresh fruit juices and other fruit products.

Caledon and around *p237*

ᛘ **The Coffee Nook**, 16 Donkin St, T028-2122744. The oldest coffee shop in town, closed evenings. Also sells local crafts.

ᛘ **Dassiesfontein**, on the N2 between Caledon and Bot River, T028-2141475. 0830-1730. Country restaurant and farm stall selling homemade bread, cheese and biltong, tables in the cottage decorated with antiques, local dishes such as bobotie and bredie, good chicken and game pies.

Greyton *p238*

ᛘᛘ **Greyton-on-Main**, 31 Main St, T028-2549722, Sat and Sun 1200-1500, Thu-Sat 1800-late, no dinner on Sun. Housed in an old trading store with a lovely bar and blue porcelain on the tables, à la carte or set menu, unusual European dishes such as sauerkraut and mash, plus a fine cheeseboard and the chef's special chocolate mousse.

Swellendam and around *p238*

Most local restaurants are closed Sun evening; be prepared to eat by 2100.

ᛘᛘᛘ **Klippe Rivier Country House**, see Sleeping, page 244, T028-5143341, breakfast and dinner, booking essential. Popular restaurant, delicious Cape haute cuisine served in a classic Cape Dutch manor and manicured gardens, good wine list. Recommended.

ᛘᛘ **The Connection**, 132 Voortrek St, T028-5141988. Pleasant restaurant serving light lunches, and meatier dinners such as venison, hearty soups, some Italian dishes, outdoor tables on terrace.

ᛘᛘ **Herberg Roosjie van de Kaap**, 5 Drostdy St, T028-5143001. Breakfast 0800-1000, dinner 1900-2130, closed Mon. Local word has this down as the best place to eat in town. Booking essential for dinner. Cosy atmosphere in a candlelit room with thick walls and a low roof. Superb gourmet pizzas plus hearty South African fare, good steaks and seafood, fine wines. Recommended.

ᛘᛘ **Koornlands**, 5 Voortrek St, T028-5143567, lunch and dinner, closed Tue. A historic Cape Dutch cottage serving local food such as crocodile steaks, ostrich fillets, loin of kudu, guinea fowl and freshwater trout, washed down with local wines. Recommended.

ᛘᛘ **La Belle Alliance**, Swellengrebel St, T028-5142252, 0800-1700, closed evenings. Good place for a lazy lunch in a lovely setting under the trees by the stream. Popular giant breakfasts, good sandwiches, fully licensed.

ᛘᛘ **Mattsen's Steak House**, Voortrek St, T028-5142715. Busy restaurant serving excellent, good-value steaks, popular with tour groups. Recommended. Close to the *Oefeningshuis* (tourist office).

ᛘᛘ **Old Mill Restaurant and Tea Garden**, 241 Voortrek St, T028-5142790, see Sleeping. 0700-late. Good afternoon teas, waffles and pancakes, outside tables in pretty gardens with chickens pecking around, romantic candlelit tables inside for dinner, South African dishes such as Karoo lamb or local curries.

ᛘᛘ **Zanddrift**, Swellengrebel St, T028-5141789, next to the museum. An old Cape Dutch farmhouse interior, closed in evening, steaks, pasta, salads, local wines, a good place to sample a typical large South African breakfast, good value. Recommended.

ᛘ **Coffee Shop at the Old Gaol**, Drostdy Museum, T028-5143847. Daytime licensed café serving light meals, coffee and cakes, homemade lemonade, and local specialities such as melktert.

Festivals and events

Caledon *p237*

Mar The rather unusual Beer and Bread Festival is held in a large marquee near the

Wild Flower Garden. Live music is laid on in the evenings, and plenty of local farm produce is available.

Sep To coincide with the annual bloom of wild flowers, Caledon holds a **Wild Flower Festival**. It is an excellent opportunity to see the plants which make up the Cape fynbos, including protea, erica, gladioli and iridaceae. The principal display hall is in Hope St, a short walk from the town museum.

Activities and tours

Caledon and around *p237*

Mountain biking

The Klein Swartberg is a popular venue for mountain biking and an annual rally is held here. Contact the tourist office for details.

Swellendam and around *p238*

Gliding

4 km to the south of the town is the **Swellengrebel Airfield**. The Langeberg Mountains provide excellent thermals.

African Wings, T072-3472093. Flights by regular glider, motorglider, and microlight.

Golf

9-hole course, Andrew Whyte St, in the lee of the Langeberg Mountains, T028-5141026.

Tour operators

Bontebok Tours, 91 Voortrekker St, T028-5143650, www.bontebok.co.za. Excellent local travel agent, organizes a range of local tours plus trips to Bontebok and Marloth parks, birdwatching trips, township and walking tours. Also acts as local information office and has internet access.

Breede River Dream Cruises, T028-5421049, www.rivercruises.co.za. A range of riverboats with onboard sleeping, aimed at fishermen, can negotiate 50 km of the river.

Felix Unite River Adventures, T021-6701300 (Cape Town office), www.felix unite.co.za. Professional outfit that runs trips from Cape Town to the Breede River, with overnight stays in bush camps, restored Voortrekker ox wagons, or A-frame houses.

Two Feathers Horse Trails, T082-4948279, www.twofeathers.co.za. 1-hr to overnight horse-riding trips in De Hoop Nature Reserve.

Umkulu, T021-8537952 (Cape Town), www.umkulu.co.za. Another operator that will take you to the Breede River from Cape Town for a day's float, some wine tasting, and an overnight at a local lodge.

Transport

Caledon and around *p237*

Car

Continuing east from Caledon, the N2 passes through rolling wheat fields towards **Mossel Bay**. From Caledon you can also deviate inland to the villages of **Genadendal** and **McGregor**; the R406 makes a convenient loop. Alternatively take the R316 south towards **Bredasdorp** into the heart of Overberg country. The R319 rejoins the N2 just before **Swellendam**.

Bus

Greyhound, T012-3231154, www.grey hound.co.za, **Intercape**, T086-1287287, www.intercape.co.za, and **Translux**, T011-7743333, www.translux.co.za, serve Caledon and **Swellendam**. Buses stop at the Caledon Hotel and Spa and the Swellengrebal Hotel in Swellendam and run daily to **Cape Town** (2 hrs); and **Durban** (24 hrs) via **Port Elizabeth** (9 hrs).

Swellendam and around *p238*

240 km to **Cape Town**, 225 km to **George**, 560 km to **Port Elizabeth**, 270 km to **Knysna**.

Bus

The Baz Bus, T021-4392323, www.bazbus.com, stops daily in Swellendam and can take you as far as **Port Elizabeth** in a day. From **Cape Town** it arrives about 1200 allowing plenty of time to see the sights in the afternoon. From **Port Elizabeth** it arrives around 1800.

Directory

Swellendam *p238*

Banks Standard Bank, 32a Voortrek St; ABSA, 14 Voortrek St. **Useful telephone numbers** Ambulance, T10177; Hospital: T028-5141140; Police, T10111.

Garden Route

The Garden Route is probably South Africa's most celebrated area, a stretch of coast heralded as one of the country's highlights. The publicity it receives has made it hugely popular, and few visitors to Cape Town miss it. The area is undeniably beautiful, with a 200-km stretch of rugged coast backed by lush mountains, however, some feel that its merits are over-hyped. Officially the route runs from Heidelberg in the west to the Tsitsikamma National Park in the east, though the most popular stretch is the coast from Mossel Bay to Storms River in Tsitsikamma National Park. The region is separated from the interior by the Tsitsikamma and Outeniqua mountain ranges. In contrast to the dry and treeless area of the Karoo on the interior side of the mountains, rain falls all year round on the Garden Route, and the o cean-facing mountain slopes are covered with luxuriant forests. It is this dramatic change in landscape, which occurs over a distance of no more than 20 km, that prompted people to refer to the area as the Garden Route.

The larger towns, such as George and Knysna, are highly developed tourist resorts, while other areas offer untouched wilderness and wonderful hikes, including one of the most famous in the country, the Otter Trail. This runs along the coast in Tsitsikamma National Park, one of the most popular national parks in South Africa. There is a second national park, Wilderness, which is also very popular. If hiking isn't your scene, the beaches are stunning, offering a mix of peaceful seaside villages and livelier surfer spots, and there are various attractions hugging the N2 to distract the motorist. Finally, the Garden Route is coming into its own as an adventure destination and there are numerous activities on offer from bungee jumping to blackwater tubing. » *For Sleeping, Eating and other listings, see pages 273-290.*

Garden Route

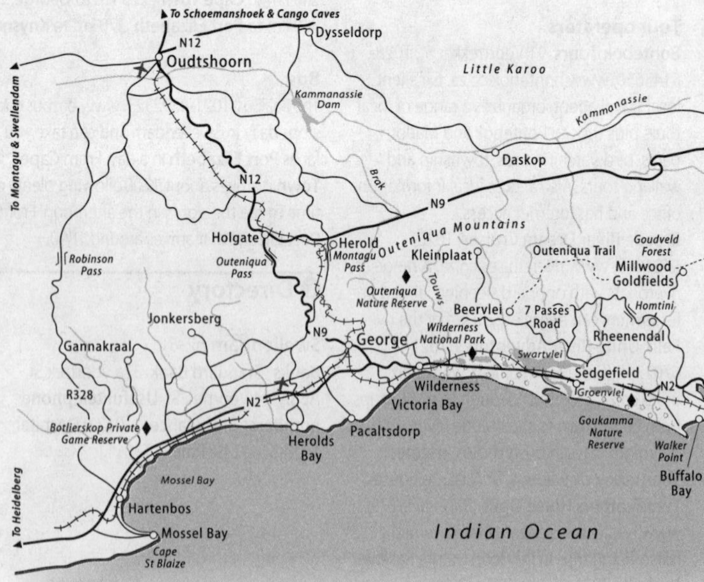

Ins and outs

The most direct route from Cape Town to the Garden Route is along the N2. It's an easy 365-km drive and you may break your journey in the attractive town of Swellendam or at the Gouritz River bridge bungee jump, 10 km out of Albertina. To get the most out of the Garden Route you really need a car, and whilst it's quite easy to drive the full length of the Garden Route in a day, most visitors either choose a base for exploring the area, or spend a day or two in several places of interest along the way. Many of the attractions are in between the major resorts so it's good to have the flexibility to stop when you want. The area's popularity means that good-value accommodation is difficult to find, and gets booked up months in advance, especially during peak season. It is advisable to avoid the area during the two weeks over Christmas and the New Year, and at Easter. For the rest of the school holidays most of the self-catering accommodation will still be fully booked, but bed and breakfasts or hostels should have a free room – call in advance to be sure. For more information about the Garden Route visit www.capegardenroute.org or www.gardenroute.com.

Background

Travelling along the coast, the vegetation is lush and green compared to the interior, but this hides the fact that the majority of the Knysna and Tsitsikamma forest was completely destroyed by the early settlers. What remains today is only a small fraction of the indigenous forest, and this is threatened by the encroachment of alien species. The recent history of the region is closely linked with the search for timber for the growing population in the Cape. It only took a few years for the small patches of forest in Hout Bay, Rondebosch, Newlands and Kirstenbosch to be depleted, and the first white colonists to reach Mossel Bay in 1711 came looking for wood. During the 1850s the forests around the Humansdorp area were exploited, but it was not until a road was cut through to the Keurbooms River in 1867 that the Tsitsikamma forest came under threat.

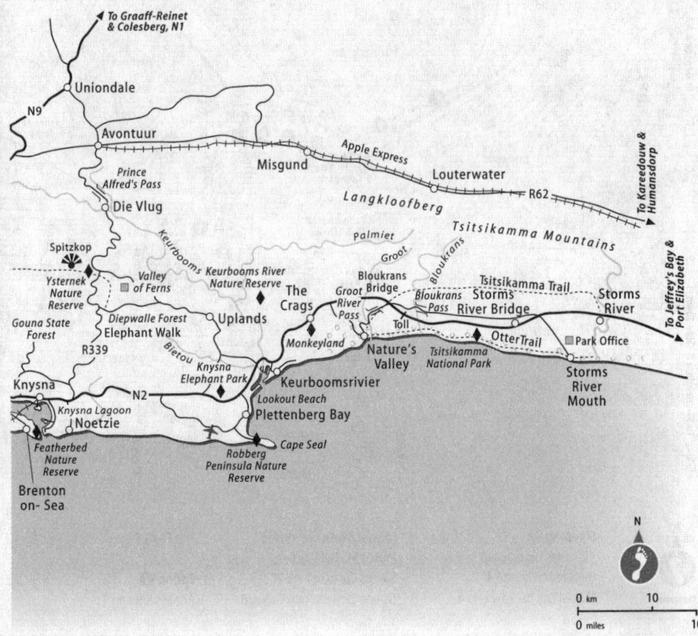

In 1880, Comte De Vasselot de Regne, a French forestry scientist of international repute, introduced the idea of preserving the indigenous forest. However, it was only as late as 1938 that over-exploitation ceased to be a problem, when all remaining woodcutters were pensioned off. The first exotic species were planted in 1891; red gum and cluster pine were planted near Bloukrans to replace sections of the forest damaged by the great fire. The supply of timber for the industry is now based entirely upon fast-growing exotic species such as slash pine, monterey pine, karri gum and Australian blackwood. However, these species are having a negative effect on indigenous species – their fast water absorption has starved other trees, in effect suffocating indigenous species. Some areas have started to remove the exotic aliens to control the problem. Today only 65,000 ha of the original forest remain along the Garden Route, most of which is in Tsitsikamma National Park and around Knysna.

Mossel Bay

» pp273-290. Colour map 7, grid B2.

Built along a rocky peninsula which provides sheltered swimming and mooring in the bay, Mossel Bay is one of the larger and less appealing seaside towns along the Garden Route. During the school holidays the town is packed – it receives one million domestic visitors in December alone – but for the rest of the year it is just another dull coastal town. A fact often overlooked in promotional literature is that since the discovery of offshore oil deposits, Mossel Bay is also the home of the ugly Mossgas natural gas refinery and a multitude of oil storage tanks. The town has a number of Portuguese flags and names dotted around, thanks to the first European to anchor in

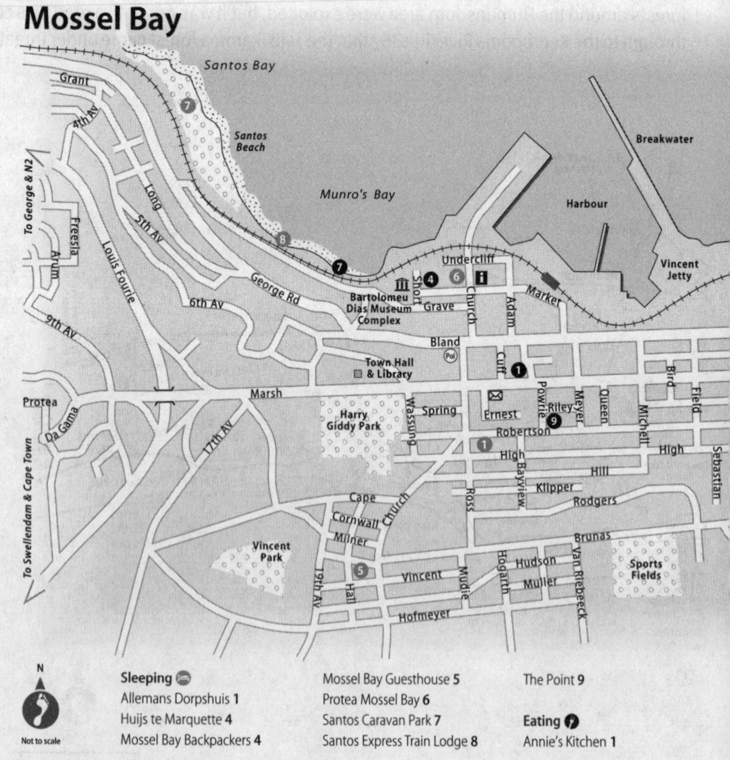

the bay – Bartolomeu Dias, who landed in February 1488. His efforts to communicate with local herdsmen were met with stone throwing, but Vasco da Gama, who moored in the bay in 1497, had more luck; he managed to establish trading relations with them. The bay's safe anchorage and freshwater spring ensured that it became a regular stopping- off point for other seafarers. The town was named by a Dutch trader, Cornelis de Houtman, who in 1595 found a pile of mussel shells in a cave below the present lighthouse.

Ins and outs

Mossel Bay Tourism Bureau ⓘ *corner of Church and Market Sts, T044-6912202, www.visitmosselbay.co.za, Mon-Fri 0800-1800, Sat and Sun 0900-1700*, provides information and acts as a central reservations office for accommodation.

Cage diving to see great white sharks is possible in Mossel Bay – see page 285.

Sights

Many of the local attractions relate to the sea and reflect the bay's importance to early Portuguese navigators and Dutch explorers. All the museums are on one site known as the **Bartolomeu Dias Museum Complex** ⓘ *T044-6911067, www.diasmuseum.museum.com, Mon-Fri 0900-1700, there's a tea shop on site in a restored 1830s cottage.* Here you'll find the Culture Museum, the Shell Museum, an Aquarium, the Maritime Museum, some Malay graves, and the original freshwater spring that attracted the early sailors, which still flows into a small dam. The displays in the Maritime Museum are arranged around a full-size replica of Bartolomeu Dias's caravel. Also here is a tree with a fascinating past, the **Post Office Tree**, a giant milkwood situated close to the freshwater spring. History relates that in 1500 a letter was left under the tree by a ship's captain. A year later it was retrieved by the commander of the Third East India Fleet en route to India. Messages were also left carved in rocks and left in old boots tied to the branches. The tree has been declared a national monument and it is still possible to send a postcard home from here – all mail dispatched from the Post Office Tree is franked with a special commemorative stamp and makes a great souvenir.

In the middle of the bay is **Seal Island** which can be visited by cruises departing from the harbour. The island is inhabited by colonies of African penguins and Cape fur seals (the best month to see seal pups is November). It's also possible to see great white sharks and small hammerhead sharks which prey upon the seals. Between September and November the warm waters of the bay are often visited by southern right, humpback and brydes whales while calving. Another vantage point for viewing whales and dolphins is **The Point** at the end of Marsh Street. Close by is the 20-m high **St Blaize Lighthouse**, built in 1864, one of only two remaining continuously manned lighthouses in South Africa. Ask the lighthouse keeper if he will show you around.

Mossel Bay
Huckle
Daley
Beach
Kloof
Lazaretto Cemetery
Bland
Muir
Lower Cross
Marsh
Upper Cross
Montagu
Lazaretto
Point
Cape St Blaize Cave
St Blaize Lighthouse
The Point
Bats Cave
Cape St Blaize
St Blaize Trail
Indian Ocean

Café Gannet 4
Coach House 9
Jazzbury's 5
Kingfisher 6
Pavilion 7
Tidals 6

Touring the Garden Route

If you don't want to self drive, there are a number of other options for exploring the Garden Route. The **Baz Bus**, T021- 4392323, www.bazbus.com, offers a very adequate service and drops and picks up at Garden Route hostels every day. Mainline buses also operate a daily service, but most departures and arrivals are in the middle of the night and it's not as economical as the Baz Bus. For those on a budget and short of time, the **Bok Bus**, T082-3201979, www.bokbus.com, is a comprehensive award-winning five-day tour of all the major attractions along the Garden Route starting and finishing in Cape Town. The tour visits most of the adventure activities and accommodation is in hostels or you have the option to upgrade to guesthouses. Prices start at R3100. There are numerous coach and minibus operators running short tours along the Garden Route that appeal to a wide range of age groups and offer a variety of accommodation alternatives. These include:
African Eagle, T021-4644266, www.daytours.co.za.
Cape Rainbow, T021-5515465, www.caperainbow.com.
Eco-Tours, T021-7885741, www.ecotourssa.co.za.
Green Rhino, T021-7947365, www.greenrhino.co.za.

The **St Blaize Trail** is a perfect introduction to the spectacular coastline that you are likely to encounter along the Garden Route. This is a 13.5-km walk along the cliffs and rocky coast west from Mossel Bay. The official trail starts from Bats Cave, just below the lighthouse; the path is marked by the white image of a bird in flight. As you walk further from the town the scenery becomes more and more spectacular. You can leave the coast at Pinnacle Point, and follow a path inland to Essenhout Street. This cuts about 5 km off the walk. The path ends by a group of houses in Dana Bay. From here you will have to organize your own transport back into town, so it helps to have a mobile phone to call a taxi from Mossel Bay. A helpful map is available from the tourism office. You are rightly warned to be careful in places during strong winds, as there are some precipitous and unprotected drops from the cliff tops. Khoi-San articles dating back 80,000 years were recently discovered in Cape St Blaize Cave – they were not open to the public at the time of writing, but check at the tourist office for more information.

Botlierskop Private Game Reserve

ⓘ *To get there turn off the N2 on to the R401 to the northeast of Mossel Bay, the Klein Brakrivier turnoff, and follow signs for 25 km, T044-6966055, www.botlierskop.co.za.* This private reserve is situated on a 2400 ha game farm, which is home to 24 different species of animals and a wide variety of birds. A former farm, Botlierskop was bought in 1996, and the new owners saw the opportunity to reintroduce wildlife in this area. After four years of recovering from domestic farming, it was opened in 2000. The land has been restocked and wildlife includes the rare black impala, rhino, elephant, lion, buffalo, giraffe, mountain zebra and eland. Activities include game drives, quad biking, nature walks, picnics and helicopter flips. The most exciting activity is elephant-riding and this is the only place elephant back rides are offered on the Garden Route. Expect to pay in the region of R500, no children under six. The two elephants are orphans who survived a culling program in the Zambezi Valley in Zimbabwe. There is luxurious accommodation available (see Sleeping, page 273) or you can visit for the day, though booking is essential. Check out the website for prices and programmes.

The milkwood tree

Four white milkwood (*Sideroxylon inerme*) trees in South Africa have been proclaimed as national monuments. All milkwoods are protected to such an extent that a permit is required before an individual can even prune a tree on their land. Their name is derived from the milky latex found in the fruit and the bark. The flowers have a very distinctive smell which attracts insects, which in turn attract birds. They also bear fruit which, when ripe, turns a purple colour and is eaten by birds and baboons. These beautiful shade trees are found all along the Pacific coast in many shapes and sizes. In the harshest of conditions they may only grow into a shrub-like bush; the largest tree is on a farm near Bredasdorp: it has a spread of 20 m, a trunk girth of over 3 m, and is thought to be over 1000 years old. The most famous specimen is the Post Office Tree in Mossel Bay which must be at least 500 years old. Milkwoods were one of the species that early settlers singled out for economic use: their wood is hard and durable and was used for building boats, bridges and homes. These days the threat to their survival comes from alien vegetation in the forests. During a bush fire, alien plants burn fiercely and any milkwoods close by may die as a result of the intensity of the heat. Thick alien growth also prevents the germination of milkwood seed and the growth of the saplings.

George and around

» pp273-290. Colour map 7, grid B2.

Often referred to as the gateway to, or the capital of, the Garden Route, George owes its status to the fact that it has an airport. It is also an important junction between the N2 coastal highway and the N9 passing through the Outeniqua Pass into the Karoo. It lies in the shadow of the Outeniqua Mountains, but unlike the majority of towns along the Garden Route, it is not by the sea. The town itself is a mostly modern grid of streets interspersed with some attractive old buildings and churches. While it is pleasant enough, it has little appeal compared to other towns along the coast; the main reason overseas visitors come here is to play golf. George has several outstanding golf courses and received worldwide attention in November 2003 when it hosted the President's Cup Golf Tournament. More recently it hosted the inaugural Women's World Cup of Golf.

Ins and outs

There's a very helpful **Tourism Bureau** ⓘ *124 York St, T044-8019295, www.tourismgeorge.co.za, Mon-Fri 0800-1700, Sat 0900-1200*, with a wide range of information on the Garden Route. But like many offices along the Garden Route, they only promote accommodation which pays a fee to the office.

Background

The first settlement appeared here in 1778 as a forestry post to process wood from the surrounding forests. In 1811 it was formally declared a town, and named after King George III. It was at this time that its wide tree-lined streets – Courtenay, York and Meade – were laid out. For the next 80 years the town remained the centre for a voracious timber industry. Much of the indigenous forest was destroyed supplying wood for wagons, railway sleepers and mine props. Some of the trees came to be known as **stinkwoods** because of their odour when freshly cut. Few remain today; they are slow growing and endemic to South Africa.

Sights

Within the town itself there are only a few sights of interest. On the corner of Cathedral and York streets is **St Mark's Cathedral**, consecrated in 1850. The building has an unusually large number of stained-glass windows for its size, and gave George its city status. Many of the windows were designed by overseas artists of limited fame. In 1911 a bible and royal prayer book were given to the church by King George V. The interior of the **Dutch Reformed Mother Church** at the north end of Meade Street reflects the town's early history as a centre for the timber industry. The pulpit is carved out of stinkwood and took over a year to create. The ceiling was built from yellowwood, and six yellowwood trunks were used as pillars.

In front of the tourist office, housed in the King Edward VII library, is an ancient oak tree known as the **Slave Tree**. It is one of the original trees planted by Adrianus van Kervel in the early 1800s and has been declared a national monument. The tree acquired its name because of the chain embedded in the trunk with a lock attached to it. The story of the chain can be traced back to when a public tennis court was in use next to the library (now the information office), and the court roller was secured to the tree to prevent playful children from rolling it down the street. The **George Museum** ⓘ *is housed in the old Drostdy on Courtenay St, T044-8735343, Mon-Fri 0900-1630, Sat 0900-1230, coffee shop*, has displays on the timber industry as well as musical instruments and a collection of old printing presses. In the Sayer's Wing is an exhibition devoted to former President PW Botha, who was a member of parliament for George for 38 years. The **Outeniqua Transport Museum** ⓘ *Mission St, just off Knysna Rd,*

The mountains create an impressive backdrop to the Dutch Reformed Mother Church when viewed from the corner of Courtenay and Meade streets.

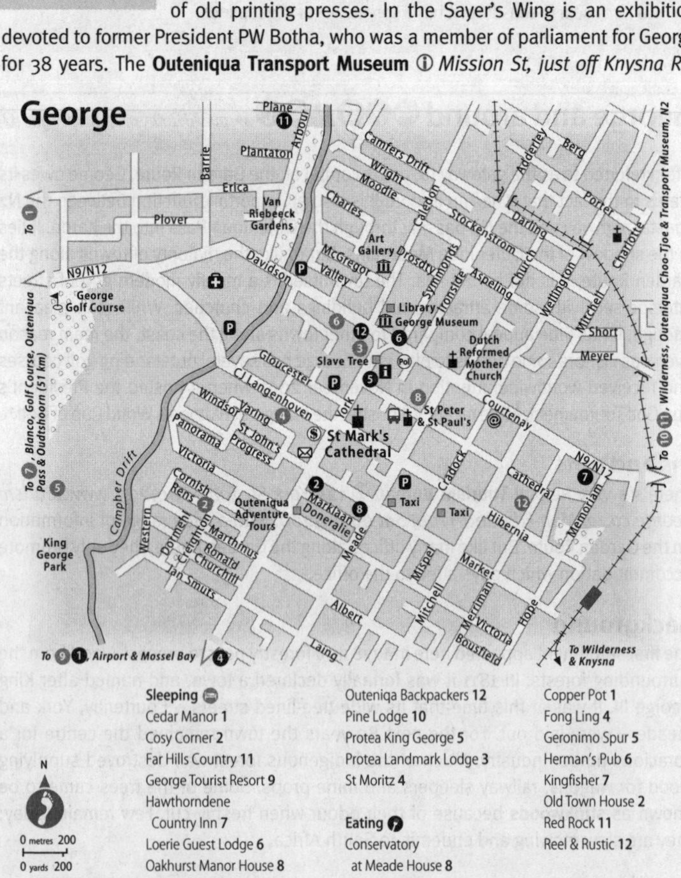

To44-8018274, Mon-Sat 0800-1800, has an interesting display outlining the history of steam train travel, as well as vintage cars and flight memorabilia. It is adjacent to the new platform from which the **Outeniqua steam train** departs.

Victoria Bay ➔ *Colour map 7, grid B2.*

If you are based in George and wish to spend a quiet day by the sea, this small resort is only 9 km or 15 minutes' drive away. Victoria Bay (2 km off the N2) is an excellent place to surf during the winter. It has a narrow cove with a broad sandy beach, a grassy sunbathing area, and a safe tidal pool for children. There's only one row of houses with some of the best-positioned guesthouses in the region. There's nowhere to buy food here, but astonishingly, the accommodation options are served by **Mr Delivery** who picks up from about a dozen takeaway joints and restaurants in George.

Little Karoo and Montagu Pass

The N2 continues from George to Wilderness, but if you have been travelling along the coast from Cape Town, a short diversion into the Little Karoo is well worth the effort. Starting in George, the most direct route is the N9 via the **Outeniqua Pass**. Having reached the summit (799 m) it quickly becomes apparent why the narrow coastal belt is referred to as the Garden Route. The dry undulating terrain is in stark contrast to the lush coastal region, no more than 15 km away. From the top of the pass it is 35 km to **Oudtshoorn**, the capital of the Little Karoo, known for its ostrich farms and the **Cango Caves** (see page 304).

Returning from Oudtshoorn, an alternative and scenic route through the mountains is via **Montagu Pass**, the fourth pass over the Outeniqua range. It was opened in 1847 and took over four years to complete. Travelling on the N12 from Oudtshoorn, look out for a left turn just before the road starts to climb up to Outeniqua Pass. This is the N9 and will be signposted to Uniondale and Willowmore. After several kilometres, look out for a right turn for Herold and Montagu Pass. Before the road starts to climb it goes through a fertile valley full of hops and fruit trees. The area is ideal for hop growing since it is sheltered from strong winds and rarely has hail. Harvest time is during February and March. This road is gravel so take care after rain. For much of the route there is a low stone wall along the side of the road, and several stretches are single track. Fortunately, very little local traffic uses this road. Near the summit the road passes under a narrow bridge – the railway line linking George with Oudtshoorn – an amazing engineering feat when you look out across the valley below. Halfway along the road are the ruins of a blacksmith's shop, and before the road links up with the N12 back into George you'll see the old toll house.

Outeniqua Choo-Tjoe

ⓘ *Departs Railway Museum in George at 0930, arrives Knysna at midday. Departs Knysna at 1415, arrives in George at 1700. Return journey R65, R45 children under 16, free for children under 6. Snacks are available on the train. 24-hr information line To82-2346332, www.transnetheritagefoundation.co.za. Reservations, George To44-8018288, Knysna To44-3821361. This is a popular excursion and you must book at least 48 hrs in advance during summer.*

When this line opened in 1928, it was considered the most expensive in the world – today it's billed as the most beautiful.

One of the most popular and enjoyable day trips is a ride on a steam train between George and Knysna. This picturesque branch line was opened in 1928 and is the train that appears in many of the South African tourist brochures with the famous curved bridge across the mouth of the Kaaimans River. The 67-km journey gives you an extraordinary view of some spectacular coastal scenery and forests, passing through Wilderness National Park and along the Goukamma Valley. The journey ends crossing Knysna Lagoon via a long bridge. Between August and May, there are daily trains from Monday to Saturday (none on Sunday) in each direction, stopping at Wilderness, Sedgefield and Goukamma. Between May and August there are trains on Mondays, Wednesdays and Fridays.

Seven Passes Road

One of the most enjoyable drives in the region, the Seven Passes Road (or the Old Passes Road), is the name given to the original route between George and Knysna. It starts 3 km out of George, just before Pine Lodge. The route was surveyed and built by Thomas Bain in 1867, and like so many of his engineering projects is still in use today. Much of the road follows the foothills of the Outeniqua Mountains. When it was built the engineers had to cut their way through dense forest and negotiate the fast-flowing rivers coming out of the mountains. The seven passes which give the road its name are: the Swart River, Kaaimans, Touw River, Hoogekraal, Karatara, Homtini and Phantom. At each pass the road winds down the gorges to a narrow bridge at the bottom. The stone bridges over the Silver and Kaaimans rivers have been declared national monuments.

After crossing the Swart River, which flows out of the Garden Route dam, the road rises through the forest onto a plateau. Some 5 km from the turning is the entrance to Saasveld, a college of forestry founded in 1905. The descent to the Kaaimans River was a major obstacle for Bain in 1867. Loaded wagons slid on their brake shoes to the bottom before being hauled up by 32 oxen on the other side, the ground so soft that the wheels had gouged out 3 m-deep channels. Shortly after the road crosses the Silver River, there is a junction with White Road for **Wilderness**. After crossing the fourth river, Touw, the road reaches turnings to Woodville, Bergplaas and Kleinplaat forest stations. Just before Woodville there is a turning north leading to a giant yellowwood tree which is thought to be more than 800 years old. It is 31 m high and has a girth of 9 m. A picnic site and a short trail into the forest have been laid out close by. At Bergplaas there is a right turning which leads down to the lakes, **Langvlei** and **Rondevlei**, before joining the N2 outside **Sedgefield**.

The next two passes are the **Hoogekraal** and **Karatara**. The village of **Karatara** was established in 1941 as a centre for woodcutters who could no longer practice their skills as attitudes towards the forests and trees changed. The **Homtini Pass** is a beautiful wooded valley which ends by the turning for the village of Rheenendal. After another 1 km there is a left turning signposted for Millwood, Goldfields and Bibby's Hoek. The rest of this route into Knysna is described in the West of Knysna section (see page 262).

Wilderness and around

» pp273-290. Colour map 7, grid B2.

This appealing little town is an ideal base for exploring the Garden Route and has a superb swathe of sandy beach. Check locally for demarcated areas for swimming and surfing. Children should be supervised in the sea as there are strong rip currents. One of the safest spots for swimming is in the Touw River mouth. Except for the few hectic weeks at Christmas and New Year, Wilderness is generally very relaxed and has an excellent range of accommodation. The advantage of staying here is that you are also within a day's drive of all the interesting sights of the Little Karoo. The highlight, however, is Wilderness National Park, a quiet, well-managed park, with three levels of self-catering accommodation available and a campsite.

The town itself doesn't have much of a centre, but stretches instead up the lush foothills of the Outeniqua Mountains and along leafy streets by the lake and river. The supermarket, restaurants, post office and tourist office are by the petrol station, where the N2 crosses the Serpentine channel. The **Outeniqua Choo-Tjoe** steam train stops at the station on the beach side of the main road.

Ins and outs

Wilderness Tourism Bureau ⓘ *Leila's Lane, turn left by the post office, T044- 8770045, www.wildernessinfo.co.za, Mon-Fri 0830-1800, Sat 0800-1300, Sun 1500-1700*, is a very helpful office, especially when it comes to finding good-value accommodation during the peak season. You can also book the **Outeniqua Choo-Tjoe** steam train here if you're not doing the full return journey between George and Knysna.

Background

The first European to settle in the district was a farmer, Van der Bergh, who built himself a simple farmhouse in the 1850s. It was in 1877 that the name was first used, when a young man from Cape Town, George Bennet, was granted the hand of his sweetheart only on condition that he took her to live in the wilderness. He purchased some land where the present-day **Wilderness Hotel** stands and promptly named it 'wilderness' (of dense bush and forest) to appease his new father-in-law. At this time the only road access was from the Seven Passes Road between George and Knysna. Bennet cut a track from this road to his new farmhouse. In 1905 Montagu White bought the homestead from Bennet and converted it into a boarding house. It was not a great success: the area was undoubtedly beautiful, but the swimming was dangerous and access was still a problem.

When the property changed hands in 1921 the farmhouse-cum-boarding house had further alterations made to it and so the Wilderness Hotel came into being. In 1907 the railway line from Mossel Bay reached George and six years later, Oudtshoorn. It was not until 1928 that the great engineering feat of building the link between George and Knysna was completed. This is the route the **Outeniqua Choo-Tjoe** steam train still runs along, including the famous curved bridge across Kaaimans River. By 1928 a second hotel had been built by the river, which is now

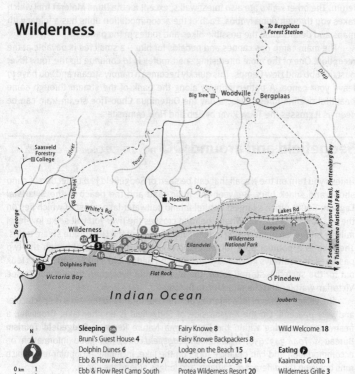

Wilderness

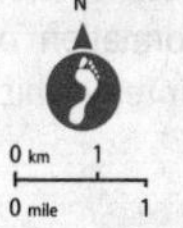

Sleeping
Bruni's Guest House 4
Dolphin Dunes 6
Ebb & Flow Rest Camp North 7
Ebb & Flow Rest Camp South & Park Office 19
Fairy Knowe 8
Fairy Knowe Backpackers 8
Lodge on the Beach 15
Moontide Guest Lodge 14
Protea Wilderness Resort 20
Villa Sentosa 17
Wild Welcome 18

Eating
Kaaimans Grotto 1
Wilderness Grille 3

 known as the **Fairy Knowe Hotel.** In 1985 the original Wilderness Hotel was destroyed in a fire – the new building is the smart four-star hotel of the same name.

Wilderness National Park → *Colour map 7, grid B2.*

ⓘ 4 km east of Wilderness, off the N2, a gravel road drops down the edge of the hill to the main camp next to a river. The camp reception, T044-8771197, www.sanparks.org, 0800-1300, 1400-1700, school holidays and Dec and Jan 0700-2000, has a map of the camp and useful information on the surrounding countryside. The daily conservation fee is R60, R30 for children. A small shop (0800-1300, 1400-1700) sells drinks, groceries and firewood. The nearest supermarkets and restaurants are in Wilderness.

This is one of the most relaxing places to stay along the Garden Route. Since the accommodation is provided by SAN Parks it is also excellent value, especially for four or more people. The main attraction is the water and the birdlife in the reed beds but there are some excellent hikes as well and a beautiful sandy beach.

The park covers 2612 ha and incorporates five rivers and four lakes as well as a 28-km stretch of the coastline. The series of freshwater lakes is situated between the Outeniqua foothills and sand dunes which back onto a beautiful, long sandy beach. As this is such a stunning and unique ecosystem, the land around the national park is also protected by SAN Parks – this area is referred to as the National Lake Area. The four lakes are known as Island, Langvlei, Rondevlei and Swartvlei. There is a bird hide on Langvlei and Rondevlei. There is also a second parks office beside Rondevlei.

There are two ways in which to enjoy the beauty of the surrounds, on foot or in a canoe. You can cover more ground by walking, but canoeing is ideal for seeing birds. There are five trails in the park. The **Pied Kingfisher Trail** is a circular route which can be completed in four hours. It follows the river in one direction and the beach on your return. The other walks are also forest walks, except for the **Dune Molerat** trail which takes you through dune fynbos. Each of the accommodation units has a folder with maps and details of all the possible hikes and routes in the park.

The main camp has canoes and pedalos for hire – a small fee is payable at the reception. One of the more interesting short routes is to continue up the Touw River past the Ebb and Flow Camps. This quickly becomes a narrow stream and you have to leave your canoe. A path continues along the bank of the stream through some beautiful riverine forest. Twice a day the **Outeniqua Choo-Tjoe** steam train can be seen as it crosses the Touw River by Ebb and Flow campsites.

Sedgefield and around » *pp273-290.* *Colour map 7, grid B2.*

Unless you turn off the N2, all that can be seen of Sedgefield is a collection of curio shops and snack bars. Between the main road and the beach is the **Swartvlei Lagoon**, South Africa's largest natural inland saltwater lake, most of which lies on the inland side of the N2. Where the road crosses the river you will see a low-level railway bridge, an ideal setting to take photographs of the Outeniqua steam trains. The lake is a popular spot for watersports and birdwatching, although the two pastimes don't always go well together. Around Sedgefield's lakes and forests look out for the secretive starred robin, the blue mantle flycatcher, the difficult-to-see Victorian warbler and the rare African finfoot.

The village itself is of little interest, but the country around the lakes is spectacular and very peaceful. On the Knysna side of Sedgefield is another lake, **Groenvlei**, a freshwater lake lying within the Goukamma Nature Reserve. **Sedgefield Tourism Bureau** ⓘ *T044-3432658, www.tourismsedgefield.co.za*, has good information on accommodation and can organize tours on the lake, including a popular ferry which runs between the different restaurants and lodges around the shore.

Goukamma Nature Reserve

ⓘ *Gates open 0800-1700, T044-8025310, www.capenature.org.za, entry for day visitors R20.*

Considering the number of nature reserves and national parks along the Garden Route, this delightful reserve has had a relatively low profile. The reserve was established to protect 2230 ha of the hinterland between Sedgefield and Buffalo Bay. This includes Groenvlei or Lake Pleasant, a large freshwater lake, and a 13-km sandy beach with some magnificent sand dunes covered in fynbos and patches of forest containing milkwood trees. The **Goukamma River** estuary is the main attraction in the eastern part of the reserve. Groenvlei was originally a river estuary, but it has been cut off from the sea by the large sand dunes. The lake is now fed by natural drainage and springs, and is surrounded by reed beds which are excellent for birdwatching. Rowing boats can be hired to paddle into the reed beds and take you closer to the nesting birds. More than 75 species have been identified. Look out for a few small mammals such as blue duiker, bushbuck and bontebok.

Ins and outs There are two points of access, one at each end of the reserve. Just east of Sedgefield, look out for the turning for the Lake Pleasant Hotel and the Groenvlei Bushcamp. Beyond the hotel the road divides; take the left turning by the dunes which takes you to the bushcamp and the Groenvlei Conservation Station. A 4-km hiking trail starts close by which runs along the lake shore. If you are feeling energetic, there is a 14-km trail starting from the same point, which takes you across the reserve to the Goukamma River in the eastern sector, although this leaves you with the problem of return transportation. On any of the walks in the reserve, always carry plenty of drinking water and keep an eye out for snakes, especially among the sand dunes. The second point of access is much closer to Knysna. Look out for the Buffalo Bay signpost where the N2 crosses the Goukamma River, and the railway crosses the N2.

There is a picnic spot by the river. This is where the hike across the reserve ends. There is a third hike which leads down to the beach and along the coast. Be very careful if you go into the sea as there are dangerous rip currents. If you plan on hiking, pick up a *Cape Nature Conservation* map from the nearby **Lake Pleasant Hotel.**

Knysna and around

» pp273-290.

Colour map 7, grid B2.

Knysna (the 'K' is silent) is the self-proclaimed heart of the Garden Route. It is no longer the sleepy lagoon-side village it once was – far from it – but is nevertheless a pleasant spot to spend a day or two. The town itself is fully geared up for tourists, which means a lot of choice in accommodation and restaurants, as well as overcrowding and high prices. It remains quite an arty place though, and many craftspeople have gravitated to the region, plenty of whom display their products in craft shops and galleries. Nevertheless, development is booming, with a slick waterfront complex, complete with souvenir shops and fast-food outlets, setting the pace. If you're trying to choose between Knysna and Plettenberg Bay as a base, Knysna offers more amenities and activities, while Plett is far more relaxed and has the better beach. Both get very busy during high season.

Ins and outs

Getting there and around **Baz Bus** has a daily service between Cape Town and Port Elizabeth, from where it continues to Durban five times a week. Mainline buses stop at Knysna daily on the route between Cape Town and Durban. Translux has a service between Knysna and Johannesburg and Pretoria via Bloemfontein. The best way to arrive is by the **Outeniqua Choo-Tjoe** train (for details, prices and reservations see page 255), which runs between Knysna and George and sweeps across a bridge over the still waters of the lagoon. This can also be used as a cheap option for travelling between the two towns; an advantage it has over some of the bus services is that the station at each end of the line is in the town centre; in Knysna the station is in Remembrance Avenue close to the lagoon and the waterfront. The centre of town is compact and it is easy to find your way about, although you'll need transport to see the sights. » *For further details see Transport, page 290.*

Tourist information Knysna Tourism ① *40 Main St, T044-3825510, www.visitknysna.com, www.tourismknysna.co.za, daily 0900-1700*, can make reservations for accommodation, tours and public transport. Helpful and professional office well clued-up on the region. For more information on Knysna also visit www.knysna.org.

Background

The Hottentots named a local river in the area by a word that sounded like Knysna to the early Europeans, and it's generally believed to mean a place of wood or leaves. In 1804 George Rex, a timber merchant, purchased the farm Melkhoutkraal, effectively taking ownership of all the land surrounding the lagoon. It was rumoured he was the first and illegitimate son of England's King George III. By 1817 the Knysna Lagoon was being used by ships to bring in supplies, and later to take away timber. The vast, indigenous forests just outside Knysna became an invaluable source of timber for buildings, ships and wagons. In 1870, Arnt Leonard Thesen and his family moved from Norway to Knysna and set up the first trading store and counting house, and by 1881 the settlements of Melville and Newhaven united to form the new town of Knysna. The timber industry continued well into the 20th century but unfortunately wiped out much of the natural forest on the coast, so whilst there are still tracts of Knysna forest, the region undoubtedly looks very different to what it did 150 years ago.

Sights

Although there are a couple of sights and museums in the town, Knysna's highlights are its natural attractions. The main feature of the town is the **lagoon**, around which much of Knysna life revolves. **The Heads**, the rocky promontories that lead from the lagoon to the open sea, are quite stunning. The **Knysna National Lakes**, over 15,000 ha of protected area, are also wonderful to explore, comprising islands, seashore and beach. This fragile ecosystem is bound to suffer from the ever-expanding tourist industry; of particular concern is the rich variety of aquatic life in the lagoon. This has not been helped by the construction of large retirement residential suburbs, such as Belvidere Estate, Thesen Island and Leisure Island – the latter two should never have been built upon. One of the striking features of Knysna is the location of the sprawling township, which is at the top of the hills above the town. From a boat trip on the lagoon you can look back at the town; all the sleek modern and luxurious development in the foreground, and quite by contrast the tight cluster of shacks at the very top of the hill.

The **Knysna Museum** ① *Queen St, T044-3825510, Mon-Fri 0930-1630, Sat 0930-1200, small entrance fee*, is housed in the Old Gaol – the first public building built by the colonial fovernment in the 1870s. Most of the collection focuses on fishing methods used along the coast, with a variety of nets and tackle on display. Unless you are a devoted angler this is not going to take up too much of your time. The highlight is in fact a fish, or to be more precise, a *Coelacanth*. This is a prehistoric fish that was believed to be extinct, but a live specimen was famously caught by a fisherman in 1938. There is also an art gallery, tearoom and gift shop.

Millwood House ① *Mon-Fri 0930-1630, Sat 0930-1230*, is a single-storey wooden building similar to those that once made up the gold-mining community of Millwood (see page 263). The house was originally built in sections and re-erected here. It is now a national monument, and houses the local history museum, including a display depicting the goldrush days. Next door is **Parkes Cottage**, a similar wooden house, which was moved three times before arriving at its present site. Originally erected in Millwood village, it was moved into Knysna when the gold ran out. In 1905 it was moved to Rawson Street, and then finally in 1992 it was moved to its present site to house the extension to the local history museum.

There are two **St George's Churches** in Knysna, the old and the new. Both ran into financial difficulties during construction. To complete the old church the Bishop of the Cape Colony, Robert Gray, persuaded six local businessmen to come up with the necessary £150. The church was consecrated in October 1855. The interior has a timbered ceiling and a fine yellowwood floor. In the 1920s it was decided that a second church needed to be built to accommodate the local congregation. It was 11 years between the foundation stone being laid and the church being consecrated by Bishop Gwyer of George in April 1937. Construction had been delayed due to lack of funds. The community was very proud of the fact that all the materials used in the construction were local – the stone for the walls was quarried from the other side of the lagoon in the Brenton hills. Most of the interior fittings are made from stinkwood, and commemorate local worthies.

Featherbed Nature Reserve ⓘ *T044-3821693, www.featherbed.co.za, daily 1000, R220 adults, R100 children*, is the unspoilt western side of **The Heads.** This is a private

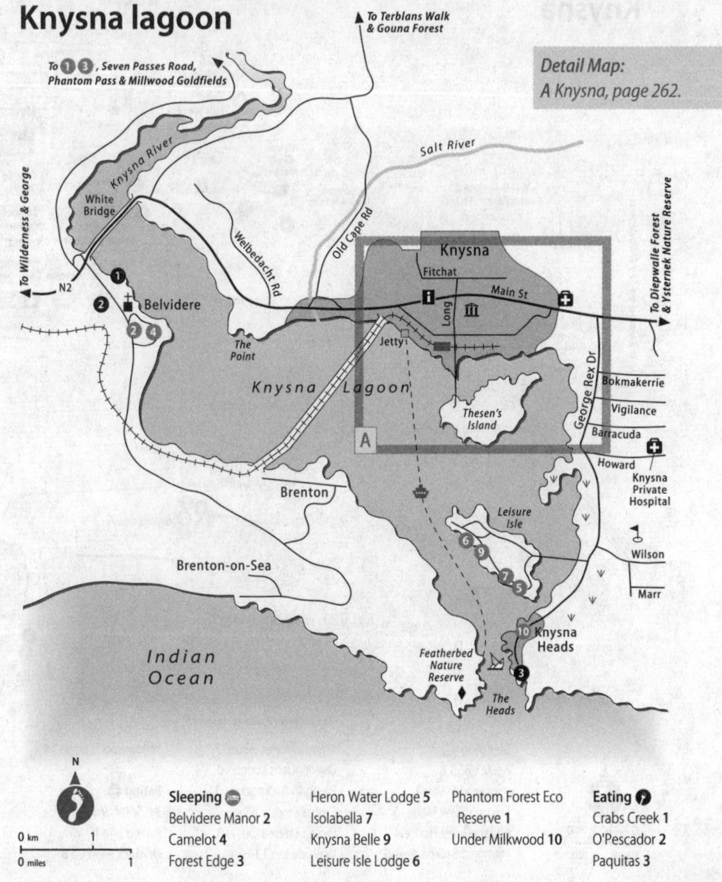

nature reserve that can only be reached by the **Featherbed Co** ferry which runs from the John Benn Jetty, at the Knysna Quays. The reserve is home to South Africa's largest breeding herd of blue duiker (*Cephalophus monticola*), an endangered species. Also of interest is a cave once inhabited by the Khoi, which has been declared a national heritage site. This four-hour excursion includes return ferry trip, 4WD vehicle-ride up the western promontory of the Knysna Heads and optional 2 km guided nature walk through the forest, onto the cliffs, into the caves and along the spectacular coastline. It ends with a buffet lunch under some Milkwood trees before returning to Knysna. The Featherbed Co also offers shorter 90 min cruises to the Heads and back, R70 adults and R30 children, and evening cruises with dinner on the paddle cruiser, R250.

West of Knysna » pp273-290.

Belvidere, Brenton and Brenton-on-Sea

These villages, 12-14 km from town on the western shores of the lagoon, are in many ways really smart suburbs of Knysna. Brenton has the great attraction of having the nearest sandy beach (Brenton-on-Sea), making it very popular during the school holidays. There is a fine hotel and a limited selection of seaside cottages. Belvidere is primarily a leafy residential suburb along the banks of the river where it enters the

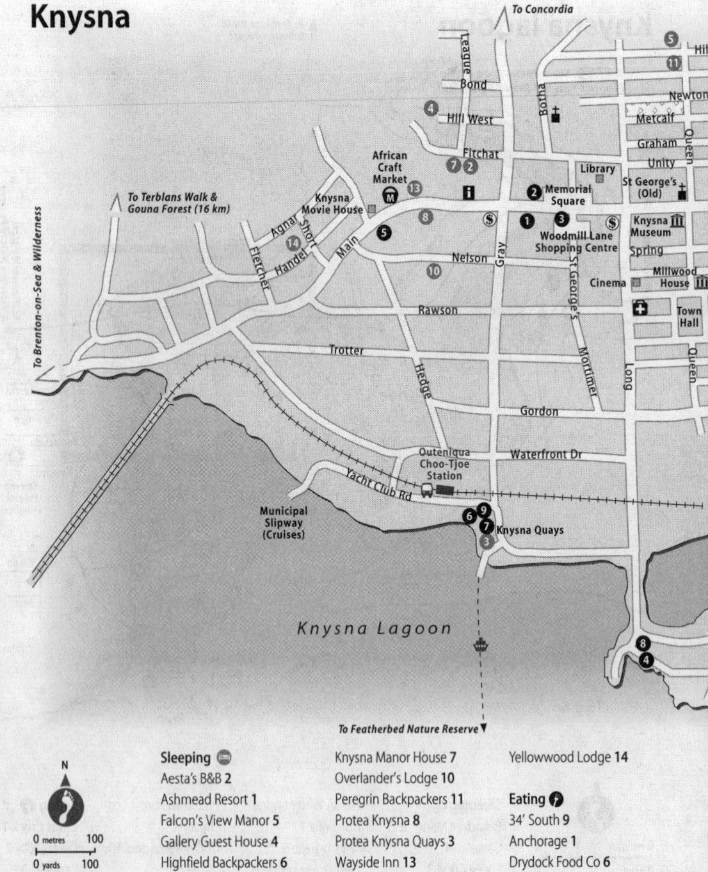

lagoon. A large proportion of the village is made up of the relatively new Belvidere Estate, a prestigious development on 67 ha, made up of large houses and gardens.

The small village church, **Belvidere Church**, is a popular attraction in the area and is a miniature replica of a Norman church. It was built in 1855 from local stone and timber, with picturesque stained-glass windows and stinkwood fittings. The rose window on the west side was installed in 1955. Further along the road is the seaside resort of Brenton-on-Sea.

Some of the glass in the window of Belvidere Church is from the bombed ruins of Coventry Cathedral in England.

Knysna Forest and Millwood Goldfields

On the southern slopes of the Outeniqua Mountains, behind Knysna, are the remnants of the grand forests that first attracted white settlers to the region. No longer a single expanse, the patches go under a variety of names which can be confusing: Diepwalle Forest, Ysternek Reserve, Goudveld State Forest, and Millwood Creek (and Jubilee Creek) Nature Reserve. As a whole, these state forests are often referred to as the **Knysna Indigenous Forests**. The indigenous forests are noteworthy for the variety of birdlife and their magnificent big trees. Species of special interest include the yellowwood, assegai, stinkwood, red alder, white alder and the Cape chestnut. A variety of short walks has been laid out in the forests. In some areas horse riding and mountain biking is allowed. The tourist office produces a good trail map.

About 25 km from Knysna, in the **Goudveld State Forest**, are the remains of an old mining town, **Millwood** ⓘ *to reach the mine, take the Phantom Pass road out of Knysna, just before the village of Rheenendal take a right turn, signposted for Millwood, Goldfields and Bibby's Hoek, 0600-1800*. This was the site of a minor goldrush in the 1880s, just before the gold was discovered at Pilgrim's Rest and Johannesburg. The first gold was discovered here in 1876 when a local farmer picked up a nugget in the Karatara River. This triggered the usual manic influx, and by 1887 Millwood had a court building, three banks, 32 stores, six hotels and three newspapers. By 1900 most people had left as the reefs became too difficult to mine. Today only one building survives, along with some mining machinery which has remained untouched for over 60 years.

For a long time abandoned and forgotten, Millwood is gradually being developed into a tourist attraction, with its perfect combination of the mystical fascination with gold and the beauty of the lush surrounding forest. The only original building still standing is a museum and tearoom called Materolli, after the Italian immigrants' mispronunciation of the name originally given to the house by the family who owned it – Mother Holly's, from a Brothers Grimm fairy tale. Recently recovered mining relics, including the handle of a sluice box and a pair of pliers, are on display in the museum as well as some more unusual items, such as dung from the Knysna elephants. Some of the mining equipment has been restored and is displayed near the museum, including a stamp mill and wheeler pan (weighing 3½ tons). Further up the slope is the shaft and a short Co-Co Pan rail track. In addition to the mine buildings, there are a few picnic spots and short paths leading into the forest – you only have to walk a few metres before being completely enveloped by trees. The museum offers guided tours, focusing on the remarkable history of the town, visiting the graveyard, mining sites, town square and reduction works display.

East of Knysna

» pp273-290.

Diepwalle Forest and Elephant Walk

ⓘ *Before setting out you must sign in at the forest station where maps are on offer. There is no charge but the hike is only open 0600-1800.*

Starting from the Diepwalle forest station is the 18-km Elephant Walk, an easy-going, level hike that gives a clear insight into the forest environment. The trail is marked by elephant silhouettes and takes around seven hours to complete. The hike is made up of three loops, but it is possible to shorten the walk by completing only one or two loops. The three paths are simply known as Routes I, II and III, and are 9-, 8- and 6-km long, respectively. Apart from the (very slim) possibility of spying the rare Knysna elephant (see page 265), of which there are three on record at present, the main attractions are the giant forest trees, particularly the Outeniqua yellowwood. There are eight such trees along the full trail – the largest, at 46 m, is known as the **King Edward VII Tree**, and stands just off the R339 by the Diepwalle picnic spot at the end of Route I and the start of Route II. The end of the **Outeniqua Trail** meets with Route III.

To get there from Knysna, follow the N2 towards Plettenburg Bay. After 7 km turn onto the R339 and the Diepwalle forest station is about 16 km on a gravel road. The R339 passes through the middle of the forest en route to the **Ysternek Nature Reserve**, see below.

Noetzie and Brackenhill Falls

Noetzie is a small village on the coast with an outlandish collection of holiday homes built to look like castles from medieval Europe, complete with towers and battlements. On the curiosity scale they rate quite high, but unfortunately you can only see them from the outside, as they are all private homes. A further 5 km beyond the Noetzie turning is another turning to the right; a gravel road passes through a eucalyptus and pine plantation to a picnic spot which overlooks the Brackenhill Falls. This is where the Noetzie River plunges into a narrow gorge with flourishing plants growing in the spray on the steep sides.

Ysternek Nature Reserve

About 25 km from Knysna, as the R339 makes its way north over the Outeniqua Mountains into the Karoo, this reserve comprises a band of montane forest which was once typical of the whole region. Today only a few patches remain and the 1212-ha Ysternek Reserve exists to conserve an area rich in mountain fynbos and wet mountain forest, with some impressive tree ferns. The area is administered by the Diepwalle State Forest, but apart from a special picnic spot and a few paths, the region remains unspoilt. The picnic spot is known as the *Dal van Varings*, Valley of the Ferns, deep in the forest. From here you can walk to a high point, **Spitzkop** view, which overlooks the canopy of surrounding forests – on a clear day you can see as far as Humansdorp. Late spring and summer, from October to May, are the best months for walking in the forest.

Invisible elephants

No guide to Knysna would be complete without a mention of the Knysna elephants. They have come to represent the last stand of wildlife against man in the region. Just over 100 years ago the forests were full of wild animals. Today the elephants live deep in the forest and few people will see them. Little is known about their numbers or their characteristics. They belong to the same species as the savanna elephant but as a result of living in the forest their lifestyle and habits have changed, and they are thought to now resemble the forest elephant found in the equatorial jungle of central Africa. These days it's thought that there are about three individuals left but they are very rarely spotted.

The Terblans Nature Walk through the Gouna Forest, 16 km north of Knysna, is a short trek through an area thought to be frequented by the Knysna elephants. Follow the bushpig markers. Happy hiking – you may just see more than the Knysna lourie.

Knysna Elephant Park

ⓘ *T044-5327732, www.knysnaelephantpark.co.za, daily, tours every half hour, bookings not required, 0830-1630.*

On the N2 20 km from Knysna and 10 km before Plettenburg Bay, this small park is a refuge for orphaned elephants. Visitors are taken on tours around the forest area and are allowed to touch and play with the little elephants. Although the animals are 'free range' they are very used to human contact, making it a wonderful experience for children. Longer walks with the elephants can also be arranged and the newest option here is sleeping with the elephants, and a large self-catering flat has been built above the elephants' boma where they sleep at night; see Sleeping page 278. This is also the only realistic chance you'll have of seeing elephants in the area – the fabled indigenous ones are far too elusive.

Plettenberg Bay

» *pp273-290. Colour map 7, grid B3.*

Plettenberg Bay, or 'Plett', as it is commonly known, is one of the most appealing resorts on the Garden Route. Although it is modern and has little of historical interest, the compact centre is attractive and the main beach beautiful. Plett has become fashionable in recent years, and during the Christmas season the town transforms. Wealthy families descend from Johannesburg and the pace can get quite frenetic – expect busy beaches and long queues for restaurant tables. For the rest of the year the pace is calmer and the resort becomes just another sleepy seaside town. There are three beaches that are good for swimming, but the coastline is spoilt by a multi-storey hotel built without much thought on a sandbar between two of the three beaches.

Ins and outs

Getting there For short trips to other towns along the Garden Route the Baz Bus represents the best value and most convenient schedule and has a daily service in either direction between Cape Town and Port Elizabeth. Mainline buses stop at the Shell Ultra City out of town on the N2. » *For further details, see Transport page 290.*

Tourist information Plettenburg Bay Tourism ⓘ *in the Melville's Corner shopping centre on Main St, T044-5334065, www.plettenbergbay.co.za, Mon-Fri 0900-1700, Sat 0900-1300, slightly longer hours during the peak summer season*, is a helpful office with quite a detailed website.

Background

In 1630 a Portuguese vessel, the **San Gonzalez**, was wrecked in the bay. This was 20 years before Jan van Riebeeck's arrival at the Cape. The survivors stayed here for eight months, during which time they built two smaller boats out of the wreckage, and one of the boats managed to sail up the coast to Mozambique. The survivors were

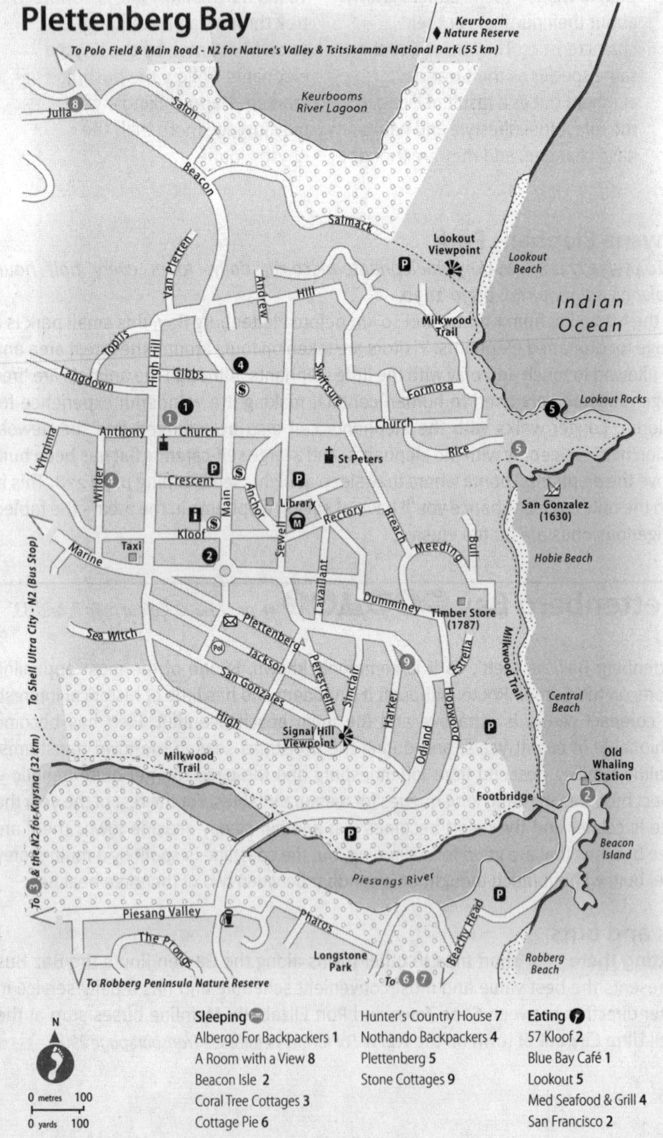

eventually returned home to Lisbon, but they left behind a sandstone plaque on which they had inscribed the name *Baia Formosa*. Today a replica can be seen in Plett in the same place that the first was left by the sailors. (The original is now on show in the South African Museum in Cape Town.) The Portuguese had a number of names for the bay, but none stuck for very long. Later the Dutch also gave the bay several different names, such as Content Bay and Pisang River Bay; it was only in 1778 when Governor Joachim van Plettenberg opened a timber post on the shores of the bay, and named it after himself, that a name stuck.

Plettenberg remained an important timber port until the early 1800s when the Dutch decided to move operations to Knysna since it was a safer harbour. For a period the bay became famous as a whaling station but all that remains is a blubber cauldron and slipway. Most of the buildings were destroyed in a fire in 1914.

Nearby are three designated trails that make a pleasant alternative to the beach.

Sights

The tourist office gamely tries to promote some sights to visit but the attraction of this area is the sea and the outdoors. Aside from the three beaches, Robberg, Central and Lookout, there is excellent deep-sea fishing and, in season, good opportunities to spot whales and dolphins, particularly southern right whales from June to October. Plett climbs up a fairly steep hill; there are many elevated land-based vantage points as well as regular boat tours offering closer encounters with the marine life. The nearby **Keurbooms River lagoon** (see page 268), is a safe area for bathing and other watersports, and the dunes around the lagoon are now part of the **Keurboom Nature Reserve**. In town itself, the main streets are just a collection of modern shopping malls and restaurants, but there are a few old buildings still standing which represent a little of the town's earlier history: St Andrew's Chapel, the remains of the Old Timber Store (1787), the Old Rectory (1776), the Forest Hall (1864) and the Dutch Reformed Church (1834). Also look out for the polo field with its lush grass and stylish white pavilion.

Hiking

Milkwood is a 3- or 5-km trail in and around the town. Follow the yellow footprints. The walk starts from the car park off Marine Drive and takes you via Piesangs River lagoon, Central beach, and Lookout beach. At this point the shorter route turns back through the centre of town via some of the historic buildings, while the longer route continues via Keurbooms Lagoon and round the back of town.

There are some recommended walks in the **Robberg Peninsula Nature Reserve** ⓘ *T044-5332125, www.capenature.org.za, 0700-1700, till 2000 in Dec and Jan. Permits are available at the entrance gate, R20, R10 child*. There are three possibilities ranging from 2-9 km on this loop along the peninsula which forms the western boundary of Plettenberg Bay. Follow the 'seal' markers. Walking is easy thanks to boardwalks, and there are plenty of prominent viewpoints from which it is possible to see whales, seals and dolphins in the bay. Allow at least four hours for the full route.

East of Plettenberg Bay » pp273-290.

The N2 continues east from Plettenberg Bay, but don't expect to travel too fast as there are a number of attractions and sights in rapid succession that are worth stopping for.

Keurbooms River Nature Reserve

First up, 7 km east of Plett is Keurbooms River Nature Reserve. Taking a sailing trip upstream on the **Keurbooms River Ferry** (see Activities and tours, page 287, for further details), is a great way to spend a few hours. You are ferried 5 km along the river through a spectacular gorge overhung by indigenous trees and other flora. At the furthest point from the jetty there is an optional 30-minute walk, with a professional guide, through the forest. This is the ultimate eco-experience and a relaxing way of being introduced to the plants, sights and sounds of the forest. Make sure you are wearing sturdy footwear if you intend to join the walk.

The only public transport that stops in Nature's Valley is the Baz Bus.

The Keurbooms River is also a safe designated area for canoeing and waterskiing and it is possible to hire canoes from the **Nature & Environmental Conservation office** ⓘ *on the east side of the Keurbooms River Bridge on the N2, T044-5332125, a double canoe costs R70 per day, if you just want to picnic next to the Keurbooms River it's R5 per person*, or you can go on an overnight trail up the river. This is a 14-km round journey through a pretty gorge where you've got a good chance of spotting kingfishers and fish eagles. As the gorge narrows further up the river, you leave behind the pleasure boats and waterskiers and reach a section of river that is seldom used by other boaters. You overnight at the **Whiskey Creek Hut**, a stilted log cabin (see Sleeping, page 280, for further details).

Monkeyland

ⓘ *T044-5348906, www.monkeyland.co.za, daily 0800-1700, free entry as far as the Banana Gialla restaurant, guided tour R80, children under 12 R40, to get there, turn off the N2 at the Forest Hall turning, Monkeyland is a further 2 km down the road.*
At the settlement known as The Crags 16 km east of Plettenburg Bay (just after the BP filling station) is the well-signposted turning to Monkeyland. As the name suggests, this is a primate reserve with lemurs, apes and monkeys from several continents where the attractions are free to move about in the living indigenous forest. Most are rescued pets. Visitors are advised to join a guided walk which takes in various waterholes in the forest. Guides have a keen eye for spotting animals. One of the highlights here is the Indiana Jones-style rope bridge that spans 118 m across a canyon, offering glimpses of species that spend their entire lives in the upper reaches of the forest. The primates themselves also use this bridge (supposedly the longest of its kind in the southern hemisphere). If you don't wish to join a tour, the day centre has a good viewpoint and the restaurant serves a tasty lunch. Great for kids. Next door and also run by Monkeyland is **Birds of Eden**, www.birdsofeden.co.za. A 2.3-ha mesh dome spanning more of the same forest with 1.2 km of walkways, 900 m of which is elevated, that go past waterfalls and dams. Along the same principle as Monkeyland, previously caged birds have been released into a natural environment and visitors, who are permitted to wander around without a guide, can get a bird's eye view of macaws, cockatoos, parrots and louries.

If you are in a hurry, stay on the N2 – this is a good stretch of road, although there is a toll of around R10. The more spectacular route is via the village of Nature's Valley along the old R102, a beautifully forested road that branches off the N2 just after The Crags. Look out for ververt monkeys in the trees.

Nature's Valley → *Colour map 7, grid B3.*

This small village has one of the most beautiful settings along the Garden Route. Since the N2 toll road was opened in 1984, most traffic bypasses this sleepy community. The village is surrounded on three sides by the western section of the **Tsitsikamma National Park** (see page 269). The approach by road is particularly spectacular. The R102, dropping 223 m to sea level via the narrow Kalanderkloof Gorge, twists and turns through lush green coastal forest. At the bottom is a lagoon formed by the sand dunes blocking the estuary of the **Groot River**. A right turn leads into the village, made up of a collection of holiday cottages and one shop that is an all-in-one restaurant, bar and **tourist information bureau** ⓘ *T044-5316835, www.natures-valley.co.za*. Note that there are no banks in Nature's Valley. There are several braai spots on the sandy beach, but be warned that swimming in the sea is not safe. Canoes, rowing boats and yachts can all be used on the Groot River and lagoon, but powerboats are prohibited.

Groot River and Bloukrans Passes

As the road starts to climb out of the Groot Valley it passes the **Nature's Valley Rest Camp** on the right. This is the only camp at the western end of the Tsitsikamma National Park (see page 280 for booking details). Many visitors will end up here because it is one end of two of the Garden Route's most spectacular hiking trails, the **Tsitsikamma Trail** and the **Otter Trail**. Look out for a poem by JP Rudd, *Ode to a tree*, on a stone slab underneath the magnificent yellowwood directly across the road from the entrance to the De Vasselot Nature Reserve. From the top of the Groot River Pass the road continues for 6 km before crossing a second river valley, the Bloukrans Pass. Here it descends 183 m into the narrow gorge before crossing the river and climbing up again. The R102 rejoins the N2 highway 10 km further on and crosses the **Bloukrans River Bridge**. Just after the bridge is a turning to the left that leads to a viewpoint at the top of the Bloukrans Gorge. The bridge is apparently the highest in Africa, and the drop into the gorge is quite spectacular. But the main reason for stopping is the **Bloukrans Bungee Jump** ⓘ *T042-2811458, www.faceadrenalin.com, daily from 0900-1700, booking not essential but recommended, bungee jump R590 which includes the bridge walk*, at 216 m the highest commercial bungee in the world. The first rebound is longer than the previous holder of the record, the 111-m bungee jump at Victoria Falls. It's a hugely exhilarating experience and the free fall once you've leapt from the bridge lasts seven seconds, travelling over 170 kph before you reach the maximum length of the bungee cord. The new event at Bloukrans is the Flying Fox, R150, a 200-m cable slide from a platform on land to the centre of the bridge arch. If you cannot muster up the courage to do either of these, than you can go on a guided bridge walk for R50. This involves walking out to the bungee platform along the caged walkway underneath the bridge where a guide tells you how the bridge was built and a little bit about the surrounding area. This is not for anyone who suffers from vertigo, but if you want to support a mate that's doing a jump, it's a great way to feel some of the fear they are experiencing when standing on the lip of the bungee platform. Also at the top of the gorge is the Tsitsikamma Forest Village, a fairly new sustainable initiative to help local people make and sell curios to the very many passing tourists. Shops are in a collection of attractive reed Khosian huts, and you can buy items such as candles or homemade paper.

Storms River Bridge → *Colour map 7, grid B3.*

Storms River Bridge is a further 5 km along the N2 from Bloukrans. There is a viewing platform to look down into the river gorge. Next to the bridge is the **Total Village**, a popular stopover with petrol pumps, curio shops, a restaurant, small museum and the Tsitsikamma information office. It is worth stopping briefly here to pick up some local tourist leaflets, especially if you have plans to hike in the region. **Tsitsikamma Information** ⓘ *T042-2803561, www.tsitsikamma.info*. This is a helpful office and can provide information and local bookings for a whole variety of adventure activities. Note Storms River Village is a further 8 km along the N2, not to be confused with Storms River Mouth which is in the Tsitsikamma National Park.

Tsitsikamma National Park » *pp273-290.*

Colour map 7, grid B3.

This is one of the most popular national parks in the country, second only to Kruger. It consists of a beautiful 80-km stretch of lush coastal forest and is known for its excellent birdlife. Not only is the forest protected, but the park boundaries reach out to sea for 5½ km in the eastern sector. No boats are allowed in this area, nor is spearfishing permitted and no shells (even dead ones) may be removed or disturbed.

Ins and outs

Getting there The turn-off for Tsitsikamma and the **Storms River camp** is on a straight stretch of road, about 4 km after the Storms River Bridge, easy to miss if driving fast. A surfaced road leads down to the reception centre on the coast. The last part of this drive is a beautiful, steep descent through lush rainforest, a marked contrast to the coniferous plantations along the N2 toll road. If you are travelling along the R102, the turning is just beyond the sawmill at Boskor. If you are approaching from the Port Elizabeth side, the turning is 4 km after the small village of Storms River.

The **Nature's Valley camp** can only be reached from the R102; when approaching from Knysna take the Nature's Valley turning at Kurland (R102). If you miss this turning you cannot turn off the N2 toll road until it meets with the other end of the R102, at which point you are only 8 km from the turning for Storms River camp. When approaching from Port Elizabeth look out for signs for Nature's Valley, R102. Nature's Valley Rest Camp is clearly signposted 3 km outside the village of the same name.

Park information The **Storm River Mouth** gate opens 0530-2130, T042-2811607. **De Vasselot** gate opens 0700-2100. Office hours are 0800-1300, 1400-1800, T042-5411607. The daily conservation fee including vehicles is R80, R40 child. The shop is open daily 0800-1800 and stocks gift items as well as groceries, wine and beer. **Tiger's Eye Restaurant** is open 0730-1000, 1200-1500 and 1800-1930, but you must make reservations for evening meals by 1700. Other facilities include a swimming pool, card telephone and occasional film shows on the park ecology.

Best time to visit The best time to visit is between November and February. Bear in mind that although this is midsummer, you can expect rain at any time. Annual rainfall is in excess of 1200 mm; June and July are the driest months, while May and October are the wettest.

Background

The park stretches 80 km along the coast between Nature's Valley and Oubosstrand. For most of its length it is no more than 500 m wide on the landward side. At the western end, where the Otter Trail reaches the Groot River estuary, the park boundary extends 3 km inland. It was established on 4 December 1964 in response to an appeal for the creation of more marine parks and reserves, made during the First World Conference on National Parks in Seattle in 1962. The main administrative office is at Storms River camp, which is almost the midpoint of the park. Apart from the short walk to the Storms River suspension bridge, the land east of the office is closed to the public. In the immediate vicinity of the camp there are several other short hikes which provide ample opportunity to explore the forest and look out for birds. West from the camp is the famous **Otter Hiking Trail** (see box, page), which follows the coastline all the way to De Vasselot, the second park camp at the western extremity of the park. The rest of the parklands are inaccessible to the public. To the west of Nature's Valley is the 'De Vasselot' section.

Vegetation and wildlife

A cross-section of the coastlands would reveal the Tsitsikamma Mountains, 900-1600 m, whose slopes level off into a coastal plain or plateau at about 230 m, and then the forested cliffs which plunge 230 m into the ocean. The slope is only precipitous in a few places; elsewhere along the coast it is still very steep, but there is enough soil to support the rainforest which the park was in part created to protect. The rainforest is the

The Otter Trail

This is one of South Africa's best hiking trails, managed by South African National Parks (SAN Parks), and it was also the first of its kind to be laid out. The 41-km trail is unidirectional; it runs between Storms River Mouth rest camp in the Tsitsikamma National Park and the village of Nature's Valley at the western end of the national park. It takes five days and four nights to complete, and closely follows the coast – care should be taken near the cliffs. None of the sectors are that long, but it is still fairly strenuous in parts since you have to cross 11 rivers and there are steep ascents and descents at each river crossing. The Bloukrans River crossing presents the most problems. Check tide tables, you will at least have to wade, or even swim across. So waterproofing for your rucksack is vital. The longest stretch is between Oakhurst and André huts, which can take seven hours to complete, although it is only 14 km in length. Apart from the natural beauty and the birdlife the trail passes some fine waterfalls and Strandloper caves. Look out for the fine large old hardwood trees which have escaped the dreaded axe.

last remnant of a forest which was once found right along this coast between the ocean and the mountains. The canopy ranges between 18 m and 30 m and is closed, which makes the paths nice and shady; if you want to take photos you'll need fast film. The most common species of trees are milkwood, real yellowwood, stinkwood, Cape blackwood, forest elder, white pear and candlewood, plus the famous Outeniqua yellowwood, a forest giant. All are magnificent trees which combine with climbers such as wild grape, red saffron and milky rope to create an outstandingly beautiful forest.

In the forest itself 35 different bird species have been recorded, while in the park as a whole over 220 species have been identified. The most colourful bird in the forest is the **Knysna lourie,** *Tauraco corythaix*. Its call is a korr korr korr, and in flight it has a flash of deep red in its wings, with a green body and distinctive crest. In the vicinity of the Storms River campsite and the Groot River estuary you will see an entirely different selection of birds: over 40 species of seabird have been recorded here. The most satisfying sighting is the rare **African black oystercatcher**, with its black plumage and red eyes, beak and legs.

With such steep slopes and dense forest you will only come across a few small mammals. The species that do occur include caracal, bushbuck, blue duiker, grysbok, bushpig and the Cape clawless otter. The **blue duiker** is the smallest antelope in South Africa – the adult male stands less than 30 cm high and weighs about 4 kg, although the female is slightly bigger. They live in forest and thick bush along the coast, feeding on forest fruits and flowers that are dropped from the canopy by feeding monkeys, or birds such as the Knysna lourie or rameron pigeons. Each animal lives alone in a territory of about 6 ha in extent. The most likely time to see them is at dawn or dusk in an open clearing – ask the park rangers about recent sightings. The **Cape clawless otter** is also very rare and considered an endangered species. It feeds on fish and sea crabs, emerging from its den in the early evening. You will be very lucky to catch a glimpse of either of these mammals.

Hiking in the park

Otter Trail Permits are available from **SAN Parks** ⓘ *Pretoria, T012-4289111, www.sanparks.org*. Bookings can also be made in person at the offices in Cape Town and Durban (see page 44). This is a very popular hike, booking opens 13 months in advance; your best chance of a permit is a cancellation during school term time. The offices also provide excellent maps which are packed full of background information and advice to help make your experience an enjoyable one. The route is marked with painted otter footprints. Only 12 people can start the trail each day; groups should consist of a minimum of four. It costs R500 per person, which includes four nights in the hiking huts as well as the permit. There are four overnight camps: Ngubu, Scott, Oakhurst, and André. At each site there are two log huts, each sleeping six people in bunk beds; mattresses and firewood are provided. Take time to enjoy the trail, respect the environment and leave with positive and happy memories.

Nature's Valley Rest Camp Across the Groot River from the camp are six trails in the Grootkloof Forest. There are a number of large trees here and the birdlife is excellent, although there's the usual problem of catching sight of them in the first place. The best spots are in clearings and along streams. Note that there are a large number of streams in the forest which can be difficult to cross after heavy rains. South of the camp the river estuary broadens into a lagoon which is a popular spot for watersports. Fortunately no powerboats are allowed on the water, and exploring the limits by canoe is great fun.

Storms River Camp There are four different trails in the vicinity of the camp. The most popular, and strongly recommended, is a 1-km walk along a raised boardwalk from the restaurant block to the mouth of the Storms River. The last part of the walk involves a steep descent – there is a solid handrail, but the wooden steps can be slippery after rains, as can other parts of the walk. At the bottom is the suspension bridge which appears in many pictures promoting the Garden Route. The views from this point are excellent, especially at midday when there is a clear view of the narrow river gorge extending back inland. The path continues on the other side of the bridge, and from here you can climb the hill for superb views; there are over 300 steps and the path is narrow and steep. Look out for identification labels on the trees as the path winds through the forest. This is a great opportunity to see the trees which a century ago were in great demand for household furniture and building projects – much of the reason for the extensive deforestation in the area. Allow at least an hour for the walk to the bridge and back.

The other trails close to the camp are the **Lourie Trail**, 1 km through the forested slopes behind the camp; the **Blue Duiker Trail**, 3.7 km further into the forest; and the **Waterfall Trail**, a 3-km walk along the first part of the **Otter Trail** – hikers without a permit have to turn back at the waterfall.

The latest addition to the park is the **Dolphin Trail**, a three-day guided trail. This is a far more upmarket hike – luggage is transported from one night stop to the next, accommodation is in luxurious lodges, all meals are included (with pre-packed picnics for lunch), and the entire hike is professionally guided. This trail is much more expensive, at R2700 per person for three days. For more information and reservations contact SAN Parks, or one of the hotels used on the trail that are listed on the website www.dolphintrail.co.za.

Behind the restaurant is the rather unusual **Underwater Trail**, which can be completed with scuba equipment or a mask and snorkel. You can see a good cross-section of the marine life found along the south coast, but conditions are not ideal, so few people complete the trail. If you do want to give it a go, the best time of year is in the summer, although conditions are rough for most of the year and visibility is rarely more than 10 m. The water is fairly cold, so be sure to wear a wetsuit. **Stormsriver Adventures** (see page 287), can arrange guided trips and rents equipment.

Storms River Village → *Colour map 7, grid B3.*

Storms River Village lies 8km east of the Storms River Bridge, 4 km from the entrance to Tsitsikamma National Park, and 1 km south of the N2. Administratively, this is the first town in the Eastern Cape Province, but it is also regarded as the first and last town along the Garden Route, hence its inclusion here. This small village of around 40 houses has several accommodation options catering for visitors to the park and hikers wishing to head for the inland mountains. It's also a stop-off for the Baz Bus and the starting point for many of the adventure activities in the region. The small supermarket and liquor store are useful for those self-catering at Tsitsikamma. Note that the village is nowhere near the sea.

Sleeping

Mossel Bay *p250, map p250*
During busy periods, especially in December, contact the **Mossel Bay Tourism Bureau** to confirm overnight accommodation. It acts as a central reservations office for registered members, T044-6912202.

L **Botlierskop Private Game Reserve** , T044-6966055, www.botlierskop.co.za. 12 luxury tented suites on wooden platforms, good views over river and mountains, some have private jetties for fishing, decorated in a colonial theme with 4-poster beds, rates include game drives and walks, and all meals. An all-round safari experience close to the Garden Route.

A-B **Mossel Bay Guesthouse**, 61 Bruns Rd, T044-6912000, www.mosselbaygh.co.za. Friendly guesthouse with 4 en suite double rooms with sea views and M-Net TV. Heated pool and wooden deck with ocean views where breakfast is served in summer, and small pub. The house is tucked back from the town centre up the hill.

A-B **Protea Hotel Mossel Bay**, corner of Church and Market St, this is part of the museum complex and was formerly known as the Old Post Office Tree Manor, T044-6913738, www.oldposttree.co.za, www.proteahotels.co.za. Comfortable hotel rooms and self-catering suites in a smart manor house which is the third-oldest building in Mossel Bay. Outdoor dining area with views across bay, swimming pool, popular and always recommended by visitors, check for seasonal discounts.

B **Allemans Dorpshuis**, 94 Montagu St, T044-6903621, allemans@telkomsa.net. In the heart of town, lovely old-fashioned hotel in a fine restored Victorian town house with the original iron balcony at the front. 6 beautifully furnished rooms with en suite showers and polished wooden floors. French and German spoken.

B **Huijs te Marquette**, 1 Marsh St, T/F044-6913182, marquette@pixie.co.za. A comfortable house which has been very thoughtfully decorated, 12 en suite rooms, relaxed atmosphere, lounge with fireplace, evening meals on request, swimming pool, secure parking, wheelchair friendly. Recommended.

B **The Point**, Point Rd, T044-6913512, www.pointhotel.co.za. Large, ugly construction but in an unbeatable location, right on the rocks below the lighthouse. All 48 rooms have sea views and private balconies, are en suite and have satellite TV. **The Lighthouse** restaurant and bar caters for most. There is a rock pool just outside which is good for swimming.

C-E **Mossel Bay Backpackers**, 1 Marsh St, T044-6913182, www.gardenroute adventures.com. Part of Huijs te Marquette, dorms and double rooms, some camping space, TV room, convenient location 300 m from the beach and close to some bars, travel centre can organize activities, popular.

C-E **Santos Caravan Park**, on the George road 2 km from town centre, T044-6912915. Large well-grassed park, limited shade, some self-catering chalets, not the place to stay when full, but fine at the quiet time of year, right on the beach.

D **Santos Express Train Lodge**, T044-6911995, www.santosexpress.co.za. Converted train carriages set 30 m from the sea on Santos beach with tiny rooms sleeping 4, sun deck and an onboard pub and restaurant serving seafood, lamb on the spit and braais. Baz Bus stop.

George *p253, map p254*
L **Fancourt Hotel and Country Club**, 6 km from George airport, T044-8040000, www.fancourt.com. This is an exclusive upmarket resort and thanks to the President's Cup being hosted here in November 2003, it is one of the world's leading golf destinations. Set on more than 500 ha of land, Fancourt encompasses 4 outstanding 18-hole golf

courses, 2 of which were designed by Gary Player. There are rooms in the 19th-century manor house or newly refurbished garden suites and studios overlooking the golf courses. Health spa, gym, tennis courts, 2 outdoor pools, 1 indoor heated pool, 5 superb restaurants. Golf open to members and guests only. Special packages are sometimes published on the website.

AL **Far Hills Country Hotel**, off the N2 towards Wilderness, T044-8890000, www.farhillscountryhotel.fsnet.co.uk. A large comfortable country hotel in the lee of the Outeniqua Mountains. 51 tastefully decorated rooms with fireplace and balcony, some with superb views across the forest, but a bit cramped. Café, **Country Cuisine** restaurant with – rather surprisingly – a sushi bar, open terrace, lounge, bar and swimming pool. Very attentive service for such a big hotel. More suited to an overnight stop than a holiday base.

A-B **Cedar Manor**, 3 Cedar Av, T044-8745462, www.cedarmanor.co.za. Fully restored Cape Dutch home, very elegantly decorated with antiques and fine china, the only 5-star B&B in George, complimentary cell phone rental, airport transfers and liquers on arrival. 3 en suite bedrooms in the main house and a self-catering garden cottage, superb views of the mountains, swimming pool. No children under 12.

B **Oakhurst Manor House**, corner of Meade and Cathedral Sts, T044-8747130, www.oakhursthotel.co.za. Luxury town inn in the design of a classic Cape Dutch house with thatched roof, 25 smart, individually decorated en suite rooms, large restaurant, lounge and ladies' bar.

B **Pine Lodge**, Knysna Rd, T044-8711974, www.pinelodgegeorge.co.za, close to Pick 'n' Pay. Large resort close to Victoria Bay, suitable for families with 46 self-catering chalets with 1-3 bedrooms, M-Net TV, telephone, and braai area. Restaurant, bar, tennis courts and swimming pool.

B **Protea Hotel King George**, King George Drive, T044-8747659, www.protea hotels.co.za. Smart Victorian hotel situated close to the 11th fairway of the George Golf Course, 60 comfortable rooms, good restaurant, pub, 2 swimming pools, the usual quality of service expected in a Protea.

B-C **Loerie Guest Lodge**, 91 Davidson Rd, T044-8744740, www.loerielodgeco.za. Modern buildings with 22 large and comfortable en suite rooms, a neat garden with a swimming pool and sun deck.

B-C **St Moritz**, 16 Varing Rd, T044-8745993, www.stmoritz.co.za. Award-winning restaurant with 6 guest rooms attached (see Eating page 282). 4 bedrooms in the main house and 2 garden suites, 1 has a whirlpool, swimming pool.

B-E **George Tourist Resort**, York St, T044-8745205, www.george-tourist-resort.co.za. Huge complex with self-catering chalets, rondavels and caravans. Shady sites with power and water, indoor pool and outdoor heated pool, gym, sauna, tennis courts, crazy golf, shop, laundry, room for 300 caravans! Double the price during peak season.

C **Cosy Corner**, 12 Rens St, T044-8740710, www.cosy-corner.co.za. B&B with old-fashioned flowery rooms, TV, en suite, dinner available on request, garden views, no children under 10, owners Susan and Cedric are also tour guides so know all there is to know about the area.

C **Hawthorndene Country Inn**, Langenhoven Rd, T044-8744160, hawthorndene@mweb.co.za. Family-run country inn with 26 en suite rooms, pool, a good restaurant and bar with big TV screen and live music at the weekends.

C **Protea Landmark Lodge**, 123 York St, T044-8744488, www.proteahotels.co.za. Large hotel in an attractive Cape Dutch-style building. Good location on the main road, with 50 standard but comfortable a/c rooms more geared to the business traveller, restaurant and bar.

C-E **Outeniqua Backpackers**, 115 Merriman St, T044-8747807, www.outeniqua-backpackers.com. Newish hostel with 20 dorm beds and a couple of doubles, bright and airy, some with mountain views, braai area, breakfasts, DSTV and internet. Only backpacker option in town. Baz Bus stop. You can hire bikes and they'll drop you off at the top of Montagu Pass for the ride back down.

For an explanation of the sleeping and eating price codes used in this guide, see inside the front cover. Other relevant information is found in Essentials pages 42-47.

Victoria Bay *p255*

A-B Lands End, The Point, T044-8890123, www.vicbay.com. 2 double en suite rooms with TV, 2 self-contained apartments with sun deck, self-catering, or breakfasts served on an open veranda only 6 m from the ocean, beautiful location, fishing and surf equipment hired out, golf at Fancourt can be arranged, extras such as laundry, wine cellar, and a glass of sherry on arrival, ask for Rod or Shanell.

B The Waves, 6 Beach Rd, T044-8890166, thewaves@intekom.co.za. A superior B&B right on the beach, 3 double rooms with en suite bathroom, balconies and sea views, 1906 historic building, friendly, low-key place, a more pleasant location than the centre of George, 2 separate family cottages available (B&B or self-catering). Recommended.

C Sea Breeze, T044-8890098, www.seabreezecabanas.co.za. 36 units, modern development of self-catering flats and chalets with M-Net TV, 300-m walk to the beach which has a safe tidal pool, good for families, bedding supplied but you have to bring your own towels and dishcloths.

Wilderness *p256, map p257*

A Dolphin Dunes, Buxton Close, T044-8770204, www.dolphindunes.co.za, approaching from George, turn right off the N2, 2.5 km after the Caltex petrol station. A fine upmarket purpose-built guesthouse with 8 tasteful, double en suite rooms, fridge, TV, telephone, splash pool, private access to the beach. 2 rooms have a self-catering option and wheelchair access.

A Protea Wilderness Resort, T044-8771110, www.proteahotels.co.za. Smartest hotel in the area, large with over 150 stylish en suite rooms with TV, restaurant, beauty spa, 2 swimming pools, bowling green, giant chess board in the grounds, great views all round. If you are not staying here, pop in for the very good-value Sun lunch from 1230-1500.

B Bruni's Guest House, 937 8th Av, Wilderness East, T044-8770551, www.brunis.co.za, close to the Holiday Inn. 4 en suite double rooms in a thatched house perched on the dunes with sweeping views of the ocean, German spoken.

B Fairy Knowe, Dumbleton Rd, T044-8771100, www.fairyknowe.co.za. 42 rooms, some thatched rondavels, peaceful forested location on Touw River, close to Wilderness National Park, birdwatchers will enjoy regular visits by the Knysna lourie, restaurant, bar, canoes, pedalos and tennis.

B Moontide Guest Lodge, Southside Rd, T044-8770361, www.moontide.co.za. 8 en suite thatched cottages, one of them a honeymoon suite, set under milkwood trees in a beautiful garden overlooking the lagoon. Each cottage has been tastefully decorated with kilims and fine furniture. Easy access to the hiking trails in the national park, a short walk from the beach and a good spot for birdwatchers. A well-appointed and well-run guesthouse. Recommended.

B Villa Sentosa, T044-8770378, overlooks the Serpentine channel. An elegant retreat with 6 luxurious rooms housed in a magnificent modern house, set in the hills behind the national park. All the rooms have large windows providing plenty of light and panoramic views. Spacious lounge with plush furnishings, heated swimming pool surrounded by a sun deck with views towards the ocean, B&B, can also organize picnic hampers, airport transfer. Recommended.

B-C The Lodge on the Beach, 45 die Duin, T044-8770263, www.pinklodge.co.za. B&B or self-catering in a great position right on the beach, 7 spacious a/c en suite rooms, 1 with self catering facilities, all facing the ocean, spot whales or dolphins from your bed, rolling lawns, a very relaxing spot. Shame about the hideous bright pink colour.

C-D Fairy Knowe Backpackers, just off Waterside Rd, T044-8771285, fairybp@mweb.co.za. A great set-up in 2 farmhouses surrounded by gardens and milkwood trees, clean attractive rooms, dorms and doubles, bar, great breakfasts, nightly camp fires and braais. Also has a travel desk. A very relaxing place to rest up for a few days. Baz Bus stops here, or you can travel by the Outeniqua Choo-Tjoe steam train from George or Knysna. The station is a request stop so tell the conductor you wish to get off at Fairy Knowe station. Recommended.

E The Wild Welcome, 479 10th Av, T044-8771307, www.wildwelcome.com. Hostel just 100 m from the beach, with dorms, double rooms and camping. TV, video, pool, free surfboards and mountain bikes. Only open Dec-Feb when the friendly European owners visit South Africa. Baz Bus stop.

Wilderness National Park *p258, map p257*

Accommodation is laid out in 2 camps divided by the railway and the Serpentine River channel: **Ebb & Flow Rest Camp, North** and **Ebb & Flow Rest Camp, South**. All the park's accommodation must be vacated by 0900. Arriving visitors can have access from 1200. Reservations through **SAN Parks** Pretoria office, T012-4289111, www.sanparks.org. Bookings can also be made in person at the offices in Cape Town and Durban (see page 44). For reservations under 72 hrs or cancellations contact the park reception directly, T044-8771197.

Ebb and Flow Rest Camp, South, on the Touw River close to Wilderness village, has 33 units in total:

B Cottages, 2 bedrooms and sofa bed, bathroom, partially equipped kitchen, lounge, modern bungalows with no appeal when you compare them with the log cabins.

B Log Cabins, self-catering cabins on stilts, all have views across the river and the reed beds, 2 bedrooms, bathroom, kitchen, comfortable lounge area and a veranda, lots of character. Good value for 4 people especially with a seasonal discount.

B-C Forest cabins, sleeping 2 or 4, fairly basic but with en suite bathroom and partially equipped kitchen, communal kitchen also available.

D Campsite Thick grass with patches of good shade on the banks of the river, beautiful setting and good facilities, an excellent campsite with 59 caravan and camping sites, full of character as long as it is not too full.

Ebb & Flow Rest Camp, North, a short walk from the office, this is a smaller camp beside the Touw River where it emerges from the hills. A beautiful and peaceful spot but its geography means that cold air collects in the narrow valley, and the sun only reacher the camp for a few hours.

C-D Huts 12 1-room rondavels with 2 single beds, 2-plate electric stove, fridge, cooking equipment, plus a shower, for 2 people, or a cheaper option with no en suite shower.

D Camping 45 caravan and camping sites on the banks of the Touw River, plenty of grass and shade, wash block, no communal kitchen but braais, some sites with electric points.

Sedgefield and around *p258*

As with all villages along this stretch of coast, prices are considerably higher at Christmas and rooms need to be booked well in advance. There is a choice of overnight stops and holiday cottages in the village and around the lakes.

AL Lake Pleasant, east of Sedgefield on the edge of Groenvlei, T044-3492400, www.lakepleasanthotel.com. This comfortable 5-star hotel has had a major overhaul and now belongs to the South African Mantis chain of luxury hotels. Set right on the lake, with 36 rooms with en suite bathroom, opening onto gardens, all with lake views. Smart lounge furnished with antiques, library, cigar bar, restaurant with a menu to match the setting – great lunch stop if you're passing through. Swimming pool, tennis court, gym, health spa. Perfect for birdwatchers with some hides by the lake, rowing boats for hire. Recommended.

B-C Groenvlei Bushcamp, reservations, Goukamma Nature Reserve, T044-8025310, www.capenature.org.za. Throughout the reserve, hidden away in the milkwood forest, are a number of thatched family en suite houses sleeping 8-9, and 3 double thatched chalets with communal bathrooms, living area and kitchen linked by boardwalks, furnishings made from wood or reeds. All are a short walk to the lake where you can swim and watch the sun set. There is no electricity; light is provided by gas or paraffin lamps. Bring all your own food and bedding. A beautiful setting with particular attention paid to the environment. Recommended.

B-C Sedgefield Arms, Pelican Lane, off the N2 in the village centre, T044-3431417, www.sedgefieldarms.co.za. A comfortable mix of self-catering cottages suitable for 2-6 people with patio and braai, or B&B. Attached restaurant and lively English theme pub, good spot for lunch on the lawn, bar with big sports screen, swimming pool, all set in leafy gardens, good value and fun atmosphere.

D-F Landfall Resort, T/F044-3431804. Well-maintained campsite with plenty of shade and grass. 2-bedroom fully equipped self-catering cottages that sleep 6 people are also available. This is an excellent campsite right on the estuary, a short distance from the beach. A good, cheap option.

Knysna *p259, maps p261 and p262*
It is difficult to find accommodation during the Christmas and New Year period unless you book 6 months in advance. As one of the most popular holiday centres along the Garden Route, there is plenty of choice of accommodation, both in type and location, but it's generally more expensive than in other towns along the Garden Route. The list below is far from comprehensive. Remember you'll be paying a premium to stay over school holiday periods. The centre of Knysna is on the northern margin of the lagoon. To the east of town, George Rex Drive leads to Leisure Island and The Heads. Along and off this road are a number of guesthouses and B&Bs. For something different, and especially recommended for families, self-catering houseboats (**A**) are available for hire on the Knysna Lagoon. All eating and sleeping equipment is included, and you do not need to have any nautical experience. They are very easy to operate and allow you to explore the lagoon at leisure. Contact **Lightleys Holiday Houseboats**, T044-3860007, www.houseboats.co.za.

AL-A Isolabella, Cearn Dr, Leisure Isle, T044-3840049, www.isolabella.co.za. Italian-run villa with wrap-around balconies in a commanding position overlooking the lagoon.

A Falcon's View Manor, 2 Thesen Hill, T044-3826767, www.falconsview.com. Small upmarket hotel with 9 spacious en suite double rooms (non-smoking) with TV, tastefully decorated and furnished to an exceptional level of comfort, relaxing on the veranda overlooking the lagoon is a perfect way to spend a day, swimming pool, neat gardens, intimate bar, a classic Victorian house. No children under 10. Recommended.

A-B Knysna Belle, 75 Bayswater Dr, Leisure Isle, T044-3840511, www.knysnabelle.co.za. 6 very stylish individually decorated en suite rooms, 1 with a Victorian bath tub, very good breakfasts, swimming pool, lovely balconies to relax and enjoy the views of the lagoon, mountain bikes and a rowing boat available to rent out, no children under 6.

A-B Leisure Isle Lodge, 87 Bayswater Dr, Leisure Isle, T044-3840462, www.leisureisle lodge.co.za. Award-winning guesthouse with spacious rooms, comfortable lounge and bar, heated swimming pool, views across bay, gardens stretch to waterfront, a short drive from The Heads.

B Aesta's B&B, 21 Fitchat St, T044-3824879, www.aestas.co.za. Nice views from several spacious and attractive rooms, swimming pool, walking distance from the tourist office and shops and restaurants on the main road, well-run medium-sized B&B.

B Heron Water Lodge, 33 Cearn Dr, Leisure Isle, T044-3840624, www.heron.co.za. A friendly and comfortable B&B with 4 spacious en suite double rooms, 2 of the rooms overlook the lagoon in a separate wing. Sun deck, bar, swimming pool, generous filling breakfasts. Recommended.

B Knysna Manor House, 19 Fitchat St, T044-3825440, manor@absamail.co.za. A peaceful Victorian stone house with good views of the lagoon, a short walk from town centre, 11 en suite rooms with TV but decor is a bit frilly.

B Protea Knysna Quays, Waterfront Dr, T044-3825005, www.proteahotels.co.za. Usual large state-of-the-art hotel, with comfortable a/c rooms, restaurant, cocktail bar, lounge, attractive swimming pool. Great location next to the Waterfront and station.

B Under Milkwood, T044-3840745, www.milkwood.co.za. 16 self-catering log chalets at Knysna Heads set in a grove of milkwood trees, can sleep 6 people, excellent kitchen facilities. Not all have views of the lagoon. Plenty of light, relaxing sun deck, recommended if you plan to spend a week in the district. Out of the town, but still close to all the amenities.

B Wayside Inn, 48 Main St, T044-3826011, www.waysideinn.co.za. Smart set-up in the centre of town with a Victorian theme. 15 luxury rooms with iron beds and sisal carpets, fans, fine African art on show, private balconies, wicker furniture, TV, superior picnic hampers can be made to order. Several readers have commented on the lack of a lounge area. Friendly staff.

B Yellowwood Lodge, 18 Handel St, T044-3825906, www.yellowwoodlodge.co.za. Lovely guesthouse in one of Knysna's older houses with 10 thoughtfully decorated rooms. Ask for an upstairs room – they have relaxing balconies with views of the lagoon and Heads. Delicious buffet breakfasts, immaculate garden, swimming pool, strictly non-smoking household, no children under

10. Loses some of its appeal when full, look out for the flagpole.

B-C **Gallery Guest House**, 10 Hill St West, T044-3822510, www.galleryguesthouse.co.za. 2 double and 2 twin rooms in an old house overlooking the lagoon. Breakfast is served on the peaceful balcony. Owner Lolly is an artist.

B-D **Ashmead Resort**, George Rex Dr, T044-3841166, www.ashmeadresort.co.za. 66 log cabins and modern brick cottages set in mature gardens overlooking lagoon, B&B or self-catering, bright lobby and lounge, stark restaurant, bar, miniature golf, swimming pool, popular domestic family holiday venue.

C-D **Highfield Backpackers**, 2 Graham St, T044-3826266, www.highfieldsbackpackers.co.za. Quiet backpacker hostel set in 2 town houses, dorms and doubles, pub that also offers tapas-style snacks, kitchen, courtyard with pool, travel centre. A bit of a rabbit warren but the new owners have done much to spruce up the place and there are some neat new en suite doubles.

D-E **Overlander's Lodge**, 11 Nelson St, T044-3825920, www.overlanders.co.za. Large dorms, clean bathrooms, TV room with good video collection, small swimming pool, well-stocked kitchen, pool table, good for camping, scooter and bike hire. They have recently taken over the house next door with much quieter doubles and twins and another 2 kitchens. Fun atmosphere but not to everyone's liking - the parties can be raucous.

D-E **Peregrin Backpackers**, 16 High St, T044-3823747, peregrin@cyberperk.co.za. Great backpacker lodge in a large town house. Colourful dorms, double rooms, camping, kitchen, bar, garden with small pool, TV room, very friendly and helpful staff, fun party place. Recommended, despite the limited bathroom space. The Baz Bus drops and picks up at all of Knysna's backpackers daily.

West of Knysna *p262*

AL **Belvidere Manor**, Duthie Dr, Belvidere, T044-3871055, www.belvidere.co.za. 30 smart cottages arranged around a swimming pool in shady gardens, private verandas with views across the lagoon, sleeping 2-4 people. Some have a study; all are individually furnished and have log fires. The manor house, from 1834, houses the reception, an elegant dining room and the Bell pub. Friendly and attentive staff.

B-C **Camelot**, 28 Lower Duthie Dr, Belvidere Estate, T044-3871393, www.camelot.co.za. 2 large upstairs suites with views across the lagoon, TV, fridge, breakfast served outside during the summer, peaceful location, secure parking, good value. Recommended.

Knysna Forest *p263, map p261*

L **Phantom Forest Eco-Reserve**, T044-3860046, www.phantomforest.com. Signposted from the Phantom Pass road. This lodge is a fairly new addition to the Knysna area and offers ultra-stylish accommodation in a superb collection of 14 luxurious and eco-friendly 'tree suites' set in the forest high above the lagoon. Each has a private terrace and luxurious bathroom - the showers are open to the forest. Individual houses are connected by walkways to the excellent restaurant, bar, lookout points, beauty spa, and pool. Attentive, helpful staff, the perfect place to experience the forest. Highly recommended.

B-C **Forest Edge**, just past the Rheenendal Post Office, turn right at the Bibby's Hoek sign. At the entrance to the state forest, turn left for 1.5 km, the lodge is the last property on this road, T082-4561338, www.forestedge.co.za. 2 holiday cottages, self-contained and fully equipped, sleeping 4-5 people, overlooking a picturesque dam. Linen and towels are provided and there is a fireplace, telephone, braai facilities and outdoor hot shower. Mountain bikes available for hire, you can walk straight into the forest from here.

Knysna Elephant Park *p265*

AL **Elephant Boma**, T044-5327732, www.knysnaelephantpark.co.za. Large self-catering apartment with picture windows over the *boma* where the elephants sleep, so you can fall asleep to their nightly sounds (and smells!), and see them when they are out and about. Modern and comfortable with 4 twin-bedded rooms, and 2 extra beds in the lounge, 3 bathrooms, DSTV.

Plettenberg Bay *p265, map p266*

During Christmas it is difficult to find a bed unless you have booked well in advance. Along with Knysna, there is an unbelievable transformation here during the midsummer holiday rush. For the rest of the year, hotels and B&Bs cry out for guests. In an effort to attract visitors during the winter months, discounts are offered so it's worth checking these out when choosing somewhere to stay.

L **Hunter's Country House**, 10 km towards Knysna, T044-5327818, www.hunterhotels.com. 23 thatched suites with fireplace, antique furnishings and private patio, 3 dining rooms, 2 swimming pools, conservatory, antique shop, forest chapel for weddings, one of South Africa's top country hotels, which has won awards for food and service, a special place to treat yourself to. Recommended.

L **The Plettenberg**, 40 Church St, Lookout Rocks, T044-5332030, www.plettenberg.com. 40 a/c rooms, lounge and dining rooms furnished with antiques, superb food and wine, swimming pool, beauty spa, smartest in area, everything you would expect in a small, exclusive top-class 5-star hotel, but very expensive. Request a room with ocean views, some of them look over the car park.

AL **Beacon Isle**, Beacon Isle Crescent, T044-5331120, www.southernsun.com. Multi-storey building dominating the bay, right on the water between 2 beaches, 200 rooms, 3 excellent restaurants, swimming pool, tennis, also a timeshare resort. A superb location but an eyesore on Plett's sweeping beach.

AL-A **Stone Cottages**, corner of Harker and Odland Sts, T044-5331331, www.stonecottage.co.za. Beautifully restored 19th-century cottage, tastefully decorated rooms with high ceilings and gleaming wooden floors, antiques and old photographs, fully equipped for self-catering, sleeps 5 in 3 bedrooms, panoramic views of the ocean, deck with jacuzzi overlooking the main beach. Close by is a smaller modern, cheaper self-catering cottage for 2, with TV and DVD in the lounge, decor in the same theme as the older cottage. A good option for families or friends travelling together, and price per person is reasonable.

A **Cottage Pie**, 16 Tarbet Ness Av, T044-5330369, www.cottagepie.co.za. Homely but upmarket guesthouse offering well-appointed rooms, very comfortable and cosy. Pool, bougainvillea bedecked terrace. Slightly out of town, but only 100 m to Robberg Beach. Healthy or full English breakfasts served, evening meals on request. Friendly owners Frik and Nerine are happy to arrange excursions. Recommended, though pricey in the height of season when rates double.

B **A Room with a View**, 5 Julia Av, T044-5331836, www.roomwithaview.co.za. Near the beach with, as the name suggests, good views, 4 en suite rooms with TV, fridge, heater and fan, special touches like fruit bowls and glasses of sherry, lovely garden terraces where you can take breakfast.

B **Coral Tree Cottages**, off the N2 11 km from Plett towards Knysna, T044-5327822, www.coraltree.net. Good self-catering option if you have a car, 6 spacious and nicely furnished thatched cottages with 1 or 2 bedrooms, satellite TV, fully equipped kitchen, patio and braai area, set in lovely green woodlands full of flowers. Good as a base for a few days as Knysna is only 25 km away.

C-D **Nothando Backpackers**, 5 Wilder St, T044-5330220, www.nothando.co.za. Dorms, double rooms, B&B, in a central location. Clean, cheap and friendly, with extras like hairdryers in the bathrooms, plus offering plenty of activities with discounts. Beds have duvets, some rooms are en suite. Small kitchen, large TV lounge, **Far Side** bar with braai and pool table, African meals available.

C-E **Albergo For Backpackers**, 8 Church St, T044-5334434, www.albergo.co.za. Centrally located hostel with sea views. Dorms, double rooms and camping area, garden with hammocks and bonfires, 2 kitchens, travel centre. Video room, bar and pool table. Will pick up from buses at the Shell Ultra.

East of Plettenberg Bay *p267*

AL **Hog Hollow Country Lodge**, 18 km east of Plettenberg Bay at the Crags off the N2 main road, T044-5348879, www.hoghollow.com. One of the finest lodges along the Garden Route set in a private nature reserve, with 15 suites, all with ceiling fans, minibar decorated with locally made wall hangings and woodcarvings, each with its own wooden deck with hammock overlooking the Matjies River gorge and Tsitsikamma Mountains. There is a spacious lounge with open fireplace for log fires in the winter months. Good evening meals are served around a communal table in a relaxed manner. Swimming pool with stunning views, library/lounge in the main house. The lodge also organizes 3-hr boat trips around the bay to view whales and dolphins, and there are a number of walking trails through the forest surrounding the lodge which are very popular with birdwatchers. Recommended.

B **Whiskey Creek hut**, Keurbooms River Nature Reserve, T044-8025310, www.capenature.org.za. R460 per night midweek, R600 per night weekends, for 1-4 people and includes canoe hire. The stilted log cabin has 10 basic bunks, hot water, flush toilets, bedding on request, and a fully equipped kitchen with outside braai facilities. There's no electricity but solar energy fuels the fridge and lights. The hut is only accessible by canoe and it's a delightfully isolated spot.

B-C **Protea Hotel Keurbooms River**, on the Keurbooms River 8.5 km east from Plett, T044-5359300, www.proteahotels.co.za. Modern and functional but very comfortable hotel set in indigenous gardens, 61 en suite rooms with TV and kettles, swimming pool, bar and restaurant with charming wooden deck with outstanding river views.

B-D **Aventura Plettenberg**, 6 km east of Plett on the Keurbooms River, T044-5359309, www.aventura.co.za. 28 neat wooden self-catering chalets nestled along the riverbank, plus 112 camping and caravan spots with excellent facilities, though can get very crowded in season. Swimming pool, canoes and pedalos for hire, tennis and volleyball courts, good all-round family option.

Nature's Valley *p268*

Surprisingly Nature's Valley has hardly any accommodation and sleeping is limited to only 2 establishments.

AL-A **Tranquility Lodge**, 130 St Michaels Av, next to the Nature's Valley shop and pub, T044-5316663, www.tranquillity lodge.co.za. This is a new spot and already readers have recommended it. Lovely reed and timber lodge in pretty gardens, 7 en suite rooms, 1 of which is a honeymoon suite with spa bath, double shower and fireplace, very nicely decorated throughout with lots of lounging areas. The owner is also a chef and meals can be taken together with other guests in the dining room, or alone in a tree house. There's a swimming pool, outside hot pool, each room gets its own double kayak to explore the lagoon, a complimentary bridge walk at the nearby Bloukrans Bridge is included in the price, and finally it's registered with BirdLife as a birder-friendly establishment.

C-D **Hiker's Haven**, 411 St Patrick's St, T044-5316805, www.hikershaven.co.za. A large stone guesthouse with thatched roof, 3 double rooms with individual garden access, 12-bed dorm in the loft which connects to a TV lounge and bar area, self-contained kitchen. However we've had consistently bad reports from budget travellers about rude service, and this only makes a listing as it the one choice for budget travellers.

Groot River and Bloukrans Passes *p269*

B-C **Tsitsikamma Forest Village**, T042-2811450, www.tsitsikamma.org.za. 16 brand-new self-catering log chalets, some on stilts with kitchen, braai area, lounge and veranda, suitable for families. Also here is the **D-E Bloukrans Backpackers Lodge**, offering a good range of accommodation including 2 dorms sleeping 8, and some double rooms, modern and comfortable communal kitchen and lounge area with DSTV and a pool table. The Baz Bus stops here though a car is useful as there are no amenities in the vicinity and only a coffee shop on site. Despite being cosy inside the chalets and backpackers' lodge, this is a bleak spot in winter.

Tsitsikamma National Park *p269*

This is a very popular national park, particularly with South Africans, so during the school holidays it is almost impossible to find accommodation here. Reservations must be made up to 12 months in advance. Fortunately there is plenty of accommodation along the Garden Route. If you're staying in Knysna, for example, the park can still be reached within a 1-hr drive. There are also several private lodges close to the main entrance (see below).

All of the park's accommodation must be vacated by 0900. Arriving visitors have access from 1200. There are 2 rest camps in the park: **Storms River Mouth**, the main camp with a full range of facilities, and **Nature's Valley**, a very basic camp close to the settlement of the same name. Reservations, through the **SAN Parks** office in Pretoria, T012-4289111, www.sanparks.org. Bookings can also be made in person at the offices in Cape Town and Durban (see page 44), www.sanparks.org. For cancellations and reservations under 72 hrs contact the Storms River Mouth camp directly, T042-2811607. Credit card bookings are accepted over the phone. Seasonal discounts apply to all forms of accommodation in May-Aug.

Storms River Mouth

On a narrow strip of land between ocean and forested hills, this is one of the most beautiful settings of all the national parks.

A **Log Cabins**, with 2 bedrooms sleeping a maximum of 6 people, fully equipped kitchen with fridge and stove, bedding provided, bathroom, lounge area.

B **Oceanettes**, with 2 bedrooms, fully equipped kitchen, bathroom, lounge, a little less smart and comfortable, but ideal when you are likely to spend most of the day outdoors.

C **Forest Cabins**, sleeping 2, very basic, shared ablution block.

D **Camping**, terraced lawns in a beautiful location right on the shoreline, exposed when the wind blows. There are a few shady trees, and it is a real thrill to peer out of your tent at dawn and watch the waves crashing on the rocks right in front of you. There are twice as many places for caravans as for tents, braai sites but no electric points, laundry and central wash blocks.

Nature's Valley Rest Camp

This camping and caravan site is 40 km west of Storms River Mouth. The site is set in an indigenous forest on the banks of the Groot River, and has recently been upgraded. Accommodation is in C **Forest huts**, which are very basic with 2 beds and electricity, or D **Campsites**. Both of these share the wash block, hot water, laundry, no electricity, no shop or restaurant, all supplies can be bought in Nature's Valley village, 3 km away.

Storms River Village *p272*

A **The Armagh**, T042-2811512, www.the armagh.com. Comfortable graded guest-house with 7 double rooms including a honeymoon suite with en suite facilities and private patios, guest lounge, craft shop and pool. Views and walks from the lodge are good and the garden is full of birds. Attached **Rafters** restaurant has a good local reputation with tasty buffets. Run by Johan and Marion who will tell you everything there is to know about the area. Recommended by readers.

A-B **Tsitsikamma Lodge**, 2 km east of the village along the N2, T042-2803802, www.tsitsikamma.com. Luxurious selection of 32 timber log cabins, including several honeymoon suites. Each log cabin has an en suite bathroom with spa bath, TV, telephone. Set in forested grounds and colourful gardens, cosy restaurant serving buffet lunches, swimming pool. The short 'strip-tease' trail into the forest brings you to some enticing cool pools. The whole complex is of a high standard and well run, the ideal base from which to start the Otter Trail as the management will transport you to the start and collect you at the end after 4-5 days for a small fee, a very useful service.

C-E **Tube 'n Axe**, corner of Darnell and Saffron Sts, T042-2811757, www.tube-n-axe.co.za. 4-bed dorms and some doubles set in a forested garden with plenty of room for camping. The rustic bar has a pool table and braai pit. Breakfast and dinner available. Shuttles to the Bloukrans Bridge Bungee, and they rent out quad bikes and mountain bikes. The **Stormsriver Adventures** office is a stone's throw away so there's plenty to keep the adventurer occupied for a couple of days. Baz Bus stop.

Eating

Mossel Bay *p250, map p250*

TTT-TT **Admirals**, in the new **Garden Route Casino** at Pinnacle Point south of Mossel Bay off the N2, T044-6067777, www.gardenroute casino.co.za. 1200-1500, 1800-2300. Great-value buffet in the main casino restaurant, over 120 dishes, plus Mongolian stir-fry bar where you make up your own plate of food before the chef cooks it in front of you, plenty of seafood and roasts, cold meat and cheese platters, and desserts including homemade ice cream. Recommended for the very hungry.

TT **Café Gannet**, Market St, T044-6911885, next to **Old Post Tree Guest House** and museum. 0700-2300. A well-established seafood restaurant, popular all year round since the tour buses stop here, seafood grills and pizza from a wood oven, sometimes oven-roasted shark, enjoyable bay views from a shady outdoor terrace, mixed reports on quality of the food.

ΨΨ The Coach House, 3 Powrie St, T044-6911177. Closed Sun. Pasta and seafood, recommended for line fish, one of the best in town. Outside tables in the garden.

ΨΨ Jazzbury's, 11 Marsh St, T044-6911923. 1100-1500, 1800-2300, closed Sat lunch. A popular restaurant serving good-value traditional meals such as potjes and bredies, ostrich steaks, seafood and a delectable dessert trolley. Eat at tables on the patio or inside the cosy bar. Recommended.

ΨΨ Kingfisher, The Point, T044-6906390. Modern development overlooking the beach, seafood platters and combos, good grilled fish served with rice and chips, some meat dishes, indifferent service. There is an attached pizza and pasta restaurant downstairs.

ΨΨ Pavilion, Santos Beach, T044-6904567. The ideal spot for lunch, just stroll up straight from the beach onto the old wooden veranda and enjoy a steak or light lunch while watching the boats sailing in the bay. Bustling atmosphere.

ΨΨ Tidals, The Point. Seafront tavern built on the rocks overlooking the ocean, cool rooms with high ceilings and plenty of light, recommended for pub lunches. Mossel Bay's liveliest drinking spot. Open late at weekends.

Ψ Annie's Kitchen, Marsh St. One of several cafés in the area serving coffee, breakfast and cheap hot lunches throughout the day.

George *p253, map p254*

As well as the town restaurants, **Fancourt Hotel and Country Club** has superb top-range restaurants open to non-guests.

ΨΨΨ Copper Pot, 12 Montagu St, Blanco, T044-8707378, www.copperpot.co.za, 1800 for dinner. Excellent and elegant seafood restaurant in a renovated 1920s house with wooden floors and art on the walls, surrounded by a herb garden. Very fresh grilled fish, as well as slightly different dishes – try the Mauritian curry. Award-winning wine list. Recommended.

ΨΨΨ Reel and Rustic, corner of York and Courtenay Sts, T044-8840707, 1130-1500, 1830-late, closed Sat lunch. Popular seafood restaurant with smart decor serving good fresh cajun and creole dishes and decadent desserts. Vegetarians need to book ahead. Award-winning wine list.

ΨΨΨ St Moritz, 16 Varing Rd, T044-8745993, www.stmoritz.co.za, dinner only. An emphasis on good-quality French cuisine, plus some seafood options. Recommended for anyone missing a more European-style meal. An elegant place with a sliding door out to a pool and tables in the rose garden. Vegetarians should inform the restaurant when booking, which is essential. Also a quality guesthouse (see Sleeping page 274).

ΨΨ Fong Ling, 69 Fichat St, T044-8840088, 1130-1400, 1730-2130, closed Sun Mar-Sep. Over 70 authentic Taiwanese and Chinese dishes, some exotic seafood dishes, good-value set menus, cheaper snacks such as won ton or shrimp chips.

ΨΨ Kingfisher, 1 Courtenay St, T044-8733127, 1200-2230. Fresh seafood dishes, renowned for prawns and fish and chips, some meat dishes including good ostrich, also has a fine selection of pasta and pizzas and a sushi bar. Good range of wine and whiskies.

ΨΨ Old Town House, corner of Market and York Sts, T044-8743663. 1200-1500, 1800-late, no lunch on Sat, closed Sun. Local specialities such as lamb shank and venison pie, plus steak, seafood and grills, and very good homemade desserts, good-value wine list.

ΨΨ Red Rock, Red River Centre, T044-8733842, 1100-1400, 1700-late. A good selection of pizza, pasta, steaks and seafood, vegetarians are well looked after, lawn and playground for kids, gets more alcoholic as the evening wears on.

ΨΨ-Ψ The Conservatory at Meade House, 91 Meade St, T044-8741938. Mon-Fri 0745-1630, Sat 0830-1500. Quality restaurant set in one of the oldest homes in George, dine in the conservatory or in the pretty gardens, very extensive a la carte menu for breakfast, lunch and afternoon teas, also has a well-stocked shop of gifts and books.

Ψ Herman's Pub, 70 Courtenay St, T044-8732052, near the museum. Grill house serving good pub meals in 2 old train carriages, also with outside seating which is a good place to watch the world go by.

Wilderness *p256, map p257*
Wilderness does not have a large choice of restaurants but most hotels and hostels offer meals. The majority of domestic visitors will self-cater.

TTT Kaaimans Grotto, in a cave next to Kaaimans Railway Bridge, T044-8771001, www.kaaimansgrotto.com. This is a unique dining experience where tables are set up on a wooden deck in a huge natural cave next to the railway bridge and overlooking the ocean. It's an evening excursion which includes a short train ride along the Wilderness and Victoria Bay beaches, a buffet meal in the cave, and live entertainment. Only open during summer, email ahead or ask at the tourist office to find out when the next event is on .

TT Wilderness Grille, George Rd, T044-8770808. Seafood, steaks and pizza, good breakfasts, outdoor leafy terrace, pop in throughout the day and you'll get something substantial to eat though service is somewhat slow.

Knysna *p259, maps p261 and p262*
Knysna is well known for its seafood, especially its excellent oysters which are cultivated in the lagoon. During the peak season, it is not uncommon to wait an hour or more before getting a table – be sure to book ahead at the better-known restaurants.

TTT O'Pescador, Brenton Rd, T044-3860036. Long-established and popular Portuguese restaurant, traditional cosy decor, Mozambique prawns or try the spicy fish dishes, peri peri chicken or grilled sardines. Portuguese wines. Booking advised in season. Recommended.

TT 34' South, Knysna Quays, T044-3827268, 0830-2200. Snacks and meals daily in a deli-style seafood restaurant, make up a meal from the packed fridges or buy takeaway items including cook books, wine and homemade goodies. Recommended.

TT Anchorage, T044-3822230, Main St, in the Garden Route Centre. Closed Sun in winter. Seafood platters, prawns, oysters and steaks all washed down with excellent draught Mitchell's beer.

TT Crabs Creek, T044-3860011, 8 km from Knysna, 200 m off the N2 on the Belvidere road. A mock-Tudor building beside Knysna River, secluded country pub in a garden of oak trees, pleasant outdoor terrace overlooking the river, sensible prices, good selection of wines, mostly seafood but of a very high standard, one of the better restaurants in the area, good value. Recommended.

TT Drydock Food Co, Knysna Quays, at the Waterfront, T044-3827310. 1130-2230. Modern restaurant with good views from the 2nd floor, mostly seafood but steaks and vegetarian options too, oysters, fish with pickles, slightly different twists on standard dishes, try west coast mussels with white wine, pickled ginger and lemongrass.

TT Knysna Oyster Co, Thesen's Island, T044-3826942, Mon-Sat 1000-2100, Sat 1000-1700. This restaurant is on Thesen's Island, right next to the oyster farm that has been in operation since 1949, you need to drive across the causeway to get there from town. Once on the island, take a left just after the timber factory. The seafood restaurant is perhaps the best place to try a dozen of Knysna's famous oysters washed down with a glass of champagne. It's one of Kynsna's must-dos but unfortunately the service is dire. Despite this, recommended.

TT La Loerie, 57 Main Rd, T044-3821616, 1830-late, closed Sun. Cosy, candlelit, family-run restaurant serving excellent seafood dishes and some meat choices. The seafood paella is excellent. Good value and recommended by readers as the best in town.

TT Oyster Catcher, Knysna Quays, T044-3829995. Another place to try oysters, at working quays with a backdrop of busy boats coming and going. If oysters aren't your thing, try the tapas or nachos. Good cocktails and vegetarian choices.

TT Paquitas, George Rex Dr, Knysna Heads, T044-3840408, 1200-2200. Relaxed family restaurant and vibey pub, burgers, pizza, pasta, seafood and steaks, but the main reason for coming here is for the stunning views of The Heads and the long beach where kids can play.

TT Zanzibar's, Main Rd, T044-3820386. Stylish Cuban-themed bar and restaurant, nice seating on a terrace overlooking Main Rd, selection of Cuban and Tex-Mex dishes, cocktails dance floor and pool tables, open nightly until late in season.

T Ile de Pain Bread & Café, The Boatshed, Thesen's Island, T044-3025707. Tue-Fri 0700-1700, Sat 0700-1500, Sun 0900-1330.

Superb bakery and coffee shop emitting lovely warm smells of freshly baked goodies, such as croissants and pastries. Good coffee, fresh fruit salad, cheeses and olives, good spot for a light brunch or lunch.

Tin Roof, corner of Main and St George's Rds. Cavernous upstairs drinking joint, with a few bar snacks available early in the evening, live bands at the weekends and during holiday season, long wooden bar, pool tables, outside balconies for conversation, rocks to the early hours.

Plettenberg Bay *p265, map p266*

All the hotels have their own restaurants and bars and you can pre-order meals at the backpacker hostels. Those listed here are all within walking distance of the town centre.

57 Kloof, Melville Shopping Centre, corner of Main St and Marine Dr, T044-5335626. 0830-2200. Modern decor and floor-to-ceiling windows highlighting great views, good range of meat and fish dishes, some with an Asian slant, large fresh salads, and unusual breakfasts such as eggs hollandaise.

The Lookout, T044-5331379, 0900-2300. Popular seafood restaurant perched on the rocks above Lookout Beach, perfect location, excellent seafood, soups, salads and steak, also has a busy bar, lively, bustling atmosphere. You can watch surfers share a wave with a dolphin from the terrace. Recommended.

The Med Seafood and Grill, Village Sq, T044-5333102. Established 20-year-old European-style bistro with alfresco dining on the leafy patio. A la carte seafood, good light lunches, huge seafood platters, and the odd vegetarian dish. Nice ambience.

Blue Bay Café, Lookout Centre, Main St, T044-5331390, 0800-late. Seafood, pasta and sandwiches, light deli lunches, good coffee. Helpful and knowledgeable waiters complement a vibey ambience.

San Francisco, Melville Shopping Centre, corner of Main St and Marine Dr. Coffee shop and restaurant serving excellent breakfasts, sandwiches and salads, good coffee, shady seating on outdoor terrace overlooking the bustle of Marine Drive.

Out of town

The following restaurants are a short drive from the town centre along the N2 highway.

Hunter's Country House (see Sleeping page 279), 10 km towards Knysna, T044-5327818. Excellent food served in a rambling thatched house, pricey but worth it, recommended for special occasions, booking essential. Tea on the veranda is quite special.

The Islander, 7 km towards Knysna, T044-5327776. Famous for the night-time seafood buffet served up under a boma in tropical surrounds, some poultry and meat dishes, booking essential. Closed Sun and other nights when they're not so busy during winter - phone first and check for opening hrs out of season.

Entertainment

Knysna *p259, maps p261 and p262*

Cinema

Knysna Movie House, Pledge Sq, Main St, T044-3827812. Daily shows of new releases.

Shopping

Mossel Bay *p250, map p250*

The **Ocher Barn** has a variety of shops. The **Liberty Shopping Centre** on Bland St contains most of the shops you'll need including chemists, bookshops, a wine store and a **Pick 'n' Pay** supermarket. **Jacana Curios**, Market St, next to the museum, sells African curios from all over the continent.

George *p253, map p254*

George has a legacy of fine craftsmanship. Quality leather goods and wood furniture are a particular speciality in the town.

Arts and crafts

El Sole, 81 Market St, T044-8735758. Shoes, belts, bags in ostrich, buffalo and various other leathers.

Strydom Gallery, Marklaan Centre, T044-8744027, daily 0900-1700. An art shop with interesting exhibits as well as pieces for sale from a cross section of South African artists and sculptors, organizes delivery worldwide.

Shopping malls

Marklaan, between Market and Meade Sts. Mall in converted store rooms arranged around open square. There is a coffee shop plus a couple of curio shops. A farmers' market is held Fri 0700-1000 in the square.
St George's Mall, at the southern end of York St, new slick mall with the usual clothes and food shops, Ster-Kinekor cinema and restaurants.
Garden Route Mall, out of town on the junction with the N2 is the location of the new R400-million, 125-store Garden Route Mall presently being constructed.

Knysna *p259, maps p261 and p262*
Keeping in tune with Knysna's reputation as a cultural arts and crafts centre are a number of galleries and craft shops. Check at the tourist office for special exhibitions. There is a good **African craft market** on the side of the road as you enter Knysna on the N2 from George, with an extensive range of carvings, baskets, drums and curios. There is also a cluster of expensive curio shops at the **Knysna Quays**.
Birds of Africa, Waenhout St. Carved wooden birds.
Bitou Craft, Woodmill Lane Centre, Main St. Local arts and crafts.
Metalcraft Gallery, 19 Clyde St. Modern pieces.
Metamorphosis, 12 Main Rd. Interesting selection made from recycled cans and other materials.
Model Shipyard, Knysna Quays, T044-6911531. Hand-crafted model ships and maritime antiques. There's another branch at the Waterfront in Cape Town.

Plettenberg Bay *p265, map p266*
There is a wide range of souvenir shops reflecting the town's popularity with domestic visitors. The only products which could be regarded as a speciality of the area are those made from wood and paintings.
African Market, Main St. Crafts and clothing.
The Art House, 1 Melville's Corner, Main St. Crafts, fabrics and pottery.
Lookout Art Gallery, Main St.
Old Nick's, T044-5331395, www.oldnickvillage.co.za, on the N2 3 km outside Plettenberg Bay going east. Group of galleries, craft workshops and studios, with a weaving museum, shops and a restaurant. Look out for the ceramics and Zimbabwean sculpture at the **Porcupine**.

Activities and tours

Mossel Bay *p250, map p250*

Diving

The best time for diving is between Dec and the end of Apr. During this period the sea is at its calmest and conditions in the bay are clear and safe. Close to Santos Beach are 4 recognized dive sites but none could be considered spectacular. All can be reached from the shore. For experienced divers, the **Windvogel Reef**, 800 m off Cape St Blaize, is highly recommended. The reef is fully exposed to the ocean and should therefore only be dived when the sea is calm. There are drop-offs and a few caves. Soft corals and colourful sponges are plentiful. The maximum depth is 27 m. (See also Essentials, page 54.)
Electro Dive, based at the **Protea Hotel**, Mossel Bay on the waterfront, T044-6907103, elecdive@mweb.co.za. Equipment hire and boat charters, also offer PADI courses.

Shark cage diving

Shark Africa, T044-6913796, www.shark africa.co.za, cage diving R1200, to view from the boat R900. Offers cage diving and snorkelling in pursuit of a great white shark on a 15-m catamaran aptly named *Shark*. You do not have to be a qualified diver and this trip is open to anyone. Apparently the youngest person in the cage was a 5-year-old, and the oldest was 87. The trip is 4-5 hrs long and includes lunch and drinks.

Tour operators

Romonza, T044-6903101, romonza @mweb.co.za. Runs daily pleasure cruises from Vincent Quay in the harbour off Bland St. Look out for the blue tent. The most popular outings are to Seal Island (see p251), a boat carrying up to 50 people leaves on the hour 0900-1700, advanced booking is advised. The sunset cruise lasts 2 hrs and includes champagne and seafood snacks. Another popular trip is a breakfast cruise. This is an invigorating way to start the day: a full cooked breakfast and fresh fruit included in the price. Romonza also offers the only licensed boat-based whale watching in Mossel Bay, Jun-Oct.

George *p253, map p254*

Golf

Fancourt Hotel and Country Club, T044-8040040, www.fancourt.com. 4 gold courses including the par 71, 5935-m, championship links course designed by Gary Player, open to members and hotel guests only. This was the location of the President's Cup tournament in 2003. At the time of writing 3 more golf courses were under construction; Oubaai Golf Estate, Kingswood Golf Estate and Le Grande George.
George Golf Course, CJ Langenhoven St, T044-8736116. Par 72, 18 holes, 5852 m course surrounded by trees.

Hiking

There are over 20 recognized hiking trails around George and Wilderness, many on private farmland. Check out www.tourismgeorge.co.za for contact details.

Tour operators

Outeniqua Adventure Tours, T044-8711470, www.outeniquatours.co.za. Minibus tours to sights along the Garden Route or Klein Karoo, can also organize cycling tours.
South Cape Travel, 111 York St, T044-8746930, www.southcapetravel.co.za. Very helpful local travel agent. Book flights, bus seats, local tours.

Wilderness National Park *p258, map p257*

Eden Adventures, T044-8770179, www.eden.co.za. A good-value adventure tour operator that organizes daily trips to the national park. Activities on offer include kayaking, kloofing, mountain biking nearby, abseiling, rock climbing and walking tours. The guides are very knowledgeable about the environment and are happy to answer endless questions. Recommended.
Windmaster Paragliding, T072-1526093, www.paraglidingsa.com. Around Sedgefield and Wilderness are many thermic sites, perfect for paragliding. Best conditions are Oct-Jun, though training conditions are best Jan-Apr. This company offers introductory courses, tandem flights and the full pilot's course that takes 2 weeks. They can arrange accommodation.

Knysna *p259, maps p261 and p262*

Golf

There is an 18-hole, par-73 course off George Rex Drive, T044-3841150.

Tour operators

Deep South Eco Adventures, T044-3822010, www.deepsoutheco.com. Arrange half-day mountain bike tours in the forests around Knysna.
The Heads Adventure Centre, George Rex Drive, T044-3840831, www.headsadventurecentre.co.za. PADI courses from their dive centre at Knysna Heads, equipment rental, daily trips to reefs and to the *Paquita* wreck in the lagoon. Also, amongst many other activities, abseiling at the Heads, paintball, canoeing and kayaking on the Knysna River. A very professional company.
Knysna Forest Tours, bookings in the Knysna Railway Station, T044-3826130, www.knysnaforesttours.co.za. Half- and full-day guided hikes, or overnight trails along the coast or in local nature reserves. For the less active they offer a short guided drive into Knysna forest to see the Big Tree, a 650-year-old yellowwood.
Mountain Biking Africa, bookings in the Knysna Railway Station, T044-3826130, www.mountainbikingafrica.co.za. Guided mountain-bike trails around the remaining tracts of indigenous forest in the area, easy rides, lots of downhills, bikes and refreshments included.
SEAL Adventures, office in the **Protea Hotel** at Knysna Quays, T044-3825599, www.sealadventures.co.za. Stands for sea, earth, air and land, adventure operator that offers abseiling and rap jumping at the Knysna Heads, canoeing on the lagoon, and quad-bike trails through the forests. Or do all of the

above in 1 exhilarating day as the Awesome Foursome. No under 16s, no-one over 110kg.
Springtide Charters, Knysna Quays, South Jetty, T082- 470 6022 (mob), www.springtide.co.za. 3-hr sunset cruises on a 50-ft sailing boat including a stop for a swim.

Plettenberg Bay *p265, map p266*

Diving and snorkelling

Conditions are best for diving during the winter months of Sep and Oct. The average water temperature is 16-18° with visibility 5-10m. There are not many tropical fish but due to an abundance of planktonic matter there is a colourful reef life. One of the more exciting dive sites is Groot Bank, about 12 km northeast of Hobie Beach. The reef is 35 m offshore and is best reached by boat. The maximum depth is 25 m and there is a whole variety of rock formations to explore, including tunnels and caves. There is a good chance of seeing parrotfish, ragged-tooth sharks and steenbras. At the southern end of Plettenberg Bay is the wreck of the *MFV Athina*, a Greek trawler sunk in 1967. It should only be dived in the calmest of conditions. For those who enjoy snorkelling, there is a popular spot in front of the Beacon Isle Hotel known as Deep Blinders – behind the reef is a sandy area where you might see stingrays. Inflatables leave from the hotel.
Beacon Isle Adventure Centre, T044-5331158, in the **Beacon Isle Hotel**. Runs daily dives and rents equipment.
Tsitsikamma Divers, Central Beach, T044-5336260.

Fishing

There are several good rock-angling sites along the coast – Beacon Island, Robberg Beach, Loockout Rocks and Nature's Valley. Elf, galjoen and steenbras are the most frequent catch. Deep-sea fishing is also possible.
Matata Fishing, T044-5331230. Deep-sea and river fishing.

Golf

Goose Valley Golf Estate, T044-5335082. A newly established and challenging 18-hole golf course designed by Gary Player with good ocean views.
Plettenberg Bay Country Club, T044-5332132, www.plettgolf.co.za. Lush 18-hole course in the middle of a private nature reserve, Piesang Valley. Tennis and bowls also available.

Horse riding

Equitrailing, Wittedrift Rd, T044-5330599. Lessons as well as trails through the forest from 1 hr to overnight. Note horse riding is not permitted on the beaches around Plett.

Whale and dolphin watching

There are several companies who organize whale- and dolphin-watching trips in season. Trips are about 2 hrs and cost R275-300 per person. Some of them can also arrange sea-kayaking.
Dolphin Adventures, T083-5903405 (mob), www.dolphinadventures.net.
Ocean Blue Adventures, T/F044-5335083, www.oceanadventures.co.za.
Ocean Safaris, T082-7845729, www.oceansafaris.co.za.

East of Plettenberg Bay *p267*

Boat Trip

Keurbooms River Ferries, T044-5327876, www.capenature.org.za, daily summer trips, 1100 and sundown; times change seasonally, so phone ahead to check, boat trip plus walk lasts for 2½ hrs, adults R70, children R35, lunches, picnics and drinks can be organized in advance, the ferry departs from the jetty on the east side of the Keurbooms River Bridge on the N2, each ferry can carry up to 30 people, they are shaded and have a toilet on board, highly recommended for nature lovers.

Bungee jumping

Bloukrans Bungee Jump, see page 269 for details.

Storms River Village *p272*

Tour operators

Stormsriver Adventures, T042-2811836, www.stormsriver.com, office is unmissable in the centre of the village thanks to the piles of equipment lying around, from inflatable inner tubes to mountain bikes. An excellent local operator who organizes a staggering number of tours in the Tsitsikamma region, including guided hikes, abseiling, mountain-bike trails, boat cruises, snorkelling and scuba diving, bass and fly fishing, and dolphin watching. One of the most popular activities is black water tubing, which starts with a steep descent by rope ladder to the Storms River canyon followed by a float on a giant inner tube to the suspension bridge within the Tsitsikamma National Park. The 'black water' refers to a stretch of river where you float under 2 overhangs of rock so close together, it's almost like floating through a cave. For the less adventurous they also operate guided 4WD tours in the Tsitsikamma Forest. This professional and fun company comes highly recommended. Each activity is described on their website.

Tsitikamma Canopy Tour, T042- 2811836, www.treetoptour.com. A fantastic way to see the forest from a new angle, which involves climbing up into the trees and gliding between 10 different platforms on a steel rope, the longest of which is 80 m, giving extraordinary views from high above the ground. Excellent for birdwatching, and the Knysna loerie may be spotted. Departure times are every 45 mins 0800-1545 in summer and 0830-1445 in winter, the excursion lasts around 3 hrs and costs R390.

Transport

Mossel Bay *p250, map p250*

394 km to **Cape Town**, 55 km to **George**, 116 km to **Knysna**, 80 km to **Oudtshoorn**, 206 km to **Tsitsikamma**, 375 km to **Port Elizabeth**. The N2 bypasses Mossel Bay, almost halfway between Cape Town and Port Elizabeth.

Bus

All mainline buses stop at the Shell Truck Stop at Voorbaai, on the N2 7 km from Mossel Bay. The Baz Bus is the only service that goes right into town.

Greyhound, T012-3231154, www.greyhound.co.za, **Intercape**, T0861-287287, www.intercape.co.za, and **Translux**, T021-7743333, www.translux.co.za, all stop here daily on the Cape Town-Durban route. **Cape Town** (6 hrs), **Durban** (19 hrs) via **Port Elizabeth** and **East London** (13 hrs).

Intercape and Translux, also have a daily service between Mossel Bay and **Johannesburg** and **Pretoria** (16 hrs).

Baz Bus, T021-4392323, www.bazbus.com. Budget bus running between **Cape Town** and **Durban**. Daily service in either direction between **Cape Town** and **Port Elizabeth**. 5 times a week between **Port Elizabeth** and **Durban**. Towards **Cape Town** the Baz Bus arrives in Mossel Bay 1500-1600, towards **Port Elizabeth**, 1400-1500.

Car hire

Garden Route Speedster Car Hire, Two Fields Farm, Albertina, T028-7352410, newks@mweb.co.za, 51 km from Mossel Bay towards Cape Town on the N2. For those who want to explore the Garden Route in style, this company rents out convertible Porsche Speedster replicas (very shiny red sports cars) for R475 per hour excluding mileage, but there's a high deposit of R10,000.

Taxis

Jordan Taxis, T044-6911191.

George *p253, map p254*

420 km to **Cape Town**, 320 km to **Port Elizabeth**, 61 km to **Knysna**, 55 km to **Mossel Bay**, 93 km to **Plettenberg Bay**, 151 km to **Tsitsikamma**, 60 km to **Oudtshoorn**.

Air

George airport is 10 km from the town centre and you'll need to take a taxi, George Taxis, T044-8708146. For general airport information, T044-8769310. If you wish to leave your car at the airport there are a few lock-up garages available.

SAA, reservations T011-9785313, www.flysaa.com, have several daily flights between George and **Cape Town** (1hr), **Durban** (2½ hrs), and **Johannesburg** (1hr 50 mins).

Nationwide, reservations T0861-737737 (in South Africa), T011-3447200 (from overseas), www.flynationwide.co.za, also has daily flights between George and **Johannesburg** (1hr 50 mins).

The budget no-frills airline **Kulula.com**, www.kulula.com, has several daily flights between George and **Johannesburg** and flights from George to **Cape Town** daily except Mon and Sat, and Cape Town to George daily except Sat. Reservations only through the website.

Bus

All buses stop in St Mark's Sq. **Greyhound**, T012-3231154, www.greyhound.co.za, **Intercape**, T0861-287287, www.intercape.co.za, and **Translux**, T021-7743333, www.translux.co.za, run daily to **Cape Town** (6 hrs) and **Durban** (18 hrs) via **Knysna** (1hr), **East London** (9 hrs) and **Port Elizabeth** (4 hrs).

Translux and Intercape also have a daily service between George and **Johannesburg** (14 hrs) and **Pretoria** (16 hrs) via **Bloemfontein** (9 hrs).

Baz Bus, T021-4392323, www.bazbus.com. Daily service in either direction between **Cape Town** and **Port Elizabeth**. Drops off at McDonalds. Towards Cape Town it arrives around 1400-1500, and towards Port Elizabeth 1500-1600.

Car hire

Avis, airport T044-8769314, www.avis.co.za. Budget, corner of Mitchell and Courtenay St, T044-8736259, airport T044-8769216, www.budget.co.za. Hertz, airport T044-8014700, www.hertz.co.za.

Taxi

George Taxis, T044-8708146.

Train

The railway station is in the centre of town at the east end of Market St. The **Outeniqua** Choo-Tjoe runs between George and **Knysna**, T044-8018288, (see page 255 for further details).

Wilderness *p256, map p257*

Bus

Translux, Greyhound and Intercape all stop at Wilderness, 20 mins before or after **George**. The daily Baz Bus, T021-4392323, www.bazbus.com, will collect and drop off at Fairy Knowe Backpackers and Wild Welcome. From **Port Elizabeth** it arrives 1300-1400 and from **Cape Town** 1500-1600.

Train

The Outeniqua Choo-Tjoe steam train stops here on its journey between **Knysna** and **George**. There is 1 train in each direction every day except for Sun during summer, and on Mon, Wed and Fri during winter. Towards **Knysna** (2 hrs), 1005; towards **George** (40 mins), 1614. Tickets must be bought in advance (see p255 for further details).

Sedgefield *p258*

Bus

Greyhound, Intercape and Translux services stop at the Shell garage, 15 mins to **Knysna**. See Knysna transport, below, for timetable and contact details. The Baz Bus, T021-4392332, www.bazbus.com, will stop in Sedgefield if requested in advance. See Knysna transport for details.

Knysna *p259, maps p261 and p262*

932 km to **Bloemfontein**, 500 km to **Cape Town**, 61 km to **George**, 1,350 km to **Johannesburg**, 100 km to **Mossel Bay**, 120 km to **Outdshoorn**, 32 km to **Plettenberg Bay**, 244 km to **Port Elizabeth**, 90 km to **Tsitsikamma National Park**.

Car hire

Parking in Knysna (a bit of nightmare) relies on a pre-paid card system. There are units on the street where you insert your card for payment. Cards are available from various shops and outlets including the tourist office. Despite paying for parking, remember it is still important to pay your car guard for watching over your car. Budget, T044-3820303, www.budget.co.za. National Car Rental, T044-8740899, www.nationalcar.co.za.

Bus

All buses stop outside the railway station. Greyhound, T012-3231154, www.greyhound.co.za. Intercape, T0861-287287, www.intercape.co.za. Translux, T021-7743333, www.translux.co.za. All run daily to **Cape Town** (8 hrs), **Port Elizabeth** (3½ hrs), and **Durban** (18 hrs). Intercape and Translux also have a daily service between Knysna and **Pretoria** and **Johannesburg** (14 hrs), via **Bloemfontein** (11 hrs).

Baz Bus, T021-4392323, www.bazbus.com. Daily service in either direction between **Cape Town** and **Port Elizabeth**. Heading towards Cape Town expect to be picked up around 1230-1330, towards Port Elizabeth 1630-1730. Drops and picks up at all the hostels.

Taxi

Bennies Taxi, T083-7285181.

Train

Outeniqua Choo-Tjoe steam train running between Knysna and **George** (2½ hrs). Station is on Remembrance Av close to the lagoon. For background details, prices and reservations see page 255. In summer, there is 1 train a day to George at 1415, except Sun. In winter it runs Mon, Wed and Fri. Trains stop at **Sedgefield** and **Wilderness**. You must book at least 48 hrs in advance, T044-3821361.

Plettenberg Bay *p265, map p266*

525 km to **Cape Town**, 93 km to **George**, 32 km to **Knysna**, 171 km to **Mossel Bay**, 236 km to **Port Elizabeth**, 55 km to **Tsitsikamma National Park**.

Air

There used to be daily flights between Johannesburg and Plettenberg Bay, and the airport is 10 km from town. However, these were recently suspended by SAA as the airport was considered too small for their aircraft. Whether flights will resume in the future remains to be seen.

Bus

Mainline buses depart from the Shell Ultra City on the N2 out of town. Most of the hostels offer shuttles into town, or you will have to arrange a taxi with your hotel. Remember though that some of the buses pass through in the early hours of the morning.

Greyhound, T012-3231154, www.greyhound.co.za, **Intercape**, T0861-287287, www.intercape. co.za, and **Translux**, T021-7743333, www.translux.co.za, all stop here daily on the Cape Town-Durban route. **Cape Town** (8½ hrs) daily, **Durban** (17½ hrs) daily via **Port Elizabeth** (3½ hrs).

Intercape has a service between Plettenberg Bay and **Pretoria** and **Johannesburg** (14 hrs) daily via **Oudtshoorn** (2 hrs), and **Bloemfontein** (11 hrs).

Baz Bus, T021-4392323, www.bazbus.com, departs daily to **Port Elizabeth** and **Cape Town**. Continuing on from **Port Elizabeth** to **Durban**, the service runs 5 times a week. Towards Cape Town expect to be picked up 1200-1300, to Port Elizabeth, 1730-1800.

Directory

Mossel Bay *p250, map p250*

Useful telephone numbers Ambulance: T10177, T044-6911911; **Private hospital**, Bay View, T044-6913718, **Police**, T10111, T044-6912222; **Sea Rescue**: T044-6904322, T082-9905954 (mob).

George *p253, map p254*

Banks All the principal banks, **First National**, Nedbank, Standard and ABSA Bank are in York St and the shopping malls. **Internet** J & D Internet Kafee, corner of Cradock and Courtenay Sts, T044-8740008, internet café with full range of digital services. **Post office** York St. **Useful telephone numbers** Medi Clinic, T044-8746777. Police, Courtenay St, T044-8034579, T10111.

Knysna *p259, maps p261 and p262*

Banks All the banks have branches on Main St and ATMs can be found in the Knysna Quays and other shopping centres. **Internet** Internet access can be found at a few spots around town including the tourist office, the Knysna Movie House, at the Knysna Quays and at all the backpacker hostels. **Laundry** Wash Tub, 20 Gray St, reliable laundry service, ironing and dry cleaning, closed Sat afternoons and Sun. **Useful telephone numbers** Ambulance, T10177; **Private hospital**, T044-3841083, with a casualty department; **Police**, T10111, T044-3026600; **Sea rescue**, T044-3840211.

Plettenberg Bay *p265, map p266*

Banks First National, 22 Main St. Nedbank, Nedbank Pl, Main Rd. Standard, 17 Main St. **Internet** There is an **Internet Café**, just next to the Melville Shopping Centre, on Main Rd. **Post office** Plettenberg St, by police station. **Useful telephone numbers** Private hospital - with a casualty: T044-5330212. Police: T10111.

Great Karoo

The Great Karoo is a vast, ancient plateau covering nearly a third of the total area of the country. It is a beautiful and extraordinary region, as much for its history as for its remarkable emptiness. Today, the landscape is a parched expanse of baked red earth inhabited by tough merino sheep and their even tougher owners. Endless plains stretch between stark mountain ranges, with little but the characteristic steel windmills peppering the horizons. Hundreds of millions of years ago, however, this was an enormous swamp inhabited by dinosaurs, making it a key palaeontological site. More recently, the region has played a significant historical role, as the Voortrekkers penetrated the interior with their ox wagons, evidence of which can be seen in a handful of perfectly preserved Victorian settlements. *» For Sleeping, Eating and other listings, see pages 297-299.*

The Koup » *pp297-299.*

The 'Koup' refers to the southern districts of the Great Karoo, traversed by the N1 highway between Cape Town and Johannesburg. Travelling east from the Hex River Valley, the countryside quickly becomes arid and seemingly barren, with vast stretches of uninhabited semi-desert stretching to all horizons. Despite the area's arid appearance there is a surprisingly abundant supply of underground water, brought to the surface by the windmills which dot the plains. The most common vegetation is the Karoo bush which forms the staple diet of the merino sheep bred here. Most of the farms are used for sheep, although more and more are being converted into game farms for game viewing and hunting. The sheer scale of the area is remarkable – the average farm size is over 20,000 ha, which makes popping round to the neighbours an arduous task. The isolated Karoo towns have a great sense of history, with many preserved 19th-century buildings, as well as a delightfully slow pace of life. Although rather off the beaten track, visitors often end up spending the night in one of these towns while en route to Cape Town or Johannesburg. None of them warrant a special visit, but have an hour or two's worth of distractions if you want to take a break from driving. Note that if you arrive in South Africa in either Johannesburg or Cape Town and tour the country, the likely route back to your starting point (to meet return or onward flights) will be along the N1. If you don't want to fly, you can negotiate this route by returning a hire car or travelling by mainline bus.

Information about the Karoo can be found at www.centralkaroo.co.za.

Climate

The dry summer months are oppressively hot. During and after the rains, however, the countryside takes on an entirely different appearance. The first rains arrive in the winter months, although centres such as Graaff-Reinet and Colesberg receive their rains in late summer. If you plan to hike in the region remember that summer daytime temperatures frequently exceed 40°C, while in the winter the nights get very cold and snow can fall on the mountain peaks.

Touws River → *Colour map 8, grid B1.*

As the railways moved further inland from Cape Town, this became an important depot for locomotives, bringing about the growth of the town in the 1870s. However, since electrification its importance as a railway centre has all but gone. The area has become a graveyard for old **steam engines** – an impressive if somewhat eerie open-air museum. In its early days the station was known as Montagu Road; its present name was taken up in 1883. In addition to the steam engines, look out for a pair of concrete pillars behind the town hotel, the Loganda. They were used to mount astronomical instruments to view the transit of **Venus**. On 6 December 1882 a British astronomer took readings to help calculate the distance between the sun and earth.

Aquila Private Game Reserve

ⓘ *Off the R46 south of Touws River, T021-4054513 (Cape Town), www.aquilasafari.com.* This is a private reserve which in the last few years has had a rather staggering R25 million spent on it, mostly through the relocation of large animals. It's also the closest game reserve to Cape Town (less than two hours' drive) with lion, giraffe and rhino. It is set among 4500 ha of mountains, rivers, valleys and kloofs which make up the southern Karoo highlands and is now home to a wide range of species, many of which were relocated from other parts of the country. As well as the above these include buffalo, black and blue wildebeest, zebra, a variety of antelope, bat eared fox, mountain leopard, crocodile, ostrich, black backed jackal and hippo. It has the largest breeding herd of white rhino in the Cape and in February 2005 the first white rhino was born at the reserve, thought to be the first rhino born in the Cape for perhaps over 200 years. Aquila also has a huge natural wetland, which is home to 172 species of birds including several breeding pairs of the rare and endangered black eagle. There is luxury accommodation on the reserve (see Sleeping page 297) but you can also visit for the day for a safari and lunch, for around R1300 per person, less if you're in your own car.

Before the arrival of Aquila, the unemployment rate in Touws River was 97%. Today the reserve is the single biggest employer in the region and provides for around 180 families. It also coordinates regular fundraising activities in Cape Town and has raised approximately R60,000 to date, for blankets, clothes and basic necessities for the people of Touws River.

Matjiesfontein → *Colour map 8, grid C1.*

In 1975 the entire village of Matjiesfontein was declared a national monument – small surprise considering the excellent state of repair of its Victorian houses. There is little to the town itself, other than a couple of dusty streets lined with perfectly preserved period houses, the highlight of which is the famous **Lord Milner Hotel**, resplendent with turrets and adorned balconies. The history of the settlement is a reflection of the life of a young Scot, Jimmy Logan, an official on the Cape Government Railways in the 1890s. He originally came here hoping that the dry air would cure a chest complaint. He found the climate so beneficial that he decided to settle permanently. As an ex-railwayman he quickly saw the opportunity to supply water to steam trains from his farm. While the engines took on water, he served the passengers cool drinks and meals as back then the trains had no dining cars. Today, the luxurious **Blue Train** still stops here for lunch. So successful was his business that he built the fashionable Lord Milner Hotel, attracting rich and influential guests who suffered from lung complaints. These included Cecil Rhodes and the Sultan of Zanzibar. During the Anglo-Boer War the town became a military headquarters and a marshalling ground for troops. Logan financed a regiment and served in the war – the hotel's turrets were used as lookout posts. Jimmy Logan lived here until his death in July 1920. Another famous resident was the writer and feminist Olive Schriener, whose first novel *The Story of an African Farm* was set in the Karoo. She lived in a Matjiesfontein cottage from where she corresponded with friends including George Bernard Shaw and William Gladstone.

Today the town is a popular stopover for travellers between the Cape and Johannesburg. There is a small town museum, the **Marie Rawdon Museum**, in the old jail under the railway station. The **cemetery**, 11 km to the west, has some interesting

The Karoo's name comes from Karusa, a Khoi word which means dry, barren, thirstland.

monuments and tombstones dating from the 1900s. Visit the hotel for **tourist information** ⓘ *T023-5613011, www.matjiesfontein.com*; they can arrange tours through the streets on an old double-decker London bus.

Laingsburg → *Colour map 8, grid C1.*

Laingsburg, another small town on the N1, started life as a staging post for coaches on a farm belonging to Stephanus Greeff. When the railway arrived, plans for a town were drawn up and in 1879 it was named Laingsburg after the John Laing, a Cape government official. Sadly, little of the original centre remains after a huge flood in 1981 washed away most of the town, though the magistrate's court and the old post office survived. The library contains a collection of photographs taken after the flood. For information visit the **Municipality offices** ⓘ *Van Riebeeck St, T023-5511019, www.centralkaroo.co.za/laingsburg.*

N1 northeast

After crossing the Dwyka river, you reach the small settlement of **Prince Albert Road**. Turning south on the R328 takes you to Prince Albert (45 km), over the **Swartberg Pass**, and to the **Gamkaskloof Valley**, a secluded valley known as 'The Hell' (see page 306). The next settlement of note along the N1 is **Leeu-Gamka**. The name means 'lion', a sad reminder that the last Cape Lion was shot here in 1857, making the species extinct.

Beaufort West

» *pp297-299. Colour map 7, grid A2.*

This is the largest and oldest of the Central Karoo towns, but despite its history it is an unattractive place. Most of its energies seem devoted to servicing those travelling from Johannesburg to Cape Town – the N1 passes right through town, lined with petrol stations and fast-food joints. It is known as the 'oasis' town, hard to believe when you see hot, dusty streets but, thanks to the presence of the Nuweveld Mountains to the north, its 150 mm annual rainfall is far higher than other towns in the Karoo. Beaufort West was named after the fifth Duke of Beaufort, father of the Cape governor, Lord Charles Somerset. It was established in 1818 to try and control gun smuggling and general lawlessness in the region. In 1837 it became South Africa's first municipality. Before the railway reached the town in 1880, all of the locally produced merino wool had to be transported to the coast by wagon across the Swartberg Mountains. The earliest route was via Meiringspoort Pass (see page 308), one of several magnificent passes which link the Great Karoo with the Little Karoo.

The country around Beaufort West is home to the largest variety of succulents in the world. In the town itself, there are more different species than in all of Great Britain. Pear trees provide welcome shade as you walk along the pavements; some of the trees date back to the 1830s. The **Beaufort West Tourism Bureau** ⓘ *57 Donkin St, T023-4151488, www.tourism.beaufortwest.co.za, Mon-Fri 0900-1700, Sat 0900-1200,* is an efficient, well-run office and they have prepared some useful material on the region and its major sights.

Sights

The tourist office provides a *Stroll Through Our Town* leaflet that takes about an hour and covers the main sights. The old Town Hall (1867) on Donkin Street houses the **Beaufort West Museum** ⓘ *T023-4152308, Mon-Fri 0830-1245, 1345-1645, Sat 0900-1200, R5*. This has a couple of above-average collections relating to two of the town's most famous past residents – Dr Christiaan Barnard and Dr Eric Louw. Dr Louw was the MP for Beaufort West for many years and rose through the government's ranks to become South Africa's Foreign Minister between 1957 and 1963. The late Dr Barnard is known throughout the world for his pioneering work with heart transplants.

The N1 to Johannesburg

The N1 covers the distance between Cape Town and Johannesburg via Bloemfontein in just over 1400 km, most of which runs through the Great Karoo. With a couple of drivers the journey can be made in one day but you need to leave early to arrive in either Cape Town or Johannesburg before dark. Alternatively, many people break their journey in one of the regional towns in either the Free State or Western Cape that have no shortage of accommodation for motorists on this route.

Recommended overnight stays are Beaufort West (roughly a third of the way from Cape Town), Colesberg (approximately halfway), or Kimberley and Bloemfontein (almost two-thirds of the distance from the Cape to Gauteng). Much of the N1 has recently been upgraded to a four-lane highway and tolls may be introduced soon. The road is long and straight, and much of the Karoo scenery is featureless – be wary of getting tired behind the wheel and take frequent breaks. The towns have large petrol stations that usually also have a shop and a restaurant, such as Wimpy, but remember there are some big distances between the centres so fill up with fuel when you can. The road is heavily used by trucks and mainline buses and at times can be very busy – over the few days at the beginning of the Christmas holidays some 500 cars an hour leave Jo'burg with Gauteng families bound for the Cape. One sad peculiarity about this road is the prostitutes that you may notice hanging around the truck stops or petrol stations. These are mostly very young, black and impoverished girls who sell themselves to the truck drivers. They spend their lives on the road sleeping in the truck drivers' cabs and could quite feasibly travel between Johannesburg and Cape Town several times a week. The National Roads Agency in conjunction with local health authorities has recently set up mobile clinics on the N1 to provide healthcare and AIDS awareness to both the truck drivers and prostitutes. Finally, if you are driving through the 'boring' Karoo – pull over to the side of the road, switch off the engine of your car and take a moment before the next truck comes rumbling by. The space and silence is deafening.

He performed the world's first at Groot Schuur hospital in Cape Town in 1967. The displays include awards and trophies given to each, along with some of their personal effects. There is also a replica of Dr Barnard's heart transplant theatre. Next door is the **Dutch Reformed Mission Church** and the **parsonage** in which Dr Barnard spent his childhood. In the next street are some fine examples of Karoo Victorian single-storey houses. These are all private homes; similar buildings can be seen in Matjiesfontein and other Karoo towns. In the **cemetery** is the grave of Stefanus Marais, a member of a group of Voortrekkers from Beaufort West who fought in the Battle of Blood River in Natal in 1838, as well as the graves of several British soldiers killed during the Anglo-Boer War.

Karoo National Park » *pp297-299. Colour map 7, grid A2.*

Only 5 km from Beaufort West, this national park was created to conserve a representative area of the unique Karoo environment. There are two other conservation areas in the Karoo, each preserving a slightly different ecosystem: the Karoo Nature Reserve near Graaff-Reinet; and the Karoo Mountain Zebra Park at

Cradock. Despite limited human presence the environment of the Great Karoo has undergone radical change during the past 150 years and the protected areas are now recognized as important conservation centres as well as popular tourist destinations.

Ins and outs

Getting there The main entrance is signposted off the N1 highway 5 km southwest of Beaufort West. The entrance gate is beside the highway and the road takes visitors straight to the park office and accommodation facilities. The gates are open 0500-2200; it is 7 km from the main entrance to the reception office, T023-4152828, which is open 0730-2000. The daily conservation fee per person, which also covers the vehicle, is R60, R30 children. Next to the office is the **Rest Camp** (see Sleeping page 298), which has a restaurant open 0800-2030, and shop open 0730-2000, selling frozen meat, firewood and booze. The office has trail and park maps as well as pamphlets detailing the main attractions within the park, and every evening except Sunday there is a slideshow. There is a bird hide near the dam close to the camp.

Climate The Karoo is semi-desert, which means extremes – very hot days in summer (average for January is 32°C) with temperatures often reaching over 35°C, and warm days in winter but very cold nights (from June to August frost is common, and snow falls on the mountain peaks). March and April are regarded as the wet months, although the rainfall only averages 250 mm annually.

Springbok are present in large numbers – a reminder of the once-massive herds that could stretch for several kilometres, which crossed the Karoo on annual migrations.

Background

The 70,000-ha national park was proclaimed in September 1979 after a lengthy and concerted effort by local residents to conserve the Karoo environment before farming practices totally destroyed it. The success of the campaign was primarily due to the efforts of a local farmer, William Quinton. The municipality donated over 7000 ha, and funds raised by the Nature Foundation were used to purchase two farms, Stolshoek and Puttersvlei. The success of the park is attributed to the efforts of the first warden, Bruce Bryden and his wife Helena. Between 1977 and 1980 they saw to the removal of all the old farm fences and ripped out as much alien vegetation as possible. This was not without opposition; local farmers feared the reserve would become a protected breeding ground for predators which would then prey upon their sheep. The numbers of caracal and jackal have increased, but so too have the smaller mammals they traditionally prey on, so they now have less need to hunt the farmers' sheep. The park has modern chalets and camp sites in a scenically situated camp.

The current boundaries of the park encompass an area of Karoo plains, which merge into mountain slopes and a high plateau. The **Nuweveld Mountains** in the north of the park are nearly 2000 m high. The vegetation in the low-lying areas is a mixture of grasses and shrubs such as honey-thorn and the common acacia karroo. On the steep slopes a sourgrass known as renosterbos (*Elytropappus rhinocerotis*) and harpuis flourish. The flora can be studied along the specially laid out Bossie Trail. Note the difference in vegetation cover between areas within the park and the neighbouring farms. The over-grazed farms have little grass cover and small, unpalatable shrubs.

Look out for the tent tortoise; it is well camouflaged and looks like an inverted egg box.

Wildlife

There is a surprisingly diverse range of game and smaller wildlife in the park. Records list 174 species of birdlife, 38 species of reptile, 37 types of gecko and lizard, and five different species of tortoise (this is the largest number in a conservation area in the world). In another effort to help restore the area to its previous state, antelope such as eland, black wildebeest, gemsbok, Cape mountain zebra, springbok and red hartebeest have been moved into the park. The reserve is also home to two endangered species: the **black rhino** and the **riverine rabbit**. While the statistics are impressive, actually spotting most of these animals requires a degree of patience, effort and, of course, luck.

Hiking in the park

There are three short day walks known as the **Fossil Trail**, 400 m, the Pointer's Hiking Trail, 10 km, and the **Bossie Trail**, 800 m. Each of these explores a different aspect of the park. The most interesting is the the Fossil Trail along which you can see fossils in situ. It has been adapted for the blind as well as people in wheelchairs: Braille boards tell the 250-million-year tale of the region. The trails all start from near the environmental educational centre where further information about the park is on display.

Driving in the park

Visitors in 4WDs are allowed to drive on certain short tracks in the park. The park also has its own vehicle for hire, and day trips with a nature guide and lunch included can be organized. Other trips on offer include night drives and overnight tours. The trails are rough, slippery and steep in parts and previous experience with a 4WD is essential. There are a few rough roads open for game viewing, but given the mountainous conditions you cannot go too far. Walking remains the best way to enjoy the park.

East to Colesberg

» pp297-299.

Hanover → *Colour map 7, grid A3.*

Hanover is the midway point between Cape Town and Johannesburg on the N1 and there is a sign marking its geographical importance. Once you have reached here during a long day on the road, remember it is another 700 km in either direction.

Three Sisters → *Colour map 7 grid A2.*

This tiny settlement is 78 km north of Beaufort West and there's nothing here except an Ultra City for petrol and refreshments. It is however the junction of the N1 and N12. The N1 continues to Johannesburg via Bloemfontein whilst the N12 goes to Johannesburg via Kimberley. The N1 is slightly shorter as far as mileage is concerned.

If you want to break the journey by exploring one of these two cities, it is at Three Sisters that you will have to choose which road to follow.

Colesberg → *Colour map 4, grid B2.*

Colesberg actually lies in the Northern Cape but for ease of reference it is included here. The town is situated at the base of a distinctive landmark, **Cole's Kop** (1700 m), visible from 40 km away. This rounded rock outcrop was a very important landmark for early settlers, who moved inland across a largely featureless region. In those days it was called Toringberg – Towering Mountain – although some insist it meant Magic Mountain. The town was then named after Sir Lowry Cole, Cape Governor in 1830.

The tourist office is on Murray St, T051-7530678, www.colesberginfo.co.za.

The town is an important junction between the N9 which heads south towards Port Elizabeth and George, and the N1, which cuts right through the centre of town. Many of the town's oldest buildings are found along here, and turning off the N1 takes you to further clusters of Victorian houses tucked between a couple of picturesque hills. In its early days, this was a classic frontier town with illicit trade in a wide range of commodities, especially gunpowder and liquor. During the Anglo-Boer War it was close to the front and several battles were fought in the vicinity. The surrounding hills are named after the British regiments who held them: Suffolk,

New Zealand, Worcester and Gibraltar. The town itself was captured by the Boers and for four months was part of the Free State territory.

Today Colesberg is the centre of two very successful businesses: horse breeding and sheep farming. Many champion racehorses have been bred around the town, due mainly to the soil type which yields high-quality grasses and other fodder. The legendary golfer Gary Player owns a nearby stud farm. The majority of visitors are just passing through along the N1 – the town springs to life in the early evening as people arrive, there is a burst of action as bills are settled and fuel tanks filled in the morning, and then Colesberg reverts to a peaceful farming town for the rest of the day.

There are a few historic buildings mainly along **Bell Street**. The flat-roofed cottages which line the street were built between 1860 and 1870, and have today been attractively restored. There is also an old flour mill which was operated by horses and was the country's last working horse mill until it was recently turned into a pub. The street is named after Charles Bell, a surveyor who is known in philatelic circles for designing a rare Cape Triangular stamp issued in September 1853. There are four churches around town. The most interesting is the **Church of the Province** (1848), designed by the wife of the first Bishop of Cape Town, Lady Grey. She had intended it to be a cathedral, but only the chancel was built. The **Dutch Reformed Church** (1866) is a characteristically grand, whitewashed building.

From Colesburg the N1 enters the Free State and heads north to Bloemfontein.

The **Colesberg Kemper Museum** on Bank Square is a short walk from the Central Hotel, and contains an interesting photo collection, objects relating to the Anglo-Boer War and a 19th-century toy collection. It is a fine, solid two-storey structure built in 1862 to house the Colesberg District Bank, later absorbed by the Standard Bank. Look out for the pane of glass in the museum on which the letters 'DP' have been scratched. In 1866 John O'Reilly, a diamond trader and transport rider from the Northern Cape diamond fields, brought a stone to the Colesberg magistrate, Lorenzo Boyes, who told O'Reilly that the scratching seemed to confirm that the stone was indeed a diamond. This was the first recognized stone to be found in South Africa. The diamond was 21.25 carats, and was bought for £500 by the Cape's governor, Sir Philip Wodehouse.

Sleeping

Touws River *p291*

L1-L2 **Aquila Game Lodge**, Aquila Private Game Reserve off the R46 west of Touws River, T021-4054513 (Cape Town), www.aquilasafari.com. Tastefully decorated luxury cottages with en suite bathrooms, outdoor showers, ceiling fans, fireplaces, and mini-bars. Raw materials such as rock, river pebbles, natural wood, reeds and thatch have been used wherever possible to maintain a natural look. Cigar Bar and Boma Restaurant, horseback safaris or traditional game drives included in the price, check out the website for details of packages.

C **Loganda**, T023-3851130. The main town hotel, in a 1960s dreary-looking block, but with 15 fairly comfortable rooms, some with a/c, a restaurant, beer garden, pub with DSTV and swimming pool.

Matjiesfontein *p292*

B **Lord Milner**, T023-5613011, www.matjiesfontein.com. The original old Victorian town hotel is very much part of the town's history. The 53 large rooms are filled with antiques, as is the lounge and entertainingly old-fashioned dining room, which serves good-value meals. There are cheaper rooms in the garden. Don't miss the wonderfully atmospheric old bar. Recommended.

Beaufort West *p293*

All the best-value lodges and hotels are fully booked months in advance by families from Gauteng, especially at the beginning and end of the long Christmas holidays. For the rest of the year trade is much quieter, although there is a continual flow of people driving between the Cape and Gauteng. Room rates increase during school holidays.

B **Beaufort Manor**, 13 Bird St, T023-4152175, www.beaufortmanor.co.za. 16 modern and attractive en suite rooms with private entrances opening onto a courtyard where there is a swimming pool, 5 open-plan self-catering cottages with a/c sleeping up to 4 which are good value for a family, located next to a pond with ducks and swans, very good restaurant and bar, 3-course Karoo dinners, famous for their lamb.

B **Lemoenfontein Game Lodge**, 2 km north of Beaufort West and 4.5 km off the N1 on the De Jager's Pass road, T023-4152847, www.lemoenfontein.-co.za. A luxury lodge with 13 en suite rooms with modern decor, swimming pool, country cooking in the dining room on a wooden deck, game drives and hiking on the farm where giraffe and zebra are present as well as a number of antelope.

B **Matoppo Inn**, corner of Meintjies and Bird Sts, T023-4151055, www.matoppoinn.mrinfo.co.za. Set in a quiet residential street, this was originally the 1834 *drostdy* (magistrate's house), now converted into a luxury guesthouse with high ceilings, beautiful yellowwood floors, comfortable rooms furnished with antiques, traditional Karoo candlelit dinners, neat garden with swimming pool. Cecil Rhodes stayed here on the way to what was then Rhodesia. Recommended.

C **The Flight Deck**, based in Beaufort West's old airport terminal building, 12 km north on the N1, T023-4143444, airport@telkomsa.net. 4 rooms, 3 en suite, 1 with private bathroom, with fans, heaters, enjoy sundowners and breakfast in the control tower with great views over the Karoo. Simple accommodation but something different. The airport is still operational for private planes.

C-D **Formula 1**, 144 Donkin St, T023-4152421, www.hotelformula1.co.za. Clean, modern, cheap option, characterless, 52 small rooms, drive in late, sleep, and drive out early.

C-D **Young's Budget Accommodation**, 156 Donkin St, T023-4143878, youngshh@intekom.co.za. 36 en suite budget rooms decorated in country style, with TV, coffee-making facilities, fans and heaters, 24-hr security and reception, safe parking, big swimming pool, braai facilities and excellent Mac Young's Restaurant, see Eating. Recommended.

C-E **Wagon Wheel Country Lodge**, 500 m north of town centre on the N1, T023-4142145, www.wagonwheel.co.za. Friendly country motel with simple rooms to suit most groups and some camping pitches, TV, bar, cheap restaurant with filling meals, swimming pool, disabled facilities, laundry service. Booking essential as it's a popular and good-value stopover for motorists on the N1.

Karoo National Park *p294*

Rest Camp, reservations through SAN Parks Pretoria office, T012-4289111, www.sanparks.org. Bookings can also be made in person at the offices in Cape Town and Durban (see page 44). For cancellations and bookings under 72 hrs, for campsite reservations, and for general enquiries, phone the camp reception direct, T023-4152828. The camp is at the entrance gate to the park where there is a shop selling basic groceries, an à la carte restaurant, laundry and a stunning bright-blue swimming pool. The accommodation here is superb, even by SAN Parks standards.

B **Cottages**, 20 spacious self-catering thatched cottages (Cape Dutch style) grouped around the swimming pool, sleeping 3-6 people, kitchen, lounge with highly unusual furnishings for parks accommodation – ornate clocks on the wall, Persian rugs, bellows and coal scuttles by the fireplace! One cottage is wheelchair and visually impaired friendly.

E **Campsite**, 24 grassy caravan and camping sites, good clean ablution blocks, kitchen unit, power points, maximum of 6 per site.

Hanover *p296*

C **Hanover Lodge**, corner of Queen and Mark Sts, T053-6430019. Excellent family-run hotel and guesthouse, good-size rooms, secure parking, children under 15 free, restaurant serves good bar meals even for late arrivals, discounts available out season.

Colesberg *p296*

B **The Lighthouse**, 40 Church St, T051-7530043, www.karoolighthouse.co.za. Popular good-value guesthouse with 1 self-catering cottage and 10 comfortable en suite rooms, furnished with antique farm furniture, well managed, good reports, booking essential, swap driving tales in the communal lounge.

B-C Colesberg Lodge, 32 Church St, T051-7530734, www.colesberglodge.co.za. A large old town hotel with 52 en suite double or family rooms with a/c or fan, rather faded but adequate, restaurant serving standard but filling meat and veggie dishes, swimming pool.

C-E Van Zylsvlei, on the Philippolis road 6 km north of town, T051-7530589, www.overnight.co.za. Roadside motel with 19 rooms in rondavels, hearty farm breakfasts and dinner on request, swimming pool and bar, 4 stands for caravans or tents, grassy and shady, electric points, shops at nearby petrol station.

D-E Colesberg Backpackers, 39 Church St, T/F051-7530582. Friendly hostel with dorms and doubles plus camping space. Kitchen, meals on request, laundry, splash pool, veranda perfect for a cold beer at the end of a hot day's driving. A welcome budget stopover on the long road from Johannesburg to Cape Town.

E Caravan Park, Church St, T051-7530040. Not very shady, quite a lot of sand, reservations needed for holiday period, good washblocks, easy walk to all shops and services.

Eating

Beaufort West *p293*

Town hotels have restaurants and most guesthouses also welcome non-residents for evening meals, given sufficient notice.

Mac Young's, 156 Donkin St, T023-4144068. Bustling restaurant decorated in tartan, including the carpet, serving steaks from a charcoal grill, plus pizza, pasta and seafood. One of their more unusual dishes is haggis, the last dish you'd expect to find in the middle of the Karoo.

Matoppo Inn, (see Sleeping), T023-4151055. Fine 4-course Karoo dinners served in a historic setting, available for non-guests if pre-booked, also open for breakfast 0700-0900.

Wagon Wheel Country Lodge, (see Sleeping, p297), T023-4142145. Light lunches, bar snacks and quality à la carte evening meals, huge menu, big portions and great value. The bar has a fireplace and TV, good place to wind down after a day's driving.

Transport

Beaufort West *p293*

Bus

Greyhound, T012-3231154, www.greyhound.co.za, **Intercape**, T0861-287287, www.intercape.co.za, and **Translux**, T021-7743333, www.translux.co.za, all stop at Beaufort West (and the other Karoo towns along the N1) on the Cape Town-Johannesburg/Pretoria route, though they often arrive and depart at awkward times during the night. The town is surprisingly quiet from as early as 2100, it is unlikely anyone will be around to help if you haven't reserved a seat. Buses stop at the Engen Garage. **Cape Town** (6 hrs) daily via **Worcester** (4 hrs). **Johannesburg** and **Pretoria** (12 hrs) daily via **Bloemfontein** (6 hrs) or via **Kimberley** (6 hrs).

Train

Spoornet, T0860-008888, www.spoornet.co.za. Daily to **Cape Town** (9 hrs), Tue to **Durban** (27 hrs) via **Bloemfontein** and **Harrismith**. Daily to **Pretoria** (17 hrs) via **Kimberley** (7½ hrs). Trains stop here for almost 30 mins.

Colesberg *p296*

778 km to **Cape Town**, 226 km to **Bloemfontein**, 625 km to **Johannesburg**.

Bus

Many services depart at awkward times in the middle of the night. Buses arrive in Colesburg 4 hrs after leaving Beaufort West and stop at the Shell Ultra City for 20 mins.

Train

Spoornet, T0860-008888, www.spoornet.co.za. There is a daily service between **Johannesburg** and **Port Elizabeth**. Change at Bloemfontein for other train services to **Durban**, **Kimberley** and **Cape Town**. **Johannesburg** (10 hrs) via **Bloemfontein** (6 hrs) and **Port Elizabeth** (7 hrs).

Little Karoo

Unlike the Great Karoo to the north, the Little Karoo is not a flat, dry and empty landscape; instead, it is made up of a series of parallel fertile valleys, enclosed by the Swartberg Mountains to the north and the Langeberg and Outeniqua Mountains to the south. It is an especially rewarding region to explore and much of it is hardly visited by tourists. The Cango Caves are a big attraction, as are the ostrich farms, but further afield lies spectacular and peaceful countryside, dotted with a multitude of small, historic villages. Here are some of the most dramatic kloofs and passes in South Africa (there are 14 in all) with excellent hiking and the springtime allure of bright patches of flowers.

The majority of the passes, constructed in the late 19th century, were surveyed and built by Thomas Bain, a truly remarkable engineer. Perhaps the greatest testament to his work is that almost every pass he constructed is still in use today along almost identical lines. A fairly new tourist initiative is 'Route 62', a beautiful stretch of road following the R62 from De Rust in the east to Montagu in the west and passing a few wine estates on the way – it is marketed as the longest wine route in the world. » *For Sleeping, Eating and other listings, see pages 309-312.*

Climate

The climate of the Little Karoo is markedly different from that of the coastal Garden Route, and yet it is no more than 30 km further inland. The principal reason for this is the mountains which act as a barrier to the weather moving inland. In the summer it is hot and dry and daytime temperatures of 40°C are not uncommon. During the winter you can expect to see snow on top of the Swartberg Mountains. Average annual rainfall is about 300 mm; water has to be carefully managed and farmers need to irrigate crops.

Vegetation and wildlife

There are several nature reserves managed by Cape Nature Conservation in the region, including Anysberg, Towerkop, and Swartberg. For the botanist, the region is one of the best environments in the world for succulents. There are many fascinating small plants which have adapted to scorching hot sunshine, erratic limited rainfall and rocky shallow soils. Aloes, lilies, geraniums and fynbos vegetation dot the landscape. A rare red variety of protea (*Aristata protea*) grows only in the Seweweekspoort Valley. The guided tours in Gamkaberg Nature Reserve are some of the most informative outings, and will leave you with a greater appreciation of the uniqueness of the Karoo landscape.

For more information on the region visit www.tourismlittlekaroo.co.za.

Around Oudtshoorn, you'll see ostrich peering at you over fences everywhere you turn. When explorers from the Cape first came to the valley, they found it to be teeming with buffalo, elephant, rhino, lion, hippo, kudu, and the now-extinct quagga. Today only a few leopard remain in the remote hills; the more common antelope can be found in the reserves. The **Gamkaberg Nature Reserve** is home to the rare Cape mountain zebra, as well as antelope such as steenbok and klipspringer. Antelope can also be seen in the **Swartberg Nature Reserve**.

Oudtshoorn

» *pp309-312. Colour map 7, grid B2.*

By far the largest settlement in the Little Karoo, this is a pleasant administrative centre which still retains much of the calm of its early days. It is a major tourist centre thanks to the nearby Cango Caves and the countless ostrich farms surrounding the town. Oudtshoorn itself is appealing, with broad streets, smart sandstone Victorian houses, many of which are now B&Bs, and a good choice of restaurants.

Oudtshoorn Tourist Bureau ⓘ *Baron van Rheede St, T044-2792532, www.oudtshoorn.com, Mon-Fri 0800-1800, Sat 0830-1300*, has a well-informed, enthusiastic and helpful team and is worth a visit for details on accommodation and the less well-known sights of the Karoo.

Background

In 1838 a small church was inaugurated on the Hartebeestrivier Farm to serve the farmers who had settled along the banks of the Olifants and Grobbelaars rivers. Nine years later the village of Oudtshoorn was founded when land was subdivided and sold by the surveyor J Ford. The town was named after Baron Van Rheede van Oudtshoorn, who died on his way to the Cape to take up the post of governor in 1773. In 1858 the first group of British immigrants settled in the village.

When visiting during the dry season it is easy to see how for many years the supply of water to the new settlement restricted its growth. A severe drought in 1865 persuaded many established farmers to move on and most made the long trek to the Transvaal. In its early days, water was brought to the town in barrels and then sold to households at sixpence a bucket. But the local farmers learnt to cope with this handicap and many of South Africa's early irrigation experts came from the region. When you cross the Grobbelaars River in the centre of town during the dry season, all the bridges and culverts seem redundant but they provide ample evidence of how much water can pass through when it rains. If you have time, walk across the Victorian **Suspension Bridge** where Church Street crosses the river; this is now a protected national monument.

Oudtshoorn

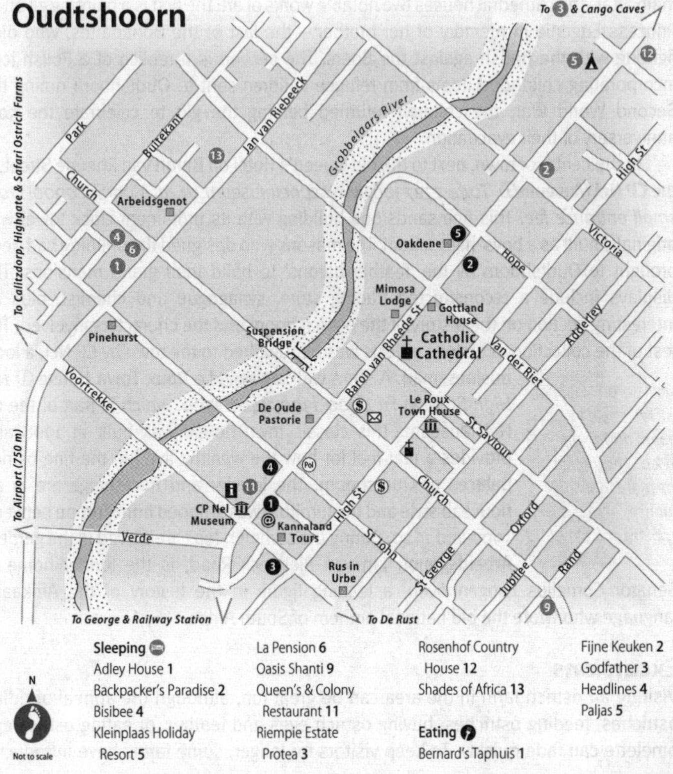

Sleeping
Adley House 1
Backpacker's Paradise 2
Bisibee 4
Kleinplaas Holiday Resort 5
La Pension 6
Oasis Shanti 9
Queen's & Colony Restaurant 11
Riempie Estate Protea 3
Rosenhof Country House 12
Shades of Africa 13

Eating
Bernard's Taphuis 1
Fijne Keuken 2
Godfather 3
Headlines 4
Paljas 5

It was the advent of two ostrich-feather booms (1865-1870 and 1900-1914) that truly established the town, and led to the erection of the fine sandstone buildings and 'ostrich palaces' that now line Oudtshoorn's streets. For a period of almost 40 years it was the most important settlement east of Cape Town. At the peak of its fortunes, ostrich feathers were selling for more than their weight in gold – little wonder that so many birds were bred. The boom attracted a large Jewish community, most of which had emigrated from Lithuania to escape the Tsarist pogroms. But when the good years finished, few chose to remain. While ostrich farming no longer brings in as much wealth, it remains an important business in the Karoo. Today, it is the production of specialized agricultural seed which contributes most to the region's wealth.

Sights

The two major reasons for coming here are the ostrich farms and the superb Cango Caves. There are also several nature reserves and scenic drives, which are introductions to the diversity of the landscape.

Within the town limits there is little to see aside from appreciating the sandstone Victorian buildings. There are several **ostrich palaces** in town, which unfortunately are not open to the public. They are still worth a look from the outside since their ornate exteriors were very much part of their design. Most examples are in the old part of town on the west bank of the Grobbelaars River. Look out for **Pinehurst**, St John Street, designed by a Dutch architect, and **Gottland House**, built in 1903 with an octagonal tower. Other buildings of note include **Mimosa Lodge**, **Oakdene** and **Rus in Urbe**. Unfortunately many fine Victorian buildings were demolished in the 1950s.

The **Catholic Cathedral**, on Baron von Rheede Street, is a fascinating modern cruciform building with splendid stained-glass windows and a chapel beneath the main altar. The cathedral houses two notable works of art: the first is a painting given by Princess Eugenie in memory of her brother – the last of the Bonapartes, who died fighting with the British against the Boers. The second is a replica of a Polish icon incorporating childhood items from refugee children sent to Oudtshoorn during the Second World War; the children returned bearing the gift to celebrate the 50th anniversary of their evacuation.

In the centre of town, next to the old Queen's Hotel on Baron van Rheede Street, is the **CP Nel Museum** ⓘ *T044-2727306, www.cpnelmuseum.co.za, Mon-Sat 0900-1700, small entrance fee*. This fine sandstone building with its prominent clock tower was originally built as a boys' high school. The masons who designed the building had been brought to Oudtshoorn by the 'feather barons' to build their grand mansions. The displays include a reconstructed trading store, synagogue and chemist, plus an interesting section on the history of the ostrich boom and the characters involved. The rest of the collection of historic objects was bequeathed to the town by CP Nel, a local businessman. A short walk away is **Le Roux Town House** ⓘ *146 High St, Mon-Fri 0900-1300, 1400-1700*, which is part of the CP Nel Museum. This classic town house was built in 1908 and provides a real feel for how the wealthy lived in the fine ostrich palaces of Oudtshoorn. The interior and furnishings are in art nouveau style and the furniture was shipped from Europe between 1900 and 1920. During the summer, teas are served in the garden.

The Klein Karoo National Arts Festival is held in Oudtshoorn during the first week of April, when there are more than 200 performances of music, dance, poetry and plays.

Arbeidsgenot, Jan van Riebeeck Road, is the former home of Senator Cornelius Langenhoven, a leading figure in the history of the Afrikaans language who wrote the old national anthem of South Africa.

Excursions

Visiting an ostrich farm in the area can be great fun, although the appeal of riding ostriches, feeding ostriches, buying ostrich eggs and leather, or eating ostrich-egg omelette can fade quickly. To keep visitors for longer, some farms have introduced

Ostrich facts and figures

The ostrich (*Struthio camelus*) has been around since the Pliocene period, and has changed little in the intervening eight million years. Here are some ostrich-related facts with which to impress your friends:

→ A giant ostrich-feather fan was discovered in Tutankhamen's tomb.
→ The Oudtshoorn area has 97% of the world's ostrich population.
→ The shell can withstand the weight of a human adult.
→ Incubation, 42 days, is carried out by both birds; the male sits at night, the female during the day.
→ Each egg can weigh more than 1 kg, they make good omelettes, and can feed 20 people in one go.
→ It takes two years for the chick to mature.
→ The best-quality feathers are produced by birds aged between three and 12 years.
→ Plucking occurs every nine months: about 1 kg of feathers is removed.
→ Over 80% of the feathers are exported.
→ Their skin makes excellent handbags and wallets.
→ The meat once used only for biltong is now popular in Europe and America because it is almost fat free.
→ The male bird has a vicious kick and a sharp toenail – beware!

different species. Visiting the farms or the Cango Caves without your own transport can be surprisingly tricky. There are no longer any tour companies that organize daily trips, although it is possible to find a guide through the tourist office. Otherwise, you might want to hire a car for the day.

Cango Ostrich Farm ⓘ *T044-2724623, www.cangoostrich.co.za, daily 0800-1700, R40, R15 children, tours every 15 mins, duration 45 mins*, in the Shoemanshoek Valley, is particularly convenient as it is on the way to and from the Cango Caves. The farm attractions are also within walking distance of each other. You can interact directly with the birds, sit on or ride them, buy local curios and sample Karoo wines and cheeses.

Wilgewandel Holiday Farm ⓘ *T044-2720878, www.wilgewandel.co.za, daily 0800-1500, small entry fee*, is also in the Shoemanshoek Valley, 2 km before the Cango Caves. It offers you the chance to ride a camel around the farm, R20, R12 children – a pleasant change from all those ostriches. There are also lots of attractions for children such as farmyard animals, a pet area, bumper boats and a restaurant serving anything from tea and scones to crocodile and ostrich steaks.

Highgate Ostrich Farm ⓘ *T044-2727115, www.highgate.co.za, daily 0800-1700, R30, children R15, tours every 15 mins, duration 1½ hrs*, is 10 km from Oudtshoorn off the R328 towards Mossel Bay. This very popular show farm, named after the London suburb of Highgate, has been owned by the Hooper family since the 1850s. It has won prizes in the last few years for its high standards, and is very well run and better organized than other farms. You will learn everything there is to know about the bird, and can then try your hand at riding (or even racing!) them. Snacks and drinks are served on the porch of the homestead. Guides speak German and Dutch.

Safari Ostrich Farm ⓘ *T028-2727311, www.safariostrich.co.za, daily 0730-1700, adults R30, children R15, tours every 30 mins, duration 1 hr*, 6 km from Oudtshoorn on the Mossel Bay road, has the usual array of ostrich rides, educational exhibits and curio shops. There is also a smart homestead known as Welgeluk. The house was built in 1910, and is a perfectly preserved example of an ostrich palace. There are roof tiles from Belgium, teak from Burma and expanses of marble floors, proof of the wealth and influence the short-lived boom brought to Oudtshoorn families. Unfortunately, the house is closed to visitors; the closest you can get is the main gate.

Cango Wildlife Ranch ① *T044-2725593, www.cango.co.za, daily 0800-1700, R35, children R20, tours every 30 mins, duration 1 hr*, is 3 km along the R328 towards Cango Caves and is a popular stop for tour groups. There are mixed opinions on this place since it is in effect a zoo which mainly stocks the most appealing animals – including pygmy hippos, leopards, cheetahs and, oddly, jaguars, pumas and two rare white Bengal tigers that produced three cubs in 2003. (And also some of the more unappealing such as an albino python.) However the ranch is a leading player in conservation and breeding, particularly with cheetah and wild dog, and the enclosures are very spacious. After walking safely above the animals, you have the choice of spending a little more to pet a cheetah, or you can visit the restaurant.

Still on the unusual animal farm theme is **Cango Angoré** ① *T028-2726967, daily 0900-1700, R40, R20 children , guided tours*, a working Angora-rabbit show farm with a restaurant and tea garden. Children can pet the fluffy bunnies, try spinning their wool, and have donkey cart rides. Sadly, the farm is becoming increasingly overpriced. The farm is 15 km from Oudtshoorn on the R328 towards Cango Caves, take the turning by Cango Potteries.

North of Oudtshoorn

Following the R328 north, the road passes several ostrich farms and then follows the Grobbelaars River Valley towards the Cango Caves (see below). 15 km from Oudtshoorn is the little village of **Schoemanshoek** in a lush valley with small farms and homesteads and some good places to stay.

Cango Caves » *Colour map 7, grid B2.*

Tucked away in the foothills of the Swartberg Mountains 28 km from Oudtshoorn, the Cango Caves are a magnificent network of calcite caves, recognized as among the world's finest dripstone caverns. In 1938 they were made a national monument. Despite being seriously hyped and very touristy, they are well worth a visit. Allow a morning for a round trip if based locally; if you have a car it is possible to visit them and Oudtshoorn on a day trip from towns along the Garden Route such as Mossel Bay, George and Wilderness.

Ins and outs

The caves are 28 km north of Oudtshoorn along the R328, clearly signposted from the centre of town. The road goes straight to the caves; you have to turn left for the Swartberg Pass and Prince Albert. A range of facilities has been developed in the middle of this sparsely inhabited wilderness. There is a restaurant, a crèche, several curio shops and a small money exchange. The caves are usually around 20°C, so a T-shirt and shorts will be fine. Wear shoes with reasonable grip, as after rain the floors can become a little slippery. It is a criminal offence to touch or take anything from inside the caves. Please adhere to these rules and be careful not to touch the rock formations – the acidity of the human sweat that is left from by wandering hands has already caused considerable damage. Eating, drinking and smoking are also forbidden inside. The caves are open daily 0900-1700; you can only enter on a tour (see Oudtshoorn Activities and tours, page 312) – these run until 1600. During the holidays it gets very crowded and nearly 200,000 people pass through the caves each year. Each tour has a maximum number of people, so you may have to wait an hour or more. It's a good idea to get here early in the morning to avoid queues.

Cave tours

ⓘ *T044-2727410, www.cangocaves.co.za. There are 2 tour options: the standard tour starting every hour from 0900, with the last tour at 1600, 1 hr, R40, R25 children, and the adventure tour starting at half past every hour 0900-1530, 1½ hrs, R55, R35 children.*

The only access to the caves is on a guided tour: the short tour takes in two chambers and provides a brief insight into the cave complex; the most popular tour takes in six caves, while the adventure tour follows narrow corridors and involves some crawling. During the tours, each section is lit up and the guide points out interesting formations and their given names. Although one small chamber is still lit in gaudy colours, the rest are illuminated with white light to best show off the formations. These are turned off behind you as you progress further into the system as research has shown that continued exposure to light causes damage to the caves.

The caverns are not just a beautiful series of bizarre formations, but represent over a million years of slow chemical processes. The Cango cave system is known as a phreatic system, the term given to caves which have been chemically eroded by underground water. Once the caves had been exposed to air, the first deposits started to form – these now make up the incredible stalagmites, stalactites and flowstones visitors can see. The timescale of some of the formations is mind-boggling; many of the pillars took hundreds of thousands of years to form, while the oldest flowstone is over a million years old.

The standard one-hour tour is a good introduction to the caves and allows you to see the most impressive formations. It is, however, aimed at tour groups, so visitors with a special interest may find it rather simplistic. The adventure tour lasts for 1½ hours, is over 1 km long and there are over 400 stairs. This can be disturbing for some people, since it involves crawling along narrow tunnels, and at the very end climbing up the Devil's Chimney, a narrow vertical shaft. It leads up for 3½ m and is only 45 cm wide in parts – definitely not for broad people. If at any stage you feel you can't go on, inform the guide who will arrange for you to be led out. Although strenuous, this tour allows you to see the most of the caves, and gives a real feeling of exploration.

Swartberg Nature Reserve » pp309-312.

Just before the Cango Caves is the turning for the Swartberg Pass and Prince Albert that travels through the Swartberg Nature Reserve. The reserve encompasses 1,291,000 ha of mostly state-owned land and includes the area around Swartberg Pass and the Gamkaskloof Valley (below). The main attractions here are the mountain fynbos and a varied birdlife. Animals likely to be spotted include kudu, baboon, klipspringer, and dassie. Leopard and caracal also occur in the region but are rarely seen. The mountains behind the Cango Caves are 2000-3000 m high and have a maze of trails snaking through them. The longest trail, the **Swartberg Hiking Trail**, is 60 km long and takes five days. There are three overnight huts at Ou Tol, Bothashoek and Gouekrans, with bunks, showers and braai facilities. Permits and maps are issued by the **Cape Nature Conservation** ⓘ *George, T044-8025310, www.capenature.org.za.* Water has to be carried between huts during the day.

Some of the original cottages in the valley have been restored as accommodation by Cape Nature – see Sleeping page 310.

Swartberg Pass → *Colour map 7, grid B1.*

One of the most spectacular passes in South Africa, the Swartberg Pass is a national monument in recognition of the engineering genius of Thomas Bain (see page 300). Following severe floods in 1875 which closed Meiringspoort and Seven Weeks Poort and washed away parts of the road, farmers in the region petitioned the government in Cape Town to build a reliable road across the Swartberg. After the first contractor went bankrupt Bain finished the job. It was built between 1881 and 1888 using convict labourers. The route is 24 km long; the top of the pass is 1585 m and the summit is often closed in winter due to snow. The road today follows much the same route and care must be taken. It is very steep: the road climbs 1000 m within 12 km, and there are very sharp, blind hairpins. As you descend towards Prince Albert there are plenty of shaded picnic sites to pause at and enjoy the views.

Gamkaskloof Valley: The Hell

ⓘ *Three kilometres past the summit of Swartberg Pass, coming from Oudtshoorn, is a gravel road to the left signposted 'The Hell' in the Gamkaskloof Valley. The Otto du Plessis road is suitable for a saloon car but be sure to take care driving here. The road is narrow and steep in parts and there are many blind bends. In all, it is 58 km to the start of the valley; allow at least 1½ hours each way. Note that there are no shops or fuel. Gamkaskloof is 16 km long with two seasonal rivers criss-crossing the road.*

This is one of the more unusual places to visit in South Africa. It is an isolated valley, which is hidden away in the mountains, and whose residents have managed to avoid the change going on all around them. For more than 50 years these European immigrants were the forgotten people. They paid no taxes, had no schoolteachers and made their own clothes. It was only in 1963, 126 years after the first Europeans built their homes here, that a road was built connecting the valley to the outside world. Prior to this all provisions had been brought in by pack donkeys from Prince Albert.

It was during the Great Trek that farmers searching for a place free of the influence and interference of British officials decided to settle in the kloof. Amongst the last people to leave the valley were their descendants. The last farmer, Piet Swanepoel, left the valley in 1991. An account written in 1955 in Karoo, by L G Green, relates an accurate image of conditions in the valley. "Calitzdorp is the nearest village, but 'The Hell' can be reached in comfort only by helicopter. It has no road, nothing but a track for pack-donkeys. As there are only about 20 families living in the kloof, the road-makers have by-passed this solitude. You must leave your car at Matjiesvlei farm and struggle along the Gamka River banks on foot for two or three hours, sometimes knee-deep in water, to meet white people who have never seen the outside world."

Prince Albert → *Colour map 7, grid B1.*

This old village lies on the edge of the Swartberg Mountains and only 2 km from the start of the scenic Swartberg Pass. Canals from these hills bring water to the gardens, helping to give an oasis feel to the settlement. There is an old watermill on the edge of town. A few minutes walking about the village quickly gives one an impression of life at the turn of the 20th century during the hot summers of the Karoo. Fortunately, many of the homes from this period have survived in a good state of repair. Reflecting the richness of the landscape is the **Frans Pienaar** collection of fossils, one of the largest in the world, housed in the local museum. There is also an excellent private mineral collection which can be viewed by appointment. Tourist information for the area can be found at the **Frans Pienaar Museum** ⓘ *Church St, T023-5411366, www.patourism.co.za*. There is a supermarket, general shops, an excellent market next to the museum on Saturday mornings selling homemade cheese, pickles, olives, dried fruit, bread and cakes, plus a couple of restaurants.

The town holds the annual Olive Food and Wine Festival on the last weekend of April with a street market, music, a half marathon and cycle races.

West of Oudtshoorn » pp309-312.

The main road through the Little Karoo to the west of Oudtshoorn is the R62, a beautiful stretch which is now marketed as **Route 62**. After 52 km you reach Calitzdorp, a small farming centre. Take the old road which follows the Olifants River to visit the **Gamkaberg Nature Reserve** and **Calitzdorp Spa**. North from Calitzdorp is a gravel road to Groenfontein along the Nels River Valley. This route is narrow and full of tight bends, and should not be travelled after heavy rains in an ordinary road vehicle. Eventually it joins up with the R328, Oudtshoorn – Prince Albert road. A loop back to Oudtshoorn via the Cango Caves is a possible circuit. Continuing west from Calitzdorp, the R62 crosses the Dwyka River. After 24 km is a turning north to Seven Weeks Poort. Soon after this you pass the mission stations of Amalienstein and Zoar. It is another 21 km to Ladismith. The area around Ladismith is good for hiking.

Calitzdorp → *Colour map 8 grid C1.*

Until the branch line from Oudtshoorn arrived in 1924, this settlement remained a small service stop for farmers. The village is now a successful agricultural centre and an important area for port production in South Africa. It is possible to visit a couple of port farms, and a **port festival** is held every July (T044-2133314). At harvest time, fresh fruits are sold along the wide roads of the village. The village is also known for the warm healing waters at Calitzdorp Spa, 22 km towards Oudtshoorn on the old cement road (see above). When the first farms were established in the area, the surrounding plains were full of game. Sadly today only the early farm names survive as a reminder. The helpful **tourist office** ⓘ *Voortrekker St, T044-2133775, www.calitzdorp.co.za*, has some good leaflets on the area as well as information about the wineries.

Anysberg Nature Reserve

This is one of the newer reserves in the region, reflecting the need to protect the Karoo. Created in 1988, the area covers 34,000 ha and has a rich and varied fauna and flora along with some well-preserved Khoisan paintings in the Anysberg hills. The further you explore into the wilderness, the more likely you are to see elusive wildlife such as scrub hare, black-backed jackal and the caracal. There are some spectacular gorges which are home for birds such as the black eagle and the pale chanting goshawk. During dry periods the dams provide a focal point for both wildlife and birds. Walking is allowed but no trails have been marked out.

Ins and outs The reserve is on the northern fringe of the Little Karoo. There are two possible routes to the campsite and offices. From the north, travelling along the N1 highway between Touws River and Beaufort West, take the turning at Laingsburg. For the first 25 km the road is surfaced. Take a right turning onto a good dirt road (signposted Ladismith). After another 25 km another right turning takes you into the hills towards the nature reserve. The camp is 23 km from here. From Calitzdorp it is about 120 km to the reserve via the small settlement of Ladismith on the R323 dirt road. This is a beautiful drive as the road climbs up into the Swartberg Mountains over the Seven Weeks Poort and Garcia passes.

Barrydale → *Colour map 8, grid C2.*

This is the centre of a small farming community set in a fertile valley between the Little Karoo and the Breede River Valley. It's a quiet rural town where the odd cow or sheep can occasionally be seen munching on someone's garden lawn. The surrounding farmland is a colourful mix of vineyards and wild flowers and in the spring the hillsides are covered with *mesembryanthemums*. The area also produces peaches, apricots, apples and brandy. The local wine cooperative has been a great success

Anysberg Horse Trail

This is a gentle two-day circular horse trail through the Anysberg Nature Reserve, suitable for inexperienced riders. At first glance the horses appear to be feral as they spend their days grazing on the mountainside, but a whistle from a staff member will soon have them reporting to the tack room for duty. This experience is quite unique and the trail goes through traditional Karoo countryside with the ever-present backdrop of the looming mountains. In the relative silence of clpping hooves, you are likely to get close to mammals and the big raptors that inhabit the reserve. At the overnight spot you sleep on a mattress under the stars in a makeshift camp next to your mount, where water is available and meals are cooked over an open fire. Cooking equipment, mattresses and firewood are included in the price but you bring your own food. Everyone is responsible for their own horse, including cleaning and feeding it. Riders are restricted to a body weight of 95 km and 5 kg of luggage. The ride is limited to six riders and costs R430 per person. Reservations through T028-4255020, bredasdorp@capenature.co.za, www.capenature.org.za.'

and any meal eaten in the locality should be accompanied by their Chardonnay. For tastings visit the **Barrydale Wine Cellar** ⓘ *on the R62 towards Montagu, T028-5721012, www.barrydalewines.co.za, Mon-Fri 0800-1700, Sat 0900-1300*. For information contact the **Barrydale Information Office** ⓘ *1 Van Riebeeck St, T028-5721572, www.barrydale.co.za.*

Tradouw Pass

Running parallel to the Langeberg Mountains, the R62, or Route 62, continues west along the course of the Kingna River to Montagu, 66 km. To the south, the R324 passes over the spectacular Tradouw Pass through the Langeberg Mountains to join the N2 11 km west of Swellendam. When opened in 1873, the pass provided an important trade link for the farmers of the Little Karoo with Port Beaufort at the mouth of the Breede River. As with many civil engineering projects of the time, convict labour was used to build the road, under the direction of Thomas Bain. Halfway up the remains of the prisoners' camp can still be seen.

Road engineer Thomas Bain built 13 road passes in the southern Cape in the 1800s.

East of Oudtshoorn » pp309-312.

De Rust → *Colour map 7, grid B2.*

This well-preserved village 35 km from Oudtshoorn along the N12 has a number of classic Karoo homes. Surprisingly it is world renowned for its rare pelargoniums from which geraniums were first grown. If you have time, the wine farm **Domein Doornkraal** has tastings and sales. Information is available from the **tourist office** ⓘ *Schoeman St, T044-2412109, www.derust.org.za*, which also a curio shop and internet café.

Continuing along the N12, the road through the **Meiringspoort Pass** in the Swartberg Mountains is worth the petrol; so too is the 60-m **Meiringspoort waterfall.** This can be reached via a short path from the car park. The road through the mountains was built by AG de Smidt, the son-in-law of the famous road builder Thomas Bain. It was opened in 1857, but because it more or less followed the course of the River Groot, it suffered considerable damage during the rains and by 1885 had been completely washed away. Funds collected at the toll gate were never sufficient to pay for repairs. The tar road still survives today along the base of the gorge, and crosses the river 30 times. The 17-km drive is one to be savoured as the vast sandstone cliffs loom above you. After the pass, the road splits; the N12 continues to Beaufort West approximately 120 km away, and the R407 eventually ends up at **Prince Albert**, 90 km away. You can then return to Oudtshoorn (72 km) via the scenic Swartberg Pass along the R328.

Sleeping

Oudtshoorn *p300, map p301*

For a town slightly off the main tourist trail, Oudtshoorn has a good and varied choice of accommodation. However, if you plan to stay at a guesthouse or B&B, book in advance. If you are interested in staying as a guest in someone's home in a township, this can be arranged through **Hazel's Homestays**, T044-2724380, hazelhomestay@absamail.co.za, or through the tourist office.

AL Rosenhof Country House, 264 Baron van Rheede St, T044-2722232, www.rosenhof.co.za. 12 a/c rooms with DSTV, swimming pool, beautiful rose garden, beauty spa, gym, jacuzzi, sauna, the 2 suites have their own pool and patio. Great thought and care has gone into choosing the furnishings of this restored Victorian house, and the fabrics and the ornaments create a comfortable homely atmosphere. Not quite small enough for real privacy but still of a very high standard. Recommended.

A Hlangana Lodge, 51 North St, T044-2722299, www.hlangana.co.za. An excellent lodge with 12 double and 6 triple rooms in a pretty, low building, a/c, TV, safe, mini-bar, saltwater pool, mountain bikes for hire, attentive and friendly hosts. Recommended.

A-B Queen's Hotel, 5 Baron van Rheede St (next to CP Nel Museum), T044-2722701, www.queenshotel.co.za. Historic hotel set in tidy gardens in the centre of town. 60 a/c rooms, en suite, stylish and comfortable. Good restaurant on 1st floor with balcony, serves a buffet lunch on Sun and some interesting South African dishes. Has a swimming pool, tennis courts, curio shop, laundry service and secure parking. A comfortable and friendly hotel which is owned and run by the Barrow family, good value with discounts during quiet periods. Recommended.

B Adley House, 209 Jan van Riebeeck Rd, T044-2724533, www.adleyhouse.co.za. A comfortable B&B in a fully restored 1905 house built during the ostrich boom, set in large grounds a short distance from the town centre. 12 rooms, all with en suite bathroom, M-Net TV, mini-bar, heaters in winter. Excellent evening meals available, 2 swimming pools. Recommended.

B La Pension, 169 Church St, T044-2792445, www.lapension.co.za. A well-furnished B&B set in large garden with shady fruit trees. 7 rooms in the Cape Dutch-style house, TV, 2-bed self-catering garden flat, sauna, swimming pool. Ask for Len or Jean.

B Riempie Estate Protea, Baron van Rheede St, T044-2726161, www.proteahotels.co.za, 3 km from town centre. Mix of thatched rondavels and double a/c rooms surrounded by farmland. 40 a/c rooms, 2 non-smoking rooms. The restaurant offers tasty country cuisine. Swimming pool, horse riding, mature shady gardens.

B Shades of Africa, 238 Jan van Riebeeck Rd, T044-2726430, www.shades.co.za. A new building which has been decorated with some fine examples of African art and textiles. 4 very stylish en suite double rooms by the swimming pool set in indigenous gardens, a/c, TV, country or vegetarian breakfasts, use of the kitchen, no children under 12.

B-C Kleinplaas Holiday Resort, 171 Baron van Rheede St, T044-2725811, www.kleinplaas.co.za. 56 simple brick-built fully-equipped self catering chalets each with own braai and carport. Caravan and camping pitches with plenty of shade (**E**), electric points, swimming pool, shop, laundry.

C Bisibee, 171 Church St, T044-2724784, www.bisibee.co.za. 4 rooms, all with en suite bathroom, B&B, swimming pool. One of the friendliest welcomes you will receive in South Africa. Breakfast will keep you going all day, outstanding evening meals, recommended to us every year by other visitors.

C-E Backpacker's Paradise, 148 Baron van Rheede St, T044-2723436, www.backpackersparadise.hostel.com. Spotless lodge set over

4 houses, with a mix of dorms and doubles, camping, volleyball court, well-stocked kitchen, pub with pool table, nightly ostrich braais, splash pool, email facilities, within walking distance of shops, free town pick-up, and a daily pick-up from the Baz Bus in George. Plenty of activities can be organized from here. Recommended.

D-E **Oasis Shanti**, 3 Church St, T044-2791163, oasis@mailbox.co.za. Clean and quiet hostel with a good range of rooms, including singles, doubles, triples and uncrowded dorms, and some space for camping. Swimming pool with braai area, ostrich-egg breakfasts, nightly ostrich braais and also vegetarian meals, TV lounge, bicycle hire, good travel advice especially about hiking in the region.

North of Oudtshoorn *p304*

AL-A **Altes Landhaus**, 13 km north of Oudtshoorn towards the Cango Caves, T044-2726112, www.alteslandhaus.co.za. Award-winning guesthouse in a Cape Dutch homestead, 10 en suite double rooms, some with a/c and TV. Each room is decorated with antiques and has its own special character, evening meals with fine wines available on request, salt pool in garden with pool bar, German spoken, recommended.

A-B **De Opstal**, 12 km north of Oudtshoorn off the road to Cango Caves, T044-2792954, www.deopstal.co.za. A working ostrich farm that offers tours, with 20 en suite double rooms, some of which are converted farm buildings and stables circa 1830 with plenty of character, some have a/c and/or fireplaces, swimming pool with sun loungers, restaurant and bar. Check first there's not a wedding on.

B **Oue Werf**, 13 km north of Oudtshoorn, T044-2728712, www.ouewerf.co.za. Old 1857 farmhouse with 6 comfortable en suite rooms and 2 self-contained cottages in the grounds, with swimming pool, plus boating on farm dam, evening meals on request; an ideal base from which to explore the area.

C-E **Cango Mountain Resort**, 7 km before Cango Caves is a turning off the R328, the resort is 3 km down the road (the road follows the Oude Murasie Valley and can be followed all the way to De Rust, see page 308), T044-2724506, www.cangomountain resort.co.za. A large resort with 21 fully equipped self-catering chalets with TV, 70 caravan and 40 camping sites, electric points, shop and swimming pool suitable for children. A peaceful spot next to the Koos Raubenheimer Dam, where there are some pleasant braai spots among the oak trees.

Swartberg Nature Reserve *p305*

Efforts have been made by **Cape Nature Conservation** to restore some of the houses scattered throughout the Gamkaskloof Valley, also known as The Hell. Reservations, T044-8025310, www.capenature.org.za.

B-C **Self-catering cottages**, sleeping 4-8 are very good value for families or groups. For a detailed description of each cottage, and a little bit of history about the individual former residents, check out the website. Each has solar lighting, gas stoves and fridges but no electricity. Bedding and cooking and eating equipment are provided but you need to bring food and towels. Rates are higher at the weekends.

D **Camping**. There are 10 camping sites with a braai and cold showers, tents only, caravans cannot access here. You can swim in the Gamka River. All-round recommended for a rustic and remote few days.

Prince Albert *p306*

Although there is little choice, this is an ideal base for the many hiking trails in the area.

B **Saxe-Coburg Lodge**, 60 Church St, T023-5411267, www.saxecoburg.co.za. A well-preserved Victorian house with 4 a/c rooms and 1 garden self-catering cottage, honeymoon room has spa bath, meals on request, swimming pool. The pub lounge is a relaxing place to end the day by the fire. Richard and Regina can offer advice on hiking. French and German spoken.

B **Swartberg Hotel**, 77 Church St, T023-5411332, www.swartberg.co.za. 13 rooms plus 5 garden rondavels, delightful restored Victorian home, over 150 years old, with antiques, restaurant, South African dishes a speciality, bar with roaring fire in the winter, swimming pool. Recommended.

B-C **Dennehof**, 5 mins from the village on the R328, T023-5411227, steynria@mweb.co.za. Authentic rustic accommodation in 2 self-contained Karoo-style cottages, each with 2 double rooms with bathrooms, a/c and TV. Large garden with views of the Swartberg, swimming in the summer months in a country dam. The main house is a well-preserved Cape Dutch farmhouse, the oldest in the village. B&B or self-catering, evening meals on request, friendly and helpful hosts who are also tour guides, can arrange tours to The Hell. Recommended.

Calitzdorp *p307*

A-B **Port Wine Guest House**, 7 Queen St, T044-2133131, www.portwine.net. A smart guesthouse in a historic Cape thatched building from the 1830s surrounded by vines. 8 en suite double rooms with 4-poster beds and open fires, swimming pool, evening meals available on request taken under the vines. The owners can tell you all you need to know about the region. If you have the time, try to arrange a visit to their ostrich farm. Recommended.

C **Welgevonden Guest House**, St Helena Rd, T044-2133642, welgevon@telkomsa.net. A peaceful country guesthouse. 4 rooms with chintzy furnishings and en suite bathrooms, communal lounge and kitchenette. Lush gardens, swimming pool, part of a Chardonnay farm, enjoy the comfort of a family home, evening meals by arrangement.

Anysberg Nature Reserve *p307*

B **Anysberg Cottages**, reservations through Cape Nature Conservation T028-4255020, www.capenature.org.za. 5 restored labourers cottages with no electricity, light is from candles and lamps, gas fridge, basic kitchen, braai, and communal ablution block, bring bedding, towels and food. This is where the Anysberg horse trails start.

Barrydale *p307*

B **Rietfontein Guest Farm**, off the R62 between Barrydale and Ladismith, 12 km from the main road, T028-5512128, www.rietfontein.co.za. Lovely rural retreat set in the foothills of the Touwsberg Mountains on a working farm, 3-self catering cottages sleeping 5-6, no electricity but paraffin lights are supplied, well furnished and equipped, telescope for star gazing at the main house, the swimming pool pump is powered by solar energy.

C **Dandelion Guest House**, 12 Van Riebeeck St, T028-5721539, www.dandelion.co.za. Delightful Cape Dutch-style thatched cottage with outside wooden stairs to rooms in the roof, 2 comfortable but tiny en suite rooms with lots of character, 1 garden rondavel, swimming pool, B&B, evening meals on request.

De Rust *p308*

B **De Gat**, 7 km from De Rust on the R341, T044-2412406, www.diegat.co.za. B&B with 5 en suite rooms in garden units separate from the main house, which is a lovely farm homestead dating back to around 1800 and a national monument. It's also possible to sleep overnight in the ox wagon. Traditional Karoo dinners on request, swimming pool.

C-D **Olivier's Rust**, 9 Schoeman St, T044-2412258, www.derust.org.za. 8 self-catering, fully equipped modern brick chalets sleeping 2-4, garden, pool, braai area, attached **Herrie's** coffee shop where you can get a light meal until 2100 and homemade bread.

Eating

Oudtshoorn *p300, map p301*

Most of the hotels have their own bar and restaurant, which tend to stay open a little later than the restaurants in town.

TTT **Colony**, Queen's Hotel, 5 Baron van Rheede St, T044-2792414. 1800-2300. Excellent restaurant set in this historic hotel. Menu has a very wide range of local dishes, such as Karoo lamb, springbok steak and ostrich. Balcony overlooking the main street, good atmosphere and service, crisp white linen. Recommended.

TT **Bernard's Taphuis**, Baron van Rheede St, T044-2723208, dinner only, closed Sun. Large central restaurant, good place to try traditional local dishes such as Karoo lamb and ostrich steak on an outside terrace.

TT **Fijne Keuken**, 114 Baron van Rheede St, T044-2726403, Mon-Fri 1130-1600, 1730-2200, Sat and Sun 1730-2200. A fine menu served in a cosy converted town house with tables in several rooms and on the outside terrace. Variety of ostrich dishes including good steaks and a more affordable ostrich stroganoff served with pasta. Good service, popular and bustling place. Recommended.

TT **The Godfather**, 61 Voortrekker Rd, T044-2725404, 1800-2300, closed Sun. Good game menu with springbok steaks and ostrich, plus pizza and good Italian fare, tasty meals but a little more expensive than elsewhere. The bar here is also a good place for a nightcap.

Headlines, Baron van Rheede St, T044-2723434. Mon-Sat 0800-1500, 1745-2300, Sun 1100-1500. Coffee shop and restaurant specializing in ostrich dishes of all kinds from ostrich-egg omelettes to ostrich-liver pâté. The Bushmen Kebab is a favourite with ostrich, venison, crocodile, pork/beef fillet and chicken on one skewer.

Paljas, 109 Baron van Rheede St, T044-2720982. 1000-1600, 1700-2300, closed Mon. Pan African cuisine, a good selection of Cape Malay curries, Karoo roasts, West Coast seafood, and a few unusual Zulu and Xhosa dishes, extensive wine list, a good place to try a 3-course meal with a lot of different flavours.

Calitzdorp *p307*

Rose of the Karoo, 21 Voortrekker Rd, T044-2133133, closed Sun. A group of buildings surrounding a vine-covered courtyard with a cosy restaurant with fireplace open all day until 2200 for freshly home-cooked food and famous for their chicken pie, a delicatessen, a curio shop, and 2 overnight family en suite rooms sleeping 4 (C) with fridge and kettle.

De Rust *p308*

Jam Tarts, just out of town on the R62 towards Ladismith, T028-5721154. Attached to an eccentric gift shop, sells homemade jams and deli products. The varied menu includes Spanish omelettes, Moroccan dishes and organic salads.

The Plough, corner Schoeman and Burger Sts, T044-2412020. 0800-1500, 1800-2100, closed Mon and dinner Sun. A good spot for Karoo lamb and traditional dishes, fresh salads and vegetables, old-fashioned sticky desserts and excellent farm-style breakfasts from a full English to a bowl of highland oats with brown sugar, fresh cream and a tot of whiskey!

Shopping

Oudtshoorn *p300, map p301*

Baron van Rheede St is lined with curio shops selling every ostrich by-product imaginable, from expensive leather purses to feather dusters and tacky enamelled eggs. One such emporium is **Kuriopik**, on the High St. For arts and crafts try **De Oude Pastorie**, 43 Baron van Rheede St.

Activities and tours

Oudtshoorn *p300, map p301*

Backpacker's Paradise, 148 Baron van Rheede St, T044-2723436, www.backpackersparadise.hostel.com. Plenty of activities can be organized from this backpackers. Mountain biking to the Swartberg Pass leaves daily at 0830 when you are driven to the top and enjoy the long ride downhill. On the way back to Oudtshoorn, you can stop at the Cango Caves and all the other attractions along the R328. They can also organize overnight trips to the 'The Hell', wine tastings and cave trips.

Horse Trek Africa, T044-2724509, www.horsetrekafrica.co.za. Multi-day horse-riding trips in the Karoo for experienced and fit riders.

Swartberg Adventures, 56 St Saviour St, T044-2793037, www.swartbergadventures.co.za. Local company that can arrange a number of activities in the Swartberg region, including quad biking through the Swartberg Pass, abseiling, hiking and kloofing.

Transport

Oudtshoorn *p300, map p301*

172 km to **Beaufort West**, 510 km to **Cape Town**, 60 km to **George**, 245 km to **Montagu**, 93 km to **Mossel Bay**.
There is a station here but no trains stop.

Bus

Translux, T011-7743333, www.translux.co.za. Buses depart from the Queen's Riverside Mall. Daily to **Knysna** (2 hrs), **Johannesburg** and **Pretoria** (14 hrs) via **Kimberley** (7 hrs) or via **Bloemfontein** (5 hrs).

Intercape, T0861-287287, www.intercape.co.za. Daily service to **Johannesburg** and **Pretoria** (14 hrs) via **Kimberley** (7 hrs) or via **Bloemfontein** (5 hrs).

Directory

Oudtshoorn *p300, map p301*

Banks Branches of the major banks are along High St or Baron van Rheede St.
Useful telephone numbers Ambulance: T10177; Private hospital, Medi-Clinic, T044-2720111; Police, 10111.

Eastern Cape

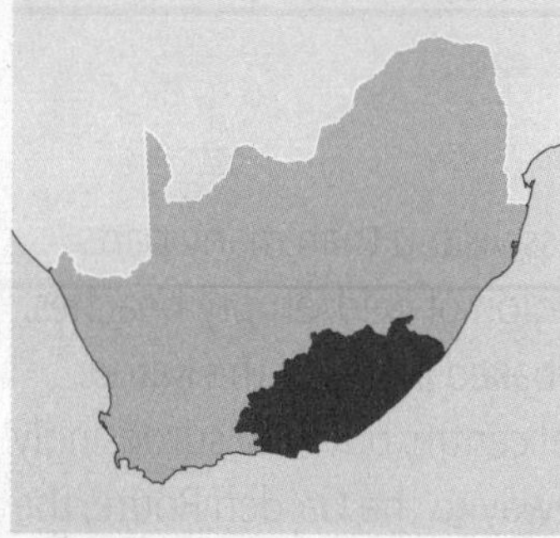

Footprint features

Introduction

The Eastern Cape, although far less visited than many parts of South Africa, is a fascinating region of wild, empty beaches, forested mountains and the sun-baked plains of the Karoo. Port Elizabeth is a major industrial centre, but with surprisingly good beaches, and acts as a gateway to the Garden Route, the lush coast stretching towards Cape Town, and Tsitsikamma National Park. A short drive from here is Jeffrey's Bay, where the long beach and perfect waves attract surfers from around the world.

To the north is a variety of game reserves and national parks, including the recently extended Greater Addo Elephant National Park, now the third largest game reserve in the country where lion have been introduced among its famously large herds of elephant. It's now the only place in South Africa where you can see the Big Seven - elephant, lion, rhino, buffalo, leopard, whale and shark. The Mountain Zebra Reserve is a haven for the endangered mountain zebra, and in Shamwari Game Reserve – a conservation success story – you can also catch a glimpse of the Big Five. Further inland lie the mystical landscapes of the Amatola Mountains and the sharply contrasting Karoo, with its surreal semi-desert conditions and quirky 19th-century towns.

During the Apartheid era the eastern region was referred to as the Transkei, the former homeland for the Xhosa people. These days the area is known as the Wild Coast because of its rugged, virtually deserted coastline. The area is far less developed than much of South Africa's coast, and most of the people live in rural settlements and work on the land. Instead of full-blown resorts, there are small seaside villages backed by protected stretches of verdant coastal forest and windswept dunes.

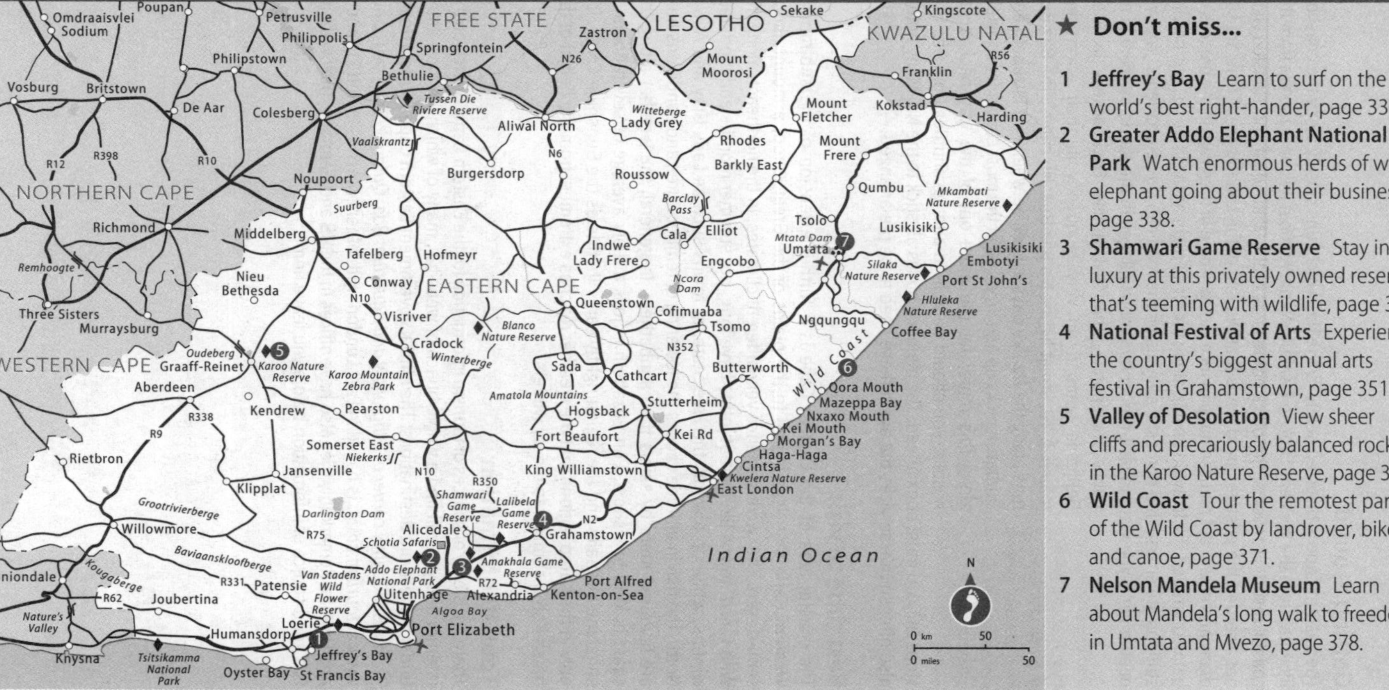

★ Don't miss...

1 **Jeffrey's Bay** Learn to surf on the world's best right-hander, page 333.

2 **Greater Addo Elephant National Park** Watch enormous herds of wild elephant going about their business, page 338.

3 **Shamwari Game Reserve** Stay in luxury at this privately owned reserve that's teeming with wildlife, page 340.

4 **National Festival of Arts** Experience the country's biggest annual arts festival in Grahamstown, page 351.

5 **Valley of Desolation** View sheer cliffs and precariously balanced rocks in the Karoo Nature Reserve, page 357.

6 **Wild Coast** Tour the remotest parts of the Wild Coast by landrover, bike and canoe, page 371.

7 **Nelson Mandela Museum** Learn about Mandela's long walk to freedom in Umtata and Mvezo, page 378.

Ins and outs

Getting around

The Eastern Cape is bisected neatly by the N2, which runs closely along the coast on its route from the Western Cape to KwaZulu Natal. At most it is only 100 km from the coastal resorts. For years, the black homelands of the Wild Coast and Transkei were not awarded the pristine tarred roads that the rest of the country was. There are still many gravel and dirt roads in the province though some of these are in the process of being upgraded. Try to avoid driving along the N2 at night as facilities such as service stations are sparse and domestic animals on the road can cause accidents. You will need a car If you want to visit the more remote villages in the Karoo as there is no public transport – the **Owl House Backpackers** in Nieu Bethesda sums it up very eloquently in their advertising material: 'No street lights. No Baz Bus. No crime'. The **Baz Bus** runs along the N2 five days a week between Port Elizabeth and Durban. It picks up and drops off at the most convenient hostels along this route; for the more out of the way backpacker hostels, you should be able to arrange shuttles from Baz Bus stops but you must book ahead. The mainline buses all stick to the N2. Many hotels also offer shuttle services but again these need to be pre-arranged.

Compared to the other provinces in South Africa, a little planning ahead is needed if you are travelling around the Eastern Cape by public transport.

Best time to visit

The coastal area of the Eastern Cape is a further extension of the subtropical Western Cape that rises inland to the plains of the Great Karoo, a mountainous semi-desert. The two experience very different climates. In the northeast, along the Wild Coast, towns like Port St Johns have long, hot summer months and moderate winters, while up towards the Free State, at towns such as Lady Grey and Aliwal North, the rise in altitude causes the lowering of temperatures and conditions here are favoured more by skiers than sunbathers. In general, the weather along the coast is kind to visitors. Port Elizabeth enjoys a daily average of seven hours of sunshine annually and the region rightly earns its title as the Sunshine Coast. It's only in the Karoo regions that the weather reaches extremes, from the height of the harsh Karoo summer to the icy winters.

Tourist information

There are plenty of sources of tourism information for the Eastern Cape. Search on the internet and you will find a whole bunch of websites, many of which we have listed under the relevant destinations. The official government **Eastern Cape Tourism Board** ⓘ *Tourism Centre, corner of Longfellow and Aquarium Rds, Quigney, T043-7019600, www.ectourism.co.za*, is based in East London, with other branches in Port Elizabeth and Umtata. Remarkably they also have offices in the US and Germany. Their website is a good source of information before you leave home.

Port Elizabeth

→ *Phone code: 041. Colour map 7, grid B4.*

Port Elizabeth – usually referred to as 'PE' – is a major port and industrial centre, the biggest coastal city between Cape Town and Durban. The centre of town, known as 'Central', is an attractive grid of Victorian houses and green spaces (burnt brown in summer) but the rest of the city – a modern sprawl of shopping malls, office blocks and apartments – is less aesthetically pleasing. The main tourist area is along the long beaches of Algoa Bay, and although the endless soft-sand beaches are enticing, the holiday flats and apartment blocks creeping onto the flat land behind them are less so. Nevertheless, Port Elizabeth is celebrated for its long hours of sunshine and the warm waters of the bay, making it a good place to try some watersports.

The city's other great draw is its proximity to a number of game reserves. The most popular, open for game viewing, are the Greater Addo Elephant National Park and the Shamwari Game Reserve. These offer the opportunity to see the Big Five without having to worry about malaria. Although Shamwari is a private reserve with some very smart camps, it is open to the public for day visits so long as you book in advance. Combine this with the fact that you can fly back to Cape Town in less than an hour and it becomes obvious why Port Elizabeth is rapidly growing as a popular tourist destination. » *For Sleeping, Eating and other listings, see pages 323-331.*

Ins and outs

Getting there

Port Elizabeth Airport, 4 km from the city centre along Alister Miller Drive, receives several flights daily from major South African centres. Visitors staying at Humewood Beach and Summerstrand can reach the airport without having to negotiate the city centre by way of an elaborate ring road and flyover system. There is no public transport from the airport into town but most major hotels provide a courtesy bus; alternatively, there are airport shuttle services to any hotel and taxis at the airport. The mainline **railway station** is on the edge of the town centre on Station Street, by the harbour. Port Elizabeth is served by **Greyhound, Intercape**, and **Translux** buses, and it is the overnight spot for the **Baz Bus** on the route between Cape Town and Durban, which calls in at most of the backpackers. » *For further details, see Transport, page 330.*

Southern right whales visit the bay June to November, while humpback whales calve and feed their young May to December.

Getting around

Local buses depart from **Market Square Bus Station**, beneath the Norwich Union Centre Building on Strand Street. The **Algoa Bus Company** ⓘ *T080-1421444 (toll free)*, operates a regular service between the beachfront, city centre, St George's Park, Rink Street, Greenacres and the Bridge Shopping Complex – Route O.

Tourist information

Nelson Mandela Bay Tourism ⓘ *Donkin Lighthouse Building, Belmont Terr, T041-5858884, www.nmbt.co.za, Mon-Fri 0800-1630, Sat-Sun 0930-1530*, is a useful office that can book accommodation and advise on nightlife, tours and travel throughout the Eastern Cape. There is also an office in the Boardwalk, T041-5832030. **Eastern Cape Tourist Board** ⓘ *15 Annerley Terr, Central, T041- 5857761, www.ectourism.co.za*, has excellent regional information and their website is very informative. **Eas'capism.com** ⓘ *Boardwalk Centre, beach entrance, T041-5832030, www.eascapism.com, daily 0800- 2200*, is a private tourism information service with an **Avis** car hire desk on site. It has a very comprehensive website and can book tours, transfers and accommodation.

Background

In 1497, Vasco da Gama noted the 'Bay' on one of his voyages. It was later named Baia de Lagoa, referring to the lagoon situated at the mouth of the Baakens River. For hundreds of years, however, Port Elizabeth was referred to on navigational charts only as "a landing place with fresh water". The city was established in 1820 when the first British settlers arrived. The town became a port and a trading centre catering for the early settlers who were gradually moving inland. During the first half of the 20th century, Port Elizabeth expanded and became an important trading and manufacturing city. The main exports were mineral ores, citrus fruits and wool. Ford General Motors opened its first assembly plants here in the 1920s. Today, with a population of around 1.5 million it is South Africa's fifth largest city, and one that is currently reinventing itself as 'Nelson Mandela Bay'. Although not official this will perhaps be formally its new name in a few years time. As an industrial city it is understandable that tourists don't want to spend a great deal of time here. However, with the massive growth in tourism along the Garden Route, the city has become a convenient point for visitors to start or finish their journey.

PE or Nelson Mandela Bay, is fondly referred to as 'Ibhayi' by Xhosa speakers, 'Die Baai 'by Afrikaners and 'The Bay' by English speakers.

Port Elizabeth

Sights

Central

The 5-km **Donkin Heritage Trail** has been created to show visitors the most important monuments, buildings, gardens and churches around the city centre. An excellent guidebook is available from the information office and contains 47 places of historical interest. A few of the more interesting buildings are mentioned below – they are not in the order you might come across them on the trail. The trail starts in Market Square opposite the City Hall, simply follow the useful signs.

Market Square is probably PE's most attractive corner, with a couple of fine buildings and the beginning of bustling Govan Mbeki Avenue. **City Hall** was built between 1858 and 1862; the clock tower was added in 1883. While part of the hall is still used by the council, it is also now a lecture and concert hall for public performances. Look out for a replica of the Diaz Cross in Market Square. This was donated by the Portuguese Government to commemorate the arrival of Bartholomeu Diaz in Algoa Bay in 1488. The **Main Public Library** ⓘ *T041-5858133, 0900-1700*, dominates the northwestern corner of Market Square. This fine early Victorian building, with its terracotta façade shipped out from the UK, dates from 1835 and started life as a courthouse. It was not until 1902 that it was officially opened as the public library. Outside by the road is a fine marble statue of Queen Victoria, erected in 1903. Once inside, visitors have the opportunity to view some beautiful early books.

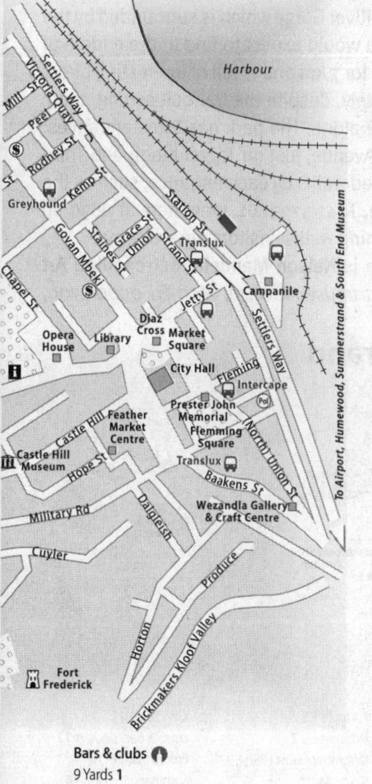

The **Prester John Memorial** stands in Fleming Square, behind City Hall. It is dedicated to the mythical king-priest and the Portuguese explorers who discovered South Africa. It was unveiled in 1886 and is thought to be the only monument in the world depicting Prester John. The monument is in the form of a large Coptic cross.

The **Campanile** ⓘ *Tue-Sat 0900-1230, 1330-1600, Sun-Mon 1400-1700*, is a 53-m bell-tower close to the docks down by the railway station. It was built to commemorate the landing of the 1820 settlers and was once the highest structure in PE. The views of the city and harbour remain impressive though, and if you're fit you can climb up 204 stairs to the observation room at the top. It contains the largest carillon of bells in the country as well as a chiming clock, and the tower is a useful reference point on the coast.

South of City Hall, near the Translux bus station, is the **Wezandla Gallery and Craft Centre** ⓘ *27 Baakens St, T041-5851185, www.wezandla.com, Mon-Fri 0900-1700, Sat 0900-1300*, hard to miss with its brightly painted exterior. This is an interesting collection of African art: wire and wood sculptures, woven baskets, pottery, crafts and curios. Many of the items are the work of local craftsmen and there are a reputed 25,000 items for sale.

Donkin Reserve is a public park in Central, high up on a hill with views of Govan Mbeki Avenue and the harbour. On the inland side of the park is the fine façade of the **Edward Hotel**; on the other side is a lighthouse and an unusual pyramid. The lighthouse dates from 1861 and is today home to the **Nelson Mandela Bay tourist office**. The rest of the lighthouse building can be opened on request. The odd-looking pyramid is actually a memorial erected by Sir Rufane Donkin in memory of his wife, Elizabeth, after whom the city was named. Local folklore is rather more sinister and suggests that her heart was buried in the pyramid. Rufane Donkin, a British colonialist and the former Cape Governor, was sent to administer PE in the late 19th century, but his wife Elizabeth never saw the town.

South of Donkin Reserve, **Castle Hill Museum** ⓘ *7 Castle Hill Rd, T041-5822515, Mon 1400-1700, Tue-Fri 1000-1300, 1400-1700, small entrance fee*, is housed in one of the oldest buildings in the city. It was built in 1827 for the Reverend Francis McCleland as the Rectory. The cottage has been restored to look like an early-Victorian home, complete with a slate roof, yellowwood floors and 19th-century furniture and household goods.

Continuing south on Belmont Terrace, is **Fort Frederick** ⓘ *daily, sunrise to sunset, free*. This was the first stone building in the Eastern Cape, completed in 1799. From its high point it overlooks the mouth of the Baakens River. It was built to stop any French troops from landing in the rivermouth but had the effect of helping the rebels at Graaff-Reinet. No shot has ever been fired from, or at, the fort.

Running through the town is the Baakens River Gorge which is surrounded by the well-kept, 54-ha **Settler's Park** – not what you would expect to find in the middle of South Africa's fifth largest city. The valley runs for 7 km and is full of interesting birds, plants and even some small buck. Unfortunately, despite the tranquil setting, there are occasional muggings, so don't come here alone. The park has three entrances: How Avenue, just off Park Drive; Chelmsford Avenue, just off Target Kloof; and Third Avenue, Walmer. Look out for the recommended walks by each entrance, such as the 8-km **Guinea Fowl Trail. Birdlife Eastern Cape**, T041-3793201, meet here at 0830 on the first Saturday of each month for birdwatching walks; visitors are welcome.

On the western fringes of the city centre is **Nelson Mandela Metropolitan Art Museum** ⓘ *1 Park Dr, T041-5861030, www.artmuseum.co.za, Mon-Fri 0900-1700,*

Humewood & Summerstrand

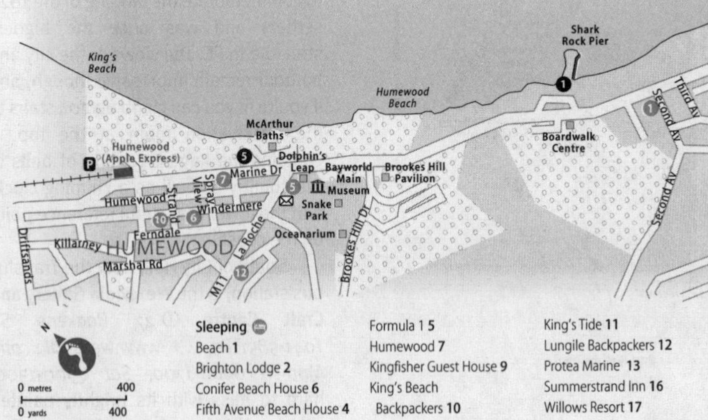

Sat-Sun 1400-1700, first Sun of every month 0900-1400, free. Formerly the King George VI Art Gallery, most of the collection on display is of 19th- and 20th-century British art, but there are also some good monthly contemporary exhibitions, accompanied by films and lectures. Other displays include a collection of oriental miniatures as well as pottery and sculpture.

The **Horse Memorial** standing on the corner of Russell and Cape roads was created after the Boer War. Between 1899 and 1902 thousands of horses died, more often through fatigue and starvation than from being slain in battle. The inscription on the memorial reads: "The greatness of a nation consists not so much in the number of its people or the extent of its territory as in the extent and justice of its compassion." The statue shows a man kneeling in front of a horse with a bucket in his hands making as if to feed or quench the horse's thirst.

Outside Central

Most visitors head for Port Elizabeth's beaches which lie to the east of the city centre in the suburbs of **Humewood** and **Summerstrand**, where there are a number of typically seaside attractions and facilities. There are also other beaches and a couple of game reserves within striking distance of the city.

In Humewood, **Bayworld** ⓘ *off Marine Dr, T041-5860650, www.bayworld.co.za*, comprises the Main Museum, Oceanarium and Snake Park (the Snake park was closed for renovation at the time of writing). The **Main Museum** ⓘ *daily 0900-1630, small entrance fee*, is a mix of natural and cultural history. Look out for the southern right whale skeleton, and the fully rigged models of early sailing ships. There is also a collection of objects collected from wrecks in and around Algoa Bay. The rest of the collection focuses on fossils and early man. The **Oceanarium** ⓘ *0900-1245, 1345-1700, R30, children R15, dolphin and seal shows daily 1100 and 1500, certified divers can dive in the shark tank on Wed at 1430, book ahead on T041-5835316*, has over 40 species of fish, as well as a ragged tooth shark tank, rays, turtles and African penguins. The most interesting part of the complex is the dolphin research centre, with seal and dolphin presentations which children will enjoy.

Also in Humewood is the **South End Museum** ⓘ *corner of Humewood Rd and Walmer Blvd, T041-5823325, Mon-Fri 0900-1600, Sat-Sun 1400-1700*. This museum is dedicated to the South End suburb, which was destroyed when the Group Areas Act in 1950 led to the forcible removal of the cosmopolitan population of the area. South End was one of the prime areas of the city because it was close to the centre of town, the beachfront and the harbour. During Apartheid, not only the blacks, Indians and coloureds were forcibly relocated from the city, but the Chinese too.

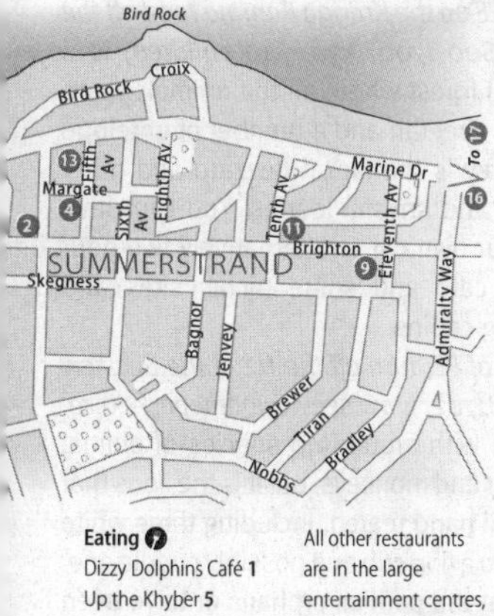

Townships

The townships around PE can be visited on a tour (see page 329). Walmer and New Brighton townships have been in existence since the 1800s when the region was mostly farmland. The **Red Location** in New Brighton is an area of tin shacks and got its name from the rusted corrugated iron used to build the shacks. Others surrounding the city are **Swartkops**, **Kwa-Zakhele** (meaning 'place to build yourself' in Xhosa) and **Motherwell** on the road to Addo, which

Eating
Dizzy Dolphins Café 1
Up the Khyber 5

All other restaurants are in the large entertainment centres, marked on the map

Sunshine Coast beaches

A combination of natural conditions and man-made developments means that the Algoa Bay beaches around Port Elizabeth form one of the most popular stretches of coast in South Africa. The water is clean, warm and calm for most of the year, making it an ideal spot for watersports.

The two main northern beaches are **New Brighton** – a good spot for swimming and fishing, with changing rooms, lifeguards, and a promenade – and **Bluewater Bay**, a long stretch of white sand with good swimming, but the lifeguards are only present during summer. To get to there by car, take the N2 towards Grahamstown and follow the signs.

There are six southern beaches which come right up to the city centre. **King's Beach** is the closest, lying between the harbour and Humewood. Being so close to the city it can get very busy, but the swimming is safe, boogie-boarding is allowed and there are lifeguards and changing facilities. This is probably the best beach for families as there is a go-kart track, mini-golf, children's playground, swimming-pool complex, and plenty of kiosks and snack bars. In contrast, **Humewood** is a quieter beach, which has been awarded the Blue Flag, the swimming is good and there is plenty of shade. The next beach, **Hobie Beach**, is marked by Shark Rock Pier. In the evenings this is a busy area due to the presence of The Boardwalk, an entertainment centre (see Bars and clubs, page 326). The swimming is safe and throughout the year there are local body surfing, beach volleyball and boardsailing competitions. Next up, **Pollock Beach** is one of the better surfing spots. Beyond the lighthouse at Cape Recife, **Sardinia Bay** is the most beautiful beach near the city and a marine reserve popular for snorkelling and scuba diving. Dolphins are often seen close to the beach on this stretch of coastline.

is reputedly the largest township in the Eastern Cape with its origins from the 1980s when the city's population swelled with people looking for work.

Game parks

Kragga Kamma Game Park ⓘ *15-min drive from PE on the Kragga Kamma road off the N2, T041-3794195, www.kraggakamma.com, 0800-1700, R30, R10 children*, is a private game reserve is in a lush tract of coastal forest where all the animals roam free. These include rhino, buffalo, giraffe, zebra, cheetah and a number of antelope including the shy nyala. The resident bird of prey is the jackal buzzard and other species include fish eagles, yellow billed kites and Knysna loeries. You can drive around the small network of gravel roads in your own car or alternatively two-hour guided game drives are on offer. There's a café and some picnic sites and accommodation in the way of safari tents and log cabins.

Seaview Game and Lion Park ⓘ *25 km west of PE, turn off the N2 at the Seaview sign, the park is 7.5 km towards the sea, T041-3781702, www.seaviewgamepark.co.za. 0900-1700, R30, R15 children*, is a wildlife park with around 40 species of animal including giraffe, zebra, wildebeest, impala, duiker and monkeys, but it is the lions that most people come to see. In total there are 55, all hand reared, including three white lion and, for an extra fee, visitors can get close up to a lion cub and possibly cuddle one. Except for the lions, many of the animals arrive at the park as orphans or have been injured and wherever possible are rehabilitated and returned to the wild. There are nature trails and self game drives, a restaurant and curio shop and a few stands for caravans and tents.

Sleeping

During the last few years Port Elizabeth has experienced a rapid expansion in tourist accommodation. Much of this has been in the seaside suburbs of Humewood and Summerstrand, and if you're looking for something close to the beach, it's perfect. The seafront area, however, is a modern and ugly stretch of high-rise blocks and shopping malls. The centre, around the Donkin Reserve, has more character and is far more appealing with a number of quiet back streets lined with some finely restored Victorian houses.

Central *p319, map p318*

B **Protea Hotel Edward**, Belmont Terr, T041-5862056, www.proteahotels.co.za. This building is a fine example of late 19th-century architecture and is one of Port Elizabeth's famous landmarks, its elegant façade bordering the Donkin Reserve. There are 110 comfortable double rooms with en suite bathroom, telephone and TV, some with good city views. The **Causerie** restaurant is rather fussy but nevertheless an excellent carvery. There is also a bar, lounge, laundry service and secure covered parking.

B **Millbrook House**, 2 Havelok Sq, T041-5853080, millbrook@eastcape.net. A delightful B&B in a leafy square in the centre of town. Victorian house with wrought-iron balconies, peaceful setting, perfect for seeing the sights. Family-run with 5 charming en suite rooms, with ceiling fans, TV with M-Net, clean, bright and airy. Small garden with splash pool, lounge, free airport pick-up. The owners are very friendly and welcoming. Excellent value. Recommended.

C **Calabash Lodge**, 8 Dollery St, T041-5856162, www.calabashlodge.co.za. Clean and comfortable guesthouse cum upmarket backpackers (though no dorms) in an ideal location for central sights. En suite double and family rooms, breakfast of homemade muffins and muesli, free pick-up from airport, station and bus terminal. Friendly, helpful, also run an excellent tour company offering ½-day trips to Addo and some worthwhile township tours. Recommended.

D **Port Elizabeth Backpackers**, 7 Prospect Hill, T041-5860697, pebakpak@global.co.za. Attractive old Victorian building with bright and airy dorms, some doubles, well-equipped kitchen, spacious lounge with fireplace, good location, small backyard, good travel centre.

D-E **Base Camp**, 58 Western Rd, T041-5823285, pebasecamp@yahoo.com. Large, functional backpackers in a good location in the centre of town. Double-storey Victorian building with Oregon floors and a fireplace in the dorm. Range of rooms with shared bathrooms and doubles with en suite bath or shower, TV, telephone, decent furnishings. Clean and practical place, good buffet breakfasts, kitchen, bar, and pool table. On the Baz Bus route and can provide free pick-up and drop-off from the airport.

D-E **Jikeleza Lodge**, 44 Cuyler St, T041-5863721, www.highwinds.co.za. Double rooms, dorms, 1 family room, kitchen, pleasant backyard, internet access, free pick-up across town, close to shops and some restaurants. Helpful set-up, keen to organize transport and tours.

Outside Central *p321, map p320*

The leafy suburb of Walmer is on the far side of St George's Park and southwest of the centre and is convenient for the airport, but not for the beach.

L **Hacklewood Hill Country House**, 152 Prospect Rd, Walmer, T041-5811300, www.pehotels.co.za. Luxurious guesthouse housed in a late-Victorian manor house full of antiques and paintings, 8 a/c tasteful double rooms, each with massive en suite bathrooms and DSTV. In the beautiful gardens is a swimming pool and tennis court, plus secure covered parking. Elegant dining room where you'll need to brush up on the use of silverware, and some special touches which make this a fine choice: guests, for example, are encouraged to select their wine from the impressive cellar. Advance booking essential during the peak season, no children under 14.

B-C **Oak Tree Cottages**, 112 Church Rd, Walmer, T041-5813611, www.oaktree.mrinfo.co.za. A well-run B&B with 5 double rooms with en suite bathroom, TV, kettle, fridge, and microwave, swimming pool, shady gardens, laundry, secure parking.

C **King George Guesthouse**, 2 King George Rd, Millpark, close to the cricket ground in St

George's Park, T041-3741825, www.kinggeorge.co.za. A mock-Tudor family home with plenty of space for guests. 8 double rooms with en suite bathroom, mini-bar and TV. There is also a study and a lounge, plus sizeable gardens with a swimming pool. Extra meals available on request.

C **Kragga Kamma Game Park**, 15-min drive from PE on the Kragga Kamma road off the N2, T041-3794195, www.kraggakamma.com. Family self-catering thatched lodges and chalets, with lounge, kitchen and undercover braai area, cheaper pre erected tents on platforms also with self catering facilities. All scattered around a pretty forest area where overnight guests are likely to encounter animal activity during the night.

Humewood and Summerstrand

AL **King's Tide**, 16 Tenth Av, Summerstrand, T041-5836023, www.kingstide.co.za. PE's first luxury boutique hotel, very stylish with 10 beautifully decorated suites, extravagant bathrooms, good gourmet breakfasts, dinner on request, bar, comfortable and friendly.

A **The Beach**, Marine Dr, Summerstrand, T041-5832161, thebeach@pehotels.co.za. Luxurious, low-rise hotel right on the beach. 58 well-appointed rooms, 3 restaurants, bar with ocean views from the patio, golf, large pool, laundry, secure parking, tidy gardens, good service, just across the road from Shark Rock pier and adjacent to the Boardwalk Centre, a short drive from the centre.

A-B **Protea Hotel Marine**, Marine Dr, Summerstrand, T041-5832101, www.marinehotel.co.za. Large, unattractive high-rise block just across from the beach. 66 a/c rooms and 7 suites with DSTV, comfortable but unimaginatively furnished, some rooms have great views of Pollock Beach and Algoa Bay. The **Connaught** restaurant has a good local reputation.

B **Brighton Lodge**, 21 Brighton Dr, Summerstrand, T041-5834576, www.brightonlodge.co.za. A very comfortable guesthouse where each of the 9 bedrooms has been decorated from a different period, all have en suite bathrooms, TV and a private entrance, walking distance from the Boardwalk and the beach. Recommended.

B **Conifer Beach House**, 39 Windermere Rd, Humewood, T041-5855959, www.conifer.co.za. Pretty house and garden with 4 self catering units with private entrances and patios, wooden floors, white linen, stylish furniture, TV, breakfast available, friendly hosts, recommended by readers.

B **Humewood**, 33 Marine Dr, T041-5858961, humewood@intekom.co.za. Attractive old-fashioned seaside building right on King's Beach. 91 rooms, most of which are sea-facing with small private balconies. Restaurant, bar, the morning coffee shop has a pleasant ambience and some seats on a terrace overlooking the street, though lacks a proper garden for children to enjoy.

B **Kingfisher Guest House**, 73 Brighton Dr, Summerstrand, T041-5832150, www.kingfisherpe.co.za. Family-run B&B close to the beach, with 6 en suite double rooms with en suite bathrooms, private entrance and patio, TV, fridge, microwave and toaster, lounge, disabled facilities, laundry, swimming pool and peaceful garden to relax in.

B **Summerstrand Inn**, Marine Dr, Summerstrand, T041-5833131, www.hotsummer.co.za. Large hotel with 237 spacious a/c rooms, TV, views of Humewood Golf Course, leafy gardens offer privacy around the pool area. **Palm Grill** restaurant, cosy **Boodles** bar, courtesy bus offered.

B-C **Fifth Avenue Beach House**, 5th Av, Summerstrand, T041-5832441, www.fifthave.co.za. Guests can stay in the main house or in a neat complex with a balcony overlooking the swimming pool. 10 double rooms with TV, garden has a tropical feel with several mature palm trees, 200 m from the beach. A friendly and good-value set-up. Recommended.

C-D **Formula 1**, Marine Dr, T041-5856380, www.formula1.co.za, corner of La Roche and Marine drives, next to the Oceanarium. Soulless basic modern accommodation units where the shower and loo are in a sort of cubicle in the corner, but clean and good value in an emergency. 88 basic rooms, same price for 1-3 people, breakfast packs can be bought in the lobby.

C-E **Lungile Backpackers**, 12 La Roche Dr, Humewood, T041-5822042, www.lungile-backpackers.co.za. Lively lodge set in a fine modern house about 10 mins' walk from Humewood Beach and the beachfront nightlife. Dorms in the main house and double rooms in separate wooden cabins at the back. Also has a garden with pool, TV and video lounge, bar, pool table, laundry, and a clean kitchen. Free use of surfboards. Great value. Recommended.

C-E Willows Resort, Marine Dr, Schoenmakerskop, T041-3661717, www.madibabayresorts.co.za. A large, self-contained complex with more than 70 caravan sites, and 70 sea-facing self catering chalets and rondavels with TV. Café serves snacks on the site during the day, plenty of extras for children: tidal pool, trampolines, mini golf, children's playground, rock fishing, tractor rides, quad bikes, tennis courts, and in season a crèche. Very popular in summer.

D-E King's Beach Backpackers, 41 Windermere Rd, Humewood, T041-5858113, www.backpackafrica.co.za. Set 2 blocks back from the beach and close to restaurants, bars and clubs. Comfortable dorms, slightly cramped double rooms set in individual buildings in the garden, and camping space on the lawn. Excellent kitchen facilities including free bread and jam, TV and video lounge, internet access, laid-back bar, travel centre. However have had recent reports about poor service from staff.

Eating

Port Elizabeth claims to have the highest per capita ratio of restaurants in South Africa, which for tourists means a wide choice without the inflated prices of Cape Town or Johannesburg. There are 2 purpose-built entertainment centres, **Brooke's Hill Pavilion** and **The Boardwalk**, where you will find a wide selection of restaurants and bars under one roof. These are similar to modern shopping malls – there is ample parking and visitors can feel more secure than they would wandering the streets at night. Away from these centres, most of the restaurants are either in the old city centre or close to the seafront in the suburbs of Humewood and Summerstrand.

Central *p319, map p318*

TT Causerie, Protea Hotel Edward, Belmont Terr, T041-5862056. Good for a buffet and carvery (on Sun) served in an old fashioned atmosphere, good value and plenty to eat.

TT Rome, 63 Campbell St, facing Russell Rd, T041-5862731. Well known for their pastas and pizzas which are cooked in a traditional Italian wood-burning oven. Generous portions served in a friendly manner, fun atmosphere, good value, check for the special daily pizzas. Recommended.

TT Royal Delhi, 10 Burgess St, T041-3738216, 1200-2330, closed Sun and Sat lunchtime. A very popular local curry house serving a full range of Indian dishes, famous for its messy crab curry. Large groups can eat in their own separate dining room.

TT Sabatino's, 35 Westbourne Rd, T041-3731707. 1200-1500, 1800-2200. Italian option where the quality of the food is matched by the ambience and attentive service. Recommended.

Outside Central *p321, map p320*

TTT Hacklewood Hill Country House, 152 Prospect Rd, Walmer, T041-5811300. Elegant dining room in a luxury guesthouse, open all day for breakfast, lunch, and dinner, romantic candlelit 4- to 5-course dinners, you'll need to know how to use the silverware, with wine suggestions for each course. Recommended for a special treat for couples, very romantic and intimate.

TTT Kyoto, Boardwalk Centre, T041-5831160. 1100-1400, 1800-2200, closed Mon-Tue lunch. PE's only upmarket Japanese restaurant, sit in a tatami – low tables in booths with cushions on the floor, or eat at the sushi bar, comprehensive menu and excellent service in Japanese inspired decor.

TT 34' South, Boardwalk Centre, T041-5831085. 1000-2200. Fabulous deli with all sorts of treats from olives to cookery books, chrome and glass decor, make up meals from the counters or chooses a selection of tapas, tables outside on the wooden deck.

TT Blackbeard's Tavern, Brookes Hill Pavilion, corner of Marine Dr and Brookes Hill Dr, Summerstrand, T041-5855567, closed Sun, reservations advised, dinner only. An à la carte seafood restaurant which has been run by the same family for 3 generations. Great ocean views and impressive fish tank displays, extensive range of seafood, steak, Italian, vegetarian and poultry dishes. Recommended.

TT The Connaught, Protea Hotel Marine, Marine Dr, Summerstrand, T041-5832101. A quality restaurant serving good seafood and meat dishes. Excellent all-you-can-eat carvery on Sun.

₶ **Lai Kung**, Boardwalk, Summerstrand, T041-5831123. 1130-2300. Large Chinese restaurant with a huge range of good-value dishes, plenty for vegetarians, quick service.

₶ **The Mediterranean Seafood House**, Dolphin's Leap, 9 Marine Dr, T041-5823981, 1200-1500, 1800-2130. Fashionable seafood restaurant overlooking the beach. Good grilled fish, calamari, sushi, some meat dishes, a Chinese stir-fry table where you make up your own meal and it's cooked in front of you, balcony with outdoor tables, good service. Booking essential at weekends.

₶ **Tapas al Sol**, Brookes Hill Pavilion, T041-5840660. Lively tapas bar, serving a limited range of tapas, plus steaks, pasta and salads. Turns into a boisterous bar and club at night.

₶ **Zorba's**, Dolphin's Leap, 9 Marine Dr, T041-5863804. 1800-late. Greek restaurant specializing in mezze and seafood. Romantic interior, good food, bar stays open after the restaurant has closed, non-smokers are advised to book as they get the smaller area.

Dizzy Dolphins Café, 1 Shark Rock Pier, T041-5834536. Trendy cocktail bar and restaurant serving seafood, steaks and salads. Popular with a young, lively crowd.

Up the Khyber, McArthur Baths complex, King's Beach. Cheap curries, burgers and steaks in a great setting right above the beach with casual wooden tables on the veranda. Try the rather unusual oxtail curry.

Cafés

Café Dulce, Boardwalk, Summerstrand, T041-5831193, and at Dolphin's Leap, Marine Drive, Humewood, T041-5823958. Great coffee shops open 0900-2200, selling tasty sandwiches, salads, milkshakes, ice creams; gets more alcoholic as the day gets longer.

Kafeehaus Maran, Brookes Hill Pavilion, corner of Marine Dr and Brookes Hill Dr, Humewood, T041-5855328. Good coffee, cakes and snacks.

The Verandah, Beach Hotel, Marine Dr, Humewood, T041-5832161. Attractive Mediterranean-style patio serving snacks and light meals.

Bars and clubs

Port Elizabeth *p317, map p318 and p320*

Port Elizabeth has a good choice of late-night bars and clubs, often offering meals in the early evening and live music or DJs later. As in all cities, clubs change regularly – for up-to-date information about what is the happening venue, ask at one of the backpackers or the waiters at **Tapas al Sol**. As in most South African cities, the biggest night out is Wed, although Fri and Sat come a close second. Some places have dress codes – this usually means no shorts, vests or sandals.

Most of the nightlife is focused at 2 major entertainment centres, **The Boardwalk** on Marine Drive by Shark Rock Pier and **Brookes Hill Pavilion** on the corner of Beach Rd and Brooke's Hill Drive in Summerstrand. These areas are safe to walk about at night, which is much of their appeal. In Central, the busiest area is along **Parliament St**, where there are a number of informal Kwaito clubs, but expect to attract quite a bit of attention if you're white and but be wary of walking here at night – stick to taxis.

9 Yards, Donkin St, T041-3929822, www.9yards.co.za. Wed and Sat, 2100-late. Hugely fashionable club with upstairs cocktail bar, stylish decor, expensive drinks and a well-heeled crowd. Its main appeal is its relaxed ambience and live DJs.

Barney's Tavern, The Boardwalk, T041-5834500. Atmospheric bar with live music every night as well as on Sat-Sun afternoons on 'The Deck'.

Tapas al Sol, Brookes Hill Pavilion, T041-5862159, www.tapas.co.za. Tapas bar and pub with extended happy hour on Thu, DJs on Fri and Sat, sometimes live SA rock bands.

Entertainment

Port Elizabeth *p317, map p318 and p320*

Cinema

All the latest releases from Europe and the US are shown, check the local newspapers for screenings. The main cinemas are: **Cinema Starz**, Boardwalk Complex, T041-5832000; **Nu-Metro**, Walmer Park Shopping Complex, T041-3671102; **and Ster-Kinekor**, The Bridge Mall, Cape Rd, T041-3630577.

Theatre

There are regular concerts and plays performed by local musical and performance groups. Check out the press for details or contact the Computicket call centre, T041-5863177, www.computicket.co.za.

The most popular venues in the city are: **The Feather Market Centre**, Baakens St, Central, T041-5855514; **The Opera House and Barn**, Whites Rd, Central, T041-5862256; and the **Ford Little Theatre**, Castle Hill Rd, Central, T041-5863625.

Festivals and events

Port Elizabeth *p317, map p318 and p320*

Feb Shakespearian Festival, a selection of plays are put on at the Mannville Open-Air Theatre in St George's Park. The theatre is named after the late Helen and Bruce Mann, who instituted the festival. A most enjoyable way to pass a summer's evening. **Prickly Pear Festival**, at Cuyler Manor Museum in Uitenhage, 34 km northwest of Port Elizabeth, on the last Sat in Feb. With over 250 products on sale, crowds of over 25,000 turn up each year to enjoy food such as pancakes, ginger beer, *potjiekos*, jam, spitbraais, fish braais, curry bunnies, and homemade pudding.

Easter Splash Festival, www.splashfestival.com, 4-day beach festival over the Easter weekend with watersports, surfing competitions, live music and fireworks. Very popular annual event that attracts 200,000 daily and fundraiser for the Community Chest.

Apr Arts and Crafts Fair, held in Walmer Town Hall. An annual event designed to provide local artists with their first opportunity to display and sell their products. A good place to find some unique pieces at bargain prices.

Oct Addo Rose Show, a massive display with over 25,000 blooms on show, including new varieties. An enjoyable day out for anyone keen on gardens.

Nov Evening Post Mini Marathon, a 10-km fun run to help raise money for charity.

Dec Opening of the Summer Entertainment Programme, very much for families. The mayor gets the show rolling by turning on the Christmas lights and there is a firework display on the beach. There is also a 4-day ski-boat race from Port Elizabeth to East London.

Shopping

Port Elizabeth *p317, map p318 and p320*

Flea markets

Art in the Park, St George's Park, located along Park Drive. An open-air exhibition of craft stalls and local art on the first Sun of every month.

Humewood Beachfront, between the King's Beach parking area and McArthur's Baths, Sat and Sun but everyday over school holiday periods.

Shopping malls

Like all South African cities, Port Elizabeth has its share of modern shopping malls where not just shops but banks and post offices are located. Most well-known chain stores have relocated from the city centre to these malls. Shops are open Mon-Fri 0900-1800, and longer over the weekend, restaurants and cinemas until 2200-2300.

Bridge Shopping and Entertainment Centre, Langenhoven Dr, Greenacres, is a giant upmarket centre, built over a main road with great views from its elevated position. There are 8 cinemas, ATMs, restaurants, coffee shops and fast food outlets, plus a smart fashion mall for those with spare cash.

Other shopping centres include: **Greenacres Shopping Centre**, adjacent to Bridge Shopping Centre; **Pier 14 Shopping Centre**, 444 Govan Mbeki Av, North End, a central location but more downmarket than the others; and **Walmer Park Shopping Centre**, Main Rd, Walmer.

Activities and tours

Port Elizabeth *p317, map p318 and p320*

Port Elizabeth has excellent facilities catering for sports, especially watersports, golf, tennis, yachting and athletics. It is also a great city in which to watch sport and is often dubbed by locals as 'Sport Elizabeth'.

Boat trips

Algoa Bay is world renowned in sailing circles and there are 2 prestigious yacht clubs in the city, www.pebyc.co.za. There are 2 prevailing winds which produce either very rough and choppy conditions or calm and flat conditions. Southern right whales mate and calve between Jul-Oct in the bay, humpback whales pass by during Jun-Jul, and again in Nov-Dec, and the sardine eating Bryde's whale is present through most of the year. Also be on the look out for Cape fur seals, penguins, bottlenose dolphins, gannets and cormorants.

Diving in Nelson Mandela Bay

There are a number of good dive sites around Port Elizabeth and the best time for diving is during the winter months of May to September when average visibility is 8-15 m. There are a variety of dive sites from colourful reefs, drop-offs, to shipwrecks and soft corals. The best diving in the area is around **St Croix Islands**, 20 km from Port Elizabeth harbour. The average dive is along a slope with a maximum depth of 30 m, where there are a few caves and gullies. The islands and the surrounding waters are protected and fishing and spearfishing are not permitted and it is forbidden to land on the islands. A consequence of this has been a flourishing population of jackass penguins, gulls, terns and cormorants on land, while the surrounding waters are rich in marine life, providing a plentiful diet for the birds. Other popular local dives are **Thunderbolt Reef**, **Sardinia Bay**, **Devil's Reef**, **Roman Rock** and **Philip's Reef**. There are also some good wreck dives at the **Pati**, on Thunderbolt Reef; the **Inchcape Rock** wreck – this steel hull from 1902 suffers from poor visibility; the **Western Knight** wreck (experienced wreck divers only); and the **Haerlem** wreck, a navy vessel sunk in 1987 to 21 m specifically for divers. The tourist office has a useful leaflet, *Dive Port Elizabeth*, outlining the major dive sites. The following dive operators can organize daily trips:
Ocean Divers International, 10 Albert Road, Walmer, T041-5815121, www.odipe.co.za.
Pro Dive, Walmer Park Shopping Mall, T041-3687880, www.prodive.co.za. Pro Dive can also organize cage diving in the shark tank at the Oceanarium.

Polani Ocean Cruises, T041-5832141, www.polani.com. Offers breakfast and sunset cruises on an 65-ft schooner.
Raggy Charters, T041-3782528, www.raggycharters.netfirms.com. Runs marine life watching trips into the Algoa Bay and to islands that form the marine section of the Greater Addo National Park, beachfront cruises from 1 ½-3 hrs, and half- or full-day fishing trips using a variety of craft.

Cricket

Port Elizabeth is home to the **Eastern Province Cricket Board**. Matches are played at **St George's Park Cricket Oval**, also now known as the 'Crusaders Ground', ticket enquiries, T041-5864259, leighd@cricket.co.za. The first Test match played here was between South Africa and England on 12 Feb 1889, which was also the first Test match to be played in Africa. St George's is a pleasant old stadium with a capacity for 22,000 and an enjoyable venue to watch cricket. The 2 ends are known as the Duckpond End and the Park Drive End. There has been a cricket club here since 1843. Semi-final matches were played here during the 2003 Cricket World Cup.

Football

Between Feb and Oct there are afternoon games every weekend. There is a fundamental sporting division in South Africa: rugby and cricket is for whites; soccer is for blacks. These ridiculous divisions mean that local whites often discourage white visitors who want to see a match – ignore them, but contact the tourist office about safety issues for visitors. The principal venues are the Gelvandale Stadium in Liebenberg Rd; the **Westbourne Oval** in Westbourne Rd; the **Moore Dyke Playing Fields** in Schauder and the **Gelvandale Playing Fields**, in Stanford Rd. For match details contact **The South African Football Association (SAFA) Eastern Cape**, T041-4513716, safaep@telkomsa.net. Port Elizabeth is expected to be the venue for some important matches in the 2010 Football World Cup and a new 60,000 stadium is being built.

Golf

There are several golf courses in and around the city, but the best bet for visitors is the **Port Elizabeth Golf Club**, T041-3743140, pegolf@wmeb.co.za, accessed from Westview Dr, Mill Park, a 100-year-old beautifully maintained 18 hole/par 73 course, or the **Humewood Golf Club**, T041-5832137, www.humewoodgolf.co.za, Marine Dr, Summerstrand, rated as one of the top 10 courses in the country, 18 holes/72 par with a very elegant clubhouse.

Horse racing

There are 2 major racecourses, **Arlington** and **Fairview**, both managed by East Cape Racing, T041-3721859, ecrpromark@intekom.co.za. There are races every Fri afternoon at both of the 2 courses throughout the year.

Horse riding

Note that some of these are a 30-min drive from the city centre.
Heavenly Stables, Sardinia Bay Rd, T041-3661038. Beach rides and trails.
Rothman Place, Lovemore Park, Sardinia Bay, T041-3675234. 35 years established, beach and trails rides, lessons.

Mountain biking

There are a number of mountain bike trails around the city. The **Baakens River Trail** is a 23-km circuit right in the middle of Port Elizabeth in a unique valley; although surrounded by an urban environment, it has plenty of examples of indigenous vegetation. The trail starts from the car park at Dodds Farm, off 9th Av, Walmer, and ends at Abelia Crescent in Sunridge Park. Concrete bollards with a bicycle painted on them mark the trail. The **Swartkops Trail** is a 22-km circular route in the Swartkops Valley Nature Reserve, an 850-ha reserve on the northern outskirts of town. The reserve was created in 1993 to protect an area of threatened valley bushveld as well as local bird-breeding colonies. This is a much more difficult trail with sections where some riders are likely to push their bikes up the escarpment. You will need to wear a helmet and have a full puncture repair kit – do not ride this trail alone. The route is marked by a blue arrow and bicycle motif on concrete bollards; the start is at the Corobrik brick factory next to the Bramlin-Markman Highway.
Beachbreak Adventure Centre, 3rd Av, Central, T041-3640830. Organized trips and mountain-bike rental.

Rugby

Port Elizabeth is home to the Eastern **Province Rugby Union**, T041-5835252, www.elephantsrugby.co.za, founded in 1888. Matches are played at Telkom Park, which has a capacity of around 34,000.

Surfing

Good waves on this stretch of coast aren't restricted to **Jeffrey's Bay**. The Pipe in **Algoa Bay** is one of the most popular spots, as is **Millars Point** further to the west. One drawback of the waves closer to town is the crowded beaches and the industrial backdrop.
Beachbreak Adventure Centre, (see Mountain biking, above). The best people to talk to about local conditions. Sells and rents surfing gear as well as mountain bikes.

Swimming

The beaches around Port Elizabeth are very clean, but the sea temperature rarely gets above 21ºC. Away from the large hotels there are a couple of excellent municipal swimming pools.
McArthur Baths, King's Beach Promenade, T041-5863412, Sep-Apr daily 0700-1700. Tidal pool, children's water-chute, splash pool, freshwater pool, permanent lifeguard, restaurant and snack bar.
St George's Park Baths, St George's Park, T041-5857751, Sep-Apr Mon-Fri 0700-2100, Sat 0900-1800, Sun 1030-1800. Olympic-size pool with diving facilities, children's pool, restaurant, snack bar.

Tour operators

Most of the companies offer a similar range of local tours; shop around, and apart from the price, check what sort of vehicle you'll travel in (in the summer it's not much fun being stuck in the back of a Land Rover without a/c), how many people will be in the group, and if the price includes entrance fees, guides and refreshments. In general, there are 3 types of tours on offer: historical town tours which may involve walking; township tours, which are growing in popularity; and wildlife tours, with visits to one or more of the local game reserves (Greater Addo Elephant National Park and Shamwari Game Reserve are the most popular). For a full list of tour operators, contact the tourist office.

Calabash Tours, 8 Dollery St, Central, T041-5856162, www.calabashtours.co.za. Excellent city tours, including visits to various townships, visits to local artists and self-help projects, and evening shebeen tours. Also runs tours to Greater Addo Elephant National Park, Shamwari Game Reserve and visits to the beaches. Minimum 2 people. Good value, highly recommended, this company was joint winner of the 2004 Responsible Tourism Award at the World Travel Market in London.

Friendly City Tours, T041-5851801, T083-2709739 (mob). Historical and sightseeing tours of Port Elizabeth's monuments. Trips last up to 1½ hrs plus longer visits to Addo.

Fundani Cultural Tours, 69 Theko St, Kwa-Magxaki, T/F041-4631471, cultours@iafrica.com. Cultural tours of the townships, tours last 2-3 hrs and cost from R330 per person. They generally involve visits to places of historical and cultural importance, viewings of local art and a stop at a shebeen for a drink and a meal. Travel is by minibus taxi, and they now have their own township B&B in New Brighton for overnight stays.

Shield Tours, T041-4535513, www.shieldtours.co.za. Historical tours and trips to the game parks.

Xhosa Tours, T072-7606881, xts@webmail.co.za. Township tour operator also based in New Brighton.

Windsurfing

Experienced windsurfers have the opportunity to go out at Noordhoek, where they are totally exposed to the ocean swell, but it is important to check the tides. There are excellent reef breaks and cross-shore conditions when the southwest wind blows. Off Hobie Beach the conditions are much calmer, particularly when there is a southwest wind. Be careful at all times to avoid the designated public bathing areas. The Swartkop River Mouth is a good area for beginners as the conditions are calm. Some of the hotels on the beach front in Summerstrand and Humewood have equipment to rent out to residents.

Transport

Port Elizabeth *p317, map p318 and p320*

72 km to **Greater Addo Elephant National Park**; 643 km to **Bloemfontein**; 763 km to **Cape Town**; 295 km to **East London**; 124 km to **Grahamstown**; 246 km to **Graaff-Reinet**; 79 km to **Jeffrey's Bay**; 1,050 km to **Johannesburg**; 150 km to **Port Alfred**; 74 km to **Shamwari Game Reserve**.

Air

Port Elizabeth airport is 4 km from the city on Alister Miller Dr, T041-5077319. There are several daily connections with the other major cities on **South African Airways (SAA)**, **Kulula**, **Comair** and **Nationwide** (see p37 for contact details). For airport shuttles into the town centre, contact **Pembury Tours**, T041-5812581, or alternatively there are plenty of taxis at the airport. Several car hire groups have a desk in the terminal, see below for contact numbers.

Bus

Long distance Baz Bus, T021- 4392323, www.bazbus.com. Provides the best budget bus travel service along the coast between Cape Town and Durban. Port Elizabeth is the midway point where the bus stays overnight. In other words, if you start the day in Cape Town and are heading towards Durban, Port Elizabeth is the furthest you can get in a single day. There is a daily service to **Cape Town** and it runs 5 days a week to **Durban**. The Baz Bus arrives in Port Elizabeth from both Cape Town and Durban 2100-2200 and departs 0630-0730.

The 3 mainline bus companies have daily departures linking the other major cities. Reservations can be booked through **Computicket**, Greenacres Centre, T041-3630576, www.computicket.co.za, or at the opera house, T041-5858648.

Greyhound, T041-5864879, www.greyhound.co.za. Coaches arrive/depart from the rear car park, 107 Govan Mbeki Av, and in front of Edgars at the Greenacres Shopping Centre. **Intercape**, T041-5861165, www.intercape.co.za. Coaches arrive/depart from the office in the Flemming Building behind the Old Post Office, corner of Flemming and North Union Sts. **J-Bay Sunshine Express**, T042-2932221. A 24-hr door-to-door minibus

The Apple Express

This historic narrow gauge steam train, similar to the Outeniqua Choo-Tjoe in the Western Cape, carries tourists on day trips through some beautiful countryside. The service is operated by a voluntary, non-profit making society formed solely for the restoration and maintenance of the famous narrow gauge trains. The trains run on a track which is only 61-cm-wide. The 310-km line runs between Port Elizabeth and Avontuur in the Langkloof, which includes a branch line to Hankey and Patensie. The train stops to allow passengers to stretch their legs and buy a cool drink from the Apple Tavern buffet coach in the middle of the train. Much of the line has been restored and renovations have started at the stations. The service is still quite irregular with trips running roughly every second weekend of the month, usually to Thornhill and back, R120, R60 children. Information is available at Humewood Station, T041-5072333, www.apple-express.com, or through Nelson Mandela Bay Tourism. In recent years Spoornet has run the Amazing Train Race where teams of 10 runners running in relay try to beat the train 74 km to Lourie.

service to **Jeffrey's Bay**. Also available for group hire – a group of surfers can hire the bus for a day to take them to a particular bay which can only normally be accessed by private transport. **Translux**, T041-3921333, www.translux.co.za. Coaches start/finish their journey by the railway station in the centre of town, then stop at the office, Ernst and Young Building, Ring Rd, Greenacres. If arriving by bus check with your hotel which is the most convenient stop for their location.

Car hire

Avis, airport T041-5017200, toll free T0861-021111, www.avis.co.za,. **Budget**, airport T041-5814242, toll free T0861-016622, www.budget.co.za. **Imperial**, airport T041-5811268, toll free T0861-131000, www.imperialcarrental.co.za. **Tempest/Sixt Car Hire**, airport T041-5811256, toll free T0860-031666, www.tempestcarhire.com. **Thrifty**, airport T041-5811259, toll free T0861-002111, www.thrifty.co.za.

Taxi

Hurters Radio Cabs, T041-5855500. Local company that rather astonishingly has been operating in PE for 75 years.

Train

The railway station is in the town centre on Station St, just off Strand St which runs parallel to Govan Mbeki Av. Information T041-5072662, reservations T0860-008888, www.spoornet.co.za. There are services between PE and **Johannesburg** and **Bloemfontein**. Train schedules and fares are published on the website.

Directory

Port Elizabeth *p317, map p318 and p320*
Embassies and consulates Germany, 11 Uitenhage Rd, T041-4872840, Mon-Fri 0830-1230. UK, 5th floor, First Bowring House, 66 Ring Rd, Greenacres, T041-3638841, Mon-Fri 0900-1230. **Internet** You can access the internet at all the backpacker lodges and some hotels. Otherwise, there is **Fantasia Internet** at the Bridge Shopping Centre, T041-3634681. **Medical services** Netcare **Greenacres Hospital**, Ring Rd, Greenacres, T041-3907000, private hospital. **St George's Hospital**, Park Dr, Central, T041-3926011. **British Airways Travel Clinic**, 19 Westbourne Rd, Central, T041-3747471, www.travel clinic.co.za. **Post office** Main Post Office: 259 Govan Mbeki Av, T041-5084039, Mon-Fri 0800-1700, Sat 0830-1300. **Useful address and telephone numbers** Immigration: corner of Stone and Lavinia Sts, T041-4871026, for visa extensions, Mon- Fri 0800-1500. **Police**, T10111. **Surf and Sea Rescue**, T041-5073911.

West of Port Elizabeth

From Port Elizabeth the N2 heads west for around 190 km to Storms River and the Tsitsikamma National Park at the eastern end of the Garden Route. Although Tsitsikamma is officially in the Eastern Cape and Storms River marks the provincial boundary, we deal with it in the Western Cape chapter along with the rest of the Garden Route. This stretch of road is nowhere near as scenic as the Garden Route itself, though there are a few attractions if you veer off the N2. These include the modern town of Jeffery's Bay, famous for its internationally good surf, a few interesting nature reserves, and the tranquil village of St Francis Bay and its neighbour, the upmarket resort of Cape St Francis. ▸▸ *For Sleeping, Eating and other listings, see pages 335-337.*

Van Stadens Wild Flower Reserve

ⓘ *The reserve has a visitor centre, nursery and a picnic site. 0800-1700. For more information contact the reserve manager, T041-9560155.*

The N2 from Port Elizabeth to Humansdorp passes directly through the middle of the wild flower reserve. The turning into the reserve is 35 km from Port Elizabeth. Established to protect and propagate indigenous flora, the area is also worth visiting for its butterflies and birds. The best time to visit is between February and August when many of the plants are in bloom. Plants to look out for include ground orchids and proteas. The southern part of the reserve is an interesting area of forest with ironwood and wild pomegranate trees, as well as a rare tree species, the Cape star-chestnut.

There are two short walks through the different ecosystems of the reserve: the **River Walk**, 3 km, passes the nursery and follows the course of the Van Stadens River; the **Forest Walk**, 2 km, enters an area that has been replanted with proteas. From the highest point of the walk there are views of riverine forest in the valleys and gorge below.

Langkloof

Three mountain ranges lie to the north of the N2 and Jeffrey's Bay: the **Kouga**, the **Baviaanskloof** and the **Grootwinterhoek**, known collectively as the 'Langkloof'. The region became the meeting point of San hunter-gatherers and Khoi pastoralists – known collectively as the Khoisan. Their rock art stands testament to their existence in overhangs and caves throughout the area.

At 270,000 ha, the Langkloof is the third largest wilderness region in South Africa.

One of the most fascinating routes to take through the Langkloof is to follow the R331 from Thornhill on the N2, 92 km west of Port Elizabeth, along the Baviaanskloof River Valley between Patensie and Willowmore. The road meanders through a landscape dominated by the red sandstone hills on either side. The hills are rich in proteas, ericas, orchids and the 'drie-bessie-bos', an endemic plant which can only be seen in this area. As the road climbs further up the river valley, the scenery becomes more rugged with the mountains rising to over 1600 m. The mountains are a maze of cliffs and ravines inhabited by baboons and tortoises; the trails here pass through thick areas of woodland where you can see the unique Baviaanskloof cedar. Views from the top of the mountains look over the acacia woodland to the fruit farms in the valleys below. Eland and Cape mountain zebra have recently been reintroduced, and kudu, bushbuck, klipspringer and baboon are present.

This region offers some of the wildest areas for hiking in the Eastern Cape, and hikes here are strenuous and involve some long climbs. Summers here are too hot for long hikes so it makes sense simply to drive through the area. March to November is cooler and more suitable for hiking. For information check out www.baviaans.co.za or www.baviaanskloof.net, or go to the **Tolbos Country Shop and Restaurant** ⓘ *on the R331 in the Gamtoos Valley, roughly 30 km north of the N2, T042-2830437.*

Jeffrey's Bay

» pp335-337. Colour map 7, grid B4.

Jeffrey's Bay, or 'J-Bay' as it's known locally, is surf central. Home to the 'perfect wave', this is an internationally acclaimed surfing spot and a major playground for self-respecting surf rats. In the evenings, the local bars buzz with talk of supertubes and perfect breaks. Waves can get big, sometimes as high as 3 m giving rides of over three minutes, but J-Bay is surprisingly renowned for its safety. Unsurprisingly, J Bay attracts more than its fair share of long-term resident travellers, but away from the beach, there's little going on in town. There are numerous surf shops selling a wide range of boards and wetsuits, as well as Billabong and Quiksilver factory outlets, but when surf's up don't be surprised to find many of the local businesses closed.

> *For hourly information on surfing conditions, swell maps, satellite images, moon and tide data, weather forecasts and wave graphics visit www.jbaytv.co.za.*

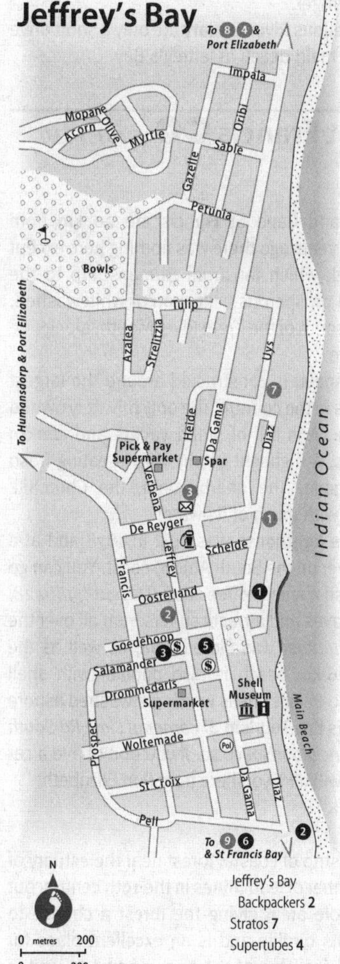

Sleeping
Beach Cabanas 3
Diaz 15 Holiday Apartments 1
Guesthouse 8
Island Vibe 9
Jeffrey's Bay Backpackers 2
Stratos 7
Supertubes 4

Eating
Breakers 1
De Viswijf 2
Die Walskipper 6
Le Grotto 3
Sunflower Café 5

Ins and outs

Getting there If you don't have a car the **J-Bay Sunshine Express**, T042-2932221, will bring you here on request from Port Elizabeth. The town is served by the **Baz Bus** (for further details, see Transport page 337). The nearest drop-off for the mainline buses (**Greyhound** and **Translux**) is in Humansdorp.

Tourist information Jeffrey's Bay Tourism ⓘ *corner of Da Gama and Darommedaris Rds in the Shell Museum complex, T042-2932923, www.jeffreysbaytourism.com, Mon-Fri 0830-1700, Sat 0900-1200*, are helpful and enthusiastic, although backpacker hostels offer the best practical information about surfing.

The origins of Jeffrey's Bay date to 1894, when a trading post was established here by Joseph Avent Jeffrey, a whaler from the island of St Helena. The trading post received goods by sea and supplied settlers living inland in the Langkloof. Little of the original settlement remains and today Jeffrey's Bay is a sprawl of unattractive bungalows and holiday homes. Out of season in summer, when most of the coast is at its liveliest, the resort is a quiet and desolate place and there's little of the surfing scene or nightlife you might expect. In winter, however, when the waves are at their best, the town comes back to life. July is also when the **Billabong Pro J-Bay** surf competition is held – with prize money amounting to US$250,000 which draws surfers from across the globe and the town gets packed out. This is a major surfing event, and you'll get to see some of the best surfers in the world compete. Visit www.billabongpro.com.

Sights

The waves here are definitely the main attraction, but as an alternative, the **Shell Museum** makes for an interesting visit. The collection is incredibly large and has many rare examples of Indo-Pacific and southern Cape shells found on nearby beaches. The position of Jeffrey's Bay along the coast happens to coincide with the meeting point of two opposing ocean currents, which explains why so many unusual shells have been found on the local beaches. Some shells have been carried all the way down the western coast of Africa. The collection was put together over a 30-year period and left to the town by Charlotte Kritzinger.

Aston Bay, **Paradise Beach** and the **Kabeljous River Estuary** are only a short drive away and make a pleasant change from the main beach in Jeffrey's Bay.

St Francis Bay and Cape St Francis » pp335-337.

Colour map 7, grid B4.

The adjoining villages of St Francis Bay and Cape St Francis are 20 km from Humansdorp, just off the R330. Less than 40 years ago there was nothing here except fine, white-sand beaches and a mule track which ran from Humansdorp to the lighthouse at Cape St Francis. These days a prosperous collection of whitewashed, thatched holiday homes line the beach just south of the Krom River Mouth, alongside an 18-hole golf course and a shopping centre.

A modern marina development, **The Canals**, is constructed around the largest manmade web of canals in the country. The only privately owned harbour in South Africa, it is full of smart yachts and *chokka* (calamari) fishing boats. A highlight of any visit is eating fresh calamari on the quayside. The nearby dam, the Churchill, supplies Port Elizabeth with much of its water.

This bay was named by the Portuguese explorer Manuel Perestrelo in 1575. St Francis is the patron saint of sailors.

The **Cape St Francis lighthouse** was built in 1878 and at a height of 27.75 m is the tallest stonework tower on the South African coast. You can go on a tour of the lighthouse, where there is also a small **coffee shop** ① *T042-2980428, daily 0900-1630*. The bay is famous for its waves and attracts surfers from all over the world. In 1963 the surfing movie *Endless Summer* was filmed here, as well as the remake *Endless Summer II* in 1992. The 16-km beach is also popular with shell collectors who come in search of the rare Indo-Pacific shells which are washed ashore by currents. For information, contact **St Francis Bay Tourism** ① *corner of Lime Rd South and St Francis Dr, T042-2940076, www.stfrancistourism.co.za.* If you don't have a car the **J-Bay Sunshine Express**, T042-2932221, will take you here from Port Elizabeth.

Maitland Nature Reserve

Facing St Francis Bay, the reserve is a small strip of coastal forest near the estuary of the Maitland River. This was the site of a number of lead mines in the 19th century but as these were abandoned so was the whole area, giving the forest a chance to recover. The reserve is now renowned for its birdlife and is an excellent place for seeing paradise flycatchers and Knysna louries. One of the best months to visit is October, when many of the forest plants are either flowering or in fruit.

The 3-km **Sir Peregrine Maitland Trail** is a leisurely walk through forest along an old wagon trail; the 9-km **De Stades Trail** covers the length and breadth of the reserve, passing through small areas of dune forest and open grassland.

Sleeping

Jeffrey's Bay *p333, map p333*

As the best-known surfing spot in South Africa, Jeffrey's Bay attracts large numbers of surfers from all over the world. Consequently, there is a good range of budget accommodation here. Each backpacker place has its own scene and you're bound to come across people who are staying there for the whole season.

AL **Diaz 15 Holiday Apartments**, 15 Diaz Rd, T042-2931779, www.diaz15.co.za. 8 2- or 3-bedroom luxury self-catering apartments, with fully equipped kitchens with microwave, large lounge with open balcony overlooking the beach, 2 bathrooms, TV with M-Net, linen included, towels available on request, perfect for families looking for a high standard of comfort right on the beach, walking distance to the shops and restaurants. Very popular, so you'll need to book several months in advance.

B **The Guesthouse**, 17 Flame Cres, Wavecrest, T042-2931878, theguesthouse@eastcape.net. Variety of accommodation available: a self-contained thatched cottage which can sleep up to 4, with a fully equipped kitchen and TV; a honeymoon suite with an oval bath and champagne on arrival in your room; plus 3 other double rooms with bathrooms. Set in a secure walled garden, close to the beach and a shopping centre. The owner offers excellent advice, information and hospitality. Recommended.

B **Stratos**, 11 Uys St, T042-2931116, www.stratos-za.com. A modern brick house on the seafront set in a quiet residential district. 8 luxury double rooms with en suite shower/bath, TV, 4 of which have sea views, non-smoking room, solar-heated swimming pool. Swiss owners, Italian, French and German spoken.

B-C **Supertubes**, 6, 10-12 Pepper St, T042-2932957, www.supertubesguesthouse.co.za. Laid-back B&B set 30 m from the beach and supertubes wave, 14 en suite double rooms with balcony, or more luxurious suites with extras like a/c and heated towel rail, set across 4 houses. Meals are available on request or there's a kitchen and dining area for guests' use.

C **Beach Cabanas**,118 Da Gama Road, T042-2932820, www.beachcabanas.co.za. Located 150 m from the beach, small attractive swimming pool surrounded by palms, smart modern flats on 2 storeys with kitchenette, heater, fan and TV, good breakfasts. One reader reports excellent service and friendly and helpful owners.

C-E **Island Vibe**, 10 Dageraad St, T042-2931625, www.islandvibe.co.za. This hostel has an excellent location at the top end of Jeffrey's Bay, perched high up with views across 2 beaches, steps down to the beach. Dorms, doubles, and camping, kitchen, bar, café serving set evening meals and good breakfasts. The place has a big surfer scene, so don't expect to get much sleep. Music from the bar pumps out through the night. Very popular and perfect for a couple of day's partying. The new and quieter **Beach House** has en suite doubles and open-plan kitchen and lounge with great sea views. Rents out bikes, canoes, fishing rods and, of course surfboards. A new activity is a walking tour to the local township. Also has a good travel centre and internet access, and is the location of **Jeffrey's Bay Surf School** (see Activities and tours, below). If you stay here you get 10% off in the Billabong factory shop. Offers a free pick up from buses in Humansdorp and is a Baz Bus stop. All in all, recommended to get a genuine feel of what J-Bay is all about.

D-E **Jeffrey's Bay Backpackers**, 12 Jeffrey St, T042-2931379, www.jeffreysbaytourism.com. This was the first backpacker place to open in Jeffrey's Bay. It is well run and remains popular, but there are rather too many rules to follow. It does have a good location in the centre of town, close to Main Beach, small dorms, 5 double rooms, camping in garden, off-street parking, reductions can be negotiated for long stays, well-stocked and clean kitchen, bedding provided, hires out surfboards and bikes. Baz Bus stop and pick ups can be arranged from Humansdorp.

For an explanation of the sleeping and eating price codes used in this guide, see inside the front cover. Other relevant information is found in Essentials pages 42-47.

St Francis Bay and Cape St Francis *p334*

AL The Sands @ St Francis, 8 Frank Rd, T/F042-2941888, www.thesands.co.za. Smart, comfortable guesthouse just a few mins from the beach. Attractive thatched house with 5 en suite a/c rooms, bathrooms have jacuzzi bath tubs and separate showers, each with its own timber deck overlooking the beach, some with private outside shower and jacuzzi. Swimming pool, sun deck, steam room, beauty therapies on request, breakfast and gourmet dinners served in a very unusual octagonal restaurant with thatched roof and glass walls with a 360-degree view. Recommended, but pricey.

A The Beach House, 4 Frank Rd, T042-2941225, www.stfrancisbay.co.za. Beautiful guesthouse set right on the beach. 4 luxurious and stylish rooms, 2 with ocean views, 2 overlooking the pool, excellent breakfasts, also evening meals by prior arrangement, attentive unfussy service. Recommended.

A-B Port Hotel, at the marina, T042-2940015, www.porthotel.co.za. Modern upmarket hotel in the heart of the Port St Francis marina overlooking the fishing boats and yachts, Mediterranean architecture, a range of 40 well furnished rooms with DSTV from standard twins to penthouses, several restaurants, swimming pool.

B Cape St Francis Resort, Da Gama Rd, Cape St Francis, T042-2980054, www.capestfrancis.co.za. Good value holiday resort with a range of accommodation, superior thatched cottages with 3 bedrooms, kitchen and lounge, en suite chalets with 1 bedroom, 110 caravan and camping sites (**D**), ablution blocks and self-catering facilities, **Park Off Pub** and **Joe Fish Restaurant**. The on-site adventure centre can organize a number of activities from boat rides to deep-sea fishing.

B Thatchwood, 63 Lyme Rd, T042-2940082, www.thatchwood.com. Smart and comfortable thatched guesthouse overlooking the local golf course with private access across the fairways to the beach. 7 double rooms with en suite bathroom and TV, meals served on the lawn or from an open dining room, bar.

B-C Port View Place, Leighton Hullet Dr, Port St Francis, T042-2941553, www.portviewplace.co.za. Towards the back of the marina development, small B&B with 4 tastefully decorated en suite rooms, a 2-bedroom apartment, spacious lounge, breakfast on balcony with harbour views.

C Seal Point Backpackers, Da Gama Rd, Cape St Francis, T042-2980284, www.seals.co.za. Great-value upmarket backpacker lodge (no dorms) 400 m from the beach, with well-kept self-catering apartments, each with TV, en suite bathrooms and open-plan kitchen, plus balconies with sea views. Good restaurant and bar downstairs serving cheap meals, braai area, pool, popular with surfers. Organize booze cruises on the canal. Will pick up from the Baz Bus at Humansdorp by prior arrangement. .

Eating

Jeffrey's Bay *p333, map p333*

TT Breakers, Ferreira St, T042-2931801. Fairly smart seafood restaurant right on the beach, slightly more expensive than other restaurants in town but good fresh dishes and comprehensive wine list. Note that the kitchen closes at 1430, so late lunches aren't an option.

TT De Viswijf, 55 Diaz Rd, T042-2933921. 1100-1500, 1700-late, closed Sun evenings. Enclosed deck overlooking the surf and fishing boats, wide selection of seafood and steaks, and specials such as *potjies*, unusual dishes such as curried tripe and occasional game meat.

TT Die Walskipper, Marina Martinique Harbour, out of town towards St Francis Bay, T042-2920005, Tue-Sat 1200-2100, Sun 1200-1500. As befits a popular surfing venue, this open-air restaurant with a corrugated-iron roof and shade cloth attracts a fun crowd on the beach. During the winter months the owners bring coal stoves to the beach. The menu consists of good local dishes with fresh ingredients and homemade breads. Steaming seafood platters with plenty of 'white gold' (calamari) is the go, served up on enamel plates, and drinks are distributed in tin mugs. Recommended.

Le Grotto, Jeffrey's St, T042-2932612. 1100-late. Popular corner restaurant serving fresh seafood, steaks and burgers, good catch of the day, famous for its 1-kg steaks.

Sunflower Café, 20 Da Gama Rd, T042-2931682, daily 0800-2300. Café and restaurant serving great range of light meals, including plenty for vegetarians. Delicious milkshakes and homemade cakes, good evening meals such as grilled calamari or pasta. Internet access and local artwork on permanent display. Recommended.

St Francis Bay and Cape St Francis *p334*

There are several coffee shops and restaurants in the **Village Shopping Centre** on St Francis Drive in the middle of St Francis Bay.

Big Time Taverna, 740 Grande Comore, T042-2941309. 1200-1500, 1800-late, closed Mon. Overlooking the Kromme River and canals, well heeled restaurant aimed at wealthy Johannesburg holiday-makers, traditional Greek blue and white decor, excellent service and renowned for its seafood.

Joe Fish, pub and restaurant at the **Cape St Francis Resort** (see Sleeping, page 336), T042-2980054,1130-late. Excellent seafood, especially the calamari steaks, or try the spare ribs, alfresco terrace around the swimming pool or cosy pub with fireplace.

Activities and tours

Jeffrey's Bay *p333, map p333*

Horse riding

Papiesfontein Beach Rides, T082-5749396 (mob), beachrides@mweb.co.za. Rides through the local countryside and along the beach.

Sandboarding

Aloe Afrika, T042-2933941, aloe@agnet.co.za. There are some big dunes around Jeffrey's Bay – perfect for sandboarding. Trips run daily and include boards and tuition.

Surfing

Jeffrey's Bay Surf School, based at **Island Vibe Backpackers**, T042-2934214, www.islandvibebackpackers.com. Beginner lessons run daily year-round and include wetsuits, beginners' boards and tuition, advanced lessons using video sessions to see what you did right or wrong, ask about the 7-day learn to surf packages which include accommodation and meals.

Transport

Jeffrey's Bay *p333, map p333*

78 km to **Port Elizabeth**, 20 km to **Cape St Francis**, 20 km to **Humansdorp** (N2), 206 km to **Knysna**, 1,062 km to **Durban**.

Bus

Baz Bus, T021-4392323, www.bazbus.com. Backpackers' budget service that calls in at hostels to collect/drop off. They should have room to carry your surfing equipment but let them know in advance. Coming from Cape Town, Jeffrey's Bay is the last drop-off, arriving 2030-2130, before the bus crew spend the night in Port Elizabeth. If you want to travel further east than Port Elizabeth, you'll have to depart the next morning. Travelling from Jeffrey's Bay to **Cape Town** the Baz Bus picks up 0830-0900 and arrives in Cape Town later that night.

Greyhound and Translux pick up and drop off at **Humansdorp**, 20 km from Jeffrey's Bay on the N2 on the service between **Cape Town** and **Durban**. From here, you have to hitch or take a local taxi. It may be possible to arrange for your accommodation to collect you for a small charge but remember some of the departure and arrival times are either late at night or in the early hours of the morning.

J-Bay Sunshine Express, T042-2932221. A local door-to-door service running only to/from **Port Elizabeth**. Expect to pay R60 per person one way if there are other people on the bus. If you are alone, the cost will be considerably more. Booking ahead essential.

Port Elizabeth to East London

There are two routes to East London from Port Elizabeth. The quickest is on the N2 via Grahamstown. An alternative route is to take the R72 coastal road, but there are three very compelling reasons for following the N2: a visit to the wonderful Greater Addo Elephant National Park; to visit the string of new private game reserves including the superb Shamwari Game Reserve; and to see the old colonial town of Grahamstown.

▸▸ *For Sleeping, Eating and other listings, see pages 346-352.*

Greater Addo Elephant National Park

▸▸ *pp346-352. Colour map 7, grid B4.*

The original elephant sector of the Greater Addo Elephant National Park, proclaimed in 1931, covered 12,000 ha, when only 11 elephants remained in the area. Since 2000, the park has been undergoing a process of expansion. New land purchase has been made possible by funds from the government and overseas donors. This process, as well as the rehabilitation and fencing of the new land, is still underway. When the expansion is finished, the park will cover 292,000 ha and it will be the third largest conservation area in South Africa. The park now encompasses five neighbouring game reserves and wilderness areas and stretches from the Indian Ocean to the Little Karoo and incorporates five different habitat biospheres.

The weather here is usually warm and dry and visits to the park are enjoyable all year round.

At the coast is a belt of coastal dunefields and forest. The 200-m Alexandria Dunefield, the largest active dunefields in the world after the Namib Desert, now falls within the park and the 120,000-ha marine reserve adjoining Addo includes many islands that are home to the largest population of African gannets and the second largest population of penguins. With the reintroduction of lion in October 2003, it is now possible to see the Big Seven – elephant, rhino, lion, buffalo, leopard, whale and great white shark – in a malaria-free environment. This expansion of the park is one of the most exciting and ambitious conservation projects ever undertaken, and Addo is set to become a highlight of the Eastern Cape.

Addo is home to the densest population of elephant on earth.

Today this finely tuned ecosystem is sanctuary to a breeding herd of over 420 elephants, 450 Cape buffalo, 40 black rhino, hippo, cheetah, leopard, lion, a variety of antelope species, as well as the unique flightless dung beetle – unique to the park and found wherever there's elephant dung. Over 185 species of birds have been recorded here. The relative flatness of the bush and the large number of elephant present mean that they are easily seen. To add to this, there are a couple of waterholes which can be accessed by car. Visitors will often see several herds drinking at one time – this can mean watching over 100 elephant – a magnificent experience. Although you'll see them at any time of year, one of the best times to visit is in January and February, when many of the females will have recently calved.

Ins and outs

Getting there Addo's main park entrance is 72 km from Port Elizabeth and can be reached by taking the R335, which is well signposted off the N2 from Port Elizabeth to Grahamstown. At the time of writing, a new access road into the park was being constructed. This road will feed off the N2 highway near Colchester, travel through the new southern block of the park and join up with the existing tourist roads in the park. Most visitors head for the area where the elephants are found which is south of the main camp. There is a network of good gravel roads if you are in your own car or you can book day and night drives, game walks, and horse rides through reception. Booking ahead is essential. The coastal section and Alexander Dunefield is south of the N2, and there are access points to the beach off the R72. The northern section is best visited from the **Darlington Lake Lodge**, see page 346.

Park information T042-2330556, www.addoelephantpark.com, www.sanparks.org, R80, R40 children. Entrance gates daily 0700-1900; the wildlife viewing area is open 0600-1800 in summer and 0700-1730 in winter, though times vary according to season so check with reception; office 0700-2000; restaurant 0800-2100, serves light snacks and meals; shop 0800-1900, sells a selection of groceries, meat, bread and wines; petrol (no diesel) 0730-1700; laundry, telephone and postal services are also available. There is a swimming pool and tennis court at the main camp and a hide at a game viewing waterhole that is floodlit at night. The park's other hide tends to be busier as it is near the restaurant, but it is good for birdwatching as it overlooks a small dam.

Note that in the elephant-watching area it is illegal to leave your vehicle anywhere other than at signposted climb-out points.

Alexandria Trail

Permits for the Alexandria trail are available through SAN Parks, www.sanparks.org. Alternatively contact the main reception office at Addo, T042-2330556. Maximum 12 people, a popular trail over weekends. Take precautions against ticks.

On the coast to the south of Alexandria between the Bushman's River and the Sundays River mouths is the part of the park that is dunes and coastal forest. There is no large game here but this is the habitat of the hairy-footed gerbil which is unique to this area. The forests are good for birdwatching and along the coast it is possible to see dolphins and the Damara tern. There are many easy trails passing along the beach and into the forest. The longest hike, for which permits are necessary, is the Alexandria Trail. It is 36 km long and is a marked two-day circular track – be warned that the markers can be blown over in strong wind and get buried in the sand. The first day takes you from the base camp at Langebos through forest down to the coastal dunefield which extends for 120 km up the coast. The hiking can be tough along the windy dunes but worth it for the fine isolated beaches. One night is spent in the hut at Woody Cape. In the morning the trail then heads back across farmland in the Langevlakte Valley and back to Langebos.

The Alexander dunes are the highest sand dunes south of the Namib Desert and in some places reach heights of 150 m.

East of Addo

» pp346-352.

Schotia Safaris

To the east of Addo, 55 km from Port Elizabeth, and just north of the junction of the N2 and N10, is **Schotia Safaris** *T042-2351436, www.schotia.com*. This is a private game reserve on the edge of Addo with 15 types of antelope, several smaller species such as warthog, monkeys and genets, and lion, hippo, giraffe and rhino. Schotia is also known for its huge open-air dining *lapa* – reputedly the largest in South Africa – built of reed and thatch, which is supported by several large Schotia trees. The lodge here has three double units (see Sleeping, page 347) and if you are staying overnight all game activities are included; day and night game drives into Addo are also available. It is also possible to visit as a day visitor between 1600-2200 and the package includes afternoon and evening game drives and a buffet dinner and drinks for around R650. Alternatively, you could combine the above day visit with a morning safari to Addo and pick-ups can be arranged from Port Elizabeth if you don't have a car. Check out the website for options and prices.

Shamwari Game Reserve → *Colour map 7, grid B5.*

ⓘ *From Port Elizabeth, follow the N2 towards Grahamstown. After 65 km take a left turn, signposted Shamwari. This gravel road is the R342; after 7 km take a right turn. It is then a further 2 km to the entrance. From Grahamstown, the R342 turning is about 58 km along the N2, T042-2031111, www.shamwari.com, daily tour at 1200, booking essential, expect to pay in the region of R650.*

This is a privately owned reserve which in many aspects resembles the reserves of Mpumalanga along the boundary of Kruger National Park. In 1990 Adrian Gardiner, a successful businessman from Port Elizabeth, bought the property and read up on historical accounts of the Eastern Cape, which described the region as one of the richest wildlife zones in Africa. Reports dating back to the 18th century indicate a time when vast herds of Cape buffalo and zebra, wildebeest, black rhino, leopard and lion freely roamed the hills and valleys. However, by 1853 early settlers had wiped out most of the game and cleared vast areas of forest for farmland. When Gardiner bought the property all that remained was a dry, eroded dust bowl, but in the last decade natural grasses and bush flora have been planted and many species of game reintroduced. Once decimated by overgrazing and drought, the landscape has been transformed into big game country. Today the park has been well stocked with game from all over the region including black rhino, elephant, buffalo, leopard, lion and antelope of all sizes. Wild dog have recently been introduced, last seen in the area over 200 years ago. The reserve covers an area of 20,000 ha; there are six different lodges within the boundary, which are part of the same operation.

Day visitors are welcome but you must make advance reservations for the half-day tour. It includes a game drive by 4WD, lunch at the **Shamwari/Born Free Conservation Centre**, overlooking the Bushman's River, and a visit to the **Kaya Lendaba**, a traditional African Healing Village that is helping to preserve methods and recipes, most of which would otherwise have been lost.

Amakhala Game Reserve

ⓘ *Off the N2 approximately opposite the turning for Shamwari Game Reserve (see above), the road is well signposted, T042-2351608, www.amakhala.co.za.*

This is another of the Eastern Cape's successful new game reserves. The 6000-ha reserve was created in 1999 as a joint conservation venture between neighbouring farms and today has six independently owned lodges. All are owner-managed by the descendants of the original families who arrived here as British settlers from 1820. The lodges offer various styles of accommodation, including two colonial homesteads, two classic bush lodges, an historic inn, a settler farmhouse and an authentic ox-wagon camp; see Sleeping, page 348, for details. The reserve has been stocked with rhino, elephant, cheetah, buffalo, giraffe, black wildebeest, zebra and over 16 antelope species. These can be seen on day and night drives, and on game walks arranged from the lodges for overnight guests (around R300). There is also the opportunity to go on a cruise or canoe trip on the Bushmen's River. Day visitors are welcome and safaris commence in the early afternoon with a two hour game drive followed by a sunset cruise on the Bushman's River with cheese and wine, a four-course dinner is served in a bush *lapa*, and the excursion ends with a short night game drive, all for just under R700 per person. The day visit is not recommended for children under 12 due to the long programme.

Amakhala means aloe in Xhosa, named after the vibrant orange flower that is common in the area.

Lalibela Game Reserve

ⓘ *22 km from Shamwari and 24 km east of Grahamstown off the N2, T041-5812332, www.lalibela.co.za.*

This is a private game reserve covering 18,000 ha and spanning four ecosystems that are home to the Big Five as well as cheetah, hyena, hippo, giraffe, zebra, warthog and numerous species of antelope. Wild dog are to be released here in 2006. A number of scientific research projects are currently being conducted on the reserve working with the Zoology Department of Rhodes University. There are four luxury lodges (see Sleeping page 348), and another is to open in 2006. There is a day programme that includes lunch, dinner and games drives but it must be booked in advance.

Grahamstown

» pp346-352. Colour map 7, grid B5.

Grahamstown is first and foremost a student town. At the top end of the high street is one of the country's major centres of learning, **Rhodes University**. The presence of the university has a significant impact on this small town and during term time the pubs and bars are packed with students. It is a pleasant enough place to wander around and there are a number of interesting little shops along the high street.

Despite the English feel to the town centre the other side of the valley is dominated by a poor, dusty and badly serviced township where the majority of the African residents live. The proximity of the two sides of town makes the contrast more apparent than in some of the bigger towns and cities where the townships are some distance from the centre.

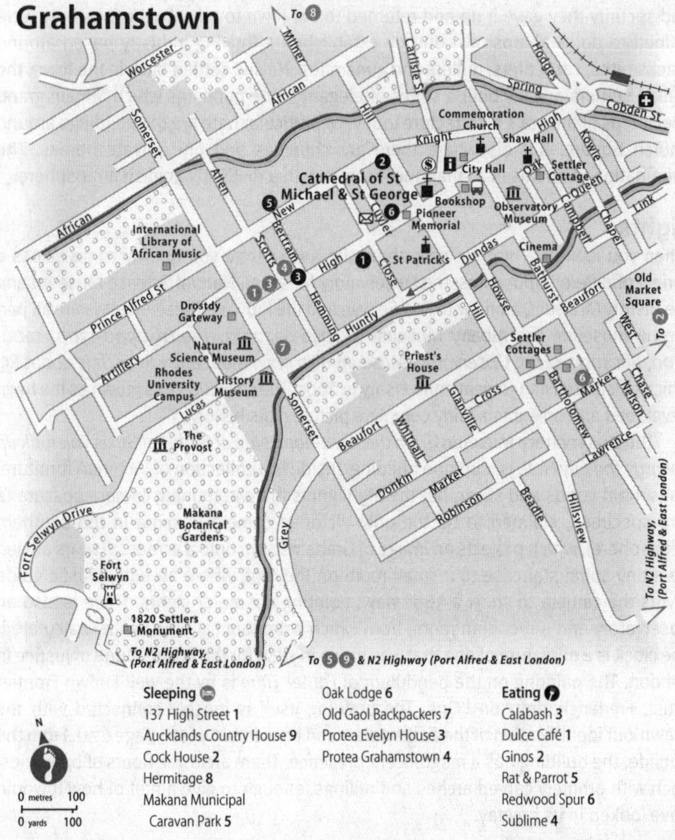

Ins and outs

Getting there The town has good transport links and is served by Greyhound and Translux buses. ▸▸ *For further details, see Transport, page 352.*

Tourist information Grahamstown Tourism ⓘ *63 High St, T046-6223241, www.grahamstown.co.za, Mon-Fri 0830-1300, 1400-1700, Sat 0830-1200*, is a well-organized centre with accommodation booking facilities for the entire region. The staff can arrange and book a variety of local tours. There is also a **Translux** desk. A worthwhile local scheme is 'Step-On Guides' under which locally registered guides join you in your own vehicle and show you around the various sights.

Background

Grahamstown was established around a fort which had been built here after the Fourth Frontier War. It was founded in 1812 and named after Colonel Graham. Within two years it was a busy border settlement. The 1820 settlers began to arrive after the end of the Fifth Frontier War, during which Grahamstown had been besieged by Xhosa warriors. Despite the continual threat of armed conflict and problems of security, the town had evolved into the second largest settlement in the whole of southern Africa by 1836.

Rhodes University has 70 major buildings on a 195-ha campus with approximately 3,200 students and 1800 staff.

One factor behind the town's rapid growth was that the majority of the 1820 settlers were ill-prepared to be farmers, let alone in an environment of which they had no knowledge. As soon as they realized farming was not going to bring them wealth and security they gave it up and returned to the town to take up the jobs they were trained to do. Grahamstown quickly established a thriving industry based around blacksmiths, carpenters, millers and gunsmiths. Having settled back in the town, the skilled settlers quickly built a series of elegant stone buildings which remain grand specimens of the era's architecture today. Of particular note are the buildings around Church Square, but elsewhere there are churches and fine private homes. The culmination of all this is a smart town centre with a distinctly English atmosphere.

Sights

When you look at a map or walk about the town centre you quickly come across a variety of different museums: the Observatory Museum, Natural Science Museum and the History Museum, along with Fort Selwyn and the Provost. These displays are all part of one museum, the **Albany Museum** ⓘ *T046-6222312, Tue-Fri 0900-1300, 1400-1700, Sat 1000-1400, Observatory Museum also open Mon; entry to each is about R5*, which celebrated its 150-year anniversary in 2005. The collection has grown as the town developed and presents a fairly complete picture of its history.

The **Observatory Museum** ⓘ *on the right-hand side of Bathurst St, as you look up towards the City Hall*, is a unique building. Inside is a collection of Victorian furniture, household goods and silver, but the highlight is the entertaining camera obscura (a rare specimen, claimed to be the only Victorian camera obscura in the southern hemisphere), which projects an image of Grahamstown onto a screen. Visitors are led up a tiny spiral staircase to a small room on the roof, where an enthusiastic guide pivots the camera to show a 360° view, pointing out major sights. There is also an observatory and a meridian room, from which astronomical time can be calculated. The clock is a miniature of one that was made in 1883 for the Royal Courts of Justice in London. The painting on the pendulum of *Father Time* is by the well-known Frontier Artist, Frederick Timpson I'Ons. The building itself is loosely connected with the drawn-out identification of the *Eureka* diamond back in 1869 (see page 671). From the outside, the building has a magnificent presence. There are three floors of balconies, each with ornately carved arches and railings, enough to give a hint of how it would have looked in its heyday.

The **Natural Science Museum** is on Somerset Street. Most of the displays are aimed at children. Some of the more interesting exhibits include a large iron meteorite which came down in a shower in Namibia, a Foucault pendulum and some dinosaur fossils. There are regular temporary exhibitions, and this is one of the main venues for the Scifest, a science and technology festival held in March. There is a café in a courtyard at the back.

The **History Museum** is in a building opposite the Natural Science Museum on Somerset Street. It houses an interesting collection outlining the area's history, including beadwork displays from the Eastern Cape, traditional Xhosa dress, 1820 settler history and some art galleries, with regularly changing contemporary exhibitions.

The **Provost**, off Somerset Street, at the western end of town in the botanical gardens, is a quadrangle building with a double-storeyed tower at its apex. It was built in 1837 by the Royal Engineers to act as a military prison; their actual instructions were to build a "fortified barrack establishment". A lot of thought went into the overall design of the complex as the architects sought to of the time sought to come up with a design where, from the central tower, it would be possible to view as many prisoners as possible with minimal manpower. In January 1838 the first 20 convicts were brought here. They were mutineers, and after they had shot one of their officers, Ensign Crowe, they were executed on the parade grounds. The building was proclaimed a national monument in 1937.

Fort Selwyn ⓘ *open by prior appointment only*, is on Fort Selwyn Drive, at the western end of town close to the Settlers Monument. During the sixth Frontier War in 1834 parliament decided that it would be necessary to protect the barracks. The Royal Engineers who built the fort were commanded by Major Charles Jasper Selwyn. Between 1841 and 1868 the fort was used as an artillery barracks and a semaphore link – a mast was erected in the northeast corner – but then the army gave up using the building in 1870. During the Anglo-Boer War the fort served in the defence of Grahamstown, but by the 1920s it had once more been left to run down and become overgrown. It was not until the 1970s that the building finally got the restoration work it deserved and this was due to it being proclaimed a national monument. Although it stands on the property of the Department of Nature and Environmental Conservation, it was given to the Albany Museum to use as exhibition space to further promote the history of Grahamstown.

The **1820 Settlers Monument** is, oddly, a large modern office block with rather a totalitarian feel to it. There is a series of rooms which include a conference hall, theatre and a restaurant. It overlooks the city and completely dominates its surrounds on Gunfire Hill. It was opened in July 1974, but in 1994 disaster struck and fire gutted the whole complex. The memorial is surrounded by the **Makana Botanical Gardens** ⓘ *daily 0800-1630*, which were laid out in 1853 with displays of indigenous plants. The botanical garden has a recreation of a nostalgic old English garden, but more interestingly there is a huge collection of aloes, cycads, proteas and tree ferns. Assuming you're not afraid of ghosts, try to catch a glimpse of Lady Juana Smith, the Spanish wife of Sir Harry Smith who reputedly haunts the gardens.

The **International Library of African Music (ILAM)** ⓘ *Prince St, follow signs from gate opposite Rhodes University Theatre, T046-6038557, www.ilam.ru.ac.za, by appointment only, Mon-Fri 0830-1245, 1400-1700*, is a research centre for traditional African music, and houses a fascinating collection of musical instruments; there are over 200 traditional African instruments from across the continent.

The **Cathedral of St Michael and St George** occupies its rightful position in the centre of town on Church Square. The style of this building is early English Gothic, a 13th-century style which the Victorians chose to revive in the late 19th century. Like similar buildings in Europe, the cathedral took generations to complete. Work started in 1824 and the first usable form was opened in 1830 as a single-room church. In 1952 the Lady Chapel was completed and so the cathedral had taken 128 years to build.

 Look out for the memorial tablets which together provide a vivid history of Grahamstown as the frontier of the empire.

The **Priest's House**, on Beaufort Street, was built as a residence for the bishop and the clergy of the Catholic church. It is one of the finer buildings in Grahamstown and like the Observatory Museum has a connection with the identification of the Eureka diamond. Because of this connection, the De Beers Group rescued the house in 1981, helped to partially restore the building and then oversaw the establishment of the **National English Literary Museum** ⓘ *To46-6227042, Mon-Fri 0900-1230, 1430-1630*. These days the research carried out behind the scenes is proving to be an important component in the understanding of the role of English as a national language of South Africa. There is a comprehensive collection of scholarly books, articles and press-clippings as well as a good bookshop. The house is also of interest. The façade is typical of the Cape during the 1800s – flat, with a colonnaded neo-Georgian portico.

The **Shaw Hall** is behind the Observatory Museum, but still in the High Street. It was inaugurated in 1832 as a Methodist Church, with three galleries and room for over 800 members. Once the Commemoration Church had been completed in 1850, the first building was turned over for use as a meeting hall. The Reverend William Shaw was a local missionary worker. The most important role the building played was on 25 April 1864 when the Governor of the Cape Colony, Sir Philip Wodehouse, convened a session of parliament in the hall. This was part of a programme of tacit support for a movement that was trying to break away from the western part of the province and set up an independent government. Although nothing ever came of the idea, it was a clear indication of how serious the government took the threats of secession, since this was the only time that the Cape parliament ever sat outside of Cape Town.

Excursions

The **Thomas Baines Nature Reserve** ⓘ *Eastern Cape Nature Conservation, To46-6227216*, offers canoeing, fishing, sailing and windsurfing at Settlers Dam. The reserve is named after the famous 19th-century artist who left a valuable record of the rich diversity of fauna and flora in the region, including the now-extinct quagga. There are 15 km of dirt tracks which pass through fynbos and bushveld inhabited by bontebok, black wildebeest, buffalo, eland, impala and white rhino. Picnic sites with braai facilities and toilets are provided at Settlers Dam. The reserve is 12 km from town next to the Great Fish River Reserve Complex.

Port Alfred to King Wiliamston

⏩ *pp346-352. Colour map 7, grid B5.*

Port Alfred

Port Alfred can be reached along the R72 coast road from Port Elizabeth or on the R67 from Grahamstown. It consists almost entirely of holiday homes and bungalows nestling into dunes. It is one of the largest holiday resorts on this stretch of coastline and overlooks large expanses of water in all directions: the Kowie River, the lagoon and the smart Royal Alfred Marina, where many local people keep their powerboats. The town's history is closely linked to the 1820 settlers and there is a small **Methodist Church** 1 km out of town whose cemetery makes for an interesting visit. Many of the names on the gravestones are those of original settlers.

Port Alfred gets fairly busy at the weekends during term time when students from Grahamstown University come to the coast to play.

The weather on this coast is mild all year round and Port Alfred has a wide range of facilities to offer tourists. Walks through the dune forests are always pleasant but for the more intrepid, there is a scuba-diving school which organizes trips to nearby reefs, as well as facilities for canoeing and game fishing. The **Fish River Casino** and **St Francis Spa** are both nearby and are popular excursions from town. For information contact **Port Alfred Tourism Information Centre** ⓘ *Causeway St, T046-6241235, www.portalfred.net, Mon-Sat 1030-1630.*

The **Oribi Hiking Trail** ⓘ *reservations for accommodation and information on walks from Oribi Haven, T046-6482043, www.oribihaven.co.za*, is a network of guided trails on Kasouga Farm, 3 km from Port Alfred. The farm has two B&B two-bedroom cottages known as **Oribi Haven**, which overlook the ocean. All the trails are relatively easy walks across rolling dunes. The longest possible walk here is around 20 km, but the guides are flexible and quite happy to go on shorter walks to specific areas. The wildlife which inhabits the area is mostly small mammals like the bushpig, duiker and jackal. The range of birdlife is a mixture of coastal and grassland species.

Kowie Nature Reserve

ⓘ *Permits for the Kowie Canoe Trail and overnight hut are available from the tourist office. Only 12 people are allowed on the trail at any one time. The trail is very popular and can get fully booked up to 6 months in advance, especially over weekends. However, it is always worth checking to see if there have been any last minute cancellations or no shows. R85 per person, including the hire of a 2-person canoe.*

This reserve lies along the banks of the Kowie River, about 5 km from Port Alfred on the Bathurst road. It passes through a thickly forested canyon and offers walking trails and a well-run canoe trail, which has turned this into one of the most popular nature reserves in the region.

The **Kowie Canoe Trail** is about 24 km in total and takes two days to complete. The first day is spent paddling 22 km up the Kowie River from Port Alfred to the forests of the Kowie Nature Reserve where you then spend the night in the reserve hut. On the second day you can attempt the 8-km walking trail, following yellow 'footprints' followed by canoeing back to Port Alfred. One of the more popular parts of the hike is a steep climb up the escarpment from where you are rewarded with a perfect view of the horseshoe bend in the river below. Look out for the small mammals found here, such as duiker and bushbuck; both are very shy and well camouflaged. There are plenty of shorter walks across the gentle hills and through the forests along with a number of picnic sites, braai facilities and toilets.

Make a note of when the tide will be coming in and going out and try to plan your trip to coincide with the flow each time. This will make the journey far more fun and less tiring.

King Williamstown

→ *Colour map 7, grid B6.*

King Williamstown, more commonly known simply as King, is 56 km northeast of East London. The London Missionary Society established a mission station here in 1826 and over the years the town has grown into an important commercial centre. The town is best known as the birth and burial place of Apartheid activist Steven Biko who was put under house arrest in the town between 1974 and 1977 before he was arrested at a road block near Grahamstown, outside his restricted area. After his arrest he was taken to Port Elizabeth and intensively interrogated until he died of a brain haemorrhage in police custody on 12 October 1977. Diplomats from 13 counties joined mourners at his funeral in King Williamstown but not a single South African was made accountable for his death. His grave with a lovingly tended polished tombstone lies in the **Steve Biko Remembrance Garden** on the edge of town on the road to Port Elizabeth. It's a moving place and the grave is much humbler than expected for such an important figure in South African history. The **Amathole Museum** ⓘ *Mon-Fri 0900-1630, Sat 0900-1300, small entry fee, T043-6424506, www.amat hole.org.za*, on Alexander Street is a good place to get a feel for Xhosa history with good displays on how the British crushed the Xhosa during the various frontier wars. There's also some contemporary art including bus, bikes and cars made from wire, and some dusty old stuffed mammals.

Greater Addo Elephant National Park *p338*

Some of the accommodation is run by SAN Parks while others are private concessions within or at the edge of the park.

SAN Parks accommodation

Reservations through SAN Parks, T012-4289111, www.sanparks.org, see page 44 for details. Bookings need to be made well in advance, especially during school holidays. For late bookings or cancellations less than 72 hrs phone Addo reception direct, T042-2330556.

AL-D **Addo Rest Camp**, next to the entrance gate and park reception. There are 61 units in total each fully equipped for self catering; some have a/c and braai facilities.

Guest cottages (AL), have 6-beds with 2 en suite a/c bedrooms, fully equipped kitchen and a living room. There are only 2 such cottages, known as Hapoor and Domkrag.

Bungalows (B), are suitable for 4 people, bathroom plus a kitchen.

2-bed huts (C) are simple units with a shower, fridge and toilet. There is a fully equipped communal kitchen.

Camping (D), a maximum of 6 people can occupy any 1 campsite. The grounds are well grassed and there is plenty of shade. Communal kitchens have hot plates, power points and hot water.

B **Narina Bush Camp**, is next to the Witriver in the Zuurberg Mountains approximately 22 km (gravel road, 40 mins' driving) from the main rest camp and park reception. This is a tented camp with 4 2-bed tents and must be booked as 1 unit, towels and bedding are provided, open lapa/braai area, kitchen with gas stove, fridge, paraffin lamps, cutlery, crockery and cooking utensils, 1 shower with hot water from a paraffin cylinder geyser, and 1 toilet. Because of no electricity the guests have to arrive at least 2 hrs before sunset but no later than 1800 as they still have to carry their food and clothing to the camp from the car park, crossing a river and walking 400-500 m through the forest. A torch is essential. The camp can also be reached on horseback on Basuto pony/Boerperd crossbreeds. All the necessary equipment is provided, but it is important to book in advance through reception at the park entrance, T042-2330556. If you want to go on horseback, departure time is no later than 1100 from the top of the Zuurberg Mountain, approximately 16 km gravel road from the main rest camp (25 mins' driving).

E **Alexandria Hiking Huts**, there are 2 huts on the Alexandria hiking trail (see page 339), both sleeping 12 people on bunks and mattresses; the hut at base camp has toilets and cold showers; at the overnight hiking hut at Woody Cape you'll be using rainwater to wash with.

Private accommodation

L2 **Gorah Elephant Camp**, central reservations T044-5327818, www.hunterhotels.com. This luxurious camp has a private concession covering 4500 ha but can also access the rest of the park. Accommodation is in 11 huge, luxurious tents with a colonial theme, complete with 4-poster beds, en suite bathrooms and terraces overlooking the park. Relaxing boma area with rock swimming pool, meals are served in a superbly renovated coach house, overlooking a waterhole frequented by elephant, buffalo and antelope. The price includes all meals, guided game drives and night drives.

A **Darlington Lake Lodge**, situated next to Darlington Dam in the northern tip of Addo, 180 km north of Port Elizabeth on the R75 to Graaff Reinet, T/F042-2433673, www.darlington.co.za. 12 double rooms with en suite facilities furnished in a colonial style, meals are served outdoors in a traditional boma. Wide range of activities on offer around the dam, walking trail, horse rides, 4WD game-viewing trips, fishing and boat cruises. A tranquil spot to enjoy the little visited furthest reaches of the new part of the park.

A **Elephant House**, on the left of the R355, 5 km before Addo's main gate, T042-2332462, www.elephanthouse.co.za. Exclusive 8 room lodge decorated with the owners private collection of antiques and Persian rugs, good food, qualified guides conduct excellent daily game drives into the park on open

Land Cruisers as well as day visits to the various private game reserves in the area.

A-B **Protea Hotel Addo**, T042-2330583, www.proteahotels.co.za, 32 km north of the main entrance on the Zuurberg Mountain Pass, access on the R335. There are 36 double rooms; some are in the original 1850s manor house while the rest are delightful individual spacious lodges under traditional thatch in the Zuurberg Village. Restaurant and pub with magnificent views, swimming pool, tennis, conference centre, chapel for weddings.

B **Africanos Inn**, corner of Main and Zuurberg Rds, Addo, 10-min drive from the park gate, T042-2330605, www.africanos-inn.co.za. An excellent new spot to stay if you cannot get accommodation in the park, 10 very spacious and modern motel-style rooms, each with lounge area, tea tray and DSTV, the barn is used for weddings and some times live music, great restaurant and bar with a long menu, swimming pool, can organize day and night drives into the park. Recommended.

Schotia Safaris *p339*

L4 **Tooth and Claw Lodge**, east of Greater Addo National Park, 55 km from Port Elizabeth, just north of the junction of the N2 and N10, T042-2351436, www.schotia.com. 3 double en suite chalets with fireplaces, hidden in the bush so very private and aimed at honeymooners, all meals and game drives included in the price, transfers from Port Elizabeth can be arranged. No electricity, but lamps will be lit for you in the evening.

Shamwari Game Reserve *p340*

There are 6 luxury camps within the reserve – all are expensive. Each is completely self-contained and independent of the others. All offer morning and evening game drives, walking safaris with an armed guard, and visits to the Shamwari/Born Free Conservation Centre. Current rates per person are R2500-R5500 though in some of the lodges rates drop between May-Oct. Reservations: T042-2031111, www.shamwari.com.

L4 **Eagles Cragg Lodge**, the most central of the 6 camps. This is a restored settler's cottage which has been divided into 9 rooms with twin beds and an en suite bathroom, private deck and plunge pool. Lodge facilities include a dining area, library, business centre, lounge, bar, and beauty spa.

L4 **Lobengula Lodge**, at the northern extremity of the reserve, the most luxurious of the 6 complexes, with thatched roof and decorated to the highest standard. 6 rooms and a maximum of 12 guests can stay here. 5 rooms have en suite bathroom and outside shower plus a/c and underfloor heating; the 6th room is the most expensive option in the whole of the reserve - the Pretorius Suite. Separate lounge with super a/c and fan, plus underfloor heating, private plunge pool, and outside shower. The swimming pool has a sunken cocktail bar and there's a small gym, beauty spa and steam bath.

L3 **Bayethe Tented Lodge**, stone-walled and thatch-roofed main lodge with viewing deck and dining boma, accommodation is 9 double a/c tented suites, with en suite bathroom, outside shower, private plunge pool and deck.

L2 **Bushman's River Lodge**, a small lodge at the centre of the reserve. The 4 double rooms are beautifully decorated in an ethnic theme and set in restored settlers' cottages. Plunge pool and a personal ranger service.

L2 **Riverdene Lodge**, the latest addition to Shamwari, has 9 a/c en suite rooms, with separate lounges. The lodge has elegantly furnished lounges, a sunroom, a rim flow swimming pool with sun deck and poolside bar, the dining room opens onto a spacious outdoor barbecue area.

L1 **Long Lee Manor**, the Edwardian manor house near the main entrance on the western side of the reserve. Largest of the 6 camps, although it never feels crowded. The 30 rooms here are in the Manor House, Palm Court or Sidbury Suites, with underfloor heating, ceiling fans, a/c, TV, telephone. Facilities include 2 swimming pools, a floodlit tennis court, a beauty spa, and down by the Bushman's River, at a point known as the hippo pool, is a covered *lapa* where guests can watch the animals drink while they enjoy a meal.

For an explanation of the sleeping and eating price codes used in this guide, see inside the front cover. Other relevant information is found in Essentials pages 42-47.

Amakhala Game Reserve *p340*
Game activities such as walks, drives or cruises are included in the price at the more expensive lodges, and are available at extra cost at the less expensive ones. All rates are full board and in most you eat with the host families. All of them have swimming pools. Reservations for all the lodges T042- 2351608, www.amakhala.co.za.
L2 Leeuwenbosch Country Lodge, built in 1908 and set in its own lovely garden, traditional country house with 4 en suite doubles and 1 suite, cellar pub with full size antique billiards table.
L2 Safari Lodge, intimate thatched lodge with stylish safari décor, unique luxurious huts with double baths and outdoor showers, outside terraces with open fire in the evening, rim flow pool.
L2 Shearers Lodge, set in the grounds of Leeuwenbosch, originally built in 1930 and used for shearing and classing wool, and now beautifully converted into 4 luxury en suite bedrooms, one with a private lounge. All the rooms open on to a wide colonial veranda overlooking the gardens and chapel.
L1 Woodbury Lodge, 4 modern stone and thatched cottages designed to blend in with the natural surroundings, good views from the wooden decks, central dining room and braai area, lounge and bar.
AL Cararvon Lodge, an 1857 farm where guests are accommodated in the historic farmhouse or the elegantly restored Edwardian cottage, rooms with wrought iron beds, some with fireplaces, private lounges, farm-style meals.
AL Reed Valley Inn, 4 en suite rooms in historic buildings that once were the rest stop for the mail wagon in the 19th century, set on a working farm, farm style breakfasts and 3 course dinners in the main dining room, babysitting can be arranged.
AL Witmos Oxwagons, authentically restored ox-wagons comfortably fitted out as bedrooms, with white starched coverings, adjoining private reed and wood bathrooms, central thatched entertainment and dining area.

Lalibela Game Reserve *p340*
Rates for all the 4 luxurious lodges in the reserve are in the region of R2500 per person per night but are all inclusive of meals, drinks and game drives. Each lodge has a large lounge, viewing deck, swimming pool, and an outdoor dining 'boma' and indoor dining area. There are special arrangements for children who are kept entertained by childminders whilst parents go on game drives and are offered their own 'kiddie's' game drives. Reservations T041-5812332, www.lalibela.co.za.
L4 Idwala Lodge, the newest of the lodges in Lalibela, smart modern African décor and rustic colours, 4 thatched units, each in a private setting in the bush perched high up on a rocky outcrop.
L4 Lentaba, 8 thatched chalets with large beds with white linen, safari decor and antique African art throughout, good views from the hilltop location.
L4 Mark's Camp, thatched and stone cottages, sleeps 20 in 4 doubles and 3 family units, private decks overlooking a waterhole, a fire is lit at the outside boma to sit around with drinks after dinner.
L4 Tree Tops, 8 luxury safari tents perched high on thatched platforms at 'tree top' level, joined by raised walkways with fantastic views, really feels like you are staying in a treehouse.

Grahamstown *p341, map p341*
Some residents in Grahamstown township offer overnight accommodation in their homes (**D**). Most is in brick houses with a hospitable Xhosa family. The tourist office can arrange this.
A The Cock House, 10 Market St, T046-6361287, www.cockhouse.co.za. Beautifully restored 1820s national monument with 9 double rooms with en suite bathrooms, 1 self-catering flat, special touches include electric blanket and homemade biscuits. Luxurious guesthouse with a good à la carte restaurant attached with a comfortable lounge and library. Peter and Belinda have clearly made a good impression – Nelson Mandela has stayed here twice. The first floor veranda is a particularly fine feature. Recommended.
A Protea Hotel Evelyn House, 115 High St, T046-6222366, www.proteahotels.co.za. A very fine guesthouse in a local landmark

building dating from the 1800s. 4 double rooms, 2 luxury suites, 1 with jacuzzi, a/c, laundry service, M-Net TV, swimming pool, sauna, gym, secure off-street parking. Well-appointed accommodation. Recommended.

A-B Protea Hotel Grahamstown, 123 High St, T046-6222324, www.proteahotels.co.za. Rather unattractive building but in a good location on the High St. 27 rooms with en suite bathrooms, TV, lounge. **Calabash** restaurant has a good local reputation, cocktail bar with pool table and darts, laundry service, secure parking, comfortable town hotel within a short walk of the shops and sights.

B 137 High Street, 137 High St, T046-6223242, www.137highstreet.co.za. Stylish hotel in a good location close to restaurants and sights. 7 luxurious rooms, en suite bath or shower, good service, attractive old building, restaurant downstairs serving excellent breakfasts and snacks, as well as more substantial meals.

B Aucklands Country House, T046-6222401, www.aucklands.co.za. A fine country house 8 km from the town centre off the N2 towards Port Elizabeth. 6 spacious rooms with en suite bathrooms, set in 14 ha of beautiful grounds with a swimming pool, tennis court, croquet lawn, and resident herd of blesbok. Horse riding and hikes nearby. Excellent gourmet meals, friendly owners. An extremely well-run establishment. Strongly recommended.

B The Hermitage, 14 Henry St, T046-6361503. Beautifully restored house, a fine example of a villa built in the 1820s by an early British settler. 1 double elegant suite with en suite bathroom and sitting room with TV, private entrance. The neat gardens complement the house, breakfasts served on a veranda. Good value, strongly recommended, ask for Bea or Dick.

B Oak Lodge Hotel, 95 Bathurst St, T046-6229123, oaklodge@albanyhotels.co.za. Large old building with23 rooms, TV lounge, gardens, swimming pool, braai area, bar, secure parking. Tours arranged. A short walk from the town centre.

C-E Makana Municipal Caravan Park, Grey St, T046-6036072. On the outskirts of town on the N2 heading towards Port Elizabeth, an easy walk to town. 48 sites for tents or caravans, communal ablution block and laundry room. The chalets and rondavels sleep up to 5 in each though you will need to bring your own bedding. They are good value, reserve in advance.

D Old Gaol Backpackers, Somerset St, opposite the Albany Museum, T046-6361001, oldgaol@imaginet.co.za. An unusual and excellent place to stay. This is the only backpackers in Grahamstown, and is housed in an old Victorian gaol. Double rooms are in individual cells, complete with thick stone walls, domed ceilings, and tiny barred windows. The dorms are housed in the communal cells. There is also a lounge with kitchen, TV room, the **Gallows** pub and restaurant, and you can sunbathe in the old exercise yard. The building is listed, so no work can be done on the original structure. While this gives the place a run-down (and rather too authentic) feel with original prisoners' graffiti on the walls, the cells are spotless and the beds comfortable. Highly recommended as an atmospheric and unique backpackers.

Port Alfred *p344*,

AL Halyards, Royal Alfred Marina, off Albany Rd, T046-6242410, www.riverhotels.co.za. Smartest hotel in Port Alfred, provides luxury accommodation in a nautical theme for the wealthy set during peak holiday periods. During quiet periods, however, you should find bargain room rates on offer. 35 spacious a/c rooms with all mod-cons, good views of the marina. 2 restaurants, bar, swimming pool, spa, gym, wooden decks, pleasant grounds.

B Royal St Andrews Lodge, 19 St Andrews Rd, T046-6241379, hilander@border.co.za. Across the road from the golf course, Tudor mock exterior with 14 bright and modern rooms, doubles and family rooms, and self-catering chalets, swimming pool with wooden deck, the **Thistle** restaurant and **Highlander** pub, good-value small, friendly hotel.

B-C The Residency, 11 Vroom Rd, T046-6245382, www.theresidency.co.za. Turn-of-the-20th-century settler's house, with wooden floors and ball and claw baths, 4 en suite rooms furnished with cottage-type items, breakfasts are taken on the wrap-around veranda, German spoken.

C-E **Medolino Caravan Park**, 23 Stewart Rd, T/F046-6241651, www.caravanparks.co.za/medolino. This is a medium-size park with 48 sites, well grassed and plenty of shade, electric points, electric lights, well-equipped laundry and 2 heated pools. 5 self-catering log cabins sleeping 4-6, tents are allowed and you can hire a caravan, disabled access.

D **Station Backpackers**, 1 Pascoe St, T046-6245869, www.thestation.co.za. A fairly new backpackers housed in Port Alfred's old station, now a national monument. Doubles, dorms, The Station restaurant and bar which is very popular locally, internet access, the Baz Bus will drop you here.

Kowie Nature Reserve *p345*

E **Horseshoe Reserve Hut**, a simple hut sleeping up to 12 people. You'll need to bring bedding and all camping supplies; the only cooking facilities are a braai area. Book through the tourist office in Port St Alfred .

King Williamstown *p345*

B-C **Dreamers Guest House**, 29 Gorden St, Hospital Hill, T043-6423012, www.dreamersguesthouse.co.za. Neat house on a quiet street, colourful gardens, 4 en suite rooms and 1 family unit, lunch and dinner on request, large pool and patio area. Can arrange visits to nearby Xhosa villages.

C-D **Grosvenor Lodge**, 48 Taylor St, T046-6421440. Modern business hotel with 19 rooms, extras include a/c and satellite TV, restaurant, bar, 10 cheaper rooms in a guesthouse around the corner. Very average but one of the only options in town.

Eating

Grahamstown *p341, map p341*

Many of the quality restaurants in town are in the main hotels. There are also plenty of cheap cafés and takeaways catering to the large student population and the town features the usual Wimpy and KFC.

TT **Calabash**, 123 High St, T046-6222324, 1200-1400, 1700-2300. Popular traditional South African restaurant specializing in Xhosa hotpots, various South African dishes and a regular menu of seafood, steaks and venison. Daily specials at lunchtime.

TT **The Cock House**, 10 Market St, T046-6361287, 1200-1430, 1900-late, closed Sun lunch, set meals on Sun evening. Excellent restaurant which is part of a smart town guesthouse (see Sleeping page 348). Plenty of attention is given to presentation and quality of the country cuisine. If you don't fancy eating then enjoy a beer in the cosy yellowwood bar with a light snack. One of the most popular spots in town so booking advised.

TT **Ginos**, 8 New St, entrance is from the car park behind on Hill St, T046-6227208, 1100-2300. 20 year old family run restaurant, good selection of pizza and pasta dishes, and some meat dishes and regular specials, very popular though the decor is slightly dated.

TT **Redwood Spur**, 97 High St, T046-6222629, 1100-2300. Predictable steak, ribs, Tex Mex, chain restaurant, one of the few options open Sun. Good service from clean-cut students working here part time.

TT **Sublime**, 65B New St, corner of Somerset St, Mon-Sat 1030-2230. Upmarket sandwich and trendy coffee shop by day, fresh bread and a wide range of filings, at dinner light meals such as stir fries, good choice for vegetarians.

T **Dulce Café**, 112 High St, open all day until 2200 except Mon when it closes at 1700. Café and ice cream parlour, excellent sandwiches made to order, ice cream sundaes, milkshakes and salads.

T **Rat & Parrot**, 59 New St, 1100-late, closed Sun. A popular bar which is big with students on Wed and Sat nights, gets quite rowdy once a few rounds of shooters have been passed around, wide range of beers and alcoholic drinks, big screen TV for major sports, bar snacks including good *potjies*.

Port Alfred *p344,*

TTT **The Halyards**, Halyards Hotel, Royal Alfred Marina, T046-6242410. One of the smartest options with a nautical decor, good seafood and traditional meat dishes, good service and views across the marina, need to dress up a bit.

TT **Barnacles**, Royal Alfred Marina, T046-06245330, 1100-late. Popular pub overlooking water, good steaks and seafood, cheaper pizzas, nightly live music and karaoke.

Buck & Hunter, 9 Main St, T046-6245960, 1130-late. Relaxed pub/restaurant serving good seafood, steaks and pub lunches in wildlife-themed decor, the odd special dish such as duck, gammon and game, and good vegetarian options like butternut bake.

Butlers Riverside Restaurant, 25 Van der Riet St, T046-6243464, 1100-late. Restaurant-cum-pub with a lively atmosphere. Pub snack menu served on the open deck overlooking the river, or eat inside in a slightly more formal setting with a more pricey menu. The fresh fish is excellent, menu and blackboard items change according to the whim of the chef.

Guido's on the Beach, West Beach, T046-6245264, open daily till late. The restaurant serves great pizzas and pasta dishes along with seafood and steaks. Busy and boozy bar upstairs with views across the waves.

Festivals

Grahamstown *p341, map p341*

Check with the local tourist office for the exact dates and programme details.

Mar In late Mar the town hosts a large Scifest, www.scifest.org.za, which features some 600 events: lectures, game drives, laser shows, robotics competitions, science olympics, interactive exhibitions, and a film festival. Attendance now exceeds 35,000 visitors a year.

Jul At the start of the month there's the famous 10-day **Standard Bank National Festival of Arts**, T046-6227115, www.nafest.co.za. This is one of the top cultural events in the country. Over 50,000 visitors are attracted to the town to watch a range of shows, which include theatre, dance, fine art, films, music, opera and an increasing variety of traditional crafts and art, plus a huge range of fringe shows. There's something for everyone from techno raves to medieval banquets. The centre of the festival is the 1820 Settlers Monument. During this period accommodation gets booked very quickly, so book several months ahead, or phone the tourist office to check if any private homes are letting out rooms. During the festival the whole atmosphere of the town changes, so if you are in the country at this time it is well worth a visit.

Activities and tours

Greater Addo Elephant National Park *p338*

Addo Elephant Back Safaris, in the north of the Greater Addo Elephant National Park in the Zuurberg Mountains, on the Toevlugt Farm. 1.5 km before Addo's main gate, turn left at the Zuurburg sign. The farm is 34km from this turn off. T042-2351400, www.addoelephantbacksafaris.co.za. Here there is the opportunity to walk with three tame elephants through the bush and forest. The walk is not strenuous and at an enjoyable pace and allows visitors to observe the elephant's habits close up and in their natural surroundings. After the walk there is the opportunity of a short ride on them to the waterhole, where you can watch the elephants swim. Snacks or lunch are provided.

Grahamstown *p341, map p341*

There are several local registered guides who will take you on historical tours, birdwatching or game viewing, on foot or in your own vehicle. Contact the tourist office for recommendations.

Bee's Tours, T046-6225051. A range of tours with a Satour registered guide from 1 hr to a full day. Combine a historical tour of the city with a visit to the township. Supports a township trust teaching unemployed people work skills. Will also arrange day trips to Port Elizabeth or Addo, or in fact anywhere that you would like to go from Grahamstown, minimum 2 people, about R150 per hr.

Frontier Country, T046-6228054, www.frontiercountry.co.za. 1- to 4-day trips in the Eastern Cape starting from Grahamstown or Port Elizabeth, half-day tour of the town and township, frontier village tour, Addo, can also arrange abseiling and horse riding in the region.

Umthathi Training Project, at the Spoornet Station Building, T046-6225051, hadeda@

imaginet.co.za, organizes half-day tours to the large township in Grahamstown which is known as **Rhini**, or Grahamstown East, and lies to the east of the town across the river. Not surprisingly, most local whites will never have visited this part of their town and will know very little of it. Tourists, however, are offered a choice of township tours, with visits to a 'traditional' Xhosa family for a meal, as well as visiting craft centres and shebeens.

Port Alfred *p344*

Diving

Keryn's Dive School, small boat harbour, T046-6244432, keryn@compushop.co.za. Fishing charters and dive courses available, plus daily dives for certified divers. The nearby reef has some fine corals and there are some popular wreck dives, but the water is not warm, nor is the visibility that good.

Golf

The **Royal Port Alfred Golf Course**, T046-6244796, www.rpagc.co.za, has a magnificent view of the sea. This 18-hole, 72-par course was laid out between 1907 and 1915 and was given royal status from King George V.

Horse riding

The roads that access the most beautiful and remote beaches and river valleys are poor, which means that horses are often the best mode of transport. If you have never ridden before, this is a good place to learn.

Rufanes River Horseback, T046-6241669, T082-6971297 (mob). Trails through rolling hills, milkwoods, dunes and along beaches. Experienced guides, can pace to any level including children. They also have mountain bike trails on their farm.

Three Sisters Farm, 15 km along the R72 towards East London, T046-6751269. Beach trails, forest dune trails, family outings, as well as 2- to 3-day safaris with game viewing on horseback.

Transport

Grahamstown *p341, map p341*

Bus

Greyhound, T046-6222235, www.greyhound.co.za. Buses depart from the corner of Bathurst and High St by the conference centre. **Translux**, T046-6223241, www.translux.co.za. Coaches depart from outside the Frontier Hotel, Bathurst St. The town tourist office acts as a local booking agent. Buses stop in Grahamstown on the **Cape Town-Durban** route.

Port Alfred *p344*

Bus

Minilux, T043-7413107, runs a service from Settler's City Motors on Beaufort St, between Grahamstown and **East London** and **Port Elizabeth**. The Baz Bus stops at Station Backpackers 5 times a week.

King Williamstown *p345*

Bus

Greyhound, T012-3231154 www.greyhound.co.za. Coaches depart from the Engen One Stop (Wimpy), Cathcart St. Translux, T011-7743333, www.translux.co.za. Coaches depart from the BP service station on Alexander Rd. Buses stop in King Williams- town on the **Cape Town-Durban** route.

Directory

Grahamstown *p341, map p341*

All the major banks have branches in the Pepper Grove Mall on African St, where there are also internet cafés.

Port Alfred *p344*

Banks Standard Bank and First National, both in Govan Mbeki Av.

Useful telephone numbers

Ambulance, police or fire: T10111.

Eastern Cape Karoo

The surreal Karoo landscape, clear air and desert sunsets are evocative of the very heart of South Africa. The archaic scenery, created from sedimentary rock around 250 million years ago, is rich in fossils and San paintings. This is an area of vast open spaces studded with scrub and cacti, craggy mountains looming in the distance. Despite its barren appearance, this is mainly a farming area, known for its sheep, cattle, angora goats and horses. The most beautiful place to experience the Karoo is in the Valley of Desolation next to the historic town of Graaff-Reinet. The fastest route north into the Karoo is via the N2 from Port Elizabeth past Addo, which connects with the N10 heading to Cradock and Middelburg. The R63 leaves the N10 at Cookhouse and heads west to Somerset East and Graaff-Reinet. For more information on the region visit www.karoo heartland.co.za. ▸▸ *For Sleeping, Eating and other listings, see pages 357-360.*

North of Port Elizabeth ▸▸ *pp357-360.*

Somerset East → *Phone code: 042 . Colour map 7, grid A4.*

Somerset East is a neat agricultural town typical of the Karoo and was founded and named after Lord Charles Somerset, Governor of the Cape in 1815 on a farm that produced horse fodder for the cavalry on the frontline of the many skirmishes going on at the time. The town has a few historical buildings and faces the Bosberg Mountains. The **Somerset Museum** ⓘ *Mon-Fri 0800-1700, small entry fee,* recreates the atmosphere and lifestyle of a Victorian parsonage. It is set among beautiful rose gardens, the petals of which are used to make rose petal jam which is on sale in the museum shop. The **Walter Battiss Art Museum** ⓘ *Mon-Fri 0900-1700*, is also here and has the world's largest collection of this South African artist's work. For information contact **Blue Crane Tourism** ⓘ *88 Njoli Rd, T042-2431448, www.somerseteast.co.za.*

Cradock → *Phone code: 048. Colour map 7, grid A4.*

This small Karoo town is made up of an attractive grid of wide roads lined with Victorian bungalows. It was once a frontier town and has three Victorian churches. The **Dutch Reformed Church** on Stockenstroom Street was opened in 1868 and is based upon London's St Martin in the Fields, on Trafalgar Square. Cradock is now better known for its connections with the author Olive Schreiner who wrote *The Story of an African Farm*. The **Olive Schreiner House** ⓘ *9 Cross St, T048-8815251, Mon-Fri 0800-1245, 1400-1630, small entrance fee*, illustrates aspects of her life. There is also a trail leading to her grave on Buffelskop Mountain, off the R390, 25 km south of the town. **Cradock Spa** ⓘ *Marlow Rd, 0645-1930, R5*, is a series of indoor and outdoor pools set around natural sulphurous springs. From here, there are also two short circular hiking trails. The 10-km **Fish River Trail** follows the Fish River into town, crossing over the bridge and returning on the opposite bank. The **Eerstekrantz Trail**, 5 km, is a hike up the mountain opposite the spa resort. The surrounding farms support the ubiquitous silver windmills, a distinguishing feature of the Karoo.

The Cradock Library is home to a copy of an 1869 first edition Encyclopaedia Britannica.

For information contact **Cradock Tourism** ⓘ *Stockenstroom Rd, T048- 8812383, www.cradock.co.za, Mon-Fri 0830-1230, 1400-1600*. The office is very helpful and has a good collection of maps and accommodation listings.

Mountain Zebra National Park → *Colour map 7, grid A4.*

ⓘ T048-8812427, www.sanparks.org, gates open Oct-Apr 0700-1900, May-Sep 0700-1800, R60, R30 children.

The plains and mountains of this Karoo landscape support a wide variety of mammals including black wildebeest, kudu, eland, mountain zebra, red hartebeest, springbok, buffalo, black rhino and caracal. The Rooiplat Plateau is a particularly good area for seeing the zebra. Over 200 species of bird have been recorded here including many raptors and the endangered blue crane and, less appealingly, this is also the home of the giant earthworm. Buffalo were introduced in 1998 and black rhino in 2001, which put a stop to hiking in the reserve. Game viewing can be done by car during the day on the 37 km of tracks which cross the reserve.

The national park was established in 1937, when the mountain zebra was facing extinction and there were only five left on 65 sq km of land, four of which were male. There are now over 300 of them here, making it the largest herd of mountain zebra in the world. After breeding, many are relocated to other parks in South Africa. There are currently several studies being done to create a greatly enlarged reserve which will protect several different environments in the area.

Ins and outs The park is 280 km from Port Elizabeth and 25 km west of Cradock in the foothills of the Bankberg. The reserve is signposted from the Cradock to Middelburg road.

Park information There is a park camp with a fully licensed à la carte restaurant (open 0700-1900), which also serves snacks; and a shop, 0700-1900, which sells a good range of groceries, wines, curios, books and firewood. The camp also has a swimming pool (resident guests only), post office, telephones and petrol. For accommodation details see Sleeping page 358. Also visit www.sanparks.org.

Nieu Bethesda → *Colour map 7, grid A3.*

This small village has become famous through the work of Helen Martins and her Owl House. Helen was a local eccentric who lived a hermit-like existence, devoting her time to her art and the study of eastern philosophies. She was born in the house in 1898, and when she reached her fifties and when her parents died, she embarked on an extraordinary 25-year transformation of the house. Then in old age with crippling arthritis and poor eyesight – and considering her decoration of her house complete – she took her own life in 1971. Most of the surfaces on the inside of the house are decorated with finely ground glass of many colours, and in the pantry are rows of jars of crushed glass that Helen carefully graded by colour and weight. The light and colour of the glass is highlighted further by the myriad of candles, lamps and strangely shaped mirrors. At the back of the house is an enclosed area known as the Camel Yard, filled with hundreds of sphinxes, camels and other figures made from cement and glass. Her remarkable house and its grounds, along with much of her art is now a **museum** *ⓘ T049-8411603, www.owlhouse.co.za, daily, May-Oct 0900-1700, Nov-Apr 0800-1800, R10, children R8*, which attracts some 13,000 visitors a year.

The village has a collection of other artists' galleries, one shop, two restaurants, and no street lights. If you are self-catering it is better to stock up elsewhere and there is no petrol available here. There are a couple of good accommodation options, or as it is only 50 km from Graaff-Reinet, it can easily be visited in a day though you'll need to have your own form of transportation. There is an **information office** *ⓘ T049-8411401, www.nieubethesda.co.za.*

Traffic was once so infrequent in Nieu Bethseda that certain streets were allowed to be used for growing potatoes.

Graaff-Reinet

» pp357-360. Colour map 7, grid A3.

Founded in 1786, Graaff-Reinet is the oldest town of the Eastern Cape and lies between the Sneuberg Mountains and the Sundays River. The town was originally described as "nothing more than a collection of mud huts", but years of prosperity from farming are reflected in the local architecture – over 220 of the town's historical buildings have been declared national monuments. Today it is surprisingly smart,

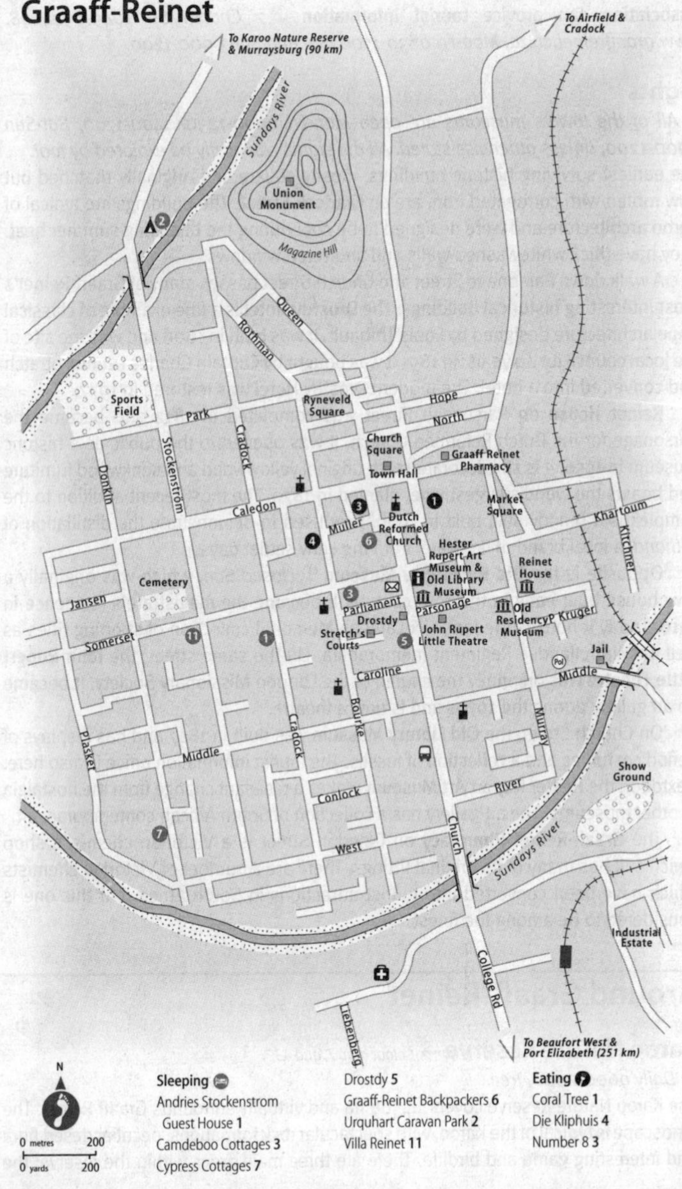

 with row upon row of perfectly restored houses, leafy streets and a quiet, bustling atmosphere. Nevertheless, Graaff-Reinet remains a small provincial town. Remember that this is deep Karoo country so don't expect much in the form of entertainment; some locals even claim that there are still lions in the area.

The town was originally established as an administrative centre to control the frontier districts for the government in the Cape. Mauritz Woeke was sent as governor or landrost in 1785. He chose the site of Graaff-Reinet because of its water supplies and fertile soils. The town grew to become an important trading centre on the new frontier and there was a boom in sheep farming during the 1850s, when English settlers first brought merino sheep to the region. The **Graaff-Reinet Publicity Association** can provice **tourist information** ⓘ *7 Church St, T049-8924248, www.graaffreinet.co.za, Mon-Fri 0830-1700, Sat and Sun 0900-1200.*

Sights

ⓘ *All of the town's museums are open Mon-Fri 0900-1230, 1400-1700, Sat-Sun 0900-1200, unless otherwise stated. All the sights can easily be explored by foot.*
The earliest surviving historic buildings, mostly square and originally thatched but now roofed with corrugated iron, are on **Cradock Street**. The buildings are typical of Karoo architecture and were designed to be cool during the blistering summer heat. They have thick whitewashed walls and shuttered windows.

A walk down Parsonage Street and Church Street passes many of Graaff-Reinet's most interesting historical buildings. The **Drostdy Hotel** is a fine example of classical Cape architecture designed by Louis Thibault. It was built in 1806 and was the site of the local council for 40 years. In 1855 it was bought by Captain Charles Lennox Stretch and converted into a hotel. The modern Drostdy Hotel was restored in 1977.

Reinet House on Parsonage Street was completed in 1812 and became the parsonage for the Dutch Reformed Church. It was opened to the public as a historic museum in 1956. It is still decorated with original yellowwood and stinkwood furniture and boasts the world's largest vine, planted in 1870. The most recent addition to the complex is a brandy still, built in 1990, now used to demonstrate the distillation of *withond*, a local brand of fire-water from the early settler days.

Opposite is the **Old Residency Museum** ⓘ *closed Sun*, which was originally a townhouse built early in the 19th century. It became the magistrate's residence in 1916. Today it houses the Jan Felix Lategan Memorial collection of sporting rifles as well as Middellandse Regiment memorabilia. On the same street, the **John Rupert Little Theatre** was originally the church of the London Missionary Society. It became an art gallery during the 1970s and is now a theatre.

On Church Street, the **Old Library Museum** was built in 1847 and has displays of period costumes and a collection of fossils. The tourist information office is also here. Nextdoor, the **Hester Rupert Art Museum** makes a pleasant change from the nostalgia of other museums. The art gallery has a collection of South African contemporary art.

The **Graaff-Reinet Pharmacy** on Caledon Street is a Victorian chemist's shop which still has many of its original fittings. There are a number of Victorian chemists which have been converted into tourist attractions in South Africa, but this one is considered to be among the finest.

Around Graaff-Reinet

Karoo Nature Reserve → *Colour map 7, grid A3.*

ⓘ *Daily 0600-2000, free.*
The Karoo Nature Reserve covers 14,500 ha and virtually surrounds Graaff-Reinet. The landscape is typical of the Karoo, with spectacular rock formations, peculiar desert flora and interesting game and birdlife. There are three main areas within the reserve: the

Valley of Desolation to the west; a game drive area to the north; and the eastern hiking area. To reach the park, take the road towards Murraysburg past the 1000-ha dam, which has picnic sites and is a popular place to sail and windsurf.

The **Valley of Desolation** is a national monument within the Karoo Nature Reserve. The bizarre rock formations were formed millions of years ago by weather erosion. Sheer cliffs and precariously balanced columns of dolerite rise 120 m from the valley floor. From the entrance to the Valley, drive up to the first viewpoint which has fabulous views of the Karoo in all directions to the horizon. Looking out over the harsh landscape gives you a good idea of the overwhelming obstacles that the Voortrekkers managed to overcome. If you continue up the road, you come to a car park and a short 1½-km hike, with stunning views of the mountains and the chance of seeing black eagles and dassies. Back down off the main road, is the 19-km game drive, where you may see Cape buffalo, kudu, mountain zebra and springbok. The **Eerstefontein Day Walks** start at the Spandau Kop Gate. There is a choice of three walks of 4 km, 11 km or 14 km. The walks pass through a wilderness area where you can see black wildebeest, kudu and springbok. Permits are required and can be bought at the gate; the trails are marked by lizard emblems. The **Driekoppe Trail** is an overnight trail that passes through the mountainous eastern area of the reserve. This area is rich in wildlife, and hikers can see klipspringers, kudu, mountain reedbuck and mountain zebra. The overnight hut sleeps 10 hikers. The trail must be booked in advance through the **Department of Nature Conservation** ⓘ *Bourke St, Graaff-Reinet, T049-8923453*. Information on the trails can be found at www.graaffreinet.co.za.

Kalkkop Impact Crater

ⓘ *Follow the N9 towards Aberdeen for about 30 km; at Aberdeen, turn left onto the R338 until you reach a right-hand turn marked as Aberdeen Rd. From here there is a dirt track that leads to the crater, follow the signs.*

A short distance from Graaff-Reinet are the weathered remains of a giant crater created by a meteorite more than 200,000 years ago. Research has shown the original hole to have been several hundred metres deep. Over time the crater has been filled with limestone deposits, but the circular ridge, with a diameter of 640 m, is still visible.

Sleeping

Somerset East *p353*

C Locomotive Lodge, accessed from the N10 near Cookhouse about 30 km east of Somerset East, T042-2472292, T082-6362036 (mob). Farm B&B with 8 rooms in an old railway station, breakfast is served in the ticket office, kitchen, TV lounge.

C-D Somerset Hotel, 83 Nojoli St, T/F042-2430557, leon_melson@ananzi.co.za. Simple town hotel built in the 1800s with tin roof, plain but good value doubles and singles with TV, cheaper rooms without bathrooms, friendly pub where you can meet the Karoo farmers, adequate restaurant on site.

Cradock *p353*

B Die Tuishuise, 36 Market St, T048-8811322, www.tuishuise.co.za. Characterful guesthouse based in a series of historical buildings on Market St, each restored and decorated to reflect the British and Dutch settlers' lifestyles a century ago. All of the houses have a fully equipped kitchen and lounge and are ideal for families or 2 couples travelling together. All rooms have en suite bathrooms and the staff are very friendly and helpful. Delicious, huge breakfasts are served in a Victorian dining room. A good evening meal can be had in the **Victoria Manor Hotel** (see below) at the end of the street. Has won numerous awards, recommended, almost worth a detour alone.

B Heritage House, 45 Bree St, T048-8813210, heritagehouse@isat.co.za. Delightful 180-year-old farmhouse with 3 comfortable and stylish double rooms, all en suite, and 2 airy cottages set on wide lawns. Electric blankets provided in winter. The owners are animal lovers so don't be surprised to see dogs, cats, rabbits or a rescued springbok foal tottering around the garden. Good breakfasts, friendly owners, the perfect spot to relax and soak up the Karoo atmosphere. Recommended.

B **Victoria Manor Hotel**, corner of Market and Voortrekker Sts, T048-8811650, reservations also through www.tuishuise.co.za. Lovely old town inn set in a 3-storey whitewashed Victorian building built in 1840. Full of character, with old-fashioned furnishings, a very good restaurant serving Karoo dinners, bar, tea room and attached curio shop.

C **Palm House**, 26 Market St, T048-8814229, metcalf@eastcape.net. Old-fashioned Victorian bungalow with 3 rooms, en suite, no smoking, old-style furnishings, high ceilings, log fires in winter, lovely old dining room, TV lounge, good breakfasts, very friendly owners.

Mountain Zebra National Park *p354*

Reservations through SAN Parks, T012-4289111, www.sanparks.org. See page 44 for details. For late bookings or cancellations within 72 hours or arrival, phone the reception direct on T048-8812427.

A **Doornhoek Guest House**, a restored Victorian farmhouse built in 1836, registered as a national monument. The house sleeps up to 6 people in 2 cast iron double beds and 2 single beds; all en suite. The house is decorated in a Victorian style, with pine floors, stained-glass windows, open fireplaces, a fully equipped kitchen. To complete the feeling of isolated luxury, the house is set in its own valley.

B **Cottages**, these 19 self-catering cottages are rather more functional. Each has 2 bedrooms, a bathroom, living room and a partially equipped kitchen.

D **Campsite**, has 20 caravan and camping sites set amongst good shade trees. There is a communal wash block and kitchen facilities. A maximum of 6 are allowed on each site. Some sites have power points.

Nieu Bethesda *p354*

B **House Number One**, 1 Cloete St, T049-8411700. Attractive old-style guesthouse, 3 very comfortable spacious rooms with antique furnishings, polished wooden floors, en suite, lounge, dining room, and veranda.

D-E **Owl House Backpackers**, Martin St, T049-8411642, www.owlhouse.info. Pleasant budget alternative with creatively decorated dorms and double rooms, cottage, camping, kitchen, bar and home-cooked meals. The friendly owners can organize tours to the Valley of Desolation and the Mountain Zebra National Park, and for a small fee they will pick you up and drop you off in Graaff-Reniet.

Graaff-Reinet *p355, map p355*

A **Andries Stockenstroom Guest House**, 100 Cradock St, T049-8924575, www.stockenstrom.co.za. This guesthouse was originally built in 1819 and has been restored and lavishly decorated. 6 en suite, a/c double rooms, swimming pool, and a superb dining room (residents only, closed Sun, TTT) serving an imaginative selection of haute cuisine Karoo meals including kudu, springbok, ostrich and guinea fowl with a French twist. The chef was trained at the *Ritz* in Paris.

A **Drostdy Hotel**, 30 Church St, T049-8922161, www.drostdy.co.za. Beautifully restored building designed by Louis Thibault in 1804. The rooms are at the back of the main house in an appealing complex of 19th-century cottages known as Stretch's Courts, originally the homes of emancipated slaves. There are 51 slightly fussy rooms, but all en suite and a/c. The public areas are decorated with antiques and paintings. The **Camdebo** and the **Court Room** restaurants have a good reputation (see Eating. There's a secluded garden where you can have pre-dinner drinks, a pool, secure off-street parking, and they have their own golf course 6.5 km out of town. Recommended.

A-B **Villa Reinet**, 83 Somerset St, T049-8923489, www.villa-reinet.co.za. A guesthouse set in an old church hall (a national monument) with broad corridors, high ceilings and comfortable furnishings. There are 2 a/c double rooms with en suite bathroom and large French doors leading onto a garden and splash pool, and 6 a/c garden cottages with hammocks. Breakfast is served in the cosy kitchen or under a pear tree in the garden. French speaking.

B **Cypress Cottages**, 80 Donkin St, T049-8923965, www.cypresscottage.co.za. 2 whitewashed Karoo single-storey cottages, 3 en suite bedrooms in each, communal lounge and dining room full of antiques, large garden, good for families, B&B.

C **Camdeboo Cottages**, 16 Parliament St, T049-8923180, www.camdeboocottages.co.za. A group of national monument 19th-century buildings which have been converted into 8 self-catering cottages built around a courtyard with a swimming pool and braai; meals available on request. Hot water bottles provided in winter, coffee shop on the premises. Centrally located. Recommended.

C-E Urquhart Caravan Park, at the edge of town next to the Karoo Nature Reserve, T049-8922136. Large park with clean, modern facilities for campers and caravans. There are a couple of chalets next to the Sundays River, some with kitchen, and very simple but excellent value rondavels, though you need to bring your own bedding and towels.

D Graaff-Reinet Backpackers, 8 Church St, T049-8925334, www.graaffreinetback packers.co.za. Dorms, doubles, triples, quads with shared bathrooms, neat modern and clean, good central location, internet access, laundry, bike hire, budget meals and braais available, and a communal kitchen.

Eating

Cradock *p353*

Cradock has its fair share of chain steak restaurants, or try the hotels.

TT Lemoenhoek, Mortimer Rd, 6 km out of town along the R337, T048-8812514. Excellent meals in the most unlikely of places, well worth the stop. Mix of quality Karoo dishes with a continental touch. Fine wines also on offer.

Nieu Bethesda *p354*

TT Die Waenhuis Pub & Grub, corner of Hudson and Martin Sts, T049-8411627. Tue-Thu 1100-1430, 1700-late, Fri-Sat 1100-late. Cosy pub wonderfully decorated with papier mâché animal lamps, stews and pies, hearty country cooking and big portions, large TV screen for important sports matches.

T The Brewery and Two Goats Deli, Pienaar St, T049-8411602. 1200-1430 low season, 1000-1600 high season. Simple rustic café with wooden benches, best known for its home brewed beer and fresh goat's cheese, excellent ploughman's platters with pickles, cheese and cold meat, eat in or takeaway.

Graaff-Reinet *p355, map p355*

One of the best restaurants is at the **Andries Stockenstroom Guest House** (see Sleeping page 357), but you have to be staying there to eat.

TTT Die Kliphuis, 46 Bourke St, T049-8922345, kliphuis@elink.co.za. Daily for breakfast and dinner. One of Graaff-Reinet's most beautiful historical buildings (1857), serves dinners of Karoo lamb or springbok are served in a traditionally decorated dining room with a roaring fire, grow their own vegetables and herbs. There are also 2 rooms here in the **B** range with Victorian bathrooms overlooking a Karoo garden with fruit trees and a pomegranate hedge.

TTT Drostdy, 28 Church St, T049-8922161. Two excellent romantic and elegant restaurants set in the historical **Drostdy Hotel**. Beautiful setting with high ceilings, polished wooden floors and candle light. Great nightly buffets with a fine range of local Karoo dishes, the à la carte menu is much more expensive but superb. Need to dress up a bit or there is a light more casual menu in the garden.

TT Coral Tree, 3 Church St, T049-8925947, closed Sun and for a couple of hrs each afternoon. Great location opposite the church. Very popular restaurant serving a good range of typical Karoo dishes – try the Karoo lamb or kudu steaks. Recommended.

TT Number 8, 8 Church St, T049-8924464, 11-late, closed Sun. Very popular pub and grill house, good simple steaks and fish and chips, TV showing sports, special kids dining room with toys, busy local watering hole.

Activities and tours

Nieu Bethesda *p354*

Tour operators

Ganora ExcursionsT049-8411302, www.ganora.co.za. Excellent small operator that specializes in trips to view ancient San rock art, as well as walking trails and fossil walks on their farm 7 km from Nieu Bethesda towards Middleburg. They also have a large stone cottage to rent out that sleeps 6. Recommended.

Graaff-Reinet *p355, map p355*

Tour operators

Irhafu Tours, T082-8442890 (mob), irhafutours@yahoo.com. Specializes in tours to the local township, the birthplace of the late Robert

Sobukwe, the former president of the Pan Africanist Congress. R80 for 1½ hrs.

Karoo Connections, 7 Church St, T049-8923978, karooconnections@intekom.co.za. Well-organized local tour operator offering a wide range of trips, including guided town historical walks, township tours, trips to San rock art, and Karoo farm visits.

Transport

Cradock *p353*

Bus

Intercape, T0861-287287, www.intercape.co.za, and **Translux**, T011-774333, www.translux.co.za. Cradock is on the **Port Elizabeth-Johannesburg** route.

Train

Spoornet, T0860-00888, www.spoornet.co.za. Cradock is on the **Port Elizabeth-Johannesburg** train routes.

Graaff-Reinet *p355, map p355*

251 km to **Port Elizabeth**, 90 km to **Murraysburg**.

Bus

Intercape, T0861-287287, www.intercape.co.za, and **Translux**, T011-774333, www.translux.co.za, stop in Graaf Reinet daily on the **Cape Town-Queenstown-East London** route. Buses stop at the Engen garage on Church St.

Cape Midlands and East London

→ *Colour map 7, grid A5.*

From King Williamstown the N2 heads back to the coast to East London. To the north of the city is the mountainous region lying between Stutterheim and Fort Beaufort, which is a beautiful area of rolling hills, lush indigenous forests and waterfalls. These are the Amatola Mountains and the region is referred to as the Cape Midlands. Sadly, some areas have now been replaced with pine plantations. Nevertheless, there remains an abundance of unharmed forest, criss-crossed with trails and perfect for hiking. The principle centre of the region is the coastal city of East London. It's predominantly an industrial city, though useful for stocking up on provisions for travel up the Wild Coast.

▸▸ *For Sleeping, Eating and other listings, see pages 365-371.*

Ins and outs

Getting there From King Williamstown to Queenstown there are two routes. The first follows the R63 west to Fort Beaufort and then heads north along the R67 to Queenstown. The second route heads north via Stutterheim and Cathcart via the N6. The Amatola Mountains can be reached from both sides. Further south the N2 runs through East London on its way to the Wild Coast. East London and Queenstown are connected by bus services running inland along the N6 from East London to Bloemfontein and Johannesburg. ▸▸ *For further details, see Transport, page 370.*

Best time to visit The mountains are at their best in spring or autumn; in winter it can get very cold and it is not unusual to have snow in May. Most of the rain tends to fall during the summer months. On the coast the climate is mild and sunny all year round.

Hogsback

▸▸ *pp365-371. Colour map 7, grid A5.* *Altitude: 1200 m.*

The quiet village of Hogsback lies in the centre of the Amatola Mountains, surrounded by rolling hills covered in forest reserves. The village itself has no real centre, but is made up of a string of cottages, hotels, tea gardens and craft shops dotted along several kilometres of gravel road. Tucked away down the side lanes are some beautiful gardens, more reminiscent of rural England than inland Africa. Among the early settlers was Thomas Summerton, a market gardener from Oxford, and his attempts to recreate the English countryside can still be seen in apple orchards, avenues lined with hazelnut, berry fruits and the flowering plants that have spread throughout the area. It's one of the few places in South Africa where berries thrive: red, white, and black currents, blackberries, raspberries, loganberries, strawberries and English gooseberries. As you can imagine the local people have gone into bottling overdrive and there are some delicious jams for sale in Hogsback's crafts shops. Lookout for **Oak Avenue**, an avenue of grand oak trees planted in the 1880s, which are still used for church services at Easter and Christmas when worshippers are seated on logs placed across the road. A new attraction in Hogsback is the labyrinth at **The Edge** (see Sleeping, page 366) which is an 11-circuit labyrinth, similar in design to the labyrinth in the Chartres Cathedral in France. The total distance of the walk to the centre and out is 1.4 km and the circumference is 91 m. There is a helpful **tourist office** ⓘ *Stormhaven Crafts, Main Rd, T045-9621050, www.hogsbackinfo.co.za, Mon-Fri 1030-1230, 1500-1700, Sat 1030-1230.*

The beautiful surroundings and slow pace of life makes Hogsback a delightful spot to rest up for a few days and explore the forests.

There are several theories as to how the area got its name. One is that a peak in the Hogsback range resembles the back of a hog when viewed from a particular angle. The other is that the founder was a Captain Hogg who had been based at Fort Mitchell. The Xhosa name for the peaks is *Belekazana* (to carry on the back), as another view from a different angle resembles a woman carrying a child on her back. Three peaks can be seen from the village, Hog One (1836 m), Hog Two (1824 m) and Hog Three (1937 m). The highest peak in the region lies to the north of Hogsback and is known as Elandsberg (2019 m).

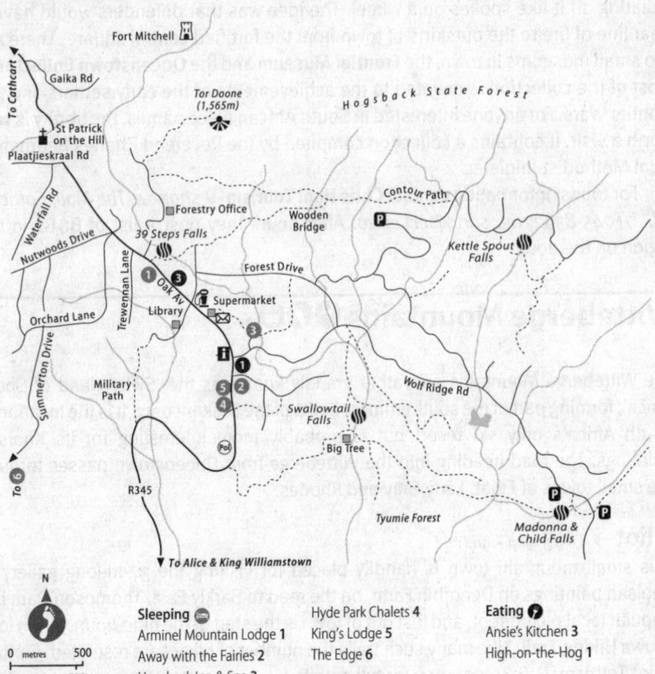

Local hikes

One highlight in the surrounding forests are the spectacular **waterfalls**. The most popular falls are known as Madonna and Child, Kettle Spout and the 39 Steps Falls. The Madonna and Child falls are a 30-minute walk from a car park on Wolfridge Road, 5 km from the village centre. The easiest falls to visit are the 39 Steps, which are 10 minutes' walk from the end of Oak Avenue. Look out for a green pig with a red triangle. If you're staying at **Away with the Fairies** (see Sleeping, page 365), there's a good one-hour walk to the Swallowtail Falls, where you'll pass an impressive 'big tree' and see plenty of vervet monkeys and birdlife.

A short distance from the centre of the village is the church of **St Patrick on the Hill**. The original chapel dates from 1935. Just beyond the church is a track off to the right, Gaika Road, which leads up to the viewpoint **Gaika Kop** (1963 m). The path is not very easy to follow – get a local map from one of the hotels before you set off.

Some of the finest views are from **Tor Doone** (1565 m), weather permitting. The easiest path follows the fire break at the end of Oak Avenue. Look out for markers with a yellow pig and a single green stripe; the contour path is marked with a green pig and yellow dot. Allow a minimum of two hours to get to the top.

Note that if you are here during the winter months the weather gets very cold at night. Even in summer, the nights are cold and a warm clear morning can quickly develop into low cloud and thunderstorms which may take a day or two to clear. If in doubt, check with local people who should be able better to interpret the vagaries of the weather.

Queenstown → *Colour map 7, grid A5.*

Queenstown is the largest town in the Cape Midlands and was named after Queen Victoria. Like many settlements in the area, it only started to thrive once the Frontier Wars had ended. However, the central square in the town was designed with defence in mind. Known today as the Hexagon, the square has six main streets radiating off it like spokes on a wheel. The idea was that defenders would have a clear line of fire to the outskirts of town from the fortified central square. There are two small museums in town, the **Frontier Museum** and the **Queenstown Collectors'**. Most of the collection is devoted to the achievements of the early settlers and the Frontier Wars. For anyone interested in South African place names, the library is well worth a visit. It contains a collection compiled by the Reverend Charles Pettman, a local Methodist minister.

For tourist information contact **Chris Hani Tourism** ⓘ *shop 14, The Mall, Cathcart Rd, T/F045-8392265, sarto@eci.co.za*. After hours they post a list of B&Bs in the region on the door.

Witteberge Mountains » *pp365-371.*

The Witteberge Mountains are rather grandly known as the 'Switzerland of South Africa', forming part of the southernmost limits of the Drakensberg. It is the location of South Africa's only ski resort but is probably more interesting for its Khoisan paintings. The road heading into the Witteberge from Queenstown passes through the small towns of Elliot, Lady Grey and Rhodes.

Elliot → *Colour map 7, grid A6.*

This small mountain town is handily placed for visiting the 32-m-long gallery of Khoisan paintings on Denorbin Farm, on the road to Barkly East. Thompson Dam is a popular local picnic spot, and just out of town is the start of the nine-hour, 39-km long **Ecowa Hiking Trail**. Like many such trails the number of hikers are restricted. Contact **Elliot Tourism** ⓘ *T045-9311011*, for full details.

Barkly East → *Colour map 4, grid B4. Altitude: 1183 m.*

Barkly East is nestled among the southern Drakensberg foothills. It's very close to Tiffindell, South Africa's only ski resort (see below), and there are snowfalls on the mountains here most winters. This area attracts skiers in winter and fly fishermen in the summer. The small **Barkly East Musuem** ⓘ *White St, T045-9710299, www.barklyeast.co.za*, has a collection of exhibits of the early settlement of the region, and displays of the Boer War. The museum also provides tourist information.

Rhodes → *Colour map 4, grid C5.*

Rhodes is a peaceful little mountain village overlooked by **Ben MacDhui** (3000 m), with a Herbert Baker designed stone school house, a Victorian hotel, a general store and one pay phone. If you arrive here in winter bring lots of warm clothes – while electricity did arrive a few years ago, there is still no central heating, though hotels will provide electric blankets. For information contact the **Rhodes Hotel** (see Sleeping, page 366).

Originally known as Rossville, the village was renamed by town leaders after the mining magnet and imperialist, Cecil John Rhodes, in the hope that he would make a substantial contribution to the town's finances. He obliged by donating a wagonload of pine trees that still decorate the streets, and £500 which promptly disappeared at the same time as the town clerk.

Tiffendell

The village is a one-hour drive from the ski resort at Tiffindell, the most popular ski area in South Africa, but the skiing is not up to much compared to other places in the world and the main slope is only 650 m long. The drive to Tiffendell through some scenic mountain passes is only by 4WD, though ask at the **Rhodes Hotel** (see Sleeping page 366) about transfers. There is a ski lift, snow-making machines and ski hire. Depending on the snow the resort is usually open from the end of May to the beginning of September. The **Snow Festival** takes place in at the end of July when there are skiing and snowboarding races. The resort is also popular during the summer with fly fishermen, mountain bikers, grass skiers and riders. For tourist information contact T011-7879090, www.snow.co.za. Accommodation is available at the resort, see Sleeping page 366.

Tiffindell is southern Africa's only ski resort located on the slopes of the highest mountain in the Eastern Cape, the 3001 m Ben Mc Dhui on the border with Lesotho.

Lady Grey → *Colour map 4, grid B4.*

Lady Grey lies in a forested sandstone valley surrounded by the high peaks of the Witteberge, often covered with snow in winter. The town dam is used for picnics, swimming and trout fishing. Tourist information is available at the **Home Coffee Shop,** T051-6030176. The **Karringmelkspruit Vulture Reserve** is 12 km south of Lady Grey on the road to Barkly East. Over 500 Cape vultures breed on the cliffs of this reserve.

Aliwal North → *Colour map 4, grid C4.*

Aliwal North lies on the south bank of the Orange River and was founded by Sir Harry Smith, governor of the Cape, in 1849 and named after his victory over the Sikhs at Aliwal in India. The 'north' bit was added, as at one time Mossel Bay on the coast was to be named Aliwal South. In the south of the town is a **Concentration Camp Memorial** commemorating the 715 Afrikaner people (mostly children) who died in terrible conditions in the camps set up by the British during the Boer War. The town's hot springs have been turned into the **Aliwal North Holiday Resort** ⓘ *T051-6332951, daily 0800-2200, R15*, with Olympic-size outdoor pool, indoor hot pools, saunas and a gym; the rather pungent waters are supposedly therapeutic for rheumatism and arthritis but the whole complex is rather run down and is due to be refurbished. **Buffelspruit Nature Reserve** lies to the east of town, where a limited number of game animals can be seen. Contact the local municipality for **tourist information** ⓘ *97 Somerset St, T051-6333567*.

Coelacanth – back from the dead

The discovery of a living coelacanth off the coast of East London in 1938 provided scientists with a link to prehistoric times. At first it was thought that they shared a common connection with lungfish and land vertebrates; on closer examination it became obvious that the fish had hardly changed since the Devonian period, 350 million years ago. It had been assumed that it had become extinct after some 290 million years. The fact that a living specimen was trawled from the deep destroyed this theory but the fish became known as a living fossil.

Named *Latimeria chalumnae*, this lobe-finned fish grows to about 1.5 m and can weigh 68 kg. It is bright blue and produces large quantities of oil and slime. Its four fins resemble legs and these have some rotating movement which allows them to crawl along the seabed. They have very powerful jaws.

More fish have been found near the Comoros Islands which lie to the north of the Mozambique Channel between Madagascar and mainland Africa. After all the excitement, it turned out that the Comores had been eating coelacanth for years. So much for coming back from the dead!

East London

» pp365-371. Colour map 7, grid B6.

East London is South Africa's only river port and a major industrial centre, with an economy based on motor assembly plants, textile and electronics industries. Nevertheless, the city centre has a certain energetic appeal to it, as well as a handful of attractive historical buildings. There are also surprisingly beautiful beaches which get very busy with domestic tourists over Christmas. Nahoon Beach is best known for its excellent surfing, and the city has attracted a real surfing community in recent years. Despite this, most travellers only pass through on their way to other coastal resorts or to the Amatola Mountains.

Ins and outs

Getting there **East London Airport** is 11 km from the city centre, T043-7060306. **East London Bus Shuttles** ⓘ *T082-5693599 (mob), www.elbusshuttle.com*, operates an airport shuttle service to the centre of town. **East Coast Shuttle** ⓘ *T043-7403060*, operates from the airport to the resorts on the Wild Coast. The larger car hire companies have desks at the airport. The **train station** ⓘ *T043-7002129*, is on Station Street. There are bus services to most South African cities with **Greyhound, Intercape, Minilux** and **Translux.** The **Baz Bus** also stops here. » *For further details, see Transport page 370.*

Tourist information The main tourist office covers the region from East London to King Williamstown and is known as **Buffalo City Tourism** ⓘ *King's Entertainment Centre, Esplanade, T043-7226015, www.visitbuffalocity.co.za, Mon-Fri 0815-1630, Sat 0900-1400, Sun 0900-1300*. The main office of **Eastern Cape Tourism Board** ⓘ*T043-7019600, www.ectourism.co.za,* is also located here.

Background

East London was originally founded as a military camp on the banks of the Buffalo River in 1847 and its strategic position as a port was soon recognized. Sir Harry Smith, the British governor, ambitiously named it London, and its two main thoroughfares are still Fleet and Oxford streets. Later it was renamed the Port of East London, and then simply as East London – not after London's East End but because the port was on the eastern bank of the river.

Sights

The town centre is a modern, bustling place, but there are several historical monuments: the Colonial Division Memorial is in front of the City Hall; the German Settler Memorial is on the Esplanade; and there are War Memorials on Oxford Street.

The **Ann Bryant Art Gallery** ⓘ *T043-7224044, Mon-Fri 0900-1700, Sat 0930-1200, free*, is on St Marks Road off Oxford Street, in an interesting Edwardian building dating from 1905. The collection was originally mostly of British artists but now has many fine contemporary South African works. An arts and crafts fair is held here on the first and second Sunday of each month.

The **East London Museum** ⓘ *Oxford St, T043-7430686, Mon-Fri 0930-1700, Sat 1400-1700, Sun and public holidays 1100-1600, small entry fee, coffee shop*, has a surprisingly interesting range of natural history exhibits. The highlights of the museum include the world's only dodo egg, and the coelacanth that was trawled up off the Chalumna River in 1938. The coelacanth, known as the fossil fish, was thought to have been extinct for 80 million years until it was rediscovered earlier this century (see page 364). The museum also has some good displays on Xhosa culture and customs, as well as a section devoted to Nguni beadwork.

Also on Oxford Street, outside the City Hall, is a monument to honour Steven Bantu Biko was unveiled by Nelson Mandela on 12 September 1997. At the time this marked the 20th anniversary of his death while in police custody.

Gately House ⓘ *1 Park Gates Rd, T043-7222141, Tue-Thu 1000-1300, 1400-1700, Sat-Sun 1500-1700, small entry fee*, was built in 1876 by John Gately, one of East London's first mayors. The house was donated to the city in 1966 and is now a town house museum decorated with original Victorian furnishings.

On the Esplanade is the **Aquarium** ⓘ *T043-7052637, 0900-1700, R15*. This is the oldest aquarium in the country with over 400 fresh water and marine species on display. There's a seal show twice daily at 1130 and 1530 and feeding times are half an hour before. There's also a whale deck with a telescope – a blue flag flies when whales are sighted.

The **Lock Street Gaol Shopping Complex** is on Fleet Street. Formerly a prison, built in the 1800's this was South Africa's first women's jail, whose most famous inmates were Winnie Madikizela-Mandela (ex-wife of Nelson Mandela) and Daisy de Melker, who was accused of poisoning two husbands and a son. The original gallows can still be seen. It is now home to shops and offices; check out the African curios shop for a good selection of items to take home.

West Bank Village

West Bank Village is the oldest surviving area of East London with some interesting old buildings on Bank Street and near the entrance to the harbour. **Hood Point Lighthouse** ⓘ *T043-7003056, Mon, Wed, Fri 1400-1600, Sat 0900-1100, small entry fee*, was built in 1895 and is a typical Victorian lighthouse with a steel upper gallery and keyhole windows. **Fort Glamorgan** is a vaulted brick building on Bank Street, closed to the general public though devotees of Victorian military architecture can get permission to visit the fort through Major Du Toit on T043-7311610. The fort was built in 1847 during the Seventh Frontier War to defend the supplies that were being sent to the inland garrisons from the Buffalo River Mouth.

Sleeping

Hogsback *p360, map p361*

In addition to the options listed below there are more than 20 different self-catering establishments. If you plan to hike in the region, these may be more convenient than staying in a lodge or hotel where meal times are fixed. Contact the local tourist office for further details. Be sure to book ahead during local school holidays.

B **Arminel Mountain Lodge**, Main Rd, T045-9621005, arminel@webmail.co.za. 23 log cabins with en suite facilities, excellent restaurant serving meals based on local fresh produce. Room rates include evening meals. Extensive gardens with great mountain views, swimming pool, tennis. The management is very friendly and keen to further promote this beautiful area which few overseas travellers visit. Recommended.

B **Hogsback Inn & Spa**, Main Rd, T045-9621006, www.hogsbackinn.co.za. Old-fashioned rural retreat with 28 comfortable (if chintzy) rooms. There is a good restaurant and a cosy, traditional pub, swimming pool, tennis court and spa facilities such as jacuzzi, massage and hairdresser, all set in 7 ha of grounds with the Tyume River flowing through. Log fires greatly add to the ambience. Very friendly and a good place to meet local folk.

B-C **Hyde Park Chalets**, 1 Dinwiddie Lane, T/F045-9621069, www.hydepark chalets.co.za. Self-catering set-up with comfortable chalets, double rooms, en suite bathrooms and kitchens, log fires, individual braais, swimming pool, nice green surrounds facing the mountains.

B-C **King's Lodge**, Main Rd, T045-9621024, www.kingslodge.co.za. 22 rooms with en suite bathroom, popular restaurant, bar, fine wood-panelled lounge and reception area. Large garden with a swimming pool and tennis court. Self-catering rooms available.

C **The Edge**, off Woodside Rd, T045-9621159, www.theedge-hogsback.co.za. 10 self-catering rondavels with log fires and feather duvets in a stunning setting perched on a cliff with spectacular views, surrounded by waterfalls and meadows filled with mushrooms and butterflies. If not staying, visit the **Tea Thyme** tea room to enjoy homemade goodies and the mountain views. Recommended.

D-E **Away with the Fairies**, T045-9621031, hogsback1@iafrica.com. One of the best backpackers in the country, a friendly, relaxed and well-run place. Well-kept, brightly painted dorms, double rooms, one new caravan (sleeps 2), well-equipped kitchen, clean bathrooms and cosy lounge with fireplace. The surrounding gardens are beautiful and a nesting ground for the Cape parrot of which there are only 300 left in the world, with plenty of camping space and a gate that leads to forest trails. There's a lively bar, great breakfasts and evening meals, daily guided walks and sundowner trips, regular shuttles to **Sugarshack** in East London and **Buccanneers** in Cintsa. Everyone feels very welcome and that there's always plenty to do from rock climbing to mountain biking. Highly recommended.

Queenstown *p362*

B **Carthews Corner**, 1 Park Av, Blue Rise (a suburb above the railway line), T/F045-8381885. Very smart B&B, with 8 rooms in garden cottages, swimming pool, secure parking, braai facilities, ask for Linda.

C **Hotel Hexagon**, 4 Hexagon Rd, T045-4513015. Standard but comfortable 2 star town hotel with 49 rooms, en suite, TV, restaurant, bar and café.

Witteberge Mountains *p362*

B **Umtali Country Inn**, 47 Dan Pienaar Av, Aliwal North, T/F051-6332400, www.getaway-gateway.com. Smart lodge with 33 newly renovated rooms with a/c, underfloor heating and DSTV, lovely swimming pool, generous meals served in the restaurant with fireplace, within walking distance of the **Aliwal North Holiday Resort** where the hot pools stay open until 2200.

B-C **Mountain View Country Inn**, 36 Botha St, Lady Grey, T051-6030421. A pleasant rural retreat in a Victorian building with a lovely view over the town towards the mountains. 12 family and double rooms with en suite bathroom, nicely decorated, excellent homemade food, especially the scones and marmalade, and friendly pub.

B-D **Tiffindell**, T045-9749004/5, www.snow.co.za. 170 guests are accommodated in centrally heated rooms within 100 m of the ski slope and the main restaurant and bar. There is a choice of private chalets, en suite rooms, budget rooms with shared ablution facilities, or luxury self-catering accommodation in wooden cabins sleeping 6.

C **Kenmure Guest Cottage**, off the R58, Barkly East, T045-9719072, cretchley@eci.co.za. B&B, 3 rooms decorated with chintzy embroidery, pretty 1.5-ha garden, clay tennis court and pool, dinner on request.

C **Rhodes Hotel**, corner of Miller and Sauer Sts, Rhodes, T045-9749305, rhodeshotel@

lbrand.com. Charming old-style hotel restored to resemble the original hotel of more than a century ago, 9 en suite rooms with antiques and electric blankets, B&B rates, good home cooking, tennis court, local tours, fly-fishing and horse riding organized.

C Walkerbouts Inn, 1 Vorster St, Rhodes, T045-9749290, www.walkerbouts.co.za. Also known as Rhodes Backpackers though there are no dorms. 6 comfortable and spacious en suite rooms with electric blankets, B&B, cosy pub with pizza oven and local beer on tap.

C-D Rose Garden, 10 Dampier St, Elliot, T045-9311158. Tidy and friendly B&B, en suite rooms with TV, tea and coffee, fresh fruit, electric blankets, dinner can be arranged.

East London *p364, map p367*

There is not a great deal of interesting accommodation in East London and most is in old beachside block hotels. The majority of backpackers staying in East London are here for the surf. Others tend to move on to the far nicer Cintsa, 38 km up the coast.

A Blue Lagoon, Blue Bend Place, Beacon Bay, T043-7484821, www.bluelagoonhotel.co.za. 76 en suite rooms in what used be a timeshare resort on the Beacon Bay headland overlooking the sea and estuary with stunning views. Some 2-bedroom apartments and 3-bedroom townhouses with kitchenette and lounge set in large grounds full of palms, 2 restaurants and bars, swimming pool, squash and tennis courts.

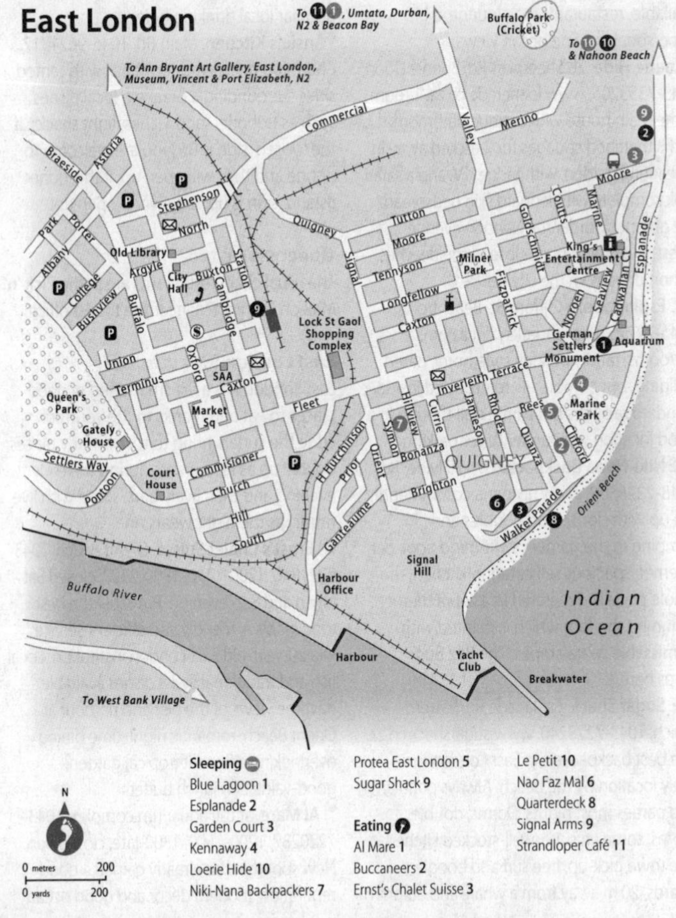

A-B **Protea Hotel East London**, 27 Inverleith Terr, T043-7223174, www.proteahotels.co.za. Comfortable city centre option aimed at business travellers, with 80 rooms, some of which are more luxurious and thus more expensive, TV, lounge. **Kasbah** restaurant serves à la carte French dishes, also **El Bistro** coffee shop, 3 bars, secure covered parking.

B **Garden Court**, corner of Esplanade and Moore Sts, T043-7227260, www.southernsun.com. This is a **Holiday Inn** which is undergoing rebranding. Modern block set back from the beach, 173 standard a/c rooms, with balcony, some have views of the beach, restaurant, bar, swimming pool, curio shop, secure parking, on the seafront.

B **Kennaway Hotel**, Esplanade, T043-7225531, www.osner-resorts.co.za. A large modern block overlooking Orient Beach, with 103 rooms, non-smoking room available, restaurants, bar, lounge, a bit impersonal but fine ocean views.

B **Loerie Hide**, 2b Sheerness Rd, Bonnie Doon, T043-7353206, www.loeriehide.co.za. 1 room in the main house with antique bathroom, and 3 thatched cottages for 2 tucked away in a beautiful garden, with fridge, TV, and a safari look complete with leopard skin bedspread, the grounds border the Nahoon riverine forest, swimming pool, close to the beaches, a short drive from the city centre.

B-C **Esplanade**, 6 Clifford St, Beachfront, T043-7222518, esphotel@iafrica.com. 74 rooms, family holiday style hotel, dated building, but completely refurbished inside, standard facilities but a little dull though in a good location with under cover parking.

D-E **Niki-Nana Backpackers**, 4 Hillview Rd, T043-7228509, www.nikinana.co.za. Friendly set-up with dorms and doubles and camping in the garden, swimming pool, bar, internet, spacious self catering kitchen, the whole place is decorated in a zebra theme, including the roof which is painted with unmissable zebra stripes. The **Baz Bus** stops here.

D-E **Sugar Shack**, Esplanade Rd, Eastern Beach, T043-7228240, www.sugarshack.co.za. The best backpackers in East London in a lively location by the beach. Always popular and parties most nights. Dorms, double rooms, some en suite, well-stocked kitchen, free town pick-up, free surf and boogie boards, 20 m away from a whale and dolphin watching tower, good value daily adrenaline-fuelled activities organized. Ideal location with a number of local pubs and clubs in walking distance. Recommended. Runs a shuttle to **Away with the Fairies** in Hogsback.

Eating

Hogsback *p360, map p361*

The main hotels include dinner in their room rate, so there is not much of a choice for eating out at night. If staying at a guesthouse, check if evening meals are available.

TT **High-on-the-Hog**, Main Rd. The only local restaurant, with good nightly specials. Great soups (don't miss the creamed butternut), steaks and pasta dishes, and friendly bar.

TT **Purple Chameleon**, **Kings Lodge**, Main Rd. Simple pub serving hearty lunch and dinner, focus on steaks and burgers, popular local drinking hole.

T **Ansie's Kitchen**, Main Rd, T045-9621317. Charming rustic wooden shack with tented sides surrounding a braai pit, local dishes such as bobotie, sandwiches, light snacks. If the 'closed' sign is up, you are welcome to phone and they will open up. If the 'gone fishing' sign is up, they won't open up!

Queenstown *p362*

The usual chain restaurants are in the **Pick 'n' Mall** on Cathcart St, near the tourist office.

East London *p364, map p367*

East London has a fair smattering of good places to eat and thanks to the youthful edge the surfers bring to town, many places double up as restaurants during the early evening and then lively bars, some with live music, as the night wears on.

TTT **Ernst's Chalet Suisse**, Orient Beach, T043-7221840, 1200-1430, 1800-2300, closed Sat lunch and Sun evening. Probably the best food in town, friendly and efficient service in a 20-year-old East London institution. Local fish and traditional Swiss dishes available, daytime views of the pier and harbour at Orient Beach, romantic night-time dining overlooking a floodlit tropical garden, good-value Sun lunch buffet.

TT **Al Mare**, at the aquarium complex, T043-7220287, 1200-1500, 1800-late, closed Sun. New spot that has already gained a good reputation, modern decor and good ocean views, daily specials, Mediterranean influenced dishes, pizza and pasta.

🍴🍴 **Buccaneers**, Eastern Beach, Esplanade, T043-7435171, 1100-late. Popular pub and grill house, serving steaks, seafood and salads, the mood at lunchtime is more business orientated then it gets very lively at night with live music and a thumping bar. Very popular venue for surfers and backpackers, on the beach close to the **Sugar Shack** backpackers.

🍴🍴 **Le Petit**, 54 Beach Rd, Nahoon, T043-7353685, 1200-1400, 1800-2200, closed Sat lunch and Sun. Classic French dishes, pub lunches and game including ostrich and crocodile (and frog's legs). A la carte or good value 3-course set menu. Watching the chef prepare flambé dishes is fun.

🍴🍴 **Nao Faz Mal**, Windsor Cabanas, T043-7432225, dinner only, closed Sun. Authentic Mozambican and Portuguese all-you-can-eat buffet with a wide range of dishes, relaxed place, good seafood and peri-peri chicken, popular place so book ahead. Recommended for the very hungry.

🍴🍴 **Quarterdeck**, Orient Pavilion, Esplanade, T043-7435312, 1200-1430, 1800-2300, closed Sat lunch and all day Sun. A busy seafood dining room and bar with German beer on tap and live music Wed, Fri and Sat. Good value, shares a kitchen with the more upmarket **Ernst Chalet Suisse**. Great if you are on a tight budget but want to eat well.

🍴🍴 **Strandloper Café**, 95 Old Transkei Rd, T043-7354570, 1830 for dinner, closed Sun. Surprisingly good seafood in a small, quiet and unremarkable restaurant from both local waters and further afield, such as imported New Zealand green-lipped mussels and Norwegian salmon. This is the place to go for seasonal oysters and crayfish.

🍴 **Signal Arms**, train station, Station St, T043-7436882, closed Sun. Steakhouse and busy pub serving the likes of bangers and mash and liver and onions with an above average choice of imported beers, giant TV screens for sport, and occasional live music. Nothing fancy, but the majority of residents keep coming back. Always a good sign.

Shopping

Hogsback *p360, map p361*

There is a supermarket, a bottle store and a petrol station in town (but no banks). Otherwise, there are several craft shops which sell gifts as well as delicious locally made jams. When you first arrive in the village you are likely to be greeted by local Xhosas selling their crafts. Look out for the clay animals: kudu, horses and hogs are the most common. These items are not found elsewhere in South Africa.

East London *p364, map p367*

Vincent Park Centre, Devreux Av, 5 km from the city centre, follow Oxford St and turn right onto Devreux Av just after the museum. This is a modern South African shopping mall where you will find a full complement of shops, plus banks, post office, multi-screen cinema showing the latest blockbuster releases, and restaurants. It holds an arts and crafts market every Sun 0900-1300.

Activities and tours

Hogsback *p360, map p361*

Trout fishing is popular in the dams and rivers belonging to the Wild Trout Association members, 50 farmers in the region who allow access to their land for fishing. Fly fishing can be arranged through a day permit system run from **Walkerbouts Inn**, T045-9749290, dave@wildtrout.co.za, www.wildtrout.co.za.

East London *p364, map p367*

Cricket

The East London cricket ground, **Buffalo Park**, is South Africa's newest international venue. It is a short distance from the beach and is the smallest of the current Test match grounds in the country, with a capacity of 16,000. Ticket enquiries T043-7437757, ticket sales through **Computicket**, www.computicket.co.za.

Diving

The best time of year for diving is during the winter between May-Aug. The dives around **Nahoon Bay** and **Three Sisters** are 8-15 m deep, over pinnacles, ledges and caves. The reefs are colourful and have soft corals, sponges and reef fish. Nahoon Reef is good for snorkelling but popular with surfers.

Border Undersea Club, T043-7482958, T083-2829138 (mob). Alan Grimmer can offer information on dive courses and trips.

Surfing

The best-known surf break is **Nahoon Reef**, with a reputation for having the most consistent break in the country. Easterns, in front of the Sugar Shack backpackers, is the most consistent beach break in the area, with regular tubes. The best surf information is to be found at the Sugar Shack and the other backpacker's hostels, most of which will hire out surfboards and offer lessons to beginners.

Tour operators

Amatola Tours, T043-7430472, www.touringsa.co.za. Local and city tours from 2 hrs to full day.
Imonti Tours, 26 Venice Rd, Morningside, T043-7413884, imontitours@absamail.co.za. City and township tours.

Transport

Queenstown *p362*

Bus

Buses depart from Shell Ultra City on Cathcart St. Greyhound, T012-3231154, www.greyhound.co.za. Translux, T011-7743333, www.translux.co.za. Queenstown is on the **Johannesburg-East London** route.

Train

Spoornet, T0860-008888, www.spoornet.co.za. Queenstown is on the **Johannesburg-East London** route, daily except Wed and Sat. Full timetables and fares can be found on the website.

Witteberge Mountains *p362*

Bus

Buses depart from Balmoral Hotel on Somerset St in **Aliwal North**. Contact details for **Greyhound**, and **Translux**, same details as for Queenstown, above. Aliwal North is on the **Johannesburg-East London** route.

East London *p364 map p367*

From East London it is 584 km to **Bloemfontein**, 1099 km to **Cape Town**, 674 km to **Durban**, 395 km to **Graaff-Reinet**, 1002 km to **Johannesburg**, 310 km to **Port Elizabeth**, 207 km to **Queenstown**, 235 km to **Umtata**.

Air

Kulula, T0861-585852, www.kulula.com. Flies daily between East London and **Johannesburg** (1 hr 45 mins) SAA, reservations, T011-9781111, www.flysaa.com. Flies daily between East London and **Durban** (1 hr 10 mins), **Johannesburg** (1 hr 45 mins), **Port Elizabeth** (50 mins), and **Cape Town** (1 hr 35 mins).

Bus

Local For information and timetables on local bus services: T043-7221251.

Long distance Baz Bus, T021-4392323, www.bazbus.com. A hop-on, hop-off service for backpackers that runs between **Port Elizabeth** and **Durban** 5 days a week. The bus will collect and drop off at any of the local backpacker hostels.

All the long distance buses depart from Windmill Park on Moore St. **Greyhound**, T043-7439284, www.greyhound.co.za. Translux, T043-7001999, www.translux.co.za. Both have services to **Durban** (9 hrs) daily via **Umtata**, **Kokstad** and **Port Shepstone**; **Cape Town** (14 hrs) daily via **Port Elizabeth** and **Knysna**; and to **Johannesburg** and **Pretoria** (14½ hrs) daily via **Bloemfontein** (7 hrs). **Intercape**, T043-7222254, www.inter cape.co.za, has a service to **Cape Town** (14 hrs) via **Port Elizabeth** (4 hrs). There is no direct service to **Johannesburg/Pretoria** but you can change buses in Port Elizabeth.

Minilux, T043-7413107. Coaches depart from the tourist office, 35 Argyle St and from Major Sq in Beacon Bay going to **King Williamstown**, **Grahamstown**, **Port Alfred** and **Port Elizabeth**.

Car hire

Avis, airport T043-7361344, toll free T0861-021111, www.avis.co.za.
Budget, airport T043-7361084, 9 Breezyvale Rd, T043-7362364, toll free T0861-016622, www.budget.co.za.
Hertz, airport T043-7362116, 165 Jan Smuts Av, Greenfields, T043-7025700, toll free T0861-600136, www.hertz.com.
Imperial, airport T043-7362230, toll free T0861-131000, www.imperialcarrental.co.za.

Taxi

Border Taxi, T043-7223946.

Train

The railway station is in the town centre on Station St, which runs parallel to Oxford St. Information T043-7002719, reservations T0860-008888, www.spoornet.co.za. There are services between East London and **Johannesburg** (20 hrs), via **Queenstown** (4½ hrs) and **Bloemfontein** (13 hrs). Fares and schedules are published on the website.

Directory

East London *p364, map p367*
Banks Branches of Standard Bank, First National and ABSA have ATMs and exchange facilities along Oxford St and in the shopping malls. Remember that if travelling on to the Wild Coast, that there are no banks in the small resort towns. **Internet** There are a few spots around town or try. **Cyber Lounge**, 58 Beach Rd, Nahoon or the backpackers. **Medical services** East London Private Hospital, 32 Albany St, T043-7223128. Medicross Hospital, T043-7210105. British Airways Travel Clinic, St James Rd, Southernwood, T043-7437471. **Useful telephone numbers** Ambulance: T10177. Police: T10111.

Wild Coast

The coastline region that stretches roughly 280 km from East London to the Umtamvuna Nature Reserve next to Port Edward in KwaZulu Natal was once the former Transkei independent homeland during the Apartheid years. These days it is known as the Wild Coast and is a largely rural area of rolling grasslands wedged between the Great Kei River in the south and the Umtamvuna River in the north. Its inland borders are the Drakensberg and the Stormberg mountains, and dotted between are small villages, brightly painted kraals and endless communal pastureland. It remains a traditional area populated by the Xhosa, who still practise customs such as dowry payments and initiation ceremonies. The Great Kei River was originally the border between South Africa and the Transkei, and as the N2 crosses the Kei River 65 km north of East London, the difference in the standard of living between the two areas is striking. Years of overpopulation and under-investment have taken their toll in the former Transkei. The landscape is deforested and seriously eroded and away from the N2 the roads are in poor condition compared to the rest of the country. There are few tourist amenities here and you will get a more realistic picture of the poverty that still blights South Africa. Nevertheless it is a beautiful region to explore and the coastline itself is rugged and peaceful, with a number of caves, beaches, cliffs and shipwrecks to explore. ▸▸ *For Sleeping, Eating and other listings, see pages 380-384.*

Ins and outs

Getting there and around The N2 is the Wild Coast's main road and is well surfaced. However, it doesn't run along the coast but runs from East London up to 100 km inland until it meets the coast again at Port Shepstone in KwaZulu Natal, from where it heads north to Durban. The towns along the N2 have thriving economies based around transport. There are abundant petrol stations, basic supermarkets and one or two small hotels, but these mainly for commercial clientele so there are very few frills. Consequently the towns along the N2 are utilitarian and scruffy and always thronged with traffic. The long distance buses stick to the N2, and the **Baz Bus** only deviates to Port St Johns. The coast itself is the area's main attraction and there is a fine selection of isolated seaside accommodation between East London and Port St Johns. A number of roads lead from the N2 to the coastal resorts, often by way of ramshackle villages, and although there has been a lot of road resurfacing going on in the Eastern Cape in the last few years, many of these are gravel. If driving, it is always a good idea to check on the latest state of the road, as the region is prone to seasonal flooding.

 Tourist information Arriving at a resort without a reservation is not a good idea as they are often at the end of long and difficult roads. Remember most resorts are fully booked during the holiday season. All towns along the N2 have public telephones, so even with a last-minute decision it is possible to phone ahead and to check on the condition of the road. For more information on visit www.wildcoast.org.za.

Wild Coast Holiday Reservations ① *To43-7436181, www.wildcoastholidays.co.za*, is an excellent central reservations service that can provide advice on accommodation. This can be very useful when trying to find out about some of the more remote hotels. An excellent way of seeing the most inaccessible areas of the Wild Coast is by doing a tour of the rural regions. » *For further details, see Activities and tours, page 384.*

East London to Kei Mouth » *pp380-384.*

The coast immediately to the north of East London has been named the 'Romantic Coast' by the local tourist board, and its relative wildness makes the statement ring true. Although the coast is being developed for tourism there are still considerable stretches of the coastline which are protected nature reserves. There are thick dune forests and windswept open beaches stretching to wild waves. The coastal resorts nearest to East London can get crowded during the South African school holidays, but for the rest of the year it is quite surprising how isolated and quiet this coast really is.

Before heading for the coast from the N2, remember to take petrol, food, cash and everything you think you will need – the nearest shop or bank could be 100 km away.

Ins and outs

Getting around The resorts of Gonubie, Cintsa, Haga-Haga, Morgan's Bay and Kei Mouth are all within an hour's drive of East London. Public transport to these resorts is virtually non-existent, but as the hoteliers on the coast regularly visit East London to collect supplies, you can often get a lift to the coast by telephoning ahead. The **East Coast Shuttle** ① *To43-7403060*, runs a service from East London to the coastal resorts, but requires a minimum of six passengers. Do not drive through the former Transkei (roughly East London to Port Shepstone) after nightfall. Some of the roads are rough and even on the N2 there is the danger of hitting a stray animal.

Gonubie → *Colour map 7, grid B6.*

This tourist resort overlooks the Qunube (Gonubie) River and the lagoon. It is only 20 km northeast of East London and has become a popular suburb with commuters. Its main attraction for tourists is that it offers a wide range of sporting facilities including some of the best diving along this coast. The beach here has large dunes, is safe for swimming in the sea and in the tidal pool, and its possible to spot dolphins and whales from the 500 m boardwalk overlooking the beach. For information contact **Buffalo City Tourism** in East London, see page 364.

Kwelera Nature Reserve lies 10 km to the north of Gonubie and is an area of sand dunes and dune forest facing the sea. The highest dune here rises just over 250 m above sea level. The forests are inhabited by vervet monkeys, bushbuck and numerous forest birds. There is a small picnic site which is popular with local visitors who come here to fish and surf. This nature reserve is part of the Strandloper Trail, see page 376.

Inkwenkwezi Game Reserve

The best time of year for spotting birdlife is from September to November; the wild flowers are best from August to September.

① *33 km from East London. Take the N2 towards Umtata and turn off at the Brakfontain exit, turn left into the East Coast Resort Rd. A sign for the reserve is 20 km on the left side. To43-7343234 www.inkwenkwezi.com.*

This private 100-sq-km coastal game reserve has a combination of forest dunes and bushveld, and is home to an impressive range of imported game, including rhino, lion, wildebeest, giraffe, warthog, Eastern Cape kudu and an abundance of birdlife. Visitors leave their cars at the entrance and are transported around the reserve by 4WD. A range of trips can be organized, including night drives, horse riding, and walking trails. Expect to pay around R500 for a four-hour game drive with lunch, and R600 for a four-hour

isiXhosa

Most of the Eastern Cape is populated by the Xhosa and the predominant language is isiXhosa. This is especially true in the Wild Coast region as this was the former Transkei homeland during the Apartheid years. In total it is spoken by approximately 7.9 million people, or about 18% of the South African population. Several letters of the language are represented by a click and even the word isiXhosa has a click in it. There are three main clicks; the first is the dental click, which is made with the tongue on the back of the teeth, the second is the lateral alveolar click, which is made by the tongue at the sides of the mouth, and the third is the postalveolar click, which is made with the body of the tongue on the roof of the mouth.

The spelling of place names in South Africa, especially in the more remote areas, can sometimes be inconsistent. Place names are derived from so many languages, which then have often become corrupted or Anglicized. Though sometimes the process goes in the opposite direction, with English names taking on a distinctly local flavour. For instance, there is a primary school in the Wild Coast called Gwadu Senior Primary. The Gwadu is a corrupted form of the word 'guardian'. It is not unusual to find the same place having slight variations in spelling in different books or maps and on signposts. Added to this is that some places in the Eastern Cape are reverting back to their isiXhosa spellings, though this may take a while to reflect on road signs and maps. Cintsa is now spelt Chintsa, Qolora Mouth and Qolora River is now Qholorha, Qora is now Qhorha, and Umtata is now spelt Mthatha. Whilst on the Wild Coast, and especially if you go off the beaten track, you will invariably encounter the Xhosa people. They will be most delighted if you try out a few words of isiXhosa.

English	isiXhosa
Hello	molo
Good morning	intsasa emnandi
Good night	ubusuku obumnandi
How are you?	Unjani?
Good-bye	sala kakuhle
Please	enkosi
Thank you	enkosi kakhulu
Yes	ewe
No	hayi

night drive with dinner. There's also a restaurant that serves a good Sunday lunch, R80, with a terrace overlooking the reserve, and a tented camp (see Sleeping, page 380).

Cintsa → *Colour map 7, grid B6.*

The combined villages of Cintsa East and Cintsa West nestle on lush hills rolling down to a lagoon and a wide stretch of deserted beach. Although popular during the Christmas holidays, the resort is blessedly isolated for the rest of the year and offers relaxing outdoor activities such as canoeing and horse riding. There are a couple of backpacker hostels which lay on more adventurous pursuits including kloofing and surfing, but the main appeal here is lazily exploring the shell-strewn beach, forests and tranquil lagoon. A large development planned for Cintsa is the Chintsa River Golfing Estate, with construction due to go ahead mid-2006. The project is expected to include an 18-hole golf course, 650 holiday/time share homes and a large hotel. Time will tell how it will change the face of Cintsa.

Haga-Haga → *Colour map 7, grid A6.*

Further along the coast lies this tiny seaside resort, 72 km from East London and 27 km from the N2. The road travels through fields of pineapples. With a rocky coastline, good beaches and a lagoon to swim in, it is ideal for hiking and fishing. Its name is said to be derived from the sound the waves make as they wash the shoreline. With only a shop and hotel, this is a peaceful spot to spend a few days and lose track of time. The best place for tourist information is the **library** ⓘ *29 Mariner's Way, T/F043-8411645.*

Morgan's Bay → *Colour map 7, grid A6.*

This is a perfect resort 90 km from East London for a peaceful beach break and a taste of the Wild Coast. The village itself is tiny and somewhat isolated and has little more than a hotel with pub and restaurant, the local store, a bottle shop, a couple of curio shops and a petrol pump. The surrounding countryside is a nature reserve and is a great place for hiking along the cliffs or strolling along the miles of white sandy beach where deep currents wash up unusual shells. The bay is regarded as one of the most beautiful in the country. Called Double Mouth, it consists of a lagoon formed by two small rivers backed by a line of sandstone cliffs. The beach with a lighthouse here was voted in the top 10 beach walks of South Africa by the South African outdoor magazine *Getaway*.

Kei Mouth → *Colour map 7, grid A6.*

This quiet seaside resort has a couple of supermarkets, some curio shops, a butcher, two bottle stores and a petrol station. Nearby are some municipal tennis courts and a golf course.

The **Kei River** was formerly the border between the two former homelands of Ciskei and Transkei, now all part of the Eastern Cape. The river is navigable upstream for a short distance by boat or canoe, although sandbanks make it difficult at times. A popular river trip is to **Picnic Rock**, about 8 km upstream. The journey passes a private game reserve where it is possible to spot game. The cliffs around **Cob Hole** on the eastern side of the river are quite dramatic and the patches of forest further on are rich in birdlife. There is a spot on the eastern bank of the river with a small creek and a landing stage. The path from here climbs up a riverbed through forest and at the end of the trail is a deep pool with two waterfalls where you can swim – this is Picnic Rock.

North from Kei Mouth » pp380-384.

There are two possible routes leading on from Kei Mouth. The *Pont* is a **car ferry** ⓘ *0630-1730, R30 per car,* which crosses over the Kei River. After crossing on the *Pont*, the R366 heads uphill for 9 km where it joins the R48/1 at Kentani. The road then divides, heading inland to Butterworth or seawards to Qolora Mouth. All these roads have recently been tarred and are in excellent condition.

Kentani

Kentani itself is a tiny settlement but it has a huge history. It was the site of the final battle of the Frontier Wars between the Xhosa and the settlers in 1878. The Xhosa warriors had been told by their witchdoctor that he had made them impervious to bullets. Therefore they stormed a fort of colonial troops but were mown down by heavy fire. Three hundred warriors died, with a loss of only two of the English forces.

Butterworth → *Colour map 7, grid A6.*

This is the first town that the N2 passes on its way through the old Transkei. It is a hectic and unappealing stretch of supermarkets and discount stores, and has little to keep

Strandloper Trail

The term Strandloper derives from the Dutch; *Strand* meaning beach and *Loper* meaning walker. This is a popular five-day 55-km hike along the coast from Kei Mouth to Gonubie, overnighting in huts. It's an ideal walk for anyone looking for a peaceful but energetic few days along the coast and the trail passes through Kwelera Nature Reserve so there is a good chance of seeing some wildlife.

The trail runs in one direction and starts at the manager's station at Cape Morgan at Kei Mouth where you are issued with a permit. The trail is clearly marked with painted yellow footprints and can be walked at any time of year, though the best weather is between February and May, which have warm windless days. Hikers are issued with a tide table to assist in crossing the Quko, Kwenxura, Kwelera and Gonubie rivers. You need to take strong watertight bags and rope in your pack.

The four huts along the trail; Beacon Valley, Cape Henderson, Pumphouse and Double Mouth, have water and ablution facilities. All have braai places except at Cape Henderson which is in a state forest and no fires are permitted. Take all necessary equipment. The huts are included in the cost of the trail, but there is the option to upgrade and stay in resorts at Morgan's Bay and Haga-Haga, or at the backpacker hostel in Cintsa.

The trail is limited to 12 people and the cost is around R360 per person. The trail is managed by the **Strandloper Ecotourism Board**, T043-8411046, www.strandlopertrails.org.za. Bookings can be made online. There are several other hikes along the Wild Coast; visit www.wildcoast.org for more information.

you there for long. Founded as a Wesleyan mission station in 1827, it is the oldest town in the Transkei, although little of its history is evident today. At the end of the Frontier Wars in 1878, traders began to settle here and the town has grown to become a small industrial centre. Just outside of town, there is one attraction worth stopping for: the **Bawa Falls** on the Qolora River are spectacular after the rains when the water drops over 100 m. From Butterworth, the N2 continues north to Umtata, 135 km.

Qolora Mouth → *Colour map 4, grid C5.*

Qolora Mouth has a private airstrip and is accessible by light aircraft. The alternative is to travel the 16 km from the *Pont* over the Kei River or come directly from Butterworth. There are two holiday resorts here on a beautiful stretch of headland overlooking a spacious beach and the Qolora Lagoon where the Qolora River widens before spilling into the sea. There is a hike up the **Gxara River Heads**, 4 km inland, to the pool where Nongqawuse, a young Xhosa girl, saw visions and communed with her ancestral spirits. She heard voices telling her that the dead would rise and destroy the European invaders if the Xhosa destroyed all their cattle and crops. This disastrous prophesy lead to the deaths of thousands of people through starvation, and Nongqawuse had to spend the rest of her life in hiding. She is buried on a farm near Alexandria.

Nxaxo Mouth

The road heading north from Kentani goes to Nxaxo Mouth, which lies at the confluence of the Nxaxo and Nqusi rivers. The area has a lagoon and is dotted with swamps and islands. The estuary is rich in birdlife and there are hiking trails through a small strip of coastal forest to a colony of crowned cranes. Listen for the distinctive calls of groups of trumpeter hornbills which inhabit the forest.

Mazeppa Bay → *Colour map 7, grid C5.*

This small holiday resort is named after the *Mazeppa*, a coastal trading ship that used the bay as a point to unload trading goods. There is a suspension footbridge to the island from where you can see Clan Lindsay Rocks, the site where the *Clan Lindsay* was wrecked in 1898. **First Beach** is good for swimming, and the waves on this stretch of coast attract local surfers. Just back from the beach are the shell middens left by strandlopers. August is a busy month when many people come here for the shark fishing. The nearby **Manubi Forest** has 7 km of trails passing through patches of yellowwood and sneezewood trees. A 4-km hike north along the coast leads to the grounded wreck of the *Jacaranda*, a 2000-ton Greek ship that ran aground in 1971.

Qora Mouth → *Colour map 4, grid C5.*

The N2 highway continues north from Butterworth until it reaches Idutywa. There is a turning at Idutywa to Willowvale, 32 km, from where there is a road which passes the village of Nyokana and leads to Qora Mouth, 66 km from Idutywa. This road has recently been tarred. Qora Mouth is a small collection of houses, hardly large enough to be called a village, and is known for its kob fishing. The rivermouth here marks the ecological boundary between the sundu palms whose habitat lies to the south of the river and are characteristic to KwaZulu Natal, and the lala palms which only grow to the north. At the mouth of the river is a lagoon and a fine swathe of beach.

Coffee Bay → *Colour map 4, grid C6.*

At the mouth of the Nenga River, Coffee Bay is easily accessible on a tarred road and is well known for its good surf, making it a major stop on many backpacker routes. Nevertheless, development has been low key and it remains a quiet and laid-back place. The name Coffee Bay comes from the coffee trees which grew here briefly in the 1860s after a ship ran aground with a cargo of coffee beans. The **Hole In The Wall** is a famous natural feature and well worth a visit. An enormous tunnel has been eroded by the sea through a cliff which lies just offshore. The local Xhosa call it izi Khaleni, which means 'place of thunder'. At high tide the sound of the waves clapping can be heard throughout the valley. A small holiday resort has sprung up by the beach here.

Umtata

» *pp380-384. Colour map 4, grid C5.*

It is believed that a clan of the Tembu tribe had a custom interring their dead by casting them into the river with the entreaty '*mThate Bawo*' (Take him, Father) and that from this verb the name the river on which Umtata was founded was named. Today Umtata is a sprawling, unattractive modern town full of cheap supermarkets and discount liquor stores with a small grid of historical buildings at its core. Founded in 1871, it was the capital of Transkei from 1976 to 1994 and has grown to be a busy administrative centre. The N2 passes through the city centre where some of the oldest buildings are located, including the City Hall built in 1908 and the Bhunga (parliament) Building dating from 1927. The latter is now home to the **Nelson Mandela Museum**, the latest addition to the city's (limited) sights, but definitely worth a stop for an understanding of how homelands such as the Transkei were created under the Apartheid system, and to learn more about the formidable man himself.

Ins and outs

Tourist information **Eastern Cape Tourism** ⓘ *corner of York Rd and Victoria St, T047-5315290, www.ectourism.co.za, Mon-Fri 0800-1630*, can provide information on local nature reserves.

The former site of the Transkei parliament, is the **Nelson Mandela Museum** ⓘ *Bhunga Building, Owen St, T047-5325110, www.nelson mandelamuseum.org.za, Mon-Fri 0900-1600, Sat 0900-1230, free*. The museum was officially opened by the great man himself on 11 February 2000, to coincide with the 10th anniversary of his release from prison. The displays provide a moving insight into Mandela's life and his struggle against Apartheid, focusing on his autobiography, *Long Walk to Freedom*. There are extracts of the book complemented by photography, personal items, letters and video footage, including a short excerpt from an interview he gave in 1961. Other displays include international awards and honorary degrees that he received, portraits and sculptures of him, and diplomatic gifts he received during his term of office, including a boxing glove signed by Mohammed Ali and George Foreman (Mandela used to box in his youth).

Other components of the museum are Mandela's primary school and birthplace. The **school** consists of two rondavels and a hut in the tiny rural village of Qunu, where Mandela lived as a youth. The graves of his parents and his son and daughter are also here, along with his new house, which can be photographed from the outside but not visited. Today the rondavels form the **Community Museum and Cultural Centre**. Mandela's **birthplace** at the former Transkei village of Mvezo on the other side of the N2 where there are the remains of the homestead where he was born and some photographs on display, including one of Mandela burning his pass book. The staff at Umtata are very enthusiastic about the museum and are happy to answer questions. If you don't have your own transport, they will also arrange a tour from Umtata to Qunu and Mvezo, a short drive south on the N2. A recommended experience.

Back in Umtata, a block north of the Nelson Mandela Museum on Victoria Street, is the **Transkei Museum**, which features local displays of traditional dress, local crafts and stuffed animals.

Port St Johns

» pp380-384. Colour map 4, grid C6.

This small, peaceful town on the banks of the Mzimvubu River has a laid-back atmosphere which may have something to do with the fact this is a major cannabis-growing area. Its bohemian feel has attracted many artists and, more recently, backpackers. Consequently, there's a good selection of budget accommodation here, much of which is self-catering. There aren't many restaurants but local produce such as papaya, avocado pears, pecans, macadamia nuts and fresh fish is sold on the beach.

Portuguese ships stopped here to pick up water on their journeys up the coast and the town itself is named after the *Sao Joao* which was wrecked here in 1552. A trading post was built in 1846, and in 1878 the British established a military outpost here and built Fort Harrison. When the Transkei was an independent homeland, much of Port St John's 'green gold' (cannabis) was sent to the gold mines of Johannesburg.

Second Beach is the most attractive beach: a beautiful stretch of soft sand, backed by smooth, forested hills. As a pleasant contrast to most beaches visited by tourists, the majority of sunbathers and swimmers here are black. There are two nature reserves within easy reach of town: Silaka (see below) and **Mount Thesiger**, which has a small herd of wildebeest belonging to an unusual sub-species which has no mane. The warm, sulphurous springs at Isinuka are just outside of town.

The **tourist office** ⓘ *T047-5641187, www.portstjohns.org.za/tourism*, is on Town Entrance Square, just to the right as you enter the town.

Silaka Nature Reserve

→ Colour map 4, grid C6.

ⓘ *Open to day visitors 0600-1800. For overnight stays, see Sleeping page 383.*

This reserve is on a gravel road 6 km south from Port St Johns and lies in a forested

Huberta the Hippo

Huberta the hippo is one of the most famous wild animals in South African history. She was born in the Mhlatuze Lagoon near the modern-day port of Richard's Bay in Zululand, and in 1928 inexplicably decided to head off on an 800-km trek down the coast. This incredible journey took three years, and her story was followed by newspapers around the world. She walked through the middle of Durban, looking into shop windows while pedestrians dived for cover, and continued down what is today the Wild Coast. Huberta arrived in Port St Johns in March 1930, and seemed to like it – she stayed for six months and lived in the river.

Despite its name (*Mzimvubu*, meaning 'home of the hippo') none of her ilk had been seen in the river for years. It was a lively six months for the residents of the town as Huberta wandered through gardens, grazed on lawns, upset a few boats, and things only calmed down after her departure in September. There was national mourning at the end of the year when news flashed around the world that a pair of trigger-happy farmers had shot Huberta in a river in the Eastern Cape. Her remains can be seen at the Amathole Museum in King Williams Town. There has never been another hippo in the Mzimvubu River.

valley that stretches from Second Beach to Sugarloaf Rock. Although the reserve is small, the tropical atmosphere of the trails weaving through the tangle of thick forest is unmissable. Blesbuck, blue wildebeest and Burchell's zebra have been reintroduced. There is a beautiful stretch of rugged coastline and just off the beach is Bird Island, a breeding colony for sea birds. Interesting rock pools occur on the shore surrounding the island, which may be reached at low tide. At the estuary opposite Bird Island, an attractive pebble beach is surrounded by driftwood and aloes, which grow almost to the sea.

Hluleka Nature Reserve → *Colour map 4, grid C6.*

ⓘ *Open to day visitors 0600-1800. For overnight stays, see Sleeping page 380.* Some 30 km south of Port St Johns, on a good dirt road, this reserve covers 772 ha of evergreen forest, lagoon, saltmarsh and rocky seashore. The Hluleka River flows through and out of the forest into an open area where large coral trees, quinine trees and Natal figs grow along its banks. A network of paths has been laid out from which you can see wildlife, including blesbuck, blue wildebeest, Burchell's zebra, which have been recently introduced, and Cape clawless otter and monitor lizards. The birdlife here is particularly rich and the African jacana, black duck, Cape batis, dabchick, green pigeon, long crested eagle, olive bushshrike and yellow-throated longclaw have all been seen here.

North to Port Edward and Durban » pp380-384.

Mkambati Nature Reserve → *Colour map 5, grid C1.*

ⓘ *Sunrise to sunset, small entry fee, for overnight stays see Sleeping page 379.* The coastal reserve covers an area of 8000 ha between the Msikaba and Mtentu rivers. The grasslands here are known for their gladioli, ground orchids and watsonias. Large numbers of grazing herbivores such as eland, red hartebeest, blue wildebeest, blesbuck and gemsbok, have been introduced into the reserve, although only the first two species are indigenous to the area. Of the many streams running through the reserve, the Mkambati is perhaps the most beautiful with its crystal-clear pools and series of spectacular waterfalls, the impressive **Horseshoe Falls** drop down several metres into the ocean. The forested ravines along the Msikaba River are lined with thick riverine forest and the unique Pondo coconut or Mkambati palm. This is the only place in the world where it grows. Cape vultures nest on the cliffs above the Msikaba River gorge. Gurney's sugarbird, the greater double collared sunbird, the red-shouldered widow and many other woodland birds can be seen here. Canoe trips, horse riding and hiking are the best way to see this area of forested ravines and coastal grasslands.

Ins and outs The reserve lies on the coast between Port St Johns and Port Edward. The road from Port St Johns passes through the villages of Lusikisiki, Flagstaff and Holy Cross. There are plans to surface the road to Mkambati, but until that happens it is best to do the journey in a 4WD.

Sleeping

Gonubie *p373*
B **Gonubie Point Guest House**, 14 Deary Dr, T043-7404279, daphneb@mweb.co.za. Luxury sea-facing en suite rooms with floor-to-ceiling windows and spacious balcony or terrace, some with spa baths, cheaper family rooms, B&B, swimming pool, modern set-up overlooking the beach.
B-E **PSA Holiday Resort**, T043-7321022, www.psaresort.co.za. 105 caravan and camping sites set in forested dunes full of birds, a few mins' walk from the beach, ablution blocks and kitchen units, 10 fully equipped self-catering chalets overlooking the Quenera rivermouth, swimming pool.

Inkwenkwezi Game Reserve *p373*
L **Inkwenkwezi Tented Camp**, T043-7343234, www.inkwenkwezi.com. Luxury tents or chalets, some with fireplaces and fridges, bathrooms set in cave-like environments with showers to look and feel like a waterfall, rates include meals and game drives. The **Emthombeni** restaurant and bar serves Eastern Cape cuisine overlooking the river valley, it's open to non-guests for the Sun buffet lunch and Wed for dinner, and is famous for its hamburger night.

Cintsa *p374*
B **Cintsa Lodge**, 684 Fish Eagle Dr, Cintsa East, T043-7385146, www.cintsalodge.com. Attractive, modern complex with picture windows, smart swimming pool and terraces and balconies with ocean views, private walkway to the beach. 5 bright and spacious doubles in the main house, and 2 family chalets in the gardens, breakfast included, dinner on request.
C-D **Buccaneer's Backpackers**, T043-7343012, www.cintsa.com. Superb backpacker lodge set in forests overlooking the lagoon and beach. A 2-km dirt track leads to the secluded site, with a choice of dorms, doubles, fully equipped self-catering cottages and camping on platforms beneath trees. There is a lively bar, pool, kitchen, volleyball court, climbing wall, horse riding on the beach, beauty treatments and massages, free canoes and surfboards, excellent home-cooked evening meals and free daily activities. Also home to **African Heartland Journeys**, an ecotourism initiative for exploring the Wild Coast (see Activities and tours, page 384). Very relaxing spot in a beautiful setting and well run, if slightly overpriced. Recommended. Baz Bus stop.

Haga-Haga *p375*
B-D **Haga-Haga Hotel and Cabanas**, 155 Mariner's Way, T043-8411670, www.hagahagahotel.co.za. A large family-run complex situated on a rocky headland. 15 hotel rooms, 30 self-catering cabanas plus budget cottages for backpackers. Seafood restaurant, bar with pub grub, TV lounge, swimming pool, tennis, fishing, safe tidal pools. Good rates for full board and a recommended family option.

Morgan's Bay *p375*
B-E **Morgan's Bay Hotel**, Beach Rd, T043-8411062, www.morganbay.co.za. This is a family-run hotel which markets itself as

an affordable family resort, great if you are travelling with kids, it was voted in the top 10 family holidays by the South African outdoor magazine *Getaway*. There are 33 good-value rooms; prices vary with the tourist season but the service maintains its high standard throughout the year and off-season is excellent value. Swimming pool, views across the bay, gardens which extend down to the beach. Inside there is a comfortable lounge, a quiet reading room, a dining room with an extensive breakfast buffet and an à la carte menu in the evenings. Travellers with children have the option of a separate dining room and child minders. There is also a caravan and camping park with 31 sites.

C-E **Mitford Lodge**, 14 Beach Rd, follow the road past the **Morgan's Bay Hotel**, T043-8411510, www.morgansbay.co.za. Excellent choice of rooms, sleeping 2-6, to suit most budgets. Comfortable en suite rooms, self-catering chalets, and a backpacker lodge is also attached. **Krans Kombuis Bar and Restaurant**, home-cooked meals, pub and internet access.

Kei Mouth *p375*

B **Kei Mouth Beach Hotel**, T043-8411017, www.keimouthbeachhotel.co.za. A neat complex right on the beach with 38 doubles and family en suite rooms with TV, a restaurant, 2 bars, and swimming pool. The pool and gardens are protected from the sea breeze by mature tropical trees. Nearby you can go fishing, horse riding, canoeing and play golf. Ask about the good-value all-inclusive package deals.

Qolora Mouth *p376*

B **Seagulls Beach Hotel**, T047-4980044, www.seagulls.co.za. Beachfront hotel with 29 double rooms with en suite bathroom, TV, private patio, some with sea views. The rooms are in small single storey units dotted around the grounds. Restaurant, bar, swimming pool, direct access to a sandy beach. The central reception block houses a TV lounge, snooker table and the **Anchor Inn** bar. Guests can enjoy canoeing, windsurfing and fishing in the nearby lagoon. Further afield it is possible to go horse riding and play golf.

B **Trennery's**, T047-4980004, www.trennerys.co.za. 45 thatched chalets set in large shady gardens full of mature trees, seafood restaurant, swimming pool, canoeing, golf, boating, tennis, fishing, bowls, snooker table and a small shop. Excellent value given that all meals are included in the rates and there are good value weekly specials. An all-round holiday resort in one of the finest settings along this stretch of coast. Recommended.

Nxaxo Mouth *p376*

A **Wavecrest**, T047-4980022, www.wavecrest.co.za. An excellent hotel in a beautiful setting on the edge of a lagoon, with 35 thatched bungalows, bar, seafood restaurant, tennis, watersports, deep-sea fishing, private airstrip. Off season full board packages start from around R360 per person, good value, recommended.

Mazeppa Bay *p377*

B-C **Mazeppa Bay Hotel**, T047-4980033, mazeppabayhotel@sanet.co.za. Accommodation is a mix of doubles, family rooms and rondavels, all with sea views and private surrounds. The central building has a restaurant, the **Red Blanket** bar which serves snacks, a TV lounge, snooker table and terrace. The whole complex sits on a green ridge covered with tropical vegetation, overlooking a broad sandy beach. Also prides itself on having its own island, accessible by an ancient swing bridge. Anglers have a choice of rock, lagoon or river fishing. Less luxurious but cheaper than some of the other Wild Coast resorts.

Qora Mouth *p377*

B **Kob Inn**, T047-4990011, www.kobinn.co.za. Isolated, comfortable hotel set on rocks above the sea. Accommodation is in 10 thatched cottages with 1 or 2 bedrooms and en suite bathroom. There is a restaurant specializing in seafood, and a bar. The swimming pool is perched on rocks overlooking the ocean, and the extensive gardens are surrounded by coastal forest. There are a couple of shady beaches nearby plus the Qora River which is ideal for canoeing. Deep-sea fishing trips can be organized from the hotel.

Coffee Bay *p377*

A-E **Hole In The Wall Hotel and Holiday Village**, T047-5750009, www.holeinthewall.co.za. Set by the beach, this, large resort has a selection of accommodation to suit all budgets, 26 en suite double rooms in garden thatched rondavels, 28 self-catering whitewashed units with 2 bedrooms sleeping up to 8, 10 campsites and a backpackers lodge with 9 cheaper doubles and 3 dorms set further up the hill, (backpackers and campers can use the hotel facilities). Swimming pool, bar, restaurant, pool tables, volley ball court, TV lounge, nightly seafood braais. With notice will pick up from the Baz Bus in Umtata.

B Ocean View Hotel, T047-5752005, www.oceanview.co.za. Comfortable set-up perched on a headland above the main beach, 29 double rooms with terraces and sun loungers, 50 m from the beach, swimming pool, bar, restaurant, rates include breakfast and dinner. Golf and horse riding nearby, deep-sea fishing charters. Trips can be arranged to a traditional Xhosa village.

C-E The Coffee Shack, T047-5752048, www.coffeeshack.co.za. Daily shuttle to Shell Ultra City in Umtata to hook up with the mainline buses and Baz Bus. Popular party place set right on the beach. Mix of dorms and doubles in thatched rondavels, camping, good kitchen facilities, **Bablaza** pub which gets very noisy at night, great seafood and African suppers and big breakfasts, plenty of activities on offer, free surfing lessons. Great spot for a couple of wild days by the beach. Recommended.

D-E Bomvu Paradise, T047-5752073, www.bomvubackpackers.com. Another party lodge set in tropical gardens with decks and hammocks. There are dorms, double rooms and campsites, a restaurant and a bar, be wary of the space cakes. An alternative place, with yoga lessons, drum sessions, monthly full-moon parties and Xhosa song and dance performances. Strong emphasis on surfing – claims to have the only surf shop on the Wild Coast.

Umtata *p377*

It is far preferable to stay in nearby Coffee Bay or Port St Johns and visit Umtata when passing through. There is no backpacker accommodation here and the centre of town is not particularly safe at night.

B-C Garden Court Umtata, (part of the **Holiday Inn** chain), 3 km north on the N2, T047-5370181, www.southersun.com. 116 a/c rooms, TV, swimming pool, restaurant, bar, slot machines, comfortable but unremarkable concrete block, 1 km from Nduli Game Reserve.

Port St Johns *p378*

A Umngazi River Bungalows and Spa, about 25 km west of the town, off the R61 back towards Umtata.T047-5641115, www.umngazi.co.za. Thatched luxury bungalows facing the estuary surrounded by mangrove forest, restaurant, bar, dine in the wine cellar, shop, swimming pool, wide range of watersports including sunset cruises up the river and night fishing, conference centre, beauty spa, fly-in packages, award winning resort, good value for families, full board rates.

B-C The Lodge, Second Beach, T/F047-5641171, thelodge@wildcoast.com. B&B, 3 double rooms, good sea views from the wooden veranda. The location and view are something to write home about – over a long lazy day or 2. Also has a reputation for quality food and wine.

B-E The Jetty, 5 km from the town centre by the river, T047- 5641072, www.the jetty.co.za. A small, peaceful guesthouse with 4 double rooms, 3 self-catering units and 2 campsites each with their own ablution block, all set in beautiful gardens on a bank of the Umzimvuba River full of avocado and lychee trees where the rare Cape parrot feeds. B&B or self-catering possible in a communal kitchen, no bar. Perfect location for a few relaxing days, and the owners offer wheelchair-friendly fishing. Recommended.

C Gwyneth's Barn, First Beach, T/F047-5641506, 8501@mrinfo.co.za. Short walk from the beach. Self-catering units in 1 cottage and 1 tree house for 4-8 people. Well equipped with all mod cons, including satellite TV for sports junkies. The units are set in wild gardens with private terraces and a braai area. Great atmosphere.

C-D Outspan Inn, Main Rd, T047-5641057, www.outspaninn.co.za. A local favourite with 9 double rooms, 4 self catering units and a backpackers dorm room, at the mouth of the Umzimvubu River. The restaurant and pub has a good reputation and is worth visiting, and there's a swimming pool. Reception also act as an unofficial local information centre.

Backpacker hostels

Backpackers will find plenty of accommodation and things to do in Port St Johns.

C-D **Ikaya Le Intlabati**, Second Beach, T047-5641266, ikaya@telkomsa.net. A fine, small guesthouse-cum-backpackers, one of the last places at the end of the dirt road on Second Beach, the name means house on the beach in Xhosa. The building is surrounded by tropical indigenous bush, and the gardens extend down to the beach. A mix of singles, doubles, and triples and 1 cottage sleeping 4, self-catering or meals, pre-book a pick-up from Umtata. Next door is a hand-dyed clothing workshop – **Jakotz Clothing**. Worth a visit if you're planning on spending some time in PSJ. Secure parking.

C-E **The Island Backpackers Lodge**, 341 Berea Rd, First Beach, T047-5641958, www.theislandbackpackers.co.za. Friendly and well-run backpacker lodge with a good range of rooms, including dorms and some comfortable en suite doubles. There's a restaurant and chill-out room, plus a TV room, internet access, bar, camping and shuttles to Second Beach, Baz Bus stop, no children.

D-E **Jungle Monkey**, 340 Berea Rd, First Beach, T047-5641517, junglemonkey@iafrica.com. Next door to **The Island**, dorms, doubles, camping, bar, TV room, bright murals and rambling garden with hammocks and swings, Baz Bus stop.

E **The Kraal**, Mpande, T082-8714964, www.thekraal-backpackers.co.za. Signposted from road to Port St Johns. The Kraal is a 20-km drive along a bad dirt road, but is well worth the trip. Set on an isolated hill above a beach and lagoon, the lodge is made up of 3 traditional Xhosa rondavels with dirt floors, no electricity and 'eco-loos'. Accommodation is in dorms, or there is space for camping. Communal kitchen where you can buy all your supplies, superb meals served, hot showers, wonderful views over the sea. The Kraal built the local school which often needs volunteer teachers, call them if you're interested. A genuine retreat and perfect for experiencing village life in the old Transkei. Recommended.

Silaka Nature Reserve *p378*

Reservations are made through the tourist office in Umtata, T047-5315290, www.ectourism.co.za. 14 very simple self-catering **bungalows** (D) with 2 bedrooms, kitchen, bathroom. You will have to book in advance to stay here.

Hluleka Nature Reserve *p379*

12 self-catering **chalets** (D) on stilts with ocean or forest views, each sleeping 6 people. There is a small shop here with postal facilities. Reservations as above.

Mkambati Nature Reserve *p379*

At the time of writing **Wilderness Safaris** were planning to develop 2 upmarket game lodges in the reserve. Visit www.wilderness-safaris.com for the latest information.

A **Wild Coast Sun**, accessed from the R61 north of the reserve, near Port Edward, T039-3059111, www.sun-international.com. Modern, brash, luxury hotel with 245 rooms, pool, casino, cabaret, cinema, championship golf course, beach and watersports, at an undeniably good location with miles of sweeping beach. Once part of the Transkei and only 90 mins' drive from Durban, this used to be the place gamblers from KwaZulu Natal would come when gaming was only legal in the homelands.

Eating

Most eating along the Wild Coast is in the hotels and resorts. There is the usual range of chicken and burger chain restaurants in Umtata and Butterworth but not much else. Most of the petrol stations along the N2 have restaurants such as **Wimpy** attached. If you are self-catering along the coast, the supermarkets in East London or in Port Shepstone in KwaZulu Natal are the best places to stock up on provisions.

Cintsa *p374*

TTT **Michaela's**, T043-7385139, www.michaelas.co.za, 1130-1430, 1800-2130, closed Mon night and all day Tue. This is a remarkable restaurant perched on the top of Cintsa's biggest sand dune, reached by a short funicular train ride. If you are not fit, call ahead to check this is operating. The thatched restaurant has 2 levels with large windows and outside decks overlooking the ocean, the seafood is excellent as are the salads that make good use of seasonal fruits and vegetables. The gut-busting Sun lunch buffet is recommended.

Port St Johns *p378*

Gecko Moon, First Beach, T047-5641221. 1100-2130. Excellent German cook, specializes in fish menus, plus good wood-fired pizza.

Activities and tours

Cintsa *p374*

African Heartland Journeys, based at Buccaneer's Backpackers in Cintsa (see Sleeping page 380), T082-2696421, www.africanheartland.co.za. Sensitively run camping tours by 4WD, bike and canoe that go right into the heartland of the Wild Coast to places you could never get to otherwise. Overnight accommodation is in Xhosa villages, which is an excellent way to see how people live without roads, electricity or cars. Highly recommended. 4-day trips start from R3000.

North to Port Edward *p379*

Amadiba Adventures, T/F039-3056456, www.amadibaadventures.co.za. This is part of a government tourism development programme funded by the European Union, where coastal communities run and own the tourism initiatives. Accommodation is in mobile camps with eco-toilets and hot bush showers, and prices include 3 meals per day. There are plenty of activities available, such as hiking and swimming beneath waterfalls, and excellent 4- to 6-day horse or hiking trails up the coast and inland. Local guides are very knowledgeable about the area and much of the tour involves contact with local people. All proceeds go back into local community. Reports have been excellent and it is an organization worthy of support.

Transport

Baz Bus

From East London the Baz Bus, T021-4392323, www.bazbus.com, runs along the N2, stopping at **Cintsa** before turning off at **Umtata** to the coast and **Port St Johns**, from where it continues on to **Port Edward** in KwaZulu Natal. It runs the same route in reverse. For the 100 km or so journey to Coffee Bay hostels will collect backpackers from the Baz Bus at the Shell Ultra City on the N2 outside Umtata for a small fee and by prior arrangement. Hotels may also pick up guests by prior arrangement. Minibus taxis also run to both resorts, and leave from Circus Triangle in town. It is not advisable to try and hitch this route. Avoid driving here after dark, as there have been violent incidents.

Umtata *p377*

Air

KD Matanzima Airport is 17 km from the city centre, information T047-5360632. SAA, reservations, T011-9781111, www.flysaa.com, operates direct flights between Umtata and **Johannesburg** (90 mins) 3 times a day.

Bus

Greyhound, T012-3231154, www.greyhound.co.za. **Intercape**, T0861-287287, www.intercape.co.za. **Translux**, T011-7743333, www.translux.co.za. All the long-distance buses stick to the N2 and Umtata is on the Cape Town-Durban route. **Cape Town** (18½ hrs) via **Port Elizabeth** (7 hrs) and **East London** (3 hrs). **Durban** (6 hrs) via **Port Shepstone** (4½ hrs).

Car hire

Avis, at the airport, T047-5360066, www.avis.co.za.

Budget, T047-5012800, www.budget.co.za, Caltex Fort Gale, Sutherland St.

Directory

Umtata *p377*

Medical services St Mary's Private Hospital, 30 Durham St, T047-5312911. 24-hr service.

KwaZulu Natal

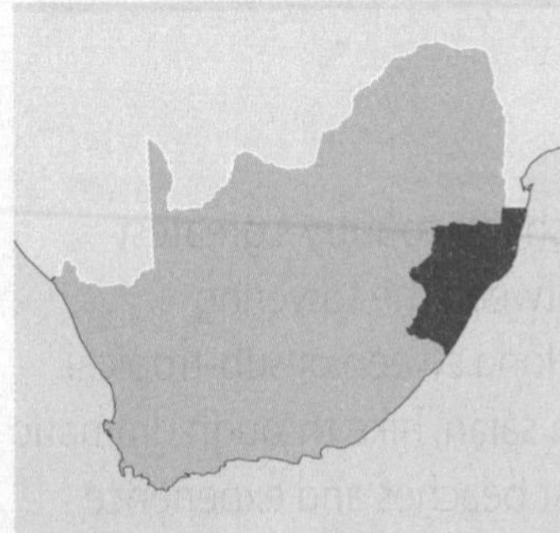

Footprint features

Introduction

KwaZulu Natal manages to squash the country's greatest diversity into a wedge of land between the towering Drakensberg Mountains and the long sweep of sub-tropical coastline. Here, visitors can go on safari, hike through dramatic wilderness, surf the country's best beaches and experience South Africa's strongest African culture. The mountains in the uKhahlamba-Drakensberg National Park soar to over 3000 m, offering the country's finest hiking on an extensive network of remote trails. Zululand, rich in history and evocative landscapes, draws visitors both for its traditional Zulu lifestyles, and the superb game reserves, some of the finest in South Africa. Hluhluwe-Imfolozi Game Reserve is the best known and has become famous for its rhino conservation programme, which has brought the rhino back from the brink of extinction. Maputaland, lying to the north of Zululand, is an extraordinary area of undisturbed African wilderness, with remote game parks and pristine coastlines, far off the usual tourist trail. The variety of wildlife experiences on offer here is on a par with Kruger – but without the crowds. The landscape of the central region, dotted with small industrial towns and rolling farmland, makes up in history what it lacks in scenic drama. This area, better known as the Battlefields, still bears the scars of the Zulu Wars: the Zulu-Boer War, the Anglo-Zulu War and the Boer War. There are dozens of battlefield sites, but the most evocative are those at Isandlwana, Rorke's Drift and Blood River. For a more light-hearted alternative, KwaZulu Natal's beaches are some of the most beautiful in the country. While those around Durban and to the south are heavily developed, the coastline extending from the north towards Maputaland is relatively wild, with long empty sweeps of white sand backed by thick tropical dune forests – an excellent place for interesting wildlife encounters.

★ Don't miss...

1 **Durban nightlife** Hang out with Durban's cosmopolitan locals in the safe and trendy areas of Berea or Morningside, crammed with stylish bars and restaurants, page 403.
2 **Gateway Shopping Mall** Visit the largest shopping mall in the Southern Hemisphere, with floor space equivalent to 17 rugby pitches, page 404.
3 **Battlefields tour** Hear the haunting stories of the Zulu and Boer wars amid the expansive plains of central KwaZulu Natal, page 430.
4 **uKhahlamba-Drakensberg National Park** Hike through Southern Africa's most spectacular mountain range, a UNESCO World Heritage Site, page 440.
5 **Hluhluwe-Imfolozi Game Reserve** Search for rhino in the rolling hills of Hluhluwe-Imfolozi, once the hunting grounds of King Shaka, page 472.
6 **Greater St Lucia Wetland Park** Take to the murky waters in search of hippos, or head to the beach to watch turtles lay their eggs, page 475.
7 **Sodwana Bay** Dive the world's southern-most coral reefs in search of tropical fish, sharks and turtles at South Africa's top scuba destination, page 490

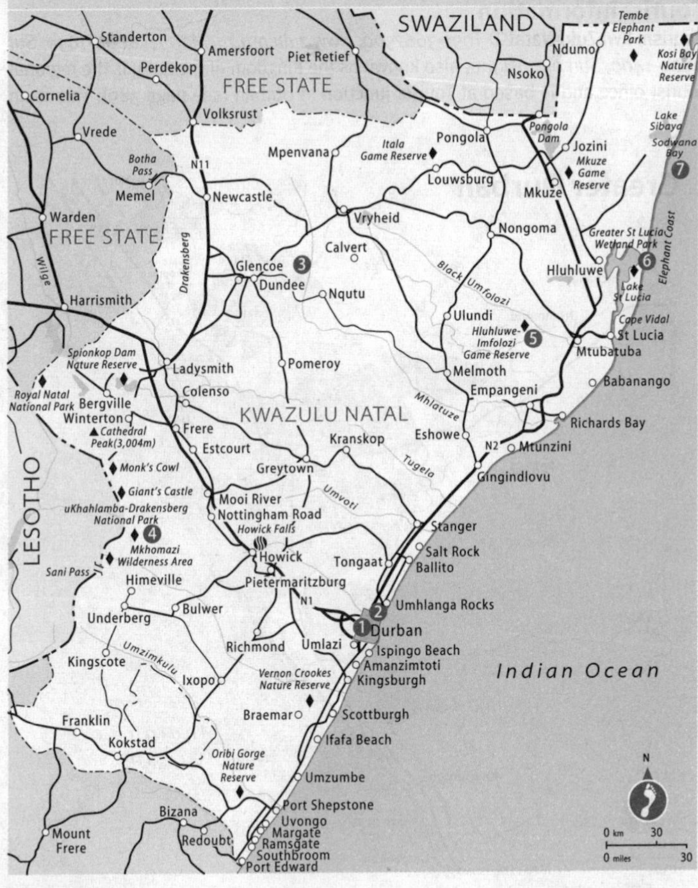

Ins and outs

Getting around

Travel within KwaZulu Natal is uncomplicated; the main areas of interest are connected by either the N2 or the N3. The **N2** runs along most of the coast from Port Shepstone in the south, through to Durban, Zululand and Maputaland in the north, before heading inland north to Mpumalanga, past Swaziland. The **N3** heads inland from Durban towards Pietermaritzburg, skirting the Battlefield Route to the east and the uKhahlamba-Drakensberg National Park in the west, eventually reaching Gauteng. The **Baz Bus** is convenient for exploring the province as it runs all the way along the coast as far as Mkuzi before heading inland to Swaziland. A second service runs from Durban towards Gauteng through the Drakensberg. All the main centres are linked by mainline bus services, so KwaZulu Natal can quite feasibly be visited by local transport, though you may want to consider a hire car for some of the national parks and game reserves. To the north, the roads in Maputaland are gradually being surfaced but there are still vast tracts of wilderness which are best explored in a 4WD. The most accessible reserve is Sodwana Bay where the colourful tropical reefs have become South Africa's most popular diving destination. The battlefield sites in the centre of the province are isolated and best experienced on a guided historical tour (see page 439).

Tourist information

Tourism KwaZulu-Natal ⓘ *T031-3667500, www.zulu.org.za, Mon-Fri 0800-1630, Sat 0900-1400, Sun 0900-1300*, also known as the Kingdom of the Zulu, is the regional tourist office and is based at **Tourist Junction** in Durban (see page 389). This is an

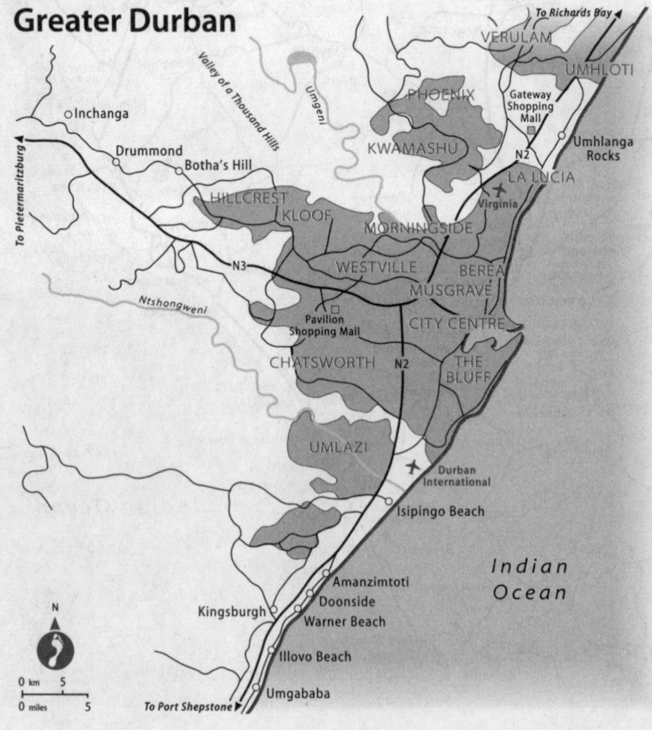

excellent office with a huge range of information on the province, as well as an attractive curio shop.

KZN Wildlife ⓘ *PO Box 13053, Cascades 3202, Pietermaritzburg, T033-8451000, www.kznwildlife.com*, is the central reservations office for all the accommodation within the various nature reserves and conservation areas throughout the KwaZulu Natal. This includes many of the Drakensberg resorts, as well as excellent wildlife reserves such as Itala and Hluhluwe-Imfolozi. All the parks' offices are open October to March 0800-1900 and April to September 0800-1800. Reservations can be made six months in advance and some of the popular camps are fully booked during the local school holidays. Credit card and online bookings are accepted. Note that accommodation in huts must be booked through KZN Wildlife whereas campsites are booked directly through the campsite manager or reception by phone.

Do not confuse KZN Wildlife with SAN Parks (see page 44). SAN Parks is responsible for parks such as Kruger, Tsitsikamma and Addo Elephant Park.

Durban

→ *Phone code: 031. Colour map 5, grid B2.*

The sprawling conurbation of Durban is Africa's largest port, and although its appeal is not immediately apparent – few original buildings survive and it can feel hectic and overcrowded – it boasts wide beaches, an extensive beachfront and a steamy tropical climate. The city also has one of the country's most interesting cultural mixes – it it is hoome to South Africa's largest Indian population and a hugely swelled Zulu presence which doesn't always sit comfortably with what was once a white centre. Away from the CBD are attractive suburbs, where tropical foliage spills from ornate balconies and the fast pace of city life is all but forgotten.

▸▸ *For Sleeping, Eating and other listings, see pages 399-406.*

Ins and outs

Getting there A limited number of international flights fly direct into **Durban International Airport** ⓘ *T031-4516758, www.airports.co.za.* Car hire desks can be found in both the domestic and international terminals. There is a **tourist information office** ⓘ *T031-4081000, daily 0630-2100*, in the domestic arrivals hall, and several mobile phone rental shops. The airport is 16 km from the city centre and transport into Durban takes about 30 minutes. Many backpacker hostels offer free airport collection/transfer service. Alternatively there are several private companies providing airport transfer services departing from the departure terminal such as **Super Shuttle,** T031-4651606, **Coastal Motor Services,** T031-4655573. Behind Durban railway station on NMR Avenue (M12) is the terminal for major long-distance coaches run by **Translux, Intercape** and **Greyhound.** ▸▸ *For more detailed information, see Transport, page 405.*

Getting around Durban has developed into South Africa's largest sea port and is also one of its main tourist centres. The approach to Durban passes through coastal tourist resorts, industrial areas, townships and eventually reaches the CBD. The extensive beachfront and the most important landmarks are within easy walking distance in the city centre. **Mynah,** T031- 3073503, is a frequent local bus service that runs between the city centre, the beachfront and Berea and Morningside, R3; very useful if you want to get to town from the suburbs, or from the north or south of the city centre. There are taxi ranks next to the City Hall and on the beachfront.

Tourist information **Durban Africa** ⓘ *Tourist Junction, Station Building, 160 Pine St, T031-3044934, www.zulu.org.za, www.bookabedahead.co.za, Mon-Fri 0800-1630, Sat 0900-1400, Sun 0900-1300*, is the city tourist information service, which is very helpful

24 hours in Durban

Head down to the **Golden Mile** at dawn: except for the few early-rising surf fanatics and muscular lifeguards limbering up, you will have the wide promenade, sandy beaches and crashing waves to yourself before the crowds, holiday resort tackiness and humidity set in. Breakfast at one of the small cafés where the surfers congregate to swap wave stories.

Explore the Indian shopping district off **Grey Street**, an exotic, cross-cultural, shopping experience, where the tangy aroma of eastern spices mingles with the colourful fabrics, trinkets and jewellery in the courtyard bazaars. When entering the **Juma Masjid Mosque** on Grey Street, the largest in the southern hemisphere, make sure you remove your shoes. Relish the cool tranquillity here before heading back on to Durban's hectic streets. Enjoy an African shopping experience at **Victoria Market**, where curios and souvenirs can be haggled over, and sample a famous Durban bunny chow at one the traditional food stalls.

Afterwards, cCatch the bird show at **Umgeni River Bird Park**, the only one of its kind in the world. Some of South Africa's largest and rarest birds, including the Blue Crane, are on display in this innovative show.

Sink a couple of cold Castle lagers and watch the sun go down on the deck of the **Bat Café** in the small craft harbour. If you're lucky you may catch some township jazz here before heading to one of Durban's top Indian restaurants to sample a fine Durban curry. The best are the **Jewel of India**, with cushions and low tables where you can kick off your shoes and relax, and **Ulundi**, where days of colonial Natal are echoed through turbaned waiters and rattan furniture.

Florida Road in Morningside and **Musgrave Road** in Musgrave are Durban's current hip and happening café-lined streets. Take your pick of trendy late-night bars, pubs, open-air restaurants and live music venues, all conveniently located along these two suburban streets.

and produces a range of brochures, including accommodation, restaurant and events guides. It also offers hotel and tour bookings, coach and rail bookings, foreign exchange, a curio shop, a café, and runs extremely good city tours. There is a smaller tourist office on the Golden Mile seafront at **Joe Kools** ① *T031-3322595, Mon-Fri 0830-1630, Sat and Sun 0900-1600*; and another at Durban Airport, see page 389.

Safety Safety has been a long-standing issue in downtown Durban. Although safety standards plummeted in the late 1990s, a number of initiatives in recent years, such as the development of the waterfront and upgrading of local housing, has improved the situation a great deal. Nevertheless, it's sensible to keep your wits about you – stick to busy areas, don't carry valuables and avoid looking like a tourist. Most importantly, avoid walking around downtown after dark. The suburbs are safe to walk around.

Background

The area around the bay was once covered with mangroves and inhabited by pelicans, flamingos and hippos. The earliest inhabitants were members of the Lala tribe who fished in the estuary, and hunted and grew crops in the fertile tropical forests along the coast. The first Europeans to land here were Portuguese explorers en route to the east. On 25 December 1497, Vasco da Gama sighted land and called it Natal, though this was probably off the coast of present day Eastern Cape. The Portuguese cartographer Manuel Perestrello mapped the coast of Natal in 1576, but it was nearly 200 years after the earliest European sighting that the first trading ships arrived. In 1684 the *Francis* began a new era when she sailed to Natal to buy ivory.

After the relative success of the first trading expedition, the Dutch East India Company planned to open a trading post here (after buying land off Chief Inyangesi for 1000 guilders worth of beads, copper rings and iron). But after a few technical hitches involving the estuary's sandbars, trade was never really developed and in 1730 the Dutch established an alternative trading station at Delagoa Bay.

The first British traders arrived in 1823 on the *Salisbury*, spurred on by news of Shaka, the powerful chief of the Zulus and his Empire. Lieutenant Francis and George Farewell arrived in the Bay of Natal and were blown over the sandbars in a storm. They returned in May 1824, with Henry Francis Fynn and a group of other adventurers, and set up their first camp in what is now known as Farewell Square. Henry Fynn was the first European trader to make contact with Shaka. Fynn and the other adventurers claimed (falsely) to be envoys of King George and were well received. Fynn became a favourite of the royal household after he helped Shaka recover from a stab wound sustained during a battle. In thanks Shaka granted Fynn a huge tract of land, over 9000 sq km.

Fynn and his young colleague Nathaniel Issacs ran this area as their own personal fiefdom, taking many Zulu wives and fathering dozens of children. Fynn declared himself King of Natal and wielded power in the same brutal manner as his infamous neighbour, Shaka. Even though Fynn and his men broke many Zulu laws, including the prohibition on all but the king from trading in ivory, they were treated with great respect by Shaka (though the chiefs they bought the ivory from were invariably executed).

The area remained undeveloped, however, with just a few dozen European settlers, and the British refused to annex the region. It was not until the establishment of the Voortrekker republic of Natalia in 1838 that the British felt their interests to be under threat. The capital of Natalia was in Pietermaritzburg, but settlements had also been established at Weenen and Durban, giving the Voortrekkers access to the sea. The possibility of a viable independent Voortrekker republic wasn't acceptable to the Cape Colony and an expeditionary force was sent from the Cape in 1842. Although they were besieged by the Voortrekkers on their arrival, by June of that year the parliament in Pietermaritzburg had accepted British rule. The Cape Colony annexed Natal in 1844, and the security given by becoming part of the Cape Colony encouraged many new settlers in search of land to come to Durban.

The development of the sugarcane industry in the 1860s encouraged the growth of Durban as a port and gave the city one of its most unique characteristics. Initially the sugarcane industry suffered from a lack of cheap labour, so the planters imported a large number of indentured labourers from India, who lived in conditions not dissimilar to slavery. After working off their five-year indenture contracts some returned home, but a number remained in Natal. Many continued farming and eventually came to dominate the local fruit and vegetable market. Others established small businesses and gradually built up important trade connections with India. These ex-indentured labourers were joined by a number of more affluent traders, mainly from Gujarat, who arrived direct from India to set up a business.

With the development of the Golden Mile in the 1970s, Durban was promoted as a seaside resort for white holidaymakers, particularly for families from Gauteng. During Apartheid, the extensive beach was split according to colour – black people were permitted to walk the length of the whole beach but, on the whites-only Addington Beach, they were not allowed to sit down or go into the sea. The late 1980s, however, saw a huge influx of workers from Zululand, transforming the fabric of the city. With the end of Apartheid came another influx: that of black holidaymakers, which gave the city the tag of 'Soweto-on-Sea' – a phrase used by both whites and blacks. However, divisions still remain: far fewer white people holiday in Durban, while the city centre has taken on a distinctly African feel.

Durban centre

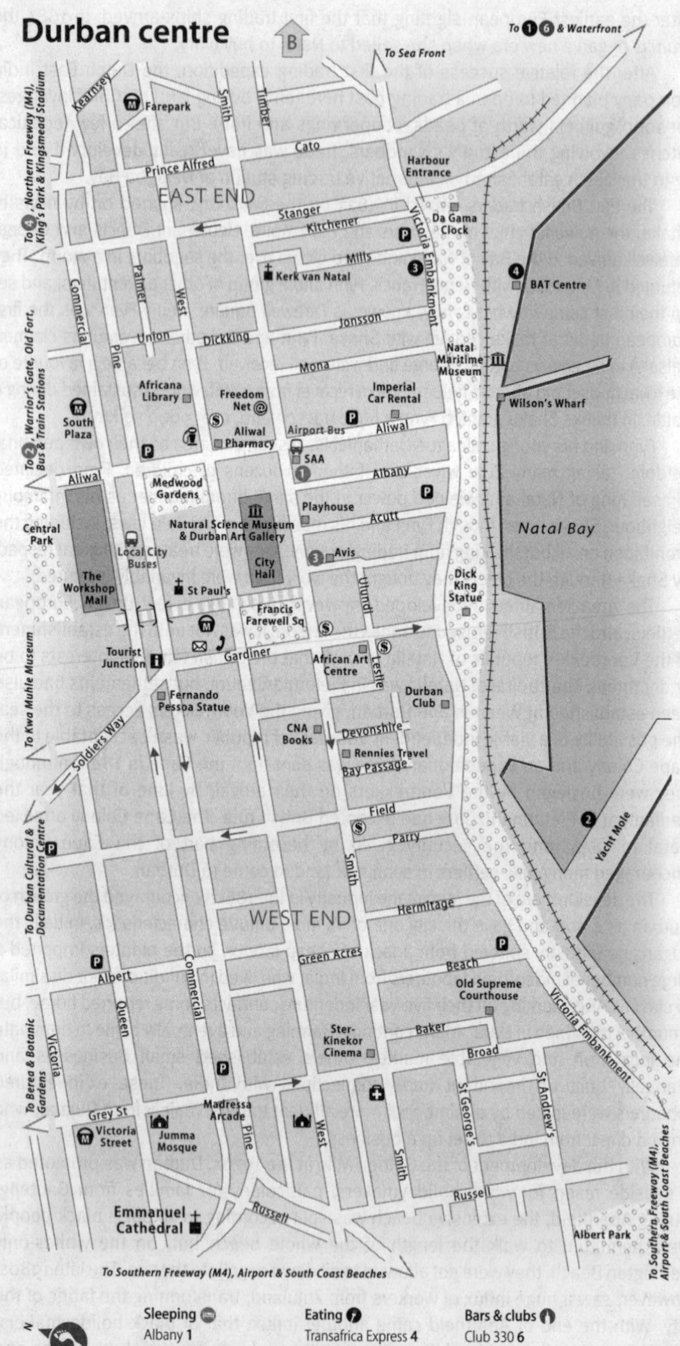

Sleeping	Eating	Bars & clubs
Albany 1	Transafrica Express 4	Club 330 6
Durban Hilton 4	Famous Fish Co 1	
Formule 1 2	New Café Fish 2	
Royal 3	Roma Revolving 3	

Sights

The main areas of interest to tourists are the **city centre** around Farewell Square, the **Indian district** around Queen and Grey streets, and the beachfront **Golden Mile**.

City centre

The small area surrounding City Hall between Commercial Road and Smith Street in central Durban is one of the city's more interesting spots. The colonial buildings and gardens offer a striking contrast between Durban's past and the present. High-rise office blocks tower over the remains of Durban's colonial history, where pastel coloured art deco buildings are dwarfed by mirrored skyscrapers. The city centre's eclectic mixture of architectural styles is the responsibility of Lord Holford, the town planner who developed the city centre during the 1970s. Lord Holford was originally from South Africa but became one of England's most notorious town planners when he created many of the soulless city centres built in England during the 1960s. He returned to South Africa to help redesign city centres as part of the Apartheid programme; his work destroyed the bustling Indian atmosphere of the city centre when thousands of Indians were moved out. The original plans for the new centre involved the demolition of the City Hall and the old railway station, but vociferous protests by conservationists prevented this.

The best way of seeing the major sights in the city centre is on one of the guided tours run by the tourist office.

Francis Farewell Square is the hub of this area and is named after the first British settler who built his home here out of wattle and daub in 1824. Today the square has bustling street market, but at night it resembles, rather incongruously, a Victorian cemetery as this is where most of Durban's commemorative statues have been placed. There is a cenotaph to those who died in both world wars, a memorial to the dead of the Boer War and statues of Queen Victoria, in commemoration of her diamond jubilee, and Natal's first two prime ministers.

The **City Hall**, on Smith Street, faces directly onto the Francis Farewell Square. This is one of Durban's most impressive buildings and reflects the town's municipal might at the turn of the 19th century. The neo-baroque building was completed in 1910 and in its day was one of the British Empire's finest city halls in the southern hemisphere. The main entrance is on Farewell Square and the hall inside is decorated with an interesting collection of portraits of Durban's mayors. What is particularly appealing about the building are the palms lining the street outside. You will also find the Natural Science Museum and Durban Art Gallery here.

The **Natural Science Museum** ⓘ *T031-3112256, Mon-Sat 0830-1600, Sun 1100-1600, free entry, gift shop and coffee shop*, has a grand colonial entrance adorned with palm trees. Inside is an assortment of scientific displays, including a huge gallery of stuffed African mammals. More interestingly, the museum also houses an extremely rare Dodo skeleton and South Africa's only Egyptian mummy. The KwaZuzulwazi Science Centre has an excellent series of displays dedicated to the Zulu culture.

The **Durban Art Gallery** ⓘ *T031-3112265, Mon-Sat 0830-1600, Sun 1100-1600, free*, on the upper floor of City Hall, has a superb collection of work by South African artists dating from the beginning of this century. This was one of the first galleries in South Africa to collect black art, and it remains an important cultural centre. It also hosts regularly changing exhibitions of contemporary art and handicrafts, and the Durban RedEye arts festival takes place here several times a year.

The Playhouse is directly opposite the Smith Street entrance to the City Hall. It was built in 1935 and was originally used as a bioscope, which seated 1900 people. The lounge bar became popular with visiting sailors during the 1970s and was notorious for its heavy drinking sessions and occasional fights. The cinema was eventually forced to close after a fire and has now been restored and converted into an arts complex with five theatres.

St Paul's Church was originally built in 1853, and was rebuilt in 1906 after a fire. The church is purely British in architectural style and inside there are commemorative plaques to Durban's early settlers. The chapel of St Nicholas on the left side of the aisle was part of the Mission to Seamen between 1899 and 1989. Reverend Wade, who was rector of the church between 1952 and 1961, was the father of tennis one-hit-wonder Virginia Wade, who won the ladies singles title at Wimbledon in 1977.

The **post office**, built in 1885, was originally Durban's first town hall. There is a plaque on the southern corner of the building, which commemorates Winston Churchill's speech after his escape during the Boer War.

The grand structure that is now home to **Tourist Junction** is Durban's old railway station. The building, modelled on a traditional British Victorian railway station, was completed in 1899 and is one of the few left standing in South Africa.

The **Fernando Pessoa Statue** is directly opposite Tourist Junction on the other side of Gardiner Street. The bronze statue commemorates Fernando Pessoa who lived in Durban during the early years of his life between 1896 and 1906. On his return to Portugal he lived in poverty while teaching English in Lisbon but went on to become Portugal's most celebrated and complex modern poet.

The Workshop, also on Commercial Road, lies directly behind the old railway station and is an enormous shopping mall that has been built inside the old train sheds. With the transition of major shops to the Pavilion and Gateway malls in the suburbs, the Workshop has suffered a decline in recent years and is starting to look shabby.

Around 500 m north of the Workshop, on Ordnance Road, near Warrior's Gate, is the **Kwa Muhle Museum** ⓘ *T031-3112223, Mon-Sat, 0800-1600, free*, housed in the Old Pass Office. It's a fascinating and moving exhibition of what it was like to be an African under the old regime and is also known locally as the Apartheid Museum. There is a collection of waxwork figures in hostels along with a series of photographs of incidents and riots of the past 25 years. Another display features the Indian merchants of Grey Street; here you can learn more about the first trade union, the Grey Street mosque, Victoria Street beer hall, the Bantu Social Centre and bunny chow (see page 401). One of the exhibits is on the 'Durban System': a method for Durban's city council to raise revenue to finance the administration of African affairs during Apartheid without using a penny of white-tax payer's money. They gave themselves the monopoly on brewing sorghum beer, which they sold for a fine profit in African-only public beer houses.

The **Moth Museum of Military History** ⓘ *Old Fort Rd, T031-3073337, Tue-Sun 1100-1500, free*, has a large collection of military memorabilia from the First and Second World Wars and battlefield relics from the Anglo-Boer and Zulu wars.

Indian district

The area around Victoria Street, Queen Street and Grey Street is one of the oldest areas of Durban still standing. The pastel-coloured shopping arcades were built in the 1920s and 1930s by Indian traders. Originally they were designed so families could have their homes over their shops. In 1973, however, legislation was introduced which prohibited Indians from living in the area, though not from trading. Family labour living above the shops was seen as integral to their success and the legislation was deliberately introduced in an effort to reduce their competition with white-owned businesses. With the new legislation, much of the residential population was forced to move out to Chatsworth or Phoenix; the wealthier traders moved to Westville.

The Indian district is a good 20-minute walk west from the centre down Commercial Road or Pine Street, or take a taxi to Victoria Street.

Thankfully the new residential rules did not succeed in destroying the Indian-owned businesses and many have continued to prosper. A number of original shops are still here, selling spices, saris and other goods from India, but it is now very much a commercial, rather than residential, area.

Durban Cultural and Documentation Centre ⓘ *corner of Epsom Rd and Derby St, T031-3097559, daily except Sat*, is well worth a visit if you're interested in the history of the Indian Community in South Africa. There are displays on the indentured Indian community, Gandhi in South Africa, culinary art and traditional clothing.

Victoria Street Market ⓘ *T031-3064021, Mon-Sat 0600- 1800, Sun 1000-1600*, is on the corner of Queen Street and Victoria Street. The original market was destroyed in 1973 by fire and has been replaced by a modern market. The new concrete building is rather dingy, but there are over 170 stalls inside selling curios, leather goods, fabrics, copper and spices. The main attraction of the stalls here are the spices and dried beans imported from India. Upstairs are a variety of food stalls serving up delicious snacks such as bunny chow, samoosas and Durban curries. It gets extremely busy, so beware of pickpockets and don't take anything valuable with you.

The entrance to the **Madressa Arcade** is on Grey Street. The bazaar-like arcade was built in 1927 and houses shops selling luggage, CDs and Indian fabrics.

The **Juma Masjid Mosque** ⓘ *corner of Queen St and Grey St, T031-3060026, open to all outside of prayer times*, was also built in 1927 and claims to be the largest mosque in the southern hemisphere, despite the fact that Muslims are a minority in Durban, which is largely Hindu. The dress code must be adhered to: no shorts for men and women should wear long skirts or trousers and cover their shoulders; leave your shoes at the door.

Victoria Embankment

The Victoria Embankment was originally built in 1897 and was a grand and desirable residential area facing a beautiful stretch of beach. Very little of this remains today, and at first glance the Embankment seems like any other busy road lined with skyscrapers. There are still a few sights worth seeking out, though. At the eastern end of the Embankment is the ornate **Da Gama Clock**. A good example of late-Victorian design, this large cast-iron clock was erected to commemorate the 400th anniversary of Vasco da Gama's discovery of the sea route to India in 1487.

A short walk further on at the junction of Gardiner Street and the Victoria Embankment is the **Dick King Statue** which commemorates Dick King's epic 10-day ride to Grahamstown in 1842 whilst Durban was under siege. The **Durban Club** is on the opposite side of the embankment and was built in 1904. This is one of the few original buildings left on the Victoria Embankment, a grand edifice which gives an inkling of what the Victoria Embankment once looked like.

Wilson's Wharf is a modern development overlooking the harbour, home to a couple of cafés, a fish market and three boats which house the **Natal Maritime Museum** ⓘ *entrance is on the docks opposite the junction of Aliwal St and the Victoria Embankment, T031-3112230, Mon-Sat 0830-1600, Sun 1100-1600, small entry fee*. Visitors can walk through the minesweeper, the *SAS Durban*, and the two tugs, the *Ulundi* and the *JR More*.

Just beyond the Maritime Museum is the excellent non-profit making **BAT (Bartle Arts Trust) Centre** ⓘ *on the harbour front, T031-3320451*, which recently celebrated its 10th anniversary. This is a popular arts centre with a concert hall and a bar and restaurant, as well as several little shops selling excellent contemporary Zulu weavings, wood-cut prints and handmade shoes. Above the **Trans Africa Express** restaurant is a gallery which hosts cutting-edge exhibitions, such as by local cartoonist Themba Siwela. The centre hosts nightly events, from live jazz to poetry readings.

Beachfront

The most popular seafront area extends along the length of Marine Parade. Traditionally known as the **Golden Mile,** it's a favourite with South African holidaymakers. The beachfront is lined with high-rise hotels, gardens and a promenade;

Durban beach

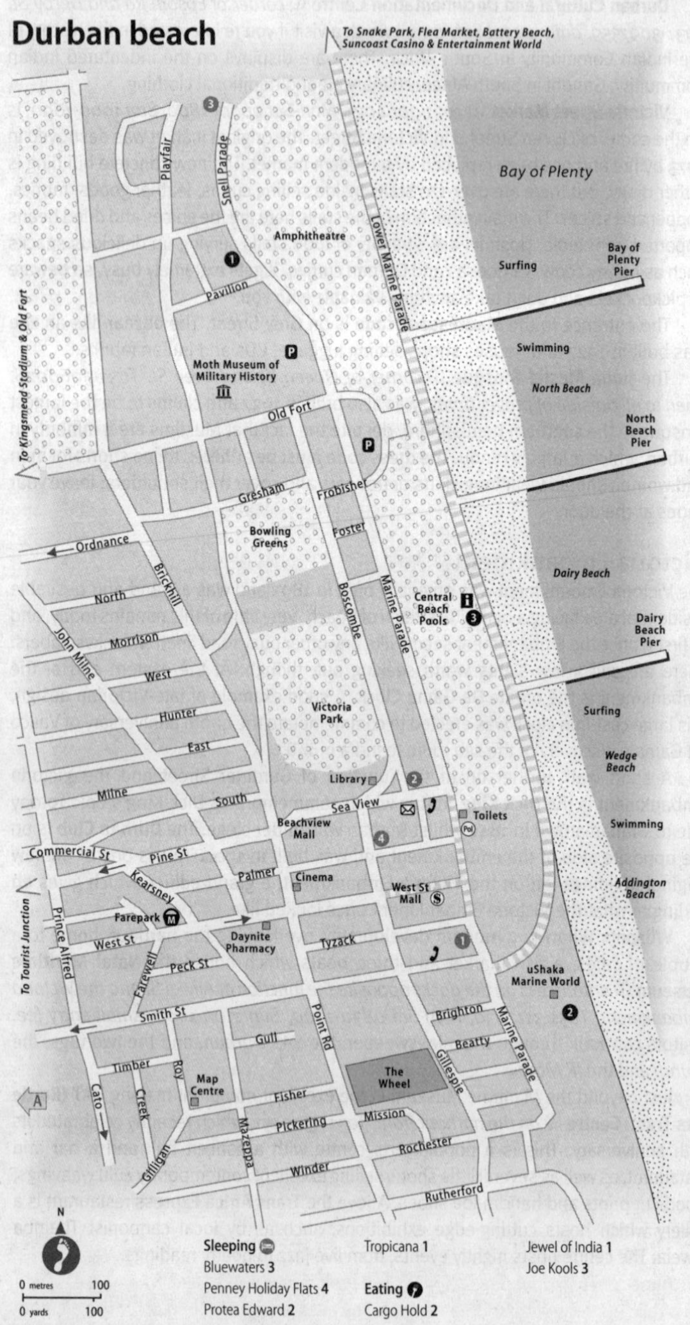

behind is a built-up urban area which had become distinctly insalubrious in recent years. Recent developments, however, have upgraded housing, brought in investment and improved safety here, although it's still best avoided at night. There's a police station on the promenade and a high police presence.

The beaches, all of which are impressive stretches of long, golden sand, are divided into areas designated for surfing, boogy boarding and swimming. All are protected with shark nets and lifeguards are on patrol daily 0800-1700. At the northern end of the Lower Marine Parade is a **flea market**, a hive of activity at weekends, with stalls selling Indian snacks and curios.

The beachfront area is not safe to wander about after dark; see Safety page 390.

The promenade along Lower Marine Parade and Snell Parade has numerous tourist attractions. Running from north to south, the entertainment starts with the flea market and the **Snake Park** ⓘ *0900-1630, small entry fee*. The park has a large collection of snakes from around the world with daily snake handling demonstrations several times daily, and feedings at weekends. Nearby are several stands where extravagantly dressed rickshaw drivers wait for tourists. The options are either a quick and painless photograph with the driver, or a photograph and ride up and down Marine Parade, usually costing around R20.

The leading attraction here, however, is **uShaka Marine World** ⓘ *1 Bell St, T031-3288000, www.ushakamarineworld.co.za, Nov-Mar 0900-1800, Apr-Oct 0900-1700, Wet 'n' Wild R60, SeaWorld R85, combined ticket R125; free entry to Village Walk*. This enormous waterpark is the largest in Africa, and has the fourth largest aquarium in the world. The park is split into three areas: SeaWorld is an impressive underground aquarium; Wet 'n' Wild has a huge choice of impressive waterslides and rides; and Village Walk is a retail village filled with shops and restaurants. The highlight in SeaWorld is the phantom ship, where visitors walk through glass tunnels surrounded by ragged-tooth sharks and game fish. Each corridor has a different theme, and there is a range of presentations in pools surrounding the ship throughout the day. There's also a dolphinarium, a seal pool, dive tank and a snorkel reef. Another free zone is the uShaka Beach, which hosts a variety of activities such as beach volleyball and surfing, and has 24-hour security.

Battery Beach

Heading 1 km north of Snell Parade and the Golden Mile, Battery Beach is perhaps the most attractive of Durban's beaches, with good swimming and fewer crowds. It's also the location of the **Suncoast Casino and Entertainment World**, with slot machines, cinemas, a selection of bars, takeaway joints, themed restaurants and a car park for 2000 vehicles. There's a boardwalk linking the complex to the beach where you can sunbathe or rollerblade on the sundeck.

Berea

This residential district, to the west of the city centre, is one of Durban's oldest and most attractive. Fine white-washed mansions and Victorian bungalows line the quiet streets, and this is one of the best places to head for restaurants and nightlife. On Sydenham Road, in Upper Berea, are the **Botanic Gardens** ⓘ *T031-2011303, daily 0730-1715, until 1745 in summer, free entry. A free tour leaves from the information centre on the last Sun of every month at 0930*. The gardens were founded in 1849, making them, supposedly, the oldest botanical gardens in Africa, and cover almost 15 ha. There are some impressive avenues of palms crossing the park, an ornamental lake, an orchid house and an information centre. The tea garden, open 0930-1615, is a pleasant place to relax. The KwaZulu Natal Philharmonic Orchestra performs by the lake on Sundays during summer.

Three other smaller parks are **Mitchell Park**, at the end of Musgrave Road, which are public gardens with an open-air café, aviaries and a few animals; the adjoining

 Jameson Park, with extensive rose gardens and a good view of Durban from the top; and the **Japanese Gardens**, on Prospect Hall Road in Durban North.

The **Campbell Collection** ⓘ *220 Marriott Rd, T031-2073711, main house open to the public by appointment only Tue and Thu 0800-1300, free entry*, is a museum and African library in a Cape Dutch house built in 1914, which still has most of its original decorations. There are some fine examples of Cape furniture and early South African oil paintings, displays of African sculpture, weapons, musical instruments and a rare collection of paintings by Barbara Tyrrell. Most of the paintings are of Africans dressed in traditional clothes from the 19th century; the paintings form part of a unique record of what people wore before contact with European settlers.

Chatsworth

Reached from the N2 south of the centre, the **Hare Krishna Temple of Understanding** ⓘ *south of the centre on Ambassador Rd, T031-4033328, daily, free entry*, opened as an ashram in 1969, but the futuristic marble temple set in extensive ornamental gardens was only opened to the public in 1975. There is a good vegetarian restaurant here, serving everything from light snacks to large curries.

Nature reserves

Durban's suburbs hold a number of natures reserves, most with walking trails which provide a welcome respite from the bustle of the city. **Burman Bush Nature Reserve** ⓘ *Windermere Rd, Morningside, T031-3122773*, is a relatively small reserve, with an important patch of dense coastal bush and a large population of vervet monkeys. On the opposite side of the Umgeni River is the **Umgeni River Bird Park** ⓘ *T031-5794600, daily 0900-1700*, which has over 3000 exotic and indigenous birds, from flamingos to macaws. There is a free flight show where large birds such as owls, raptures and vultures fly over the heads of the audience to perches at the top of the open-air auditorium. **Kenneth Stainbank Nature Reserve** ⓘ *96 Coedmore Av, Yellowwood Park, T031-4692807, daily 0600-1800, small entrance fee*, is a fairly large area of woodland and grassland next to a dam with an impressive array of game including impala, zebra, duiker and bushbuck. There is a mountain bike trail and 13 km of walking trails.

Information centres at the reserves stock maps and guides detailing walking trails.

Excursions

Durban's motorway network opens up a range of day trips within driving distance of the city centre, although good public transport connections are limited to the south coast, Pietermaritzburg and Umhlanga.

To the north, inland along the N3, is the Valley of 1000 Hills, Pietermaritzburg, the Natal Midlands and the Battlefields. To the south on the N2 are the surfing beaches and tourist resorts heading to Port Shepstone and Margate. To the north along the N2 lies Umhlanga and the coastal resorts of the north coast, whilst just inland from the N2 is the historical Zulu town of Eshowe.

Valley of 1000 Hills

The Valley of 1000 Hills, a peaceful area named after the dozens of hills which fold down towards the Umgeni River, is an easy 35-km drive from Durban. Follow the N3 north out of the city and leave at the Westville/Pavilion Mall exit. Join the old Pietermaritzburg road (R103) and drive through the suburbs of Kloof and Hillcrest. Here you will pick up signs for the Valley of 1000 Hills Meander which runs through the villages of Botha's Hill, Drummond, Monteseel and Inchanga. The **Comrades Marathon**, a gruelling 90 km between Pietermaritzburg and Durban, follows this route in June. For information contact **1000 Hills Tourism** ⓘ *Old Main Rd, Botha's Hill, T031-7771874, www.1000hills.kzn.org.za.*

Two excellent nature reserves are located in this area. **Krantzkloof Nature Reserve** ⓘ *152 Kloof Falls Rd, T082-9318335, daily 0600-1800*, has a forested gorge and three waterfalls. **Shongweni Reserve** ⓘ *Shongweni Dam, T031-7691283, daily 0600-1800 winter, 0500-1900 summer*, is a good place to see birds with over 200 species on record. Mammals include wildebeest, giraffe, warthog and kudu; both white rhino and buffalo have recently been re-introduced. There are 15 km of self-guiding hiking trails, and activities include morning and evening game drives, horse riding and canoeing.

> *The Valley of 1000 Hills was supposedly named by the writer Mark Twain on a visit to South Africa at the end of the 19th century.*

Between Durban and Pietermaritzburg the landscape quickly climbs some 700 m over a series of rolling hills characteristic of the suburbs around the two cities. From Botha's Rest, there are many viewpoints on the R103 from where you can see the valley unfold. The fertile hills are dotted with villages, farms and encroaching townships closer to Durban. The valley has historically been a Zulu stronghold and, in the early 19th century, was a refuge for dispossessed Zulus who had lost their farmland through battle further north.

The R103 runs along the lip of the valley; tourism has gone into overdrive along this route, with a variety of craft shops, restaurants, B&Bs, guesthouses, farm stalls and several Zulu cultural villages. The most popular of these is **PheZulu Safari Park** ⓘ *T031-7771000, several Zulu shows daily*, at Botha's Hill. There are commanding views of the valley from here, a reptile farm, a small game park with zebra and antelope, curio shops, the **Crocokraal** restaurant which specializes in croc steaks, and the **Mbizo** restaurant, which serves traditional *potjies* (stews), open Sundays only. The main attraction here is the Zulu show, where visitors are taken into traditional beehive shaped huts and Zulu beliefs, rituals and artefacts are explained. There follows an impressive dancing display.

The Umgeni Steam Railway's **1000 Hills Choo-Choo** ⓘ *T031-3048666 or T082-3536003 (mob), 2 daily departures at weekends, tickets from Kloof Station, R65 per person return*, is a vintage 1912 steam train that runs along a line built 1877-1880. On departure days there are two round trips, between Kloof Station and Inchanga, and it's a leisurely way to enjoy the scenery.

Sleeping

Central Durban and the beachfront have a wide selection of accommodation, although safety issues have caused a decline in tourist numbers here in recent years. Current safety measures mean that it's much safer now, but it's best to avoid walking around the centre after dark. Safer, more attractive and with a wider range of restaurants are the suburbs of Morningside and Berea. For assistance contact the Accommodation Reservation Service, Tourist Junction, 160 Pine St, T031-3043868, www.bookabedahead.co.za.

City centre and the beachfront

p393 and p396, maps p392 and p396

AL Royal Hotel, 267 Smith St, T031-3336000, www.theroyal.co.za. The hotel originally built on this site in 1842 was made of wattle and daub; it now has luxurious 5-star service, 251 rooms, a/c, DSTV, pleasant decor, an attractive outdoor pool, and 6 restaurants including an excellent Indian restaurant, a grill and a theatre supper club (see Eating, page 402).

AL-A Durban Hilton, 12-14 Walnut St, next to the International Conference Centre, T031-3368100, www.hilton.com. All the trappings you'd expect from a modern 5-star 'name' city hotel. A relatively recent addition, popular with conference delegates. 327 rooms, restaurant, bar, gym, pool, curio shop.

A Protea Hotel Edward, 149 Marine Park, T031-3373681, www.proteahotels.co.za. Large luxury hotel on the Golden Mile, with 100 a/c rooms, en suite with M-Net and minibar, 2 restaurants, bar, pool and deck, secure covered parking, one of the most luxurious of the beachfront hotels.

B Bluewaters, 175 Snell Parade, North Beach T31-3277000. 250 rooms, standard modern beachfront hotel, rooms have dated decor (lots of frills and swirly fabrics) but are comfortable with DSTV, en suite bathrooms, a/c, plus excellent views of the beach. Restaurant, indoor pool, hairdressing salon.
B Tropicana, 85 Marine Parade, T031-3681511, www.tropicanahotel.co.za. 80 a/c rooms, fairy spacious but with uninspiring decor, all are en suite and have M-Net TV and internet access. Large pool area, 2 restaurants, plus the popular **Clippers Café Bar** which serves light meals on the terrace. Swimming pool, secure covered parking.
B-C Albany, 225 Smith St, T031-3044381, www.albanyhotel.co.za. Classic art deco hotel, 72 simple, functional rooms, en suite, a/c, M-Net TV, rooms have views over gardens. Restaurant, 2 bars, central location opposite City Hall and Playhouse.
C Penney Holiday Flats, Rydal Mount, 130 Gillespie St, T011-8492384, www.penney holidayflats.co.za. Simple self-catering apartments set in a high-rise block a couple of streets back from the beach. Some have great views. All have en suite bathrooms, a/c, DSTV and kitchen facilities. Secure undercover parking. Avoid walking here at night.
D Formule 1, next to the railway station and long-distance coach station, T031-3011551, www.accorhotels.com. Modern, clean, budget rooms for up to 3, ideal for late arrivals but nothing to keep you there other than sleeping. Book to guarantee a room as there are few budget options.

Durban suburbs *p397*
The suburbs are far more appealing than the centre, both for their attractive, historical architecture and the wide choice of restaurants and bars, all within safe walking distance of each other.
AL Quarters, 101 Florida Rd, Morningside, T031-3035246, www.quarteres.co.za. 4 historic homes have been converted to create this boutique hotel. Refreshingly modern feel, 25 bedrooms, cool white walls and dark red fabrics, black and white photographs on the walls. Excellent on-site brasserie serves meals throughout the day, shaded courtyard, modern bar. Some of the rooms have a small veranda overlooking palm-shaded gardens, but some are slightly cramped, and are set on a busy corner. Good location close to restaurants.
A 164, 164 St Thomas Rd, Musgrave, T031-2014493. Stylish boutique hotel in the centre of Musgrave. Luxurious rooms with polished wooden floors, fashionable decor, simple colour palette, Victorian bathrooms, DSTV. Secure parking, swimming pool set in gardens, delicious cooked-to-order breakfasts, attractive bar with ocean liner decor. Low-key, friendly service, excellent value for what is one of the best guesthouses in Durban. Recommended.
A Westville, 124 Jan Hofmeyr Rd, Westville T031-2666326, www.threecities.co.za. Luxury hotel aimed at business travellers and tour groups, 42 a/c rooms, TV, the **Cape Southeaster** restaurant (renowned for its good Cape and French cuisine), swimming pool, squash courts, big sports bar.
B Riverside Hotel, Northway, T031-5630600, www.threecities.co.za. Large modern hotel overlooking the river, with spacious rooms, a/c, DSTV, dark wood furniture. Friendly service and a great restaurant and popular bar, secure parking. Some noise from traffic, very popular with tour groups.
B Rosetta House, 126 Rosetta Rd, Morningside, T031-3036180, www.rosetta house.com. 4 luxury a/c double rooms, cool tiled or wood floors, country inn-style furnishings, en suite, TV, some rooms have separate entrance. Secure parking, a fine old town house set in tranquil gardens. Close to the restaurants on Florida Rd.
B-C Elephant House, 745 Ridge Rd, Berea, T031-2089580, elephanthouse@mweb.co.za. The building housing this small B&B is said to be one of the oldest in Durban, and got its name from once having come under attack from elephants. Peaceful and friendly, 2 double rooms, a/c, en suite, TV. Guest lounge, laundry and attractive, quiet tropical gardens. Meals available on request.
B-C Ridgeview Lodge, 17 Loudoun Rd, Berea, T031-2029777, www.ridgeview.co.za. 7 double rooms each with a/c, en suite bathrooms, TV, phone with email connection

For an explanation of the sleeping and eating price codes used in this guide, see inside the front cover. Other relevant information is found in Essentials pages 42-47.

Bunny chow

One of the more popular and delicious takeaway meals in Durban is bunny chow: half a loaf of bread with the middle scooped out and filled with curry. The scooped out bread is then used instead of a spoon to soak up the sauce. The dish was originally created by innovative chefs for black caddies, commonly known as bunnies, who were not allowed to use the crockery and cutlery at certain exclusive, white-only golf clubs in the old Apartheid days.

and private patios. An elegant house with excellent guest facilities. Secluded lush gardens with swimming pool and good views. Close to restaurants and shops. Airport transfer can be arranged.

C Bali on the Ridge, 268 South Ridge Rd, Glenwood, T031-2619574. Close to the University of Natal, spectacular views of the city and harbour, elegantly furnished with pieces from Bali, attractive polished wooden floors, stylish a/c rooms, TV, bar fridge, pool.

C Tripple Five, 555 Essenwood Rd, Berea, T031-2096787, www.triplefive.co.za. 4 a/c en suite double rooms set in 2 separate apartments, extremely comfortable, with well-equipped kitchens, lounges, balconies, both have DSTV. Garden with jacuzzi, dining area, B&B or use the self-catering kitchen, secure off-street parking.

Backpackers

The Baz Bus collects and drops off from all backpacker hostels 5 times a week.

C-D Durban Backpacker's, 17 Promenade, Glenashley, T031-5621591, www.durban backpackers.com. Great location set just back from the beach, north of the city centre. Smart set up with mix of en suite doubles and self-catering dorms. Most rooms have floor-to-ceiling glass windows with ocean views. Prices include breakfast. Lively bar, home-cooked meals, comprehensive travel centre, pool, internet, DSTV, secure parking. To get here follow the M4 through Durban North; after Virginia Airport take the Aubery Drive exit to the beach. Recommended.

C-D Hippo Hide, 2 Jesmond Rd, Berea, T031-2074366, www.hippohide.co.za. A small, upmarket backpackers set in a pretty tropical garden, double rooms, some en suite with TV, one en suite dorm with attached self-catering kitchen, relaxed atmosphere, rock pool, outside bar and pleasant deck, close to shopping centres and restaurants on Musgrove Rd. Good info desk which can help with tours and bookings.

C-D Tekweni Backpackers, 169 Ninth Av, Morningside, T031-3031433, www.tekweni backpackers.co.za. One of the liveliest, most popular hostels in Durban, 2 km from the beach, bus station and town. Dorms and double rooms, small swimming pool and bar out front, space for a couple of tents, laundry facilities, internet access. Often in a party mood, quieter doubles next door. The excellent **Tekweni Ecotours**, T031-4632576, www.tekwiniecotours.co.za, is based here.

D Anstey's, 477 Marine Dr, Bluff, T031-4671192, www.ansteysbeach.co.za. The Bluff is the section to the south of Durban that sticks out to sea on the opposite side of the entrance to the port. Another beachside hostel, with dorms, self-catering apartments sleeping 4, bar with pool table, meals. Family run but with a surf vibe, so lively. Can arrange city tours of Durban, beach horse rides and surfing lessons. The lodge is opposite the cave rock, thought to be the most hollow wave in South Africa – surf dudes should head here.

D Nomads, 70 Essenwood Rd, Berea, T031-2029709, www.durban.co.za/nomads. Spacious dorms and doubles, self-catering facilities, **Bambooza** bar, swimming pool, pool table. Friendly backpackers in a safe area within easy walking distance of shops, bars and restaurants. The owners can offer travel advice and are knowledgeable about the area.

Eating

A wide choice of restaurants, bars and cinemas can be found in the Gateway shopping mall, see page 404.

City centre *p393, map p392*

TTT New Café Fish, Yacht Mole, Victoria Embankment, T031-3055062. Set right on the water with yachts moored within arms reach, upstairs bar great for a sundowner, a basket of calamari and view of the working harbour. Downstairs is the more formal restaurant, seafood a speciality, very popular, outdoor deck in summer.

TTT Royal Grill, Royal Hotel, 267 Smith St, T031-3336000. One of 6 restaurants in this upmarket hotel. This is the hotel's 70-year-old flagship restaurant, serving excellent steaks in an opulent setting with chandeliers, soaring ceilings and potted palms. An elegant, colonial dining experience.

TTT Ulundi, Royal Hotel, 267 Smith St, T031-3336000. Closed Sun. Also based in the **Royal Hotel**, this is regarded as one of the best Indian restaurants in town. Top end curries with a feel of colonial Natal, turbaned waiters, rattan furniture, ceiling fans, tandoori grills and traditional Durban curries. Good choice for vegetarians.

TT Famous Fish Co, King's Battery, Point Waterfront, T031-3681060, www.thefamousfishco.com. A popular outfit right by the port, slightly out-of-the-way location, but worth finding and with secure parking. Simple set-up with a seafaring theme and an attractive wooden deck overlooking the boats. Excellent choice of seafood, including memorable specials such as a Durban crab curry served in a *potjie*. Also good grilled seafood platters. Book ahead in summer.

TT Roma Revolving, John Ross House, Victoria Embankment, T031-3682275, www.roma.co.za. Closed Sun. Old-fashioned and kitsch concept, this long-running Italian restaurant is set on the 32nd floor, with a revolving floor offering excellent city views. Italian dishes, seafood and pasta, heavily laden dessert trolley, good value 3-course set meals, unparalleled views.

T Transafrica Express, in the BAT Centre, Victoria Embankment, T031-3320804. Relaxed, trendy venue with a deck overlooking the harbour. African menu, including Congo crocodile curry and 'funky chow' – a bunny chow served in warm olive bread. Fashionable, arty crowd, gets very busy in the evenings when there's live music on in the auditorium. Also has jazz on the deck on Fri and Sun afternoons.

Beachfront *p396, map p396*

TTT Cargo Hold, uShaka Marine World, T031-3288065, www.ushakamarineworld.co.za. Great location, popular with families, spread over 3 floors in the phantom ship, with a glass wall looking into the shark tank, with ragged tooth sharks sidling by as you eat. Impressive menu, including good seafood, steaks, warm salads and Mediterranean starters. Reservations essential.

TTT Jewel of India, Holiday Inn Elangeni, 63 Snell Parade, T031-3378168. Large restaurant with traditional Indian decor. Attractive side room with cushions and low tables where you can kick off your shoes and relax with a drink. Tasty North Indian dishes served with tandoori breads.

T Joe Kools, North Beach, T031-3329697. Superb views of North Beach, large restaurant and pub with a set of wooden decks overlooking the sand. Standard pub fare, range of burgers, pizza, pasta, fried seafood (calamari and fish and chips) and club sandwiches. Perfect for people-watching, turns into a lively bar at night.

Durban suburbs *p397, map p388*

Durban's most popular night time hubs are Florida Rd in Morningside and Musgrave Rd in Berea, both lined with bars and restaurants.

TTT Christina's, 134 Florida Rd, Morningside, T031-3032111. Open for dinner Wed-Sat, breakfast, teas and lunch Tue-Sat. This restaurant is linked to a chef's training school, offering a weekly changing menu. Excellent standard of French cuisine in the evenings, international, themed buffets at lunch and superb breakfasts. Superb cheese board, good deserts and interesting wine list. Outdoor shaded patio is pleasant in the summer.

TT Bean Bag Bohemia, 18 Windermere Rd, Greyville, T031-3096019. Hugely popular set-up, with a vibey bar on the ground floor and smarter tatty-chic restaurant upstairs, in an old converted Durban town house. Quirky decor, great menu with a Mediterranean bias, mezze platters, pasta and steak. Popular cocktail evenings on Weds. Recommended.

TT Bistro 136, 136 Florida Rd, Morningside, T031-3033440. Classic bistro atmosphere and French and Swiss menu. Smart, traditional setting, award-winning wine list, good oxtail and roast duck, and a luxurious lobster bisque. Plenty of loyal local regulars.

Café 1999, corner of Silverton and Vasue Rds, Berea, T031-2023406. Sheltered outdoor eating area and relaxed, stylish interior. Modern European food, excellent salads, Italian-style mains, great coffees and cakes, too. Young, well-dressed crowd.

Indian Connection, 485 Windermere Rd, Mornigside,T031-3121440. Traditional suburban home which has been converted into a modern, stylish Indian restaurant. Refreshingly free of the usual curry house decor, the interior is pure white with wooden floors. Mix of north and south Indian dishes, choice of tandooris, tikkas and biriyanis, plus local coconut prawn curries, friendly service and a trendy, urban crowd.

Mykonos, 156 Essenwood Rd, Berea, T031-2025636. Lively atmosphere with Greek music and dancing. Simple decor, excellent value eat-as-much-as-you-can buffet with an extensive selection of dishes, including great roast lamb and grilled prawns.

Vestige, 225 Musgrave Rd, corner of St Thomas St, Morningside, T031-2017767. Fashionable, low-key restaurant on a street corner with tables on the veranda outside or in the funky, white and airy interior. Long menu, with good specials such as grilled crayfish or Durban prawn curry, and delicious salads, pasta and open sandwiches – the spicy butternut salad is excellent. Laid-back, friendly service, good value. Recommended.

Legends Café, Musgrave Centre, Musgrave Rd, T031-2010733. Simple café serving a mix of stirfries and Mexican dishes, the inside is decorated with posters of movie stars, bar and kitchen open late.

Bars and clubs

Durban *p389, maps p392 and p396*

Make sure you get a taxi to and from the clubs on Point Rd as walking is not recommended.

Bean Bag Bohemia, 18 Windermere Rd, Greyville, T031-3096019. The trendy bar on the ground floor is one of the most popular in the area. Great cocktail menu including a long list of martinis, popular cocktail nights on Weds. Arty, stylish crowd.

Club 330, 330 Point Rd, T031-3377172. Open Fri and Sat 2200. One of South Africa's top nightclubs and something of an institution. Huge area, with a number of dance floors playing a mix of techno and house in the main rooms, and with funkier beats elsewhere. Hosts big-name international DJs, and has a range of one-off special events.

Joe Kools, North Beach, T031-3329697. Right on the beach opposite one of the most popular surf sites, outside terraces which liven up with live DJs at night, very popular bar with the surfing fraternity.

Roman Lounge, 201 Florida Rd, Morningside, T031-3039022. Recently re-opened gay bar, with a trendy, mixed clientele. Packed at weekends, good music.

Society, Hollis House, Florida Rd, Morningside. Recently converted historical house, now home to an ultra-stylish lounge bar, popular with well-heeled fashion types. Good cocktails, light meals, the place to go for a bout of posing.

Entertainment

Durban *p389, maps p392 and p396*

Cinema

The following are multi-screen cinemas.

Nu Metro, www.numetro.co.za, at Suncoast Entertainment World, Snell Parade, T031-3283333, and the Pavilion mall in Westville, T031-2650001.

Ster-Kinekor, Musgrave Centre, Musgrave Rd, Berea, www.sterkinekor.co.za.

Theatre

Catalina Theatre, Wilson's Wharf, Victoria Embankment, T031-3056889 for information. 175-seater venue for comedy and music.

The Playhouse, 231 Smith St, T031-3699555 for information. Shows regular performances in 5 auditoriums: the Opera, Loft, Drama, Studio and Cellar Supper Theatre. An eclectic range of shows ranging from Shakespeare to contemporary political satire and modern dance.

The Royal Backstage, Royal Hotel, 267 Smith St, T031-3336000. A cabaret venue and supper theatre offering 3-course meals and various shows. Wed-Sat from 1900.

Shopping

Durban *p389, maps p392 and p396*

African Art Centre, 1st floor, Tourist Junction, Station Building, 160 Pine St, T031-3047915. This is one of the best places in Durban to buy Zulu beadwork, baskets and ceramics, at slightly marked-up prices, but excellent quality. The shop is a non-profit making outlet for rural craftspeople.

Antiques and Bygones, 437 Windermere Rd, Morningside, T031-3038880, www.antiquesandbygones.co.za. Sells a range of silver jewellery and European antiques.

BAT Centre, Victoria Embankment, T031-3320451. Superb arts and crafts shops selling a variety of goods, from contemporary Zulu art and jewellery to traditional wood cut prints or handmade shoes.

Matombo Art Gallery, Tourist Junction, T031-3049968. Good quality but expensive stone sculptures from Zimbabwe.

Victoria Street Market, corner of Queen and Victoria Sts, T031-3064021. This modern, rather dingy market is crammed with over 170 stalls selling African curios, leather goods, fabrics, copper and spices. The main attractions are the spices and dried beans imported from India.

Village Walk, uShaka Marine World, 1 Bell St, T031-3288000, www.ushakamarineworld.co.za. The shopping arm of this huge marine park, with a wide range of shops, including chain stores and independent boutiques, surf shops and a mix of fast food outlets.

Suburban shopping malls

Gateway, north out of town in Umhlanga Rocks, T031-5662332. This vast complex is supposedly the largest shopping mall in the southern hemisphere – easily believable once you step inside. There's a huge variety of shops and restaurants, 18-screen cinema, IMAX theatre, impressive climbing and abseiling wall, an artificial surf wave and the world's only manmade double point break (for those who understand surf jargon), plus a championship skateboard park.

Musgrave Centre, 115 Musgrave Rd, Berea, T031-2015129. Over 110 shops with a mix of trendy boutiques and national chain stores. A craft and curio market is held on level 5 of the car park on Sun.

Pavillion, T031-2650558, Westville. 320 shops and restaurants, and a multi-screen cinema. It's always busy – an estimated 1 million people visit this mall each month.

Activities and tours

Durban *p389, maps p392 and p396*

Cricket

Kingsmead, T031-3329703, dolphins@natalcricklet.co.za, tickets from www.sacrickettickets.co.za. Home to the KwaZulu Natal provincial cricket team, Kingsmead is a modern stadium with large grandstands. All of Durban's big matches are played at this popular venue, and it was host to some Cricket World Cup matches in 2003. The weather for matches is generally good but being close to the sea there is always a chance of rain or poor visibility.

Diving

Operators dive from Durban or can arrange trips to other sites such as Sodwana Bay or the Aliwal Shoal. Visibility is at its best during the winter months.

Dive Nautique, T082-5532834 (mob), www.divenautique.co.za. PADI and NAUI, equipment rental and sales, courses, single dives and dolphin-watching boat trips.

Meridian Dive Centre, T031-5732190.

Golf

Windsor Park Municipal Golf Course, next to the Umgeni River just north of Durban, T031-3122245. 18 holes, phone for teeing off times for visitors as competitions are held here regularly, equipment can be hired here by the day or by the week. There are also a number of newer golf courses further north or south along the coast.

Horse racing

Race meetings are held at one of KwaZulu Natal's 3 racecourses operated by the Golden Circle Turf Club: **Greyville**, T031-3141500; **Clairwood Park**, T031-4691020; and **Scottsville**, T033-3453405. Each has regular stands and an indoor buffet restaurant overlooking the course for which you will need to dress up a bit. Night racing is held at Greyville only. Phone ahead for times.

Paragliding

Blue Sky Paragliding, T031-7651318. Flights Wed-Sun in the Valley of 1000 Hills, weather permitting.

Surfing

There are several designated surfing and boogie boarding beaches along the seafront, and a number of surf shops on the South Beach promenade have boards for hire.

Surf Zone, Ocean Sports Centre, North Beach, T031-3685818. Rents out surf- and body boards by the hour (R40), half-day (R70) or full-day (R100), plus organizes surf lessons from R180 for an hour.

Tour operators

Durban Africa, Tourist Junction, T031-3044934. The tourist office runs a range of walking tours through the city Mon-Fri, from R50 per person. Tours must be booked a day in advance and are a good, safe way of getting to know the city.

Durban Ferry Services, T031-3011953, ferry@worldonline.co.za. Sundowner cruises and harbour tours.

Far and Wild Safaris, 477 Essenwood Rd, T031-2083684, www.africasafari.co.za. Large operator offering luxury safaris to Hluhluwe-Umfolozi, plus longer tours and fly-in day trips.

Islamic Propagation Centre, T031-3060026. Guided tours of the mosque on Queen St.

Jikeleza Tours, T031-7021189, www.jikeleza tours.co.za. Township tour starting at the Kwa-Muhle Museum to understand the nature of Apartheid, before visiting the Umlazi or Nanda township. Also evening trips with local guides for drinks at the township shebeens, plus wider city tours.

JNC Helicopters, T031-5639513. Helicopter tours of Durban.

Strelitzia Tours, T031-2672273, www.stre litzatours.com. A comprehensive range of tours in the province 1-3 days with regular departures. City tours and day trips to townships, Valley of 1000 hills.

Tekweni Ecotours, at Tekweni Backpackers, 169 Ninth Av, Morningside, T031-4632576, www.tekweniecotours.co.za. Budget tour operator offering a huge range of tours. Regular tours to Hluhluwe-Umfolozi and St Lucia game parks, scuba-diving trips, tailor-made bird trips, and city, Valley of 1000 Hills, and township day tours. There are also a number of cultural day and overnight trips to Zululand. Consistently good reports.

Watersports

Chalupsky Paddling, T031-3037336. Kayaking trips along the coast and out at sea.

Durban Charter Boat Association, Fuelling Jetty, Yacht Mole, T031-3011115. Offers a wide range of boats, for small speed boat diving trips and deep-sea shark fishing to luxury booze cruises.

Transport

Durban *p389, maps p392 and p396*

Air

Durban is a practical alternative point of arrival in South Africa to Johannesburg. **Comair/ British Airways**, T011-9210222, www.com air.co.za, has several daily flights to **Johannesburg** and **Cape Town**. South African Airways (SAA), central reservations T011-9781111, www.flysaa.com, has a number of daily flights to **Cape Town** and **Johannesburg**, as well as to other principal South African cities. **Nationwide**, T0861-737737, www.flynationwide.co.za, flies from Durban to **Port Elizabeth**, **Cape Town** and **Johannesburg**. Kulula, T0861-585852, www.kulula.com, flies to **Johannesburg** and **Cape Town**. One Time, T0861-345345, www.1time.co.za, flies to **Johannesburg**.

Airline offices Air Zimbabwe, Musgrave Centre, Musgrave Rd, T031-2016061-5. **Comair/BA**, airport, T031-4507009. **East Coast Airways**, Virginia Airport, T031-5649344. Private air charters. **Lufthansa**, 66 Kensington Dr, Durban North, T031-5646684. **Nationwide**, airport, T031-4089300. **Singapore Airlines**, 305 Musgrove Rd, T031-2024303. **South African Airways**, airport, T031-4502210, reservations T031-2501111. **Swazi Express**, T031-4081115/6.

Bus

Greyhound, T011- 2768500, www.grey hound.co.za, regular buses run to **Cape Town** via Umtata, East London, Port Elizabeth, Knysna and Swellendam, or via Harrismith, Bloemfontein and Beaufort West; **Pretoria** and **Johannesburg**; **Richards Bay**.

Intercape, T0861-287287, www.inter cape.co.za, runs to **Bloemfontein**, **Johannesburg** and **Pretoria**.

Margate Mini Coach, T039-3121406, after hours T082-4559736 (mob), departs Durban Station Translux Terminal, advance booking essential, to **Margate** (2 hrs), departs up to 3 times per day, fewer services at the weekend, via Durban Airport, Scottburgh, Hibberdene and Port Shepstone; expect to pay R80 return.

Translux, T0861-589282, www.translux.co.za, runs to **Cape Town** via Bethlehem and Bloemfontein, or via **Port Elizabeth**, **Johannesburg** and **Pretoria**.

Baz Bus, T021-4392323, www.bazbus.com, has services to **Port Elizabeth**, **Johannesburg** and **Pretoria**, via Northern Drakensberg, or via Zululand and Swaziland.

Car hire

Avis, www.avis.co.za, T08610-21111; also at the airport, T031-4081777, toll free T08610-2444. **Berea Car & Bakkie Hire**, 331 Berea Rd, T0800-333811, www.berea.co.za. **Budget**, www.budget.co.za, 108 Ordnance Rd, T0860-016622; also at the airport T031-4081888. **Hertz**, www.hertz.com, 13 The Avenue East, toll free T0861-600136; also at the airport, T031-4694247. **Imperial**, www.imperialcarrental.co.za, 34 Aliwal St, domestic reservations T031-2631260; also at **Durban Airport** T031-4690066, toll free T0800-131000. **Tempest**, 47 Victoria Embankment, T031-3685231, also at **Durban Airport** T031-4690660.

Taxi

Taxis must be booked in advance: **Eagle**, T031-3378333; **Mozzie Cabs**, T086-0669943; **Zippy Cabs**, T031-2027067.

Train

Trains for Durban arrive at the **New Durban Station**, NMR Av, T0860-008888, www.spoornet.co.za. The country's longest route, from Durban to **Cape Town** (36 hrs), leaves weekly, and runs via **Bloemfontein** and **Kimberley**. The route to **Johannesburg** (13 hrs), via **Pietermaritzburg** (2 hrs) and **Ladysmith**, (6 hrs), leaves daily, except Tue and Sat.

Directory

Durban *p389, maps p392 and p396*

Banks

ABSA, T0800-111155. **First National**, T0800-111722. **Nedbank**, T0800-110929. **Standard Bank**, T0800-020600. **American Express**, Pavilion Mall, T031-2651455/6; 213 Musgrave Rd, T031-2028733, Mon-Fri 0800-1700, Sat 0830-1200. **Rennies**, 333 Smith St, T031-3055722. Foreign exchange and Thomas Cook representative, Sanlam Centre, Musgrove Rd, T031-2027833, The Pavilion, Westville, T031-2650751. **Mastercard**, T0800-990418. **Diners Club**, T0800-112017.

Consulates

Belgium, 2 Sunrise Close, Morningside, T031-3032840. **Germany**, 4 Devonshire Pl, T031-3055677. **Italy**, 14th floor, Embassy House, 199 Smith St, T031-3684388/9. **Mozambique**, 320 West St, T031-3040200. **Netherlands**, Standard Bank Building, 135 Musgrave Rd, Berea, T031-2020461. **Sweden and Norway**, 702 Musgrave Centre, 115 Musgrave Rd, Berea, T031-2076900. **United Kingdom**, 19th floor, The Marine, 22 Gardiner St, T031-3052929. **USA**, 31st floor, Old Mutual Building, 303 West St, T031-3057600.

Hospitals and medical services

Emergencies T10177. **Addington Hospital**, (Principal State Hospital), Erskine Terrace, South Beach, T031-3272000. **Entabeni Private Hospital**, 148 South Ridge Rd, T031-2041377. The **Travel Doctor**, 45 Ordnance Rd, International Convention Centre, T031-3601122, F3601121. Vaccination centre and a good place to pick up anti-malarials. **South Beach Medical Centre**, Rutherford St, Point, T031-3323101. A multi disciplinary centre, open 24 hrs. Practical central location. **Emergency** pharmacy T031-2073946, T031-3056151.

Internet

The **Freedom NetCentre**, 385 Smith St, T031-3073461, has 65 terminals and is open 0800-2400. **Durban Online**, Ushaka Village Walk, T031-3371818, has numerous outlets in the shopping malls and most of the backpackers offer internet access.

Useful telephone numbers

City Police T10111. Police Tourism Unit T031-3682207. Sea Rescue T031- 3618567. Weather T082-2311603.

KwaZulu Natal coast

The stretch of coast directly north of Durban is a mix of built-up holiday resort and city suburb, from which locals commute to the city centre. To the south, the coastal resorts have more of a holiday feel. Much of this stretch has undergone considerable development and is extremely popular with domestic tourists. ▸▸ *For Sleeping, Eating and other listings, see pages 414-419.*

South of Durban ▸▸ *pp414-419.*

The landscape south of Durban includes a fertile subtropical region stretching from the southern tip of the Drakensberg Mountain Range to the Indian Ocean. The Umzimkulu, the Umkomaas and the Elands rivers wind their way from the Drakensberg escarpment through the rolling hills of KwaZulu Natal to the sea. This was one of the first areas to be settled by the British during the 19th century and continuous agricultural development has left its mark on the landscape. Some of South Africa's largest pine and eucalyptus plantations extend for mile after mile around Harding, while, nearer to the coast, sugarcane and banana plantations dominate the scenery. A strip of subtropical forest runs down the coast bordering onto the beach. Excellent roads also make the Strelitzia and Hibiscus coastlines among South Africa's most popular holiday destinations.

Dolphin watching and scuba diving on the Aliwal Shoal and on the reefs south of Port Shepstone thrill an ever-growing number of enthusiasts. A wide range of sporting facilities, including numerous golf courses and tennis courts, are available at the resorts. The main attractions inland are the nature reserves at Oribi Gorge and Umtamvuna.

Amanzimtoti → *Colour map 5, grid B2.*

The Srtrelitzia Coast is one of the more built-up areas south of Durban. Driving down the N2, the road passes Durban's international airport and goes through an extensive industrial belt. Amanzimtoti, or 'toti', only 22 km south of Durban, is effectively a suburb, a huge built-up holiday resort with little to keep you in town. The Zulu name translates as 'sweet waters', as described by Shaka. Thousands of locals spend their annual holiday here, swimming, soaking up the sun and partying. A wide range of holiday accommodation is available among the high-rise flats and holiday homes facing the beach. **Inyoni Rocks** and **Pipeline Beach** are the two main beaches for swimmers and sunbathers, behind which is a busy main road. On the outskirts of town is a large chemical factory and an explosives factory. However, the lagoons beyond Amanzimtoti have been spared the relentless pace of development and these havens of tropical vegetation are sanctuaries for the coast's prolific birdlife.

Kingsburgh to Scottburgh → *Colour map 5, grid B1.*

Between Amanzimtoti and Umgababa are a series of coastal resorts and beaches known collectively as Kingsburgh. The 8-km stretch is known for its good beaches and is popular with surfers and jet-skiers. Travelling down the coast from Amanzimtoti, the first beach you reach is **Doonside**; across the Little Manzimtoti River is **Warner Beach**. **Winkelspruit** is one of the more developed parts of the area. Across the Lovu River is **Illovo** beach, which is backed by a lagoon at the mouth of the river. **Karridene** is at the mouth of another river, the Msimbazi. **Umkomaas** is the last resort in this area, next to the **Empisini Nature Reserve**, where a small dam has been built on the river which attracts an interesting variety of birdlife. The reserve can be reached by taking the Umkomaas and Widenham exit off the N2.

Scottburgh → *Colour map 5, grid B1.*

Scottburgh is 35 km south of Durban and has become one of the busiest resorts on the Strelitzia coast. The beach by the estuary of the Mpambanyoni is protected by shark nets and is very popular. The beaches are connected by a seafront miniature railway. There is a **tourist office** ⓘ *library centre, Scott St, T039-9761364, www.scottburgh.co.za.*

The **Aliwal Shoal** lies just north of Scottburgh, and after Sodwana Bay is one of South Africa's most popular diving areas (see page 418). The shoal is a haven for marine life and offers a good selection of dives on wrecks and on the reef. The caves attract ragged tooth sharks each winter.

Hibiscus Coast » *pp414-419.*

There is less industrial development along this stretch of coast, which stretches from Scottburgh to Port Edward, but the overall impression as you drive down the coast is of a long line of caravan parks and holiday homes, set in a lush subtropical strip of forest. The ocean is the highlight here. During the warm winter months billions of sardines travel close to the beaches, attracting dolphins, sharks, game fish and birds, and the ocean teams with life.

Vernon Crookes Nature Reserve

ⓘ *Reservations through KZN Wildlife, T033-8451000, www.kznwildlife.com, sunrise to sunset, R10.*

From the N2, the R612 heads inland towards Ixopo. Eight kilometres after passing Umzinto, there is a signpost to the Vernon Crookes Nature Reserve. The road passes through eucalyptus and sugarcane plantations as it heads towards a typical African landscape of grassland and thornveld, which supports 56 species of mammals.

This is one of the best reserves to see blue wildebeest, eland, impala, nyala, oribi, reedbuck and zebra near to the south coast. The wide range of habitats here supports over 300 species of birds. The best time of year to see the reserve's wild flowers is during the spring in September and October – there are some magnificent displays of orchids, lobelias and watsonias. A network of dirt roads crosses the park and there are picnic sites, a dam and viewpoints. Guided walks and night drives are available throughout the year.

Umzumbe Village

This is a small, pleasant village exactly 100 km south of Durban with a great backpackers' place to chill out at by the sea. It's also a good spot for dolphin watching and scuba diving. Driving from Durban, turn off the N2 at Hibberdene and follow the R102. Turn right at the sign for Umzumbe Fairview Mission and look out for the sign after about 1 km. It's also on the Baz Bus route.

Port Shepstone → *128 km from Durban. Colour map 5, grid C1.*

Located at the mouth of the Umzimkulu River, Port Shepstone is the largest town on the south coast and is more of an industrial centre than a tourist resort. **Hibiscus Coast Tourism** ⓘ *Princess Elizabeth Dr, T039-6822455, www.hibiscuscoast.kzn.org.za.*

The **Banana Express** ⓘ *T039-3157065, www.bananaexpress.co.za, trains depart from next to Shark's Den Restaurant, Aug-Feb Thu and Sat at 1000, Dec and Jan daily, R60, tickets available from the station kiosk or tourist office,* is a vintage steam train which runs from Port Shepstone as far as Paddock station, 39 km from the coast (the station is listed as a national monument). The narrow gauge railway was opened in 1907 and is one of the few remaining steam journeys in South Africa. The route from Port Shepstone follows the coast for about 6 km before the track starts to wind its way up into the green hills covered with banana and sugarcane plantations.

South of Port Shepstone

The towns and villages on this southernmost stretch of coast are the last of the chain of resorts that feel like seaside holiday camps before the R620 enters the Wild Coast (see page 371). Hiking in Umtamvuna Nature Reserve, diving on Protea Banks and the reefs off Shelly Beach, and whale and dolphin watching are the highlights of this region.

Shelly Beach is 5 km south of Port Shepstone on the R620. It is quite a large suburb with one of the region's biggest shopping malls and has a wide variety of shops, restaurants and a cinema. The beach here is popular as a launch site for various fishing and diving charters.

Uvongo, 12 km south of Port Shepstone, is built on cliffs looking out to sea and is one of the more pleasant resorts on the south coast. The beach, protected by shark nets, is safe for swimming and surfing. The waterfall at the nearby **Uvongo River Nature Reserve**, open from sunrise to sunset, is a pleasant place for a picnic. The 23-m-high waterfall tumbling over cliffs into the beachside lagoon is the reserve's main feature. At the rear of the beach are some steps to a viewpoint overlooking the falls.

South Coast

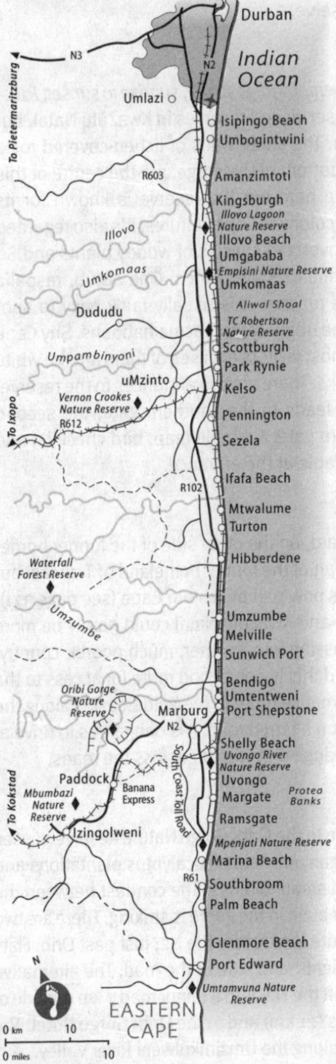

Margate → *Colour map 5, grid C1.*

Originally a palm-fringed stretch of and, the town began to be developed in 1919 and is now a highly developed family resort, popular with holidaymakers from Gauteng. The beach is excellent and was recently awarded the Blue Flag. From the junction with the South Coast Toll Road, the link road immediately enters the tourist zone passing the mini golf and holiday homes on the way into town. In the centre, high-rise flats are crammed in towards the beachfront, which gets very crowded during school holidays. For information contact **Hibiscus Coast Publicity Association** ⓘ *Panorama Pde, Margate Beachfront, T039-3122322, www.hibiscuscoast.kzn.org.za.*

Ramsgate is 2 km south of Margate and is now practically a suburb, but the beach here is a little quieter and has shark nets so is popular for surfing. It has a tidal pool for swimming, with pedalos and canoes for hire.

Southbroom

Southbroom is a popular resort with subtropical trees coming down to the beach. It mainly consists of private holiday homes belonging to wealthy Gautengers and can feel deserted out of season. There is safe swimming in a tidal pool just down the coast at Marina Beach, a beautiful 5-km stretch of sand and rolling dunes.

The **Riverbend Crocodile Farm and Art Gallery** ⓘ *Old National Rd, T039-3166204, daily 0900-1630, feeding time Sun 1500, small entry fee*, breeds around 200 Nile crocodiles. There is also a snake house, with snake handling demos every day at 1430. This tourist complex also has a tea garden, a restaurant, farm stall and an art gallery.

Mpenjati Nature Reserve ⓘ *sunrise to sunset, R10*, is 20 km west of Margate and 12 km south of Southbroom and is popular with windsurfers, canoeists and fishermen. The reserve covers a small area of coastal forest and wetlands along the edge of the lagoon and is good for spotting wetland and woodland birds including a resident pair of breeding fish eagles. There are some leisurely walking trails along the Mpenjati River and around the lagoon, with two picnic spots.

Port Edward → *Colour map 5, grid C1.*

This small tourist resort has a large palm-fringed beach backing onto tropical forest. There are shark nets here and good swimming and surfing. It is a convenient place to stay when visiting Umthamvuna Nature Reserve.

Umtamvuna Nature Reserve

ⓘ *8 km north of Port Edward towards Izingolweni, T039-3132383, sunrise to sunset, R10.* This is the southernmost and one of the lesser visited reserves in KwaZulu Natal, but has some of the finest hiking in the region. The sheer walls of lichen-covered rock, dropping down into thick rainforest at the bottom of the gorge, are the centre of this dramatic landscape. There is no big game here but the reserve is known for its displays of wild flowers in the spring and its colony of Cape vultures. It's also regarded as one of the world's top plant spots with over 330 species of woody plants and 80 herbaceous plants, of which 30 are endemic to South Africa. One shrub, raspalia trigyna, is very rare and only found in this reserve. It is usually fairly easy to spot bushbuck, blue and common duiker, and the ubiquitous chacma baboons. Shy Cape clawless otters inhabit the reserve but the most visitors ever see of them are the white calcareous droppings found along river banks. There are two entrances to the reserve: the first turning, off the Izingolweni road, leads to the southern gate; the second turning 5 km further on leads to the northern gate. A simple map, bird checklist and some ecology information leaflets are available at the entrance.

Towards the Wild Coast

The Wild Coast lies to the south of Port Edward, on the other side of the former border over the river Umtamvuna. This used to be part of the former homeland of Transkei but since the abolishment of the homelands it is now part of Eastern Cape (see page 371). The contrast between the former homeland and KwaZulu Natal could hardly be more marked – crossing the old border is like crossing into another, much poorer, country. Road conditions deteriorate immediately and this is not a good route for access to the Wild Coast unless you have a 4WD. The alternative route to the Wild Coast is along the N2 via Kokstad and Umtata to Port St Johns on a tarred road. It is dangerous to drive at night because of the goats, cattle and stray dogs that wander across the roads.

West from Port Shepstone

The road heading inland from Port Shepstone to the Oribi Gorge Nature Reserve passes through an extensive agricultural area of sugarcane fields, eucalyptus plantations and cattle pastures, crowded with Zulu huts and smallholdings. The contrast between the outlying farmland and the untouched African bush in the gorge is striking. There are two routes to Oribi Gorge (21 km). The fastest route is to follow the N2; just past Oribi Flats East there is a signpost to the park on the right-hand side of the road. The alternative route is slightly longer and involves turning off the N2 onto a minor road 7 km outside of Port Shepstone. This road leads to Oribi Flats (21 km) and to the **Oribi Gorge Hotel**. The road passes through some rugged scenery along the Umzimkulweni River Valley.

The **Soobramanya Temple** is a tiny green building with a corrugated iron roof 1 km before the Portland Cement Factory. This is an enchanting place to break your journey; apart from the beautiful views over subtropical woodland, a stop here offers a rare insight into Natal's history. The temple was built around the turn of the 19th century by Indian labourers working on the nearby sugar plantations and is a good example of early Natal temple architecture. The site has all the traditional elements of a South Indian shrine: there is a Kodi pole, a lingam stone and a fig tree in the courtyard in front of the main building, while inside the shrine are the bronze statues representing the deities of the Hindu pantheon.

Oribi Gorge Nature Reserve → *Colour map 5, grid C1.*

ⓘ *21 km west of Port Shepstone via the N2, 0630-1930, R10.*

Established in 1950 to protect this area of thick woodland and towering cliffs where the Umzimkulu and Umzimkulweni rivers meet, the Oribi Gorge Nature Reserve is 24 km long and 5 km wide. The views from the top of the sandstone cliffs, some of which are up to 280 m high, look out over the forest, which clings to the sides of the ravines below. The cliffs provide nesting sites for birds of prey, and the forest, home to the African python, is so thick that although leopard live here they are never seen. One of their prey, the Samango monkey, can sometimes be seen in small groups. Favouring dense, evergreen jungle, the Samango has a dark brown face and longish hair. Birdlife here is prolific, with over 250 species present, including Knysna louries, narina trogons, trumpeter hornbills and five kingfisher species. Ironically, oribi are not common and are very rarely seen.

Don't leave valuables in your car when you walk to the edge of the gorge as cases of petty theft have been reported.

Samango Falls, **Hoopoe Falls** and **Lehr's Falls** are the most spectacular waterfalls in the gorge and are best seen after heavy rain when vast quantities of water come crashing down into the ravines below. There are several clearly marked hikes, from 1 km to 9 km. A series of tracks lead to viewpoints over the gorge. There are stunning views from **Oribi Heads, Horseshoe Rock**, **Camel Rock** and the **Overhanging Rock.**

A tarred road winds down 4 km from the hutted camp to a picnic spot next to the bridge crossing the Umzimkulweni River. There are some impressive views of the gorge. The Umzimkulweni River is not safe to swim in as it is infected with bilharzia but there is a pleasant swimming pool in the camp. The camp shop sells wildlife books, souvenirs, charcoal, firewood and a limited range of food. Fresh meat, vegetables and cheese are available from a farm shop just by the entrance to the reserve. The nearest petrol station is 4 km away in Paddock.

North of Durban (Dolphin Coast)

▸▸ *pp414-419.*

The area north of Durban, between Umhlanga and Tugela Mouth, is known as the **Dolphin Coast**, thanks to the bottlenose dolphins that frolic in the waves year-round. It is also known as the Sugar Coast, thanks to the rolling sugar plantations backing the sea. Like the coastline to the south of Durban it is possible to miss many of the sights and small coastal settlements if you remain on the N2 highway. The inland towns of Verulam, Tongaat and Stanger, tucked between vast rolling sugar plantations, have large resident Indian populations and are processing centres for the area's industry, with few attractions for tourists.

The old coast road, however, runs parallel to the sea passing through the beach resorts of Umhlanga Rocks, Ballito and Salt Rock, attracting vast crowds of holidaying South Africans in summer. After Umhlanga Rocks, most of the resorts are far smaller than those found on the south coast and appeal to more upmarket holiday makers, but the area is developing quickly. Nevertheless, it feels more relaxed and far less developed than the south coast, with crowds thinning out the further you get from Durban. The beaches are beautifully wild stretches of soft sand, pounded by impressive waves (but remember to check if they're protected by shark nets before going for a dip). Away from the water, locals flock to the impressive golf courses, although a quieter choice are the numerous tropical nature reserves; seldom overrun with visitors, these well-run protected areas provide some fine birdwatching opportunities.

Umhlanga Rocks → *Colour map 5, grid B2.*

Sugar Coast Tourism Association ⓘ *Chartwell Dr, T031-5613978, www.sugarcoast.kzn.org.za, Mon-Fri 0800-1630, Sat 0900-1200*, arranges accommodation and provides advice on visiting the nature reserves. It also has maps and brochures.

The upmarket holiday resort of Umhlanga Rocks is a short drive north of Durban – these days it is virtually a suburb of the city, although its sprawl of concrete highrises makes it feel more like a Spanish Costa. The main attraction here away from the beach is **Gateway**, South Africa's premier shopping mall, allegedly the largest in the southern hemisphere (see page 404).

Umhlanga Rocks beach is a beautiful stretch of wave-lashed sand, although day visitors have little chance of seeing it, thanks to the belt of highrises stretching along its length. Access to the water is almost exclusively through resort complexes and hotels, and there's no beachfront area. Nevertheless, South Africans flock to the hotels and condominiums, and the area has a buzzing atmosphere in high season. **Umhlanga Lagoon** lies just to the north of town, where there are beautiful expanses of wetland, forest and an unspoilt, open beach yet to be concreted over by the developers.

The town's name means 'Place of Reeds' in Zulu after the reeds that are washed down the river to the north and onto the pristine beaches. The area was once covered with dune forest; today, only small pockets of original vegetation have been preserved in surrounding nature reserves. In the 19th century, the land was part of a large sugar estate, Natal Estates Ltd, owned by Sir Marshall Campbell. The estate was managed from Mount Edgecombe in the interior; a track was built from here to the coast and local farmers began to lease small plots on the beach and build holiday cottages. The first cottage was built in 1869 and was known as the Oyster Box, today the **Oyster Box Hotel**.

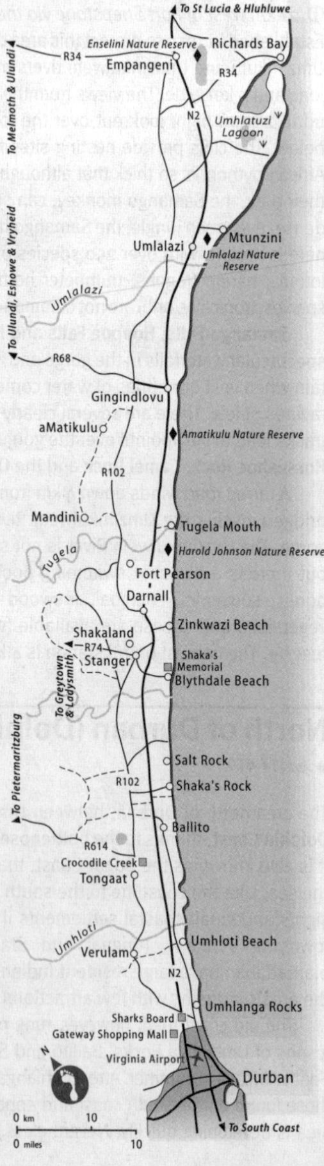

A popular local landmark is the **Umhlanga Lighthouse**. The distinct red and white, circular concrete tower stands 21 m above the beach and acts as a fixed point to help ships, waiting to dock in Durban harbour, confirm their exact position in the outer anchorage. The lighthouse tower has stood here since November 1954, occupying the centre point on the beach, right in front of the **Oyster Box Hotel**. The lighthouse has never had a keeper; instead it is operated by the owner of the **Oyster Box Hotel** from controls in the hotel office.

The **Sharks Board** ⓘ *Herrwood Dr, T031-5660400, www.shark.co.za, display hall and curio shop Mon-Fri 0800-1600, tour and video Tue-Thu 0900 and 1400, Sun 1400, R20*, set inland from the resort, studies the life cycles of the sharks that inhabit the sea off the coast of KwaZulu Natal and investigates how best to protect bathers with various forms of netting. Umhlanga Rocks became the first beach to erect shark nets in 1962, following a series of attacks along the whole coast in December 1957. Today the Sharks Board is responsible for looking after more than 400 nets, which protect nearly 50 beaches. Tours at the Sharks Board begin with a 25-minute multimedia video show on the biology of sharks and their role as top predators in the marine food chain. This is followed by a stomach-churning shark dissection. The display hall has a variety of replicas of sharks, fish and rays, including that of an 892 kg shark. It is also possible to accompany researchers on the Sharks Board boat as they go about their daily servicing of the shark nets off Durban's Golden Mile (R150).

Hawaan Nature Reserve is 4 km north of Umhlanga Rocks at the end of Newlands Drive. During the 1920s, William Alfred Campbell, son of Sir Marshall who had founded the sugar estates, used to stage an annual hunt in this unique forest environment. It was not until 1980 that 60 ha were protected as part of the nature reserve. Within the reserve there are 4 km of leisurely guided walks through an unusual area of mature coastal forest. The trails are not open to the public but walks can be organized with the **Wildlife Society**, T031-5612030. The area is rich in birdlife and you can also see bushbuck, duiker and vervet monkeys.

Crocodile Creek ⓘ *T032-9443845, daily 0930-1700, out of season closed Sat, small entry fee*, is between Umhlanga and Ballito; turn off the Old Main Road (R102) close to Maidstone Golf Course. This crocodile centre has regular hands-on guided tours viewing its population of over 9000 crocodiles, as well as snakes, tortoises and small monkeys. Between December and March, it is possible to see baby crocs hatching. The curio shop sells goods made from the skins and the coffee shop has crocodile on the menu.

Ballito and around → *Colour map 5, grid B2.*

The small-scale, largely low-rise resort of Ballito is far more attractive than Umhlanga, with easy access to the long beach and attractive accommodation nestled in lush vegetation stretching up the hillside. At the entrance of town, just off the coast road, is the new **Sangweni Tourism Centre** ⓘ *T032-9461997, www.thedolphincoast.co.za*, a useful stop-off with information on the Dolphin Coast area. Most visitors to Ballito are South African holidaymakers, who settle in for a bucket-and-spade holiday every summer. If you're passing through, it's a pleasant enough spot for a day or two by the beach, but stick to the southern, less developed end.

North of Ballito, **Salt Rock** is named after a rock where the Zulus used to collect salt, and is similar to Ballito, while nearby **Shaka's Rock**, also developing fast, is named after the cliff from which Shaka is said to have thrown his enemies to their foamy deaths. There is good snorkelling at Tiffany's Reef and Sheffield Reef, but neither resort holds much appeal other than for those after a sand and sea holiday.

Tongaat, Verulam and Stanger

Inland from Umhlanga Rocks, the R102 passes through the towns of Verulam, Tongaat and Stanger, which collectively form the heart of KwaZulu Natal's sugar processing industry. The descendants of the indentured labourers, who were brought here from India in the 1860s, give the region a distinct Indian atmosphere and, although the towns are now predominantly industrial centres, the Hindu temples and Indian markets are interesting. Accommodation is available here, but the beach resorts on the coast are more pleasant places to stay.

In Tongaat, the **Juggernath Puri Temple** is 23 m high and can be seen from miles away. There are no windows in the tower, but inside, as the eye adjusts to the darkness, the Vishnu statue gradually becomes visible. **Shri Gopalal Temple** is just outside of Verulam on the road to the Packo food factory. The temple was opened by Gandhi in 1912, and catered for wealthier and more educated Gujurati immigrants. **Subramanyar Alayam Temple** is set in a beautiful tropical garden just north of town as you reach the railway bridge. A good time to experience the atmosphere of the temple is at weekends when many weddings are held.

It is customary to remove your shoes before entering the temple buildings.

Stanger is a busy commercial centre surrounded by extensive sugar plantations. The original settlement here was founded by Shaka as a capital and was known as KwaDukuza. At its height there were up to 2000 beehive huts surrounding Shaka's royal kraal. Shaka was murdered here by his half-brothers Dingaan and Umhlangana on 22 September 1828. A monument was erected in Shaka's memory in 1932, which today has become the focus point for the small **King Shaka Visitor Centre** ⓘ *T032-5527210, Mon-Fri 0830-1700, Sat 1900-1300, free*. Here, visitors can watch a short audio-visual display on Shaka's life, and have a nose around his memorial garden and tea room. For further information on Shaka, see page 716.

Harold Johnson Nature Reserve

ⓘ *T031-4861574, daily 0600-1800*

Just over 20 km north of Stanger on the N2, a signposted dirt track leads through sugar plantations up to the entrance of this 100-ha reserve, where there is a parking area and a picnic site. In the reserve are the remains of **Fort Pearson**, which was used as a base from which British troops invaded Zululand in 1879. The **Ultimatum Tree**, the other attraction here, was where Shepstone read out the ultimatum to Cetshwayo's *izindunas* (warriors) giving them 20 days to disband their armies, pay fines in cattle and conform to the coronation vows that Shepstone had imposed. These demands and others were totally unreasonable to the Zulus but non-compliance with the ultimatum was used by the colonial authorities as an excuse for war.

In the reserve, wildlife includes red and grey duiker, bushbuck, impala, vervet monkey and over 110 species of butterfly, which can be sought out on 7 km of walking trails. The **Muthi Trail** gives an interesting insight into the medicinal uses of various traditional plants used by the Zulu people; a booklet can be bought at the entrance. There's also a small cultural **museum** ⓘ *at the picnic site, R10*, portraying traditional Zulu dress and culture.

Sleeping

Kingsburgh *p407*

C **Angle Rock Backpackers**, 5 Ellcock Rd, Warner Beach, T031-9167007, www.anglerock.co.za. Smart backpackers' place in a great beachside location, with octagonal-shaped dorms and double rooms. Also has camping, excellent kitchen, laundry facilities, snooker table, swimming pool in a private garden full of palm trees and a great tropical feel. Owners organize diving at the Aliwal Shoal, free use of surfboards and fishing rods, recommended as the place to stay south of Durban, call in advance for pick ups from Durban stations and airport.

Albert Luthuli, who won the Nobel Peace Prize in 1960, was restricted to living in Stanger as punishment for his political activities with the ANC. He died here in 1967.

Scottburgh *p408*

B-C **Cutty Sark**, beachfront, T039-9761230, www.cuttysark.co.za. Modern, slightly dated hotel in a lovely beachside location. 55 rooms, TV, 2 restaurants, bar, swimming pool, tennis and squash courts, gym, in 6 ha of well-kept tropical gardens. Horse riding on the beach and diving can be arranged from here. Popular family hotel.

C **Blue Marlin Resort**, 180 Scott St, T039-9783361, www.bluemarlin.co.za. Large resort on a hill overlooking the beach, pool, gardens, games room, 2 bars, inclusive of buffet meals, 120 spacious and functional rooms, has weekly specials for senior citizens so, as you can imagine, activities lean towards bingo, bowls and bridge.

D-E **Scottburgh Caravan Park**, seafront, T039-9760291, www.scottburghcaravanpark.co.za. Giant caravan park, over 300 sites stretching along 1 km of beach, designed to cater for families during school holidays. The park has several swimming pools and has good sports facilities. Gets very busy with families during holidays, but provides functional accommodation in a great setting out of season.

Umzumbe Village *p408*

D-E **Mantis & Moon**, Station Rd, T039-6846256, www.mantisandmoon.net. Rustic backpackers set in lush jungle, with dorms, doubles and camping dotted between wild banana trees, also has newer tree house, with double rooms. Pool table, candle-lit bar, great music, home-cooked food, free use of surf boards, courtyard with a wild garden, outdoor hot tub, rooftop deck. Recommended.

Port Shepstone *p408*

B **Kapenta Bay**, 11-12 Princess Elizabeth Dr, T039-6825528, www.kapentabay.co.za. 50 units, all 3 room self-catering suites with 2 bathrooms, bland modern block overlooking the beach, large swimming pool, secure parking, typical resort set-up and popular conference venue.

C-E **Pepper Pots**, 60 Commercial Rd, T039-6950852. Family-run set-up, smaller and less sprawling as the usual beachside resorts. Self-catering chalets, backpackers dorm, caravan and campsites, bar, restaurant, TV lounge, walking distance to the beach.

South of Port Shepstone *p409*

B **Ayton Manor**, 2½ km inland from Shelly Beach, after driving under the N2, take the first right, T039-6850777, www.aytonmanor.co.za. B&B and self-catering guest lodge with 6 rooms and 2 family suites set in a fine country house on a sugar estate, rather over-the-top decor (frills, heavy curtains), private balconies and separate entrances, TV, fridge, microwave, bar, pool, children will like the working farmyard. Popular with golfers.

D **Greyfare**, 38 Frere Rd, Shelly Beach, T039-3157446, greyfare@saol.com, ask for Arlene. 6 modern spacious flats for 1-4 people, private balconies or secluded patios, fully equipped, TV, lovely small pool and garden, breakfast available on request, walking distance to beach, shops and cinema, cheap rates, good value for money.

Margate *p409*

B **Kenilworth-on-Sea**, Marine Dr, T039-3120342, kenilworthonsea@intekom.co.za. Guest lodge nestled in 1 ha of tropical gardens with good sea views near the beach, 30 rooms, a/c, TV, en suite, dinner and breakfast, private parking, swimming pool, children's playground, pool table, table tennis, scuba diving/training.

B **Margate Hotel**, 71 Marine Dr, T039-3121410, info@margatehotel.co.za. 69 a/c en suite rooms, TV, **Keg** pub and restaurant, swimming pool, tennis, comfortable but run-of-the-mill family hotel set in mature gardens overlooking the beach. Discounts in low season.

B **Wailana Beach Lodge**, 436 Ashmead Rd, T039-3144606, www.wailana.co.za. Luxury lodge located 1 km to both Ramsgate and Margate centres, easy walking distance to all amenities, nice gardens with hammocks and pool, B&B, 5 stylish en suite rooms, TV, fan, lovely private sun decks with ocean views, evening meals on request, much more friendly than the standard holiday flats.

B-C **Beach Lodge Hotel**, Marine Dr, T039-3121483. Recently renovated hotel with 35 a/c rooms, TV, plus modern self-catering units, all with well-equipped kitchens, diners area, TV, DVD player. Restaurant serving buffet breakfast, bar, large swimming pool, secure parking.

D-E **Margate Backpackers**, 14 Collis St, Manaba Beach, T039-3122176. Despite its name this is closer to Port Shepstone; Manaba Beach is off the R620. Dorms, doubles plus camping in the garden. Bar and pool table. Easygoing set-up, Baz Bus stop, free pick-ups from Port Shepstone. A colourful old-style town house with the ideal veranda to chill on. Short walk from the beach, can arrange surfing and diving.

Southbroom *p409*

B-C Nature's Cottage, Churchill Rd, T039-3168533, natcot@iafrica.com. Charming log house encircled by large verandas with cane furniture, set in a patch of indigenous forest. 3 bedrooms, 2 of which open up on to the deck, separate dining room, 2 Victorian bathrooms overlooking trees, lounge with TV, video and CD player, fully fitted kitchen with deep freezer and separate scullery. Great place for families (over 13s only) or groups of friends. Recommended.

Port Edward *p410*

B Estuary Country Hotel, 1 km before Port Edward on the N2, clearly signposted, T039-3132675, www.estuary.co.za. 24 en suite a/c rooms in a restored Cape Dutch manor house, most with balcony overlooking the estuary, TV, bar, pool, health and beauty spa, close to a safe swimming beach. The **Fish Eagle Restaurant** is open to non-residents, ownership by an Austrian family, interesting and varied South African and European menu.

C-E Ku-Boboyi River Lodge and Backpackers, 4 km north of Port Edward in Leisure Beach on the R61, T039-3191371, www.kuboboyi.co.za A bright hilltop lodge with good views over the ocean and beach. Dorms, doubles decorated in an African theme, plenty of space for camping, pool, sunny veranda, B&B. The owner, Eric, is a chef and cooks exceptionally good value gourmet meals each night.

Oribi Gorge Nature Reserve *p411*

C-D Oribi Gorge Hotel, T039-6870253, www.oribigorge.co.za. 18 double rooms, separate cottage for backpackers, small family hotel, restaurant, snooker, gym, country pub, curio shop, swimming pool. The hotel, built in the 1870s, is a colonial building encircled by a veranda. The restaurant serves burgers, steaks, pies and pub food. There is a pleasant beer garden where you can eat outside under the trees. The gorge can be seen from viewpoints on farmland adjoining the hotel, which is only 17 km from the hutted camp. A number of activities can be arranged from here with **Wild 5 Adventures** (see page 419). Follow the scenic route through the gorge and, on leaving the reserve, head towards Port Shepstone. The hotel is on the northern side of the gorge and is clearly signposted.

B-E Oribi Gorge Camp, reservations through **KZN Wildlife**, T033-8451000, www.kznwildlife.com. 6 huts with 2 beds in each, a 7-bed chalet, plus 3 tent sites. The huts and chalet are equipped with fridge, kettle, toaster, crockery and cutlery but no cooking facilities. Bring all food and drinks with you. There's also a communal braai area, lounge with satellite TV and a swimming pool with sundeck for use by all guests and campers.

Umhlanga Rocks *p412*

In addition to hotels and B&Bs, there is a large selection of holiday apartments, most of which are rented out by the week. During the off season it may be possible to organize shorter lets in the middle of the week.

Umhlanga & Coastal Letting, at the Caltex service station on Lighthouse Rd, T031-5615838, www.getcoastal.co.za, offers short and long term lets as well as time share. Contact well in advance if you are planning on renting a family-size apartment during any local school holidays.

AL Beverly Hills Sun Inter-Continental, Lighthouse Rd, T031-5612211, www.southernsun.com. 95 rooms in a smart hotel overlooking the beach, a/c, TV, choice of top-end restaurants including the **Sugar Club** and **Cabin** cocktail bar, swimming pool, fitness centre, tennis and squash courts, afternoon tea served daily.

B Oyster Box, Lighthouse Rd, T031-5612233, www.oysterbox.co.za. The area's first hotel building dates from the 1940s and was always popular with British travellers visiting the colonies. The hotel retains its elegant colonial atmosphere to this day but has been in need of refurbishment in recent years. 80 rooms, a/c, TV, restaurant (serving oysters), swimming pool, tennis, 2 bars. Spectacular setting behind the dunes, the beach and the lighthouse, with a nice terrace for tea or a sundowner.

D Cathy's Place, 18 Stanley Grace Cres, T031-5613286, cathysbb@mweb.co.za. Homely B&B run by the affable Irish Cathy, en suite doubles and singles in modern bungalow or 1 self-catering family cottage in the garden, TV, swimming pool. 5 mins' walk from the beach and shops, can arrange airport pick-ups.

D Honeypot , 11 Hilken Dr, T031-5613795, sugarfld@iafrica.com. Smart B&B rooms with TV, bar, fridge and email access. Dog and child friendly. Satour accredited.

D Jessica's, 35 Portland Dr, T031-5613369, hallgren@iafrica.com. Close the beach and shops, this small B&B has comfortable cottages in the garden, with M-Net and tea-making facilities, overlooking the pool.

Ballito and around *p413*

AL Zimbali Lodge, just off coast road, south of Ballito, T032, 5381007, www.suninternational.com. Luxurious lodge set in the grounds of a country club and golf course, stretching along the coast just south of Ballito. Golf carts ferry guests around the estate, between the sport facilities, spa, posh restaurants and opulent rooms, which have polished wooden floors, huge beds, balconies and all mod cons. All set in beautiful tropical forest. Stunning pool area and direct access to the beach.

B Boathouse, 33 Compensation Beach Rd, Ballito, T032-9460300, www.theboathouse.com. Luxury guest house right on the beach, 22 beautifully decorated rooms, the floor-to-ceiling windows have a boat rail with life rings attached, TV, phone, a/c, the bar is a great place to have a sundowner and spot dolphins. Recommended.

B-C Shortens Country House, Compensation Rd, Ballito, T032-9471140, www.shortenshotel.com. Country house located next to **Umhlali Country Club** (with 18-hole golf course, tennis, squash, pool). The house is 5 mins from the beach, with attractive a/c en suite rooms in garden units. Good restaurant and pretty tea garden.

C-E Salt Rock, Basil Hluett Dr, Salt Rock, T032-5255025, www.saltrockbeach.co.za. A big block overlooking the beach but a friendly hotel with a beautiful location, restaurant, bar and swimming pool. Popular local haunt for rugby fanatics on Sat nights, expect a rowdy time during the playing season. Caravan and camping park attached.

D Beach House, 3 Osborne Dr, Salt Rock, T/F084-5815573. Recently renovated double rooms with en suite facilities, TV, internet access, garden, swimming pool, sundeck overlooks the beach, secure parking. Recommended.

D-E Dolphin Holiday Resort, Ballito, T032-9462187, www.dolphinholiday resort.co.za. Basic caravan park with shady campsites. You can't see the sea from here but it's only a couple of mins' walk to the beach.

Harold Johnson Nature Reserve *p414*

There are 6 shady sites for tents or caravans with a tap, braai pit and ablution block. Come fully prepared as there are no other facilities. Reservations are made directly with the campsite office, T032-4861574.

Eating

Amanzimtoti *p407*

¶ Clearwaters Spur, 97 Beach Rd, T031-9038813. Busy Western-style saloon bar with enormous steaks, roast chicken and beer.

¶ Keg & Hedgehog, 417 Kingsway, T031-9037390. A lively pub atmosphere serving a wide range of food from steaks to the Keg chain's famous foot-long pies. Good setting in an old house with sea views.

South of Port Shepstone *p409*

¶¶¶ Stephward Estate, 17 Peter St, Uvongo, T039-3155926. Part of a guesthouse with a tea garden and upmarket restaurant serving à la carte lunches and dinners in the dining room or al fresco.

Margate *p409*

¶¶¶ La Capannina, Marine Dr, T039-3171078. Authentic Italian restaurant, the chef actually comes from Italy, known for slow roast lamb and tripe stew, plus good fried prawns. Open Tue-Sun lunch and dinner, closed Sat lunch.

¶¶ The Bistro, T039-3144128, Marine Dr, Ramsgate. Closed Sun out of season. Colonial-style restaurant serving traditional cuisine, such as a good rack of lamb, roast duck, as well as grilled seafood and curries. Customers can bring their own wine.

¶¶ Eat & Meet, Granada Building, Marine Dr, T039-3122213. Seafood restaurant, vast menu and large portions, including good fresh grilled seafood, and occasional buffets.

Ÿ 7 Seas, William O'Connor Dr, T039-3174349. Beachfront restaurant and bar with live music. Good spot for a sundowner.

Ÿ Larry's, corner of O'Connor Dr and Panorama, beachfront, T039-3172277. Pizza restaurant with a long menu, some salads and pasta choices, with seating on a busy terrace overlooking the beach.

Ÿ The Waffle House, Marine Dr, Ramsgate, T039-9424. Sweet and savoury waffles on a terrace next to Ramgate Lagoon, breakfast waffles until 1100, next door is the Gaze Gallery exhibiting the work of local artists.

Umhlanga Rocks *p412*

ŸŸŸ The Cabin, Beverly Hills Hotel, Lighthouse Rd, T031-5612211. Pricey dinner and dance in an extravagant blue and gold stateroom, every evening except Sun.

ŸŸŸ Razzmatazz, Cabana Beach Hotel, 10 Lagoon Dr, T031-5615847. Closed Sun. 5-star prices in a 5-star hotel serving excellent food, unusual game and seafood dishes, such as lemongrass-steamed langoustines, and a great setting on an outdoor deck overlooking the ocean.

ŸŸŸ The Sugar Club, Beverly Hills Hotel, Lighthouse Rd, T031-5612211. Sundower terrace overlooking the sea, and a smart dining room with good fresh seafood dishes and a romantic atmosphere.

ŸŸ Al Firenze, 21 Ray Paul Dr, T031-5725559. Pasta and seafood with a lively terrace. Takeaways available.

ŸŸ Cottonfields, 2 Lagoon Dr, T031-5612744. Popular bistro and bar, freshly cooked Natal seafood and meat dishes cooked in *potjiekos*, traditional cast iron pots.

ŸŸ Lord Prawn, Umhlanga Plaza, T031-5611133. Recommended for its simple seafood dishes, including fish and chips, served on a terrace overlooking a small road.

Ÿ Ninos, Umhlanga Plaza. Good spot for lunch at shady tables on the pavement, with a wide choice of sandwiches and salads and excellent daily specials. Friendly service.

Ballito *p413*

ŸŸŸ Mariner's, Valenti Centre, Compensation Beach Rd, T032-9461858. Excellent but pricey seafood, with good prawn curries and fresh linefish, served in a mall setting. Non-smoking.

Entertainment

Margate *p409*

Funworld, Marine Dr, T039-3120741. 3-screen cinema, bowling alley, pool, arcade games.

Shopping

Umhlanga Rocks *p412*

The enormous Gateway shopping mall lies uphill from the coast in Umhlanga (see page 404). The other malls in the area are far smaller and more manageable, such as Granada Centre, on Chartwell Dr, and La Lucia Mall, on Armstrong Rd. In town, there is a small selection of craft and souvenir shops.

Activities and tours

Scottburgh *p408*

Aliwal Dive Charters, 21 Harvey St, Umkosaas, T039-9732233, www.aliwalshoal.co.za. Boat dives and courses, snorkelling and whale and dolphin watching boat trips; also offers good value accommodation and has a restaurant.

Meridian Dive Centre, Cutty Sark Hotel, T039-9732813, www.meridiandive.com. Wide range of dives, lots of shark dives including cage diving, also organizes longer dive trips along the coast or to the cape.

Margate *p409*

Being the main tourist centre on the south coast, Margate is a good place from which to organize activities. Fishing is allowed off the pier and off Margate Rocks and there are plenty of tackle shops in town. Designated surfing and boogie-boarding areas are on Main Beach and at Lucien Point. Boards can be hired from a number of shops in town. Main Beach is shark-protected and therefore the safest and most popular for swimming.

African Dive Adventures, T039-3171483, afridive@iafrica.com. Offers a wide range of diving courses, and specializes in shark dives. Dives take place at the Protea Banks where schools of hammerhead and Zambezi sharks are regularly seen.

Margate Country Club, T039-3120571, Tue-Sat 0800-1700, Sun 1400-1700. 18-hole golf course, visitors welcome. Green fees R120.

Oribi Gorge Nature Reserve *p411*
In addition to its hiking trails, Oribi Gorge is also the ideal location for adventure sports. **Wild 5 Adventures**, T039-6870253, www.oribigorge.co.za, based at the **Oribi Gorge Hotel** (see page 416) offers whitewater rafting trips, in conventional rafts or large inner tubes on the Umzimkulu River, and abseiling from Lehr's Waterfall, the last 66 m being a free abseil during which you can feel the spray of the falls on your back. Also has the Wild Swing, a 75-m freefall and a 100-m outward swing over the falls, and the Wild Slide, a 120-m steel cable slide over Lehr's.

Umhlanga Rocks *p412*
Diving
There are 2 interesting wreck dives at the *T-Barge* and the *Fontao*. Both sites are at around 20 m deep where visibility is good. The boats were sunk to create artificial reefs and provide habitats for tropical fish.
Dive Nautique, at the Surf Lifesaving Club on the beachfront, T082-5532834 (mob). Offers local dive charters and can also organize dolphin viewing boat trips.

Golf
Zimbali Country Course, just off coast road, south of Ballito, T032-5381007, www.suninternational.com. 18-hole championship course designed by Tom Weiskopf.

Ballito and around *p413*
La Mercy Microlight Flights, La Mercy Airfield, T084-2663359 (mob). Short flights over Umhlanga Lagoon, ideal for whale spotting; lessons also available.

Transport

Port Shepstone *p408*
Bus
Baz Bus, T021-4392323, www.bazbus.com, runs between **Durban** and **Cape Town**. Greyhound, T011-2768500, www.greyhound.co.za, runs to **Cape Town** (25 hrs) and **Durban** (1½ hrs). Margate Mini Coach, reservations T039- 3121406, after hours T082-4559736 (mob), runs between **Durban** and **Margate**. Translux, T011-7743333, www.translux.co.za, runs regular buses to **Cape Town** and **Durban** (1½ hrs).

Margate *p409*
Air
Margate Municipal Airport is 2 km from the town centre, T039-3120560. The **Margate Mini Coach** service calls in at the airport to meet incoming and departing flights. The only scheduled service is operated by **SA Airlink**, central reservations, T011-9781111, www.saairlink.co.za, to **Johannesburg**, operating most days.

Bus
Margate Mini Coach, reservations T039-3121406, after hours T082-4559736 (mob), runs to **Durban** (2 hrs), via **Port Shepstone**, **Hibberdene**, **Scottburgh** and **Durban Airport**.

Car hire
At the airport: Avis, T039-3120094; Budget, T039-3173202; Imperial, T039-3121346.

Port Edward *p410*
The Baz Bus, T021-4392323, www.bazbus.com, stops here en route to Durban or Port Elizabeth.

North of Durban *p411*
Bus
Greyhound, T011-2498900, www.greyhound.co.za, has a regular service between **Durban** and **Pretoria** via Richards Bay, Vryheid, Piet Retief and Evander.

Car hire
Forest Drive, 40 Forest Dr, La Lucia, Umhlanga Rocks, T031-5628433, offers low cost daily rental rates but a very small amount of free mileage.

Taxi
Dolphin Coast Taxis, T032-5259449.

Directory

Umhlanga Rocks *p412*
Banks Branches of all the major banks can be found in the shopping malls. **Medical services** Ambulance, T10177. **Post office** Tanager St, next to civic offices, open Mon-Fri 0830-1630, Sat 0800-1200. **Useful telephone numbers** Ballito Lifeguards, T031-9461963.

Pietermaritzburg and the Natal Midlands

➔ *Colour map 5, grid B1. Altitude: 647 m.*

This attractive city, the capital of the Colony of Natal in the late 19th century, was named after the Voortrekker leaders Gert Maritz and Piet Reteif, who settled here in 1838 after the Battle of Blood River; today it is the joint capital of KwaZulu Natal with Ulundi. It markets itself as a distinctly English city and, despite its largely African population and bustling street life, its red-brick buildings do give it a strikingly similar look to a provincial English town centre. An important trading centre for the local farming industry, Pietermaritzburg is also home to the University of Natal and a number of technical colleges, giving it a young, studenty feel during term time, with a decent selection of nightlife. ➤➤ *For Sleeping, Eating and other listings, see pages 426-429.*

Ins and outs

Getting there Pietermaritzburg is only 80 km from Durban on the N3 and can easily be visited in a day. **Durban International Airport** (see page 389) is 45 minutes drive from Pietermaritzburg. **Oribi Airport** is 6 km from the centre of town and has daily domestic flights to Johannesburg, Ulundi and Durban operated by **SA Airlink**. The **railway station** is on the corner of Church and Pine streets. This is a rough part of town, so arrange to be collected in advance if you're arriving by train. Long-distance **buses** stop here on the route between Durban and Johannesburg. Pietermaritzburg lies on the Durban-Johannesburg **Baz Bus** route, via the Northern Drakensberg; **Sani Pass Carriers** runs regular shuttles to the Southern Drakensberg.

Best time to visit The climate is subtropical with heavy rainfall from December to February. The rest of the year tends to be warm and dry and makes a pleasant change from the humidity in Durban.

Tourist offices **Pietermaritzburg Tourism** ⓘ *Publicity House, 177 Commercial Rd, T033-3451348/9, www.pmbtourism.co.za, Mon-Fri 0800-1700, Sat 0800-1300, closed Sun*, is conveniently situated and has a comprehensive range of maps and leaflets as well as an accommodation service. Staff are helpful, friendly and keen to promote their city. **Capital Coach Bookings** also has a desk here for booking mainline coach tickets. The original building was completed in 1884 and used to be the local police station.

Pietermaritzburg is the location of the central office of **KZN Wildlife** ⓘ *T033-8451000, www.kznwildlife.com*. To get here, follow Commercial Street out of town towards Hilton, and follow signs for the Cascades shopping mall. The KZN offices are next to the mall in the Queen Elizabeth Park Nature Reserve.

Background

Pietermaritzburg was founded as the capital of Natalia in 1838. Originally, the town was laid out in the same way as Cape Dutch towns, with thatched houses, wide streets, large gardens and irrigation channels running down the streets. The small rural capital was a trading centre for farmers and game hunters and later became a stopover for wagon trains heading for the interior.

The republic of Natalia only lasted a few years; the British arrived in 1843 and established a garrison here, and the safety provided by the garrison encouraged other settlers to arrive from Britain and Germany. Pietermaritzburg became a prosperous Victorian town and many of its most attractive buildings date from this period. The administrative buildings of the Colony of Natal are in the city centre, but it is the quiet side streets, lined with fine Victorian houses built by wealthy merchants, which make the town so pretty. Here, the mix of bungalows and two-stored red-brick houses retain their original verandas, decorated with cast-iron lattice work, hardwood windows and brass fittings, all shaded by huge, arching jacaranda trees.

Sights

The city centre has Pietermaritzburg's most imposing Victorian buildings, civic gardens and war memorials. The old buildings are not all open to the public but it is possible to walk around most of the sites in a morning. Dominating the centre is the grand **City Hall**, which looms on the corner of Commercial Road and Church Street. Built on the site of the Volksraadsaal in 1900, it is supposedly the largest all-brick building in the southern hemisphere and is decorated with stained-glass windows.

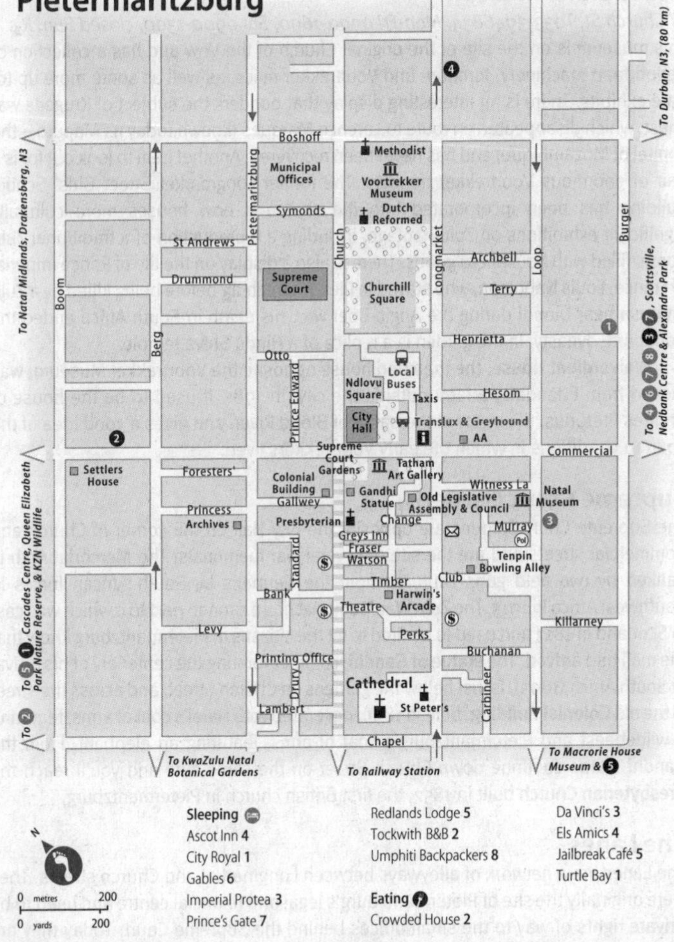

Tatham Art Gallery

ⓘ *60 Commercial Rd, T033-3421804, Tue-Sun 1000-1800, free.*

Opposite the City Hall is a similarly imposing red-brick structure, completed in 1879 and used as a post office until 1906, when it became the site of the Supreme Court. Renovation work started during the late 1980s and, in 1990, it was inaugurated as the new home for the Tatham Art Gallery.

Inside is a fairly ramshackle selection of modern and Victorian art; the original collections are of French and British Victorian art, and although the landscapes are fairly pleasant there is nothing particularly striking about them. But the gallery does have some interesting and unusual works, including a Stanley Spencer landscape called *Near Nareta, Bosnia*, and paintings by Degas, Renoir, Braque and Picasso. There is a large, highly ornate ormolu late-Victorian clock at the top of the stairs on the first floor which is worth seeing. During chiming, a screen is raised to reveal a clockwork blacksmith and some bellringers moving in time to the chimes. The South African Gallery is perhaps the most interesting, with a collection of contemporary art. These eclectic works are a refreshing change from the worthy but somewhat staid collections of Victoriana. There is a tea room on the first floor, overlooking the gardens.

Voortrekker Museum

ⓘ *Church St, T033-3946834, Mon-Fri 0900-1600, Sat 0900-1300, closed Sun, R3.*

This museum is on the site of the original Church of the Vow and has a collection of period farm machinery, furniture and Voortrekker relics, as well as some more up-to-date exhibits. There is an interesting display that ponders the subject of Kruger's war chest, which disappeared en route to Lorenço Marques (known today as Maputo – the capital of Mozambique) and has never been recovered. Another item to look out for is a pair of enormous Voortrekker trousers. The former Longmarket Street Girls' School building has been incorporated into the site, and now houses more culturally significant exhibitions on Zulu heritage, including a reproduction of a traditional Zulu home, filled with household goods. There is also a display on the life of Prince Imperial of France, Louis Napoleon, who stayed in Pietermaritzburg before being killed by a Zulu ambush near Ulundi during the Anglo-Boer war. His death in South Africa ended the Bonaparte dynasty. In the garden is a replica of a Hindu Shiva temple.

Welverdient House, the thatched house opposite the Voortrekker Museum, was moved from Edendale, a farm outside the city, in 1981. It used to be the house of Andries Pretorius, the victor at the battle of Blood River, and gives a good idea of the spartan conditions in which the early Voortrekkers lived.

Supreme Court Gardens

The Supreme Court Gardens are opposite the City Hall on the corner of Church and Commercial streets and are the site of several war memorials. The **Memorial Arch** is flanked by two field guns captured from the Germans by South African forces in Southwest Africa in 1915. The **Zulu War Memorial** has a cannon next to it which was cast in Scotland in 1812 and used to be fired to let the citizens of Pietermaritzburg know that the mail had arrived. The **statue of Gandhi**, commemorating the centenary of his arrival in South Africa (1893), is just below the gardens on Church Street, and across the street is the old **Colonial Building**, built in 1899, decorated with Natal's coat of arms, featuring a wildebeest and Pietermaritzburg's coat of arms, featuring an elephant. From the Gandhi statue continue down Church Street on the same side and you'll reach the **Presbyterian Church** built in 1852, the first British church in Pietermaritzburg.

The Lanes

The Lanes are a network of alleyways between Longmarket and Church streets. They were originally the site of Pietermaritzburg's legal and financial centre and used to be private rights of way to the small offices behind the Supreme Court. Today they are

Mahatma Gandhi in South Africa

Gandhi was asked by a journalist when he was on a visit to Europe what he thought of Western civilization. He paused and then replied: "It would be very nice, wouldn't it". The answer illustrated just one facet of his extraordinarily complex character. A westernized, English-educated lawyer, who practised law in South Africa from 1893 to 1914, he preached the general acceptance of some of the doctrines he had grown to respect in his childhood, which stemmed from deep Indian traditions – notably *ahimsa*, or non-violence. From 1921 he gave up his Western style of dress and adopted the hand spun *dhoti* worn by poor Indian villagers, giving rise to Churchill's jibe that he was a 'naked fakir' (holy man). Yet if he was a thorn in the British side, he was also fiercely critical of many aspects of traditional Hindu society. He preached against the iniquities of the caste system, which still dominated life for the overwhelming majority of Hindus. Through the 1920s much of his work was based on writing for the weekly newspaper *Young India*, which became *The Harijan* in 1932. The change in name symbolized his commitment to improving the status of the outcastes, Harijan (person of God) being coined to replace the term outcaste. Often despised by the British in India, he succeeded in gaining the reluctant respect and ultimately outright admiration of many.

Gandhi arrived in South Africa in 1893 but soon became involved in South African politics after being a victim of racial prejudice himself when he was forcibly removed from a whites-only train carriage in Pietermaritzburg. He founded the Natal Indian Congress in 1894 to fight for the freedom of the indentured Indian labourers that were working in the docks, sugar plantations and railways. He moved to a farm just outside of Durban with his family and followers in 1903, to produce a resistance magazine called *Indian Opinion*, and his fame as an opponent to the rising racial prejudice saw him negotiating with General Jan Smuts in person. Thousands of indentured workers went on strike when the government passed a law to ban Indians entering the Transvaal in 1907, which led to the Indian Relief Bill in 1914 that finally emancipated the Indians. With the fight over, Gandhi returned to England in July 1914 and never saw South Africa again.

lined with small shops and cafés and administrative buildings dating from the turn of the 19th century. From Church Street, enter the Lanes on Timber Street where you can see **Harwin's Arcade**. The arcade was built in 1904 and has a skylight running through it, illuminating the second-hand bookshops.

Timber Street leads into Longmarket Street; turn left here and return to Commercial Road. This route passes the impressive **General Post Office,** opened in 1903, and the offices of the *Natal Witness*, South Africa's oldest newspaper established in 1846. The **Old Legislative Assembly** and the **Old Legislative Council** are on the left-hand side. On the right is Witness Lane which leads to the Natal Museum.

Natal Museum

ⓘ *237 Loop St, T033-3451404, Mon-Fri 0900-1630, Sat 1000-1600, Sun 1100-1500, R5.*
The Natal Museum has a more diverse collection than many other South African museums. The natural history gallery has a considerable collection of stuffed creatures that date from the foundation of the museum. The last wild elephant shot in Natal in

1911 is on display, as are two specimens of the black and white rhino. The first treasure chest of the Colony of Natal can be found here; it is an old iron chest that used to travel around the colony by wagon and was used to collect the Native Hut Tax. The colony's finances were at times so desperate that the chest held less than a pound.

Upstairs is the relatively new 'Origins' gallery, with anthropology displays including a fascinating section on the Ashanti people of the Gold Coast. There is a wooden stool decorated with strips of gold, a sacred object which was demanded by the British as a token of surrender. The collection of brass weights is particularly beautiful; they were used for weighing gold and were moulded from natural objects such as snails, ground nuts and grasshoppers. There are also a number of archaeological displays, with examples of San rock art in a reconstructed cave, and recreations of Stone Age life. The final gallery focuses on Portuguese shipwrecks.

South of the Lanes

At the other end of Longmarket Street is **St Peter's Church**, a museum with displays of European stained glass. The church was built in 1857 after Colenso split with the Church of England. Bishop Colenso is buried in front of the altar. From here, turn left into Chapel Street, then right into Loop Street. At number 11 is the **Macrorie House Museum** ⓘ *T033-3942161, Mon 1100-1600, Tue-Thu 0900-1300, closed Fri-Sun, small entry fee*, where Bishop Macrorie lived from 1870 to 1892. The house is decorated with period furniture and houses a collection of Victorian costumes.

Beyond the city centre

Butterflies for Africa ⓘ *Willowton Rd, T033-3871356, www.butterflies.co.za, Tue-Fri 0900-1630, Sat 0930-1530, Sun 1030-1530, closed Mon, small entry fee*, is clearly signposted from the N3 towards Durban. It incorporates a large enclosed butterfly house, a butterfly garden and nursery with a maze, a craft and coffee shop, an art gallery and museum, and audio-visual presentations on the life of a butterfly. New in 2005 is the monkey house, with examples of small monkeys and a walk-through path.

Alexandra Park lies to the south of the city centre and can be reached by following Commercial Road past the Voortrekker Cemetery. The park was founded in 1863 and has large public gardens with a beautiful old cricket pavilion built in 1898. Two other interesting features here are the Victorian bandstand and a cast-iron water trough for horses. An open-air art show is held here every May.

World's View lies to the west of town and you can get to it by following the Old Howick Road (R103), past the Country Club golf course and into World's View Road. A plaque at World's View, next to the Voortrekker Road, marks the route taken by the early Voortrekkers. The short trails follow the path of an old railway line and pass through pine and wattle plantations where it is possible to see interesting birdlife and some small buck. There are magnificent views of Pietermaritzburg from the top of the hill.

KwaZulu Natal Botanical Gardens ⓘ *2 Swartkops Rd, Mayors Walk, T033-3443585, www.nbi.ac.za, daily 0800-1730, small entry fee*, was founded in 1870 and following a fine Victorian tradition has a collection of plants from all over the world. The most interesting feature in the gardens is the **Zulu Muthi Garden**, created with the help of local healers and including a traditional beehive-shaped healer's hut. This is a 'living display' to inform visitors about traditional plant-use and associated conservation issues but it is also designed as a centre where healers can attend courses in the sustainable use of traditional medicine plants. It is an ideal place for a leisurely stroll or afternoon tea next to the ornamental lake.

Queen Elizabeth Park Nature Reserve, off the Howick road on the outskirts of Pietermaritzburg (free) is small but has a network of short walking trails from which you can see blesbock, impala and zebra. The flora here is particularly interesting; the park has been a wild flower reserve since 1960 and has stunning displays of colour in the spring. The headquarters of **KZN Wildlife** is located within the park (see page 420).

Trainspotters will be interested in the **Natal Railway Museum** ⓘ *Hilton Station, T033-3431857, daily 0800-1600, small entry fee*, which is part of Umgeni Steam Railway and run by volunteers. The museum has a fine display of railway memorabilia and a number of coaches and locomotives dating from the 1930s. Some of the highlights of the museum include a sleeper coach from 1903, a bullion coach from 1937 and a 36-ton steam crane.

Natal Midlands » *pp426-429.*

The Midlands cover the region between Greytown and Richmond, Pietermaritzburg and Estcourt. The many rivers flowing off the Drakensberg escarpment have created a well-watered, fertile landscape that originally supported a large population of Zulu cattle herders and farmers in the lowlands. San migrated between here and the Drakensberg, following the herds of eland according to the changes of the seasons. Later the fertile territory attracted first the Voortrekkers and then British immigrants in the 1850s, all of whom fought for control of the land.

Today, the farms here cultivate wattle for tanning and paper pulp, and there are large horse breeding studs, cattle and sheep ranches. The N3 bisects the Midlands and the majority of traffic passes through on its way between Gauteng and Durban. However, by taking the alternative R103, the Midlands towns and countryside can be explored by following the Midlands Meander route, a tourist initiative highlighting the multitude of craft outlets, country restaurants and rural retreats, popular with South African tourists.

Ins and outs

There is an excellent map and brochure available in the region's tourist information offices promoting a series of routes for visiting the Midlands by car. The 'meander' is reminiscent of a drive through English countryside on a Sunday afternoon and is one of South Africa's local tourism success stories. Over 400 places are marked on the map and include a selection of bed and breakfasts, craft shops and restaurants. The antique shops, potteries and weavers are good places to buy gifts. Information is available from **Midlands Meander Association** ⓘ *T033-3308195, www.midlandsmeander.co.za.*

Howick → *Colour map 5, grid B1.*

The small and quiet town of Howick has grown up around what was originally a fording point across the Umgeni River on the wagon route to the interior. The original settlement was named by the colonial secretary Earl Grey after his English home of Howick in Northumberland. More recently, Howick was the location where Nelson Mandela was arrested in 1962 before being sent to jail for 27 years. The actual spot where the police arrested him is just outside of town on the R103, on a road heading towards Tweedie Junction. He was disguised as a driver for a white friend and it is thought the police stopped the car because of a tip off. There is a memorial, unveiled by Mandela himself in 1996, marking this otherwise unassuming spot in a field next to the road

The 95-m-high **Howick Falls** are popular with South African tourists, who stop off here for a break while travelling on the N3. In 1951 they were proclaimed a national monument. To the Zulu people the waterfall is known as kwaNogqaza, 'the place of the tall one'. There is a path to the bottom of the falls but beware of the slippery rocks. Above the falls is an open-air café.

The **Howick Museum** ⓘ *T033-3306124, Tue-Fri 0930-1530, Sat and Sun 1000-1300, small entry fee*, is just next to the falls and has a display of Victorian furniture and farm machinery. There is also an interesting collection of military badges. Next door is the Old Agricultural Hall, now home to an excellent craft and curio shop, **Craft Southern Africa**, T033-3305859. The hall was built in 1899 and is well worth a look.

Midmar Nature Reserve

ⓘ *From Howick the R617 crosses the N3 and passes Midmar Public Resort Nature Reserve (7 km) en route to Bulwer (90 km) and Underberg (120 km). Reserve open 24 hrs, R15.* This attractive dam is a hugely popular holiday resort with numerous sporting facilities on offer including power boating, jet-skiing, windsurfing and yachting. Sunset cruises can be organized with advance notice. There is a small shop open at weekends and peak periods where bikes, windsurfs and canoes can be hired. Day visitors are permitted.

Towards Estcourt

The fastest route north from Howick to Mooi River (37 km), Estcourt (60 km), Spionkop (92 km) and the Free State is on the N3. An alternative scenic route is to take the R103 through Nottingham Road (29 km) to Mooi River (48 km).

The Nottingham Regiment gave their name to the small farming settlement of **Nottingham Road** after being stationed near here in the 1870s. This is a quiet, rural area, known for its trout fishing and holiday farms. The **Nottingham Road Brewery Company** ⓘ *Old Main Rd, Rawdons Estate, T033-2636044, tastings and shop daily 0800-1700*, is a rustic brewery with enticingly named beers that are hand-brewed using spring water: Tiddly Toad Lager, Pie-eyed Possum Pilsner, Pickled Pig Porter. From Nottingham Road, the R27 heads west towards the Drakensberg reserves at Kamberg (48 km; see page 455) and Lotheni (70 km; see page 458). This road is a rough dirt track which can become impassable after rain; check on road conditions before starting out.

Further northwest, the **Mooi River** flows through a small farming community en route from the Drakensberg Mountains to the Tugela River. The area around Mooi River is well-known for stud farming; it's smaller than the Cape but has produced a higher proportion of winners. The Drakensberg reserves at Kamberg (42 km) and Giant's Castle (see page 452) are well signposted from here.

Estcourt → *Colour map 5, grid B1.*

Estcourt is a thriving industrial town, site of South Africa's largest sausage factory and a Nestlé factory, both of which can be visited on a factory tour, if you're that way inclined. Factories aside, there's no reason to stop in Estcourt other than to stock up if you're on the way to self-catering accommodation in the Drakensberg.

Bushman's River Tourism ⓘ *Old Civic Building, Upper Harding St, T/F033-3526253, www.bushmans.co.za, Mon-Fri 0900-1600*, is an excellent tourist office, stacked full of brochures from all over the country. Well worth a stop if you are passing through town, it also has internet facilities and a craft shop. **Greyhound** and **Translux** buses stop outside.

Fort Durnford ⓘ *T033-3523000, daily 0900-1200, 1300-1600*, has interesting displays on military history, a good section on fossils and, rather oddly, one of Africa's most complete bird egg collections, donated by a local collector. In the grounds you can look around a reconstructed Amangwane Zulu kraal. The fort itself was built in 1874 in order to protect local residents from feared Zulu attacks.

Sleeping

Pietermaritzburg *p420, map p421*
There are lots more B&Bs in town; check with the tourist office for details.

AL Redlands Lodge and Hotel, 1 George Mcfarlane Lane (off the Old Hilton Rd), T033-3943333, redlands@mweb.co.za. A luxury hotel set in a slightly surreal gated development, in a quiet suburb. Country-style pastel-coloured rooms with private balconies, bar and mediocre restaurant. Popular with business people. Comfortable with friendly service, but feels isolated.

The Midmar Mile swimming contest is held every February and attracts around 10,000 entrants. It's now the world's largest inland swimming race.

A Imperial Protea, 224 Loop St, T033-3426551, www.proteahotels.com. Part of the **Protea** chain, 70 rooms set in a historical building, comfortable rooms with DSTV, a/c, room service, secure parking, restaurant and bar, the restaurant is recommended for its game dishes, oldest hotel in town and recently refurbished but feels a little impersonal. The Imperial Crown Prince of France, Louis Napoleon, stayed here during the Anglo-Boer War.

C Ascot Inn, 210 Woodhouse Rd, Scottsville, T033-3862226, www.ascot-inn.co.za. B&B or self-catering cottages set in a large garden with 2 swimming pools. Simple, cosy decor and friendly bar and grill restaurant on site. Has become a popular conference venue.

C City Royal, 301 Burger St, T033-3947072, www.cityroyalhotel.co.za. Slightly run down but fairly spacious double rooms, with a/c, en suite facilities and TV, set in a modern, run-of-the-mill town hotel. Restaurant serving traditional food in a rather dark setting, bar, plus an open-air terrace for drinks. Secure parking.

C Gables, 216 Woodhouse Rd, Scottsville, T033-3460792, www.thegables.co.za. Comfortable B&B or self-catering units in converted stables of a former racehorse stud, with rooms set around a small garden. All units have TV. Small restaurant and bar with set meals each night.

D Prince's Gate, 227 Prince Alfred St, Scottsville, T033-3450159. 12 simple self-catering units with open plan kitchen/lounge, TV, a/c, set around a small garden. Good value, central location.

D Tockwith B&B, 208 Chapel St, T033-3425802. A small cottage with a veranda, sleeps 4, TV, swimming pool and garden, plus 2 double B&B rooms in the main house. Ask for Megan.

D-E Umphiti Backpackers, 317 Bulwer St, T033-3943490, umphiti@mweb.co.za. Backpackers hostel housed in a Victorian home bang in the centre of town, with a pleasant veranda and small, lush garden with pool. Lounge with DVDs, meals available, accommodation in dorms and doubles. Adventure tours can be arranged.

Howick *p425*

A-B Old Halliwell Country Inn, 10 km north of Howick on Curry's Post Rd, T033-3302602, halliwell@mweb.co.za. A traditional English-style country hotel and restaurant built in 1830 as a wagon stop. Each double en suite room has a fireplace, honeymoon suites with jacuzzis, underfloor heating. Cosy pub, swimming pool and golf driving range.

A-B Shafton Grange, 12 km from Howick towards Rietvlei, T033-3302386, www.shaftongrange.co.za. A fine old farmhouse built in 1852, 5 rooms with en suite facilities, lounge. The attraction here is horse riding or polo on the 52-ha farm, there are 21 stables and people from Johannesburg bring their horses here on holiday. This is also home to the South African Lipizzaner stud, which breeds the white stallions used by the Lipizzaner School in Gauteng, affiliated to the Spanish Riding School in Vienna, Austria. Any equestrian lover is welcome to visit the stables if not staying here.

B Penny Lane Guest House, 11 km from Howick on the R103 towards Lidgetton, T033-2344332, www.pennylane.co.za. 8 spacious rooms, decor varies from twee to tasteful, fan-cooled, satellite TV and heaters for the winter months. The guest lounge has a log fire and a bar with a rustic African feel, traditional meals served. Swimming pool and tennis court.

C Howick Falls Hotel, Main St, T033-3302809, fallshotel@sai.co.za. 19 simple rooms in one of Howick's oldest buildings, built in 1872. Former guests include Mark Twain and Cecil Rhodes. Don't expect too much but it's cheap, full of atmosphere and the rooms have recently been renovated, quite a good Greek restaurant on site.

Midmar Nature Reserve *p426*

A-D Midmar Camp, KZN Wildlife, T033-8451000, www.kznwildlife.com. Range of rustic cabins, en suite self-catering units, chalets and campsites, some set on the shoreline, including a 6-bed chalet equipped for the disabled, shared ablution blocks for units without bathrooms. The campsites get very crowded during the school holidays, and have shared ablution blocks. Some have electricity.

Towards Estcourt *p426*

A The Bend, 14 km from Nottingham Rd towards Kamburg on the R103, T033-2666441, www.thebend.co.za. Smart lodge set in a nature reserve with a variety of lodge rooms and cottages, spacious with attractive decor and antique furniture, country meals, indoor swimming pool, horse riding and hiking, 5 km of the Mooi River runs through this reserve, trout fishing on 6 dams. Has its own chapel for country weddings.

A Rawdons, Old Main Rd (R103), T033-2636044, www.rawdons.co.za. A luxurious, thatched English-style country hotel in a 480-acre estate. 25 double rooms, light, airy decor, en suite bathroom, TV, restaurant, swimming pool, bowls, tennis, 7 trout dams for fishing, also location of the **Nottingham Road Brewery** (see page 426).

A-B Thatchings, 12 km from Nottingham Rd on the Curry Post Rd on the other side of the N3, T033-2666275, www.thatchings.co.za. Rural guesthouse set in a huge garden. 7 en suite rooms with TV, country-style decor, fresh flowers. A la carte evening meals. Bar with snooker table, golf course nearby as well as trout fishing on the farm.

C-E Sierra Ranch, on the R622 or Old Greytown Rd, 16 km from Mooi River, T033-2631073, www.sierraranch.co.za. Huge Western-themed resort with restaurant, swimming pool, offers a wide range of sporting activities including tennis, bowls, river tubing. Accommodation is in chalets, rondavels, en suite doubles or the bunkhouse.

Estcourt *p426*

C Blue Haze Country Lodge, 6 km from Estcourt, T036-3525772, www.bluehaze.co.za. Thatched lodge located on the way to the Battlefields and mountains, overlooking a peaceful lake. 7 comfortable garden suites, swimming pool fringed by palms, cosy pub serving meals. Game trails, horse riding and river rafting can be organized.

E Wagendrift Public Resort Nature Reserve, KZN Wildlife, T033-8451000, www.kznwildlife.com. Wagendrift Dam is 5 km from the city centre on the road to Ntabamhlopem. There are 2 campsites with a total of 37 sites, ablution blocks. Also has a 4-bed self-catering chalet. The reserve is a popular holiday resort and has facilities for power boats and fishing, canoes are available for hire. There are some short walking trails and a feeding site for vultures. The remains of trenches dug during the Boer War can still be seen.

Eating

Pietermaritzburg *p420, map p421*

TTT Turtle Bay, Cascades Centre, T033-3471733. Closed Sun evenings. Fine dining choice in the Cascades Centre, with lovely terrace. Traditional dishes, fresh seafood such as crayfish and tiger prawns, plus roast duck and delicious pies. Popular afternoon teas.

TT Da Vinci's, 266 Prince Alfred St, T033-3455084. Italian menu, good value. Well-managed with a pleasant atmosphere and attentive service. Upmarket cigar bar with live music daily from 2200, jazz on Sun. One of the few places open on a Sun.

TT Els Amics, 380 Longmarket St, T033-3456524. Closed Mon, Sun, and Sat lunch. Long-running restaurant serving Catalan and Mediterranean food, delicious gazpacho and fish dishes, and decent wine list, plus tasty Italian deserts.

T Jailbreak Café, corner of Burger St and Pine St, T033-3943342. Located in the old prison that is a national monument, slightly musty but friendly café and tea garden, cakes, lunches, surrounded by number of craft shops, open 0800-1600.

Bars and clubs

Pietermaritzburg *p420, map p421*

Crowded House, Commercial Rd. Open Thu-Sat. Long-running dance club in town. Popular with the students from the university. Alternative live music and dance music.

Exclusive Lounge, Commercial Rd. Trendy nightclub and bar, popular with students, with a sofa area and nightly DJs playing R'n'B and house music.

Entertainment

Pietermaritzburg *p420, map p421*

Club Lanes, Club Lane, T033-3428220. 10-pin bowling.

Numetro, Cascades Centre near the new Grey's Hospital. 8-screen cinema.

For an explanation of the sleeping and eating price codes used in this guide, see inside the front cover. Other relevant information is found in Essentials pages 42-47.

Activities and tours

Pietermaritzburg *p420, map p421*
The tourist office has a full list of registered guides for tours of the city, Drakensberg and the Battlefields.

Countryside Tours, T033-3868753, sheph@worldonline.co.za. Local guide Dennis organizes a number of day tours around the Natal Midlands area, as well as longer tours into the Drakensberg or around the Battlefields. Minimum 2, from R180 per person for 3 hrs. The **Pietermaritzburg Tour** (3 hrs) visits the city centre, botanical gardens and parks; **Valley of 1000 Hills Tour** (3 hrs) takes in a crocodile park and Zulu dancing; **Midlands Meander** (8 hrs) includes a visit to Howick Falls and a drive around the Midlands with views of the Drakensberg.

Meet us in Africa, T033-2394607, www.meetusinafrica.co.za. Interesting tours to some of the lesser visited nature reserves near Pietermaritzburg, plus flower trips to Drakensberg. Informative company run by Carolyn and Derek McDonald who are specialist field guides and can arrange birding and flower tours to the Drakensberg.

PMB Heritage Tours, T033-2124040, www.battleguide.co.za. One of the leading operators visiting the **Battlefields Route**, a member of the British Guild of Battlefield Guides, tours are tailor made. A day trip starts at around R700. Recommended.

Transport

Pietermaritzburg *p420, map p421*

Air

Durban International Airport is a 45-min drive from Pietermaritzburg. There is also a small town airport, 6 km from the centre, on the Oribi Rd from where SA Airlink, central reservations, T011-9781111, www.saairlink.co.za, runs services to **Johannesburg**.

Car hire

Budget, Imperial Hotel, T033-3428433, www.budget.co.za. **Hertz**, at the airport, toll free T0861-600136, www.hertz.co.za. **Sixt**, T033-3462551, at the airport.

Bus

The Baz Bus, T021-4392323, www.bazbus.com, stops in Pietermaritzburg 3 times a week. **Intercape**, T0861-287287, www.intercape.co.za, runs regularly to **Durban**, **Bloemfontein**, **Johannesburg** and **Pretoria**. Greyhound, T011-2768500, www.greyhound.com, runs regularly to **Durban**, **Butterworth**, **Johannesburg** and **Pretoria**.

Luxliner, central reservations T011-9144321, www.luxliner.co.za, runs from **Durban** to **Johannesburg International Airport** via Pietermaritzburg.

Sani Pass Carriers, T033-7011017, has a daily service, except Sun, to **Underberg**, useful if you wish to get close to the Drakensberg Mountains without your own transport. The bus picks up and drops off at Ngena Backpackers and the Imperial Hotel mid-morning Mon-Sat.

Translux, T011-7743333, www.translux.co.za, coaches depart from the Premier Caltex service station on Commercial Rd to **Cape Town**, **Durban**, **Johannesburg** and **Pretoria**.

Taxi

Yellow Cabs, T033-3971910.

Train

The railway station is on the corner of Church and Pine Sts, www.spoornet.co.za. Trains running between Durban and Johannesburg stop here daily except Tue and Sat.

Estcourt *p426*
Greyhound, T011-2768500, www.greyhound.co.za, runs services to **Durban**, **Johannesburg** and **Pretoria**.

Directory

Pietermaritzburg *p420, map p421*
Banks Rennies Foreign Exchange, Park Lane Centre, Commercial Rd, T033-3943968. Standard Bank, 211 Church St, T033-3452421. **Internet** Hive Media Café, Nedbank Centre, 50 Durban Rd, Scottsville, T033-3428988. **Medical services** Mediclinic, T033-8453700.

Battlefields Route

The vast, open landscapes of northern KwaZulu Natal are as evocative as one would hope, with rolling plains and savannah grasslands stretching to the horizons, studded with flat-topped acacias, mysterious rock formations and granite koppies. This landscape forms the stage upon which three major wars have been fought, and the battlefields of the clashes between Boers, Britons and Zulus can all be visited. Don't expect self-explanatory sights, however – many of the battlefields are marked by little more than small commemorative plaques, and you'll need a good guide to really bring the history of the area to life. This area also provides an eye-opening glimpse into the lives of rural Zulus, the roads passing numerous traditional subsistence kraals, with their thatched rondavals, herds of goats and waving children. The poverty of these remote areas can be striking after the affluence of the coastal resorts.

The best way to appreciate the history of the battles is to go on an organized tour; with a decent guide it can be surprisingly tear-jerking. The major sites can be visited in a day. Two of the best museums are the Siege Museum in Ladysmith and the Talana Museum in Dundee. Of the wars fought between the Voortrekkers and the Zulus, the most interesting battlefield site is Blood River, east of Dundee. Two of the most interesting historical sites of the Anglo-Zulu War are Isandlwana and Rorke's Drift; the latter has a good museum, making it the best site to visit without a guide. The most interesting Boer War sites to visit are Talana, the Siege of Ladysmith and Spionkop.

» For Sleeping, Eating and other listings, see pages 438-440.

Ladysmith and around » pp438-440.

→ Colour map 4, grid A6

Ladysmith is a quiet rural town surrounded by cattle and sheep ranches, with little more than a run-down shopping complex, a handful of Victorian buildings and the Siege Museum – a good place from which to start a visit to the Battlefields Route. In recent years, the town centre has undergone something of a transformation, and today has a vibrant African feel to it, although it remains an unattractive place to stay. The siege aside, Ladysmith is perhaps best known as being home to Ladysmith Black Mambazo band, the phenomenally popular South Africa band. The region lying to the south of Ladysmith is where many of the Boer War Battlefields are located. The Siege Museum in Ladysmith will help to arrange tours or provide a detailed map of the battlesites.

Ins and outs

Getting there Ladysmith is on the N11 and is well connected to the highway network. The N11 heads north to Newcastle (100 km), Volksrust (153 km) and into Mpumalanga. Some 26 km south of Ladysmith, the N11 connects with the N3, which in turn leads north into the Free State and south to Durban. The N11 also connects at this junction with the R616 leading to the Northern Drakensberg.

Tourist information **Ladysmith Tourist Information Office** ⓘ *Siege Museum, Murchison St, T036-6372992, www.ladysmith.co.za, Mon-Fri 0900-1600, Sat 0900-1300*, has a good selection of maps and leaflets on the Battlefields. The bureau is also very helpful with accommodation suggestions and advising on battlefield tours.

Background

The Voortrekkers first arrived in 1847 and established a small republican settlement on the banks of the Klip River. However, it was only a matter of months before the area fell

Ladysmith Black Mambazo

Ladysmith Black Mambazo is one of the best known South African musical groups of all time, outselling both the Beatles and Michael Jackson in their homeland. Internationally they were relatively unknown until Paul Simon 'discovered' the band on a visit to Johannesburg and collaborated with them on his album *Graceland*, which sold millions of copies worldwide and brought them instant fame. One of the band members, Joseph, gave Paul Simon the Zulu nickname *Vulindlela*, 'he who has opened the gate'.

As a child, Joseph had worked as a simple herd boy in the Ladysmith area. In 1961 he formed the group Ladysmith Black Mambazo, meaning the black axe of Ladysmith. At their first concert in Soweto the band became an immediate hit and each member received the princely sum of R5.28.

under the British sphere of influence. British settlers began to arrive during the 1850s to farm in the area. Ladysmith grew in importance as a trading centre because it was on the trail connecting the diamond and gold mines of the interior, Kimberley and Barberton, with Port Natal on the coast. Ladysmith is most famous for being besieged by General Piet Joubert for 118 days during the Boer War (see box page 432). The British garrison of 12,500 men was cut off from the outside world for the duration of the siege.

Sights

Ladysmith's historical monuments are on the main square by the town hall on Murchison Street. The **town hall**, on the corner of Murchison and Queen streets, is a classic Victorian municipal building which was completed in 1893. During the siege, it was converted into a hospital until the clock tower was hit by a six-inch shell. The town

Ladysmith

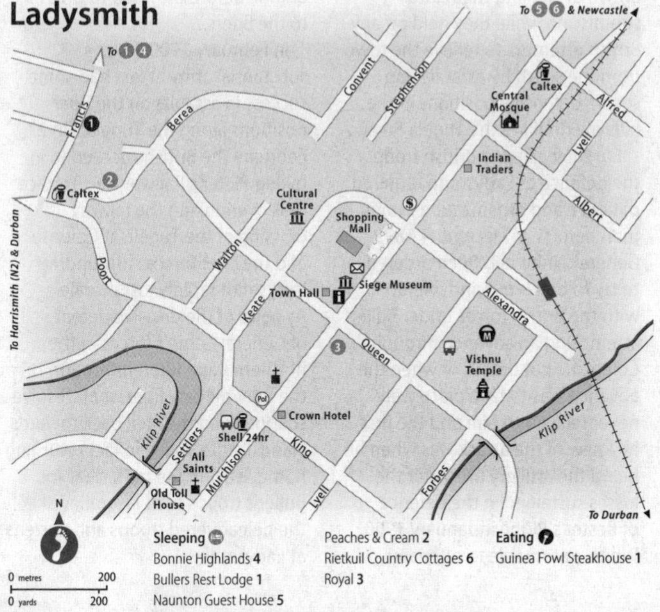

Sleeping
Bonnie Highlands 4
Bullers Rest Lodge 1
Naunton Guest House 5
Peaches & Cream 2
Rietkuil Country Cottages 6
Royal 3

Eating
Guinea Fowl Steakhouse 1

The siege of Ladysmith

The siege of the British in Ladysmith by Boer forces lasted from early in the Anglo-Boer War, October 1899, until February 1900 – 118 days in total. The British forces in northern Natal, under General White, had been forced to withdraw into Ladysmith after a series of defeats at the hands of Boers from both the Free State and Transvaal. The Boer forces had taken up positions in approximately a six-mile radius around the town but made few attempts to defeat decisively the 10,000 remaining British troops. The Boers, under the command of Piet Joubert (ably assisted by his tactically-minded wife), did make one major assault on the British defences at Bester's Ridge on 6 January 1900. The British were, however, able to repulse the Boer attack, although it succeeded in placing a further strain on their already stretched resources.

The Boer forces decided to concentrate on starving out the British or shelling them into submission while they held off any British attempts to relieve the town from the south by establishing secure defensive positions in the hills overlooking the Tugela River.

For the besieged British troops the defence of Ladysmith required patience and organization rather than heroics. In December 1899 General White had been ordered to try to break-out and join up with the British forces under Buller attempting an advance through Colenso – but details of when the advance was to take place were never relayed to him and the first he knew of the attack was when he heard the artillery fire. After the losses sustained in the defence of Bester's Ridge in January 1900, White was unable to offer any support to General Buller's forces in their attempts to relieve Ladysmith and all his troops could do was sit tight and survive the bombardment as best they possibly could.

Conditions for the town's inhabitants, whether military or civilian, were harsh. Food and other provisions were in short supply and what was available became exceptionally expensive. Tins of condensed milk, for example, could fetch up to a pound and bottles of whisky seven pounds. One source of comfort for the civilians and wounded was that the Boer commanders allowed them to set up a camp and hospital at Intombi, some four miles southeast of the town, so that they were spared the heavy artillery bombardment of the town centre. News of Buller's numerous blunders at Colenso, Spion Kop and other battles along the Tugela did nothing for morale, however, and many inhabitants felt it was only a matter of time before they had to give in to the Boers.

In February 1900 Buller's substantial army at last had some success in assaults on the Boer positions along the Tugela. On 27 February the British succeeded in taking Pieter's Railway and Terrace Hills overlooking the railway crossing of the Tugela at Colenso and the Boer forces surrounding Ladysmith rapidly lost morale. As news of the decisive defeat of General Conje's forces in the northern Cape filtered through to the Boer military lines, their resolve snapped and they fell back towards Elandslaagte, many in fact returning home, leaving the path clear for Buller's troops to at last relieve the beleaguered troops and citizens at Ladysmith.

hall was repaired in 1901 after the end of the siege. There is a small museum here with a gallery of photographs illustrating Ladysmith's history up to the present day. The **Siege Museum** ⓘ *Murchison St, T036-6372992, www.ladysmith.co.za, Mon-Fri 0900-1600, Sat 0900-1300, small entry fee*, is next to the town hall. This is a fascinating museum, with one of the country's largest collections of South African military memorabilia, including reconstructions of scenes from the Siege of Ladysmith and the Boer War. There are displays of weapons, uniforms and household goods that were used during the siege, with explanations in English, Afrikaans and Zulu.

A walk around the town centre to see these sights will take less than two hours.

There are four field guns on Murchison Street just outside the museum: **Castor** and **Pollux** are the two guns sent from Cape Town at the outbreak of the Boer War for the defence of the town; **Long Tom** is a replica of the Creussot Fortress Guns, which were used by the Transvaal Republic to bombard Ladysmith from the surrounding hills. The Boers destroyed the original gun at Haenertsburg when Kitchener's Fighting Scouts threatened to capture it. The last gun is a German **Feldkanonne**, which was captured in German Southwest Africa and sent back as a war trophy.

Walking south down Murchison Street will take you past two historical hotels which are still in use. The **Royal Hotel** was built before the siege during the gold and diamond rushes of the interior. During the siege it was used by the press corps as a base. The **Crown Hotel** is the site of Ladysmith's first hotel, which was built of wattle and daub. The earliest battlefield tours, on horseback, could be booked here in 1904. Further down Murchison Street, on the corner with Princess Street, is the **Old Toll House** where wagon drivers paid a toll before entering town.

Walking north up Murchison Street to the junction with Albert Street, visitors can see what is left of the old Indian district. Before the introduction of the Group Areas Act this used to be a thriving trading area. **Surat's House**, **Seedat's** and **Asmal's Stores** were all magnificent buildings in the 1920s. These fell into disrepair when the Indian traders were forcibly relocated to the 'Oriental Plaza'. Next door are two buildings from the same period: the **NGR Institute**, a magnificent structure built in 1903 to house railway workers, and the **Central Mosque**, completed in 1922, with its beautiful fountain and courtyard surrounded by palm trees.

A refreshingly non-historical site is the new **Cultural Centre** ⓘ *25 Keate St, behind the town hall, T036-6372231, Mon-Fri 0800-1600, small entry fee*. Housed in a restored Victorian house, there is a collection of cultural and natural history exhibits, a township shack and a tribute to the Drakensberg Boys' Choir. There is also a hall dedicated to **Ladysmith Black Mambazo** – the world-renowned group that became South Africa's most successful band (see box page 431). The music-filled hall contains the footprints of the members of the band eternalized in concrete, and life-size cut outs of the band on a mock-up stage. The curio shops sells the band's CDs.

Colenso

An easy excursion from Ladysmith, the town was named after John William Colenso, the Anglican Bishop of Natal from 1853 to 1883. The first advance by British troops trying to break the siege at Ladysmith was foiled here by General Louis Botha in a battle fought along the Tugela River. It was to be a further two months before Ladysmith was relieved. The small **RE Stevenson Museum** ⓘ *open on request, ask at the municipal offices next door for the key*, concentrates on the Battle of Colenso, with exhibits of weapons, medals and photographs. There are also two vintage steam engines and a steam tractor.

One of Ladysmith's first industries was a lard factory set up by two Scotsmen who culled the region's vast herds of zebra and melted down their fat.

Weenen Game Reserve

ⓘ *20 km south of Colenso on the R74. From Durban take the N3 to the Estcourt junction and follow the R74 to the reserve, 25 km. From Ladysmith follow the R74 to Colenso and then on to Weenen. Oct-Mar 0500-1900, Apr-Sep 0600-1800, R12.*

The 6500-ha reserve is the core area of the much larger **Thukela Biosphere Reserve**. The reserve has been hailed as a conservation success as it has succeeded in converting heavily eroded farmland into an area where the flora and fauna indigenous to the Natal Midlands have been re-established. The vegetation is mostly grassland, interspersed with acacia woodland. One of the great attractions are the black and white rhino. Other more common species include elephant, kudu, giraffe, zebra, eland and buffalo. This is a good reserve for birdwatchers; more than 250 species have been recorded including korhaans, blue crane and the scimitarbilled woodhoopoe. Thukela has short walking trails, picnic sites, a 47-km network of game viewing dirt roads, 4WD trails and the Isipho Hide, which can be rented at night for game viewing.

Dundee and around

» pp438-440. Colour map 5, grid A1.

The R602 leaves the N11 26 km north of Ladysmith and shortly passes the village of **Elandslaagte**, where there is a signpost leading to the site of the Battle of Elandslaagte. On 21 October 1899, British forces abandoned the village and the railway station. They had kept it open to enable the Dundee garrison to retreat back to Ladysmith. The R602 continues to Dundee through a vast treeless plain with plateaux rising up in the distance. The small mining and farming town of **Glencoe**, just before Dundee, is named after the village in the Highlands of Scotland, from where some of the first miners originated.

The modern town of Dundee built up around the coal mining deposits which were first exploited here on a large scale in the 1880s. The town centre unfortunately fell victim to South Africa's town planners, and is today a rather dull grid of modern streets lined with sleepy shops. Although it provides a convenient base from which to explore the battlefield sites at **Isandlwana, Rorke's Drift** and **Blood River**, it might be preferable to stay one of the more remote lodges away from town.

Ins and outs

Tourist information Tourism Dundee ⓘ *Civic Gardens, Victoria St, T034-2122121, www.tourdundee.co.za, Mon-Fri 0900-1630*, is a helpful office with information on accommodation and excellent advice on how best to view the battlefields depending upon your time, budget and level of interest. Ask about personal tour guides.

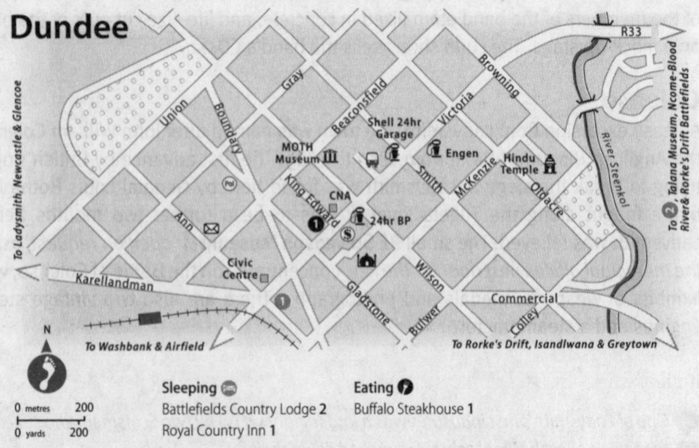

Sights

The **MOTH Museum** ⓘ *corner of Beaconsfield and Wilson Sts, open by appointment through the tourist office*, is one of the best private collections of military memorabilia in South Africa and includes pieces from the Anglo-Zulu War. The museum can usually only be visited on an organized tour.

The **Talana Museum** ⓘ *1 km north of town on the R33, T034-2122654, www.talana.co.za, Mon-Fri 0800-1630, Sat and Sun 1000-1630, R10*, has been built on the site of the Battle of Talana Hill, which took place on 20 October 1899 and was the first major battle of the Boer War. British forces had been sent to Dundee to protect the coal field from the advancing Boers. General Lucas Meyer, moving down from the Transvaal, took the hill and began bombarding the British. The counter attack succeeded in forcing the Boers off the hill but only at great cost to the British, who lost 255 soldiers including their commanding officer General Penn Symons. A self-guided trail visits the remains of two British forts and the Boer gun emplacements, passing a cairn where General Penn Symons was wounded.

The main building is a modern museum with good displays on the Zulu Wars and the Anglo-Boer War. The industrial section includes the **Consol Glass Museum**, which has an extensive display of glass products, which were once produced here, illustrating the changes in taste from highly decorative Victorian vases to the crisp designer products of today. The **Chamber of Mines Coal Museum** has re-created scenes of early mining in Dundee with many of the original tools on display. The **Miner's Rest** restaurant and curio shop is housed in a typical miner's cottage of the 1920s in the gardens behind the new building.

Many of the outlying buildings are original. The **Peter Smith Cottage** has been restored and decorated with period furniture, while the workshop and stables outside have a collection of original blacksmith's tools and several wagons. **Talana House** has historical displays on the lifestyles of the Zulus and the early settlers in Dundee, with interesting bead collections. Both these buildings were used as dressing stations during the Battle of Talana Hill.

Battlefield excursions

The battlefield sites around Dundee can easily be visited on day trips. The major sites are clearly signposted and can be reached from Dundee or Ulundi. However, the sites themselves are often little more than a war memorial in a windswept field; they are isolated and accessed along dirt roads. Allow enough time to return in daylight as the bad roads and wandering cattle make it dangerous to drive at night. The best way to appreciate the sites and the epic events that took place in this region is to take a guided tour with a qualified historian. ▸▸ *For further details, see Activities and tours, page 439.*

Ncome-Blood River ⓘ *48 km from Dundee, T034-2718121, Mon-Fri 0800-1600, Sat and Sun 0900-1600, R15*, is the site of a replica *laager* that commemorates the dreadful battle between the Zulus and the Boers on 16 December 1838. The 64 wagons are made of bronze and include replica bronze spades, lamps and buckets, all slightly larger than life-size, and there is a small museum, the Ncome Museum, on site. There is also a café serving drinks, snacks and selling a selection of historical leaflets. To get to the site, take the R33 northeast as far as Dejagersdrif, where there is a turning on the right leading to Blood River. The last section of the journey is on a dirt road.

Isandlwana ⓘ *80 km southeast of Dundee, T034-2718165, Mon-Fri 0800-1600, Sat and Sun 0900-1600, R15*, is where the 24th Regiment were defeated by 25,000 Zulu warriors on the 22 January 1879. This is perhaps the most epic of the great Zulu War stories, where the Zulu army sat silently in a valley out of sight of a small British regiment (which thought the Zulus were elsewhere), waiting for the signal to attack. A British patrol stumbled across them, upon which the impis leapt to their feet and

Blood River

The year 1838 had been a difficult one for the Voortrekkers in Natal. In February their leader Piet Retief was beaten to death at the Zulu king Dingane's kraal and shortly afterwards about 500 members of a Voortrekker party at Bloukrans River were killed in a Zulu ambush. The majority of the dead were in fact 'coloured' servants but subsequent generations of Boers honoured the defeat by naming the site *Weenen* – meaning 'weeping'. Voortrekker attempts at reprisals against the Zulus similarly failed and in a battle near the Buffalo River Piet Uys, another Voortrekker leader, was killed. It was only with the arrival of Andries Pretorius and a party of 60 experienced commandos later in the year that Voortrekker fortunes began to take a turn for the better.

On 9 December Pretorius set out with 468 men and three cannons to confront Dingane's army. Before setting out he reportedly stood on a gun carriage and made the famous vow that if God gave them victory "we would note the date of victory to make it known even to our latest posterity in order that it might be celebrated to the honour of God". Many historians doubt if the vow was ever really made; certainly it was not commemorated until many years after the event. Nevertheless the vow has taken on an important place in Afrikaner traditions.

On 15 December Pretorius' scouts reported a heavy Zulu presence nearby and he ordered the column to move their wagons into the tried and tested Voortrekker defensive laager. This involved lashing all the wagons together into a ring and protecting all cattle, horses and stores in the centre. This allowed trekkers to hide in and under the wagons and fire out at any approaching attackers. Pretorius had formed his laager on the banks of the Ncome River with a deep gully to the rear and an open plain to the front. He placed the three cannons at points along the perimeter of the laager to give them a clear line of fire across the open ground. Early in the morning of 16 December the Zulu army, estimated at about 10,000, began its attack.

Wave upon wave of Zulu soldiers charged the laager but their short spears, so effective in hand to hand combat, were useless against the trekkers' rifles and the grapeshot from the cannons. Finally the Zulu attack faltered and Pretorius sent out a party of mounted commandos to pursue the shattered Zulus. The trekkers were merciless and shot every Zulu in sight, including more than 400 hiding in a small ravine. No prisoners were taken and around 3000 people were killed. No trekkers had been killed and only three were injured – including Pretorius who was stabbed in the hand. So many Zulu soldiers were shot whilst trying to flee back across the Ncome River the waters ran red – hence the name Blood River.

stormed over the lip of the hill, descending upon the small regiment in the characteristic 'horns of the buffalo' manoeuvre. Within just two hours, 1329 of the 1700 British soldiers were dead. Today, it is an atmospheric spot, with white-painted cairns marking the places where British soldiers were buried, and a self-guided trail taking in the memorials, starting with the relatively new memorial to the Zulu dead, represented by a giant bronze replica of a Zulu victory necklace. To reach the site, take the R68 west, passing through Vant's Drift and Nqutu; the dirt road leading to Isandlwana is clearly signposted south of Nqutu.

Rorke's Drift ⓘ *42 km from southeast of Dundee, T034-6421687, daily 0900-1600, R10*, is clearly signposted off the R68 between Dundee and Nqutu. Made famous by Michael Caine and his memorable performance in the movie *Zulu*, this site was a Swedish Mission next to a ford over the Buffalo River. In 1879, the mission consisted of two small stone buildings, a house and a storeroom, which was also used as a church, and these were commandeered by the British at the start of the war and converted into a hospital and a supply depot. Only 110 men were stationed there on 23 January 1879, when two survivors of Isandlwana arrived warning about an imminent attack. Four thousand Zulus arrived 1½ hours later and launched the assault on the mission station. The British refused to surrender, and succeeded in defending the mission from behind a makeshift barricade of grain bags and biscuit boxes. The ferocious attack was resisted for 12 hours before the Zulu impis withdrew, losing around 400 men; 17 British officers were killed. The mission station has been converted into a fascinating little museum which illustrates scenes from the battle and outlines the lives of the men who were awarded the Victoria Crosses. Just beyond the museum there is a cemetery and a memorial to those who died.

Newcastle and around

» *pp438-440. Colour map 5, grid A1.*

This major industrial town is supported by surrounding coal and steel mines. It was established in 1864 by a Dr Sutherland from Newcastle in England who was trapped on the swollen banks of the Ncandu River during his honeymoon. To pass the time he planned a township for the site, named streets after the then government, and filed his plan on return to Pietermaritzburg. There is little in this modern town to attract tourists, although the nearby mountain range, which rises to over 2000 m, has become a popular destination for South African hikers.

Ins and outs

Newcastle is well connected by road and rail and local taxis will take hikers out to the farms that organize private hiking trails. **Tourism Newcastle** ⓘ *Town Hall, Scott St, T034-3153318, www.tourismnewcastle.co.za, Mon-Fri 0900-1600, Sat 0930-1530*, has a useful range of brochures and information on hiking and birdwatching.

Sights

Fort Amiel ⓘ *Memel Rd, Mon-Fri 1000-1600*, was built in 1876 and used for military operations until 1902. It was built by a detachment of the Staffordshire Volunteers (80th regiment) and named after their commander Major Charles Frederick Amiel. It was used as a hospital during both Anglo-Boer wars. After the original plans for the fort were found in a London museum in 1985 the fort was completely rebuilt. The museum houses displays on the Boer War and has an interesting section on Rider Haggard. There is a Boer War cemetery just outside.

Majuba Battlefield is 43 km from Newcastle on the N11 to Volksrust. The site is signposted from the highway. A 2-km dirt road leads to the battlefield where there is a caravan park, a youth hostel and a small museum. Majuba is the site where the British were defeated by the Boers in 1881. There is a short trail (45 minutes) heading up Majuba Mountain from where there are spectacular views of Volksrust, Newcastle and the surrounding countryside. The N11 continues north from here into Volksrust and Mpumalanga Province.

The defence of Rorke's Drift is one of the epic tales of British military history. 11 Victoria Crosses were awarded here, the most ever awarded at a single battle.

Sleeping

Ladysmith *p430, map p431*

B Bullers Rest Lodge, 61 Cove Cres, T036-6376154, www.bullersrestlodge.co.za. B&B accommodation in a family-run lodge, set in a thatched house with fine views of the mountains. Chalets with double and single rooms, with en suite facilities. The Boer War Pub on site has a fine collection battlefield artefacts. Located near the site of the Naval Gun Shield. Recommended.

B Royal Hotel, 140 Murchison St, T036-6372176, www.royalhotel.co.za. A busy central hotel with an interesting history. 71 en suite rooms, could do with an update, TV, a/c, grill restaurants, and the **Tippsy Trooper** pub, swimming pool and garden.

C Peaches & Cream, 4 Berea Rd, T036-6311233, pc.bb@mweb.co.za. Centrally located old-fashioned B&B, family-run, with 8 en suite rooms with TV. Small pool, dinner served on request, friendly management.

D Bonnie Highlands, 10 Tozer St, T036-6378390. 5 double rooms in a fine old town house with good views of the surrounding area. The homely rooms are set along a shady veranda. Evening meals on request. The peaceful gardens are the perfect place to relax after a day exploring the Battlefields.

D Naunton Guest House, 4 km from town centre off the Newcastle Rd (N11), T036-6313307, nauntons@telkomsa.net. 6 double rooms with en suite facilities in a farmhouse, a self-catering unit sleeping 2, DSTV, cosy pub with pool table, evening meals available on request, swimming pool. A pleasant alternative to suburban B&Bs.

D Rietkuil Country Cottages, 12 km out of town off the Newcastle Rd (N11), T036-6319021. 4 self-catering cottages sleeping up to 6, fully equipped. All with private patio, braai facilities and set in fine gardens with mountain views and swimming pool, undercover parking. Evening meals available on request.

Weenen Nature Reserve *p434*

D Cottage, reservations through KZN Wildlife, T033-8451000, www.kzn wildlife.com. 5-bed self-catering cottage, 2 bedrooms, fully equipped modern bungalow near the campsite below. Also has 12 pitches for tents and caravans near the entrance gate, 7 with electricity points, shared ablution block. There's also a game-viewing hide overlooking a waterhole. Small shop sells a limited range of food.

Dundee and around *p434, map p434*

LL Isandlwana Lodge, Islandlwana, 80 km southeast of Dundee, T034-2718301, www.isand lwana.com. Superbly constructed luxury lodge with awesome views over Isandlwana and the rolling grasslands. The stunning wood, thatch and stone double-storey building sensitively blends in with the landscape and is built into the rock that the Zulu commander stood on the start of the Isandlwana battle. 13 tastefully decorated rooms, with huge beds, stylish mirrors and fashionable stone bathrooms, plus private balconies with views over the battle site. The smart dining room, also with brilliant views, has Zulu chefs. Rob Gerrard is the resident historian, offering excellent battlefield tours – his storytelling will provide a startlingly moving insight to the battles (R300 per person). Rates include all meals. Recommended.

L Fugitive's Drift Lodge, approximately 50 km south of Dundee towards Greytown on the R33, T034-6421843, www.fugitives-drift-lodge.com Home to famous battlefield guide David Rattray, this lodge offers traditional accommodation and excellent guided tours. Bedrooms are stylish and comfortable and have private verandas. There are also rooms in an annex cottage. The lounge and dining room is filled with Battlefields memorabilia. The original Battlefields experience. Recommended.

A Penny Farthing, Greytown Rd, T034-6421925, www.pennyf.co.za. This farmhouse is 31 km south of Dundee on the R33, with a choice of rooms in either the old fort, the colonial sandstone farmhouse or the garden cottage. Luxury B&B catering for up to 14 guests and offering battlefield tours with resident guide, plus hiking, swimming pool. Reservations essential.

B Royal Country Inn, 61 Victoria St, T034-2122147, www.royalcountryinn.com. 27 a/c en suite double rooms in a mock-Tudor building over 100 years old, with well-preserved pressed iron ceilings and wrought-iron fittings, opening onto a peaceful garden. Decent meals served in the à la carte restaurant, a bar decorated with Zulu and Boer War memorabilia, and a tea garden.

C **Lennox Cottage**, a few kilometres out of town off the R68 towards Nqutu, T034-2182201, lennox@dundeekzn.co.za. A comfortable spacious guesthouse with 10 doubles with en suite bathrooms. Plenty to keep yourself occupied in the gardens, a swimming pool, tennis court, plus a snooker room. Owned by a former Springbok rugby player. This has been recommended as an ideal base for exploring the battlefields.

C-E **Battlefields County Lodge** overlooking Talana Hill battlefield site, T034-2181641, www.battlefieldslodge.co.za. 30 en suite rooms in quiet bungalows, plus camping and dorms, use of a kitchen and lapa area with bar where evening meals are served. Can organize battlefield tours in English, French, or German, or alternatively take a tour with a Zulu guide for a different perspective.

Newcastle and around *p437*

Many of the farms offering hiking trails have camping facilities and overnight huts.

B **Haggard's Hilldrop**, 15 Hilldrop Rd, 3 km out of town, T034-3152098, www.haggards hilldrop.co.za. Beautiful house which used to be the home of Sir Rider Haggard, whose novel *Jess* (1887) was based on his experiences at Hilldrop. The house is now a national monument set in 3 ha of indigenous forest and gardens. 25 en suite double rooms, stylish decor, some rooms under thatch, TV, pub, log fires, large pool, evening meals on request. Request the forest rooms, which have private balconies and separate entrances. Recommended.

B **Majuba Lodge**, 27 Victoria St, T034-3155011, www.majubalodge.co.za. Self-catering chalets, fully equipped, DSTV, kitchen facilities, set around a main building where meals are served, swimming pool, gym and a driving range for golfers, friendly set-up, but avoid if there is a big conference going on.

C **Cannon Lodge**, Allen St, T034-3152307, cannonlodge@crazyweb.co.za. 22 double rooms with en suite facilities, motel-style set-up, all rooms have phone, a/c, TV, room service, basic decor. Attached to The Cannon pub and restaurant, very popular with locals, and next door to a gym.

Eating

Ladysmith *p430, map p431*

Ƴ-ƳƳ **Royal Hotel**, 140 Murchison St, T036-6372176, has an old-fashioned carvery restaurant, serving a selection of steaks, pub lunches, and with the occasional large, good value buffet dinner. Friendly, laid-back staff.

Ƴ **Guinea Fowl Steakhouse**, Shop 13, Marco Centre, Francis Rd, T036-6378163. Steakhouse, known for their excellent ribs. Good value and friendly, with outdoor tables spilling onto the pavement.

Ƴ **Santa Catalina Spur**, Oval Shopping Centre, T036-6311260. The usual family chain restaurant serving reliable if uninspiring portions of steak, ribs and chicken, plus a salad bar and baked potatoes.

Dundee and around *p434, map p434*

ƳƳ **Buffalo Steakhouse**, 5 King Edward St, T034- 2124644. It may be a small town, but the meat and portions are big at this run-of-the-mill steak house. Steaks and grills, plus a small selection of healthier options.

Newcastle and around *p437*

Ƴ **The Cannon**, Allen St. Bar and restaurant attached to a hotel, large menu and portions. Outside terrace. Busy at the weekend, open late, very popular with local families.

Shopping

Dundee and around *p434, map p434*

ELC Craft Centre, Rorke's Drift museum. Sells locally produced Zulu crafts: baskets, ceramics and dyed cloth as well as replica spears. Mon-Fri 0800-1600, Sat 0900-1600.

Activities and tours

Battlefield tours can be organized from the tourist offices in Ladysmith and at the Talana Museum in Dundee. Expect to pay around R300 per person for a half-day tour and R500-800 for a full-day tour with a guide in your own vehicle.

Ladysmith *p430, map p431*

Battlefield tours

Evan Jones, T034-2124040. Battlefield tours plus cultural tours and adventure tourism.

Dundee and around *p434, map p434*

Battlefield tours

David Rattray, T034-6421843. Leading expert on the region; he took Prince Charles on tour in 1997. If you can't afford a personal tour guide, buy David's tapes/CDs at the Talana Museum for a self-guided tour.

Paul Garner, T034-2121931, garner@xsinet.co.za. Enjoyable tales of the San paintings found in the area.

Rob Gerrard, T034-2718301, www.isandlwana.com. Based at **Isandlwana Lodge**, offering excellent tours of Isandlwana, Rorke's Drift and walks between the 2, known as the Fugitive's Trail, providing a nail-biting account of the area's history. Recommended.

Transport

Ladysmith *p430, map p431*

Bus

Greyhound, T011-2768500, www.greyhound.co.za, regular coaches to **Johannesburg** and **Pretoria**, **Durban** and **Cape Town**.

Train

www.spoornet.co.za. Trains from **Johannesburg** and **Pretoria** most days, en route to **Durban**. Also trains to **Cape Town**.

Newcastle *p437*

Bus

Greyhound, T011-2768500, www.greyhound.co.za, coaches to **Durban**, **Johannesburg** and **Pretoria**.

Train

www.spoornet.ci.za, trains to **Durban** and **Johannesburg**.

Directory

Ladysmith *p430, map p431*

Medical services La Verna Private Hospital, T036-6310065.

uKhahlamba-Drakensberg Park

→ *Colour map 5, grid A4.*

The Drakensberg Mountains, which rise to 3000 m and extend 180 km along the western edge of KwaZulu Natal, form the backbone of the uKhahlamba-Drakensberg Park, and determine the border with Lesotho. This formidable mountain range is one of South Africa's most staggeringly beautiful destinations, and in November 2001 it was awarded the status of a World Heritage Site by UNESCO, both for its diverse flora and fauna and its impressive San rock paintings. The greater uKhahlamba-Drakensberg Park extends from the Royal Natal National Park in the north to Sehlabethebe National Park, part of Lesotho, in the south. The protected area is 180 km long and up to 20 km wide. Almost the entire range falls within protected reserves managed by KZN Wildlife (see page 389). Despite going through a series of name changes over the years, this conservation body has looked after the region's natural heritage for decades and succeeded in striking a balance between protecting the fragile resources and giving visitors an opportunity to appreciate all the mountains have to offer. There are numerous points from which to explore the Berg, ranging from fully equipped holiday resorts and luxury hotels to campsites, mountain huts and isolated caves. ▸▸ *For Sleeping, Eating and other listings, see pages 459-468.*

Ins and outs

Getting there and around **Baz Bus,** T021-4392323, www.bazbus.com, runs through the Drakensberg three times a week en route between Johannesburg and Durban, stopping at Olivershoek Pass and Winterton. In the southern Drakensberg **Sani Pass Carriers,** T033-7011017, runs to/from Underberg/Sani Pass and Pietermaritzburg.

There is little in the way of public transport, so the best way of exploring the area is by car. The most popular resorts are within two to three hours' drive of Johannesburg, Pretoria or Durban, accessed from the N3 and then a network of minor

The border with Lesotho

In the Drakensberg area the border between South Africa and Lesotho follows the watershed along the top edge of the escarpment. As there are no boundary markers it is quite possible that you will inadvertently enter Lesotho once you reach the summit plateau. It is therefore essential to carry your passport with you at all times in case you meet one of the mounted border patrols on the Lesotho side.

roads heading west into the mountains. The popular sights and resorts are well signposted. Those in the far south are best approached via Underberg on the R617 from Pietermaritzburg, or the R626 from Kokstad. The Central Drakensberg resorts, and the reserves around Monk's Cowl and Cathedral Peak, are signposted from Winterton and Bergville, off the N3, along the R74 and then onto the R600. The Northern Drakensberg resorts can be reached by taking the N3 as far as the Northern Berg turning. From here the R74 goes through Winterton and Bergville, and on to the Royal Natal National Park. The Battlefields Route lies to the northeast (see page 430). *For further details, see Transport, page 468.*

There have been a number of carjacking incidents in the Drakensberg. Beware when driving down isolated roads and always take local advice.

Tourist information There are a number of information offices in the area. The **Drakensberg Tourism Association** ⓘ *Municipal Building, Thatham Rd, Bergville, T036-4481296, www.drakensberg.kzn.org.za, Mon-Fri 0900-1700*, provides information on the whole region. The accommodation office can be contacted on T036-4481557. The **Central Drakensberg Information Centre** ⓘ *Thokozisa, on the R600, 13 km west of Winterton, T036-4881207, www.cdic.co.za, daily 0900-1700*, is an arts, crafts and tourist centre, which has a coffee shop and restaurant and stocks useful maps and brochures. It can also help arrange accommodation.

Entry fees An entry fee, which includes a community levy and an emergency rescue levy, is payable each time you enter a protected area administered by **KZN Wildlife**. This fee is included in the cost of accommodation within the parks so only day visitors pay an entry fee at the gate. Current rates for day visitors are R20-25 depending on the park.

Best time to visit The weather in the Drakensberg can be divided into two main seasons: summer and winter. Although the weather tends to be pleasant all year round, the altitude and the mountain climate shouldn't be underestimated. Climatic conditions can change rapidly and snow, fog, rain and thunderstorms can develop within minutes, enveloping hikers on exposed hillsides.

Winter (May to August) is the driest time of the year and also the coolest. There will always be some rain during the winter months which, when it's cold enough, will occasionally fall as snow. Daytime temperatures can be as high as 15°C, while at night temperatures will often fall below 0°C. Despite the risk of snow, this the best season for hiking.

Summer (November to February) is the wettest time. The mornings tend to be warm and bright, but as the heat builds up clouds begin to collect in the afternoon. The violence of the thunderstorms when they break is quite spectacular, usually accompanied by short bursts of torrential rain. Daytime temperatures average around 20°C and the nights are generally mild with temperatures not falling much below 10°C. The summer is a less popular season for hiking, although the landscape is greener and the wildlife more abundant.

Cave paintings

The sandstone caves of the Drakensberg are one of the best places in the world to see rock art. Most of the surviving paintings are on the walls of rock shelters. There are traces of paintings on exposed rocks but they have been heavily weathered. The paintings tend to be quite recent and are probably only 200 to 300 years old, but they do form part of a long- standing tradition. The earliest cave paintings in Southern Africa date from 28,000 years ago.

The pigments used by the San were made from natural ochre mixed with blood, fat or milk. Artists would carry their pigments in antelope horns hanging from their belts. The San here were particularly prolific and there are hundreds of caves throughout these mountains which are covered with layer upon layer of paintings. Some of the most beautiful of South Africa's cave paintings can be found in the Drakensberg.

There have been numerous attempts at interpreting the meaning of these paintings. One of the more outlandish theories held by European archaeologists at the beginning of this century was that they had been drawn with the help of migrating Carthaginians. Other more recent theories hold that the paintings are either little more than well-executed graffitos illustrating scenes from daily life or that they were used in sympathetic magic.

The most recent research has drawn from ethnographic records from the end of the last century and interviews with the remaining San people in this century. The eland features largely in San mythology and is one of the most frequently painted subjects. It seems unlikely that the eland were painted as part of a hunting ritual using sympathetic magic as the eland is not often found in food debris from archaeological excavations. It is thought that the eland in some way represents god.

The most prevalent current theory holds that the paintings of human figures dancing which show people with nose bleeds hallucinating geometric patterns, are people taking part in shamanic rituals who are in a state of trance.

There are also other paintings which seem to deal with more mundane matters. The scenes of San collecting wild honey, hunting pigs or being chased by a leopard reveal aspects of a way of life which has now disappeared.

Background

San The earliest human inhabitants of the Drakensberg were the San who lived here as hunter-gatherers. Evidence of their time here is the rock art which can be seen in numerous caves and rock shelters throughout the range. It is thought that groups of San would gather at certain points in the year at these sites to exchange goods, arrange marriages and carry out shamanic ceremonies.

For the rest of the year they dispersed into smaller family groups moving slowly in search of food. The women gathered edible plants and looked after children while men hunted. Part of the reason for the success of their lifestyle was its relative simplicity. The few goods that they needed could be made from local materials – hides for clothing, bones, flint and wood for tools, and hunting poison from crushed insects and plants.

Anthropological studies of modern hunter gatherers in Australia and the Amazon estimate that they only spend about 20 hours a week collecting enough food to survive. Considering the relative abundance of food, it is thought likely that the Drakensberg San had a similar working week, dedicating much of the rest of their time to rock painting, singing and dancing.

The San came under increasing pressure towards the middle of the 19th century as new settlers established themselves on their land. Opportunities for hunting decreased as European immigrants shot such large numbers of game, and gradually the San were forced to adapt. They were driven further and further into the mountains, and eventually abandoned their stone tools and hunting poisons in favour of horses and guns and became cattle rustlers. Their raids on farms in Natal were so successful that the raiders were often hunted down and shot.

Attitudes of Europeans towards the San during 19th century couldn't be more different from the rather romantic view in which they are held today. They were seen, at best, as pests, were often shot on sight and were captured and forced into slavery. The last records of San being seen in the Drakensberg date from 1878 just before the Natal government began auctioning plots of land at the base of the mountains themselves.

Colonial The first Europeans to see the Drakensberg were a group of Portuguese sailors whose ship was wrecked on the Transkei coast in 1593. They had decided to head inland on their way back to Lourenço Marques and reported having seen snow-covered mountains in the distance.

Almost 250 years later the first hunters, missionaries and farmers began to arrive. The Voortrekkers arrived from the north, moving down into Natal through what was later to be called Oliviershoek Pass while the settlers from the Eastern Cape moved up from the south. As the land gradually fell under their control, the Drakensberg's natural resources were subject to the settler's rapacious exploitation. The timber and sheep farming industries were particularly successful in the short term, but their effects on the delicate ecosystem of the Drakensberg were eventually to lead to the creation of the national park.

Modern The first area of the park to receive protection was the Giant's Castle Game Reserve in 1903. Over the years more land was acquired and given protected status.

One of the main reasons for creating a national park here is that the Drakensberg escarpment is the source of many of the rivers which flow through Natal. The Tugela, the Mkhomazi and the Mzimkhulu are three of the most important sources of water in Natal. During the 1950s, damage caused by deforestation and overgrazing was proved to be affecting the water supply. The indigenous vegetation of the Drakensberg was shown to play an essential role in holding water from torrential seasonal rain and preventing flash floods. The root systems in the soil release the water gradually throughout the year providing Natal with a regular water supply. The park now protects a unique area of Afro-montane and Afro-alpine vegetation and access to this delicate ecosystem is restricted in order to prevent further damage. In 2001 UNESCO named the park a World Heritage Site, in recognition of its universal environmental value to mankind.

Landscape

The Drakensberg are divided into two areas known as the High Berg and the Little Berg. The **High Berg**, covering the area which rises steeply up to the plateau, is the more interesting of the two with its spectacular scenery of high peaks and cliffs. The top of the escarpment averages around 3,000 m in altitude and forms the western boundary of the park along the watershed between Natal and Lesotho. The **Little Berg** lies at lower altitude and consists of the spurs of sandstone which stretch out towards the plains of Natal. The landscape here is of rolling hills and grassland divided by forested ravines. The Little Berg is the most popular area for hiking and many of the KZN Wildlife resorts are located here.

Originally the Nguni people called the mountains uKhalamba or the 'Barrier of Spears', an apt description of the escarpment that rises sharply from the rolling hills of Natal.

Drakensberg snakes

There are only three poisonous snakes in the Drakensberg, all of which will do their best to avoid people. The **puff adder** and the rinkhals or **spitting cobra** are the most likely to be disturbed whilst basking as they are more common at lower altitudes. The **berg adder** lives higher up and is therefore less frequently encountered.

The venom of all three snakes is potentially lethal, although deaths in fact are very rare. The best course of action is to always be aware of where you are stepping and to avoid contact with them at all costs.

In the unfortunate event of a snake bite take the victim to a hospital as soon as possible (for further advice see Health, page 57).

Wildlife and vegetation

The different wildlife habitats in the Drakensberg vary according to altitude, which can range from the subtropical at around 1000 m to the Afro-alpine at over 3000 m. The wealth of plantlife in the Drakensberg is quite staggering: over 1500 plant species have been identified here, among which 350 are endemic. By far the best time of year to see the veldt is during the spring, when the grass is green and lush and many of the orchids, irises and lilies are in flower. Plants on the high plateau are hardy, small alpine plants consisting mostly of grasses, shrubs and succulents.

The **wildlife** is not as easy to spot as in some of South Africa's other wildlife reserves. Numbers are relatively low, and viewing wildlife is more the preserve of enthusiastic naturalists rather than casual observers. The large mammals you might see include eland, baboon, and some of the small antelope such as klipspringer and duiker. Red hartebeest, blesbok, bushbuck and oribi are present but are seen less often as they only inhabit certain areas. Leopard, lynx, serval, aardvark, aardwolf and porcupine are thought to be present but are almost never seen, even by park staff or regular hikers.

Birdlife in the Drakensberg is particularly rich, as it is possible to visit several different ecosystems within a relatively small area. Over 300 species have been recorded here, most of which live below 2000 m. The best time to see the birds is during the summer when they are courting and nesting. This is their most active time of year and their most colourful, as the birds will be in their breeding plumage.

The rarest birds live at higher altitudes on the summit plateau, and include the orange-breasted rockjumper, the Drakensberg siskin, the bald Ibis, the Cape vulture and the lammergeyer. Conditions are so harsh in this environment that only 54 species have been recorded here. The environment in the Little Berg is less extreme and many species of bird common to other parts of KwaZulu Natal can be seen here.

Hiking

Trails vary between short, well-marked strolls to challenging hikes at high altitude, lasting several days. The majority of visitors to the Drakensberg prefer to complete a number of day hikes and stay overnight in KZN Wildlife camps.

Experienced hikers have compared some of the longer trails to hiking in the Himalayas, where several days are spent in isolated wilderness areas at altitudes of up to 3000 m. Some of the longer hiking trails can last up to 10 days crossing through isolated and challenging mountain passes such as the Mnweni and Ifidi, which are among the wildest and most beautiful trails along the Northern Berg. Planning ahead is essential for longer hikes as overnight caves and mountain huts have to be booked in advance. It is recommended that all overnight hikers read **KZN Wildlife**'s brochure *It's Tough at the Top – Hiking Safely in the Drakensberg*.

Permits Permits are necessary on all longer walks and are available from camp offices for a small fee. Maximum group size is 12 people and the minimum size is three. Hikers intending to stay overnight in the mountains must fill in the **Mountain Rescue Register**, carry detailed maps and be equipped to deal with extreme weather. Mountain registers are located at all the trail heads and should be filled in even for short day walks.

Hazards The most common problems to watch out for are the effects of intense sunlight at high altitudes. Sunstroke and dehydration are best avoided by wearing a sun hat, using a high protection factor suncream and by carrying enough water. It's worth considering going on a guided hike, as registered guides will be well versed in mountain safety. Contact any of the tourist offices in the Drakensberg region who will be able to arrange a guided hike.

Equipment and supplies See page 51 for a full list of recommended hiking equipment. Note that **camping stoves** are essential for overnight hikes as fires are not allowed in the park. Petrol is available for multi-fuel stoves from some of the larger resorts. **Camping gas** and other fuels should be bought in advance from a camping shop in a large urban centre such as Durban or Pietermaritzburg. It is better to buy meths from a pharmacy than a supermarket, as it is much better quality.

Resort shops and the local stores up in the mountains have a limited selection of tinned **food**. It's best to bring lightweight dry food from Durban or Johannesburg. Fresh produce can be bought in the towns en route to the mountains.

Some hikers choose not to carry a tent if they have booked accommodation in caves or mountain huts. However, these are not always marked accurately on maps and they can be difficult to find, so it's sensible to have a tent as a backup in case you get caught out at nightfall. On overnight hikes a **trowel** or a spade is necessary for digging toilets to prevent litter and pollution. Dig a hole at least 30 m away from streams and make sure everything is properly buried.

The most exciting Drakensberg hikes are the ones up to the summit plateau. The **clothing** you carry with you should protect you from the weather you are likely to encounter over 3000 m. An anorak made from waterproof breathable fabrics like Goretex will be useful all year round, while in winter layers of thermal underwear, fleece, a woolly hat and gloves should prepare you for sub-zero temperatures. Even on short day hikes in the Little Berg a waterproof jacket and a sweater are invaluable.

Maps A map, a compass and a good knowledge of map reading are essential for hiking in the Drakensberg. **KZN Wildlife** produce a series of six comprehensive 1:50,000 maps, which usefully also cover the Lesotho side of the mountains. Contact KZN Wildlife in advance.

Activities and tours

Hiking, horse riding and mountaineering are the traditional Drakensberg sports but newer activities like mountain biking and hang-gliding are becoming very popular. Many of the larger resort hotels also offer a wide range of sporting facilities such as tennis, squash, golf and swimming. ▸▸ *For further details, see Activities and tours, page 466.*

Staying in the park

There is a huge choice in the area, including within **KZN Wildlife** accommodation and in private establishments on the fringes of the park. KZN Wildlife offers a wide range of facilities, from luxury lodges and chalets through to campsites, mountain huts and caves. All of the KZN Wildlife camps are basically self-catering and although there are some camp shops which sell food, the choice is limited. It is far better to come prepared and buy your food beforehand in the nearest large town.

 The area bordering the national park is increasingly being developed for tourism and a number of self-contained holiday resorts and timeshares have sprung up. These tend to offer numerous sporting and entertainment facilities but they are sometimes rather distant from the Drakensberg Mountains themselves. There is also a good selection of B&Bs, which can offer better value.

Reservations for **KZN Wildlife**, T033-8451000, www.kznwildlife.com. Bookings can be made by telephone or online; camping reservations must be made directly with the officer in charge of the campsite, see individual areas for details.

Northern Drakensberg » *pp459-468.*

The scenery of the Northern Berg is exceptional in its grandeur, and is perhaps the most photographed section of the range. The Royal Natal National Park is the most popular of all the resorts in the Drakensberg, and although there are some good hikes outside the park, they don't really compare with the sheer majesty of those within its boundaries.

Ins and outs

From Royal Natal National Park the R74 heads east to Bergville (41 km) and Winterton (62 km). The R615 heads north off the R74, 14 km from the park gates. After 11 km it reaches the top of Oliviershoek Pass from where it is a further 37 km to Harrismith.

Royal Natal National Park

The highlight of a visit to the park is the first view of the massive rock walls that form the **Amphitheatre**. The **Eastern Buttress** (3009 m) is the southernmost peak of the 4 km of cliff face, which arcs northwards towards the **Sentinel** (3165 m) forming an impressive barrier. On the plateau directly behind the Amphitheatre is **Mont-aux-Sources** (3299 m) named by French missionaries in 1836. This mountain is the source of five rivers: the **Elands** which flows into the Vaal; the **Khudeda** and the **Singu** leading into the Orange/ Gariep River in the Free State; and the **Tugela** and the **Bilanjil** which lead into Natal.

The most impressive of these is the Tugela which plunges over the edge of the Amphitheatre wall, dropping around 800 m through a series of five falls. The gorge created by the waters of the Tugela is a steep-sided tangle of boulders and trees which at a point near the Devil's Tooth Gully has bored straight through the sandstone to form what appears to be a tunnel around 40 m long.

The national park was established in 1916 when farms around the Amphitheatre were bought by the government to protect the land. Tourism started around this time and the park has been popular since then. Queen Elizabeth II visited the park in 1947, five years before she became Queen; since then, the national park and the (now closed) hotel are prefixed by the word 'Royal' in memory of this visit.

Ins and outs The park can be reached on tarred roads from Harrismith (60 km) or Bergville (40 km). The route is well signposted from the N3. Note that the number of day visitors is controlled to prevent overcrowding in the park; however, this only tends to be a problem at weekends and on holidays. The **visitor centre** ⓘ *T036-4386303, daily 0800-1630, R25 per person*, has a gift shop that sells a good selection of books, T-shirts, a very limited range of tinned goods, curios, alcoholic and soft drinks, maps and sometimes fresh trout. Petrol is also available here.

Michael Caine and the film crew stayed at the Royal Natal National Park Hotel, now closed, during the filming of Zulu *in the early 1960s. The film set was close to the Amphitheatre.*

Hiking There are over 130 km of walking trails around the Royal Natal National Park, many of which are easy half-day strolls. Even the hikes that don't climb up to the top of the escarpment wind through beautiful countryside of grassland dotted with patches of yellowwood forest and proteas set against the stunning backdrop of the Amphitheatre. The visitor centre sells hiking maps and a leaflet describing the many possible walks around the park. Permits are also available here. Soil erosion has increasingly become a problem as more and more hikers visit the park. In an attempt to control erosion some paths may be closed to hikers.

The 20-km hike up to **Mont-aux-Sources** (3299 m) can be completed in a strenuous day's walk. The path starts at Mahai Campsite and heads steadily uphill following the course of the Mahai River. The path climbs steeply around the eastern flank of the Sentinel (3165 m). Just after the Sentinel Caves is the notorious chain ladder, built in 1930, which takes you up a 30-m cliff face. Once on top, Mont-aux-Sources is only 3 km away and involves no more serious climbing. The views from the top of the escarpment are splendid as they stretch out over KwaZulu Natal. The hike up to Mont-aux-Sources is restricted to 100 people per day because it is so popular.

The walk up the **Tugela Gorge** is a 14-km round trip which begins at the car park below Tendele Camp. The path heads up the gorge and follows the Tugela River passing through shady patches of yellowwood forest. Higher up along the valley there are rock pools which are ideal for swimming in. After around 6 km at the entrance to the gorge there is a chain ladder; from here you can either wade through the gorge or climb up the ladder and walk along the top. There are magnificent views here of the Devil's Tooth, the Eastern Buttress and Tugela Falls. Beware of heavy rain on this walk as flash flooding through the gorge is extremely dangerous.

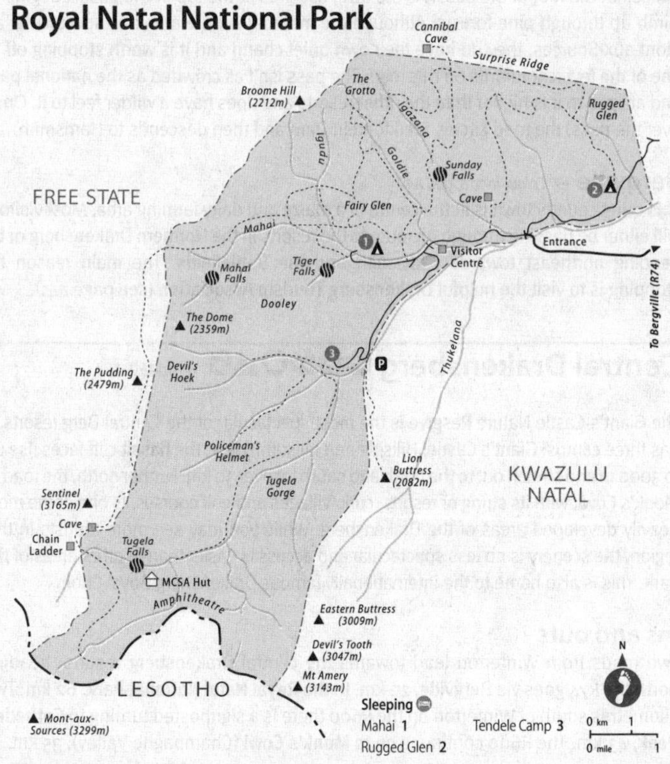

Cannibal Cave

This large cave overlooking a quiet valley is accessible on foot either from Mahai Campsite or Rugged Glen. The remains of some San paintings can still be seen.

During the Zulu wars, refugees escaped into the mountains and lived in the caves. Times were so turbulent that people were unable to plant crops and, as game became scarcer, the refugees were forced to eat passing travellers or even their own children. Rumour has it that the bodies were hung up from the cave roof to keep them fresh, to save them for later.

The cannibals lived here for around 20 years, eventually becoming such a threat that they were hunted and killed by the Zulus.

The 8-km trail to **Cannibal Cave** heads north from the road leading to **Mahai Campsite.** The route follows the Goldie River for 1 km before crossing over and following the ridge north again until it passes close to Sunday Falls. The path then rises over Surprise Ridge and on to the Cannibal Cave. The walks from the **Rugged Glen Campsite** are over rolling hills and although there are some good views of the amphitheatre, they don't compare with the hikes from the Thendele and Mahai camps.

Oliviershoek Pass

Oliviershoek Pass was named after Adriaan Olivier who was one of the first Voortrekkers to descend from the Orange Free State in the 1830s. He claimed a farm for himself at the foot of the pass. As the R615 ascends to the top of the pass it begins to climb up through pine forests. Although the mountains here aren't as spectacular as Mont-aux-Sources, they do have their own quiet charm and it is worth stopping off at one of the few restaurants on this road. The pass isn't as crowded as the national park and at 1730 m it is higher than the other resorts and does have a wilder feel to it. Once over the pass, the road circles Sterkfontein Dam and then descends to Harrismith.

Bergville → *Colour map 5, grid A4.*

This quiet country town is in the centre of a maize and dairy farming area. Most visitors will either be passing through en route to the resorts in the Northern Drakensberg or be heading northeast towards Ladysmith and the Battlefields. The main reason for stopping is to visit the helpful **Drakensberg Tourism Association** (see page 441).

Central Drakensberg » *pp459-468.*

The Giant's Castle Nature Reserve is the most spectacular of the Central Berg resorts. It has three camps: Giant's Castle, Hillside and Injisuthi. Here, the basalt cliff faces rise up to 3000 m and stretch out to the north and south for over 30 km. Further north, the road to Monk's Cowl, with its string of resorts, curio villages and golf courses, is one of the most heavily developed areas of the Drakensberg. While you may see more tourists in this region, the scenery is no less spectacular and access is easier than in other areas of the park. This is also home to the internationally famous Drakensberg Boys' Choir.

Ins and outs

Two roads from Winterton lead towards the central Drakensberg resorts: heading north the R74 goes via Bergville, 22 km, to the **Royal Natal National Park**, 62 km. Two kilometres south of Winterton on the R600 there is a signposted turning to **Cathedral Peak**, 43 km. The R600 continues on to **Monk's Cowl** (Champagne Valley), 35 km. To

African Wildlife

Introduction

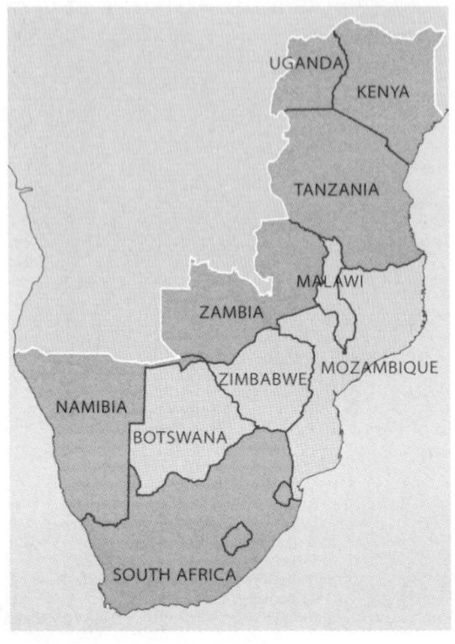

A large proportion of people who visit Africa do so to see its spectacular wildlife. This colour section is a quick photographic guide to some of the more spectacular mammals found in east and southern Africa (it covers the countries shown on the map here). From the 'Big Nine', once thought by hunters to be the ultimate 'trophies' on safari and now most prized of all by those who shoot with their cameras, to the more everyday warthog, and from the wildebeest to the tiny Kirk's Dikdik antelope, which stands at a mere 40 cm at the shoulder, here we give you pictures and information about habitat, habits and characteristic appearance to help you when you are on safari. It is by no means a comprehensive survey and some of the animals listed may not be found throughout the whole region (where this is the case, we have listed the areas where they occur). For further information about the wildlife of the country, see the Land and environment section of the Background chapter.

The Big Nine

Hippopotamus *Hippopotamus amphibius* (below). Prefers shallow water, grazes on land over a wide area at night, so can be found quite a distance from water, and has a strong sense of territory, which it protects aggressively. Lives in large family groups known as "schools".

Black Rhinoceros *Diceros bicornis* (bottom right). Long, hooked upper lip distinguishes it from White Rhino rather than colour. Prefers dry bush and thorn scrub habitat and in the past was found in mountain uplands. Males usually solitary. Females seen in small groups with their calves (very rarely more than four), sometimes with two generations. Mother always walks in front of offspring, unlike the White Rhino, where the mother walks behind, guiding calf with her horn. Their distribution has been massively reduced by poaching and work continues to save both the Black and the White Rhino from extinction. You might be lucky and see the Black Rhino in: Etosha NP, Namibia; Ngorongoro Crater, Tanzania; Masai Mara, Kenya; Kruger, Shamwari and Pilansberg NPs and private reserves like Mala Mala and Londolozi, South Africa.

White Rhinoceros *Diceros simus* (bottom right). Square muzzle and bulkier than the Black Rhino, they are grazers rather than browsers, hence the different lip. Found in open grassland, they are more sociable and can be seen in groups of five or more. More common in Southern Africa due to a successful breeding program in Hluhluwe/Umfolozi NP, South Africa.

Reticulated Giraffe *Giraffa reticulata* (right). Reddish brown coat and a network of distinct, pale, narrow lines. Found from the Tana River, Kenya, north and east into Somalia and Ethiopia. Giraffes found in East Africa have darker coloured legs and their spots are dark and of an irregular shape with a jagged outline. In southern Africa the patches tend to be much larger and have well defined outlines, although giraffes found in the desert margins of Namibia are very pale in colour and less tall – probably due to a poor diet lacking in minerals.

Leopard *Panthera pardus* (below). Found in varied habitats ranging from forest to open savanna. They are generally nocturnal, hunting at night or before the sun comes up to avoid the heat. You may see them resting during the day in the lower branches of trees, see picture page ii.

Common Zebra (Burchell's) *Equus burchelli* (right). Generally has broad stripes (some with lighter shadow stripes next to the dark ones) which cross the top of the hind leg in unbroken lines. The true species is probably extinct but there are many varying subspecies found in different locations across Africa, including: Grant's (found in East Africa) Selous (Malawi, Zimbabwe and Mozambique) and Chapman's (Etosha NP, Namibia, east across Southern Africa to Kruger NP).

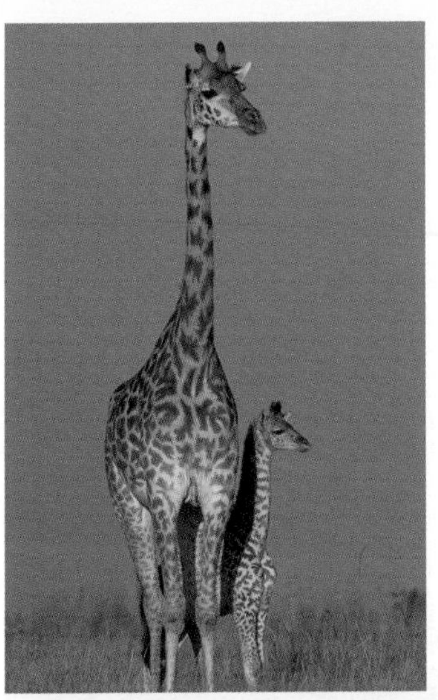

Common/Masai Giraffe *Giraffa camelopardis* (left). Yellowish-buff with patchwork of brownish marks and jagged edges, usually two different horns, sometimes three. Found throughout Africa in several differing subspecies.

Cheetah *Acinonyx jubatus* (below). Often seen in family groups walking across plains or resting in the shade. The black 'tear' mark is usually obvious through binoculars. Can reach speeds of 90 km per hour over short distances. Found in open, semi-arid savanna, never in forested country. Endangered in some parts of Africa, Namibia is believed to have the largest free-roaming population on the continent. More commonly seen than the leopard, they are not as widespread as the **lion** *Panthera leo* (see picture on front page of this section).

Grevy's Zebra *Equus grevyi* (left). Larger than the Burchell's Zebra, with bigger and broader ears and noticably narrower white stripes that meet in star above hind leg. Lives in small herds. Generally found north of the equator. A further zebra species, the **Mountain Zebra** *Equus zebra zebra*, is found in the Western Cape region of South Africa on hills and stony mountains. It is smaller than the two shown here and has a short mane and broad stripes.

■ **Lion** *Panthera leo* (page i). The largest (adult males can weigh up to 450 pounds) of the big cats in Africa and also the most common, lions are found on open savanna all over the continent. They are often not at all disturbed by the presence of humans and so it is possible to get quite close to them. They are sociable animals living in prides or permanent family groups of up to around 30 animals and are the only felid to do so. The females do most of the hunting (usually ungulates like zebra and antelopes).

■ **Buffalo** *Syncerus caffer* (below). Were considered by hunters to be the most dangerous of the big game and the most difficult to track and, therefore, the biggest trophy. Generally found on open plains but also at home in dense forest, they are fairly common in most African national parks but, like the elephant, they need a large area to roam in, so they are not usually found in the smaller parks.

■ **Elephant** *Loxodonta africana* (bottom and page xvi). Commonly seen, even on short safaris, throughout east and southern Africa, elephants have suffered from the activities of war and from ivory poachers. It is no longer possible to see herds of 500 or more animals but in southern Africa there are problems of over population and culling programmes have been introduced.

Larger antelope

■ **Gemsbok** *Oryx gazella* 122cm (below). Unmistakable, with black line down spine and black stripe between coloured body and white underparts. Horns (both sexes) straight, long and look v-shaped (seen face-on). Only found in Southern Africa, in arid, semi-desert country, though the very similar **Beisa Oryx** *Oryx beisa* occurs in East Africa. ■ **Nyala** *Tragelaphus angasi* 110cm (bottom left). Slender frame, shaggy, dark brown coat with mauve tinge (males). Horns (male only) single open curve. The female is a different chestnut colour. They like dense bush and are usually found close to water. Gather in herds of up to 30 but smaller groups more likely. Found across Zimbabwe and Malawi. ■ **Common** *Kobus ellipsiprymnus* and **Defassa** *Kobus defassa* **Waterbuck** 122-137cm (bottom right). Very similar with shaggy coats and white marking on buttocks. On the common variety, this is a clear half ring on rump and round tails; on Defassa, the ring is a filled in solid white area. Both species occur in small herds in grassy areas, often near water. Common in east and southern Africa.

Greater Kudu *Tragelaphus strepsiceros* 140-153cm (right). Colour varies from greyish to fawn with several vertical white stripes down the sides of the body. Horns long and spreading, with two or three twists (male only). Distinctive thick fringe of hair running from the chin down the neck. Found in fairly thick bush, sometimes in quite dry areas. Usually live in family groups of up to six, but occasionally larger herds of up to about 30. The **Lesser Kudu** *Strepsiceros imberis* 99-102 cm, looks similar but lacks the throat fringe and has two conspicuous white patches on the underside of the neck. Unlike the Greater Kudu, it is not found south of Tanzania.

Topi *Damaliscus korrigum* 122-127cm (below). Very rich dark rufous, with dark patches on the tops of the legs and more ordinary looking, lyre-shaped horns.

Sable Antelope *Hippotragus niger* 140-145cm (right) and **Roan Antelope** *Hippotragus equinus* 127-137cm. Both similar shape, with ringed horns curving backwards (both sexes), longer in the Sable. Female Sables are reddish brown and can be mistaken for the Roan. Males are very dark with a white underbelly. The Roan has distinct tufts of hair at the tips of its long ears. Found in east and southern Africa (although the Sable is not found naturally in east Africa, there is a small herd in the Shimba Hills Game Reserve). Sable prefers wooded areas and the Roan is generally only seen near water. Both species live in herds.

Hartebeest. In the Hartebeest the horns arise from a boney protuberance on the top of the head and curve outwards and backwards. There are 3 sub-species: **Coke's Hartebeest** *Alcephalus buselaphus* 122cm, also called the **Kongoni** in Kenya, is a drab pale brown with a paler rump; **Lichtenstein's Hartebeest** *Alcephalus lichtensteinii* 127-132cm, is also fawn in general colouration, with a rufous wash over the back and dark marks on the front of the legs and often a dark patch near shoulder; the **Red Hartebeest** *Alcephalus caama* (left), is another subspecies that occurs only throughout Southern Africa, although not in Kruger NP. All are found in herds, sometimes they mix with other plain dwellers such as zebra.

Brindled or **Blue Wildebeest** or **Gnu** *Connochaetes taurinus* (above) 132cm is found only in southern Africa; the **White bearded Wildebeest** *Connochaetes taurinus albojubatus* is found in central Tanzania and Kenya and distinguished by the white 'beard' under the neck. Both often seen grazing with Zebra.

Eland *Taurotragus oryx* 175-183cm (left). The largest of the antelope, it has a noticeable dewlap and shortish spiral horns (both sexes). Greyish to fawn, sometimes with rufous tinge and narrow white stripes down side of body. Occurs in groups of up to 30 in both east and southern Africa in grassy habitats.

Smaller antelope

Bushbuck *Tragelaphus scriptus* 76-92cm (top). Shaggy coat with variable pattern of white spots and stripes on the side and back and two white, crescent-shaped marks on front of neck. Short horns (male only) slightly spiral. High rump gives characteristic crouch. White underside of tail is noticeable when running. Occurs in thick bush, especially near water. Either seen in pairs or singly in east and southern Africa.

Thomson's Gazelle *Gazella thomsonii*, 64-69cm (above) and **Grant's Gazelle** *Gazella granti* 81-99cm. Superficially similar, Grant's, the larger of the two, has slightly longer horns (carried by both sexes in both species). Colour of both varies from bright to sandy rufous. Thomson's Gazelle can usually be distinguished by the broad black band along the side between the upperparts and abdomen, but some forms of Grant's also have this dark lateral stripe. Look for the white area on the buttocks which extends above the tail on to the rump in Grant's, but does not extend above the tail in Thomson's. Thomson's occur commonly on plains of Kenya and Tanzania in large herds. Grant's Gazelle occur on rather dry grass plains, in various forms, from Ethiopia and Somalia to Tanzania. Not found in southern Africa.

Kirk's Dikdik *Rhynchotragus kirkii* 36-41cm (top left). So small it cannot be mistaken, it is greyish brown, often washed with rufous. Legs are thin and stick-like. Slightly elongated snout and a conspicuous tuft of hair on the top of the head. Straight, small horns (male only). Found in bush country, singly or in pairs. East Africa only.

Steenbok *Raphicerus campestris* 58cm (top right). An even, rufous brown colour with clean white underside and white ring around eye. Small dark patch at the tip of the nose and long broad ears. The horns (male only) are slightly longer than the ears: they are sharp, have a smooth surface and curve slightly forward. Generally seen alone, prefers open plains, often found in more arid regions. A slight creature which usually runs off very quickly on being spotted. Common resident throughout southern Africa, Tanzania and parts of southern Kenya.

Bohor Reedbuck *Redunca redunca* 71-76cm (bottom left). Horns (males only) sharply hooked forwards at the tip, distinguishing them from the Oribi (see next page). It is reddish fawn with white underparts and has a short bushy tail. They usually live in pairs or otherwise in small family groups. Found in east and southern Africa. Often seen with Oribi, in bushed grassland and always near water.

Klipspringer *Oreotragus oreotragus* 56cm (bottom right). Brownish-yellow with grey speckles and white chin and underparts with a short tail. Has distinctive, blunt hoof tips and short horns (male only). Likes dry, stony hills and mountains. Only found in southern Africa.

■ **Common (Grimm's) Duiker** *Sylvicapra grimmia* 58cm (below). Grey fawn colour with darker rump and pale colour on the underside. Its dark muzzle and prominent ears are divided by straight, upright, narrow pointed horns. This particular species is the only duiker found in open grasslands. Usually the duiker is associated with a forested environment. It's common throughout southern and eastern Africa, but difficult to see because it is shy and will quickly disappear into the bush.

■ **Oribi** *Ourebia ourebi* 61cm (bottom left). Slender and delicate looking with a longish neck and a sandy to brownish fawn coat. It has oval-shaped ears and short, straight horns with a few rings at their base (male only). Like the Reedbuck (see previous page) it has a patch of bare skin just below each ear. They live in small groups or as a pair and are never far from water. Found in east and southern Africa.

■ **Suni** *Nesotragus moschatus* 37cm (bottom right). Dark chestnut to grey fawn in colour with slight speckles along the back, its head and neck are slightly paler and the throat is white. It has a distinct bushy tail with a white tip. Its longish horns (male only) are thick, ribbed and slope backwards. This is one of the smallest antelope, lives alone and prefers dense bush cover and reed beds in east and southern Africa.

Springbuck *Antidorcas marsupialis* or **Springbok**, 76-84cm (below). The upper part of the body is fawn, and this is separated from the white underparts by a dark brown lateral stripe. It is distinguished by a dark stripe which runs between the base of the horns and the mouth, passing through the eye. This is the only type of gazelle found south of the Zambezi River and you will not see this animal futher north. You no longer see the giant herds the animal was famous for, but you will see them along the roadside as you drive between Cape Town and Bloemfontein in South Africa. They get their name from their habit of leaping stiff-legged and high into the air.

Impala *Aepyceros melampus* 92-107cm (bottom). One of the largest of the smaller antelope, the Impala is a bright rufous colour on its back and has a white abdomen, a white 'eyebrow' and chin and white hair inside its ears. From behind, the white rump with black stripes on each side is characteristic and makes it easy to identify. It has long lyre-shaped horns (male only). Above the heels of the hind legs is a tuft of thick black bristles (unique to Impala) which are easy to see when the animal runs. There's also a black mark on the side of abdomen, just in front of the back leg. Found in herds of 15 to 20 in both east and southern Africa, it likes open grassland or sometimes the cover of partially wooded areas and is usually close to water.

Other mammals

There are many other fascinating mammals worth keeping an eye out for. This is a selection of some of the more interesting, or particularly common, ones.

■ **African Wild Dog** or **Hunting Dog** *Lycacon pictus* (right). Easy to identify since they have all the features of a large mongrel dog: a large head and slender body. Their coat is a mixed pattern of dark shapes and white and yellow patches and no two dogs are quite alike. They are very rarely seen and are seriously threatened with extinction (there may be as few as 6,000 left). Found in east and southern Africa on the open plains around dead animals, they are not in fact scavengers but effective pack hunters.

■ **Brown Hyena** *Hyaena brunnea* (above). High shoulders and low back give the hyena its characteristic appearance. The spotted variety, larger and brownish with dark spots, has a large head and rounded ears. The brown hyena, slightly smaller, has pointed ears and a shaggy coat, and is more noctural. The spotted hyena is only found in east Africa and the brown hyena is only found in southern Africa. Although sometimes shy animals they have been know to wander around campsites stealing food from humans.

■ **Spotted Hyena** *Crocuta crocuta* 69-91cm (middle right).

■ **Warthog** *Phacochoerus aethiopicus* (left). The warthog is almost hairless and grey with a very large head, tusks and wart-like growths on its face. It frequently occurs in family parties and when startled will run away at speed with its tail held straight up in the air. They are often seen near water caking themselves in thick mud which helps to keep them both cool and free of ticks and flies. They are found in both east and southern Africa.

■ **Chacma Baboon** *Papio ursinus* (opposite page bottom). An adult male baboon is slender and weighs about 40 kg. Their general colour is a brownish grey, with lighter undersides. Usually seen in trees, but rocks can also provide sufficient protection, they occur in large family troops and have a reputation for being aggressive where they have become used to man's presence. Found in east and southern Africa.

■ **Gorilla** *Gorilla gorilla* (left) are not animals you will see casually in passing – you have to go and look for them. They are sociable animals living in large family groups and have a vegetarian diet. Gorillas are the largest and most powerful of the apes. Adult males reach an average height of 150-170 cm and weigh from 135 to 230 kg. They occur only in the forests in the west of the region in Uganda, Rwanda and DR Congo.

reach **Injisuthi**, take the turning to Loskop off the R600, before reaching Loskop there is a dirt road on the right. Follow the signposts to Injisuthi from here. Heading southeast, the R74 crosses the N3 to **Estcourt**, 43 km.

Winterton → *Colour map 5, grid A4.*

This village is an important centre for dairy farms as well as being the last place to stock up on supplies for visitors to Cathedral Peak or Monk's Cowl. It's worth stopping here for a look around its pleasant tree-lined streets and small museum, and to gather some local information. The petrol station and the supermarket are on the junction of the R74 with the road leading into the centre of village. Nearby in Thokosiza is the **Central Drakensberg Information Centre**, a major arts, crafts and tourist centre, see page 441.

Spionkop Dam Nature Reserve

ⓘ *14 km north of Winterton on the R600. Office T036-4881578. Oct-Mar 0600-1900, Apr-Sep 0600-1800, R15.*

This 6000-ha game park is a popular tourist resort for boating and fishing. Almost all the game here has been reintroduced and there is a good chance of seeing white rhino and buffalo. With this in mind visitors must be careful when walking in the open around their campsite. Other animals one can expect to see include giraffe, kudu, mountain reedbuck, waterbuck, blesbok, impala, zebra, eland, duiker and steenbok. The area is particularly rich in birdlife and more than 270 species have been recorded here. Anglers can fish the reservoir from the dam or from the shore.

The **Battle of Spion Kop**, 24 January 1890, was yet another embarrassing defeat for the British at the hands of the Boers and had a marked impact upon British public opinion. In an attempt to relieve the beleaguered British troops at Ladysmith (see page 432), General Warren attempted a direct assault on the Rangeworthy Hills to dislodge the Boer positions. He decided to occupy the highest peak on the ridge – Spion Kop. However, this meant that the shallow British defences were exposed to Boer gun fire from all sides and soon suffered heavy losses. A brigade under General Lyttelton came to Warren's assistance but General Buller disastrously reversed the decision, ordering all British forces to retreat down from Spion Kop and back across the Tugela. Some 1750 British troops were either killed, wounded or captured at Spion Kop compared to about 300 Boers. The famous battlefield overlooks the dam and is clearly visible from the reserve. It can be reached on one of the self-guided trails.

Cathedral Peak → *Colour map 4, grid B6.*

ⓘ *Signposted from Bergville and Winterton. The road is tarred and is usually passable even after rain. T036-4881880, reception at Mike's Pass daily 0600-1800. Shop and information office daily 0800-1630. R20 per person, vehicles to Mike's Pass R35.*

Cathedral Peak is the main point of access to some of the wildest areas of the central Drakensberg, and provides some of the most spectacular scenery for hikers. Driving into the area, the road passes traditional Zulu villages and dips through leafy valleys, with the views gradually opening up as you get closer to the park. The park itself is ringed by dramatic peaks with views of the Cathedral Spur and Cathedral Peak (3004 m), the Inner and Outer Horns (3005 m), and the Bell (2930 m). An alternative to hiking round the peaks is to drive up Mike's Pass, suitable for saloon cars, from where there are spectacular views of the Little Berg.

The sheltered valleys in this area are thought to have been one of the last refuges of the San in the Drakensberg. This is one of the best places to see a large number of

In 1906 Liverpool Football Club named the home stands at Anfield 'Spionkop' in memory of those who died here during the Boer War. The stands are still called 'the Kop' to this day.

San cave paintings found in the Drakensberg; the Rock Art Centre at Didimi makes a good starting point. Leopard's Cave and Poacher's Cave in the Ndedema Gorge have especially good galleries of paintings.

An earlier name for Cathedral Peak was Zikhali's Horn, named after Zikhali who escaped to Swaziland after his father was killed by Dingaan. During the years that he and his tribe spent in Swaziland they assimilated many aspects of Swazi culture. Swazi influences can still be seen today in the way that traditional huts are built in this region.

Hiking The Cathedral Peak area is growing in popularity with hikers. There is a good network of paths heading up the Mlambonja Valley to the escarpment from where there are trails heading south to Monk's Cowl and Injisuthi or heading north to Royal Natal National Park. The campsite at Mike's Pass or the **Cathedral Peak Hotel** are good bases from which to set out exploring the area on a series of day walks. Maps are available in the information office and show a number of walks departing from the hotel. For keen hikers there are designated caves and mountain huts on the longer trails. The 10-km hike to the top of **Cathedral Peak** (3004 m) is one of the most exciting and strenuous hikes in this part of the Drakensberg, and the views from the top of the Drakensberg stretching out to the north and south are unforgettable.

Northern & central Drakensberg

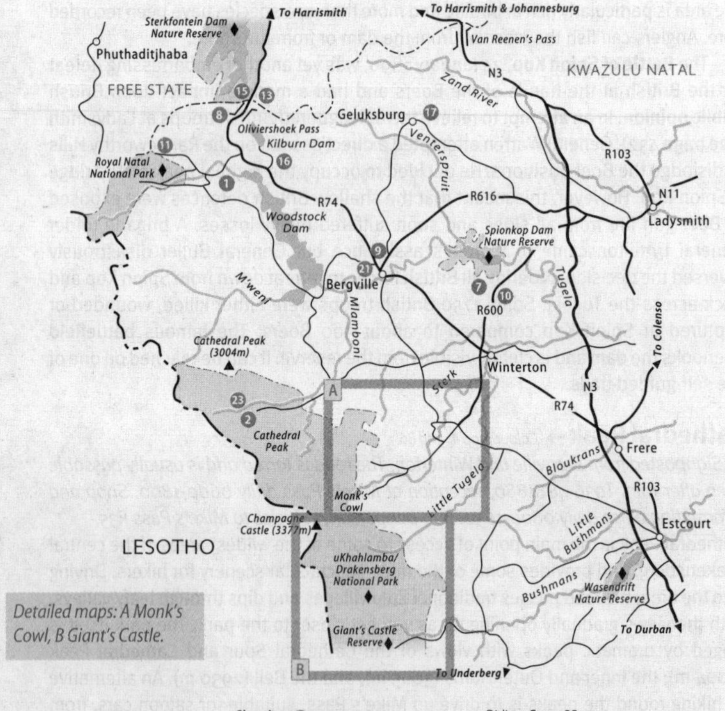

Sleeping
- Alpine Heath 1
- Amphitheatre
- Backpackers 13
- Bingelela Lodge 21
- Caterpillar & Catfish 15
- Cathedral Peak 2
- Cavern 11
- Didima Camp 23
- Drakensville Berg Resort 16
- Homestead Guest House 17
- Iphika Tented Bush Camp 7
- Little Switzerland 8
- Sandford Park Resort 9
- Spionkop Lodge 10

N

0 km 10

0 miles 10

Cave paintings An excellent introduction to San rock art in the area is at the relatively new **Rock Art Centre** ① *Didima Camp, just past the entrance to the park, T036-4888025, ndumemi@kznwildlife.com, 0800-1300, 1400-1600, small entry fee.* The stylish thatch building holds a series of displays interpreting the art found in the surrounding mountains. A key thread in the museum is the eland, a vital aspect in San mythology and culture, with some life-size replicas in the entrance. The museum begins with an introduction to the culture and lifestyle of the San, with a look at archaeological finds, quotes from some of the last San descendants, and descriptions of the symbolic meaning of some of the most famous paintings. At the back of the museum is a replica of an open-topped cave, complete with starry sky and fake camp fire, where recordings of San folklore stories are played. This leads to the auditorium, an impressive structure built to look like a rock overhang, where you can watch an interesting 15-minute audio-visual show on the history of the San and their cave paintings.

From the reception at Mike's Pass, regular tours leave to visit the main sites in the area. Visitors are driven into the mountains and then are guided on a two-hour round trip to see some of the finest caves (R65 per person; call ahead to check availability). There are also several caves within walking distance of the **Cathedral Peak Hotel** (accessible with a guide only; call the hotel to book, see page 461). Mushroom Hill has two particularly interesting scenes, one of two mythical human figures with animal heads and hooves holding what are thought to be early musical instruments, and the other depicting a more lighthearted scene of some San scrambling away from an irate leopard. Xeni Shelter, 2 km beyond Mushroom Rock and also easily reached from the hotel, shows a group of people and a few antelope. Ladder Shelter shows San ladders with a small picture of a man climbing up the rock face.

Junction Shelter has a number of interesting scenes of men crossing on a rope bridge, a baboon hunt and some human figures dancing. Eland Cave is a large cave with many splendid paintings; more mysteriously, a San hunting kit was found here in the 1920s, which can now be seen at the Rock Art Centre.

Monk's Cowl → *Colour map 4, grid B6. See also map page 452.*

① *T036-4681103. Park gates Oct-Mar 0700-2000, Apr-Sep 0600-1800. Camp office daily 0830-1230, 1330-1600. R20 per person.*

The road to Monk's Cowl passes through one of the most developed areas of the Drakensberg. Looking down from Monk's Cowl the view of KwaZulu Natal is dotted with hotels, golf courses and timeshare developments and the area is locally dubbed 'Champagne Valley'. However, **Champagne Castle**, **Monk's Cowl** and **Cathkin Peak** are still impressive features in this landscape and several interesting long distance hikes begin from here.

The nearest shop to Monk's Cowl is opposite the Champagne Sports Resort (9 km).

The **Drakensberg Boys' Choir School** is on the right of the R600 towards Monk's Cowl and is one of the most beautiful locations for a school in the whole of South Africa. The school is highly accredited in its own right, but is most famous for the choir that has performed all over the world over the last three decades. Boys aged between nine and 15 have performed in front of the Pope and 25,000 people at the Vatican City, sung with the Vienna Boys' Choir in Austria, and have been proclaimed top choir three times at the World Festival of Choirs. The choir has even received a special award at Disney's Magic Kingdom. Most audiences expect only classical choral renditions but the boys sing anything from Beethoven to Freddy Mercury. For further details, see Entertainment, page 466.

Just before the **Champagne Castle Hotel**, turn off the R600 to reach **Falcon Ridge** ① *T082-7746398 (mob), bird shows Sat-Thu at 1030*, a rehabilitation centre for rescued birds of prey, mostly injured through flying into power lines. The daily show is a big attraction, and you can don a glove and have your photo taken with a large raptor.

 Hiking The short hikes around Monk's Cowl get busy as so many tourists visit here for the day. A map is available from the office and the paths are clear and well signposted. Places to visit include **Nandi's Falls** (5 km), **Sterkspruit Falls** (2 km), and **The Sphinx** (3 km). The paths cross areas of proteas and some woodland.

The hike up to **Champagne Castle** (3377 m) is a 20-km, two-day hike which involves a steady slog uphill, but no climbing skills are needed. From the camp, the trail rises up and follows the Mhlawazini Valley circling around Cathkin Peak and Monk's Cowl. There is a campsite just below Gray's Pass. A path winds steeply up the pass for 2 km to the top of the escarpment. From here it is possible to walk to the top of Champagne Castle or to visit the cliffs at Vulture's Retreat where a colony of Cape vultures breed.

Giant's Castle Reserve

→ *Colour map 4, grid B6.*

This reserve was established in 1903 when there were only 200 eland left in the whole of KwaZulu Natal. Over the years, the reserve has successfully helped the eland population in the Drakensberg to recover and at present there are around 600 in the reserve. Blesbok, mountain reedbuck and oribi are some of the other mammals you are likely to see. Rolling hills of sourveld grasslands dominate the landscape of the reserve, with the Drakensberg escarpment towering over the main camp. A wall of basalt cliffs rise up to over 3000 m and the peaks of **Giant's Castle** (3314 m), **Champagne Castle** (3248 m) and **Cathkin Peak** (3149 m) can be seen on the skyline. The grasslands below the cliffs roll out in a series of massive hills, which give rise to the Bushman's River and the Little Tugela River. On the drive to the main camp from the park gates, the road passes through a cutting which exposes layers of brown, red, yellow and purple rock. These are the **Molteno Beds**, layers of sandstone deposited 200 million years ago where plant and dinosaur fossils have been found.

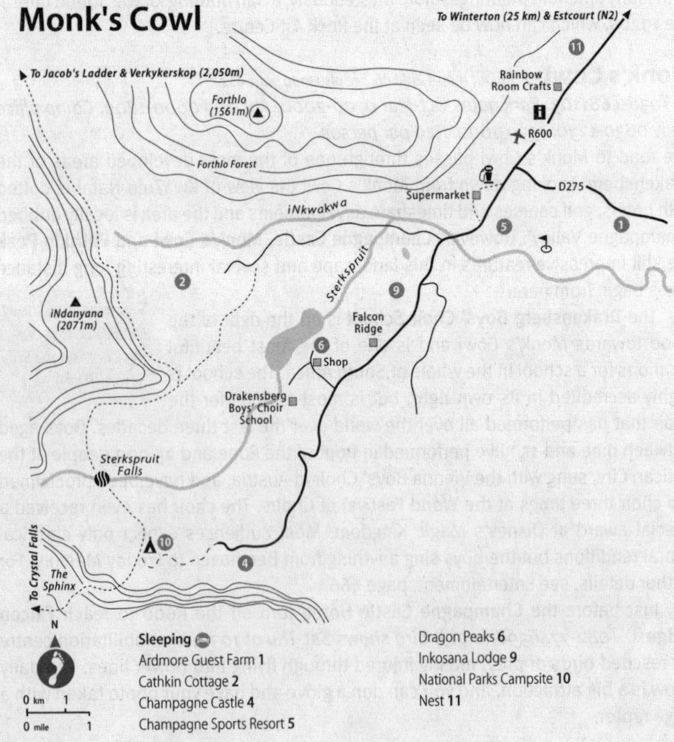

Ins and outs The road to Giant's Castle is signposted from Mooi River (64 km) and Estcourt (65 km) on the N3. The road from Estcourt is tarred for most of the way while the mostly dirt road from Mooi River should be avoided in wet weather. From Mooi River take the road to Ncibidwana Store, 46 km, and then follow the signs.

Giant's Castle camp and around ⓘ *T036-3533718. Park gates Oct-Mar 0500-1900, Apr-Sep 0600-1800. Camp office daily 0800-1230, 1400-1630, R25.*
The area around the camp has a network of short paths through riverine forest and wetlands which supports many species of birds. The malachite kingfisher, Gurney's sugarbird and the various sunbirds are often spotted here and grey duiker can sometimes be seen walking around the camp.

There are numerous interconnected hikes crossing the reserve. The shorter walks explore the forests and river valleys within a few kilometres of the camp, whilst the longer ones take up to three days and can reach areas as far afield as Injisuthi. A comprehensive leaflet detailing the hiking choices is available from the camp office.

The **Main Cave** is half an hour's walk from the camp and has a large wall covered in paintings and a simple display on the archaeology of the cave and the San who lived there. The cave must be visited with a guide; book at the main office, T036-3533718.

The 7-km hike up to **World's View** (1842 m) follows a path north along a ridge overlooking the Bushman's River. The climb up to the top is not too strenuous and the views looking over Wildebeest Plateau to Giant's Castle and Cathkin Peak are well

Giant's Castle Reserve

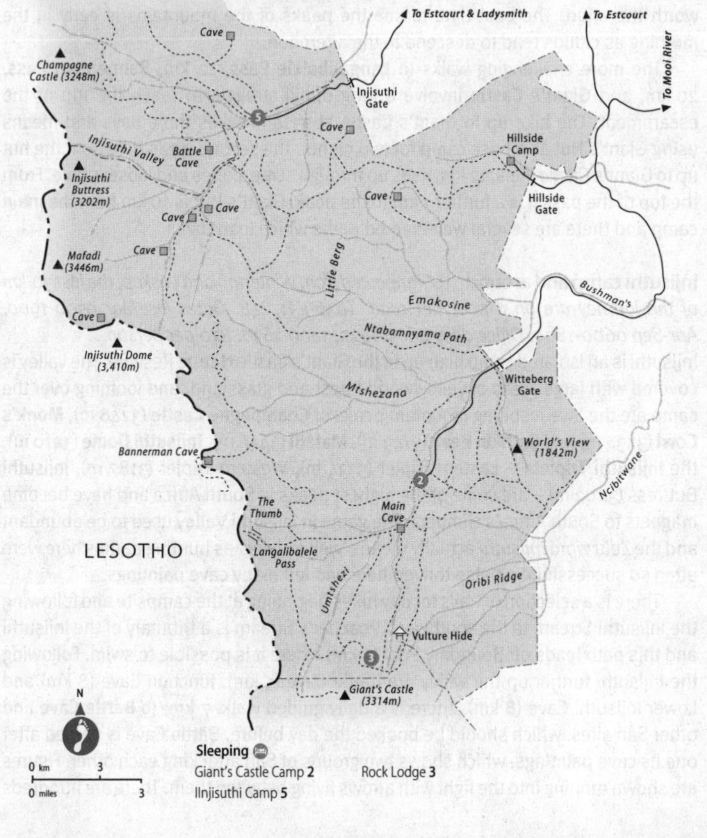

Sleeping
Giant's Castle Camp 2
Injisuthi Camp 5
Rock Lodge 3

Lammergeyers

Lammergeyers are one of the world's rarest vultures, living mainly in isolated high mountain areas in the Pyrenees, the Atlas Mountains of Morocco and the Middle East. However, there are around 200 pairs of lammergeyers in the Drakensberg and Lesotho, and a visit to the hide at Giant's Castle is one of the best ways to see them.

They live on a diet of dried bones, waiting for a carcass to be cleaned by other vultures before they will start to feed. The lammergeyer flies off with bones from the carcass and drops them onto rocks below. The bones crack open enabling the bird to feed on the bone marrow inside.

The lammergeyer is a rare and endangered species, under threat from local farmers, who leave poisoned carcasses out in the wild to kill jackals. The carcasses attract vultures who, in their turn, are poisoned.

The **lammergeyer hide** ⓘ *T036-3533718, May-Sep Sat and Sun only, R130 per person, minimum per party R400,* is a popular attraction and advance booking is necessary. Up to six people are driven up to the hide in the early morning but must make their own way back to the camp on foot. In addition to the lammergeyer you can expect to see the lanner falcon, jackal buzzard, Cape vulture and the black eagle.

worth the effort. The best time to see the peaks of the mountains is early in the morning as clouds tend to descend in the afternoon.

The more challenging walks to **Langalibalele Pass**, 12 km, **Bannerman Pass**, 20 km, and **Giant's Castle** involve a long uphill struggle to reach the top of the escarpment. The hike up to Giant's Castle at 3314 m takes three days and means using Giant's Hut as a base camp for two nights. The second day's hike from the hut up to Giant's Castle Pass, 12 km, rises up through scree slopes and loose rubble. From the top of the pass it is a further 1 km to the peak. Giant's Hut is 10 km from the main camp and there are several well-marked paths which lead to it.

Injisuthi camp and around ⓘ *Signposted from Winterton and Loskop, the last 30 km of the journey are on a poor dirt road. T036-4317848. Gates Oct-Mar 0500-1900, Apr-Sep 0600-1800. Office daily 0800-1230, 1400-1630. R20 per person.*
Injisuthi is an isolated camp high up in the Giant's Castle Nature Reserve. The valley is covered with large areas of yellowwood forest and grassland, and looming over the camp are the awe-inspiring mountain peaks of **Champagne Castle** (3248 m), **Monk's Cowl** (3234 m) and **Cathkin Peak** (3149 m). **Mafadi** (3446 m), **Injisuthi Dome** (3410 m), the **Injisuthi Triplets** – Eastern Triplet (3134 m), Western Triplet (3187 m), Injisuthi Buttress (3202 m) – are some of the highest peaks in South Africa and have become magnets to South Africa's climbers. The game in Injisuthi Valley used to be abundant and the Zulu word *Injisuthi* actually means 'well-fed dog' as hunting parties here were often so successful. San also thrived here and left many cave paintings.

There is a selection of trails for day hikes beginning at the campsite and following the Injisuthi Stream to the southwest. Poacher's Stream is a tributary of the Injisuthi and this path leads off Boundary Pool (3 km) where it is possible to swim. Following the Injisuthi further up the valley are Battle Cave (5 km), Junction Cave (8 km) and Lower Injisuthi Cave (8 km). There is a daily guided walk, 7 km, to **Battle Cave** and other San sites, which should be booked the day before. Battle Cave is named after one its cave paintings, which shows two groups of San attacking each other. Figures are shown running into the fight with arrows flying between them. There are hundreds of other paintings on the cave walls of animals that used to live here, including a family of lions, numerous eland and rhebok, an elephant and an antbear.

Giant's Castle is a three-day hike from Injisuthi following the contour path south. The trail can be exhausting but it does pass through spectacular mountain scenery including Popple Peak. Reservations for sleeping at Lower Injisuthi Cave and Bannerman Hut have to be made beforehand.

Kamberg Nature Reserve

ⓘ *48 km from Nottingham Rd travelling via Rosetta; the route is well signposted and only the last 19 km are on dirt roads. If travelling from Mooi River (42 km) on the N3, take the turning to Rosetta, T033-2637312. Gates Oct-Mar 0500-1900, Apr-Sep 0600-1800. Office daily 0800-1130, 1400-1530. All visitors must report to the office on arrival. R20.*

The reserve was established on farmland in 1951. The scenery is not as spectacular as at some of the other resorts, however, the Clarens Sandstone around Kamberg does have its own special appeal, and there is some good San rock art within the reserve. The reserve is at relatively low altitude, the highest point being **Gladstone's Nose** at 2265 m, and is therefore known for its birdlife with over 200 species recorded here.

Kamberg is probably best known for its trout fishing; there is a hatchery open to the public and several dams stocked with brown and rainbow trout which can be fished all year round. The Mooi River can only be fished during the season between September and April. Food and petrol are not for sale at the camp. The nearest shops and petrol station are 42 km away in Rosetta.

The trails around Kamberg are quite leisurely and involve no steep climbs. The **Mooi River Trail**, 4 km, has been designed with wheelchair access in mind, and is a relaxing stroll past willows and eucalyptus trees along the banks of the Mooi River. Longer trails, such as the hike up to **Emeweni Falls**, are detailed in a booklet available in the camp office.

There are several rock art sites in the reserve, but the two main sites worth visiting for the variety and quality of the paintings are Game Pass Shelter and The Kranses. **Game Pass Shelter** is approximately a 7-km walk from Kamberg. The sheer number of paintings here is impressive. Among the many scenes on the rock wall is one of a human with hooves instead of feet holding the tail of a dying eland. This is thought to have shamanic meaning and to be connected to a trance-like state. Just outside the shelter there are some fossilized dinosaur footprints. An impressive **San Rock Art Interpretation Centre** ⓘ *T033-2637312, daily 0830, 1100 and 1330, R40 per person, book in advance*, provides visitors with an insight into the lifestyle of the San hunter-gatherers. There's an audio-visual presentation followed by a guided walk to the Game Pass Shelter that takes about 2½ hours. The centre also has a small restaurant.

The walk to the **Kranses** group of caves is a 12-km round trip. Apart from these there are also several other interesting caves to visit. The Kranses has a long sheltered rock wall covered in paintings of eland. Among these are some smaller scenes showing a group of people, some of whom are carrying shields. It is known that the San didn't use shields so they must be paintings of cattle herders, possibly the Amazizi, who moved up into the Drakensberg and lived peacefully with the San.

Southern Drakensberg

» *pp459-468.*

The southern section of the Drakensberg is the least visited part of the mountain range, although the scenery here is no less spectacular, and offers some excellent walks – particularly around Cobham. The area is best known for the Sani Pass, a spectacular track crossing over to the mountains to Lesotho, reaching 3000 m at its highest point. The main towns in the south are Underberg and Himeville – both are convenient stop-off points for stocking up on supplies.

Ins and outs

Underberg is the main access point to the Southern Drakensberg resorts. Both Underberg and Himeville are sleepy farming villages but have a good variety of pubs, restaurants and shops, and are convenient stop-offs for provisions en route to the KZN Wildlife camps or the Sani Pass. Despite its relative isolation, **Sani Pass Carriers** offers transport to/from Underberg, which helps make this beautiful area of the Drakensberg accessible for budget travellers.

Always make sure you have warm clothing as conditions can change very quickly in this area. Try and hike in groups of three or more people.

Southern Berg Escape ⓘ *7 Clock Tower Centre, Main Rd, Underberg, T033-7011471, www.drakensberg.org*, produces a leaflet with information on activities and accommodation in the Southern Drakensberg, and can book accommodation.

Towards Underberg

Bulwer is a small village in the foothills of the Drakensberg set among pine plantations. There is little of interest for tourists here but it is one of the few centres for paragliding and hang-gliding in the Drakensberg and was host to the national championships in 2002. ▸▸ *For further details, see Activities and tours, page 466.*

From here the R617 begins to climb, offering spectacular views of the mountains in the distance. Twenty kilometres beyond Bulwer towards Underberg, a sign marks the turning to the **Reichenau Mission.** This old Catholic mission station was originally run by Trappist monks; the highlight here is the Zulu Mass held every Sunday. The church has no organ so all the hymns are purely choral and the singing is amazing. Most of the people here are Zulu speakers and only the local nuns and priests speak English. Guides are available for the local rock art sites and fishing is permitted in the trout dam.

Underberg → *Colour map 4, grid B6. See also map p464.*

This small market town was founded in 1886 and is still very much the main service centre for this part of the Drakensberg. The junction with the road to Himeville is where the banks, supermarkets and the tourist information office can all be found.

Himeville → *Colour map 4, grid B6.*

Founded in 1893, Himeville is a small prosperous village reminiscent of England. Arbuckle Street runs through the village centre where there is a supermarket, post office, museum, hotel and petrol station. **Himeville Arms** is the main hotel; its distinctive Tudor architecture wouldn't be out of place in an English village. There is a small **museum** ⓘ *T033-7021184, Tue-Sun 0930-1230*, in the old fort and prison. It is an early sandstone building with exhibits on settler history and one of the better displays on San.

Himeville Nature Reserve ⓘ *day visitors R15*, is set on the outskirts of Himeville, where there are two dams surrounded by grassland. The 105-ha protected area is a home for waterbirds and the occasional blesbok and black wildebeest; look out for three different species of crane which have been bred here in captivity.

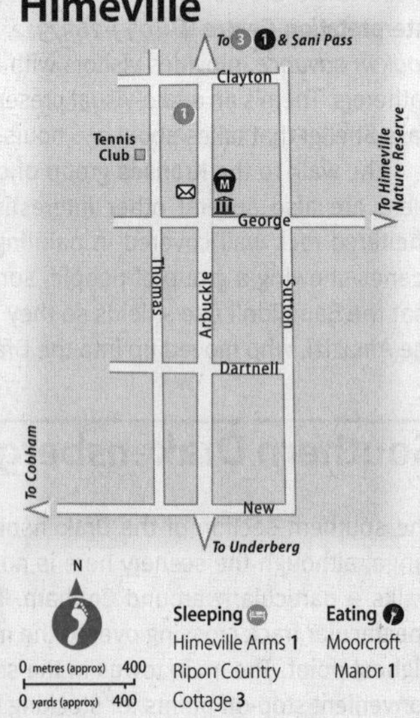

Cobham

ⓘ *T033-7020831. Park gates Oct-Mar 0500-1900, Apr-Sep 0600-1800. Office daily 0800-1630. R20. There is a curio shop at Cobham; otherwise plan on being totally self sufficient. The nearest shops and supermarkets are in Underberg.*

On the road between Underberg and Himeville, a signposted turning leads down a dirt road (D7) to Cobham (14 km). This is a fascinating wilderness area and is an ideal base for many exciting hikes. The land rising up towards the escarpment has been gouged with steep sided gorges filled with thick yellowwood forest. The view above the cliffs of the escarpment is of the Giant's Cup, lying between Hodgson's Peaks, and the Drakensberg stretching out to the north and south. The Mzimkulu River rises here and flows to Port Shepstone. This area is relatively undisturbed by human activity and the clean waters of the high Drakensberg streams are a sanctuary for Cape clawless otters and spotted-necked otters. People rarely see them, as they are very shy animals, but they tend to be active at dusk and dawn. White droppings on riverbanks are a sign of their presence; the distinctive colour comes from the calcium of the crab shells that make up a large proportion of their diet.

Hiking There are five hikes of various lengths in the reserve, most of which leave from the campsite, including the Gxalingenwa River Trail, Ouhout Trail, Troutbeck Loop, Emerald Stream Trail and the Pholela River Trail. The camp office has full information on all hikes available. Most notable is the Giant's Cup Hiking Trail, a 60-km five-day trail.

Note that hiking permits for the Sani Pass area (see below) including the Giant's Cup Hiking Trail are available from Cobham. Caves should also be reserved here. For your own safety, a mountain rescue register must be filled in. Nights at Cobham are cold all year round, so it is a good idea to bring some warm clothing.

Sani Pass → *Colour map 4, grid B6.*

The road from Himeville to Sani Pass (15 km) rises steadily through rolling hills covered in grassland and patches of pine plantation until it passes the **Sani Top Chalet** and the 3000 m peaks on the escarpment come into view. **Hodgson's Peaks**, at 3256 m and 3229 m, the **Twelve Apostles** and **Sani Pass**, at 2874 m, are at their most beautiful after snow. Flora and fauna have adapted to this harsh environment and some of the Drakensberg's rarest species can be found here. The road is one of the most dramatic in Africa and is the only route leading into Lesotho on its eastern border with South Africa.

Sani Pass was originally used by traders transporting goods by mule into Basutoland. A trading post was opened in the 1920s at Good Hope Farm at the bottom of the pass, which was the closest store to Mokhotlong in Lesotho. Then the Sani Pass was little more than a bridle path, but it was upgraded to a road in 1955 after the first 4WD Land Rover managed to complete the ascent. Maize and trade goods, including a fair number of guns, were taken up, while wool and hides were taken down. Trade still continues on this route, although these days most traders supplying shops in Lesotho have their own 4WDs and prefer to drive to the larger warehouses in Pietermaritzburg to stock up on goods. The Good Hope trading post closed in 1990 but the remains of the buildings can still be seen at the bottom of the pass.

The border ⓘ *South African border post daily 0800-1600; Lesotho border post daily 0700-1700. Access to the pass is restricted to 4WD vehicles, motorbikes, mountain bikes and pedestrians.*

In spite of its isolation you should expect full border formalities at Sani Pass. The crossing is normally quick and easy. The road is so rough that saloon cars are not allowed past the border post. If you are hiking, the walk between the two border posts takes about three hours.

Interestingly, there are no customs and immigration officials at this border and all formalities are conducted by the police. This could be due in some part to the high incidence of *dagga* (marijuana) smuggling. Some overnight hikers on the KZN Wildlife trails have reported coming across Lesotho smugglers with great bags of *dagga* hiding in the mountains so they can cross into South Africa undetected by night.

Tours and hikes The pass is a popular attraction with tourists, and organized trips to the top of the pass and over the border to Lesotho are available from Underberg, the **Sani Pass Hotel** and **Sani Lodge.** Travellers are taken up by Land Rover; the road is terrifyingly steep and winding but the views are outstanding. The tours are a good way to discover local history and wildlife and include a visit to a Basotho village to see sheep shearing, maize cultivation or beer making. A picnic lunch in the Black Mountains or lunch at the **Sani Top Chalet** is included; don't miss a glass of warming mulled wine at the pub at the Sani Top Chalet – at 2874 m it is the highest pub in Africa.

Hiking permits for the Sani Pass area are available from Cobham (see page 457). For your own safety, a mountain rescue register must be filled in. The most rewarding hike in this area is the day hike up to the top of Sani Pass at 2874 m. There is a car park at the South African border post from where it is a further 14-km hike to the top. The trail is quite straightforward and just involves following the road. A number of shorter walks visit **Gxalingwena, Kaula** and **Ikanti Shelter.** These cave-like dwellings are home to a number of San rock paintings. New regulations stipulate that for the protection of the paintings, they must only be visited with a registered guide. These can be arranged from the **Sani Pass Hotel** or **Sani Lodge,** where survey maps are also available for a deposit of R50.

Mkhomazi Wilderness Area

Vergelegen

ⓘ *T033-7020712, entry fee R15, overnight hiking permits R30.*

Vergelegen is one of the most remote reserves in the Drakensberg National Park and as such receives fewer visitors than most other reserves. Thaba Ntlenyana on the Lesotho side of the border is the highest mountain in Southern Africa at 3482 m and can be seen from the top of the escarpment in the reserve. The rugged mountain terrain here makes this an ideal base from which to explore the mountains on some of the most inaccessible and demanding hiking trails in the Drakensberg. Permits are needed for hikes which leave from Vergelegen. Hikers can register at the camp office.

Facilities such as petrol or basic food supplies are not available at Vergelegen; visitors should be completely self-sufficient.

Lotheni

ⓘ *T033-7020540. Park gates Oct-Mar, 0500-1900, Apr-Sep, 0600-1800. R20.*

The reserve can be reached either from Himeville or from Nottingham Road; both access routes are along rough dirt tracks which can become impassable during heavy rains. The most popular route is the signposted dirt track from Himeville which heads north for 45 km towards **Lotheni Store** and the reserve. The Nottingham Road track heads southeast for 60 km to **Lotheni Store,** from where there is a signposted turning for the last 10 km to the reserve. There is a camp shop here which sells hiking maps and permits; otherwise the nearest shop is **Lotheni Store,** 14 km from the entrance to the camp. Petrol is not available here.

The landscape at Lotheni is mainly rolling grassland rising up towards the High Berg and Redi Peak at 3298 m. The grassland is interspersed with patches of protea woodland, tree ferns and the rare Berg bamboo. The demand for timber in the first half of this century resulted in most of the indigenous woodland being cut down leaving large areas of grassland. The land was then used for grazing and as farmland until the 1950s when it was bought by the KwaZulu Natal Parks Board. The original farmhouse (at the camp) was built in 1905 and is now the **Settlers' Homestead Museum** where the lifestyle of the early settlers has been recreated. Wagons, farm tools and period furniture are on display here.

Streams cutting down through the rock have formed narrow wooded gorges, which have been stocked with brown trout. The trout season lasts from September to April and during these months accommodation at weekends can be fully booked. Spring is also a popular time for visitors who come to see the magnificent wild flowers. There are three leisurely day hikes and two overnight trails in the reserve, for which maps can be bought in the camp shop. During hot weather it is worth remembering that it is safe to swim in the Lotheni River when it is not in flood. There are some natural pools a short walk from the camp although the water flowing straight off the mountains can be icy.

Garden Castle

ⓘ *Entrances at Drakensberg Garden (34 km from Underberg) and Bushmen's Nek (45 km from Underberg), both signposted off the R626, T033-7011823. Park gates Oct-Mar 0500-1900, Apr-Sep 0600-1800. R20. Overnight hiking fee R30.*

Garden Castle is the southernmost reserve in the Drakensberg Park, a wild area with few visitors, home to eland, grey rhebok and reedbuck. The landscape consists mostly of grassland with patches of proteas and tree ferns. There are many tarns in this part of the Drakensberg where waterbirds and wildlife can be seen. There are magnificent views up into the mountains on a clear day, with the mountain peaks of **Walker**, at 3322 m, **Wilson**, at 3342 m, and the **Rhino**, at 3051 m, towering over the reserve.

Overnight hikers must complete the Mountain Rescue Register before starting their hike and make sure they sign in on return. The office has a small shop which sells basic supplies, permits and hiking maps, otherwise the nearest shops are in Underberg. Petrol is not available here.

There are plenty of huts and caves to spend the night in, but no fires are allowed anywhere within the Garden Castle Reserve.

The highest peaks in this area, which can be hiked in a day via a strenuous 11-km trail, are **Mashai Pass** (peak 3313 m) and **Rhino Peak** at 3051 m. **Engagement Cave** and **Sleeping Beauty Cave** are only 4 km from the Parks Board office and are easily visited in a morning. There are many options for day hikes around Bushman's Nek to various caves.

Sleeping

Royal Natal National Park

p446, map p447

A-C Thendele Camp, camp office open daily 0800-1600, advance bookings on T033-8451000, www.kznwildlife.com. Stunning location with unrivalled views of the Amphitheatre from a cluster of chalets, cottages and a lodge sleeping 4-12. The cottages and lodge have cooks who prepare food supplied by the guests, while the chalets are self-catering with fully equipped kitchens, a coal fire, a private terrace and braai overlooking the Amphitheatre. The camp's setting makes it one of the most popular in the entire Drakensberg, so must be booked months in advance. There is also a curio shop here selling books, T-shirts, jackets, boots and other souvenirs.

Camping

E Mahai, T036-4386310. The spacious campsite has pleasant lawns and is bordered by large pine trees and a stream. 60 sites, most with power points, 2 wash blocks, washing machines, and an area for open camping, good views of the Drakensberg and footpaths leading straight up into the hills make this campsite very popular (it can be crowded and noisy at weekends).

E Rugged Glen, T036-4386310. Small campsite to the north of the park, with 15 sites shaded by pine trees and a central ablution block, some with power points. There are no other facilities here.

Oliviershoek Pass *p448, map p450*

AL-A Little Switzerland, look out for the signposted turning off the R74 next to the petrol station, just below Oliviershoek Pass, T036-4386220, www.lsh.co.za. 66 thatched cottages and self-catering chalets set in a 2000-ha reserve, this large luxury resort offers a choice of sporting facilities including riding, fishing, canoeing, tennis and swimming. Recent additions include indoor heated pool, health and beauty centre, and gym. Geared towards South African families.

A Alpine Heath, below Oliviershoek Pass, follow signs along the R74, also known as Cavern Berg Rd, T036-4386484, www.threecities.co.za. A fully self-contained and well-established resort, with a large conference village, and offering a range of activities. 100 self-catering chalets with 3-bedrooms, lounge, 2 bathrooms, and private patio, TV. Facilities include 2 pools, gym, sauna, tennis, squash, restaurant.

A The Cavern, 10 km, follow the signs heading off the R74 towards the Royal Natal National Park, T036-4386270, www.cavern.co.za. The resort is a large complex set among gardens and woodland offering accommodation in 55 luxury thatched cottages. A wide range of activities are on offer including horse riding, bowls, swimming and a weekend disco. Rates include all meals and guided hikes. A superb location, with well-kept mature gardens and an overall friendly and welcoming atmosphere; good choice for families.

A-B Montusi Mountain Lodge, follow signs along R74 towards Royal Natal National Park, T036-4386243, www.montusi.za.net. Attractive series of luxury chalets, with large bedrooms and plush sitting rooms with large TVs, fridge, private terrace with staggering views towards the Amphitheatre. The chalets are surrounded by lawns, and there's a good restaurant and small bar on site. The owners run a choice of daily guided walks to the Royal Natal park, including San rock art walks. Fly-fishing, horse riding, pool, cycling, flying trapeze on attached grounds.

B Caterpillar & Catfish, at the top of Oliviershoek Pass, T036-4386130, www.cookhouse.co.za. A pine panelled mountain lodge in a restored trading post, tucked under large pine trees with great views. Decorated with African antiques, stripped pine and handmade furniture. 8 comfortable en suite bedrooms, and 10 self-catering units in the gardens sleeping 2-3. Massage room for weary hikers, huge buffet breakfasts, guided hikes to some fascinating rock art, fishing in a well-stocked trout dam. Beautifully decorated piano bar and 24-seater restaurant specializing in trout and fusion cooking. Popular with groups from Gauteng for Sun lunch, gaining a fast-growing reputation. Recommended.

B-E Drakensville Berg Resort, from Oliviershoek Pass, the turning is on the left towards Jagersrust, T036-4386287, www.drakensville.co.za. A large all-purpose holiday camp with 70 self-catering chalets for couples, plus family units and more upmarket B&B rooms. Sporting facilities include waterskiing, fishing, riding, tennis, squash and mini golf. There's also a camping and caravan park set under big shady trees.

D-E Ampitheatre Backpackers, 17 km, at the top of Oliviershoek Pass, T036-4386106, www.amphibackpackers.co.za. Excellent backpackers and the highest hostel in the country with fantastic views. Has 2 venues, one at the top of the pass, the other closer to Royal Natal National Park. Main building is a converted sandstone house, log fires, dorms, doubles and camping, hearty home-cooked meals, packed lunches to take with you on over 30 hikes in the area. On the Baz Bus route. Recommended.

Bergville *p448, map p450*

B-C Homestead Guest House, off the R616 towards Ladysmith, T036-4481328, www.thehomestead.co.za. 14 double rooms with en suite facilities in a mock Tudor building, TV, swimming pool, good value as rates include breakfast and dinner, an ideal

For an explanation of the sleeping and eating price codes used in this guide, see inside the front cover. Other relevant information is found in Essentials pages 42-47.

location from which to explore either the Battlefields or the mountains.

B-C Sandford Park Resort, on the R616 to Ladysmith, T036-4481001, www.sandford.co.za. One of the finest lodges in the region, this resort has grown up around a hotel dating back to 1852. There are 50 charming en suite rooms, some in separate rondavels, with tasteful furnishings. Neat gardens around the house, large swimming pool, horse riding, hiking and canoeing, plus a popular restaurant and bar. Rates are for dinner, B&B. Good base from which to explore both the Drakensberg and the battlefields.

C Bingelela Lodge, a short drive out of town towards Woodstock Dam, T036-4481336, bingelela@mweb.co.za. 10 units in comfortable, rustic, thatched cottages, a honeymoon suite with spa bath, swimming pool, attached à la carte restaurant serving good standards of South African cuisine.

E Bergville Caravan Park, T036-4481273, on the R74 just south of town. There are 10 bungalows, 2 rondavels and a campsite next to the Tugela River, in the low season and during the week the resort offers large discounts on accommodation, the river is popular for canoeing.

Winterton *p449*

C Lilac Cottage, 10 Springfield Rd, T036-4881025, purple@futurenet.co.za. Homely B&B with accommodation in 2 garden cottages, sleeping 2-10, all with en suite bathrooms and TV. Braai area, small pool, trampoline and children's play area. Meals served in the **Purple House** restaurant.

C Swallow's Nest, 1 Bergview Dr, T035-4881009, swallowsnest@telkomsa.net. Double rooms, with fans and heaters, shared bathroom, separate toilet. Plus a garden cottage that can sleep 4, with a fridge and microwave, and a family room sleeping 4. TV lounge for communal use, breakfasts served in the homely dining room. All set in a landscaped garden. A short walk from the **Bridge Lodge** restaurant for evening meals. Good value, recommended.

Spionkop Dam Nature Reserve *p449*

B Spionkop Lodge, on the R600 between Winterton and Ladysmith, T036-4881404, www.spionkop.co.za. This delightful country lodge makes for an excellent base from which to explore the surroundings. 15 comfortable double rooms, fully inclusive, set on a farm close to Spionkop. Owner Raymond Heron is a vivid story teller and excellent guide to the area. Can also arrange canoe rides on the nearby Tugela River, birdwatching trips to Spionkop Dam and horse riding (including Battlefield tours on horseback). Recommended.

D Iphika Tented Bush Camp, KZN Wildlife, T033- 8451000, www.kzn wildlife.com. Can sleep up to 4 in 2 large 2-bed tents and also has a stone and thatch lounge area with fireplace and kitchen. It is set on the slopes of Spionkop Mountain overlooking a small waterhole and it is possible to go on game walks from here; Spionkop battlefield is a short walk away, up a steep slope.

D-E Bungalows, KZN Wildlife, T033-8451000, www.kznwildlife.com. 3 chalets, each with 3 twin bedrooms and fully equipped kitchen. Visitors need to bring their own food and drink. The closest shops are in Winterton, 14 km away.

Camping

30 sites next to the dam with power points, slip ways for launching of boats, popular with anglers. Reservations direct with the officer, T036-4881578.

Cathedral Peak *p449, map p450*

A-B Cathedral Peak Hotel, at the end of the road past the entry gates, T036-4881888, www.cathedralpeak.co.za. An all-round resort, popular for weddings in its own stone chapel, traditionally used as a base by hikers and climbers because of its stunning location close to the high peaks of the Drakensberg. 90 luxurious double rooms, several restaurants and bars, 3 swimming pools, 9-hole floodlit golf course, horse riding, squash, jogging and mountain bike trail, 10-m climbing tower, gym, beauty spa, and tennis. It is one of South Africa's most popular destinations and booking in advance is essential all year.

B-C Didima Camp, on the road leading into Cathedral Peak, just before **Cathedral Peak Hotel**, KZN Wildlife, T033-8451000, www.kznwildlife.com. The camp is themed around the art of the San people and the thatched chalets have been designed to look like caves. 63 2-bed self-catering units built back to back so can be converted into 4-bed units using a connecting door, 1 6-bed chalet and a honeymoon suite. All have satellite TV and fireplace, and there's a central restaurant, bar and small shop. The conference centre/wedding chapel has a full height glass wall framing a view of Cathedral Peak. Also the location of the **Rock Art Centre** (see page 451).

Camping

There are 21 sites opposite the information office This is a secluded campsite up in the mountains with a quiet, tranquil feel to it. The facilities here are simple: there is only an ablution block for campers. The campsite is popular so it is advisable to book up to a month in advance. Camp gates are open daily from 0600-1800, and until 2100 on Fri. There are also at least 15 caves near here in which hikers can camp. They should be booked well in advance. Reservations through the officer in charge, T036-4888000.

Monk's Cowl *p451, map p452*

All the accommodation listed below is outside the park and signposted off the R600. The distances shown are from each hotel to the entrance to Monk's Cowl.

A **Champagne Castle**, 2 km, T036-4681063, www.champagnecastle.co.za. Traditional Drakensberg resort in a spectacular mountain setting, with 47 luxurious rooms plus some self-catering cottages, set in the main lodge and annexes with thatched roofs, surrounded by attractive leafy grounds. Restaurant, horse riding, tennis, swimming pool.

A **Champagne Sports Resort**, 9 km, T036-4681088, www.champagnesports resort.com. Large sporty resort with beautiful views, attracting weekenders from Gauteng and Durban. 62 newly refurbished rooms with bright furnishings, stylish bathrooms and private balconies. Impressive 18-hole golf course, large buffet restaurant, sports bar, 4 swimming pools, tennis, squash, horse riding, gym and beauty salon. Also has timeshare bungalows. Pleasant, typically South African family resort.

A **The Nest**, 13 km, T036-4681068, www.the nest.co.za. 55 guestrooms in thatched rondavels with private verandas and views of the mountains, bright furnishings and wood furniture. Restaurant, bar, guest lounges, swimming pool, bowls, horse riding. Rates include all meals as well as afternoon tea; good base for exploring the area.

B **Ardmore Guest Farm**, T036-4681314, www.ardmore.co.za. Superb views with lovely gardens overlooking a dam. Mix of B&B, full board or self-catering in 8 double en suite rooms. Popular with anglers for the dam fishing, where you can also canoe. Good local reputation for home-cooked meals, plus known for its ceramic art studio – worth a visit, with a tea garden on site. Recommended by several readers.

B **Dragon Peaks** , 4 km, T036-4681031, www.dragonpeaks.com. Mix of B&B and self-catering chalets with TV, plus a camp and caravan site. Popular restaurant with outdoor lapa area. Good facilities for families, including 2 swimming pools, tennis, and horse riding, plus a wide range of organized entertainment. There is a small supermarket here and a petrol pump.

C-D **Inkosana Lodge**, 7 km, easy access via a good surfaced road, T036-4681202, www.inkosana.co.za. Simple lodge with fine views towards the mountains, set in a large garden with a swimming pool. 4 small dorms, double rooms, some en suite, rondavels and camping. Large dining area with hearty homemade meals on request, kitchen available for self-catering. Tours, email access, laundry, horse riding, evening meals, large modern bungalow. Guided hikes lasting up to several days can be organized from here. Free collection from the Baz Bus in Winterton. Short walk to shops and restaurants.

D **Cathkin Cottage**, 13 km, after the **Drakensberg Sun** hotel, turn right into Yellowood Dr, T036-4681513, www.cathkin cottage.co.za. Simple double rooms and family units with en suite facilities and private entrances. Some rooms have fridge and TV, small pool and pretty garden. Good breakfasts served. Secure parking. Val and Ian can organize guided walks.

Camping

There are 15 pitches, some with electric points, and an ablution block bordered with indigenous trees and shrubs next to the camp office. Reservations for this campsite should be made through the officer in charge, T036-4681103.

Giant's Castle Reserve *p452, map p 453*

B Rock Lodge, KZN Wildlife, T033-8451000, www.kznwildlife.com. Up the valley and secluded from the hutted camp, sleeping up to 6 people with TV, luxurious lodge with its own cook that prepares food brought by the guests. Uninterrupted views of the Giant's Castle peaks, and the highlight is the honeymoon suite built into the side of a massive rock.

B-D White Mountain Resort, on the road to Giant's Castle and Hillside from Estcourt, T036-3533437, www.whitemountain.co.za. Family holiday camp, full-board rooms, self-catering chalets, dorms, camping and caravan sites, pool, bar, restaurant. The resort is self-contained and offers a wide range of organized activities, but is a long distance from the higher parts of the Drakensberg. There is a small supermarket and petrol is also available.

C Giant's Castle camp, KZN Wildlife, T033-8451000, www.kznwildlife.com, Recently revamped camp, 50 chalets with between 2 to 6 beds, lounge and dining area and fully equipped kitchen. Self-catering or fully catered. Shop sells a wide range of books and curios but only a limited selection of dried and frozen food. The camp is popular all year and accommodation tends to be full at weekends. **Izimbali** restaurant and pub. Swimming in summer is permitted in the Bushmen's River below the camp.

C-E Injisuthi camp, KZN Wildlife, T033-8451000, www.kznwildlife.com. 16 6-bed chalets, fully equipped for self-catering with gas stove and fridge, no plug points. Also basic 8-bed dormitory cabins. Electricity between 1730 and 2200 only. There is no shop here so visitors need to bring all supplies with them.

Camping

There are 20 sites at Injisuthi camp that can accommodate 120 people, 3 2-bed pre-erected tents, and shared ablution blocks. Reservations direct, T036-3553775. **Lower Injisuthi Cave**, **Upper Injisuthi Cave** and **Grindstone Cave**, can all be used by hikers for overnight stops but should be reserved in advance. No fires allowed, very basic facilities. Come well-equipped. Reservations T036-3553775.

Mountain huts

There are 4 mountain huts about 4-5 hrs walk from Giant's Castle camp: Giant's Hut, Centenary Hut and Bannerman Hut sleep 8 people each, and Meander Hut sleeps 4. All the huts are at an altitude of around 2000 m and can get very cold at night. Bunks and mattresses are provided. Reservations through **KZN Wildlife**, T033-8451000, www.kznwildlife.com.

Kamberg Nature Reserve *p455*

It is possible to camp on overnight hikes but you need to be fully equipped.

C Main Camp, KZN Wildlife, T033-8451000, www.kznwildlife.com. 7 self-catering chalets with 2-6 beds. Kitchenettes and a communal lounge area.

D Stillerus Rustic Cottage, 8 km from the main camp, KZN Wildlife, T033-8451000, www.kzn wildlife.com. 1 cottage with 8 beds, for a minimum of 6. Self-catering and fully equipped with a gas stove, a fridge and gas lighting. Bring your own bedding.

E Drakensberg International Backpackers Lodge, T033-2637241, wildchild@telkomsa.net. The actual address is 'Grace Valley Farm' on the Highmoor Rd; there are signposts but call for directions if you don't have a good road map. 18 dorm beds, 2 double rooms, camping, TV lounge, kitchen, bar, email facility, laundry service, horse riding, evening meals provided. Lovely farm surrounded by mountains. Owned by Lionel who runs local tours, pick-up from the Baz Bus at Mooi River Wimpy, also offers shuttle service to Durban for groups.

Towards Underberg *p456*

E Reichenau Mission, T033-7012976, www.reichenau.co.za, halfway between Bulwer and Underberg, 2 km of gravel road off the R617. A simple guest cottage sleeping up to 20. Bed linen provided. There is a large kitchen with cold water, gas cooker, fridge and cutlery, a lounge and dining area. You either need to bring your own food or give advance notice for Western-style or traditional Zulu food to be prepared.

Underberg *p456, map p464*

B-C Elgin, Bushman's Nek Valley, T033-7011918, www.elginholidayfarm.co.za. 4 luxurious suites set in wings attached to a farmhouse, en suite, TV, attractive decor. Also has a self-catering log cabin sleeping 10, all set on a working farm, with organic dairy and vegetables for sale.

C **Rocky Mountain Lodge**, T033-7011676, www.rockylodge.co.za. 4 self-catering log cabins sleeping 2-12 people, B&B also an option. Magnificently positioned on a mountain plateau, with beautiful views and a peaceful setting overlooking the Mzimkulu River. Private feel with cosy log fires.

D **Torridon**, on the road to Bushman's Nek, T033-7011637, www.torridon.co.za. B&B in a quiet location, double rooms for up to 8 people, the lodge overlooks the Mzimkulu River, trout fishing and swimming.

Himeville *p456, map p456*

C-D **Ripon Country Cottage**, contact the Rose & Quail, T033-7021154, www.ripon cottage.com. Self-catering or B&B accommodation on a rose and cherry farm north of Himeville, sleeps up to 10, fully self-catering, popular with 4WD owners.

C-E **Himeville Arms**, Arbuckle St, T033-7021305, www.himevillehotel.co.za. Old-fashioned, 100-year-old hotel. Rooms can be rather gloomy in summer, but are cosy in winter thanks to well-stocked log fires. Cheaper backpacker beds available in shared rooms. Good lunchtime bar menu in the **Arms Pub**, plus 2 restaurants.

Cobham *p457*

Reservations for campsites, trail huts and caves should be made through the Cobham officer in charge T033-7020831. The campsite here is very basic with an open area for setting up tents and you need to be totally self-sufficient. There are 8 toilets but no showers though campers may swim in the river below the campsite if it's not too cold.

Sani Pass *p457*

A-B **Sani Pass Hotel**, Sani Pass Rd, 22 km from Underberg, T033-7021320, www.sani passhotel.co.za. A large resort hotel offering accommodation either in the hotel building or in luxury cottages in the gardens. Sporting facilities include squash, fly-fishing, tennis, bowls, riding and swimming. The restaurant has a reasonably priced set menu. Beautiful location, but slightly overpriced.

C-D **Sani Top Chalet**, top of the pass, next to the Lesotho border post, T033-7021158 or T082-7151131 (mob), www.sanitop chalet.co.za. A combination of double rooms in the main building or backpacker bunks in rondavels out back. You can camp but you'll need thermals. The hotel has a licensed pub (the highest in Africa) and dining room warmed by roaring wood fires, overlooking the dramatic road below. Fantastic hikes and pony trekking to some awesome viewpoints along the escarpment. When it does snow it is possible to hire skis from the hotel.

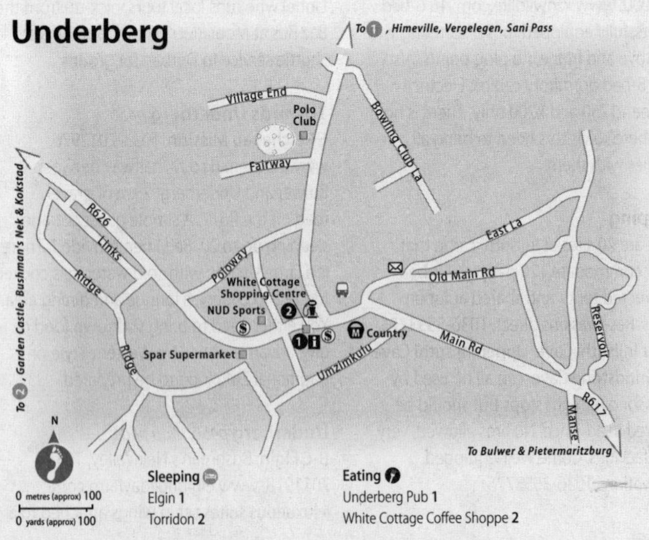

They are currently building more upmarket accommodation on site.

D-E Sani Lodge, 19 km from Underberg on the Sani Pass road, call for collection from Underberg, T033-7020330, www.sanilodge.co.za. If you are coming from Pietermaritzburg, travel with Sani Pass Carriers, see page 468 for details, who drop off here. This is one of the best backpackers away from the big towns in South Africa. There are 4 small dorms, 5 large double rooms with pine ceilings and good insulation, 2 private rondavels, a 22-bed dorm, and plenty of space to pitch a tent, outside hot shower with tremendous views of the mountains. Large kitchen, comfortable lounge with open fire for the winter months when it can get very cold, and a veranda with a superb uninterrupted view of the Drakensberg escarpment. Great meals served. Run by Russell and Simone who are experts on hiking in Lesotho. Simone also offers aromatherapy massages. Recommended.

Mkhomazi Wilderness Area
p458, map p

Reservations for all accommodation are made through **KZN Wildlife**, T033-8451000, www.kznwildlife.com.

C Lotheni, 2 self-catering cottages with 6 beds, and 12 self-catering bungalows, with 2 or 3 beds. All the accommodation is fully equipped; there are 2 freezers in the camp kitchen which can be used by guests, electricity from 1700-2200 only.

C Simes Rustic Cottage, sleeps 10, although the minimum charge is for 6 people. The small dam nearby has been stocked with brown trout and is exclusively for the use of visitors staying at the cottage. The cottage has a gas supply but visitors are expected to bring their own bedding, gas lamps and torches.

Camping

The 10 sites at **Lotheni**, T033-7020540, are a secluded 2 km from the hutted camp and it's a beautiful spot. The only facility is an ablution block with hot and cold water. It is possible to camp overnight within the **Verlegen** reserve on long-distance hikes.

Garden Castle *p459*

There are 3 rustic huts on the Giant's Cup Hiking Trail. Each can accommodate up to 30 people. During the winter months hikers are strongly advised to stay in these huts as there can be heavy snowfalls and very cold conditions. There are 10 camping sites and an ablution block near to the park entrance as well as 12 caves in the park available to hikers. Campsites, caves and huts should be booked in advance through the camp office T033-7011823.

B-D Penwarn Country Lodge, T033-7011417, www.penwarn.com. 2 luxury lodges close to Bushman's Nek, 25 km from Underberg. Choice of en suite bedrooms or simple self-catering log cabins. This is a comfortable mountain farm offering a wide range of activities: canoeing, fly-fishing, clay pigeon shooting, archery, mountain biking and hiking. Excellent food served in a colonial-style restaurant, and a homely atmosphere during the winter months.

Eating

All the large mountain resorts have restaurants and bars on site. Much of the other accommodation is self-catering; as a result there is a lack of choice for eating out in the region.

Bergville *p448*

Candles & Antiques, T036- 4481339. Craft shop with a little coffee shop, good for a simple sandwich or tea and cake.

Winterton *p449*

Purple House, 10 Springfield St, T036-4881025. The restaurant attached to **Lilac Cottage** (see Sleeping page 461). South African home-cooked meals, light lunches, afternoon teas and cool drinks.

Thokosiza Centre, T036-4881273, on the R100, 13 km west of Winterton. Coffee shop and restaurant in this cultural/craft/tourist centre, popular spot for a light lunch or mid-afternoon tea, with pleasant wooden tables on a shady deck. Closed evenings.

Underberg *p456, map p464*

Underberg Pub, Underberg Hotel, Main Rd. Pub grub and bar meals just like a pub in England. This is where the local farmers come to drink, there's sport on the satellite TV, rock music and plenty of beer, for a good meal try the freshly grilled trout.

White Cottage Coffee Shoppe, White Cottage Shopping Centre, T033-7011589. A rustic tea room serving light snacks.

Himeville *p456, map p456*

Moorcroft Manor, Sani Rd, T033-7021967. Restaurant within a luxury lodge, stylish dining room with beautiful terrace. Suitably upmarket menu with a French feel. Bookings are essential.

Entertainment

Monk's Cowl *p451, map p452*

Drakensberg Boys' Choir, T036-4681012, concerts@dbdchoir.co.za. During term-time, the choir performs on Wed at 1530 in the school's impressive auditorium. Bookings are essential.

Festivals and events

Underberg *p456, map p464*

Apr/May Splashy Fen Festival, www.splashyfen.co.za. A popular music festival held on Splashy Fen Farm. Over the years it has increased in size and it now attracts a broad selection of modern musicians as well as South Africa's folk crowd.

Shopping

Bergville *p448*

There are several supermarkets in town to stock up in before heading into the reserves. The shops at the campsites stock only the most basic supplies. Outside the centre, look out for farms selling fresh produce.

Tevreden Cheese, take the R74 out of the village towards the Northern Berg, take a left turn after approximately 7 km, T036-4481840. Cheesemaking farm with tastings, a good spot to stock up before a hike.

Winterton *p449*

There are several craft shops along the R600 to Champagne Valley and Monk's Cowl.

Cheesery, 6 Springfield Rd, T036-4881296. Farm shop specializing in various cheeses, free tastings.

KwaZulu Weavers, 12 km west of Winterton on the R600, T036-4881098, www.kwazuluweavers.com. Colourful handwoven rugs made from wool and mohair. Attached is a popular handmade candle shop.

Rainbow Room, off the R600 just after the Nest Hotel, heading towards Monk's Cowl, T036-4681801. An unusual selection of handmade crafts; unfortunately, the larger pieces are a bit too big to take home for overseas visitors. Run by Inger.

Thokozisa, on the R600, 13 km west of Winterton, T036-4881273. A one-stop tourist centre (the **Central Drakensberg Information Centre** is here) with shops selling arts and crafts and wines, and a coffee shop.

Cathedral Peak *p449, map p450*

The shop at Mike's Pass sells a limited range of basic groceries, otherwise the nearest supermarket is at Winterton. Petrol can be bought at the **Cathedral Peak Hotel**.

Giant's Castle Reserve *p452, p 453*

Petrol is for sale by the main gate. There is a farm shop next to the park gates selling fresh and smoked trout, otherwise the nearest supermarket is in Estcourt.

Underberg *p456, map p464*

There are a number of craft shops and a coffee shop in the **White Cottage Shopping Centre**, a mini shopping mall with a rather twee white picket fence.

Activities and tours

uKhahlamba-Drakensberg Park *p440*

Climbing

The Drakensberg is a relatively undiscovered mountain range – due largely to the sports boycott imposed on South Africa during the Apartheid era. Today, the mountains are becoming increasingly accessible and present challenging climbing.

Mountain Club of South Africa, T082-9905877 (mob), www.kzn.mcsa.org.za. A useful source of information.

Fishing

Trout were introduced into the rivers of the Drakensberg around the turn of the last century and over the years fly-fishing has become popular. Fishing licences are available from **KZN Wildlife**, T033-8451000, www.kznwildlife.com.

Golf

In good weather, the backdrop for each is spectacular. Green fees are very reasonable; call in advance to check on availability of equipment hire. There are courses at the **Cathedral Peak Hotel**, T036-4881888, 9 holes; **Monk's Cowl Country Club**, T036-4681300, 9 holes; and the **Champagne Sports Resort**, T036-4681088, 18 holes. The **Hlalanathi Golf Club**, T036-4386852, 9 holes, is in Royal Natal National Park.

Hang-gliding and paragliding

Wildsky Adventures, Bulwer, 50 km west of Pietermaritzburg, T082-7488637, www.wildsky.co.za. Courses or one-off tandem glides. Also offers a number of other activities, including abseiling, horse riding or fishing, and has simple accommodation in log cabins available to those who are undertaking paragliding courses.

Helicopter flights

There is an airfield opposite the **Champagne Sports Resort** (see page 462) from where you can take short helicopter flights over the mountains. Bookings can be made at the **Cathedral Peak Hotel, Champagne Sports Resort**, or the **Drakensberg Sun**. A 20-min scenic flight should cost R490 per person; book at hotel reception.

Horse riding

The full length of the Berg is negotiable on horseback, by way of trails and bridleways. Riding is available in the KZN Wildlife parks of **Rugged Glen** and **Spionkop** and can be arranged at the parks offices. Trips into the mountains of the **Royal Natal National Park** are available from Rugged Glen and cost roughly R50 per hour. The rides are very popular during the holiday period and it is best to book in advance at the stables, T036-4386422. Day trips on horseback are also available from the hotels at **Sani Pass, Drakensberg Gardens, Bushman's Nek** and **Coleford Nature Reserve**. In the **Royal Natal National Park**, trips from many of the large resort hotels on the boundaries of the national park offer riding as an activity, and several include overnight adventure rides for groups of 5 or more into the parks. Contact the local tourist office or ask the people where you are staying to point you in the direction of the nearest operator, of which there are many. **Khotso Horse Trails**, Bergvlei Farm, 10 km from Underberg towards Drakensberg Gardens, T033- 7011502, www.khotso trails.co.za. Mountain rides for beginners and advanced riders, specialist adventure rides and cattle round-ups. Accommodation is available in dorms in a log cabin with shared kitchen and bathroom or in self-catering thatched chalets.

Ice climbing

In winter, there is the possibility of ice climbing the **Lotheni Falls**, which are usually frozen from mid-June to mid-Aug. This is strictly for experienced mountaineers only, with full equipment, including an ice pick. Contact one of the regional tourism offices, or camp office at Giant's Castle, T036-3533718, for details.

Mountain biking

Mountain biking has become hugely popular in recent years. 3 areas of the Drakensberg have designated biking trails: **Cathedral Peak, Champagne Valley** and **Underberg**. There are 70 km of dirt roads in the Cathedral Peak area which can be used by mountain bikers. The routes are by no means extreme but they pass through some spectacular scenery. The views from the top of Mike's Pass are as exhilarating, as is the 5-km ride back down.

The route from Underberg to **Sani Pass** and back is one of South Africa's epic mountain bike rides. The 20-km climb up to the Lesotho border is a challenging ascent along a trail cut out of the rock. The altitude at the highest point of the trail is around 2800 m from where there are spectacular views over the sheer cliffs and gorges of the Mkhomazana Valley. There are also a number of more sedate rides around Underberg itself.

A 75-km Mountain Bike Challenge is held at **Giant's Castle** annually on the last Sun in Apr. Check www.ultimatemtb.org.za for further details.

Tour operators

Most of the Drakensberg National Park is more or less inaccessible to travellers who have not hired a car. Based in Underberg, **Major Adventures**, T033-7011628, www.majoradventures.com, **Sani Pass Tours**, T033-7011064, www.sanipasstours.com, and **Thaba Tours**, T033- 7012888, www.thabatours.co.za, all offer daily 4WD day trips to the top of Sani Pass. **Drakensberg Adventures**, Sani Pass Lodge, T033-7021401, www.sanilodge.co.za. Great selection of tours in area, including an overnight trip into Lesotho. Russell is a formidable guide for the Sani Pass excursion and local hikes. On offer are 4WD tours, hikes to San rock art, horse riding and visits to local Zulu families where you can spend the night. Guided climbs of Thabana Ntlenyana (Africa's 2nd tallest mountain) also organized.

Transport

Northern Drakensberg *p446, map p450*
Baz Bus, T021-4392323, www.bazbus.com, runs from **Ampitheatre Backpackers** in Oliviershoek Pass to **Johannesburg** and **Durban**.

Central Drakensberg *p448, map p450*
Baz Bus, T021-4392323, www.bazbus0.com, runs in both directions between **Johannesburg** and **Durban**, drops off and picks up outside of the First National Bank in Winterton.

Southern Drakensberg *p455*
Sani Pass Carriers, bookings T033-7011017, runs between **Underberg**, **Himeville**, **Sani Pass** and **Pietermaritzburg**. The minibuses pick up from **Sani Lodge**, **Sani Pass Hotel**, the **Himeville Arms** and the **Underberg Hotel**, every morning, and drop off and pick up from the **Ngena Backpackers** and the **Protea Imperial Hotel** in Pietermaritzburg. They arrive back in Underberg early the same afternoon.

Directory

Bergville *p448*
Banks First National Bank, South St, T036-4481037. **Useful telephone numbers** Police T10177.

Zululand

Zululand, homeland of Shaka and one of the most evocative regions of South Africa, will forever be associated with the classic movie starring Michael Caine as the redoubtable British officer fighting Zulu warriors. Today, this region – extending from the northern bank of the Tugela River up to Mkuze and Maputaland – is rather more peaceful and offers long, unspoilt beaches, excellent game reserves and a chance to experience traditional Zulu culture. Gone are the vast herds of migrating elephant, wildebeest and springbok, victim in part to the many battles fought over this wealthy province. Despite being one of the more traditional areas of South Africa, it has thriving industrial cities and vast areas of sugarcane and eucalyptus plantations. However, game reserves at St Lucia and Hluhluwe-Umfolozi are still natural magnets for tourists and around six per cent of KwaZulu Natal is managed by KZN Wildlife as conservation areas. For more information on the region visit www.zululand.kzn.org.za. ▸▸ *For Sleeping, Eating and other listings, see pages 481-487.*

Elephant Coast ▸▸ *pp481-487.*

Ins and outs

The route into the Zulu heartland follows the N2 north from Stanger to the village of Gingindlovu. From here the R68 goes inland to Eshowe (26 km), Ulundi and the Battlefield sites (see page 430), while the N2 continues up the coast to Mtunzini, Empangeni, Richards Bay, Hluhluwe-Umfolozi, St Lucia and Maputaland. This is the most popular area of Zululand, and was recently renamed the Elephant Coast – thanks to the reintroduction of elephant in sections of the Greater St Lucia Wetland Park. There are a number game farms in the area offering luxury accommodation, while scuba diving and deep-sea fishing are available in the coastal resorts. The region has a subtropical climate; it is hot and humid from December to March and warm and dry from April to November.

Gingindlovu and around → *Colour map 5, grid B2.*

Gingindlovu was originally a military kraal established by Cetshwayo after the Battle of Ndondakusuka where he defeated his half-brother Mbulazi and gained control of the Zulu Kingdom. Today Gingindlovu is a small commercial centre surrounded by farmland and sugarcane plantations.

Six kilometres from Gingindhlovu on the coast is the entrance to **Amatigulu Nature Reserve** ⓘ *T032-4530155, open sunrise to sunset, R10*. The reserve is 100 km from Durban and covers approximately 2000 ha of forested dunes overlooking the sea and is a beautiful place to combine game watching with a beach holiday. Unlike the other small reserves in this area, Amatigulu does have some big game since giraffe, zebra and waterbuck have been reintroduced; it is the one of the few places to see animals grazing close to the sea. Bush baby and large-spotted genet are frequently seen around the camp at night and the Nyoni River attracts the elusive African finfoot and other unusual waterbirds. There are game drives and walking trails but the most interesting way to see the reserve is by canoeing up the Amatigulu River; canoes can be hired from the camp office. A newer addition in the reserve is a whale-watching tower built on the dunes.

Eshowe and inland » *pp481-487. Colour map 5, grid B2.*

Eshowe is a historical inland town named after the sound of a breeze passing through bushes. Situated on a hill, the town has pleasant views over Dlinza forest and is an administrative centre for the surrounding sugarcane growing region. Although there's little within town for visitors, this makes a good base for taking a cultural tour of Zululand. The historical origins of Eshowe are based around a kraal called Eziqwaqweni which was established here by Cetshwayo. In 1860 the Norwegian missionary, Reverend Oftebro, was allowed to open a mission station here which was occupied by the British in 1879 while they planned an attack on Ulundi. The Zulus briefly gained the upper hand here when they laid siege to the garrison for 10 weeks. Eshowe was relieved by Lord Chelmsford in April 1879, but not before the Zulus had managed to burn the mission station down.

Dlinza Forest ⓘ *T035-4744029, www.zbr.co.za/boardwalk, Sep-Apr daily 0600-1800, May-Aug daily 0800-1700, small entry fee includes guide*, is next to the municipal caravan park. It is a 250-ha area of dense hardwood forest, ferns and creepers where Shaka supposedly hid his wives and children during attacks. There are two short walking trails here through orchids, wild plum and milkwood trees, and knarled vines that are clearly labelled, which in turn attract a number of birds and butterflies. Dhlinza is great for birdwatchers, with 65 species recorded in the forest, including the endangered spotted thrush and Delegorgue's Pigeon. A recent addition, and the first of its kind in South Africa, is a 125-m wheelchair-accessible aerial timber boardwalk, which takes you through the treeline to the 20-m viewing platform that overlooks the canopy of the forest.

On Fort Nongqai Road is the **Zululand Historical Museum** ⓘ *daily 0900-1600, entry by donation*. Fort Nongqai was built in 1883 and served as a residence for the Natal Native Police who acted as bodyguards for Sir Melmoth Osborn, the Resident

Gingindlovu means 'the swallower of the elephant', although the British used to call it 'Gin-Gin-I-love-you'.

for British Zululand. It is a square fort with high towers on each corner. The museum has displays on John Dunn and his 49 wives and on the Bambata rebellion, as well as a number of Zulu items. John Dunn was the first European settler in what is now KwaZulu Natal. He became an honorary chief and was granted land by the Zulus, ruled at the time by Cetshwayo. His 49 wives gave him 117 children. Given this statistic, not surprisingly the surname Dunn is still very common in this region.

The northern KwaZulu Natal coast is a low risk malarial area.

Vukani Collection Museum ⓘ *T035-4745274, Mon-Fri 0900-1500, small donation*, is housed in a purpose-built centre in the grounds of Fort Nongqayi. While there are antique items on display, this is actually an exhibition of the Vukani Association – a body of over 1000 Zulu craftspeople run and owned by the crafters themselves to manage the pricing and quality of their products. It is quite probably the largest display of Zulu art in existence with some 3000 to 4000 pieces on display. Some of the exhibits are by award-winning artists and include carvings, pottery, colourful basketry, and the famous Zulu beadwork.

Zululand game reserves

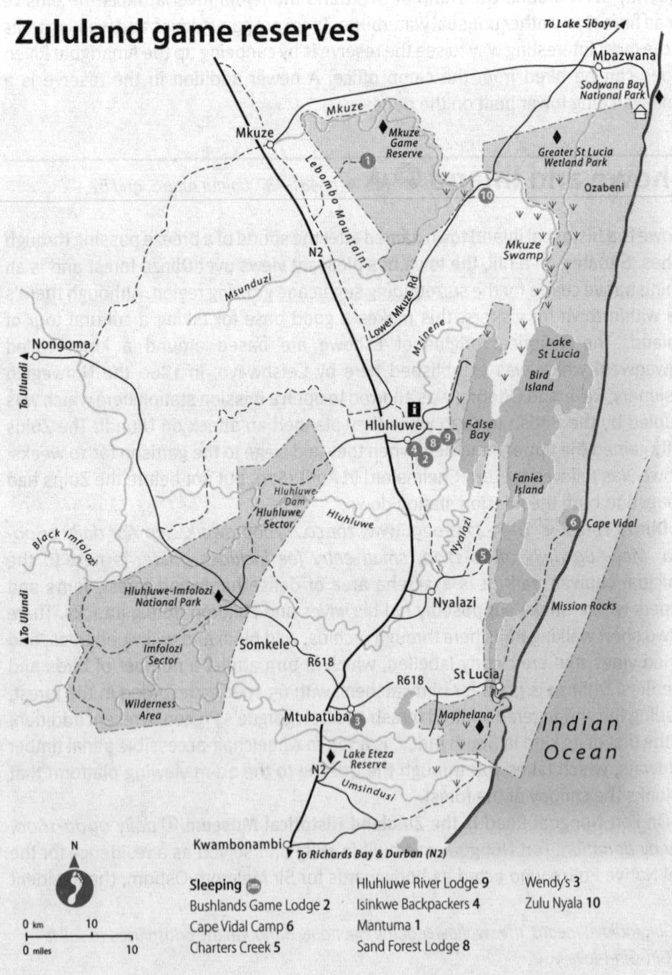

Sleeping
Bushlands Game Lodge 2
Cape Vidal Camp 6
Charters Creek 5
Hluhluwe River Lodge 9
Isinkwe Backpackers 4
Mantuma 1
Sand Forest Lodge 8
Wendy's 3
Zulu Nyala 10

North of Eshowe

From Eshowe the R66 heads north through the **Nkwalini Valley** to **Melmoth** (52 km). **Shakaland** ⓘ *signposted off the R66, 14 km north of Eshowe, T035-4600912, www.shakaland.com, 2- to 3-hr tours throughout the day, R250*, is a very popular Zulu theme park with daily cultural shows, which include Zulu dancing and tours of a traditional village where tribal customs such as spearmaking, the beer ceremony and Sangoma rituals are explained. This is a reconstruction of a 19th-century village but it doesn't give a very authentic insight into how the Zulu people live today. However, the food isn't bad and a lunch in the **Shisa Nyama Restaurant** is included.

The **Protea Simunye Zulu Lodge** is about 30 km out of Eshowe; look out for a left turning, marked with a wagon wheel and a large 'S', on to the D256. This road will take you to another popular Zululand stop, a lodge hosted by the Biyela clan, offering a marginally more authentic introduction to Zulu culture. Follow the gravel road for 12 km until you reach an old trading store. This is the assembly point for guests before they are taken down to the lodge on horseback (for accommodation, see page 481). West of Melmouth, Central Zululand is famous for its rich cultural heritage. The museums and battlefield sites are the main attractions and are the best way to gain an insight into the region's history. » *For further details, see pages 430-440.*

! The R66 north of Eshowe is notorious for having one of the highest rates of carjacking in KwaZulu Natal province.

Mtunzini and around » *pp481-487.*

→ *Colour map 5, grid B2*

Mtunzini means 'the shady place' and is a pleasant town at the mouth of the Umlalazi River facing the lagoon, 18 km from Gingindhlovu, set in an area of coastal forest and mangrove swamps. John Dunn, who had become a Zulu chief in his own right and was one of Cetshwayo's advisors, lived here with his 49 wives and 117 children.

Umlalazi Nature Reserve

ⓘ *132 km north of Durban, 1 km east of Mtunzini, daily 0500-2200, R10.*

Signposted from the N2, this is a small nature reserve but it is popular with South African tourists and, when full, can accommodate at least 300 people, who come here for fishing, windsurfing and the beaches. There are no shark nets. The natural ambience of the 1028-ha reserve is best felt when it is less crowded and it is easier to appreciate the long tropical beaches and walks along the banks of the lagoon and mangrove swamps. There's good fishing in the lagoon and Mlalazi River but crocodiles and sharks are present. Other wildlife includes red, grey and blue duiker, and bushbuck.

Empangeni and around » *pp481-487.*

→ *Colour map 5, grid B2*

Empangeni is named after the Zulu word of 'pangaed' meaning grabbed – due to many people being taken by crocs on the banks of the Mpangeni River, on which the town is situated. Shaka grew up in this area before the Norwegian Missionary Society mission station opened in 1851. The town has developed into a busy industrial centre and has been pulping wood since the first eucalyptus plantations were established in 1905. While many visitors pass through on their way between St Lucia and the Battlefields, there is nothing to merit a stop. Nor is there any reason to follow the R34 east from Empangeni, crossing the N2, towards Richards Bay (18 km), although those using Richards Bay airport might pass through this flat plantation landscape, loomed over by clusters of pylons and the ugly chimneys of industrial complexes. The N2, meanwhile, allows a quick escape north to St Lucia (80 km), and Hluhluwe-Umfolozi (106 km).

 Ins and outs This area is undergoing a series of name changes. Officially Empangeni and Richards Bay, 18 km away, have now joined together as one municipal area, referred to jointly as the city of **uMhlathuze**. It will be some time before this change is reflected on maps or signposts so, for the purposes of this guide, the old names are used, despite the fact that the towns share many of the same facilities.

Game reserves

Thula Thula Private Game Reserve ⓘ *T035-7928322, www.thulathula.com*, west of Empangeni and north of the small village of Heatonville, makes for an excellent stopover for those who have missed the larger parks further north. Take the R34 for 8 km before turning onto the road to Heatonville, which is a further 10 km. Thula Thula is signposted down a gravel road from Heatonville. The reserve is a large private game reserve in the Enselini Valley, originally part of King Shaka's hunting ground. It was converted from farmland in 1964, and the present owners offer exclusive accommodation, game drives and bush walks through rolling, acacia-covered thornveld. Some of the larger mammals you can expect to see are white rhino, elephant, giraffe, kudu, nyala and other antelopes and, if you're lucky, a leopard. Cheetahs are being introduced in 2006, and there are plans to take down the fences between here and Hluhluwe-Impfolozi National Park, creating a huge wildlife area, and bringing the Big Five to Thula Thula.

Enselini Nature Reserve ⓘ *T035-7920034, 17 km north of Empangeni on the N2, sunrise to sunset, free*, is a small, 293-ha reserve on the banks of the Enselini River, run by KZN Wildlife. The **Nkonikini Trail**, 7 km, passes along raised platforms over the swamp and through grasslands where game has been reintroduced. Here you can see hippo, crocodile, giraffe, nyala, waterbuck, wildebeest and zebra. The shorter **Mvuvu Trail** passes through similar terrain. This is an interesting reserve to visit and a good chance to break the monotony of driving through the vast plantations that line the N2. At the reception centre there is a picnic site, where maps and information leaflets are available.

Richards Bay → *Colour map 5, grid B2*

Richards Bay, a modern rash of a town, focuses entirely on its enormous industrial port, soon to be the largest in Southern Africa. The port exports mineral ores and coal, and massive tankers arrive here to discharge oil for Gauteng through the oil pipeline; this is the first port of call for ships coming from Asia and Suez. Characterized by a series of vast industrial plants and featureless highways (albeit skirting around a pretty series of canals and a lagoon), the only reason for coming here is to use the small airport (see page 487), and then hire a car to speed up the coast to the parks.

Hluhluwe-Imfolozi National Park » *pp481-487.*

→ *Colour map 5, grid A2.*

This is one of Africa's oldest game reserves and one of the few parks in KwaZulu Natal where you can see the Big Five. What were traditionally two reserves have been joined into one national park. Hluhluwe is named after the umHluhluwe or 'thorny rope', a climber which is found in the forests of this area. The aerial roots hanging from the sycamore figs where the Black Umfolozi and the White Umfolozi rivers meet give the area its name. Imfolozi is named after 'uMfula walosi' or the 'river of fibres'. The park has a variety of landscapes – thick forests, dry bushveld and open savannah – that are home to a number of species of game, including healthy populations of rhino and the rare nyala. What is unusual about the park is the hilly terrain, which provides a great vantage point for game viewing.

Ins and outs

Getting there Hluhluwe-Imfolozi is 280 km north of Durban just off the N2. There is a turning at Mtubatuba leading west on the R618 (50 km) to the **Imfolozi sector** ⓘ *Oct-Mar 0500-1900, Apr-Sep 0600-1800, office daily 0800-1230, 1400-1630, conservation levy (per day) R90*, and a turning opposite the exit to Hluhluwe village, which leads (14 km) to the northern Memorial Gate entrance to the **Hluhluwe sector** ⓘ *same hours and levys as above, camp reception at Hilltop daily 0700-1930*. This is an easy park to visit on a day trip if you are staying in the Maputaland or St Lucia regions.

Best time to visit The best time to see the park is between March and November. The park's vegetation is lush during the summer months, when the weather is hot and humid, but this makes it more difficult to see the game. During the winter months the climate is cool and dry and you might even need a sweater in the evenings. Animals congregates at the waterholes and rivers at this time of year and the lack of vegetation makes it easier to see them.

Background

The confluence of the Black and White Umfolozi rivers is where the Zulu king Shaka dug his hunting pits. Once a year game was driven into the area and would fall into the pits, where it was speared by young warriors eager to prove their courage. Consequently, Hluhluwe-Umfolozi was established as a protected area as long ago as 1895. Since then the park has suffered a number of setbacks, such as temporary de-proclamation and the massive slaughter of thousands of game animals in a campaign to eliminate tsetse fly. Aerial spraying of the chemical DDT eventually eliminated the tsetse fly but at great cost to the environment. In 1947 the newly

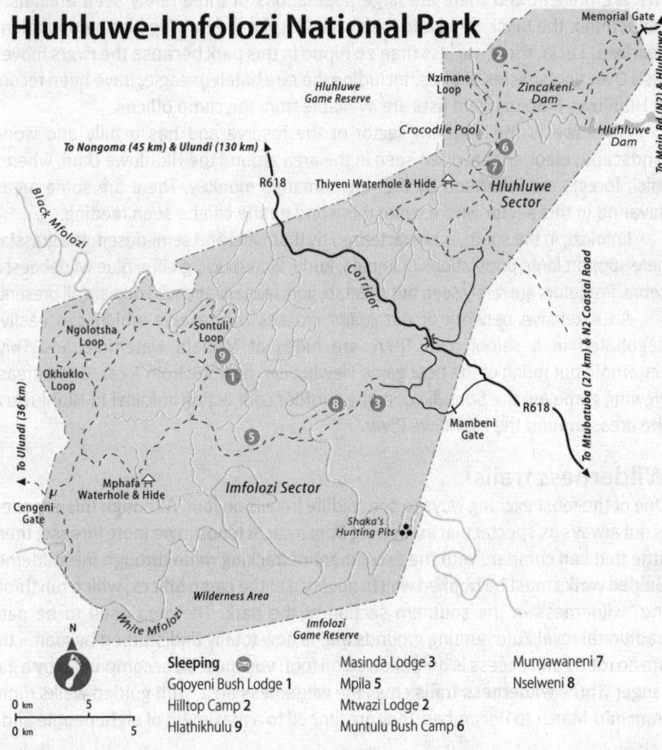

Saving the rhino

The biggest conservation success story for Hluhluwe-Imfolozi is the white rhino, which has been brought back from the brink of extinction. It is estimated that in 1900 the entire world population of southern white rhinos was only 20, all of them living in this area. Southern Africa is the genetic home for the white rhino and all populations in the world have their origins here.

The early protection of the rhino from hunting allowed numbers to grow to such an extent that, since the 1950s, surplus rhino have been transferred to other areas as part of the internationally famous 'Operation Rhino'. As a result, the population of white rhino in South Africa has grown from around 500 in the 1950s to 6000 today.

Hluhluwe-Imfolozi is now focusing on saving the black rhino, whose numbers in Africa over the last decade have dwindled from 14,000 to a mere 1550. At least a quarter of the world's population of black and white rhino are found in this park.

formed **Natal Parks, Game and Fish Preservation Board** took control of the park and reintroduced locally extinct species such as lion, elephant, rhino and giraffe.

Wildlife

This is one of the best reserves in KwaZulu Natal for seeing wildlife, and one of the finest in the world for seeing rhino. The varied landscapes of Hluhluwe-Imfolozi provide a wide range of habitats which support large numbers of big game. The Big Five are present and there are large populations of three rarely seen animals: the white rhino, the black rhino and the nyala. Despite the thriving hippo populations in nearby St Lucia, there are less than 20 hippo in this park because the rivers move too fast. Over 300 species of birds, including the rare bateleur eagle, have been recorded in Hluhluwe-Imfolozi; bird lists are available from the camp offices.

Hluhluwe is the northern sector of the reserve and has a hilly and wooded landscape; elephant are often seen in the area around the Hluhluwe Dam, where the thick forests are inhabited by the rare samango monkey. There are some areas of savanna in this sector where white rhino and giraffe can be seen feeding.

Imfolozi, in the south, is characterized by thornveld and semi-desert; the grasslands here support large populations of impala, kudu, waterbuck, giraffe, blue wildebeest and zebra. Predators are rarely seen but cheetah, lion, leopard and wild dog are all present.

An extensive network of dirt roads crosses the reserve which can easily be negotiated in a saloon car. There are hides at Mphafa waterhole and Thiyeni waterhole but much of the best game viewing can be done from a car. Good areas for viewing game are the Sontuli Loop, the corridor connecting Imfolozi to Hluhluwe and the areas around the Hluhluwe River.

Wilderness trails

One of the most exciting ways to see wildlife here is on foot. Although this experience is not always as spectacular as viewing from a car, it tends to be more intense; there is little that can compare with the excitement of tracking rhino through the wilderness. **Guided walks** must be booked well in advance at the camp offices, which run through the wilderness in the southern section of the park. The area used to be part of traditional royal Zulu hunting grounds and is now totally undisturbed by man – there are no roads and access is only allowed on foot; you must be accompanied by a game ranger. Three **wilderness trails** cross the wilderness area, with guided walks running from mid-March to December. They are limited to a maximum of eight people and are extremely popular, so should be booked well in advance. Food, drinks, water bottles, cutlery and cooking equipment, bedding, towels, day packs, backpacks and donkey bags are all provided by KZN Wildlife. The trails cover about 15 km per day and cost from R1320 to R2580 per person for up to three nights (accommodation is in tented camps in the wilderness area). There are also three self-guided walks in the Imfolozi sector. Reservations for all accommodation and wilderness trails within the park can be made up to six months in advance through **KZN Wildlife** ⓘ *T033-8451000, www.kznwildlife.com.*

Hluhluwe

→ *Colour map 5, grid A3.*

Hluhluwe is a small village in an area surrounded by large luxury game farms. It is a good base to explore the region as it is within easy reach of many of the local game parks and is only 15 km from St Lucia's False Bay. An international game auction is held here annually by KZN Wildlife. There are a couple of craft villages in the area; **Dumazulu Traditional Village**, a short drive from Hluhluwe, is one of the better ones, with displays of Zulu dancing, spear making and basket weaving.

Passengers using the **Baz Bus**, T021-4392323, www.bazbus.com, are dropped off and picked up outside the tourist office. **Hluhluwe Tourism Association** ⓘ *next to the Engen garage, Main St, T035-5620353, www.hluhluwe.net, Mon-Fri 0800-1700, Sat 0900-1300*, acts as a booking agent for the area.

Greater St Lucia Wetland Park

» *pp481-487.*

→ *Colour map 5, grid A3*

The Greater St Lucia Wetland Park was declared a World Heritage Site in 1999, the first place in South Africa to be awarded this status. The protected area is the largest estuarine lake system in Africa, with a variety of flora and fauna which compares favourably with the Okavango Delta or Kruger National Park. The birdlife is outstanding, with a staggering 420 species recorded here. But despite drawing a huge number of visitors throughout the year, the town remains small and low-key, with an appealingly languid, tropical atmosphere.

Ins and outs

Getting there and around The area now known as the Greater St Lucia Wetland Park consists of a number of formerly separate nature reserves and state forests. These are still referred to locally under a bewildering array of old and new names, but the greater area is considered to be South Africa's third largest park. The entire 328,000-ha reserve starts south of the St Lucia Estuary and stretches north to the border of Mozambique, and is about 280 km in length. The terrestrial section of the park varies from 1 km to 24 km wide, and the marine section extends 5 km out to sea, protecting 155 km of coastline.

In the southern region, accessible from St Lucia, the park falls into three main areas: **St Lucia Public Resort and Estuary National Park**, which is a good area to see crocodiles, hippo, impala, waterbuck, wildebeest and zebra; the coastline up to **Cape Vidal**, 32 km north of St Lucia, with the beautiful Cape beach; and the **western shore** of the lake, which is much quieter than the other two and affords the opportunity to explore the lake by boat.

The Greater St Lucia Wetland Park also encompasses **Maphelana** to the south (see page 479), accessed from Kwambonambi, and all the coastal parks to the north, from Sodwana Bay to Kosi Bay Nature Reserve on the border of Mozambique. » *For further details, see Maputaland, page 488.*

Tourist information For information about the Greater St Lucia Wetland Park, visit the St Lucia office of **KZN Wildlife** ⓘ *Pelikan Rd, near Eden Park campsite, T035-5901340, www.kznwildlife.com, daily 0800-1300, 1400-1600.* It has a small selection of brochures and can help with accommodation and trail information; reservations should be done well in advance, though (see below).

Staying in the park Reservations for all self-catering accommodation and wilderness trails within the park can be made up to 12 months in advance through **KZN Wildlife Reservations**, T033-8451000, www.kznwildlife.com. There are only limited supplies available in the camp shops so it is essential to bring your own food. The nearest supermarket is in St Lucia, unless you are staying at Charters Creek or one the camps around False Bay, in which case the nearest shops are in Hluhluwe. ➡ *For further details, see Sleeping, page 484.*

Best time to visit

Each season in the wetlands has its own attraction. From November to February there tends to be more rain making the vegetation greener. June to August is the best time for birdwatching as this is the breeding season. The best months for walking are March to November when it is less hot and humid. The school holidays are always a popular time for South African tourists to visit and accommodation at these times should be booked well in advance.

Natural hazards When hiking around the lake, watch out for hippos – they kill more people than any other mammal in Africa. If you come across one on land, retreat and, if possible, try and climb a tree. Also keep an eye out for snakes and crocodiles; avoid the water's edge. When swimming in the sea, stay well away from the estuary, which is inhabited by crocodiles and Zambezi sharks. Note that most self-guided trails in the area have been closed following the reintroduction of elephant. St Lucia is a malarial area and prophylactics should be taken.

Background

The land now occupied by the park has had human inhabitants since the Early Iron Age. Archaeological excavations have uncovered the remains of settlements and middens, and large areas of forest and dunes are thought to have been cleared to provide charcoal for iron smelting. St Lucia was named by the Portuguese explorer Manuel Perestrello in 1575, although European influence in the area was minimal until the 1850s. Up to that time the area was inhabited by a relatively large population of Thongas and Zulus who herded cattle and cultivated the land.

Professional hunters began visiting the lake in the 1850s in search of ivory, hides and horns which were at one point the Colony of Natal's main source of income. So successful were these hunters that within 50 years the last elephant in this region had been shot. Amongst the big game hunters here were William Baldwin, Robert Briggs Struthers, 'Elephant' White and John Dunn who recorded having shot 23 seacows in one morning and a total of 203 seacows in the following three months. Hunting parties would kill hundreds of elephants, crocodiles and hippos on each expedition.

During the 1880s the British government annexed St Lucia in a move which would foil the Boers from the New Republic in their search for access to the sea. It was after this that land was distributed to settlers and that missions were founded at Mount Tabor, Cape Vidal and Ozabeni.

St Lucia Lake, along with Hluhluwe-Umfolozi, was one of the first game reserves to be established in Africa in 1895. Further moves to protect wildlife also took place in 1944 with the addition of False Bay Park to the protected areas, and in 1975 South Africa signed the international RAMSAR Convention to protect wetlands. It was then that the Greater St Lucia Wetland region was declared. More recently, land was

St Lucia

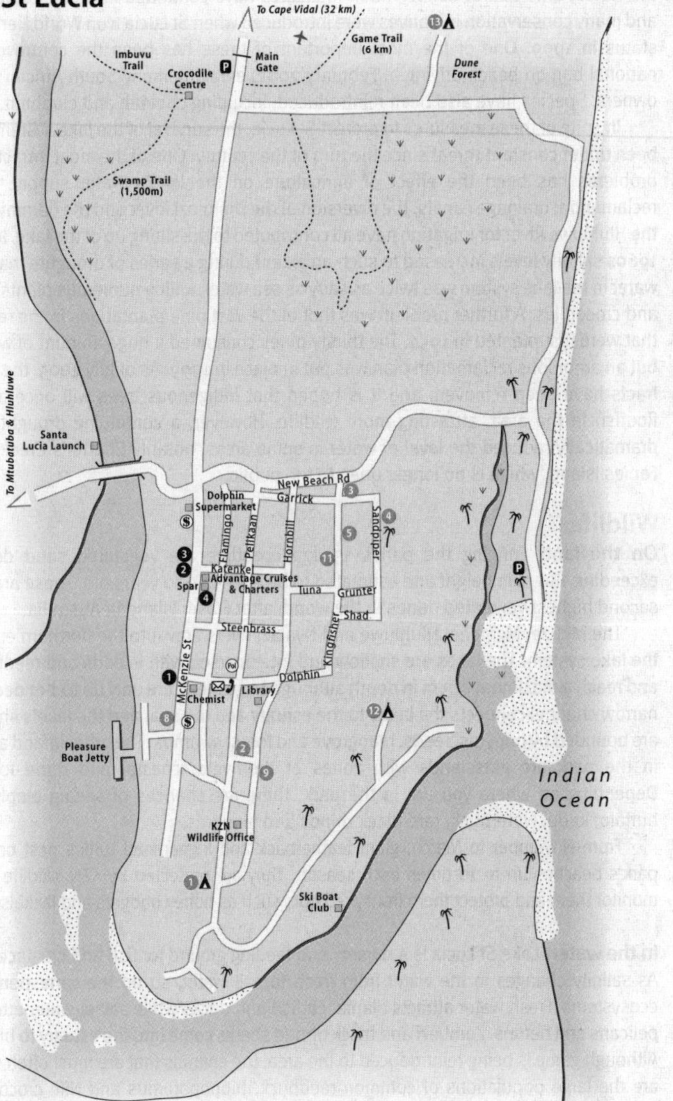

To Cape Vidal (32 km)
Game Trail (6 km)
Imbuvu Trail
Crocodile Centre
Main Gate
Dune Forest
Swamp Trail (1,500m)
Santa Lucia Launch
To Mtubatuba & Hluhluwe
New Beach Rd
Garrick
Dolphin Supermarket
Flamingo
Pelikaan
Hornbill
Sandpiper
Katenkel
Advantage Cruises & Charters
Spar
Tuna
Grunter
Shad
Steenbrass
Kingfisher
Dolphin
McKenzie St
Chemist
Library
Pleasure Boat Jetty
Indian Ocean
KZN Wildlife Office
Ski Boat Club

Sleeping

African Ambience 2
Bibs Backpackers 8
Eden Park 1
Elephant Coast House 3
Iphiva 13
Lalapanzi Guest Lodge 4
Maputaland Guest House 5
Seasands Garden Cottages 9
Sugarloaf Camp 12
Wetlands Guest House 11

Eating

Alfredos 1
Greek Sizzler 2
Quarterdeck 3
St Pizza 4

 recovered by the park in 1987 when the Eastern Shores State Forest was returned to the Natal Parks Board. Conservation measures have continued in the last decade, and many conservation initiatives were introduced when St Lucia won World Heritage status in 1999. One of the most important of these has been the controversial national ban on beach driving in February 2002, enraging many South African 4WD owners. Species have also been reintroduced, including cheetah and elephant.

In spite of these measures to protect St Lucia, the survival of the lake system has been under constant threat since the turn of the century. One of the most intractable problems has been the effect of agriculture on the lake's water supply: land reclamation, drainage canals, the diversion of the Umfolozi River and the damming of the Hluhluwe River for irrigation have all contributed to the silting up of the lake. In the 1960s salinity levels increased to such an extent during a series of droughts that the water in the lake system was twice as salty as sea water, killing numerous plants, fish and crocodiles. A further problem was that of the vast pine plantations in the region that were first planted in 1954. The thirsty pines consumed a huge amount of water, but an ambitious reclamation plan was put in place in 1999. As of July 2005, the pine tracts have been removed, and it is hoped that indigenous trees will once again flourish in the area, attracting more wildlife. However, a continuing drought has dramatically reduced the level of water in some areas, notably Charter's Creek and Fanies Island, which is no longer open to the public.

Wildlife

On the land Fringing the park's 155-km coastline are vegetated sand dunes exceeding 180 m in height and estimated to be over 30,000 years old. These are the second highest vegetated dunes in the world, after Fraser Island in Australia.

The Mkuze, Mzinene, Hluhluwe and Nyalazi rivers flow into the northern end of the lake system. The lakes are shallow and interspersed with islands and reedbeds and reach a maximum of 3 m in depth although large areas are only up to 1-m deep. A narrow channel connects the lakes to the estuary and the sea, and the lake's shores are bounded by papyrus, reeds, mangrove and forest swamps. The other inland areas in the park are grasslands with zones of thornveld, coastal and dune forest. Depending on where you are in the park, there are chances of seeing elephant, buffalo, kudu, waterbuck, rare black rhinos and leopards.

From November to March, giant leatherback and loggerhead turtles nest on the park's beaches up to 10 times each season. They are protected by KZN Wildlife who monitor them and protect them from predators such as honey badgers and jackals.

In the water Lake St Lucia is a nursery and feeding ground for fish and crustaceans. As salinity changes in the water from fresh to salt water, so do the corresponding ecosystems. Fresh water attracts tilapia, catfish and ducks while saltier water attracts pelicans and herons. Zambezi and black tipped sharks come into the estuary to breed. Although game is being reintroduced to the area, the animals that are most often seen are the large populations of common reedbuck, hippopotamus and Nile crocodile. There are an estimated 2000 crocs in the entire lake system, and it is thought that is the only place in the world where sharks and crocodiles share the same water.

In the air The birdlife is the main attraction here, and the fish eagle, easily spotted, has become the unofficial symbol of the area. Other species often seen around the water include kingfishers and weaverbirds, and large numbers of unusual migrant birds can also be spotted. Southern African waterbirds migrate depending on regional droughts between Bangweulu and Kafue in Zambia, the Okavango Delta in Botswana, the Zambezi Delta in Mozambique and the wetlands of Maputaland and St Lucia. The St Lucia waters are high in nutrients and support large populations of pinkbacked and white pelicans, greater and lesser flamingos, ducks, spoonbills and ibises.

The pelicans arrive every autumn to feed on migrating mullet in the Narrows, north of St Lucia Village. Around 6000 pelicans nest at the northern end of the lake where visitors can see their courtship displays.

Maphelana → *Colour map 5, grid A3.*

ⓘ *Head east from Kwambonambe to the Kwambonambi Lighthouse, from where it is a further 50 km to Maphelana along a narrow sand track. Oct-Mar 0600-1900, Apr-Sep 0600-1800; office daily 0800-1230, 1400-1630. R20 per person.*

Maphelana National Park was established in 1897, but was later handed over to the Department of Forestry. After the campaign waged by the Wildlife Society of Southern Africa, the threat of strip-mining the titanium-rich dunes was averted. It is now the southernmost part of the Greater St Lucia Wetland Park. The Maphelana Camp is tucked away in a sheltered bay on the south bank of the Umfolozi River and is popular with fishermen who can launch their speedboats here. There is a safe beach for swimming and licences are available to collect mussels, oysters and crayfish. Swimming or wading in the Umfolozi River is prohibited as there are too many crocodiles.

4WD vehicles are recommended for the track to Maphelana but vehicles with high road clearance can also get through in dry weather.

St Lucia → *Colour map 5, grid A3.*

The holiday resort of St Lucia lies to the south of Lake St Lucia and is surrounded by the Greater St Lucia Wetland National Park. St Lucia is the largest seaside holiday destination on this part of the coast and is particularly popular during the South African school holidays. Although it can get very busy around Christmas, it remains a sleepy provincial town off season, making a pleasant base from which to explore both the wetlands and the nearby wildlife parks.

Many visitors come for a day trip, to explore the narrow reaches of the estuary leading up to the lake. Boats leave regularly from the jetty at the far end of McKenzie Street, usually seating around 20 people and taking a two-hour tour upriver. These provide an excellent introduction to the wetlands, with chances of seeing large pods of hippos, crocodiles and prolific birdlife.

Ins and outs The end of the R618 leads directly into the centre of the resort on McKenzie Street, which is lined with supermarkets, banks, restaurants, handicraft shops and boat charter companies. Continuing down past the end of McKenzie Street, the road leads to the large KZN Wildlife office to the left, and the jetty from which river cruises leave to the right.

The best source is **Advantage Cruises and Charters** ⓘ *corner of McKenzie St and Katonkel Av, close to the Spar, T035-5901180, www.zululink.co.za, daily 0700-1900*, a booking agent for all local activities and accommodation. St Lucia is the main tourist centre in this part of Zululand and is a good base to stock up on supplies before staying in self-catering accommodation either in the Greater St Lucia Wetland or in game reserves at Hluhluwe-Imfolozi and Mkuzi. For information on the Greater St Lucia Wetland Park, see page 476.

Beaches

The beaches lying to the east of St Lucia are large swathes of pristine white sand backed by dune forest, which stretch all the way to Cape Vidal. Visitors swim here at their own risk as there are dangerous currents, no shark nets and no lifeguards. Swimming is prohibited in the estuary and within 100 m of the river mouth as the strong unpredictable currents, sharks and crocodiles make it too dangerous.

St Lucia Public Resort and Estuary national parks

These areas directly surround St Lucia village. There is a 12-km network of self-guided trails, which start in the area near the Crocodile Centre (see below). As the trails extend from the Indian Ocean to the estuary they cross several different habitats such as dune forest, grasslands, mangroves and swamps. The trail leading from the Crocodile Centre to the estuary takes you to some good hippo-viewing riverside spots. The grasslands to the north of the village are a source of ncema grass, traditionally used by Zulus to make sleeping and sitting mats. The cutting season starts on 1 May when thousands of people come for the annual harvest.

The **Crocodile Centre** ⓘ *T035-5901386, Mon-Fri 0800-1630, Sat 0830-1700, Sun 0900-1600, snake demonstration Sat 1400, crocodile feeding Sat 1500, R20,* is next to the entrance gate to Cape Vidal, where a small display highlights the important role crocodiles play in the ecosystem of the park. The Nile, long snouted and dwarf crocodiles that are kept here in pens are all endangered in the wild and are part of an international breeding programme to protect them. KZN Wildlife routinely releases Nile crocodiles back into Lake St Lucia. The curio shop here is one of the best in St Lucia with a good selection of books and leaflets on the area. The **Zulu & I** restaurant is also here.

Cape Vidal

ⓘ *32 km north of St Lucia, T035-5909012. Gates Oct-Mar 0500-1900, Apr-Sep 0600-1800; office daily 0800-1230, 1400-1630. R20 per person, R35 per vehicle.*

Cape Vidal makes an easy and pleasant day trip from St Lucia. A road heads north from the park gates (near the crocodile centre), passing through an area that was until recently pine forest but is now returning to indigenous wilderness. Elephants were recently reintroduced here, and the area is also home to kudu and cheetah.

Only 100 vehicles per day are allowed past the gate at Cape Vidal; the speed limit in the park is 40 kph. Beach driving is not allowed.

Mission Rocks is 16 km from St Lucia, signposted off the dirt road. Snorkelling and scuba diving are allowed here but there are no facilities so it is essential to bring your own equipment. The rock pools here are full of life and are best seen at low tide.

Cape Vidal is an area of vegetated dunes along what must be one of the most spectacular beaches in KwaZulu Natal. The sand is pure white and the Indian Ocean is warm and inviting; the rocks just off the beach are teeming with tropical fish and the shallow water is safe to snorkel in. Thanks to the daily limit of cars into the reserve, the beach is never crowded even at the busiest of times. The camp has facilities for launching powerboats and is popular for game fishing, but as Cape Vidal marks the beginning of a marine reserve that stretches north to the Mozambique border, anglers require permits and many fish are on a tag and release system.

Exploring the park

Mount Tabor is the starting point the three-day **Mziki Trail** ⓘ *T033-8451000, or T035-590002 (local office), www.kznwildlife.com, advance booking essential,* operated by **KZN Wildlife**. Hikers sleep at the self-catering Mount Tabor base camp, which is reached by foot from Mission Rocks (2 km), and go out on three full-day hikes accompanied by armed game guides. Each day, a different loop is completed: the 10-km **South Coast Loop** passes through dune forest before reaching the sea at Rangers Rocks. From here the trail returns along the coastline to Mission Rocks before heading back to Mount Tabor through dune forest. Kudu are often seen on this trail. The 10-km **Mfazana Pan Loop** crosses the road to Cape Vidal and heads for the hides at Mfazana Pan, from where it turns north through grassland to the shore of Lake St Lucia. At 18 km, the **North Coast Loop** is the longest day hike. It heads north along Mount Tabor Ridge to Bokkie Valley and then returns back along the coast past Bat's Cave and on to Mount Tabor.

Ticks and mosquitoes can be a problem on the trail.

Western shores

The camps on the western shores are smaller and less often visited than the coastal areas of the park. Access to these camps is via the N2 north of St Lucia.

Charter's Creek ⓘ *20 km north of Mtubatuba on the N2, take the signposted turning 18 km to Charter's Creek, the last 6 km are on a dirt road, T035-5509000, Oct-Mar 0500-2000, Apr-Sep 0600-2000, office daily 0800-1230, 1400-1630, R20 per person, R35 per vehicle*, has a boat launching area and is popular with fishermen who come here in search of kob which can grow up to 20 kg in weight. Low water levels, however, mean that the launch area has been closed for some time. The introduction of elephants also means that there are no longer any self-guided trails here.

Fanies Island ⓘ *follow the signs to Charter's Creek from the N2; before reaching Charter's Creek, take the signposted turning north for 13 km*, had been closed to the public for the better part of a year at time of writing, thanks to low water levels. Check with the KZN Wildlife office in St Lucia for updates.

False Bay ⓘ *from the N2, take the turning to Hluhluwe village, the road continues 15 km to the park, T035-5620425, Oct-Mar 0500-2000, Apr-Sep 0600-2000, office daily 0800-1230, 1400-1630, R20 per person, R35 per vehicle*, is the northernmost camp on the lake and is a good place to see flamingos and pink-backed pelicans during the breeding season from December to April. The accommodation here is more basic than at the other camps but this is offset by the splendid landscape. The surrounding sand forests are similar to Mkhuze Game Reserve and are inhabited by the rare suni antelope and nyala. The banks and marshlands along the Hluhluwe River are rich in birdlife. A viewing platform near the camp looks over the lake. Launch tours are currently unavailable due to low water levels.

Sleeping

Gingindhlovu and around *p469*

E **Inyezane Backpackers**, T/F035-3371326, inyezane@ethniczulu.com. Dorms, doubles and singles located in rondavels, kitchen and dining area. The whole site is on an expansive sugar farm, a short walk from the huts is a large dam, swimming here is not possible because of bilharzia. We've had mixed reports about the management.

E **Zangozolo Tented Camp**, Amatigulu Nature Reserve, KZN Wildlife, T033-8451000, www.kznwildlife.com. 6 2-bed tents are connected by wooden walkways, both have proper beds, on raised wooden platforms overlooking the sea, a shared ablution block, dining area, and fully equipped kitchen with gas stoves, fridge and freezer, there is no shop here so bring all your own food and supplies.

Eshowe and inland *p469*

A **Protea Simunye Zulu Lodge**, T035-4503111, www.proteahotels.com. You must be at the trading post by 1530, from where you travel for 1 hr on horseback, donkey or ox wagon (disabled guests can request a 4WD drive transfer). The lodge is simple and traditional with rooms in thatched stone huts and open-air rock baths lit by candles and oil lamps. In the evening, music, singing and dancing is performed by local people. Rates include all meals, guides and demonstrations.

B **Shakaland Protea**, T035-4600912, www.shakaland.com. If you are staying the night the Shaka experience continues in the adjacent Protea hotel, where Zulu dancers escort you to your beehive-shaped hut. The evenings are spent sampling the local brew tshwala around the campfire while being entertained with dancing and story telling. The en suite huts are huge and have all mod cons.

C **Amble Inn**, 116 Main St, Eshowe, T035-4741300, ambleinn@corpdial.co.za. Friendly guesthouse with 11 comfortable rooms overlooking a pool. The dining room offers hearty English meals like roast beef and Yorkshire pudding or steak and kidney pie for lunch and dinner.

D **Kwabhekithunga/Stewarts Farm**, 36 km from Eshowe on the R34 towards Empangeni, T035-4600644, info@stewartsfarm.com. Rather than having been built especially for tourists like many similar

Zulu 'experiences' in the area, this village is the real home of Chief Mbhangucuza Fakude, his 4 bothers and their extended families. Accommodation is in Zulu beehive-shaped huts, all en suite, with bright and colourful interiors and electricity. Bar and swimming pool on site. For an extra R165 per person, visitors are treated to a 'cultural experience' – Zulu dancing and singing, and a taste of Zulu food and home-brewed beer. Pre-booking is essential. Recommended for a feel of real Zulu life.

E Zululand Backpackers, 38 Main St, T035-4744919, www.eshowe.com. At the back of the **George Hotel**. Dorms, kitchen, showers, double rooms, camping possible, M-Net TV, pool table, internet, swimming pool, close to shops and banks, Baz Bus stop. Has an excellent reputation for organizing local tours, such as visits to traditional Zulu weddings, mountain bikes available for hire. Recommended.

Mtunzini and around *p471*

B Trade Winds, 12 Hely Hutchinson Rd, T035-3402533, www.tradewindscountry inn.co.za. Well-established, small town hotel with 26 rooms, a/c, TV, restaurant, swimming pool and à la carte restaurant,

C Highfield Country Home, 7 km from town off the N2, however, you must get to it from Mtunzini on the old Durban road, T035-3401731. 5 double rooms with lovely Victorian bathrooms, TV, meals on request, pool, set in a beautiful farmhouse in 4 ha of parklands, sea views, ask for Willie or Sarco. International visitors return here year after year. Recommended.

C Mtunzini Forest Lodge, T035-3401953, www.goodersonleisure.com. 22 beach chalets set in attractive dune forest right by the beach, sleeping up to 6 people in rustic log cabins. Swimming pool for guests' use; meals available.

E Xaxaza Caravan Park, at the top of town, T035-3401843, xaxaza@mtunzini.co.za. Standard caravan park with decent facilities, including electrical points and clean ablutions, a significant distance from the beach.

Empangeni and around *p471*

There is little accommodation in the town itself, and it doesn't make a very pleasant stop over; head along the R34 inland instead.

L Thula Thula, Thula Thula Private Game Reserve, T035-7928322, www.thula thula.com. Family-run exclusive safari lodge with 7 luxury thatched chalets decorated in an ethnic style, set on rolling lawns and surrounded by forests ringing with bird calls. Rates are all-inclusive of meals and game drives, and the excellent French food is served in an outside boma, with tables sets around a fire. Guests can also relax in the large, thatched bar area, overlooking the pool. Recommended.

Richards Bay *p472*

B The Ridge – Jacks Corner, Davidson St, T035-7534312, www.jackscorner.co.za. A good choice if you're passing through Richards Bay, this upmarket guesthouse has 6 tasteful rooms set around a pool, with views of the ocean and harbour. Restaurant and bar on site.

Hluhluwe-Imfolozi National Park *p472, map p473*

All reservations through **KZN Wildlife**, T033-8451000, www.kznwildlife.com.

Imfolozi sector

L1 Masinda Lodge. Luxury 9-bed hosted lodge, fully-inclusive of meals and safari activities. The 4 en suite rooms can be booked individually, lounge and dining room, drinks served around a bush fire. Beautiful setting with good views of the bush.

A Gqoyeni Bush Lodge, 8-bed bush lodge, 4 thatched cottages, each with 2 bedrooms, on stilts connected by raised wooden walkways to the living area with lounge, dining area and kitchen, the camp has its own viewing platform overlooking the Mfolozi River where there are good chances of seeing crocodiles, lions and elephants in the summer.

A Hlathikhulu, 8-bed bush camp, rustic decor, lovely setting overlooking the Black Mfolozi. 4 2-bed en suite chalets, a central lounging area and kitchen linked by wooden boardwalks, cook and game guide.

A-B Mpila Camp. Centrally situated in the heart of Imfolozi, Mpila Camp commands magnificent views over the wilderness area to the east and the Msasaneni Hills to the west. 12 1-bed self-catering thatched cottages, 2 self-contained 3-bed cottages

(cook on hand to prepare food supplied by guests), 6 self-catering chalets sleeping up to 5. Also has a luxury tented camp with 9 units of walk-in tents (self-catering). The shop stocks basic provisions and petrol station.
B **Nselweni**. A wonderfully atmospheric reed and thatch bush lodge raised on stilts just above the floodplain of Mfolozi River. 4 2-bed units, shared ablutions, lounge, dining area, fully equipped kitchen. Cooks will prepare meals, but guests must bring all their own food and drinks.

Hluhluwe sector
AL **Mtwazi Lodge**. Original thatched house which was home to the park's first warden. 3 double bedrooms, shared lounge, dining room, cook (no need to bring food) and a game guard.
AL **Muntulu Bush Camp**, 4 2-bed units in this rustic bush lodge, linked by wooden walkway to a central lounge and dining area, all overlooking the Hluhluwe River, verandas. Cooks are on hand to prepare meals, but guests must bring all food. There is also a game ranger on site.
AL **Munyawaneni**, 8-bed bush lodge on the banks of the Hluhluwe River in a good area for seeing elephant and nyala, who come to drink at the secluded waterhole that can be seen from each of the 4 en suite rooms. Boardwalks link the accommodation units to a central lounge and kitchen. Again, cooks can prepare meals but guests must bring food.
A-C **Hilltop Camp**, the main camp was recently refurbished and offers 4 types of accommodation. At the top end are 20 **2-bed chalets** (A) with 2 bedrooms, 2 bathrooms and fully equipped kitchen; slightly cheaper are the 7 **2-bed chalets** (B), with fully equipped kitchen, and the 20 2-bed rest huts (not self-catering) with fridge and kettle. The cheapest options are the 20 **2-bed rest huts** (C), with communal kitchen and ablution block. This is the largest and most accessible of the camps and has a fabulous hilltop location, with sweeping views over much of the park and parts of Swaziland. Although this doesn't have the exclusivity of the smaller bush camps, the central lounge, restaurant, bar, pool and veranda are welcome at the end of the day. Game drives and guided walks can be arranged here.

Hluhluwe *p475*
AL **Bushlands Game Lodge**, T035-5620144, www.goodersonleisure.com. 20 luxurious a/c wooden cabins set in lush gardens overlooking the swimming pool. Boardwalks link the cabins to the central eating boma and lounge. Rates are all inclusive. The lodge is signposted from the N2. Fly-in package deals from Johannesburg and Durban are available; they last up to 4 days and include visits to the game reserves, scuba diving and game fishing tours.
AL **Hluhluwe River Lodge**, 15 km from Hluhluwe village off the road to False Bay Park, T035-5620246, www.hluhluwe.co.za. 8 double A-frame thatched chalets with great views and swimming pool. Also has 2 family chalets and 2 luxury honeymoon chalets, with open bath area and private viewing deck. Central lodge houses a dining area, bar, lounge, curio shop and library. Recommended.
A **Gazebo Safari Lodge**, a short drive from Hluhluwe village, off the road to False Bay, T035-5621066, www.gazebo.co.za. 12 double en suite rooms, TV, a/c, verandas with stunning views of the bush. Restaurant, bar, lounge, beautiful swimming pool and deck, boma area where meals are served in summer, game drives to nearby reserves.
A **Zulu Nyala**, 15 km on the Mzinene Rd, T035-5620177, www.zulunyala.com. Set within a private game reserve, 53 twin a/c rooms, restaurant, 2 bars, curio shop, pool, tennis, clay-pigeon shooting. Also 10 luxury 'Hemmingway'-style tents in the extensive gardens. Also on this reserve is the **Heritage Hotel**, set in a lovely 1940s colonial home.
B **Hluhluwe Hotel**, 104 Bush Rd, T035-5620251, www.hluhluwehotel.co.za. 67 a/c rooms, TV, tennis, swimming pool and volleyball, smart modern hotel decorated with African motifs, 2 restaurants serving an à la carte menu or a buffet, occasional performances of Zulu dancing in the evenings around the pool, can organize safaris to the local parks.
B **Sand Forest Lodge**, 10 km from Hluhluwe village off False Bay Rd, T035-5622509, www.sandforest.co.za. A quality game farm within an ancient sand forest. 4 a/c self-catering cottages, en suite double room, kitchenette, veranda overlooks a neat lawn with acacia trees; variety of

simpler self-catering log cabins on stilts in the forest with separate kitchen. Central bar, swimming pool and thatched lapa. Game walks and drives with resident guide plus visits to Zulu villages. Good value and peaceful setup.

E Isinkwe Backpackers, look out for the 'Bushlands' turning on the N2, 40 km north of the St Lucia/Mtubatuba turning, the lodge is a further 2 km down this road, T035-5622258, www.isinkwe.co.za. The Baz Bus stops here. A neat hostel with 40 beds in dorms, double rooms and camping. Swimming pool and a bar area for star gazing. Rustic set-up, has done much to create employment for local people. Great homemade meals served up most nights, or self-catering in the kitchen. Laundry. Well-organized day trips in a 4WD to all the local sights and transfers to Sodwana Bay.

Maphelana *p479*

B Maphelana Camp, KZN Wildlife, T033-8451000, www.kznwildlife.com. 10 recently renovated 5-bed log cabins, self-catering, with kitchen, bathroom, dining room and lounge. The cabins are set on a large forested dune with views over a large beach and the sea.

Camping

Maphelana Camp, 45 sites, ablution blocks. Electricity is restricted to generator times. Basic supplies are available at the camp site; petrol is not available. Campsite reservations T035-5901407.

St Lucia *p479, map p477*

Accommodation is cheap by international standards, however, there is almost always a shortage of beds so book well in advance.

B African Ambience, 124 Pelikaan St, T035-5901212, www.africanambience.com. Delightful new guesthouse in a quiet thatched house a few blocks from the centre. Bright and airy TV-free rooms have chunky wooden furniture and ethnic fabrics, with huge beds and attractive bathrooms. Downstairs rooms have private terraces, and there is a garden with a rock pool. An excellent, peaceful choice. Recommended.

C Elephant Coast House, corner of Garrick and Kingfisher Sts, T035-5901888, www.elephantcoastbnb.co.za. 5 spacious rooms with balconies overlooking a large garden (where hippos sometimes come to graze) with a small fenced off terrace and pool. Rooms are large and sunny, with tiled floors and vaguely ethnic decor, but no TVs. Friendly service, big breakfasts served in the large dining area, TV lounge, secure parking. Recommended.

C Lalapanzi Guest Lodge, 7 Sandpiper St, T035-5901167. Large double rooms with en suite facilities and fridge full of cool drinks. TV lounge, self-catering facilities, swimming pool, lush tropical garden, secure off-street parking.

C Maputaland Guest House, 1 Kabeljou St, T/F035-5901041, www.maputaland.com. 5 rooms, TV lounge, B&B, swimming pool set in a large tropical garden in a quiet suburb away from the main drag. Recommended. Wide selection of wildlife tours organized from here. German speaking.

C Seasands Garden Cottages, 135 Hornbill St, T035-5901082, www.seasands.co.za. Fairly large hotel, offering a mix of B&B rooms and self-catering cottages set in tropical gardens. Attracts groups and some conferences, but remains a popular choice. Restaurant, swimming pool and extensive gardens.

C Wendy's, Riverview, just off the R618 in Mtubatuba, 10 km west of St Lucia, T035-5500407, www.wendybnb.co.za. Well outside town, but in an excellent location for access both to St Lucia and Hluhluwe-Imfolozi. Family-run guesthouse surrounded by tropical gardens, with spacious double rooms filled with quirky and antique furniture, and Victorian-style bathrooms. Good food served in the little restaurant. Range of activities organized, from game drives and fishing to tours of the wetlands. Very friendly and welcoming. Recommended.

C Wetlands Guest House, 20 Kingfisher St, T/F035-5901098, www.stluciawetlands.com. Family-run B&B set in quiet street close to the centre. 6 large a/c rooms with en suite bathroom, 1 family unit, with high ceilings

For an explanation of the sleeping and eating price codes used in this guide, see inside the front cover. Other relevant information is found in Essentials pages 42-47.

and wood floors which help keep things cool in the summer. Guest lounge with bar and TV. Self-catering flat also available. Large swimming pool with child protection fence.

E **Bibs Backpackers**, 310 McKenzie St, T035-5901056, www.bibs.co.za. Small dorms, double rooms, twins and camping. Great kitchen and self-catering area, Spar shop next door for supplies, evening meals on request. Braai area, rock swimming pool, relaxing gardens with hammock and bar area, Zulu dancing on Sat nights, email/internet access. Well-organized guided day trips to Hluhluwe and other local sights. Free transfer to beach, beach fires at night. On the Baz Bus route.

Camping

There are 3 **KZN Wildlife** campsites on the edge of town, reservations T035-5901340. Each has a shop selling a wide range of guides and curios and a restaurant.

Eden Park, in a small forest to the south of town, 20 sites, ablution block.

Iphiva, near the Crocodile Centre, 88 sites, ablution blocks and laundry facilities.

Sugarloaf Camp, close to the beach and estuary, 92 sites, swimming pool, ablution blocks, laundry facilities.

Cape Vidal *p480*

The small shop at Cape Vidal has a couple of narrow shelves stocked with food. Petrol and firewood are also on sale in the camp. If you are staying overnight stock up in St Lucia.

B-D **Cape Vidal Camp**, KZN Wildlife, T033-8451000, www.kznwildlife.com. 5- to 20-bed log cabins, all are self-catering with fully equipped kitchens, dining rooms, terraces and bathrooms. These represent great value for a group. All the cabins are set under trees on the dunes 200 m from the beach.

Camping

Cape Vidal Camp, T035-5909012. 50 sites set among the pines. Shared ablution blocks, power points and an area for cleaning fish. It gets overcrowded with fishermen here during the high season. The minimum charge of R288 per day is expensive by local standards and there are better options closer to St Lucia town.

Western shores *p481*

C-D **Charters Creek**, KZN Wildlife, T033-8451000, www.kznwildlife.com. 7-bed cottage, 2-bed self-catering chalet, 14 rest huts with 2-4 beds, communal lounge, ablution block, 2 kitchens. Each unit is fully equipped.

D **Dugandlovu Rustic Camp**, False Bay, KZN Wildlife, T033-8451000, www.kznwildlife.com. 4-bed huts, cold showers, paraffin lamps, gas cookers, freezer, braais, firewood, bring your own bedding, fully equipped kitchen. There is a small shop selling cold drinks and tinned food, petrol is available.

Camping

Charters Creek, reservations T035-5509000. 10 sites with electricity, ablution block. Nearby main camp also has a shop and swimming pool.

Lister Point, False Bay, T035-5620425. 38 sites next to the lake, electricity points, ablution blocks.

Eating

Decent restaurants in this area are limited to the hotels. If you find yourself in Richards Bay, there is a wider choice.

Richards Bay *p472*

TTT **The Grill Fish**, Tuzi Gazi Waterfront, T035-7880110. Offers views of the harbour and quality seafood, including excellent grills and a decent winelist.

Hluhluwe-Imfolozi National Park *p472, map p473*

There is a good restaurant at **Hilltop Camp** in the Hluhluwe sector, serving full English breakfasts, buffet meals, light snacks and braais, open until 2100. The tables on the shady outdoor terrace are in a superb setting overlooking the reserve; the game burgers are highly recommended.

St Lucia *p479, map p477*

TT **Alfredos**, McKenzie St, T035-5901150. Good Italian food at this cheap and cheerful set-up, with occasional live music and tables inside and out. Easy-going, fun atmosphere.

TT **The Greek Sizzler**, 37 McKenzie St, T035-5901554. Hugely popular local restaurant serving steaks, seafood and a couple of Greek specials at tables spilling out on to the pavement. Friendly Greek management.

Quarterdeck, McKenzie St, T035-5901116. Great wooden deck overlooking the road, with a large (more beery) interior. Good selection of fresh grilled seafood, as well as burgers and salads. Popular cocktail bar downstairs.

St Pizza, 13 McKenzie St, T035-5901048. Ever-expanding pizza joint with wooden tables strung out on a large deck overlooking the street. As well as good thin-crust pizzas, the seafood specials are filling. Wide choice of wines and beers, and a good atmosphere in the evenings.

Shopping

Richards Bay *p472*

There are a number of shopping malls in the centre of town, the largest of which is the **Boardwalk**, where facilities include banks, chemists, supermarkets, restaurants, a wide range of shops, a cinema and a branch of **Rennies Travel** (Thomas Cook agent, foreign exchange).

Hluhluwe-Imfolozi National Park *p472, map p473*

In the Imfolozi sector there are souvenir shops selling gifts and books on natural history at Masinda and Mpila Camps. Otherwise there are no shops in the reserve so it is necessary to bring all your own food and other supplies; the nearest shop is in Mtubatuba. Petrol is sold at Mpila Camp.

In the Hluhluwe sector there is a curio shop at **Hilltop Camp** and a small supermarket, but it only has limited basic supplies. Petrol and oil are on sale.

Hluhluwe *p475*

Ilala Weavers, Thembalethu Craft Village, T035-5620630, is a quality handicraft shop selling traditional basketwork and beadwork, decorated with geometric patterns.

St Lucia *p479, map p477*

There is a large, modern **Spar** on the main street – McKenzie St – which sells a good range of supplies. In season, women often peddle fresh tropical fruit from stalls along this street.

Cape Vidal *p480*

There is a small shop selling a good range of wildlife identification books, T-shirts, souvenirs and limited supplies of food.

Activities and tours

Eshowe and inland *p469*

Tour operators

KZN Kaleidoscope, T035-4742348, ahbird@netactive.co.za, run by Henry Bird. Out-of-the-way tours to Zulu graves and battlesites, or a day tour of all the major sites including lunch and wine for around R300.

Zululand Eco-adventures, based at Zululand Backpackers, T035-4744919, www.eshowe.com. Run by Graham Chennells, a registered guide involved in community projects for many years. Unusual cultural tours of the surrounding countryside moving from village to village, no shows are visited, see contemporary traditional life as it is. Interesting projects include the Eshowe Skills Centre, a papermaking project, and the Rotary Classroom Project (the building of 2000 classrooms in the region). Graham is the former mayor of Eshowe who has intimate knowledge of the Zulu people. Highly recommended for more of an insight into Zulu traditions than the usual all-singing all-dancing tourist traps.

Hluhluwe-Imfolozi National Park *p472, map p473*

Night drives, R180, and game walks, R150, can be booked through the camp office. There are 3 self-guided walking trails and daily guided walks with a game guard from Mpila camp lasting 2-3 hrs. No children.

Zululand Adventures, T035-5500681, www.zululand-adventures.com. Morning and afternoon game drives run by the cheery Gavin to Hluhluwe-Imfolozi National Park, including lunch or sundowners. Good on history of the park and very knowledgeable and enthusiastic about the area. Also offers day-long fishing trips off the coast.

Hluhluwe *p475*

Dinizulu Safaris, T035-5620025, www.dinizulu.co.za. An established family outfit with excellent knowledge of Zululand and its parks.

Isinkwe Tours & Safaris, at Isinkwe Backpackers, T035-5622258, www.isinkwe.co.za. Tours in open-top 4WDs to Hluhluwe-Imfolozi, St Lucia and Mkuze, including breakfast and a braai lunch. Good value.

St Lucia *p479, map p477*
Advantage Charters, T035-5901180/590-1259, www.zululink.co.za. A wide choice of boat rides, including 2-hr estuary trips, costing from R120. Whale-watching trips run Jun-Nov when humpback, mink and occasional southern right whales travel along the coast heading for the warmer breeding waters of Mozambique. Expect to pay around R500, 80% of which is refundable if no whales are spotted. If you don't have a car, this is a good value tour operator for day trips to Cape Vidal and deep-sea fishing. New for 2006 are shark cage diving trips, offering the chance of seeing hammerhead, Zambezi and bull sharks, costing R600 for a 4-hr trip.
Santa Lucia, T035-5901340, www.kznwildlife.com. 80-seater double-storey launch with a bar departs from the jetty next to the bridge at 0830, 1030, 1430. The tour lasts for 90 mins and travels up the estuary past thick banks of vegetation as far as the Narrows. There is a good chance of seeing hippos and waterfowl. Migrating mullet are often seen leaping out of the water during the autumn when they move from the lake into the sea.
Shaka Barker Tours, McKenzie St, T035-5901162, shakabarker@stlucia.co.za, is the only operator licensed to run trips to see the turtles laying at Leven Point, which is normally a restricted area. It's not uncommon to see crocodiles and snakes, as well as turtles, on the beach. This is a very special wildlife experience conducted in an eco-friendly way and highly recommended. The tour departs at 1830 and returns at 0300 the following morning. 4-10 people are required and advance booking is essential. Expect to pay R500, which includes supper and night drives in search of genets, leopard, bush babies, chameleons and hippos.

Transport

Empangeni and around *p471*
Greyhound, T011-2768500, www.greyhound.co.za. Coaches depart from the museum in Turnbull St, towards **Durban**, **Johannesburg** and **Pretoria**.

Richards Bay *p472*
Air
There is a small airport at the northern edge of town, 5 km from the centre. SAA, T011-9781111, www.flysaa.com, has daily flights to **Johannesburg**.

Bus
Greyhound, T011-2768500, www.greyhound.co.za, has regular coaches to **Durban**, **Pretoria** and **Johannesburg**.

Car hire
All offices at the airport: Avis, T035-7896549, Budget, T035-7860986, Imperial, T035-7860309, Hertz, T035-7861201.

Taxi
Zululand Taxis, T035-6682108.

St Lucia *p479, map p477*
Passengers using the Baz Bus can be dropped off at Bib's Backpackers on Mackenzie St.

Directory

Richards Bay *p472*
Banks Ned Bank and Standard Bank are both on Bullion Blvd. **Medical services** Central Pharmacy T035-7893910. The Bay Hospital, Krugerrand CBD, T035-7806111.

St Lucia *p479, map p477*
Banks First National Bank, T035-5901008, and Standard Bank, T035-5901044, are on McKenzie St.

Maputaland

Named after the Maputa River, which flows through southern Mozambique, Maputaland covers an area of 9000 sq km stretching north from Lake St Lucia to the Mozambique border and east from the Indian Ocean to the Lebombo Mountains. One of South Africa's least developed regions, Maputaland has preserved a traditional African atmosphere. The land is unsuitable for intensive modern agriculture and the small farmsteads which dot the landscape are connected by a rough network of roads.

The climate varies from being tropical in the north to subtropical in the south, and this has created a fascinatingly diverse range of ecosystems, from the forested Lebombo Mountains at 700 m to the low lying expanses of the coastal plain. Maputaland's features include Lake Sibaya – South Africa's largest freshwater lake – as well as mangrove swamps, coral reefs, dune forest, riverine forest and savannah. And seeing Maputaland's last wild elephants from a Land Rover in Tembe or diving on the reefs at Sodwana Bay are among South Africa's ultimate wilderness experiences.
» *For Sleeping, Eating and other listings, see pages 496-498.*

Ins and outs

Getting there Maputaland is well connected by road on the N2 highway. By car it is only a three-hour drive from Durban or six hours from Johannesburg. From Hluhluwe, leave the N2 at the Ngwenya-Sodwana exit, the Lower Mkuzi Road runs along the southern boundary of Mkhuze Game Reserve and passes a number of luxury private game lodges. The tarred road continues on to Mbazwana and Sodwana Bay (90 km) (see page). Passengers using the **Baz Bus,** T021-4392323, www.bazbus.com, are dropped off and picked up at the **Ghost Mountain Inn** (see Sleeping, page 496). » *For further details, see Transport, page 498.*

Mkuze → *Colour map 5, grid A2.*

This small modern town next to the N2 has a supermarket, bank, petrol station and the office of **Maputaland Tourism** ⓘ *Kingfisher St, T035-5731439, www.maputaland.co.za, Mon-Fri 0900-1730, Sat 0930-1330,* just off the N2, on the right side of the road as you drive into town.

From Mkuze there is a dirt road heading south parallel to the N2 which leads to the turning to **Mkuze Game Reserve** (20 km). There is also an alternative northern route on dirt roads from Mkuze to Sodwana Bay (120 km), passing through Ubombo, Tshongwe and Mbazwana. The drive to Mkuze passes through sisal plantations before entering a beautiful rustic area. The road winds through gently rounded hills dotted with aloes and acacias. Donkeys and cows graze on the meadows at the side of the road and wander about freely. The road is in good condition but after rain it is crossed by numerous streams.

A further 10 km along the N2 from Mkuze is the exit for **Jozini** (the N2 continues north towards Lavumisa, 40 km, on the frontier with Swaziland). Jozini is the last place of any size before the reserves in northern Maputaland; it is a good idea to fill up on petrol and buy any last minute supplies while you are here. The road east from Jozini crosses the Lebombo Mountains and the Maputaland coastal plain.

Mkuze Game Reserve » *pp496-498.*

ⓘ *Clearly signposted from the N2, 335 km from Durban and 145 km from Richards Bay, T035-5739001, Oct-Mar 0500-1900, Apr-Sep 0600-1800, office daily 0800-1230, 1400-1630. R35 per person, plus R35 per vehicle.*

The reserve, established in 1912 and covering an area of 40,000 ha, has a flat and dry landscape of open grasslands, dense forests, coastal dunes and pans. The area to the north is tropical whereas the southern part of the reserve is more temperate. The protected area conserves a representative cross-section of the Maputaland ecosystem. Mkuze is not visited as often as Hluhluwe-Imfolozi (see page 472) as there are not as many rhinos, but it offers opportunities to go on guided bush walks and see some of Maputaland's more unusual animals.

There is some frozen food for sale in the curio shop and a selection of books on natural history and postcards. It's also a good place to pick up some informative leaflets on birds, trees, walks and drives. There's petrol is for sale at the entrance gate. Reservations for camping sites should be made here.

Wildlife

Mkuze is an excellent place to see some of Maputaland's big game. Elephant, giraffe, blue wildebeest, eland, kudu, black and white rhino, cheetah, leopard and hyena are all present in the reserve. It is also one of the best places to see the shy nyala antelope – nearly 8000 live here. As part of the Mozambique coastal plain, Mkuze attracts many tropical birds often seen further north. Over 450 species have been recorded here, representing 7% of the world's total number of species. Look out for

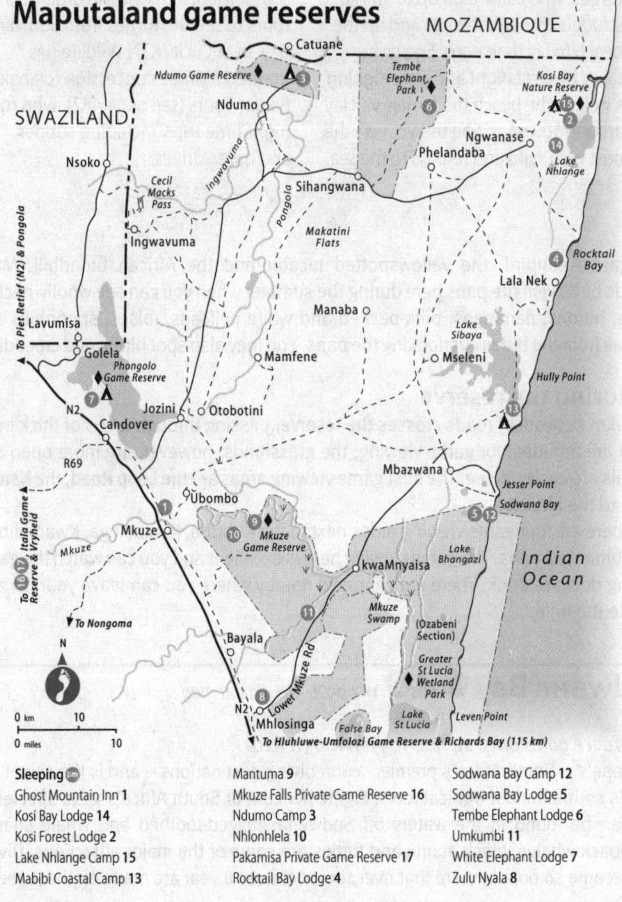

Sleeping
Ghost Mountain Inn **1**
Kosi Bay Lodge **14**
Kosi Forest Lodge **2**
Lake Nhlange Camp **15**
Mabibi Coastal Camp **13**
Mantuma **9**
Mkuze Falls Private Game Reserve **16**
Ndumo Camp **3**
Nhlonhlela **10**
Pakamisa Private Game Reserve **17**
Rocktail Bay Lodge **4**
Sodwana Bay Camp **12**
Sodwana Bay Lodge **5**
Tembe Elephant Lodge **6**
Umkumbi **11**
White Elephant Lodge **7**
Zulu Nyala **8**

Maputaland turtles

Five species of turtle can be found off the Maputaland coast but the loggerhead and the leatherback turtles are the only ones to breed here. The turtles arrive between October and February migrating vast distances from as far afield as Madagascar, Kenya and the Cape. There are two theories as to how the turtles return to the beaches where they were born after spending at least 15 years at sea. One proposes that the turtles are guided by the earth's magnetic fields, while the other holds that they use their sense of smell to find the right beach.

After mating offshore the female turtles, who can weigh up to 900 kg, struggle through the surf and up the beach to lay their eggs. Egg laying takes place at night and after digging a hole in the beach the female will lay around 100 eggs. She then covers the nest with sand and returns to the sea.

Incubation takes around 60 days, the tiny turtles then hatch together and dig their way to the surface. Few hatchlings live to become adults and the threat of being eaten by predators begins immediately with ghost crabs and jackals waiting to catch them before they can reach the sea. About one turtle in every 500 will survive.

The Maputaland Marine Reserve has played a vital role in rescuing the loggerhead and the leatherback from extinction. The beaches along this coast are an important breeding area and years of protection have finally resulted in increasing the numbers of turtles returning each year to breed.

In season, KZN Wildlife organizes tours to see the turtles from Sodwana Bay. In St Lucia, KZN Wildlife has granted a single concession to Shaka Barker Tours (see page 487), who run night time trips, including supper and game drives.

Neergard's sunbird, the yellowspotted nicator and the African broadbill. Many aquatic birds visit the pans here during the summer when you can see woolly-necked storks, herons, flamingos, pink-backed and white pelicans, ibises, spoonbills and jacanas from the hides overlooking the pans. You may also spot hippo and crocodile.

Exploring the reserve

A 100-km network of roads crosses the reserve, passing through areas of thick bush which are not ideal for game viewing; the grasslands, however, are more open and animals are easier to see. The best game viewing areas are the **Loop Road**, the **Nsumo Pan** and the **airstrip**.

There are four game viewing hides next to the Kubube, Kumasinga, Kwamalibala and Kumahlala pans. The game viewing here is excellent and you can watch the game coming down to drink. There are car parks nearby where you can leave your car and walk to the hides.

Sodwana Bay » *pp496-498. Colour map 5, grid A3.*

ⓘ *Entrance gates open 24 hrs, T035-5710051; R20.*

Sodwana's is South Africa's premier scuba diving destinations – and is the site of the world's southernmost tropical reefs. Eighty per cent of South Africa's 1200 species of fish can be found in the waters off Sodwana; ragged-toothed and whale sharks, humpback whales, black marlin and turtles are some of the major attractions. Diving has become so popular here that over 100,000 dives a year are made on these reefs.

Ins and outs

Getting there Sodwana Bay is 350 km from Durban and is well signposted from the N2, approaching from the south on the N2 take the Ngwenya/Sodwana Bay exit. The road is tarred and goes through **Mbazwana** en route to Sodwana Bay (80 km). This small village has mushroomed in recent years. There is a colourful market selling fruit and handicrafts. It is 15 km from here to Sodwana Bay along a tar road.

From the N2 in the north take the turning to Jozini and Mbazwana. Follow the dirt road to Sodwana Bay (120 km), passing through Ubombo, Tshongwe and Mbazwana. The dirt road to Sodwana can be tackled without a 4WD but the stretch between Mbazwana and Lake Sibaya can be difficult after rain.

Best time to visit Sodwana is popular with visitors all year round. Divers prefer April to September, whereas fishermen tend to congregate here in November and December. December and January are the best times to see the turtles laying their eggs. Sodwana gets very crowded during the school holidays when the accommodation is fully booked months in advance.

Diving

The coral reefs at Sodwana lie just offshore and teem with colourful tropical fish. Among some of the more unusual sightings are the loggerhead, leatherback and hawksbill turtles, honeycomb moray eels, dolphins, whale sharks, stingrays, humpback whales and black marlins. **Two Mile Reef** is very popular with divers. It is 1½ km long and nearly 1 km wide, with depths ranging from 9 m to 34 m. There are numerous dive sites to explore here and anemones, triggerfish, sponges and fan-shaped gorgoniums can be seen in this area of overhangs and caves. The dives at **Five Mile Reef** and **Seven Mile Reef** are at around 22 m, and both are renowned for their corals. Access to Five Mile Reef is limited, but it is worth trying to get on a dive to see this protected area with its delicate miniature Staghorn Coral Gardens. **Nine Mile Reef** is only open for a limited number of dives and is well known for its soft corals. There are some large caves which can shelter pyjama sharks. Depths range from 5 m to 24 m. » *For more detailed dive facts and recommendations, see Essentials, page 54.*

The closest snorkelling site to Sodwana is on **Quarter Mile Reef**, 500 m off Jesser Point. Further south are **Algae Reef** (5 km) and **Adams Reef** (10 km). These are shallow rocky reefs with good visibility inhabited by tiny tropical fish.

Heading north from Mbazwana » *pp496-498.*

Lake Sibaya → *Colour map 2, grid C6*

From **Mbazwana** a track heads to the remote northern coastal reserves, but this route can only be negotiated with a 4WD. Lake Sibaya, 20 km north of Sodwana, is the largest freshwater lake in South Africa and was previously connected to the sea. The lake is now surrounded by swampy reed beds and patches of forest which provide varied habitats for the many species of birds which can be found here. A long strip of thickly forested dunes runs between the Indian Ocean and the lake. Tropical birdlife is Lake Sibaya's main attraction and kingfishers, cormorants and fish eagles are often seen, as are the lake's hippos and crocodiles.

! This is an endemic malaria area.

Lala Neck, Rocktail Bay and Black Rock

Continuing north past the forest station of **Manzengwenya** there is a dirt track running parallel to the coast which leads to three secluded beach resorts: **Lala Neck** (8 km), **Rocktail Bay** (12 km) and **Black Rock** (20 km). These are renowned for being among the ultimate game fishing sites in South Africa. **Lala Neck** and **Black Rock** have clear waters that offer spectacular opportunities for snorkelling and diving, with good chances of seeing turtles and sharks as well as hundreds of colourful tropical fish. There are no facilities here (other than one upmarket place to stay) but there is a day entry fee of R20 per person.

Ndumo Game Reserve » pp496-498. Colour map 2, grid C6.

ⓘ Park gates Apr-Sep 0600-1800, Oct-Mar 0500-1900; office daily 0800-1300, 1400-1600. R35 per person, plus R35 per vehicle.

Ndumo is a low lying and humid tropical floodplain renowned for its magnificent birdlife and large numbers of crocodiles and hippos. This is one of the wildest and most beautiful reserves in South Africa and its verdant wetlands have been compared with the Okavango Delta.

The area had been heavily hunted since the 1850s. Early hunters left records of having seen large herds of game here, but within 50 years a huge proportion of them had been shot. One of the species which has recovered well is the nyala which was hunted here by Courtney Selous. He visited this region at the turn of the century to capture nyala for London Zoo.

Ins and outs

Getting there and around From Jozini the road heads directly north to Ndumo. The reserve is 14 km beyond the village of Ndumo on a rough dirt road and lies along the border of Mozambique. The roads are in good condition and visitors can drive around the reserve in their own cars or travel by Land Rover with a guide. There are five game viewing hides to stop at and a leaflet is available for a self-guided car trail.

Wildlife

The reserve was initially established in 1924 to protect the hippos which lived here. As human activity has decreased the animal population of the park has increased dramatically. Some species have been reintroduced and the varied flora of the reserve, which includes numerous pans and reedbeds interspersed with patches of riverine forest and mixed woodland, provides habitats for many different species.

The pans at Banzi and Nyamithi are fascinating areas to experience the atmosphere of an African tropical swamp. There are many waterbirds to look out for on the pans including some rare tropical species at the southern limit of their habitats. Thousands of birds congregate here in the evenings and it is possible to see flocks of flamingos, geese, pelicans and storks.

Buffalo are occasionally seen in the swampy areas of the reserve, but nyala, hippo and crocodiles are present in large numbers. The vegetation in the rest of the reserve is quite thick and makes game viewing difficult. Black and white rhino, leopard and suni antelope thrive in these thickets but they are very rarely seen. A good way to see Ndumo is on one of the tours organized by the reserve. It is possible to go on five different guided walks with a game ranger.

Tembe Elephant Park » pp496-498. Colour map 2, grid C6.

ⓘ 72 km from Jozini. Park gates Apr-Sep 0600-1800, Oct-Mar 0500-1900. R35 per person, plus R35 vehicle.

The reserve was established in 1983 to protect this area's elephant population, which had declined to just 130. They used to migrate over the border into Mozambique but suffered greatly at the hands of poachers; scars left by poachers can still be seen on some of the older elephants. This herd is reckoned to be the only indigenous elephants in KwaZulu Natal. The 30,000-ha protected area at Tembe is a vast impenetrable wilderness of sand forest, thick bush and the Muzi Swamp. This is a very special place to visit, but you will need to plan well in advance, given the strict access controls.

Ins and outs

Getting there Tembe lies on the border with Mozambique between Ndumo Game Reserve and Kosi Bay. It is 72 km from Jozini and although the road is tarred as far as the entrance to the park, the roads inside are so rough that only 4WDs are allowed in.

Wildlife

In addition to overnight visitors staying in the luxury lodge (the only accommodation within the park), only a further five groups of day visitors in a 4WD are allowed into the park each day. Each group is accompanied by a park ranger and there are good chances of seeing Tembe's abundant game and birdlife. Some of the more common species to be seen include giraffe, elephant, waterbuck, zebra, nyala and buffalo. Lion have been introduced to the park, now making it home to the Big Five. If you are lucky you may see the small, shy, suni antelope and a leopard. There are two hides in the reserve: one at Ponweni by Muzi swamp, this overlooks an elephant crossing point; the second overlooks Mahlasela Pan. There is also a self-guided walk within the Ngobazane enclosure area.

Kosi Bay Nature Reserve » pp496-498. Colour map 2, grid C6.

ⓘ *96 km from Jizini. Park gates open Apr-Sep, 0600-2000, Oct-Mar 0500-2000. R20 per person, R15 per vehicle.*

Kosi Bay is one of South Africa's favourite wilderness destinations. The protected area is over 25 km long and consists of four lakes separated from the sea by a long strip of forest-covered dunes. Lakes Amanzimnyama, Nhlange, Mpungwini and Sifungwe are part of a fascinating tropical wetland environment. Lake Amanzimnyama is a freshwater lake with darkened due to decomposing plants. The shores of the lakes are bordered with reedbeds, ferns, swamp figs and umdoni trees. Five species of mangrove thrive in the estuary, where local fishermen have built traditional fishing traps.

Kosi Bay is home to South Africa's only remaining estuarine hunter-gatherer tribe, the Tembe-Thonga, whose traditional fishing traps you can see across the estuary.

Ins and outs

Getting there and around From Jozini head north as if going to Ndumo but stay on the road through the villages of Sihangwana and Ngwanase, from where the entrance gate to Kosi is around 10 km to the north. There is a rough dirt road leading to the park though a 4WD is not necessary. However, access to Kosi Mouth itself is through deep sand for which a 4WD is needed. The nearest petrol station and supermarket are at Kwangwanase.

Best time to visit The tropical climate here can be debilitatingly hot and humid. The best time to visit is in August and September, which are the coolest months and tend not to be so humid.

Wildlife

The lakes are inhabited by hippos and crocodiles, which can be seen basking in the sun around Lake Amanzimnyama. There are no large mammals here but you are likely to see samango and vervet monkeys. The tropical climate is a boon to reptiles and two species of monitor lizard, the Rock and the Nile, are often seen. Many of the snakes which live here are poisonous. The gaboon adder, boomslang, green mamba and forest cobras are all found here.

Many aquatic birds are attracted to the lakes and over 200 species have been spotted here. Rarities include the palmnut vulture and Pel's fishing owl.

The research station at Bhanga Nek has been tagging turtles and protecting nesting sites since 1963. Leatherback and loggerhead turtles arrive on these beaches after lengthy journeys from as far away as Madagascar and the Cape.

Exploring the reserve

A four-day trail, recently taken over by the local community, can be booked on T072-1871516 (mob). The trail is 34 km long and is probably the best way to see the Kosi Bay Nature Reserve. Hikers are accompanied by a guide who leads the group through the entire ecosystem. The distances covered every day are quite short so this gives ample time to relax and enjoy the atmosphere of the lakes. The trail is very popular and can be fully booked up to six months in advance, a maximum of 10 people are allowed on each trail. More information can be found at www.kznwildlife.com.

Northwest along the N2 » pp496-498.

Returning to the N2 via Jozini, the highway heads northwest towards Phongolo and Swaziland. The Phongolo dam can be seen lying to the east with the Lebombo Mountains in the background. The entrance to the Phongolo Game Reserve is clearly signposted off the N2.

Phongolo Game Reserve → Colour map 2, grid C5.

ⓘ *The reserve is accessed from the right of the N2 approximately 20 km before the town of Phongolo. Park gates summer 0500-1900, winter 0600-1800. R18 per person, plus R20 per vehicle.*

This large area of bush surrounding the dam has been declared a biosphere reserve and large game was recently reintroduced. These include white rhino, elephant, giraffe, blue wildebeest and zebra that now live alongside resident nyala, kudu, impala, suni antelope, reedbuck and warthog. The dam itself has significant populations of hippo and crocodile, and the elusive tiger fish that lures fishermen every year for the annual tiger fishing competition. The landscape is rolling grasslands interspersed with acacias and patches of thick bush. There is a beautiful stretch of lush riverine woodland along the Phongolo River and the dam itself attracts thousands of aquatic birds during the winter months (probably the best time to visit as the tracks within the reserve become impassable after rain in the summer months). Interestingly, this was the site of the first game reserve in Africa, proclaimed by Paul Kruger in 1894, which comprised 17,400 ha of farmland between Swaziland, the Lebombo Mountains and the Phongolo River. The Anglo-Boer War doomed the existence of the reserve but the Phongolo Game Reserve was reinstated in 1964.

Crossing into Swaziland

The N2 continues to **Golela** and the border with Swaziland. From here it is possible to head north into Swaziland through **Lavumisa**. This is not a very interesting place and most people pass straight through. Fuel and snacks are available here and there is a basic hotel. Continuing on into Swaziland is relatively easy as this is one of the busiest crossings into Swaziland, with many local buses plying the route between Lavumisa and Manzini. The **border** post is open daily 0700-2200. You will need a valid passport. If you are driving a hired car, make sure you get a letter from your car hire firm confirming that you may take the car out of South Africa. The alternative route into Swaziland is to head west into Mpumalanga along the N2 towards **Piet Retief**.

Itala Game Reserve

» pp496-498. Colour map 5, grid A2.

ⓘ 74 km east of Phongolo, 400 km north of Durban and 500 km from Johannesburg. T034-9075105. Park gates Oct-Mar 0500-1900, Apr-Sep 0600-1800. Reception office at Ntshondwe Camp, daily 0700-1930. R35 per person, plus R30 per vehicle.

The R69 heads west off the N2 at Candova. The gravel road goes as far as Magudu. From there the R69 is tarred leading to the Itala Game Reserve. This section of the R69 is a fascinating drive through rural Zululand, passing through low lying grasslands and cattle-ranching country. In November and December, after the rains, the countryside is green and lush and rich in birdlife. Many private game reserves and farms have recently opened, stocking their land with game bought at the annual game auctions that occur in the area. The reserve was established in 1972 after the Natal Parks Board began buying farms on the land lying between the top of the escarpment at Louwsburg and the Phongolo River Valley. After years of overgrazing the land had seriously deteriorated and very little wildlife remained. In the last 30 years Itala has been transformed into one of KwaZulu Natal's most spectacular reserves.

The rivers at Thalu and Mbiso camps are not infected with bilharzia and are safe for swimming.

Ins and outs

Getting there From Durban, travel north on the N2 as far as Phongolo. From here take the R66 and then the R69 for 73 km and the park entrance is near the village of Louwsburg. From Gauteng the easiest route is via the N2 to Phongolo, though the park can also be approached via Vryheid from the Battlefield region.

Getting around There is a network of dirt roads looping around the reserve which offer good game viewing by car. Large herds of grazers are often seen on the grasslands near the airstrip look out for white rhino and tsessebe and particularly cheetah, which favour grass airstrips because of their openness. There are also some self-guided walking trails passing through forest.

Best time to visit The climate is warm all year round but it can get cold in the evenings from May to August when there are occasional frosts. Most of the rain falls in the summer months of November, December and January.

Wildlife and vegetation

The reserve's landscapes are mostly large areas of low lying grasslands at 400 m rising up through steep sided forested valleys to granite cliffs at 1450 m. The streams rising in these mountains flow down into the Phongolo River. The steeply rising terrain has created several different ecosystems from deep narrow valleys and boulder outcrops to cliff faces, with an interesting diversity of wildlife. Twenty new species have been reintroduced into the reserve including a herd of young elephant and the only herd of tsessebe in Natal. Animals commonly seen include eland, giraffe, kudu, blue wildebeest and zebra. The following animals are present here but are rarely seen: cheetah, white rhino, elephant, klipspringer, leopard, nyala and black rhino. For visitors wanting to see the park on foot, guided day hikes (as well as self-guided trails) can be booked at reception.

Some 320 species of bird have been recorded here, including black eagle, bathawk, bald ibis, martial eagle and brown-necked parrot. Some interesting plants to look out for in season are the flowering aloes trees, unmistakable in June and July when they come into bloom. Their large orange flowers are an important source of nectar at this time of year and they attract birds and insects.

Mkuze *p488*

B **Ghost Mountain Inn**, T035-5731025-7, www.ghostmountaininn.co.za. Next to the northern entrance to Mkuze. 52 rooms, a/c, stylish decor, TV, restaurant, spa and swimming pool. Good value safari packages. The inn also owns **Moyeni Lodge**, a remote self-catering lodge sleeping up to 8, very private, set up in the mountains with impressive views.

Mkuze Game Reserve *p488*

The prices for the following are for the whole lodge or cottage; when split among a group, they are quite good value. Reservations through **KZN Wildlife**, T033-8451000, www.kznwildlife.com. Camping is booked directly, T035-5730001.

A **Umkumbi**. There are 4 en suite safari tents each containing 2 beds and a fridge. Thatched wood and reed lounge, dining area and bar overlooking a natural pan. There is a cook here to prepare your meals and a game guard to take you on guided bush walks. The bush camp is open Nov-Mar only as it is in a controlled hunting area.

A-D **Mantuma**. The main camp with a variety of cottages, including 2 7-bed cottages with 3 bedrooms, 2 bathrooms and fully equipped kitchen; 5 4-bed en suite bungalows with 2 bedrooms and fully equipped kitchen; 4 3-bed en suite chalets with fully equipped kitchen; 10 2-bed and 3 3-bed tents raised on a wooden deck with en suite bathrooms and communal open plan kitchen; 6 3-bed rest huts with communal kitchen and ablution block. This is the largest camp, the buildings are set among natural gardens and are not fenced off from the reserve so game does sometimes wander through. There is also a pool, shop, and game drives and guided walks can be arranged.

C **Nhlonhlela**. This luxury 8-bed bush lodge looks out over the fever trees and Nhlonhlela Pan. There is a central lounge and kitchen where a cook will prepare your meals and there's a game guard for guided bush walks.

Sodwana Bay *p490*

The supermarket sells petrol and oil and stocks bread, tinned food and beach gear. Freezer drawers are available for hire and should be booked in advance, but at R30 for 24 hrs they are expensive.

B **Sodwana Bay Camp**, KZN Wildlife, T033-8451000, www.kznwildlife.com. 10 8-bed and 10 5-bed self-catering fully equipped log cabins, some recently renovated.

B **Sodwana Bay Lodge**, T035-5716000, www.sodwanadiving.co.za. Accommodation is in 20 twin-bedded reed and thatch huts on stilts overlooking woodland, restaurant serving seafood (what else), bar, pool, game fishing trips available. The lodge offers a number of all-inclusive diving package deals plus a full range of PADI courses, with a fully equipped dive shop and learning pool.

D-E **Gwalagwala** is a large campsite with 286 basic sites in the main section which can become very crowded, plus 33 luxury sites with their own water and electricity supplies. Camping is booked directly T035-5710051/3.

Heading north from Mbazwana *p491*

L2 **Rocktail Bay Lodge**, 12 km north of Manzengwenya along a dirt track running parallel with the beach. A luxury bush camp with 11 A-frame chalets set on stilts among dunes and coastal forest a few hundred metres from the beach and the Indian Ocean. A wide range of activities available including birdwatching, diving, snorkelling, swimming, fishing and 4WD trips to nearby beaches and Lake Sibaya. The highlight of a stay here is a night-time search for egg laying turtles on the beach just below the lodge. Reservations through **Wilderness Safaris**, Johannesburg, T011-8830747, www.wilderness-safaris.com.

E **Mabibi Coastal Camp**, Lake Sibaya, reservations, T035-4741504, taryn@isibindafrica.co.za. 10 sites, each with shadecloth gazebo, ablution block, no electricity. The camp is set in one of the most isolated stretches of the Coastal Forest Reserve and is the ideal place for an idyllic tropical beach holiday. It lies on the strip of forested dunes between Lake Sibaya and the sea, and a path connecting the camp to the beach passes through thick tropical forest rich in birdlife. Lying just offshore is a fascinating area of rarely visited coral reefs and rock pools, but it's only possible to visit here in a 4WD. Report to the office on arrival, which closes at 1600. The nearest petrol and supplies are 60 km away at Mbazwana. There have been reports of hijackings in the area, so exercise caution when driving.

Ndumo Game Reserve *p492*

C **Ndumo Camp**, KZN Wildlife, T033-8451000, www.kznwildlife.com. 7 2-bed rest huts, with a/c and private verandas. Lovely setting overlooking the Phongolo floodplain, surrounded by tropical vegetation. Well-equipped kitchen, swimming pool. Cook on hand to prepare meals (but guests must bring their own food). Game drives can be arranged from here.

Camping

8 sites near the hutted camp, with kitchen and ablution block, T035-5910004.

Tembe Elephant Park *p492*

L1 **Tembe Elephant Lodge**, T031-2670144, www.tembe.co.za. The bush camp consists of upmarket tents raised on wooden platforms tucked away in secluded areas. There are hot showers with glass walls that look out over the bush, small pool with thatched roof and relaxing veranda. Rates include meals and game drives, which are also available to day visitors by prior arrangement.

Kosi Bay Nature Reserve *p493*

L2 **Kosi Forest Lodge**, reservations T035-4741473, www.zulunet.com. Luxury all-inclusive safari camp within the reserve. 16-bed lodge, with individual reed and thatch suites, beautiful hardwood floors, open-air bathrooms, very secluded – popular with honeymooners. Excellent restaurant, bar, swimming pool. Beautiful setting, range of activities on offer including turtle-watching trips, canoeing and diving.

B **Kosi Bay Lodge**, 500 m from the lake, 500 m from the bay itself outside the reserve, T035-5920392. Restaurant, swimming pool, pub, self-catering also an option, in A-frame chalets with communal ablution block or 2-bed reed en suite huts. The lodge runs trips to the eastern shore of the lake from where you can hike 5 km to the beautiful beaches. One of the cheaper options in the region.

B-C **Camp**, KZN Wildlife, T033-8451000, www.kznwildlife.com. There are 3 thatched cabins here with either 6, 5 or 2 beds. All 3 are fully equipped and fully equipped for self-catering.

Camping

15 pitches and an ablution block among the trees near Lake Nhlange, T035-5920236.

Northwest along the N2 *p494*

L2 **Mkuze Falls Private Game Reserve**, near the village of Mahlangasi, access off the R66, T034-4141018, www.mkuzefalls.com. Super luxury in 8 thatched chalets with private plunge pool and open-air showers, 1 safari suite, or 5 en suite tents with a/c, mosquito nets, all accommodation has fantastic views of the waterfall on the Mkuze River, personal attentive service, all inclusive with meals and game drives. The reserve is home to the Big Five.

AL **Pakamisa Private Game Reserve**, off the R66, T034-4133559, www.pakamisa.co.za. 2500-ha estate, 8 spacious luxury rooms designed in a Spanish villa style with private balconies, terrace restaurant overlooking the Pakamisa Mountains, dinners 'out bush' can be arranged, horse riding, game drives and walks, clay pigeon shooting, swimming pool. Rates are all inclusive.

AL **White Elephant Lodge**, next to the dam Phongolo Game Reserve, T034-4132489, www.whiteelephant.co.za. A luxurious, all-inclusive 5-star game lodge. The 8 elegant safari tents have a colonial theme and en suite open-air baths. Lots of activities on offer, including game drives, guided mountain biking, boat cruises, tiger fishing, rhino walks and short flights in a 6-seater plane.

A **Pongola Country Lodge**, 14 Jan Mielie St, Phongolo, T034-4131352, www.pongola countrylodge.co.za. Hardly a country lodge as it's next to an industrial area in the village but pleasant enough inside. 44 rooms, some on the small side, en suite, TV, a/c, phone, parking outside of the rooms, pool, extensive gardens, restaurant, bar. Slightly overpriced for what it is.

C-E **Pongola Caravan Park**, 219 Hans Meyer St, PO Box 539, Phongolo, T034-4131789. 9 self-catering chalets, TV, a/c, shady and grassed caravan and camping sites, all sites have electric points, spotless ablution block, mini golf course, small kiosk with basic camping supplies, ideal base for exploring the region as well as Swaziland.

Camping

Phongolo Game Reserve, T034-4351012. 20 basic sites next to the dam, ablution block, cold water only.

Itala Game Reserve *p495*

Reservations through **KZN Wildlife**, T033-8451000, www.kznwildlife.com.

AL **Ntshondwe Lodge**. Sleeps 6 in 3 luxurious en suite double bedrooms, small plunge pool, viewing deck, all-inclusive, hosted, catered safari lodge. Ingeniously camouflaged in a jumble of boulders and flowering plants and trees. Game drives and walks are available.

C-D **Ntshondwe Camp**. 25 2-bed and 12 4-bed self-catering chalets, with fully equipped kitchens, a lounge and dining room. Also 28 2-bed en suite units with no cooking facilities. There's a shop, restaurant serving meals and takeaways, bar and a pool. The camp shop sells limited tinned and dried food, wildlife books and charcoal and petrol is on sale next to the main gates. The nearest shop is in Louwsburg (5 km).

Bush camps

The camps are all self-catering but are supplied with bedding and have a fully equipped kitchen; the lodges are thatched and built from natural materials. The camps are set by themselves in the bush and guests can game watch from the comfort of their verandas in front of the huts or go on a game walk accompanied by a guard. The bush camps are only available for single group bookings.

B **Mbizo**. Sleeps 8 in 2 lodges with a shared lounge, kitchen and viewing deck. Overlooks the rapids on the Mbizo River. Guests must supply their own food.

B **Mhlangeni**. Sleeps 10 in 2 lodges, and is set in a rocky area overlooking the Ncence River well away from the busiest areas of the park and is renowned for its game viewing. A central open plan lounge and kitchen with its own sundeck provide wonderful views. Guests supply food which is cooked by the resident cook.

B **Thalu**. 4-bed camp with kitchen, lounge and viewing deck on the banks of the Thalu River. Guests supply food, which is cooked by the resident cook.

Camping

Campsite, Main camp, T034-9832540. Ablution block with 1 toilet and cold showers only. Maximum 20, tents only, caravans not permitted. Animals can be seen wandering around and it's a great place for wilderness camping.

Activities and tours

Sodwana Bay *p490*

Coral Divers, T033-3456531, www.coraldivers.co.za, is consistently recommended. PADI courses from open water to dive master and include dorm accommodation, equipment but no meals or park entry fees. Open water courses start from R1850. It has its own backpacker resort at Sodwana with bar, restaurant, deck, pool, TV room and internet access, and will pick you up from Hluhluwe for an extra R100.

Ghost Mountain Inn, T035-5731025, www.ghostmountaininn.co.za, offers a range of all-inclusive safari tours in the area, ranging from 1-5 days. **Tribe Africa Tours**, is also based here, T035-5731474. Professional local operator, canoe trips, game drives, specialist birding safaris, snorkelling trips to a lagoon near Kosi Bay, cultural tours.

KZN Wildlife. Turtle-viewing trips are held nightly Dec-Jan, R90 per person and should be booked at reception. There is also a 5-km self-guided walking trail through the coastal forests and dunes.

Transport

Sodwana Bay *p490*

This is a relatively remote part of the coast and until recently it was only accessible to people with 4WDs.

The **Baz Bus**, T021-4392323, www.bazbus.com, drops passengers off at the Isinkwe Backpackers near **Hluhluwe** on its way north to **Swaziland**.

Gauteng

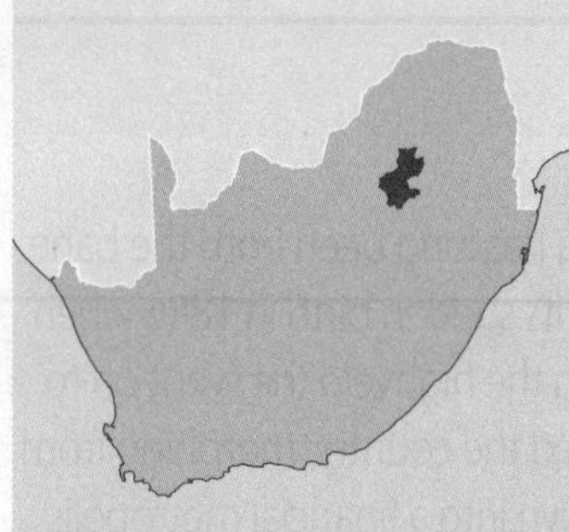

Footprint features

Introduction

Loud, brash and rich, Johannesburg has long been both the bane and lifeblood of South Africa. Since its sudden birth in 1886 when a hapless Aussie discovered gold on the highveld (he went on to sell his plot for £10), it has dominated the country, morphing from a rough and debauched frontier town into a financial metropolis with a good deal of debauchery still imbedded in its fabric.

Built on a high plateau surrounded by the world's richest gold mines, Johannesburg dominates Gauteng – both in size and in wealth. The highrise city centre is surrounded by some 600 suburbs: to the north lie the realms of the wealthy and white, while in the southwest is the vast township of Soweto. Although the city has suffered from much-publicized high crime rates, it is now dusting off its dodgy reputation and drawing back visitors for the first time in over a decade. Crime-busting regeneration programmes have seen areas like rundown Newtown transformed and filled with restaurants and shops, while recent additions include one of South Africa's finest museums, the Apartheid Museum. The northern suburbs are an enclave of posh boutiques, good restaurants and the country's most sophisticated nightlife, while Soweto now attracts more tourists than Kruger National Park.

50 km to the north is the capital of the state, Pretoria. Although connected by an almost unbroken ribbon of development, the two cities couldn't be more different. Pretoria is staid and conservative, with wide streets lined with jacaranda trees which bloom a ladylike purple in spring. The centre feels peaceful and orderly, with attractive sandstone buildings and large, tidy parks. Pretoria has long been a centre of Afrikanerdom, best summed up by the sombre Voortrekker Monument. But its conservative feel has mellowed of late, with a lively student population and the influx of a multilingual diplomatic community.

★ Don't miss...

1 **Newtown** Stroll through this rejuvenated corner of downtown Johannesburg, stop for a coffee with well-heeled locals or catch a play at the Market Theatre, page 507.

2 **Apartheid Museum** Get a real insight into the country's past at this superb and often harrowing exploration of the Apartheid regime, page 508.

3 **Soweto** Explore South Africa's most famous township – now a city in its own right – and learn about the country's history of segregation, page 510.

4 **Melville nightlife** Join South Africa's most mixed and fashionable crowd in the cafés, restaurants and bars of buzzing Melville, page 520.

5 **Rosebank Mall** Grab a paper and munch on a fat breakfast before exploring the Sunday African craft market, page 521.

6 **Voortrekker Monument** Take in this controversial monument of Afrikaner culture, a vast granite block perched on a hill overlooking Pretoria, page 530.

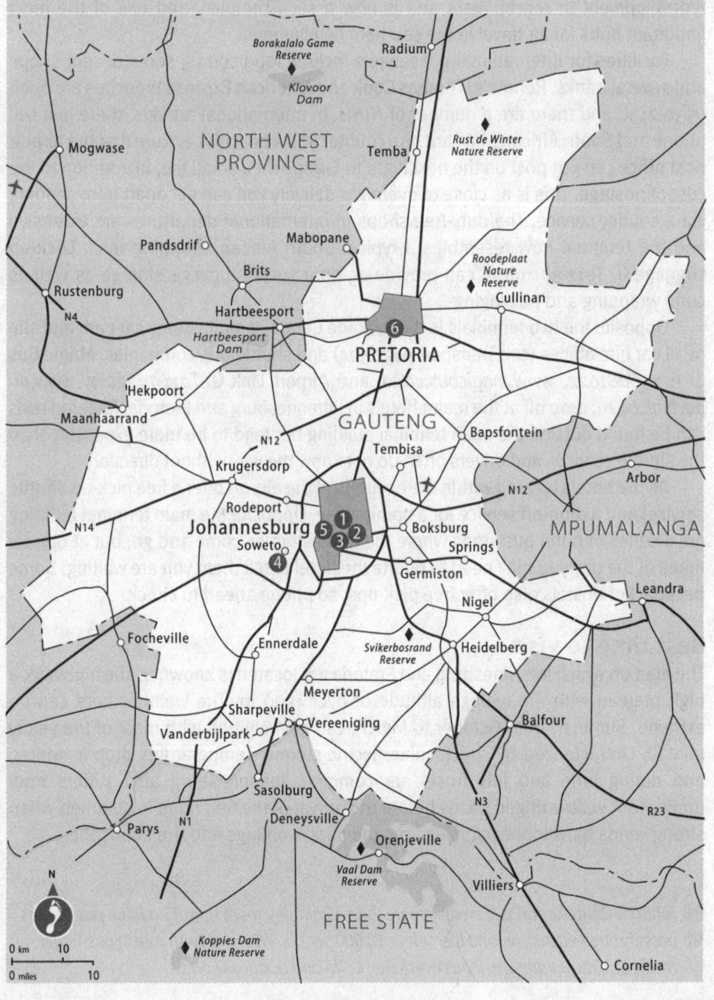

Ins and outs

Neither Johannesburg nor Pretoria merit more than a couple of days' exploration; if you're on a tight schedule, a day or two will cover the major sights and give you time to explore the excellent shopping and dining opportunities, some of the best in Africa. However, it is the area's history, and its excellent museums, which give a real feel for the country's troubled past – and for the shape of its future.

Arriving by air

Johannesburg International Airport ⓘ *Kempton Park, To11-9216262*, is 24 km from the city centre and 35 km from the northern suburbs on the R24, roughly halfway between Johannesburg and Pretoria. Both cities can be reached by car in 30 minutes. There are two terminals, one catering for international flights and the other for domestic flights. The terminals are next to each other, and at time of writing, passengers have to walk between the two (along a safe pavement), taking about five minutes, but a new building is being constructed to connect the two. The airport has been undergoing steady redevelopment in recent years and is now a slick complex, and one of the most important hubs for air travel in the southern hemisphere.

Facilities for international passengers include food courts, some decent shops and several banks. **Rennie's/Thomas Cook** and **American Express** branches are open 0530-2130 and there are a number of ATMs. In international arrivals, there is a cell phone and South African SIM card hire counter and a post office. Note that the airport post office can put post on the next flight to Europe for a small fee, in addition to the cost of postage. This is as close to overnight delivery you can get apart from sending via a courier service. The duty-free shops in international departures are extensive and the terminal now resembles a typical South African shopping mall. **Lock-up Luggage** ⓘ *To11-3901804*, can provide 24-hour secure luggage storage as well as curio wrapping and packaging

Opposite the two terminals is the **Parkade Centre**, a multi-storey car park and site of all car hire offices (see Transport page 524) and shuttle bus companies. **Magic Bus** ⓘ *To11-6081622, www.magicbus.co.za*, and **Airport Link** ⓘ *To11-7922017, www.airportlink.co.za*, drop off at the major hotels in Johannesburg and Pretoria. Metered taxis can be found outside the main terminal building but tend to be more expensive than the shuttle services and drivers often do not know the way without direction.

All the hotels located within the environs of the airport offer a free pick-up shuttle service, and a drop-off service for a nominal fee. Opposite the main terminal building are a series of hotel bus stops where the hotel shuttles come and go, but at quieter times of the day you may need to phone the hotel to tell them you are waiting. Some backpacker hostels also offer free pick-ups, so phone ahead to check.

Best time to visit

The area on which Johannesburg and Pretoria are located is known as the highveld, a high plateau with an average altitude of over 1500 m. The weather here can be extreme. Summer, from October to March, can get very hot, with most of the yearly rainfall, characterized by spectacular electric storms. Temperatures drop in winter, and during June and July frosts are common. Johannesburg also suffers from unpleasant yellow-tinged hazes before the arrival of the first rains in summer, when strong winds blow loose particles from the mine workings into the atmosphere.

Johannesburg Airport is served by more than 45 airlines, more than 11 million passengers pass through each year, and it employs 18,000 people. With a growth rate in passenger traffic of 10% per annum, it has overtaken Cairo and Dubai airports.

Arriving at night

Johannesburg International Airport is open 24 hours but most flights from Europe arrive in the early morning. If you do happen to arrive at night, you will find the airport perfectly safe, some restaurants and shops stay open and banking hours are until 2130. There are also ATMs. Shuttle buses will collect you at any time though it is worth arranging this in advance, as the shuttle desks at the airport close at night. The same is true for the car hire companies. There are several hotels within a few kilometres of the airport that will collect you for free if you phone ahead.

Tourist information

The **Gauteng Tourism Authority** ⓘ *1 Central Place, corner of Jeppe and Henry Nxumalo Sts, Newtown, T011-8322780, www.gauteng.net*, is responsible for information for the whole province. It's a fairly new office with only has a small selection of maps and brochures, but its staff are very helpful and will advise you on sites and attractions. **Johannesburg Tourism Company** ⓘ *Grosvenor Corner, 195 Jan Smuts Av, Parktown, T011-2140700, www.joburg.org.za*, is a rather odd set-up, with limited information in the walk-in office, but an excellent website. For information on Pretoria contact the **Tshwane Tourism Information Bureau** ⓘ *T012-3581430, www.tshwane.gov.za, Mon-Fri 0800-1600, 24-hr information line T082-2392630.*

Johannesburg

→ *Phone code: 011. Colour map 2, grid B3.*

Johannesburg is the largest financial, commercial and industrial centre in South Africa. Barely over a 100 years old, the discovery of gold transformed this deserted heartland into a vast urban sprawl and made it one of the wealthiest cities in the world. The gold rush brought in settlers from all over the world multiracial and cosmopolitan city, but Apartheid changed all that. Forced relocations altered the fabric of Johannesburg, creating deep divisions in society that still remain evident today. Despite Apartheid's demise, Johannesburg is still on the whole segregated, albeit no longer by legal requisite. The city centre and neighbouring suburbs, such as Hillbrow, are largely home to the urban black population, a condensed area of overcrowded high-rise flats where poverty and crime is rife. Soweto is a vast, sprawling township of government housing and informal settlements, home to the majority of Johannesburg's black commuters. Most white residents, on the other hand, live in the leafy and affluent northern suburbs.

But things are changing. Soweto has become a city in its own right, with new affluent suburbs and a fast-growing middle class, while a breed of wealthy, successful black people – known locally as "Buppies" (Black Upwardly-mobile People) have moved into what were until recently the reserves of rich whites. The notorious city centre, meanwhile, is undergoing extensive regeneration programmes, with streets being cleaned up and close-circuit cameras deterring casual criminals. But while crime rates have dropped considerably, safety remains an issue, with most visitors, like most well-off locals, confining themselves to the safe suburbs and numerous shopping malls. ▸▸ *For Sleeping, Eating and other listings, see pages 513-524.*

Getting there For detailed information on Johannesburg International Airport, see Arriving by air, page 502. The **railway station** and the **main bus terminal** are at the Park City Transit Centre. » *For further details, see Transport, page 523.*

Getting around Although public transport is improving in the city, it is still advisable to stick to private transport, hire cars and metered taxis. Locals rely mainly on minibus taxis, thousands of which ply the centre throughout the day, but these are not recommended for visitors due to high accident rates and issues of crime. The new **metrobuses** ⓘ *T011-8382125, www.mbus.co.za*, are a far safer option, running along 80 routes in and around the city from 0600 to 1900. Tickets run on zones; the central zone is by the bus terminus in Gandhi Square (formerly Vaderbijl Square) at the corner of Main and Rissik streets. A single tickets costs from R2.70. If you hire a car, plan your route before setting out and always carry a map – the system of one-way streets and snaking highways can be utterly bewildering. The **Gautrain**, a new high-speed rail link between Johannesburg and Pretoria via the airport and Midrand is due to begin construction in early 2006; it should be completed within a couple of years.

Greater Johannesburg

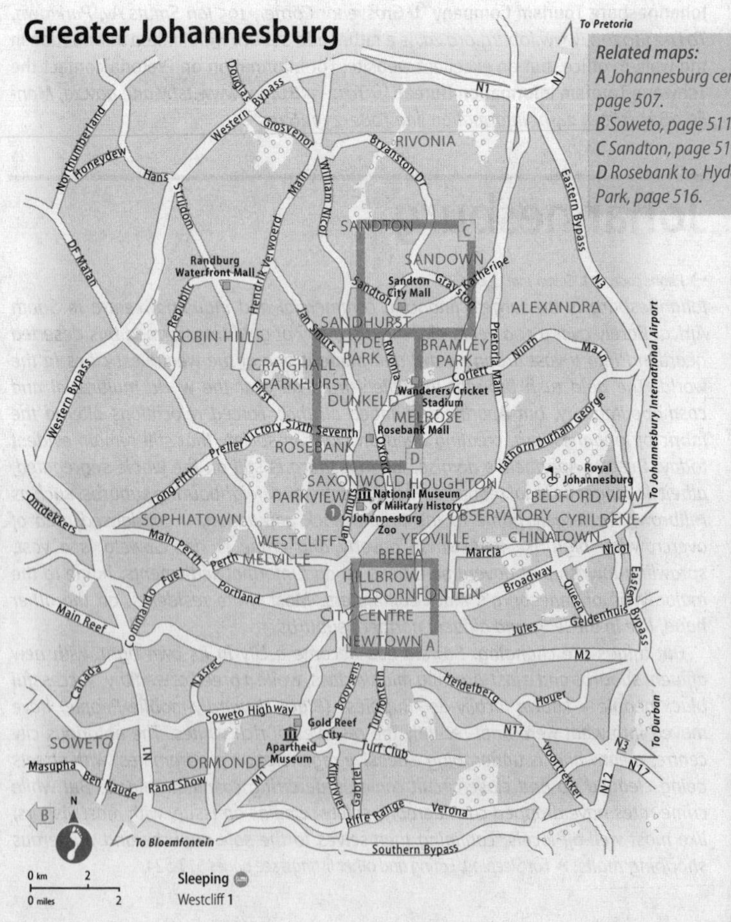

Orientation The once-prosperous central business district is today a hectic muddle of abandoned office blocks, market stalls and concrete flyovers. Crime remains a problem here and most businesses have moved out to the safer northern suburbs, although recent regeneration projects are starting to draw back investment. A visit to the city centre is well worthwhile for an insight into how Johannesburg has developed over the decades, although it is recommended that you go on an organized tour.

Johannesburg's affluent suburbs are in the northern part of the city. Clustered around the main freeway to Pretoria, the M1, they feel far removed from the hectic bustle of the centre. These are the safest areas in town and home to most of the city's tourist accommodation.

The largest of Johannesburg's suburbs feels very different. The infamous township of **Soweto** lies southwest of the city, named because of it's location – South West Township. Soweto is linked to the city by a number of freeways that carry hundreds of thousands of commuters to the city centre and northern suburbs each day. Adjoining Soweto to the south, are smaller townships where other communities were relocated during Apartheid; coloured people were forced to move to **Eldorado Park**, and Indians were moved to **Lenasia**.

Tourist information **Gauteng Tourism Authority** ⓘ *1 Central Place, corner of Jeppe and Henry Nxumalo Sts, Newtown, T011-8322780, www.gauteng.net, Mon-Fri 0800-1700*, is the main source of information in the city centre. There are also kiosks in Rosebank (T011-3272000, daily 0800-1800), Sandton (T011-7849596, daily 0800-1800) and Johannesburg International Airport (T011-3903602, daily 0600-2200). All have a selection of maps and brochure and can help with accommodation. **Johannesburg Tourism Company** ⓘ *Grosvenor Corner, 195 Jan Smuts Av, Parktown, T011-2140700, www.joburg.org.za, Mon-Fri 0800-1700, Sat 0900-1300*, has limited information but an excellent website.

Background

The city centre of Johannesburg is surrounded by some 600 suburbs covering approximately 500 sq km. The population of greater Johannesburg is roughly 3.2 million excluding Soweto. As it is almost impossible to estimate the population of Soweto due to the constant arrival of people from rural areas and illegal immigrants looking for work, the population of greater Johannesburg including Soweto is put at somewhere between six and eight million.

Much of Johannesburg's fabric was formed by the actions of the Apartheid regime from the mid-1950s. The thriving multi-racial conurbation (see page 509) was changed dramatically with the advent of the Group Areas Act, which forcibly relocated the city's black population from the centre to specially built townships outside town, such as Soweto. The most infamous forced removal was the bulldozing of an area to the west of Johannesburg called Sophiatown. This was an area of slum housing near to the city centre and was home to a diverse population of Africans, coloureds and 'poor whites'. During the 1940s and 1950s there was a huge outburst of a new African urban culture in Sophiatown, based mainly on the influence of American jazz musicians. This cultural explosion attracted bohemian whites and a huge number of African writers, journalists and politicians. To the Apartheid planners, the area stood for everything they opposed. In the mid-1950s the entire population was removed and the bulldozers were sent in. A new white suburb was built over the ruins and, in a gesture that was crass even by the standards of Apartheid, they named the new suburb Triomf – Afrikaans for 'triumph'.

Since the mid-1980s this forced movement of Africans from the city centre to the townships has been reversed. The breakdown of influx controls led to the rapid growth

24 hours in Johannesburg

Start the day with a sumptuous breakfast at **Fourno's Bakery** – they open at 0700 but the chefs have been busy baking pies, breads, and pastries from midnight. It's a great place to watch Jo'burg's high-fliers conduct power breakfasts over trendy coffees.

Don't miss a mind-expanding morning tour of **Soweto**, South Africa's oldest and most famous township. Drop in at Mandela's former home which is now a museum, drink a cool Castle lager in a shebeen, and visit the memorials dedicated to the struggle against Apartheid.

Lunch at **Rosebank Mall** before hitting the shops. Jo'burger's love their shopping malls and Rosebank has an excellent African Craft Market and a lively rooftop flea market on a Sunday.

Take an afternoon drive out to the **Lion Park**, where you can get close to a number of lions and play with some cubs, then go to the **Lesedi Cultural Village**. After the two-hour tour of four authentic African villages recreated from the Xhosa, Zulu, Pedi, and Sotho tribes, enjoy traditional dancing from over 60 performers around a large fire and a dinner of game meat such as impala or crocodile.

Crack open a good bottle of South African wine at the stylish **Blues Room** in Sandton, one of the best jazz and blues venues in Gauteng, before heading to **Melville**, Jo'burg's hip and happening nightlife district – two streets of bars, restaurants, and late night lounges where all the trendy people go to be seen.

If you're feeling peckish in the wee small hours, try the nachos at **Catz Pyjamas**, Jo'burg's original 24-hour bistro and cocktail bar.

of the African population of Johannesburg city centre, especially in Hillbrow, which has one of Africa's highest population densities. Since the end of Apartheid this trend has continued and has been bolstered by the arrival of new immigrants from outside South Africa's borders. Tens of thousands of Nigerians, Congolese and Zimbabweans have flooded, often illegally, into the centre, suburbs and townships. The population has mushroomed in the last decade, with a growth of around 23% since 1996.

The inner city has suffered from soaring crime rates in the last two decades, although much is being done to reverse the trend. While the mid-1990s saw much of central Johannesburg being deserted, with business and offices moving out to the northern suburbs, and the city being tagged as the murder capital of the world, the local government has clamped down in recent years. Massive raids on apartment blocks in Hillbrow have ousted thousands of illegal immigrants. An extensive network of CCTV cameras, a huge new Metro police force and numerous regeneration projects have made the centre far safer. Improved border security arrangements with neighbouring countries have blocked the traffic in stolen cars to other African countries, and the rate of car hijackings has been reduced considerably. A recent study showed that street crime in general has dropped dramatically, and you're now more likely to be a victim of violent crime in the Cape than in Johannesburg. The first of the regenerated areas was Newtown, where the streets were pedestrianized and the Mary Fitzgerald Square upgraded; the area is now filled with restaurants and shops and is attracting businesses back to the centre, including the new Gauteng tourism office. This is acting as a model for other parts of town, and it's hoped that the centre will once again become as safe as it once was.

Improved security is drawing back visitors, but its sensible to take common-sense precautions. Johannesburg is still not yet a city which can be casually explored on foot, and the best way of seeing the sights is probably on a guided tour.

Sights » pp513-524.

City centre

The **Newtown** area, once the cultural heart of Johannesburg, has, after years of deterioration, once again become a popular spot with locals. A huge regeneration project, which saw the introduction of closed circuit cameras, a police presence and the revamping of Mary Fitzgerald Square into a smart cobbled square, has transformed the area. Shops and cafés are moving in fast, and this is the site of the new **Gauteng Tourism Authority** office, see page 505. Unlike the rest of the city centre, it is safe to wander around Central Place. There is safe parking on the eastern part of Mary Fitzgerald Square, just in front of the Africa Museum.

The **Africa Museum** ⓘ *121 Bree St, T011-8335624, Tue-Sun 0900-1700, free*, is one of the city's major museums, but despite its reputation it is rather run down and disappointing. Housed in the city's former fruit and vegetable market, it attempts to explain the black experience of living in Johannesburg. There are displays on the struggle for democracy and on life in the goldmines and the townships, with mock-ups of an informal settlement. On the second floor is a gallery dedicated to San rock

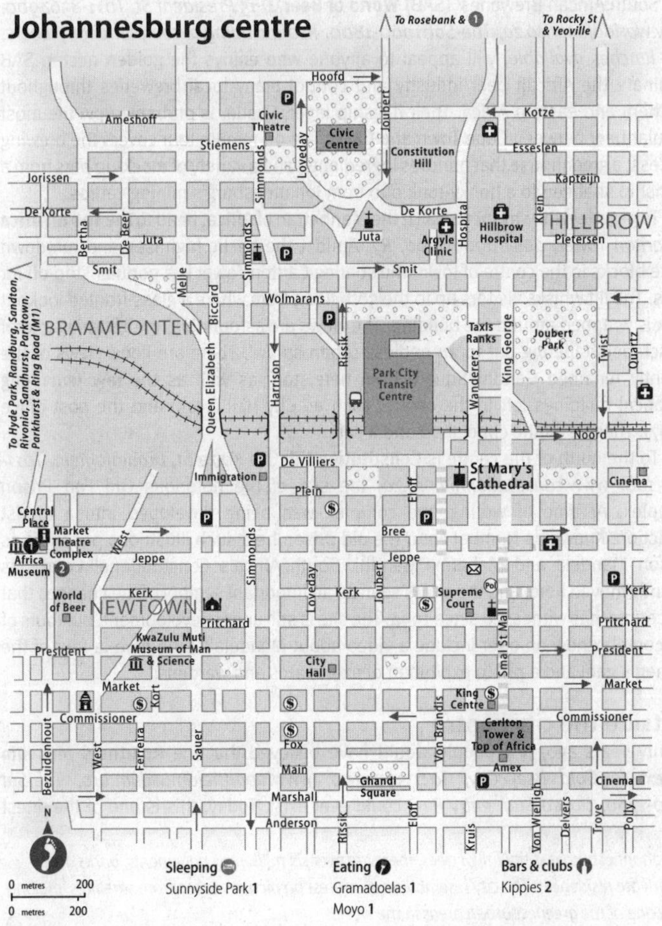

 art, but some of the displays seem to be missing. The most popular gallery is called 'Tried for Treason', with some interesting original editions of newspapers dating from treason trials in the 1960s, although the displays pale in comparison to those of the Apartheid Museum (see page 508). Perhaps most rewarding is the ground floor gallery, with changing temporary exhibitions, including some excellent photography shows. There is a small café and gift shop by the entrance.

The **Market Theatre Complex**, next to Museum Africa, is the main hub of the area's regeneration. As well as the theatre, there is the **Market Theatre Mall** (a series of small craft shops), and a couple of popular restaurants and bars, with stalls strung along the street selling Zulu beadwork, jewellery and crafts. At weekends, the market expands into Central Place, which also holds special events and occasional live music. The theatre itself is one of the best and most established in Gauteng.

The **KwaZulu Muti Museum of Man and Science** ⓘ *corner of Diagonal (14) and President St, T011-8364470, Mon-Fri 0730-1700, Sat 0730-1300*. This isn't actually a museum but a *muti* shop which has been on this site since 1897. *Muti* is a form of witchcraft practised exclusively by witch doctors, and this shop is crammed with products used in traditional herbal medicine and magic. The ingredients on sale include leaves, seeds and bark, as well as more specialized items like monkey skulls, dried crocodiles and ostrich feet.

South African Breweries' (SAB) **World of Beer** ⓘ *15 President St, T011-8364900, www.worldofbeer.co.za, Tue-Sat 1000-1800, R10 including 2 complimentary beers, pub lunches available*, will appeal to anyone who enjoys the golden nectar. SAB dominate the African beer industry and control many local breweries throughout southern and eastern Africa. Their flagship lager, Castle, is probably now the most popular beer between Cape Town and Cairo. The 90-minute tour covers the brewing process, a greenhouse that nurtures ingredients, and a variety of mock-up bars from a township shebeen to a honky-tonk pub from Johannesburg's mining camps.

To get a feel for why locals call it the Manhattan of Africa, head to the **Top of Africa** ⓘ *Carlton Tower, daily 0900-1700, R7*. Amidst the hectic highrises and run-down office blocks in the centre of town, the soaring Carlton Tower is a popular stop-off for tours. The lift whisks visitors up to the 50th floor, from where a glass-fronted lookout deck is wrapped around the building. The views are astounding, the glittering grid of skyscrapers tapering out to an endless urban sprawl. There are good views of the recently renamed Gandhi Square from here, too, as well as the few remaining historical buildings left in the centre, such as City Hall (1915) and the post office (1897). There is a little curio shop and a café.

To the north of the centre is **Constitution Hill** ⓘ *1 Kotze St, Braamfontein, T011-3813100, www.constitutionhill.org.za*, the site of the notorious Old Fort Prison Complex. At time of writing, the complex was being developed into a tourist attraction. Known as Number Four, the old prison held such illustrious prisoners as Nelson Mandela and Mahatma Gandhi. South Africa's Constitutional Court has recently moved here, and the site is seen as an important symbol of the changes that the country has witnessed since 1994. The site is still under development, but tours of the complex now on offer include a video about Mandela's time here, a tour of the women's gaol and a photo exhibition of ex-inmates and wardens.

Outside the city centre

Twenty years ago, few people would have believed that the **Apartheid Museum** ⓘ *next to Gold Reef City, T011-3904700, www.apartheidmuseum.org, Tue-Sat 1000-1700, closed Sun, entry R25*, could ever exist. Today, this is one of the finest

Johannesburg is a city full of trees, there are over six million on pavements, parks and private residences. The city resembles a rainforest on pictures taken from satellites, making it one of the greenest urban areas in the world.

City of gold

The high plateau on which Johannesburg was built was originally an arid place inhabited by a few Boer farmers grazing cattle and cultivating maize and wheat. This harsh and isolated landscape was transformed after the discovery of gold in 1886. During the 1880s, prospectors began arriving in the Eastern Transvaal attracted by reports of gold in Barberton and the mountains of the Eastern Drakensberg. George Harrison arrived from the Cape and travelled north to look at an abandoned gold mine on a farm in the Witwatersrand. He was employed to build a farmhouse at Langlaagte but in his free time he continued his search for gold. He discovered Main Reef in March 1886 and travelled to Pretoria to register his claim. Within weeks hordes of prospectors and fortune hunters began to arrive and officials of the Pretoria government were quickly sent to inspect the diggings and to lay out plans for a town.

Johannesburg expanded at a phenomenal rate and within three years had become the largest town in the eastern Transvaal. Confidence in Johannesburg's future was so great that traders in other regions of South Africa dismantled their wood and corrugated-iron buildings and transported the component parts to reassemble them in the new boom town. The *Star* newspaper relocated to Johannesburg from Grahamstown and transported its printing press across the veld by ox wagon. The gold rush attracted people from all over the world and Johannesburg became a cosmopolitan town where vast fortunes could be made overnight. Gambling dens, brothels and riotous canteens lined the streets and hundreds of ox-drawn wagons arrived daily to deliver food, drink and building supplies.

The mines expanded as new technologies opened up the deeper deposits of gold and Johannesburg was gradually transformed from being a gold rush boom town to being a large modern industrial city.

museums in the country and an excellent insight to what South Africa – past and present – is all about. This extraordinarily powerful museum was officially opened by Nelson Mandela in April 2002 and has already become the city's leading tourist attraction. The museum is divided into 'spaces' which follow the birth of Apartheid to the present day. When paying your entry fee you are issued with a random white or non-white ticket that takes you through two different entry points to symbolize segregation. The building itself has an innovative design to reflect the cold subject of Apartheid – harsh concrete, raw brick, steel bars and barbed wire.

The museum begins with a 15-minute video, taking you briefly through Voortrekker history to the Afrikaner government of 1948 which implemented Apartheid. The 'spaces' are dedicated to the rise of nationalism in 1948, pass laws, segregation, the first response from townships such as Sharpeville and Langa, the forced removals and the implementation of the Group Areas Act. From here, exhibits cover the rise of Black Consciousness, the student uprisings in Soweto in 1976, and political prisoners and executions.

The reforms during the 1980s and 1990s are well documented including President FW DeKlerk's un-banning of political parties, Mandela's release, the 1994 election, sanction lifting, and the new constitution. One of the most interesting 'spaces' is the House of Bondage, named after a book of photographs published in 1967 by Ernest Cole and banned in South Africa at the time. A white photographer, he managed to class himself as coloured in order to go into the townships and take the pictures. The black and white photographs are both tragic and beautiful. The exhibitions effectively use multimedia, such as television screens, recorded interviews and news footage, all providing a startlingly clear picture of the harshness and tragedy of the Apartheid years. Allow several hours for a visit.

The **Johannesburg Zoo** ⓘ *Jan Smuts Av, Parktown, T011-6462000, www.jhbzoo.org.za, daily 0830-1630, R32*, has over 400 different species of birds and animals set in an area of parkland and gardens. The ponds attract free ranging aquatic birds, which come here to breed. All the enclosures have recently been upgraded and the night tours to see the nocturnal animals are fun, ending with marshmallows and hot chocolate around a bonfire. There is a small restaurant here for light meals and drinks.

Near to the Johannesburg Zoo is the **South African National Museum of Military History** ⓘ *20 Erlswold Way, Saxonwold, T011-6465513, www.militarymuseum.co.za, daily 0900-1630, R10*. This building has exhibits on the role South African forces played in the Second World War including artillery pieces, aircraft and tanks. There is a more up-to-date section illustrating the war in Angola with displays of modern armaments including captured Soviet tanks and French Mirage fighter planes.

Gold Reef City ⓘ *Northern Parkway, Ormonde, T011-2486800, www.goldreefcity.co.za, Tue-Sun 0930-1700, mine tours 0930 and 1330, R70 includes all rides, R45 for mine tours, casino open 24 hrs*, is built on the site of one of Johannesburg's gold mining areas, but today has developed into a garish theme park with rides, amusement arcades and a gaudy casino. Of greater interest are the original miners' cottages and the tour of the gold mine. The tour drops to a depth of about 220 m (720 ft), taking you down No 14 Shaft, one of the richest deposits of gold in its day.

Northern suburbs

The hills to the north of the city centre are criss-crossed by wide avenues, lined with posh shopping malls and large houses with well-tended gardens. Here, homes are surrounded by high walls, topped with razor wire and guarded by dogs and armed response units. **Rosebank**, a few kilometres north of the city, and **Sandton**, further north off the M1 to Pretoria, are the most popular areas. To the east of Rosebank are the trendy suburbs of **Melville**, one of the few places in Johannesburg with a street restaurant and bar scene, as well as **Parkhurst** and **Parktown**.

Soweto

ⓘ *The new Soweto Tourism Information (STIC) office is located on the recently opened Walter Sisulu Square in Kliptown, Soweto, T011-9453111. It's recommended to only visit Soweto on a guided tour; see Activities and tours, page 522, for further details.*

They used to say that when Soweto sneezes, the whole country catches cold.

The most popular excursion from Johannesburg is to the (in)famous township of Soweto, lying 13 km south-west of Johannesburg city centre. Home to some four million people, Soweto has mushroomed into a city in its own right. Short for South West Township, people first moved here in 1904 from Sophiatown where there was an outbreak of plague. The township increased in size dramatically in the 1950s and 1960s when black peoples were forced forcibly to relocated from the city centre into designated areas outside the city. Since then, the population has soared, bolstered by immigrants from rural areas, as well as from Nigeria, Mozambique, Zimbabwe and other African countries.

Today Soweto covers an area of 135 sq km, but despite its size and population, it still has only one hospital, one fire station and 350 schools. The Baragwanath Hospital claims to be the largest hospital in the world, with over 5000 beds and

On his release from prison, Mandela insisted on moving back into his house in Soweto, but eventually its small size and the difficulty of keeping it secure put too much of a strain on him and he moved out of the township.

20,000 employees. It is estimated that half of Soweto's residents were born here and it also attracts unfortunate attention for it's large proportion of AIDS patients and victims of street violence.

Despite its reputation, Soweto feels remarkably ordinary. Large areas are given over to tidy rows of affluent suburban houses. Like in any other South African city, there are districts and suburbs and shopping centres. The streets are well maintained, there are banks and golf courses and a football stadium. Yellow commuter trains trundle to Johannesburg and Mercedes cruise between smart homes with well-tended gardens and satellite dishes. Soweto allegedly has the highest concentration of millionaires in the country and one of the most successful BMW dealerships. The flip-side, much like in any other city in the country, is that there are also areas of squatter camps and informal housing, where unemployment is as high as 90%. Rudimentary two-roomed government-built houses make up the majority of township homes, and many still don't have basic amenities such as running water, electricity and sanitation. For every 7000 people who live in these areas, there are approximately 90 toilets and five taps, and every house sleeps between 10 and 68 people. The government has pledged to improve the situation, but efforts are hampered by an estimated influx of 20,000 people flooding into Soweto every month, fleeing rural poverty and desperate for jobs. And signs of Soweto's troubled history are everywhere. Two cooling towers dominate the skyline, which once spewed out smoke while producing electricity for Johannesburg's white suburbs; Soweto, meanwhile, had no electricity until 1986.

Most tours of Soweto take in a handful of important historical sites. First stop is usually the excellent **Hector Pieterson Museum** on Moema Street. This modern museum stands two blocks away from where thirteen-year-old Hector Pierterson was shot dead by riot police during a peaceful school demonstration on 16th June 1976. This event, captured on camera in an image that shocked the world, sparked the final ten-year battle against Apartheid causing townships across the country to rise up in bitter revolt. Outside the museum is a memorial to Hector, marked by the iconic image of his body being carried by a friend. Inside, the museum is similar to the Apartheid Museum, using multimedia exhibits, films, newspapers, personal accounts and photographs to piece together what happened on and around that date.

Soweto

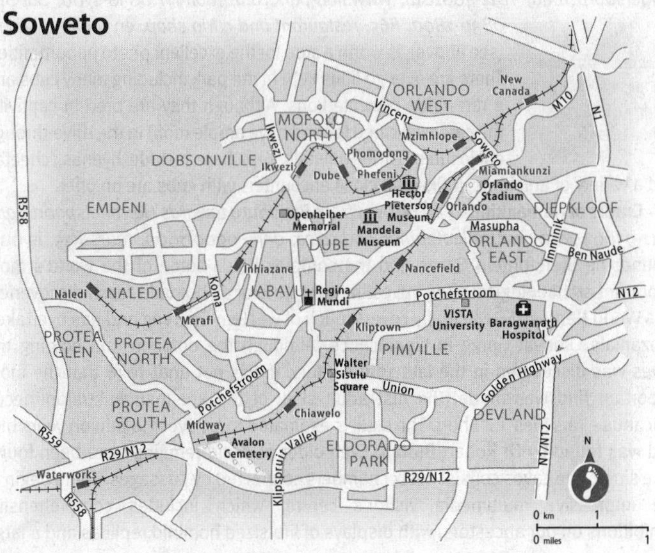

A few blocks away is **Vilakazi Street**, the only street in the world to have been home to two Nobel Peace Prize winners, Nelson Mandela and Desmond Tutu. The home where Nelson and Winnie Mandela lived before he was incarcerated is today a small museum. The house is a diminutive three-roomed house, regularly rebuilt after attacks from the South African Defence Forces. Visitors are led through the small living room and into the bedroom, with its odd fur-covered bed. The house is crammed with pro-Winnie propaganda (she suffered a fall from grace in the mid-1990s after numerous incidents of corruption and violence); she now owns the house after legal wranglings with her ex-husband. Guides reverently point out the few personal belongings left by Mandela, including three pairs of his shoes. Further down the road is the home of Archbishop Desmond Tutu, hidden behind high walls. Next door is a good restaurant, **Sakhumuzi**, often visited by tour groups but also a popular drinking hole with well-heeled Sowetans.

Also worth visiting is **Regina Mundi**, to the southwest, off Potchesfstroom Street, the largest church in Soweto, and an important site of demonstrations in the 1980s. You can still see bullet holes in the ceiling, a lasting testament to shots fired by police. Old photos of government attacks are pasted outside, and, if you're lucky, you'll catch the choir practising inside.

Excursions from Johannesburg

Lesedi Cultural Village ⓘ *on the R512, 12 km north of Lanseria Airport, T012-2051394, www.lesedi.com, tours at 1130 and 1630, R260 per person including meals*, is an easy day-trip from Johannesburg or Pretoria. Four African villages have been recreated from the Xhosa, Zulu, Pedi, and Sotho tribes and there are two tours daily (each lasting two hours). These include an audio-visual presentation on all aspects of tribal life of the 11 ethnic groups that live in South Africa, as well as music, singing and traditional dancing from over 60 performers around a large fire in an amphitheatre. The morning tour includes lunch and the afternoon tour includes a dinner of game meat such as impala or crocodile. Lesedi is the Sotho word for 'light'. For those who wish to extend the experience, the **Protea Hotel Lesedi**, www.proteahotels.com, is part of the cultural village and provides en suite accommodation in traditional bomas or rondavels decorated with Ndebele crafts.

The **Lion Park** ⓘ *30 mins' drive from Johannesburg on the Old Pretoria-Krugersdorp road, T011-4601814, www.lion-park.com, Mon-Fri 0830-1700, Sat-Sun 0830-1800, R65, restaurant and curio shop*, en route to Lesedi (see above), is worth a stop for the excellent photo opportunities. There are over 70 lions kept in the park including many cubs and a rare pride of white lions. Although they are bred in captivity, they are well cared for and have ample room in the drive-through enclosures. Other animals kept here include hyenas, cheetah and a variety of antelope. Walks and close encounters with cubs are on offer.

The lions are accustomed to vehicles and don't think twice about strolling right up to a car. Keep windows at least half closed.

Cradle of Humankind ⓘ *off the N14 from Randburg towards Hartbeetspoort Dam, T011-9566342, www.cradleofhumankind.co.za, daily 0900-1600, tours R35*, is built around the Sterkfontein Caves and the complex holds some of the world's most important archaeological sites, revealing over 40% of all hominid fossil discoveries. This World Heritage Site actually covers much of western Gauteng and has overtaken Tanzania's Olduvai Gorge in significance. Although the dolomite hill holding the caves was discovered in the late 19th century, it was not until 1936 that the most important find was made, the first adult skull of the ape-man Australopithecus africanus - 'Mrs Ples' for short. The skull is estimated to be over 2.6 million years old, and was found by Dr Robert Broom. Even older hominid remains have been found here since. The caves consist of six chambers connected by passages. Tours begin in the impressive multimedia visitor's centre, which includes comprehensive exhibitions on our ancestors, with displays of life-sized hominid replicas and a large amphitheatre. Tours then pass through the six caves, taking in the archaeological sites. There is a craft market and a choice of restaurants on site.

The recently-renamed **Walter Sisulu Botanical Gardens** ⓘ *30 mins' drive from the city centre on the banks of the Emmarentia Dam in Roodepoort, T011-9581750, www.sanbi.org, daily 0800-1700, exit closes 1800, small entry fee*, is a pleasant place to visit for a quiet stroll away from the bustle of the city. The gardens are planted with oaks, cherry trees and a mixture of exotic and indigenous plants. The nursery, with over 2,500 species of succulent plants, is a fascinating area and the nearby ponds attract birds, including yellowbilled ducks, Egyptian geese and crested grebes.

Sleeping

Most of the city's best hotels are in the safe areas of Sandton, Rosebank, Parkhurst and Melville. Accommodation tends to be pricey; there's a wide selection of luxury hotels, but little in the lower price bracket other than hostels.

Near the airport

There are several airport hotels within a few kilometres, all providing free pick-ups. The closest are:

AL Airport Sun Intercontinental, T011-9615400 This smart 5 star hotel is conveniently located directly opposite the terminal buildings. You can push your trolley from the airport into your room, flight arrival and departure airport TV information throughout the hotel. Gym and beauty salon available for passengers on long waits between flights.

A-B City Lodge, Sandvale Rd, Edenvale, T011-3921750, www.citylodge.co.za. Modern, well-run hotel for the business traveller, restaurant, pool, 4 km from the airport.

Backpacker hostels

D-E Airport North South, 1 Boompieper Av, Birch Acres, T011-3934393, www.northsouth backpackers.co.za. Owned by the same couple as North South Backpackers in Pretoria, this lodge is 10 km from the airport and offers free pick ups and transfers. Dorms, doubles and twin rooms, bar area, swimming pool, lapa area. Well run with a good travel centre.

D-E In Africa Lodge, 20 Swartkops Cres, Buurendal, Edenvale, T011-6095874, inafricabac@worldonline.co.za. A small hostel in a private house near the airport (5-min drive) run by pleasant couple who can arrange a choice of tours in the country. Free transport to/from the airport. There's a dorm, some smart double rooms and a garden with pool.

E Airport Backpackers, 3 Mohawk St, Rhodesfield, Kempton Park, T011-3940485, www.airportbackpackers.co.za. Only 2 km from the airport close to the end of the runway, so planes fly low overhead. Dorms, double rooms and camping. Internet, swimming pool, free pick-up and drop-off, free basic breakfast. Festival Mall nearby, but little else to do in area.

Northern suburbs *p510, maps p514 and p516*

L The Grace, 54 Bath Av, Rosebank, T011-2807200, www.thegrace.co.za. Beautiful luxury hotel set right next to Rosebank Mall (with a convenient passage connecting to it). Large rooms spread over 9 floors, some with great city views, decorated in country-style fabrics, with pretty pale-green colour themes, dark wood and colonial prints on the walls. Excellent restaurant, popular for brunch, serving contemporary South African cuisine, plus good extras such as free neck massages for new arrivals, and complimentary tea and cakes in the afternoon. Business centre with free internet access, and efficient friendly service. Recommended.

L Melrose Arch, Melrose Arch, T011-2146666, www.africanpridehotels.com. A trendy addition to the northern suburbs, with stylish rooms, lots of chrome, bare-brick walls and flat-screen TVs. Smart bar and restaurant. The location is slightly odd, within a gated development, but shops and restaurants are a safe stroll away.

L The Michelangelo, 135 West St, Sandton Sq, T011-2827000, www.michelangelo.co.za. 242 super-luxury rooms, includes a variety of giant suites, residents' lounge, restaurants, bar, heated swimming pool, fitness centre, shops, one of the best luxury options of Sandton, which has contributed to the area becoming one of the smartest centres of Johannesburg. Plenty of restaurants, shops and offices in the immediate surrounds.

L **Sandton Hilton**, 138 Rivonia Rd, Sandton, T011-3221888, www.hilton.com. Big business hotel with 329 luxury rooms, including the latest Hilton feature – a separate executive floor with its own lounge-cum–club room where business folk can breakfast and have snacks throughout the day. 2 restaurants, bar, health club, swimming pool, tennis court, extensive conference facilities, all set in a beautiful landscaped garden, close to smart shopping malls in Sandton.

L **Saxon**, 36 Saxon Rd, Sandhurst, T011-2926000, www.thesaxon.com. Voted the 'World's Leading Boutique Hotel' every year since it opened in 2000. 26 suites including one named after Nelson Mandela, who spent 7 months here working on his book *Long Walk to Freedom*. Set in 2 ha of beautifully tended grounds, gigantic heated swimming pools, state of the art gym, 2 wine cellars. Expensive by South African standards.

A **A Room with a View**, 1 Tolip St, corner of 4th Av, Melville, T011-4825435, www.aroomwithaview.co.za. As the name would suggest, beautiful views over leafy Melville from this delightful hotel. 13 rooms in 2 buildings; those in the newer building, designed to look like an Italian villa, have bare-brick walls, soaring ceilings and stylish, colourful furnishings, as well as huge beds, slate-tiled bathrooms and private balconies. Those in the older house have carved wooden bed frames and polished wooden floors. Legendary breakfasts, pleasant pool and very friendly service. Highly recommended.

A **Rosebank**, corner of Tyrwhitt and Bath Avs, Rosebank, T011-4472700, www.rosebankhotel.co.za. Large mid-range independent hotel with 318 a/c rooms and suites, renowned Chinese restaurant, swimming pool, gym, sauna, 2 bars, popular for conferences, within walking distance of Rosebank's shopping malls.

A **Westcliff**, 67 Jan Smuts Av, Westcliff, near to Johannesburg Zoo, T011-6462400,

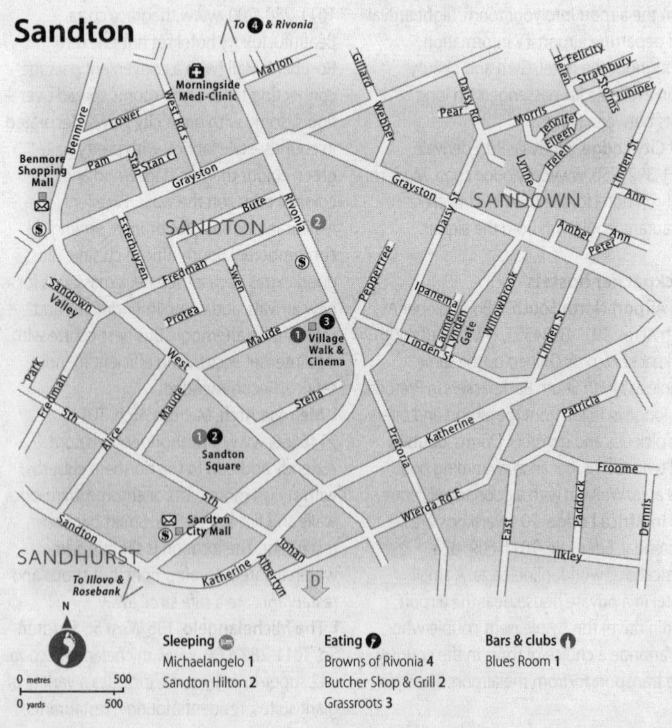

www.westcliff.orient-express.com. A bright pink Mediterranean-style hillside village on a 3-ha estate, with 106 a/c rooms and 14 suites, 2 heated swimming pools, floodlit tennis court with resident coach, gym, health spa, old-fashioned charm in the cigar bar and restaurant, great views of the northern suburbs and zoo.

B **Protea Wanderers**, corner of Corlett Dr and Rudd Rd, Illovo, T011-7705500, www.proteahotels.co.za. Directly opposite Wanderers cricket stadium. Quality hi-tec modern hotel, but lacking in character. 230 rooms have individual office station with faux African and sporting motifs, and sound proofing. Pleasant pool area except for the traffic noise from the busy road below.

B **Sunnyside Park**, Prince of Wales Terr, Parktown, T011-6437226, www.legacy hotels.co.za. 104 rooms, restaurant, swimming pool, converted Victorian mansion declared a national monument, with new annexes set in picturesque gardens, an unusual find this close to the city. Decent restaurant. Pleasant old-fashioned atmosphere but not great service.

C **Mercure Inn**, corner of Republic and Randburg Waterfront roads, T011-3263300, www.accorhotels.com. 104 rooms with lots of extras including fridge, modem point, and internet station with keyboard attached to the TV. Narrow rooms and minuscule bathrooms but comfortable and excellent value for money. Avoid if there is a conference on. Breakfasts only, arrangement with 4 restaurants in the adjacent Randburg Waterfront mall to bill your hotel account.

Backpacker hostels

C-D **Backpackers Ritz**, 1A North Rd, Dunkeld West, T011-3257125, www.backpackers-ritz.co.za. One of Johannesburg's best established long-running hostels. Large house in a secure neighbourhood with garden and swimming pool. Dorms, double rooms, travel desk, Soweto and city tours, internet access, individual safes plus long term baggage storage, helpful place to start your visit to South Africa from. Meals available. Close to shops and entertainment at Hyde Park and Rosebank, all in a safe suburb, 30 mins from airport, free pick-up, call before leaving home. Recommended.

E Africa Centre , 65 Sunny Rd, Lakefield-Benoni, T011-8944857, afrcentr@global.co.za, www.africacentre.co.za. Dorms, doubles and twins. Laundry, shared kitchen, meals available, bar with pool table, garden with pool, sauna and Jacuzzi, internet access. Travel services and airport pick-up.

F Rockey's of Fourways, 22 Campbell Rd, Craigavon, Sandton, T011-4654219, www.backinafrica.com. This well-established backpacker hostel relocated a few years ago to the growing suburb of Fourways, within walking distance of the Fourways Mall. Doubles and 30 dorm beds in large comfortable house. Camping available in 1 ha of gardens, large pool, lively pub with open fire, meals available, internet access, free airport pick-up. Has a good travel centre.

Rosebank to Hyde Park

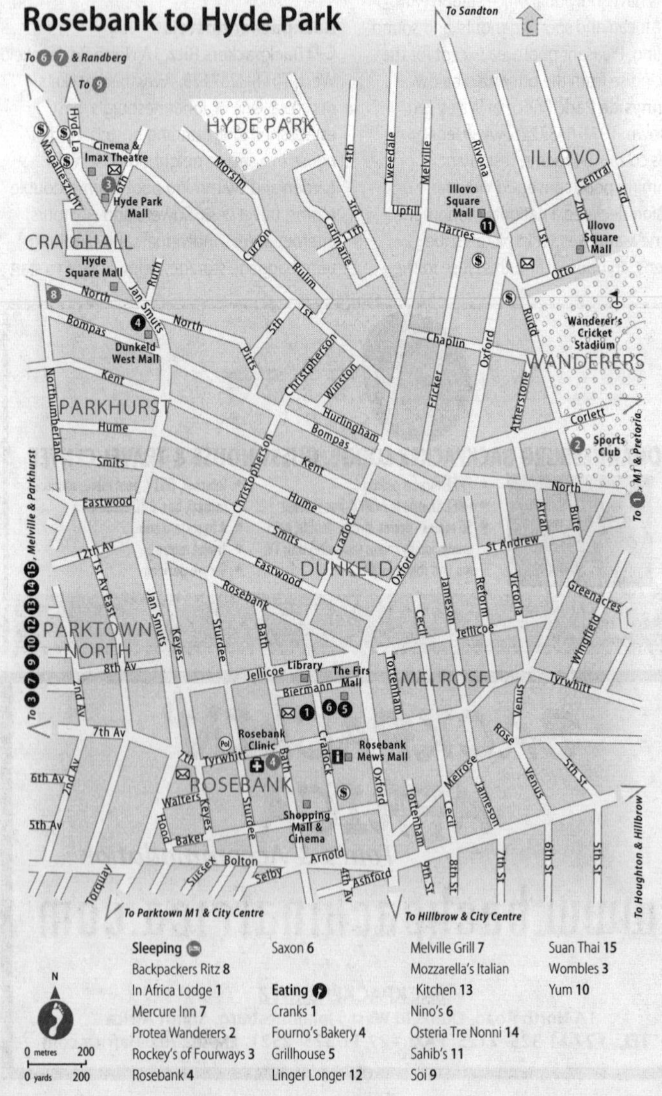

Sleeping
Backpackers Ritz 8
In Africa Lodge 1
Mercure Inn 7
Protea Wanderers 2
Rockey's of Fourways 3
Rosebank 4
Saxon 6

Eating
Cranks 1
Fourno's Bakery 4
Grillhouse 5
Linger Longer 12
Melville Grill 7
Mozzarella's Italian Kitchen 13
Nino's 6
Osteria Tre Nonni 14
Sahib's 11
Soi 9
Suan Thai 15
Wombles 3
Yum 10

Eating

Johannesburg *p503, maps p507, 514 and p516*

Many of Johannesburg's restaurants and bars are within the confines of a shopping mall. The best place in town for lively streetside restaurants and bars is the trendy suburb of **Melville**, in the northern suburbs off the M1. The streets around 7th St are lined with popular bars, fashionable restaurants and kooky cafés. Most appealing is the fact that its safe to park and wander around here, even at night.

General

TTT **Browns of Rivonia**, 21 Wessels St, Rivonia, T011-8037605, closed Sun. Meals served in the courtyard of an old farmhouse, expensive but extensive menu includes roast lamb, salmon timbale, mustard sirloin and crêpes. Impressive wine list, too.

TTT **Linger Longer**, 58 Wierda Rd, Wierda Valley, Sandton, T011-8840465, closed all day Sun and lunch on Sat. One of Johannesburg's top restaurants and something of an institution – it's been going for 43 years – serving an imaginative mix of old fashioned and contemporary cooking, from seafood casserole to lemon pepper filet. Attractive homely setting.

TTT **Yum**, Gleneagles Road, Greenside, T011-4861645. Generally regarded as one of Jo'burg's finest restaurants. Stylish, minimalist interior, smart crowd and fabulous contemporary cuisine, including inventive dishes such as crab ravioli, apricot-glazed duck and bitter chocolate tart.

TT **Melville Grill**, corner of 3rd Av and 7th St, Melville, T011-7262890. Upmarket, slick steak house, serving the best steaks in the city. The interior has low lighting and wooden floors, white tablecloths and red walls. Different cuts and prices are chalked up on the walls, and the menu includes details such as how long a cut was aged and if the meat is free range. Simple salad starters, and a couple of fish and poultry choices, followed by warm chocolate brownies. Good, unpretentious service. Recommended.

TTT **Yum**, 26 Gleneagles Road, Greenside T011-4861645. Tiny restaurant with a tiny menu, but widely regarded as one of Jo'burg's top restaurants. Minimalist interior and modern cuisine, with some weird (but delectable) choices including a roast duck with bitter chocolate. Good location, on Greenside's restaurant strip.

TT **Butcher Shop & Grill**, Sandton Sq, Sandton City, T011-7848676/7, www.butchershop.co.za. The sawdust on the floor fools nobody – this award-winning steakhouse is a top-quality restaurant and shouldn't be missed by meat-lovers. The Butcher Shop is famous for its aged steaks, and although there are a few outlets around the country, this is the original and gets through 5 tons of steak each week. The menu is, obviously, focused on steak and other grills: when available, there's a specially aged T-bone which is cut to order. There's also a selection of seafood, and a good range of starters and deserts, but literally nothing for vegetarians other than a couple of salads.

TT **Café Flo**,116 Greenway Rd, Greenside, T011-6466817. Pavement dining in this little cult restaurant. A young, fashionable crowd come here for Flo's imaginative home-cooked meals, including a delicious lamb and aubergine pizza and malva pudding with custard. The connected **Ova Flo** has also opened next door.

TT **Grillhouse**, The Firs, Oxford Rd, Rosebank, T011-8803945. Popular for its melt in the mouth fillets and succulent sauces. Exposed brick and green leather furniture, excellent service and a lively atmosphere. Opposite and under the same ownership is **Katzy's** late night piano bar and cigar lounge, which has live music most nights and is fast making its way onto Jo'burg's nightlife circuit. Vast selection of Cognacs and malt whiskies. You would never know you're in a shopping mall.

TT **Wombles**, 17 3rd St, Parktown North, T011-8802470. Closed lunch Sat and Sun. A relative newcomer, Wombles has fast gained an excellent reputation for its matured steaks. The setting is attractive colonial style, with dark wood tables, high-backed chairs and white linen table cloths. It's a simple menu, with traditional starters like grilled mushrooms, or chicken liver salad, followed by a choice of cuts and sauces. There's also a fair choice of poultry, fish and even a couple of vegetarian dishes. Service is friendly and relaxed.

African

ⴸⴸⴸ Carnivore, 69 Drift Boulevard, Muldersdrift, 30 mins' drive (approx 30 km) from Johannesburg centre on the N14, some hotels and backpackers arrange transport out here, T011-9506000. This has become something of an institution and is the ultimate 'African' eating experience. Rustic decor, zebra skin chairs and a large central fire pit characterizes the interior. Meals consist of eat-as-much-as-you-can, with slabs of game carved off Masaai spears onto cast iron plates. There's a choice of at least 10 different types of meat every day, which usually includes ostrich, crocodile, warthog zebra, kudu and impala as well as beef of pork. If vegetarians can bear it, they actually have a good choice, including *aviyal*, a mix of vegetables cooked in spicy coconut sauce.

ⴸⴸⴸ Gramadoelas, Market Theatre Complex, Bree St, Newtown, T011-8386960, closed Sun and Mon lunch. One of the best places to get a full overview of Southern African dishes is at this long-standing favourite, set in the renovated Market Theatre Complex. The faux-ramshackle decor adds to the atmosphere, and there are tables outside in summer. Starters include fried *mopani* worms served in peri-peri sauce, and to follow you can try *sosaties* (spicy kebabs), *bobotie* (sweet and spicy ground beef pie), or a range of dishes from further afield such as Morocco or Ethiopia. A delicious desert is the sticky malva pudding, or *melktert* (milk tart). This is also the place to try home-brewed sorghum beer or *mageu* (fermented milk).

ⴸⴸⴸ Moyo, Melrose Sq Melrose Arch, T011-6841477. Popular new chain of trendy African-themed restaurants springing up around South Africa. This outlet is in chi-chi Melrose Arch, and is spread over 3 floors, with rustic, candlelit ethno-fashionable decor, and pan-African cuisine, including good Moroccan tagines. Live music in the evenings. There also a branch in Newtown, next to **Gramadoelas**.

Mediterranean

ⴸⴸⴸ Osteria Tre Nonni, 9 Grafton Av, Craighall, T011-3270095, closed Mon and Sun. Expensive but sophisticated north Italian cuisine, homemade pasta, fresh seafood, best tiger prawns in the city, rich creamy sauces, reservations recommended.

ⴸⴸ Mozzarella's Italian Kitchen, 6c 7th St, Melville, T011-4826910. In the heart of vibey Melville, this romantic restaurant, lit by candles and fairy lights, stretches through 2 bungalows overlooking bustling 7th St. Big portions of well-cooked pasta, oven-baked pizzas and traditional Italian mains draw in lots of couples, especially on Thu and Fri.

ⴸⴸ Primi Piatti, Upper Level, The Zone, Rosebank Mall, T011-4470300. Stylish Italian chain, with colourful, industrial-style decor and lively staff. Huge portions of imaginative pasta, excellent wood-fired pizzas and big salads. **Primi Studio**, attached, is a lounge bar with big comfy sofas and music, perfect for relaxing after a meal.

Indian

ⴸ Sahib's, 83 4th St, Melville, T011-4826670. Simple, cheap and slightly run-down curry house, but refreshingly unpretentious, with a wide range of bunny chows, roti wraps, tandoori grill, and biryanis, Good value buffet lunches at weekends.

Oriental

ⴸⴸⴸ Daruma, Sandton Sun/Towers Hotel, T011-7805157/9. Formal Japanese restaurant that serves some of the best sushi in town. The food is presented delicately in a low-key stylish modern dining room, hung with Japanese art. Extensive menu, fairly pricey.

ⴸⴸ Cranks , Shop 162, Rosebank Mall, next to the African Craft Market, T011-8803442. Delicious Vietnamese and Thai dishes are served in this eccentric Asian eatery, well situated in the popular Rosebank mall. The decor is in itself worth a visit, with Barbie and Ken dolls dangling from the ceiling in compromising positions. Freshly prepared Thai, including green chicken curry and pad thai, and some spicy Vietnamese dishes. Asian beer plus Thai schnapps and soothing herbal teas. Live blues performed Sat and Sun.

ⴸⴸ Soi, corner of 7th and 3rd Av, Melville, T011-7265775. Excellent Thai and Vietnamese cuisine in this low-lit, trendy restaurant. Wide selection of curries, pad thai noodles and interesting dishes like 'angry duck' – perfect for those with fiery tastes. Fashionable, friendly serving staff, stylish, understated decor and a chatty crowd make this one of the best places on the Melville drag. Recommended.

Jo'burg's Chinatown

Johannesburg's Chinatown is a vibey strip of neon-lit Chinese supermarkets and restaurants in a less than salubrious part of the city located on Derrick Avenue, Cyrildene, just east of Observatory. To get there you are going to have to rely on a good-natured taxi driver or know someone who knows Jo'burg well. From the northern suburbs it involves a drive through Hillbrow and along the notorious Rockey Street, before it turns into Observatory Street and follows through to Cyrildene. To drive through Hillbrow and along Rockey Street after dark is an education in itself though ill-advised – these are areas renowned for high crime and the streets can feel menacing. Once at Chinatown, there are car guards and vehicles are looked after safely for a tip. Walk up and down Derrick Street until you find a restaurant that takes your liking or otherwise one that's not already full. Most are small eateries with formica top tables, plastic chairs, fluorescent lights, takeaway counters, unbelievably kitsch decorations on the walls, and sometimes dead ducklings hanging in the window. Some only seat several people at a time whereas others have the luxury of four or five tables. Regional dishes include Szechuan, Shanghai, Hong Kong, Taiwanese, and there's sushi, Mongolian and Korean for good measure. The food is delicious and you're not going to get more authentic Chinese dishes anywhere else in Africa. It's hugely popular with the Chinese community, always a good sign that the food is good, few menus are written in English, and it's best to ask for a selection of dishes to share. Order Chinese beer or tea to drink, or bring your own wine; of the few restaurants that serve wine, it's chateux-le-cardboard (5-litre box wine) by the glass. The most delightful aspect of this eating experience is asking for the bill: hardly any of the staff in the restaurants speak English and they simply write the total down on the paper tablecloth or a napkin, only cash is accepted and it's ridiculously cheap. Arrive early, most kitchens close at 2100.

Suan Thai, corner of 3rd Av and 7th St, Melville, T011-7827801. Another Melville quality restaurant, authentic Thai cooked dishes including great curry (try the duck and prawn), tom yam soup and Mozambican crab. Good vegetarian options. Mango and coconut ice cream for dessert, live jazz some Sun evenings.

Vegetarian

There are few specific vegetarian restaurants in Jo'burg, but most menus have expanded in recent years to include at least a couple of meat-free dishes.

Grassroots, Village Walk mall, Sandton, T011-8836020. Healthy eating from this shopping mall restaurant, serving only vegetarian and vegan dishes, and fully organic. Pastas, salads, bagels, cakes that lean towards the fruity, nutty, leafy and grainy type of cuisine. Pumpkin and leek soup and hash browns are recommended.

Cafés

Fourno's Bakery, Dunkeld West Centre, Jan Smuts Av, T011-3252110, Mon-Fri 0700-1800, Sat-Sun 0700-1400. Cheap eats with a number of branches around the city. Range of pastries, cakes, croissants, quiches and pies. Big, greasy breakfasts, simple lunches, a good-value bakery-cum-greasy-spoon.

For an explanation of the sleeping and eating price codes used in this guide, see inside the front cover. Other relevant information is found in Essentials pages 42-47.

Nino's, 22 Cradock Av, Rosebank, T011-4474758, daily 0700-1800. Large, open, street side eating area, reasonably priced coffee and build-your-own panini sandwich bar, opposite the Rosebank craft market, good place to start the day with a fat 3-egg omelette.

Bars and clubs

Johannesburg *p503, maps p507, 514 and p516*

Entertainments listings are published in the weekly *Mail and Guardian*, with a useful 'Gig of the Week' review and online listings on www.mg.co.za.

Bassline, 7 7th St, Melville, T011-4826915, nightly except Mon until 0200. Popular South African jazz venue with Cuban and Latin sounds at weekends. Cover charge of around R40-60.

Blues Room, Village Walk, Sandton, T011-7845527, www.bluesroom.co.za, closed Mon. One of the best jazz and blues venues in Gauteng, this is a stylish basement bar and restaurant, catering for music lovers who are after a decent meal. There's live music on every night and the pace picks up later on when diners take to the floor for a dance. The American-style dishes are named after blues legends.

Catz Pyjamas, corner of 3rd and Main Sts, Melville, T011-7268596. Jo'burg's original 24-hr bistro and cocktail bar, rather shabby these days with a funky atmosphere (avoid the food though). It's open throughout the day but pretty lackluster – the atmosphere really only picks up late in the evening, carrying on until the early hours.

Cool Runnings, 4th Av, Melville. The popular Jamaican-themed chain of bars/clubs comes into its own at this Melville branch, which is one of the most popular bars around. There's loud music every night, when a young crowd gathers to work its way through the extensive cocktail list. There are occasional drumming sessions held in the bar.

Jolly Roger, 10, 4th Av, Parkhurst, T011-4423954. Landmark put on the main stretch in popular Parkhurst, with an excellent balcony perfect for watching the area's stylish locals swan up and down 4th Av. Good draught beer and pizza specials, plus live music at weekends.

Kippies, Market Theatre Complex, Bree St, Newtown, T011-8333316. Recently revamped legendary jazz venue in Newtown, famous for its township jazz and serving light meals.

Monsoon Lagoon, at Caesar's Casino next to the airport, T011-9281290, Tue-Sat 2000-late. One of Jo'burg's biggest and brashest clubs is this huge special events venue, regularly hosting TV and fashion parties. It's an upmarket mainstream club (over 23s only) covering several floors with a number of dance floors, bars, and lounges. It's lavish and totally over the top – great for a big night out.

Ratz, 7th St, Melville, T011-8033555. Friendly drinking hole with a couple of sofas and high tables dotted around in front of the wooden bar. Gets packed on Fri nights, and serves decent cocktails, but is more of a low-key beer joint for students.

Statement, 7th St, Melville, T011-4825593. One of a handful of gay bars in the area, with a very young and well-dressed crowd. Colourful, understated decor and excellent apple Martinis attract a mixed crowd.

Xai Xai, 9b 7th St, Melville. Super-trendy lounge bar with a Mozambique theme. Great cocktails, low-level sofas, good looking punters and chilled music make this a relaxing and stylish setting for a few pre-dinner drinks.

Entertainment

Johannesburg *p503, maps p507, 514 and p516*

Computicket, T011-3408000, www.computicket.com. A central booking agency for tickets to the cinema, theatre, concerts, sports events and city tours. Note that international credit cards are not accepted online or over the phone; you can pay by international credit card at kiosks, located in most of the large shopping malls. If you're heading to one of the downtown theatres, its best to travel by taxi and pre-order one for after the show. The Market Theatre area is safe, but don't wander away from Bree St.

Cinema

All the latest Hollywood, European and home-grown releases can be seen at multi-screen cinemas in shopping malls.

Check local newspapers for listings. All of the major shopping malls have multi-screen cinemas, run by **Nu Metro**, T011- 3254257, www.numetro.co.za, or **Ster-Kine Kor**, T011-4457700, www.sterkinekor.co.za.
IMAX Theatre, Hyde Park Mall, Hyde Park, T011-3256182. Giant screen with surround sound system, showing films on wildlife, mountains, deserts and seas. 4 shows daily during the week, 5 at the weekends.

Theatre

Civic Theatre, Loveday St, Braamfontein, T011-8776800. Modern theatre complex with 4 auditoriums, frequent performances of South African plays, visiting international ballets and classical orchestras.
Market Theatre, Bree St, Newtown, T011-8321614. 3 auditoriums, famous for its community theatre and controversial political plays during the 1980s.

O Shopping

Johannesburg *p503, maps p507, 514 and p516*

African art

Art Africa, 62 Tyrone Av, Parkview, T011-4862052, Mon-Fri 0900-1800, Sat 0900-1500. Great place to pick up inexpensive gifts, strong emphasis on recycled art products. Some of the most interesting pieces include flowers made from recycled plastic, and baskets woven from telephone wire. There are also some genuinely rare antiques from across Africa.
African Craft Market of Rosebank, Cradock Av, Rosebank, T011-7885530, Tue-Sun 0900-1700. The former street traders of this area have now been housed in one ethnic-inspired building in the centre of the popular Rosebank Mall. Curios from all over Africa are for sale at over 140 stalls. Credit cards are accepted and shipping can be arranged. It's a lively spot, with street performers and musicians, and on Thursday evenings African food is served and there's a dance show.
Kim Sacks Gallery, 153 Jan Smuts Av, Parkwood, T011-4475804, Mon-Fri 0900-1700, Sat-Sun 1000-1500. A selection of quality ethnic art from all over Africa is on show in this gallery, housed in a lovely old home and regarded as one of the top galleries in the city. There is a good range of and contemporary South African pieces, including prints, sculptures, beadwork, and ceramics.

Camera equipment

Kameraz, Rosebank Mews, Oxford Rd, Rosebank, T011-8802885, www.kameraz.co.za, Mon-Fri 0800-1700, Sat 0800-1400. One of the largest dealers in new and second-hand camera equipment in Gauteng. New and used accessories and lenses, and specialists in insurance claims. On the first Sun of every even month they hold a flea market of second-hand equipment, and on the first Sun of every odd month, an exhibition and sale of work from local photographers.

Camping equipment

Cape Union Mart, Hyde Park Mall, Jan Smuts Av, T011-3255038, www.capeunionmart.co.za and 14 other branches in Johannesburg's various shopping malls, plus one at the airport. Excellent shop selling outdoor equipment, practical clothing, backpacks, mosquito nets, and a great range of walking shoes.

Gold

Scoin Shop, U24a, Sandton City Mall, T011-7848551, www.sagoldcoin.com. Krugerrands, South Africa's famous gold coins, can be bought here as an investment or souvenir. It also produces collector's coins such as the Mandela Medallion.

Shopping malls

Johannesburg has a abundance of vast, modern shopping malls filled with shops, restaurants, cinemas and bars. There are over 20 malls around the city, some of which are so enormous and extravagant that they are worth visiting in their own right. In most, the shops open 0900-1800, while the restaurants and cinemas stay open until 2200 or 2300.
Hyde Park, Jan Smuts Av, Hyde Park, T011-3254340. Luxury shopping aimed at ladies who lunch. Also home to the city's only IMAX theatre, plus 2 other cinemas, and the excellent **Exclusive Books** has an outlet here.
Rosebank, corner of Cradock and Baker Sts, Rosebank, T011-7885530. One of the more pleasant malls with a large open-air plaza

lined with cafés, ideal for sitting in the sun and watching people go by. Flea market on the roof every Sun selling crafts and snacks. Also home to the excellent **African Craft Market** (see box page 506).

Sandton City, corner of Sandton Dr and Rivonia Rd (attached to Sandton Sq by a walkway), T011-8832011. Massive double-storey mall featuring all of South Africa's chain stores, cinemas, African art galleries, and hypermarkets. The opulent Sandton Sq has international exclusive stores and trendy restaurants around an attractive square.

Activities and tours

Johannesburg *p503, maps p507, 514 and p516*

Cricket

Wanderers' Stadium, 21 North St, Illovo, T011-7885010, www.wanderers.co.za, tickets from www.sacrickettickets.co.za. This is one of South Africa's premier cricket grounds and regular international matches are played here in season.

Football

FNB Stadium, Nasvec Rd, Ormonde, T011-4943522, tickets in person from **Computicket** (only South African credit cards are accepted online or by phone), or in person at the stadium. Johannesburg is, first and foremost, home of the country's greatest soccer teams, and the FNB Stadium, on the outskirts of Soweto, is the best place to see a match. More popularly called Soccer City, it is the largest of Johannesburg's stadiums and home of the South African Football Association. This will be the venue of the opening match and the final of the 2010 FIFA World Cup (following a proposed R300 million facelift).

Golf

There are numerous golf courses around Johannesburg and several of South Africa's top courses are open to visitors midweek.

Glendower Club, Marais Rd, Bedford View, T011-4531013, glengolf@mweb.co.za. Beautiful location in a bird sanctuary, tough course with 85 bunkers, 20 mins from the city centre.

Houghton Golf Club, 2nd Av, Lower Houghton, T011-7287337. One of the country's top courses; many major tournaments are held here including the South African Open.

Royal Johannesburg Golf Club, Fairway Av, Linksfield North, T011-6403021. Century-old club with 2 courses, East and West. South African Open held on the East Course, 30 mins from the city centre.

Wanderers Golf Club, Rudd Rd, Illovo, T011-4473311, www.wanderersgolf club.co.za. One of the oldest courses in South Africa, quite challenging, hosts the South African PGA Championship, next to the cricket ground, just north of Rosebank.

Rugby

Ellis Park, Staib St, Doornfontein, T011-4028644, www.elispark.co.za. This is the home of the Gauteng Strikers and the Cats, and matches are played regularly during the season. The stadium seats 50,000 spectators and it can be a rowdy day out, with fans bringing their braais and beers with them. It's also home to Kaizer Chiefs soccer club.

Tour operators

Emthunzini Tours, T011-9850085, kktsheola@postnet.co.za. Soweto-based operator, making this a good choice for township tours. Also has full-day trips which include the Apartheid Museum and city centre, plus longer tours out of the city.

Jimmy's Face to Face Tours, T011-3316109, www.face2face.co.za. One of the original Soweto tour operators, with a focus on climbing out of the minibuses and meeting local people. Good for exploring on foot.

JMT Tours, T011-9806038, www.jmt tours.co.za. Relative new-comer but has received some good reports. Half-day Soweto tours, trips to Lesedi, Sun City, Cullinan mines and longer grips to Kruger.

Joburg Tours, T011-7869749, www.joburg tours.co.za. City tours, township tours (including to Alexandra Township) and excursions to the Cradle of Humankind and various animal sanctuaries.

Karabo Tours, T011-3257125, karabotours@ iafrica.com. Affordable in-depth Soweto tours with a guide who was an active 12-year-old in the 1976 school children uprisings. Also offers historic Pretoria tours, Gold Reef City, Lion Park and comprehensive Johannesburg city tours.

Lords Travel & Tours, T011-7915494, www.lordstravel.co.za. Range of set and tailormade city tours, Soweto, Sterkfontein Caves, Botanical Gardens, Lion Park, Lesedi, expect to pay in the region of R350 for a day tour, further afield packages to Pilanesberg and Sun City and Kruger from R3920.

Transport

Johannesburg *p503, maps p507, 514 and p516*

Air

Johannesburg International Airport is southern African's biggest transport hub and one of the largest airports in the world, with numerous daily flights connecting to all major cities domestically and internationally.

South African Airways, (SAA), central reservations T011-9781111, www.flysaa.com has countless daily flights run in conjunction with its subsidiary, **SA Airlink**, covering the entire country.

Comair/British Airways, T011-9210222, www.comair.co.za, has several daily flights to all major cities.

Nationwide, T0861-737737, www.fly nationwide.co.za, has daily flights to **Cape Town**, **Durban**, **George**, **Port Elizabeth**, and **Kruger**.

Kulula, T0861-585852, www.kulula.com, flies to **Durban** and **Cape Town**.

One Time, T0861-345345, www.1time.co.za, flies to **Durban**.

Airline offices Air Botswana, T011-4476078. **Air France**, T011-7701600. **Air Malawi**, T011-6220466. **Air Namibia**, T011-3902876. **Air Tanzania**, T011-3902664/5. **Air Zimbabwe**, T011-6157017. **American Airlines**, T011-3255777. **British Airways**, T011-4418600. **Cathay Pacific**, T011-7008900. **Delta Airlines**, T011-4824582. **Egypt Air**, T011-8804126. **Emirates**, T011-8838420. **Ethiopian Airlines**, T011-2898114. **Kenya Airways/KLM**, T011-8819696. **Lufthansa**, T0861-842538 (toll free SA), **Malaysia Airways**, T011-8809614. **Nationwide**, T0861-737737. **Qantas**, T011-418550. **SAA & SA Airlink**, T011-9781111. **Singapore Airlines**, T011-8808560. **Virgin Atlantic**, T011-3403400.

Bus

Local Magic Bus, T011-5480822, www.magicbus.co.za and **Airport Link Shuttle**, T011-7922017, www.airport link.co.za, run shuttle services to the major hotels in Johannesburg and Pretoria.

Long distance Translux, Intercape, Greyhound, and all the smaller bus companies depart and arrive from the Park City Transit Centre, which is also where the railway station is, in central Johannesburg. The surrounding area has long had a bad reputation for muggings. Although crime levels have dropped in the area, be extra vigilant in and around the terminal. Don't go wandering outside with a backpack on your back. Many of the buses depart and arrive late at night or early in the morning, so make sure you have pre-arranged a pick up – most of the backpacker hostels offer free transfers.

All the bus companies listed below have frequent departures between Johannesburg and Pretoria throughout the day (1 hr). You cannot pre-book this short journey, but it is never a problem to get a standby ticket; expect to pay around R110.

Greyhound, T011-2768500, www.grey hound.co.za, has regular departures to **Bulawayo**, **Cape Town** via **Bloemfontein**, **Durban** via **Newcastle** and **Ladysmith**, **Durban** via **Vryheid** and **Richards Bay**, **Harare** (Zimbabwe) via **Polokwane/ Pietersburg** and **Masvingo** (Zimbabwe), **Nelspruit** (4 hrs), **Port Elizabeth** via **Bloemfontein** and **Grahamstown**, and **Maputo** (Mozambique) via **Nelspruit**.

Intercape, T0861-287287, www.inter cape.co.za, has regular departures to: **Durban**, **Cape Town** via **Bloemfontein**, **Port Elizabeth**, **Plettenberg Bay**, **Upington** via **Kuruman**, **Maputo** (Mozambique) via **Nelspruit**, and **Gaborone** (Botswana) via **Rustenburg**.

Translux, T0861-589282, www.translux. co.za, has regular departures to: **Blantyre** (Malawi) via **Harare**, **Bloemfontein**, **Bulawayo** (Zimbabwe), **Cape Town** via **Kimberley** and **Bloemfontein**, **Durban**, **Maputo** (Mozambique) via **Nelspruit**, **Knysna** via **Kimberley** and via **Bloemfontein**, **East London** via **Bloemfontein**, **Harare** (Zimbabwe), **Lusaka** (Zambia) via **Harare**, and **Port Elizabeth** (14 hrs).

Luxliner, T011-9144321, toll free T0800-003537, runs a daily service from the Parkade Centre at Johannesburg International Airport, to **Margate** via **Durban**.

Budget buses Baz Bus, reservations T021-4392323, www.bazbus.com. The best option for backpackers See Essentials, page 39 for full details of the service.

Car hire

Phone the toll-free numbers for nearest branch.
Avis, T0861-021111, www.avis.co.za.
Britz Africa, T011-3961860, www.britz.co.za. Contact for camper vans and motorhomes for travel in and beyond South Africa. Good all-inclusive deals.
Budget, T0861-016622, www.budget.co.za.
Imperial, T0861-131000, www.imperialcarrental.co.za.
Hertz, T0861-600136, www.hertz.com.
Leisuremobiles, T011-7921884 , www.africanleisure.co.za. Camper vans and fully equipped safari 4WD.
U-Drive, T011-3925852, www.udrive.co.za.

Taxi

Some of the malls have taxi ranks outside.
Rose Radio Taxis, T011-4039625/403-0000, www.rosetaxis.com. A recommended radio taxi company, with metered fairs.

Train

Local Local trains run between Johannesburg and Pretoria every 30 mins, but it is best avoided due to problems of crime. The **Gautrain**, a new high speed rail link between Johannesburg and **Pretoria** via the airport and Midrand is due to begin construction in early 2006; it should be completed within a couple of years.

Long distance The railway station is in the Park City Transit Centre. Central reservations, T086-0008888, www.spoornet.co.za. Even though rail travel is relatively slow the train service is popular and seats should be reserved well in advance. There are services (usually daily excluding Weds and Sat) to East London, Musina, Komatipoort, Bloemfontien, Durban and Port Elizabeth.

Luxury The main operators of epic luxury train journeys are **Blue Train**, T021-3348459, www.bluetrain.co.za, and **RovosRail**, T012-3158242, www.rovos.co.za.

Directory

Johannesburg *p503, maps p507, 514 and p516*

Banks American Express, Sandton City Mall, T011-8849195; 33 Bath Av, Rosebank, T011-8808382; Eastgate Mall, Bedfordview, T011-6223914; Hyde Park Mall, T011-3254424. **Rennies Travel**, toll free T0800-115514 to find the nearest branch. There are **Rennies Travel** and **American Express** bureaux de change at Johannesburg International Airport, open daily 0500-2100. All the major banks have foreign exchange facilities, most shopping malls will have a bank where you can cash traveller's cheques and change money or withdraw money from your credit card at an ATM. **Embassies and consulates** Botswana, T011-4033748. Canada, T011-4423000. France, T011-7785600. **Mozambique**, T011-3272938. **Swaziland**, T011-4032050. **UK**, T012-4217733 (Pretoria). **United States**, T011-6448000. **Hospitals** North Sandton Medi-Clinic (private) T011-7092000, Rosebank Clinic (private) T011-3280500; Netcare (24-hour medical services and ambulances) T0800-002609. **Rosebank Vaccination Station**: 63 7th Av, Parktown North, T011-7882016, Mon-Fri 0730-1800, Sat 0830-1300. Useful stop to update vaccinations and pick up anti-malarials. **Internet** All of the shopping malls now have internet cafés; you will also be able to access the internet in most hostels and hotels. **Post office** Postnet, T0800-110226, toll-free for customer services. **Useful addresses and numbers** Air Mercy Ambulance: T011-6428000. **Ambulance**: T10111. **Fire Brigade**: T10111. **Police**: T10111. **Metro police**: T011-4032625. **Emergency number from cell phones**: T112. **VAT refund**: T011-4847530.

Pretoria

→ *Phone code: 012. Colour map 2, grid B3. Altitude: 1363 m.*

The name Pretoria was given to the new settlement by Marthinus Wessel Pretorius, in memory of his father, Andries Pretorius, who had led the Voortrekkers in the bloody massacre of the Zulus at Blood River. Today it is the administrative capital of South Africa and the third largest city in the country. Despite being almost joined to Johannesburg 56 km to the south by a band of green belt towns, the atmosphere of each city couldn't be more different. While Johannesburg was built on gold and industry, Pretoria's was founded on the Voortrekker period of South Africa's turbulent past and retains a rather stern, bureaucratic atmosphere – albeit softened by a large student population. While it is safer than Johannesburg, downtown Pretoria, like most major cities in South Africa, has gone through a transformation in recent years. With the demise of Apartheid, black South Africans are again permitted to live and work freely within the city centre, and it has much more of an African feel about it.

▸▸ *For Sleeping, Eating and other listings, see pages 531-536.*

Ins and outs

Getting there The centre of Pretoria is about 45 km from Johannesburg International Airport. The easiest way to travel to and from the airport is to take an airport shuttle service. There is a Metro commuter train service between Pretoria and Johannesburg but high crime levels means you should avoid it. **Intercape, Greyhound** and **Translux** have several departures between the two cities per day. The new high-speed **Gautrain** will link up Pretoria, Johannesburg and the airport, but this in unlikely to be completed for several years. ▸▸ *For further details, see Transport, page 535.*

Getting around Most of Pretoria's sights lie in the surrounding hills. While there is a good local bus service, it does not connect between the various monuments in the city's suburbs. The easiest way to appreciate the city sights is either on a guided tour or with a hire car. During the day, taking a municipal bus that runs between the centre and suburbs is a safe and cheap way of getting about town. **Church Street** is Pretoria's main through road, running from east to west, and at 26 km long is considered to be one of the world's longest streets. From the city centre it leads east to **Arcadia** where many of the embassies and the Union Buildings are located. To the south of here is **Sunnyside,**

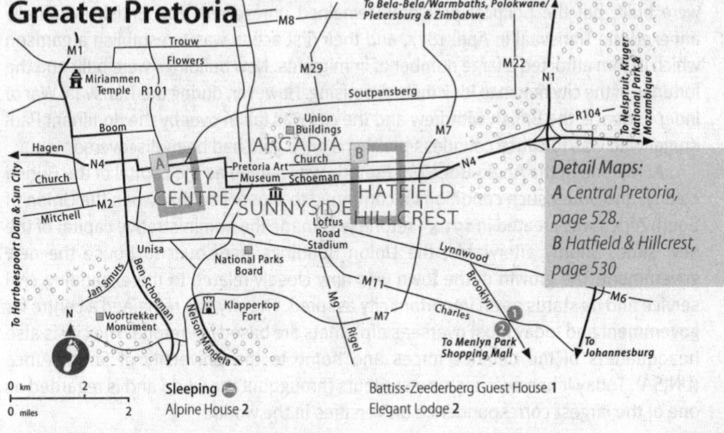

 which until recently was home to most hotels and nightlife. However, the area has suffered a decline in recent years, with increasing crime rates. Many restaurants, hotels and backpacker hostels have relocated to the safer suburbs of **Hatfield** and **Brooklyn** a few kilometres further east where the colleges, universities and sports stadiums are located. Both are attractive suburbs, dotted with parks and gardens, and streets lined with Pretoria's distinctive jacaranda trees.

Best time to visit Pretoria has a pleasant climate with warm to hot summers and mild sunny winters. In winter the daily temperature averages 19°C, the days are still and the skies are clear and cloud-free. In the evening it can get cool. The average annual rainfall is 741 mm, usually falling between November and March. The best time to visit is during the spring when the jacarandas are in full bloom.

Tourist information The **Pretoria Tourist Rendezvous Centre** is in the Old Netherlands Bank Building, Church Square. Also Located here is the **Tshwane Tourism Information Bureau** ⓘ *T012-3581430, 24-hr information line T082-2392630, www.tshwane.gov.za, Mon-Fri 0800-1600, closed weekends*. While there isn't the usual desk and helpful staff found in most local tourist offices, this bureau does produce a couple of useful maps, highlighting the major sights in the city.

The Pretoria office of **South African National Parks (SAN Parks)** ⓘ *643 Leyds St, Muckleneuk, reservations T012-4265000, www.parks-sa.co.za*, is the head office and handles all bookings for accommodation and special long-distance hikes such as the Otter Trail in Tsitsikamma National Park.

Background

From the outset, Pretoria has been closely involved with political upheaval in South Africa, culminating in the inauguration of President Nelson Mandela at the Union Buildings on 10 May 1994. In August 1854, work began on building a church right by today's Church Square – this was to be the beginnings of the town. The first streets were laid out by Andries du Toit, a self-taught surveyor, while the first suburb was known as Arcadia, which was developed by Stephanus Meintjes who in turn was commemorated by naming the hillock nearby, Meintjeskop.

During the 1860s, as the city was steadily growing, Marthinus Pretorius, who had been made president of the republic, tried to unite the Orange Free State with the Transvaal. He failed, resigned as president and was replaced by the Reverand Thomas Francois Burgers in 1870. Under Burgers, the city developed and schools and parks were built, but the political problems remained unresolved. The British eventually annexed the Transvaal in April 1877, and their first action was to establish a garrison which in turn attracted a large number of immigrants. New buildings were built and the fortunes of the city began to look more promising. However, during the Transvaal War of Independence, the British withdrew and the city was taken over by the dominant Paul Kruger who was to cause countless problems once gold had been discovered.

At the end of the Anglo-Boer War Pretoria was named as the capital of the British colony, and under such conditions it continued to prosper so that when the Union of South Africa was created in 1910, Pretoria was made the administrative capital of the new state. Shortly afterwards, the Union Buildings were built to house the new government. The growth of the town was now closely related to the expanding civil service and its status as an important city assured. The city has remained a centre for government and today most overseas diplomats are based in Pretoria. The city is also headquarters of the defence forces and home to the University of South Africa (UNISA). Today it has over 125,000 students throughout the world and is regarded as one of the largest correspondence universities in the world.

Like Johannesburg, Pretoria has large township areas to the northwest and northeast of the city. The greater Pretoria area covers over 1600 sq km and the population is estimated at 1.6 million. The metropolitan council has recently reorganized itself to unite the previously segregated areas under one council administration. The greater area is now called Tshwane, which means 'we are the same'. Technically this is the new name for Pretoria but like other regional name changes in South Africa, it will be some time before this is widely recognized.

Sights » pp531-536.

Pretoria's sights are spread between the city centre, around Church Square, and in the suburbs, and can easily be seen in a day. Most popular is the controversial Voortrekker Monument, although there are also a couple of decent museums and historical buildings worth visiting. The other major attractions are the glitzy distractions of Sun City, a couple of hours' drive away and often visited as a day trip. Johannesburg and its outlying attractions such as Soweto and Walter Sisulu Botanical Gardens are dealt with in the Johannesburg section (see page 512) but are easily accessed from Pretoria.

In the centre

The oldest buildings in Pretoria are clustered around Church Square, once a Voortrekker marketplace. Today it is the heart of the city and is a popular meeting spot for locals, with suited businessmen stopping on the grass for lunch and hawkers selling roasted mealies to passers by. A rather unattractive statue of a grim-faced, grizzled Paul Kruger stands in the middle, surrounded by fluttering flocks of pigeons and flanked with important late 19th-century banks and government offices. The most interesting of these is the **Palace of Justice**, where Nelson Mandela and other leaders of the ANC were tried during the notorious Treason Trials of 1963- 1944. On the southwest side is the Raadsall, or parliament, and the Old Netherlands Bank building now houses the tourist office.

Every spring the appearance of the city is transformed by 60,000 flowering jacaranda trees, covering the parks and gardens in a mauve blanket.

The **Transvaal Museum** ⓘ *Paul Kruger St, T012-3227632, daily 0800-1600, R10*, is a typically dusty natural history museum. It was founded in 1892 and moved into its current premises in 1912. Today, the museum serves as a research and documentation centre for the fauna of southern Africa, one of the leading centres for zoological research in the country. The displays, focusing on geology and stuffed animals, are spread over a series of halls, including the Austin Roberts Bird Hall, a showcases the varied birdlife of southern Africa and a collection of semi-precious stones. More interesting perhaps is the fact that the world-renowned hominid fossil, 'Mrs Ples' (*Australopithecus africanus transvaalensis*), is kept here, although sadly the public doesn't have access to it. Opposite the museum is **City Hall**, dating from 1935, a grand building fronted by broad square, with a fountain and a statue of Andries Pretorius on horseback.

The **Treaty of Vereeniging** ending the Anglo-Boer War (1899-1902) was signed in **Melrose House** ⓘ *275 Jacob Maré St, T012-3222805, www.melrosehouse.co.za, Tue-Sun 1000-1700, R5, small café in the converted stables*, on 31 May 1902, between the British High Command and Boer Republican Forces. The house was originally built in 1886 for George Heys, who made his fortune from trade and a stagecoach service to the Transvaal. It is regarded as one of the finest examples of Victorian domestic architecture in South Africa; marble columns, stained-glass windows and mosaic floors all help create a feeling of serene style and wealth. The house was restored after being bombed by right-wingers in 1990. Today the grounds are used for classical concerts.

Kruger House Museum ⓘ *Church St West, T012-3321266, Tue-Sat 0830-1600, Sun 1100-1600, R16*, is where President Kruger lived between 1884-1901. Now a museum, it displays a fairly diverting collection of his possessions, as well as objects relating to the Anglo-Boer War. At the back of the house is the state coach and his private railway carriage.

Central Pretoria

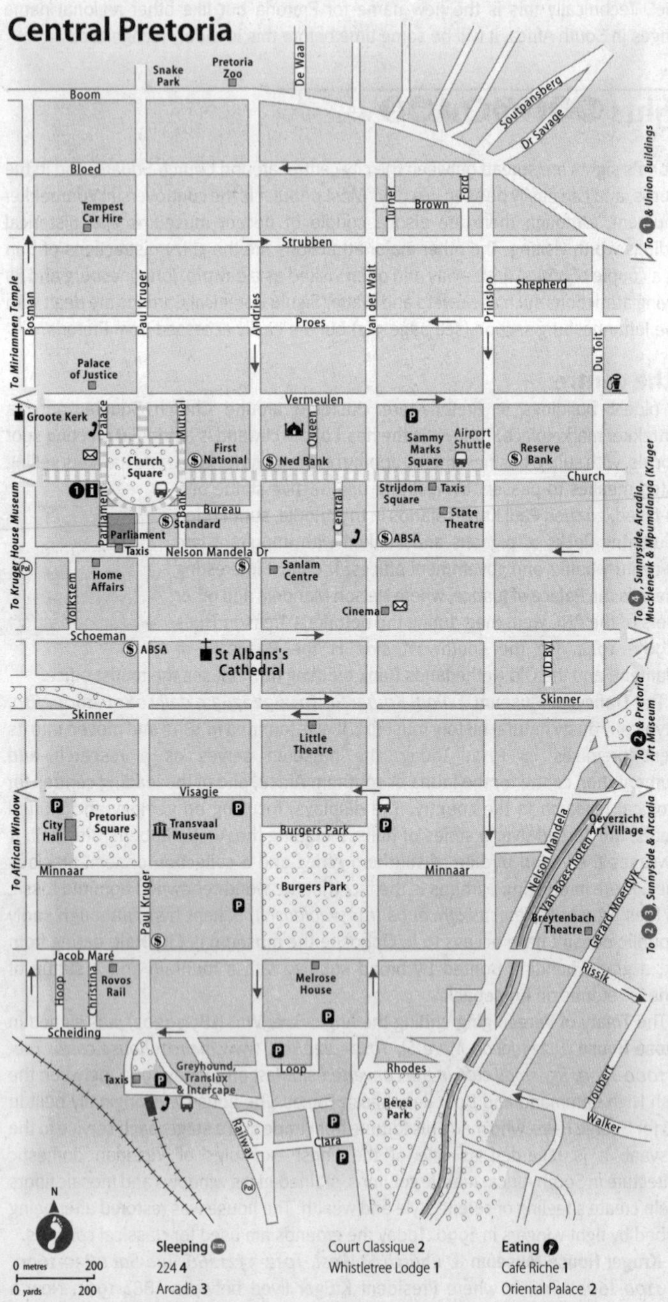

Pretoria Zoo ⓘ *corner of Paul Kruger and Boom Sts, the entrance is on Boom St, T012-3283265, summer 0800-1730, winter 0800-1700, R30*, now known officially as the National Zoological Gardens, is heavily involved in research and conservation. This is South Africa's largest and best designed zoo and is surprisingly spacious.

Difficult to miss if you are walking about in the centre of town **Strijdom Square** is a sprawling open square that used to be dominated by a massive bust of JG Strijdom, covered by a curved concrete roof. The roof, thought of as something of an architectural feat, collapsed on 31 May 2001, 40 years to the day from when it was built. Strijdom was prime minister between 1954-1958 when the government started to place heavy restrictions on the ANC and banned the Communist Party – his statue doesn't seem to be missed much today. The square, flanked by the tall ABSA Bank building and the State Theatre, remains a popular meeting place at lunchtime.

Burgers Park ⓘ *between Van der Walt and Andries Sts, winter 0600-1800, summer 0600-2200*, is the most central of Pretoria's city parks. This fine Victorian park was first laid out as a botanical garden in the early 1870s, and is today a popular meeting place where visitors relax in the shade of rubber trees, palms and jacarandas. The 'florarium' houses a collection of exotic plants in contrasting environments, from subtropical flowers to succulents from the Karoo and Kalahari regions. Elsewhere in the garden is a statue of remembrance for the officers of the South African Scottish Regiment who were killed during the First World War.

African Window ⓘ *149 Visagie St, between Bosman and Schubart Sts, T012-3246082, daily 0900-1700, free, the main entrance hall contains a curio shop and restaurant*, promotes itself as a centre of 'living' culture. There are good temporary exhibitions as well as displays on San rock art and information on the history and development of the Hananwa people from the Blue Mountain before the arrival of the first Europeans in Africa.

Sunnyside and Arcadia

Pretoria Art Museum ⓘ *in Arcadia Park, T021-3441807, Tue-Sat 1000-1700, Wed 1000-2000, Sun 1400-1800, closed Mon, guided tours, www.pretoriaartmuseum.co.za, R5*, teas and light meals available, houses a fine collection of South African art as well as a selection of run-of-the-mill 17th-century Dutch paintings. The collection includes works by Pierneef, Frans Oerder and Anton van Wouw. It also houses interesting temporary exhibitions, including photography.

The magnificent red sandstone complex of the **Union Buildings** ⓘ *Church St, Arcadia, T012-3002000*, sits proudly on top of Meintjeskop overlooking the city centre. This is the administrative headquarters of the South African President, most famous for being the site of Nelson Mandela's speech after his inauguration president on 10 May 1994, when the grounds in front of the building where packed with thousands of well-wishers. The building, designed by Herbert Baker, who also designed St George's Cathedral and Rhodes Memorial in Cape Town, was completed in 1913. Baker went on to help Edwin Lutyens in the planning of New Delhi, India. (The Union Buildings in Pretoria influenced his designs for the new Government Secretariat and the Imperial Legislative Assembly). The formal gardens below the buildings are pleasant to walk about, but the best reason for coming here is for the city view. Look out for the statues of South Africa's famous generals: Botha, on horseback, Hertzog and Smuts. Also found on the hill is the Pretoria War Memorial, Delville Wood Memorial and the Garden of Remembrance.

Eight people were shot dead in Strijdom Square by right-wing activists in the early 1990s, led by Barend Strijdom who shot at a minibus taxi and who rather curiously lends his name to the square.

Miriammen Temple ⓘ *follow the N4, Proes St, from the city centre for 2 km, turn right into 7 St, daily all day*, is a pleasant reminder of the importance of the Indian population in South Africa. The temple is one of the oldest (1905) buildings in Pretoria. The imposing *gopuram*, or tower, is a 12.5-m-high layered structure of brightly-painted gods, goddesses and demons interspersed with white layers of stones. he temple is devoted to Miriammen, the Hindu goddess of infectious diseases such as smallpox. You are free to enter most areas but remember to remove your shoes.

South of the city is the looming granite hulk of the **Voortrekker Monument** ⓘ *south of the city, just off the R28, T012-3266770, www.voortrekkermon.org.za, daily 0800-1700/1800, small entrance charge*, a controversial Afrikaner memorial. The monument, a 40 m cube, was completed in 1949 after 11 years of work. It is a sombre and unattractive structure, a windowless block dominating the landscape, but one of particular significance to Afrikaners. It was built to commemorate the Great Trek of the 1830s, when the Afrikaners struck inland from the Cape with just their ox wagons and little idea of the trials that lay ahead of them. Inside is the cavernous Hall of Heroes, guarded by a carved head of a buffalo above the entrance, thought to be the most dangerous animal in Africa, with 27 marble friezes around the walls depicting both

Hatfield & Hillcrest

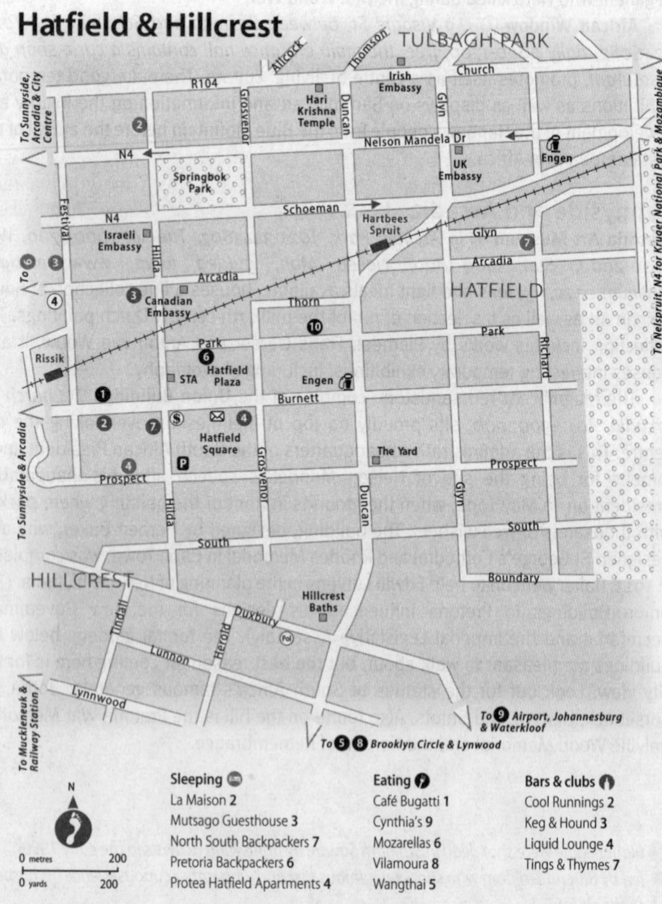

the trek and scenes from the Zulu wars, including a seriously suspect portrayal of the Battle of Blood River (see page 717), where the Afrikaners are shown as brave soldiers and the Zulus as cowardly savages. The monument was, until recently, the site of a huge annual celebration on 16 December, the date of the battle (known as the Day of the Covenant). At exactly midday on this date a ray of sunlight falls onto a large slab of stone in the centre of the basement (rather like a tomb), spotlighting the carved words: "Ons Vir Jou, Suid Afrika" (We are for you, South Africa). The fact that this date celebrated the bloody massacre of Zulus proved, unsurprisingly, hugely controversial, and after the end of Apartheid, this national holiday was renamed the Day of Reconciliation. Today, the celebrations are very low key indeed. For impressive views of the surrounding countryside and to the city, take the lift to the viewing area around the roof. In the basement are some displays of life during the Great Trek. Outside, the surrounding wall recreates the circular laager of 64 ox-wagons that can be seen at the site of the battlefield.

The best reason for coming to **Klapperkop Fort** ⓘ *daily 0800-1700, off the R28 on J Rissik Dr, small entry fee*, is to enjoy the excellent views from this high vantage point. You can walk around the battlements but the rest of the fort is closed to the public. A separate building houses a museum on South Africa's military history. There is an old steam locomotive in the car park, plus a couple of tanks in the grounds. The fort was built to guard the southern entrance to the town, but no resistance was put up when the British entered the town in May 1900.

Parks and gardens

Pretoria, known as the Garden City, is well known for its parks and gardens and the city takes much pride in its magnificent open space.

Jan Celliers Park, also known as Protea Park, is west of Queen Wilhelmina Road in Groenkloof and is the furthest park from the city centre. The park is on a natural slope and is made up of rock gardens, mixed borders, groups of trees and a water garden; two ponds are linked by a series of 14 small waterfalls. Aside from being a relaxing spot for a wander, the park is worth visiting if you are keen on wild flowers and wish to see some of South Africa's indigenous flora close up.

Springbok Park, in contrast, has a much more informal layout. Located between Schoeman and Pretorius streets in Hatfield to the east of the city centre towards the N1, this park was declared a national monument in 1979. It was first planted in 1905 when WH Lanham was planning the suburb of Hatfield. A stream flows through the grounds and there are some fine trees from different regions of the country.

Venning Park is a neatly planned garden known for its immaculate rose beds. Like Springbok Park it is found between Schoeman and Pretorius streets, but slightly closer to the centre of town. An avenue of palm trees ends beside a pleasant tea garden and restaurant; the park is close to the diplomatic enclave and many families come here at weekends.

Sleeping

Pretoria *maps p525, p528 and p530*
As in many South African cities, must of the best accommodation is found in Pretoria's suburbs.

A Court Classique, corner of Schoeman and Beckett Sts, Arcadia, T012-3444420, www.courtclassique.co.za. Practical choice in the suburb of Arcadia, range of suites aimed at families or business travellers, all are spacious, en suite and have kitchenettes, set around landscaped patios with water features, swimming pool, restaurant bar and conference centre.

A La Maison, 235 Hilda St, Hatfield, T012-4304341, www.lamaison.co.za. 6 large en suite bedrooms, old fashioned decor, grand white Victorian mansion, close to many diplomatic missions, restaurant is highly regarded lush gardens, swimming pool, roof-top terrace.

A Whistletree Lodge, 1267 Whistletree Drive, Queenswood, T012-3339915/6, www.whistletree.co.za. Award-winning guesthouse close to the Union Buildings. 2 en suite rooms elegantly decorated, private balconies, attractive lounge with traditional, sumptuous furniture, and high ceilings, landscaped gardens and pool, tennis court, sauna, cocktail bar, dinner and snacks on request.

A-B Protea Hatfield Apartments, 1080 Prospect St, Hatfield, T012-3626105, www.proteahotels.co.za. 28 en suite suites, TV, a/c, pleasant decor, pool area, bar, great location in the throng of shops, restaurants of Hatfield.

B-C Alpine House, 268a Alpine Rd, Menlo Park, T012-8110169, www.alpinehouse.co.za. 2 self-catering units, both with 2 bedrooms, open plan kitchen, private lounge with DSTV, undercover parking, tasteful contemporary decor, stylish furniture. B&B available.

B-C Arcadia, 515 Proes St, T012-3269311, www.arcadiahotel.com. 139 a/c rooms with TV, quality city centre hotel, clean, well managed and aimed at business travellers and tour groups. Restaurant, bar, coffee shop, lounge, gym, undercover parking, part of the **Arcadia** shopping complex, close to embassies and a short walk to the Union Buildings.

A-B Mutsago Guesthouse, 327 Festival St, Hatfield, T012-4307193, www.mutsago.co.za. Smart 2-storey home surrounded by lush tropical gardens, good-sized pool with deck chairs set around it. 14 rooms with an African theme, murals painted on the walls depicting Zulu homesteads, African-print fabrics on the beds, all en suite, TV and minibar.

C Battiss-Zeederberg Guest House, 3 Fook Island, 92 20th Street, Menlo Park, T/F012-4607318, http://battiss.co.za. Guesthouse set in original home of the artist Walter Battiss, and much of his character is still evident around the house – his murals remain on the walls and the floors as a reminder of his love for San paintings. 4 double rooms with lofty ceilings, shiny wood floors and large French windows opening on to a leafy courtyard, en suite, TV, fans, kitchenette. You'll need your own car to get into town, but it's a short drive from the N1 and Menlyn Park shopping mall (see Greater Pretoria map, p525).

C Elegant Lodge, 83 Atterbury Rd, Menlo Park, T012-3466460, www.elegantlodge.co.za. Attractive business hotel with easy access to the N1 and Menlyn Park Mall. 16 a/c rooms, comfortable furnishings, en suite, TV, internet line, small pleasant restaurant, escape the traffic on the main road in the pretty courtyards.

C That's It, 5 Brecher St, Clydesdale, T012-3443404, www.thatsit.co.za. Neat B&B set in a family home in a quiet suburb. 4 simple and pleasant rooms, white-washed walls and blue-and-white fabrics, thatched lapa in the tropical gardens, swimming pool, TV lounge, useful location if you need to apply for visas one of the nearby foreign embassies.

C-D Hotel 224, corner of Schoeman and Leyds St, T012-4405281, www.hotel224.com. Huge concrete block offering 224 single and double a/c rooms, rooms are dated and on the small side, DSTV, video channel, restaurant, bar, secure parking, short walk from the Union Buildings, free transfers.

Backpacker hostels

F North South Backpackers, 355 Glynn St, Hatfield, T012-3620989, www.northsouthbackpackers.com. Clean and airy lodge with well-tended gardens and spotless pool within a few mins' walk of the shops and restaurants at Hatfield Sq. Doubles (one with its own TV) and dorms, bar with fireplace, pool table, helpful with booking tours. Will pick up from Johannesburg airport if arranged in advance.

F Pretoria Backpackers, 425 Farenden Rd, Clydesdale, T012-3439754, www.pretoriabackpackers.net. The oldest backpacker hostel in town, recently relocated and thoroughly renovated. 2 houses around the corner from each other, 2 small dorms, several very comfortable doubles in garden huts or in the main house, stylishly decorated with a guesthouse feel, lovely tropical gardens with fish ponds and gazebos, pool, travel desk. Organize local tours of Pretoria, Sun City/Pilansberg, Lesedi Cultural Village. Will collect from Johannesburg airport. Staff will accompany guests to football and rugby matches at Loftus Stadium. Recommended.

Eating

Pretoria *maps p528 and p530*
In a city as spread out as Pretoria, the restaurants tend to be found in or near the large shopping malls (see Shopping, p534). The city centre has plenty of sandwich bars and fast food outlets serving office workers during the day, but few places to eat in at night. The best places to go in the evening are **Hatfield** and **Brooklyn**.

TTT La Madeleine, 122 Priory Rd, Lynnwood, T012-3613667, closed Mon, Sun and Sat lunch. Long-standing top restaurant, running for over 20 years. Fine cuisine and a pleasant, airy setting, classical French cuisine, dishes including Provençal lamb and confit of duck, award-winning wine list. Reservations recommended at weekends.

TTT Vilamoura, 273 Middel St, Brooklyn, T012-3461650, lunch Mon-Fri, dinner Mon-Sat. Highly rated for its Portuguese-style seafood, smart restaurant favoured by the well-heeled social set. Relaxed setting, prawns are a house speciality, good seafood platters. Pricey. Also has branches in Jo'burg and Cape Town.

TT Cynthia's, Maroelana Centre, near **Pretoria Country Club**, in Maroelana, in the southern suburbs off the N1, phone for directions, T012-4603220, closed Sat lunch, Sun evening and most of Dec. Popular local restaurant, rural feel to decor and menu, traditional meat dishes, some seafood and game. Extensive wine list.

TT Oriental Palace, Colosseum Hotel, 410 Schoeman St, Arcadia, T012-3222195. Authentic Indian restaurant, chefs from Pakistan and north India who prepare genuine curries, good tikka and tandoori, delicious and great value dhal, tandoori breads and kulfi. Everything halaal, no alcohol.

TT Wangthai, 281 Middel St, Brooklyn, T012-3466230. Authentic and elegant Thai restaurant, huge menu, lots of choice for vegetarians, not cheap but excellent food, sister restaurant in prestigious Sandton Square in Jo'burg.

T Mozzarellas, Hatfield Sq, Hatfield, T012-3626464. Good value Italian pizza and pasta, tables spilling from the brightly-painted interior onto lively Hatfield Square, popular with students, good selection of pasta and decent pizzas, plus seafood and steaks.

Cafés and coffee shops

Café Bugatti, Burnett St, Hatfield. Popular spot, especially with the brunch crowd on Sun mornings. Alfresco tables plus a bar and restaurant inside. Great sharing platters, breakfasts and brunch, plus light meals, friendly service.

Café Riche, Church Sq (southwest corner), T012-3283173. Restored historical building, feels like a Parisian café, great views over the square, range of breakfasts, light meals and late night dinners, thought to be the oldest café in Pretoria. Atmospheric spot.

Bars and clubs

Pretoria *maps p525, p528 and p530*
Again, by far the best areas to head for in the evening and at weekends are **Hatfield** and **Brooklyn**, both to the east of the town centre. Ask the taxi to take you to Hatfield Sq, from where there are dozens of places to explore within a short walk of each other.

Boston Tea Party, Menlyn Park, T012-3653625, 1800-late, closed Sun-Mon. This is a large conference centre during the day, but at night it transforms into a popular venue with a mix of live music, comedy, and dancing with DJs spinning records. Impressive place holding up to 1000 revellers.

Cool Runnings, Burnett St. One of the chain of bar-cum-restaurants that attract a young studenty crowd, loud and raucous evenings, live reggae music on Sun. Always busy at the weekend, garish cocktails and imported beers.

Devine Lounge, Menlyn Park Mall, T012-3681361. Award-winning wine list, cocktails, a plethora of sofas, great jazz on Sun, shopping mall setting but doesn't feel like it. Serves good meals, too.

Hillside Tavern, 320 Hillside Rd, Lynnwood, T012-3481402, closed Sat lunch. Pub and steak restaurant, substantial bar with wide choice of beers and ciders, revamped to look like a traditional English country pub.

Keg & Hound, 1077 Arcadia St, Hatfield. Good choice of imported beers, plus a snack menu. Popular pub atmosphere among the local university students, late nights at the weekend.

Liquid Lounge, 141 Burnett St, Hatfield. Stylish late-night cocktail bar, music has a chilled vibe, more popular with young professionals than the usual student crowd.

Tings & Thymes, just off Burnett St in Hatfield Plaza, Hatfield, T012-3625537. Small bar with mix of live music, can get very crowded, best to arrive mid-evening to guarantee a table, great cocktails, middle eastern and vegetarian meals, fun place.

Entertainment

Pretoria *maps p525, p528 and p530*

Computicket, T083-9158000, www.computicket.com. Advance booking for all events, has kiosks in Hatfield Plaza and Menlyn Park malls.

Cinema

Drive-in, on the rooftop of the shopping mall, Menlyn Park. Showings nightly at 1930 and 2130. If you don't have your own car, you can hire a renovated original Chevvy or Chrysler convertible.

IMAX, Menlyn Park, T012-3681186. Giant screen with wrap-around sound, showing wildlife and landscape films.

NuMetro, at Menlyn Park, T012-3681301, www.nutmetro.co.za, 15 screens; and at Hatfield Plaza, T012-3625899.

Shopping

Pretoria *maps p525, p528 and p530*

Most of Pretoria's shopping is limited to its large shopping malls: **Brooklyn Mall**, 338 Bronkhorst St, New Muckleneuk, T012-3461063; **Hatfield Plaza**, Park St, Hatfield. A lively flea market is held here at the weekend; **The Tramshed**, corner of Van der Walt and Schoeman Sts, though avoid this area after dark; **Sanlam Centre**, Andries St, in the town centre.

Menlyn Park, Atterbury Rd, Menlo Park, clearly seen from the N1, T012-3488766. Pretoria's premier mall for 'shopper-tainment', with 300 shops and restaurants, 15-screen cinema, IMAX theatre, bowling alley, and unique drive-in cinema. Its architectural focal point is its large tent-like roof that can be seen from far away.

Oeverzicht Art Village, between Gerard Moerdyk St, Kotze St and Van Boeschoten Lane, T012-4402320. This is a delightful small pocket of old Pretoria, a mix of galleries, antique shops and restaurants. All the houses date from 1895-1920 and have been restored. At the south end of Gerard Moerdyk St is the Breytenbach Theatre.

Activities and tours

Pretoria *maps p525, p528 and p530*

Cricket

Centurion Park, 23 km from the centre of town, off the R21 to Johannesburg, enquiries 012-6631005, info@ncu.co.za, tickets from www.sacrickettickets.co.za. The ground where international matches for Pretoria are now played is 23 km from the centre of town, off the R21 to Johannesburg. The ground, home to the Northern Transvaal provincial cricket team, is a modern circular stadium dominated by a huge single grandstand. The rest of the boundary is made up of grass banks which are great fun for picnics and braais.

Rugby

Pretoria is the home town for the **Northern Transvaal Rugby Union**, T012-3444011.

Loftus Versveld Rugby Stadium, Kirkness St, Sunnyside. The main rugby stadium, also the venue for occasional football matches.

Tour operators

Apart from city tours, the most popular day trips from Pretoria are to **Sun City**, **Pilansberg National Park** and the **Gold Mines**. Expect to pay in the region of R350 per person for a half-day tour of the city, which takes in the major sights such as the Voortrekker Monument and Union Buildings.

Rennies Travel, 15 Sanlam Centre, T012-3202240. National chain, all purpose travel agent plus Thomas Cook bureau de change, useful for reconfirming flights.

Travel the Planet, Church Sq, T016-4232467, www.traveltheplanet.co.za. A reservation and booking service, offering a range of tours in and around Pretoria and further afield.

Ulysses, T012-6634941, www.ulysses.co.za. Daily city tours in a distinctive purple open-topped bus. Also has trips to Pilanesberg, Sun City and Cullinan Diamond Mine.

Transport

Pretoria *maps p525, p528 and p530*
Exercise caution about the bus stand and train station as muggings have occurred in this area. Pretoria is 500 km to the Zimbabwe border (**Beitbridge**), 474 km to **Bloemfontein**, 1492 km to **Cape Town**, 688 km to **Durban**, 1060 km to **East London**, 1078 km to **Harare** (Zimbabwe), 58 km to **Johannesburg**, 530 km to **Kimberley**, 1406 km to **Knysna**, and 1133 km to **Port Elizabeth**.

Air

See page 523 for flight details for Johannesburg International Airport. **Magic Bus**, T011-5480822, www.magicbus.co.za, and **Airport Link Shuttle**, T011-7922017, www.airportlink.co.za, both drop off at the major hotels in Johannesburg and Pretoria.

Bus

Local Municipal buses run between the city centre and the suburbs. Timetables are available in chemists and from the service information office in Church Sq, T012-3080839. **Translux, Greyhound**, and **Intercape** buses run between Pretoria and Johannesburg (1 hr). Although they are long distance coaches, there are several departures throughout the day. They cannot be pre-booked but seats are always available; expect to pay around R100 standby. You can then connect with other buses or trains at Johannesburg's Park City terminus.

Long distance The bus stand is to the left of the railway station (as you face it) in the 1928 Building. **Translux, Greyhound** and **Intercape** all have an office here, open during normal office hours.

Greyhound, T011-2768500, www.greyhound.co.za, has regular departures to **Bulawayo, Cape Town** via **Bloemfontein, Durban** via **Newcastle** and **Ladysmith, Durban** via **Vryheid** and **Richards Bay, Harare** (Zimbabwe) via **Polokwane/ Pietersburg** and **Masvingo** (Zimbabwe), **Nelspruit** (4 hrs), **Port Elizabeth** via **Bloemfontein** and **Grahamstown, Maputo** (Mozambique) via **Nelspruit**.

Intercape, T0861-287287, www.intercape.co.za, has regular departures to: **Durban, Cape Town** via **Bloemfontein, Port Elizabeth, Plettenberg Bay, Upington** via **Kuruman, Maputo** (Mozambique) via **Nelspruit**, and **Gaborone** (Botswana) via **Rustenburg**.

Translux, T0861-589282, www.translux.co.za, has regular departures to: **Blantyre** (Malawi), via **Harare, Bloemfontein, Bulawayo** (Zimbabwe), **Cape Town** via **Kimberley** and **Bloemfontein, Durban, Maputo** (Mozambique), via **Nelspruit, Knysna** via **Kimberley** and via **Bloemfontein, East London** via **Bloemfontein, Harare** (Zimbabwe), **Lusaka** (Zambia) via **Harare**, and **Port Elizabeth** (14 hrs).

Luxliner, T011-9144321, toll free T0800-003537, runs a daily service from the Parkade Centre at Johannesburg International Airport, to **Margate**, via **Durban**.

Budget buses Baz Bus, T021-4392323, www.bazbus.com, is the only budget transport for backpackers which will pick up and drop off at hostels in Pretoria. See page 39 for details of the service.

Car hire

Phone the toll-free numbers for the nearest branch.
Avis, T0861-021111, www.avis.co.za.
Budget, T0861-016622, www.budget.co.za.
Hertz, T0861-600136, www.hertz.com.
Imperial, T0861-131000, www.imperialcarrental.co.za.
Tempest, T0861-002111.

Taxi

Taxis in front of the railway station, on Prinsloo opposite the tourist office, and on Church St by Strijdom Sq. You cannot wave down a taxi, restaurants and clubs will always order one by telephone. Most are reliable and should use their meters with a minimum of fuss.
A-Class, T012-3228147.

Train

Local Not all of the long distance trains depart from Pretoria. If you are going to Durban, East London, Bloemfontein, or Port Elizabeth you will have to start your journey from Johannesburg. There are plenty of Metro commuter trains throughout the day between Pretoria and Johannesburg but avoid this service.

Long distance: There is a booking office to the right in the main railway station building. Central Reservations, T086-0008888, www.spoornet.co.za. Regular trains to Musina, Komatipoort and Cape Town.

Directory

Pretoria *maps p525, p528 and p530*

Banks American Express, 306 Brooklyn Mall, Bronkhorst St, T012-3463580; **Rennies Travel**, agents for Thomas Cook, Sanlam Centre, corner of Andries and Pretorius streets, T012-3202240. There are **Rennies Travel** and **American Express** bureau de changes at Johannesburg International Airport, open daily 0500-2100. All banks have outlets in the many shopping malls dotted about the suburbs and have foreign exchange facilities where you can cash TCs and change money or withdraw money from your credit card at an ATM. **Embassies and consulates** Australia, T012-3423740. Belgium, T012-4403201. **Botswana**, T012-4309640. **Canada**, T012-4223000. Denmark, T012-4309340. **Finland**, T012-3430275. **France**, T012-4251600. Germany, T012-4278900. **Ireland**, T012-3425062. **Israel**, T012-3480470. **Japan**, T012-4521500. **Lesotho**, T012-4607648. Malawi, T012-3420146. **Mozambique**, T012-4010300. **Namibia**, T012-4819100. Netherlands, T012-3443910. **Swaziland**, T012-3441910. **UK**, T012-4217500. **USA**, T012-3414000. **Zambia**, T012-3261854. Zimbabwe, T012-3425125.

Hospitals Wilgers Hospital, T012-8070019; Zuid-Afrikaans Hospital, (private) T012-2430300. **Internet** There are numerous internet cafés in all the malls, an in and around Hatfield Sq. Most backpacker hostels and hotels offer internet access.

Useful address and telephone numbers Ambulance: T10177. **Dept of Home Affairs**, corner of Maggs and Petrolieum Sts, Waltloo, T012-8108911. Visa extensions will take 10 working days. You will need to produce an onward ticket and proof of funds. **Police**: T10111.

North West Province

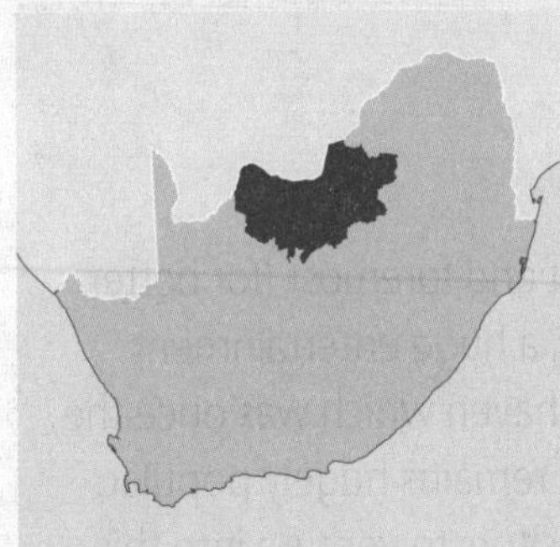

Footprint features

Introduction

North West Province is known first and foremost (for better or worse) as the home of Sun City, a huge entertainment complex and one-time gambling haven which was once the most visited site in South Africa. It remains hugely popular, and is the most likely reason for visitors to venture into this dry and stark state. Much of North West Province is visually unremarkable, made up of flat Kalahari grasslands and dotted with lonely farming communities which were some of the most important agricultural centres in the 19th century. This was once the Western Transvaal, one of the areas where the Voortrekkers settled at the end of the Great Trek, and towns such as Mafikeng and Rustenburg have a fascinating history.

Gambling and history aside, the best reason for visiting is the region's excellent game parks, all at a malaria-free altitude of 1000-2000 m. The well-publicized Pilanesberg National Park is easily accessible, lying incongruously close to Sun City, while Madikwe Game Reserve is one of the finest parks in the country, offering excellent accommodation and the chance of seeing the Big Five just a few hours from Johannesburg and Pretoria.

A more low-key attraction and a big draw for locals are the Magaliesberg Mountains, less than one hour's drive from Pretoria. Although made up by a fairly bland series of bush-covered hills, they are filled with wild hiking trails and dotted with comfortable holiday resorts. Further west are numerous private game farms, which provide an insight into life in the bushveld on the edge of the Kalahari.

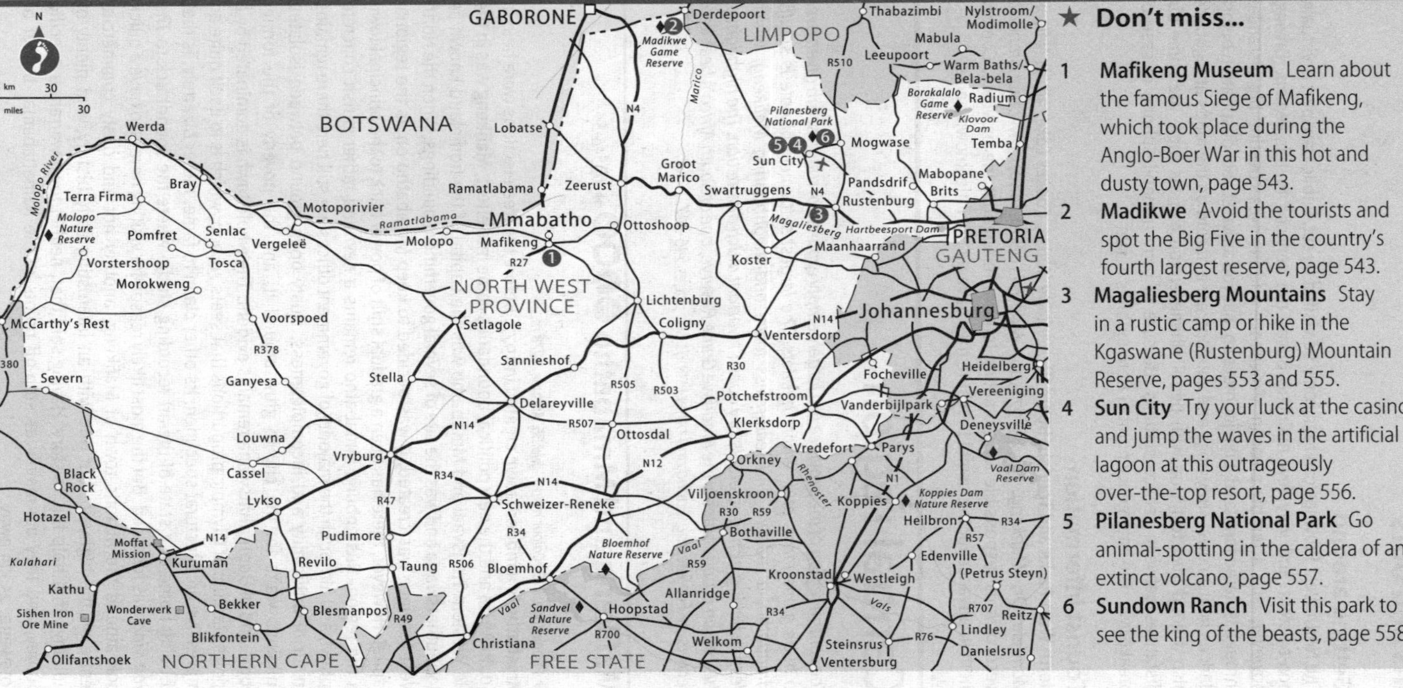

★ Don't miss...

1. **Mafikeng Museum** Learn about the famous Siege of Mafikeng, which took place during the Anglo-Boer War in this hot and dusty town, page 543.
2. **Madikwe** Avoid the tourists and spot the Big Five in the country's fourth largest reserve, page 543.
3. **Magaliesberg Mountains** Stay in a rustic camp or hike in the Kgaswane (Rustenburg) Mountain Reserve, pages 553 and 555.
4. **Sun City** Try your luck at the casinos and jump the waves in the artificial lagoon at this outrageously over-the-top resort, page 556.
5. **Pilanesberg National Park** Go animal-spotting in the caldera of an extinct volcano, page 557.
6. **Sundown Ranch** Visit this park to see the king of the beasts, page 558.

Ins and outs

Getting around

The North West Province can really only be visited by car. Public transport is virtually non-existent and very few mainline buses run services to this region. Driving, however, isn't a terribly pleasant experience and involves covering big distances through isolated farmland. Plan journeys so that you arrive at your destination before dark as goats, cows, stray dogs and antelope are a hazard on the roads at night. It's also a good idea to fill up with petrol whenever you can, as there are some big distances between service stations. Be sure to carry a mobile phone in case of breakdown. The emergency number from mobiles is 112.

Tourist Information

North West Parks and Tourism Board ⓘ *Heritage House, Cookes Lake, 30/31 Nelson Mandela Dr, Mafikeng, T018-3971500, Mon-Fri 0800-1640, www.tourismnorthwest.co.za*, is responsible for promoting tourism throughout the province. Contact them in advance for the useful brochure they have on the little-known parks.

Central region

The central region of the province is a largely empty expanse of rough scrub given over to huge game farms and remote hamlets. The largest settlement of note is scruffy Mmabatho, a modern and featureless town, and neighbouring Mafikeng, which despite having a chequered history doesn't warrant much distraction. The highlight of this region is undoubtedly the Madikwe Game Reserve, one of South Africa's best-kept secrets. » *For Sleeping, Eating and other listings, see pages 546-547.*

Mafikeng and Mmabatho » *pp546-547.*

→ *Phone code: 018 . Colour map 1, grid B6. Altitude 1,278 m.*

Mmabatho is a modern town created in 1977. Before the free elections were held in South Africa and the new political boundaries came into effect, **Mafikeng** was in the old Western Transvaal and Mmabatho was the capital of the homeland known as Bophuthatswana and was the site of several government buildings. When the North West Province was created, it was decided to keep Mmabatho on as the regional capital. However, there has been a gradual shift of power back to the principal town in the region, Rustenburg. Mmabatho remains a new and rather garish concrete sprawl, and although the majority of government offices are still here there remains an air of artificiality and incompleteness. Dusty open ground between isolated buildings waits for the city to grow around it, and the poverty of the former homeland of Bophuthatswana remains evident. The whole town is dominated by a sports stadium of Olympic proportions that seats 70,000, which is in itself quite an impressive architectural specimen. Its other claim to fame, rather bizarrely, is that of being home to a state-of-the-art recording studio where the soundtrack to *The Lion King* was recorded. But the most likely reason for visiting here is to have a quick look around the historic town of Mafikeng, another hot and dusty commercial centre on the highveld, but one with an interesting early history, and plenty of buildings that help tell its story. Having said that, neither town warrant a specific journey, and they act mainly as stop-off points to the Ramatlabama border of Botswana, 25 km away.

There are several different sources of tourist information in the two towns. For local and regional information call in at the **North West Parks and Tourism Board** ⓘ *Heritage House, Cookes Lake, 30/31 Nelson Mandela Dr, Mafikeng, T018-3971500, Mon-Fri 0800-1640, www.tourismnorthwest.co.za*. The Mafikeng Museum (see page 543) is also a useful centre for finding out what to do in the town.

Background

Mafikeng was founded as a British administrative centre in 1885, when Sir Charles Warren was sent to the region with a military force to occupy and bring peace to this frontier territory. Only 20 km away was the Goshen Republic, an independent state created by a group of European mercenaries who had been given farms by the local Rolong tribe. The name of the new settlement came from the Tswana *maFikeng*, 'place of boulders'. The surrounding territory became known as British Bechuanaland, with Mafikeng as the centre for the local farmers, traders and hunters. At the time this was still very much frontier territory, occupied by a rough crowd and policed by the tough Bechuanaland Border Police.

On 14 October 1899, a Boer force under the command of General JP Snyman besieged the town, and so started the period of events that was to put the town on the map. The Siege of Mafeking lasted 217 days until 17 May 1900, when the town was relieved by a combined force of Rhodesian troops from the north and Imperial troops from the south. At the time, the siege captured the imagination of the British public in England – the Anglo-Boer War was the first war to be reported in such detail, with pictures, cartoons and newspaper articles. It was during the siege that the British commander, Colonel RSS Baden-Powell, made his name and conceived the idea for the Boy Scout movement (see box, page 542).

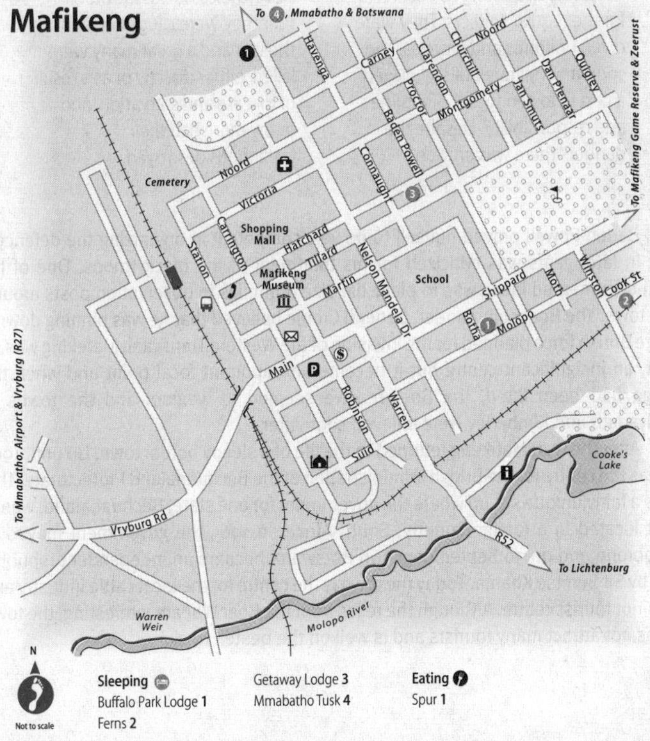

Siege sidelines

During the long days of the seven month Siege of Mafikeng (which lasted from 13 October 1899 to 17 May 1900), the English schoolboys in this colonial town started to become undisciplined – especially when their school closed because of the daily bombardment of the town by artillery shells. The commander of the town's British forces, Colonel Baden-Powell, whose small force was having difficulty defending the town, had an idea. He organized boys, aged between nine and 15 years, into a disciplined Siege Cadet Corps and put them to non-combat use. Their tasks included carrying supplies and messages between the front line and command posts, delivering post within the town, assisting the aged, and acting as observers for the regular soldiers. They were given uniforms and bicycles, and sport and military drills all played a part in fostering self-discipline and responsibility. Despite the dangers there was only one casualty during the siege among the cadets, that of nine-year-old Frankie Brown, who was killed by an exploding shell; his grave can be seen in Mafikeng cemetery. Baden-Powell went on to found the Boy Scout movement at Brownsea in southern England in 1907. He said of the boys of Mafikeng, "These lads proved by their achievements that, if trusted, boys can be relied upon to act as men when needed."

The impact of the war between Briton and Boer on the majority of the southern African population is also often forgotten. Neither side made much use of African soldiers directly, though a great many were employed (or forced to work) as porters, transport handlers and messengers. Nevertheless it was inevitable that they were caught up in the war and a great many were killed, either directly or as a result of disease and starvation, and many more had their livelihoods destroyed.

Baden-Powell proved himself to be very competent in organizing the defences, but in later years was criticized for his treatment of the black troops. One of his well-documented ideas was to place life-size dummies in observation posts around the town. The Boer commander, General Cronje believed that he was pinning down a large British force planned for the invasion of the Western Transvaal. Mafeking was, in fact, an insignificant centre but it became an important focal point and when the siege had been lifted, the Boer resolve seemed to weaken and the towns of Ladysmith and Kimberley were relieved soon after.

After the war, Mafikeng returned to the life of a sleepy border town. Up until 1965 it was the centre for the British administration of the Bechuanaland Protectorate. This was a fairly unique set-up where the government for one state, Bechuanaland, was in fact located in a foreign country, South Africa. In 1965 the government moved to Gaborone and on 30 September 1966 Botswana became an independent republic, led by Sir Seretse Khama. Today the town is the centre for the local cattle industry and a minor tourist centre. Although the relics from the Boer War are interesting, the town does not attract many tourists and is well off the beaten track.

Sights

The **Mafikeng Museum** ⓘ *corner of Martin and Robinson Sts, Mafikeng, T018-3816102*, has an excellent series of displays relating to the Siege of Mafeking, as well as some informative exhibits which trace the history of the region along with the culture of the indigenous peoples. **Mafikeng Cemetery** contains the graves of British servicemen, the Town Guard and South African troops. The most prominent grave is that of Andrew Beauchamp-Proctor, South Africa's most highly decorated First World War airman. **Kanon Kopje** is the site of a fort on the southern banks of the Molopo River built during a conflict between the Goshen Republic and the Barolong Boo Tshidi. The fort has been restored along with some cannon and guns and there are panoramic views out over Mafikeng.

The **Mafikeng Game Reserve** ⓘ *T018-3815611, 0700-1800, R15*, lies at the edge of town, though the entrance is 10 km out on the Zeerust road. The reserve, covering 4600 ha of open Kalahari grassland and acacia thorn scrub, contains large populations of plains game, buffalo, and giraffe and is a good place to try and see white rhino. There are various tracks through the reserve, dotted with picnic sites, and the main circuit takes only two hours.

North of Mmabatho

▸▸ *pp546-547.*

Botsalano Game Reserve

ⓘ *Follow the R52 Ramatlabama border road north from Mmabatho for 30 km; the park is signposted, T018-3862433, Apr-Aug 0800-1700, Sep-Mar 0600-1800. Hunting is still permitted in the reserve and between Apr and Aug it may well be closed.*

Like many of the game reserves in the North West Province, this is a little-known park in beautiful countryside, stocked with a good range of wild animals. The 5800-ha reserve is set in typical Kalahari country – open grasslands with patches of acacia and karee woodlands. It is well known locally for its successful breeding of white rhino. You can also hope to see gemsbok, eland, springbok, steenbok, giraffe, jackal, hartebeest, zebra, kudu, duiker, warthog and impala. Hiking is allowed and there are several waterholes and dams which are ideal spots for game viewing.

Zeerust

→ *Colour map 1, grid B6.* *Altitude 1187 m.*

Zeerust is a small centre for the local sheep and cattle industry, with little of interest in the town, although it does serve as a useful overnight stop between Gauteng and Gaborone. The commercial centre is along Church Street, where you will find banks to change money, supermarkets, and snack bars at the 24-hour petrol stations. Among these is a Woolworths with a food hall, a godsend in these remote parts.

Madikwe Game Reserve

▸▸ *pp546-547. Colour map 1, grid A6.*

Madikwe is the fourth largest game reserve in South Africa. Although the reserve lies entirely within South Africa, it is only 35 km from the Botswana capital, Gaborone. The northern limits of the park are marked by the international border, while the southern limits coincide with the Dwarsberg Mountains. Most of the park sits between the main road to Botswana and the Marico River to the east. Covering over 60,000 ha, it has the second largest elephant population and it lies in a malaria-free zone. At present the park is not open to day visitors, but offers excellent accommodation and activities. There are plans to open a section of the park to day visitors once internal roads have been improved sufficiently. Visitors must book through one of the lodges/camps listed under Sleeping, page 546.

Ins and outs

Getting there If you are driving from Gauteng, take the N4 west through Magalies, Swartruggens. At Zeerust turn right onto the R49 following signs to Gaborone. After about 100 km, just before the border crossing, turn right onto a sand road for 12 km to the Tau Gate. There are other gates at Derdepoort and Abjaterskop. Visitors should establish entry points before arrival; gates are opened by arrangement for pre-booked visitors. Entrance fees are included in the rates for the lodges. **Madikwe Charters** ① *T011-8054888, www.madikwecharters.com*, flies daily to and from the park to Johannesburg (50 minutes). The lodges pick up from the Madikwe airstrip.

Best time to visit Most of the rain falls during the summer between November and March. Up to 600 mm is expected in the south, but as you move across the plains northwards, the annual rainfall averages about 100 mm less. During the summer it can get very hot during the day – this is not ideal weather for walking. During winter it is dry but gets very cold at night.

Wildlife

One of the great features of the reserve is its diverse geology which has resulted in a broad mix of habitats suitable for a wide range of animals. In the northern part of the reserve the land is a level savannah plain. Running across the middle of the park and, in effect, dividing it in two, is the **Tweedepoort Escarpment**. Above the escarpment is an undulating plateau covered with dense vegetation, a marked contrast to the grasslands below. At the southern edge is a more extensive range of rocky mountains, the **Dwarsberg Range**. These are similar in appearance to the Magaliesberg but have been severely eroded over the years, the highest point being only 1228 m. The final distinct environment is provided by the perennial **Marico River** along the eastern boundary, where an aquatic and well-vegetated environment exists.

Madikwe Game Reserve

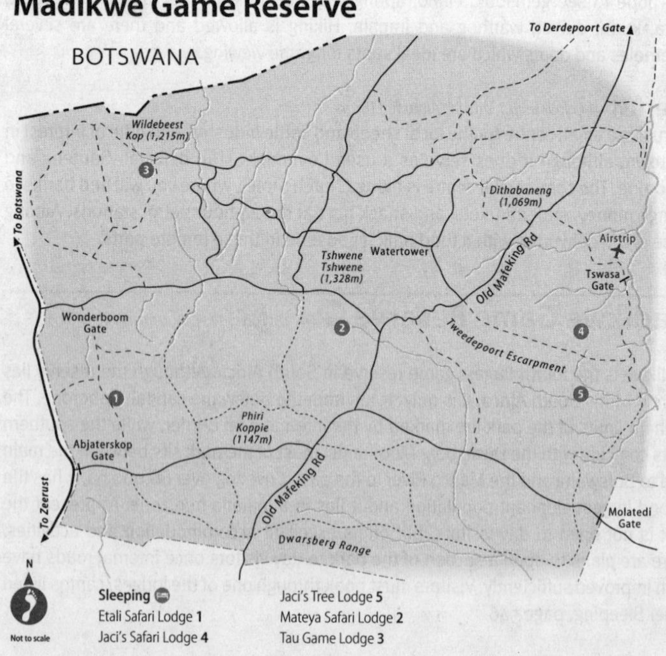

Sleeping
Etali Safari Lodge **1**
Jaci's Safari Lodge **4**
Jaci's Tree Lodge **5**
Mateya Safari Lodge **2**
Tau Game Lodge **3**

Crossing into Botswana

There are several border crossings between the North West Province and Botswana. The most commonly used is **Pioneer Gate** (24 hours), 56 km northeast of Zeerust, the route most of the haulage trucks take along on the N4 between Pretoria and Gaborone, and part of the Great Kalahari Highway that stretches all the way to Walvis Bay in Namibia. The **Ramatlabamba** (0600-2000) border post is on the R503 26 km north of Mafikeng, which is more convenient if coming from the Cape or interior of South Africa. Around 70 km east of Mafikeng is the **Makgobistad** border post which, despite being more remote on a minor road, is open 24 hours so is an alternative to Ramatlabama if crossing at night.

Intercape buses use the Pioneer Gate border post on the service between Pretoria and Gaborone – the Botswana capital is only 102 km north of the border. All the borders are easy to cross and formalities at customs and immigration are quick and courteous. If you are in a hire car, ensure that you have documentation from the car rental company that allows you to take a car out of South Africa. Botswana is part of the Southern Africa Development Community (SADC) customs agreement so if you are in your own car travelling on a carnet, you do not need to produce your carnet here and won't need to until you reach Zimbabwe or Zambia which are outside SADC. You simply fill out the car's details in a book. On the Botswana side you will have to pay for temporary third party insurance but this costs very little. There are bureaux de change at the border where you can change rand into Botswana pula, and small duty-free shops (mostly booze and cigarettes).

In South Africa it is customary to drive within the yellow line, or hard shoulder of a road, to let an overtaking car pass more easily. The signs on the Botswana side of the border declare: "Unlike South Africa, in Botswana, we do NOT drive in the yellow lines, it destroys the edges of our roads."

When the area was being prepared for inclusion within a game reserve, only a few of the indigenous species had survived the years of hunting and farming, as well as an outbreak of *rinderpest*. Back in 1836 the hunter William Cornwallis came across the first known sable in the Marico Valley and wrote of large herds of elephant and prides of lion frightening the local farmers. In 1991, Operation Phoenix was launched – one of the largest game translocation programmes in the world. By 1996 more than 10,000 animals from 28 species had been successfully released into the reserve.

Animals now present in the park include elephant, zebra, lion, buffalo, white rhino, spotted hyena wild dog, steenbok, duiker, kudu, leopard and cheetah. Visitors are able to view these animals during game drives or on morning walks with a guide and experienced tracker. A special feature of the reserve is the introduction of community projects, which is allowing local communities to benefit from, and contribute to, the ecological management of the reserve. Another project planned for the future is the development of the Heritage Park conservation corridor that will join Madikwe with Pilanesberg. This proposed conservation estate will allow bigger migration for the animals, creating a prime eco-tourism destination. It's expected to take 20 years to achieve.

There are fewer cheetah in South Africa than spots on a single animal. Cheetah are found in Madakwi, Pilanesberg and Kruger national parks, some breeding centres and zoos, a number of private game reserves and on farmland mainly in the northern regions of the country.

Sleeping

Mafikeng and Mmabatho
p540, map p541

A **Mmabatho Tusk**, Nelson Mandela Dr, Mmabatho, T018-3891839, www.tusk-resorts.co.za. Recently renovated upmarket hotel complex with several restaurants, swimming pool, casino and health centre with spa and sauna facilities. Once an important gambling centre when gaming was illegal in the rest of South Africa, but it now looks somewhat out of place next to the dusty townships.

B **Buffalo Park Lodge**, 59 Molopo St, corner of Botha and Molopo Sts, T018-3812159. Modern guesthouse with 20 simply decorated rooms, mix of double and twin rooms, all with TV, en suite, very popular bar and restaurant, home-cooked meals and a good Sun lunch.

B **Ferns**, 12 Cook St, Mafikeng, T018-3815971, www.ferns.co.za. A modern quality guesthouse with 24 double rooms with pleasant decor, a/c, en suite bathroom or shower, TV. Guest lounge, bar, laundry service, swimming pool, secure parking. Good value. The smart restaurant is probably one of the better places to eat at in town.

C **Getaway Lodge**, 39 Tillard St, Mafikeng, T018-3811150. Friendly guesthouse in a good, central location. 33 en suite rooms, recently renovated, with TV, fridge, good reasonably priced restaurant and relaxing gardens. Very welcoming staff who can advise on what to do in the area.

Botsalano Game Reserve *p543*
Reservations T083-3401851 (mobile)

D **Mogobe Tented Camp**, 4 tents with 2 beds in each, bedding supplied, there is a fully equipped kitchen. The camp is in a typical shady thicket overlooking Mogobe Dam, in a central position.

E **Campsite**, next to the main entrance gate, open campsite and picnic area with basic amenities.

Zeerust *p543*

B-D **Abjaterskop**, Rustenburg Rd, T018-6422008, abjaters@gds.co.za. Mix of guestrooms and rondavels set in gardens, this is the most comfortable and friendly option in town despite looking a bit dated. 19 a/c rooms, with en suite bathroom, TV. Camping and caravan site and much cheaper accommodation in 10 simple rondavels with showers round the back. Restaurant, bar serving home-distilled peach schnapps, lounge, swimming pool, gardens, secure parking, rates include breakfast.

C-D **Marico Bushveld B&B**, 5 President St, T018-6423545. Pretty B&B with 9 en suite rooms, TV, bar, secure motel style parking, evening meals on request.

Madikwe Game Reserve *p543, map p544*
Madikwe is a low-density tourism facility and the luxury lodges are built as far away as possible from each other. There are at present 21 lodges run under various concessions; below are a selection. Rates include all meals and game activities.

L4 **Etali Safari Lodge**, T012-3460124, www.etalisafari.co.za. 8 luxury a/c thatched chalets joined by wooden boardwalks, rooms are a blend of contemporary earth colours and crisp white linen, each with a deck and outdoor jacuzzi, the main lodge has a pool, outdoor gym, pampering in the Wellness Centre, or beauty therapists will give guests a massage on their private sun deck after a day of game driving, outside eating around a fire, cuisine is African and Asian using organic vegetables.

L4 **Jaci's Safari Lodge** and **Jaci's Tree Lodge**, T014-7789900, www.madikwe.com. Both lodges regularly win awards. The **Safari Lodge** has 8 large thatched suites with gauze walls, double-poster beds, handcrafted stone baths, outside shower, private plunge pool, viewing deck, personal safari guide for all game drives, walks, and information. The **Tree Lodge** comprises 8 treehouses on stilts up to 4 m from the ground, built in the arms

For an explanation of the sleeping and eating price codes used in this guide, see inside the front cover. Other relevant information is found in Essentials pages 42-47.

of giant leadwood or tambotie trees, outdoor jungle shower and stone bath, private decks, linked by raised boardwalks, central outside *boma* for eating, set on a circular candlelit table around a fire.

L4 Mateya Safari Lodge, T014-7789200, www.mateyasafari.com. 5 enormous, super-luxurious, thatched suites, en suite bathrooms and open-air showers, each with its own pool and deck with views of the plains and a waterhole below. The lodge is decorated with a valuable African art collection with pieces from as far away as Cameroon and Ghana, the library has 3500 books, the wine cellar has 7000 bottles, and there are 40 staff to look after the whims of only 10 guests.

L3 Tau Game Lodge, T011-13144350, www.taugamelodge.co.za. 30 luxury chalets with en suite bathrooms, private wooden view/sun deck, swimming pool, not as luxurious as some of the lodge but comfortable nevertheless. The chalets are arranged in an arc looking out onto a large seasonal waterhole, allowing good game viewing. Also has a conference centre

A Mosetlha Bushcamp, T011-4449345, www.thebushcamp.com. Good value alternative to the luxury camps. Offers rustic accommodation in an unfenced camp without electricity. 9 simple, raised wooden cabins with oil lamps, shared outdoor safari showers, bush food cooked over an open fire. The camp is in the middle of the park close to the Tswene Tswene Hills, game drives or guided walks are available twice a day, the guides are exceptionally good. Friendly and well run.

Eating

Mafikeng and Mmabatho

p540, map p541

Apart from the obligatory **Spur**, found in most of South Africa's small towns, there are very few eating options in either town. Unusually, however, most of the guesthouses have their own decent, à la carte restaurants, which are reasonably priced and open to non-residents. These are where local people go out to eat.

Shopping

Mafikeng and Mmabatho

p540, map p541

Mega City is a modern shopping centre close to the parliament buildings in Mmabatho. This obviously once had grand ambitions of being a typical South African modern mall, but is far too big for the number of shops required for the region. Many units within the mall now stand empty. Outside the main entrance is a small selection of Botswana curio sellers with some marula, mopane and ebony carvings.

Transport

Mafikeng and Mmabatho

p540, map p541

217 km to **Gaborone**, 287 km to **Johannesburg**, 320 km to **Kimberley**, 200 km to **Rustenburg**, 156 km to **Vryburg**, 70 km to **Zeerust**. Public transport is almost non-existent and there are no scheduled flights, buses or trains; you will need a car to explore this region.

Air

Mafikeng Airport, T018-3851140, is 17 km north of town. There are currently no scheduled flights here.

Bus

There are regular minibus taxis running between Mafikeng railway station and **Mega City** shopping centre that depart when full.

Zeerust *p543*

Bus

Intercape, T0861-287287, www.intercape.co.za, buses stop here daily.

Western region

Very few tourists visit the flat, featureless plains of the western half of the North West Province. This empty corner of South Africa holds little of interest, and the arrival of visitors can stir up quite a bit of interest amongst the sleepy inhabitants of the ancient farming communities dotted around the region. Most visitors to the area are actually just passing through en route to Botswana, where things liven up again over the border. However, some people choose to break the journey in Vryburg, the biggest town in the region. ▸▸ *For Sleeping, Eating and other listings, see page 549-550.*

West to Stella

After leaving Mafikeng, the R49 leads across a large expanse of unremarkable savannah broken only by the occasional stands of acacia trees. For most of the year this is a hot and dusty region, in desperate need of rain. Most of the country is given over to farming cattle, maize and groundnuts. Stella, 181 km from Mafikeng, is the largest settlement between Mafikeng and Vryburg. This is a typical, quiet farming centre where nothing much seems to be going on when you drive through. However, every October the town wakes up for the national **Cattle and Beef Festival** which attracts farmers from all over the country.

If driving, be careful not to fall asleep at the wheel, and always look out for wild animals suddenly running out in front of the car.

Vryburg

▸▸ *pp549-550. Colour map 1, grid C5.*

No matter which direction you approach from, the size of Vryburg often takes visitors by surprise, appearing as it does in the middle of a vast area of flat dry savannah. This is an important cattle centre where an auction is held every Friday.

North West Province Western region

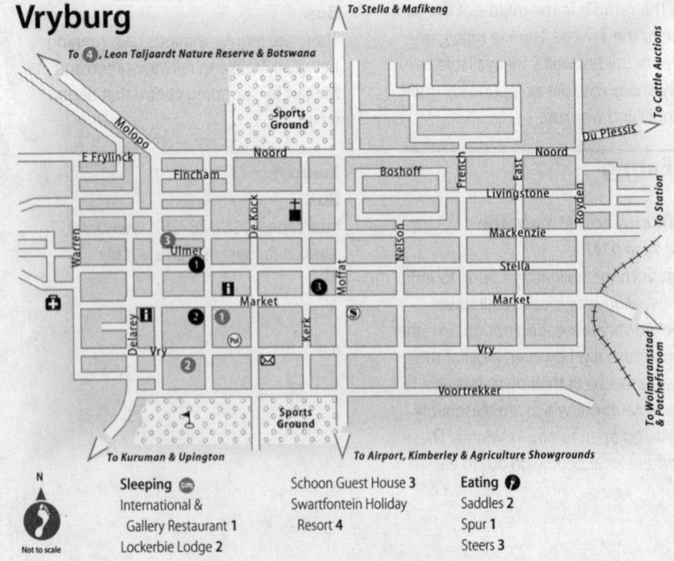

Background

The early history of Vryburg is interesting in so far as it provides a vivid picture of life along the frontier of the British empire. Before the arrival of any organized form of authority in the region, there was a protracted war between the Tlapin people of Chief Mankwarane and the Koranna Khoikhoi, led by David Massouw. In an effort to win the conflict, Massouw offered a collection of European mercenaries farms as their share of the loot and eventually 416 farms were given away. Shortly afterwards, in August 1883, the ex-mercenaries proclaimed their block of farms to be a new (short-lived) independent republic, which would be known as Stellaland. The capital of this new republic was Vryburg, the 'town of freedom'.

Sights

Leon Taljaardt Nature Reserve ⓘ *5 km from the town centre, to the left off the Botswana road, Apr-Aug 0700-1500, Sep-Mar 0700-1800, small entrance fee*, is the municipal game reserve. It's a small, pleasant reserve stocked with a mix of species including buffalo, white rhino, black and blue wildebeest, eland, gemsbok, impala, red hartebeest, Burchell's and mountain zebra and waterbuck. Accommodation is provided by **Swartfontein Holiday Resort**, see Sleeping, below.

Molopo Nature Reserve

» *pp549-550. Colour map 1, grid B5.*

ⓘ *250 km north of Vryburg, 7 km west of the village of Vostershoop. To make sure that you are allowed to visit the park contact the park office, T053-922 ask for Vorsterhoop 1722, or T082-8738780 (mob). Gate times 0600-1800, R15. This is a non-malarial region.*

This is a remote reserve on the Botswana border, proclaimed in 1988. Lying on the fringes of the Kalahari, the climate is hot, dry and dusty, and feels very much off the beaten track. Although the region is not well known for its wildlife, it is home to huge herds of antelope. One border of the 24,000-ha park is made up by the Molopo River, which is also the international border with Botswana. The river rarely flows only every few decades, but there is plenty of water in the ground which keeps the area's vegetation.

The park is in an area of dry thornveld, and supports a mix of wildlife including gemsbok, red hartebeest, kudu, springbok and eland; if you are very lucky you may also see cheetah, leopard and brown hyena. Unsuprisingly, given the remoteness and the fact that few tourists visit here, few facilities have been developed. The network of roads is only suitable for 4WD vehicles. Walking is allowed anywhere in the park with prior permission. Always carry sufficient water, and avoid walking in the summer.

Sleeping

Vryburg *p548, map p548*

B International, 43 Market St, T053-9272235, international@mega.co.za. 40 a/c rooms with en suite bathrooms, TV, M-Net, **Gallery** restaurant, popular local pub, swimming pool. Average and outdated.

B-C Lockerbie Lodge, Vry St behind the International, T053-9272302. 29 doubles with en suite bathroom, comfortable lounge with an open fire for winter, self-catering kitchen, pool. This hotel, now a listed historical building, was established in 1890 and was used by Cecil Rhodes.

C-D Schoon Guest House, 14 Ulmer St, T053-9273576. 5 double rooms, some en suite, others with shared bathroom. Cosy TV lounge, bar fridge, swimming pool, braai area, secure parking. A quiet base for exploring the area, with a very helpful service providing picnic/braai hampers, this is a well-run and friendly guesthouse. Recommended.

D-F Swartfontein Holiday Resort, 5 km from town off the R378, T053-9274261. 14 a/c self-catering chalets with 2 or 4 beds, kitchen with fridge but no oven, braai facilities, dining area, swimming pool, peaceful, shady camping sites, acts as the accommodation for the adjacent Leon Taljaardt Nature Reserve (see page 549).

Molopi Nature Reserve *p549*
All reservations: T082-8738780 (mob). If you wish to stay here you have to be completely self-sufficient. The **Motopi Camp** is suitable for 8 people on a self-catering basis; Phiri Camp has 9 campsites over a wide area.

Eating

Vryburg *p548, map p548*
Vryburg has the usual range of chain steakhouses and little else; vegetarians may struggle to find something to eat. **Spur**, **Saddles** and **Steers**, are around Market St. The only venue offering anything different, is **Gallery**, T053-9272235, the principal town restaurant and pub in the **International**.

Transport

Vryburg *p548, map p548*
250 km to **Botswana** (Bray), 420 km to **Johannesburg**, 212 km to **Kimberley**, 156 km to **Mafikeng**, 400 km to **Upington**.

Eastern region

The eastern region of the province gets the lion's share of visitors, thanks to the extravagant attractions of Sun City and the excellent Pilanesberg National Park, where stocks of game readily stand to attention for camera-toting safari enthusiasts. Surrdoung the historic town of Rustenburg are the gently rolling Magaliesberg Mountains, which, thanks to their proximity to the urban sprawl of Pretoria and Johannesburg, are a popular weekend retreat offering a number of good country hotels and nature reserves. It's a scenic region for sports and outdoor pursuits and the mountains are ideal for hiking. ▸▸ *For Sleeping, Eating and other listings, see pages 558-562.*

Pretoria to Botswana

The N4, which heads westwards from Pretoria, is a toll road and therefore avoided by most local traffic, which sticks to an alternative route via the R27. The N4 has been recently upgraded, with most of the tract between Gauteng and Botswana being well maintained tar broken up by frequent toll gates. This road is part of the planned Trans-Kalahari Highway (the Botswana section has been completed), which will eventually link Pretoria with Walvis Bay in Namibia.

Hartbeespoort Dam → *Colour map 2, grid C2. Altitude 1200 m.*

The proximity of Johannesburg and Pretoria (35 km) has made this dam in the Magaliesberg Mountains a popular watersports resort and weekend retreat. Around the shoreline are marinas and large private homes overlooking the lake. For information contact the **Hartbeespoort Dam Information Shop** ⓘ *Damdoryn crossroads next to the curio market, T012-2531567, www.hartbeespoortdam.com, Tue-Sun 1000-1700*.

The dam was built in 1923 in a narrow gorge where the Crocodile River cuts through the Magaliesberg Mountains. There are two major canals which conduct water away from the dam into a series of smaller canals that irrigate the farmlands around Brits. The old main road from Pretoria runs through the village of **Schoemansville** on the north shore of the lake before crossing the dam wall and continuing to Rustenburg and Sun City. There is a **Snake and Animal Park** ⓘ *T012-2531162, daily, 0800-1700, R45,* which remains a popular attraction for visiting families from Gauteng, but alongside the collection of reptiles are chimpanzees, panthers and Bengal tigers, making it unpleasant and zoo-like. Also here is the **Hartbeespoort Dam Cableway** ⓘ *on the R513 towards Pretoria, T012-2531706, R15, 2.3 km link to one of the highest points of the Magaliesberg Mountains.* There was an accident here in 2004, but the cableway remains popular.

Brits → *Colour map 2, grid B2.*

Brits is a medium sized industrial centre surrounded by highly productive farmlands irrigated from the Hartbeespoort Dam. It is also, incidentally, the sole source in Africa of the production of optical fibres. However, most visitors steam past Brits on their way west and are only likely to pass through town if heading north to the little-known Borakalalo Nature Reserve (see below), one of several excellent reserves tucked away in the province. The **De Wildt Cheetah Centre** ⓘ *T012-5041921, www.dewildt.org.za, R165, tours Tue, Thu, Sat and Sun at 0830 and 1330; booking ahead is recommended*, is an important breeding centre and is famous for being the first such place where a cheetah was successfully born in captivity.

Borakalalo Nature Reserve » *pp558-562. Colour map 2, grid B2.*

ⓘ *T012-7291008, Apr-Aug 0600-1900, Sep-Mar 0500-2000, R15.*

This is a pleasant nature reserve north of Pretoria, primarily known for the excellent fishing in the Klipvoor Dam (permits are issued at the gate). The reserve surrounds the dam and the area on the northern shore has been restocked with a variety of wild animals so that visitors have a choice of hiking, game viewing and fishing. There is a small shop at the main gate.

Ins and outs

Getting there From Brits, take the R512 and then the right turning signposted Lethlabile. After Lethlabile follow the signs for Jericho. At Jericho take a right at the T-junction and then the first left signposted Legonyane. The reserve is signposted along this road. There is no petrol available here, so fill up in advance.

Best time to visit The reserve receives most of its rain during the summer months, October to April; the summer temperatures range from a very hot 37°C to an average 20°C in the evening. During winter it can get very cold at night.

Wildlife

At 13,000 ha this was, for a time, the second largest national park in the former Bophuthatswana. It is closer to Pretoria than Pilanesberg National Park, yet it receives far fewer visitors. Since the reserve was proclaimed in 1984, there has been a complete restocking programme in order to replace the animals that once roamed the plains: white rhino, buffalo, giraffe, zebra, eland, elephant, hippo, buffalo, nyala, leopard, crocodile, jackal, tsessebe, gemsbok and roan antelope. There are over 350 species of bird in the park – enough to keep any keen ornithologist happy. Several sturdy hides have been built where you can enjoy viewing the wildlife without being stuck inside a car.

The Moretele River flows through the park which encompasses the 800-ha **Klipvoor Dam**. The dam contains carp, bream and barbel. To the southwest of the dam is the game-viewing area, where 50 km of gravel roads have been cut through the open savannah woodland. There is also another small dam, **Sefudi Dam**, where animals may be seen drinking.

Hiking trails

One of the most rewarding experiences in the park is to follow one of the self-guided walks through the riverine forest along the banks of the Moretele River. These vary from 1-4 km in distance. Guides are available for the longer walks, which are usually made in the early morning and last up to three hours.

Rustenburg » pp558-562.

→ *Phone code 014. Colour map 2, grid B1. Altitude 1,160 m.*

Rustenburg, or 'castle of rest', is one of the oldest towns in the region and was an important centre under the Transvaal Republic. Today, much of its old charm has disappeared and it is little more than a scruffy, sprawling crossroads between Gauteng, Sun City and Pilanesburg. Nevertheless, its proximity to Johannesburg and Pretoria on the one hand, and the Magaliesberg Mountains and the Kgaswane (Rustenburg) Mountain Reserve on the other, means that hotels are often full and it's a good to book in advance. If you're heading to Sun City, Pilanesberg or Madikwe, it's best to head straight through.

Ins and outs

Getting around The only bus that stops in Rustenburg is the regular **Intercape** service that runs between Pretoria and Gaborone in Botswana. There is little in the way of public transport, and a hire car is essential for exploring the area. Two or three days should be enough to take in the Magaliesberg, Sun City and Pilanesberg; many visitors do the lots in a single day trip from Johannesburg or Pretoria.

Tourist information **Rustenburg Tourism Information and Development Centre** ⓘ *corner of Nelson Mandela Dr and Kloof St, T014-5970904, on the outskirts of town, clearly visible when approaching from the Pretoria side on the N4, Mon-Fri 0730-1800, Sat 0800-1200*, is staffed by a friendly and enthusiastic team, although take their accommodation recommendations with a pinch of salt – their enthusiasm has been known to oversell shoddy establishments. The office also has some useful maps and leaflets for the **Magalies Meander**, www.magaliesmeander.co.za, a self-drive route through the mountains. This is a satellite office for the **North West Parks and Tourism Board** so they can also provide information on the whole region.

Background

The first white settlers were a group of burghers who had followed the Voortrekker leader Andries Pretorius from the Cape. Among the first Voortrekkers to start farming on the northern slopes of the fertile Magaliesberg in the mid-1800s were AH Potgieter and Casper Kruger, the father of the future president of the Transvaal, Paul Kruger.

During the short existence of the Boer Republic, Rustenburg was the capital before the government moved to Pretoria. On 16 March 1852, the town was the scene of the reconciliation between Andries Pretorius and Hendrik Potgieter, two of the leaders of the splintered Voortrekkers' Great Trek. This was an important step within the republic, as Pretorius had gone to the Orange Free State and Potgieter to the Eastern Transvaal and Mozambique. Reconciling their differences helped unify the two states (Orange Free and Transvaal) as a strong force against the British.

Sights

Despite being the third oldest town in the region and an important historic settling point for the Voortrekkers, there is very little of historical interest within Rustenburg. Two exceptions are **Hervormde Church Square**, which was the site of the reconciliation between Andries Pretorius and Hendrik Potgieter, and the **Statue of a Voortrekker Girl** in Plein Street opposite the Hervormde Church. The candle in the girl's hand represents the introduction of Christianity to the area.

Excursions

Paul Kruger Country House Museum ⓘ *18 km northwest of Rustenburg, off the R565 towards Sun City, look out for a left turning just after Phokeng, T014-5733218,* *www.rali.co.za, daily 1000-1600, R15*, is at Boekenhoutfontein, the farm where Paul Kruger lived as an obscure farmer before he became the president of the Transvaal Republic from 1883 until the end of the Anglo-Boer War. Four buildings have been preserved and restored as museums to the life of Paul Kruger and the earliest farmers in the Transvaal. The oldest building is a cottage built in 1841 by the first owner of Boekenhoutfontein, a single-storey building with a thatched roof and stone patio out front. When Paul Kruger moved here in 1863, he built a new thatched homestead for his family, known as the 'Pioneer House'. To its right stands the main homestead, a double-storey stone building built in 1872 in typical Eastern-Cape style. The house contains many of Kruger's possessions along with an assortment of period furniture from other homes. The fourth house, built for Kruger's son Pieter, dates from 1892.

Of the original 500-ha farm, 32 ha have been kept as part of the museum. The gardens have been partially restored and visitors are free to stroll around looking at the birds and plants; picnic areas have been laid out. The old **Rustenburg Museum** has moved here and has a small but interesting collection of local historical items. The statue of Paul Kruger which used to stand in front of the information office in Rustenburg has also been moved to Boekenhoutfontein. Sculpted in bronze by a French artist, Jean Archand, the statue was discovered in Paris in 1919 by General Louis Botha and General Jan Smuts. It is of the president sitting grumpily in his arm chair during his last days in exile in France.

Magaliesberg Mountains » *pp558-562.*

Colour map 2, grid C1.

The Magaliesberg are a range of flat topped quartzite mountains which extend roughly from Pretoria to just beyond Rustenburg. In 1977 the area was declared a Natural Heritage Site, and the entire area is one of the most visited in South Africa. Much of the mountains have been parcelled off into private resorts, but there remain some pockets of indigenous landscapes, notably in the excellent Pilanesberg Park and Kgaswane (Rustenburg) Mountain Reserve.

Ins and outs

Getting around Approaching Rustenburg from Pretoria, the main road splits into a one-way system by the showgrounds. If you drive straight through town on Van Staden Street, take a right at the junction with Malan Street. This road becomes the R510 and goes north across the plains to Pilanesberg. After 51 km take a left turn, follow this road for a further 5 km past a couple of factories and take a right turn by the petrol station. The entrance to **Pilanesberg National Park** and **Manyane Camp** is just on the left. If you are heading for **Sun City** follow Nelson Mandela Street straight out of town, past the golf course to your left, and then take the right turning on the R565, signposted Phokeng and Sun City. Shortly before Sun City is left turn for Pilanesberg National Park. The entrance to Sun City is just after a large shopping mall by the staff housing complex. To explore the **Magaliesberg** take the R30 shortly before entering the town from Pretoria. This road leads up into the mountains to **Olifantsnek**, a gap in the Magaliesberg created by the Hex River. There are plenty of hotels and resorts along this road.

Background

When the first white hunters came to the region they named the hills the 'Cashan Mountains', a corruption of Khashane, the name of the local chief. They were renamed by the Voortrekkers who called the range after another local leader, Mohale, but whose name they misspelled as Magalie.

The region witnessed a number of bloody battles during the 19th century. The first major conflicts were between Mzilikazi, leader of the Ndebele, and the local peoples when he arrived here from modern day KwaZulu Natal. A few decades later, the mountains were the scene of several important battles during the Anglo-Boer War. One of these was the Battle of Nooitgedacht on 13 December 1900, in which the British forces suffered their heaviest defeat since their arrival in July 1900. Three hundred men were killed and a similar number taken prisoner, and the Boers managed to seize 70 full wagons, 200 tents, ammunition, 300 mules, some cattle and over 400 horses. The gorge where the battle took place is just off the R560 close to Hekpoort.

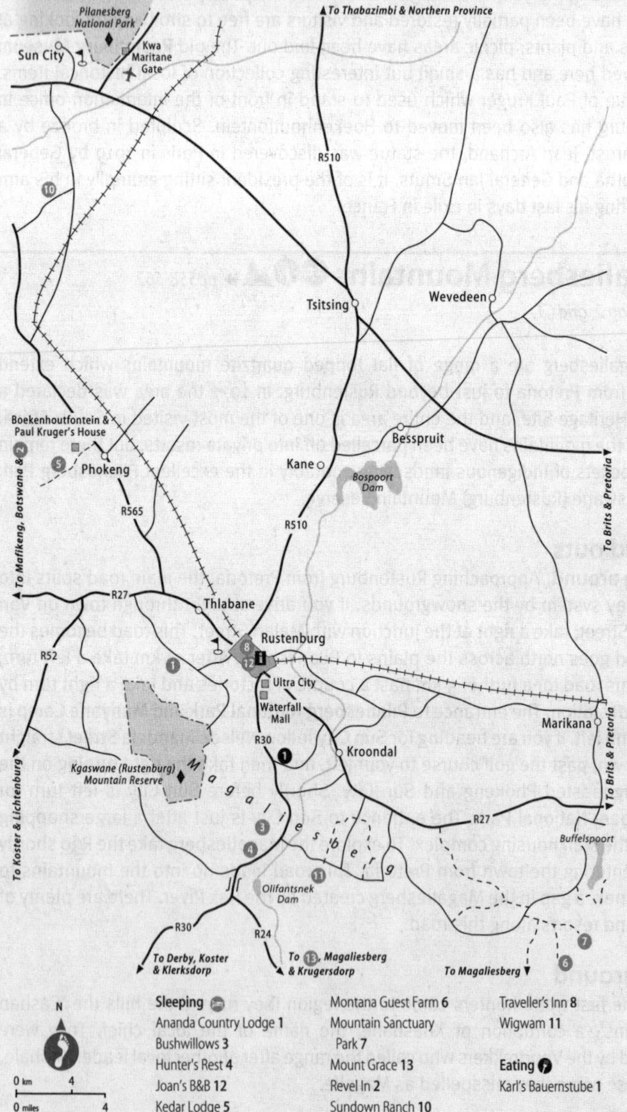

Wildlife and vegetation

The range is about 160 km long, reaching 1852 m at its highest point – which is actually no more than 400 m above the surrounding countryside. The difference in elevation is, however, sufficient to ensure that the hills receive a relatively high rainfall and are far greener than the plains, with some remaining stands of forest. Most of the wild animals that once lived in the hills have long since been hunted out. An exception can be found on the ledges on the south-facing cliff faces, which are important nesting sites for the endangered Cape vulture. The north-facing slopes are no more than a gentle climb, cut by mountain streams and leafy gorges. The range forms the natural divide between the cool highveld to the south and the warm bushveld to the north.

Kgaswane (Rustenburg) Mountain Reserve

 ▸▸ *pp558-562. Colour map 2, grid B1.*

ⓘ *T014-5332050, Sep-Mar 0530-1900, Apr-Aug 0600-1830, R15 per person, R10 per car.* This popular mountain reserve stretches along the summit and the northern slopes of the Magaliesberg range, 400 m above Rustenburg, providing excellent hiking territory. The reserve is an important recreational area for visitors from Johannesburg and Pretoria, just over 100 km away, and school buses are a regular sight. Because it is so close to the large cities, the number of visitors is tightly controlled and anyone wishing to camp or enjoy the longer hiking trails needs to book up to six months in advance.

Ins and outs

From the centre of Rustenburg, follow Wolmarans Street (from the junction with Van Staden by the municipal offices) through the residential suburbs to the very end where it then curves to the left and becomes Boekenhout Road. Follow this road out of town until you come to a T-junction, turn left (the right is signposted to the **Ananda Hotel**). Shortly after passing Rustenburg Kloof, just before the entrance gates to the **Orion Safari Lodge**, is a right turn to the main gates of the reserve. The reserve is not clearly signposted in the centre of town.

Wildlife

The land was originally part of Rietvallei farm, which belonged to President Paul Kruger. The reserve was proclaimed in 1967 after the council had been given the land by one of Kruger's descendants. In 1981 the nature reserve was extended to include an adjoining farm to the east and today the total area protected is 4257 ha. From the top of the reserve you can see the flat bushveld to the south, while the ridge of the mountains disappears east towards the Hartbeespoort Dam and Pretoria.

Some of the species of antelope found here include grey duiker, klipspringer, mountain reedbuck, impala, oribi, waterbuck, steenbuck, kudu, zebra and red hartebeest. Jackal, leopard, hyena and caracal are also known to live in the mountains. There are also raptors which live high up along the rocky cliff faces. Scops owl, martial eagles and black eagles can be viewed along with an important breeding colony of the endangered Cape vulture.

Hiking

There are currently three marked hiking trails in the reserve. Two of the trails are open for day visitors; the third trail requires spending a couple of nights in the reserve. For information on the trails, visit www.tourismnorthwest.co.za/kgaswane. Detailed maps are available at the reserve office.

Sun City

» pp558-562. Colour map 2, grid B1.

Tucked between dusty plains and rolling bushveld is the surreal highrise, neon-lit resort of Sun City, one of the most-visited sights in the country. Much like Las Vegas in the US, the resort was built around gambling and today comprises a vast complex of four hotels, linked by a skytrain, and extravagant recreational facilities, including a fake sandy lagoon and a constructed tropical rain forest. The result is both staggeringly impressive and laughably tacky – all good fun if you take it with a pinch of salt.

Ins and outs

For details of how to get to Sun City, see Ins and outs page 553. There is a daily entrance fee for day visitors, R50 per person, part of which is redeemable in tokens to spend inside. The **Welcome Centre** ⓘ *T014-5571544, daily 0800-2000*, is in the middle of the complex and is a good place to start and pick up a map. The free skytrain runs throughout the complex, and shuttle buses run to and from the car park. Day visitors can join a tour of The Palace of the Lost City, costing R55.

The complex has four hotels, numerous restaurants and fast food outlets, two golf courses, a water park, a man-made rainforest, a crocodile park, an aviary, a lake offering watersports, a cultural centre, casinos and the Superbowl, a large entertainment hall which most recently was host to Westlife.

Background

The first part of the complex was opened in 1979, when the central features were the Sun City Hotel and a golf course designed by Gary Player. Much of the appeal of Sun City was its gambling licence: the hotel was in the homeland of Bophuthatswana where gambling was legal, unlike in the rest of South Africa at that time. Wealthy whites travelled to what were then the designated black homelands to gamble, and like many other casino resorts from the Apartheid era, the contrasts between the luxury of the resorts and the impoverished areas around them were (and to some extent, still are) stark.

In the same year Pilanesberg National Park opened. A year later the second phase was complete – the 284-room **Sun City Cabanas** opened, aimed at families. In 1980 the famous **Sun City Million Dollar Golf Challenge** was founded, and over the years this has attracted most of the world's top golfers. In 1984 the third hotel was opened, the five-star **Cascades**, surrounded by waterfalls, streams and a tract of forest. In 1992 came the icing on the cake: the **Lost City** and the **Valley of the Waves** (see Sights and activities below).

With the change in gambling laws, visitor numbers dropped sharply in the 1990s, but these have crept up again as the focus has switched from gambling to family entertainment, golf and conferences. Although it's far removed from the culture and landscapes that draw most tourists to South Africa, Sun City's glitz and garishness is fascinating and well worth a day's visit.

Sights and activities

The complex focuses on the newest and most excessive addition to the Sun City stable, the **Palace of the Lost City**, a magnificent hotel completed in 1992. The vaguely Moorish construction is characterized by soaring dome-capped towers ringed by prancing statues of antelope; you can only actually reach the hotel if you're staying there, but regular tours are held for day visitors. Below the hotel is the **Valley of the Waves**, reached by a bridge that trembles and spouts steam during mock earthquakes (every 30 minutes). This stunning artificial sandy lagoon, complete with desert island and palm-lined soft white sand, has a wave machine capable of creating metre-high waves. Day visitors have to pay R40 to enter the Valley of the Waves, accessed from the entertainments centre, but this doesn't seem to put anyone off – the beach gets completely packed at weekends, with noisy music pumping out of loudspeakers and every large wave bringing forth a yell of jubilation from the crowds. Smaller swimming pools dotted around the lagoon are quieter.

A welcome retreat lies around the hotel and lagoon, the impressive 25-ha **man-made forest**. Remarkably lush and quiet, the forest was originally made up of 1.6 million plants, trees and shrubs, and the rainforest component includes three layers with creepers and orchids growing in the canopy. Although the moulded cement rocks and perfectly pruned paths give it a distinctly Disney feel, the plants have attracted prolific birdlife and the walking trails, lasting up to 1½ hours, allow a real sense of isolation from the resort.

Elsewhere, an abundance of activities is available to guests. There are two 18-hole golf courses, including the Gary Player course, home to the annual **Nedbank Golf Challenge**, one of the world's great championships with a prize of US$2 million. At **Waterworld**, guests can try parasailing, waterskiing and jetskiing. There is a horse-riding centre, tennis, mini golf, squash, a gym and spa, mountain biking trails, jogging routes, 10-pin bowling and numerous swimming pools (the more peaceful of which are located in the hotels).

Close to the entrance is **Kwena Gardens Crocodile Sanctuary** with over 7000 crocs, including the three biggest captive Nile crocodiles in the world. Nearby is the **Cultural Village**, a new incentive where guests are shown around mock-ups of villages of eight tribal groups, with dancing and singing displays and a Shebeen serving pan-African cuisine. There's also an aviary, a bird of prey centre, several cinemas, a casino, a vast hall filled with slot machines, and countless restaurants and bars.

Pilanesberg National Park » *pp558-562. Colour map 2, grid B1.*

ⓘ T014-5555354, www.tourismnorthwest.co.za/pilanesberg, Nov-Feb 0530-1900, Mar-Apr 0600-1830, May-Aug 0630-1800, Sep-Oct 0600-1830, R20 per person, R15 per car. This is a malaria-free zone

This is the fourth largest national park in South Africa, and was created in 1979 to complement the new luxury development being built at Sun City. The two have been closely linked ever since.

Ins and outs

Follow directions for Sun City. If coming from Johannesburg it is quicker to take the N1 north until it joins the N4 and then head west for Rustenburg. From Rustenburg, the R510 heads north towards Sun City Airport and the park. Pretoria is about 140 km from the park. It can be visited as a long day trip from Pretoria, but most visitors stay at least one night in the region and combine a trip to Pilanesberg with Sun City.

Background and sights

The area earmarked for the park in the 1970s was home to a large number of Tswana people, but these were either coerced into leaving or forcibly removed – a hugely controversial move, but one that was not reported at the time. On a more positive note, the area's re-introduction of game has been heralded as a huge success. The stocking was known as Operation Genesis, a complex and ambitious project. The animals came from all over southern Africa: elephant and buffalo from Greater Addo Elephant National Park, black and white rhino from the Natal Parks Board, eland from Namibia, Burchell's zebra and waterbuck from the Transvaal and red hartebeest from the Northern Cape and Namibia. As a transition zone between the Kalahari sandveld and the bushveld, it was also the natural habitat for a number of rare species already in existence, including brown hyena, Cape hunting dog and sable antelope. As you drive around the 55,000-ha reserve you now have a good chance of seeing all the large animals including rhino, elephant, lion, cheetah, buffalo and the occasional leopard. More than 7000 animals have now been successfully introduced.

The park encompasses the caldera of an extinct volcano, which is geographically similar to the Ngorongoro Conservation Area in Tanzania. The crater is surrounded by three concentric rings of hills and in the centre is a lake, **Mankwe Dam,** where you can see crocodile and hippo. The hills are broken up with wooded valleys, which gradually give way to open savannah grasslands. This variety of habitat is ideal for wild animals and it is a rewarding birdwatching environment where over 340 species have been recorded, some of which are extremely rare. A number of walk-in viewing hides have been constructed. Excellent tar and gravel roads traverse the park and maps and game check lists are available at each of the four gates; Manyane, Bakgatla, Bakubung and Kwa Maritane – the latter being the closest to Sun City.

Sleeping

Hartbeespoort Dam *p550*

B-C **Berg & Dam**, 90 Scott St, T012-2530522, www.bookeasysa.com. 3 linked guesthouses, with a choice of B&B, self-catering or semi-self-catering (ie rooms with microwaves). All come with TV, en suite, spacious rooms, a/c and heating. Pretty gardens, secure parking, meals on request, welcoming staff. Great choice but very popular, often booked up months in advance. Recommended.

B-C **Waterside Country House**, 70 Waterfront Rd, T012-2530123, T082-4443904 (mob). Rather jumbled collection of 9 self-catering units dotted around the owner's back garden. Fridge, microwave, TV, meals on request. Close to the dam. Prices drop considerably out of season.

C-E **The Ring Oxwagon Inn**, T012-2591506, www.thering.co.za. 6 chalets attached to historical, restored and furnished ox-wagons, sleeping up to 6, en suite bathroom, homely restaurant, swimming pool, cheaper beds available in a backpackers dorm built out of an old double-decker bus, situated high up in the hills with nice views and hiking trails.

D **Squires on the Dam**, 1 Scott St, opposite the snake and animal park, T012-2531001. A simple set of 7 rooms attached to the Squires on the Dam restaurant. Plain, basic en suite rooms with TV.

Borakalalo Nature Reserve *p551*

For reservations contact T012-7291008.

C **Phudufudu Safari Camp**, tented camp, 6 upmarket tents, fully self-catering. Set in a secluded corner, shaded by large trees, shared ablution block, central dining area and lounge overlooking a small waterhole, fully equipped kitchen with freezer, plunge pool.

D **Moretele Camp**, 2 camps of semi-permanent tents with basic furnishings, including gas lamps and fridge. Self-catering facilities and shared ablution blocks, bring everything you need with you including towels, and all eating and cooking utensils.

E **Campsite**, a basic, rustic camp beside the dam, primarily used by anglers, camping sites have a braai area and a water tap, the central washblock is made from reeds, hot water and clean washing and toilet facilities, the camp has no electricity or fridges.

Rustenburg *p552, map p554*

Most of the local hotels are located beyond the built-up area towards the Magaliesberg Mountains. Within town, the choice is fairly dire. A new Protea hotel was being planned at time of writing. Far more attractive are the fine country resort hotels in the Magaliesberg range, or the (albeit pricey) hotels in Sun City and Pilanesberg National Park.

A **Kedar Lodge**, 20 km from Rustenburg towards Sun City on the R565, T014-5733218, kedar@rali.co.za. A peaceful group of cottages next to the historic farm of President Kruger, with 27 double rooms with en suite bathroom, open log fires, plunge pools, rustic stone shower rooms. Zebra and ostrich within the grounds, small restaurant and bar. Good value dinner, B&B rates. Fishing trips can be organized from here.

C **Sundown Ranch**, 33 km from Rustenburg centre, on the R565, T014-5731000, www.sundownlionpark.com. 10 km from Sun City and Pilanesberg National Park. 101 double hotel rooms set within 1600 ha of grounds, 2 restaurants, swimming pool in a pleasant palm courtyard, outdoor bar, tennis courts, squash, bowls, horse trails and a lion park, where visitors can play with lion cubs.

C-D Bergsig Lodge, 7 Peperboom Av, T014-5971139, bergsigl@mweb.co.za. Friendly B&B with handful of double rooms and a couple of singles with en suite facilities, ceiling fans, TV lounge, M-Net, separate entrance, braai area, swimming pool, well-kept garden with shady corners, ideal for local sights and town centre, secure parking. Well-run and good value.

D Joan's B&B, 61 Wildevy Av, Protea Park, T014-5932086, joansbnb@mweb.co.za. Straightforward B&B in a private home in a peaceful residential district, with good value singles, but be sure to call in advance to guarantee a room. Full English breakfasts included in the price.

D Traveller's Inn, 99 Leyds St, T014-5927658, travinn@mweb.co.za. Basic guesthouse with bare but comfortable rooms all with tiled floors, TV, ceiling fans and en suite bathrooms (most with showers). Pub attached serving meals. Secure parking and friendly staff, but don't wander around this area at night.

E Revel In, 38 km west of Rustenburg off the N4 towards Swartruggens, turn right at Bokfontien and travel up a dirt road for 6.5 km, T072-2257182, www.revelin.co.za. A hostel and campsite set on a beautiful remote farm. Hiking trails to natural springs, bar with a reggae feel, stone and thatch rustic bungalows, some with sunken baths made from rock, open fires, a bunkhouse with 16 dorm beds, also has some treehouses homemade furniture, pool, self-catering kitchen. The owner is promoting this place as an outdoor music festival venue to compete with Rustlers Valley in the Free State. Several festivals are held throughout the year and draw revellers from the big cities. At other times you might have the place to yourself.

Magaliesberg Mountains *p553, map p554*

AL Mount Grace, approaching Magaliesberg village on the R24 towards Johannesburg T014-5771350, www.grace.co.za. 80 double rooms with en suite bathrooms, rooms are in a variety of thatched cottages set in 4 ha of beautiful gardens with lakes and waterfalls, swimming pool, tennis, library. Excellent food. Sumptuous spa with set of hydro pools, natural stone walls and thatch roof, most treatments such as massages, scrubs, hand and foot grooming are conducted outside beneath olive trees. Spa and restaurant open to non-guests. Recommended.

B Hunter's Rest, 14 km from Rustenburg on the R30, T014-5372140, www.hunters rest.co.za. 91 spacious rooms with private patio, arranged up the side of the hill, bit of a hike from the furthest room to the restaurant. Bar serves good range of imported beers and has an English pub feel, large swimming pool, well-kept garden, curio shop, huge range of activities including tennis, sauna, squash, fitness centre, horse riding and 9-hole golf course. Good for families.

C Ananda Country Lodge, 8 km from Rustenburg, T014-5971966, anandacl@ mweb.co.za. 68 hotel rooms, thatched chalets and a shady campsite, all set in the lee of the Magaliesberg, restaurant, bar, 3 swimming pools, tennis courts, bowls, squash, golf nearby, though often overrun with conference delegates.

C Wigwam Holiday Hotel, 14 km from Rustenburg centre, T014-5378000, www.wig wam.co.za. Mix of large a/c rooms or one of 7 rather hideous 'wigwam' units which sleep up to 5. Restaurant, bar, neat colourful gardens, large holiday resort that can sleep up to 270, recreational facilities include: 2 swimming pools, 4 tennis courts, 9-hole golf course, squash court, games room, mini golf and a choice of hikes behind the complex.

C-D Montana Guest Farm, T014-5340113, www.montanagf.co.za. 8 self-catering chalets, some with thatched roofs, well-equipped kitchens, surrounded by the natural woodlands of the Magaliesberg, swimming pool, pub and games room, no restaurant, bring all your own food, a small and friendly retreat with some excellent local hikes.

C-E Mountain Sanctuary Park, T014-5340114, www.mountain-sanctuary.co.za. A private nature reserve in the mountains 35 km from Rustenburg. Simple rest camp, visitor numbers are controlled and there are strict regulations to preserve and maintain this mountain wilderness, so early booking is advised even for day visits. Accommodation consists of self-catering chalets, fully equipped and furnished (but bring your own bedding, towels, soap and food), caravans for 2-4 people, and a shady campsite. Stunning pool built from natural stone on the lip of the valley, offering fantastic views.

Guests have access to over 1000 ha of hiking country. Horse trails offered.

E **Bushwillows**, 12 km from Rustenburg, off the R24, T014-5372333, wjmcgill@lantic.net. A modern family home at the end of a long woody lane, with 4 double rooms with fans, 2 with en suite bathroom and own entrance, upstairs 4-bed family suite, TV guest lounge, swimming pool in the mature gardens, B&B only (but there's a good restaurant at the end of the road), run by the affable Bill.

Kgaswane (Rustenburg) Mountain Reserve *p555*

E **Hiking Huts**, reservations T0145332050. 4 huts sleeping 4, between the 2 bedrooms is a communal seating and dining area. Meals have to be cooked by wood fire over a braai, cooking pots, buckets to collect water and 2 lamps are provided. There is also a veld toilet close by. During the winter months you'll need a sleeping bag.

Sun City *p556, map p554*

The whole complex is part of the **Sun International Group**, central reservations T011-7807800, www.suninternational.com. None of the rooms are cheap, but all are of a very high standard. the hotels listed below must be booked through central reservations. Off-season packages are sometimes available.

AL **The Cascades** has the best of both worlds: it has 5-star amenities but is neither over the top nor over-run with families. The 242 a/c rooms were recently renovated in muted colours, with dark wood furniture and olive and beige fabrics. M-Net TV, minibar, stylish bathrooms, 24-hr room service. All rooms face the forest and pools with thrashing waterfalls and tinkling streams. Auditorium seating 6000. The main restaurant is **The Peninsula**, a smart international restaurant with a weekend buffet. **The Grotto** is a trendy Italian and seafood restaurant overlooking the pool. There are 2 bars, **Vistas** and **Grotto**.

AL **The Palace of the Lost City**, is the central point of the complex and is both impossibly kitschy and beautifully lavish. 338 a/c rooms spread across a string of airy courtyards, each overlooking fountains and sculptures of game. The entrance is marked by a super-sized sculpture of cheetahs hunting, surrounded by lakes and tinkling fountains. The lobby is a palatial hall lined with vast columns, leading to a variety of restaurants and elegant bars. It's all totally over the top, and has attracted so many goggling visitors that only guests are now allowed entry, unless you're on a pre-paid tour. **Villa del Palazzo**, with classic northern Italian cuisine, is an excellent restaurant overlooking the pools; **Crystal Court** has Californian-style cuisine, live piano music and is surrounded by jungle (smart dress code); elsewhere in the hotel there are 3 bars and a poolside snack bar and bar; there is a selection of shops, a beauty spa, and a heated swimming pool.

AL **Sun City**, this is the original hotel which was refurbished in 1995. 341 a/c rooms overlooking the swimming pool and lush lawns; plenty of choice on the restaurant front: **The Harlequin**, à la carte, in the casino, casual dress; **The Calabash**, carvery and salad bar; **Sun Terrace**, fastfood during the day, formal restaurant at night; 2 cocktail bars.

AL **Sun City Cabanas**, 144 standard cabanas for 2 people; 236 family cabanas which can accommodate 4, all are fully a/c, TV, en suite bathrooms. The cottages are set in neat gardens close to a lake and Waterworld, with a kid's petting farmyard and adventure playground in the grounds. This is the best value option available, and has families firmly in mind. **Morula** restaurant serves steaks and grills; **Palm Terrace** is an informal carvery; **Famous Butcher's Grill** has more of those steaks and a vegetarian's nightmare; **Pool Bar** and **Boathouse Bar**, both casual dress, serve snacks during the day.

Pilanesberg National Park *p557, map p561*

There are several camps within the park operated by different concessionaries, but advance booking is essential.

The following 3 lodges are part of the **Legacy Hotels Group**, central reservations T0800-468357, www.legacyhotels.co.za.

L3 **Tshukudu Game Lodge**, in the middle of the park on the slope of a steep rock outcrop. Small lodge, 6 stone thatched chalets built into the rock, slate floors, wicker furniture and a fireplace, beds on an elevated platform, sunken double bath with a view, lounge area with bar fridge, books and magazines. Chalets are linked to the main lodge by a steep, winding stone staircase. From the top you have clear views across the park and a floodlit waterhole, restaurant, bar, swimming pool.

AL Bakubung Lodge, on the edge of the park, 10 km from Sun City. Large complex, 76 rooms, 66 chalets all with en suite bathroom, restaurant, bar, curio shop, tennis court, swimming pool, game drives and hikes are extra, price includes all meals, there are superb views of the surrounding bush and a waterhole with resident hippos, a free shuttle runs to Sun City every couple of hours.

AL Kwa Maritane, a smart bush lodge with 90 a/c rooms and 54 self-catering chalets, each with a TV, high thatched ceilings, and a private veranda. Restaurant, outdoor braai. Nearby waterhole, with underground hide reached via a 180-m tunnel from the lodge. Game drives and guided walks, 2 swimming pools, floodlit tennis courts, table tennis, sauna, gym. There is a free shuttle to Sun City.

The 2 other camps are run by **Golden Leopard Resorts**, T014-5551000, www.goldenleopard.co.za.

B-E Bakgatla Resort, at the northwest of the park close to the Bakgatla Gate. 58 self-catering chalets, sleeping a maximum of 5 people, all are a/c and are fitted with a kitchen, en suite bathroom, lounge area plus a private patio and braai area. At the centre of the complex is a large swimming pool, picnic site and kiosk. There is also a limited number of caravan and campsites available. The campsites have a central kiosk plus a small bar.

C-E Manyane Resort, 300 m from the Manyane Gate. 60 2- to 6-bed self-catering thatched chalets with kitchen, lounge, bathroom, braai, couple of swimming pools among the chalet. Behind the chalets is a caravan and campsite, electric points, clean washblocks and shade trees. Central restaurant block open for all meals, bar, central swimming pool, children's play area. The camp is in open savannah grasslands with a few trees dotted about. Can get very busy during school holidays. There is a day visitors' complex with a shop, picnic area, swimming pool, a couple of walk-in aviaries, a 4WD track, walking trails, and mini-golf.

Eating

Rustenburg *p552, map p554*

There is little choice in the town centre and most restaurants are in the shopping centre environs of the **Waterfall Mall** on the edge of town on the R30, where there's a predictable

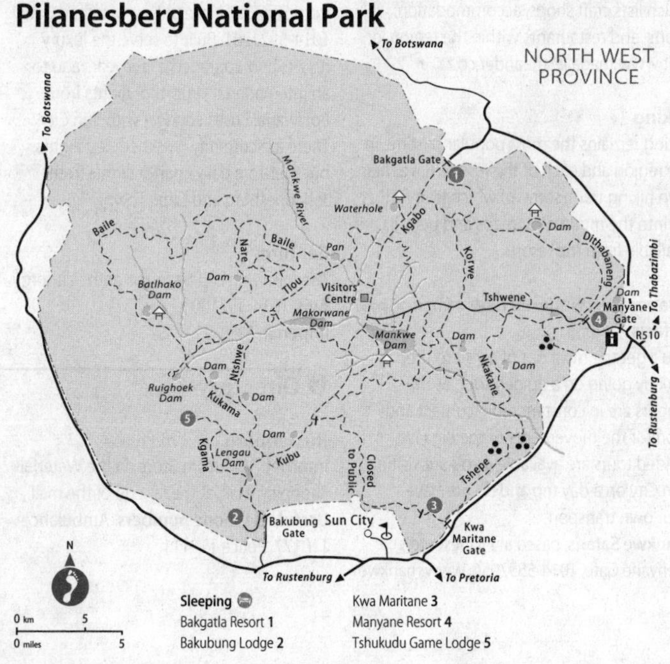

range of pasta, steak and fastfood joints. Otherwise, there are some fine restaurants in the Magaliesburg Mountain resorts.

Magaliesberg Mountains *p553, map p554*
Karl's Bauernstube, 5 km from Rustenburg on the R30, turn off the Pretoria road by the Ultra City, T014-5372128, closed Mon, Sat lunch, Sun evening. Country pub and restaurant with an Austrian menu including pork knuckles, schnitzels, plus game, duck and seafood. Good for pub lunches, shady terrace for alfresco eating. Simple self-catering rondavels or camping, and swimming pool out back.

Activities and tours

Rustenburg *p552, map p554*
Rustenburg Travel, Steen St, T014-5920251. Useful local booking agent, can also organize domestic and international flights and car hire.

Magaliesberg Mountains *p553, map p554*
Most of the holiday resorts are equipped with a complete range of sports facilities, including golf courses, tennis courts and gyms. Pick up a map for the 'Magalies Meander' at the tourist office in Rustenburg, which lists craft shops, accommodation, sports, and restaurants within the region, or visit www.magaliesmeander.co.za.

Hiking
Hiking remains the most popular pastime in the region and each of the resorts have their own hiking trails, some of which lead further up into the mountains. Maps and permits are available from the resorts.

Pilanesberg National Park *p557, map p561*
Safaris
You'll get the most out of a visit to the park by going on a guided tour, as the rangers are in constant radio contact and monitor the movements of the Big Five. Guided tours are available if you are visiting Sun City on a day trip and do not have your own transport.
Mankwe Safaris, based at Pilanesberg's Manyane Gate, T014-5557056, www.mankwesafaris.co.za. Runs 3-hr game drives in the morning, afternoon and at night, around R250 per person, plus 3-hr walking trails, R300 per person, maximum 8 in a group.
Pilanesberg Elephant Back Safaris, T014-5525020, www.gametrac.co.za. Similar set-up in Kruger, 5 elephants that can carry 2 riders plus the guide. Silently travelling through the bush on elephant back is a unique game-viewing experience. The ride is about 1 hr but the whole excursion lasts 2-3 hrs, interaction with the elephants is encouraged. Pick-ups from Sun City.

Transport

Rustenburg *p552, map p554*
48 km to **Sun City** via R27 and R565, 200 km to **Mafikeng**, 130 km to **Zeerust**, 105 km to **Pretoria**, 112 km to **Johannesburg**.

Bus
Intercape, central reservations T0861-287287, www.intercape.co.za, buses stop here en route to **Gaborone** from **Pretoria**.

Sun City *p556, map p554*
Air
Pilanesberg International Airport, 10 km from Sun City, close to Kwa Maritane Gate, T014-5521261. Built to serve the luxury resorts and upgraded a few years ago to an international airport for flights from Botswana. Buses connect with Sun City. There are currently no scheduled flights, but there are daily charter flights from Johannesburg and Cape Town.

Car hire
The following can be found at the airport:
Avis, T014-5571000.
Imperial, T014-5521767.

Directory

Rustenburg *p552, map p554*
Internet Vodacom Store, in the Waterfall Shopping Mall, at the far end of the mall.
Useful telephone numbers Ambulance T10177. Police T10111.

Mpumalanga

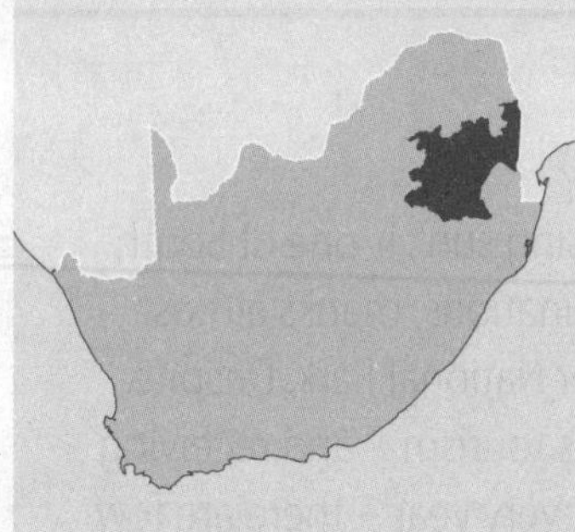

Footprint features

Introduction

Mpumalanga, the 'place of the rising sun', is one of South Africa's most popular tourist destinations, thanks almost entirely to the magnificent Kruger National Park. Despite being completely geared towards tourism – and receiving a staggering one million visitors every year – there are few places in Africa offering such excellent game viewing. It's a vast area, roughly the same size as Wales and with a bewildering variety of habitats. While it's entirely possible to see the Big Five in one afternoon, a longer stay allows visitors to fully appreciate the wilderness of the park – and to escape to its less-visited corners. Fringing the national park are large private reserves where game wanders unrestricted by fences; also here are some of the world's most luxurious safari lodges.

The rest of the province is understandably eclipsed by Kruger, but the area west of the park is well worth a detour. The forests and waterfalls of the Eastern Drakensberg make a pleasant change from the heat of the Lowveld. This mountainous area is dotted with quiet agricultural towns, clustered along the top of the spectacular Blyde River Canyon, the third largest in the world. A handful of viewpoints open up stunning vistas to the Lowveld shimmering to the horizon, but the depths of the canyon can only really be explored on foot. Further into the mountains is the historical gold-mining town of Pilgrim's Rest, a string of restored miners' cottages nestling in a quiet valley. The gold-rush story continues in the Victorian town of Barberton, set in the hills close to Swaziland.

★ Don't miss...

1 **Matsulu township** Hook up with Zozi, an enterprising and entertaining guide, who offers an extraordinary insight into African rural life on the edge of Kruger, page 576.
2 **A guided night drive** Join an organized tour with a game ranger to gain a deeper understanding of the wildlife in Kruger National Park, page 583.
3 **Pilgrim's Rest** Pan for gold or join in the festivities at the National Gold Panning Championships at the end of November, page 607 and page 615.
4 **Pancakes in Graskop** Harrie's was the first pancake house in town but there are now plenty to choose from, page 608 and page 614.
5 **Blyde River Canyon** Take a photo from the Three Rondavels, where a lip of rock juts out over the third largest canyon in the world, page 610.
6 **The Bookcase, Sabie** This secondhand bookshop is one of the best in South Africa, stuffed full of interesting books and collector's items, page 615.

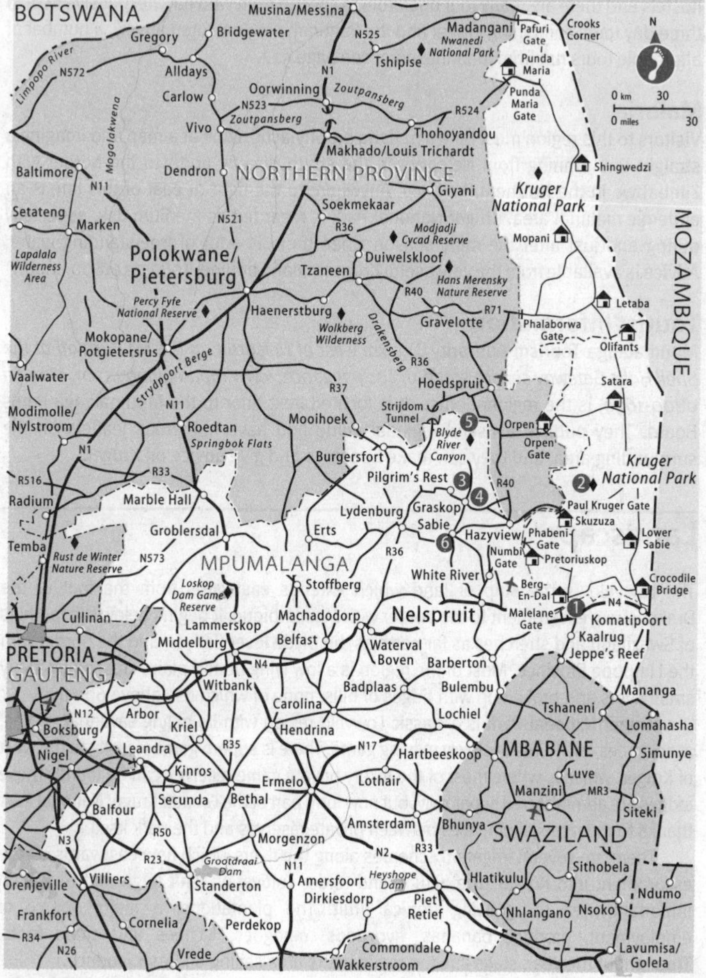

Ins and outs

Getting there

Kruger Mpumalanga International Airport (KMIA) is 25 km from the centre of Nelspruit towards Kruger, 10 km from the Maputo corridor (N4) and a short drive from Kruger's Numbi and Malelane gates. The airport is served by national airlines as well as a number of small private charter companies flying visitors into the private game reserves. » *For further details, see Ins and outs, page 567, and Transport, page 577.*

Getting around

The two main areas of interest in Mpumalanga are the Kruger National Park and the eastern Drakensberg, or Panorama Region, famous for the Blyde River Canyon. The public transport network doesn't link the towns and sights effectively, so the best way to visit the more isolated beauty spots is to hire a car, and it's possible to do a leisurely circuit in two or three days. For budget travellers, the **Baz Bus** picks up and drops off at backpacker hostels in Nelspruit. From here it is possible to arrange pick-ups by other hostels and there are many tour operators to choose from who run inexpensive two- to three-day tours combining Kruger and the Panorama region. Alternatively, a number of affordable tours run from Johannesburg, see page 522.

Malaria

Visitors to this region must take a malaria prophylactic. Look at a map and imagine a straight line running from Nelspruit in the south directly north to the border with Zimbabwe in the Northern Province. Anywhere to the right or east of this line is an endemic malarial area. Kruger National Park is regarded as medium risk, especially during and just after the rainy season when there is a lot of free-standing water. Advice is available from the very useful Kruger malaria hotline, T082-2341800 (mob).

Tourist Information

Mpumalanga Tourism Authority ① *5 km west of Nelspruit on the N4 (turn off at the Shell Halls Gateway service station), T013-7527001, www.mpumalanga.com, Mon-Fri 0800-1630*, is the regional office. It is located next door to the Mpumalanga Parks Board. They publish a useful regional guide and have numerous leaflets on the surrounding area, and they can make bookings and give advice on Kruger.

Landscape

The Lowveld is the strip of land which extends eastwards from the foot of the Drakensberg escarpment to the border with Mozambique. It begins below the foothills of Swaziland and stretches as far north as the Blyde River Canyon and the border with the Limpopo Province. Most of the region is a low lying humid plain, crossed by many small rivers and broken up with ridges of hills, none of which rise above 600 m.

Kruger National Park is a classic Lowveld region with its rolling savannah plains, acacia trees and herds of slowly moving game. There is superb game viewing to the west of Kruger, which is where most of the luxury private game reserves can be found. These lodges are administered separately, but now form part of the Greater Kruger National Park thanks to the removal of fences between private reserves and the park itself.

There are several irrigation schemes along the rivers which flow eastwards off the escarpment into Kruger. The actual land under cultivation isn't large, but this is an important area for growing tropical fruit. The plantations, a major source of employment, produce bananas, avocados, mangoes, lychees and citrus fruits. Throughout the year, stalls line the roads in the area selling off fresh produce.

Nelspruit and around

→ *Phone code: 013. Colour map 2, grid B5. Altitude: 716 m.*

Nelspruit developed around the railway when the line between Pretoria and Lourenço Marques (now Maputo) was completed in 1891. Briefly the capital of the Transvaal Republic after Paul Kruger abandoned Pretoria in 1900 during the Boer War, Nelspruit is now the industrial centre of the Lowveld and a processing point for the fruit, tobacco and beef farms of the surrounding region. The town has a sleepy, tropical feel with broad, modern streets lined with acacias, bougainvillea and jacaranda trees. Although there's little to keep you here, most visitors to the region pass through at some point. ▸▸ *For Sleeping, Eating and other listings, see pages 572-577. For places north of Nelspruit, see pages 603-616.*

Ins and outs

Getting there Nelspruit has good transport links, with an important international airport and good train and bus links. There are great facilities here for tourists planning trips to Swaziland, the Panorama region and Kruger National Park, as well as across the border to Mozambique (there is a daily train service between Pretoria/ Johannesburg and Komatipoort, the border post with Mozambique). The **Baz Bus** runs from Johannesburg, Pretoria and Swaziland. **Greyhound, Intercape** and **Translux** all operate services from Johannesburg and Pretoria to Maputo in Mozambique, which stop in Nelspruit. ▸▸ *For further details, see Transport, page 577.*

Getting around Nelspruit has excellent road links to Mpumalanga's major tourist attractions. The nearest entrance gates to Kruger are less than 80 km away on the N4

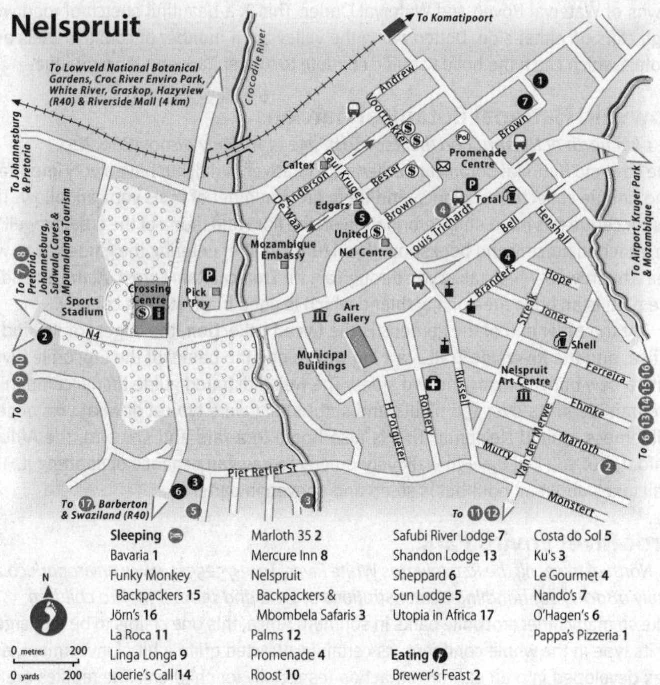

Sleeping
Bavaria 1
Funky Monkey Backpackers 15
Jörn's 16
La Roca 11
Linga Longa 9
Loerie's Call 14
Marloth 35 2
Mercure Inn 8
Nelspruit Backpackers & Mbombela Safaris 3
Palms 12
Promenade 4
Roost 10
Safubi River Lodge 7
Shandon Lodge 13
Sheppard 6
Sun Lodge 5
Utopia in Africa 17

Eating
Brewer's Feast 2
Costa do Sol 5
Ku's 3
Le Gourmet 4
Nando's 7
O'Hagen's 6
Pappa's Pizzeria 1

(east), and the R40 through White River (north), and a day trip to see the southern sector of the park is quite feasible. The gold rush town of Barberton is 43 km to the south on the R40, and a visit here could be combined with a day trip over the border to Swaziland. The mountain villages of Sabie and Graskop are equally accessible and make a pleasant change from the heat of the Lowveld. All these places have an excellent range of accommodation and there is little reason to stay in the centre of town. The shopping centres in town are convenient for stocking up on food and equipment before setting off to stay in self-catering accommodation in Kruger.

Orientation Nelspruit has grown rapidly in recent years and it has a prosperous air with a new sprawl of well-off suburbs surrounding the city centre. New business parks and a number of shopping malls have been built in the area, especially along the road to White River. As a consequence, Nelspruit has extended its municipality by joining with neighbouring White River and Hazyview to form the Mbombela Municipal Region (meaning, appropriately, 'a lot of people put together in a small space'). Mbombela is now the provincial capital of Mpumalanga Province.

Tourist information **Lowveld Tourism Association** ⓘ *Crossing Centre, at the junction of the N4 and the R40, just west of the centre, T013-7551988, www.lowveldinfo.com, Mon-Fri 0800-1700, Sat 0800-1300*, is the main tourist office for the entire region. It can organize car hire, safaris, game drives and accommodation in Kruger.

From Gauteng to Nelspruit

The journey east along the N4 from Gauteng crosses a bland, sprawling area of cattle ranching country, broken up by industrial towns like Witbank and Middleberg. There's little to break the monotony of the drive, other than a couple of looming coal-fired power stations. At **Machadodorp** the views improve, where the road starts to drop into the Elands River Valley and the vista opens up over the Lowveld, passing through the towns of Waterval Boven and Waterval Onder. This is a beautiful stretch of road with high cliffs on either side. Dotted along the valley are a number of country hotels and motels which catch the holiday traffic en route to Kruger Park and Mozambique.

Lowveld National Botanical Gardens

ⓘ *1 km north of Nelspruit on the R40. T013-7525531. Daily 0800-1800. R10.*

The Lowveld National Botanical Gardens are relatively small but have a very important and unique collection of plants, and there are a number of trails you can follow. The visitor centre has interesting information on the flora and fauna of the area, as well as an attached nursery and bookshop. If you turn left after entering the gardens you will see a boardwalk which takes you through a 3-ha **Tropical Rain Forest**. At the far end of the path is an open area of marshland which is good birdwatching country.

At the other end of the gardens is the **Cycad collection**, the largest of its kind in Africa, and the **Riverside Trail** – a 1 km walk along the banks of the Crocodile River, with a new bridge linking the two sides. The well-illustrated guide that accompanies the trail identifies over 130 plants and shrubs that were typical of what was once a wilderness around Nelspruit. This is also home to a rare and shy bird, the African finfoot, but you will have to walk very quietly to have any chance of spotting it. The trail takes about an hour but is steep and uneven in parts.

Croc River Enviro Park

ⓘ *North of town, off the R40 towards White River, T013-7525511, www.enviropark.co.za. Daily 0800-1700; handling demonstrations at 1100 and 1500. R30, R10 children.*

Like so many other crocodile parks in southern Africa, this one claims to be the largest of its type in the whole continent. Its certainly attracted quite a bit of investment, and has developed into an exciting attraction (especially for children). The reptiles are on show in a variety of houses, each with a different environment, rather like the greenhouses in a botanical garden. The turtle pond, crocodile pool and fishpond are linked by a cascading waterway. Inside the tropical house is a 9-m waterfall and an aquarium with some dwarf crocodiles from Central America. The reptile gallery houses 88 indigenous and exotic species. Visitors can view two snake pits from the safety of an elevated walkway. There is also a desert house with a realistic desert landscape.

Sudwala Caves

ⓘ *36 km north west of Nelspruit, follow the N4 westwards, turn onto the R539 (towards Sabie) after 30 km and follow the signs for the caves, T013-7334152. A 90-min tour departs every 30 mins 0800-1600. R36.*

The entrance to the caves is on a forested hillside in the Houtbosloop Valley. Only the first 2.5 km of the cave system has been explored and it is thought that the passages could lead much further into the mountains. A tour explores the first 600 m of the cave system, where the stalactites and stalagmites are lit by coloured spotlights. The rock formations have been given biblical names, such as Lot's wife, Devil's pulpit and the weeping Madonna. One of the most interesting formations is the Gong, which resonates through the cave chambers when struck. Keen cavers can organize a special visit to the Crystal Chamber, which takes five hours and must be booked in advance.

Towards Komatipoort and Mozambique

▸▸ pp603-616.

The N4 heads east from Nelspruit to Komatipoort (104 km), past the villages of Kaapmuiden, Malelane and Hectorspruit. The road follows the Crocodile River Valley through an area of fruit plantations at the bottom edge of Kruger National Park. This valley is one of the hottest areas of South Africa with year-round temperatures averaging between 25 and 30°C.

Malelane → *Phone code: 013. Colour map 2, grid B5.*

A dusty town with a sprawling shopping centre, Malalane is the hub of a sugarcane and fruit growing area. There's not much to the town itself but thanks to it's proximity to Kruger there are a number of excellent game lodges along the Crocodile River around this region. Indeed, it's common for buffalo and elephant to cross the river here and graze in people's gardens. The R570 continues north through the village to the entrance to Kruger Park at Malelane Gate. Information is available at the **Kruger Park South Tourism Association** ⓘ *Daph's Leather Shop, Spar Mall, T013- 7901193, malelaneinfo@mweb.co.za*. It's a helpful private office with a collection of brochures and will book local accommodation.

The Matsamo/Jeppes Reef border crossing into **Swaziland** (open 0700-1800), is 38 km south of Malelane on the R570.

Komatipoort → *Altitude: 137 m. Phone code: 013. Colour map 2, grid B5. 104 km from Nelspruit.*

Komatipoort is the last town in South Africa before the main road enters Mozambique at Lebombo. The town has always been close to the border between the two countries and has grown over the years as the trade and the transport of goods between the coast and the interior has increased.

In the early days, Komatipoort was just a campsite by the river crossing but as soon as the railway arrived in 1890, it quickly developed into a permanent settlement. Travelling from Lourenço Marques (today Maputo), this was the only place where the railway could pass through the Lebombo Mountains. The Nkhomati Accord was signed here in March 1984 between Samora Machel, President of Mozambique and PW Botha, Prime Minister of South Africa. The accord intended to promote peace and co-operation between the two countries but met with limited success as Mozambique, along with the rest of Africa, was still a staunch opponent to the Apartheid regime and supported sanctions. Not far from here on the Komati flats is the **Machel Memorial** which is a national monument marking the site where President Samora Machel tragically died in a plane crash in 1986. Joaquim Chissano succeeded him and his widow Graca Machel went on to marry Nelson Mandela a few years later.

Mahatma Gandhi was imprisoned in Komatipoort in 1907, before escaping to the coast.

Today, the town is an important marshalling yard for the railways and a popular centre for supplies for visitors to Kruger National Park (**Crocodile Gate** is only 9 km away). Lying at the foot of the Lebombo Mountains at the confluence of the Komati and Crocodile rivers and little over 60 km from the Indian Ocean, the climate here is tropical and humid, with high summer temperatures and rainfall. Fortunately, the streets are shaded by poinciana and jacaranda trees, which provide essential shade. There are supermarkets in the town centre along Rissik Street.

Mozambique border

ⓘ *Daily 0600-2200. Most visitors require visas for Mozambique, which are issued at the border, US$25 or R170. South African passport holders do not need a visa.*
The South African border post is at **Lebombo**, 3 km out of town. There is a viewpoint on a hill by the border from where one can look into Mozambique, striking for the rolls of barbed wire that stretch along either side of the border to prevent people crossing illegally. There is a new toll road between Nelspruit and Maputo; the journey between the two cities takes around two and half hours. Komatipoort is 96 km from Maputo. Note that most hire car firms do not allow vehicles into Mozambique. If you are in your own vehicle, you will need a carnet de passages and third party insurance.

Barberton

» *pp603-616. Phone code: 013. Colour map 2, C5.*

This quiet colonial town, 43 km from Nelspruit, is a pleasant place to spend a day or two, and offers a surprising amount to do and see, including a couple of community projects and several museums. The Swaziland border is only 43 km away. It has an interesting gold mining past and, unlike the gold mining town of Pilgrim's Rest near Sabie, which is completely devoted to tourism, the old corrugated iron roofed mining buildings in Barberton are very much part of the working commercial town. Lone Tree Hill, on the outskirts of Barberton, is one of the most popular hang gliding centres in South Africa. It is set in the De Kaap Valley where some of the oldest sedimentary rock formations in the world have been found (4200 million years). The Makhonjwa Mountains around Barberton are covered in grasslands and woods and are an extension of the southern Drakensberg.

The road into Barberton passes the Emjindini township before entering the quiet, wealthy, garden suburbs on the edge of town. An old abandoned mining centre, suitably named Eureka City, is tucked up in the hills at the back of the working Sheba mine (visits can be arranged in a 4WD vehicle). The main sights in town are all within walking distance and the hiking trails start from the edge of town.

Ins and outs

Tourist information Barberton Information Bureau ⓘ *Market Sq, T013-7122121, www.barberton.info, Mon-Fri 0800-1300, 1400-1630, Sat 0830-1200*, is a friendly and helpful office with good information on tours and accommodation in the area. Check here for up-to-date information on excursions to Swaziland.

In the 19th century Cockney Liz, a notorious prostitute and resident of Barberton, would dance on a snooker table every night whilst being auctioned off to the highest bidder.

Background

The De Kaap Valley was originally known as the 'Valley of Death' due to the many prospectors who had died here of malaria. Barberton is famous for being the site of one of South Africa's first large-scale gold rushes. Pioneer Reef was discovered in 1883 by 'French Bob' and by 1886 over 4000 claims were being worked in the valley. Barberton became a wild frontier town of corrugated iron shacks, gambling dens and whisky bars.

The town soon developed into a wealthy hub. South Africa's first gold stock exchange opened here in 1887 and many of Barberton's most attractive colonial buildings were built during the gold rush. Unfortunately, the gold rush only lasted a few years – the stock market crashed after too many speculators were sold shares in bogus companies and investors lost fortunes in the Transvaal and Britain. By the outbreak of the Boer War, Barberton had been virtually abandoned by the miners who had moved on to Witwatersrand. However, in recent years the industry has been revived and four gold mines operate within the area: Sheba, Fairview, New Consort, and Agnes, providing employment for much of the local community.

Sights

The historical sites within the town have been clearly mapped out by Barberton's tourism initiative as the **Heritage Walk**, and are all within walking distance of Market Square. Pick up a map at the tourist office. The walk starts from the Barberton

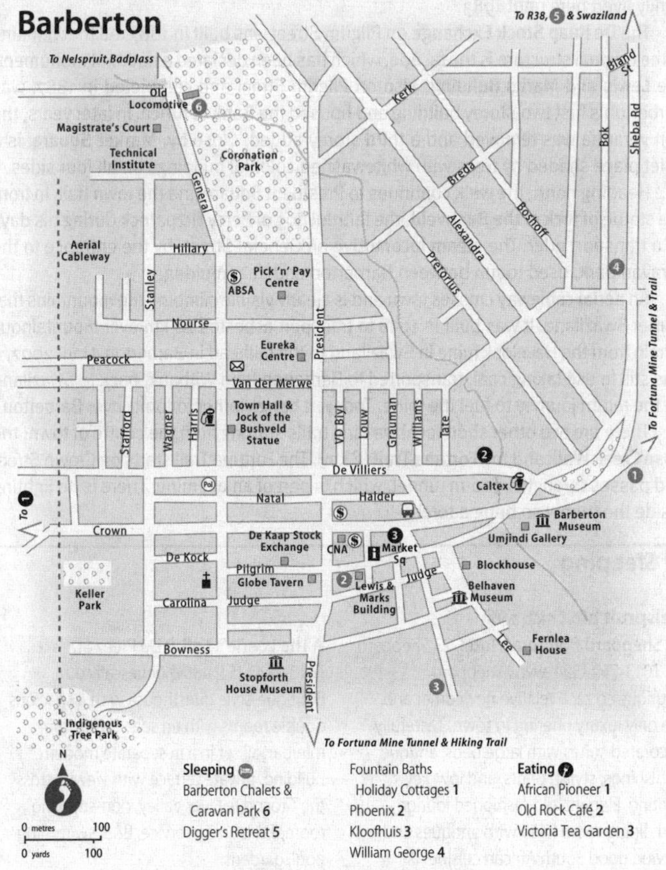

Museum and ends at the Steam Locomotive. The sights have been listed below in order of the walk. Only Belhaven House Museum and Stopforth House Museum have an entry fee, R10 per person, but you only need pay once to cover entrance at both.

Barberton Museum ⓘ *36 Pilgrim St, T013-7124280, daily 0900-1600*, is the town's local history museum with displays on geology, mining, and cultural history of the area, including some displays on Swazi history. **The Blockhouse**, on the corner of Lee Road and Judge Street, is a small fort built in 1901 during the Boer War as part of the defence of Barberton. It is made from wood and corrugated iron and is one of the earliest examples of its kind. **Belhaven Museum** ⓘ *Lee Rd, several tours daily*, is a large, early Edwardian mansion built in 1904 and set in mature gardens. The interior is decorated with period furniture and gives an interesting insight into the comfortable lifestyles of Barberton's middle class. **Fernlea House** ⓘ *Lee Rd, Mon-Fri 0830-1300, 1330-1600*, was built in the 1890s from wood and iron. The house is in a beautiful setting at the bottom of a wooded valley on the edge of Barberton. It is decorated with period furniture and has displays on Barberton's famous botanists.

The walk passes **Rimer's Creek**, the site where, on 24 June 1884, David Wilson the mining commissioner, broke a bottle of gin over a rock to christen the new town of Barberton. At the time, Rimer's Creek was a popular recreational spot for the townsfolk, particularly on Wednesdays when it was frequented by the barmaids of the town.

To the west, **Stopforth House** ⓘ *18 Bowness St, several tours daily*, belonged to James Stopforth, a baker and a general dealer, and was built in 1886. The Stopforth family lived here until 1983.

The **De Kaap Stock Exchange** on Pilgrim Street was built in 1887. All that remains of the original structure is the façade, which has been declared a national monument. The **Lewis and Marks Building**, also on Pilgrim Street and completed in 1887, was Barberton's first two-storey building and housed the **Bank of Africa**. In later years, the iron veranda was removed and a third storey added. Close by, **Market Square**, is a quiet place shaded by trees with whitewashed colonial buildings on all four sides.

Heading north, the walk continues to President Square and the town hall. In front is a statue of **Jock of the Bushveld**, the faithful dog of Percy Fitzpatrick during his days as a transport rider. The **steam locomotive** on General Street, by the entrance to the caravan park, used to run between Barberton and Kaapmuiden.

An **aerial cableway** crosses town and is clearly visible climbing the mountains that border Swaziland. It was built in 1938 to transport asbestos 20 km over mountainous terrain from the Havelock mine in Swaziland to the railhead in Barberton. Until 2002, it was still in use taking coal, transported to Barberton from Witbank, back to Swaziland on the return journey to fuel the mine. Today, it hangs rather forlornly over Barberton.

There are two other short local walking trails starting from the centre of town; the **Rose Creek Walk** and the **Fortuna Trail** (2 km). The Fortuna Trail starts on Crown Street and passes through a 500-m tunnel, which is part of an old mine. There is no lighting inside the tunnel so bring a torch.

Sleeping

Nelspruit *p567, map p567*

AL Sheppard Boutique Hotel, 23 Sheppard Dr, T013-7523394, www.sheppardboutique.co.za. A relative newcomer and the only luxury offering in town. Tastefully decorated suites with large beds, antique furnishings, stylish prints, and low-key lighting. Elegant, old-fashioned lounge and dining room filled with antiques and serving good South African cuisine.

A The Loerie's Call, 2 Du Preez St, T013-7441251, info@loeriescall.co.za. Boutique-style guesthouse with 4 spacious double rooms with en suite bathroom, minibar, all set in a in separate modern building, private terrace with views across the Crocodile River Valley, non-smoking room, TV, laundry service, B&B, swimming pool, gardens.

A Mercure Inn, corner of Graniet St and N4, T013-7414222, www.mercure.co.za. Part of a successful quality French chain. 104 luxury self-catering, single-storey units, TV, a/c, airport transfers, large conference facilities. Spacious lounge and bar, attractive pool area, harps on a bit about having the largest pool in Nelspruit. Good quality, with the benefit of having self-catering facilities.

A-B Shandon Lodge, 1 Saturn St, quite a distance from the town centre, follow Ferreira St out of town, T013-7449934, www.shandon.co.za. Fine colonial-style house on a hilltop suburb, 5 mins' drive from town. Each room opens up onto a shaded veranda running around the house, with views over the small pool and terrace overlooking the countryside. 7 large double rooms with en suite shower, country-style decor with green and yellow fabrics, separate seating area, M-Net TV, tea and coffee facilities with homemade biscuits. Pleasant bar, meals on request, huge breakfasts served in the cool dining room. Friendly, family-run with lots of advice on the area. Recommended.

B Bavaria, 45 Zebrina Cres, T013-7411703, www.marilize@hppmc.co.za. Homely guesthouse set in a converted home surrounded by tropical gardens, in a quiet suburb just west of town. 9 en suite luxury rooms with bright, African-themed decor, all rooms have M-Net TV, tea and coffee facilities and work stations. Breakfasts served in bright breakfast room overlooking garden. Pool, bar, laundry, car hire can be arranged.

B Jörns , 62 Hunter St, T013-7441894, www.jorns.co.za. Large guesthouse run by a German couple, 9 comfortable rooms, all en suite and some with corner bath in the bedroom. Lounge, bar, swimming pool with beautiful views over the Lowveld, koi fishpond in the tropical garden.

B The Roost, 21c Koraalboom St, T013-7411419, theroost@mweb.co.za. Spacious old house 8, smart double rooms with en suite bathroom, TV, M-Net, overhead fans, swimming pool, set apart from the main house, conference facilities, secure parking, plenty of atmosphere. Recommended.

C La Roca, 56 van Wyk St, T013-7526628, laroca@worldonline.co.za. Recently refurbished guesthouse with 4 double rooms with en suite bathrooms, 2 single rooms, each with a private balcony or patio with views across the Lowveld, TV, bar fridge, ceiling fans, lounge, lovely swimming pool surrounded by boulders, will collect from town centre and airport.

C Linga Longa, Karee Cres, T013-7511942, rogers@lantic.net 8 elegantly decorated bedrooms with private entrances with fan or a/c, TV, bar fridge, lovely verandas, pool, jacuzzi, tasteful house in the suburbs.

C Marloth 35, 35 Marloth St, T013-7524529, eggink@lantic.net. Simple double rooms with en suite bathroom, microwave and fridge in all rooms, set away from main house, private, swimming pool, braai, secluded gardens, family run B&B set in a quiet residential suburb. Nothing special but good value.

C Palms Guest House, 25 van Wijk St, T013-7554374, thepalmsnelspruit@absamail.co.za 3 double rooms, 3 single rooms all with en suite bathroom, TV, M-Net, lounge areas, B&B, all meals available on request, swimming pool, sauna, gardens, secure parking, comfortable and relaxing.

C Utopia in Africa, 6 Daleen St, T013-7457714, www.utopiainafrica.com. B&B in a stylish house in quiet suburb. Open-plan layout with thatched roof and 5 large, sunny bedrooms, stylishly furnished, all en suite with balconies. Full English breakfasts served, elevated pool with views of a nearby nature reserve, secure parking, no children under 14.

D Promenade, Louis Trichardt St, T013-7533000. A smart hotel in a Spanish-style hacienda, 71 a/c rooms with en suite bathrooms, TV, non-smoking room available. Restaurant, bar, terrace overlooks a small pool, tastefully designed interior, secure parking, but suffers from a lack of recreational space. Many of the mainline buses stop here.

D-E Safubi River Lodge, 45 Graniet St, 2 km from the city centre, T013-7413253, www.safubi.co.za. Self-catering chalets, with fully equipped kitchen, bathroom, lounge, TV, secure parking, braai in the garden, set in 16 ha of bushveld on the banks of the Gladdespruit river. Also a 40-site camping and caravan park. Large peaceful and secure, swimming pool plus communal kitchens for self-catering and coffee shop serving breakfast and light meals. Good value.

E Funky Monkey Backpackers, 102 van Wyk St, T013-7441310, funkymonkeys@yebo.co.za.

Dorms, double rooms and camping, with rooms spread through a spacious house adorned with bright artwork. Swimming pool and pool table, fully licensed bar. Lorna knows plenty about the local area and can organize trips to Kruger or Blyde River Canyon, Good travel centre which can arrange Kruger and Mozambique trips.

E Nelspruit Backpackers, 9 Andries Pretorius St, T013-7412237, www.nelback.co.za. Mix of dorms and double rooms in a good location next to a nature reserve. Kitchen, laundry, bar, pool table, swimming pool, close to restaurants and pubs in the Sunpark Centre. Free pick-up service from town, on the Baz Bus route. Excellent base from which to explore the area. Day trips to Blyde River Canyon and Kruber, see Tour operators page 576 for details.

F Sun Lodge, 7 de Villiers St, T013-7412253, sunlodge@absamail.co.za. Garden chalet plus double room in main house, dorms, pool set in colourful lush gardens, close to shops and restaurants. This used to be a guesthouse but with the addition of a dorm room is reinventing itself as a backpackers, on the Baz Bus route.

Malelane *p569*

AL Thanda-Nani Game Lodge, the turning is 11 km east of Malelane, clearly signposted on the left of the N4, T013-7924543, www.thandanani.com. 6500-ha private luxury game farm with 10 a/c stylish double rooms with en suite bathrooms, set in thatched rondavels. Lounge and dining area set under an open thatched area, attractive pool, game drives with chance of seeing range of wildlife including black and white rhino and a fairly tame herd of zebra that wander through the grounds. Enjoyable variation on the full-on Kruger experience.

A Serenity Mountain and Forest Lodge, T013-7527361-5, www.serenitylodge.co.za While most of the lodges in this region are on the fringes of Kruger and the Crocodile River, this lodge is in an unusual location in a patch of rain forest high up in the hills in the opposite direction, 12 km off the R570 toward the Jeppe's Reef border with Swaziland. 2 camps of luxury thatched chalets overlooking the trees, en suite, private verandas overlooking the butterfly-filled forest, all linked by walkways in the trees. Unusual sunken bar. Hiking and 4WD trails through forest. Beautiful spot that combines the highlights of Kruger with somewhere a little different to stay, recommended.

B Selati 103 Guest Cottages, 103 Selati Crescent, in a suburb north of town, T013-7900978, www.selati103.co.za 9 garden cottages, self-catering or B&B, colourful decor, TV, large swimming pool, comfortable option before entering Kruger Park.

B-C Bezuidenhout Guest House, in a quiet suburb north of town, T013-7900978, www.bezuidenhoutbnb.co.za. 8 smart rooms in double B&B rooms or self-catering units, each with a/c, kitchenette and en suite bathroom, thatched house in pleasant gardens, swimming pool.

Komatipoort *p569*

B-C Tree's Too, 11 Furley St, T013-7908262. 6 large, spotless a/c en suite rooms under thatch, all with separate entrance and set in lush tropical gardens under palm trees. Lounge, pleasant pool area, small **Gecko's** restaurant serving breakfast, lunch and dinner. English-owned. Recommended.

Barberton *p570, map p571*

B Fountain Baths, 48 Pilgrim St, T013-7122707, www.fountainbaths.co.za. Mix of B&B double rooms and self-catering units sleeping 2-4, simple decor with wooden floors, garden with swimming pool, peaceful setting edging on to the hills. Good attached restaurant.

C Digger's Retreat, 14 km out of town, signposted just off the R38 to Kaapmuiden, T013-7199681, diggersretreat@mweb.co.za 18 double rooms or thatched rondavels. A la carte restaurant, **Old Gold Rush** pub with themed decor, swimming pool. Hiking, bird-watching and 4WD trips can be arranged.

C Kloofhuis, 1 Kloof St, T013-7124268, www.kloofhuis.co.za. Central location just behind Bellhaven House, a short walk from the tourist office. Fine Victorian home with wrap-around veranda. 3 rooms, doubles and

For an explanation of the sleeping and eating price codes used in this guide, see inside the front cover. Other relevant information in found in Essentials, pages 42-47.

twins, en suite or shared bathroom. Homely setting, floral decor, relaxing place to stay.

D **Phoenix Hotel**, 20 Pilgrim St, T013-7124211, phoenix@soft.co.za. Historical town hotel dating from the gold rush; apparently Paul Kruger was entertained here after meetings with the miners. The hotel was so popular in its day that on occasions guests had to sleep on or under the billiards table. Today it's looking rather dated, with lots of chintz and swirly carpets. A/c, bar lunches and à la carte restaurant, 3 pool tables, **Jocks Tavern** is a lively bar.

D **William George House**, 1 Bok St, T/F013-7125886, wilgohouse@telkomsa.net. Pretty colonial house with 50 m of covered veranda. 8 double en suite rooms, TV, minibar, pool, B&B but choice of early breakfast or takeaway brunch, evening meals on request,

D-F **Barberton Chalets & Caravan Park**, General St, T013- 7123323, www.barbertonchalets.co.za. Self-catering chalets sleeping up to 6, serviced daily, caravan spots and campsite set in the neatly maintained shady gardens with a swimming pool, tea garden, shop and laundrette.

Eating

Nelspruit *p567, map p567*

The centre of town gets very quiet at night, with just a handful of restaurants open for evening meals.

Costa do Sol, ABSA Sq, Paul Kruger St, T013-7526382. Closed Sun and Sat lunch. Well-established restaurant set in a mall, specialising in Mozambique seafood that arrives fresh from the coast daily, Italian and Portuguese dishes, pizzas and pastas, seafood platters and best known for their giant prawns; good winelist that includes some Portuguese wines.

Le Gourmet, 24 Branders St, T013-v 7551941. Closed Sun and Mon and only open for lunch Tue and Sat. Provincial French-style cuisine in intimate surroundings and pretty garden, excellent wine list.

Brewer's Feast, on the corner of the N4, T013-7414674. Cheap and cheerful roadside restaurant open all day and well into the night serving truck drivers and passing tourists, budget takeaway meals. Huge menu, and bargain breakfasts.

Ku's, Sunpark Mall, corner of General Dan Pienaar and Piet Retief Sts, T013-7413989. Economically priced Chinese dishes, takeaway service, close to some of the backpackers and other budget accommodation, and O'Hagen's pub, so popular for a cheap night out.

Nandos, 46 Brown St, T013-7551481. Best of the bunch of the standard chains in town, with delicious peri-peri chicken served with chips, and an outdoor veranda overlooking the street.

O'Hagen's, Sunpark Mall, corner of General Dan Pienaar and Piet Retief Sts, T013-7413584. Good Irish theme pub chain, wide selection of imported beers, open-air terrace and music, standard pub meals.

Pappa's Pizzeria, 56 Brown St, T013-7551660. Simple wooden chalet-style building serving wood-fired pizzas which are a little on the small side, but the selection of delicious pastas are a good bet. Friendly service, enjoyable wooden deck and live acoustic music in the evenings.

Malelane *p569*

Casa Portuguesa, behind the Toyota service station on the N4, T013-7901344. Fancy tablecloths indoors, or outside courtyard with fountain, popular with Afrikaner farmers for the fresh Mozambique peri-peri prawns.

Barney's Pub and Grill, Impala St, T013-7901294. Town pub popular with local game rangers, standard but filling meals, regular pool competitions, laid-back place for a few beers.

Komatipoort *p569*

For a small town this is quite a happening place for bars and restaurants and is well-known for its seafood, which arrives daily from Mozambique.

Tambarina Comida, 48 Rissik St, T013-7937110. A fun restaurant decorated in bright colours with a lovely courtyard shaded by mango trees, and serving good Portuguese cuisine and seafood. If you can't make it to the coast, the meals here are the next best thing. Guests from **Crocodile Bridge** camp in Kruger Park often dine here.

The Border Country Inn, T013-7937328. A hotel restaurant 1 km from the border, pleasant outdoor setting on a leafy terrace (watch the mosquitoes at night), indifferent service, but excellent prawns and calamari.

Hippo's, 81 Rissik St, T013-7938155. Popular bar and restaurant, with fat sofas and reasonably priced menu, open all day for snacks and coffees, closes when the last person leaves.

Barberton *p570, map p571*

Fountain Baths, 48 Pilgrim St, T013-7122707, www.fountainbaths.co.za. Attached to the guesthouse, this new restaurant has a weekly menu serving smart, contemporary South African cuisine mixed with traditional favourites. Decent wine list.

Old Rock Café, 73 de Villiers St, T013-7126264. Family pub and grill with large-screen TV, gets very busy during big games. Standard pub menu with range of steaks and burgers, some seafood and salads.

Victoria Tea Garden, Market Sq, T013-7124985. Charming open-air café under a white gazebo serving toasted sandwiches, juice and light snacks, open until late afternoon. Close to the tourist office, a good place to start the Heritage Walk around town.

Shopping

Nelspruit *p567, map p567*

Crossing Centre, at the junction of the N4 and the R40, just west of the centre. A variety of shops and banks, including a **Woolworths** food shop and a **Clicks** pharmacy.

Riverside Mall, 5 km out of town on the White River road. A wider selection than the Crossing Centre and proudly boasting to be the largest shopping centre in Mpumalanga, with a variety of shops, restaurants and a **Nu Metro** 8-screen cinema. Next door is the Emnotweni Casino.

Activities and tours

Nelspruit *p567, map p567*

Vula Tours, T031-7412826, vula@soft.co.za. Affordable day trips to Kruger, the Panorama region, and Sudwala Caves. Expect to pay from R550 per person per day.

Place of Rock, T013-7515319, www.placeofrock.co.za. Wide range of day and overnight trips to Kruger, the Panorama region and elsewhere, for a variety of budgets.

Green Rhino, T013-7511952, www.greenrhino.co.za. National adventure operator. Tours from 2-4 days throughout the region.

Mbombela Safaris, **Nelspruit Backpackers**, 9 Andries Pretorius St, T013-7412237, www.nelback.co.za. Will pick up from anywhere in Nelspruit if you are staying elsewhere. 2-day/1-night Kruger tour, from R850 per person, longer tours available, free night's stay at the backpackers if you book a Mbombela safari.

Malelane *p569*

Zozi's, T013-7788849, T082-6681577 (mob). An enterprising and entertaining local female guide who runs tours of the Matsulu township on the edge of Kruger. The site of the village was originally inside the park's boundary, but in 1968 the fences were removed and people were relocated from neighbouring farms to form the Matsulu community. Today, it's not uncommon to have an elephant stride through the village. Zozi shows you around in a taxi, and visits include a *shebeen* (pub), a hairdresser's where the art of African plaiting is demonstrated, a witch doctor who will 'throw the bones', and a school. This excellent tour not only gives insight into African rural life, but also shows how the local people manage to live alongside the animals. Great fun and highly recommended. A 3-hr tour costs R100, or R150 including a meal.

Barberton *p570, map p571*

African Pioneer Mining Tours, based at the **African Pioneer Restaurant**, 7 km from Barberton on the Agnes Rd, follow Crown St out of town, T013-7128002, andreab@soft.co.za. Underground tours of the 120-year old Pioneer mine, plus gold-panning demonstrations and the chance of trying it yourself. Lunch included at the at the African Pioneer restaurant, which has a pool where diners can swim. This company also supports the **Umjindi Jewellery Project**, an initiative by the municipality to teach young people from disadvantaged communities jewellery design and manufacture.

Eureka City Ghost Town Tours, General St, T013-7125055, eurekacitytours@barberton.info. With sufficient numbers of people, this tour departs from Barberton daily at 0900 and returns at 1630. Transport is in a 4WD open-sided vehicle and includes drinks and informative guide. The road is very bad and you are not permitted to drive here yourself. Visit Eureka City, the abandoned mining town, and walk a short way underground into the gold mine itself. The drive goes through some spectacular mountain scenery and is recommended for an all-round historical picture of the region.

Transport

Nelspruit *p567, map p567*

Air

Nationwide, T0861737737, www.flynationwide.co.za, has flights to **Cape Town** and **Johannesburg**. SA Airlink, T011-9781111, www.saairlink.co.za, has flights to **Johannesburg**, **Cape Town** and **Durban**.

Bus

Baz Bus, T021-4392323, www.bazbus.com has services towards **Johannesburg**, **Pretoria** and **Swaziland**. Greyhound, T011-2768500, www.greyhound.co.za has buses to **Pretoria**, **Johannesburg**, **Durban** and **Mozambique**. Translux, central reservations, T011-7743333, www.translux.co.za, runs buses to **Pretoria**, **Johannesburg** and **Maputo**.

Car hire

All offices are at the **Kruger Mpumalanga International Airport** terminal building, 25 km from Nelspruit: **Avis**, T013-7501015, www.avis.co.za; **Budget**, T013-7509150, www.budget.co.za; **Hertz**, T013-7509150, www.hertz.co.za; **Imperial**, T013-7502871, www.imperialcarrental.co.za.

Rail

The Komati Express between **Pretoria/ Johannesburg** and **Komatipoort** (border post with Mozambique) stops daily in Nelspruit.

Taxi

City Bug, T013-7414114.

Komatipoort *p569*

Bus

The buses between **Pretoria/Johannesburg** and **Maputo** stop at the border post.

Rail

The Komati Express is the daily service running between **Pretoria/Johannesburg** and **Komatipoort**. The train connects with a shuttle service to the border, which links with the train to **Maputo** .

Barberton *p570, map p571*

There is no public transport to Barberton. Without a car, the only (expensive) option is take a taxi from Nelspruit.

Directory

Nelspruit *p567, map p567*

Banks American Express, Riverside Mall, T013-7570400. There are branches of all other banks in the Riverside Mall and the Crossing Centre. **Internet** Alpha Internet Café, Riverside Mall. **Consulates** Mozambique Consulate, CVA building, Bester St, T013-7532089, Mon-Fri, 0830-1500. Visas take 3 days but can be issued on the same day or within 24 hrs for an extra fee, you will need to bring 2 passport-size photos and then fill in the application form at the embassy. Expect to pay in the region of US$15 but double this for same day issue. Alternatively visas are now issued at all Mozambique borders, costing R170 or US$25. South African passport-holders no longer need visas. **Medical services** Ambulance, T10177. Chemist, after hours, T013-7525721. **Rob Ferreira Hospital**, T013-7413031. **Medi-clinic**, T013-7590645. **Travel agent** Harvey World Travel, Riverside Mall, T/F031-7570883. Reliable national chain of general travel agents, flight sales. **Useful telephone numbers** Police, T10111, T013-7591000.

Komatipoort *p569*

Banks First National, Rissik St, open for foreign exchange. FX Bureau de Change, at the Komati Oasis service station just before the border, T031-7907457, Mon-Sat 0700-1700, Sun 0700-1300.

Barberton *p570, map p571*

Useful telephone numbers Ambulance, T013-7125002. Police, T10111.

Kruger National Park

→ Colour map 2, grid B5

Kruger Park is the king of South African game parks and one of the best game-viewing areas in all of Africa. The figures speak for themselves: 507 bird species, 114 reptiles, 49 fish, 34 amphibians, 147 mammal and over 23,000 plant species have been recorded here. The region itself is enormous, extending from the Crocodile River in the south to the Limpopo in the north, from the wooded foothills of the eastern escarpment to the humid plains of the lowveld. It certainly fulfils most visitor's fantasies of seeing magnificent herds of game roaming across acacia-studded stretches of savannah, and of course is home to the Big Five. The park is 60 km wide and over 350 km long, conserving 21,497 sq km, an area the size of Wales or Israel. Despite its size, it is very well developed, with a good network covering 2600 km of roads and numerous camps, making a Kruger safari relatively hassle free.

Don't expect to have the park to yourself, however. Kruger receives over one million visitors a year and the park camps cater for up to 5000 visitors a day. Nevertheless, despite the huge number of people passing through, Kruger has managed to maintain its wild atmosphere. Only 5% of the park is affected by the activities of the visitors and only a few areas in the south come close to the overcrowding seen in East Africa's game parks.

While much of the park is designed for self-driving and self-catering, it is also possible to stay in an ever-expanding choice of top-end private reserves, which are popular with first-time visitors as all game drives are led by rangers, so you can leave the animal-spotting to the experts. The fences that once split Kruger from the private reserves have now all come down, so game can roam freely between the national park and private concessions. Moreover, the fences between the countries bordering South Africa have also come down in the last few years: the demolition of fences between Kruger and Mozambique's Limpopo National Park and Zimbabwe's Gonarezhou have created the Great Limpopo Transfrontier Park – a conservation area straddling a staggering 35,000 sq km. » *For details of the private game reserves along the park's western boundary, see pages 594-603.*

Ins and outs

Getting there and around

Air **SA Airlink** flies between Johannesburg and **Kruger Mpumalanga International Airport, Phalaborwa Airport** and **Mala Mala Airfield** (available only to guests of Mala Mala). **SA Express** and **Kulula** fly to **Kruger Mpumalanga International Airport**. Kruger Mpumalanga International Airport is the largest airport in the area, located 22km from Nelspruit. Phalaborwa is just outside the park and within easy reach of many of the entry gates. There is also an airfield by Skukuza Camp within the park, and Marulaneng/Hoedspruit has the **Eastgate Airport**, but there are no scheduled flights to either at present. You may, however, find yourself passing through these airports if you have booked an all-inclusive package with one of the private game reserves. Some of the luxury game lodges also have their own landing strips for chartered flights.

! The park is in an endemic malaria area. Take anti-malarial medication and use insect repellent. Malaria hotline, T082-2341800.

Road Most people arrive in Kruger by road, either on a tour or in their own vehicle. There are nine entry gates and numerous options of approach. Which area you end up staying in will depend to a large extent on where you are coming from. Petrol is available at all the camps during office hours, and the mark-up on litre prices is not as

unreasonable as you'd expect (although note that credit cards aren't accepted).
There is a speed limit of 50 kph on the surfaced roads in the park. **Kruger Emergency Road Services** is based at Skukuza, T013-7355606, or T072-4564937. The service is not equipped to do any major repairs, but if you break down within the park they will tow you to the nearest garage outside the park.

Orientation

The information provided in the following section is intended as a guide for the whole of the national park. Given its huge size, many visitors to Kruger concentrate on one area of the park on each visit. Unless you are staying for more than a couple of nights, it is impossible to combine effective game viewing and visit all the areas. For the purposes of this guide, the park has been divided into three areas: Southern, Central and Northern, with a description of each of the different camps within these areas.

Best time to visit

Each season has its advantages. The park looks its best after the summer rains when the new shoots and lush vegetation provide a surplus of food for the grazers. Migratory birds are attracted and display their colourful breeding plumage, and this is a good time to see courtship rituals and nesting. The animals look their best thanks to their good diet, and mammals give birth to their young. The disadvantages of summer are that the thick foliage and tall grasses make it harder to spot animals and daytime temperatures can rise to a sweltering 40°C; afternoon rains are also common.

The winter months are good for game viewing because the dry weather forces animals to congregate around waterholes and there is less foliage for them to hide in. However, the animals tend not to be in their best condition. The winter months of June, July and August are more comfortable with daytime temperatures of around 30°C, but nights can be surprisingly cold at this time of year with temperatures at times dropping to 0°C. This is a good time of year to visit the northern areas of the park which can be unbearably hot in the summer.

Kruger is at its most crowded during the South African school holidays (see page 20). Accommodation within the park will be completely full and the heavy traffic on the roads can detract from the wilderness experience.

Arriving

Most of the camps are at least an hour's drive from the nearest entrance gate so always make sure you arrive in time to get to the camp. At the park gate, your reservation will usually be checked before you are allowed in, especially during the busy periods when all the accommodation, including campsites, gets booked up. You could be fined if you arrive at the camp gate after it has closed. **Conservation fees** are R120 per adult per day, and R60 per child under 16. South Africans get a substantial discount. **Camp receptions** are open daily April to June 0800-1800; March, September and October 0800-1830; November to February 0800-1900.

Background

The first area of what was to become Kruger National Park was officially protected in 1898 by President Kruger when he established the Sabie River Game Reserve. This consisted of what is now the southern sector of Kruger, the area extending between the Crocodile and the Sabie rivers. The area's early inhabitants were San and the Baphalaborwa tribes, who had little impact on the region's wildlife but did leave their mark in cave paintings throughout the area.

The game reserve was established to protect wildlife from the threat of 'biltong hunters' who were visiting the lowveld in ever increasing numbers during the dry

Kruger National Park opening times

National Park gates		Camp gates	
January	0530-1830	January	0500-1830
February	0530-1830	February	0530-1830
March	0530-1800	March	0530-1800
April	0600-1730	April	0600-1730
May-August	0630-1730	May-August	0630-1730
September	0600-1800	September	0600-1800
October	0530-1800	October	0530-1800
November	0530-1830	November	0430-1830
December	0530-1830	December	0430-1830

season. Hunters had already slaughtered vast herds of animals throughout South Africa and this was an early attempt to preserve an undisturbed wilderness. A single police sergeant at Komatipoort was given the daunting task of protecting the entire area from poachers.

It was re-proclaimed by the British in 1903, increasing the size of the park with both the Shingwedzi Game Reserve, the area between the Letaba and the Luvuvhu rivers, and the 5000 sq km of unworked ranches between the Sabi and the Letaba rivers. The new area under protection covered roughly the same area as Kruger does today. However, numerous factions threatened the survival of the park: hunters wanted access to the park, soldiers returning from the First World War expected land for sheep farming; prospectors looking for gold, coal and copper wanted mining rights; and South Africa's vets were campaigning for a mass slaughter of wildlife to prevent the possible spread of tsetse fly.

The seeds of creating a self-financing national park open to visitors were unwittingly sown by South African Railways, when they opened a new tour running from Pretoria to Lorenço Marques (today Maputo) which stopped in the reserve for game rangers to take visitors into the bush. The first tourists arrived in 1923 and the visits became such a popular feature of the holiday that park visits were used as publicity by the railways. Public support for a national park empowered the conservationist lobby and public access was finally allowed in 1926.

The first cars arrived in 1927 and were able to travel by road through Sabi Bridge between the Olifants and Crocodile rivers. Visitors were expected to fend for themselves and made their own thorn bush camps to stay in. The animals reacted well to visitors in cars as long as they stayed inside them, but night driving was stopped almost immediately as too many animals were being killed. The first camp was built for tourists at Pretoriuskop after the chaos of the early years when tourists had been known to spend the night in trees hiding from predators.

By 1946, 38,000 tourists a year were visiting Kruger and in 1947 Princess Elizabeth and Princess Margaret visited the park on their royal tour of South Africa where they stayed in the first luxury lodges. The publicity surrounding the tour ensured that a visit to Kruger became a fixture on every tourist's trip to South Africa. By 1955 over 100,000 people were visiting each year.

The land area available to the park's wildlife has increased considerably in the last two decades. In 1994 the game fences between the private reserves on Kruger's western border were taken down, allowing animals to roam freely in an extra 2000 sq km of bush. Even more significantly, 2001 saw the removal of the fences between the international borders, creating the Greater Limpopo Transfrontier Conservation Area. This now incorporates Parque Nacional do Limpopo in Mozambique and Gonarezhou National Park in Zimbabwe, forming one of the largest conservation areas in Africa. The Mozambique section of the park can now be accessed from the Giriyondo border gate.

Staying in the park

Kruger has 12 main rest camps, five bushveld camps, two bush lodges and four satellite camps, owned and managed by **South African National Parks** (SAN Parks), head office in Pretoria. Although there is a choice in the type of accommodation available, all the room rates are very reasonable. If you're looking for luxury, Kruger's private concessions offer some of the finest camps in Africa. There are also now a handful of private luxury lodges within Kruger, such as **Tinga Private Lodge** and **Jock Safari Lodge**. The SAN Parks website, www.sanparks.org, has excellent information on all the lodges within Kruger. » *For details of private reserves outside the park, see pages 594-603.*

Reservations

The direct line for each camp is included with the description of the camp. This number can only be used for making a last-minute booking, up to 48 hours prior to arrival. All other bookings should be made through **SAN Parks** ⓘ *T012-4289111, www.sanparks.org*. Once you are in the park it is always worth calling a day ahead or in the early morning to see if there have been any cancellations. The camp receptions will also be able to change your reservations to another camp if there is availability.

Main public camps

The majority of overnight visitors stay in one of the 12 main public camps in the park at **Berg-en-Dal, Crocodile Bridge, Lower Sabie, Pretoriuskop, Skukuza, Letaba, Mopani, Olifants, Orpen, Satara, Shingwedzi** and **Punda Maria**. Most of the accommodation is in the form of chalets or cottages, which can sleep between two and 12. If you are self-catering, you'll have the choice between a separate fully equipped kitchen, a kitchenette or the use of a communal kitchen. The units with just a kitchenette do not have any cutlery or crockery. All accommodation comes with a refrigerator, bedding and towels. If in doubt, always check when booking exactly what you will be getting. More precise details of the choices are listed under the separate entry for each of the camps.

Some of the older camps feel a little outdated, but the grounds are universally clean and well-kept. The facilities from one camp to the next vary but in most cases they include a shop selling basic self-catering supplies, a petrol pump, a restaurant or cafeteria, laundrette, toilets and hot showers, braai areas with seating, public telephones and an office with information on the other camps. During the school holidays, the atmosphere in the larger camps can feel like holiday camps, and you can easily forget you are in the middle of a game reserve.

Private camps

Private camps offer secluded luxury accommodation and are smaller and more remote than public camps, without facilities such as shops, restaurants, or petrol stations. These camps are ideal for a large group of friends, since the whole camp has to be taken with each booking. The two main private camps are **Boulders**, which sleeps 12, and **Roodewal**, sleeping 19. Reservations should be made well in advance as they offer exceptionally good value if the maximum number of people stay in the camp. The camps are located away from the main public camps but are close enough for visits to the shops for supplies. Although they are privately owned, all bookings are dealt with by **SAN Parks**, as for any other accommodation within the park.

Major James Stevenson-Hamilton

James Stevenson-Hamilton, Kruger's first game warden, was appointed at the end of the Boer War. He established his headquarters at the end of the railway on the branch line from Komatipoort to the Sabie River. The headquarters were then called Sabie Bridge and have grown to become Skukuza camp.

He began his work with two other rangers and spent years patrolling the reserve on horseback and on foot. His main duties were to encourage a healthy game population and to rid the park of poachers. However, his deep love of the African bush inspired him to campaign to increase the size of the park and to ensure the continued protection of the wildlife within its borders. He retired in 1946 after working in Kruger for 44 years.

James Stevenson-Hamilton's philosophy was that man's attempts to manage the park only interfered with natural processes. He believed that all the creatures within the park deserved to live regardless of temporary effects and that the balance of nature would always be preserved.

Bushveld camps

The five bushveld camps at **Biyamiti**, **Shimuwini**, **Talamati**, **Bateleur** and **Sirheni** are smaller and offer more of a wilderness experience than the main camps, but they also have far fewer facilities. Staying in these camps is one of the best ways to experience Kruger, but it does involve a degree of advanced planning. The chalets are all self-catering with fully equipped kitchens; bedding and towels are provided, and each chalet can sleep up to four people.

Campsites

Although most of the main public camps have a separate area for caravans, tents and camper vans, there are two separate campsites at **Maroela** and **Balule**. The only facilities here are washblocks and communal kitchen facilities – there are no power points.

Eating

The camp restaurants are open daily for breakfast (0700-0900), lunch (1200-1400) and dinner (1800-2100). Some of the camps also have a bar. At small camps, or when there are fewer guests, you will be asked to order your evening meal in advance.

Shopping

Camp shops are open 0800-1800 daily from April to June; 0800-1830 daily during March, September and October and 0800-1900 daily from November to February. The closer you are to Skukuza (the largest camp), the fresher the produce stocked in camp shops. Most shops stock firewood and braai lighters, bread, frozen meat, tinned vegetables, jams, biscuits, beer, wines, spirits, cool drinks, books and a few curio items. If you don't have a cool box in your car and you are self-catering, it is still possible to buy all you need for a meal from the shops each day.

Other facilities

Some of the camps have **swimming pools** for residents, a good option if you choose to base yourself at a camp for several days in summer and want to relax during the midday heat. Camping areas have **laundry blocks** and hot, clean **showers**. The **communal kitchens** have power points, instant boiling water machines, electric rings and a sink. It is your responsibility to clean up after yourself. Always secure rubbish to minimize the risk of baboons raiding the bins. There is a **bank** and ATM at Skukuza.

Wildlife, activities and tours

Wildlife management

Although Kruger appears impressively wild, many aspects of the ecosystem are carefully monitored and controlled by the park authorities. Windpumps, for example, have been built at waterholes in dry areas so that game congregates in large numbers, and a number of species have been reintroduced. White rhinos were first reintroduced in 1961; the programme has been so successful that there are now over 2000 in the park. Black rhino were reintroduced in 1971, 40 years after they had last been seen here. Other animals which have been re-established include tsessebe and roan.

Game viewing

Kruger is, of course, home to the Big Five: lion, elephant, buffalo, black rhino and leopard. The highest concentrations and variety of game are around **Lower Sabie**, **Satara** and **Skukuza**. The best times for game viewing are after dawn and just before dusk, as animals tend to rest during the heat of the day.

There is a network of tarred and dirt roads linking the camps and looping through the best game-viewing areas. They are only open to the public during daylight hours and are subject to speed limits, which are monitored by radar. Game viewing takes time and it is best to drive below 20 kph to maximize your chances of spotting animals. Although there is a temptation to head for the most isolated dirt tracks and to neglect the tarred roads, this can be mistake as cars are quieter on tarred roads and the animals living near them are more used to traffic. The run-off from tarred roads also makes the vegetation greener and attracts more animals. Driving around Kruger can be very tiring, so it's a good idea to visit one of the get-out points (marked on park maps) and to spend time game viewing at a waterhole.

Kruger shops sell a wide choice of identification guides. Their own publications, including the map, travel guide and the comprehensive *Find it* guide are an excellent introduction to the geology, history, vegetation and wildlife of Kruger.

Game drives

A guided tour with a game ranger can increase your chance of game spotting and provides a deeper understanding of the wilderness. Most camps offer guided day and night drives. Both are very popular and should be booked in advance at camp reception as soon as you arrive. A drive costs from R110 per person, depending on the camp and time of day. Night drives are an added attraction as private vehicles are not allowed outside the camps after sundown. These usually depart around 1700. Make sure you have warm clothing as temperatures drop in the evenings. The drives finish in time for guests to have an evening meal at the camp restaurant. Some camps also offer a late drive after dinner, departing at 2030 and lasting for up to three hours.

Guided walks and mountain biking

A number of camps offer two- or three-hour walks in the morning or afternoon accompanied by an armed game ranger. Groups are kept small – up to eight people – and the rangers are trained in field guiding. These provide an excellent way of getting close to smaller animals and are a thrilling way of exploring the bush. A new mountain biking guided trail is now on offer at Olifants camp, costing R315 for a morning ride.

Wilderness trails

A relatively new initiative are a series of seven wilderness trails, offering three-day guided walking safaris. Seeing the park on foot is the most exciting way to experience the wilderness, and places on the hiking trails are booked up months in advance. A maximum of eight people go on each trail and they are accompanied by an armed ranger. Hikers spend every night at the same rustic bush camp and go out on day walks. Food, water bottles, sleeping bags, rucksacks and cutlery are all provided.

The wilderness trails are run twice a week on Sunday and Wednesday and last for two days and three nights, costing R2240 per person. For reservations contact **South African National Parks** (SAN Parks) offices; bookings can be made up to a year ahead and places fill up quickly. The best time of year for hiking is from March to July when the weather is dry and daytime temperatures are cooler.

Bushman Trail This is a good area for seeing white rhino and wild dogs and the walks also visit nearby San paintings. The camp is in an area of mountain bushveld, southwest of Kruger in an isolated valley surrounded by koppies. Hikers stay in thatched bush huts. Hikers check in at Berg-en-Dal which is an hour's drive by Land Rover from the camp.

Napi Trail Passes through a variety of habitats following the banks of the Biyamiti River through thick riverine bush and crossing through mixed woodlands. This is a good area for seeing both the black and white rhinos, duiker, jackal, kudu and giraffe. Hikers check in at Pretoriuskop.

Metsi-Metsi Trail The camp is in an area of mountain bushveld near the N'waswitsontso River. The trail also visits areas of marula savannah where many plains animals are seen. Hikers check in at Skukuza.

Nyalaland Trail Passes through a vast expanse of mopane scrub, dotted with baobabs, aloes and koppies. The wildlife here is unique to this sector of the park and nyala are often seen. The birdlife here is spectacular. The hutted camp is shaded by kuduberry trees next to the Madzaringwe Stream. Hikers check in at Punda Maria.

Olifants Trail Crosses through a region of classic African plains. It is excellent for seeing large herds of buffalo, wildebeest and zebra. The hutted camp overlooks the Olifants River and is 1½ hours by Land Rover to Letaba. Hikers check in at Letaba.

Sweni Trail Southeast of Satara overlooking the Sweni River and crossing through knobthorn and marula savannah where large herds of buffalo, wildebeest and zebra can be seen. The interesting species to spot are cheetah, lion, kudu, sable and steenbok. Hikers check in at Satara.

Wolhuter Trail Passes through lowveld savannah where it is possible to see some of the rare species such as lions, cheetah, black and white rhino, roan, sable and wild dog. The trail is named after the park ranger Harry Wolhuter, who killed a lion with his knife in 1903. The bush camp has wooden huts and is near the Mlambane River. Hikers check in at Berg-en-Dal.

Driving into Mozambique

The Mozambique section of the park can now be accessed from the Giriyondo border gate, situated 45 km northeast of Letaba on the eastern boundary of Kruger Park. There is a limit of 250 cars per day and they must be 4WD vehicles, as the roads on the Mozambique side are still being developed. The border post is open from October to March 0800-1600 and April to September 0800-1500. Entry is R50 per person plus R50 per vehicle. South African passport holders do not need a visa; foreign visitors should apply for a visa before travelling if they plan on spending more than 30 days in Mozambique. Facilities on the Mozambique side remain very basic, although there have been a few new initiatives including a self-drive 4WD eco-trail, the Machampane wilderness trail (with a new luxury bush lodge) and Massingir hiking trail, for hikers willing to carry their food in and rubbish out.

Tours

Organized tours of Kruger are widely available throughout South Africa and can be booked in all major cities. The variety of tours on offer can be baffling, so it is a good idea to shop around. Prices vary according to the quality of accommodation, the length of the tour, additional destinations, and whether you travel by minibus, open air game vehicle or air-conditioned coach. There are dozens of companies offering tours; the tourist offices at Nelspruit (see page 566 and page 568) have a list of operators. See also Activities and tours, page 603.

Camps in southern Kruger

The greatest concentrations of game and most of Kruger's large camps are in southern Kruger and many visitors only ever see this section of the park. The landscape here is far more varied than the rest of the park and therefore supports a wider range of animals.

Ins and outs

The entrance gates at **Crocodile Bridge** and **Malelane** are on the southern boundary of the park and are clearly signposted from the N4 running between Nelspruit and Komatipoort. The entrance gates at Numbi, Paul Kruger and **Phabeni** are on the southwestern boundary. **Numbi Gate** is signposted off the R538 between Nelspruit and Hazyview; **Paul Kruger Gate** is on the R536 from Hazyview.

Berg-En-Dal

ⓘ *Near the entrance at Malelane Gate, T013-73561106 for last-minute reservations (maximum 48 hrs before arrival).*

This large, modern camp has a rather austere, institutional feel to it. It is set in a hilly landscape, wooded with acacias, marulas and jackalberry overlooking the Matjulu Dam. **Facilities** include a swimming pool, in-camp trail, environmental centre showing wildlife films, petrol station, camp shop, restaurant, telephones and laundrette; open to day visitors. The camp accommodates 300 guests when full and offers day walks and day and night game drives. The **cottages** (B) at this camp are slightly larger than at the other camps and sleep six to eight people. There are also three-bed **bungalows** (B)and 70 **camping** and caravan sites with ablution blocks and kitchen units.

Biyamiti

ⓘ *26 km to Crocodile Gate, 45 km to Malelane.*

This bushveld camp is in the far south of Kruger on the banks of the Mbiyamiti River set in an area of crocodile thorn thicket. The camp sleeps 70 people in 15 one- or two-bed **cottages** (B) with kitchen. Day walks and night drives can be booked at reception.

Crocodile Bridge

ⓘ *34 km to Lower Sabie, 175 km to Orpen, 125 km to Pretoriuskop, 127 km to Satara, 77 km to Skukuza, T013-7356012 for reservations (maximum 48 hrs before arrival).*

This small camp is next to the park's southern gate set in acacia woodland. There is a hippo pool on the dirt road to Malelane where elephant and other animals come to drink. The camp has 18 three-bed **self-catering chalets** (B), plus eight **safari tents** (C), and two **camping** and caravan sites, with ablution block and kitchen units. Facilities include a petrol station, camp shop, cafeteria, telephones, laundrette; open to day visitors. Night drives and game walks can be booked at reception; day drives are open to people staying outside the park.

Lower Sabie

ⓘ 113 km to Berg-en-Dal, 141 km to Orpen, 53 km to Paul Kruger Gate, 213 km to Phalaborwa, 90 km to Pretoriuskop, 342 km to Punda Maria, 93 km to Satara, 43 km to Skukuza, T013-7356056 for last-minute reservations (maximum 48 hrs before arrival). The region around Lower Sabie is part of a classic African savannah landscape, with grasslands, umbrella thorn and round leaf teak stretching off into the distance. This is one of the best regions for seeing game, particularly rhino. Game is attracted here by water at the Mlondosi and Nhlanganzwani dams and the camp overlooks the Sabie River. The accommodation here is impersonal but the camp itself is fairly peaceful. Facilities include the **Ingwe Restaurant**, a bar, shop, petrol station, laundrette, phones and swimming pool. Day walks and night drives can be booked at reception.

Accommodation is provided in large four- five- or seven-bed **cottages** (A-B) with two bathrooms and a kitchen; two- or three-bed **chalets** (B) with bathroom, fridge and hot-plate; two-bed **rondavels** (B) with bathroom and fridge; two-bed **huts** (C), with bathroom and fridge; small, two-bed **cottages** (C) with a/c, fridge, veranda, ablution block; one-bed **huts** (D) with a/c, fridge and ablution block; one-bed **safari tents** (C) with ablution block, plus **camping** and caravan sites, with ablution blocks and kitchen facilities.

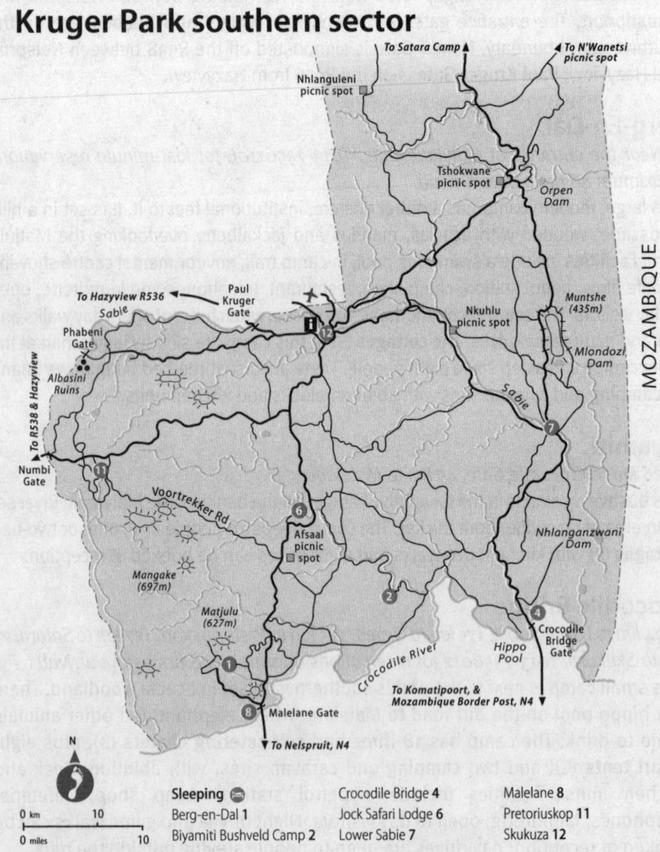

Malelane

ⓘ *Check in at Berg-en-Dal.*

Malelane is a luxury satellite camp to Berg-en-Dal, set in a rugged area of mountain bushveld on the banks of the Crocodile River on the southern boundary of the park. It has five luxury four- and five-bed **cottages** (A), with bathroom and solar-powered communal kitchen unit, plus **camping** and caravan sites with ablution block and kitchen unit.

Pretoriuskop

ⓘ *Near Numbi Gate, 92 km to Berg-en-Dal, 125 km to Crocodile Bridge, 90 km to Lower Sabie, 184 km to Orpen, 140 km to Satara, 49 km to Skukuza, T013-7355128 for last-minute reservations (maximum 48 hrs before arrival).*

This is the oldest camp in Kruger and is also the third largest, with a fairly institutional feel. The game drives around Pretoriuskop pass through marula woodland and tall grassland, with good game-viewing areas to the north along the Sabie River and to the south along the Voortrekker Road, which follows the original wagon route through the veld. Rhino are often seen close to Numbi Gate. More animals congregate in this area in the summer than in the winter but it is always a rewarding area for game. Facilities include a restaurant, cafeteria, swimming pool made out of natural rock, petrol station, shop, laundry; day walks and night drives can be booked at reception. It is also possible to join a night drive at Numbi Gate if you are staying outside the park in the Hazyview Area.

There are 142 sleeping units: six-, eight- and nine-bed guest **cottages** (B), with two bathrooms and a kitchen; four-bed **cottages** (B) with one bathroom and a kitchen; two- to four-bed **bungalows** (B) with bathroom, fridge and hot plate; two-, three-, five- and six-bed **huts** (C) with a/c, fridge and ablution block, plus 45 **camping** and caravan sites with ablution blocks and kitchen units.

Skukuza

ⓘ *72 km to Berg-en-Dal, 77 km to Crocodile Bridge, 43 km to Lower Sabie, 137 km to Orpen, 213 km to Phalaborwa, 49 km to Pretoriuskop, 342 km to Punda Maria, 93 km to Satara, T013-7354152 for last-minute reservations (maximum 48 hrs before arrival).*

Located on the south bank of the Sabie River, Skukusa is Kruger's largest camp and the administrative centre of the park. The camp has grown to such an extent that it resembles a small town and you can forget that you're surrounded by a national park. In spite of all the development, Skukusa is still at the centre of Kruger's prime game-viewing area and is a good base for game drives. The road heading northeast towards Satara has high concentrations of game and this region is said have one of the densest concentrations of lion in Africa – and the densest populations of cars in Kruger.

Facilities here cater to almost every need and include a supermarket, petrol station, car wash, restaurant, bank, post office, telephones, doctor and laundrette. There is also an open-air cinema showing wildlife videos in the evenings, a good information centre and library, and a small nursery selling indigenous plants including baobabs. Day walks and night drives can be booked at reception and there's a 9-hole golf course. **Kruger Emergency Road Services** is also based here.

Skukusa accommodates over 1000 people in four-, six- and eight-bed **cottages** (AL), with two bathrooms and kitchen; two-, three- and four-bed **cottages** (B) with one bathroom and kitchen; two-bed **chalets** (B) with one bathroom and kitchen; three-bed **chalets** (B) with bathroom, fridge and hot-plate; three-bed **bungalows** (C), with bathroom and fridge; three-bed **huts** (C) with bathroom and fridge; four-bed **safari tents** (C) with ablution block, kitchen units, plus 80 **camping** and caravan sites, ablution blocks and kitchen units.

Camps in central Kruger

The central area of Kruger is quieter than the south. There are large areas of flat mopane woodland inhabited by herds of buffalo, elephant, wildebeest and zebra. The camp at Olifants is in a spectacular location.

Ins and outs

Orpen Gate and **Phalaborwa Gate** are on the western boundary. Orpen Gate is on the R531 from Acornhoek and Phalaborwa is on the R71 route from Pietersburg and Tzaneen.

Kruger Park central sector

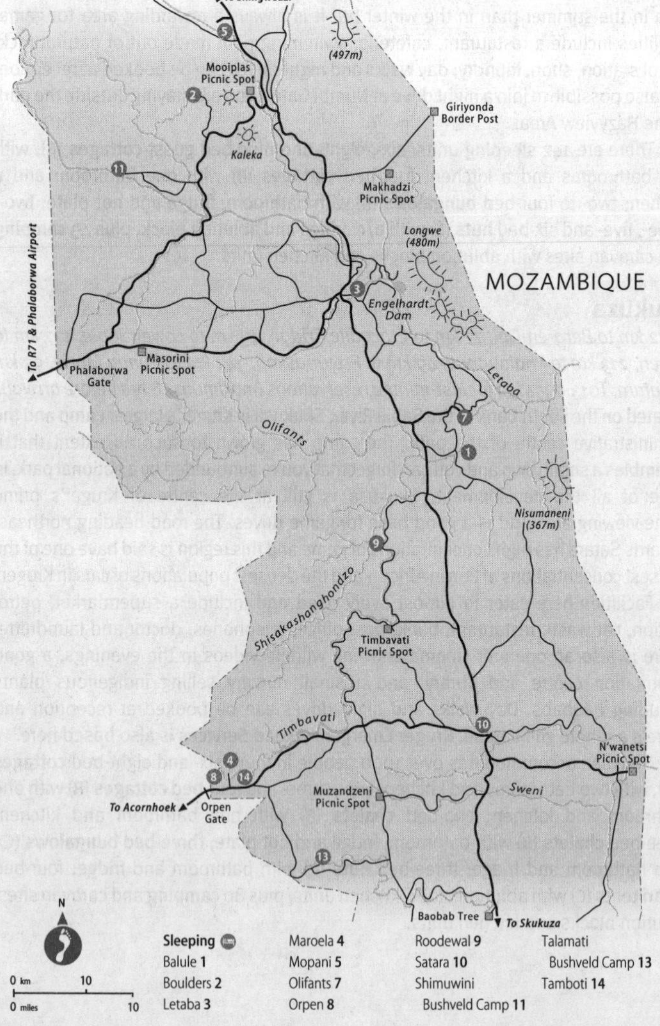

Balule

ⓘ 11 km from Olifants where visitors must check in. T013-7356306 for last-minute reservations (maximum 48 hrs before arrival).

Balule is on the banks of the Olifants River and is one of Kruger's wildest camps. It is little more than a patch of cleared bush surrounded by an electrified chain link fence; visitors can see animals wandering by only metres away. There are six three-bed **huts** (D), with an ablution block but no electricity and 15 basic caravan and **camping** sites, with ablution block and braai sites; firewood is on sale here. The only cooking facilities here are the braai sites and the smell of barbecued meat attracts hyenas who patrol the fence all night in search of scraps (but don't under any circumstances feed them).

Boulders

ⓘ 54 km to Letaba, 31 km to Mopani, 54 km to Phalaborwa Gate; check in at Mopani, the camp must be booked as a single unit.

This unfenced private camp is in an area of acacia, knobthorn and mopane woodland. The camp blends in beautifully with its environment and is set amongst massive granite boulders. The four thatched **bungalows** (C) are raised on stilts and have a veranda from which to observe the wildlife wandering through the camp. Each sleeps three people and has a communal kitchen and solar power.

Letaba

ⓘ 234 km to Berg-en-Dal, 117 km to Orpen, 51 km to Phalaborwa, 176 km to Punda Maria, 69 km to Satara, 162 km to Skukuza, T013-7356636 for last-minute reservations (maximum 48 hrs before arrival).

Letaba is one of the larger public camps in central Kruger and is a pleasant, neatly laid-out camp on the banks of the Letaba River. The restaurant is in a magnificent setting for watching the game come down to drink. Some interesting species can be seen here, most notably the large herds of elephant, but the list also includes cheetah, lion, ostrich, roan, sable, steenbok and tsessebe. There is good game viewing to the east of Letaba along the river and at Engelhardt Dam. The two hills rising in the distance to the east of the dam are Longwe, 480 m, and Mhala, 465 m. They are flanked by some beautiful round-leaf teak woodland and baobabs. Middelvlei windmill is 20 km north of Letaba on the H1-6 and provides the only source of water for miles around. Facilities include a mini supermarket, good restaurant, laundrette, petrol station, museum with exhibits on Kruger's elephants (see box, page 590) and Kruger Emergency Road Services. There is a short nature trail around the camp and day walks and night drives can be booked at reception.

Accommodation is available in six-, eight- and nine-bed **cottages** (C) with two bathrooms and kitchen; two- and three-bed **chalets** (B) with bathroom, fridge and hot plate; three-bed **bungalows** (C) with bathroom and fridge; four-bed **huts** (C) with a/c, fridge and veranda; four-bed **safari tents** (D) with ablution blocks and kitchen units, plus a large, shadeless **campsite**, with 35 camping and caravan sites with ablution blocks and kitchen units.

Maroela and Tamboti satellite camps

ⓘ Check in at Orpen Gate, 4 km.

These are both satellite camps to Orpen. Maroela large camp ground is on the south bank of the Timbavati River, and has 20 camping and caravan sites, ablution blocks and kitchen units. There are no other facilities here, but there is a shop at Orpen Gate where you check in and where you can also arrange day walks and night drives. Not far from Maroela, Tamboti is a tented camp on the banks of the Timbavati River, offering accommodation in 40 furnished safari tents for two to four people. This is the ideal spot for people looking for a complete bush experience without having to bring all the equipment. There is no restaurant or shop.

The 'Magnificent Seven'

The herds of elephant that roam around Kruger, migrating from east to west, are one of the park's biggest attractions. The population was estimated at 7500 in 1992, having grown substantially from the 986 elephants found during the aerial census of 1959.

Elephants have voracious appetites and will eat bark, fruit, leaves and roots. The damage caused by feeding elephants is easy to spot and they have played an important role in the creation of the African landscape. However, too many elephants feeding in a restricted area can cause serious damage to trees and shrubs.

The air-conditioned **Prospectors Museum** at Letaba camp in central Kruger has an amazing exhibition devoted to elephants. A small theatre shows wildlife videos and a large hall has displays related to the life cycle of the elephant.

The most impressive section of the museum, however, focuses on the 'Magnificent Seven'. These were Kruger's finest elephants who became famous for their exceptionally large tusks. The skulls and tusks are on display, accompanied by a photo of the elephant and a map showing each animal's range.

Mopani

ⓘ *281 km to Berg-en-Dal, 47 km to Letaba, 86 km to Olifants, 74 km to Phalaborwa Gate, 258 km to Punda Maria, 209 km to Skukuza, T013-7356535 for last-minute reservations (maximum 48 hrs before arrival).*

This is one of Kruger's largest public camps set on a rocky hill overlooking the Pioneer Dam. It is only a few kilometres south of the Tropic of Capricorn, set on a seemingly endless plain of mopane shrub. The accommodation at Mopani has been made from natural materials and is more pleasant and spacious than some of the older camps. Choose from an eight-bed **cottage** (B); six-bed **cottages** (B) with kitchen, or two- and three-bed **bungalows** (B) with kitchen. Facilities include swimming pool, nature trail, petrol station, shop, restaurant, bar overlooking the dam, cafeteria, laundrette; night drives can be booked at reception.

Olifants

ⓘ *219 km to Berg-en-Dal, 147 km to Lower Sabie, 102 km to Orpen, 158 km to Paul Kruger Gate, 83 km to Phalaborwa Gate, 212 km to Punda Maria, 147 km to Skukuza, T013-7356606 for last-minute reservations (maximum 48 hrs before arrival).*

This peaceful camp is in a spectacular setting high on a hill overlooking fever trees and wild figs lining the banks of the Olifants River. The game drives in the immediate area pass through flat mopane woodland in the north and a hilly area of rocks and woodland in the south where klipspringer are often seen. Olifants is one of Kruger's most attractive camps, blending into the surrounding woodland. Facilities include a restaurant, shop, information centre, wildlife films, petrol, laundrette, open to day visitors; night drives can be booked through reception. This is the only camp in Kruger offering guided mountain biking trails. A thatched veranda perched on the edge of the camp looks down into the river valley and is a superb place for game viewing. The thatched accommodation, shaded by large old sycamores and sausage trees, encompasses eight-bed **cottages** (B); four-bed **cottages** (B) with kitchen; two-bed **chalets** (B) with kitchen or bathroom, fridge and hot plate and three- or two-bed **bungalows** (B) with bathroom and fridge.

Orpen

ⓘ *Just beyond Orpen Gate, T013-7356355 for last-minute reservations (maximum 48 hrs before arrival).*

Orpen is a small camp just past the entrance gate on the western central plains, set amongst acacias, marulas and aloes. The road passing along the Timbavati River offers a chance of seeing game and the area around the camp is known as a good place to see leopard, lion and cheetah. There are six-bed **cottages** (B) with bathroom and three-bed **huts** (D) with ablution block. A communal cooking area is available for all the accommodation. Facilities include a petrol station, camp shop, and day walks and night drives can be booked at reception.

Satara

ⓘ *15 km from Berg-en-Dal, 127 km from Crocodile Bridge, 69 km from Letaba, 93 km from Lower Sabie, 48 km from Orpen, 104 km from Paul Kruger Gate, 140 km from Pretoriuskop, 245 km from Punda Maria, 93 km from Skukuza, T013-7356306 for reservations (maximum 48 hrs before arrival).*

Satara, Kruger's second-largest camp looks rather like a motorway service station in the middle of the bush, although the institutional atmosphere of the accommodation is softened by its trees and lawns. Satara is set in the flat grasslands of the eastern region, which attract large herds of wildebeest, buffalo, kudu, impala, zebra and elephant. There is good game viewing on the road to Orpen.

Accommodation is available in guest **cottages** (A-B) sleeping six, eight or nine, with one or two bathrooms and kitchen; two- or three-bed **bungalows** (B) with bathroom, fridge and hot plate; and on 74 **camping** and caravan sites, with ablution blocks, kitchen units. Facilities include petrol station, car wash, Kruger Emergency Road Service, camp shop, cafeteria, restaurant, laundry, day walks and night drives can be booked at reception.

Shimuwini

ⓘ *66 km to Letaba, 118 km to Olifants, 52 km to Phalaborwa*

This bushveld camp is set in a region of bushwillow and mopane woodland, with less of a concentration of wildlife, compared to the south of Kruger. However, this is still an interesting wilderness area with a good variety of wildlife. The private access road leading to Shimuwini follows the Letaba River where elephant can sometimes be seen bathing and the riverine forest around the camp is good for birdwatching.

The camp overlooks the Shimuwini Dam. Visitors to the camp have private access to the dam which is surrounded by giant sycamore trees. There is a hide here from which to see crocodiles, hippo, waterbuck and waterbirds. The camp consists of a row of four- and six-bed thatched **cottages** (B) with kitchen and veranda, shaded by appleleaf trees and acacias. The camp can accommodate up to 70 visitors and offers day and night game drives.

Talamati

ⓘ *30 km to Orpen Gate.*

This rustic bushveld camp is set on the banks of the Nwaswitsonto River which is normally dry. The grassland and acacia woodland along the western boundary attract kudu, giraffe, sable and white rhino. Klipspringer can be seen on the rocky outcrops. There are two hides in the camp for game viewing and birdwatching. The camp accommodates 80 visitors in two-, four- and six-bed **cottages** (B), with bathroom and kitchen, and offers day and night game drives.

Camps in northern Kruger

This is a dry and remote region that is rarely visited by tourists. As there is no year-round water supply, there isn't the same density of animals as in the south of Kruger, but the area does support animals unique to this part of Kruger, including Sharpe's grysbok, tsessebe, sable and nyala.

The **Luvuvhu River** offers some of the best wildlife viewing in the area. The river banks are lined with ironwood, ebony and sycamore fig – huge pythons thrive in the thick forests, and some of the largest crocodiles in Kruger can be seen in the Luvuvhu River. The bridge over the Luvuvhu is an excellent spot for birdwatchers after heavy rains. Many birds are attracted to the fruit trees, and some of the more unusual species which can be seen here are the Cape parrot, Basra reed warbler, tropical boubou and

Kruger Park northern sector

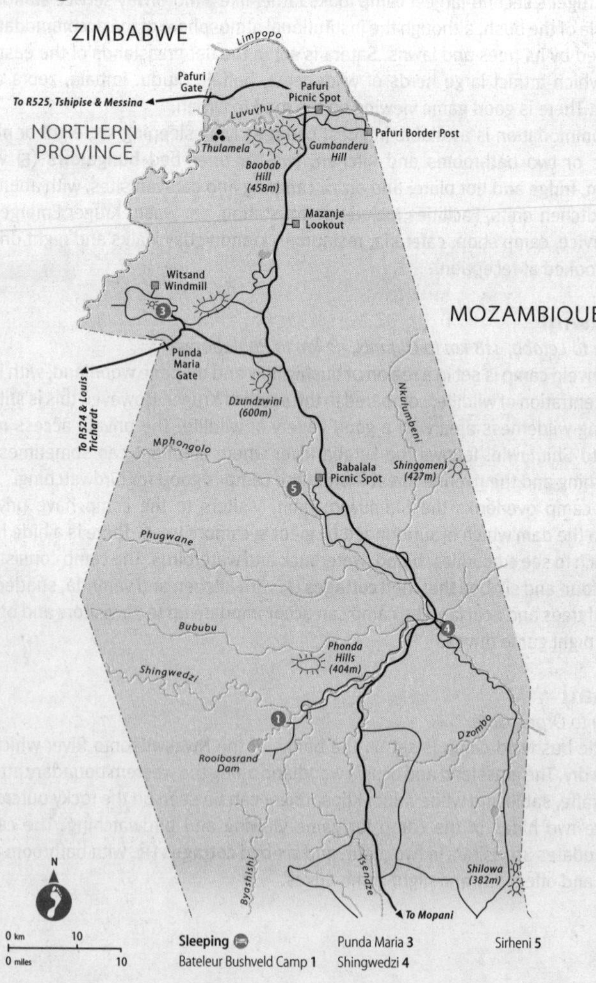

yellowbellied sunbird. There are also two interesting raptors here, Ayre's eagle and Dickinson's kestrel. A good location is the picnic site at Mooiplaas between Letaba and Shingwedzi, which overlooks a waterhole on the Tsende River where game can be seen.

Close to the Luvuvhu River, in the northern corner of Kruger Park, is the late Iron Age site of **Thulamela**. This is an important archaeological site that has forced people to reconsider their understanding and interpretation of the local regional history. Sidney Miller was responsible for the excavation project, which was sponsored by the Gold Fields Foundation. Aside from clearing all the vegetation and collecting items such as spearheads, pots, beads, bracelets and harpoons, the team embarked upon an ambitious project of rebuilding some of the stone walls, which had originally been built over 400 years ago. The whole site lies on the top of a sub-plateau which is reached after a steep 25-minute climb. It is estimated that more than 1500 people lived here. The stone enclosure was a royal palace, which, during its heyday in the Khami period, was an important commercial centre of a powerful agro-pastoral kingdom. Evidence collected at Thulamela points towards a thriving metal-working community producing spearheads and hoe blades in iron, as well as more delicate items from copper and gold. Guided walking tours to Thulamela depart from the Pafuri picnic spot twice daily. Bookings can be made at Sirheni, Shingwedzi, Punda Maria and Pafuri Gates.

To the east, **Gumbandevu Hill** used to be a traditional centre for rain makers, where offerings of livestock and snuff were given in return for rain. The sounds of a goat being sacrificed at the base of the hill helped to summon the spirits that made rain. The hill is still thought to be haunted and is always greener than the surrounding area.

Ins and outs

Punda Maria Gate and **Pafuri Gate** are in the far north of the park. Punda Maria Gate is on the R524 and can be reached from Louis Trichardt. Pafuri Gate is in the far north and can be reached on the R525 from Venda.

Bateleur

ⓘ *37 km to Shingwedzi, T013-7356843 for last-minute reservations (maximum 48 hrs before arrival).*

Bateleur is an isolated bushveld camp surrounded by a vast area of mopane and acacia woodland with the Phonda Hills (400 m) lying to the north. Visitors to the camp have exclusive access to the two nearby dams, Rooibosrand and Silverfish, both of which are good areas for game watching, especially for sable and nyala. There is a viewing platform nearby overlooking a waterhole which is best seen after the rains. The camp is solar powered and accommodates up to 34 visitors in four- and six-bed **cottages** (B) with kitchens. Day and night game drives are available.

Shingwedzi

This is the most northerly large camp in the national park. Brick units are arranged in a large circle, looking in on an open area, which has no grass, just a shady area of short mopane trees. The best game viewing in this area is around Kanniedood Dam and the riverine forest along the banks of the Shingwedzi. Many animals from the surrounding areas come here for water. There is a bird hide south of the camp on the S134 overlooking the river.

Accommodation comprises one four-bed **cottage** (A-B) with kitchen; two-bed **chalets** (B-C) with bathroom and fridge or kitchen; two-bed **bungalows** (C) with bathroom and fridge; three-bed **huts** (D), with fridge, veranda, ablution blocks and kitchen facilities.

Punda Maria was named after the zebra that Captain JJ Coetzer saw when he first arrived here; he mistakenly believed 'punda maria' to be the Swahili word for zebra. In fact, it's 'punda milia', but the first name has stuck.

 Facilities include a restaurant, cafeteria, shop, petrol, information centre, swimming pool and laundrette. Night drives and guided walks can be booked at reception. The restaurant has a pleasant outside terrace where one can sit during the day and look out over the Shingwedzi River. The **campsite** is well away from the cottages and chalets. It has plenty of space, but there is limited shade and virtually no grass.

Punda Maria

ⓘ 8 km from the Punda Maria Gate, 415 km from Berg-en-Dal, 176 km from Letaba, 130 km from Mopani, 201 km from Phalaborwa Gate, 71 km from Shingwedzi, 342 km from Skukuza, T013-7356873 for last-minute reservations (maximum 48 hrs before arrival).
This peaceful camp, hidden by dense woodland, is the northernmost large public camp in Kruger and by far the most pleasant. It is situated in a unique area of sandveld dotted with baobabs, white seringa and pod mahogany. There are spectacular views of the surrounding landscapes from the top of Dzundzwini (600 m) and good game viewing near the camp on the Mahonie Loop and up by the Witsand windmill. Look out for nyala and kudu. The game drive north to Pafuri passes through mopane shrubveld inhabited by roan, sable and tsessebe. The bridge over the Luvuvhu River is a top place for birdwatchers, where many species of bird are attracted to the fruit trees along the banks of the river. This is the only area in the park where you can see and enjoy Mopani Forest. The short Paradise Flycatcher nature trail loops around the camp.

Accommodation is available in four-bed **cottages** (B) with kitchen; two-bed **chalets** (B) with kitchen – some of the chalets date from the 1930s but are still adequately comfortable; two-bed **bungalows** (B) with bathroom, fridge, ablution block and communal kitchen, plus a camping and caravan park, with ablution block, braai sites and communal kitchen. Note that this is a small camp and is often fully booked at weekends. Facilities include restaurant, bar, shop and petrol. The food in the restaurant is better than other camps, but meals must be ordered in advance.

Sirheni

ⓘ 28 km to Shingwezi, 48 km to Punda Maria, T013-7356860 for reservations (maximum 48 hrs before arrival).
This is a bushveld camp overlooking Sirheni Dam, surrounded by mopane and acacia woodlands. This region is better known for birdwatching than game viewing and, although game is present, it is not found in the same concentrations as in southern Kruger. The road approaching the camp from the south on the S66 passes through the alluvial plains and riverine forest of the Mphongolo River, inhabited by leopard, nyala and waterbuck. It is signposted off the H1-7. The camp accommodates up to 80 visitors in four- and five-bed **cottages** (C) with kitchen, and offers day and night bush drives.

Private game reserves » pp599-603.

The reserves fringing the western border of Kruger offer some of the most exclusive game viewing in the world. Here you have the chance of seeing the Big Five and exploring the natural environment of Kruger from the comfort of a private 4WD, with the promise of luxury accommodation and superb cuisine at the end of your game drive. Each lodge has its own secluded setting, providing an enjoyable 'in the wild' experience. But the biggest advantage of staying in the private reserves are the excellent game guides, who provide a fantastic introduction to the bush – usually with far better game-spotting skills, too, which means you'll see much more than if you were self-driving.

Ins and outs

Access to the lodges is straightforward. Guests are collected from either **Phalaborwa Airport**, **Eastgate Airport** at Marulaneng/Hoedspruit, or **Kruger Mpumalanga International Airport** near Nelspruit (scheduled flights or charter flights are usually included in packages) and driven by safari vehicle to the lodge. Alternatively, a charter by light aircraft will take you directly to those lodges that have a private airstrip, or you can drive yourself – it takes around six hours from Johannesburg.

Reserves

There are now numerous private reserves, each holding countless game lodges. The best-known private reserves include **Klaserie**, **Timbavati**, **Thornybush**, **Mala Mala**, and **Sabi Sabi**, which together form the largest private game area in the world. The first three are in Limpopo, but are included here together with the Mpumalanga reserves. Within these reserves are several smaller reserves, which have been incorporated into a single wilderness area; some still retain their original name which can be a bit confusing. For example, Idube Game Reserve and Londolozi Game Reserve are now both part of the much larger Sabi Sand Game Reserve. In the last decade, the fences between all these reserves have been removed, including, most significantly, the western Kruger National Park fence. This development has helped, in part, to restore natural east-west migration routes and has created the **Greater Kruger National Park**. Despite a confusing range of names for reserves and camps, they all now fall into this greater area.

Game viewing

Game viewing is, of course, the main activity in all the lodges. Days normally begin with an early-morning game drive, returning in mid- to late-morning for breakfast. Guests can then either choose to go on a game walk or relax by the pool before lunch. When the worst of the day's heat has passed, the vehicles set off on an other game drive, returning for dinner. Optional night drives are usually also available.

Game viewing can vary from lodge to lodge, depending on how many vehicles patrol an area and, of course, how much effort the rangers put into showing visitors around. Nevertheless, game viewing is always dependent on luck, and staying in a five-star private game lodge does not mean that you will be guaranteed better animal sightings than if you were travelling around Kruger in a hire car and staying in a SAN Parks campsite. The benefits, however, are that you will have a personal and knowledgeable guide, and you're unlikely to come across many other tourists.

Lodges

Most guests spend between two and three days at a lodge to get the most out of game viewing. Prices vary considerably, and can range from fairly expensive, old-fashioned lodges, to full-on luxury living, with extravagant accommodation, sumptuous cuisine and a variety of extras such as butler service. Most lodges are fairly luxurious, however, and in between outings you can appreciate the full extent of your surroundings: most camps have platforms overlooking a waterhole or a river, there are usually comfortable lounge areas, libraries of books and magazines about wildlife, and most lodges have swimming pools. Recent additions to some camps include gyms, spas and conference facilities.

Special deals are often available, and it is worth looking out for fly-drive packages and discounts out of peak season. The daily cost of staying at a lodge can vary from R2000 to R8000 for two people sharing, though rates can soar to over R25,000; prices include all meals, game walks and game drives. Reservations should be made well in advance because, despite high prices, the most popular lodges get fully booked very quickly.

Luxury bush camps & safari lodges

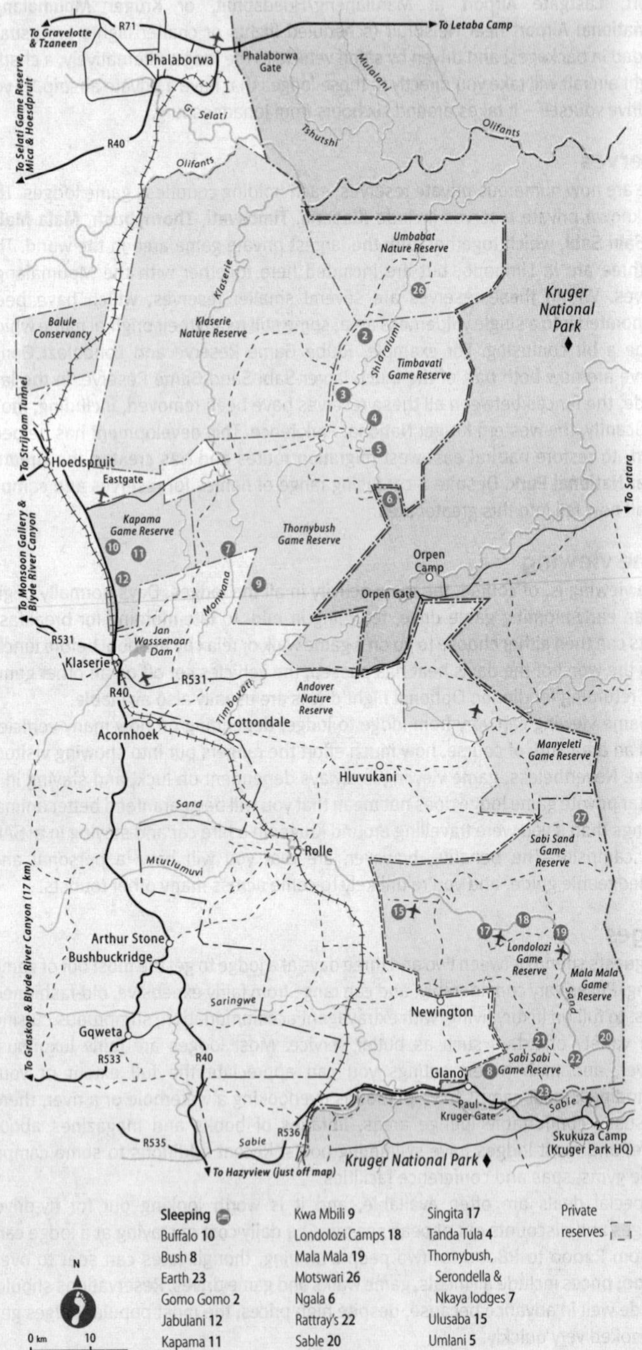

The Olifant hermit

In the early years of the park the region was a massive wilderness which attracted hermits. During the 1940s a hermit lived naked by the Olifants River for five years. He made his home in enlarged aardvark holes and lived off fruit and game. The park authorities left him in peace, partly because there were not enough people to catch him – he could run and hide too well through the bush – and partly because he wasn't causing any trouble.

However, he was eventually caught, after he began stealing equipment from the rangers. A group of them tracked him to his shelter and surprised him late one night while he was sleeping next to his fire. The hermit escaped but the rangers recovered the knives, pots and pans that he had stolen.

Finally, an anti-poaching patrol caught up with him after surprising him on the banks of the Olifants River. He stumbled whilst trying to escape and the rangers grabbed him and tied him up. He was prosecuted for poaching and committed to a lunatic asylum.

There are far too many lodges to list in full, but below is a selection – be sure to shop around while choosing where to stay. Most reserves have good websites.

Timbavati Game Reserve

Timbavati extends from Orpen to the region just south of the Olifants River. As well as large herds of elephant, giraffe, blue wildebeest, zebra and impala, this area is known for its white lions, although these have largely become assimilated in to the larger lion population. Open savannah, riverine forest, acacia, marula and mopane woodlands support a tremendous variety of wildlife including 350 species of bird. The reserve was created in the 1950s from a group of privately owned farms where hunting was banned. Game, such as cheetah, sable and white rhino, was reintroduced to re-establish populations which were originally present in this area. There are a number of luxury lodges and camps dotted about the reserve. You can get to the lodges in the northern part of the reserve via the turning 7 km south of Marulaneng /Hoedspruit off the R40. The nearest airport is **Eastgate**, although many of the lodges have private airstrips. Camps in the southern areas are accessed by the turning 9 km north of Klaserie at Kapama, off the R40.

Kapama Private Game Reserve

Kapama Private Game Reserve is one with the easiest to access as it's right next to **Eastgate** airport near Marulaneng/Hoedspruit in Limpopo Province. The reserve covers approximately 13,000 ha of prime big game territory, with five luxury lodges within its borders. A highlight here are the elephant-back safaris offered at **Camp Jabulani**, the first operation of its kind in South Africa following a successful programme at Victoria Falls in Zimbabwe. Twelve fully trained African elephants arrived at Kapama in early 2002, after being relocated from Zimbabwe. Guests are seated on canvas-covered saddles positioned behind an experienced elephant handler. From this vantage point, you are able to view game from a close proximity as the elephants move silently and in a single file through the bush. The reserve also offers game drives, clay pigeon shooting, bush walks, birdwatching from a bird hide on the banks of a large dam, sundowner cruises, traditional dancing, hot air ballooning and quad biking. All the activities are exclusively for the guests at the luxury lodges within the reserve.

The railway lions

The entrance gate to Sabi Sand at Newington used to be the site of a layby on the Selati railway line, and the graves of the construction workers who died of malaria or were killed by wild animals can still be seen here. This area is known for its lions. When the railway was still running, the threat to passengers waiting for trains was so serious for that they were provided with ladders by the railway company so that they could climb to safety in the trees, where the lions couldn't reach them.

Thornybush Nature Reserve

Thornybush started life as a private farm sharing a border with Timbavati. It was converted into a private game reserve of 11,500 ha and is now part of the Greater Kruger National Park. There are five game lodges here. The main entrance is 9 km north of Klaserie off the R40; look out for the signs for Kapama and the Hoedspruit Cheetah project. The nearest airport is **Eastgate** at Marulaneng/Hoedspruit.

Mala Mala Game Reserve

Mala Mala was one of the first private reserves to identify and cater for the top end of the luxury market. It has three camps, with an excellent reputation for combining luxury service and game viewing; rates for the main camp start at over R5000 per person. Guests have exclusive access to over 50 km of riverfront along the Sand river, offering some of the best game viewing in South Africa thanks to the fact that this is a perennial river. Seeing the Big Five is a central part of the Mala Mala experience and guests get a certificate to authenticate their sightings.

The camps in the south of the reserve are approached from the R536, the Hazyview to Skukuza road. For the lodges to the north, turn off the R40 about 15 km north of Hazyview. It is at least a further 50 km to the accommodation.

Sabi Sabi Game Reserve

Sabi Sabi Private Game Reserve is a relatively small area of land in the extreme south of the block of contiguous reserves which stretch all the way from the Olifants River to the Sabie River. To get there, follow the R536 from Hazyview to Skukuza, turn off at Glano. Although it is now part of the Greater Kruger National Park, the collection of private lodges and camps in Sabi Sabi couldn't be more different than the Skukuza camp across the Sabie River. Sabi Sabi has an excellent reputation by virtue of being the only private reserve on the perennial Sabie River. It is also home to some of the most fashionable lodges.

Sabi Sand Game Reserve

Sabi Sand has the highest density of lodges and game-viewing vehicles and is slightly more crowded than Timbavati or Thornybush. However, the Sand River has water all year round, which does attract large numbers of game. The reserve was established in 1934 by the owners of farms in this area but the first lodge wasn't opened to the public until 1962. The quality of the game viewing here is superior to that of Kruger and the rangers are extremely knowledgeable about the wildlife and don't just concentrate on the Big Five. Some of the most famous private concessions are within Sabi Sand, including Londolozi and Ulusaba. The game-viewing experience here is intended to give visitors a deeper understanding of the wilderness. To reach the reserve, turn off the R40 about 15 km north of Hazyview; this is the same road for Mala Mala Game Reserve. It is at least a further 50 km to the accommodation.

Timbavati Game Reserve *p597, map p596*

L3 Ngala, T011-8094300, www.ccafrica.com. Ngala is a long-running favourite amongst the area's luxury lodges. The lodge is on the Timbavati Flood Plain, a region known for its herds of elephant and prides of lion. Visitors in this part of the reserve experience 2 contrasting ecosystems; the open savannah grasslands, and the magnificent mopane woodlands. The range of habitat means that the birdlife in this area is particularly interesting and varied. The 20 a/c thatched cottages, filled with antique furnishings, and the luxury Safari Suite with its own lounge, dining area, swimming pool, and private Land Rover, are all set in an area of mopane woodland overlooking a waterhole. Meals are served on the open decking area overlooking the waterhole, or in a lantern-lit lapa area. The food here is particularly good, and the game rangers very knowledgeable. Recommended.

L2 Motswari, T011-4631990, www.motswari.co.za. One of the smaller luxury camps, located in the northern region of Timbavati, with exclusive access to a large area. Game viewing can be from a jeep, on foot or at hides overlooking waterholes. Lodge facilities include a traditional open-air eating *boma*, a spacious lounge and bar overlooking a beautiful dam, an art gallery exhibiting original wildlife art, a fully equipped conference room and a refreshing swimming pool. The lodge accommodates 30 guests in 15 luxury en suite bungalows. All bedrooms have a/c and overhead fans, with magnificent bush and river views from the beds.

L2-L1 Tanda Tula, T021-7946500, www.tandatula.co.za. Set in an area of thick acacia woodland, is not ideal country for seeing the Big Five but you will see some of the more unusual animals. This is one of the oldest lodges and with only 16 guests offers a more personal service. The accommodation consists of thatched bungalows and luxury east African safari tents furnished with wicker furniture and Victorian bathrooms. The bar on the veranda overlooks the swimming pool and a waterhole. In the evenings, weather permitting, barbecued dinners are held in the dried-up river bed in front of the camp.

L1 King's Camp, T013-7554408, www.kingscamp.com. An exclusive camp which enjoys easy access with Johannesburg via Eastgate Airport. 10 luxury en-suite, a/c thatched suites, with mini-bar and outdoor showers, lounge-dining room, bar, swimming pool, gym, game-viewing platform and deck overlooking a very active waterhole. After a night drive guests enjoy dinner in the *boma*, wine cellar, or out bush under canvas.

L1 Umlani Bush Camp, T012-3464028, www.umlani.com. Accommodates 16 guests in en suite reed and thatch rondavels lit by paraffin lamps with open-air bathrooms. This is a lowveld area where kudu, nyala, giraffe, elephant, lion and white rhino can be seen. Game drives are run during the day and in the evenings but the emphasis is on the game walks. There is a treehouse overlooking a waterhole which is good for birdwatching.

AL Gomo Gomo Game Lodge, T013-7523954, www.gomogomo.co.za. A relatively simple bush camp, one of the less expensive options around. Here the emphasis is very much on enjoying the bush and the wildlife, rather than the luxury and the food and drink. A friendly camp where guests enjoy traditional South African fare under the open sky. There are 6 thatched rondavels with en suite bathrooms and 3 luxury tents, the gardens are an interesting collection of aloes and other indigenous plants. Game drives and bush walks included.

Kapama Game Reserve *p597, map p596*

L4 Buffalo Camp, T012-3680600, www.kapama.co.za. Built on the theme of an east African safari camp of bygone days, 8 luxury canvas tents, each sleeping 2 guests, set on stilts in the upper reaches of tall trees, overlooking a seasonal river. Each tent is interconnected to other tents by wooden walkways high above a sandy river bed.

L4 Camp Jabulani, T012-4605605, www.campjabulani.com. Relatively new camp offering guests opulent accommodation and elephant-back safaris. 13 fully grown elephants are used, which were relocated from Zimbabwe following a threat to their safety during election time. 6 stylish suites, with private decks and splash pools, butler service, open showers.

L4 **Kapama Lodge**, T012-3680600, www.kapama.co.za, 20 luxurious thatched chalets set in indigenous gardens. Winding timber walkways link the reception area, conference room, lounge, library and dining room. The tea deck is a relaxing venue for watching an abundance of birds in the balmy evening, while the lounge offers a warm, cosy welcome on cool winter evenings.

Thornybush Nature Reserve *p598, map p596*

The first 3 lodges listed below are all part of the same company and are very close to each other. Refer to **Thornybush Lodge** on the map. Reservations: T011-8837918, www.thornybush.co.za.

L2 **Nkaya Lodge**. Similar to Serondela (below), but slightly less expensive. The camp has 4 a/c suites which can be converted into singles if need be, each of the thatched chalets have been built well apart to ensure privacy, the central lounge area has a large fireplace sunken into the floor and a high roof, dinners are eaten in a reed *boma* under the stars.

L2 **Serondella Lodge**. A delightful small lodge with just 4 a/c suites connected by wooden walkways which meet up at the **Eagle's Nest** restaurant. The lounge is at the centre of the camp where elephant, rhino and antelope can be seen visiting the waterhole and there is a secluded hide for birdwatching and game viewing.

L2 **Thornybush Game Lodge**. The largest lodge in the reserve but you can still enjoy a relaxing and private time in the bush here. The lodge has 16 a/c rooms with en suite bathrooms, the bar and the *boma* are a popular feature beside the Monwana River. Discuss with the camp rangers how you would most like to enjoy your game viewing; night drives, bush walks and morning drives are all possible, and there is a swimming pool.

L1 **Kwa Mbili Game Lodge**, T015-7932773, www.kwambili.com. A pleasant small lodge that offers comparatively cheap accommodation for the region. Game drives in open vehicles or bush walks are on offer, all in the company of experienced game rangers and trackers. The lodge has choice of thatched chalets or safari tents, all with en suite bathrooms, simple decor. Meals are served around a camp fire or on the open veranda where there is also a bar and a lounge area, plus a swimming pool.

Mala Mala Game Reserve *p598, map p596*

There are 3 camps to choose from, each with its own character. Reservations: T011-4422267, www.malamala.com

L4 **Rattray's**. Original farmhouse dating from the 1920s when the area was a cattle ranch belonging to Harry Kirkman. Kirkman was one of Kruger's first game rangers and the house is decorated with early photos, hunting rifles and old maps of the Transvaal. Appealing colonial atmosphere, 8 luxury suites each with private veranda and plunge pool, antique furnishings, satellite TV and internet access. Swimming pool, gym, massage room.

L3 **Sable Camp**. In the southern corner of the reserve, away from the **Main Camp**, is the most intimate of the 3 camps. Just 5 luxury suites, and one 2-bedroom suite, colonial theme, beautiful setting overlooking the Sabie River. Deck and swimming pool with views, meals served outdoors. Excellent game viewing from here – the camp is very close to Kruger Park headquarters at Skukuza.

L2 **Mala Mala Main Camp**. The accommodation consists of 18 ochre coloured thatched rondavels, extremely spacious, each with a his and hers bathrooms, a/c, heating, and minibar. Lounge area is decorated with elephant tusks, hunting rifles, spears and African memorabilia. The whole camp is set in a shady wood beside the river; good meals served. Swimming pool.

Sabi Sabi Game Reserve *p598, map p596*

The 3 lodges that are part of Sabi Sabi Private Game Reserve have won multiple awards as 'Best Game Lodge in Southern Africa'. In some, rates are as high as R11,000 per person sharing per night. Reservations: T011-4833939, www.sabisabi.com.

L4+ **Earth Lodge**. Set on the banks of the Sabie River, this innovative lodge feels like an ultra-trendy boutique hotel set deep in the African bush. The design cuts into the earth, which means that the lodge is virtually invisible, with smooth stone and grass-covered roofs blending into the surroundings. Stylish decor with muted colours, natural materials, private plunge pool. Bar area made up of the roots of trees, and meals are served in an open-air *boma* cut into the ground.

L4+ Selati Lodge. The most expensive and exclusive of the 3 camps. 8 stone and thatch chalets, colonial theme, antiques and four-poster beds. The camp is lit with oil lamps at night, but electricity was recently introduced to provide ceiling fans and a/c. Meals served on deck or boma.

L4 Bush Lodge. Set amongst trees along the banks of the Msuthlu River, overlooking a waterhole. There are 20 a/c thatched chalets and 5 luxury suites, with ethnic decor, plus a swimming pool, spa, meals served in open-air boma. The main building is decorated with African art and animal trophies.

Sabi Sand Game Reserve *p598, map p596*

There are numerous lodges within the reserve. Several of the concerns who operate private lodges have more than one camp, providing you with a choice in style as well as price. The camps have been grouped under their collective names.

Londolozi

Along with Mala Mala, Londolozi is one of the best known and most exclusive luxury game lodges in the region. The highlight of a game drive here is the opportunity to see leopards. Leopards are some of the most elusive creatures but in Londolozi they are used to game viewing vehicles. There is an emphasis on finding the Big Five, but the rangers here are also willing to spend time searching for other animals. Londolozi operates 5 camps along the banks of the Sand River. All are run by **Conservation Corporation Africa**, T011-8094300, www.ccafrica.com, which works on the principles of luxury eco-friendly safaris that benefit local communities.

L4 Bateleur Camp. 8 luxurious chalets on the site of an old hunting camp built in 1926. All have private plunge pools and wooden decks, colonial decor. A focal point in the bathrooms are the capacious tubs with uninterrupted views of the surrounding bush. The camp has a well-stocked wine cellar, a library (with internet access), historical photographs of the reserve, spacious deck which incorporates an ancient ebony tree with views of the Sand River, and there is a large swimming pool.

L4 Tree Camp. One of the best game lodges in Africa. The camp consists of 6 thatched chalets each with en suite facilities and private view platforms high in the trees above the Sand River. The furniture is made from old railway sleepers of beautifully polished hardwoods giving the camp a luxurious but ethnic feel. It is set amongst the rocks in a patch of riverine forest and has a platform on stilts over the river.

L3 Founders Camp. 5 chalets and 1 suite secluded in dense riverine forest overlooking the Sand River. The a/c chalets with their wooden decks feature a personal bar and the suite has a stone-laid outdoor shower. Charming and intimate, the dining area at Founders Camp overlooks the Sand River, with a walkway leading to a thatched viewing deck where guests can relax while game and bird viewing. The boma is adjacent to the camp's swimming pool. There is a covered sitting area, with a well-stocked drinks cabinet.

L3 Pioneer Camp. Sitting on a gentle rise in the landscape with elevated views of the reserve and breathtaking river views, the camp consists of 3 suites and 3 chalets all of which are furnished in classic safari style. The suites have a fireplace, and all have a personal bar, and en suite bathrooms with baths and indoor and outdoor showers. The intimate guest area provides a unique interactive experience with the kitchen, sitting and dining areas all being open plan. The camp has a swimming pool and boma where evening meals are enjoyed under the stars.

Ulusaba

Owned by Virgin boss Sir Richard Branson, Ulusaba has 2 camps, the **Safari Lodge** and the more expensive **Rock Lodge**. Both are hugely expensive and offer game drives and bush walks. Pampering is available for guests in the Aroma Boma beauty spa. Reservations: T011-3254405, www.ulusaba.com

L4+ Rock Lodge. In an extraordinary setting on a kopje 200 m above the reserve. The views of the plains below are spectacular. Pathways lead down the rock face to a veranda from where you can see the animals coming to drink at the Ulusaba dam. The lodge has 10 spacious a/c rooms with en suite bathrooms and colourful furnishings; there is a rock pool surrounded by a sundeck, and meals are served on the deck.

L4+ **Safari Lodge**. 10 thatched chalets built on elevated wooden platforms shaded by wild fig trees. Some of them can only be reached by rope swing bridges. Each chalet has an outside shower, and there is also a rock pool above the river where guests can swim.

Singita

This private game reserve has 5 lodges that are generally regarded as some of the finest in South Africa – they have won the Condé Nast Traveller Best Hotel award for several years running. The company has also been awarded the Fair Trade in Tourism stamp. Reservations: T021-6833424, www.singita.com

L4+ **Boulders**. Impressive lodge built of curving thatch and stone moulded into the rock. Set on the banks of the Sands River. Luxurious suites, stone theme, natural decor and cool, neutral colours, beautiful views from the beds. Spa, sun deck, swimming pool, attractive lounge, meals served on deck.

L4+ **Castleton**. Stone lodge for groups of 12 or families. 6 en suite chalets, colonial decor, the main lodge has a lounge and dining area.

L4+ **Ebony**. Suites nestling in the shade of jackleberry trees on the banks of the Sand River. Stunning decor, spacious suites with a mix of antiques and splashes of vibrant colour, open-plan bathrooms, plunge pools and private decks. Super-stylish lounge area, excellent meals served outdoors on deck. Gym and beauty spa available.

L4+ **Lebombo**. A modern and stylish lodge built of glass, steel and stone. Fashionable alternative to the usual colonial or ethnic themes, the suites, linked by walkways, have sleek decks, designer furniture, infinity pool with white loungers, trendy bar area.

L4+ **Sweni**. Smallest of the lodges, with just 6 suites built on stilts. Decor is dark wood, ethnic fabrics and earthenware with splashes of bright lime. Attractive suites tucked way in the trees with views over the bush, stylish dining room with floor-to-ceiling windows.

Kruger Park concessions *p581, map p586*
Several concessions have been granted to private camps within the old boundaries of the Kruger National Park.

L4 Jock Safari Lodge, T013-7355200, www.jocksafarilodge.com. The camp is in an area of mixed woodland between Malelane and Skukuza. This used to be a national park camp and was the first to be turned over to private hands. The 12 cottages have been refurbished to the highest standard and are decorated with prints of the original illustrations from the novel, *Jock of the Bushveld*. Each has its own private viewing deck and outside showers overlooking the Mitomeni and Biyamiti rivers. Rock swimming pool. Rates include game drives, bush walks, and all meals.

Activities and tours

Tour operators

Bundu Safaris , T011-6750767, www.bundusafaris.co.za. Budget backpacker camping tours, with regular departures from Johannesburg. 4- to 8-day overland tours including Kruger; they have their own camp in the park from where is possible to go game walking.

Mozaic Travel, T011-9074511, www.mozaictravel.com. Specialist in Mozambique travel, offers tours through to the Mozambique side of the park, overnighting in a new luxury camp on the Machampane river.

Spurwing, T011-6736197, www.spurwingtourism.com. Luxury tours using 4WDs and top end lodges, Kruger and Panorama region, ex Johannesburg or Durban.

Viva Safaris, T011-4768842, www.vivasafaris.com. 3-5 day budget and camping tours, owns its own lodges with a range of accommodation, also has walking safaris and fly-ins.

Wildlife Safaris, T011-7914238, www.wildlifesaf.co.za. 3-day Kruger tours from R3250, 4-day Kruger/Panorama tours from R3920. Also 2-day Pilanesberg and Sun City tours. Knowledgeable and friendly guides, recommended.

Panorama region → *Colour map 2, grid B5.*

The road north of Nelspruit gradually climbs up into the eastern Drakensberg, generally referred to as the Panorama region. The region is dotted with small towns, popular with local tourists who come for the craft shops and restaurants, but the main reason for a visit is the spectacular Blyde River Canyon, the third largest canyon in the world. The mountains provide blessed relief from the heat on the plains of the Lowveld. Although there is no longer a centralized tourist information service, the website www.thepanorama.co.za has useful information on accommodation and restaurants in the region. *For Sleeping, Eating and other listings, see pages 611-616.*

White River → *Phone code: 013. Colour map 2, grid B5. Altitude: 800 m.*

This small country town is at the centre of a citrus fruit-growing area; fresh local produce includes macadamia nuts, pecans, cashews, avocados, lychees and mangoes. The first settlers here were Boer cattle ranchers who arrived in the 1880s, at the end of the Anglo-Boer War a settlement was created to accommodate a new farming community made up of newly demobilized soldiers. There's little in the town itself, although the Motor Museum and Orange Winery attract a fair share of South Africa tourists. **Lowveld Tourist Information** ⓘ *T013-7501073, www.lowveld.info,* has a small office on the Hazyview road, just past the bridge before town.

The **Local History and Motor Museum** ⓘ *Casterbridge Farm, 2 km from town on the Hazyview road, T013-7502196, daily 0900-1630, R20*, has small displays on local history, but more impressive is the collection of over 60 vintage cars. One of the most remarkable cars on display is a 1912 Willy's Overland, which was purchased by a Mr Brandt in 1924. Legend has it that he parked his beloved car in a room in his house and, presumably in an eccentric effort to preserve it, bricked up all the doors and the windows. Many years later, after his death, Mr Brandt's grandson unearthed the vehicle and it was restored in 1997. Also at the farm is a shopping centre.

In the heart of the Nutcracker Valley, a short distance from White River, **Rottcher Wineries** ⓘ *T013-7513884, Mon-Fri 0800-1700, Sat and Sun 0800-1500; tours 1000 and 1400*, incorporates a nuttery, macadamia nut farm and nut factory, as well as the orange winery, which produces a range of orange liquors. For children there is a riding school offering pony and horse rides each day.

Hazyview → *Phone code: 013. Colour map 2, grid B5. 58 km from Nelspruit.*

Hazyview lies on the banks of the Sabie River in the hot lowveld country on the southwestern border of Kruger, surrounded by banana plantations. The town is a convenient stop on the way to Kruger, and is only 16 km to Numbi Gate and 10 km to Phabeni Gate. There is a wide range of accommodation from caravan parks to luxury private game reserves, useful if you'd rather not stay in the park itself. Information is available from **Golden Monkey Big 5 Reservations** ⓘ *Perry's Bridge Trading Post, Main Rd, T013-7378191*, which acts as an agent for a range of tour operators in the region.

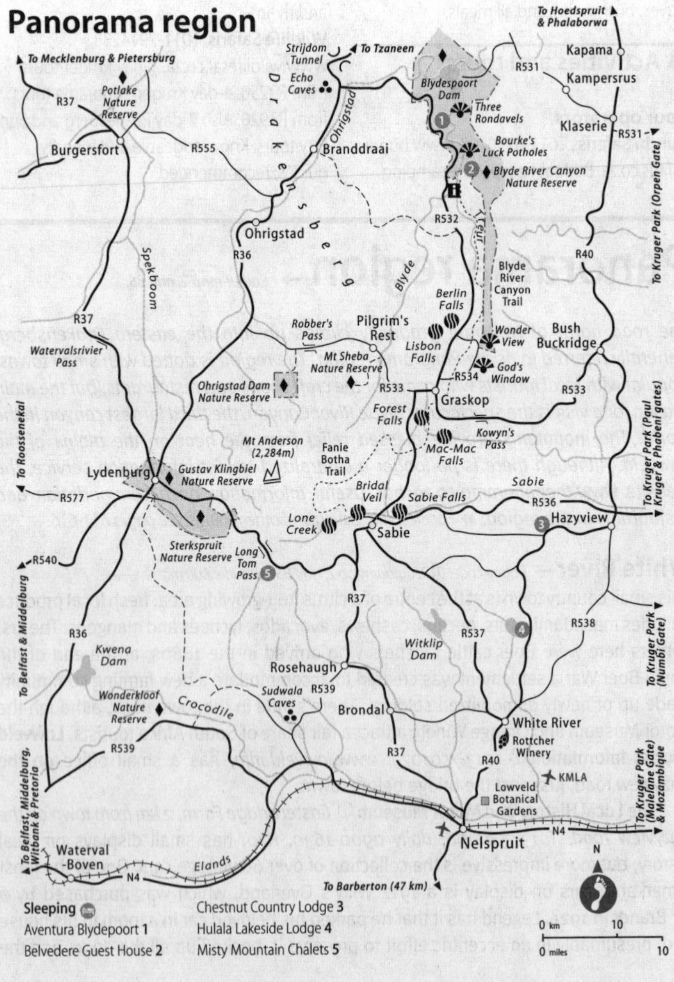

Sabie → *Phone code: 013. Colour map 2, grid B5. Altitude: 1,020 m.*

Once a gold mining town, Sabie has little left to show of its glistening age and is now a prosaic timber-processing centre. Nevertheless, it has a pretty setting, ringed by mountains, pine and eucalyptus plantations, and it attracts a fair number of visitors who flock to its main road, lined with pleasant craft and coffee shops.

Prospectors first found gold in the region during the 1870s, but it wasn't until 1895 that gold was discovered at Sabie. The land here belonged to a big game hunter named Glynn who found the gold while on a picnic at Lower Sabie Falls. Glynn and his friends began shooting at a row of empty bottles on an outcrop of rock – the bullets chipped away at the rock revealing flecks of sparkling gold. This led to an influx of fortune hunters who came and camped on the banks of the Sabie River. In the process, many indigenous forests were chopped down to meet the demand for mine props and firewood. Fortunately, the farsighted mine manager, Joseph Brook Shires, realized that manmade forests were necessary and planted the first trees in 1876. Planting continued into the next century, creating forestry jobs during the 1930s depression.

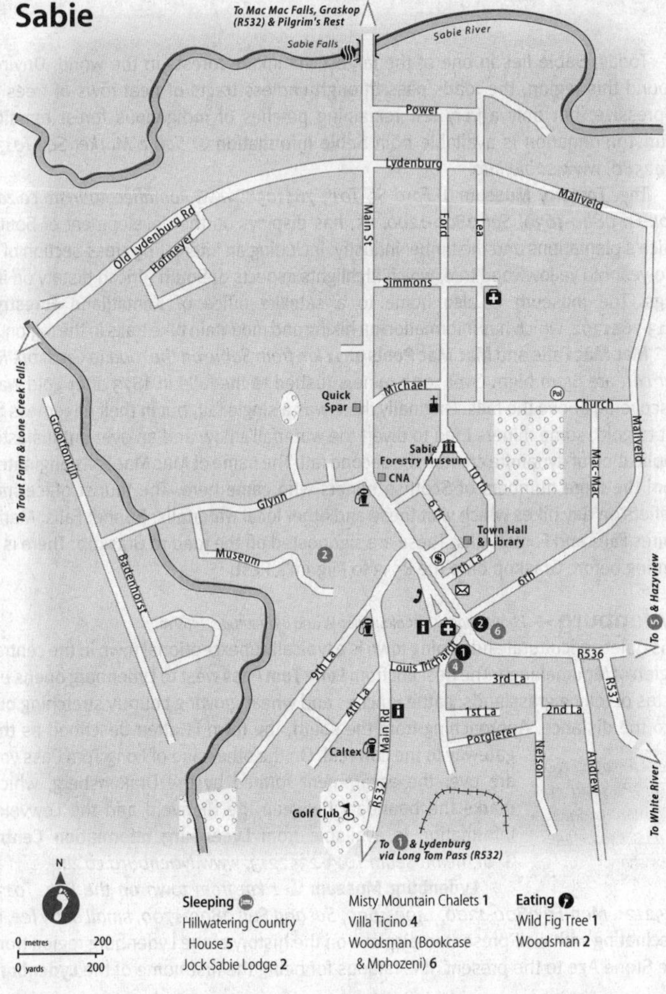

Lydenburg Heads

The Lydenburg Heads are a collection of seven clay heads that date back to AD 590. They are unique pieces in the history of South African art and some of the earliest sculptures of the human form. The clay heads have only ever been found in this region and it is thought that they may have been used in initiation ceremonies.

The heads were first discovered in 1957 by Ludwig von Bezig on a farm near Lydenburg. Ludwig was 10 years old when he found the pieces of pottery but it wasn't until five years later that he became interested in archaeology. He returned to the farm several times between 1962 and 1966, where he found the pieces of the broken heads. When they were reconstructed he had seven heads of different sizes, one of which had the snout of an animal.

The heads on display in the Lydenburg Museum are replicas of the originals, now in the South African Museum in Cape Town.

Today, Sabie lies in one of the largest manmade forests in the world. Driving around this region, the roads pass through endless tracts of neat rows of trees – impressive, but only a very few remaining patches of indigenous forest remain. Tourist information is available from **Sabie Information** ⓘ *Sabie Market Sq, T013-7642580, www.sabie.info.*

The **Forestry Museum** ⓘ *Ford St, T013-7641058, www.komatiecotourism.co.za, Mon-Fri 0800-1630, Sat 0800-1200, R5*, has displays on the development of South Africa's plantations and the timber industry, including an interesting cross-section of a 250-year-old yellowwood tree, which highlights aspects of South African history on its rings. The museum is also home to a satellite office of **Komatiland Forestry,** T013-7641392, which has information on hiking and mountain bike trails in the region.

Mac Mac Falls and **Mac Mac Pools** ⓘ *11 km from Sabie on the road to Graskop, R5 per car*, are 65 m high. Over 1000 miners rushed to the falls in 1873 after gold was discovered above the falls. Originally there was a single fall, but in their eagerness to get to gold, some miners tried to divert the waterfall's flow and an over-enthusiastic application of dynamite created the second fall. The name of Mac Mac Falls originates from the large numbers of Scottish miners who came here. The tourist office has leaflets on day hikes which visit these and other local waterfalls: Bonnet Falls, Maria Shires Falls and Forest Falls. These are signposted off the road to Graskop. There is a turning before Graskop onto the R533 to Pilgrim's Rest.

Lydenburg → *Phone code: 013. Colour map 2, grid B4. Altitude: 1469 m.*

This quiet agricultural and mining town is a typically unexceptional town in the central region of Mpumalanga. The descent from **Long Tom Pass** west to Lydenburg opens up vistas of rolling grasslands, cattle ranches and wheat-growing country stretching out into the distance. Approaching from the south, the town is often described as the gateway to the Lowveld. On the other side of Long Tom Pass you are over the escarpment formed by the Drakensberg, which marks the boundary between the Highveld and the Lowveld. Information is available from **Lydenburg Information Centre** ⓘ *at the museum T013-2352213, www.lydenburg.co.za.*

Beware of fog at the top of Long Tom Pass and, in the winter months, note that the pass is sometimes blocked by snow.

Lydenburg Museum ⓘ *1 km from town on the R37, T013-2352121, Mon-Fri 0800-1300, 1400-1600, Sat and Sun 0800-1700, small entry fee*, is fascinating with well-presented displays on the history of the Lydenburg region from the Stone Age to the present. It is famous for being the first home of the **Lydenburg**

Heads (see box, page 606), and has displays illustrating South African history before the arrival of the Voortrekkers. This is the best local museum in the region, and superior to most local history museums in the country. The museum also distils its own *mampoer* – a local brew similar to brandy or schnapps – ask for a taster.

Several short hiking trails lead from the museum into the adjoining 2200-ha **Gustav Klingbiel Nature Reserve,** where you have the opportunity to view some small antelope and a vulture's restaurant. Staff at the museum can direct you to some Iron Age sites and the remains of some early trenches from the Boer War.

Pilgrim's Rest

▸▸ *pp611-616. Colour map 2, grid B4.*

Pilgrim's Rest, a tiny mining town dating from the late 19th century, has been totally reconstructed as a living museum to preserve a fascinating part of South Africa's cultural heritage. It's a pretty spot, with a row of miners' cottages with their corrugated iron roofs and wooden walls lining the main street, nestling in a lush, leafy and utterly quiet valley. It's easy to imagine how it must have once looked, with a magistrate's court, church, local newspaper and schoolhouse. However, it's all almost too perfect, and the artificial atmosphere is exacerbated by the coach loads of tourist which pitch up throughout the day. Many of the reconstructed cottages today house gift shops and cafés, and a large craft market is held at the entrance to the village. The best time to see Pilgrim's Rest is early in the morning or in the late afternoon after the day-trippers have gone and the locals creep back onto the streets and into the bars. Although most of the buildings are strung out along one long street, the settlement has a very clear division between Uptown and Downtown, but both now attract tourists.

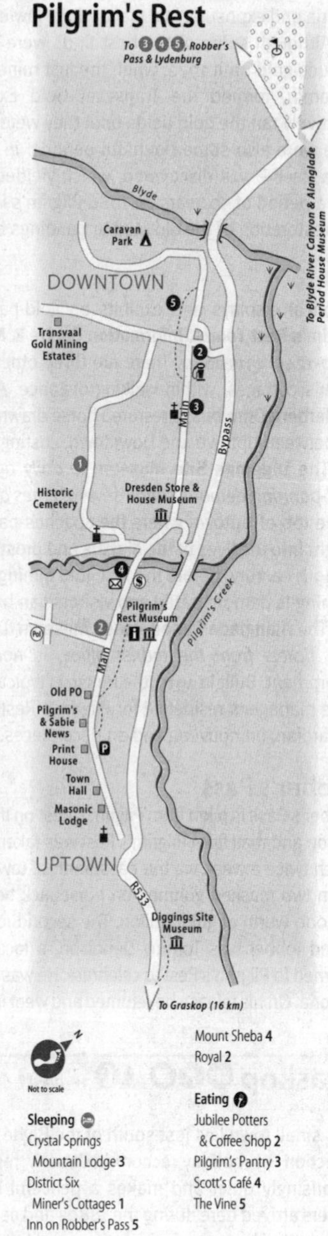

Background

The history of Pilgrim's Rest is a fascinating tale of gold fever in southern Africa during the late 19th century, as prospectors opened up new areas in search of a fortune. The town was named by one of the first prospectors,

William Trafford, because he believed that his wandering days in search of gold had finally ended and yelled out "the pilgrim is at rest!". The first gold was found by Alec 'Wheelbarrow' Patterson, in a fertile valley then known as Lone Peach Tree Creek, in September 1873. Once Trafford announced that he had also found gold, the newspapers quickly spread the word and by the end of the year more than 1500 prospectors had pitched their tents along the creek. Life was far from easy for these fortune seekers, who slept on grass mattresses in makeshift tents, often sick with malaria and exposure, in a place where lawlessness and violence was rife.

Although some of the best finds were made in 1875, the region continued to produce gold until 1972, when the last mine was closed. In 1881, a financier, David Benjamin, formed the Transvaal Gold Exploration and Land Company, which effectively ran the gold fields until they were closed. Although there were poor years there were also some bountiful periods: in the 1890s a particularly rich reef – the Theta Reef – was discovered, which yielded more than five million ounces of gold over a period of 50 years. In 1986 Pilgrim's Rest was declared a National Monument and restoration of the old mining buildings began.

Sights

Historical displays and exhibits on gold-panning techniques can be found at the **Pilgrim's Rest Tourist Information Centre & Museum** ⓘ *Main St, T013-7681060, daily 0900-1245, 1315-1630*. There are three other small village museums, housed in old miner's cottages, within walking distance. Alternatively, you can take a ride on the **Zeederberg Omnibus**, a restored horse drawn coach now pulled by a tractor that runs 1 km between Uptown and Downtown, costing R3 each way.

The **Diggings Site Museum** ⓘ *daily 0900-1245, 1345-1600, guided tour with gold-panning demonstration several times daily, R10, tickets from the tourist office*, is at the top of Uptown where the coaches park. A visit here helps visitors to gain an insight into the lives of the diggers and prospectors during the gold rush at the end of the 19th century, before the first gold mining company took control of the town. Gold panning is demonstrated and visitors can have a go themselves.

The **Alanglade Period House Museum** ⓘ *guided tours only, daily 1100 and 1400, R20, tickets from the tourist office*, is north of the village on the Mpumalanga escarpment. Built in 1915, the house is typically early 20th century and was the official mine manager's residence for Pilgrim's Rest up until 1972. Today it is furnished with Edwardian, art nouveau and art deco pieces.

Robber's Pass

Robber's Pass is 9 km from Pilgrim's Rest on the R533 and rises 650 m in only 9 km. Gold bullion and mail from Pilgrim's Rest was taken to the commercial banks in Lydenburg by coach twice a week via the pass north of town. The first major robbery took place here when two masked gunmen on horseback held up the stagecoach and made off with £10,000 worth of gold bullion. The second robbery in 1912 was not as successful. The armed robber was Tommy Dennison, a local barber, who carried out the crime and returned to Pilgrim's Rest to celebrate. He was soon arrested and spent five years in jail in Pretoria. On his release he returned and went into business at the Highwayman's Garage.

Graskop

» pp611-616. Phone code: 013. Colour map 2, grid B5.

This small town lies just south of the Blyde River Canyon, but despite having a large selection of holiday accommodation, restaurants and craft shops, it remains surprisingly quiet and makes a peaceful base from which to explore the region. Miners arrived here during the 1880s and established a camp, but modern Graskop is surrounded by forestry plantations and is an important centre of the timber industry.

Today Graskop attracts fame as being home of the South African stuffed pancake – the famous **Harrie's** restaurant started it all, and the stuffed sweet and savoury pancakes are renowned throughout the country. Local residents have capitalized on this reputation, and there is now a line of pancake houses along the main street.

Information is available in the private **information office** ⓘ *Louis Trichardt St, T013-7671377, daily 0800-1700*. Run by the chatty Brendan, who can help with a wide variety of information on the region. For accommodation bookings, visit the private **Graskop Tourism Office** ⓘ *Spar Centre, T013-7671833, www.wildaventures.co.za*.

Climate

Graskop is 1000 m higher than the Lowveld at the bottom of the escarpment and temperatures here are normally up to 8°C cooler; night-time temperatures in winter often go below 0°C and even in summer a sweater can be useful. This is also one of the wettest regions in South Africa but most of the rain falls during torrential thunderstorms in the summer months. This is the best time of year to see the waterfalls; the force of the water crashing into the pools below is spectacular.

Around Graskop

The road east goes over **Kowyn's Pass** a few kilometres from Graskop. Before descending towards the Lowveld it passes **Graskop Gorge**, where adrenaline junkies try out the **Big Swing** (see Activities and tours, page 615), and there are views looking up to **God's Window** (see page 610). This is a fruit-growing area of mangoes and lychees, which are sold at stalls on the side of the road in season.

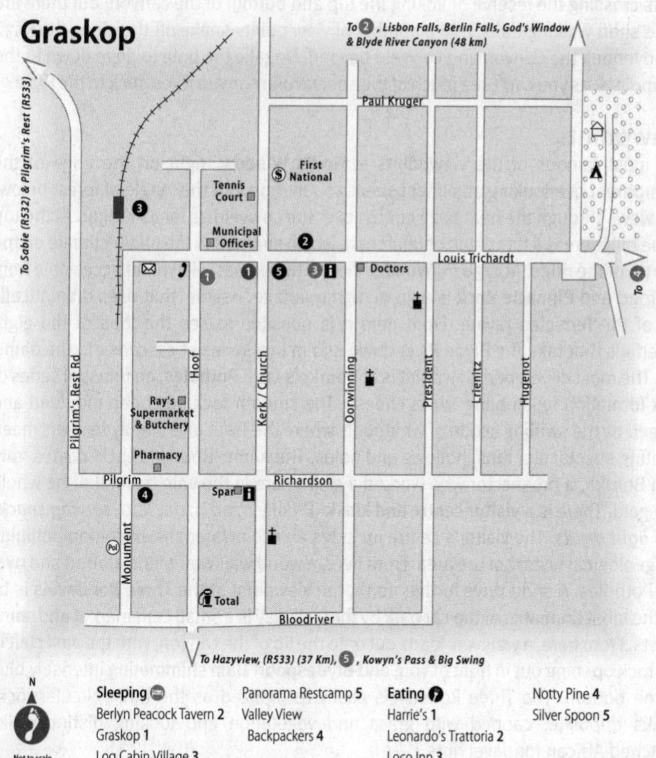

Jock of the Bushveld Trail is an 8-km circular trail starting from within **Graskop Holiday Resort**. Along the trail you will pass a magnificent 500-year-old bearded yellowwood tree as well as several eroded sandstone formations mentioned in the story of *Jock of the Bushveld*; the walk can be completed in three hours.

Berlin Falls and **Lisbon Falls** are further north on the R532 heading straight out of Graskop. Berlin Falls are 45 m high, and the water cascades into a circular pool surrounded by forest. At 92 m, Lisbon Falls are the highest in the area, and the river is separated into three streams as it plunges into the pool below.

Blyde River Canyon

» *pp611-616. Colour map 2, grid B5.*

The Blyde River Canyon is the third largest in the world after the Grand Canyon in the USA and Fish River Canyon in Namibia. It is the product of the Blyde River, which tumbles down from the Drakensberg escarpment to the Lowveld over a series of waterfalls and cascades that spill into the **Blydespoort Dam** at the bottom. Blyde means 'river of joy', and the river was so named after Hendrik Potgieter and his party returned safely from Delagoa Bay (Mozambique) in 1844. Voortrekkers, who had stayed behind at their camp, first named the river Treur River ('river of mourning'), under the mistaken impression that the party had been killed, so when Pogieter returned, they had to rename it.

The winding canyon is 26 km in length and is joined by the similarly spectacular 11 km **Ohrigstad Canyon** near Swadini. The 27,000 ha **Blyde River Canyon Nature Reserve** extends from God's Window down to the far side of the Blyde River dam. The canyon drops down 750 m, and for most of its length it is inaccessible. There are no roads crossing the reserve or linking the top and bottom of the canyon, but there are some short walking trails, and a number of view points snake off the along the R532 and overlook the Canyon and Lowveld beyond. Do take the time to drive down to the viewpoints, as you can't see much of the spectacular canyon if you stick to the R532.

Viewpoints

The most famous of the viewpoints is **God's Window**, right on the edge of the escarpment overlooking an almost sheer 300 m drop into the tangle of forest below. The views through the heat haze stretch over the Lowveld as far as Kruger. At the top of the hill there is a tiny patch of rainforest, which survives in the micro-climate on the very tip of the ridge. At 1730 m, **Wonder View** is the highest viewpoint accessible from the road and **Pinnacle Rock** is a 30 m high quartzite 'needle' that rises dramatically out of the fern-clad ravine. From here it is possible to see the tops of the eight waterfalls that take the Blyde River down 450 m in a series of cascades to the dam.

The most developed viewpoint is at **Bourke's Luck Potholes**, an unusual series of rock formation resembling Swiss cheese. The smooth rock has been moulded and formed by the swirling action of whirlpools where the Treur and the Blyde rivers meet, creating spectacular dips, hollows and holes. The name 'Bourke's Luck' comes from Tom Bourke, a prospector who worked a claim here in the vain belief that he would find gold. There is a **visitor centre and kiosk** ⓘ *daily 0700-1700, R20, serving snacks and light meals*. The visitor's centre includes an eco-awareness exhibition outlining the geological history of the area. From here, a wood walkway winds around and over the Potholes. A short drive further north, the viewpoint at the **Three Rondavels** is by far the most dramatic. At the car park by the walkway is a small craft market and some toilets. From here, a walkway leads out onto the lip of the canyon, with the vast cleft in the rock opening out in front of you, and **Blydespoort Dam** shimmering intensely blue at the bottom. The Three Rondavels easily recognized as the three circular rocky peaks opposite, capped with grass and vegetation and looking distinctly like thatched African rondavel huts.

North into Limpopo

The R532 continues north from the top of the canyon until it joins the R36 and the road descends through the **Strijdom Tunnel** and north to Marulaneng/Hoedspruit and Phalaborwa. **Echo Caves** ⓘ *T013-2380015, www.echocaves.co.za, daily 0830-1630, guided tours take 45 minutes, R30*, are on the R36 continuing south to **Ohrigstad**. The caves extend 2 km into the mountain and are known for the echoes produced when the stalactites are tapped. Many human bones have been found inside, proving that at one time they were inhabited. A tour takes 45 minutes, and there are lights and rails throughout the caves, although you might have to crawl to get to the further reaches of the caves, such as the spectacular Crystal Palace cave.

You could easily spend a few days exploring the lower section of the **Blyde River Canyon Nature Reserve** around the dam on the Limpopo side of the Strijdom Tunnel. Once you have passed through the tunnel the road quickly descends and you will immediately notice the rise in temperature. You can either continue to Marulaneng /Hoedspruit and into Kruger Park via Phalaborwa or Orpen Gates, or take the R36 to Tzaneen, where another region awaits you. At present hardly any of this area has been touched by tourism. ▸▸ *For further details, see the Limpopo chapter, pages 617-646.*

Sleeping

White River *p603*

AL Hulala Lakeside Lodge, 22 km from White River on the R40 towards Hazyview, T013-7641893, www.hulala.co.za. Situated on a peninsula in a lake that gives the feeling of being on an island, this lodge has 25 luxury suites, private lounge, fireplace, TV, secluded patios overlooking the garden or lake, fine dining in the restaurant, pool, 2 bars. Choice of canoes, rowing boats, specially adapted boats for anglers, or the nightly sundowner cruise. A romantic setting, recommended for couples. The completely secluded honeymoon suite has its own pool.

A Balcony Manor, 51 Frank Townsend St, T013-7512024, www.balcony.co.za. 2 double a/c rooms with en suite bathroom, TV, non-smoking, 2 suites, all set in a fine old double-storey house with an elegant upstairs balcony, a mix of modern fittings with antique furnishings, old fashioned and comfortable. Each room has its own unique character, mature gardens, swimming pool, very ornate.

B Greenway Woods, T013-7511094, www.greenway.co.za. 50 luxury chalets set in the beautiful countryside focussed on a championship golf course, swimming pool. Each chalet has 2 bedrooms, 2 bathrooms, open fireplace in the lounge, a popular conference venue, relatively new, needs to age a bit before developing the full character of the location. Prices depend on how many people share a chalet.

B iGwalagwala, 5 km to the south of town off the R40, T013-7501723, www.igwalagwala.co.za. 8 garden suites, each with own entrance and private terrace, simple decor with cool tiled floors, 1 self-catering unit, large swimming pool, beautiful mature gardens. Good breakfasts served.

B-C Karula, Old Plaston Rd, 1 km from town centre, T013-7512277, www.karulahotel.co.za. 44 double rooms with en suite bathroom, TV, restaurant, bar, swimming pool, tennis, billiard room, a slightly dated, old-fashioned hotel but nevertheless it is popular and has an excellent local reputation. Rates include set dinner.

Hazyview *p604*

A Hippo Hollow Country Estate, 3 km from Hazyview off the R40 en route to Paul Kruger Gate, T013-7376628, www.hippohollow.co.za. A selection of 37 semi self-catering thatched cottages with private balconies overlooking the Sabie River populated with hippos, stylish, understated decor, large bathrooms, each has a gas braai, kitchenette and kettle. Also has 26 en suite hotel rooms, good restaurant, bar, curio shop, 2 swimming pools. Watch the hippos on the lawn at night. Kruger game drives can be arranged for those without a car.

B Rissington Inn, 2 km from Hazyview on the R40 White River road, T013-7377700, www.rissington.co.za.

14 comfortable en suite cottages, some with outside showers, Victorian baths and private verandas overlooking the countryside. Neat gardens, views of the river, swimming pool. Best known for its good à la carte restaurant that is also open to non-guests, pub and outside eating on the veranda, great breakfasts and brunch, good vegetarian dishes. Also has attached internet café. Recommended.

C **Chestnut Country Lodge**, 11 km out of Hazyview off the R40 to White River and Nelspruit, T013-7378195, www.chestnutlodge.co.za. A comfortable rural retreat with 13 individually-designed double rooms with en suite facilities, simple decor, TV, each with a private patio, all set on a 48-ha farm. Evening meals available on request. Swimming pool with deck where sundowners are served, homely lounge with reference library bar. 15 mins' drive from Numbi Gate. Off-season special deals.

D **Big 5 Backpackers**, just south of Hazy view on the R40 towards White River, T083-5246615 (mob), www.big5backpackers.co.za. Dorms with thatched roof, double rooms, camping, swimming pool, laundry, comfy lounge and deck area with braai. Kruger park and Panorama tours can be organized, collection from the Baz Bus and mainline buses in Nelspruit.

D **Kruger Park Backpackers**, junction of R40 and the road leading to Numbi Gate, T013-7377224, www.krugerparkbackpackers.com. Dorms and doubles set in Zulu huts, en suite bathrooms, painted in bright tribal designs, lounge, bar, pool table, swimming pool, meals using home grown organic produce, camping available. Kruger and Drakensberg tours are organized from here. Will collect Baz Bus passengers from Nelspruit at no extra charge if you book one of their tours.

Sabie *p605, map p605*

B **Hillwatering Country House**, 50 Marula St, T013-7641421, www.hillwatering.co.za. Country house set in a beautiful garden on the outskirts of Sabie, 5 en suite rooms with private terraces and mountain views, simple, homely decor, breakfast is served outside in summer, other meals on request.

B **Misty Mountain Chalets**, 24 km from Sabie, at Long Tom Pass on the R532, T013-7643377, www.mistymountain.co.za. 23 self-catering or B&B chalets in a beautiful mountain setting, all linked to a cosy pub and restaurant, veranda with small infinity pool and stunning views, the endangered blue swallow nests on the site.

C **Villa Ticino**, Louis Trichardt St, T013-7642598, www.villaticino.co.za. German-owned guesthouse with 5 double rooms with en suite bathroom, B&B, outdated decor but comfortable, TV lounge, swimming pool, non-smoking, pleasant gardens with a superb view across the valley and forests, , central, next door to **Wild Fig Tree** restaurant.

C-D **Jock Sabie Lodge**, off Main St, T013-7642178, www.jock.co.za. 2.5 ha of attractive lawns, with wide choice of accommodation including self-catering log cabins with 2 bedrooms, 10 en suite hotel rooms, backpackers dorm sleeping 40, camping and caravan sites. Restaurant, bar, pool, wheelchair friendly, very popular with South African families.

D **The Woodsman**, next door to the restaurant and bookshop of the same name, 94 Main St, T013-7642015, www.thewoodsman.co.za. 12 suites set in an uninspiring block, but very comfortable inside with dark wood furniture, en suite bathrooms, TV, tea and coffee-making facilities. Restaurant and pub serving Greek Cypriot dishes, with pleasant deck overlooking the valley, underground parking, walking distance to restaurants and shops.

Lydenburg *p606*

D **Laske Nakke**, 2 km on the Dullstroom road, T013-2352886, hartzlcr@intekom.co.za. Self-catering chalets or budget en suite B&B rooms, camping and caravan park, 2 pools, bar, simple restaurant. Don't be put off by the sad looking concrete blocks, the good value rooms are fine inside.

Pilgrim's Rest *p607, map p607*

B **Crystal Springs Mountain Lodge**, T013-7685000, www.crystalsprings.co.za. A holiday resort high up in the hills off the R533 north of Pilgrim's Rest, large number of luxurious self-catering chalets set in 5000 ha of mountain bushveld, plus larger lodges sleeping up to 8, popular **Pointer's Rest** restaurant, bush *boma* braais, a full range of sporting activities including hiking, tennis, squash, birdwatching, health spa, gym, game drives, indoor and outdoor heated swimming pools. An all round resort in a convenient location to explore the region, rates drop considerably off-season.

B Inn on Robber's Pass, 17 km above Pilgrim's Rest on the R533 heading towards Lydenburg, T013-7681491, innonrp@global.co.za. 4 self-catering cottages plus 6 double rooms with en suite bathrooms in the converted stables, restaurant with a long gleaming wooden bar and fireplace which is put to good use during the winter, snack meals served in the pub, trout dams for fishing, excellent quiet rural retreat.

B Mount Sheba, 19 km from Pilgrim's Rest off the R533, T7681241. Set in the Mount Sheba Nature Reserve. 25 double rooms with en suite bathrooms, lounge, **Potted Owl** pub, **Chandelier** restaurant, a luxury retreat high up in the hills. Rates include dinner and breakfast. Cheaper rates in the low season.

B The Royal, Main St, Uppertown, T013-7681100, www.royal-hotel.co.za. The original Royal Hotel is over 100 years old and dates from the time of the gold rush; it has been thoroughly restored with period-style corrugated iron roof and wooden walls. 50 rooms set around courtyards, decorated with reproduction antique furniture, floral fabrics, open-plan bathrooms and claw-foot baths, very rickety brass beds. Also has rooms in cottages spread around the village. Great restaurant serving excellent traditional buffets, popular with tour groups, also has the historical **Church Bar** filled with Victorian memorabilia. Good choice in a great central location, but let down by unfriendly service.

D District Six Miners' Cottages, T013-7681211. The cottages are on the hill above Pilgrim's Rest, 7 self-catering cottages with 4 or 6 beds, the cottages were built in 1920 and are decorated in the original style with brass bedsteads and period furniture. The best value budget accommodation in the area, book in advance.

Graskop *p608, map p609*

A-B Graskop Hotel, Hoof St, T/F013-7671244, www.graskophotel.co.za. An excellent recently-renovated hotel in the centre of town, with a range of rooms at different prices, decorated with an attractive mixture of modern and African furniture (from the shop next door), contemporary feel, the 'artist's' rooms have funky splashes of colour and modern art on the walls. Great main restaurant, worth making a detour to eat here, bar with large fireplace, swimming pool in the gardens.

D Berlyn Peacock Tavern, Berlin Waterfalls, T031-7671085. A fine old house in the country with 5 double rooms with en suite bathroom and private verandas, non-smoking room, dining room, bar, comfortable lounge, swimming pool, nearby hikes and horse riding, emphasis is on peace and privacy, no young children, open for afternoon teas.

D Log Cabin Village, Louis Trichardt St, T013-7671974, www.logcabin.co.za. 8 wooden self-catering cabins with 1 or 2 bedrooms, comfortably furnished, TV, well-equipped kitchen, small private garden with swimming pool, situated on the main road right in the middle of town. Good for families, and must be booked in advance during local school holidays.

D-E Panorama Restcamp, on the road to Kowyn's Pass, T013-7671091, www.panoramarestcamp.co.za. Holiday resort overlooking the Blyde River Canyon and has a selection of basic chalets and camping sites, kiosk selling provisions, TV and pool room, amazing swimming pool perched on the edge of the escarpment.

E Valley View Backpackers, 47 De Lange St, T013-7671112, www.yebo-afrika.nl. Located on the west of the village, this relatively new backpackers offers good dorms, comfortable doubles including in self-catering rondavels and apartments, and arranges a wide range of activities in the area plus has mountain bike rentals. Kitchen, TV room with DVD player.

Blyde River Canyon *p610, map p604*

There is a wide range of accommodation around Marulaneng/Hoedspruit in Limpopo. For further details, see page 643.

B-C Belvedere Guest House, at the start of the canyon next to the old power station, T013-7681066. Private house sleeping 4-6 in comfort, outside veranda with superb views, whole house must be taken in one booking. Take a good torch, and note that access to the house is very steep.

C-D Aventura Blyde Canyon, T013-7698005, www.aventura.co.za. Huge family resort in a great setting, with 93 self-catering chalets, campsite, youth hostel, restaurant, shop selling provisions, bar, swimming pool, golf course, view points. This is a very popular family resort and gets packed during school holidays.

Eating

White River *p603*

Injabula Boma, Greenway Woods Hotel, T013-7511094. African-themed restaurant set in a luxury hotel restaurant in a lovely setting, with a price tag to match. Good range of dishes and South African wine list, but can be overrun with conference delegates.

Ten Green Bottles , Casterbridge Farm, 2 km out of town towards Hazyview, T013-7501097. Mixed menu in pleasant, atmospheric converted farm building, located in a smartly renovated series of courtyards filled with posh food shops and boutiques and an arty cinema. Good daily specials on the blackboard; try the famous Maputo sandwich – fresh Mozambique prawns and homemade bread – or local stuffed trout with avocado. Pretty outside terrace or candlelit interior.

Hazyview *p604*

Most restaurants are located in hotels.

Digby's, Perry's Bridge Trading Post, T013-7376957. Casual restaurant set in the Perry's Bridge complex, serving a mix of South African cuisine, with a large outdoor bar area and large TV for sports events.

Stuck in the Mud, 4 km on the R536 to Sabie, T013-7378122, closed Mon and Tue. Farm pub serving hearty lunch and dinner, steaks, good salads, bagel burgers. Daily happy hour draws in the locals, and the monthly curry night is very popular.

Sabie *p605, map p605*

The Wild Fig Tree, Main St, T013-7642239. Quality restaurant serving light lunches and more ambitious meals in the evening, choice of cool interior or shaded veranda. Fresh trout, guinea fowl, crocodile, warthog, and some delicious homemade desserts, good choice for vegetarians. Attached curio shop full of overpriced but good quality items.

The Woodsman, 94 Main St, T013-7642015, www.thewoodsman.co.za. Open daily, smart restaurant and bar on the outskirts of town attached to a B&B and craft centre, emphasis on Greek food and wine, but local trout and steaks also available, sit outside on the terrace for a few beers in the evening.

Lydenburg *p606*

Digger's Grill, Jocks Country Stalls, R36 towards Dullstroom, T013-2353408. A small shopping centre with a few restaurants and takeaways, including this family restaurant which serves pizza and steaks.

Pilgrim's Rest *p607, map p607*

The Inn on Robber's Pass, 17 km from Pilgrim's Rest on the R533, T013-7681491. Meals made from fresh farm produce are served in the dining room or on the open veranda overlooking the mountains. A rare opportunity for vegetarians to enjoy good imaginative dishes. Recommended. Also has overnight rooms, see above.

The Vine, Main St, Downtown, T013-7681080. Olde world pub-cum-restaurant with small **Ladies Bar**, very popular and typical of the town, filled with tour groups during the day, hearty steaks and other typical local fare such as bobotie, ostrich neck *potje*, and oxtail and samp.

Jubilee Potters & Coffee Shop, Main St, Downtown, T013-7681151. Open 0900-1900, early closing Tue. Burgers and salads along with coffee, cakes and Blyde River trout.

Pilgrim's Pantry, Main St, Downtown, T013-7681129. Local baker also acts as a coffee shop and handicraft shop. The pancakes make for a pleasant light lunch, homemade jams, mustards, and pickles.

Scott's Café, Main St, Uppertown, 0900-1800, T013-7681061. Choice of salads and hot dishes, quality country cooking making good use of local fruit and vegetables, afternoon teas with scones and fresh cream, also an art gallery.

Graskop *p608, map p609*

Leonardo's Trattoria, Louis Trichardt St, T013-7671078. Mon-Sat. Family-run Italian restaurant on the main drag, serving standard pizzas and wide selection of pasta dishes, average quality meals but one of the few places open in the evening.

Notty Pine, 3 Pilgrim St, T013-7671030. Lunch and dinner, sophisticated set-up and

smart atmosphere, try the delicious freshly grilled trout – pan-fried and filled with sautéed onions and mushrooms is the best, in winter there is a lovely central fireplace, one of the best restaurants in the area.
Harrie's, Louis Trichardt St, T013-7671273. Wide selection of pancakes, with sweet and savoury fillings including a good chicken and mushroom or spicy butternut, and a mouth-watering banana and caramel. Also serves salads and other snacks. This is the original pancake house that somehow established a countrywide reputation; consequently pancake houses have opened up all over town.
Loco Inn, in an old railway building at the station, T013-7671961. Noisy pub set-up serving steaks and grills in the 'coachman's grill'. Most locals come here for beers.
The Silver Spoon, corner of Louis Trichardt and Kerk Sts, T013-7611039. More of those pancakes, also has huge burgers, salads and famous black forest gateau, and hosts art shows. Pleasant deck overlooking the street.

Festivals and events

Pilgrim's Rest *p607, map p607*
Sep The new **World Gold Panning Champion ships** are held annually in Pilgrim's Rest, www.sagoldpanning.co.za.
Nov The **National Gold Panning Championships** are also held here each year, when the village hosts a festival lasting 4-5 days at the end of the month.

Shopping

White River *p603*
Casterbridge Farm, www.casterbridge.co.za, 2 km from White River on the R40 to Hazyview. Upmarket group of boutiques set in converted farm buildings. Railway sleeper furniture, leather goods, art, ceramics, **Ten Green Bottles** restaurant (see above), bookshop, the **Barnyard Theatre** and cinema.
Safari Junction, across the road from Casterbridge Farm, daily 0830-1800. A small shopping centre selling African handicrafts, furniture, safari clothes and books. Nursery sells bonsais grown from indigenous trees. Delicatessen sells homemade jams, cheeses, chocolates and fresh trout. The indigenous African butterfly sanctuary is worth a look.

Hazyview *p604*
Marula Market, 5 mins from Hazyview on the R535 to Graskop. Traditional market set in the Shangana Cultural Village, with a good range of curios including clay pots, wooden sculptures and contemporary metalwork.
Perry's Bridge Trading Post, Main St. This group of shops include the Trading post curio shop with some good value African crafts as well as maps, books and gifts.

Sabie *p605, map p605*
The Bookcase, Woodsman Centre, Main St. One of the best secondhand bookshops in South Africa, stuffed with collectors' items. The African section is particularly good with turn-of-the-19th-century volumes on the great explorers and once-controversial titles from the 1950s and 1960s on the rise of Apartheid. A number of books that were banned in South Africa during the Apartheid years have resurfaced in this shop.
Mphozeni, Woodsman Centre, Main St. Large selection of African arts and crafts, jewellery and fabrics.

Graskop *p608, map p609*
Africa Silks, Louis Trichardt St, T013-7671655. Fine selection of hand-woven silk products, including hand-dyed scarves, clothes, cushion covers and bedspreads. Also has outlets in Pilgrim's Rest and Hoedspruit.

Activities and tours

Panorama region *p603, map p604*
For a the most comprehensive choice of adventure activities in the Panorama region, contact **Golden Monkey Big 5 Reservations**, in Hazyview, T013-7378191, www.big5 country.com. See also page 604.

Adrenaline activities
Big Swing, Graskop Gorge, Graskop, T072-2238155, bigswing@mweb.co.za, Mon-Sat 0900-1700, weather permitting, R250. Similar to a bungee jump, but with more of an outward swing on the descent. The free fall is 68 m and lasts 3 secs. Once the bungee cord has reached its optimum length, you are lowered down into the rain forest at the bottom of the gorge, before a 10-min walk back to the top.

Horse riding

Pilgrim's Rest Stables, Pilgrim's Rest, T013-7681465, www.pilgrimsrest stables.co.za. A variety of horse-riding trips ranging from 2 hrs to a full day. There are also some self-catering bungalows on site.

Mountain biking

Increasingly popular in the forests around **Sabie**. 13 km, 22 km, and 45 km guided and self-guided trails have been marked out by the forestry department, SAFCOL, including challenging ascents and downhill runs over loose shale and eroded gullies.

Valley View Backpackers, 47 De Lange St, Graskop, T013-7671112, www.yebo-afrika.nl, rents mountain bikes for R160 for a full day.

The Bike Doc, corner of Louis Trichardt and Main Sts, Sabie, T082-8785527 (mob), bikedoc@ lantic.net. Bikes for hire, experienced guides and offers special tours to ride on game farms on request.

Whitewater rafting

The tamest rafting routes are on the lower **Blyde River** – 3 km of mild rapids – or the **Sabie River** – 3-hr trips through well-wooded banks. A day on the **Olifants River** takes you over grade II-III rapids and the odd grade IV rapid that can be avoided if you walk around. Arguably the best river action in South Africa is at the northern section of the **Blyde River**, 8 km of intense rapids with the occasional grade V, which can also be walked around. A 5-km ferry trip on the Blydepoort Dam is usually included on this day trip. For adrenaline junkies, day or multi-day trips on Blyde River and Olifants River offer a combination of exciting rapids and gentle paddles through some spectacular scenery, over-night in either riverside bush camps, local accommodation or a combination of both. Check that operators are members of the South African River Association (SARA). Tourist offices can supply further information.

Hardy Ventures, T013-7511693, www.hardy venture.com. A wide choice of whitewater rafting and canoeing trips on a choice of 3 rivers, suited to all ages and experience.

Otter's Den White Water Rafting, T015-7955488, www.ottersden.co.za. Olifants and Blyde River rafting, including overnight trips staying at their camp on the Blyde River.

Scenic flights

The Blyde River Canyon region and the Sabie Valley look even more impressive from the air. **Helicopter** trips from 15 minutes to one hour fly right into the canyon and dip down to the various waterfalls in the region, R600- 200 per person, depending on number of people. Early morning (1-hr) **balloon** rides float wherever the wind maybe going over the Sabie Valley, R2450 per person, and **microlight** flights from Hazyview take in Graskop, God's Window, and the Sabie River. Reservations and details from **Golden Monkey Big 5 Reservations** (see above).

Transport

Panorama region *p603, map p604*

White River is 20 km from **Nelspruit** on the R40. The entrance to Kruger Park at **Numbi Gate** (35 km), is signposted off the R538 heading north towards **Hazyview** (40 km); the entrance at Paul Kruger Gate is on the R536. The R40 continues north into Limpopo Province to **Acornhoek** (56 km), **Orpen Gate** (100 km), and the private game reserves on Kruger's eastern boundary. The R536 climbs up from the lowveld around Hazyview onto the edge of the Drakensberg escarpment at Sabie. **Sabie** is 34 km west of Hazyview on the R536. **Graskop** is 24 km west of Hazyview on the R535. **Lydenburg** lies 66 km from the N4 on an important route that takes traffic from the Highveld down to the Lowveld.

Directory

Hazyview *p604*

Internet Simunye Centre, T013-7377811. **Medical services** Ambulance, T10177. **Useful telephone numbers** Police, T10111.

Sabie *p605, map p605*

Medical services Hospital, T013-7641222. **Useful telephone numbers** Police, T10111.

Graskop *p608, map p609*

Banks First National Bank Kerk St, ATM outside. **Medical services** Chemist, T013-7671055, open all hours. **Police**, T10111.

Limpopo

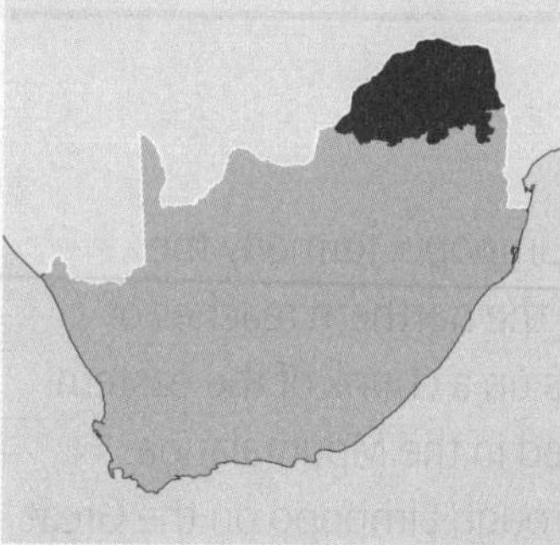

Footprint features

Introduction

Few foreign visitors see much of Limpopo, formerly the Northern Province, unless visiting the northern reaches of Kruger National Park which makes up a chunk of the eastern side of the province (and is covered in the Mpumalanga chapter). Many, however, pass through Limpopo on the Great North Road, the thoroughfare linking South Africa with the rest of the continent via its neighbours: Zimbabwe and Botswana. The importance of this route has defined development in the region but the province offers plenty more than the service stations and dusty towns dotting the highway. As well as Kruger, Limpopo has over 50 nature reserves and countless private game farms that sustain intricate African eco-systems. While much of the countryside is dry bushveld, the mountains around Makhado/Louis Trichardt and Tzaneen are green and lush, forming some of the most important agricultural districts in South Africa. The Drakensberg Escarpment is a beautiful forested area and, within the Magoebaskloof range, there are spectacular waterfalls and patches of indigenous forest, providing excellent hiking territory. Further south is a region promoted as the 'Valley of the Olifants', an area rich in wildlife and with an interesting history. To the north, the landscape opens up into dry plains dotted with tubby boabab trees, home to the fascinating Venda people, famous for their wood carvings.

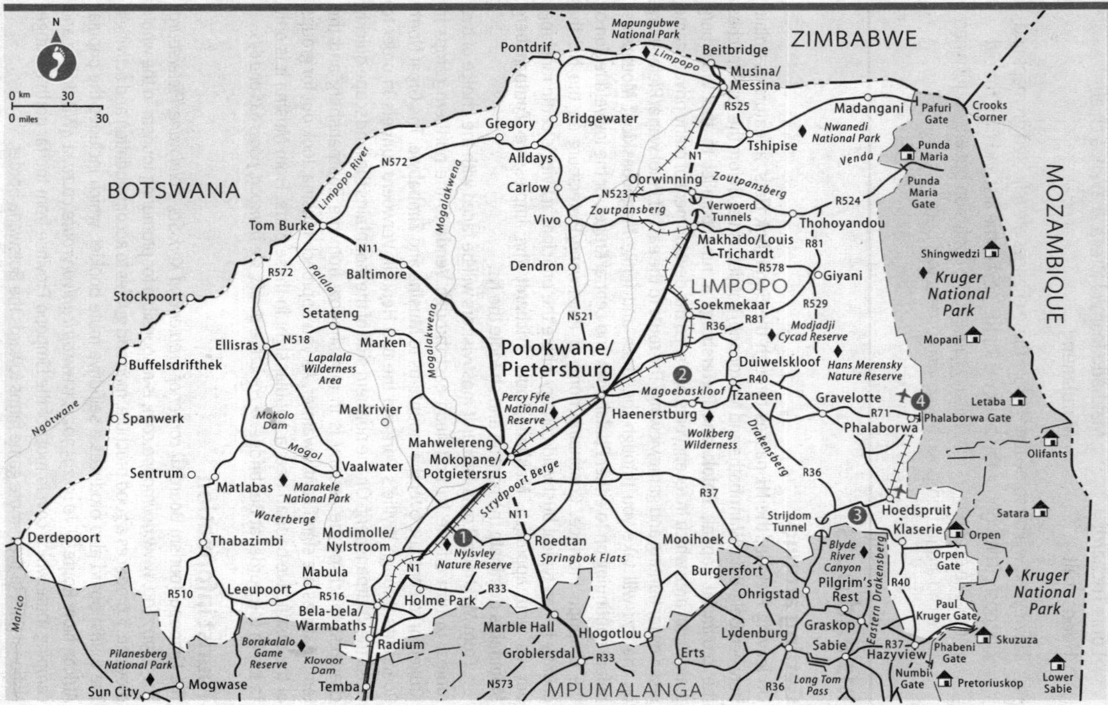

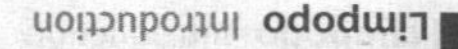

★ Don't miss...

1. **Nylsvley Nature Reserve** Go twitching at the largest and best-conserved floodplain in South Africa. It's not unheard of to see 200 species in one day, page 622.
2. **Magoebaskloof Mountains** Explore the mountains in autumn, when all the wild flowers and cherry trees are in bloom, page 637.
3. **The Trading Post** Cook your own warthog on an in-built braai at this restaurant near Hoedspruit, page 645.
4. **Golf in Phalaborwa** Have a wild round of golf on the edge of Kruger National Park, but watch out for hippos on the 17th hole, page 645.

Name change

In 2002 Northern Province was re-named Limpopo and now many of its towns and cities are also in the process of exchanging their outdated Afrikaans titles for contemporary African names as follows:

Pietersburg	**Polokwane** ('place of safety')
Messina	**Musina** ('copper')
Nylstroom	**Modimolle** ('place of spirits')
Potgietersrus	**Mokopane** (after the 1850s chief of the Tlou tribe)
Warmbaths	**Bela-bela** ('boiling place')
Louis Trichardt	**Makhado** (named after a VhaVenda chief)
Hoedspruit	**Marulaneng**

However it will be some time before these changes are reflected on maps and signposts. Throughout this book we list the new name first and then the old name. The dual names may initially cause some confusion but are useful when travelling around Limpopo as you will come across both.

Ins and outs

Getting around

On leaving Pretoria, the N1 passes through the **Springbok Flats**, a featureless plain between Bela-Bela/Warmbaths and Mokopane/Potgietersrus. Before the road reaches the provincial capital, **Polokwane/Pietersburg**, it runs parallel to the Waterberg plateau, an area which in recent years has seen the development of many private game reserves for hunting and game viewing. The route to the east of Polokwane/Pietersburg on the R71 will take you through the green and fertile **Magoebaskloof Mountains**, before continuing on to either Phalaborwa and central Kruger, or the lowveld region of the Limpopo Province. Continuing north of Polokwane/Pietersburg on the N1, the country is flat, typical bushveld country where the principal activity is cattle ranching, but as you approach **Makhado/Louis Trichardt** the impressive **Zoutpansberg Mountains** dominate the horizon and straddle the N1.

From Makhado/Louis Trichardt most visitors will be faced with the choice of two routes: to turn off the N1 and head east through **Venda** to the northern camps in Kruger; or to continue over the mountains to **Musina** and **Zimbabwe**. The Great North Road cuts through Wyllie's Port and the two Hendrik Verwoerd tunnels in order to cross the Zoutpansberg. On the northern side of the mountains the landscape quickly changes; much of the country is in rain shadow from the Zoutpansberg and the temperatures are significantly warmer. As you approach Musina, look out for groups of the distinctive baobab tree, a popular sight in these parts. From Musina it is only 12 km to the border at Beitbridge. » *For further details, see Transport, pages 635 and 645.*

Tourist information

The **Limpopo Tourism Board** ① *corner of Grobler and Kerk Sts, Polokwane/Pietersburg, T015-2907300, www.golimpopo.com*, is responsible for promoting tourism in the whole province. It produces a good brochure, map and guides to accommodation and activities. The tourist board also produces a self-drive route booklet, which includes the popular **African Ivory Route** ① *T015-2953025, www.africanivoryroute.co.za*, a 4WD driving and camping route which covers most of the Limpopo Province from the far north of Kruger National Park to the remote game farms towards the Botswana border.

Up the Great North Road

The N1, sometimes referred to as the Great North Road, is the only direct route linking South Africa with Zimbabwe and, in effect, the rest of Africa. Between Pretoria and the Zimbabwe border, the road passes through four regional centres, which are linked by bus and train. However, these towns have few local attractions, and you really need a car to explore the countryside on either side of the N1 to fully appreciate Limpopo Province. » *For Sleeping, Eating and other listings, see pages 631-636.*

Bela-Bela/Warmbaths

» *pp631-636. Phone code: 014. Colour map 2, grid B2.*

This resort town only exists because of the natural hot springs 'discovered' in the 1860s by Jan Grobler and Carl van Heerden whilst hunting in the region. (The local Tswana people called the springs *Biela bela*, 'the water that boils on its own'.) The 50°C springs bubble out of the earth at about 22,000 litres per hour and are rich in sodium chloride, calcium carbonate and are also slightly radioactive. The town is less than one hour's drive from Pretoria, and a staggering two million people visit Bela-Bela each year. The mild climate during the winter months ensures an average of 286 sunny days a year; many people retire here because of the good year-round climate. The principal springs now lie engulfed within the massive **Aventura Resort** (see Sleeping, page 631), where visitors can enrol in a variety of treatments at the spa.

Sights

There is very little of interest in town, and there's no point stopping unless you're here to take the waters. If you do stay overnight, the most popular attraction is the **Carousel Entertainment World**, 56 km from Bela-Bela on the N1 (free shuttle bus from town at weekends), a 24-hour gambling and entertainment complex on a bleak section of the highway. Otherwise, the **Thaba Kwena Crocodile Farm** ⓘ *T014-7365059, daily 0900-1600*, has over 10,000 crocs. **Bela-Bela Tourism Association** ⓘ *corner of Old Pretoria and Voortrekker Sts, Waterfront development, T014-7363694, www.belabelatourism.co.za, Mon-Fri 0800-1700; Sat and Sun 0900-1200*, is a useful municipal office that can book local accommodation. Ask here about the choice of game farms in the area, offering game drives and meals. There are also a number of shops and restaurants in the Waterfront development and a petting farm for kids.

Modimolle/Nylstroom and around

» *pp631-636. Phone code 014. Colour map 2, grid B2.*

Modimolle, meaning 'place of the spirits', is the commercial centre of the Waterberg region with a small centre shaded by jacaranda and poinciana trees. Grapes, watermelons and peaches are the principal sources of income, and stalls sell boxes of fruit at the roadside after the harvests. A grape festival is held here in January. The NTK is the largest agricultural cooperative society in the Limpopo Province, where you can see nuts being sorted and peanut butter being made.

Sights

The main attraction in the area is **Nylsvley Nature Reserve**, one of the finest birdwatching spots in South Africa. Being a quiet rural centre, Modimolle itself has little in the way of sites, although it does boast a surprising number of distinguished

The source of the Nile, I presume

The tale behind the foundation and naming of Nylstroom must rate as one of the most bizarre in South Africa. In the early 1860s a group of Voortrekkers from the vicinity of Great Marico in western Transvaal resolved to continue their journey northwards until they reached the Holy Land, which was conceived as a means of finally escaping British authority. Their route followed the southeastern edge of the Waterberg plateau until they arrived at a river in flood flowing northwards. Consulting the maps in their family bibles they concluded that the river must be part of the Nile headwaters, and so the river was named Nyl, and the presence of a nearby hill resembling a pyramid settled it. In February 1866 the village Nylstroom, 'stream of the Nile', was laid out on a farm on the southern bank of the river. In fact the river was the headwaters of the Magalakwin, which flows north into Limpopo. The 'pyramid' was an isolated hill known locally as Modimollo; coincidentally it was revered as a burial ground of local chiefs – today it appears on maps as Kranskop, 1365 m.

previous residents, including Gerhard Moerdijik, the architect that designed the Voortrekker Monument in Pretoria, and South Africa's fifth prime minister (1954-1958), JG Strijdom, who lived here while he was a member of parliament for the Waterberg constituency. His house, **Strijdom House** ⓘ *Church St, Tue-Sat 0900-1300, 1400-1700, Sun 1400-1700*, is a national monument and a museum about his life. The **Hervormde Kerk** on Calvyn Street, is also a national monument, built in 1889.

Nylsvley Nature Reserve

ⓘ *20 km out of town towards Naboomspruit. Daily 0600-1800.*

The Nyl River (see box, above) rises in the hills near Modimolle/Nylstroom and eventually spills into the Limpopo. For much of its journey, the river meanders back and forth, forming a marshy floodplain that is the largest and best conserved in South Africa. The floodplain reaches 6 km in width and extends for nearly 70 km between Middlefontein and Moordriftan. It is an important wetland ecosystem, which attracts up to 80,000 breeding birds during the rains. Consequently, this is a hugely popular birdwatching destination; it's not unheard of to see 200 of the 420 recorded species on a single day. It's home to the biggest concentration of water birds in the southern hemisphere, with species numbering just over 100, and 37 red-data species, including the critically endangered bittern. Up to 80,000 wetland birds are attracted to the area at any one time. The reserve is listed as a RAMSAR site, an internationally important habitat for waterfowl. A birdwatching festival and bird census are held here each year. Visitors are allowed to walk or ride bikes on tracks through the reserve and there are a number of bird hides, from which you may also spot eland, tsessbe, kudu, waterbuck, reedbuck, zebra, and giraffe. Even if birdwatching isn't your thing, this is a beautiful environment.

Mokopane/Potgietersrus and around

▸▸ *pp631-636. Phone code: 015. Colour map 2, grid B3.*

Mokopane is a busy centre for the surrounding agricultural area. Peanuts, cotton, wheat and oranges are major crops; the Zebediela Citrus Estate, 55 km to the southeast, is the largest citrus farms in the country and was handed back to its original owners, the Bjatladi community, in 2003. It is a modern town with few attractions, although it does have an interesting past. In 1854 the local chief, Makapan, hid in caves in the Makapan Valley with his people to escape from the Voortrekker commandos. During the siege, which lasted from 25 October to 21 November, the Boer leader Piet Potgieter was killed by the warriors of Makapan; over 1500 of the warriors and their families died from starvation during the siege. After these events, the local town changed its name from Vredenburg to Pieter Potgietersrus and, in 1935, it became Potgietersrus. In 2002 it was renamed Mokopane after the Ndebele chief.

Sights

If you do find yourself in the area with time to spare then the **Arend Dieperink Museum** ⓘ *Voortrekker Rd, T015-4912244, Mon-Fri 0800-1630, small entry fee*, is a cut above the average provincial collection. It has interesting displays on the Sotho and the early settlers of the Transvaal, as well as dinosaur fossils and a reproduction of the *Australopithecus africanus* skull found in the **Makapan's Caves**, part of an excellent palaeontological display. The **Mogalakwena Bushveld Tourism** ⓘ *Voortrekker Rd, T015-4918458, Mon-Fri 0900-1630* organized tours of the caves, which are 15 km north of the town (see page 624).

Around Mokopane/Potgietersrus

The **Game Breeding Centre** ⓘ *1 km north of town on the N1 to Polokwane/Pietersburg, T015-4914314, Mon-Fri 0800-1600, Sat and Sun 0800-1800, small entry fee*, is part of the National Zoological Gardens of Pretoria and breeds rare species such as cheetah, roan antelope, black rhino and pygmy hippos from West Africa. These are then taken to Pretoria in order to expand the national zoo's breeding programmes. It is a member of the World Zoo Organisation, which focuses on the breeding of exotic, indigenous and endangered wildlife. A network of roads run throughout the 1500-ha area of

 bushveld but dense vegetation makes game viewing difficult. At the entrance is a pleasant picnic area and small aviary. Guided tours and game drives can be organized from reception.

Fifteen kilometres northwest of Mokopane/Potgietersrus on the R518 to Marken are the **Ana Trees**, a clump of apiesdoring trees *Acacia albida* under which David Livingstone camped on one of his journeys. The biggest tree has a circumference of 6 m; they are considered a botanical rarity in this area.

Percy Fyfe Nature Reserve is an important reserve about 35 km northeast of Mokopane/Potgietersrus. Percy Fyfe was a local farmer, who in 1933 bought a few head of blesbok from the Orange Free State to try and introduce the species to the region. After he donated the farm to the state in 1954 it has been used as a sanctuary to breed threatened antelope. Roan, sable and tsessebe have all been successfully bred here and then reintroduced to parts of the Waterberg range. Addo buffalo have recently been introduced. There is a simple campsite here for overnight visitors.

Makapan's Caves

ⓘ *19 km north of Mokopane in the Makapan's Valley. Visits by guided tour only, information from Mogalakwena Bushveld Tourism Association T015-4918458.*

The caves of the Makapan's Valley are a unique archaeological site: nowhere else in the world is there such an extensive and complete record of hominid occupation. They provide a record of occupation from australopithecine times through the Stone and Iron Ages right up to the present day – over 3.3 million years.

In 1925 the first archaeological finds were made by Professor Raymond Dart. Following his discoveries, a local teacher from Pietersburg, Mr Eitzman, sent Professor Dart a collection of rocks he had found near some lime kilns close to the caves. After close examination Dart realized they had stumbled across an important site and in 1936 the caves were declared a national monument, later becoming a National Heritage Site. In total there are seven caves plus a couple of other sites all of which have yielded thousands of bones and artefacts – the Cave of Hearths, Hyaena Cave, Rainbow Cave, Historic Cave, Buffalo Cave, Ficus Cave and Peppercorn's Cave.

Polokwane/Pietersburg » pp631-636.

Phone code: 015. Colour map 2, grid B3. Altitude: 1,312 m.

The capital of Limpopo Province is a sprawling, low-rise town built on a grid system. It was founded in 1884 by Voortrekker Commandant-General Pieter Joubert as the main agricultural and industrial centre for the thinly populated province. The town is located in a shallow hollow surrounded by level grass plains, a rather dull setting, but making a practical base nevertheless. Polokwane offers alternative routes to Kruger: one via Makhado/Louis Trichardt to the northernmost entrance at Punda Maria, and the other through the beautiful Magoebaskloof to Phalaborwa.

Ins and outs

Tourist information The **Limpopo Tourism Board** ⓘ *corner of Grobler and Kerk Sts, T015-2907300, www.golimpopo.com, Mon-Fri 0800-1630*, is responsible for promoting tourism in the whole province. It has little information on the city itself, but produces a useful brochure on the province.

Climate The town enjoys a very pleasant climate; the summer temperatures are moderated by the altitude and in winter the average temperature is 20°C. Rainfall varies between 400-600 mm and falls during the summer months.

City centre

As the regional capital, the city has grown rapidly in recent years and is by far the largest centre between Pretoria and Harare in Zimbabwe. If you have spent a few days in the surrounding countryside it can come as quite a shock as you drive into the busy centre with its wide tree-lined roads, traffic jams and tall buildings.

The first stop for most visitors is likely to be the 'Irish House', home to the **Polokwane Museum** ⓘ *corner of Thabo Mbeki and Market Sts, T015-2902183, Mon-Fri 0800-1600, Sat 0900-1200, Sun 1500-1700, free.* The history of the building is as interesting as the collection it houses. The building is a prefabricated steel structure from Germany which was imported by Aug Julius Möschke after his shop had been destroyed by a fire in 1906. It is a classic example of late Victorian architecture with wrought-iron decorations topped by a fine clock tower and weather vane. During the First World War, Möschke was interned and on his return to Pietersburg he found his business to be bankrupt and was forced to sell the shop to James Albert Jones in 1920. It was Jones who named the building the Irish House and over the years it grew into a very successful local fashion shop, which imported the latest quality materials from Europe. The museum itself traces the history of the region from the Stone Age to modern times; it is a well-presented display in a spacious and airy building.

On the other side of Thabo Mbeki St from the Irish House, in the gardens which form the civic square, you will find the **Hugh Exton Photographic Museum** ⓘ *T015-2902186, Mon-Fri 0900-1530, Sat closed, Sun 1100-1300, free*, housed in the town's

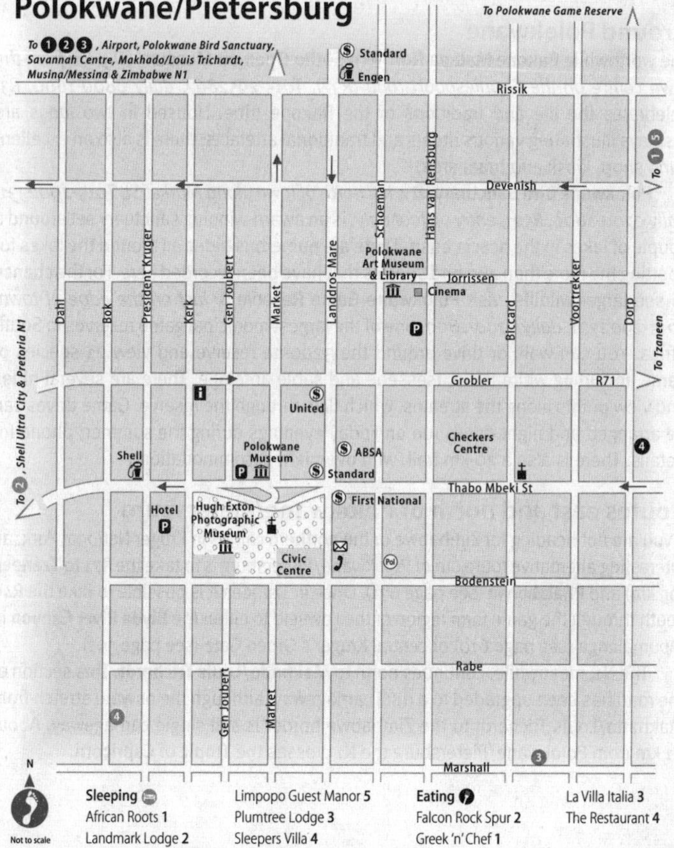

Zebra-drawn mail coach

A weekly mail-coach service between Pretoria and Pietersburg was introduced by the Zeederberg Coach Company in 1890 and was later extended north into Rhodesia (Zimbabwe). In order to deal with the problem of the tsetse fly, which causes sleeping sickness in horses, the company trained a team of zebras to pull the coaches on the eastern leg of the run through Limpopo. Although the training was fairly successful, the zebras lacked the stamina of horses and the practice was later discontinued.

first Dutch Reformed Church, dating from 1890. This is a superb collection of prints and over 23,000 glass negatives, tracing the first 50 years of Pietersburg – few towns have such a unique record of their past. Hugh Exton was a local photographer who had a studio in Pietersburg.

North of the Civic Centre on Jorrissen Street is the library, which houses the **Polokwane Art Museum** ⓘ *T015-2902177, Mon-Fri 0900-1600, Sat 0900-1200, closed Sun, free*. This has a fine collection of South African modern art and sculptures from Jacobus Botes's collection. Although lacking in funding and with poor labelling, the collection is interesting.

Around Polokwane

The worthwhile **Bakone Malapa Northern Sotho Open-air Museum** ⓘ *9 km from the town centre on the Chuniespoort road (R37), T015-2952867, daily 0800-1600, R3*, celebrates the life and traditions of the Bakone tribe. Housed in two *lapas* are displays illustrating various rituals and traditional artefacts; there is also an excellent curio shop, kiosk and braai area.

Polokwane Bird Sanctuary ⓘ *4 km north of town along Market St, T015-2902331, daily 0700-1800, R521, entry on foot only*, is an award-winning sanctuary set around a couple of lakes in the acacia bush. There are numerous hides all around the lakes for spotting the more than 280 bird species that have been recorded here. For the chance to see larger wildlife, visit **Polokwane Game Reserve** ⓘ *just on the edge of town, T015-2902331, daily 0700-1800*, one of the largest municipal game reserves in South Africa. You can walk or drive around the 3200-ha reserve and view 21 species of game, including white rhino, tsessebe and sable antelope. There are several hides and view points along the streams, which flow through the reserve. Game drives can be arranged and night drives run on Friday evenings during the summer; phone for details. There is also a 20-km trail, with overnight accommodation.

Routes east and north of Polokwane/Pietersburg

If you are not heading for Zimbabwe or the northern camps in Kruger National Park, an interesting alternative route out of Polokwane/Pietersburg is to take the R71 to **Tzaneen** (95 km) and **Phalaborwa** (see page 631). Once in Tzaneen it is possible to take the R40 south through the game farm region of the Lowveld to either the **Blyde River Canyon** in Mpumalanga (see page 610) or central Kruger's Orpen Gate (see page 591).

The N1, meanwhile, continues north to **Makhado/Louis Trichardt**. This section of the road has been upgraded to a dual carriageway, although the onward stretch from Makhado/Louis Trichardt to the Zimbabwe border is still single carriageway. About 61 km from Polokwane/Pietersburg the N1 crosses the **Tropic of Capricorn**.

Zion City

One of the most significant modern day landmarks in this region is the Zion City at Moria, 30 km from Pietersburg on the R71 towards Haenertsburg. Although there is nothing much for the visitor to see here, this is the seat of the Zion Christian Church, an entirely black denomination that has the largest following of any denomination in Southern Africa. During Easter weekend each year, up to 2,000,000 followers congregate here from all over South Africa and Zimbabwe for mass worship, when they traditionally wear white robes. The sight of such staggering numbers of people in the Pietersburg region at this time is quite extraordinary.

Makhado/Louis Trichardt and the Zoutpansberg

pp631-636. Phone code: 015. Colour map 2, grid A4. Altitude: 984 m.

The modern town of **Makhado** is another important agricultural centre, where tea, coffee, timber and sub-tropical fruits are the main crops. There's not much to see in town itself – it's a sleepy backwater that trucks rumble through on the N1 – but to the north and west is the sandstone **Zoutpansberg** mountain range, which stretches for about 130 km and reaches 1753 m at its highest point, known as Lejume. it takes its name from the salt-pan and brine spring at the western end of the range. These hills have played an important role in the early history of the region and now offer good wilderness hikes. Dotted along the high plateau are traditional Venda villages.

Many of the valleys and lakes in the Zoutpansberg are considered sacred – the best-known of these are the Phiphidi Falls and Guvhukuvhu Pool, Lwamomdo Hill, Lake Fundudzi and the Thathe Vondo Forest. These sights are difficult to find and you should enlist the services of a registered guide if you wish to visit them. This will also help ensure that you approach and treat the sights sensitively. A self-drive route, taking in the area's arts and crafts highlights, begins in Makhado – information is available from the **Zoutpansberg Tourist Office** ⓘ *corner of Songozwi St and the N1, T015-5160040, www.tourismsoutpansberg.co.za, Mon-Fri 0900-1700, Sat 0800-1300.*

The world-renowned Elim Hospital is 25 km southeast of Makhado/ Louis Trichardt on the Gyani Road.

Background

Makhado was formerly known as Louis Trichardt, after the Voortrekker leader who set up his camp near here in May 1836. He had travelled up to the Zoutpansberg with another group of Voortrekkers under Hans Van Rensburg. After arguments between the two groups, Hans Van Rensburg led his people east in search of a route to Lourenço Marques (today's Maputo in Mozambique). They disappeared into the wilderness and were never heard from again. Louis Trichardt remained in the area for a year before following Hans Van Rensburg east. This was one of the classic journeys of the Voortrekkers, taking seven months to reach Lourenço Marques. It took them two and a half months to get down the Drakensberg escarpment and by the end of their trek, 27 of the original 53 Boers had died. Louis Trichardt and his wife survived the journey but both died of malaria soon after. After his death other Voortrekkers settled in the area as ivory hunters but left after Chief Makhado (after whom the town is now named) and his vhaVenda people defeated them in 1867. Only in 1898 did the Zuid-Afrikaansche Republiek take control of the region; the town of Louis Trichardt was established the following year.

Manavhela Ben Lavin Nature Reserve

ⓘ *T015-5164534, daily 0600-1900, R30. To get there, follow the N1 8 km south of the town and look out for the Fort Edward Rd, the reserve is 5 km along this road.*

The Manavhela Ben Lavin Nature Reserve is a protected area of indigenous woodland with 18 km of walking trails, mountain biking trails and hides. The reserve is a good place for birdwatching and has giraffes, wildebeest and other game indigenous to the area. There are also some interesting archaeological sites, which have been dated to around AD 1250. Hikers and bikers are provided with a booklet that helps interpret the environment. There are some new overnight huts along the hiking trail (see Sleeping page 633), which are fully furnished. When exploring the park on foot always remember to look out for wild animals.

Hangklip Forest Reserve

ⓘ *3 km west of town, signposted off the N1.*

The Hangklip Forest Reserve is an area of indigenous forest around the base of the Hangklip, a wall of rock rising 1719 m. The top of the cliffs are some of the highest points of the Zoutpansberg. There are several day hikes here through spectacular mountain scenery, including the **Zoutpansberg Hike**, a 21-km walk, which you should allow two days to complete. Although this is a circular route all hikers must walk in the same direction and only 30 people are allowed on the trail at any one time. For further details contact **Komatiland Forestry**, a subsidiary of the **Department of Forestry (SAFCOL)** ⓘ *T013-7542724, www.komatiecotourism.co.za*, which has information on the trial, and issues permits.

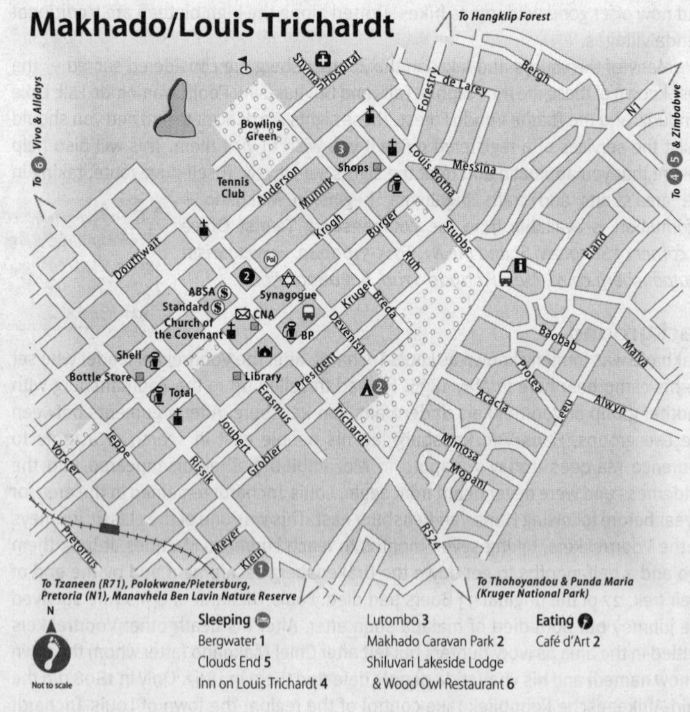

The upside-down tree

The baobab tree (*Adansonia digitata*) is the undisputed king of the African savannah and grows throughout east and southern Africa. The trees reach to about 25 m in height, with trunk diameters of up to 10 m, and live for thousands of years. This giant tree, with its enormous girth and unmistakable appearance, is surrounded by legend. One story suggests that the tree's root-like branches are a result of the gods, in a frivolous mood, planting the tree upside down. Another legend has it that if you drink water soaked in baobab seeds, you can wade across a crocodile-infested river and get to the other side unharmed. However, few people seem willing to test this theory.

Beyond Makhado

The N1 continues to the north winding through wooded valleys. After 21 km the highway passes through the Zoutpansberg, via the **Verwoerd Tunnels**. The R524 heads east from town through **Thohoyandou**, the former capital of the Venda homeland, to Punda Maria Camp (140 km), one of the most northerly camps in **Kruger National Park** (see page 578).

Venda

→ Colour map 2, grid A4.

You are only likely to pass through this former homeland region if you are heading to the northern camps of Kruger from Makhado on the R524 or from Polokwane or Tzaneen on the R81. The area has more in common with rural Tanzania or Kenya than with most areas of South Africa. Unlike Bophuthatswana in Northwest Province, which the Apartheid government proclaimed a black homeland simply because they had no use for the inadequate land, Venda is fertile and green and produces tea, bananas and mangoes. Despite this, and efforts made by the current government, the infrastructure is still poor, the roads are badly maintained, and families survive on subsistence hand-to-mouth farming.

Background

The culture of the vhaVenda is steeped in the belief of the spirit world, and there are many important sacred, and private, sites in the region. Originally from Zimbabwe, it is thought that the vhaVenda people migrated here at the beginning of 18th century. They are regarded as some of the finest artists in South Africa, and are particularly renowned for their drum making and pottery.

Thohyandou and around

Thohyandou is the former capital of the independent homeland and is the commercial and administrative centre for the district. It's name means 'head of the elephant' in tshiVenda. The town has an energetic African feel to it: business, schooling and life in general is conducted outdoors, the people are astoundingly friendly, and local produce is sold at stalls along roadsides. If you would like to explore this region in detail, go with a guide to avoid offending the vhaVenda who still uphold ancient customs and beliefs. Contact the **Zoutpansberg Tourist Office** in Makhado (see page 627) to organize a tour with a specialized local operator. » *For further details, see Activities and tours, page 635.*

Musina/Messina

» pp631-636. Phone code: 015.

Colour map 2, grid A4.

Musina is the northernmost town in South Africa and has the sleepy atmosphere of a frontier town, easily missed if you're passing through from the south. Coming from Zimbabwe, particularly at night, the effect is different: the main street is lit up and lined with shops, banks and fast food outlets. Although there's little of interest in town, it makes a reasonable base from which to explore Venda to the east. There is also a good road across to the northern camps of Kruger via Tshipise. The tourist office, **Musina Tourism** ⓘ *Information Centre, National Rd, T015-5343500*, is useful for local accommodation bookings but it's a tiny office in comparison with the larger towns.

This is your last chance to buy South African products before crossing the border into Zimbabwe, at Beitbridge, 12 km away.

The town started life as a camp, set up around the copper mines that opened in 1905. Archaeological evidence has since indicated that mines had been worked here for several centuries before they were abandoned at the beginning of the 19th century. The principal copper mines were closed over a decade ago but, fortunately for the local labour force, a new diamond-mining operation was started up in 1992, 80 km west of town; the diamond mine is today the third largest De Beer diamond mine in the world and South Africa's biggest producer of diamonds.

Mapungubwe National Park

Mapungubwe is the country's youngest and northernmost national park, developed on the South African side of the confluence of the Shashe and Limpopo Rivers, 135 km west of Musina on the road to Pontdrift. The park forms part of what will become the Transfrontier Conservation Area, covering the corner of the province which borders Zimbabwe and Botswana. It protects important San rock art sites, but is best known for **Mapungubwe Hill**, which researchers believe was the site of the first capital of the ancient kingdom of Great Zimbabwe between AD 900 and 1300. Gold and silver artefacts have been unearthed here, including the famous Golden Rhino, as well as items of Arab, Chinese, Indonesian and Indian origin – indicated important trading routes – many of which are on display at the University of Pretoria. Mapungubwe is the earliest evidence of Africa's Iron Age and was awarded World Heritage status in 2003. The park now covers 28,000 ha, and is home to a variety of wildlife, including black and white rhino, elephant, kudu, zebra, eland, waterbuck, gemsbok, giraffe and baboon. There are four camps within the park.

Facilities are still being developed in the park, but at present a series of rough roads pass through a variety of terrains, offering a range of wildlife viewing opportunities. Make sure you pick up a map at reception, as some of the roads are still being developed. There are a handful of hides overlooking pans and dams, and an interpretive centre is being built at the main entrance gate. One of the highlights of the park is its hiking trails: **Vhembe Trails** operates much like the wilderness trails in Kruger, with guests venturing out on guided day hikes from a main base camp. There are also a couple of 4WD routes going through rugged hilly terrain, including the **Tshugulu Eco Route** which covers 45 km, with a game hide en route. This is a malarial area, so take prophylactics. There are, as yet, no shops or petrol available in the park, so stock up in Musina before you visit.

It is estimated that many hundreds of thousands of Zimbabweans are living in virtual anonymity in the townships of Gauteng (see page 510), having crossed the border into South Africa illegally.

Crossing into Zimbabwe

In view of the current political climate in Zimbabwe, it is recommended that all visitors refer to the British Foreign and Commonwealth Office website, www.fco.org, for up-to-date travel advice before attempting to enter Zimbabwe.

Beitbridge border

ⓘ *Daily 0530-2230; open 24 hrs over the Dec/Jan and Easter holiday periods.* Formalities on the Zimbabwe side of the border can be very slow – during local school holidays it can take as long as five hours to clear all formalities and it gets very hot here during the summer. Avoid this border at opening time early in the morning, as this is when the buses arrive from both Johannesburg and Harare and there are lengthy queues. All returning Zimbabwean bus passengers are searched thoroughly and the procedure is time consuming. There should be no problems for tourists but be prepared for some frustrating questions and delays from the officers in Zimbabwe customs. » *For details of crossing the border by car, see Vehicle formalities, below; for public transport, see page 636.*

Facilities

There is a duty-free shop on the South African side, selling a limited range of cigarettes and spirits, and a VAT refund office. This is particularly useful for tourists who can claim back the VAT on any unused items they are taking home with them (see page 27), but expect a long wait.

Do not state your occupation to Zimbabwe custom officials as that of journalist or any other media-related job.

Vehicle formalities

At present, most hired cars from South Africa are not allowed into Zimbabwe. For those that are, **third party insurance** is required by law for all vehicles entering Zimbabwe. Short-term policies can be bought at the border posts or offices of the **AA**, who are the sole representatives of Zimbabwean third-party insurance in South Africa. Visitors from overseas countries must have an English translation of their **licence** plus a photograph. Tourists in private vehicles must also have a **vehicle registration certificate** and will normally be granted a temporary **import permit** free of charge, provided the vehicle is licensed in its home country and has the appropriate number plates. People travelling in their own vehicle on a **carnet** must get it stamped when exiting South Africa and entering Zimbabwe, as Zimbabwe is not part of the South African Development Community (SADC), shared customs agreement that covers South Africa, Namibia and Botswana.

Be wary of petty thieves, especially on the Zimbabwe side. Lock everything up and make sure anything on the outside of the vehicle is tied down. Do not under any circumstances accept help from touts in the car park who offer to sell relevant forms or 'look after' your car; all forms are available free of charge inside the border control building, and official uniformed security guards patrol the car park.

Sleeping

Bela-Bela/Warmbaths *p621*

AL **Mabula Game Lodge**, 35 km from Bela-Bela off the Thabazimbi-Rooiberg Rd, T014-7347000, www.mabula.com. 51 luxury self-catering and full board double rooms, with restaurant, swimming pool, squash, tennis, gym, sauna, bush walks, game drives, horseback trails, luxury game farm with excellent facilities, recommended for a longer break. Also has timeshares. Day visitors welcomed for game drives and lunch.

B **Château Annique**, Swanepoel St, 2 km from town, T014-7362847. 6 smart suites furnished with antiques set in a country house built by 2 Italian prisoners- of-war, attractive decor, swimming pool, immaculate landscaped gardens, private library, overall a smart exclusive bush retreat.

B-D Aventura Resort Warmbaths, T014-7362200, www.aventura.co.za. This resort contains the main Bela-Bela springs and is so vast that guests are required to wear plastic identity bracelets at all times. The caravan park alone extends for a couple of kilometres to the edge of the town. Chalets and log cabins, 94 in total, surround 3 man-made dams, and there's a standard **Protea** 45-room hotel at the entrance gate. A selection of restaurants and bars, mineral pools, spa and hydro with a full range of beauty treatments, horseriding, squash, tennis, cable water ski circuit, water slides, go-karts, quad bikes, fishing. Advance booking is essential. Day visitors permitted until 1700.

C Villa Palmeira, 9 Knoppiesdoring Av, T014-7362558. 10 en suite rooms in this comfortable guest house in a quiet suburb 2 km from the springs. En suite rooms, DSTV, internet access, set in a thatched villa surrounded by well-tended sub-tropical gardens. B&B, other meals on request, pool in garden, thatched lapa with braai.

Modimolle/Nylstroom and around *p621*

B Shangri-La , Eerstebewood Rd, midway between Bela-Bela and Modimolle on a bushveld farm, T014-7181600, www.shangri-la.co.za . Part of the **Protea** group. Geared towards conferences, but with decent accommodation in 37 thatched cottages, with en suite bathroom, spacious and tastefully decorated. Pool, restaurant, bar, tennis courts, all set in lush gardens with views of the Waterberg.

Camping

E Nylsvley Nature Reserve, T015-2889000, simple campsite with 80 spaces in a beautiful setting within the nature reserve.

Mokopane/Potgietesrus *p622, map p623*

B-C Orinoco, 66 Ruiter St, T015-4915891, www.orinoco.co.za. Local 2-star hotel, a/c double rooms with M-Net TV, restaurant, sports bar, both popular with local Afrikaners, swimming pool, special rates for families.

B-C Protea Park, 1 Beitel St, T015-4913101, ppark@mweb.co.za. 98 a/c double rooms with en suite bathroom, non-smoking rooms, TV MNet, lounge, restaurant, bar, laundry service, swimming pool set in garden in the middle of the complex with a few decorative palms, regular quality hotel.

D Oasis Lodge, 1 Voortrekker St, T015-4912124, www.oasishotel.co.za. Simple double rooms with en suite bathroom, ceiling fans, cool tiled floors, DSTV, conference facilities, restaurant, laundry service, shady garden.

Polokwane/Pietersburg *p624, map p625*

B African Roots, 58a Devenish St, T015-2970113, www.africanroots.info. Attractive converted farmhouse dating from 1928 with wrap-around veranda, owned by artists so the rooms have an interesting mix of antique furnishings and contemporary art, all are en suite with a/c, lounge and bar, deck overlooking swimming pool in garden. Recommended.

B Limpopo Guest Manor, 48 Devenish St, T015-2971656. Overpriced B&B suited to business travellers, with spacious en suite rooms, looking distinctly frayed around the edges, bar attached.

C Landmark Lodge, next to the N1 Shell Ultra City just south of town, T015-2557255, www.proteahotels.com. Part of the **Protea** chain. 80 a/c functional rooms, aimed at business travellers, TV, pool, bar, restaurant, buffet breakfast, internet provided through the TV and separate keyboard. Standard business hotel but conveniently located.

C Plumtree Lodge, 138 Marshall St, T015-2956153/4, www.plumtree.co.za. 14 double ooms in a modern house, with cool terracotta floors, white fabrics and wicker furniture, en suite bath or shower, separate lounge area with sofas, a desk and TV. Palm-shaded pool surrounded by sun loungers, breakfast is served in a bright dining room. The staff are friendly and helpful. Gets booked up quickly.

D Sleepers Villa, 20a Bok St, T015- 2915285, sleepervilla@mweb.co.za. A rather bizarre looking house with a private walled garden and 5 rooms with bathrooms (only separated with a screen), TV, lounge, meals available on request. Close to city centre.

Camping

D-E **Polokwane Game Reserve** , 5 km out of town along Dorp St, T015-2902331. 60 sites for caravans and tents, 12 rondavels, self-catering, clean ablution block, electric points, laundry.

Makhado/Louis Trichardt and the Zoutpansberg *p627, map p628*

There are a number of pleasant country hotels and farms in the area that have developed small camps for visitors.

A **Inn on Louis Trichardt**, 11 km north of Makhado, T015-5177020, iolt@iafrica.com. The tranquil setting of this guesthouse makes it a popular choice, beautiful views of the Zoutpansberg Mountains from its thatched rondavels, dotted around tended gardens. 18 rondavels have enormous beds, en suite bathrooms, TV and phone. Swimming pool in the garden, rates include dinner and breakfast. Meals are served on the terrace restaurant, also has a bar and tea rooms. Recommended.

A-B **Shiluvari Lakeside Lodge**, T015-5563406, www.shiluvari.com. A peaceful country lodge located in the Albasini Conservancy, 23 km from Makhado, with 60 ha of grounds, ideal for birdwatching, fishing and hiking. Spacious thatched double rooms and chalets overlooking a dam, attractive decor, cool tiled floors, mosquito nets over beds, separate seating area with wicker furniture. Full board rates available, **Wood Owl** restaurant and pub with fireplace is well regarded, swimming pool, Fair Trade curio shop. Boat trips organized during the day and at sunset on the dam, maximum 6 people. Recommended.

B **Bergwater Hotel**, 5 Rissik St, T015-5160262. 36 double a/c rooms with en suite bathroom, a/c, DSTV, à la carte restaurant favoured by the locals , 2 bars, lounge, swimming pool, conference facilities, a whitewashed double-storey building overlooking a pond on the edge of town.

C **Medike Mountain Reserve**, T015-5160481, medikwe@mweb.co.za. 3 unique pioneer cottages in the Zoutpansberg 37 km from Makhado towards Vivo on the R522, close to an impressive gorge cut by the Sand River. This is a Natural Heritage Site, excellent local hikes, rock paintings, mountain bike trails, a beautiful wilderness. Recommended.

C-D **Clouds End**, N1 north out of town, T015-5177021, cloudsend@mweb.co.za. 38 double rooms, a/c, en suite, TV, all in a variety of blocks dotted about the hillside, caravan park, restaurant serves good 5-course dinners, bar and spacious lounge with large open fireplace, essential in the winter months, swimming pool, floodlit tennis court, extensive grounds, even a cricket pitch. A popular hotel though old fashioned – think 1970s chintz. Rates are for dinner, bed and breakfast, excellent service, probably the best value in town.

C-D **Lutombo** , 141 Anderson St, T015-5160850,lutombo@lantic.net. 3 rooms with en suite bathroom, non-smoking, TV lounge, all meals available on request, gardens, swimming pool, good value B&B.

Camping

C-E **Manavhela Ben Lavin Nature Reserve**, T015-5164534. Range of thatched self-catering chalets and huts, plus 30 campsites, caravan park, electric points and lighting, plenty of shade, spotless ablution block. Also has luxury tents, with en suite bathrooms and attached kitchen, sleeping 4.

E **Makhado Caravan Park**, T015-5193025, www.makhado.caravanparks.com. Excellent caravan site which has one national prizes. In the middle of town next to the Indigenous Tree Park, 120 sites with electric points, hot water, plenty of shade under towering trees, lovely setting next to a meandering stream with two dams, although mosquitoes can be a problem. Walking distance from restaurants and pubs, peaceful most of the year but can get very busy in school holidays.

Musina/Messina *p630*

B-C **Ilala Country Lodge**, 2 km north of Musina, 13 km from Beitbridge border post, turn left on the R572 Pontdrift Road, lodge is 5 km after turn off, T015-5343220, rodsal@lantic.net. 10 stone and thatch chalets set in a 240-ha game estate, sleeping 4-10, furnished kitchens, en suite bathrooms, braai areas, beautiful views over the Limpopo Valley into Zimbabwe. Bush walks, swimming pool, guest dining room and lapa.

B-E **Aventura Resort Tshipise**, 37 km from Musina, 105 km from Kruger's Pafuri Gate on the R508 or R525, T015-5390634, www.aventura.co.za. Part of the **Aventura** chain, conveniently situated en route to Kruger. Tennis, swimming pools, horse riding, hiking, mini golf, hot springs, laundry, shops and restaurants on site. Self-catering rondavels, TV, braai area, large camping and caravan park with shared ablutions. Summer temperatures are regularly over 40° C.

Camping

D-E Baobab Caravan Park, on the left as you approach town from Makhado/Louis Trichardt, T015-5343504. Tent and caravan sites, some self catering chalets, electric points, laundry, well-grassed and shaded, busy over Christmas period, can get very crowded, booking advised. A greatly improved site since the management passed from the municipality into private hands.

Eating

Bela-Bela/Warmbaths *p621*

¥ O'Hagans, in the Waterfront development close to the tourist office, T014-7365068. Successful nation-wide chain with attractive setting in the Waterfront development, outdoor tables. Interior filled with mock Irish touches, menu is Irish-style pub fare. Small choice, with steaks and schnitzels, steak and ale pie and sausages and mash. Good range of local and imported beers.

¥ Tocoma Spur, in the Aventura Resort. A reliable steak house chain found in most small towns throughout South Africa. Steaks, burgers and average salad bar.

Mokopane/Potgietesrus *p622, map p623*

The restaurant scene here is limited to the standard chain outlets found throughout the country: KFC, Nando's, and **Spur**, are all on Voortrekker St.

¥ Ginello's, in the Shoprite mall. Good coffee and pancakes during the day, next door to an internet café.

Polokwane/Pietersburg *p624, map p625*

Polokwane has a couple of excellent restaurant choices which make a welcome change from the usual chains. Most standard restaurants are in the Savannah Mall on Grobler St, away from the centre.

¥¥¥ The Restaurant, 50 Dorp St, just out of the centre, T015-2911918, closed Sun. By far the best restaurant in town, if not in the entire province. Lengthy menu offering good selection of salads, steaks, good venison and a delicious prawn curry. Good wine list, too, and pleasant wooden deck spreading out from the fine old corner building. Recommended.

¥¥ Greek 'n' CheE, Savannah Mall, T015-2960662, closed Sun evening. Good Mediterranean cuisine, including pasta, risotto and meze platters, plus a couple of Moroccan dishes like couscous and lamb tagine. Makes a pleasant change from the usual steak and burger menus.

¥¥ La Villa Italia, Savannah Centre, T015-2960857. Long standing family-run restaurant, serving an excellent selection of pasta dishes (penne with prawns in white wine are the best) huge range of pizzas and substantial mains such as roast lamb. Relaxed, friendly atmosphere.

¥ Falcon Rock Spur, Savannah Centre, T015-2961991. Hugely popular outlet of the steak house chain set in the basement of the mall. Stick to the steaks; the burgers aren't great. Standard salad bar.

Makhado/Louis Trichardt and the Zoutpansberg *p627, map p628*

¥¥¥ Wood Owl, Shiluvari Lakeside Lodge, off the R578 to Elim, T015-5563406, www.shiluvari.com. Hotel restaurant with an excellent local reputation. Smart à la carte menu, using local produce such as Venda maize bread and local beef. Delicious specials, beef with mustard mash or sweet potato soup, good choice of deserts, and the decor is from the fair trade shop attached.

¥¥ Café d'Art, 129 Krogh St, T015-5165760, closed Sun. Central family-run restaurant, set in attractive old house and serving traditional South African food, including good T-bone steaks, light lunches such as soup or quiche, great deserts or afternoon tea and cakes.

Musina/Messina *p630*

The only restaurants in town are either in the hotels or the standard chains, such as **Buffalo Ridge Spur**, on Main St, which serves the usual choice of ribs, steaks and fried chicken.

Festivals and events

Bela-Bela/Warmbaths *p621*

May The town hosts an annual Tourism Festival, with a wide range of stalls, events and special offers.

Mokopane/Potgietesrus *p622, map p623*

Oct If in the area around this time, look out for the Biltong Festival, when a whole range of game biltong can be tried and bought.

Activities and tours

Modimolle/Nylstroom and around *p621*

Equus Horse Safaris, T014-7210063, www.equus.co.za. Based 60 km from town, offering exciting horse trails for experienced riders.

Friends of Nylsvley, T012-6672183. A voluntary organization for birdwatching based in Pretoria, but with a special interest in Nylsvley.

Polokwane/Pietersburg *p624, map p625*

SA Tours & Bookings, 2 Voortrekker St, T015-2956162. Comprehensive brochure with a full range of tours. Recommended.

Makhado/Louis Trichardt and the Zoutpansberg *p627, map p628*

Adventures Lifestyle, T082-3215430, www.adventurelifstyles.co.za. Wide range of adventure activities in the Zoutpansberg, including kloofing, abseiling, rock climbing and mountain biking.

Face Afrika Tours, Lommies Emporium Building, 104 Burger St, T015-5162076; facaf@mweb.co.za. Good for a complete tour of the region. Expert local knowledge. Recommended. Owner-manager Chris Olivier is a formidable character and a member of the Limpopo Tourism Board.

Kuvona Cultural Tours, T015-5563512, kuvona@mweb.co.za. Tours to the tribal sacred sites, traditional ceremonies, and villages in the Zoutpansberg and Venda. Community development through tourism.

Saddles Horse Trails, T072-5093939, ingagilf@yebo.co.za. Horse trails in the Zoutpansberg Mountain, suitable for novices, overnight at bush camps, swim bare back with the horses. Also bike and hiking trails.

Transport

Bela-Bela/Warmbaths *p621*

Rail

Spoornet, Central reservations T0860-008888, www.spoornet.co.za. Trains run between **Johannesburg** and **Musina** (11 hrs) via Polokwane and Makhado.

Modimolle/Nylstroom and around *p621*

Bus

Greyhound, T011-2768500, www.greyhound.co.za. Coaches depart from the Engen Garage for **Bulawayo** (Zimbabwe); **Pretoria** (2 hrs) and **Johannesburg** (3 hrs).

Mokopane/Potgietesrus *p622, map p623*

Bus

Greyhound, T011- 2768500, www.greyhound.co.za, runs coaches to **Bulawayo** (Zimbabwe) (9 hrs) and **Johannesburg**.

Translux, T011-7743333, www.translux.co.za, runs coaches to **Harare** (Zimbabwe) (13 hrs), **Johannesburg** and **Pretoria** (3 hrs).

Rail

T086-000888, www.spoornet.co.za. Trains runs between **Johannesburg** (and **Musina**, via Polokwane and Makhado.

Polokwane/Pietersburg *p624, map p625*

Air

Gateway Airport is 5 km north of the city centre off the N1, information T015-2880122. SA Airlink, T011-9781111, www.saairlink.co.za.

Bus

Greyhound, T011-2768500, www.greyhound.co.za. Coaches depart from Shell Ultra City on the outskirts of town, to **Bulawayo** (Zimbabwe) (8 hrs); **Harare** (Zimbabwe) (11.5 hrs); **Johannesburg**.

Translux, T011-7743333, www.translux.co.za, coaches depart from Thabo Mbeki St, to **Bulawayo** (10 hrs;) **Lusaka** (21 hrs) via Harare (13 hrs); **Pretoria** and **Johannesburg** (4 hrs).

Car hire

The following companies are located at Gateway Airport. **Avis** T015-2880171; **Budget** T015-2880169; **Imperial**

T015-2880097; Sani 4x4 Rentals T015-2880268, www.sanirentals.co.za. The latter is useful if you want to explore the Limpopo Province with a 4WD; some vehicles are equipped with roof tents.

Rail

Spoornet, T086-000888, www.spoornet.co.za. Runs trains to **Johannesburg** and **Musina**.

Makhado/Louis Trichardt and the Zoutpansberg *p627, map p628*

Bus

Coaches depart from Safari Motors, Caltex garage in Baobab St close to the tourist office. Greyhound, T011-2768500, www.greyhound.co.za, runs coaches to **Bulawayo** (Zimbabwe) (6½ hrs), **Harare** (10½ hrs), **Pretoria** (5½ hrs) and **Johannesburg** (6½ hrs).

Translux, T011- 7743333, www.translux.co.za, runs coaches to **Bulawayo** (8½ hrs), **Lusaka** (Zambia) (20 hrs), **Pretoria** (5 hrs) and **Johannesburg** (6 hrs).

Rail

Spoornet, T086-0008888, www.spoornet.co.za. Trains to **Musina** and **Johannesburg** (11 hrs).

Musina/Messina *p630*

Bus

Greyhound, T011-2768500, www.greyhound.co.za, runs coaches to **Bulawayo** (Zimbabwe) (5½ hrs), **Harare** (Zimbabwe) (9½ hrs), **Pretoria** (7 hrs) and **Johannesburg** (8 hrs).

Translux, T011-7743333, www.translux.co.za, runs coaches to **Bulawayo** (7 hrs); to **Lusaka** (Zambia) (18 hrs) via **Harare** (9 hrs), **Pretoria** and **Johannesburg** (7 hrs).

Rail

T086-0008888, www.spoornet.co.za. Trains to **Johannesburg** via Makhado, Polokwane and Mokopane.

Crossing into Zimbabwe *p631*

To Zimbabwe

Expect to pay no more than R10 for a ride to the border post from Musina. Once you have negotiated the South African side, you will either have to walk or hitch across the bridge over the Limpopo River. Allow yourself plenty of time to cross the border and find a lift towards **Bulawayo**, **Masvingo** or **Harare**. Minibus taxis to these destinations can be found waiting on the other side of Zimbabwe immigration.

From Zimbabwe

There is a minibus taxi car park just outside the South African border post gates; from here you can get a lift to **Musina** (for onward transport, see above). Alternatively you can pick up one of the mainline bus services on either side of the border that operate between Harare and **Johannesburg**. The total bus journey between these 2 destinations is around 18 hrs.

❶ Directory

Polokwane/Pietersburg *p624, map p625*

Internet Vodashop in the Savannah Centre, T015-2963907, Mon-Sat. Business Basics, Shop 17a, Middestad Centre, Market St, T2970246. **Medical services** Ambulance, T10177. Medi Clinic, corner of Thabo Mbeki and Burger Sts, T015-2903600. Pharmacy, daily 0800-2000, T015-2955737. **Useful telephone numbers** Police, T10111.

Makhado/Louis Trichardton and the Zoutpansberg *p627, map p627*

Banks Standard, ABSA and First National are on Krogh St, at 93, 98, and 295. **Medical services** Ambulance, T10177. Pharmacy, T015-5164994. **Useful telephone numbers** Police, T10111.

Musina/Messina *p630*

Banks First National, Main Rd. Standard, corner of Main Rd and Emery St. **Bureau de change**, Main Rd next to the PO, T015-5343412, daily 0700-1700. There are also bureaux de change at the service station just before the Zimbabwe border. **Internet** The Computer Shop, Main Rd, opposite Shoprite. Medical services Ambulance, T10177. Medical Centre T015-5340557. **Useful telephone numbers** Police, T10111.

East of the Great North Road

→ *Colour map 2, grid A4.*

While the area north towards Zimbabwe seems largely flat and featureless, venturing off the main north-south route leads to more varied landscapes and interesting sights. This is especially true of the region around the agricultural centre of Tzaneen, surrounded by tea plantations, lush mountains and fruit farms. Turning off the N1 at Polokwane/Pietersburg onto the R71 towards Tzaneen, the landscape changes dramatically after around 30 km, from dusty scrubland dotted with acacias and untidy villages, to forest-covered hills. This craggy range, swathed in indigenous forests and peppered with waterfalls and dams, is known as the Magoebaskloof. » *For Sleeping, Eating and other listings, see pages 641-646.*

Ins and outs

Getting there and around The best way of exploring the area is by car; there is no public transport in the region. **SA Airlink** flies between Johannesburg and **Phalaborwa Kruger Park Gateway Airport,** T015-7815823, on the edge of Phalaborwa, 2 km from the entrance to Kruger National Park. » *For further details, see Transport, page 645.*

The Magoebaskloof

» *pp641-646.* *Phone code: 015.*

Colour map 2, grid B4.

One of the best times of the year to explore this mountainous area is in spring, when the tropical valleys burst into a riot of colour. The area is best known for its cherry blossoms, and a small cheery blossom festival takes place here every year. The valleys are also famed for their orchids (over 200 species have been recorded here), and during December and January you can see bright pink and mauve 'pride of India' trees. Many of the country hotels in the area get fully booked at this time of year, as this is the most popular time for walking. Birdlife is prolific and includes Knysna and purple crested louries, several species of eagles, and the rare black fronted bush shrike. The lower slopes are cultivated with tea and banana plantations and gum tree forests, creating the effect of a rolling green patchwork quilt.

Before the region was peacefully settled, it witnessed a bloody feud between the Transvaal government and the Tlou tribe of the chief Makgoba. In 1894 the followers of Makgoba retreated into the forests refusing to pay government taxes. The European soldiers were unable to dislodge the force and it took a group of Swazi warriors, working for the government, to defeat Makgoba. The warriors beheaded Makgoba to prove to the government that they had killed him, and the mountains were named after him.

Towards Tzaneen

The small village of **Haenertsburg** is the principle centre at the western end of the mountains. There are a handful of tea gardens and craft shops in town, and Market Square is dominated by a display of over 400 species of trees from each of the five continents laid out in five rings, much like the Olympic Games logo. Information and accommodation bookings are available from **Magoebaskloof Tourism** ⓘ *Rissik St, behind the Atholl Arms, T015-2764972, www.magoebaskloof.com, Mon-Fri 0800-1700, Sat and Sun 0830-1200*. From Haenertsburg you are faced with the choice of two possible routes to Tzaneen. The R71 continues past Ebenezer Dam and winds through the beautiful, forested **Magoebaskloof Valley** before reaching **Sapekoe Tea Estates** (Middelkop). At the top of the magnificently lush tea plantation, with a spectacular view down the valley over the tea bushes, is the **Pekoe View Tea Processing Plant**

 ⓘ *T015-2765047, tours at 1100, tea garden 1000-1700.* Tour the plant, before tasting the tea in the peaceful and tranquil tea garden, along with a slice of Sapekoe's famous chocolate cake. The other option is to follow the R528 along George's Valley.

Magoebaskloof Hiking Trail

The Magoebaskloof Hiking Trail has a variety of sections, ranging from two- to five-day hikes, with six huts for overnighting. The trail is considered tough and should only be attempted by seasoned hikers. Permits must be obtained from **Komatiland Forestry** ⓘ *T013-7542724, www.komatiecotourism.co.za*, a subsidiary of the Forestry Department (SAFCOL), as each section has restrictions on the minimum and a maximum number of hikers. The website has thorough trail information, with details of overnight huts.

Tzaneen and around

» *pp641-646. Phone code: 015.*

Colour map 2, grid B4.

Tzaneen lies at the centre of a prosperous agricultural region on the eastern side of the Magoebaskloof Mountains. After the scrubby dryness of surrounding areas, this region seems gloriously green and fertile, with verdant banana plantations and sweet-smelling orange groves creating a tropical setting. Although the town itself is little more than a busy grid of chain stores and petrol stations ringed by quiet suburbs, the abundance of the area's soil is apparent in the numerous stalls selling tropical fruits – this is, in fact, South Africa's biggest producer of avocados, mangoes, tea and tomatoes. **Limpopo Tourism & Parks Board** ⓘ *on the R71, on the right hand side as you approach town*

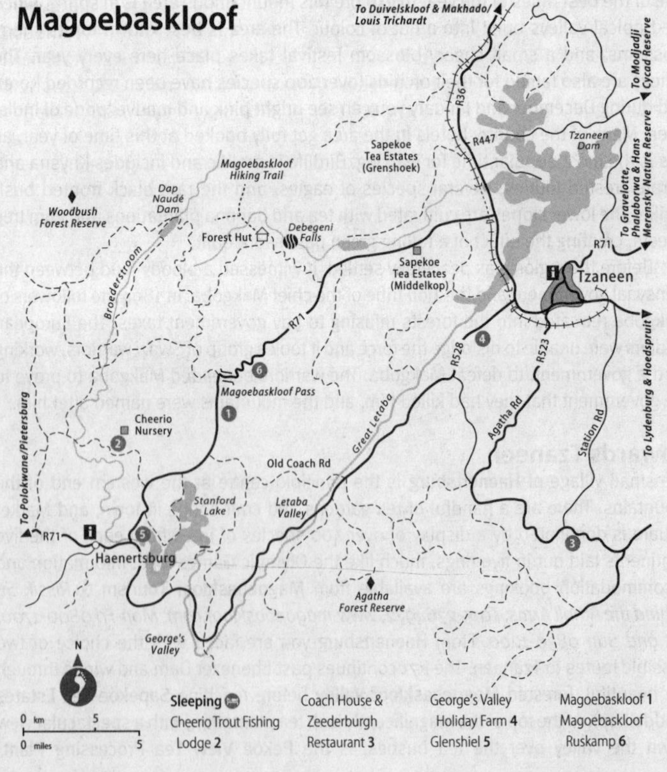

from the Phalaborwa and Kruger National Park, T051-3073582, www.golimpopo.org, Mon-Fri 0800-1700, is a very helpful office with a wealth of information on the area.

Background

Although it is now the largest town in Limpopo after Polokwane/Pietersburg, Tzaneen is a relatively young town, which only became a permanent settlement when the Selati Railway arrived in 1912. There are several versions of how the town was named. One theory suggests that the name comes from the very old Bantu word, Tsaneng, used to refer to the people in this area. The change in spelling is explained by the first German settlers transcribing the sound 'ts' as 'tz' when they wrote down the Bantu word.

Sights

Do not be deceived by its unassuming appearance, the **Tzaneen Museum** ⓘ *Agatha St, T015-3072425, Mon-Fri 0900-1600, Sat 0900-1200, donate generously for the upkeep of the building*, is one of the best provincial museums in South Africa and deserves far greater recognition and resources. The displays are a unique private collection of ethnological artefacts put together by Jurgen Witt. Crammed into three small rooms is an impressive and absorbing selection of pottery, carvings, drums and beadwork from the regional Tsonga and Venda peoples. The enthusiastic staff lead visitors around the displays, explaining certain items and providing a fascinating overview of this priceless muddle of a collection.

Modjadji Cycad Reserve

ⓘ *32 km north of Tzaneen on the R36, T015-2889000, daily 0830-1600, R20 per car, R10 per person.*

Modjadj Cycad Reserve is the home of the Rain Queen, the hereditary female monarch of the Lobedu people, who has reigned since the 16th century. The last queen, the sixth Queen Modjadi, died of AIDS in June 2005 at the age of 26. At time of writing her heir is yet to be decided; her daughter, who should by rights take the crown, is just two years old. That aside, the position of Rain Queen remains of huge importance in the area. Legend maintains that she has the power to produce rain, which is traditionally very important in this fertile region. Her powers seem to have had considerable success: the 12,000 cycads in the reserve stand at over 13 m high (normal growth in other areas is around 5 to 8 m tall). This particular species of fern, *Encephalartos transvenosus*, is thought to be billions of years old and has been protected for four centuries by the Modjadji Rain Queen. The reserve at the top of a steep hill protects these plants and surrounds the village where the Rain Queen lives. There are a few trails within the reserve and an information centre that gives up-to-date news about the monarch.

Hans Merensky Nature Reserve

ⓘ *68 km east of Tzaneen, on the R529 towards Giyani, T015-2889000.*

Hans Merensky Nature Reserve is on the southern banks of the Great Letaba River and was founded in 1954 to protect various species of lowveld antelope, in particular roan and sable. The natural vegetation is described as mopane lowveld and there is a chance of viewing giraffe, bushbu ck, zebra, impala, duiker, impala, tsessebe, hippo, leopard and blue wildebeest.

Sunland Nursery

ⓘ *68 km north of Tzaneen, just off the R526, signposted off the main road, T015-3092228, www.boabab.thi.co.za.*

The Sunland Nursery is home to what claims to the world's largest boabab tree, with an impressive 46.8 m circumference. It is said to be over 6000 years old, and the owners have built a bar into the hollow areas in part of the trunk. A couple of chalets and quadbikes are for hire.

East of Tzaneen

» pp641-646.

There are two possible routes east and south of Tzaneen: the R71 leads to Gravelotte, Phalaborwa (111 km) and the entrance to Kruger National Park at Phalaborwa Gate; the R36 heads south towards Marulaneng/Hoedspruit (120 km), the Drakensberg escarpment and Kruger's Orpen Gate. Both routes pass through the region known as the **Valley of the Olifants**, an area filled with private game reserves providing an attractively wild drive if you're passing through. If not entering Kruger, the route continues to the **Blyde River Canyon** in Mpumalanga, see page 610.

Phalaborwa

→ *Phone code: 015. Colour map 2, grid B5. Altitude: 450 m.*

This quiet Afrikaner town is only 2 km from Kruger's Phalaborwa Gate and is a convenient base from which to visit Kruger, although it's a rather dull choice compared to the reserves and camps nearby. South Africa's Amarula cream liqueur is distilled here, and you can visit the **distillery** ⓘ *T015-7817766, www.amarula.com, Mon-Fri 0900-1600, Sat 0900-1200*, for tasting and tours. It's a young town, established since 1958, when open-cast mining for minerals and copper began here. The mine is considered to be the widest man-made hole in Africa at 2 km wide and 450 m deep. Information is available from the **Phalaborwa Tourism Centre** ⓘ *Hendrick van Eck St, near the Spar, T015-7817267.*

Marulaneng/Hoedspruit and around

» pp641-646. *Phone code: 015. Colour map 2, grid B5.*

Hoedspruit is Afrikaans for 'hat creek', and the place acquired its name when, after a long trek over the mountains into the heat of the Lowveld, one of the Voortrekkers removed his hat, threw it into the cool waters of the Sandspruit River and decided to stay. Today, the town has barely expanded beyond its string of shops, banks and petrol station, and remains a sleepy outpost surrounded by game-rich country, loomed over by the Drakensberg escarpment. At the very south of Limpopo in the lowveld region, Marulaneng/Hoedspruit is close to both the private game reserves around Kruger (see page 594), and the Panorama region of Mpumalanga (see pages 603-616). There is little of interest to keep you in town itself; the main attractions and accommodation options are along the R531 towards Blyde River Canyon. **Hoedspruit Visitors Centre** ⓘ *corner of Kerk and Grobler Sts, T015-7933000*, is a private information centre which can help with accommodation, car hire and safaris.

Bombyx Mori Silk Farm

ⓘ *23 km south of Marulaneng/Hoedspruit on the R531, T015-795556. Mon-Sat 0900-1600, Sun in summer only 1100-1400; 5 daily tours. R20.*

Skilled women weavers from the local community show visitors the intricate methods of commercial silk farming and weaving at this farm. The cultivated silk, a soft creamy colour, is produced from the cocoons of the Bombyx Mori silk worm, and the farm shop sells a wide range of products: silk scarves, blankets, silk filled duvets and cushions, and there is a kiosk and tea garden.

Hoedspruit Endangered Species Centre

ⓘ *23 km south of Marulaneng/Hoedspruit on the R531, T015-7931633, info@cheetahresearch.co.za. Daily 0800-1700; 2-hr tours depart hourly 0800-1600. R75. Curio shop and tea garden on site.*

This is a unique project that conducts essential research on endangered species, in particular cheetah. There are daily standard tours lasting two hours, which begin with an informative video about the plight of endangered species, before viewing cheetah, African wild dog, ground hornbills, and the 'vulture restaurant', where wild vultures come to feed. Around 80 cheetah can be seen. The extended tour, which runs twice daily for three hours, also includes a visit to a breeding and rehabilitation camp for rhino and the rare Barbary lion. Booking is advised for both tours as many local school groups visit the centre. Game drives at the attached Kapama Game Reserve are also on offer.

Moholoholo Rehabilitation Centre

ⓘ *T015-7955236, www.moholoholo.co.za. Mon-Sat 0930 and 1500, Sun 1500. R50.* Moholoholo is a rehabilitation centre for abandoned, injured and poisoned wildlife. Wildlife is brought here from all over South Africa, and once healthy enough the animals are re-introduced back into their natural environments. There are a number of big birds such as raptors and vultures, many of which are injured from flying into power lines. Another important function of the centre is breeding and they have successfully bred and released into the wild the endangered crowned eagle, serval and many others.

Khamai Reptile Park

ⓘ *33 km south of Marulaneng on the R531, T015-7955203. Daily 0800-1700. R25.* This impressive reptile park was established 25 years ago by Donald Strydom, one of Africa's leading snake specialists, as a refuge and platform for understanding reptiles. There are numerous enclosures holding a wide variety of snakes, lizards, tortoises and crocodiles, and Donald's staff provide a good understanding of how many snakes are needlessly killed by farmers in South Africa. The park also offers a free service to people with phobias of snakes and spiders.

Sleeping

Magoebaskloof *p637, map p638*
There is a range of accommodation options in the 2 valleys; if you are not staying in the more expensive hotels they are still worth visiting for lunch or afternoon tea.

A **Glenshiel**, 2 km from Haenertsburg on the R71, T015-2764335, www.glenshiel.co.za. 15 luxury suites in a country lodge, each with an open fireplace and TV. The lodge is well known for its excellent cuisine. Tennis, swimming pool, trout fishing, delightful gardens, walking trails, good service. Worth trying to bargain on the price out of season.

A-C **Cheerio Trout Fishing Lodge**, at the Cheerio Nursery off the R71, T015-2761804, www.cheerio.co.za. Self-catering chalets or B&B in pretty rondavels, sleeping 2-5. Swimming pool and tennis court. Perfect setting with fine views across the valley. Trout fishing offered in 3 dams. The nursery here is the site of the annual cherry blossom festival.

C **Magoebaskloof Hotel**, off the R71, approximately 26 km from Tzaneen, T015-2764776, www.magoebaskloof.co.za. Recently rebuilt leisure hotel with range of self-catering units, double rooms and family rooms, all with en suite bathroom, disabled access, and some with fabulous valley views. A la carte restaurant and café, pub showing big screen sport, squash, swimming and the Samango monkey project, with viewing platforms to watch the monkeys in their natural habitat. Popular with weekending groups from Gauteng. Wide choice of walks available from here.

C **Magoebaskloof Ruskamp**, 25 km from Tzaneen on the R71, T015-3054144, www.magoebaskloofruskamp.co.za. Long-established resort with a cluster of 27 rondavels perched high up on the R71 where it climbs over a winding pass, gets a bit chilly at night. Self-catering or smaller B&B units, TV, heater, pool, sub-tropical gardens, good restaurant with a fantastic terrace overlooking the valley, but availability on the menu a bit hit and miss depending on how many people are staying.

E **George's Valley Holiday Farm**, 12 km from Haenertsburg, R528,

T015-2764817. Stunning location next to the picturesque Letaba River and dam in George's Valley. 20 camping stands, basic loos and outside showers, no electricity but paraffin lamps available, 3 simple self-catering cottages, lower rates for longer stays, lots of outdoor activities including mountain biking.

Tzaneen *p638, map p642*

Most of the accommodation options are around Tzaneen, on the road from Phalaborwa.

AL Coach House, T015-3068000, www.coachhouse.co.za. Hidden away in the forests south of Tzaneen, close to the Agatha Forest Reserve. Delightful country hotel with mountain views and colourful gardens with a swimming pool, beauty spa on site. Cosy bedrooms with en suite bathrooms, TV and private verandas with views of the mountains, and little touches like mohair blankets on the beds and homemade biscuits and fruit laid out each day. Some have log fires. Much of the fresh produce served in the restaurant is grown within the grounds, and it is possible to hire mountain bikes or walk on marked trails in the forest straight from the hotel. Excellent restaurant.

B Tzaneen Country Lodge, 17 km from Tzaneen on the R71 from Phalaborwa, T015-3043290, www.tznlodge.co.za. 25 a/c functional rooms, DSTV, bar, restaurant, room service. Large pretty gardens, outside restaurant that serves pub lunches and good pancakes, plus fancier evening meals. Popular wedding venue.

B-E Aventura Eiland, Hans Merensky Nature Reserve, 68 km east of Tzaneen T015-3868000, www.aventura.co.za This a huge resort with 103 luxury rondavels

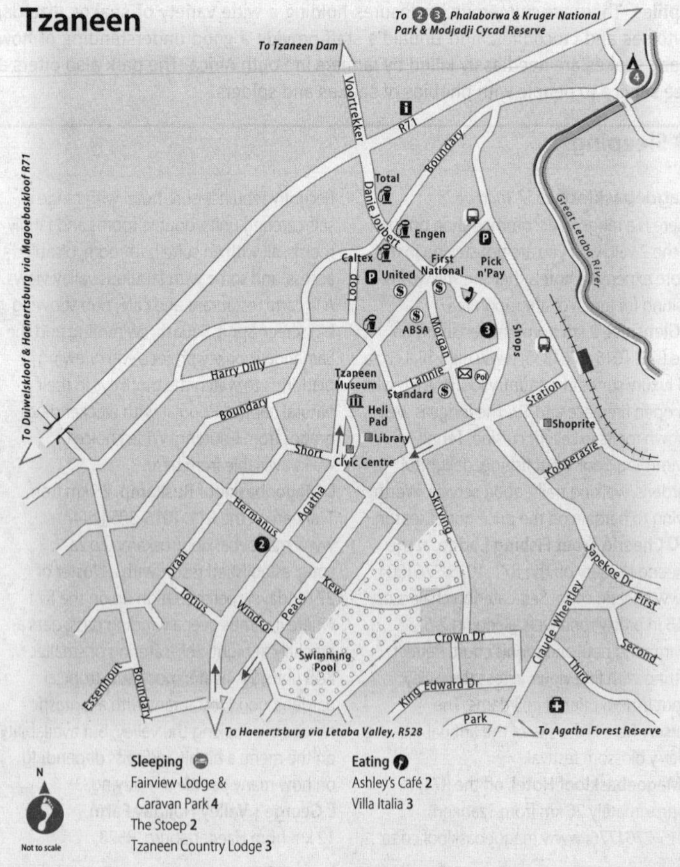

with TV, a/c, 91 2-4 sleeper self-catering rondavels, 300 stand caravan and camping park with electric points, restaurant, bar, swimming pool, sauna, mineral pools, horse riding, water park, beauty spa, gym, mini golf, and tennis. Full-on family resort with entertainment programs, aimed at the local market and overrun in school holidays.

C-E Fairview Lodge & Caravan Park, Old Gravelotte Rd, T015-3072679, fairstay@mweb.co.za. A pleasant shady complex on a series of terraces above the Letaba River, with access to a restaurant. Chalets are divided into 3 categories; avoid the cheapest ones. The newer luxury self-catering chalets are good value, just out of town on the Phalaborwa road.

D The Stoep, 4 km from Tzaneen on the Deerpark road, turn off at the Bananas for Africa farm stall on the R71 from Phalaborwa, T015-3075101. 5 double rooms with separate entrance, en suite bathroom, non-smoking room, TV, lounge, evening meals available on request, swimming pool with pleasant deck overlooking the valley, peaceful family-run farm setting.

Phalaborwa *p640*

Being so close to Kruger, this town has a wide range of accommodation options.

A Hans Merensky Estate, just out of town, at the Kruger end, off Koper Rd, T015-7813931, www.hansmerensky.com. Marketed as a golf and wildlife resort, with 18 luxury a/c chalets set around a golf course where game from Kruger casually wanders around. Excellent restaurant.

A Tulani Safari Lodge, on the R40 to Mica, T015-7815454, www.tulanisafarilodge.co.za. Set in the Balule Nature Reserve on the western border of Kruger. 25 chalets with mix of ethnic and modern decor, a/c, restaurant, bar, swimming pool, tennis, hiking trails, bush drives.

A-B Sefapane Lodge, corner of Copper and Essenhout Sts, T015-7806700, www.sefapane.co.za. 31 upmarket, thatched, self-catering chalets in a large indigenous garden. Braai boma, restaurant, swimming pool with a sunken bar, have a meet and greet desk at the airport, fly-in packages available, day trips to Kruger and other regional tours. If you don't have a car this is a good mid-range option.

B Ingwe Park, 3 km out on the Tzaneen road, T015-7813776, www.ingwepark.com. This relaxed and fun bush lodge is set in a restored old miner's camp with comfortable, self-contained bungalows, each with TV and kitchen. Swimming pool, hiking, wide range of bush trails on horseback can be arranged.

B Steyn's Cottage, 67 Bosvlier St, T015-7810836, steyncot@lantic.net. 15 a/c double rooms with en suite bathroom, TV, elegant lounge filled with fine antiques, rooms overlook a neat garden and swimming pool, excellent service, one of the best mid-range options. The La Werna restaurant is next door.

C Raintree Cottage, 1 Essenhout St, T015-7810995, www.raintreecottage.co.za. 8 a/c en suite rooms with attractive Victorian-style decor. B&B with attached tea garden, meals available, swimming pool, close to park gates, evening meals on request, friendly.

C-D Daan & Zena, 15 Birkenhead St, T015-7816049, www.daanzena.co.za. 21 funky units, individually decorated en suite double rooms, self catering units and budget rooms all decorated with whacky furniture and bright colours, with M-Net TV, a/c and tea and coffee making facilities. Swimming pool, colourful lounge, secure parking. Friendly set-up, recommended.

C-E Lantana Lodge, corner of Kiaat and Hall Sts, T015-7815191, www.lantanalodge.co.za. Well-appointed self-catering units with, a/c, DSTV, plus small, cheaper log cabins aimed at backpackers. Also has camping space. Good restaurant, garden bar, swimming pool. Can arrange tours of Kruger.

D-E Elephant Walk, 30 Anna Scheepers Av, T015-7815860, elaphant.walk@nix.co.za. A welcome backpackers close to Kruger Park which also offers good value game viewing trips into Kruger Park. Choice of 13-bed dorm, attractive double room, self-catering cottages, a flat or camping in the shady garden with separate ablution block. Fully equipped kitchen, laundry, meals on request.

Marulaneng/Hoedspruit *p640*

The accommodation listed below is at the bottom of Blyde River Canyon close to Marulaneng/Hoedspruit. For accommodation at the top of the canyon, refer to the Mpumalanga chapter. All are situated within an hour's drive of Kruger's Orpen Gate.

B **Blue Cottages**, 37 km from Marulaneng/ Hoedspruit on the R527 towards Blyde River Canyon, T015-7955114, www.monsoongallery.com. 5 bungalows, 2 suites, set in a beautiful bush garden, swimming pool, each unit is decorated with unique pieces of artwork and African antiques from the attached **Monsoon Gallery**. Self-catering possible, although the attached **Mad Dogz Café**, is regarded as the best restaurant in the area. The owner, has been instrumental in promoting the lowveld and central Kruger region as a world recognized biosphere. Recommended.

B **Blyde River Canyon Lodge**, 28 km from Marulaneng/Hoedspruit, turn off the R531 towards the bottom of the Blyde River Canyon Nature Reserve and Aventura Swadini, T015-7955305, www.blyderivercanyonlodge.com. A very intimate and individual lodge, 6 double thatched rooms with verandas, bar, pool, excellent cuisine. The building is constructed from natural materials, beautiful grounds, which the owners have gone to great lengths to keep totally indigenous, zebras, warthogs, and a blue wildebeest wander across the lawns and through the car park. Recommended.

B **Moholoholo Mountain View Camp**, from Marulaneng/Hoedspruit, turn off the R531 towards the bottom of the Blyde River Canyon Nature Reserve, opposite **Blyde River Canyon Lodge**, T/F015-7955684, www.moholoholo.co.za. A 4000-ha private reserve with wild lion, rhino and hippo. Free morning game walks with a ranger, night drives R40 pp. 9 simple, reed- wall, self-catering chalets, dining boma overlooks a waterhole, educational bush experience.

B-E **Aventura Resort Swadini**, at the very base of Blyde River Canyon off the R531, adjacent to the Blyde River Nature Reserve and dam, T015-7955141, www.aventura.co.za. Part of the Aventura chain, award-winning resort in a stunning location. 78 chalets, 180 camping/caravan stands, shops, restaurants, swimming pools, tennis, mini golf, lots of hikes and a pleasant drive to viewpoints in the reserve, boat rides on the dam. As the crow flies, there is another Aventura resort, **Blyde Canyon** only a few kilometres away at the top of the canyon (see the Blyde River Canyon section in the Mpumalanga chapter), but they are actually over 100 km apart by road.

Eating

Magoebaskloof *p637, map p638*

TT **Atholl Arms**, in front of the tourist office in Haenertsburg on Rissik St, T015-2764712, closed Mon. Breakfast, lunch and dinner, hearty country fare, Sun set lunch, cosy atmosphere. Games evening on Thu.

T **Picasso's**, a prominent wood cabin just off the main road through Haenertsburg, T015-2764724, closes at 1630. Comfortable restaurant and curio shop with a good choice of light meals. The pancakes are a speciality, but also on offer are more substantial dishes like beef stew or chicken casserole. Great local grilled trout, too. Resident African Grey parrot. Internet access.

T **Pot & Plow**, 8 km out of town on the Tzaneen Rd. Closed evenings. Popular roadside restaurant and bar, good for lunch, decent homemade pies and tasty salads.

Tzaneen *p638, map p642*

The best restaurants are in the country hotels. During the day there are a number of roadside tea gardens which serve snack lunches.

TTT **Zeederburg**, The Coach House, T015-3068000, 14 km from town. One of the finest restaurants in the region set in this top-class lodge. Colonial decor, professional service. Good local produce, including smoked trout, and delicious mains, plus some decent veggie options. Huge wine list.

TT **Ashley's Cafe**, 30 Agatha St, T015-3077270. Best restaurant in town, offering great breakfasts, coffees, salads and sandwiches at lunchtime, and larger meals in the evenings, including a good pepper steak, plus a decent cocktail menu. Pleasant balcony overlooking gardens.

T **Villa Italia**, corner of Danie Joubert and Lannie Sts, T015-3072792. Standard good value Italian, adequate pizza and pasta dishes.

Phalaborwa *p640*

TT **La Werna**, 67 Bosvlier St, T015-7810836. The best restaurant in town is this smart diner next to **Steyn's Cottage**. Meals are served by candlelight. There's an enjoyable selection of meat and poultry dishes, plus good local ingredients like trout. Beautifully decorated intimate dining room, booking advised. Recommended.

Sefepane Lodge, Copper Rd, T015-7806700. Smart lodge restaurant with indoor ethnic dining room and pleasant outdoor boma lit by lanterns and candles. Good South African fare served indoors, such as lamb potjies or bobotie, plus venison specials such as springbok. The boma is popular with tour groups; buffets served.
La Gondola, Phalaborwa Mall. Good value pasta and pizza.

Marulaneng/Hoedspruit *p640, map p*
Mad Dogz Café, on the R527, east of the junction of the R527 and R36, T015-7955425, by the entrance for the **Blue Cottages** on the main road. The food here is some of the best you'll find in the region, and this makes for a great lunchtime stop-off en route to Kruger National Park. Big, wholesome breakfasts, excellent lunches using fusion dishes, Creole chicken, spicy Thai beef and Cape Malay bobotie. The setting is lovely, with brightly-painted tables clustered under thatched roofs, surrounded by lush tropical vegetation. Recommended.
The Trading Post, 26 km from Marulaneng/Hoedspruit via Klaserie on the R531, T015-7955219, tradingpost@mweb.co.za. An attractive and unusual restaurant and pub owned by a friendly ex-game ranger . A happy combination of the traditional South African way of cooking and the French social way of eating. Each table has an in-built gas *braai*, and you cook your meat to your liking. Game platters including strips of warthog and crocodile are available, as are ready-prepared meat dishes, salads, and pizzas.

Festivals and events

Magoebaskloof *p637, map p638*
Sep The Spring Cherry and Azalea Blossom Festival, Craft Fair and Orchid Exhibition take place around Haenertsburg. The flowers transform entire valleys into blankets of colour.

Shopping

Marulaneng/Hoedspruit *p640*
Monsoon Gallery, next door to the **Mad Dogz Café** (see above), www.mansoongallery.com. Tasteful gallery selling fine African art, jewellery, cloth and antiques, plus some contemporary pieces. All the packing and shipping can be arranged from here. There is also a shop here selling items produced at the **Bombyx Mori Silk Farm** (see page 640).

Activities and tours

Phalaborwa *p640*

Golf

Hans Merensky Country Club, T015- 7813931, www.hansmerensky.com. Based around an 18-hole PGA championship golf course. Golfers negotiate wildlife on the greens while they play; watch out for the hippos on the 17th hole. Also has accommodation. Call in advance. The best times early morning or late afternoon.

Tour operators

Jumbo River Safaris, T015-7816168, www.riversafaris.co.za. Organizes a fun 3-hr boat trip on the Olifants River for ever-popular sundowners. Always a good chance of seeing game and colourful water birds. Also arranges longer Kruger safaris.

Transport

Phalaborwa *p640*

Air

Phalaborwa Kruger Park Gateway Airport, 2 km from town centre and entrance to Kruger Park, T015-7815823, has a fabulous design. The baggage reeclaim is under a thatched roof, the seats in the waiting area are rocks and the drinking fountain spouts from a tree stump.
SA Airlink, T015-7815823, central reservations T011-9781111, www.saairlink.co.za, operates daily flights between Phalaborwa and **Johannesburg** (1 hr).

Car hire

Budget T015-7815404, **Hertz** T015-7819900 and **Imperial** T015-7810376, are at the airport.

Marulaneng/Hoedspruit *p640*

Air

Eastgate Airport is 7 km from Marulaneng/Hoedspruit on the road to the Timbavati Game Reserve, T015-7933681. There are currently no scheduled flights to Eastgate, but it is used by charter companies for guest of the luxury lodges in private reserves.

Directory

Tzaneen *p638, map p642*
Internet Procom Internet Café, 18 Peace St, T015-3074836, a short distance from the commercial centre; follow the one-way street towards the swimming pool, Mon-Sat. **Medical services** Ambulance, T10177. Chemist, T015-3073790. Hospital, T015-3068500. **Useful telephone numbers** Police, T10111.

Phalaborwa *p640*
Banks Standard, Palm St; ABSA, Wilger St, ATMs and foreign exchange available. **Internet** Net-o-Mania, T015-7817812, Phalaborwa Mall, Palm St, not open evenings or Sun. **Medical services** Chemist, 24-hr, T015-7813805. Hospital, T015-7853511. **Useful telephone numbers** Police, T10111.

Free State

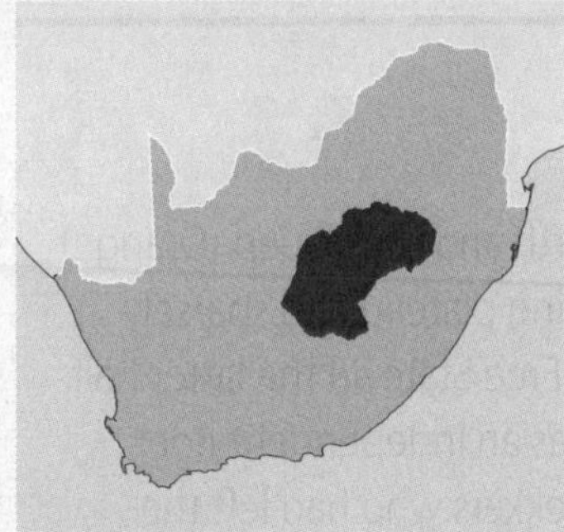

Footprint features

Introduction

Between the Vaal River to the north and the Gariep (Orange) River in the south lies an undulating plateau and sparsely populated prairie land known as Free State. In the latter half of the 19th century the region was an independent Boer Republic governed by the Voortrekkers who had left the British Cape Colony in the 1830s. During this brief period of independence, Bloemfontein developed into a fine modern capital with many grand sandstone buildings. But the discovery of diamonds at Jagersfontein and Kimberley, along with gold in the second independent Boer Republic of the time, led to the outbreak of the Anglo-Boer War on 11 October 1899, a fact that has left its mark on the province.

While there is not much to see in the arid farmlands to the west of Bloemfontein, the Maluti Mountains in the eastern Free State hold many surprises. The scenery is spectacular as it rises to meet the lands of Lesotho, scattered with dams, mountain rivers and nature reserves, and connected by pretty rural villages with a wide range of accommodation choices and activities. At the centre of this area lies the spectacular Golden Gate Highlands National Park, where, even during the summer months, the hills can sometimes be covered with snow.

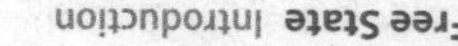

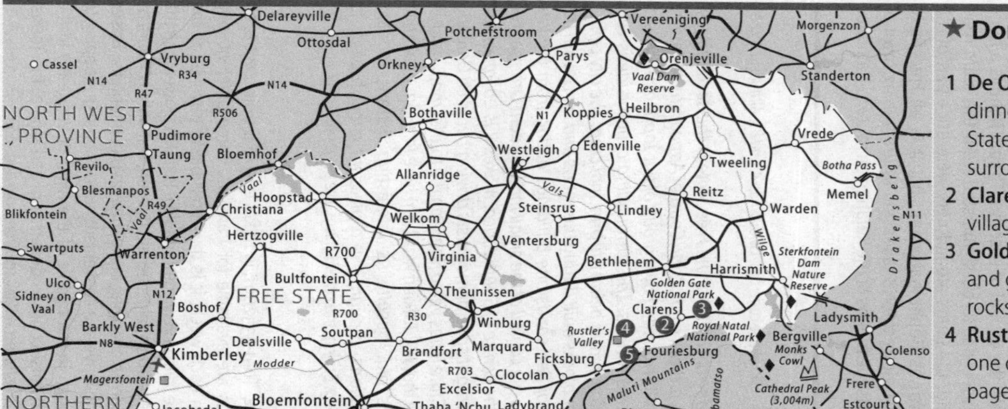

★ Don't miss...

1 **De Oude Kraal** Treat yourself to a gourmet 6-course dinner accompanied by fine wines. This is the Free State's best restaurant set on an 1885 farmstead surrounded by beautiful gardens, page 655.

2 **Clarens** Shop for arts and crafts in this small pretty village in the Eastern Highlands, page 659.

3 **Golden Gate National Park** Visit the caves, cliffs and grasslands, set against a backdrop of golden rocks, page 659.

4 **Rustler's Valley Festival** Celebrate the New Year at one of the country's most exciting music festivals, page 665.

5 **Maluti Mountains** Go horse riding across beautiful farmland in the foothills. The Free State was made for horses and there are several stables in the region, page 666.

Ins and outs

Getting around

Bloemfontein is one of South Africa's most central transport hubs for buses, flights and trains, so you will not have any trouble getting to the Free State's capital. Getting around this part of South Africa is another matter, however, and you will need a car to explore it properly. The general flow of traffic is between the Cape and Johannesburg along the N1 but there are several contrasting routes you can take from Bloemfontein.

The **N1 north** takes you across the veld to Johannesburg; most of the countryside is flat and scattered with ugly mine dumps. There is little to stop for between here and Gauteng. The **N1 south** passes by the early settler towns of the **Xhariep** region before entering the **Great Karoo**. There is a long way to go before you reach the first fertile valleys of the Cape. The **N8** to the east goes to the higher lands of Lesotho and what are known as the **Eastern Highlands**. The countryside here is the most spectacular in Free State and this is the main road to Maseru (140 km), the capital of Lesotho. **Thaba 'Nchu** is a huge township that used not to be signposted from the main road during Apartheid; the lands around here were once part of the quasi-independent homeland known as Bophuthatswana, but it is all Free State today. Finally a short trip to the west along the N8 takes you to the mining town of **Kimberley**; further west the road skirts the fringes of the Kalahari en route to Namibia.

For more information visit www.freestateprovince.co.za or www.freestateonline.co.za.

Bloemfontein

→ *Phone code: 051. Colour map 4, grid B3. Altitude: 1,392 m*

With one million residents, the provincial capital of the Free State is the sixth biggest city in South Africa and the country's judicial capital, the Court of Appeal sits here. The city is located on the highveld plains surrounded by a group of flat-topped hillocks. It has warm, wet summers and dry, cold winters. The surrounding countryside is very fertile and an important farming region, maize being the principal crop. The city centre is an interesting mix of modern tower blocks built during the 1960s and 1970s with the State's mineral wealth, and a core of fine sandstone buildings dating from the late 19th century when Bloemfontein was the capital of the small independent Orange Free State Republic. Its location right in the centre of South Africa, makes it is an important transport centre, and a popular overnight spot for motorists driving between Gauteng and the Cape. Like much of the Free State it has yet to figure on the tourist map, though fans of Lord of the Rings should note that JRR Tolkien was born here in 1892, moving to England when he was four years old. Despite its interesting history, modern Bloemfontein has few visitor attractions, though it is a pleasant enough place to spend a couple of days. ▸▸ *For Sleeping, Eating and other listings, see pages 654-657.*

Ins and outs

Getting there Bloemfontein Airport, T051-4332001, is 10 km east of the city centre, off the N8, the Thaba Nchu road. Taxis are available for transfers. Three different long distance **trains** stop in Bloemfontein each week, it is thus possible to travel to all the major towns in South Africa. While the train is very comfortable it is much slower than the bus, for example the journey from Cape Town takes 20 hrs by train, but only 11 hours by bus. Check timings carefully if you plan on changing bus or train in Bloemfontein. **Buses** starting their journey from here tend to leave at a convenient hour, but those stopping to pick up and drop off can pass through in the middle of the night or very early in the morning. **Greyhound, Intercape** and **Translux** buses depart from and stop at the Tourist Centre on Park Road (see below). ▸▸ *For further details, see Transport, page 656.*

Tourist information The **Tourist Centre** ⓘ *60 Park Rd, T051-4058489, www.bloemfontein.co.za, Mon-Fri 0800-1615, Sat 0800-1200*, is helpful with knowledgeable staff who are keen to promote Bloemfontein as a tourist destination. **Motheo District Municipality Tourism** ⓘ *next to the Tourist Centre, T051-4471362, transgariep@intekom.co.za, Mon-Fri 0730-1600*, has a range of leaflets covering most of the province including the Xhariep. It has a good selection of information on the Free State, strong supporters of cultural and community-based tourism projects.

Background

There are several theories about the name Bloemfontein, but the accepted version is that the wife of Johannes Nicolaas Brits, one of the first settlers in the area who started to farm here in 1840, planted some flowers around the fountain which was used by everyone travelling across the central plains.

In 1846 the Governor of the Cape Colony, Sir Peregrine Maitland, made a treaty with the Griqua chief, Adam Kok, by which the land between the Riet and Modder rivers be opened to European settlement. Major Henry Warden, the British resident in Griqua territory, was instructed to move to the location to co-ordinate the new settlers. He chose Bloemfontein farm and Brits received £37.10 in compensation, followed by £50 a few years later and a farm in Harrismith, which he also named Bloemfontein.

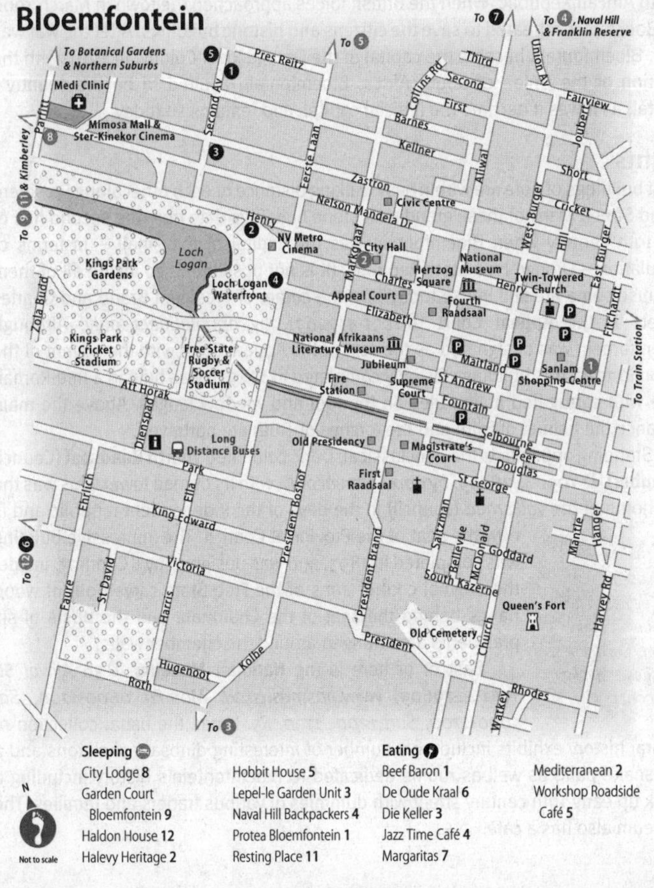

In 1848 Sir Harry Smith visited the new settlement and proclaimed the territory between the Orange and Vaal rivers as British, calling it the Orange River Sovereignty with Bloemfontein as its capital. Queen's Fort was built and the town started slowly to take shape. By 1853, Church Square and Market Square (now Hoffman Square) had been laid out. However, the surrounding countryside was still full of wild animals, which meant that travellers and farmers were in danger of attacks from lions, leopards and wild dogs. The British Government had decided the territory was hardly fit for habitation and not worth the trouble of maintaining. In 1854 the Bloemfontein Convention was signed, giving independence to the land between the Orange and Vaal rivers, and the British soldiers marched out of the town.

Josias Hoffman was the first President of the Republic of the Orange Free State and a *volksraad* (people's council) was elected to sit in the simple *raadsaal* (council chamber). This first council chamber can still be seen in St George's Street. President Johannes Brand followed him in 1863, under whom the town enjoyed 25 years of stable and prosperous independence when some fine government buildings were built. In 1890 the railway link with the Cape was finally completed and the town prospered further, though in 1904 there was a disastrous flood that cut the city in half and destroyed many buildings.

The discovery of diamonds at Jagersfontein and Kimberley along with gold, quickly led to the British wanting to re-establish control over these two regions. The Anglo-Boer War broke out and President Steyn of the Orange Free State sided with the South African Republic. When the British forces approached the town in March 1900 the Boer forces retreated to save the citizens and historic buildings. After the war was over, Bloemfontein became the capital of the Orange River Colony. In 1910, with the creation of the Union of South Africa, Bloemfontein aspired to be the country's capital; as it was it became the judicial capital, and remains so today.

Sights

Most buildings of note are within easy walking distance of each other along President Brand Street. Many of these grand sandstone buildings date from the second half of the 19th century when Bloemfontein was the capital of the small – in terms of population – Orange Free State Republic. (It is not possible to go inside all of them because some are still in use today.) On the corner of President Brand and Charles streets is the **Appeal Court** ⓘ *T051-4472631, by appointment only*. Although Bloemfontein was designated as the seat of the Appeal Court with the advent of the Union in 1910, this building was only completed in 1929. It was built in a free-Roman style with corrugated Italian tiles on the roof and window ledges. Above the main entrance the helmet of Faith and the torches of Truth are portrayed.

Standing opposite is the neoclassical, Doric columned **Fourth Raadsaal (Council Chamber)** ⓘ *T051-4478899, by appointment only*, with its domed tower. This was the last home of the *volksraad* (council) in the days of the independent republic and is now the seat of the Provincial Council. The impressive building was completed in 1893, and was designed by L Canning. Inside, the original coat of arms of the Free State carved out of wood hangs behind the seat of the Chairman, and the busts of six presidents are arranged around the chamber walls.

The Tourist Centre produces a useful map showing 'The Rose Walk through Bloemfontein', which covers the major historical sites and takes about 1½ hours.

East of of here is the **National Museum** ⓘ *36 Aliwal St, T051-4479609, www.nasmus.co.za. Mon-Fri 0800-1700, Sat 1000-1700, Sun 1200- 1730, R5*. It has the usual collection of natural history exhibits including a number of interesting dinosaur skeletons and a live snake park, as well as rooms dedicated to Bloemfontein's history including a mock up early 19th century street with dummies of various traders and families. The museum also has a café.

On the corner of President Brand and Maitland streets, is the **Old Government Building**, now the **National Afrikaans Literature Museum** ⓘ *Mon-Fri 0800-1215, 1300-1600, Sat 0900-1200, T051-4054711*, an important collection of Afrikaans literature, and original manuscripts by leading poets and novelists. The original single-storey building had a high clock tower and was built by Richard Wocke in 1875 to house a government office. A second storey was added and then in 1906 an extension designed by Herbert Baker was built at the back. Baker created the present form after a serious fire in 1908.

On President Brand Street is the **Jubileum** building. It was built in the late 1920s by boys from a local orphanage to provide a venue for reading and refreshments for young Afrikaners. A variety of entertainments were staged here, including concerts and art exhibitions, as well as political rallies.

Opposite the fire station, is the **Supreme Court** ⓘ *corner of President Brand and Fontein Sts, T051-4478837, by appointment only*. This seat of the Provincial Law Court was built in 1909 at a cost of £60,000. This is a stately and vast court building where many famous cases have been tried in recent years.

Across the river is the **Old Presidency** ⓘ *corner of President Brand and St George's Sts, T051-4480949, Tue-Fri 1000-1200, 1300-1600, Sat-Sun 1300-1700, free*. This was home to the last three state presidents before the British invasion and occupies the site where Brits erected his original farm buildings and where Major Warden built his first residence in 1846. It has now been converted into a concert hall and a museum depicting the lives of the presidents. The original stables at the back have been converted into a coffee shop.

Just around the corner is the **First Raadsaal (Council Chamber)** ⓘ *St George's St, Mon-Fri 1015-1500, Sat-Sun 1400-1700, small entrance fee*. This is a typical pioneers' building with a thatched roof, beaten dung floor and long white mud walls. It was opened in 1849 as the Government Schoolhouse, but was also used as a church and council chamber. After the creation of the Orange Free State Republic the inauguration ceremonies for the first two presidents, Josias Hoffman and Jacobus Boshof, were held here. The *volksraad*, or people's council, met here until 1856, hence the name First Raadsaal. In 1877 the building was given to the town to be used as a museum.

On Church Street, the **Twin-towered Church**, which was fully restored in 1985, is on the site of the first small church built in 1849. Inaugurated in 1880, the church played a major role as the venue for the inauguration ceremonies for the last three state presidents, JH Brand, FW Reitz and MT Steyn. In 1935 the western tower collapsed and the other tower was removed, only for residents then to complain that the absence of spires spoilt the church's appearance; so in 1942 the two spires were re-erected.

In **Hertzog Square**, outside the City Hall, is a memorial and statue of General Hertzog. He became Prime Minister of South Africa in 1929 and again in 1934. A founder member of the Afrikaans-supporting, right wing National Party in 1914, he introduced much of the legislation against non-whites.

The **National Women's Memorial** is an obelisk, 36.5 m high, built of sandstone from Kroonstad and resting at the foot of two kopjes on the outskirts of Bloemfontein on Monument Rd. On each side of the column is a bronze bas-relief depicting scenes from the suffering of women and children during the Anglo-Boer War. The monument was unveiled on 16 December 1913 to commemorate the 26,370 women and children who died in concentration camps as a result of the Anglo-Boer War.

Naval Hill was once outside the city, but is now almost completely engulfed by the expanding suburbs. The panoramic views of the city are worth the drive. At the top of this hill are the **Franklin Game Reserve**, the **Observatory Theatre** and a **White Horse**. The White Horse was laid out by soldiers during the Anglo-Boer War as a landmark for returning horsemen. There are eland, hartebeest and springbok in the reserve, and it is not uncommon to get very close to giraffe in the car park of the Observatory Theatre where they seek out shade.

South of the centre is the **Queen's Fort**, or **Military Museum** ⓘ *Church St, T051-4475478, Mon-Fri 0800-1600, free.* Following his victory over the Boers at the battle of Boomplaats, Sir Harry Smith decided to build a new fort on a more strategically situated hill, named after Queen Victoria. For the first 30 years of the Free State Republic it was left to fall into a state of disrepair. In 1879, Captain FW Albrecht was appointed to oversee the complete rebuilding of the fort and mounted four iron nine-pounder guns. During the Second Anglo-Boer War it was occupied by British troops and at the end of the war it was given to the South African Constabulary. After housing a military headquarters the building is now a museum.

Free State National Botanical Garden ⓘ *Rayton Rd, off Dan Pienaar Dr, R702, T051-4363612, daily 0800-1800, R10,* covers 70 ha on the outskirts of Bloemfontein and spans a valley between picturesque dolerite koppies. Its natural vegetation comprises tall grassland and woodland, dominated by magnificent wild olive and karee trees and is home to about 400 species of plants. From November to March most of the plants in the garden are in full leaf; from March to June the colourful autumn shades dominate. There are pleasant walks through the gardens and up to the koppies and there's a birdhide, restaurant and visitor centre. Two new demonstration gardens are being developed; one on plants with medicinal properties, and the other to show water wise gardening techniques.

Township tours

While Bloemfontein has important 'white' historical sites, the nearby townships also have significance relating to the birth of the ANC and the legacy of the struggle. To see how life is lived in these places is interesting in its own right, and tours visit cultural and art centres, shebeens (pubs), dance demonstrations, traditional restaurants, jazz clubs, and the various historical sites. There are three major townships outside Bloemfontein. Within the city limits, **Mangaung** was where the ANC was founded in 1912. **Botshabelo**, meaning 'place of refugees', is 60 km from Bloemfontein on the N8. Estimated to be the second largest in the country after Soweto, it was established when blacks were forcibly removed from the Orange Free State towns. The vision of Pretoria during the Apartheid era was to develop Botshabelo into a so called 'Golden City' for the Sotho and Xhosa people, and rapid Apartheid planning at the time made it the fastest-growing urban centre in South Africa. Beyond Botshabelo, 65 km from Bloemfontein, **Thaba 'Nchu** was originally settled by Voortrekkers and later by Chief Moroka, the founder of the Barolong tribe and an important member of the early ANC. There is a rich Tswana culture here, particularly in the villages, which are still governed by chiefs and traditional courts. ▸▸ *For further details, see Tour operators, page 656.*

Township tours are playing an increasing role in the South African tourism industry, and create jobs for local communities who have been denied the role of being involved in tourism in the past.

Sleeping

Bloemfontein *p650, map p651*

As Bloemfontein is an overnight stop for traffic between Jo'burg and Cape Town, there is a vast range of accommodation here. Look out for signs as you drive into town from the N1. The tourist centre has a full list.

AL **Halevy Heritage Hotel**, corner of Markgraaff and Charles Sts, T051-4030600, www.halevyheritage.com. Very stylish historic building dating from 1893, now completely refurbished with Victorian and Edwardian décor and reopened in 2004, 21 elegant rooms with all the mod cons, 2 bars, quality restaurant and cosy courtyard.

A **Hobbit House**, 19 President Steyn Av, T051-4470663, www.hobbit.co.za. 12 double en suite rooms with fluffy towels and duck down duvets in a superior renovated boutique hotel dating from 1925 and obviously named after Tolkien's creation, full of period furnishings. Bar fashioned out of a tree, gourmet food in the restaurant served on china and silverware, after a day of exploring the city by foot the neat garden and swimming pool are a welcome sight. A special touch is a glass of sherry and chocolate at bedtime. Recommended.

A Garden Court Bloemfontein, (this is a Holiday Inn which has been rebranded) corner of Zastron St and Melville Drive, T051-4441253, www.southernsun.com. 147 a/c rooms, non-smoking room, set around an open courtyard, restaurant, bar, swimming pool, disabled facilities, secure parking, comfortable if not predictable hotel on the outskirts of the city.

B Protea Hotel Bloemfontein, Sanlam Plaza, East Burger St, T051-4301911, www.protea hotels.com. 113 a/c rooms, TV, restaurant, bar, shops, secure parking, swimming pool, the principal hotel in the city centre, full quota of facilities but lacking in charm.

B City Lodge, corner of Nelson Mandela St and Parfitt Av, T051-4442974, www.city lodge.co.za. 50 doubles, 102 singles, a/c, good value town hotel geared for the business traveller, hence lots of small single rooms, choice of non-smoking, evening bar, pay extra for breakfast which is served in lobby lounge, small swimming pool. Rooms tend to suffer from traffic noise when you open windows.

B The Resting Place, 50 Scholtz St, T051-5225008, www.restingplace.cjb.net. A total of 23 units set around the garden or pool, doubles and family rooms, some with DSTV, microwave, a/c, safe, jet bath and Turkish bath, also self-catering chalets, breakfast on request, spacious and secure central guesthouse, children and wheelchair friendly.

C Glen Country Lodge, 20 km north of Bloemfontein on the N1, T051-8612042, www.glencountryloge.co.za. An alternative to city accommodation for drivers, 12 thatched chalets with bathrooms and kitchenettes, nestled amongst acacia trees, breakfast and dinner on request, swimming pool, lovely spot in the bush with sweeping lawns.

C Haldon House, Japie Spesery Lane, Kwaggafontein, west of the city, T051-5233607, haldon@internext.co.za. 8 en suite double rooms with TV, most have a separate entrance. This is a fine house set in a mature estate with a swimming pool and a large shade veranda. Evening meals can be arranged. Short drive from city centre. Recommended.

C Lepel-le Garden Unit, 14 Usmar St, T082-6713137, lventer22@polka.co.za. (The name means 'to lie like spoons'.) A cosy, peaceful poolside cottage, self-catering for 4 people, in a quiet suburb, private entrance, TV, the owner manages the tourist office so you'll be in good hands. Recommended.

D-E Naval Hill Backpackers, Delville Rd, north of the centre, follow West Burger St towards Naval Hill and Franklin Reserve, T051-4307266, www.navalhillbackpackers.co.za. Regular users of backpackers will appreciate the different building; here the set-up has been created in an old water pump station dating from 1901. Dorms in ingenious corrugated iron shacks within the old building, camping in the large grounds, 1 double private room with bush shower, large lounge and unusual underground eating area with pizza oven.

Eating

Bloemfontein *p650, map p651*

TTT De Oude Kraal, 35 km out of town, off the N1 to Cape Town, T051-5640636, www.oude kraal.co.za, breakfast 0715-0900, dinner 1930, lunch by arrangement only. Something a bit special, so despite its remote location booking is essential. Famous for its typical South African food, such as 'boerekos', formal 6-course dinners, fine wines, and cigars in a wonderful setting in a restored farmhouse, this restaurant is a favourite of South Africa's *Eat Out* magazine. Also offers 8 spacious garden rooms and 2 suites (**B**) each with their own bathroom and fireplace. Recommended.

TT Beef Baron, 22 Second Av, Westdene, T051-4474290, 1200-1430, 1830-late, closed Sun evening and Mon and Sat lunchtime. Well-established steakhouse, good Karoo lamb as well as mature steaks and wide range of sauces, friendly service, good wine list, wooden deck for alfresco dining.

TT Butcher's Brothers Steakhouse and Deli, Loch Logan Waterfront, T051-4301253. 1000-2200. Quality steak house with excellent cuts of beef also available from the deli along with olives and homemade pasta, excellent though expensive wine list, quick service.

TT Catch 22, Mimosa Mall, T051-4446877. 1030-2330. Good and fresh seafood, despite the distance from the sea, try the seafood paella or casserole, or snails in garlic sauce, pleasant decor and friendly staff.

Die Keller, 149 Zastron St, Westdene, T051-4487840, 1100-late. Good value restaurant and cellar bar, beer on tap, giant TV screen, fun atmosphere at the weekend.

Mediterranean, Loch Logan Waterfront, above House of Coffees, T051-4486194, 1130-2330. Wide veranda overlooking the lake and King's Park, seafood, pasta, Greek salads, vegetarians get special attention.

Jazz Time Café, Loch Logan Waterfront, T051-4305727, 1200-2400. Huge cocktail bar, outside terrace, excellent music, jazz, blues, big band, hubble-bubble pipes, extensive menu, try the *Zivas*, a Yemeni dough with a savoury filling, folded and toasted, a great place for an evening out.

Margaritas, Bays Village, 59 Milner Rd, Bayswater, T051-4363729, 1200-1430, 1830-2230, closed Mon, no lunch Sat, no dinner Sun. A good choice of fresh seafood and steaks, extensive wine list, or snacks at the English pub-style bar.

Workshop Roadside Café, 109 President Reitz St, Westdene, T051-4472761. Trendy café with a giant TV screen, packed solid when there's a rugby match on, good value for the budget-minded.

Bars and clubs

Bloemfontein *p650, map p651*

There high number of students in Bloemfontein mean there is also a large club scene. As in any city, clubs go in and out of favour quickly and often change names or move location. For the latest information ask the waiters at the **Jazz Time Café** (see above).

Shopping

Bloemfontein *p650, map p651*

An arts and crafts market is held in Kings Park on the first Sat of every month.

Loch Logan Waterfront, First Av. An attractive outdoor shopping mall next to a lake and dam in Kings Park. Some of Bloemfontein's trendiest restaurants and bars are scattered along the boardwalk on the water's edge and there is a 6-screen cinema.

Mimosa Mall, corner of Nelson Mandela and Parfitt Sts. A standard South African mall with the usual facilities, banks, food court, 4-screen Ster-Kinekor cinema, 2 internet cafés, American Express office.

Activities and tours

Bloemfontein *p650, map p651*

Cricket

International cricket matches are played at the **Goodyear Park Stadium** which is part of the complex of excellent sports facilities to the west of the city centre close to the tourist office. It has been renamed Springbok Park, but it is mostly referred to by its old name. The cricket ground is a fun, small stadium, which has yet to be spoilt by towering modern stands. Here fans can still lounge around or cook up a braai on grass banks as the game unfolds in front of them, a cool beer in hand. Tickets through **Compu ticket**, www.computicket.co.za, and contact the **Free State Cricket Union's**, T051-4475715, www.fscu.co.za, for fixtures.

Football and rugby

Free State Stadium, T051-4071700, www.fschee tahs.co.za. Also known as Vodacom Park after its sponsors, this is next door to the cricket ground in Kings Park, and is a neat modern stadium where international football and rugby matches are played. Tickets through **Computicket**.

Tours

A full-day tour visits all 3 townships, while a half-day tour visits 1 or 2, which can be combined with a half-day city tour. Contact **Motheo District Municipality Tourism** (see page 651), or **Mipa Tours**, T051-4488786.

Johan Hattingh, T051-4473447, jhattingh @anglo-boer.co.za. A recommended, knowledgeable guide for tours of the battlefields from the Boer War and the Zulu wars. He also organizes historical, tailor-made trips throughout Free State.

Transport

Bloemfontein *p650, map p651*

1000 km to **Cape Town**; 415 km to **Johannesburg**; 186 km to **Kimberley**; 157 km to **Maseru**.

Air

Airport information, T051-4473811. SAA, T011-9781111, www.flysaa.com, flies direct to **Durban** and **Port Elizabeth**, and **East London** via Port Elizabeth.

Bus
Intercape, T051-4471435, www.intercape.co.za, **Greyhound**, T051-4471558, www.greyhound.co.za, and **Translux** T051-40832422, www.translux.co.za, offices are in the tourist centre on Park Rd where the buses stop. There are daily services to just about all the other large cities including **Cape Town**, **Durban**, **Johannesburg**, and **Port Elizabeth**. Big Sky Coaches, T051-5233620, www.bigskycoaches.co.za, runs a service to **Upington**, in the Northern Cape Province, at Fri 1400 from the tourist centre; this service returns from Upington on Sun.

Car hire
Avis, airport, T051-4332331, Gysie Pienaar Motors, Nelson Mandela St, T051-4476185, www.avis.co.za. **Budget**, airport T051-4331178, www.budget.co.za. **Imperial**, airport T051-4333511, **Safari Motors**, Zastron St, T051-4474202, www.imperialcarrental.co.za.

Taxi
Silver Leaf Taxis, at the tourist centre T051-4302005, for airport transfers.

Train
Part of the original station building from 1890 still remains. Information T051-4082941, reservations T0860-008888, www.spoornet.co.za, timetables and fares are published on the website. Bloemfontein is connected to most major cities, there are services to **Port Elizabeth**, **Johannesburg**, **East London**, **Kimberley** and **Cape Town**.

Directory

Bloemfontein *p650, map p651*
Banks All the main branches are within the Mimosa Mall, corner of Nelson Mandela and Parfitt Sts. **Medical services** Ambulance, Chemist and Medi clinic, T051-4046225/6, www.medicclinic.co.za.

Eastern Highlands

The countryside neighbouring the Lesotho border, dominated by sandstone outcrops and eroded river valleys, is the most dramatic and interesting in the Free State. The hills once provided shelter for the early San hunters who lived in the region and there are some fine examples of cave paintings as a record of this past. (You will need guidance from the local tourist offices to find and see the art.) The region looks its best in the spring when the cherry orchards are in blossom. During winter there can be heavy snowfalls in the mountains. The highlands are perfect hiking country and ideal for pony trekking and there are some great accommodation options on farms and in secluded valleys. Running parallel to the Lesotho border, the R26 passes through all the towns of note in this region. For more information on the area, visit www.easternfreestate.com.
▸▸ *For Sleeping, Eating and other listings, see pages 662-666.*

Ladybrand

▸▸ *pp662-666. Phone code: 051. Colour map 4, grid B4.*

A pleasant country town surrounded by a sandstone ridge full of San paintings and hidden caves, Ladybrand is the closest South African town to the Lesotho capital, Maseru (15 km). Along with Ficksburg, the town was founded in 1867 after the war between the Boers and the Basothos to help guarantee peace in the Conquered Territory. It was named after Lady Catharina Brand, the mother of President Brand of the Orange Free State Republic. Sandstone from this area was used to build the Union Building in Pretoria. The small **Catharina Brand Museum** at 17 Church Street has an interesting feature on the **Lesotho Highlands Water Project** (see Lesotho chapter).

Ins and outs

Maloti Route Tourism Office ⓘ *Catharina Brand Museum, T051-9245131, malotiinfo@xsinet.co.za, Mon-Fri 0800-1700*. The Maloti Route covers the Free

 State's Eastern Highlands, parts of the Eastern Cape and Lesotho, so this enthusiastic tourist office is well worth going out of your way for if you are planning to travel in any of these regions. They can provide an excellent booklet and map.

Sights

There are two major **San rock painting** sites nearby that can be visited with a guide from the tourist office. One of 12 San art national monuments in the country, it is thought that they are the most concentrated San paintings in South Africa, ranging from 5000 to 250 years old. At **Modderpoort**, 15 km to the north, there is a unique cave church dating from 1869. It was built by the Anglican Society of St Augustine, a small group of monks. You can visit by prior arrangement, T051-9243318.

Ficksburg and the Rustler's Valley » pp662-666.

Phone code: 051. Colour map 4, grid B5. Altitude: 1,629 m.

Named after Cmdt-Gen Johan Fick, a hero of the Basotho wars, the town was founded in 1867 to occupy what was known as the Conquered Territory after the Basotho war. Its role was to prevent cattle rustlers coming over from Lesotho and to strengthen general control over the area. Interestingly, cattle rustling still occasionally occurs in this region. A **cherry festival**, www.cherryfestival.co.za, is held here during the third week of November each year, when you can indulge in cherry liqueur, maraschino, schnapps, and brandied cherries in syrup. These days the small town has important trade links with Lesotho, but otherwise it is only worth visiting for basic supplies and for the **tourist office** ⓘ *96 McCabe St, T051-9332130, www.ficksburg.net*, which has an exhibition on the **Lesotho Highlands Water Project**. A small **museum** ⓘ *Mon-Fri 1000-1200, 1400-1600*, commemorates the (not very interesting) life of General Fick.

Rustler's Valley is a popular destination to the north of Ficksburg in the foothills of the Witteberge Mountains. It has become famous as one of South Africa's premier festival sites. » *For further details, see Festivals and events, page 665.*

Fouriesburg to Clarens » *pp662-666.* *Phone code: 058.*

Colour map 5, grid A5.

Fouriesburg is a small, untidy town 12 km from the **Caledonspoort** border post with Lesotho. Founded in 1892, it was named after Christoffel Fourie, the local farmer who originally owned the land. For a few months during the **Anglo-Boer War**, the town was the last seat of the Orange Free State's republican government and a stronghold of the Boer forces. As a consequence it was almost destroyed by the British army.

About 2 km south of Fouriesburg is the **Meiringskloof Nature Park** (R10 per car, R20 per person). Within the park are overnight chalets and a campsite and short walks among the cliffs where there is a large open cave, '*holkrans*', once used as a hide-out during the Anglo-Boer War. For visitors with a head for heights there is a chain ladder which goes up a steep cliff face to a dam supplying water to Fouriesburg.

North of Fouriesburg

Travelling north from Fouriesburg there is a choice of two routes; 45 km direct to Bethlehem on the R26, or a much more interesting route, the R711 to Clarens, which also provides the opportunity to visit the Golden Gate National Park (see page 659).

Surrender Hill is 7 km before Clarens on the R711. The name reminds the Boers of their most devastating defeat during the Anglo-Boer War, when on 29 July 1900, 4314 Free State soldiers under General Prinsloo were cornered in the mountains and surrendered to the British. Most were sent to India as prisoners of war.

Bread basket

About 90% of the Free State is used for agriculture with about two million hectares under cultivation for crops. Of these, about 100,000 are irrigated. The Free State is aptly referred to as the 'bread basket' of South Africa, producing about 40% of the total maize production of South Africa, 50% of wheat, 80% of sorghum, 33% of potatoes, 18% of red meat, 30% of groundnuts and 15% of wool. Around 11,500 commercial farmers are farming on some 50,000 farms in the province. The other big earner is mining and the Free State produces about one third of South Africa's gold. It also has large deposits of coal, and produces approximately 80% of South Africa's bentonite (a sort of clay that used in the building trade). The mining industry is also the biggest net supplier of jobs in the province employing approximately 22% of the labour force.

Clarens

» *pp662-666. Phone code: 058. Colour map 4, grid A5.*

This village was named after the Swiss resort on the shore of Lake Geneva where President Paul Kruger died in 1904. The settlement was only laid out in 1912 and has no historical past to explore but the relaxed feel of the place makes it the ideal spot to use as a base to explore the highlands. Tourism has taken over in this tiny, pretty village and a number of galleries, craft shops, and tea rooms surround a grassed square with a few sandstone buildings and large trees. It is the closest village to the Golden Gate National Park when approaching from the west. The natural beauty of the area has attracted a number of artists to the region.

The grasslands which dominate the sandstone slopes are known for their large variety of wild flowers in the summer months.

There are five quite well-preserved **cave paintings** on a farm called Sonaapplaats, 20 minutes' walk from town. To visit these paintings, call in at the local tourist office, **Clarens Destinations** ⓘ *Market St, T058-2561542, www.goclarens reservations.co.za, daily 0900-1300, 1400-1700*, who will phone ahead to let the farm owners know you are coming. Clarens is a small community and the staff in this office are helpful, local booking agents for accommodation and activities, and know all the local artists and craftspeople. Worth a stop if you are considering buying quality pieces.

Around Clarens

Basotho Cultural Village ⓘ *from Clarens head towards Golden Gate National Park, the village is 10 km before the park gate on the right, T058-7210300, www.dorea.co.za/ecotourism, Mon-Fri 0900-1600, Sat-Sun 0900-1700, entry and 30-min guided tour R25, tea gardens, curio shop and art gallery*, is a worthwhile stop. It offers an insight into the lives of the Basotho people who have similar traditions to those people living over the border in Lesotho. Guided tours take you around a scattering of *bomas* and huts where traditional craft-making is demonstrated, local beer can be sampled, and a lively band and dancers provide entertainment.

Golden Gate National Park

» *pp662-666. Colour map 4, grid A5.*

A small (11,600-ha) national park on the edge of the Drakensberg and Maluti Mountains, the Golden Gate National Park is set in an area of massive sandstone rock formations. The eroded valleys have produced some spectacular shapes, with caves, cliffs and green grasslands against a backdrop of golden rocks. This is a particularly special place at sunset when the colours of the rocks are at their most intense. The Caledon River rises in these mountains. It is a popular park given its proximity to Johannesburg (three hours by car). The principal attractions are the hiking opportunities, the climbing and the spectacular rock formations. The Rhebok Hiking Trail is also in the park, see below.

Ins and outs

Getting there The common approach is the main road from Clarens (15 km), which is surfaced all the way through the park. As you enter the park and approach the offices the road passes through a narrow valley with giant cliffs which give the name 'Golden Gate'. The sun shining on the oxides in the sandstone produces a brilliant golden hue to the cliff face.

Tourist information A public road runs through the middle of the park so day visitors do not have to pay an entrance fee. Overnight visitors, R60, children R30. All enquiries can be dealt with at the **Glen Reenan Camp reception,** T058-2550000. Fuel is available at Glen Reenen, 0700-1730. **Glen Reenen Shop** ⓘ *daily, winter 0730-1700, summer 0700-1730*, stocks limited groceries, beer and wine, firewood and a few fresh items, maps and curios.

Climate The typical climate is cool rainy summers and cold winters with a high chance of snow. There is heavy snowfall on the high peaks while the valleys and surrounds remain untouched. Do not hike without suitable protective clothing in the winter. The park receives over 800 mm of rain annually so it is lush and green nearly all year.

Wildlife

You are unlikely to see many wild animals from the car, but once you get into the wooded valleys and the quiet hills you may well see black wildebeest, Burchell's zebra, mountain reedbuck, blesbok, eland and grey rhebok. The larger raptors favour the high rocky cliffs; look out for the bearded vulture, jackal buzzard, bald ibis and black eagle.

Rhebok Hiking Trail

ⓘ *The trail has to be booked in advance through one of the SAN Parks offices or online, www.sanparks.org, bookings open 13 months in advance.*

This popular two-day hike covers a total distance of 30 km. The path starts from the campsite at Glen Reenen and it is about 16 km to the overnight Rhebok Hut; look out for the San cave near the start of the trail. On the second day you will cover 14 km, but this includes the ascent of Generaalskop (2837 m). This is the highest point in the Free State and has views to match. On hot sunny days, the waterfall and Langtoon Dam are welcome sights near the end of the second day. The trail ends back at Glen Reenen, so you can look forward to hot showers at the end of some strenuous walking. Do not walk alone, a minimum of four people is ideal in this terrain. There are plenty of shorter day walks that have been marked out; some will take you to a peak top and back, others enable you to explore wooded kloofs. Keep an eye out for game at all times.

Horse riding

There are stables outside the park at Gladstone, 3 km from the Glen Reenan towards Clarens, T058-225 0951. Although the owners will tell you that anyone can go on these rides they are not suitable for totally inexperienced people as the horses will occasionally break into a gallop. There are plenty of horses and it is not necessary to book, just turn up around 1000, though to be certain of a ride phone ahead. Rides cost about R30 per hour.

Bethlehem

» pp662-666. Phone code: 058. Colour map 4, grid A5.

The town was founded in 1864 on a farm known as Pretoriuskloof. It is the principal town of the Eastern Free State, an important wheat-growing area and one of South Africa's biggest exporters of roses. A prominent local church minister, FP Naude, gave the settlement its name, reflecting the fact that the first settlers found that wheat flourished in the fertile Jordan Valley. It is a large town with a good range of restaurants and accommodation, but there is little here for the visitor apart from some fine examples of early sandstone buildings. The Dihlabeng Municipality **tourist office** ⓘ *9 Muller St, T058-3035732, info@bethlehem.org.za, Mon-Sat 0730-1300, 1400-1600*, has a good range of brochures including a map of the Sandstone Walking Tour which takes you around the old buildings and lasts about 1½ hours.

The **Museum of Cultural History** ⓘ *in the former Nazareth Mission Church at the top end of Muller St, T058-3033477, Fri 1000-1230, 1430-1700*, has a collection depicting the region's local history, with an early steam locomotive in the grounds.

South Africa's national hot air balloon race is held around Bethlehem annually in May.

Wolhuterskop Nature Reserve, 3 km from the town centre on the Fouriesburg road, is a small reserve where you can see several species of antelope: blesbok, eland, gemsbok, hartebeest, impala, springbok and waterbuck. Horseriding and hiking trails are possible for groups. For more information contact the tourist office.

Harrismith

» pp662-666. Phone code: 058. Colour map 4, grid A6.

Most visitors pass this town on the N3 en route to Durban. The town is dominated by a long flat mountain, the **Platberg**, 2377 m. Each year on 10 October a race is run up the mountain and along the top for 5 km before returning to the town. The origin of the race is very much part of local history. At the end of the Anglo-Boer War a Major John Belcher from the British Army referred to the mountain as 'that little hill of yours'. He was immediately bet that he could not run to the top in less than an hour. He duly won the bet, and the race, along with a trophy, was born.

The town was named after the British Governor Sir Harry Smith and nearby Ladysmith is named after his Spanish wife. The growth of the settlement was influenced by the discovery of diamonds at Barkly West and Kimberley in the 1860s, and gold on the Witwatersrand in 1886. Before the railway was built from the coast, at least 50 wagons a day used to stop over in the town.

Today it is still a popular stop for travellers between Gauteng and Durban, either overnight or for a break in one of the many service stations off the N3. Information is available from **Maluti a Phofung Visitor Centre** ⓘ *Southey St, T058-6223525, Mon-Fri 0800-1630, Sat 0930-1230*.

Around Harrismith

Sterkfontein Dam Nature Reserve, set in the foothills of the Drakensberg, 23 km from Harrismith, covers an area of more than 7000 ha with a 104-km shoreline and is one of the largest in South Africa. Most visitors come here for watersports and fishing. Hiking is possible and there are good opportunities for viewing raptors, and an interesting vulture 'restaurant' that attracts Cape and Bearded vultures. The entrance is off the R74 between Harrismith and Bergville. For those staying overnight at the reserve's resort, day trips can easily be made from here to the Northern Drakensberg (see page 446).

Ladybrand *p657*

B **Arbutus Lodge**, 19 Prinsloo St, T/F051-9242258, arbutuslodge@lbrand.com. 4 doubles, 1 garden self catering cottage in the former stables, historic sandstone house that is a national monument, B&B with high ceilings and antique furnishings, garden full of flowers, neat veranda.

B **Cranberry Cottage**, 37 Beeton St, T051-9242290, www.cranberrycottage.co.za. Smart award-winning B&B in a restored Victorian country house with additional rooms in the original ticket office and waiting rooms of Ladybrand Railway Station decorated with railway memorabilia and antiques. 24 en suite double rooms with DSTV and kettles, some with fireplaces, swimming pool. Gourmet dinners are served on the patio or in the candlelit dining room. If not staying the tea garden is still worth a visit on the way through the village. Recommended.

B **My Housy**, 17a Prinsloo St. T051-9241010, www.myhousy.co.za. A well run B&B with 7 double and 1 family rooms with en suite bathroom, TV, heaters for winter and private entrance, peaceful garden, all individually decorated thanks to one of the owners being an artist, not too sure about the teddy bears on the beds though.

D-E **Leliehoek Resort**, T051-9140654, 2 km from centre, has self-catering units, caravan and tent sites, grassed and reasonably shady, full ablution facilities, swimming pool, a beautiful quiet place near some caves with some San paintings.

Ficksburg and Rustler's Valley *p658*

Apart from the dreary **Highland Hotel**, which isn't recommended, there's a limited choice in town; many visitors choose to stay at one of the country lodges north of Ficksburg in the foothills of the Witteberge Mountains.

B-C **Bella Rosa**, 21 Bloem St, T/F051-9332623, bellarosa@telkomsa.net. 12 elegant suites make up this quality B&B set in a sandstone Victorian town house. Start the day with a delicious breakfast overlooking the mature gardens. A quiet and comfortable home decorated with antiques, pub and wine cellar, dinner on request, no young children.

C **Green Acorn**, 7 Fontein St, T051-9332746, www.greenacorn.co.za. Comfortable guesthouse centrally situated in Ficksburg, quiet and tranquil. 4 rooms with private entrances in the house or in pretty garden cottages, light and airy furnishings.

C-D **Hoekfontein Oxwagon Camp**, 10 km to the south of Ficksburg is a turning onto a gravel road, follow signs for 15 km, T/F051-9333915. Accommodation in original ox wagons arranged in a semi circle around a central eating and lounge boma. Double beds in the wagons themselves under white starched canvas roofs, also some rondavels, shared ablution block and self-catering kitchen, horse riding, ox-wagon drives, visits to San rock art and abseiling on the neighbouring cliffs. Recommended.

E **Thom Park**, corner of McCabe and Bloem Sts, T051-9332232. Plenty of grass and shade in this town centre caravan and camping site, some electric points, laundry, telephone, shops and restaurants a short walk away, but not much privacy as unshielded from the main road in the middle of town.

Rural retreats

About 15 km north of Ficksburg in the Witteberge Mountains are 3 contrasting rural retreats. Take the turning at Generaalsnek onto the S385, a gravel road winds its way into the hills (all 3 have their own signposts at each junction).

A-B **Franshoek Polo Lodge**, 15km north of Ficksburg, T/F051-9332828, www.franshoek.co.za. A luxury rural lodge, 10 rooms with 4-poster beds, thatched restaurant with cosy log fires, swimming pool. Plenty of emphasis on outdoor pursuits, including polo, rock climbing, abseiling, trout fishing, swimming pool, limited numbers, intimate atmosphere. The chef here also offers Thai cookery courses. Rates are full board.

B **Nebo Holiday Farm**, at the junction of the S384 and S385, off the R26, T051-9333947. 2- and 4-bed luxury chalets, TV, underfloor heating, plus self-catering cottages, quiet location on a sheep and cherry farm, quality restaurant and wine list, vegetarians will enjoy their meals here, swimming pool, ideal for hiking, fishing and birdwatching, everything you need to relax in comfort.

B-E **Rustler's Valley Mountain Lodge**, T/F051-9333939, www.rustlers.co.za. Mix of cottages, rooms and dorms to suit all budgets and group sizes. In the warm months camping is possible, bar, restaurant serving some of the best vegetarian food in South Africa. See also Festivals, page 665.

Fouriesburg to Clarens *p658*

B **Carolina Lodge**, 3 km along the road to the Lesotho border, T058-2230552, www.carolinalodge.co.za. 17 rooms in a holiday farm in the foothills of the Maluti Mountains, fresh farm cooking in the restaurant, bar, plenty of outdoor activities, swimming pool, tennis, horse riding, hiking and mini golf.

C **Fouriesburg Country Inn**, 7 Reitz St, T058-2230207, www.fouriesburgcountryinn.co.za. 14 rooms, the only hotel in town, the facades have been taking from the old railway buildings, a comfortable, quiet overnight stop, small rooms opening onto sheltered veranda overlooking the church, a pleasant touch is being able to go into the original sandstone wine cellar and choose your wine before dinner. Restaurant offers a selection of mixed grills and salads.

C-E **Meiringskloof Nature Park**, 2 km south of Fouriesburg, follow Fleck St out of town, T058-2230067, www.meiringskloof.co.za. Simple self-catering stone chalets and basic campsite with braai pits and power points in a beautiful kloof surrounded by sandstone cliffs with open caves, thick indigenous bush and abundant bird life. Swimming pool, horse riding, 4WD trails, a number of short hikes, kiosk selling basic groceries, popular with families.

Clarens *p659*

Clarens Destinations will fax or email a complete list of accommodation.

B **Kiara Lodge**, 14 km from Clarens on the Golden Gate National Park road, T058-2561324, www.planethotels.co.za. Pleasant en suite rooms with old world charm in a 1882 sandstone building, good Italian cuisine in the **Lord Robberts** restaurant or lighter meals in the pub, swimming pool, local activities can be arranged, wellbeing centre for all sorts of treats.

B-E **Bokpoort**, signposted 5 km out of Clarens on road to Golden Gate, a 3-km dirt road winds up into the hills onto a ridge where the farms and stables are laid out, T/F058-2561181, www.bokpoort.co.za. There are 7 self-catering chalets and a 8-bed hikers' hut and camping, the shower block has plenty of hot water when the wood fires are burning, simple dining room and bar. Well known for their excellent Western-style horse riding safaris in the Maluti Mountains, when you are treated to some superb countryside and real South African breakfasts. Recommended.

B **Country Lodge**, T/F058-2561354. 20 rooms, 4 family chalets each with 2 bedrooms, restaurant, bar, swimming pool, gardens.

B **Maluti Mountain Lodge**, Steil St, T058-2561422, www.malutilodge.co.za. 20 en suite double rooms, 4 family rondavels, with heating and M-Net TV, set in neat gardens, 2 restaurants with good country cooking, fun pub atmosphere, swimming pool.

B **Patcham Place**, 262 Church St, T/F058-2561017, patcham@netactive.co.za. 4 double rooms with en suite facilities in a timber cottage with good mountain views, TV, each has a private balcony and a separate entrance, but share a kitchen and lounge. The electric blankets and heaters serve as a reminder as to how cold it can actually get in this area during the winter months.

C **The Thistle Stop**, 58 Le Roux St, T/F058-2581003. A neat town house B&B, lounge area where tea, coffee and rusks are available, also a family self catering cottage sleeping 4, electric blankets and heaters are available in the winter months.

C-E **Clarens Inn**, Van Reenen St, T058-2561199. Family cottage sleeping 6 plus a dorm with communal kitchen with microwave, fridge, stove and coffee machine, and some space for tents. Good value, pretty spot, central location.

Golden Gate National Park *p659*

A-B **Protea Hotel Golden Gate Mountain Resort**, beside the main road that runs through the park, T058-2551000, www.proteahotels.com. Refurbished large with hotel rooms for up to 4, with bathroom and TV; in the grounds are 4-bed chalets, with bathroom, kitchenette, fridge, TV and braai facilities. The restaurant has excellent views, bar serves pub lunches, kiosk does takeaways. Professional set up and from your room you have an unimpeded view of the mountains, but unfortunately no effort was made to make the complex blend in to the otherwise uninterrupted scenery and it really shouldn't have been built in 1965 in such a naturally beautiful spot.

B **Mountain Retreat**, SAN Parks, T058-2550012, www.sanparks.org, 7 km from Glen Reenen off the Oribi Loop road. 2200 m above sea level, this new camp has double and family log cabins with kitchen, braai, TV and fireplace (pretty essential most nights), some with disabled access. Check in is at Glen Reenen where you will be given a map and directions. The last km to the camp is quite steep, but manageable in a normal car.

B-E **Glen Reenen Camp**, beside the main road that runs through the park, SAN Parks, T058-2550012, www.sanparks.org. It is always worth calling the park reception direct on T058-2550000 to check for late availability, reception hours, winter 0730-1700, summer 0700-1730. If you arrive outside these hours the nightwatchman can give keys to pre-booked guests but cannot check in those without bookings. There are 2 types of self-catering hut, each has shower, fridge, cooking utensils, one type has a TV, 2 single beds and a double bed in the loft, the other has 3 single beds in 1 room. Some have fireplaces. All accommodation has been recently refurbished and the old staff houses have been turned into 10 2-bed units. Across the road is the campsite which has plenty of shade and is beside a mountain stream, kitchen, electric points in shower block, swimming pool, a peaceful setting in a narrow, steep sided valley. Be warned it can get far too cold for camping in the winter. Some recognized hikes start from here; you can pick up a map at the shop.

E **Rhebok Hut**, SAN Parks, T058-2550012, www.sanparks.org, overnight hut on the Rhebok Hiking Trail, 3 bedrooms with 6 bunks and mattresses, coal stove, paraffin cooker, basic utensils in the kitchen, cold showers, toilets, bring a sleeping bag and food.

Bethlehem *p661*

B-D **Cam-O-rhi Game Lodge**, 17 km from Bethlehem on the R26 and S175, clearly signposted, T058-3041691, www.camorhi lodge.co.za. A selection of B&B rooms in the main house, en suite family cabins and larger self catering cottages, cheaper backpacker accommodation available in shared dormitory-style cabin, bar, restaurant, curio shop, pool, and jacuzzi. There is a variety of game including lion and white rhino in enclosures that are fenced but spacious, the lodge has successfully bred white lion. Activities include game drives, horse riding, walking trails, quad bike rides, and there are often some lion cubs to play with and feed from a bottle. Open to day visitors for an entry fee of R80 per vehicle, local people visit this place at the weekends and it's great for families, especially on Sun when if booking the excellent Sun lunch buffet the entry fee is wavered. Most of the activities need to be booked in advance, so check out the website for times and prices and plan your day/ overnight visit round these. Recommended.

B-C **Fisant, Bokmakierie and Hoephoep Guest House**, 8-10 Thoi Oosthuyse St, T058-3037144, www.fisant.co.za. Smart houses on the outskirts of town, 7 double rooms and 9 family units with en suite bathroom, some with kitchenettes for self-catering, non-smoking room available, buffet breakfasts, TV, laundry, peaceful garden, undercover parking, German spoken, well run and good value.

C **Bread House**, 14 President Vorster St, T058-3034329, www.breadhouse.co.za. 5 modern double rooms with en suite bathroom, DSTV, under carpet heating, electric blankets, homely guest lounge with fireplace, braai area, swimming pool, pool table, excellent value.

C **Die Nes**, 3 van Raalte St, T058-3034073, die_nes@nnet.co.za. 4 double rooms with en suite bathroom, bar fridge, TV. A smart B&B decorated in strong primary colours, bright, fresh and hospitable.

C **Park Hotel**, 23 Muller St, T/F058-3035191, parkh@inntic.net. 15 double rooms, 27 single rooms, all a/c and with TV, cheaper family and double rooms in old block, the new part is built around a leafy atrium. Restaurant, bar, swimming pool, secure parking, one of the best in town.

C-E **Loch Athlone Holiday Resort**, 3 km on the Fouriesburg road, T058-3034981. Popular family resort beside Loch Athlone, a large lake created by damming the Jordan River. Good value rooms out of season, but very busy during school holidays, space for 200 caravans! Self-catering chalets, restaurant, bar, TV room, laundry, tennis, mini-golf, swimming pool, all watersports available on the dam, from pedal boats to power boats.

Harrismith and around *p661*

B **Shady Pines**, 67 Stuart St, T058-6223020, www.shadypines.co.za. Comfortable and hospitable guest house in a restored house built in 1880, spacious gardens, 7 en suite rooms and 2 self-catering units, home cooked meals available, tiny chapel in the grounds for weddings.

C-E **Mount Everest Game Reserve**, 21 km northeast of Harrismith on the R722 to Verkykerskop, T058-6230235. 10 luxury log cabins and some self-catering chalets, tent sites and caravan stands, all with plenty of privacy, shop, restaurant, bar and a swimming pool, all set on a private 1000-ha reserve with the usual collection of antelope, which roam freely among the guest rondavels.

C-E **Sterkfontein Dam Nature Reserve**, on the R74 on the Oliviershoek Pass 23 km from Harrismith, T058-6223520. Chalets for 2-6 people as well as camping. The local popularity of the reserve is illustrated by there being 360 camp sites.

Eating

Ladybrand *p657*

ƳƳ **Impero Romano**, 11 Church St, T051-9241184. A surprising find for a small town this Italian restaurant comes complete with pillars and statues. The wide range of pizzas and pasta is actually cooked by an Italian.

Ƴ **Cosmo Cafe**, 30 Joubert S. A twee coffee shop serving cakes and light lunches during the day, with some outside tables.

Ficksburg and Rustler's Valley *p658*

Ƴ **The Bottling Co**, Piet Retief St, T051-9332404, closed Sun. Pub and restaurant with good choice of beer, steak, chicken and fish.

Clarens *p659*

ƳƳ **Sunnyside Guest Farm**, 12 km east of Clarens on the way to Golden Gate, 2 km off the R712, T058-2561099. Each Sun they organize an excellent braai and roast dinner along a shaded riverbank, bring your own drinks, make a reservation as this is hugely popular locally.

Ƴ **@ The Square**, adjoining the Johan Smith art gallery in the main square and owned by the artist himself. Breakfasts, light meals, good for pastries thanks to the resident pastry chef. Closed evenings.

Ƴ **Clarens Bakery and Saloon**, 280 Main Rd, T058-2561406. Open daily for milkshakes, pies, cakes, pastries, light meals, sandwiches made from fresh bread, jungle gym in the garden for kids.

Ƴ **Street Café**, T058-2561064, daily. Snack meals and afternoon teas, open-air veranda, pub open late.

Bethlehem *p661*

ƳƳ **O'Hagens**, 8 Theron St, T058-3030919. 1100-late. Good value pub/restaurant chain, English pub decor, varied menu, large portions, the very hungry can try the foot-long pies.

ƳƳ **Park Hotel**, see Sleeping page 664. Has an extensive menu, good healthy stir-frys, but slow service and dim interior.

ƳƳ **Wooden Spoon**, 12 Church St, T058-3032724. Closed Sun and pub only Mon. Restaurant and pub in the oldest building in Bethlehem, home-style cooking, lots of meat. Some overnight rooms.

Harrismith *p661*

ƳƳ **Princess & Frog**, 17 Vowe St, T058-6222476. Tue-Sat 1000-late. Unusual for the area, a cosy double-storey Victorian house, fine French cuisine, a limit of 12 people so advance booking essential.

Festivals and events

Ficksburg and Rustler's Valley *p658*

Rustler's Valley Festival One of South Africa's premier festival sites. Each year the New Year festival invites a range of different live bands and DJs to perform their latest material. A great opportunity to see some good live South African music and DJs in a safe setting. It's not Glastonbury or Roskilde, but it's an event well worth seeing if you are in South Africa at the time. For the budding musician Rustler's Valley is one of the most exciting alternative places to visit throughout the year and their website, www.rustlers.co.za, continually promotes a wide range of cultural activities and seminars for the faithful.

Shopping

Clarens *p659*
For a small village Clarens has no fewer than 18 galleries and craft shops, so its just a case of browsing around. For sale are local handicrafts and jewellery, various paintings by local artists, antiques, ceramics and decorations and furniture from as far away as Malaysia.
Art & Wine Gallery on Main, Main St. Sells wines from Stellenbosch and exhibits paintings, sculptures, ceramics and glassware.
Clarens Meander Shops, next to the Caltex garage as you approach town, has several craft shops and galleries, a farm stall selling home made treats, ATMs and a café. Also here is an information office for the **Lesotho Highlands Water Project**, ww.lhwp.org.ls.

Activities and tours

Clarens *p659*
Golf
9-hole club in the lee of the Rooiberg Hills, superb views from some holes. Guest members welcome, T058-2561255.

Horse riding
Bokpoort, T/F058-2561181, www.bokpoort .co.za (see Sleeping). The most exciting horse trails in the region. Standard route lasts for 2 days, with a night at a deserted homestead in the Maluti Mountains, the larger the group the better the value. Shorter rides also available and the Basotho ponies are suitable for young children.

Quad biking
Sethuthuthu Tours, (the name means motorbike in Sesotho), T058-2561569, or book at the tourist office. Quad-bike tours from 1 hr to a full day on guided trails connecting local farms. These trails are not for the thrill seeker as the pace is quite slow, but there are some great views over the Free State and Maluti Mountains.

Whitewater rafting
Outrageous Adventures, T083-4859654, www.outrageousadventures.co.za. Since the opening of the Katse Dam in Lesotho, part of the mammoth Lesotho Highlands Water Project to increase the feed of many South Africa's rivers, **Clarens Ash River** has experienced a surge of extra water from the new Trans Caledon Transfer Tunnel. The water exits the tunnel at 54 cu m per second and a series of rapids have developed on the river; some grade III-IV. This company offers whitewater rafting runs for around R430 per person Oct-Mar. Included in the trip is an optional 35m abseil.

Transport

Bethlehem *p661*
Bus
Translux, www.translux.co.za, and Greyhound, www.greyhound.co.za, buses stop at the Wimpy on Church St. Bethlehem is on the Bloemfontein-Durban route. For Johannesburg and Cape Town there are connections in Bloemfontein.

Train
There is a weekly service between **Cape Town** and **Durban** that stops in Bethlehem. Spoornet, T0860-008888, www.spoor net.co.za, timetables and fares are published on the website.

Northern Cape

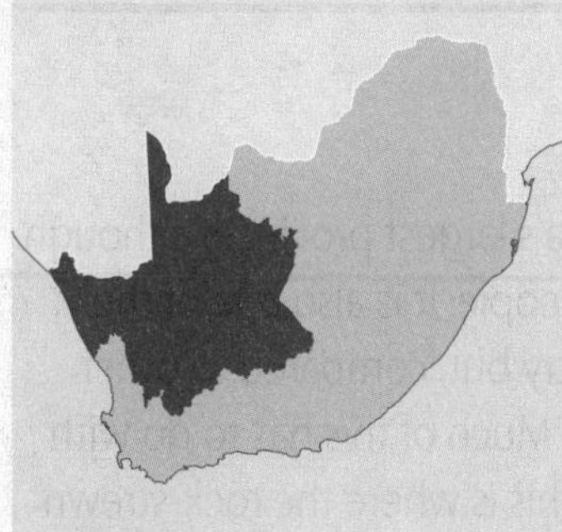

Footprint features

Introduction

The Northern Cape is South Africa's largest province, although it is home to less than a million people. It is also one of the most beautiful areas of the country but, compared to other provinces, it remains tourist-free. Much of this has to do with the sheer harshness of the area: this is where the rock-strewn semi-desert of Namakwa (Namaqualand) merges with the rolling red dunes of the Kalahari, where cruel heat pounds the parched wilderness for much of the year. But it is this sun-bleached emptiness and inaccessibility that gives the area its stark beauty, endless shimmering plains and hazy saltpans providing it with a real sense of isolation.

The state can be divided into three distinct regions: Namakwa (Namaqualand) in the west; the Kalahari lying north of the Gariep (Orange) River; and the Karoo to the south. Despite the pervasive arid conditions, it is an area of excellent game viewing, with the magnificent Kgalagadi Transfrontier Park offering one of the finest national park experiences in Africa. In spring, Namakwa (Namaqualand) becomes the main attraction, when the valleys are transformed into carpets of vibrant colour as desert flowers explode from the earth with the first rains. The Gariep River runs through much of the state; formerly the Orange River, it has recently been given a Nama name meaning 'great river'. It thunders over the surreal Augrabies Falls, the fifth largest in the world, and offers superb whitewater rafting. Lastly, this is diamond country, with the key town of Kimberley having a rich history and a number of sights, not least the colossal diamond mines themselves.

Although the summer can be oppressively hot, the winter has pleasant daytime temperatures but frost at night; the best times to visit are the more moderate seasons of spring or autumn.

★ Don't miss...

1 **Diamond mines** Don a hard hat and drop down an 800m mine shaft in Kimberley, page 675.
2 **Gariep (Orange) River** Plunge down heart-pumping rapids and meander through lush vineyards on a river-rafting trip, page 681 and page 708.
3 **Kgalagadi Transfrontier Park** Look out for gemsbok or kalahari lion among the red sand dunes of South Africa's most remote national park, page 686.
4 **Augrabies Falls National Park** Scramble through a surreal, cactus-studded moonscape around the dramatic waterfalls, page 697.
5 **Namaqwa** Follow the flower trail and watch the sombre desert burst into a carpet of colour, page 701.
6 **Ai-Ais Richtersveld Transfrontier Conservation Park** Explore the jagged mountains and sun-baked expanses in a 4WD, page 702.

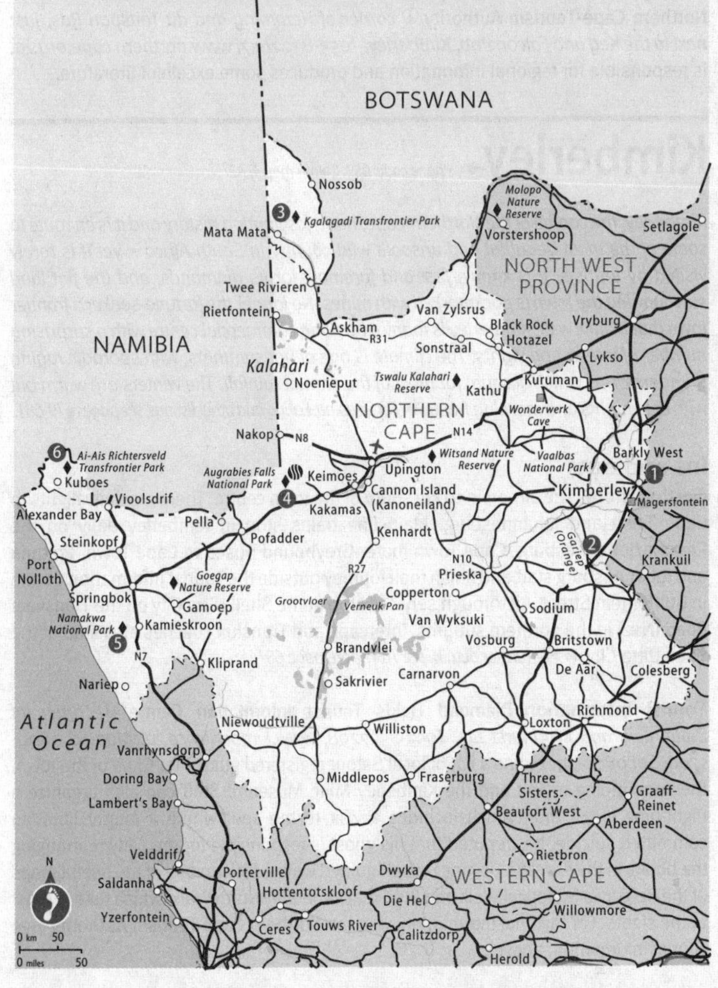

Ins and outs

Getting around

The Northern Cape is not well served by public transport and long-distance buses only run along the N7, the artery route from Cape Town to Namibia. To explore the remote settlements of the Kalahari, Namakwa (Namaqualand) or the Kgalagadi Transfrontier Park, you will need a car and you should be prepared for some challenging driving. Distances are vast, fuel needs careful attention and you need to plan your journey carefully to reach your destination before dark, as animals on the road make driving at night dangerous. Breakdowns can be a problem in remote regions, so it's useful to carry a mobile phone, and, in some areas, a 4WD is advised.

Off-roading is hugely popular in South Africa but 4WD companies are loathe to rent their vehicles to complete novices. Consider doing a one-day 4WD course in your home country before your arrival in South Africa. Alternatively, if you don't want to self-drive there are tours on offer from the regional centres.

Tourist information

Northern Cape Tourism Authority ⓘ *corner of Hemming and du Toitspan Rds, just next to the Keg and Falcon Pub, Kimberley, T053-8322657, www.northern cape.org.za*, is responsible for regional information and produces some excellent literature.

Kimberley→ *Phone code: 053. Colour map 4, A2*

Kimberley, the capital of the Northern Cape, has a fascinating history and it is en route to some of the most beautiful and unspoilt wild country in South Africa – yet it is rarely visited by tourists. It is known first and foremost for its diamonds, and the flat land surrounding the town is pockmarked with mines. No longer the fortune-seeker's frontier town that it once was, Kimberley is today a bustling commercial centre with a surprising number of interesting sights. The climate is one of hot summers, with sporadic raging thunderstorms which account for most of the annual rainfall. The winters are warm but with cold nights and morning frosts. ▸▸ *For Sleeping, Eating and other listings, see pages 679-681.*

Ins and outs

Getting there The airport is 10 km south of the town centre. There are daily flights to Cape Town and Johannesburg. Main line trains stop in Kimberley daily on the Pretoria/Johannesburg–Cape Town route. **Greyhound** buses to Cape Town, Pretoria and Johannesburg start and finish their journey outside the Tourist Information Centre in Bultfontein Street. All through services stop at the Shell Ultra City on the Transvaal Road (N12) in the northern suburbs. **Intercape** and **Translux** coaches also stop at the Shell Ultra City. ▸▸ *For further details, see Transport, page 681.*

Tourist information **Diamond Fields Tourist Information Centre** ⓘ *corner of Bultfontein and Lyndhurst Sts, T053-8327298, www.kimberley.co.za, Mon-Fri 0800-1700, Sat 0800-1200*, has a list of local Satour registered guides for tours of the town, the surrounding region and the Kimberley Mine Museum. Staff can also organize a night-time ghost tour, which includes a visit to the spot where a former librarian committed suicide. It is reputed that his ghost is responsible for regularly rearranging the books in the Africana Library. For self-guided walks, pick up one of the useful maps of the Belgravia Historical Walk and the Great Kimberley North Walk, which take in most of the sights. For regional information, visit the **Northern Cape Tourism Authority** (see Tourist information, above).

Background

The early history of Kimberley is also the tale of the discovery of diamonds: a definitive turning point in the history of the country. The first significant find was in 1866 on a farm called De Kalk, owned by Daniel Jacobs, near modern-day Hopetown. Jacobs' children gave a stone to their neighbour, Schalk van Niekerk. He in turn gave it to a trader, John O'Reilly, and asked him to find out the value of the stone. The stone ended up in Grahamstown in the hands of Dr Guyborn Atherstone, who found it to be a diamond of 21.25 carats, worth R1000 and later named *Eureka*. In 1869 Schalk van Niekerk bartered for a larger stone from a Griqua shepherd; news soon spread of this stone and public interest began to grow. It came to be known as *The Star of Africa* and, in 1974 was sold in Geneva for over half a million US dollars.

The tremendous wealth of the diamond mines in Kimberley was the basis on which the modern economy of South Africa was founded.

In 1869 the search for diamonds was divided between two areas: the wet diggings along the Vaal River; and the dry diggings on two farms some 40 km to the south. The Vaal River diggings attracted most prospectors, as the heat and drought of summer made conditions very tough on the farms at Bultfontein and Dorstfontein. In December 1870 the future of the region was finally determined when the children of Adriaan van Wyk found diamonds near their farm, Dorstfontein. The area was immediately overrun by diamond-diggers and their equipment, including a party from Colesberg led by Fletwood Rawstone, known as the Red Caps. One night a servant appeared at his master's tent with a handful of diamonds. He had found them on the slopes of a hill on the nearby farm of Vooruitzicht, owned by the brothers Diederick and Nicolaas Johannes de Beer. The hill was named Colesberg Kopje and, within just a few months, 50,000 diggers had turned the hill into a hole. Living conditions were very tough, and supplies expensive. In 1873 the name 'New Rush' was changed to Kimberley in honour of the Earl of Kimberley, British Secretary of State for the Colonies. A twin town grew up around the Bultfontein and Du Toit's pan mines, called Beaconsfield, named after Benjamin Disraeli, the Earl of Beaconsfield. In 1912 the two towns amalgamated to become a city.

As the mines delved deeper, it became clear that individual claims would have to merge; there was simply no way of keeping them separate. At one point, there were 1600 separate claims at the Kimberley mine (now known as the Big Hole; see page 673). In addition to the problems of mining logistics, the price of diamonds started falling because of over production. It was at this point that Cecil John Rhodes (see page 674) and his partner, Charles Dunell Rudd, entered the scene. Together they began buying up claims in the De Beers mine and, in 1880, they founded the De Beers Mining Company. As Rhodes and Rudd expanded their operation, they came up against a man with similar ideas, Barney Barnato. The ensuing infamous power struggle was only resolved when Rhodes gave Barnato a colossal pay-off for his Kimberley Central Mining Company. The Big Hole stopped producing diamonds in 1914 but three mines remain productive today: Dutoitspan, Bultfontein and Wesselton.

Sights » *pp679-681.*

Most of Kimberley's attractions are in some way connected to the diamond industry. Although there are some elegant Victorian buildings in town, there is far less evidence of the diamond wealth here than one might expect. Indeed, Kimberley was little more than a rough frontier settlement for much of its history, with most of the diamond wealth making its way back to the more civilized and comfortable surroundings of the Cape. Nevertheless, it is thought that in the 1890s more millionaires met together under the roof of the **Kimberley Club** ⓘ *T053-8324224, private visits can be arranged*, than anywhere else in the world. Past members include Cecil Rhodes, and Ernest and Harry Oppenheimer. The club still stands in Du Toitspan Road close to the Africana Library, and the 1891 building is now a national monument. Also on Du Toitspan Road is a **statue of Cecil Rhodes** astride his horse with a map of Africa on his lap, while just south of here, opposite the Civic Centre, are the **Oppenheimer Memorial Gardens** and the **Diggers Fountain**. This is a memorial to Sir Ernest Oppenheimer, mining magnet and erstwhile Mayor of Kimberley, featuring a fountain and a statue of five miners holding up a sieve, surrounded by a rose garden.

A subtle reminder of Kimberley's past is the irregular street pattern, which more or less runs true to the mud tracks which once criss-crossed the land between the tented camps and diamond diggings.

The suburb of **Belgravia** (see page 676) has a fine collection of Victorian houses but the rest of the city centre is made up of dull modern shops and office blocks. (There are some early pictures of the town centre at the **Kimberley Mine Museum**, along with a display on the siege of Kimberley; see page 673). Today, the town's skyline is dominated by the **Telkom tower** and the De Beers headquarters, an ugly tinted-glass building. More interesting is the equally unattractive **Harry Oppenheimer House**, near the Civic Centre. This is the main diamond sorting centre in South Africa, which was designed to allow in optimum natural light by which to judge the stones.

The pale yellow and white, Corinthian-style **City Hall** was built in 1899. From here, you can catch a **tram** ⓘ *daily 0900-1600, on the hour every hour, R5*, to the Kimberley Mine Museum. Trams played an important role in the history of public transport in Kimberley. The first passenger tramway, pulled by mule, was opened in June 1887 to bring labour from the Beaconsfield township to Kimberley. Today, the restored model in Kimberley, dating from the early 1900s, is the only working tram in South Africa.

Kimberley

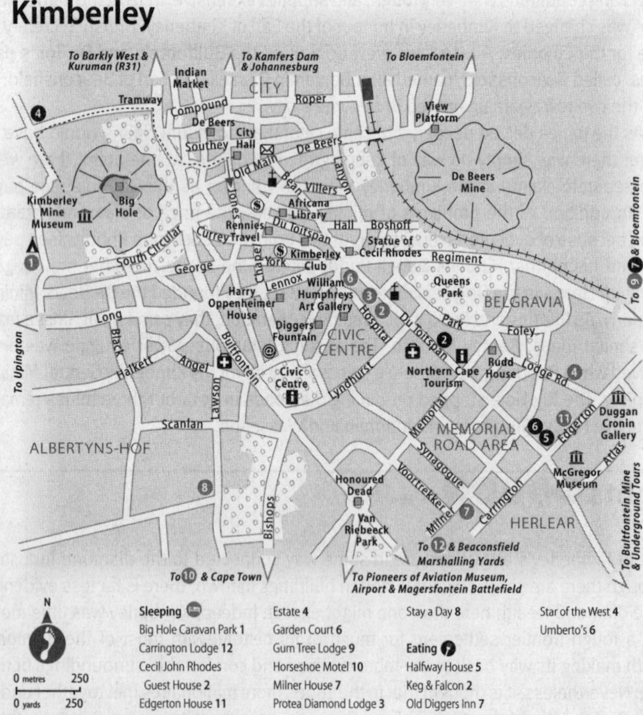

Big Hole: big statistics

It has a surface area of 17 ha and a perimeter of 1.6 km. Before the consolidation of diggings, 30,000 men dug here night and day, and for several kilometres around Kimberley you could hear the dull noise of tapping and machinery. The diggers reached 400 m down before it became impossible to mine as a group of individuals. In 1889 De Beers sunk the first shaft, extending the hole to 800 m deep. By August 1914, when the mine was closed, the mine shafts were 1100 m deep.

It is estimated that between 22 and 28 million tonnes of earth were removed to create the Big Hole. All this labour resulted in the recovery of 14.5 million carats: only 2722 kg of diamonds or less than three metric tonnes! Today, water fills the hole to a depth of over 600 m.

Africana Library

ⓘ *Du Toitspan Rd, T053-8306247. Mon-Fri 0800-1245, 1330-1630.*

The Africana Library is a major research centre and a rewarding place to visit for those with a particular interest in local history. There is a wealth of archive material on the diamond industry, missionary work in the region and early SeTswana books. Two of its most famous books are Dr Moffat's copy of his 1829 translation of the Old Testament into SeTswana, the first bible to be printed in Africa, and a first edition of Schedel's *Nuremburg Chronicle*, 1493.

William Humphreys Art Gallery

ⓘ *Cullinan Crescent, Civic Centre, T053-8311724. Mon-Fri 0830-1645, Sat 1000-1645, Sun 1400-1645. Small entry fee.*

This gallery houses one of the most important art collections in South Africa, with fine examples of 16th- and 17th-century art by British and Flemish-Dutch Old Masters. More interesting is the newer collection of contemporary South African art. There are works by South African impressionists, an excellent graphics and prints display and a few individual treasures, such as the Irma Stern portraits. Also of interest is the rock engravings collection, tracing ancient San engravings dating back to 12,000 BC with photographs and actual examples.

Kimberley Mine Museum and the Big Hole

ⓘ *Entrance on Tucker St, T053-8331557. Daily 0800-1800; allow at least 2 hrs. R20, R12 children. Shop and café.*

Sitting alongside the Big Hole, this fascinating museum is made up of a collection of 40 original and model buildings dating from the late 19th century. They have been arranged to form a muddle of streets, with sound effects such as singing or snatches of conversation playing inside the shops. Each shop or office is furnished with items dating from the early days of Kimberley, and the overall result is very effective. There are a number of professions on show, including Dr JM Osborne's dental surgery, R Bodley & Son Undertakers, Barney Barnato's Boxing Academy, EHW Awty, a well-known watchmaker, the Standard Bank and A Ciring, the Pawnbroker – the window display includes objects that have never been redeemed. One of the most impressive items is the original De Beers Directors' Private Pullman Railway Coach, a very plush carriage complete with a dining table, laid with silverware and cut glass decanters, and luxurious leather chairs. Another highlight is Sir Davis Harris' ballroom, an ingenious structure built in 1901. It is constructed entirely out of corrugated iron, with stamped steel walls made to look like smart wallpaper, fake skirting boards and metal stucco on the ceilings.

Cecil John Rhodes

Cecil Rhodes was perhaps the ultimate British imperialist and played a central role in the history of southern Africa in the years after the discovery of diamonds at Kimberley.

He was born in the English town of Bishops Stortford in 1853 and was sent to Natal at the age of 17 to work on his brother's farm and to recuperate from bouts of tuberculosis. He was not, however, suited to a farming life and soon set off for the new diamond sites at Kimberley. From humble beginnings he began to prosper, slowly buying up shares in diamond-buying concerns and through other schemes related to the diggings. With the money he earned from these businesses, he went back to England in 1872 to study for a degree at Oxford. Bad health forced him back to South Africa for a couple of years and he then alternated spells at Oxford with spells in South Africa; in 1881 he eventually managed to pass his degree. The contacts he made while at Oxford put him in an advantageous position in Kimberley and he was able to utilize British capital in his programme of gaining control of all the diamond mining activities. In 1880 Rhodes founded the De Beers Diamond Mining Company and continued to expand his commercial interests.

When diamonds were first discovered, plots were sold cheaply to the first digger to lay claim to the site but, very quickly, and especially as the diggings became deeper, one or two individuals and companies managed to buy up all the shares and monopolize the buying and selling of diamonds. By the end of the 1880s, there were only really two players left in the game: Cecil Rhodes and Barney Barnato. In 1888, with the backing of British capital, Rhodes eventually bought out Barnato – with one cheque for the sum of £5,338,650.

As befits a grand imperialist, Rhodes combined his hugely successful business career with a career in politics – indeed the two went very much hand in hand. He was first elected to the Cape parliament, as member for Barkly West, in 1880, and soon gained a reputation as an ardent supporter of British interests in South Africa and the expansion of British rule to the whole of southern Africa. In 1890 he became the colony's Prime Minister and continued to advocate British imperial expansion into remaining African controlled areas, such as Pondoland. This expansionism was driven partly by jingoistic pride in Britain but mainly by his commercial ambitions. This is clearly demonstrated in the expansion

The **Big Hole** (see also page 673) can only be seen from inside the Kimberley Mine Museum. There are two caged viewing platforms which stick out over the rim of the hole so you can look down and see the murky green lake at the bottom. It is an astounding sight when you remember that only a fraction of the hole lies above the water level, and that every piece of earth and rock was removed by hand.

Inside the **Mining Hall** are examples of the first machines used in the diamond mining industry, some of which can be made to work for 10 cents. Look out for the early photographs of the diggings as the Big Hole gradually started to take shape, providing a vivid impression of life during the heady days of the boom. For a taste of the real thing, head to De Beers Hall close to the exit. More of a bank vault than a hall, it contains a collection of uncut stones, including the 616 diamond (at 616 carats, the world's largest octahedron uncut diamond), reproductions of the world's largest cut diamonds and examples of multicoloured stones.

to the empire he is best known for – the founding of a new colony that was to take his name.

Despite Rhodes' commercial genius he had made a serious miscalculation when gold was first discovered on the Witwatersrand. Taking the advice of an American prospector who told him that the gold was not even worth getting off a horse for, Rhodes decided to sit out the initial rush to buy up the best goldfields. By the time the true worth of the new reef was apparent, Rhodes was too late to make an economic killing, though he did become involved with deep level mining activities. Frustrated by missing a golden opportunity, Rhodes began to look to the lands further to the north, beyond the Limpopo River. Gold had been mined in these areas for centuries in small-scale mines and Rhodes hoped to find another Witwatersrand. In 1888 he sent his Kimberley business partner, Charles Dunell Rudd, to secure from Lobengula, the leader of the Ndebele, mineral rights in the area they controlled. Armed with the mineral concession, Rhodes was able to secure agreement from London to set up a 'charter company' (the South Africa Company), which would not only prospect for minerals in the area but also be granted ownership of all the land and run all the administration. In 1890 Rhodes sent out a 'Pioneer Column' to lay claim to the area. Their dreams of huge gold reserves proved illusory but the country was still rich in minerals and many of the pioneers indulged in the settlers' favourite activity of land speculation.

With the failure to find a second Witwatersrand, Rhodes turned his attention back to his investments in the Transvaal. Rhodes' annoyance with President Kruger's constraints on non-Boer residents led him to make one of his worst political mistakes in backing the ill-fated Jameson Raid. This failed attempt to topple Kruger's government led to a serious breach in relations between Rhodes and Afrikaners in the Cape. He was forced to resign as Prime Minister and take a less public role in the Charter Company in Rhodesia.

At the outbreak of the Anglo-Boer War, Rhodes was staying at his house in Kimberley, where he remained throughout the siege (see page 678). His health was poor throughout much of his life and the harsh conditions during the siege did not help. He died in his Muizenberg cottage outside Cape Town in 1902; his body was transported by train and gun carriage to be buried in the Matopo Hills in present-day Zimbabwe.

Bultfontein mine

ⓘ Molyneux Rd, T053-8421321, cindy.carls@debeersgroup.com. Mine tours Thu-Tue 0800, 4 hrs; book 24 hrs in advance; no children under 16. Surface tours from the mine gate Thu-Tue 0900 and 1100, 2 hrs.

The most exciting part of the tour is when the miners are blasting – the ground and air shakes with the force of the explosion.

On the other side of town from the Big Hole are two operational diamond mines, the Bultfontein and Dutoitspan mines. It is possible to go on a fascinating underground tour of the Bultfontein mine, which allows an insight into the reality of diamond mining. Tours begin with a safety video, and you are kitted out in protective overalls, hard hat, shoes, head torch, safety goggles and an emergency oxygen provider. You then walk to the main shaft and are taken in a lift down to 820 m, a fairly unnerving experience and not for the claustrophobic. Once down, the guide walks you around key areas of the mine, including the main retrieval areas, crusher machines and mile-long conveyer belts transporting kimberlite.

You may also be taken to see 'development' sites, where the tunnels of the mines are being expanded. There are no luxuries such as dust extraction or electric light, so you really get a feel for how tough mining can be. Visitors are also taken to see the mine from the surface, which is actually a far bigger hole than the Big Hole. The tour is a superb way of experiencing the heat, dust and mud of a mine, but you are very unlikely to see any diamonds. This is reputedly the world's only underground tour of a working diamond mine.

Belgravia

Just to the east of the city centre is the residential suburb of Belgravia where many of the wealthy mines people built grand Victorian houses. There is a 2-km historical walk through the suburb, which takes you past most of the old buildings, and a map is available from the tourist office. The majority can only be appreciated from the outside, as they remain in private hands, but the best of the buildings open to the public are **Rudd House**, 5-7 Loch Road, and **Dunluce**, 10 Lodge Road. Both are national monuments and have been fully restored. They are kept closed for security reasons but they can be viewed on weekdays by prior arrangement with the McGregor Museum (see below). The first owner of Dunluce was Gustav Bonus of Dunluce, who instructed the architect to design a house fit for a member of the Diamond Syndicate. He was not disappointed; when the house was completed in 1897 it perfectly reflected the prosperity of the period. Unfortunately, it was badly damaged during the Siege of Kimberley in 1899 by a shell from the Boers' infamous 'Long Tom' gun.

Also in Belgravia is the **Duggan-Cronin Gallery** ⓘ *T053-8420099, Mon-Sat 1000-1300, 1400-1700, Sun 1400-1700, small entrance charge*, set back on Edgerton Road. The basis of this collection is a series of 8000 ethnographic photographs taken between 1919 and 1939 by Alfred Martin Duggan-Cronin, a De Beers' nightwatchman with an interest in photography.

McGregor Museum

ⓘ *2 Edgerton Rd, entrance from Atlas St, T053-8392700, www.museumsnc.co.za, Mon-Sat 0900-1700, Sun 1400-1700. Small entrance charge. Café and museum shop.*

The history of this building is worth mentioning in addition to the collection inside. The original house was built by Rhodes to serve as a hotel and a health spa, since the pure dry climate of Kimberley was thought to be healthy. During the siege of Kimberley, Rhodes lived in two rooms on the ground floor. These now form part of the museum and are furnished as he had them; note the austere surroundings preferred by Rhodes. During the next period of use, the building was converted into the very elegant Hotel Belgrave. One of the rooms upstairs has been furnished as it would have been in the 1920s. As the diamond industry fell into decline, the wealthy customers disappeared and the hotel was forced to close. In 1933 it was taken over by the Sisters of the Holy Family and turned into a school and convent. Forty years later the McGregor Museum moved its displays and offices here.

The collection is a mix of objects depicting the history of Kimberley and the northern region, and standard displays of natural history. While the latter are of little interest, the displays relating to Kimberley are reasonably absorbing.

Galeshewe

ⓘ *For tours of Galeshewe, contact the tourist office.*

Kimberley was the first town in South Africa to establish 'locations' for housing non-white mine labourers on its outskirts. Galeshewe, the resulting township, rose significantly in importance during the struggle against Apartheid, and was second only to Soweto as a centre of political activism. It was home to **Robert Sobukwe**, the leader of the Pan African Congress (PAC), who spent the last days of his life under house arrest in Galeshewe, following his imprisonment on Robben Island.

Pioneers of Aviation Museum

ⓘ *General van der Spuy Drive, 4 km from the airport, T053-8420099. Mon-Fri 1000-1530, Sun 1400-1700. Small entrance charge.*

On the site of South Africa's first flying school, this museum comprises a reconstructed hangar and a replica of the biplane used in the early days of flight training. The flying school was set up here in 1913 and the graduates went on to become the first pilots of the newly formed South African Aviation Corps, which in turn saw its first action over Walvis Bay in May 1915.

Around Kimberley

Kamfers Dam

Kamfers Dam is 5 km out of town on the N12 towards Johannesburg, partially hidden from the road by the raised railway line. This is a natural heritage site and an important area for greater and lesser flamingos; just driving past the dam allows views of the carpet of pink created by the resident flamingos. Sadly, the waters are under threat from continual agricultural pollution, and it has been predicted that the flamingos may soon disappear from here. Look out for a gravel track leading from the road under the railway line, where there is a small parking area.

Magersfontein Battlefield

ⓘ *32 km from Kimberley; follow the new road to Bloemfontein and follow signs for Modder River, T053-8337115. Daily 0800-1500. Small entry fee. Tea room and museum.*

On 11 December 1899 one of the most famous battles of the Anglo-Boer War took place here. The British force, under the command of Lt-General Lord Methuen, was defeated by a Boer force under General Piet Cronje while attempting to come to the aid of besieged Kimberley (see page 678). This was the first appearance of trench warfare and the first major defeat suffered by the British: in the first encounter 239 British soldiers were killed and 663 wounded. The Boer trenches can still be seen from the hilltop. There are nine memorials commemorating the dead, including a Celtic cross in memory of the Highland Regiment, a granite memorial to the Scandinavians who fought with the Boers, and a marble cross in memory of the Guards Brigade.

Routes west from Kimberley

Wildebeest Kuil Rock Art Centre and Nooitgedacht

ⓘ *www.museumsnc.co.za, Mon-Fri 1000-1700, Sat and Sun 1100-1600, R10.*

Both these are open-air sites display glacial geological rock formations, which have been covered in ancient San rock engravings, thought to be 1500 years old. At the **Wildebeest Kuil Rock Art Centre** ⓘ *16 km from Kimberley on the R31 towards Barkly West, T053-8337069*, there is a visitor centre, an auditorium showing a short film about the rock art and an 800-m walking trail. At **Nooitgedacht** ⓘ *31 km on the same road, T053-8420009*, display boards and a boardwalk have been developed. At both sites there is the opportunity to meet the local community of Xu and Khwe people who were granted 1200 ha of land under the Land Reform Programme. The communities shares this land, from where they produce traditional and progressive arts and crafts.

Barkly West → *Phone code: 053. Colour map 4, A2.*

The R31 passes through Barkly West, 32 km from Kimberley en route to Kuruman. The first site of the diamond rush in South Africa, the town is named after Sir Henry Barkly, Governor of the Cape when diamonds were discovered here. This is also the town Cecil Rhodes represented when he was first elected to the Cape parliament.

Siege of Kimberley

During the Anglo-Boer War, Kimberley was besieged by some 4000 Boer soldiers from 15 October 1899 to 16 February 1900. Hemmed inside the town were 500 British troops under Colonel Kekewich and about 50,000 civilians including the town's most famous resident, Cecil Rhodes, whose capture was a particularly enticing prospect for the Boers. However, they were never able to break through some carefully mounted British defences; the surrounding countryside made an attack difficult; there were few nearby hills on which to place siege guns or snipers, and the British were able to use the mine dump heaps to build secure gun placements overlooking the flat and sparsely vegetated plain on the town's outskirts.

The Boers, therefore, had to content themselves with trying to starve the town into surrender. However, the extensive stores owned by De Beers Diamond Mining Company meant that the town did not suffer from food shortages to the same extent as Ladysmith or Mafeking, and Kekewich prudently passed a military law that all food prices were to remain at pre-siege levels. Nevertheless, the town's inhabitants did suffer and, inevitably, the African population suffered the most. There were widespread reports of scurvy and very high rates of infant mortality. By the end of the siege horse meat was the main item on many menus.

Rhodes, nearing the end of his life, put the full resources of De Beers into defending the town. This included manufacturing ammunition in the mine's workshops and most impressively a big gun, inevitably nicknamed 'Long Cecil', that could return fire on the Boer siege guns. The main mine tower was also invaluable as a lookout post; messages about any Boer movements could be relayed by telephone to the outer perimeter of the British defences. This lookout also

Today, the town is tatty and run down, and you may still see prospectors using manual methods to work their claims along the **Vaal River**. In 1869, the first diamond digging area, known as Klipdrift, drew thousands of prospectors to the river. The following year the diggers at Canteen Kopje took the unexpected step of establishing the independent Republic of Klipdrift. In 1871 the Cape government decided to annex the territory to keep it out of the hands of the Transvaal government. On the north bank of the Vaal River is the steel girdered **Barkly Bridge**, which was the first bridge to span the river in 1885. The restored tollhouse serves as the local **museum** ⓘ *daily 0900-1700, small entry fee*, with a limited display on geology and archaeology. The old **pump house**, a few metres from the bridge, is now a pub.

Wonderwerk Cave

ⓘ *Signposted 42 km before Kuruman, T082-8327226. Book in advance and then stop at the homestead to collect a key. Small entry fee. Toilets, small display centre.*
Wonderwerk Cave is an important archaeological site on a private farm, set back from the road in the Kuruman Hills. The main attraction is some rock paintings and the evidence of early human habitation. The display contains interesting background material on the prehistory of the region. The cave has been extensively examined by the Kimberley museum; most of the floor has been divided into squares for research purposes and archaeologists are often at work here. It stretches back 700 m into the hillside, with a level path leading into it. The rock paintings are near the entrance. The grandparents (and their 11 children) of the current owners lived in the cave when they first settled in the region and started farming. Allow one hour for a visit.

proved invaluable as an early warning post for incoming shells: when a lookout spotted a puff of smoke from the main Boer siege gun (sited 4 miles away), a flag would be waved and buglers sited around the town would sound a warning for people to take cover. The system gave about 15 seconds' notice and undoubtedly saved many lives – though the shelling did take a heavy toll.

Relations between Colonel Kekewich and Rhodes were very poor. Rhodes was used to getting what he wanted and in early 1900 he wanted the town relieved. Rhodes could not understand why a large British army located just 20 miles away at Modder River was unable to break through and relieve the town. To the ire of Kekewich he managed to get out to the South African and British press increasingly critical statements about the performance of the British military. In February 1900 Rhodes threatened to call a public meeting, at which Kekewich was convinced he would call for Kimberley to surrender, unless they were given specific information about plans to relieve the town. Kekewich was determined that the meeting should not take place so, instead, Rhodes and 12 other leading citizens demanded that Kekewich send a message to the British Commander-in-Chief, General Roberts, calling for their immediate relief. When Kekewich refused, the two of them almost resorted to a fist fight.

Relief was not far off, however. General Roberts' arrival at Modder River with reinforcements had revitalized the British efforts. A bold plan of attack was evolved. The British cavalry completely outflanked General Cronje's Boer forces, unblocking the main advance and allowing Roberts t o relieve Kimberley. With this attack the whole impetus of the war turned against the Boers. On 16 February Kimberley was at last relieved and Cecil Rhodes (and many London stock brokers) were able to celebrate.

Sleeping

Kimberley *p670, map p672*

AL **Edgerton House**, 5 Edgerton Rd, T053-8311150, edgerton@mweb.co.za. Historic house built in 1901 with pressed ceilings, wooden floors, fireplaces, plenty of antiques, 11 a/c double rooms with en suite bathroom, some with free standing tubs and gold plated fittings, TV, all meals available, swimming pool, gardens, secure parking, a relatively large guesthouse with home comforts.

A **The Estate Private Hotel**, 7 Lodge Rd, T053-8322668, www.theestate.co.za. Luxury hotel set in a building built for Sir Ernest Oppenheimer's wife as a wedding present in 1907. 7 en suite rooms, grand furnishings such as gilt mirrors and wing-back chairs, gardens with pool, restaurant, close to sights.

B **Cecil John Rhodes Guest House**, 138 Du Toitspan Rd, T053-8302500, www.ceciljohnrhodes.co.za. Luxurious old-style guesthouse set in converted house built in 1895 that is a national monument. 7 comfortable rooms, en suite bathrooms, a/c, TV, shady tea garden, friendly management, dining room has a good reputation. Recommended.

B **Garden Court Kimberley**, 120 Du Toitspan Rd, T053-8331751, www.southernsun.com. Bland but comfortable hotel with 135 a/c rooms in a concrete block. Disabled access. Restaurant is an attached franchise steakhouse. Bar, swimming pool, sauna.

B **Protea Hotel Diamond Lodge**, 124 Du Toitspan Rd, T053-8311281, www.proteahotels.co.za. 34 large a/c rooms, with 2 double beds, minibar, clean and modern, restaurant, bar, swimming pool, good service, airport pick-up by arrangement.

B-C **Carrington Lodge**, 60 Carrington Rd, T053-8316448, www.carringtonlodge.co.za. A comfortable guesthouse with 16 en suite rooms with TV, ceiling fans and minibar. Spacious gardens with pool, hearty cooked breakfasts served in the pretty dining room, secure parking, central location.

B-C Milner House, 31 Milner St, T053-8316405, www.milnerhouse.co.za. Well-run guesthouse in a good location in Belgravia, 6 luxurious double rooms with fans, en suite bathroom, TV, phone, swimming pool, large gardens, log fires in the winter evenings, good breakfasts, internet access, an excellent B&B. Highly recommended.

C Horseshoe Motel, Cape Town Rd, T053-8325267. Large roadside motel, 58 a/c rooms, restaurant, bar, swimming pool, popular conference venue so can be very busy or empty, airport transfer service.

C-E Gum Tree Lodge, Old Bloemfontein Rd (R64), 4 km from town, T053-8328577, www.gumtreelodge.co.za. Large complex with 150 beds in dorms and doubles with communal kitchen, some self-contained flats, lounge, **Old Diggers** restaurant and bar next door, shop, TV room, swimming pool, probably the best option for budget travellers, quiet but inconvenient for the sights.

D-E Stay a Day, 72 Lawson St, T053- 8327239. Functional building with a range of rooms, from en suite with TV to dorms sleeping 8, TV lounge, breakfast room, secure parking, spotless throughout, friendly owners, but sterile and completely lacking atmosphere. One of the few budget options in town. Profits go to a local orphanage run by the Dutch Reformed Church.

E Big Hole Caravan Park, West Circular Rd, T053-8306322. Medium-sized site surrounded by mine dumps, grassy, a few young thorn trees provide limited shade, smart central washblock, clean grounds, fenced-off swimming pool, pay phones, an easy walk to the Big Hole museum, 20-min walk from town centre.

Eating

Kimberley *p670, map p672*

Kimberley is better served by pubs and bars than restaurants. There are the usual fast food outlets by the taxi stand behind the City Hall, including **King Pie**, **Steer's** and **Captain Do Regos**. There are also the standard chain steak restaurants, and a number of bars and restaurants in the **Flamingo Casino** complex just out of town on the Johannesburg road.

TT **Halfway House**, Du Toitspan Rd, T053-8316324. Historical pub with bizarre drive-in section, claiming to be where Cecil Rhodes used to ride in to sip a quick beer on his horse. Good atmosphere, simple pub meals, can get very busy at weekends.

TT **Keg & Falcon**, 187 Du Toitspan Rd, T053-8332075. Open daily. Popular English- style theme pub serving decent meals and beer on tap, varied menu from steaks to their famous foot-long pies. Part of a chain that is slightly more upmarket than most bars. Good for lunch. Rather oddly, women dining alone on a Wed night get 50% off.

TT **Star of the West**, North Circular Rd, T053-8326463. 1000-late. The oldest pub in South Africa, dating from 1873. It was originally a corrugated iron shack were thirsty miners paid tuppence for a beer and half-a-penny for a glass of wine. Bit of a tourist trap but characterful, with a long wooden bar. Tram to the Mine Museum stops outside across the road (on request). Enjoy a cool beer and a pub lunch before visiting the Big Hole. The miners still drink here.

TT **Umberto's**, 229 Du Toitspan Rd, T053-8325741. Mon-Sat 1200-1430, 1800-late. Excellent Italian restaurant just next to the **Halfway House**. Superb pizza and home-made pasta dishes, some 260 items on the menu, meat and fish a little more expensive, traditional red and white checked tablecloths and friendly service. Recommended.

T **Old Diggers Inn**, next to the **Gum Tree Lodge**, T053-8328577. Large restaurant frequented by backpackers staying next door, open all day for good-value meals, hearty portions, busy bar.

Activities and tours

Kimberley *p670, map p672*

Birdwatching

Kimberley is less known for its birds than its Big Hole but there are a number of sites around the town that are excellent for birdwatching. There are up to 30,000 flamingos on the **Kamfers Dam** (see page 677), and 50 pairs of African white-backed vultures can be spotted on the De Beers' Dronfield Farm a few km north of the city. During summer European bee-eaters breed in the suburb of West End, and saltpans and rivers in the region support populations of water birds and raptors. A number of local guides from previously disadvantaged backgrounds have been trained in the Kimberley region by **Birdlife International** and funded by the South African lottery. They will go with you in your car and be able to take you on to a number of private properties for some excellent birdwatching. Pick up a leaflet at the tourist office which has a list of the informative guides' cell phone numbers.

Cricket

International matches are played at the **De Beers Diamond Oval**, Dickenson Av, Cassandra, enquiries T053-8332601, tickets from Computicket, www.computicket.co.za. Watching a game here makes a pleasant change from the large stadiums found in the cities. The atmosphere is very relaxed and if you're lucky you may meet the players in the club bar. During the domestic season, Kimberley is home to Griqualand West.

Tour operators

Diamond Tours Unlimited, T053-8614983, www.diamondtours.co.za. Half- and full-day tours of local diamond mining sites including Barkly West, 35 km northwest of Kimberley, where old prospectors still pan by hand. Also tours to bushman rock art and battlefields.

Whitewater rafting

River rafting is not what you might expect looking out over the dry, flat countryside around Kimberley, but to the south flows the Gariep (Orange) River, one of South Africa's largest rivers. It is possible to raft the rapids between Hopetown, on the N12, and Douglas. The river flows through beautiful dolerite hills past old farms and orchards. **Aquarush**, Hopetown, 120 km south of Kimberley, can organize trips from Kimberley, T083-5861795 (mob), aquarush@mweb.co.za.

Transport

Kimberley *p670, map p672*
485 km to **Johannesburg**, 979 km to **Cape Town**, 238 km to **Kuruman**, 401 km to **Upington**.

Air

The airport is 10 km south of the town centre. There are 2 flights a day between Kimberley and **Cape Town**, and 6 flights a day between Kimberley and **Johannesburg**. For flight information, T053-85111241. For reservations, contact SAA, T011-9781111, www.flysaa.com.

Bus

Buses depart from outside the Tourist Information Centre on Bultfontein Rd. There are daily services to **Cape Town** (13 hrs), **Johannesburg** and **Pretoria** (6½ hrs). All services also stop at the Shell Ultra City on the N12, 6 km from the centre of town. **Greyhound**, central reservations, T012-3231154, www.greyhound.co.za. The local booking agent is **Tickets for Africa** at the Tourist Information Centre on Bultfontein Rd, T053-8326040. **Translux**, central reservations T011-7743333, www.translux.co.za.

Car hire

All the companies are based at the airport and are open throughout the day during the week, but only when flights arrive over the weekend. If you want to take a vehicle over the border to Namibia make sure you mention this. **Avis**, T053-8511082, www.avis.co.za. **Budget**, T053-8511183, www.budget.co.za. **Hertz**, T053-8302200, www.hertz.co.za. **Imperial**, T053-8511132, www.imperialcarrental.co.za.

Taxi

AA Taxis, T053-8614015. The main rank is behind the City Hall.

Train

For steam enthusiasts there is a collection of locomotives in perfect condition in the Beaconsfield Marshalling Yards to the south of the city centre. There are daily trains to Cape Town and Johannesburg/Pretoria. Information, T053-8382631, reservations T0860-008888, www.spoornet.co.za.

Directory

Kimberley *p670, map p672*
Banks Standard Bank, 10 Old Main St. ABSA, 69 Du Toitspan Rd. **Internet** Small World Net Café, 42 Sidney St, T053-8313484. **Medical services** 24-hr Medi-City Private Hospital, 177 Du Toitspan Rd, T053-8381111, www.kimberleymc.co.za.

The Kalahari

The Kalahari, like all great deserts, evokes images of vast lapis skies, shimmering horizons and cruel heat. The name Kalahari is derived from Kgalagadi, the San term for 'place without water'. It is at once enthralling and intimidating, begging to be explored but overwhelming in its sheer size and harshness. The landscape is semi-desert – rolling red sand dunes, salt pans, dry river beds and endless scrub – stretching from the Gariep (Orange) River to northern Botswana and west into Namibia. Despite the arid conditions, the Kalahari supports some of the best game viewing in South Africa, in the magnificent Kgalagadi Transfrontier Park. But the main draw of the Kalahari is its vast open spaces and the true wilderness of the desert; even today, travelling here evokes a real sense of adventure. For more information on the Kalahari visit www.kalahari.org.za.

» *For Sleeping, Eating and other listings, see pages 691-695.*

Ins and outs

Getting around Kuruman is the principal town in this part of the Kalahari. If you plan to travel north from here, make sure you stock up on all supplies and check the condition of your car, especially water, oil and fuel levels. The R31 north is one of only two routes to the Kgalagadi Transfrontier Park. The only other road into the park is from Upington. Each route involves stretches on gravel, although much of the road between Upington and Askam is now tarred. Note that driving on loose gravel and sand can be dangerous and these are not the best conditions in which to break down. Do not be tempted to drive too fast if the roads are empty and straight. If you have an accident you could be waiting a long time for help.

Climate As a desert, the Kalahari region is known for its extreme temperatures. Rainfall in the region is only 50 mm annually and usually arrives in dramatic but brief thunderstorms during summer. Temperatures in the northern Kalahari and along the Gariep (Orange) River often reach above 40°C during the summer, while, on winter nights, they can drop as low as 6°C – a consideration if camping.

Kuruman

» *pp691-695. Phone code: 053. Colour map 1, C4.*

This isolated northern town has two reasons for being on the tourist map: the Moffat family and their mission station; and a natural spring known as The Eye. Neither take up much time and the town itself is scruffy and unappealing, so half a day here should be more than enough on your way through. However, Kuruman is an important regional centre, so it's a good place to stock up on fuel and supplies.

Ins and outs

The **tourist office** ⓘ *Voortrekker St, T053-7121095, www.kurumankalahari.co.za*, is in an old cottage next to The Eye. This is, in fact, the old Drostdy House, once home to the local magistrate. Part of the building is given over to a tea room that serves light lunches and tea and coffee throughout the day. Birdwatchers can pick up a map and an identification list for the northern Kalahari Raptor Route. More than 50 species, 35 of which are resident, have been recorded in the region.

The Eye

ⓘ *Main St, T053-7121095. Daylight hours. Minimal entrance fee. Small café.*

The Eye, or 'die oog' in Afrikaans, is an amazing spring which has continuously produced almost 20 million litres of fresh water per day, with little variance between the

Robert Moffat

Robert Moffat is known in southern Africa for two reasons, first for translating the Bible into Tswana and secondly for his association with David Livingstone, the great Victorian explorer of the region. Moffat was born at Ormiston in Scotland into a poor family; he left school at the age of 11 and then worked as a gardener for 10 years – hardly a background to prepare him for 50 years of scholarly work in remotest Africa. After a brief theological training he was accepted by the London Missionary Society on 30 September 1816. His first posting was to Namaqualand where he immediately made a name for himself by converting an outlaw called Jager Afrikaner. In 1819 he married Mary Smith, his employer's daughter, in St George's Church in Cape Town. The first days of their marriage were spent in a wagon crossing the Karoo to Kuruman.

In 1824 Moffat persuaded the missionaries to move to the present site, which he considered to be far more suitable because of the abundant water supply, and the fertile level land was ideal for farming. It took four years to build the Moffat Homestead and a house for his colleague, Robert Hamilton. Fine materials were used and neat gardens were laid out. They wanted to show what Christianity could do. The homestead is still standing today and is the oldest building north of the Orange River.

An important part of a missionary's work was teaching. And it was when Moffat was confronted with a class "of Batswanas, Hottentots, two Bushmen and two Mantatees", that he realized the problem of language. The next 40 years of his life were dominated by translation and printing. He was the first person to print the language of the Matabele people, on his press in Kuruman, and so laid the foundations for their modern education system. His greatest feat was the translation of the Bible into Tswana. In 1857 he printed 1000 copies despite a whole range of problems. He then had to teach the Tswana people to read their own language. It was both the first time the Bible had been printed anywhere in Africa, and the first time it had been produced in a previously unwritten African tongue.

It was beyond the capacity of the Kuruman press to print the New Testament, and Moffat could find no one in South Africa to help, so the couple had no choice but to return to England, only to find out that they were famous. This helped them to raise vital funds and to get the printing done but, after three years away, they both yearned for Africa. The Moffats worked in Kuruman until 1870, when the Missionary Society persuaded them to return to England. Mary died within six months of their return but Robert Moffat continued to work for the LMS. He died 13 years later on 9 August 1883. In 1983 a bronze bust of Moffat was moved from Brixton, London, to Kuruman to mark the centenary of his death.

wet and the dry season. It was the presence of this water and the resultant river that made settlement possible in this area. The site was proclaimed a national monument in 1992. There is little to see of the spring, save for a wet, moss-covered rock, but the gardens around the clear pond are a popular and attractive picnic spot – the pond is full of large goldfish, fattened by breadcrumbs. The enormous willow trees were planted by the first magistrate in 1881. Unfortunately the grounds are not quite as peaceful as they might appear: there is a constant background noise of buried pumping equipment. The gardens around town rely on the spring water, which is fed into two 7-km-long irrigation channels, giving Kuruman the feel of an oasis during the dry season when the surrounding farmlands are burnt brown. There is an 11-km hiking trail that starts at The Eye, crosses the golf course and goes through some local villages, and ends at another small natural spring to the west of Kuruman. Ask the tourist office for a map.

Moffat Mission

ⓘ 5 km north of town on Moffat Lane; follow Voortrekker St out of town past the police station, T053-7121352, www.kuruman-mission.org.za. No public transport. Daily 0800-1700; allow at least 2 hrs. Small entrance charge.

Under the guidance of Robert Moffat (see page 683), the Kuruman Mission Station became one of the best-known missions in Africa. Today it is run by the United Congregational Church of Southern Africa, and the complex is an atmospheric and fascinating place.

The first building you come to is the **stable**, with a few portraits on the walls and an early wagon used by the mission. Turning left out of the stable, you find yourself walking parallel to a **furrow** that Moffat had dug to bring water from The Eye, 5 km away (see page 682). Across the furrow is a small garden created by Mary Moffat; it was here that explorer David Livingstone proposed to the Moffats' daughter, after she had nursed him back to health following an attack by a lion. Opposite the garden is the **Moffat Homestead**, built in 1824 and fully restored in the 1980s. Inside, the main room has a few objects on display but, overall, it is disappointing. The kitchen has been turned into a tea room and curio shop. Just beyond the homestead is the original **Mission Church**, for many years the largest building in the interior of South Africa. Despite having only nine converts when he designed the T-shaped church, Moffat planned for it to seat 800 people. The stone walls stood for seven years before timber of sufficient length could be found for the roof. Moffat found the trees on one of his journeys 350 km away in the Marico Valley. The building still has a thatch roof, dung floor and wooden pews, and the acoustics are surprisingly good.

This was the first house that Livingstone lived in when he came to Africa.

The final building of note is the **school classroom**; inside are the original wooden school benches and desks. The room is now home to the original press Moffat used to print the Tswana Bible, the first bible to be printed in Africa. The press was also used to print school books and publications for the church.

Southwest from Kuruman

» pp691-695.

From Kuruman the N14 runs 263 km west to Upington via Kathu and Olifantshoek. The only reason for stopping en route is to refuel and buy something to eat and drink, unless you wish to marvel at an opencast mine in the midst of a beautiful and fragile environment.

Kalahari Raptor Rehabilitation Centre

ⓘ 19 km from Kuruman, on the Upington road. Look out for a side road, the D3340 on the right, signposted Ulster; the farm is a further 12 km from here, T053-7123576, www.raptor.co.za. By appointment only. Small entrance charge.

This privately owned centre has a wealth of information on raptors and a chance to see the rehabilitation work on injured birds, most of which get hurt from flying into power lines. Staff can advise on the best areas for birdwatching in the Kalahari. There is also a small selection of rescued and hand-raised mammals, such as young impalas, meerkats and bat eared foxes.

Kathu → *Phone code: 053. Colour map 1, C3.*

Just off the main road (N14), this modern settlement has grown up entirely around the mining industry, first started in 1972. This is the location of **Sishen Iron Ore Mine**, a massive scar in the earth and the largest single pit open cast mine in the world. It's roughly 12 km long and 1.5 km wide, and over 28 million tonnes of iron ore is extracted each year, employing 3200 people. Everything associated with the mine is giant – the trucks that move the ore look oversized, and can carry over 170 metric tonnes. The mine is connected to Saldanha ore terminal on the west coast by a single railway line which you can see in the vicinity of Elands Bay and Velddrif. Guided tours of the mine are usually held on the first Saturday of the month; contact **Mokala Safaris** ⓘ*Kathu, T053-7232391, www.mokala.co.za*. For a small fee visitors are welcome at the mine's 18-hole golf club, T053-7392290, with clubhouse and bar, and at the adjoining recreation club, which has a swimming pool and squash and tennis courts.

Northwest from Kuruman » *pp691-695.*

Hotazel and Black Rock → *Phone code: 053.*

Travelling on the R31 from Kuruman allows you to explore more of the Kalahari region. This is a good road but it is only surfaced as far north as Hotazel, 61 km; 25 km further north is Black Rock. These are nothing more than searingly hot *dorps* but both are important manganese ore mining centres. Oddly enough, both these centres have sports clubs with tennis and squash courts, golf, even bowls, built for the miners but they can be used by visitors for a small fee, and it's not a bad idea to stop for a swim after a hot drive. From Hotazel, follow the signs for Sonstraal and Van Zylsrus, 105 km.

Tswalu Kalahari Reserve

ⓘ*off the R31 between Hotazel and Sonstraal, www.tswalu.com.*

Tswalu is a magnificent 100,000-ha reserve created by the late Stephen Boler. Over $US7 million was spent in establishing the enterprise, reputedly South Africa's largest private reserve. Today it is owned by the Oppenheimer family.

At the foot of the Korannaberg mountains, this is a region of stunning red sand dunes and typical savannah dotted with acacia trees. The park has been well stocked with wildlife, including lion, buffalo, three types of zebra, red hartebeest, blue and black wildebeest, giraffe, gemsbok, kudu and impala. A breeding programme for the rare desert black rhino has been set up and, from just eight that were introduced from Namibia in 1995, the population now stands at 19. The head count for large game has risen from 5000 to 12,000 in five years, so conservation in this region has been an incredible success. You can explore the reserve on game walks, by 4WD or on horseback. The only place to stay is the five-star lodge, which has its own plane to pick guests up from Johannesburg or Cape Town. » *For further details, see Sleeping, page 691.*

Van Zylsrus to Kgalagadi Transfrontier Park

Van Zylsrus is a typical Kalahari town: one dusty street is lined withshops and there is little of interest. From Van Zylsrus the road follows the dry course of the Kuruman River as far as **Askham**. At this point the route combines with the road from Upington, and just one (gravel) road leads a further 61 km to the gates of the Kgalagadi Transfrontier Park. After a long and dusty drive, the national park camp at **Twee Rivieren** is a welcome sight, especially the swimming pool. The total distance from Kuruman to the park gates is 385 km. It is an undeniably tiring journey but allows you to experience the vast southern fringes of the Kalahari Desert.

Kgalagadi Transfrontier Park

» pp691-695. Colour map 1, B1.

ⓘ Twee Rivieren is the only entrance on the South African side, T054-5612000. Gate/office/shop hours vary: Jan and Feb 0600-1930, Mar 0630-1900, Apr and Aug 0700-1830, May 0700-1800, Jun and Jul 0730-1800, Sep 0630-1830, Oct 0600-1900, Nov and Dec 0530-1930. Daily conservation entrance fee R120, children R60, also covers your vehicle (South Africans pay reduced rates).

Although probably one of the least visited national parks in the country, the Kgalagadi Transfrontier Park has some of the finest game viewing in Africa. It is remote and relatively undeveloped, with uncomfortably high summer temperatures, but few visitors begrudge the hot dusty roads once they've glimpsed their first lion. The roads follow the scrubby valleys of two seasonal rivers, the Auob and Nossob, and cut across red sand dunes typical of the Kalahari.

Ins and outs

Getting there From Upington, the first 190 km is an excellent tarred road followed by 61 km of fairly good gravel; allow 3½ hours to the park gates. Petrol is available at Noenieput and Andriesvale. From Kuruman, it is 385 km to the park gates, via Hotazel, Sonstraal and Van Zylsrus (see page 685). There is no direct access from **Namibia**, because the Mata Mata border gate is closed. The easiest access from Namibia is via the Aroab/Rietfontein border.

All routes on the Botswana side of the park are strictly 4WD and must be travelled in a convoy of at least two vehicles.

There are gates between the South Africa and Botswana sides. Visitors wishing to visit the **Botswana** side do not need a passport as long as entry and exit is made through the same gate. However, if you are entering the park in one country and exiting through the other, than you will need a passport. There are border posts at Twee Rivieren on the South African side and at Two Rivers on the Botswana side of the park, daily 0700-1600.

Best time to visit This is an arid region with less than 200 m of rainfall a year, falling between the summer months of January and April. In the summer it gets very hot and you should carry at least 10 litres of drinking water in your vehicle. The best months are February to May, but most of the accommodation is fully booked during these months, especially at weekends and around Easter. Camping is usually possible, although the main camp, Twee Rivieren, is likely to be very busy. Camping in winter requires warm sleeping bags as temperatures fall below zero. Always check the availability of rooms in advance – this is the end of the road and even space for tents gets fully booked. If you plan to visit during the main season, pre-book your accommodation before your arrival in South Africa.

A major advantage is that Kgalagadi is free from malaria.

Park information

The three main rest camps – **Twee Rivieren, Nossob** and **Mata Mata** – have shops which stock basic groceries but none stock fresh vegetables. Meat and bread are available at Twee Rivieren, which also has a restaurant and swimming pool. Petrol is available at all the camps; electricity is provided by generators (220V) and is available in the early morning and 1700 to 2300. From each camp guided day walks and night drives are available and can be booked at reception. There are also six unfenced wilderness camps: **Gharagab, Kielie Krankie, Urikaruus, Kalahari Tented Camp, Bitterpan** and **Grootkolk**, none of which have shops or other facilities.

The combined protected area is over 3.7 million ha, nearly twice the size of Kruger National Park and one of the largest protected areas in the world.

Due to the remoteness of the region a close record is kept of your movements and you have to sign in and out of every camp. There is a curfew on returning to the camps in the evening; if you do not make it back to the gates on time, you will be fined. When driving here you have to remember that distances are vast and you may well be delayed considerably by game viewing so some careful planning on driving times is needed. Note, too, that some tracks are one-way only (see map below). Without stops, it takes 2½ hours to drive between Twee Riveren and Mata Mata (and Kalahari Tented Camp which is 3 km from Mata Mata); Twee Riveren and Nossob, 3½ hours; Twee Riveren and Grootkolk, six hours; Twee Riveren and Kieliekrankie, 1½ hours; Twee Riveren and Urikaruus, two hours; Nossob and Grootkolk, 2½ hours; Nossob and Bitterpan, 2½ hours; Nossob and Gharagab, four hours; Nossob and Bitterpan, 2½ hours; Bitterpan and Mata Mata, two hours.

Remember there is no mobile phone reception in the park in the event of an emergency.

Although the park authorities and the Upington tourist office insist that 4WDs are not necessary, saloon vehicles can be uncomfortable on the gravel roads and prone to flat tyres. If you don't have an off-road vehicle, be sure that your car is in good condition and can deal with several days on gravel. Although Twee Rivieren has a car workshop, there is no system in place to cope with breakdowns. In the event of a breakdown, stay in the car and wait for passing cars to assist you. You will have to

Kgalagadi Transfrontier Park

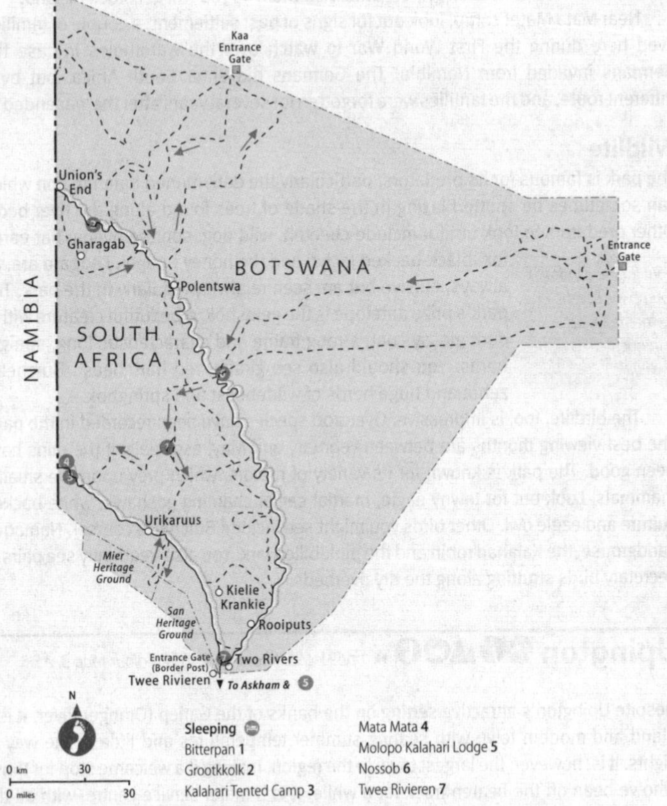

make your way back to Twee Rivieren, from where a mechanic can drive out to your car. You should never leave the gravel roads, it is easy to get stuck in the soft sand. Experienced drivers can hire a 4WD and camping equipment at the **Molopo Kalahari Lodge**, 50 km south of the gate (see Sleeping, page 693), but obviously you have to get there first. Another option would be to drive as far as the lodge in your saloon hire car, leave it there and hire a 4WD for a few days to explore the park.

Background

The area was proclaimed a national park on 3 July 1931 as part of a progressive initiative to combat the problem of poachers. Known until a few years ago as the Kalahari Gemsbok National Park, the area was adjacent to the Gemsbok National Park in Botswana. On 7 April 1999 the two parks were formally merged into a single ecological unit, now known as the Kgalagadi Transfrontier Park.

The first camp for tourists was built in 1940 near the confluence of the Auob and Nossob rivers. Most of the game viewing is along these riverbeds where the vegetation is concentrated. Thanks to the aridity of the region, vegetation remains sparse and mostly close to the ground, which is why game viewing is so good here. The rivers rarely flow but rainwater collects in the bed under the sand, which is sufficient for grasses and plants to survive. Both rivers were once thundering waterways, evident in the great width of their valleys in some areas. Between the two rivers stretch mighty red sand dunes, aligned from north to south and covered in yellow grass following good rains. These are fossil dunes, and their red tint is produced by an iron oxide coating on the white grains of sand. Between the 20 m high dunes are level valleys known as streets. Two roads cross the dunes; do not venture off them as you will get stuck in sand.

Near Mata Matat camp, look out for signs of past settlement; a couple of families lived here during the First World War to watch over the waterholes in case the Germans invaded from Namibia. The Germans did enter South Africa, but by a different route, and the families were forgotten for several years after the war ended.

Wildlife

The park is famous for its predators, particularly the dark-maned Kalahari lion which can sometimes be spotted lazing in the shade of trees found along the river beds. Other predators to look out for include cheetah, wild dog, spotted hyena, bat-eared fox, black-backed jackal and the honey badger. Leopard are, as always, elusive but are seen relatively regularly in the park. The park's prize antelope is the gemsbok, a beautiful creature with a dark glossy coat, strong frame and characteristic long, straight horns. You should also see giraffe, red hartebeest, Burchell's zebra and huge herds of wildebeest and springbok.

Look out for the windmills which pump the boreholes – these waterholes are usually frequented by some form of wildlife.

The birdlife, too, is impressive. Over 200 species have been recorded in the park. The best viewing months are between February and May, especially if the rains have been good. The park is known for its variety of raptors, which prey upon the smaller mammals. Look out for tawny eagle, martial eagle, chanting goshawk, white-backed vulture and eagle owl. Other birds you might see include Burchell's courser, Namaqua sandgrouse, the Kalahari robin and the pink-billed lark. You also frequently see pairs of secretary birds strutting along the dry riverbeds.

Upington

» pp691-695. Phone code: 054. Colour map 3, A5.

Despite Upington's attractive setting on the banks of the Gariep (Orange) River, it is a bland and modern town with searing summer temperatures and little in the way of sights. It is, however, the largest town in the region, making it a welcome stop for those who've been off the beaten track for a while. It is a major service centre, with all the usual South African shops and high-street chains, and, as such, it is an excellent place to restock your supplies. As a major entry point to the Kalahari, Upington is also a good spot to organize trips to the Kgalagadi Transfrontier Park and Augrabies Falls National Park, and it is also en route to the Fish River Canyon in Namibia to the west on the N8.

Ins and outs

Getting there There are daily flights from Cape Town and Johannesburg, and buses from Cape Town via Clanwilliam, Johannesburg and Pretoria. There is a train station but no South African passenger trains stop here and it's only used for freight. However, Namibia's railway company, **Transnamib Starline Passenger Services,** runs a service from Upington in South Africa to Windhoek twice a week. ▸▸ *For further details, see Transport, page 695.*

Tourist information **Upington Tourist Office** ⓘ *Kalahari Oranje Museum, Schröder St, T054-3326064, www.upington.co.za, www.upington.com, Mon-Fri 0800- 1730, Sat 0900-1200,* deals only with information on the town. For information on the Kgalagadi Transfrontier Park and the Kalahari in general you'll have to visit the **Green Kalahari Information Centre** ⓘ *26 Swartmodder Av, T054-3372800, www.green kalahari.co.za.* This office has a good selection of brochures on the Kalahari area.

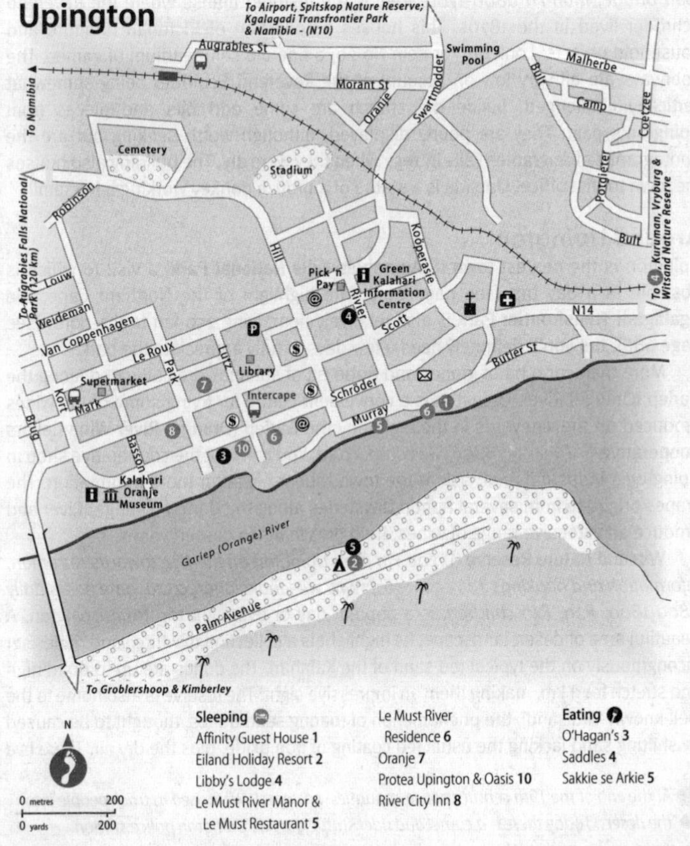

Background

The origin of the town is rather more disreputable than one might expect. In the mid-19th century the northern reaches of the Cape Colony were home to a colourful variety of outlaws and rustlers; there were no settlements, making it impossible for the police to track people into the uncharted wilderness. By 1879 the Cape government had had enough and founded a small settlement on the Gariep (Orange) River to try and exercise some control over the area. In 1884 Sir Thomas Upington, the new Prime Minister of the colony, visited the settlement, which was renamed in his honour.

The fortunes of the new settlement and the subsequent development of the district, can be attributed to the pioneering work of two men, the Reverend Christiaan Schröder and Johann 'Japie' Lutz. Together they built the first irrigation canal, constructed a pump on the river and started a pontoon ferry. After the Anglo-Boer War, Lutz built canals at Kakamas, Marchand and Onseepkans. These irrigated areas now produce cotton, lucerne, vegetables, grapes and sultanas. Today the **SA Dried Fruit Cooperative** and the **Gariep (Orange) River Wine Cellars Cooperative** are responsible for handling most of the agricultural produce in the region. Another famous resident was Scotty Smith, a legendary rogue and Robin Hood of the Northern Cape, who stole and gave to the poor. He died in Upington in 1918 during a flu epidemic and his grave is in the local cemetery.

Sights

The main building of the **Kalahari Oranje Museum** ⓘ *Schröder St, overlooking the road bridge, Mon-Fri 0800-1700, free*, is the restored manse where the Reverend Schröder lived in the 1870s. This houses a collection of Victorian furniture and household objects. Look out for item No 20, a fine old compendium of games. The doorways are all very low on account of the Reverend Schröder being somewhat vertically challenged. Inside the church are some odd bits and pieces from Upington's past. They are poorly displayed, although worth seeking out are the photographs of Augrabies Falls in 1957 when they were dry. The building also houses the town tourist office. Outside is a statue of a bronze donkey working a horsemill.

Around Upington

Upington is the nearest town to **Augrabies Falls National Park**, a visit to which is possible in a day trip (see page 697). The highlight of the Northern Cape, the **Kgalagadi Transfrontier Park** is also relatively near, lying 250 km to the north (see page 686), but you'll definitely need a few days to fully appreciate the park.

More than 1000 ha of grapes and 8000 ha of sultanas are cultivated along the Gariep (Orange) River. Upington is a convenient centre for trying some of the wines produced on the vineyards in the region by the **Gariep (Orange) River Wine Cellars Cooperative** ⓘ *T054-3378800, www.owk.co.za*. You can visit the cooperative shop in Upington's industrial area; ask at the town tourist office for more information. The grapes originate from several hundred wineries along the Gariep (Orange) River and produce an extensive range of wines, from dry whites to dessert wines.

Witsand Nature Reserve ⓘ *200 km from Upington off the N14 towards Kuruman, information and bookings T053-3131061, www.witsandkalahari.co.za, gate hours daily 0800-1800, R20, R10 children*, is a popular day or overnight trip from Upington. A beautiful area of desert landscape, its highlight is a collection of white sand dunes set incongruously on the typical red sand of the Kalahari. The dunes are up to 60 m high and stretch for 9 km, making them an impressive sight. The reserve is also home to the well-known 'Brulsand', the phenomenon of roaring sand dunes, thought to be caused by shifting sand lacking the usual red coating of iron oxide, plus the dry air. There is a

At the end of the 19th century police 'mounties' on camels were used to track people into the desert. Today there is a camel and rider statue outside Upington police station.

comfortable resort, visitors can walk freely around the reserve, and there are two 4WD trails. There is also a concealed bird-hide dug into the ground, allowing an eye-level view of a waterhole; if you're lucky you might spot the pygmy falcon which is Africa's smallest raptor. Dune boarding is a new activity here, and boards as well as bicycles can be hired from the information centre.

Closer to town, about 15 km north of Upington off the R360 (follow Swartmodder Street past the swimming pool), is the **Spitskop Nature Reserve** ⓘ *information and bookings, T054-3321336*. The 5000-ha reserve makes for a pleasant day trip and acts as a good introduction to the flora and fauna that lie further north. Here you can view a variety of wildlife commonly found throughout the Kalahari region, including springbok, eland, zebra and gemsbok. In the centre of the reserve is a *kopjie* with an observation platform and telescope. There are hiking trails throughout the reserve, the staff at reception will point you in the right direction, or you can explore the reserve in your own car.

Sleeping

Kuruman *p682*

B Eldorado Motel, Main St, T053-7122191. Bland 1960s roadside motel on the outskirts of town, 60 a/c refurbished rooms in 4 blocks arranged around swimming pool, large airy dining room with plenty of light, quiet but overpriced, more suited to business travellers.

B-C Riverfield, 12 Seodin Rd, T/F053-7120003, www.riverfield.co.za. Modern house set in large well-kept gardens, 12 en suite doubles or family rooms, TV, lounge, braai area at the back, swimming pool, self-service bar, good breakfasts, dinner available Mon-Thu, well run, the best option in Kuruman.

C Janke Guest House, 16 Chapman St, T053-7120949, janke@spg.co.za. A large modern house painted in bright yellow and purple, easily spotted from the road as you head out to the mission, 7 smart a/c en suite rooms with TV, bar, secure parking, meals by arrangement, good value and friendly.

Southwest from Kuruman *p684*

B-C Khai Appel Resort (formerly known as Gamagara Lodge), Hendrik van Eck St, Kathu, T053-7232261, www.gamagara.co.za. 1-bedroom chalets and 2- or 3-bedroom park homes, fully equipped for self catering. Swimming pool with slide. Also grassy campsite (**E**) with power points and braais. All set next to a peaceful dam, horse riding and fishing can be arranged.

B-E Red Sands Country Lodge, 15 km from Kuruman, along the N14 towards Upington, T053-7120033, www.redsands.co.za. Located on a private game farm in the hills above town that is home to several species of antelope. Selection of B&B double rooms, fully equipped self-catering chalets, camping and caravan sites, swimming pool with slide, restaurant. Gets busy during school holidays.

Tswalu Kalahari Reserve *p685*

L4 Tswalu Lodge. T053-7819234, www.relaischateaux.com/sa. Part of the Relais & Chateaux luxury hotel group. Top-notch luxury lodge, 8 beautifully appointed stone cottages with private decks, outdoor showers with views of the Kalahari, swimming pool, library. Excellent service and meals. Rates include all meals, game drives and horse riding. Air transfers from Cape Town or Johannesburg can be arranged. At over R8000 per couple per night this is a serious extravagance but a wonderful experience.

Kgalagadi Transfrontier Park *p686, map p687*

There are 3 main camps in the park: Twee Rivieren, the main camp at the entrance gate; Mata Mata, a more remote camp; and Nossob, on the Botswana border. At each main camp there is a mix of self-catering cottages plus a campsite with washing and braai facilities. There are no electric points in the campsites, but lighting is provided by generator until 2300. Check in is from 1200 but all rooms must be vacated by 0900. Reservations through SAN Parks in Pretoria, T012-4289111, www.sanparks.org, Mon-Fri. You can also contact the park direct, T054-5612000; credit card bookings are accepted over the telephone.

Six new, upmarket wilderness camp are in the process of opening. At the time of writing 3 were functional (see below) and the others (Urikaruuus, Gharagab and Kielie Krankie), were being developed. Unlike the main camps, these are not fenced but a ranger is on duty at all times. If the park is full there are several options just outside (see below).

On the Botswana side there are campsites at Polentswa, Rooiputs and Two Rivers. Bookings are made through the Botswana Parks Authority, PO Box 131, Gaborone, T+267(0)3-9180774, dwnp@gov.bw.

Twee Rivieren

The biggest of the camps with 31 units in total. Accommodation and administrative buildings are lined up on a sandy slope. A shop sells groceries, meat, bread, wine, beer and souvenirs. There is also a takeaway selling snacks, a bar with TV, a swimming pool and an overpriced (and frankly awful) restaurant. Self-catering is a far better option. Night drives and guided walks can be arranged at the information centre.

B **Chalets**, self-contained thatched cottages with a/c, sleeping 6, shower, fully equipped kitchen, no oven but braai area.

B **Cottages**, sleep 3 (2 adults and 1 child) or 4; one has wheelchair access.

E **Campsite**, dusty site but with good prefabricated shade, some trees, plus good ablutions including a laundry but no cooking facilities other than braais. Swimming pool. Can be very busy with noisy families.

Mata Mata

118 km from entrance gate, allow at least 2½ hrs travelling time. This road is one of the most beautiful in the park with some of the best game-viewing opportunities. The camp has a small shop selling groceries and firewood. Electricity is generated from 0500 for a few hours, and again 1700-2300.

B **Chalets**, self-contained chalets sleeping up to 6 in 2 bedrooms, with extra beds in dining room, shower, kitchen, no oven, braai area.

B-C **Huts**, 1 double room, shower, kitchen, no oven, braai area.

C **Park Homes**, sleep 3 or 5. Check with SAN Parks for details.

E **Campsite**, sandy plots in front of the chalets, little shade but fantastic setting, good ablution facilities, braai areas.

Nossob

152 km from the entrance gate, allow at least 3½ hrs travelling time; the first sign of the camp is a pair of white gates and a few battered trees beside the white buildings. This is the most remote camp, with the least facilities, and probably provides the best opportunity of hearing lions roar at night. The camp has recently been refurbished and there is now a predator information centre where you can organize guided game walks and night drives.

A **Guesthouse**, 2 units attached by a connecting door, sleeping 8 or 2 groups of 4. Each has 2 bedrooms, bathroom, dining room, lounge, fully equipped kitchen, enclosed veranda, good value for a group.

B-C **Cottages**, sleep 4 or 6, 2 bedrooms, 2 bathrooms, dining room, kitchen with gas stove and fridge.

E **Campsite**, ablution bock and braai pits, the whole camp overlooks a broad section of the riverbed and a waterhole.

Wilderness camps

B **Bitterpan**. Situated in the dunes, about 3 hrs from Nossob but accessible by 4WD only along sand roads. Accommodation in stilted huts sleeping 2, with en suite bathroom, built with natural materials. Walkways link the 4 huts to a communal kitchen/entertainment/braai area. There is also a 6-m-high tower allowing excellent views out over the dunes. Electricity is solar-powered.

B **Grootkkolk**. 100 km north of Nossob, this new camp is again set in red sand dunes but is more basic. 4 simple en suite chalets sleeping 2, built out of sandbags and canvas. There is a communal kitchen with fridge and hotplates, plus a braai. This camp can be accessed by saloon car.

B **Kalahari Tented Camp**. 3 km from Mata Mata, 15 fully equipped spacious tents with kitchen and bathroom, sleeping 2-4, swimming pool, overlooks a waterhole in the Auob riverbed. This camp can also be reached by saloon car.

Outside the park

During peak season park accommodation is fully booked for weeks on end. There are several other accommodation options en route to Twee Rivieren, but these are also likely to be booked up at peak times.

B-D Molopo Kalahari Lodge, 15 km from Askham, on the gravel road to the park (50 km), T054- 5110008, www.molopo lodge.com. Well-run lodge on the edge of the park, 22 en suite rondavels, 4 family self-catering chalets, and campsite set in dusty grounds, large restaurant, bar, TV lounge, swimming pool. Owners organize all-in tours around the region or you can hire 4WDs and camping equipment from here. Rates are very reasonable and children under 6 go free (including breakfast). The last stop before the park. Recommended.

C Klipkolk Guest House, Opstaan, T072-1596726 (mob). A simple B&B sleeping 12 with attached tea room set on a typical Kalahari farm. Evening meals available on request. 13 km to the border post at Rietfontein. Follow the R360 from Upington, take the R31 turning. Run by Gertuida and Hendrik who can organize tours by donkey cart to meet the local Mier people.

C Loch Broom Guest Farm, Askham, off the Kuruman road, T054-90291620. Rooms in the farm guesthouse or permanent tents under shade, a/c rondavel for 4 and an a/c family room on a working cattle and sheep farm, secluded setting, swimming pool, restaurant serving country fare, prices include dinner and breakfast.

C Rooipan Guest House, T082-4151579 (mob). Old farmhouse which has been converted into a guesthouse and tea room. Swimming pool, braai area. Evening meals on request, specializes in South African dishes. Located midway between Upington and the Kgalagadi Transfrontier Park. Ask about the 2-hr hiking trail.

Upington *p688, map p689*

A Le Must River Residence and Le Must River Manor, 14 Butler St and 12 Murray Av, T054-3323971, www.lemustupington.com. 2 elegant guesthouses set in mock Cape Dutch buildings overlooking the river. In total ,15 double rooms with en suite facilities, TV, heating and a/c, crisp white linen on the beds. The houses are filled with South African art and antiques and a large selection of books and music. Also home to the excellent restaurant of the same name (see Eating, page 694). Recommended.

A Protea Hotel Oasis, 26 Schröder St, T054-3378500, www.proteahotels.co.za. Art deco building with 32 double rooms, modern furnishings, a/c, TV, non-smoking room, designed for regular business travellers, guests can use the swimming pool at the other Protea next door which is actually much better value (see below).

B Oranje Hotel, Scott St, T054-3324177, www.oranjehotel.co.za. 51 a/c rooms with DSTV, restaurant, bar, swimming pool, comfortable but characterless modern building, often full with coach groups.

B Protea Hotel Upington, 24 Schröder St, T054-3378400, www.proteahotels.co.za. A well-run hotel, with 56 clean and spacious a/c rooms some with river view, TV. 4-bed rooms are good value. Pool at back in secluded grounds overlooking the river. Attached is a standard steak restaurant, the **Totem Creek Spur**. Both Proteas offer cheaper rates at the weekend. If you are heading for the national parks ask here about 4WD hire.

B-C Affinity Guest House, 4 Butler St, T054-3312101, www.affinityguesthouse.co.za. 20 en suite rooms, all a/c with TV and fridge, in a bright pink building. Secure parking, swimming pool, good views of the river, can arrange boat cruises. Recommended.

B-C River City Inn, Scott and Park Sts, T/F054-3311971. 29 a/c rooms, TV, bar and braai area, small gym, breakfast area but no restaurant, a newish mid-range hotel in the centre of town popular with business travellers.

C Libby's Lodge, 140 Schröder St, T054-3322661, lgerber@mweb.co.za. Peaceful B&B in the town centre, 8 en suite rooms and 1 family flat, swimming pool, covered parking, breakfast not included in price, but kitchen and braai available for guests' use.

C-E Eiland Holiday Resort, T/F054-3340286, corp@kharahais.gov.za. Good location on a large island opposite the town, a mix of 58 self-catering chalets and rondavels, good value for 4 people, campsite has plenty of large trees and grass, well kept, clean, electric points, swimming pool, restaurant, shop, telephones, a well-run municipal campsite. Has what is claimed to be the longest palm avenue (1041 m) in the southern hemisphere. The 200 palms were planted in 1935 and the avenue is a national monument. Recommended. Sundowner cruises on the river depart from here whenever there is sufficient demand.

Around Upington *p690*

Spitskop Nature Reserve, see page 691. Simple self-catering **chalets** (C) with 4 beds, and a basic **campsite** (E) at the base of the *kopjie*. Hiking, mountain-biking, canoeing.

Witsand Nature Reserve, see page 690. 10 comfortable self-catering **chalets** (B), with 3 bedrooms, all a/c, 1 bathroom, safari decor, one has disabled facilities. Small shop with basic groceries and curios, 2 swimming pools, full board packages. Also a **campsite** (E) with basic facilities, ablution block and electricity points.

Eating

Kuruman *p682*

Eating is limited in Kuruman, though there are branches of **Spur**, **Wimpy** and **KFC** on Main St. The food is good at the **Red Sands Country Lodge**, 15 km from town, so if you are staying there, stay put for dinner. There's also a small coffee shop at The Eye. For those self catering, **Pick 'n Pay** supermarket is on Beare St and **Spar** is on Main St.

🍴 **Kalahari Pub**, 63 Main Rd, T053-7121271. Pub and grill serving predictable lunches.

Upington *p688, map p689*

All South African small towns have the standard and unimaginative steakhouse chain restaurants; Upington must feature every single one of them. **Saddles** is on Market St and **Spur** is in the Protea Hotel Upington. For coffee try the **Pick 'n Pay** shopping mall and, for a late night drink, try **Scotty's Bar**, also at the Protea Hotel Upington.

🍴🍴🍴 **Le Must**, 12 Murray Av, T054-3323971, www.lemustupington.com, dinner Mon-Sat from 1800. By far the best restaurant in town and one of the best in the Northern Cape – Mandela, Mbeki and FW De Klerk have eaten here. Book ahead. Sophisticated decor, tables overlooking the riverbank, well-prepared dishes, good service, interesting local wine list priced with overseas visitors in mind. If you've been out in the desert for a few days, this is the place to treat yourself. Intriguing items on the menu include blue cheese brûlée topped with honey roasted pork, springbok shank with garlic and roast onion mash, and very unusual lavender ice cream for dessert. The chef travels all over the world for culinary inspiration. Highly recommended. It's a must!

🍴🍴 **O'Hagan's**, 20 Schröder St, T054-3312005. 1100-late. Irish theme pub and restaurant, usual steak, pasta and pies, big portions and good selection of beers.

🍴 **Sakkie se Arkie**, T082-5645447 (mob). Sundowner cruise with a braai on an attractive double storey pontoon departing from the **Eiland Holiday Resort**. If you're not staying here, enquire at reception.

Activities and tours

Kuruman *p682*

Golf

Kuruman Country Club, T053-7321242, 9-hole course. Also tennis, squash and bowls.

Paragliding

Extreme Paragliding Tours, T053-7231471. The country around Kuruman produces the ideal conditions for paragliding. During summer, with ground temperatures at around 40°C, the resulting thermals enable pilots to stay in the air for a very long time; the world record for a long distance flight was set in the district. Daily flights can be organized for experienced paragliders, who are winched up from the local airstrip.

Upington *p688, map p689*

Tour operators

Trips into the Kalahari are not cheap, as 4WDs are often essential and all equipment and provisions (including water) has to be taken along. This requires quite a bit of organization, but the rewards are well worth it. If you wish to visit the Ai-Ais/Richtersveld Transfrontier Park, it's better to organize a tour from Springbok (see page 708).

Kalahari Safaris, 3 Oranje St, T054-3325653, www.kalaharisafaris.co.za. Budget tours including 2- to 5-day trips to the Kgalagadi Transfrontier Park, 1 day trip to Augrabies Falls, rafting on the Gariep (Orange) River and trips to Witsand and Spitskop nature reserves. Pieter really knows and loves the area, making him a great guide. Recommended.

Kalahari Tours & Travel, T054-3380375, www.kalahari-tours.co.za. Well-organized and established local operator organizing a range of tours into the Kalahari, including to the Kgalagadi Transfrontier Park, Augrabies and Namakwa (Namaqualand), also offers rafting on the Gariep (Orange) River.

Transport

Kuruman *p682*
238 km to **Kimberley**, 263 km to **Upington**.

Bus
Intercape, reservations T0861-287287, www.intercape.co.za. Buses leave daily from the Leach petrol station on the main road for **Johannesburg** and **Pretoria** (7½ hrs), and **Upington** (3 hrs).

Upington *p688, map p689*
804 km to **Johannesburg**, 894 km to **Cape Town**, 401 km to **Kimberley**, 263 km to **Kuruman**, 374 km to **Springbok**, 120 km to **Augrabies Falls National Park**, 80 km to **Kakamas**, 50 km to **Keimoes**.

Air
The town airport, T054-3377900, has one of the longest runways in southern Africa. SAA, T011- 9781111, www.flysaa.com, has 2 flights a day between Upington and **Cape Town** and 3 flights a day between Upington and **Johannesburg**. These are very useful services if your time is short and you wish to visit the magnificent Kgalagadi Tranfrontier Park – you can fly in, hire a car at the airport and be in the park by the end of the day.

Bus
Intercape, T0861-287287, www.intercape.co.za. Coaches arrive/depart from their town office in Lutz St, which is a short walk from the Protea hotels. Buses run daily to/from **Cape Town** (10 hrs), via **Springbok** (5 hrs) and **Clanwilliam** (7 hrs); to/from **Johannesburg** and **Pretoria** (10 hrs) via **Kuruman** (3 hrs), and to/from **Windhoek** in Namibia (12 hrs).

Car and 4WD hire
Car hire is available at the airport: Avis, T054-3324746-7, www.avis.co.za; Hertz, T054-3373613, www.hertz.co.za; Imperial, T054-3322383, and National, T054-3321089, www.nationalcar.co.za.

If you want to hire a 4WD there are several local companies in Upington catering specifically for the wilderness regions of the Northern Cape, some also hire out camping equipment such as roof top tents. Try Kalahari 4x4, 66 Scott St, T054-3323099, www.kalahari4x4hire.co.za; Kgalagadi 4x4, T054-3377133, www.kgalagadi4x4.com; Venture 4x4, 24 Schröder St, T054-3378500 www.4x4venture.co.za, based at the Protea Oasis; or Desert 4x4, 26 Swartmodder Av, T054-3321560, desert4x4@upington.co.za.

Expect to pay in the region of R850 per day, although some packages have additional kilometre costs, which can make it very expensive; it's definitely worth shopping around. Also ask about emergency back-up. Some firms will allow you to take the vehicle into Botswana and Namibia, too.

Train
There is a service of sorts between Upington and Windhoek in Namibia run by **Transnamib Starline Passenger Services**, T+264 (0)61-2982032, www.transnamib.com.na. However as Namibia's trains are primarily used for freight, it is slow going with a lot of stops. Despite this, the passenger compartments are comfortable with airline-like seats, videos and vending machines for drinks and snacks. The service departs Upington on Thu and Sun at 0500 and arrives in Windhoek the following morning at 0700. In the other direction the train departs Windhoek on Wed and Sat at 1940 and arrives in Upington the following day at 2130 with a lengthy stop at Keetmanshoop en route. **Intercape Mainliner** bus takes 12 hrs to do the same route, compared to around 24 hrs on the train.

Directory

Kuruman *p682*
Banks First National and ABSA Bank, Beare St. Standard Bank, Voortrekker St. **Medical services** Hospital, Main St, T053-7120044. **Post office** School St. **Useful telephone numbers** Police, Voortrekker St, T10111. Tow-in-Service (24 hrs), T053-7122551, after hours, T083-2598537.

Upington *p688, map p689*
Banks First National and ABSA have branches in Schröder St, close to the hotels. **Internet** Café de Net, in the Pick 'n Pay Centre. **Medical services** Ambulance, T10177. Hospital, T054-3386100. Medi Clinic Private Hospital, T054-3388900. **Useful telephone numbers** Police, Schröder St, opposite the camel and rider statue, T10111.

West towards Namakwa (Namaqualand) and Springbok

Driving across the Northern Cape between Upington and Springbok, stop for a moment and look out over the endless horizons and stillness of the desert. Here one gets a real sense of how large South Africa is, pausing in countryside that has barely changed in thousands of years. Although stark and deserted, the emptiness has a certain beauty. The first part of the journey is particularly striking as the road follows the Gariep (Orange) River, with its band of lush vegetation along either bank. The highlight in this region is a visit to the dramatic waterfall in Augrabies Falls National Park. Once in Springbok, you will have arrived in Namakwa (Namaqualand), the name given to the arid northwest corner of the Northern Cape, starting in the south at the Doorn River bridge near Klawer and extending north to the Namibian border. The area is best known for its magnificent wild flowers, which transform the barren, rocky countryside every spring. The regional centre is Springbok, the most viable base for exploring the area. » *For Sleeping, Eating and other listings, see pages 705-708.*

Cannon Island (Kanoneiland) → *Phone code: 054. Colour map 3, A5.*

Between Upington and Keimoes there is a choice of two roads along the banks of the Gariep (Orange) River. The main road follows the northern bank, but if you take the southern road you can stop off at Cannon Island (Kanoneiland). This is the largest island on the river, 14 km long and 3 km at its widest point. These days, 1700 ha out of a total area of 2500 ha are irrigated. Before the Cape government had managed to establish control over the region, the island was a stronghold for Korana tribes who harassed the early sheep farmers. The island was named after a terrible incident when the Korana tried to fire a cannon made from the hollowed-out trunk of a quiver tree – when the smoke cleared, six of them lay dead amongst the debris.

Keimoes → *Phone code: 054. Colour map 3, A5.*

Keimoes is the local farming centre at the junction with the R27, the main road south across the Karoo to Calvinia. This is the quickest route to Cape Town but it means missing out Namakwa (Namaqualand). The name in Afrikaans means 'mouse nest' so presumably the settlement once had a problem with mice. Look out for the Persian waterwheel in the centre of town, still in use on an irrigation canal. A short 4-km drive from the centre takes you to **Tierberg Nature Reserve**, a municipal reserve covering some 160 ha which is notable for aloes and succulents. Most of the flowers are in bloom between August and September.

Kakamas → *Phone code: 054. Colour map 3, A4.*

The second most important farming centre along this stretch of the Gariep (Orange) River is Kakamas. The settlement was founded in 1893 by the Cape Parliament, as a centre for the Dutch Reformed Church to establish a colony for poor farmers who had lost everything following periods of drought and an outbreak of *rinderpest*. For tourist information contact the **Kalahari Gateway Hotel** ⓘ *19 Voortrekker Rd, T054-4310838, www.kalharigateway.co.za.*

The meaning of Kakamas is 'vicious, charging ox' and legend has it that the pasture was so poor in this region that cattle often turned on their herders.

Most of the town is strung out along the main road which runs parallel to the southern canal. The canal is one of several fed by the **Neus Weir** which irrigate the surrounding vineyards and fruit farms. The wier is 936 m long and was the first cylindrical weir with a smooth overflow to be built in South Africa. Driving along Voortrekker Road in the town centre, look out for the set of fine, giant **waterwheels**. These nine wheels were built by a local farmer, Piet Burger, to help lift water from the canals into his fields. They are still in use today and considerably more economical to operate than modern lifting methods such as pumps. Along the route of the northern irrigation canal are a couple of **water tunnels**. One tunnel is 97 m long; the second is an incredible 172 m, and both are 2 m high and 3-4 m wide. They were built in 1889-1901 by Cornish tin miners.

Pofadder and around → *Phone code: 054. Colour map 3, A3.*

The road to Springbok runs through the dusty town of **Pofadder** which is a small *dorp* (village) lying on a particularly arid stretch of road; were it not for a small natural spring it would never have come into being. There is little more here than a cluster of ramshackle houses, a petrol station, a general store and bottle shop. It is only worth a mention as it is one of the remotest settlements in the country and is the butt of much South African humour. For those South Africans who admit they have been to Pofadder, it's as good as saying that they have been to the ends of the earth. Pofadder is not actually named after the venomous snake, but after Klaas Pofadder, a cattle rustler, who based himself here during the 1860s.

To the north of here is the settlement of **Pella,** founded by the London Missionary Society in 1814, and named after the village which provided refuge for Christians in Macedonia. In 1878 the running of the station was taken over by the Catholic church. Of particular interest is the original **mission church** which has been consecrated as a cathedral. It was designed and built by Father LM Simon and Father Leo Wolf – neither had any experience or knowledge of building, so they used an encyclopaedia for reference. The cathedral comes as a welcome cool refuge, standing in a neat walled garden fringed with date palms.

Augrabies Falls National Park » *pp705-708.*

Colour map 3, A4.

ⓘ *T054-4529200. Gates: Apr-Sep 0630-2200; Oct-Mar 0600-2200. Office 0700-1900.*
The remote location of the Augrabies Falls park has saved it from mass development, and it remains one of the highlights of the north. The main reason for coming here is

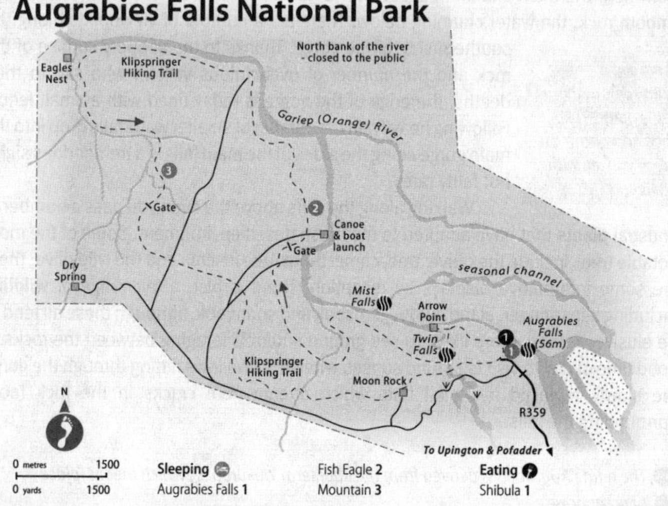

 to see the huge waterfall, although the surrounding landscape is equally impressive: a bizarre moonscape of moulded rock formations, surrounded by shimmering semi-desert. There is good hiking here, and the Gariep (Orange) River above and below the falls has some excellent whitewater rafting. » *For further details, see Activities and tours, page 708.*

Ins and outs

Getting there There is only one route into the park, the R359. From Upington, take the N14 and turn off at Alheit. From Springbok, there is a left turning before you reach Alheit. All are clearly signposted. The park is 120 km from Upington and 304 km from Springbok.

Tourist information There is a large shop stocking a selection of groceries including meat and a few fresh vegetables, plus beer and wine; open office hours. In the same building there is a restaurant with views of the falls. Petrol is available by the entrance and there are pay phones (cards only) by the reception desk.

Best time to visit March to October is the best time to visit. This area has a typical arid climate, with very hot summer days. Rain falls in autumn and, in winter, conditions are ideal for walking, although it gets very cold at night.

Landscape and wildlife

The park was created in 1966 to protect the waterfall and conserve the surrounding area, a unique ecosystem of riverine and desert environments. The landscape is typical of the arid north, seemingly barren but rich in wild plants and with a growing population of small mammals. It was extended in 1973 but not without some controversy. Around the small settlement of Riemvasmak to the northeast of the park, the residents were forcibly removed as part of Apartheid's Group Areas Act and to extend the park. The community was displaced, with the Xhosa resettled in Cape Town and the Nama people sent to South West Africa (now Namibia). However 74,000 ha of land to the northeast of the park was returned to the community in 1995 and many people have now returned to the area to live.

The impressive **waterfall** is the sixth largest in the world. Above the falls, the Gariep (Orange) River passes over a series of impressive cataracts, dropping about 100 m. From here the main channel passes over a 56-m drop into a narrow gorge of steep, smooth rock, the water churning below. There are a number of viewpoints along the southern side of the gorge. Thanks to the slippery surface of the rock and the number of over-curious visitors who slid to their deaths, the edge of the gorge is today lined with a small fence. Following heavy rains, a number of smaller waterfalls drop into the main gorge along the sides of the main falls – a tremendous sight, but fairly rare.

There are some dangerous spots at the edge of the gorge. Take care when approaching it, especially if you are with small children.

Walking along the cliffs above the river, you pass a number of unusual **plants** that have adapted to the harsh desert environment. Some of the more notable trees include the quiver tree, camel thorn, tree fuschia and the wild olive; there are some informative displays by reception. There is also a fair range of **wildlife,** including klipspringer, eland, kudu, gemsbok and springbok, although these all tend to be elusive. You are more likely to see ground squirrels foraging between the rocks. A good time of day to visit is around sunset, when the swallows flitting through the gorge are slowly replaced by small bats which stream from cracks in the rock faces surrounding the falls.

The name Augrabies is derived from the Khoi term 'oukurubes', which means 'place of great noise'.

Hiking

There is a popular three-day, 40 km hiking trail, the **Klipspringer Trail**, which is open 1 April to 30 September but is often booked up during local school holidays, (see Sleeping, page 705, for details of overnight huts). There are also several one-hour hikes which you don't have to book, each leading to a scenic point close to the camp. The walk to **Arrow Point** is perhaps the best, with superb views downstream. You need to wear shoes with a good grip, but the walk does not involve any climbing.

Game drives

There are several short game drives from the campsite; ask at reception for a map. The gravel roads take you to Echo Corner, Oranjekom, Ararat and Moon Rock. The only game you're likely to see is klipspringer and eland, but the birdlife is very rewarding, as is the unusual desert plantlife. The park also organizes guided night drives in an open 4WD, which may be a better way of learning about the flora and fauna found in the park. These can be booked at reception.

Springbok and around » pp705-708.

Phone code: 027. Colour map 3, B2.

The capital of Namakwa (Namaqualand) is set in a narrow valley surrounded by the Klein Koperberge (Small Copper Mountains) and hemmed in by *kopjies* littered with rough butter-coloured rocks. It is a modern town with little of interest within its

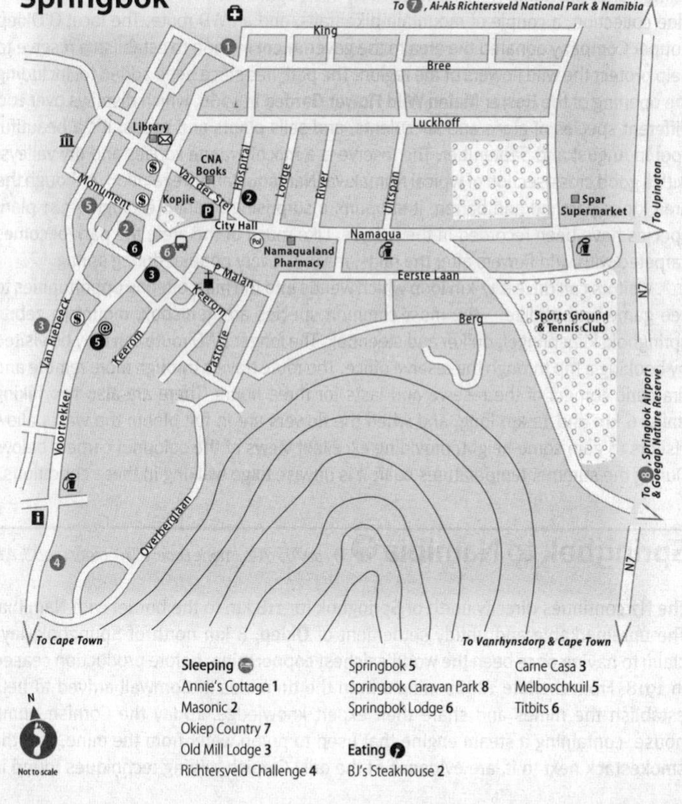

confines, but it is has an important position, straddling the N7, and is a good base from which to explore the countryside north to the Namibian border and west to the Atlantic coast. The town is quiet for most of the year but is totally transformed when the spring wild flowers start to bloom.

Namakwa Tourism Information ⓘ *Voortrekker St, on the left as you enter town, T027-7182986, www.namakwa-dm.gov.za, Mon-Fri 0730-1615; during the flower season also Sat and Sun 0830-1600*, is the main office for the Namakwa (Namaqualand) region. The staff are very knowledgeable and have a good selection of pamphlets and maps on the region, but the office sometimes closes completely out of season.

Sights

In the past, the fortunes of the town were closely linked with the **copper industry**. In 1852 the first copper mine started production; this was the first commercial mining operation of any type in South Africa. Despite several other discoveries further north, Springbok was able to develop into an important regional centre because of its abundant supply of drinking water from a spring, a rare and valuable commodity in the region before dams and pipelines were built. There is a small town **museum** ⓘ *Van der Stel St, T027-7188100 Mon, Wed and Fri 0830-1530*, outlining local history, housed in what was once a synagogue.

Goegap Nature Reserve → *Colour map 3, B2.*

ⓘ *From the centre of Springbok, pass under the N7 and turn right; just before the airport, take a left turn; it is 15 km to the gates. T027-7121880. Daily 0800-1600. Small entrance fee per car and per person. Visitor centre and café.*

Named after the Nama word for waterhole, this popular little reserve has a well-known aloe collection, a couple of mountain-bike trails, and a 4WD route. The local O'Okiep Copper Company donated the area to the government in 1960 to establish a reserve to help protect the wild flowers of the region. The park has since been added to, including the opening of the **Hester Malan Wild Flower Garden** in 1966, which displays over 100 different species of aloes and succulents, and sells plants and seeds; it's a beautiful spot in August and September. The reserve is a mix of granite *kopjies* and dry valleys, with a good cross-section of typical Namakwa (Namaqualand) vegetation. Although the area looks parched and barren, it supports a surprisingly varied ecology – 581 plant species have been recorded in the reserve. Like much of the area, the park becomes carpeted with wild flowers after the rains, making it very popular during spring.

Visitors can drive a 17-km loop which wends into the hills, offering opportunities to see game and birdlife – the most common species are gemsbok, mountain zebra, springbok, klipspringer, duiker and steenbok. The longer 4WD route can only be visited by booking a trip through the reserve office. The route travels through more remote and dramatic corners of the reserve and lasts for three hours. There are also two hiking trails, 6 km and 12 km long, and when the flowers are in full bloom the walks allow visitors to gain some height, providing excellent views of the colourful carpets below. During the summer temperatures soar; it is unwise to go walking in these conditions.

Springbok to Namibia

» pp705-708. Phone code: 027. Colour map 3, A1.

The N7 continues directly north of Springbok for 118 km to the border with Namibia. The unremarkable and untidy settlement of **Okiep**, 8 km north of Springbok, lays claim to having once been the world's richest copper mine, before production ceased in 1918. From the late 1880s miners from the tin mines in Cornwall arrived to help establish the mines and share their expert knowledge. Today the Cornish pump house, containing a steam engine that used to pump water from the mine, and the smokestack next to it, are evidence of the only Cornish mining techniques found in

Namakwa (Namaqualand) flowers

Namaqualand, now referred to as Namakwa, the 'land of the Nama people', is a scorched area of semi-desert which, for much of the year, holds little more than shimmering dust and rock-strewn mountains. However, following the spring rains the ground explodes in a riot of colour, literally carpeting the region with wild flowers. The Namakwa flowers have become a major tourist attraction and, in spring, the still valleys and sleepy towns are transformed into busy visitor hubs crowded with tour buses.

Nevertheless, the very nature of the attraction – the flowers appear in different locations from year to year – prevents the flower-viewing industry from getting too over the top. Under normal conditions, rains are expected in July and August; the further north you travel, the less rain the land receives. The occurrence and distribution of the wild flowers is determined by the interaction between temperature, light, and the timing and intensity of rainfall. As climatic factors vary from year to year, so too does the composition of the vegetation change. A late frost or intense sand storm can cause a sudden end to the flower season in an area overnight, while in the mountains, some blooms last until the end of October.

Over 4000 species have been discovered in the area, the most common of which is the **orange and black gousblom**, a large daisy. These flowers look their best when they occupy a valley floor, forming a stunning carpet of orange. On the mountainsides or rocky hills you will see **mesembryanthemums**, commonly known as vygies or sour figs. Their blossoms can be pink, scarlet, blue or yellow. Closer to Springbok are **quiver trees** (*Aloe dichotoma*), the tree from which the San made their quivers. This is a slow-growing plant which reaches a height of 7 m when fully grown. Another interesting plant to look out for is the **halfmens** (*Pachypodium namaquanum*), a strange looking succulent which has a long spine with a clump of leaves at the top; some specimens are thought to be several hundred years old. These are usually seen along the Gariep (Orange) River and on isolated granite kopjies. Before travelling to the region call the **Flower Hotline** ⓘ *T027-7182985/6, T083-9101028 (mob)*, which can advise where to find the best blooms.

the southern hemisphere. The N7 continues north to **Steinkopf** which marks the junction with the R382 that goes to Port Nolloth, Alexander Bay and the Ai-Ais/Richtersveld Transfrontier Park (see page 702).

Vioolsdrif border

The N7 continues to the Vioolsdrif border with Namibia (open 24 hours), where there is a bridge over the Gariep (Orange) River. The border crossing is pretty straightforward and, although this is the major border between South Africa and Namibia, and there is a lot of traffic, formalities at customs and immigration are quick and courteous. If you are in a vehicle it is likely to be searched, and you are not permitted to take firewood across the border. If you are in a hire car, ensure that you have documentation from the rental company that allows you to take a car out of South Africa. Namibia is part of the Southern Africa Development Community (SADC) customs agreement so if you are in your own car travelling on a carnet, you do not need to get it signed here, and you won't need to until you reach Zimbabwe or Zambia which are outside SADC. You simply fill out the car's details in a book. On the Namibia side you will have to pay for temporary third party insurance but this costs very little.

Noordoewer is the first town in Namibia, a few kilometres beyond the border, and has a petrol station, a small shop and one hotel: the **Orange River Lodge**, which has a bar and restaurant; you can also camp here. Beyond Noordoewer, it is 350 km to the next major town – **Keetmanshoop**. If you want to explore the Ai-Ais Hot Springs and Fish River Canyon before you get here then you need to stock up on provisions in South Africa; the **Spar** in Springbok is the best bet. It is worth noting that the Namibian Dollar is interchangeable with the South African Rand and both are accepted throughout Namibia, so you do not need to change money.

Port Nolloth → *Phone code: 027. Colour map 3, A1.*

Port Nolloth is an odd little town on the windswept west coast. It is an important fishing centre but, more interestingly, it is renowned for attracting fortune-seekers who trade (often illegally) in diamonds. The town was established as a harbour and railway junction for the copper industry in 1854, but it proved too shallow for the bulk-ore carriers and the trade moved north to Alexander Bay. These days it has developed into a small holiday centre – the only one on this stretch of the coast – with crayfishing and diamonds supplementing local income. The town is split into two sections, Port Nolloth being the business and fishing sector, and **McDougalls Bay**, 4 km to the south, the holiday resort. The local fishing fleets are not permitted to fish off the coast at McDougalls Bay, which is reserved for angling and crayfish diving for visitors. The beaches have a certain wild, windswept beauty to them, although the long stretches of sun-bleached sand can appear rather bleak at times and it often gets misty along the coast. Don't be deceived by the calm sea; it's very cold all year round.

Alexander Bay

The diamond industry becomes more apparent further north in Alexander Bay, by the Namibian border. Diamonds were first found here in 1925, and today the town is run by the mining company Alexkor Ltd. Alexander Bay was closed to visitors until a few years ago; today visitors can take part in diamond mine tours, although most people come here for easy access to the Ai-Ais/Richtersveld Transfrontier Park (see below). The Gariep (Orange) River estuary has been awarded RAMSAR status as an important wetland habitat for birds; more than 200 species have been recorded in the region.

If you wish to explore the diamond region, contact **Alexkor Ltd** ⓘ *Alexander Bay, T027-8311330, www.alexkor.co.za, or www.coastofdiamonds.co.za. Tours run on Thu 0800-1230; book a week in advance as you need to supply copies of your passport; no children under 18; the price depends on the size of the group*. The tour starts at the town museum and goes into the mining region to visit the workshops and mining blocks, harbour area, aswell as an oyster farm and seal colony. The **museum** itself (Mon-Fri 1000-1400) has exhibits on the history of the region's diamond industry and a video of the mine. Alexkor also runs the local **tourist information office** ⓘ *next to the gate into town, T027-8311330, www.diamondcoast.co.za.*

Ai-Ais/Richtersveld Transfrontier Conservation Park ▸▸ *pp705-708. Colour map 3, A1.*

The magnificent Ai-Ais/Richtersveld Transfrontier Conservation Park covers some of the most remote and starkly beautiful scenery in Namakwa (Namaqualand). The park is isolated and inaccessible and the terrain is rough – much of it can only be reached by 4WD. Richtersveld was proclaimed a national park in 1991. The northern boundary was the Gariep (Orange) River and the international border with Namibia. However, after much negotiation, the Richtersveld is now part of a transfrontier park, joining it with Namibia's Ai-Ais Hot Springs and Fish River Canyon over the border.

Transfrontier conservation area

The Richtersveld National Park in South Africa, and Fish River Canyon, Ai-Ais Hot Springs and the Hunsberg Conservation Area in Namibia, are now all part of the newly established Ai-Ais/Richtersveld Transfrontier Conservation Park. This is the first such park between Namibia and South Africa and the treaty was signed by presidents Nujoma and Mbeki in Windhoek in 2003. The ultimate aim is to link the Ai-Ais/ Richtersveld Transfrontier Conservation Park with the newly proclaimed Sperrgebiet National Park along Namibia's coast and then to the Lona National Park in Angola.

The park currently covers 6045 sq km and spans some of the most spectacular desert scenery in southern Africa. It contains over 50 species of mammal and there are plans to relocate other species such as black rhino or mountain zebra. The park is managed jointly by SAN Parks and the Namibian Ministry of Environment and Tourism, and sponsored by the Peace Parks Foundation (www.peace parks.org), which promotes sustainable development, conservation and political stability across the region.

By taking down fences, original migration routes for the game are re-established and park authorities from neighbouring countries are encouraged to work as a team. Other transfrontier parks include the Kalahari Gemsbok Park, between South Africa and Botswana, and the Limpopo Transfrontier between South Africa, Zimbabwe and Mozambique. Many others are in the pipeline throughout east and southern Africa.

The park encompasses a mountainous desert, seemingly barren but full of sturdy succulents, many of them endemic. These, coupled with the surreal rugged terrain, are the principal attractions of the park. Some of the most visible plants include the kokerboom (quiver) and halfmens trees, while hidden in the mountains are hundreds of different succulents. None of the larger mammals are able to survive in such a hostile environment, but you may come across klipspringer, grey rhebok, steenbok, duiker and mountain zebra; consider yourself very fortunate if you see leopard, jackal, brown hyena or caracal. Swimming and fishing (with a permit) are allowed in the Gariep (Orange) River, but you need always to be wary of the current.

Ins and outs

Getting there The easiest route is to drive north from Springbok on the N7 to Steinkopf (49 km). Take the Port Nolloth turning and follow the R382 to the coast via Annenous Pass. In Port Nolloth take the coast road north towards Alexander Bay. The park is signposted from Alexander Bay. It is a further 93 km of gravel along the Gariep (Orange) River, curving back inland to the park's office at Sendelingsdrift (see below).

Getting around None of the routes within the reserve are suitable for normal cars – a 4WD is essential. Due to its remoteness, it is not possible to visit the park on a day trip and it is recommended that you don't go alone, so try to group up with other vehicles. Fuel is available at reception at Sendelingsdrift, though not unleaded. Entry permits are issued here. Visitors must arrive before 1600 in order to reach the designated campsites before dark. If possible, buy a copy of the 1:250,000 map of the area, as the park's map leaves off many of the roads making it easy to get lost. Keep clear of all 'no entry' signs, most of which denote mining and security areas.

Tourist information The **park office** ⓘ *Sendelingsdrift, 330 km from Springbok, T027-8311506, www.sanparks.org, gate hours 0700-1800, office hours 0800-1600, R80, children R40 per day*, strictly controls visitor numbers; always call in advance. There is a small general store (weekdays only), selling cool drinks and basic provisions. The nearest shops are at Kuboes and Alexander Bay. Petrol and diesel are also available in the latter. Fresh drinking water is only available at Sendelingsdrift; make sure you have containers which can hold up to 20 litres. The park authorities advise visitors to bring gas stoves for cooking, rather than campfires, as there can be strong winds at the end of the day. All rubbish must be removed from the park so ensure you have rubbish bags. There is no mobile phone reception in the park, but if you have international roaming you can call from a few spots around Sendelingsdrift.

Best time to visit Visits in the spring and autumn avoid the climatic extremes. The region receives virtually no rainfall in the east, while the western margin is frequently covered by coastal fog known as the *malmokkie*. In summer the daytime temperatures can exceed 50°C, so this is definitely a time to avoid the area. Three hiking trails are open from 1 April to 30 September: **Vensterval Trail** (four days, three nights); **Lelieshoek-Oemsberg Trail** (three days, two nights) and the **Kodaspiek Trail** (two days, one night). Conditions are tough and for experienced hikers only. It is also possible to walk a little in the vicinity of the campsites.

Springbok to Cape Town » *pp705-708.*

As you travel south from Springbok, the N7 winds through rugged granite scenery. There are no settlements of note until you reach Van Rhynsdorp. After 66 km the road passes the small settlement of **Kamieskroon**, which has little more than a petrol station, a shop, a few houses and a couple of places to stay. During the spring many visitors stop in this area to admire the wild flowers.

Continuing south on the N7 there is little of interest until you are past Van Rhynsdorp and enter the **Olifants River Valley**. From here you can explore the West Coast fishing villages (see page 166) or the beautiful Cederberg Mountains (see page 182). Cape Town (495 km) can also easily be reached in a single day.

Namaqua National Park → *Colour map 3, B2.*

ⓘ *T027-6721948. Daily 0800-1700 during the flower season when the park can get very crowded; the best time is 1030-1600. Outside the flower season, there is little to see. R20. The information centre has a shop, tea room and toilets.*

Formerly known as the Skilpad Wildflower Reserve, the 1000-ha Namaqua National Park has some of the best flower displays in the region. The reserve is being incorporated into a larger 60,000-ha area designed to protect its unique and fragile ecosystem. Lying to the west of the N7 highway between Garies and Kharkams, it covers the area between the Spoeg and Groen rivers, allowing for the protection of the Atlantic seaboard marine ecosystems as well as the associated estuaries.

Its fine flowers have much to do with the park's location, set on the first ridge of hills in from the coast, which ensures that it receives the first rains of the season. Even in poor years, the displays here are better than in most areas. Visitors can expect to see various bulb species: *babianas*, *lapeirousias* and *romuleas*, plus duikerwortel (*Grielum humifusum*) and orange mountain daisies (*Ursinia cakilefolia*).

Access is via a gravel road, heading north and then west from the **Kamieskroon Hotel.** The entrance is 17 km from the N7. From here, a 5-km gravel road winds in a loop around the hill, which, during the flower season, is a carpet of orange. Visitors can either walk around the park or ride a mountain bike. There is also a slight chance of seeing some wildlife: klipspringer, steenbok, duiker and black-backed jackal.

Sleeping

Kakamas *p696*

B Kalahari Gateway Hotel, Voortrekker St, T054-4310838, www.kalaharigateway.co.za. 25 a/c rooms, restaurant, 2 bars, swimming pool in pleasant palm setting, comfortable, good value hotel. Very enthusiastic about the region and can advise on local activities.

B Vergelegen, from Upington the farm is located just before Kakamas before crossing the Gariep River, T054-4310976, www.augrabiesfalls.co.za. 15 comfortable rooms with a/c and heating, some have internet access, swimming pool, superb restaurant that has been rated by the South African magazine *Eat Out*, try the unusual biltong and peppadew soup, also has a farm stall and tea garden so well worth a stop even if not staying.

B-C Die Werf Lodge, Upington Rd, T054-4611635, dewerf@mweb.co.za. 13 en suite double rooms in the main farmhouse or in garden units with TV and a/c, 3 4-bed self-catering brick chalets next to a small dam where springbok roam. All meals available on request in the small restaurant.

Pofadder and around *p697*

B Diepvlei Farm Guest House, T/F027-7121578, diepvlei@netactive.co.za. A working sheep farm 125 km from Pofadder and Springbok off the Gamoep Rd. 6 doubles with shared bathrooms plus a honeymoon suite. TV lounge with log fireplace. Rates include dinner and afternoon tea served on the veranda. Although hardly local, this farm is an excellent spot to explore the countryside, and is especially good for birdwatching and fossil hunting. Recommended.

C Pofadder Hotel, Voortrekker St, T/F054-9330063. Squat, orange building on the main street, 23 basic rooms, restaurant with hot buffet in the evening, lively bar, swimming pool, secure parking, the only hotel in town.

Augrabies Falls National Park *p697, map p697*

Reservations through **SAN Parks**, Pretoria, T012-4289111, www.sanparks.org, Mon-Fri. Bookings can also be made in person at the offices in Cape Town and Durban (see page 44). For reservations under 48 hrs prior to your arrival contact reception directly, T054-4529200; credit card bookings are accepted over the telephone.

Next to the falls

Check-in is from 1200, but all rooms must be vacated by 0900. The cottages and campsite are well spaced out and private. There are 3 small swimming pools, ideal for hot summer days when temperatures can rise above 40°C. The campsite is located at the far end of the complex from the office. In between are a mix of 2-, 3- and 4-bed cottages. These are self-catering, but many guests choose to eat in the restaurant in the evening. Overall the park's accommodation here is good, and while the campsite can get crowded, it is in a beautiful setting. The shop and restaurant are in the main reception centre.

B Cottages. All 59 cottages have a/c and fully equipped, clean, comfortable units with views towards gorge, typical parks style, good value for 4 people.

D Campsite. Not all of the 40 pitches have electricity, grass patches are preserved for recreational use, which means you have to pitch your tent in the dust. The best shady spots get occupied quickly. Kitchen block has electric hot plates, laundry and an ironing room.

Klipspringer Trail

D Fish Eagle and **Mountain** are both overnight stone huts. Each sleeps 12 and is fitted with bunks, mattresses, toilets, drinking water, firewood and simple cooking utensils. There are no showers or lamps. Hikers must carry their own food, cooking pots, sleeping bag and light. Numbers are limited so it is always advisable to book in advance. The trail is closed mid-Oct to end Mar due to high temperatures.

Springbok *p699, map p699*

At present there are insufficient hotel rooms to cope with the peak seasonal demand. During spring, Aug-Oct, you should reserve accommodation well in advance. If you are unable to find a room, try to join a tour to the region; there are plenty advertized in Cape Town.

B **Annie's Cottage**, 4 King St, T/F027-7121451, annie@springbokinfo.com. Finely restored old farmhouse with immaculate polished floors, comfortable furnishings. 11 en suite double rooms, one in the attic and 2 with kitchenettes, neat and mature gardens with 40-year-old jacaranda trees, swimming pool, secure off-street parking. Annie can also organize stays on farms in the surrounding area. Recommended.

B-C **Old Mill Lodge**, 69 van Riebeeck St, T027-7181705, www.oldmilllodge.com. 8 a/c en suite rooms with queen-size bed and TV, bar, communal kitchen, lounge and braai area, self-catering or B&B, a comfortable option.

B-C **Springbok Hotel**, 87 van Riebeeck St, T027-7121161, jcb@mynet.co.za. The main hotel in town, an old building but comfortable and clean, central setting, 28 rooms, most a/c, à la carte restaurant but only serves dinner during flower season, bar.

B-C **Springbok Lodge**, Voortrekker St, T027-7121321, www.springboklodge.com. 45 rooms of various formats, most of the houses in neighbouring streets are outbuildings belonging to the lodge, look out for the deep yellow paintwork, some are double rooms, others are self-catering flats. A bizarre local institution run by Jopie Kotze, who spends his day at a table surrounded by mirrors so he can watch all the goings-on of his mini empire. The reception area is also an information centre, newsagent and curio shop, with an interesting semi-precious stone display and some old photographs on historic Springbok. In the middle of all this is the restaurant (see Eating, page 707). This popular lodge has a prime central location and is good value when compared with the larger hotels.

C **Masonic Hotel**, 3 Van Riebeeck St, T027-7121505, jcb@mynet.co.za. 26 a/c en suite rooms, TV, restaurant, bar, homely rooms, plenty of character, retains much of the original 1940s decor, helpful and friendly management. Some of the rooms are next door in a renovated Victorian cottage.

E **Richtersveld Challenge**, Voortrekker St, opposite the tourist office, T027-7121905, richtersveld.challen@kingsley.co.za. Local adventure tour operator (see page 708), also has rooms for backpackers. Some very comfortable rooms with 4 beds, 1 double room, very clean, shared bathrooms, kitchen. Also has a bunkhouse, basically a large garage with pull-down beds, but more comfortable than it sounds. Friendly management, still quite new so everything is in very good condition, gardens, braai area. Best choice for backpackers in town.

E **Springbok Caravan Park**, 2 km from town centre, on the opposite side of the N7, on the left off the road to Goegap Nature Reserve, T027-7181584. Small with 1 chalet and 2 caravans, limited shade, few power points, coin-operated washing machine, kitchen, swimming pool, small shop.

Springbok to Namibia *p700*

C **Okiep Country Hotel**, 120 km south of the border with Namibia and 8 km north of Springbok on the N7, T27-7441000, www.okiep.co.za. Pleasant en suite rooms with DSTV, parking and good country cooking in the restaurant and bar. A good overnight stop en route to Namibia.

C **Scotia Inn Hotel**, Beach Rd, Port Nolloth, T027-8518353. Modern single and double en suite rooms in a neat brick block, cheaper rooms with shared bathroom. Restaurant, bar, swimming pool surrounded by pleasant patio, secure parking.

C-E **Fiddler's Creek**, just before the border, by the police station, is a track to the left that follows the banks of the Gariep (Orange) River, 12 km from Vioolsdrift border, T027-7618953, www.bushwhacked.co.za. Beautiful shady camping on the Gariep (Orange) River, hot/cold showers in reed huts, boma for buffet meals, great little rustic bar next to the river, 3 double/twin rooms. Also the home of **Bushwhacked**, a tour operator offering full-, half-day or overnight canoeing trips on the Gariep (Orange) River, a very relaxing way to explore the scenery. A very popular New Year's Eve party is held here each year, attracting revellers and bands from Cape Town, followed by a spot of canoeing on New Years Day. Recommended.

C-E **McDougall's Bay Caravan Park**, 4 km south of Port Nolloth, T027-8511110. A delightful clutch of self-catering cottages and chalets right on the beachfront, and some sheltered sites for camping and caravans, beautiful clean beach to walk along. This is an area well known for its lobster and crayfish, so enjoy a delicious seafood braai while staying here.

Ai-Ais/Richtersveld Transfrontier Conservation Park *p702*
Reservations through SANParks, T012-4289111, www.sanparks.org, or through the offices in Cape Town and Durban (see page 44). For late availability contact reception direct, T027-8311506.
B **Tatasberg and Ganakouriep Wilderness Camps**. The former is near the river and the latter in the south of the park. Both have 4 2-bed self-catering units with hot showers, lighting, fridges and gas stoves. Caretaker.
C-D **Sendelingsdrift Restcamp**. New rest camp at the park gate with 19 chalets, 4-bed and 2-bed units, each with a/c, fridge and stoves. Porches have views over the Gariep (Orange) River. 12 campsites with shared ablutions (cold showers). Swimming pool.
D **Camping**. There are 4 designated sites within the park: **Potjiespram, De Hoop, Richtersberg** (all close to the river) and **Kokerboomkloof** to the southeast of the park. Do not sleep on the bare ground, as there are many scorpions in the park, and heavy dew in the mornings. Kokerboomkloof only has toilets, each of the other sites has toilets and cold showers. You must bring everything you might need with you, including containers to carry drinking and cooking water. 4WDs and all the necessary camping equipment can be hired in Upington (see Activities and tours, page 694) but it is strongly advised that you have experience in driving 4WDs (see Ins and outs, page 670).

Springbok to Cape Town *p704*
C-D **Kamieskroon Hotel**, Kamieskroon, T027-6721614, kamieshotel@kingsley.co.za. Well-run family hotel and handy for the Namaqua National Park which is just 17 km away. 15 rooms plus a caravan and camping park, rates include dinner and breakfast, tasty country meals. Good source of information when the flowers are in bloom and has an excellent reputation for its photographic courses during the flower season.

Eating

Augrabies Falls National Park *p697, map p697*
TT **Shibula**, at the park entrance. Open 1200-1400, 1800-2200. A surprisingly smart dining room given the location, with a choice of pricey continental dishes. Last orders are at 2030. Next to the restaurant is the cosy **Gariep** ladies bar, while downstairs is a cafeteria for drinks and light meals during the day.

Springbok *p699, map p699*
The hotels all have restaurants and there are a few fast-food options along Voortrekker St and by the petrol stations.
TT **BJ's Steakhouse**, Hospital St, T027-7122701, 1800-late. Basement restaurant with spaghetti western theme, generous portions, German dishes, boozy bar, pleasant change to hotel food. Recommended.
TT **Carne Casa**, Voortrekker St, just before the Springbok Lodge. Closed Sun. New steak-house with a vague Portuguese theme, pleasant outdoor seating, excellent steaks, also chicken dishes, schnitzels and seafood.
TT **Melboschkuil**, Voortrekker St, T027-7181600. Mon-Fri 0800-1700, Sat 0800-1300. Attractive, brightly painted restaurant in an old town house with a pleasant outdoor deck, serves a range of snacks, pasta dishes, some vegetarian options, good wine list. Attached is a curio and information shop with internet café.
T **Springbok Lodge**, Voortrekker St, T027-7121321. Part of the reception area and the curio shop is the hotel restaurant, interesting photos of the region on the walls, popular – most residents seem to eat here. Good selection and generous portions but bland food. Laid-back and slow service, settle for breakfast here and have a more hearty meal elsewhere in the evenings.
T **Titbits**, Voortrekker St, T027-7181455. A friendly pizzeria with excellent stone-baked pizzas, also range of other dishes such as pasta and steaks, breezy outdoor seating overlooking the main road.

Shopping

Springbok *p699, map p699*
Springbok has all of South Africa's main high street shops and supermarkets. Most are within walking distance of the car park below the small *kopjie* in the centre of town. **CNA Books**, Van der Stel St, stock glossy coffee-table books showing the flowers at their best. If you are self catering or heading towards Namibia, the large **Spar**, on the outskirts of

town is probably the biggest and best supermarket in the Northern Cape and a good stop for provisions, charcoal and ice. The deli counter and bakery are especially good. Remember that there are no shops for a long distance on the Namibian side of the border. All overland trucks do a big shop at the Springbok Spar before entering Namibia.

Activities and tours

Augrabies Falls National Park *p697, map p697*

Canoeing and rafting

An excellent way of experiencing the gorge at Augrabies is by rafting its rapids. The most popular stretch is the **Augrabies Rush**, an 8-km section of grade II-III rapids pulling out 300 m above the falls. Longer 2- to 5-day trails involve rafting some excellent rapids as well as calmer stretches in 2-man inflatables. The park also organizes the **Gariep 3-in-1 Adventure**. This involves descending into the gorge, canoeing for 3 km and then hiking the 4 km out of the gorge. The final 11 km back to the rest camp is completed by mountain bike. The river is still relatively uncommercial, which means that you're unlikely to see anyone on the longer trails. For more details, contact the **Kalahari Adventure Centre**, T054-4510218, www.kalahari.co.za, prices start at around R400 for the 3-hr Augrabies Rush. The centre also offers a range of rafting and back-road tours to the **Kgalagadi Transfrontier Park**. Recommended. Check their website.

Springbok *p699*

Richtersveld Challenge, Voortrekker St, T027-7121905, richtersveld.challen@kingsley.co.za. Good local operator. Overland trips, 4WD tours of Ai-Ais/Richtersveld Transfrontier Park, and boat trips on motorized inflatables on the Gariep (Orange) River. Will also rent out 4WDs for self-driving.

Ai-Ais/Richtersveld Transfrontier Conservation Park *p702*

Canoeing and rafting

Many Cape Town companies offer multi-day canoe trips on the Gariep (Orange) River through the Ai-Ais/Richtersveld Transfrontier Park in 2-man inflatable or fibreglass canoes. This is a wonderful experience. The trips pass amazing rock formations and each night is spent on the riverbank under the stars, with meals cooked over an open fire. Rapids are grades II-III. A guide boat carries all equipment but you will need a sleeping bag, sleeping mat, torch, cutlery, a plate and a cup. You will also need your passport as some nights are spent on the Namibian side.

Amanzi Trails, Cape Town, T021-5591573, www.amanzitrails.co.za. 4- to 5-day trips either catered or self-catering. You just need to bring food and drink for the self-catering option as they provide equipment such as cool boxes, kettles and braai grids.

Umkulu, Cape Town, T021-8537952, www.umkulu.co.za. 60-80 km, 4- to 6-day fully catered rafting and canoeing trips,with return transport from Cape Town included or meet them at their Vioolsdrift base camp, which has secure parking, lock-up storage, showers and a bar. The guides have years of experience on the river and come highly recommended.

Wildthing Adventures, Cape Town, T021-4235804, www.wildthing.co.za. 4- to 5-day trips, fully catered, except drinks.

Transport

Springbok *p699, map p699*

1274 km to **Johannesburg**, 554 km to **Cape Town**, 374 km to **Upington**, 401 km to **Lamberts Bay**, 256 km to **Van Rhynsdorp**, 239 km to **Ai-Ais** (Namibia), 941 km to **Windhoek** (Namibia).

Air

There is a small airfield close to Goegap Nature Reserve but it is only used by charter airlines en route to Namibia.

Bus

Intercape, central reservations, T0861-287287, www.intercape.co.za. Buses depart daily from the **Springbok Lodge** to **Cape Town** (8½ hrs) and **Windhoek** (12 hrs).

Directory

Springbok *p699, map p699*

Banks Standard, Voortrekker St. ABSA, Van der Stel St. **Internet** Melkboschkuil, Voortrekker St, has speedy internet access, Mon-Fri 0800-1700, Sat 0800-1300.

Background

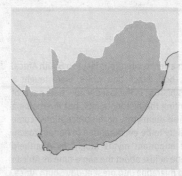

History

History, and not just modern history, is often a very contentious issue in South Africa. During the Apartheid era, schoolchildren, both black and white, were taught a particularly lopsided version of the country's history. In the last decade there have, of course, been massive moves towards rewriting the history books, but it remains a field of conflict between left and right. Not all the myths, or misconceptions, come from racist Apartheid historians and we will try to be even-handed in our approach. However, we start with one of the most important myths taught by Apartheid historians; that Europeans arrived at the Cape at just about the same time as African people were crossing the Limpopo River and migrating into present-day South Africa. It is one of the easier myths to dismiss.

Early humans in South Africa

South Africa is actually home to some of the oldest fossil human remains in the world. Three million-year-old fossil remains of an early human-like species Australopithecus africanus, have been discovered at a number of sites on the highveld. The exact way in which the evolution of the early human-like species into modern human took place is a matter of considerable debate amongst archaeologists. Whatever the exact timing and process of this evolution, by one million years ago a species that looked and behaved very much like modern humans, called Homo erectus, ranged far and wide across Asia, Africa and Europe. Within the last 100,000 years some of these groups seem to have developed still further into Homo sapiens, or modern humans. According to some archaeologists the earliest fossil remains anywhere in the world of modern man come from Klasies River mouth in Eastern Cape and Border Cave on the KwaZulu Natal border. They are dated as being more than 50,000 years old.

As elsewhere in the world, early humans in southern Africa were hunter-gatherers. They had stone tools to help with basic tasks. At first these tended to be large and multi-purpose but over time they became increasingly specialized and usually smaller. Early humans tended to live in small nomadic groups and their activities were largely dependent upon the particular environment they occupied. It is often assumed that the life of hunter-gatherers is necessarily harsh with very little leisure time, but anthropological studies of present-day hunter-gatherers indicates that this is probably not the case.

The Khoi and the San

The fossil evidence of early humans in present-day South Africa confirms that the Apartheid myth of an unpopulated land is indeed simply fiction. However, Apartheid historians were too sophisticated in telling their particular stories to be put off by the presence of a few fossils. The argument was not so much that the land was totally empty when Europeans arrived but that it was not populated by the ancestors of the present-day African population of South Africa. The fossil remains, according to this argument, were of the ancestors of a totally separate race of people who were killed by the ancestors of the present-day African population as they migrated south.

Physical anthropologists working early in the 20th century believed that all humans fell into a small number of distinct race groups that had evolved independently from early human-like species. The Khoi and San people of southern Africa, called Hottentots or Bushmen by European settlers, were believed to have been one of these totally distinct race groups and to be the direct descendants of the early humans whose fossils are found across South Africa. More recent scientific studies, especially studies of the gene pools of present-day populations, indicate that this was not the case. While Khoi and San people may look racially distinct from other African peoples, they share many of the same genes (as do Europeans with Africans and so on). However, the perception that Khoi and San people were very different from other human groups and stuck in some sort of stone-age past where little ever changed, has lived on. While Khoi and San technologies had remained relatively unsophisticated, political units small and populations sparse, it is wrong to think that when Europeans first arrived at the tip of Africa they somehow encountered primitive stone-age people. These communities had changed and adapted over time and had long established trading contacts with other groups in southern Africa.

Up until about 20,000 years ago, the ancestors of the Khoi and San people were all hunter-gatherers living in small egalitarian communities of about 20-30 people. They were nomadic and moved with the herds of wild game as they undertook seasonal migrations. Their tools were made out of stone, water was stored in ostrich shells rather than pottery and they lived in caves or simple tents. As they were nomadic they had few personal possessions and there was no concept of personal possession of land or wealth. They spoke a series of similar languages distinctive for the large number of clicks and whistling noises included in their speech.

Given their lifestyle, few of their remains have been discovered by archaeologists, with one notable exception: their famous and beautiful **cave paintings**. These are found throughout southern Africa and usually depict hunting expeditions or the trance dances through which the San believed they could communicate with their dead ancestors. These paintings were at first monochrome but over time some artists began to experiment with colour. The contents also changed over time with later paintings showing domesticated animals, especially cattle and, after the arrival of Europeans, people holding guns.

Around 20,000 years ago some of these hunter-gatherer communities underwent a huge and relatively rapid change that was to have far reaching effects on their lifestyles. At this time a number of groups, probably sited in present-day northern Botswana, acquired domesticated livestock. The first livestock they had were fat-tailed sheep. These were probably originally domesticated in North Africa and the Middle East and the southern African hunter-gatherers traded for them with the Sudanic tribes who then occupied much of eastern Africa. Later they were able to acquire cattle from Bantu groups who migrated from the forest margins of West Africa into East and southern Africa.

The arrival of domesticated livestock radically altered the social relations within hunter-gatherer communities. With livestock came the concept of ownership of property and it was possible for one or two individuals to amass wealth and prestige. The people that acquired cattle also became more politically powerful and formed into larger groups under one or two chiefs. These groups, who became known as the Khoi, migrated south from present-day Botswana and occupied the coast zone of the Cape region from the Fish River right round to Namibia. The interior was occupied by San hunter-gatherers who maintained the smaller social units and a more egalitarian society. There was a large degree of interchange between these two peoples. The San hunters often raided the livestock herds of the Khoi, especially if these herds had displaced the wild animals upon which they relied and there is some evidence that the Khoi had San working for them as servants. There was also probably a large flow of people backwards and forwards between the two categories – if San acquired livestock they could become Khoi and if Khoi fell on hard times and lost all their cattle they could end up as San.

Arrival of the Bantu speakers

There was also a large degree of contact between the Khoi and San and other African peoples living in southern Africa. Apartheid history was right when it taught that these other African peoples had migrated into southern Africa from the north but got the dates wrong by some 1,000 years. These newer arrivals, the ancestors of the vast majority of South Africa's present-day population, spoke a group of languages known as the Bantu group of languages. The people themselves are sometimes called Bantu people but this word is now associated with the racist institutions of the 1960s that used the name.

Bantu-speaking peoples began migrating into present-day South Africa about the period 500 AD, bringing with them new technologies, especially iron smelting and new domesticated livestock. The migration was not one big trek southwards but a whole series of small movements by groups of individuals setting off in search of new pastures and looking to establish new villages. Where they came into contact with San and Khoi groups occupying good pasture they tended to displace them, pushing them into the more marginal desert and mountain areas. Some groups occupied the highveld areas whilst others spread out along the fertile coastal strip that was later to become KwaZulu Natal and the Eastern Cape. The peoples who settled along the coastal strip were known as **Nguni** and were the ancestors of the present-day Zulu and Xhosa people, whilst those who settled on the highveld were eventually to become the Sotho, Tswana and other related people. When the Bantu speakers came up against organized and established coastal Khoi groups in the area between the Fish and Sundays rivers, in present-day Eastern Cape, and the drier interior Karoo and Kalahari areas on the highveld, the migration came to a halt.

Like the Khoi these newer arrivals were essentially herders and cattle were the mainstay of their economy. But they were also keen agriculturists and raised crops of millet, sorghum and other cereals and vegetables. In good rainfall years any surplus was exchanged for cattle with other people not so fortunate and in bad years cattle could in turn be exchanged for cereals. The Bantu-speaking peoples tended to form larger and more politically organized groups with clear hierarchical structures. In the dry interior they tended to form large villages around regular water supplies, whilst on the better-watered coastal strip they tended to live in more isolated homesteads. Iron smelting was an important activity and iron goods were traded over long distance exchange networks. In present-day Zimbabwe some Bantu-speaking peoples were especially successful with smelting gold and this was traded with Arabs along the east African coast and later with Europeans.

There is a good deal of trading contact between the Bantu speakers and the Khoi. The Khoi were particularly keen to get hold of iron which they used in their tools, as well as dagga (marijuana) that they enjoyed eating or drinking in tea and which did not grow well in the dry Cape. Both Khoi, San and Bantu speakers only started smoking dagga after being introduced to pipes by Europeans. This large degree of contact is reflected in the fact that some Bantu speakers incorporated the Khoi-San clicks into their language – today these clicks can be heard in both Xhosa and Zulu. There was also a degree, small but significant, of intermarrying between the Khoi and Bantu-speakers, the Xhosa in particular.

Arrival of the Europeans

Dutch, Khoi and slave society at the Cape

The first Europeans to make contact with these three different social groups in southern Africa were Portuguese sailors attempting to find routes to the spice islands of Asia. For many years the Portuguese had been pushing further and further south along Africa's western coastline and in 1487 a ship captained by Bartholomeu Dias made it around the Cape of Good Hope and sailed up the eastern coast of southern Africa as far as Algoa Bay. Ten years later another Portuguese sailor, Vasco da Gama, rounded the Cape and continued up the continent's eastern coast before heading further east, eventually to India. Over the next 200 years increasing numbers of Portuguese traders and their Dutch and British competitors began to make the journey to the east via the Cape of Good Hope. Though they occasionally stopped for fresh water and supplies in some of the more sheltered Cape bays and river mouths, the Portuguese usually tried to give a wide berth to the territory that is now South Africa. Apart from the treacherous coastline they also often encountered a hostile reception from the local inhabitants. Instead the Portuguese had trading and supply posts in present-day Angola and Mozambique where they were able to both resupply their ships on the way to their eastern empire and capture slaves to send to their American colonies.

The Dutch were the first European trading power to set up a permanent settlement in South Africa. In 1652 the powerful **Dutch East India Company** built a fort and established a supply station under the command of Jan Van Riebeeck on a site that later became Cape Town. The idea was that this was to be simply a point where passing Dutch ships could drop in to get fresh supplies and to rest sick members of their crew. The company did not envisage the settlement growing into a larger community and at first, every inhabitant was a company servant. This situation soon altered, however, when the company decided that it would allow a group of servants who had worked out their contracts to settle close by as independent farmers and supply the post with their produce. Prior to this decision all fresh supplies had been either delivered by sea or brought from the Khoi groups living in and around the Cape Peninsula. These independent settlers were known as burghers and their number was soon increased by the freeing of more servants and the arrival of new settlers from Holland and, after 1685, Huguenots fleeing French anti-protestant legislation.

With the advent of free burghers, the size of the settlement began to increase and some farmers moved out into outlying districts. This brought them into increased conflict with Khoi herders. There were a series of small skirmishes which the Dutch, with their superior weapons, easily won and the Khoi found themselves displaced from more and more land and their herds of cattle diminished. Under these circumstances some began to work for the burghers on their farms, theoretically as free labourers but in effect as little more than slaves. In this early expansion and subjection of the Khoi the seeds of a whole long history of dispossession of the established population of South Africa are apparent. As the settler farming areas expanded they came into contact with San groups whom they systematically slaughtered in revenge for their raids on settler livestock. European and Asian diseases, especially smallpox, also killed many more San and Khoi and by the end of the 18th century they had almost all been either absorbed into the settler economy as servants, pushed into the most marginal mountain and desert areas, such as the Kalahari, or exterminated.

As the settlers moved further to the east and north they encountered environments less conducive to settled agriculture and more suited to pastoralism. Many settlers adopted a life as semi-nomadic trekboers living exclusively by trading their livestock and the products of hunting with the settled colonists in the western Cape. As they moved east they also began to come into contact with Bantu-speaking Africans, in particular the Xhosa in what is now the Eastern Cape. Trading relations were established between the settlers and Xhosa and some Xhosa also came to work on settler farms in return for guns and other European imports. As well as trade, however, the settlers and Xhosa also interacted through warfare. Cattle raiding was especially common and some historians also argue that settlers also indulged in widespread slave raiding (see Mfecane section for more details about this). These battles were, however, inconclusive and a fluid and unstable boundary between the trekboers and Xhosa persisted for many years.

The other factor that began to alter the original function of the settlement was the arrival, in 1658, of a group of slaves captured from the Portuguese in Angola. The company had originally intended that there would be no slaves at the settlement but the company servants and free burghers soon became accustomed to avoiding the hardest and most menial manual tasks and demanded that they be supplied with more slaves. Unlike in the Americas most of these slaves did not come from West Africa but from Asia and Madagascar. They tended not to be owned in large numbers on huge plantations but in small groups, often less than 10, by individual farmers. The balance between the slave and free population of the Cape remained much more even than in West Indian and South American colonies.

There was, however, always a big gender imbalance in both the settler and slave populations, with far more men than women. Sexual encounters between slave owners and their female slaves, or Khoi servants, were frequent and a number of slave owners married freed slaves. Apartheid history taught that the present-day coloured population are the descendants of slaves and passing sailors, but even a cursory reading of the contemporary Dutch and other European reports of the settlement show that it it is probably more accurate to see the present-day Afrikaner and coloured population as having the same ancestry. Another fact about the present-day coloured population that is seldom recognized is that they are frequently the direct descendants of original Khoi inhabitants of the area. This is especially so in the Eastern and Northern Cape, where there was never a large slave population and certainly no sailors!

A number of slaves managed to escape from their captivity and joined up with still independent groups of Khoi and miscellaneous European and mixed race adventurers beyond the frontiers of the Dutch colony. Here they formed new and unusual political groupings who often existed by raiding both European settlers and African groups in the interior. The best-known of these bands were known as the **Griquas**. With European horses and guns they became an important political force in the South African interior right through until the mid-19th century.

Arrival of the British

During the 18th century Dutch economic and political power began to wane. Just as the Dutch had superseded the Portuguese they were themselves challenged by the rising power of the British. In 1795 the British sailed into False Bay and annexed the Dutch colony (The Battle of Muizenberg). The British were concerned that the French, with whom they were fighting in Europe, would take over the strategic port. In a general peace settlement of 1803 the colony was returned to the Dutch but in 1806 the British reconquered the territory and their sovereignty was finally accepted by other European powers in the peace settlement of 1816.

The British were only really interested in the Cape as a staging post and strategic port to protect trade with their new Asian empire. The colony was not profitable and neither the British government nor business took much interest in the new possession. There were, however, two important events in the early years of British rule that were to have crucial impacts on the subsequent history of South Africa.

The first factor was the British authorities' concern over persistent and inconclusive fighting along the colony's eastern frontier with the Xhosa. Some Xhosa groups had taken advantage of the instability in the colony to re-establish themselves to the west of the Fish River. The British decided that the only way to stop the persistent battles was to push the Xhosa back across the Fish River and establish a secure and clear frontier. During the first years of their rule they cleared the Xhosa occupying this area and tried to ban trekboers from having any contact with them. It was decided that what was needed was a group of permanent settlers on new farms in the area from which the Xhosa had been cleared in order to keep them apart from the trekboers.

In 1820 the British parliament agreed to release £50,000 to transport settlers from Britain to occupy this area. The money was used to send out 4,000 settlers, with an additional 1,000 paying their own passage to the region. These people became known as the **1820 Settlers** and formed the nucleus of the subsequent British settler community. Though the British authorities had intended that they should become farmers and hence occupy the disputed territory, most of the settlers were from urban artisan backgrounds and few had the skills or inclination necessary to become successful cultivators in the difficult and unfamiliar environment of the Eastern Cape. Most of them quickly gravitated towards the small towns, especially Port Elizabeth and Grahamstown, where they used their previous experience to become traders or skilled artisans. Their presence introduced an important new element to the equation, not least cultural, and 1820 Settler attitudes towards things such as the freedom of the press and towards the proper role of government played an important part in shaping 19th-century Cape settler society.

It soon became apparent that the British attempts to create a permanent border between the Xhosa and settlers had failed and cattle raiding backwards and forwards across the border continued. The Xhosa tried on numerous occasions to reclaim their land, occupied now by the settlers, but these attempts always failed, despite many initial successes. The **Frontier Wars** between Xhosa and settler continued for the next half century with Xhosa independence and land occupation being progressively eroded until their remaining areas (which became known as Transkei), were eventually incorporated into the Cape Colony.

The other fundamental change that British rule brought about was the **ending of the slave trade** and then the total banning of slavery. The peripheral role of South Africa in the British colonial empire and the dispersed nature of its slave population meant that it was seldom considered in debates about slavery, which instead concentrated on the massive slave plantations of the West Indies. Nevertheless, when the British parliament eventually decided to call an end to the institution that many felt was both inhumane and, more importantly, not beneficial to the empire's economy, it was also banned in South Africa. In 1834 slaves throughout the British Empire were officially emancipated, though they were to remain with their owners as apprentices until 1838. Slave owners were also offered compensation of one third of the value of their slaves. Though emancipation provided some slaves with new opportunities, in reality many of them continued to live very similar lives, carrying out the same heavy manual labour, under extremely harsh conditions, on the same Cape farms.

Nevertheless, many of the original Dutch settlers were extremely unhappy about the emancipation of slaves. To make things worse the British government, after extensive lobbying by British missionaries working in South Africa, also prevented them from introducing legislation aimed at tying both freed slaves and Khoi servants to individual farms as indentured labourers. The Dutch settlers had already been annoyed by the way their extremely loose system of administration had been reformed by the British, making it more difficult for individual farmers to impose their own law on their particular district. Many trekboers in the eastern districts also felt that the British were not quick enough in coming to their support when they had cattle raided by Xhosa groups to the east. Now they were not only losing a large proportion of their 'property' (slaves) but were being prevented from making sure they had a captive (cheap) labour supply. Though they were offered compensation at one third of the value of their slaves this had to be claimed in London. Many slave owners, therefore, sold their compensation rights to agents at usually about one fifth of the slave's value.

In response to these complaints a number of Dutch settlers decided that they would set out with their families and servants in search of new land beyond the British colonial boundaries. Between 1835 and 1840 around 5,000 people left the Cape colony and headed east in a movement that later became known as the **Great Trek**. It tended to be the trekboers from the eastern areas, who had fewer possessions and little investment in established farms who took part in this movement. The settlers taking part in the trek became known as *voortrekkers* and their experiences beyond the colonial frontiers have become fertile ground for 20th century Afrikaner nationalism. One thing not often celebrated in the national myths that grew up around the Great Trek is that accompanying the treks were a large number of Khoi servants and a small number of freed slaves still economically and socially bound to their masters/patrons.

African States and the Mfecane

The area the voortrekers were entering into was the home of numerous Bantu-speaking African chiefdoms, but at the very time they made their appearance on the scene these political groupings were undergoing unprecedented political upheaval. The causes and indeed the very nature of this upheaval is a matter of considerable debate amongst historians and for once this is not a debate between Apartheid historians and their opponents. Rather the debate is between those who believe that the turmoil was caused by wholly internal African political manoeuvrers and those who believe that external parties, especially slave raiders from Mozambique and the Cape, were to blame. Inevitably the truth is probably somewhere between the two. External factors, such as the presence of European traders interested in products such as ivory, may have lead to increased competition amongst African chiefdoms for lucrative resources, but the dynamics of the upheaval probably had more to do with internal African state formation. On balance, the evidence used by those who argue for a basically internal dynamic to the process seems to be stronger than those arguing the opposite.

Prior to the early 19th century African political units tended to be small and loyalty fluid. If there was disagreement within a chiefdom one section would simply set off and establish a new village in a new area. In the early 19th century, however, new larger and more strictly organized African political groupings (something closer to European nations), were formed. The epicentre of this new process of state formation was between the Tugela and Pongola rivers in present-day northern KwaZulu Natal and involved one of the best known pre-colonial African personalities: **Shaka Zulu**.

Before the rise of Shaka, the Zulu clan had been just one of a large number of small political groups amongst the northern Nguni people in the coastal strip below the Drakensberg escarpment. At the time of Shaka's birth there were two powerful chiefdoms in the area, the Ndwandwe and the Mthethwa, who clashed repeatedly and with unprecedented ferocity. Shaka, an illegitimate son of the head of the Zulu clan, joined the army of the Mthethwa and proved to be a highly successful warrior and quickly rose through the ranks. When his father died and with the support of the chief of the Mthethwa, he managed to overcome all his half-brothers' claims to lead the Zulu clan. With Shaka as their chief, the Zulus were transformed into a very powerful political and military force. When the chief of the Mthethwa was killed by the Ndwandwe, Shaka was able to reunite the larger chieftainship under his Zulu clan. Unlike previous chiefs who had been willing to make loose alliances with other groups, Shaka ensured that everyone who came under his leadership expressed loyalty to the Zulu alone. He vigorously enforced a rule that his followers had to follow only Zulu cultural and religious practices and speak only the Zulu dialect.

By the process of incorporating surrounding smaller groups Shaka quickly forged a very powerful Zulu state. He took on and decisively beat the Ndwandwe and then set about raiding all surrounding chiefdoms for cattle and grain. His impis, organized regiments of full time soldiers, were a new innovation amongst the Bantu speakers, as was their method of attack, which involved using short spears that were thrown or thrust from close quarters.

During the 1820s the Zulu impis became increasingly predatory, whilst at home Shaka's reign became even more autocratic and his punishment of any sign of opposition truly terrible. This lead to an era of unprecedented disruption, fighting and suffering known in the Nguni areas as the

At home, Shaka's reign of terror eventually came to an end in 1828 when he was assassinated by one of his half brothers, called Dingane. He continued many of the same domestic and external policies as Shaka, though with less vigour and skill but the Zulu chiefdom maintained its position as the most powerful African state in southern Africa until its eventual defeat by the British Imperial forces in 1879.

The mfecane had caused havoc across southeastern Africa. People's crops and cattle had been destroyed and starvation was widespread. The population of the southern highveld was decimated and survivors existed mainly in small, frightened bands. A number of larger political groups had arisen out of the chaos, such as the Zulu, the Ndebele, the Sotho, the Swazi and the Pedi, all of whom to some extent regarded large portions of highveld as either belonging to them or falling within their sphere of influence but none of them really occupied the area. This was the arena into which the voortrekers made their unexpected arrival in the late 1830s.

European expansion

The voortrekers were by no means a unified movement. In fact there were numerous splits and some of the leaders were not on speaking terms. In the early years there were a number of small autonomous communities established by the voortrekers, but these often failed because of a poor location or challenges from nearby African states. Over time, however, two separate republics were established, the Orange Free State and the Transvaal. In the 1850s the British recognized these two states' sovereignty over most of the South African highveld to the east of the Orange River. This was not, however, exactly the location to establish their republics the voortrekers had hoped for.

After leaving the Cape Colony one of the groups of voortrekers turned south and crossed the Drakensberg in search of a site for the new republic with access to the sea. In so doing they entered into the Zulu kingdom's domain. The Zulu king did not trust these new arrivals, especially as he had heard they had inflicted a defeat on the Ndebele and the Zulu killed the voortrekers leader when he came to negotiate a deal to be given land. A few months later, in the Battle of Blood River, the voortrekers extracted a terrible revenge and carved out a space for themselves south of the Tugela River. Their plans for a new republic with access to the sea were scuppered, however, when the British set up a new colony based at a site that became Durban and created the new colony of Natal.

The Natal colony was not willing to challenge the might of the Zulu kingdom to the north of the Tugela until 1879, so for many years the two separate entities existed side-by-side. During this time the Zulu kingdom was an inward-looking entity and the Natal colonists were unable to attract many Zulu labourers to work on the sugar plantations they established in the area. They therefore turned to India as a source of labour following the lead of West Indian plantation owners who had imported indentured Indian servants as a replacement labour force for the newly emancipated slaves. These indentured Indian labourers were followed by free Indian merchants and together these two groups make up the ancestry of the present-day Indian population based in Natal.

On the highveld the Boer Republics also appropriated land from African polities. The Sotho lost much of their territory in a long series of wars with the Orange Free State and eventually turned to the British for protection. A similar chain of events led to the declaration of the Bechuanaland Protectorate (present-day Botswana). Through the 19th century the Boer Republics on the highveld gradually defeated all the independent African states, the last one, the Venda, fell in 1898. The defeated African populations usually managed to maintain access to at least some land. These areas were later exclusively reserved for African occupation after it was realized that if all the land was appropriated the colonies and republics would have to find space for large numbers of African people.

Whilst voortrekers may have lodged claims to certain farms they invariably contained resident African populations. More often than not the Boers were happy to leave the African population in place and simply collect rent, either in the form of produce or labour. Later on in the century this created tensions when some landowners wanted to set up proper productive farms and had trouble getting enough labour. They often looked across at the neighbours' farms and saw a potential labour force simply getting on with its own peasant farming activities. They therefore lobbied for legislation outlawing what they described as kaffir farming. This was to become a more important issue after the 1870s when an unexpected event was to transform the South African economy and produce a new market for agricultural goods.

Mineral revolution

Despite the machinations on and beyond their frontiers the two colonies remained very much a backwater of the British empire. Wool exports from the Karoo and wine from the Western Cape created some commercial interest but other colonial possession held greater promise. But this was all to change in 1867 when alluvial diamonds were discovered near the confluence of the Harts and Vaal rivers. The flurry of interest and activity that this discovery created were just petering out when a larger outcrop of diamonds were discovered at a dry digging nearby. By 1872 20,000 Europeans and a larger number of Africans and coloureds had converged on the site that soon revealed itself as the world's richest diamond pipe and grew to become the world's diamond capital, Kimberley. At first there were numerous small individual plots at the mines but these soon became concentrated into the hands of one or two companies who bought up the claims from small entities. Eventually total control of the mines rested in the hands of Cecil Rhodes' DeBeers Consolidated Mines.

In 1886 there was a further mineral discovery in South Africa; this time it was gold on the Witwatersrand in the Transvaal Republic. Miners from across the world rushed to the new reef and capitalists were quick to make sure they got a slice of the pie. The deep level and relatively poor grade of the ore meant that it was only large capitalist organizations that could secure the investment necessary to succeed and, just as at Kimberley, mine ownership was quickly consolidated into a few hands. The main town on the Rand, Johannesburg, grew rapidly from nothing to about 75,000 white residents and many more Africans by the turn of the century.

These mineral discoveries fundamentally altered South African society. It was at the mines that many of the features that dominated life in 20th century South Africa first came into existence, in particular the pass laws, the migrant labour system, the compounds and the colour bar. The deep level diggings and the complicated process of extraction from poor gold ores meant that production expenses were high and, as the gold price was fixed internationally, the one way mining companies could ensure high profits was to hold down or reduce labour costs. The diamond mines at Kimberley provided the model of how this was to be done.

At first all labour at Kimberley was able to demand a high wage, but as the number of companies were rationalized there were fewer and fewer opportunities. White labourers began to realize that they were losing out to cheaper African labourers and pressurized the government to reduce this competition. Whilst government was unwilling to institute too overtly racist legislation, they did introduce a pass law that required all Africans present in the town to carry a pass signed either by a magistrate or a mine owner showing that they had legitimate employment. This legislation was aimed at preventing large numbers of Africans arriving at Kimberley in hope of jobs and hence pushing down wage rates.

The mines' owners, however, wanted to keep wages as low as possible and therefore to substitute more expensive white labour with cheaper African labour. The solution to this problem lay in the migrant labour system, where only male Africans came to the mines leaving their families at home on the reserves. The DeBeers mining company had quickly introduced a system whereby all African labour had to live in a single compound above the mine from which they were prohibited to leave for the duration of their contract. The official reason was that this was to prevent diamond thefts, but there were also many other advantages for the employers. As the compounds were only to house single male African labourers the company did not have to pay adequate wages to support the miner's family, who usually remained in the reserves and farmed to meet their own subsistence needs. Furthermore the mine owners could be assured of economies of scales in buying in provisions and therefore were able to feed African labourers on the site. If Africans had to buy their own food they would have needed higher wages. At first DeBeers wanted to introduce a compound system for white labourers, but because they had a political voice they were able to resist these plans.

For white labour the migrant labour system meant that they were being squeezed out of the job market by cheaper African labour. The mining companies were always nervous that white and African labour would unite, especially as many of the white labourers were experienced trade union activists. Over time there developed a sort of tacit agreement between white labour and capitalists that in exchange for the political support of labour, the capitalists would introduce a colour bar that reserved the more skilled and better paid jobs for whites only. At times this arrangement broke down, especially in the years after the First World War, but on the whole white labour never rocked the boat.

While capitalists on the Rand were able to develop a labour system that ensured wages were kept low, they were not able always to secure African labour in the quantities they required. They were, therefore, always pressurizing the respective governments to introduce policies to push more African men out of the reserves. They also went to great extents to get labour from wherever it was available, including beyond the borders of South Africa as far away as Malawi. The mine owners also decided to co-operate with one another to keep wages low and formed a Witwatersrand Native Labour Association that was to look after all recruitment of African labour. When mine owners experienced a particular shortage of labour early in the 20th century, they recruited 63,000 Chinese labourers on fixed contracts who undermined the wage levels demanded by Africans. Once the wage rate had been forced down, the Chinese labourers were simply repatriated.

One reason the capitalists felt that Africans were not entering the labour market in the numbers they required was the success that African peasant farmers were having at this time. African farmers were the first to react to the new markets created by the mines at Kimberley and on the Rand and, using new farming techniques learnt from missionaries, they increased their output of grains tremendously. Many of the successful African peasant farmers lived in the reserves, but others had managed to buy or rent land outside these areas. White farmers were not usually able to cope with the competition these new African peasants presented and lobbied government for support. This was forthcoming in the form of subsidies, soft loans and technical advice and after the turn of the century these African peasant farmers began to lose out against their white competitors. In 1913 legislation was introduced that made it impossible for Africans to buy or rent land in many 'white' areas. The depression of the 1930s was the final nail in the coffin for many peasant farmers and after that date very few struggled on. Today it seems hard to believe that there was once a highly successful African peasant class, outperforming their white neighbours, and that it was deliberately ruined by government action. The success of African farmers at this time was ignored by all school history textbooks during the Apartheid era and even today few South Africans, black or white, know that African farmers were at one time much more successful than their white competitors.

Anglo-Boer War

When diamonds were discovered at Kimberley it was not quite clear who had sovereignty over the area, with a Tswana chiefdom, the Orange Free State, the Transvaal Republic and the Griquas all claiming the area. Britain pressurized the rival claimants to undergo a process of arbitration under their direction. At the arbitration it was decided that the Griqua's claim was strongest, but the British immediately offered the Griqua leader substantial compensation if he agreed that the territory should be administered by the British. Not surprisingly, the Orange Free State, which had the strongest claim out of the two republics, was annoyed by this sleight of hand, especially as the British soon incorporated the area into the Cape Colony, but there was little they could do about it.

The Rand, on the other hand, was clearly within the Transvaal Republic. The British had annexed the Transvaal in 1877 but after a brief Boer uprising they handed control back. They must have regretted the decision when gold was discovered just five years later. The government of the Republic was primarily concerned with looking after the interests of its richer Boers, the vast majority of whom were farmers. They were a little unsure about how to treat the new mining economy. On the one hand the extra revenue from taxing the operations was clearly to be welcomed, whilst on the other they were nervous about the implications of having a large number of new immigrants, known by them as uitlanders, or foreigners, in their midst. They therefore introduced legislation restricting the franchise to white adult male naturalized citizens who had lived in the Republic for at least 14 years.

While most uitlanders were too busy trying to make their fortune to worry about politics, they did complain about the inefficiency of the Transvaal government in meeting the conditions necessary for an efficient capitalist system. British Imperialist forces were keen to get their hands on the Republic and in 1895 tried to manipulate uitlander dissatisfaction in a plot to overthrow the Transvaal government. In 1895, with the backing of the Colonial Office in London, Cecil Rhodes, then Prime Minister of the Cape Colony, tried to organize a committee of leading uitlanders to seize control of Johannesburg and declare a new government. Rhodes also arranged for a column of British police, under the control of his old friend Leander Starr Jameson, based in the Bechuanaland Protectorate, to come to their assistance. The plot, later known as the Jameson Raid, was a fiasco. The uitlander committee in Johannesburg bickered amongst themselves and did not command any mass following. Realizing this, Rhodes called off the proposed intervention by Jameson's force, but Jameson ignored his command and entered the Transvaal. When the committee learnt of this, they did belatedly declare that they had taken over Johannesburg but even in the process of doing so they entered into negotiations with the Transvaal Republic and came to an agreement. Jameson's column, therefore, had no crisis in which to intervene and were simply met and arrested by a Transvaal commando. This embarrassing incident marked the end of Rhodes' political career and helped to alienate British and Afrikaners across South Africa.

Despite the failures of the Jameson Raid the British were still keen to gain control of the Transvaal. Just four years after, Britain mounted a far better equipped, more sustained and ultimately successful bid to gain control of the whole of South Africa; the Anglo-Boer (or South African) War of 1899 to 1902. There is some disagreement among historians about the underlying cause of the war. Afrikaner Nationalist historians tend to view it simply as an example of British Imperial expressionism. Some historians of the British Empire, on the other hand, argue that it was more to do with British strategic concerns; they were worried that the Transvaal Republic could inspire Afrikaners in the Cape to rebel against the British who would, therefore, lose control of ports such as Simon's Town which were vital for protecting her sea routes.

Most historians, however, see gold as being the key. The British were, not surprisingly, keen to control the world's largest supply of gold and make sure their investment in the mines was profitable.

During the late 1890s the Colonial Office in London and the British High Commissioner in the Cape both lobbied for direct British military intervention to overthrow the Transvaal and the Orange Free State Republics. The situation grew more and more tense and in September 1899 Britain sent a large party of British soldiers to reinforce their troops. Sensing that Britain was about to invade the Transvaal, the Orange Free State decided to strike before the reinforcements arrived and on 11 October 1899 declared war on Britain in an attempt to preserve their independence. Deciding that attack was the best form of defence, they invaded both the Cape and Natal colonies.

At first the Boer Republics had great success and achieved victories in both northern Natal and the northeastern Cape. They drove back British forces and laid siege to Ladysmith, Kimberley and Mafikeng. They were, however, unable to advance much further in either colony and the general uprising of Afrikaners in the Cape that they had hoped for never materialized. Initially they held off British attempts to relieve the three towns, but with the arrival of huge numbers of British troops the fortunes changed. During 1900 the British set off on a triumphant and unstoppable advance on Pretoria and Paul Kruger, the president of the Transvaal Republic, escaped into exile via the Portuguese colony of Mozambique.

British victory seemed secure, but a number of die-hard Boers had other ideas. For the next two years they indulged in a continuous and, for the British, exceptionally frustrating, guerrilla war. The British were unable to capture the small bands of highly skilled Boer commandos so set about instituting a scorched earth policy to deny the guerrillas any help from local populations. Large numbers of Boers from areas with a guerrilla presence were placed in concentration camps to prevent them from supplying the commandos in the field with provisions. Though it was by no means a deliberate policy of the British, poor administration meant that food and medical supplies in the camps often ran out and many Boers, including many women and children, died of disease or starvation. Memories of the British scorched earth policy were often revived by Afrikaner politicians throughout the 20th century, though they conveniently forgot that the Boers tended to use very similar techniques in their battles against African chiefdoms. Also forgotten is the British policy of rounding up any African workers on Boer farms and placing them in similar concentration camps during the war.

Peace and union

The British scorched earth policy and the sheer hopelessness of their situation eventually lead many Boers to abandon the fight and return to their farms. The remaining guerrilla bands, who became known as the bitterenders, eventually surrendered to the British under the Treaty of Vereening in April 1902. The British were keen to ensure that the two defeated Boer republics were fully incorporated into a unified South Africa and therefore agreed a number of concessions for the defeated army. One of the key issues that the British were willing to concede was that any discussion of political rights for Africans be delayed until some unspecified future date.

The British hoped that after the war they would be able to substantially Anglicize the country by enforcing English as an official language and encouraging mass immigration from Britain. This policy proved to be a failure but they were successful in encouraging the four territories to agree to Union just seven years after the end of the war. One of the key sticking points in discussions over Union was the issue of African voting rights. In the Cape Africans and coloureds had the right to vote as long as they owned above a set value in property. While this excluded most Africans it did give at least some an opportunity to vote and therefore a political voice, however weak. Natal also had a property qualification but the figure was set so high for Africans that only a handful ever managed to vote. The other two Boer republics had never allowed Africans any political rights whatsoever. During the discussions over Union, which only Natal had reservations about, it was decided that the issue of voter representation for Africans would be side-stepped by entrenching a constitutional clause maintaining the pre-Union franchise arrangements in each of the four territories. With this issue solved and agreement on things such as dual official languages (English and Dutch), all sides agreed on the **Act of Union**, which was passed by the British Houses of Parliament in 1909 and the Union of South Africa came into being in 1910.

The rise of nationalism

First stirrings of African nationalism

The Act of Union, and particularly the entrenchment of the Boer republics' voting arrangements, felt like a powerful slap in the face for very many Africans. Most Africans had supported the British during the Anglo-Boer War and had assumed that their loyalty would be recognized in the post-war settlement. Though Africans in the Cape had their voting rights entrenched in the Constitution they feared that the Cape government's willingness (with British backing) to placate the two northern former republics was a very bad omen. This proved all too correct; in 1935 they had their voting rights removed by an Act which amended the Constitution.

In the early 20th century African political opposition to racist policies tended to be exceptionally moderate. During the 19th century there had been small but steady growth of the African educated middle class. They were mostly educated in mission schools, were committed Christians and employed as teachers or government clerks. They tended to look to London for support and were especially concerned about preserving their voting rights. Not surprisingly these early African political leaders were dismayed about the proposals for Union and sent a delegation to London to try to urge the British House of Commons to amend the Act. Despite receiving some support from Labour politicians they failed in this venture. In 1912 a group of African leaders called for a national convention for all African political groups in the country. This gathering in Bloemfontein marked the formation of a more organized phase in African opposition to racist legislation and lead to the South African Native National Congress, later renamed the **African National Congress.**

Despite the formation of a national opposition organization, African protest still tended to be extremely moderate. Many African leaders placed a special emphasis on education as a means to achieving political recognition. Many still believed in the old Cape liberal ideology of 'equal rights for all civilized men' and went to great lengths to prove just how civilized they were. London remained the Mecca for these early leaders and the most common form of protest was appeals to the Imperial authorities.

Over the next few decades, however, there were also a number of shorter lived, more radical, opposition movements. The most successful of these was the Industrial and Commercial Union (ICU) established by the very colourful figure, Clements Kadalie. The ICU spread rapidly through South Africa in the 1920s and was especially successful amongst farm workers. It demanded fairer wages for African workers and full political rights for all. The organization of the ICU left much to be desired, however, and just as quickly as it grew it subsided.

After the First World War a few white communists also made attempts to forge links between the white union movements and African workers. Though there were many influential Africans who came up through these Communist Party links the movement was never able to reach out to a wide range of Africans, especially Africans in the rural areas. The Party also suffered from numerous internal splits, often caused by contradictory statements coming from the international Communist leadership and from continual harassment from the police. White Unionists also resisted the attempts to form a non-racial movement and in 1922 the South African Labour Party, which represented the interests of white working class voters, entered into an election pact with the Afrikaner nationalists in the National Party.

While the 1920s had seen a great deal of protest from African peoples, especially from the ICU, the 1930s were a period of relative quiet. The international depression also affected the South African economy and many Africans found themselves unemployed or on low wages. To make matters worse the early years of the decade also saw one of the worst ever droughts, ruining the residual African farming economy in the reserves. Under these circumstances political protest seemed to be secondary to the tough job of simply surviving. During the Second World War, however, there was an upswing of African protest culminating in a series of protest movements amongst squatters outside Johannesburg and a massive African mineworkers strike. After the war African protest entered a more radical phase as younger leaders came to the forefront.

Rise of Afrikaner nationalism

It is a common misconception that Afrikaner nationalist sentiments existed right from the arrival of Van Riebeeck and that the 'Afrikaner spirit' somehow grew out of the harsh conditions of the frontier. This is a misconception that has often been fuelled by Afrikaner nationalists' versions of history. The reality is very different and, whilst Afrikaners have used the imagery of the Great Trek to help create a sense of nationalism, it was by no means an event in which all Afrikaners took part.

Class divisions were strong among both the descendants of the original settlers who remained in the Cape and those who migrated to the north. The established richer Western Cape farmers looked down both on the people who migrated to the new Republics and their poorer neighbours. Because of these deep rooted divisions it is not really correct to talk about Afrikaners as a single category prior to the 20th century, when there were potent political forces that led to increased collective nationalism. It is, therefore, somewhat of an anachronism to talk about Afrikaners, which simply means African in Dutch, prior to the 20th century. In the Western Cape it is possible to see an earlier sense of Afrikaner nationalism, but this might more accurately be called a Dutch settler identity, whilst in the two Republics the sense of nationalism was firmly tied up with an extremely local (agricultural) identity, hence the use of the term Boer, which simply means farmer in Dutch.

In the 19th century the Afrikaans language, later to become a potent symbol of Afrikaner nationalism, was regarded by the more élite settlers as a bit of an embarrassment. Because the language had developed out of a mixture between Dutch and the various languages spoken by the Khoi and slaves, it was regarded as a rather low form of dialect and its association with coloured servants was apparently the common description of a language known as kitchen Dutch. There had been one attempt to raise the profile of Afrikaans in the 1870s but it had not spread much beyond the movement's base in Paarl. During the negotiations over Union, Boer leaders were not arguing for Afrikaans to be a dual official language, they were arguing for Dutch. At the very time these negotiations were taking place, however, there was a second attempt to gain respectability for the Afrikaans language. The political climate was much more conducive to the movement and it quickly spread throughout the Cape and the two former Boer Republics.

The ravages of the war and the development of mechanized agriculture meant that many poorer Afrikaner tenant farmers were being forced off the land in the early decades of this century. They migrated to the new towns in search of work, but had few skills to offer and often ended up poor and unemployed. Their plight, often labelled 'the poor white problem', was a continual worry for Afrikaner politicians. They were especially fearful that their marginal position in the new towns was pushing them into closer contact with the growing band of African urban poor. The 'poor white problem' was a key motivation behind the deepening of segregationist policies in the urban areas, designed to keep black and white apart. During the first half of the century the nitty-gritty of segregation tended to be largely left up to local authorities to implement, with central government simply providing the legislative framework for local regulations. Nevertheless, in almost every town residential segregation and pass laws strictly regulated the daily lives of Africans.

The 'poor white problem' was also an important force behind the development of Afrikaner nationalism. As poorer Afrikaners moved to the towns they became immersed in a very different working class culture to the one they had experienced in the countryside. The Afrikaner leaders realized that if these new urban residents became part of this new urban culture they may well lose much of their separate Afrikaner identity and the Afrikaner politicians would find their support base undermined. They therefore decided that they needed to create a stronger sense of Afrikaner nationalism that would incorporate all Afrikaners, rich and poor. Historical events, such as the Great Trek, were deliberately resurrected and celebrated, the Afrikaans language was encouraged and, crucially, the Afrikaner leaders developed exclusively Afrikaner economic institutions that deliberately helped Afrikaner small businesses.

Afrikaner politics

Despite the deliberate fostering of Afrikaner nationalism the Afrikaner leadership was constantly fighting amongst itself and political parties frequently split and reformed. One of the key issues of disagreement was over the relationship between the new Union and the British Empire. After Union the British asked an ex-Boer General, Louis Botha to form the first government. He, and his close ally and successor General Jan Smuts, both strongly believed that the Afrikaners should strive to have good relations with the Imperial government and unite English and Dutch/Afrikaans-speaking white South Africans. Their **South Africa Party**, built on a coalition between the Transvaal and Cape ruling parties easily won the first election, but another important ex-Boer General, Hertzog, felt that they were too keen on maintaining good relations with the British government and formed a rival **National Party**. At first the National Party only had support in Hertzog's home province, the Orange Free State, but later he was joined by DF Malan, an ardent anti-British Afrikaner from the Cape province.

The First World War caused a further and more vicious split in Afrikaner ranks. A number of important generals resisted Botha's strong support for Britain in the war and his commitment to send South African troops to Europe. Their attempted coup failed and Botha quickly put the rebellion down, but the issue resurfaced again and again over the next few decades. A strike by white miners in 1922, which grew into a mini revolt as workers seized power in Johannesburg, was dealt with in a similar fashion by Botha's successor, Smuts. This time, however, white workers were able to gain a measure of revenge: in 1924 their support was crucial in electing a coalition Labour/Nationalist government.

Under Hertzog, Afrikaner nationalist sentiment was given an important boost by the replacement of Dutch by Afrikaans as one of the two official languages. In 1934 there even seemed a chance of forging a united Afrikaner leadership when Hertzog and Smuts joined together under a new United Party banner during the crisis caused by the great depression. This, however, was not to be, as Malan led a breakaway group to form a new 'Purified' National Party. The decision whether or not to join the Second World War caused a further split and Hertzog resigned as Prime Minister to join Malan in opposition, in so doing creating yet another version of the National Party

– this time the Herenigde (Reunited) National Party. Smuts, the ardent supporter of close ties with Britain, became the new Prime Minister and took South Africa into the war. He won an election in 1943 on the back of a wave of pro-British feeling and his international reputation grew and grew. After the war, however, he found his popularity at home waning. The economic boom caused by the war had lead to massive African urban migration and the National Party were able to use this to stir up fear amongst white, especially Afrikaner, voters. In 1948 they voted in Malan's Nationalists on an election platform promising a new ideology of Apartheid.

The Apartheid programme

What exactly was meant by Apartheid was not exactly clear in 1948; and the full programme of legislation was only really finalized in the mid-1950s. In fact the real beauty of the concept in 1948 was that it meant different things to different sections of the white voting population. The word simply means 'apart', and as such can be seen as simply a refinement of segregationist ideas that had dominated in the first half of the century. Despite the image of Apartheid created by many popularist historians and journalists, it was by no means or exclusively Afrikaner ideology. Indeed the roots of the idea can be traced back to English-speaking liberals in the early years of the century.

There was a distinct group of white South Africans who were very concerned about the plight of Africans and saw the solution as being total separation of the two races. They believed that rapid urbanization was destroying the basis of African culture and that they needed to be protected from the evils of white urban civilization. This ideology was tied up with ideas of both paternalism, that whites should be like parents to child-like Africans, and ideas of Social Darwinism, that different races were at different points along an evolutionary scale. In the middle decades of the century these ideas began to be considered by a group of Afrikaner intellectuals who saw the total separation of the races as being the only way in which whites could maintain political power over South Africa. They began to argue that if Africans were allowed to take part in the white capitalist economy they could rightly expect to be given political rights, so the solution was to keep them in a totally separate political and economic sphere where they could exercise their own rights.

This political philosophy was obviously not at all popular amongst white factory owners and farmers who relied upon cheap African labour to run their business. To these people Apartheid should be simply a way of maintaining a cheap supply of African labour with few employment or political rights that would allow the demand of higher wages. There was, therefore, a clear conflict between the ideology of Apartheid as expressed by Afrikaner intellectuals and the wishes of the average Afrikaner voter. During the early 1950s this conflict was solved by the nationalists stating that their long term aim was the total separation of races, but in the meantime they had to be practical and recognize the economic reality that white industry relied upon African labour.

Apartheid became in essence a way of ensuring a continual supply of cheap African labour whilst denying Africans any political rights. Legislation such as the Group Areas Act tightened previous segregation regulations and the government set about a massive national campaign to remove Africans from urban areas or squatter camps close to urban centres. Africans living in vibrant urban communities such as Sophiatown in Johannesburg found their homes bulldozed as they were ordered out. Those without passes were returned to the reserves, now restyled as homelands, whilst those with rights to reside in urban areas were removed to distant townships such as Soweto. Segregation of all amenities was also tightened and there became no areas of African life where the state did not intervene. In the countryside, Africans who had retained access to land either as freeholders or tenant farmers, in areas that were labelled 'black spots', were also forcibly removed to the homelands.

African opposition

Africans did not take these new assaults lying down, and the 1950s saw an unprecedented display of African political opposition to the white state. The ANC was revitalized and radicalized by the rise of a group of young militant activists, including Nelson Mandela, who had joined the ANC's Youth League in the 1940s. The organization saw that their attempts to appear moderate had not done them any favours and they could clearly not rely upon Britain to look after their interests. In 1952 the ANC launched a Defiance Campaign that used Gandhian tactics of peaceful resistance to the new Apartheid legislation. The ANC, in alliance with Indians, coloureds and a few radical whites, took the lead in deliberately breaking racist laws and offering themselves up for arrest. These peaceful protests were often met with violence from the police and many ANC members were harshly treated after arrest. Though the campaign failed, the ANC's membership mushroomed in its aftermath.

The National Party met this increased opposition with new legislation that firstly banned the South African Communist Party and then increased restrictions on the ANC and other political organizations. The banning of the Communist Party meant that many Communists now looked to the ANC as their main political organization. Some within the ANC were worried about the increased prominence of communists within the organization, especially as they tended to have very strong links with white communists, many of whom joined a newly formed white organization called the Congress of Democrats. These people were also concerned about the developing alliances with Indian and coloured organizations and wanted to maintain the ANC as an exclusively African organization. Uniting under the slogan "Africa for the Africans", they formed a splinter group within the ANC and finally broke off to form a rival Pan African Congress (PAC) under Robert Sobukwe.

Apartheid policies also made themselves felt in the homelands where the government introduced 'betterment' policies designed to shore up the faltering subsistence economy in the areas which provided food for the families of migrant workers and for the workers themselves when unemployed. The plans consisted of regulations to consolidate small plots of land and setting aside areas for farming and areas for grazing. A crucial element of the plans was the compulsory culling of African cattle when there were deemed to be too many head of livestock on grazing land. This was really the first time that the white state had intervened in the daily lives of Africans living in the reserves and many resented the fact that there was now no area of their life free from the control of the racist authorities. The compulsory culling regulations were especially resented and when the government tried to implement them there was violent resistance in a number of areas. These outbreaks were inevitably dealt with extremely harshly.

A number of urban areas also experienced bouts of violence, with African protesters displaying their frustration through rioting. In response to the growing protest the government moved to break the ANC-led alliance and put 156 of its leaders on trial for treason. The mammoth trial lasted from 1956 to 1960, eventually resulting in their acquittal. Despite the acquittal it was important in diverting the accuseds' energy away from organizing opposition. Furthermore, by the time the trial was over it had also been overtaken by other events.

In late 1959 the newly formed PAC decided to launch a massive anti-pass law campaign. The pass laws were one of the most hated Apartheid policies as they strictly controlled African mobility and were also used by the police as an excuse to stop and search any African. Their campaign was to start on 21 March 1960, in order to pre-empt an ANC led campaign due to start on 31 March 1960. The PAC called on all African men to leave their passes at home and present themselves for arrest at the nearest police station. They believed that the prison system would be swamped and the pass laws would have to be revoked. One of the main areas of PAC activity on the morning of 21 March was the southern Transvaal. At Evaton and Vanderbijlpark police stations large crowds were dispersed by police baton charges and low flying jets, but at Sharpville the crowd stayed put when they were buzzed by the jets. At 1315 there was a small scuffle and a small section of the wire fence surrounding the police station was knocked over. The police later claimed they were under extreme danger and were being stoned but this is denied by almost all eyewitness accounts. What is clear, however, is that the police suddenly opened fire on the crowd with machine guns. The terrified crowd ran for cover but the police continued to fire on the fleeing protesters. Most of the 69 dead and 180 wounded were shot in the back.

Moves towards armed resistance

The Sharpville Massacre marked a turning point in African political opposition to Apartheid. As news of the killings spread around the country Africans rioted and refused to go to work. In Cape Town there was a series of huge marches from the townships into the city centre which created panic amongst the white residents and police. The march leaders were, however, insistent that they passed off peacefully and had negotiations with the local police chief to ensure this was the case. They were rewarded with arrest and the Cape Town townships also erupted into rioting. A nationwide state of emergency was declared and the police arrested thousands of political activists from across the country. Strikers were beaten and township food supplies cut off to force people back to work. Both the ANC and PAC were banned and many of their leaders thrown into prison under new security legislation that meant they could be held without being charged. Over the next few months the unprecedented harshness of the police action broke the back of the widespread resistance. It also convinced many ANC and PAC members that non-violent action meant nothing if it was met by police brutality.

The leadership of both the PAC and ANC were concerned that they were about to lose control of their rank and file members unless they modified their position on the use of violence. The ANC leadership decided that it would establish an organized armed wing, named Umkhonto we Sizwe (Spear of the Nation), to carry out sabotage attacks on economic targets and not to threaten human lives. During an 18 month period from December 1961 the organization carried out a total of 200 attacks on targets such as post offices, government buildings, electricity sub-stations and railway lines. Despite the official policy on not putting human lives at risk a number of Umkhonto we Sizwe activists did attack policemen and collaborators. The organization was effectively neutralized by the security police in July 1963 when its headquarters at Lilliesleaf Farm in Rivonia were discovered and a number of crucial documents were unearthed. The majority of the organization's leadership, including Nelson Mandela, Walter Sisulu and Govan Mbeki, were arrested and sentenced to life imprisonment.

The PAC leadership had more ambitious and less well-organized plans for armed struggle. The PAC's armed wing, Poqo (meaning 'standing alone'), attempted to organize a general armed uprising to overthrow the white government once and for all. The leadership had little control over the individual cells and was unable to co-ordinate the armed attacks. One cell did organize an attack by some 250 men armed with makeshift weapons on the police station and prison in Paarl, but the attack failed against a police force armed with guns, and instead they attacked nearby houses, killing two people. There was also an isolated attack which killed five unarmed whites asleep in a car in the Transkei. Plans for a general uprising were effectively crushed when Potlako Leballo, one of the organization's founders and then resident in the British colony of Lesotho, stupidly boasted of the plans. As a result the PAC headquarters were raided by the British authorities and Poqo membership lists were handed over to the South Africans. Hundreds of people were arrested in a huge police operation and the PAC was effectively smashed. Despite its short-lived publicity and success, the organization was unable to reorganize effectively in exile and it was never again able to compete with the ANC for the leadership of South Africa's disposed African population.

1960s: the darkest days

With the ANC and PAC banned and their leaders either in prison or exile, political opposition by Africans to the Apartheid state was muted in the 1960s. The 'separate development' policies of the nationalists began to be applied with more rigour and economic opportunities for Africans became even more constrained. The winds of change may have been sweeping across the rest of Africa but for most South Africans the 1960s represented the darkest days.

The newly declared Republic appeared confident and strong and the National Party was able to gain support from all sections of the white electorate, English-speaking as well as Afrikaans. The economy boomed and quickly recovered from the financial crash in the aftermath of Sharpville. International capital was attracted back by exceptionally good rates of return on investment and by the promise of cheap and non-unionized African labour. Germany and France were particularly keen on grabbing a piece of the pie and began to invest heavily in South African industry for the first time. In response to this new investment the South African economy rapidly diversified and actively sought out new export markets. The South African government played an active role in the economic boom and channelled investment into state-run enterprises including, significantly, the arms industry. The National Party also set about promoting Afrikaners within the civil service and state-run industry. Over this period the economic divide between English and Afrikaans-speaking white South Africans significantly narrowed.

The economic divide between white and black, however, widened. Whilst wages in manufacturing for whites increased, Africans found theirs held down. With organized opposition smashed, the government set about fully implementing its Apartheid policies. Forced removals increased as the government set about dividing the country into clear white, Indian, coloured and African zones. The official policy was that all Africans should live within the homelands though the presence of large townships like Soweto made this policy look unlikely. Nevertheless Africans living in cities such as Pretoria with homeland areas within daily commuting distance (in reality huge distances), found themselves removed to new townships within the homeland. On occasions the government also altered the borders of homelands so that townships on the outskirts of cities were absorbed into a new administrative structure. Forced removals and natural population growth meant that the populations of the homelands increased rapidly and though these areas were officially rural, their population densities were closer to urban areas.

Apart from the insidious change of name there were important differences between the previous reserve system and the homelands. The Apartheid government attempted to allocate each and every African to one of eight tribes and then allocated them to a homeland. This proved very difficult, partly because many Africans, especially those who were long term residents in urban areas, did not identify themselves as belonging to a particular tribe and partly because, as the history of pre-colonial African groups discussed above indicates, tribal identity was often fluid and somewhat confused. Many people resisted attempts to define them as belonging to one of eight hard and fast categories and the government tacitly admitted this problem when it increased the number of possible tribes to which people could be allocated to 10.

Under the Apartheid system all Africans were supposed to express their political rights through the homeland administration. The government established totally separate bureaucracies in each homeland and then began a process of encouraging the areas to become increasingly autonomous. A number of African leaders saw that they could gain power and economic wealth through the new system and actively collaborated with the Apartheid state.

During the 1970s the South African government encouraged the homeland administrations to become independent states. They argued that this was a process that would allow Africans to enjoy full political rights in their own area. The first homeland to take independence was Transkei in 1976 and over the next five years Ciskei, Bophuthatswana and Venda followed suit. Transkei was at least a more or less unified block of land with a long coastline, but the other three were divided into numerous small blocks totally surrounded by South Africa. Their independence was never recognized by any country other than the Republic of South Africa: and they even refused to recognize each other's independence! The borders of Bophuthatswana were so complicated that neither South Africa's nor the homeland government were ever quite sure exactly where they were. Indeed just before independence the borders had to be altered when it was discovered that the South African embassy to Bophuthatswana was not actually inside the homeland. Though homeland independence was a farce it had great significance for the South Africans labelled as belonging to that particular tribe. They were now considered foreigners in the land of their birth.

The developing Apartheid programme had not just material effects on the African population but also psychological. In the late 1950s and early 1960s many African people felt that the overthrow of the racist white state was imminent. But the Apartheid state had managed to break African opposition and for almost a decade renewed resistance seemed impossible. The effects on many Africans' morale was not surprisingly extremely bad.

Union and student opposition

In the early 1970s South Africa entered a new era of opposition to Apartheid, but this time not led by organized political groups such as the ANC and PAC but by the trade unions. During the 1960s there had been very little labour unrest; only about 2,000 workers went on strike each year. Then in early 1973 there was suddenly a huge rise in strike activity and in the first three months of the year there were 160 strikes involving something like 61,000 workers. The epicentre for the strike activity was Durban but they quickly spread to other areas such as East London and then on to the Rand. These strikes were unusually successful in gaining the workers' demands; almost always this was for increased wages to reflect the recent sharp rises in the inflation rate. One reason they were surprisingly successful was that the workers refused to elect leaders to enter into negotiations with their employers, rather they simply published their demands and then struck for short periods, usually staying in the vicinity of the factory. This meant that the employers had no target on which to aim reprisals and the police could not be called in to arrest strike leaders.

The early 1970s also saw the rise of a more vocal African student protest movement. This was spearheaded by the South Africa Students Organization (SASO), which had broken away from the white dominated National Union of South African Students in 1968, under the leadership of Steve Biko. SASO had a Black Consciousness ideology which stressed the need for all black people in South Africa, Africans, Indians and coloureds, to free themselves from the mental oppression that taught them white people were somehow innately superior to blacks. SASO took this message out into the country at large and played particular attention to spreading the ideology amongst school pupils.

With the example of the striking workers before them and a Black Consciousness message in their minds school pupils began to rebel against an education system designed to make them fit only for un-skilled and semi-skilled occupations. The immediate issue around which they organized their protest was the new rules enforcing the Afrikaans language as a medium of instruction. On the 16 June 1976 a Soweto school pupils' committee organized a mass march to deliver their complaints to the local authorities. This peaceful march was met with a violent response and the police shot two of the pupils. At first the pupils fled but then many turned and started throwing stones at the police. They then went on a rampage throughout the township destroying every symbol of their oppression that they could get to, including the government-run beer halls which many pupils felt bought off their fathers' opposition to state oppression with cheap beer. The **Soweto Uprising**, as the incident soon became known, marked an important turning point in the history of opposition to Apartheid: from 16 June 1976 onwards there was constant and violent unrest across South Africa, lead by school pupils but gaining widespread support.

Rioting erupted around the country when news of the Soweto Uprising spread. The government was hard pressed to stop the unrest spreading beyond the townships but in a nationwide clampdown they eventually managed to quieten some of the protest. The SASO and school pupil leaders found themselves under arrest or harassed by the police. Many of the young people involved in the uprising escaped across the border.

ANC re-enters the scene

Though the ANC had not been involved in the organization of the school pupils' protest, their underground cells, which had been carefully and quietly organizing in the early 1970s, it did help channel escaping pupils towards the guerrilla training camps they had set up in countries like Tanzania, Algeria and the newly independent Angola. The ANC benefited greatly from this new arrival of activists and managed effectively to amalgamate them into their organization. The ANC had made better use of their time in exile than the PAC, who suffered from poor organization and internal splits. Many of the pupils were ideologically closer to the PAC but they nevertheless ended up in ANC camps. In recent years these camps have been revealed to have often been pretty brutal places and people who disagreed with the camps' leaders were sometimes dealt with extremely harshly.

Despite the government crackdown, protests continued and a generalized culture of resistance was fostered. The ANC made use of this new climate of opposition to begin to reinfiltrate South Africa. In the late 1970s they began a new campaign of sabotage, but now there was less care to avoid civilian casualties and the ANC released a statement saying they were at war with the Apartheid state and, whilst their attacks were aimed at Apartheid and economic targets, they could not promise that civilians would not be caught up in the struggle. A number of Unkhonto cells seemed to ignore these commands and bombs were set off in shopping centres and similar locations.

The ANC quickly regained legitimacy amongst Africans, many of whom had been disillusioned with the organization during its long dormant period. Black Consciousness organizations, smashed apart by the police after the Soweto Uprising, lost support to the ANC, though it could be argued that the movement had achieved its aim of increasing African pride. In August 1983 there was a large gathering of 575 community, church and similar non-governmental organizations which resulted in the formation of the United Democratic Front (UDF) which spearheaded protest throughout the 1980s. The government argued that the organization was simply a front for the ANC. This was an exaggeration but it is true that the UDF did have strong links with the ANC and that they regarded it as the government in exile and the imprisoned Mandela as the legitimate president of the country.

'Total onslaught' and destabilization

The Apartheid state was not only coming under attack from internal protest but from international criticism of the Pretoria regime. The ANC in exile had managed to foster anti-Apartheid groups in Europe and North America that began to put pressure on their governments to institute economic sanctions against South Africa. Most Commonwealth governments supported these sanctions and also instituted sporting and cultural sanctions on South Africa. The anti-Apartheid movement also started campaigns detailing the working conditions inside branches of multi-national companies in South Africa and asking individuals to boycott companies with large investments in South Africa. Despite the resistance of Margaret Thatcher and Ronald Reagan, during the 1980s these campaigns began to take effect and a number of important companies withdrew from South Africa.

This international isolation of Pretoria added to their gradual geopolitical isolation in southern Africa during the 1970s. Up until the mid-1970s South Africa had been surrounded either by states run by white settler régimes or by small states that rarely criticized their actions. However, independence for Angola and Mozambique in 1976 and Zimbabwe in 1980 changed all that. Now South Africa had hostile, left-wing, neighbours right on its doorstep, and even the previously compliant weaker states, such as Lesotho, began actively to oppose the Apartheid state. White South Africa felt increasingly vulnerable and the government argued that they were now facing a 'total onslaught' led by communists that were intent on bringing them down.

The Apartheid government reacted to this 'total onslaught' with a careful mixture of economic, diplomatic and military foreign policy designed to neutralize the threat. The exact mix of the different elements varied in each country and over time. In Angola, for example, intervention was in the form of a direct military invasion designed to overthrow the communist government. When the invasion faltered they concentrated on supplying an armed opposition movement and therefore helped to fuel a bloody civil war that has gone on more or less ever since. In Mozambique they also intervened militarily, but this time through another opposition organization that had originally been set up by Ian Smith's settler régime in Rhodesia/Zimbabwe. They encouraged their clients in Mozambique to blow up railways and pipelines running from Zimbabwe to their nearest ports. With these out of action, Zimbabwe and other landlocked central African states were forced to continue trading with South Africa in order to get access to the sea. This, in turn, gave the South Africans an important economic hold over the countries to the north.

Across the region South African guerrilla troops carried out occasional raids designed both to knock out ANC camps and to keep their neighbours in political and economic turmoil and therefore as less effective opponents. South Africa's proxy war with the rest of the region caused a huge amount of suffering to very many people, especially in Mozambique and Angola. Though these states did receive some international support the international media tended to concentrate more on events unfurling in the South African townships than on these regional events.

Reform or revolution?

In the mid-1980s South Africa's townships, simmering since the Soweto Uprising, exploded into violence. The primary target of the violence were Africans who had taken jobs as administrators in the 'homelands' or townships and African policemen. Many had their families killed and their houses burnt down and a new and horrendous form of execution was invented, called 'necklacing'. This involved placing a car tyre full of petrol over the victim's torso and then setting fire to it. The police reacted violently to unrest in the townships and shot, arrested and beat many protesters. Bus boycotts, strikes and 'stay aways' (where Africans remained at home), were frequent and often met with violence by the police.

Violence became endemic to the townships and there was a fine line between political violence and general crime. Many of the young ANC supporting comrades decided that they should take the law into their own hands and kangaroo courts were frequent occurrences. Older Africans sometimes found it hard to take orders from the youngsters and inter-generational battles broke out on a number of occasions, most violently at Crossroads squatter camp on the outskirts of Cape Town. The violence was fanned by massive new flows of illegal migrants into the towns. The government was unable to cope with the new influx of people and eventually was forced into the withdrawal of the hated pass laws. The growth of squatter camps was spectacular and no sooner had the government removed squatters from one site than they appeared somewhere else. During the 1970s wage increases in established industry had been generous, partly reflecting the move towards a more capital intensive economy and partly a result of the strikes. The downside of this was massive and endemic unemployment, especially among the young. A whole generation of young people missed all their formal education because of their involvement in 'the struggle' and their chances of employment were extremely remote. Inevitably this fuelled the violence and crime.

The worst violence took place in the townships surrounding Pietermaritzburg and Durban. These areas were within the KwaZulu 'homeland' run by Gatsha Buthelezi. Originally Buthelezi had been an ANC supporter and had even received the organization's (reserved) blessing in the establishment of a Zulu cultural organization called Inkatha. The organization, however, began to act much more like a political party and ran the KwaZulu 'homeland' administration. When ANC supporters began to challenge the 'homelands' authority this lead to violent clashes as the two organizations vied for control of the townships. This conflict has continued until the present and has involved numerous atrocities committed by both sides.

By the late 1980s the South African state had more or less lost control of large portions of the townships. The unrest and international sanctions were hitting the economy hard and South African businesses were feeling the pinch. While the state security apparatus was strengthened and numerous crackdowns were attempted, the government, fearing revolution, also undertook a programme of reform.

To some extent this programme had begun in the 1970s but it was accelerated in the early 1980s under the presidency of PW Botha. One strand of the reform process was to pull coloureds and Indians into the political process under a new tri-cameral parliament. Under a new constitution there were to be three houses in the parliament, one for white voters, one for coloureds and one for Indians. Most coloureds and Indians saw this move as an attempt to drive a wedge between them and the African population and refused to vote for the new parliament. The National Party's reform policy also lead to a new split in Afrikaner ranks and the creation of a new, more right-wing, Conservative Party. Over the 1980s the new Party was to attract more and more Afrikaner support and the National Party became increasingly reliant upon English-speaking supporters.

Botha also set about dismantling some of the segregationist policies, in particular the 'petty Apartheid' legislation that divided up facilities such as beaches. These did very little to assuage the unrest in the townships and were probably more to do with creating an international impression of reform to hold off further sanctions. Under these circumstances the National Party began to do the unthinkable and sat down to negotiate with the ANC. Business leaders were the first South African establishment figures to talk with the ANC in exile, in September 1985. With sanctions and unrest big business was being squeezed hard and Apartheid was no longer making them good profits as it had in the 1960s. The business leaders were therefore keen for a political settlement, but were obviously nervous about the intentions of an

ANC strongly influenced by communist ideology. South African ministers and eventually Botha himself met with Mandela, offering him his freedom if he repudiated the use of violence as a weapon in the fight against Apartheid. Mandela refused the offer and for a time it seemed further reform was impossible.

The late 1980s, however, saw a crucial shift in the global political scene that opened up an important window to allow a negotiated settlement. The unexpected collapse of the Soviet block suddenly made Botha's image of a 'total onslaught' seem meaningless and the ANC was no longer seen by whites as a front for Soviet-backed communist expansion into South Africa. These changes coincided with a change in leadership of the National Party and the replacement of Botha with FW de Klerk. Even though de Klerk had been regarded as a conservative he soon made it clear he was embarking on a bold new policy. The ANC was unbanned, Mandela and other political leaders were released and the process of negotiating a settlement got underway.

Modern South African politics

Constitution

South Africa's first democratic constitution was passed by the Constitutional Assembly in May 1996, the 1994 elections being held under an interim version. After ratification by the Supreme Court most of it passed into law, since some elements were returned to the Constitutional Assembly for reconsideration. The Constitutional Assembly is made up of both Houses of Parliament sitting together and constitutional provision needs to be passed by a two-thirds majority. The bi-cameral Parliament consists of a directly elected lower house (the National Assembly) and an upper house (the Senate) appointed by provincial assemblies. The National Assembly is elected via a system of proportional representation. The President is elected by members of the National Assembly and chooses his cabinet from those members.

Parliament sits in Cape Town and government ministries are in Pretoria. This geographical division dates from the Act of Union in 1910 as a way of balancing power between the two former British colonies and the two former Boer republics. This division has been criticized in recent years as government representatives have to waste time and money travelling backwards and forwards to opposite ends of the country. There are moves to relocate Parliament in Pretoria, though this will require a change in the constitution and would be strongly opposed by delegates from the Western Cape.

Significant powers are devolved to the nine provincial administrations. Provincial assemblies are also elected via proportional representation and in turn they elect members to the Senate who are specifically charged with looking after provincial interests against the power of central Government.

Provincial governments have significant scope over things such as regional planning, investment policies, social services and education. Provincial leaders are, therefore, powerful political figures and a number of politicians of national standing have decided to serve as provincial representatives rather than seek election to Parliament.

1994 elections

The African National Congress (ANC), together with its alliance partners, the South African Communist Party (SACP) and the Congress of South African Trade Unions (Cosatu) won the national vote in South Africa's first democratic elections in April 1994 by a huge majority. They gained 63% of the total vote giving them 252 seats in the National Assembly. The only other parties to win significant numbers of votes were the National Party (NP) (20.5%) and Inkharta Freedom Party (IFP) (10.8%). The

ANC's victory was based upon widespread support from the majority African population throughout the country. The only area in which its support amongst Africans was threatened was in KwaZulu Natal where the IFP received significant support from rural Zulu speakers. The IFP were unable to convert their popularity in their political heartland to any other parts of the country. The NP received widespread support from the white population and, more surprisingly, from a majority of coloured voters in the Western Cape.

Four other parties managed to secure seats, though with tiny proportions of the total vote. The Freedom Front (FF), an alliance of right-wing Afrikaner Nationalists, won nine seats with a 2.3% share of the vote, coming mainly from working-class Afrikaners fearful of the new political dispensation. The Democratic Party (DP), traditionally the party of liberal English-speaking white South Africans, were unable to expand their attraction and won a paltry 1.7% of the vote. The Pan African Congress (PAC) fared particularly badly; an organization which in the 1950s had seriously challenged the ANC's position as the most popular political organization amongst the African population received only 1.2% of the national vote, giving them just five seats. The remaining two seats were won by a newly formed political organization called the African Christian Democratic Party (ACDP) which called for the enactment of policies in line with the gospels.

In line with the interim Constitution, the leader of the ANC, Nelson Mandela, was duly elected President and set about choosing his cabinet. The constitution stated that any party who gained more than 20% of the vote was eligible to have its leader instated as a Deputy President. Mandela, therefore had two deputy presidents, Thabo Mbeki from the ANC and FW de Klerk, the leader of the NP. The selection of Thabo Mbeki as Deputy President effectively marked him as Mandela's likely successor. All other parties were invited to join the ANC in a Government of National Unity (GNU). Despite the continued antagonism between the ANC and IFP, Mongosuthu Buthelezi was given the important post of Minister of Home Affairs. A number of cabinet posts were also filled by delegates from the NP. The only party to stay out of the GNU were the DP who felt they could have more of an impact as the official opposition.

The elections for provincial assemblies resulted in the ANC winning control of seven out of the nine provinces. In a number of provinces they won huge majorities: 80% of the vote in the Free State, 83% in Mpumalanga, 85% in the Eastern Cape, 87% in North West Province, and a staggering 95% in Northern Province. Though many of these areas are associated with hardline Afrikaner nationalism it has to be born in mind that the vast majority of the population in these areas are poor, rural Africans who solidly support the ANC.

In the more populous provinces of Gauteng and KwaZulu Natal, the ANC fared less well. In KwaZulu Natal the ANC were beaten into second place by the IFP who won just over half of the votes. In Gauteng the ANC still won an impressive overall majority of 58%, but they lost seats to the NP (24%) who gained the support of the urban middle-class whites and to smaller parties such as the FF and DP. Three seats in Gauteng also went to the IFP: their only seats outside KwaZulu Natal.

In the Western and Northern Cape the NP did better than many people had expected. Their 40% in the Northern Cape was still substantially behind the ANC's 50% but in the Western Cape they managed to gain 55% to the ANC's 33%. In both these provinces the NP vote was based upon widespread support amongst coloured voters who feared an ANC government would put the interests of Africans ahead of their own. The irony of the only NP election victory being built on the back of coloured voters is quintessentially South African!

Politics since the 1994 election

The GNU's first task was to set about ratifying the interim constitution. Debate on some issues was intense. Labour rights proved to be a bone of contention between the NP and ANC while the ANC and IFP frequently clashed over the division of power between central government and the provinces. Despite their official position as part of the GNU and Buthelezi's cabinet seat the IFP boycotted much of the debate on the constitution on the grounds that the ANC had gone back on a pre-election promise to allow international mediation on the issue of KwaZulu Natal ceding from the rest of the country. Nevertheless by May 1996 all the clauses of the new constitution had been agreed and the Constitutional Assembly voted to ratify the new constitution. With the new constitution in place De Klerk announced that the NP would be leaving the GNU to become the official opposition and try to rebuild itself in order to fight the next national elections due in 1999. The NP ministers selected in 1994 left the cabinet in June 1996 and were replaced by members of the ANC. No new Deputy President was selected; effectively increasing the power of Thabo Mbeki. The IFP remained within the GNU.

In the aftermath of the election the most pressing political problem was the continuation of violence in KwaZulu Natal between supporters of the ANC and supporters of the IFP. Unprovoked attacks, revenge killings and political intrigue all continued to haunt the townships and villages of the province. Peace talks between the leaderships of the provincial parties and high-level discussions between Mandela and Buthelezi were frequently called off and when they did take place made no impact on the rate of violence. Local elections for new unitary local government structures took place throughout the country in mid-1995 but were frequently delayed in KwaZulu Natal because of the violence and allegations over fraudulent electoral rolls. The elections did eventually take place, about one year after the rest of the country and marked the beginnings of a period of significantly reduced levels of violence in the province. Buthelezi and the IFP continue to be primarily interested in provincial issues, though Buthelezi's reputation nationally has somewhat improved from its dire position in 1995-96. The local elections in KwaZulu Natal indicate that the IFP has continued to command widespread support in the rural areas, though the urban townships returned ANC local governments by big majorities.

Mandela commanded huge popular support amongst the African population and won the backing of many of South Africa's white population as well. Mbeki lacked the same mass popularity, but was seen as having aa good grasp of the major issues and is credited with being a key player in bringing peace to KwaZulu Natal. Mandela's punishing international schedule meant that Mbeki was left with many of the domestic political chores, especially dealing with the ANC's internal problems. His position as Mandela's successor left him vulnerable to accusations of manipulating internal ANC politics to strenthen his position over some of his colleagues. This was particularly the case with the easing out of Cyril Ramaphosa, who had led the ANC negotiating team during initial negotiations with the NP. Prior to the election he was seen by many as Mandela's likely successor and his decision to leave politics and join a commercial company was seen as evidence that his leadership ambitions had been frustrated.

The ANC has had its fair share of internal wranglings. In 1995 the most serious of these was over the role of Winnie Mandela (or since her divorce, Winnie Madikizela-Mandela). Since mid-1995, she has experienced a spectacular fall from grace. She was sacked from her cabinet position in 1995, and was divorced by Nelson Mandela the following year. She has faced a series of charges and convictions, including for her role in the kidnapping and murder of a 14-year-old anti-Apartheid activist; she received a six-year prison sentence, which was reduced to a fine. In 2003 she was found guilty of 43 counts of fraud and 25 of theft. Although she again managed to walk away from a prison sentence, she resigned from her positions as a Member of Parliament and President of the ANC Women's League. It seemed Madikizela-Mandela's lifestyle had finally caught up with her.

Provincial ANC governments have also had their share of problems. The Free State party was subject to a bitter split during 1996 between the then provincial premier Patrick Lekota and his Finance executive, who was investigated for corruption. The national ANC leadership stepped into the battle and redeployed Lekota as a member of the National Assembly. In the midlands region of KwaZulu Natal the local ANC leader, Sifiso Nkabinde, was expelled after he was accused of having been an informer during the Apartheid era. He has since joined Holomise's National Consultative Forum and accused the ANC of fostering violence and stockpiling weapons in the region. The Eastern Cape ANC has also had more than its fair share of problems and the national executive have intervened on more than one occasion.

The NP has very little success in repositioning itself as a non-racial centrist party. Its efforts to change its image have not been helped by the continual unearthing of more and more horror stories from the Apartheid years. Particularly damaging to the NP are the stories about covert actions taking place right up to the evening of the 1994 elections, a time when the party had supposedly thrown off its old ways and embraced democracy. The Steyn Report into the actions of the Third Force includes many disturbing allegations, including reports that SADF operatives initiated the spate of train massacres that took place on the Witwatersrand in the run up to the 1994 election. Other allegations in the report included reports that the SADF used chemical bombs against Frelimo troops in Mozambique in the late 1980s and that they stockpiled weapons in game reserves in countries as far away as Kenya.

Other reports of atrocities have come out of the hearings of the Truth and Reconciliation Commission (TRC) chaired by Desmond Tutu. These hearings were intended to be a process of national healing, but many of the wounds revealed look more like running sores. Reports of Apartheid era death camps in the South African countryside resulted in the media putting huge pressure on De Klerk to say exactly what he, and other senior NP members, knew about. Instead De Klerk went on the offensive, denying any knowledge of the camps and attacking the TRC for being 'political'. His image was tarnished by both the allegations and his reaction: his claims that ANC members had attacked his fundamental human rights by saying they did not believe his denials made him look petty, especially in the context of the gross human rights violations being continually reported in the TRC.

De Klerk also dithered over restructuring the NP. There were originally two basic visions for the party's future within the organizations. Firstly a more conservative wing, centred around the hard-line Western Cape Premier Hernus Kriel, wanted to develop the NP as the 'party of minorities' and look to maintain control of Western Cape and perhaps make in-roads in the Northern Cape and KwaZulu Natal. They argued that this approach might leave the party in constant opposition nationally but that it would allow them to retain control of at least one province. The other vision, associated with a more liberal section of the party, centred around former secretary general Roelf Meyer, wanted radically to restructure the party, looking for support amongst the African population and sought to challenge the ANC for national power. De Klerk's attempt to accommodate both visions proved to be untenable and in mid-1997 he appeared to opt for the first. Meyer was first dismissed as secretary general and then he had his task team (trying to find viable African NP leaders) disbanded.

Not surprisingly, Meyer left the party and formed an alternative organization known as the New Movement Process. He took a number of members of the Gauteng Provincial Assembly (his home province) with him to the new organization. There was some speculation at the time that he might team up with Holomise's National Consultative Forum or the Democratic Party.

In June 1999 Nelson Mandela passed the mantle of power over to his long time deputy Thabo Mbeki. In the national elections the ANC won a large victory despite a widespread feeling that they had still to deliver on promises they made when they first came to power in 1994. Although there was some violence associated with the elections it was a great triumph for the country on a continent which has so rarely witnessed fair and peaceful democratic elections.

The outcome of the election showed that people still saw the ANC as the only party capable of providing for their needs. Mbeki was always going to find Mandela a hard act to follow. He surrounded himself with a cabinet of loyal supporters, and he is regarded as an efficient if not dynamic party leader. Keeping the ANC-SACP-Cosatu alliance intact has been one of Mbeki's biggest challenges. Following the 1999 election, relations between the ANC and its alliance partners became increasingly strained over the issues of privatization, the neo-liberal growth, employment and redistribution (Gear) policy, and the government's approach to dealing with HIV/AIDS. Much to Mbeki's embarrassment, Cosatu timed a two-day general strike against privatization to coincide with the International Conference on Racism in Durban during August-September 2001. Cosatu also publicly supported a court challenge to the Government's AIDS policy by the HIV/AIDS NGO, Treatment Action Campaign. However, by February 2002 there were signs of rapprochement between the government and Cosatu, and rumours of a split were premature, although Cosatu has continued to criticise the government's AIDS policy.

Thabo Mbeki has been keen to see South Africa expand its scope of activity in regional and international affairs. Infused with Mbeki's vision for an African Renaissance, South Africa has been a driving force behind restructuring the Southern African Development Community (SADC), establishing the new African Union, and developing the New Partnership for Africa's Development (Nepad). South Africa has also been involved in efforts to solve a number of conflicts and political crises on the continent, such as the long-running war in the DRC; former president Nelson Mandela has led efforts to bring an end to political instability in Burundi. South Africa has become an articulate advocate for Third World interests and has helped to reinvigorate the Non-Aligned Movement. South Africa is usually careful to balance the concerns of smaller countries with those of the broader international community. After September 11 for example, the country voiced its opposition to terrorism, but demurred from supporting US military action. South Africa also courted controversy by declaring the contentious 2002 Zimbabwean elections free and fair, but Mbeki ultimately decided, along with the leaders of Australia and Nigeria, to recommend Zimbabwe's suspension from the Commonwealth. However, Mbeki's continued refusal to openly criticise Robert Mugabe's regime – preferring instead to stick to 'quiet diplomacy' – has attracted condemnation.

Mbeki's views on AIDS cast a shadow over the first four years of his presidency. Going against the weight of medical opinion, he questioned the link between HIV and AIDS, and the effectiveness of anti-retroviral drugs. The Department of Health's refusal to provide anti-AIDS drugs to pregnant women and rape survivors angered AIDS activists and drew widespread criticism of the government. However, the Treatment Action Campaign won a High Court case against the Department of Health in 2001, forcing it to provide the anti-retroviral drug Nevirapine to all HIV-positive pregnant women. In November 2003, the cabinet voted to provide anti-retroviral drug across the board.

The 1999 election did not dramatically alter South Africa's political landscape, except for some growth in support for the Democratic Party (DP). The DP's line on crime and tough talk from its leader, Tony Leon, won it a substantial proportion of the white vote. In an effort to unite opposition to the government in the lead up to the 2000 local elections, the DP joined forces with the NP, under the new guidance of Marthinus van Schalkwyk to form the Democratic Alliance. The Alliance was however short-lived and fell apart following in-fighting about the party's administration in the Western Cape. Van Schalkwyk became the leader of what was then known as the New National Party (NNP), and continued to develop his party as a 'party of minorities'. Efforts to expand the NNP's profile beyond the Western Cape were unsuccessful, and in 2004 it was announced the he was to become a member of the ANC, and that the NNP would be disbanded in 2006. April 2004 saw the latest set of general elections, which the ANC, led by Thabo Mbeki, won in a characteristic landslide, gaininig 69.7% of votes. Theoretically, this proportion would allow them to change the constitution, but they have pledged not to. The main opposition party, the Democratic Alliance, won an increased share of the votes (thought to be largely thanks to former supporters of the NNP switches allegiances). The NNP, meanwhile, won just 1.7% of the votes. The elections were particularly notable as 2004 marked South Africa's decade of democracy. Van Schalkwyk was appointed as minister of Environmental Affairs and Tourism, and in 2006, following March's local elections, the NNP finally folded.

Economy

South Africa is often referred to as being a First and Third World economy within one country. While it is true that parts of South African society are extremely rich and the majority are extremely poor this situation is not actually that different from many other countries classified as Third World (or developing or South countries). The well-off sections of society are bigger than in other African countries but they are not dissimilar in size and wealth to countries such as Brazil or Argentina. The overall per capita levels of wealth in South Africa are also pretty much similar to these Latin American economies (referred to as the Higher Middle Income nations in World Bank league tables).

Structure of the economy

The economy is dominated by the industries exploiting the country's extremely rich mineral resources. The mineral sector of the economy accounts for something like two thirds of export earnings, though it employs less than 10% of the labour force. Apart from the gold and diamonds for which the country is famous it also produces a range of other mineral products, including platinum and chromium (of which it is the major world producer). The country lacks oil, though it does have some reserves of natural gas. The scarcity of oil was a key issue in the Apartheid days, hence the conversion of coal into oil by SASOL.

Agricultural production also continues to make a significant contribution to the economy, especially if you add the food preparation secondary industries based on primary agricultural products. Almost one third of the workforce is in agriculture, though employment in this sector is characterized by extremely low wages and seasonal unemployment. The agricultural base is very diverse and in non-drought years, the country is a net food exporter.

The manufacturing sector of the economy has tended to suffer from low productivity levels, meaning that South Africa has found it difficult to break into lucrative export markets. The southern African regional market, where South Africa does have an advantage, is constrained by low levels of consumption and is, in any case, already pretty much saturated with South African goods. The most important local manufacturing sectors include automobile assembly, machinery, textiles, iron and steel, chemicals and fertilizers.

The tourism sector has been highlighted as a significant area of potential growth. Though there have been positive developments in many sectors of the tourism economy the country has been hampered by its reputation for high crime rates – although positive developments in the centre of Johannesburg and Cape Town have reassured many visitors. Crime is thought to be a fairly significant drain on the economy in general and is the major political issue in the country.

Recent economic developments

The ANC came to power in 1994 with the economy in a mess. Throughout much of the 1980s and early 1990s the economy had grown slower than population growth rates and in some years had contracted in absolute terms. Inflation rates were high, the rand was slipping against the major currencies, investment rates were low, productivity was low and unemployment rates were extremely high. Much of this was due to global isolation which had led the country down an economic dead end. Growth was low because of the limitations of the domestic market and the inaccessibility of export markets, difficulties in obtaining technology due to sanctions and an unskilled labour force due to the poor state of African education. Probably the only area in which South Africa was better placed than comparable economies was in the level of external debt: sanctions by international banks and finance organizations had prevented the government from borrowing heavily. Despite its stated objectives of reducing poverty, increasing equality and providing basic social services for all, the new ANC government also signalled its intentions to ensure macro-economic stability. The first post-Apartheid Minister of Finance, Derek Keys, was appointed from outside party politics and the subsequent budgets did not include the heavy public borrowing and increased taxation that many observers predicted before the election. Macro-economically the economy has been a qualified success. Economic growth rates have been running at around three to four percent per annum, inflation has been controlled and deficit spending and public borrowing have only risen slowly. The rand has continued to slip on the international currency markets, though not as catastrophically as might have been expected when currency dealing and profit repatriation legislation were revoked. A significant development for South Africa's export industries was the signing of the EU-South Africa Trade, Development and Co-operation Agreement (TDCA) in October 1999. The benefits of increased access to European markets for South African goods have become immediately apparent; South Africa's trade surplus with the EU increased four-fold between 1999 and 2001. Since 1999 the economy has experienced uninterrupted growth; it is predicted to grow around 5% year in 2006 and 2007.

The major problem area for the economy has been unemployment. Despite the fact that the economy is growing there are still more young people entering the employment market than there are new jobs being created. Although the number of jobs being created is increasing, the growth in the population means that South Africa's unemployment rate remains virtually unchanged. In September 2005, the unemployment rate was put at 26.7%.

In terms of meeting its objectives to provide basic social services for all, the government's record has been mixed. Some ministries have performed well while others barely seem to have got programmes off the ground. The much vaulted Reconstruction and Development Programme collapsed under its own weight and its functions were parcelled out to various government agencies. The provision of clean drinking water and rural electrification programmes have both been making steady progress. Provision of new housing to meet the huge urban backlog, on the other hand, is far slower. International development organizations have shown a huge amount of interest in the country and there have been some significant flows of new capital into the country from these sources.

The ANC government is beginning to show signs of reassessing the growth, employment and redistribution policy (Gear), which was criticised by trade unions as being a 'home-grown structural adjustment programme'. The 2001 budget showed a significant increase in public expenditure on social services. This may be an acknowledgment that Gear has not delivered the expected levels of economic growth. Ultimately, it is HIV/AIDS that may have the greatest impact on South Africa's economic future; a recent study predicts that by 2010, the disease may have shrunk the South African economy by between 17% and 20%. Mining and manufacturing, the two largest segments of the South Africa economy, are estimated to be effected the most by HIV/AIDS, with absenteeism due to ill health driving down profits.

Culture

Population distribution

Figures from South Africa's 2001 census show the total population to be around 48.8 million, a considerably growth from 1996, when the population was estimated to be around 38 million.

The two most populous provinces are KwaZulu Natal and Gauteng. KwaZulu Natal contains a major urban area, Durban, but higher rainfall figures also means that the KwaZulu Natal countryside is able to support a greater population density than other rural areas of the country. The legacy of Apartheid means that former homeland areas have much higher population densities than other rural areas: the scattered fragments of what was the homeland of KwaZulu Natal stretch across the province and account for much of the region's 7.7 million people.

Gauteng, the country's smallest province in area (1.4% of the total), contains 19% of the total population, the vast majority of whom are urban residents living in the towns and cities around Johannesburg.

The Eastern Cape's 5.9 million people are less urbanized. Though the province contains a major city, Port Elizabeth, many of its people live in the area that used to comprise the homelands of Transkei and Ciskei.

The Western Cape, by contrast, never contained any homeland areas. Its 4.1 million people mainly live in and around Cape Town though there is also a significant population of farmworkers and residents of small rural towns and villages.

The next four provinces in terms of population size, Northern Province, North West, Mpumalanga and the Free State, all have their population divided between smaller industrial centres, sparsely populated white rural areas and densely populated fragments of former homelands.

Finally, the Northern Cape, the largest province in area (361,830 sq km), has a tiny population of just 700,000 people widely dispersed across this semi-arid region.

Ethnic groups

South Africa's population is a true melting pot, with numerous races, religions, ethnicities and cultures which can be somewhat bewildering for visitors. While many people today resent being classified in terms or race and ethnicity – it was, after all, racial classifications which denied the majority of the population many of its basic human rights for many years – it is impossible to discuss modern South Africa without touching on these terms.

The Apartheid system recognized four major population groups (races) in the country: African, Asian, coloured and white (the terminology has changed over time). Despite the avowed non-racial nature of the present South African state, this fourfold classification remains profoundly important to South African life. This does not mean, however, that everyone fits neatly into these four categories: during the Apartheid era, huge numbers of people had their race altered by official decree. This could have profound impacts and often resulted in people being evicted from their homes and their children thrown out of schools. Within each of the four racial categories it is possible to make further sub-divisions on the basis of home language, tribe and geography – these sub-divisions (especially tribe) are even more fluid and open to debate than the fourfold racial classification.

African

The African population makes up around 75% of South Africa's total population. The terminology used to describe this section of the population has changed over the years: in the 19th and early 20th century they tended to be referred to as 'natives' while in the 1960s the Apartheid authorities adopted the term 'Bantu'. Both these names have strong connotations of racism. The word Bantu simply comes from the Zulu and Xhosa words for people but it is resented by most South Africans because of its connection to the Apartheid institutions who adopted it in the 1960s, especially in the field of education. Today it is only acceptable to use the term when discussing languages; the Bantu group of languages includes all the African languages spoken in South Africa and related Bantu languages are spoken as far away as Somalia.

The Apartheid system also designated the African population on the basis of tribe. This was not as straightforward as it might seem. Many Africans, especially those living in urban areas and those who were long-term residents on white farms, had only weak links with any tribal authority and often did not describe themselves in terms of their tribal background. Under the Apartheid system every African was allocated to one of nine different tribes, each with a designated tribal authority and a homeland. This classification system lead to many complaints and many people claimed that they did not belong to any of the tribes or that their clan constituted a separate tribe – originally there were eight designated tribes but complaints of this nature lead to the creation of a ninth.

In terms of population, the biggest African tribal group is the Zulu. The majority of Zulus live in KwaZulu Natal or in the industrial centres of Gauteng. Rural Zulus probably have the greatest ethnic identity out of the entire African population and this has been fuelled by the IFP calls for more autonomy for KwaZulu Natal. The second biggest ethnic group is the Xhosa. Under the Apartheid system they were ascribed two separate homelands: the Ciskie and Transkie, now incorporated into Eastern Cape. There is a large Xhosa population in Cape Town and on the farms of the Western Cape. Many of the ANC's leaders are Xhosa from the Eastern Cape, reflecting the area's long history of resistance politics and the education provided in the large number of mission schools in the region. These two groups together account for about 40% of the African population.

There are three ethnic groups in the country who are closely related to the populations of three neighbouring countries dominated by people of that tribe: the Tswana (Botswana), the Swazi (Swaziland) and the Southern Sotho (Lesotho). These three and the other four ethnic groups, the Shangana or Tsonga, the Ndebele, the Venda and the Northern Sotho have their populations dispersed in the previous homeland areas or mixed together in the towns and cities of the highveld.

Each one of the nine ethnic groups has an official language. Many of these are more or less mutually intelligible. The major distinction is between the Nguni languages (Xhosa, Zulu, Swazi and Ndebele) and those closely related to SeSotho and SeTswana. There are distinctive cultural activities associated with each ethnic group, though these usually only come into play at times like weddings and funerals. In the urban areas, where the majority of Africans live, many of these ethnic tribal customs have been replaced by generic amalgams of different practices. Similarly a distinctive urban African language containing words from all the languages plus English and Afrikaans has evolved in the urban areas.

White

South Africa's white population accounts for something like 13% of the total. It can be sub-divided into two main groups on the basis of home language: English speakers and Afrikaans-speaking people. The ancestors of English-speaking white South Africans first arrived in the country in 1820 and since then there has been a steady stream of new immigrants. The first English settlers to arrive were concentrated in the

 Eastern Cape but today they are to be found in every town and city. They tend to be more urbanized and more metropolitan in outlook than the Afrikaners, though this is a generalization that does not always match up to reality.

The Afrikaner population are descended from the original Dutch and Huguenot settlers who came with the Dutch East India Company. The word Afrikaner simply means African in Dutch. They account for just over half of the white population. They have a reputation for being conservative, rural and more racist than the English-speaking population. In reality the vast majority live in town and you can very often only tell the difference between an English-speaking and Afrikaans-speaking white South African from their surnames.

There are a number of other smaller communities of white South Africans, including a Jewish community descended from early 20th century immigrants from eastern Europe and a Portuguese community, many of whom came to South Africa from Moçambique and Angola in the 1970s.

Asian

South Africa has a small Asian population, accounting for about three percent of the total. It is descended from two main groups: indentured labourers brought to the sugar cane farms of Natal in the 19th century and a number of traders and their families who followed the indentured labourers. The vast majority of the Asian population are originally from South Asia and they are also often referred to as Indian. The majority of Asians still live in KwaZulu Natal though there are small Asian communities in most towns and cities across the country, especially in Gauteng. About 70% of the Asian population are Hindu and 20% Muslim. Almost all Asians speak English as their home language.

Coloured

This is probably the most contentious of the four basic racial categories used in South Africa. In some ways the coloured category just represents the rest lumped together into one group. There is a distinctive coloured cultural identity – though by no means all people classified as coloured during Apartheid would subscribe to it. Under Apartheid about 9% of the population was classified as coloured. The coloured population is concentrated in the Western Cape. Many of them are descended from slaves brought to work on the farms of the Cape during the era of rule by the Dutch East India Company and from slave owners and other white settlers. There are also many coloured people who are descended from the pre-colonial San and Khoi populations of the Cape. This is especially so in the Northern and Eastern Cape which never had large slave populations. Some coloured people, especially the 200,000 strong Malay community in Cape Town, have retained elements of their pre-slavery culture, including Islam.

On the whole, the coloured community is very closely linked (both culturally and through descent) with the Afrikaner community. About 80% of the coloured population speak Afrikaans as their home language: it surprises many visitors to discover that coloured Afrikaans speakers outnumber white Afrikaans speakers. In post-Apartheid South Africa the links between the coloured and Afrikaner communities have been increasingly stressed by people on both sides.

Music and dance

Most visitors will be familiar with the most famous of South African sounds, the rousing vocal harmony of Ladysmith Black Mambazo, made internationally famous by Paul Simon's Graceland album. It doesn't end there, though: the country has produced an incredible variety of music – little surprise given its immense range of cultures and influences. In fact, the key to understanding South African music is in realizing where it comes from. Be it the adaptation of Dutch instruments in the 17th century by Indonesian slaves, or the mutation of 1990s house music into township Kwaito, home-grown and foreign sounds mingle to produce a singularly South Africa sound. And like so much of South African culture, music is inextricably linked with the political upheavals of the last century.

Vocal harmony is the oldest music tradition in South Africa, with its roots in communal dances accompanied by elaborate call-and-response patterns. This movement, defined as gospel acapella (and known as Isicathamiya in Zulu), has long been popular in South Africa, but it was the band Ladysmith Black Mambazo who first propelled it into the international arena. The beginnings for the group were not easy; at their first concert in Soweto in the 1980s, they received the princely sum of R5.28 each. The band, however, became an instant hit, outselling Michael Jackson within months. When Paul Simon invited them to sing on his Graceland album, they were thrust into the international limelight, and they remain the most popular South African band of all time. Made up of ten male singers, including the charismatic front-man, lead singer and original founder Joseph Shabalala, the band continue to tour, and have now recorded over forty albums.

However, few musical styles have been as influential as jazz, something of a harmonious hotbed since emerging from the Johannesburg slums in the 1920s. Today, the jazz scene is once again flourishing following a turbulent few decades when many of the biggest jazz stars left South Africa under Apartheid, and is now best experienced at the Cape Town International Jazz Festival, held every March in Cape Town. Many of the godfathers of Cape Jazz, including Abdullah Ibrahim (previously known as Dollar Brand) and Hugh Masekela can be seen performing during the three-day festival, while newcomers, using a range of influences from the harmonica of migrant west African miners, to the clubbing beats of drum 'n' bass, are also making a bit impact. Every year the South African acts are complemented by the latest international recruits – 2004 saw the likes of Jamie Cullum and Alicia Keys raising the roof.

If music is the very heartbeat of this country, then dance also features as an integral part of life for many South Africans. In KwaZula Natal tourists can be treated to a traditional Zulu ceremony, while the talented *Gumboots* dance company have toured the world with their unforgettable mix of music, dance and showmanship.

Western music is hugely popular with young South Africans, and both Durban and Cape Town have significant live rock scenes. A number of home-grown talents such as rock band Just Jinger have recently made it onto the national arena, but the most popular white musician remains Johnny Clegg. In the 1970s, Clegg began performing traditional Zulu material with Sipho Mchunu, and later added a mix of western rock with to form the band Juluka. Clegg remains something of a South African legend, and still draws thousands of fans when he performs. Known affectionately as the "White Zulu", Clegg challenged the racial boundaries manifest in music under Apartheid, and blazed a cross-over trail which survives to this day. Although popular mainly amongst (liberal) white people, his tours are sell-outs and he remains a big influence on the music scene.

Kwaito

The fastest-moving force in music today is undoubtedly Kwaito, the sound of young, black Johannesburg. The style is resolutely urban, drawing on American and British house music, with slow, deep beats and electronic melodies overlaid with chanted *tsotsi* (township gangster) slang. Born from 1980s pop-influenced dance music known as bubblegum, Kwaito has a darker, edgier feel, carrying with it an unmistakable association with gangster culture. But despite its underground roots and reflection of a despondent township youth, Kwaito has become the country's definitive youth sound, led by top record label Kalawa Jazzmee and stars like Mandoza and Zola. Ubiquitous in the clubs of young black urbanites, it is also now popular in designer nightclubs – until relatively recently the reserve of the white and wealthy.

Land and environment

South Africa is a big country with an extremely diverse physical environment. The country's total land area amounts to 1,219,912 sq km (1,267,462 sq km including Swaziland and Lesotho). Contained within this land area are a wide mix of environments, ranging from tropical moist forest, through high mountains, rolling grasslands and temperate woodlands to sparsely vegetated areas of semi-desert. South Africa's natural scenery is world famous and rightly so. There are some amazingly beautiful areas which can take the breath away from even the most world weary traveller. The wild and empty beaches of the south coast, the panoramic views of the Drakensberg mountains, the wide open spaces of the Karoo and many other stunning landscapes can all leave a lasting impression on the visitor.

There are also, however, some big areas of undistinguished natural scenery and the impacts of both industrialization and Apartheid have also had their toll. This is obviously worth bearing in mind when you are planning a holiday, especially if you are only going to be there for a short period of time. If your primary interest is in South Africa's natural beauty read the following sections carefully before planning your route.

Landscape

South Africa's physical geography is dominated by one feature: a massive escarpment that runs right around the subcontinent dividing a thin coastal strip from a huge inland plateau. This escarpment is clearest in the east, where it is marked by the spectacular Drakensberg mountains, running in an arc from the Eastern Cape round to northern Mpumalanga. To the west the escarpment is confused by a jumble of beautiful mountain chains (the Cape Folded Mountains), such as the Cederberg, the Tsitsikamma, the Swartberg and the Hottentot-Hollands. The inland plateau, usually known as the highveld, is a relatively flat plain sloping gently down towards the west and north. This plain is, however, broken up by numerous geological features, resulting in isolated steep-sided hills or longer chains of higher ground.

This interior plateau forms the southernmost tip of the massive Africa continental plateau which stretches as far north as Ethiopia. This plateau was part of the ancient landmass of Pangaea (c200 million years ago), which split in two to form Gondwanaland in the southern hemisphere and Laurasia in the north. Gondwanaland later broke up to form the continents of South America, Australasia and Africa, around 135 million years ago. As it is made up of an old continental plate many of South Africa's rocks are very old and some rocks found in the Limpopo valley, Northern Province, rank with the oldest yet discovered anywhere in the world.

Other areas, such as the Witwatersrand and Barberton complexes, are also made up of ancient Precambrian rocks, about 3,000 million years old. This contrasts with rock formations in places such as the Western Cape coast which were only formed in the past 250,000 years, during the Quaternary era. Most of the country is, however, made up of sandstone and slates laid down in the Carboniferous to Jurassic periods (when Pangaea began to break up). These are commonly referred to as the Karoo sequence of rocks. The eastern portions of the Karoo sequence have been covered by an intrusion of basalt. This harder layer of rock has protected the softer Karoo sandstones from erosion and stands out as a highland area, especially in Lesotho.

The Karoo sequence is particularly rich in fossil remains. Contained in the sandstones and shales are the remains of many reptilian creatures who lived in the low-lying areas of swamps and shallow lakes. Some of these fossils have been crucial to scientists' attempts to reconstruct the way in which reptiles evolved into mammals. The best places to look for fossils is along the sides of the many steep-sided hills or koppies that dominate the Karoo landscape. The best fossils are usually found in the dull red shales, which erode easily to reveal the fossil remains.

Climate

Over most of South Africa rain falls during the southern hemisphere summer months (November-March). Rainfall tends to be in the form of intense cloud bursts, often accompanied by thunderstorms, though there can also be periods of longer rainfall. During the summer months warm and wet easterly winds sweep in from over the Indian Ocean. As these winds flow over the southeastern coast and the Drakensberg they drop much of their moisture, making these areas the wettest parts of the country with annual totals over 1,000mm. Over the highveld the moisture-bearing winds trigger rain showers and thunderstorms. In the east of the highveld these tend to be more regular but towards the west, especially in the Northern Cape, they are infrequent. Here average annual rainfall figures are usually below 200 mm per annum. The summer rains never reach the western coast of the Northern Cape province and rainfall levels here can be as low as 20mm per annum. South Africa is, on the whole, a very dry country, with something like 30 percent of the land area receiving below 250 mm a year on average. Rain may be unpopular with visitors but it is almost always welcomed by South Africans.

The only part of the country where the major rainfall does not come from summer easterlies is the Western Cape and the extreme west of Northern Cape province. Here most rain falls during the winter months as depressions over the southern Atlantic sweep north and east bringing with them frontal systems and cool rains. Late in the winter and early spring an occasional winter storm will travel further north than usual and bring with it much needed rain to the arid northwestern coastal belt. Apart from these occasional storms this area receives its moisture from mists that roll in from the cold Atlantic during the summer months.

The winter weather systems can also sometimes skirt up along the southern coast bringing rain and even snow to the Eastern Cape, Lesotho and KwaZulu Natal. Snowfalls tend to be minor and confined to light dustings of the highest peaks, though there are occasionally significant falls of a few inches or more. In the winter of 1996 a number of people had to be rescued after large snow storms in the Drakensberg.

This seasonal pattern is also highly variable from year to year. This variability tends to be most pronounced in the lowest rainfall areas: here there can be some years where the rains fail entirely. The exact reasons for this variability are a matter of considerable academic debate. There does appear to be a cycle of wet and dry years in South Africa over a period of about four to eight years. This cycle is related to a frequent, but irregular, event known as the El Niño, in which ocean and air currents in the South Pacific are reversed. This, in turn, triggers changes in the circulation of air around the southern hemisphere and results in weaker easterlies and drought in South Africa. The weather system is, however, extremely complex and involves the interaction of global and local variables, so predicting exactly how something like the El Niño will affect South African rainfall is impossible with any degree of accuracy. Global warming may also be further complicating the already complex weather systems. Beyond short range forecasting all that meteorologists can predict with any degree of accuracy is that the climate is very unpredictable.

Temperatures vary according to season, altitude and distance from the moderating influence of the oceans. During the summer months the inland plateau tends to heat up considerably, especially if the rains fail. The highest daytime temperatures are to be found in the lower lying semi-desert areas of the Northern Cape and the lowveld regions of Mpumulanga. On the highveld temperatures can also soar in summer, though they tend to be moderated by the higher altitudes. Fortunately in these inland regions the evenings tend to be significantly cooler, especially under clear skies. Travelling at night or in the early morning is a sensible and popular option in these regions during summer. The coastal fringes of Natal are also hot and sticky in summer and don't expect too much relief at night. The most pleasant area of the country during the summer months is the Western Cape, with hot but often breezy days and comfortable evenings.

During the winter the Western Cape can get very chilly, with frequent blustery storms and heavy rain. On the highveld and in the Karoo stable high pressure systems result in clear skies, warm days and cold nights. It is a combination many visitors find very comfortable especially for travelling long distances. In the highest areas of the Drakensberg winter temperatures can plummet to way below freezing at night: the best time to visit these areas is during the autumn or spring. The Natal coast remains warm throughout the year, especially in the northern subtropical areas near the Moçambique border. Winter is a good time to visit the lowveld game parks: the drier conditions make it easier to spot wildlife, especially around water holes.

Vegetation

There are a number of different ways of categorizing South Africa's vegetational zones, which are sometimes called biomes or ecozones. All these categorizations are simplifications of complex and dynamic patterns of vegetation and rarely are there clear boundaries between the different zones. Even without the influence of humans this pattern has constantly shifted with long-term trends in climate: when you add in millenniums of human impacts, mapping a set pattern of different biomes becomes an extremely difficult task.

One vegetational zone that is not difficult to classify as distinctive is the fynbos of the Western Cape. Although fynbos covers only a relatively small area it comprises one of the earth's six separate floral kingdoms. The other five floral kingdoms cover huge areas such as most of the northern hemisphere or the whole of Australia. The Cape floral kingdom is both the smallest and the richest floral kingdom in the world, with the highest known concentration of plant species per unit area. There are over 7,700 different plant species within the fynbos biome and of these over 5,000 are endemic to the Western Cape (ie they do not occur naturally anywhere else). The 470 sq km of the Cape Peninsula is home to 2,256 different plant species – more than the whole of the UK, an area 5,000 times bigger! The 60 sq km of Table Mountain alone supports 1,470 species. The richness of the fynbos is well demonstrated by its ericas or heaths, of which there are over 600 different species. There are just 26 in the rest of the world. Not surprisingly the Western Cape is a magnet for plant enthusiasts.

The word fynbos comes from the Dutch for fine-leaved plants. Almost all of the woody plants have small leaves (microphyllous) which are hard, tough and leathery (sclerophyllous). True grasses are also relatively rare and as much as five percent of the biome is covered by Cape reeds (of the Restionaceae family). Most of the plants that fill the niches usually taken up by grasses have small, thin (ericoid) leaves. Additionally, the fynbos biome contains proteas, ericas and members of seven plant families found nowhere else in the world. These include the King Protea, South Africa's national flower, the beautiful Red Disa, symbol of the Cape Province and the popular garden plants, pelargoniums, commonly known as geraniums. The largest family in number of species is Asteraceae (daisy family), with just under 1,000 species of which more than 600 are endemic. Fynbos is very rich in bulbous plants (geophytes) and many species from the family Iridaceae have become household names such as babiana, freesia, gladiolus, iris, moraea, sporaxis and watsonia.

As many of the endemic fynbos species have amazingly small ranges (sometimes as small as a football field), they are extremely vulnerable to extinction. One small housing project, for example, could wipe out a whole species. Given this and the fact that the Western Cape has fairly dense human population, it is not surprising that many of South Africa's threatened and rare plants are found in the fynbos. Almost 500 species are classified as rare, threatened or endangered. Fynbos species tend to grow fairly slowly. This is because they are in a winter rainfall region so during the summer months there is not enough water available and during the winter low temperatures restrict plant growth. The hot dry summer months also make fire a common occurrence in the biome. The fynbos plants are well adapted to fire and the biome is adapted to quickly re-establish itself after naturally occurring burns. If fire is totally restricted fynbos often loses out to plant species from surrounding biomes. If fires are too frequent, however, the fynbos plants do not have time to re-establish themselves and this can lead to local extermination of species.

Soils under fynbos tend to be extremely infertile, due partially to the chemical make-up of the underlying rocks and partially to heavy leaching that has occurred over long periods. The nutrient-poor soils produce plants that are also low in nutrients and therefore of low feeding potential for grazing animals. This means that there is a relatively low density and diversity of mammals and birds in the fynbos biome.

The western coast of South Africa also has a large number of endemic plant species. This area, stretching north into Namibia, has extremely low and erratic rainfall and the plant life reflects this. Many of the plants in this region are succulents and about 200 of these are classified as rare or endangered. When rains do come to the area there is a dramatic transformation of the vegetation. Hundreds of flowering plants lying dormant during the long dry periods burst into bloom covering the whole of the landscape in a carpet of brightly coloured flowers. This is a spectacular annual event and attracts many visitors to the region every spring, but as the flowers are reliant upon unpredictable rainfall it is impossible to say exactly when and where they will appear. The rains are expected in the spring, and once the first blooms start to appear a 'Flower Hotline' can be called for the latest information, see page 747 in the Northern Cape for full details. After a brief period of flowering the plants drop their seeds which then lie dormant until the next rainfall event.

The inland plateau of the Cape is dominated by Karoo types of vegetation. This is made up mainly from low lying shrubs and succulents, though in good rainfall years grasses can also make an appearance. There tends to be a lot of open soil between the shrubs so much of the region takes on the red tinge of the underlying soils and this can lead to some wonderful sunsets and sunrises. The low density of vegetation also makes fires a less common occurrence than in better watered regions. There are occasional areas of green along side streams and rivers and these are the only places you will see trees in the biome.

The northern highveld areas (along the Botswana border) and the lowveld areas of Northern Province, Mpumalanga and Swaziland, by contrast, have a fair number of trees. This is the classic savanna formation: areas of grassland interspersed by occasional trees. In the highveld areas the vegetation is dominated by thorny acacia woodland, often referred to as bushveld. In valley bottoms and in lowveld areas the vegetation is often dominated by mopane, which can tolerate the extremes of waterlogging and drying encountered on heavy soils. This region tends to have fertile soils and grasses have a high nutrition content. They are, therefore, heavily populated by grazing animals (both wild and domestic). The major wildlife viewing areas fall within this biome.

The remaining highveld, the KwaZulu Natal midlands, Lesotho and the inland areas of Eastern Cape are taken up by grasslands with few naturally occurring trees. The grasses grow vigorously during the hot and wet summer months and then remain dormant during the dry, cold winter. The grasslands are often divided into two different categories: sweet and sour veld. Sweetveld occurs in the areas with lower rainfall figures (400-600 mm per annum), especially on heavier clay soils. It tends to be more nutritious than the sour velds and is therefore popular for grazing, especially during the summer months. Sourveld tends to occur in the areas with rainfall above 600 mm per annum. Greater availability of water means that sourveld grasses grow rapidly, though they tend to have a lower nutritional content. Both these veld types intermingle and it is hard to draw a clear distinction between the two. The division between the Karoo and grassland areas is also hazy. During dry spells and in areas which have been overgrazed, Karoo-type shrubs expand into the grasslands while in wetter years or if grazing pressure is reduced they will retreat. On the highveld much of this grassland has been converted to agriculture or covered with factories, roads and cities.

The densely populated narrow coast strip of the Eastern Cape and KwaZulu Natal was once heavily wooded. The closed canopy subtropical forests of KwaZulu Natal can still be found in a few isolated patches but most of the area has been converted to agriculture. In the Eastern Cape the evergreen temperate forest has also been largely cut down, though some small patches are left around Knysna. The forests here give some idea of what the environment would have been like before the arrival of Europeans with commercial logging: there are some beautiful trees such as the stinkwood, Cape chestnut, yellowwood and the white and red alder. In total, indigenous closed canopy woodland accounts for only 1% of South Africa's land area, with a similar amount under commercial plantations (many of these on the Drakensberg escarpment in Mpumalanga).

Urban and rural environments

Any description of the South African landscape that leaves out the impact of humans would not give a visitor any real idea about what the place actually looks like. Though Apartheid has now come to an end its legacy is often apparent in the South African landscape and the pattern of South African cities and towns. For many years some of the most striking features of Apartheid social engineering, such as the huge rural slums that sprang up around the country, were never shown on official maps. Visitors were often shocked to suddenly encounter a massive area of slum housing way out in the countryside which they could not find on their road maps and which did not appear on any road signs. Official maps and guides are now slowly catching up with reality but the landscape itself will take much longer to transform.

Agriculture

While large areas of South Africa are given over to wildlife or wilderness areas most of the countryside is dominated by farming. The nature of the country's agricultural sector, therefore, has a huge impact on the landscape. The pattern of agriculture in South Africa is determined by two major factors: the physical environment and the legacy of Apartheid. Low and variable rainfall figures make arable farming an extremely risky business and only about 10% of the country is covered by arable crops. Maize is the country's staple crop. It is mainly grown in the Free State, the southern and eastern portions of North West, the western portions of Mpumalanga and those parts of Gauteng not covered by towns and industry. These areas comprise some of the least eventful countryside in South Africa. Maize and other grain crops, such as sorghum or millet, are also grown in the Eastern Cape and KwaZulu Natal. In these wetter areas the constraining factor is often not availability of water, but of sufficient flat land to plough amongst the broken topography. The most rewarding landscapes for a tourist are inevitably very different from the most rewarding landscapes for a farmer.

Other arable crops include wheat, grown mostly in the Western Cape and sugar cane, grown mostly in KwaZulu Natal. The Western Cape is also well known for its vineyards and fruits, such as peaches and nectarines. The lowveld areas of Mpumalanga and Northern Province are also major fruit growing areas.

The majority of the countryside is, however, given over to extensive grazing land. This accounts for something like 65% of the country's total land area, the vast majority of this given over to large enclosures of naturally occurring veld plants rather than improved and carefully managed paddocks. The wetter areas in the east, where grasses dominate over woodier Karoo shrubs, are given over mainly to cattle. The rolling hills of the KwaZulu Natal Midlands are particularly good cattle rearing country: well watered but with sufficiently cool evenings and winters to kill off disease-bearing insects that flourish in the more tropical coastal fringes and the lowveld regions. Further west, especially in the Karoo, livestock rearing is dominated by sheep and in the very driest areas by goats.

This pattern of agriculture is confused, however, by the legacy of Apartheid. Until very recently African farmers were not allowed to own or buy land outside certain prescribed areas. These areas, known as the homelands, comprised only 13% of the country and were supposed to provide land for an African population comprising 75% of the total. In these areas the population density is high and plots of land for agriculture are very small. Most of these plots are unproductive and yields from agricultural crops very low. Grazing in these areas is on common land owned by the local community. Though individual herds tend to be small the total animal population is high and includes a mixture of goats, sheep and cattle. As the grazing land is unfenced and communal herds will usually be looked after by a shepherd – usually a teenage boy, livestock are usually brought back to the village at night where they are kraaled to stop them wandering and to reduce the risk of theft.

This contrasts with the white farming areas where farms tend to be huge. Arable agriculture is highly mechanized and produces high yields. Some farms, such as the fruit growing areas, employ large numbers of seasonal labour but on the whole the number of people employed permanently on each farm is not high. On the white farms livestock are grazed in large fenced paddocks at a lower density than on the former homeland areas. Except on the dairy farms, livestock are only checked up on periodically.

These different patterns of farming produce very different looking landscapes. The former homeland areas are more densely populated with small plots of unhealthy looking maize interspersed amongst scattered homesteads. The grazing areas often look barren, especially towards the end of the winter dry season when all available forage has been eaten by livestock. The white farming areas, on the other hand, have large fields of arable crops or huge areas of grazing land. On the grazing land there will tend to be more vegetation available to the livestock, though in drought years these areas can also look pretty barren. It is unusual to see many people in the fields and paddocks of the white farming areas.

Though the restrictions on buying or renting land have now been lifted this pattern will remain for many years. Some African farmers who were evicted from white farming areas during the Apartheid era have been resettled on their original farms, but this process is very slow and the geography of agriculture is unlikely to change significantly in the conceivable future.

Living in the city

South Africa's urban geography has been largely shaped by segregation: this pattern is now changing rapidly but the legacy of residential segregation will be apparent for a very long time to come. Under the Group Areas Act different areas of each city were reserved for one of the four major population groups (white, Indian, coloured or African). Prior to the passing of the Group Areas Act in 1950 most cities and towns were already segregated to an extent. The pattern of segregation was complicated however and there were in most cities a number of areas in which the different population groups intermingled. Under the Group Areas Act the government attempted to consolidate this pattern of segregation into bigger, clearly defined blocks of land and to do away with any areas where there was a mixture of the different races. This process continued right through to the mid-1980s. The urban environment that this system created is distinctive.

Prior to the Group Areas Act much of the poorer urban population lived in slum areas near the central business areas of industrial centres. These areas were home to large numbers of Africans, Indians and coloureds and a few 'poor whites'. Under the Group Areas Act these slum areas were knocked down and new housing for whites was built in their place. The African, Indian and coloured populations were moved to new, racially segregated, planned settlements on the outskirts of cities, known as townships. These areas tend to be some distance from the city centre and are divided from the white suburbs by areas of unoccupied land. There are often only one or two access routes into the township and the streets are wide and straight: both factors were deliberately intended to make the control of unrest and protest easier to handle. The best known of these township areas is the vast residential area called Soweto, which originally stood for South Western Townships, on the outskirts of Johannesburg.

The vast majority of Africans living in urban areas still live in these townships. They tend to be made up of large areas of small uniform houses with few local urban amenities. Many of the roads in township areas are not tarred, rubbish is strewn across the streets and air pollution is horrendous. In recent years there have been a proliferation of squatter camps within the townships on areas of open ground and many of the residential plots include not just the original house but a large number of additional shacks. These townships contrast sharply with the suburbs reserved for white populations during the Apartheid years. Houses in these areas are usually large, streets are clean and often tree-lined. The fear of crime means that in areas like Johannesburg's northern suburbs many of these houses look like mini-forts.

This pattern of residential segregation will remain for many years to come. A few rich Africans, coloureds and Indians have moved into formerly all white suburbs, but on the whole these middle-class groups tend to live in small richer enclaves in the townships. The major change in the pattern of residential segregation over the past decade or so has been the rebirth of inner city African housing, resulting in areas such as Hillbrow in Johannesburg.

Industry and infrastructure

Not surprisingly the pattern of industry and infrastructure has also been affected by Apartheid. Obviously industrial development has also been influenced by matters such as the proximity to raw materials but industrial development planning has also had an influence. The main industrial centre is Gauteng where the South African industrial revolution was centred around the gold mines on the Wit watersrand. Other important industrial centres are in the major coastal port cities of Cape Town, Port Elizabeth and Durban and around secondary mining centres in the Free State and Mpumalanga.

During the Apartheid years some efforts were made to decentralize industrialization in order to provide jobs for the African population in areas closer to the homelands. The idea was to try to prevent rural to urban migration amongst the African population and to foster the plan of overall segregation. On the whole these decentralization policies were unsuccessful, though a number of labour intensive industries, such as garment manufacturers, did relocate to the borders of homeland areas to take advantage of the low wages prevalent in these areas of high unemployment.

Infrastructural development tends to reflect the pattern of racial segregation. The major cities and the smaller towns and villages of the former white rural areas are well served by roads, railways and other economic infrastructure. The former homeland areas tend to be badly served by roads and railways and other infrastructure, such as piped water, is also lacking. This pattern will again take many years to rectify.

Books

Literature

South Africa has produced internationally recognized and award- winning novelists. Probably the best known is **John Coetzee**, whose novels include *Dusklands*, *In the Heart of the Country*, *Waiting for the Barbarians*, *Life & Times of Michael K* (winner of the 1983 Booker Prize), *Age of Iron*, *Foe* and *The Master of Petersburg*. He won the Booker Prize again in 1999 for his novel, *Disgrace*. His style is stark and intellectual, but surprisingly accessible. He is one of the most brilliant commentators on the effects of Apartheid.

Another award-winning South African novelist is **Nadine Gordimer**. Her novels include *A Guest of Honour*, *The Conservationist* (winner of the 1974 Booker Prize), *Burger's Daughter*, *July's People*, *A Sport of Nature*, *My Son's Story* and *None to Accompany Me*. Her beautifully written work tends to concentrate on the way wider political/social events impact on individual lives.

Bessie Head is a widely respected South African author, though much of her work is set in Botswana where she was exiled in 1964. She wrote 3 novels – *When Rain Clouds Gather*, *Maru* and the semi-autobiographical *A Question of Power*, a collection of short stories *The Collection of Treasures*, and a portrait of the Botswanan village where she lived and eventually died at the age of just 49, Serowe, *The Village of the Rain-wind*.

Andre Brink is another internationally recognized author who has published in both English and Afrikaans. His novels in English include *A Chain of Voices*, *The Ambassador*, *Looking on Darkness*, *Rumours of Rain*, *An Act of Terror* and *A Dry White Season* (made into a Hollywood film). Like Coetzee he has published extensively on literary criticism as well as his own fiction.

All of these authors are highly recommended though their work is not always easy going.

Tom Sharpe, an Englishman who lived in South Africa throughout the 1950s, represents a very different literary genre. His novels *Riotous Assembly* and *Indecent Exposure* are both hilarious and the absurd situations and characters he conjures up seem eminently believable in the South African context.

Another novelist representing a previous generation is **Alan Paton**, internationally recognized (though some find him sentimental) for his novel *Cry the Beloved Country* but he also published *Too Late the Phalarope* and *Ah, But Your Land is Beautiful* and a collection of short stories *Debbie Go Home*.

Another well-known South African novel is **Olive Schreiner**'s *The Story of an African Farm*. When it was first published in 1883 (under the pseudonym Ralph Iron) it received notoriety for its feminist and anti-racist message. **Rider Haggard** covered very different topics. His hugely popular novels *King Solomon's Mines* and *She* have a romantic theme with an African settingand and remain popular today.

The majority of the internationally recognized South African novelists described above are white. This does not mean that there is not a tradition of novel writing amongst South Africa's African, coloured and Indian populations. The 2 earliest African novelists in the country were **RRR Dhlomo**, who wrote *An African Tragedy* (1928) and **Sol Plaatje**, who wrote *Mhudi*, completed in 1917 but not published until 1930.

There has also been a strong emergence of modern black creative writing since the end of Apartheid. Perhaps the most important black writer today is **Zakes Mda**, who for many years worked as a playwright and poet before turning his hand to novels. His first 2 novels, *She Plays with Darkness* and *Ways of Dying*, place contemporary politics in the context of family and community in modern-day South Africa. His most recent novel, *The Heart of Redness*, won the Commonwealth prize and interlaces the present with the story of Nongqawuse, a princess who brought ruin to the Xhosa people. A young author who made a significant impact before tragically committing suicide in 2005 was **K. Sello Duiker**. His novels *Thirteen Cents* and *The Quiet Violence* explore street kids in Cape Town and the life of an ostracized gay student, respectively. An insight to the physical and moral decay of life in Hillbrow is provided by the critically-acclaimed **Phaswane Mpe** in *Our Hillbrow*.

Short stories have also been a fairly popular form of literature: interesting collections include *Hungry Flames and other Black South African Short Stories*, edited by **Mbulelo Mzamane**, Harlow, Longman, 1986 and *The Penguin Book of Contemporary South African Short Stories*, edited by **Stephen Gray**, London, Penguin, 1993.

Autobigraphy and political writing

The autobiography that has received most attention is **Nelson Mandela**'s *Long Walk to Freedom*, London, Little Brown, 1994, a fascinating insight into the struggle. A number of other ANC leaders have also published autobiographies, including a posthumous publication by **Joe Slovo**, *Slovo: the unfinished autobiography*, Randburg, Ravan Press, 1995. Previous African leaders who published autobiographies include: **ZK Matthews** *Freedom for my People: Southern Africa 1901-1968*, edited by Monica Wilson, London, Collins, 1981, and **Clements Kadalie** *My Life and the ICU: the Autobiography of a Black Trade Unionist in South Africa*, edited by Stanley Trapido, London, Cassell, 1970. Autobiographies tracing the lives of less famous South Africans include **Ezekiel Mphahlele**'s *Down Second Avenue* and *Afrika my Music: an Autobiography*, Johannesburg, Ravan Press, 1984, *Bloke Modisane Blame me on History*, London, Penguin, 1990, and the highly recommended *Call me Woman* by **Ellen Kuzwayo**, London, Women's Press, 1985. There have also been collections of political speeches, articles and other writing by major political figures such as **Steve Biko**'s *I Write what I Like*, edited by Aelred Stubbs, Edinburgh, Heinemann, 1987. Others have published diaries written while in prison, such as **Albie Sachs**'s *The Jail Diary of Albie Sachs*, London, Paladin, 1990. Another interesting diary is **Sol Plaatje's** *Mafeking Diary: a Black Man's View of a White Man's War*, edited by John L Comaroff, Johannesburg, Southern Book Publishers, 1989.

History and biography

Recommended biographies include: **Peter Alexander**'s biography of the South African novelist and well-known liberal Alan Paton, *Alan Paton*, (Oxford, OUP, 1994); **William Hancock**'s biography of Jan Smuts, *The Sanguine Years, 1870-1919* and *The Fields of Force 1919-1950 (Cambridge, CUP, 1962 and 1968);* **Richard Mendelsohn**'s biography of the businessman Sammy Marks, *Sammy Marks* (Cape Town, David Philip, 1991); **Antony Thomas**'s book on Cecil Rhodes, *Rhodes: The Face for Africa* (Johannesburg, Jonathan Ball, 1996); **Donald Woods**'s book on Steve Biko – the basis for the film *'Cry Freedom'* – *Biko* (London, Paddington Press, 1978); **Ruth First**'s biography of thenovelist, feminist and anti-racism campaigner *Olive Schreiner* (London, Women's Press, 1989); and finally **Brian Willan** on Sol Plaatje, the novelist and early African nationalist, *Sol Plaatje: South African Nationalist* 1876-1932 (London, Heinemann, 1984). Biography tends to be associated with the lives of 'great men': one that is not is **Charles Van Onselen**'s *The Seed is Mine: the Life of Kas Maine, a South African Sharecropper*, 1894-1985 (Oxford, James Curry, 1996) – it is a long book but fascinating and highly recommended. **Allister Sparks** *Beyond the Miracle* (University of Chicago Press, 2004), charters the country's first decade of democracy, giving a balanced view of the governments successes and failures. **Antjie Krog**'s *Country of My Skull* (Three Rivers Press, 2000), an national bestseller, is written by the head of the SABC reporting team during the Truth and Reconciliation Commission, providing an often harrowing picture of how the commission affected those involved.

Natural history and environment

Good guides to game parks and wildlife include: **Jean Dorst** and **Pierre Dandelot** *A Field Guide to the Larger Mammals of Africa* (London, Collins); **Gordon Maclean Roberts**' *Birds of South Africa* (Cape Town, CTP); **Kenneth Newman** *Newman's Birds of Southern Africa* (Struik Publishers, 2002); **CW Mackworth-Praed** and **CHB Grant** *Birds of the Southern third of Africa* (London, Longman, 1963) and **Eve Palmer** *Field Guide to the Trees of Southern Africa* (London, Collins, 1977). General books on the environment are: **Mamphela Ramphela** (ed) *Restoring the Land* (London, Panos, 1991), **Jacklyn Cock** and *Eddie Koch* (eds.) *Going Green: People, Politics and the Environment in South Africa* (Cape Town, OUP, 1991) and **Munyaradzi Chenje** and **Phyllis Johnson** (eds) *State of the Environment in Southern Africa* (Harare, SARDC, 1994).

Lesotho

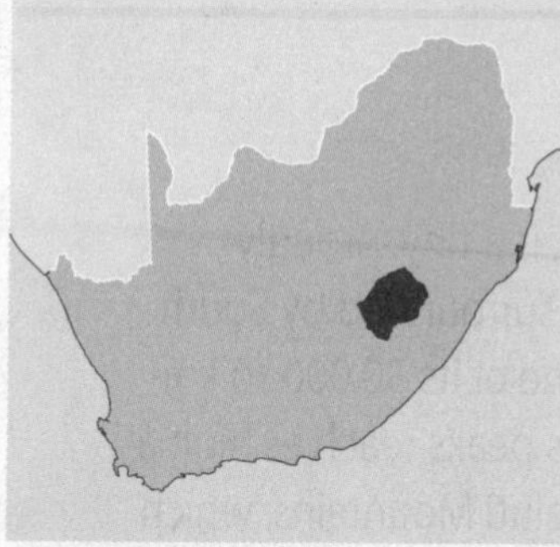

Footprint features

Introduction

Lesotho, the 'Kingdom in the Sky', is a tiny, proudly independent country completely surrounded by South Africa. Its nickname is apt – not one of its 30,000 sq km lies below 1000 m and many of its peaks reach as high as 3480 m. It is dominated by the Maluti Mountains, which cover three-quarters of the country, with the dramatic Drakensberg escarpment forming the eastern side and the border with KwaZulu Natal. To the west the land flattens out somewhat into what is know as the Lowlands. Here are most of the kingdom's towns, the small capital of Maseru, the richest agricultural land and where the majority of the population lives.

Lesotho's mountain scenery is markedly different from any of South Africa's landscapes: the mountains are more rugged, the lower slopes drier and the villages maintain a traditional subsistence lifestyle. Tourism is still in its infancy here, and heading even a little of the beaten track will allow a fascinating insight into time-honoured Lesotho customs. Herder boys roam about the mountains and farmers travel on horseback, swaddled in traditional blankets. The country's lack of fences also provides excellent hiking conditions, while trekking with mountain ponies opens up some of the most remote areas of the country.

★ Don't miss...

1 **Thaba Bosiu** Climb the mountain stronghold of the founder of the Basotho nation, Chief Moshoeshoe, page 771.

2 **Maletsunyane Falls** Take a walk from Semongkong to the highest single drop falls in southern Africa at 192 m, page 773.

3 **The road to Katse Dam** Drive from Hlotse along this spectacular and newly tarred road to take in the sweeping views from 3000 m, page 781.

4 **Morija Arts and Cultural Festival** Get into the swing of Basotho culture at the annual festival, page 783.

5 **Pony trekking** Explore the mountains from Malealea Lodge, without doing the hard work yourself, page 786.

Essentials

Planning your trip

Where to go

The most logical entry point from the east of South Africa's Free State is via the capital **Maseru**, which warrants no more than a couple of hours before venturing further into the mountains. On the day of arrival it is quite feasible to visit Maseru and perhaps a couple of the surrounding attractions such as the museum at **Morja** or the mountain at **Thaba-Bosiu**, before driving on to one of the mountain retreats in the south of Lesotho such as **Malealea** or **Semonkong** before nightfall. A few days at one of these resorts will allow you to take in a hike or pony ride, perhaps visit a waterfall or Basotho village, and enjoy the clean mountain air.

For those with more time, another day or two could be spent exploring the small towns of the Lowveld linked by a good tarred road and frequent minibuses. Lesotho's greatest attraction though is the **highlands**, and the real highlight here is to drive through one of three spectacular roads: the mountain road from Maseru to **Thaba-Tseka**; the new tarred road from **Hlotse** to **Katse Dam**; and the roof of Africa road between **Butha-Buthe** and **Mokhotlong**. All of these roads are in good enough condition during the drier months to attempt in a normal saloon car. If you have a 4WD, the last two routes can be linked in a full circle by the road between Mokhotlong and Thaba-Tseka – this is the Roof of Africa Rally route. All of these routes can be negotiated by bus or taxi though they run less frequently than in the Lowlands so some planning ahead is needed. There's another stunning drive in the far south of the country between **Moyeni (Quthing)** and **Qacha's Nek** and beyond to the **Sehlabathebe National Park**, but this is rough country and only advised for experienced drivers and sections are only suitable for 4WDs.

Depending on where you approach Lesotho, three to four days is enough time to head straight for a pony trekking and hiking centre, but at least a week to 10 days is needed to combine this with a few days travelling through the highlands. If you only have a day than take an informative day trip up the **Sani Pass** from KwaZulu Natal on the South African side.

When to go

About 85% of Lesotho's rainfall occurs in the summer months (December to February) when it also gets fairly hot, particularly in the Lowlands, though the rain turns untarred highland roads into rivers of mud. Mid-winter is popular with South Africans who are attracted by the novelty of seeing snow in the mountains, though again this is not a good time for driving as the roads are slippery with ice, nor good for hiking or pony trekking as the temperatures drop below freezing at night. On the very upper reaches of the Maluti Mountains, snow occurs all year round. The spring or autumn months (October to November and March to May) are the best times of the year to visit, when skies are clear and temperatures warm.

Language

Lesotho has two official languages, Sesotho which is spoken everywhere and English. Both are taught in schools from the fifth year of primary education so while English is spoken in Maseru and the bigger towns, in remote areas there will usually be somebody, often a school child, who speaks at least some English.

Kingdom of Lesotho missions overseas

Belgium, Boulevard General Wahis 45, Brussels, T+32 (0)2-7053976.
Denmark, Strandvejen 64H, Copenhagen, T+45 3962 4343.
Germany, Dessauer Strasse 28/29, Berlin 10963, T+49 (0)30-257 5720.
South Africa, 391 Anderson St, Menlo Park, Pretoria 0001, T012-460 7640.
UK, 7 Chesham Place, Belgravia, London, T+44 (0)20 7235 5686.
USA, 2511 Massachussets Av, Washington DC 20008, T+1 202-797 5533.

Before you travel

Visas and immigration

Holders of the following passports do not require visas for Lesotho: South Africa, Denmark, Sweden, Norway, Finland, Ireland, United Kingdom, Germany, France, Italy, Switzerland, the Netherlands, Canada, Israel and Japan. Others such as Australia, New Zealand, USA, Belgium and Austria do need visas.

People not requiring a visa will be given a one month permit with their entry stamp, although it is possible to ask for longer if you have proof of funds. To extend your permit, go to the **Lesotho Immigration Department** ⓘ *Transport Building, Assissi Rd, Maseru, T2231 7339*. It's also worth asking at the larger border posts if they will extend it for you. Visitors who require a visa can wait until they are in South Africa and then contact the **Lesotho High Commission** ⓘ *391 Anderson St, corner of Anderson and Thomas Edison Sts, Menlo Park, Pretoria 0001, T012-4607648, lesotho@global.co.za, visa office Mon-Fri 0900-1200*, or in a few cases contact the Lesotho Overseas High Commission in their own country, see box, above. When applying for a visa you must fill in an application form and provide a passport photo; processing takes 24 hours. A single entry, valid for one month, costs R400. Remember that when going back to South Africa from Lesotho, the immigration officials on the South Africa side will restamp your existing South African entry stamp so a quick border hop is not a way to extend your stay in South Africa. If your South Africa stamp has expired while in Lesotho they will give you a one- to two-week temporary stamp to allow enough time to go to one of the Department of Home Affairs offices in South Africa and extend it officially. See www.home-affairs.gov.za, to find out the nearest office.

Vaccinations

If arriving from tropical African countries you may be asked for a Yellow Fever vaccination card.

Money

Currency

Lesotho's standard unit of currency is the Maloti, divided into 100 lisente. It is exactly equivalent to the Rand, and the two are interchangeable, so you can pay in either currency. Bring sufficient Rand with you from South Africa, as this will considerably reduce money changing hassles. While the Rand is interchangeable with the Maloti in Lesotho this is not the case in South Africa. If you are due to leave Lesotho in a few days, try to get change in Rand and when you change money ask for the cash in rand.

In this chapter, Lesotho telephone numbers are given as they should be dialled within Lesotho. South African numbers are given as they should be dialled within South Africa. Other numbers are shown with their international code. See also page 765.

Exchange

Banks There are four main banks in Lesotho, the **First National Bank, Lesotho Bank 1999, Nedbank** and **Standard Bank**. All change money, although it usually involves filling out paperwork and long queues. There are now several ATM machines in Maseru, which offer a hassle-free way of getting hold of local currency. See box, page 759 for bank opening hours. Outside Maseru, most banks do not have a separate foreign exchange counter. Avoid changing money on Fridays as this is when many local people get paid, so the queues can be enormous.

! It is illegal to change money on the black market.

Credit cards These are accepted at the large international Sun hotels and can be used at ATM machines in Maseru. Some of the main branches of the banks in Maseru can advance local currency off a credit card, but this is lengthy process. Outside Maseru they are of little use.

Getting there

Air

Moshoeshoe I International Airport is 21 km south of Maseru along the Main South Road. Since the liquidation of Lesotho Air several years ago, **South African Airways,** (SAA), T011-9781111, www.flysaa.com, has been operating the route between Moshoeshoe I International Airport and Johannesburg International Airport. There are three flights per day in each direction taking 1 hour 10 minutes. There is a M20 departure tax on international flights when you leave Lesotho.

Road

As very few people visit Lesotho without also going to South Africa, the most common way of entering and leaving is by road. There is a R5 entry and R2 departure tax on all vehicles.

Overland entry is via the following border posts: **Calendonspoort** ⓘ *T051-9335674/5 (South Africa), daily 0600-2200*, is close to the town of Butha-Buthe and the South African town of Fouriesburg and is the logical border post for visitors arriving in their own transport from Gauteng or northern KwaZulu Natal. **Ficksburg/Maputsoe Bridge** ⓘ *T051-9332760 (South Africa), 24 hours daily*, is close to Ficksburg on the South African side and is one of the busiest crossings used by most of the mineworkers returning from the Witwatersrand. **Maseru Bridge** ⓘ *T051-9244002 (South Africa), 24 hours daily*, is the crossing used by visitors arriving from Bloemfontein. This border post is usually less crowded than Ficksburg/Maputsoe Bridge, so if you have your own transport and are going straight to Maseru, you might find it quicker to use the South African Ficksburg–Ladybrand road and cross at Maseru Bridge. **Van Rooyen's** ⓘ *T051-5831613 (South Africa), daily 0600-2200*, is between Mafeteng and the small Free State town of Wepener. **Makhaleen Bridge** ⓘ *T051-6731484 (South Africa), daily 0800-1800*, is close to Mohales Hoek and on the South African road to Zastron. The southernmost border crossing at **Tele Bridge** ⓘ *daily 0600-2200*, is close to the town of Quthing/Moyeni and joins up with South African roads to Sterkspruit, Lady Grey and other small Eastern Cape towns.

There are five road crossings from the eastern mountains of Lesotho into the uKhahlamba-Drakensberg National Park. **Monontsa Pass** ⓘ *T058-7131600 (South Africa), daily 0800-1600*, is a little-used crossing between the Lesotho settlement of Libono and the South African village of Phuthaditjaba near to the Golden Gate National Park in the Free State. This is the most northerly border crossing and can only be accessed by 4WD. **Sani Pass** ⓘ *T033-7021169 (South Africa), daily 0800-1600*, is a well-known scenic crossing, with poor roads only passable by 4WDs. **Qachas Nek**

Touching down

- **Business hours** **Banks**: Mon-Fri 0900-1530, Sat 0830/0900 to 1030/1100. **Businesses**: Mon-Fri 0830-1700, Sat 0830-1400. **Government offices**: Mon-Fri 0830-1300 and 1400-1630 **Post offices**: Mon-Fri 0830-1600, Sat 0800-1200. **Shops**: Mon-Fri 0800-1800, Sat 0800-1300, Sun 0900-1300.
- **IDD code** +266
- **Official time** 2 hrs ahead of GMT, 7 hrs ahead of eastern USA standard time, 1 hr ahead of Europe; 8 hrs behind Australian Eastern Standard Time.
- **Voltage** 220/230 volts AC at 50 Hz.
- **Weights and measures** The metric system is used.

ⓘ *daily 0700-2000*, was partly tarred at time of writing and traffic here is increasing. Two border crossings into the Drakensberg are totally unmanned on the Lesotho side and you can only walk or ride a horse across them: **Ongeluksnek** ⓘ *T039-2567001 (South Africa), daily 0800-1600*, and **Nkonkoana/Bushman's Nek** ⓘ *T033-7011212 (South Africa), daily 0800-1600*. If you enter Lesotho at either of these, you are required to present yourself at the nearest immigration office in Qachas Nek or Quthing to complete formalities.

As Lesotho is part of the Customs Union, visitors with South African registered vehicles do not need a Temporary Import Permit (TIP) or Carnet de Passages en Douanes. South African third party insurance is valid in Lesotho, but if in a hire car from South Africa check that your insurance covers Lesotho; some car rental companies don't include it because of Lesotho's poor road conditions (although most, these days, do). You might also need a letter of authorization from the rental company giving you permission to take the car into Lesotho. Visitors with vehicles registered outside the Customs Union will need to purchase a TIP at the border. Driving licences issued in countries outside Lesotho are valid for up to six months, provided they are printed in English or are accompanied by a certified translations. International Diving Licences are also recognized.

Touching down

Tourist information

The **Ministry of Tourism** has an office on the 7th floor of the New Post Office Building in Maseru, T22313034. The official government website for Lesotho is www.lesotho.gov.ls, which has good general information for tourists. For information about the Lesotho Highlands Water Project, visit www.lhwp.org.ls; the site also has information about the new national parks. The **Lesotho Tourist Board Office** in the Basotho Shield building, on central Kingsway in Maseru, T22312427, www.ltdc.org.ls, is extremely helpful and stocks a range of brochures and maps. If you are crossing into the country through Maseru Bridge be sure to drop in at the **Moloti Tourist Office** in Ladybrand, which also covers Lesotho in its jurisdiction (see page 657).

Local customs and laws

Greetings are very important in Sesotho culture. It is considered very rude if you do not formally greet people before addressing them and, except on busy town streets, people will expect you to greet them if you are simply passing them on a street or path. A simple "hello" will suffice – *"lumela"*. Remember not to take photographs of any Royal building or the airport, and naturally always ask first if you want to photograph people.

Getting around

Road

Many of Lesotho's roads are currently being upgraded to tarmac – ask at the tourist office for the latest developments. The main route running north-south along the lowland strip is tarred and in good repair. Other tarred routes include the road from Maseru to Roma, Maseru to Mohale Dam, Leribe/Hlotso to Katse dam, and Butha-Buthe to Mokhotlong. The quality of gravel roads varies considerably: the 'mountain road' to Thaba Tseke and the road to Semonkong are both in good condition while the routes from Thaba Tseke to Mokhotlong or Qacha's Nek are very poor in parts and get very slippery in the wet.

Petrol is readily available in the lowland centres but if you are travelling into the mountains make sure you have plenty of fuel before you leave. Distances between filling stations are long and supplies are not always reliable. You will definitely need to put anti-freeze in your car radiator in the colder months as it can freeze overnight.

Car If driving yourself through Lesotho, take local advice regarding the time a journey may take, and the possible need for 4WD and chains. The tourist office in Maseru can assist with this and can give detailed instructions of the exact route to be taken. Remember that while there have been major improvements to Lesotho's roads in recent years, all road conditions deteriorate rapidly after heavy rains, they get icy in the cooler months, and some may be blocked by snow in the winter. It is worth considering carefully what time of the year to go if you are driving. It's recommended that you carry two spare wheels and a couple of spare inner tubes if possible, though many of the villages offer cheap tyre-mending services.

Road safety in Lesotho usually leaves a lot to be desired, as the death of the King in an accident in 1996 on the Main South Road indicates. Taxi drivers are often in direct competition for passengers so rush to get to stops ahead of other drivers – which often means they take huge risks. Be especially careful when driving behind taxis as they often brake sharply to pick up passengers. Drink driving is also a problem, especially at weekends, bank holidays and at the end of the month when people have just been paid. It is probably best to avoid driving at these times. Wear your seat belt at all times; occasionally the police will use this as an excuse for imposing a fine. Always be wary of pedestrians, cyclists and livestock at the sides of the road.

Taxis and buses The lowland towns and villages are linked together by a regular and cheap (if hair-raising) taxi service. These consist of minibuses with about 16 seats or sometimes, in remote districts, of converted 4WDs. There is no set timetable for taxis; they simply set off when they are full. It is important to remember, however, that taxis stop running very early in the evening and it is more or less impossible to get one after sunset. There is very little space for baggage. The first passengers to arrive get the most comfortable seats next to the driver, though the downside is that you'll have a full view of Lesotho driving habits. Unlike most of South Africa, people talk to each other in taxis.

Larger buses cover the longer routes, especially over the gravel mountain roads. To most towns there is at least one bus a day to and from Maseru or another larger lowland centre. They usually leave about 0900 or 1000 but timetables vary with the number of passengers.

Hitching As taxis are cheap and frequent and most drivers will charge the same fare as a taxi anyway, hitchhiking in the lowlands is not usually worth the trouble. In more remote areas more or less every passing vehicle acts as a de facto taxi service –

somewhat blurring the distinction between hitching and taking a taxi. There are certain routes, however, where hitchhiking is the only alternative to walking, for example over Sani Pass into KwaZulu Natal or from Qacha's Nek into the Eastern Cape. If you are hitchhiking in the mountains make sure you have a jacket or blanket (or both) to hand – most lifts will be on the back of a pick-up or a truck and it can get very cold, especially on winter evenings. Although it's usually safe to hitchhike in Lesotho, remember to avoid hitchhiking alone.

Other transport Horses and ponies are the main form of transport other than foot for most Basotho in the mountains. You can hire ponies from a number of centres.

Sleeping

Hotels

Most main centres have one or two formal and rather soulless hotels. These often look dilapidated from the outside but are usually kept reasonably clean inside. They rarely have more than a handful of guests, so you are usually able to benefit from close attention from hotel staff. Nearly all of them have restaurants and they are often the only choice for eating, but don't expect anything other than plates of basic chicken and rice or stew and pap. As these hotels are often the centre of local nightlife for local professionals it is usually best to ask for a room away from the bar area, especially at weekends. Cheaper accommodation can be found in various farming training centres, missions, or education centres. In these you'll usually get a dorm bed, a (not always hot) shower, and perhaps a simple meal. Most are very basic but nonetheless friendly and very cheap. Lesotho has a number of well-run lodges in the mountains and foothills that provide excellent value accommodation, namely the **Trading Post, Semonkong Lodge, New Oxbow Lodge** and the **Malealea Lodge.** These are a much better alternative to the bland town hotels and it is in these resorts that you are going to get the most out of a visit to Lesotho as they also organize hiking and pony trekking.

Maseru has two international standard hotels (both part of the **Sun** chain). Neither are outstanding, but they are comfortable with a range of facilities, though expensive. There are few budget travellers' hostels in Maseru and what are available are not very nice. For the budget traveller, it is a good idea to arrive in Maseru early in the morning, spend the day in the city before heading out to cheaper accommodation in the outlying districts, some of which is only 20-30 km away. This avoids having to pay the high prices for the city hotels. Remember that most accommodation outside Maseru only accepts cash for payment.

Camping

Away from the main towns, camping is very easy if you are completely self-sufficient. You should always get permission to set up camp from the chief of the nearest village. Apart from the obvious courtesy, getting permission can also be to your advantage: you may be offered space in one of the village huts or allocated a young boy to guard your equipment. You should not pass up the opportunity of staying in a village hut: you will often be offered a fascinating experience, though a small payment should be offered.

In the densely populated lowlands it is more difficult to find a suitable camping site and you also run the risk of losing your belongings to the crowds of children who inevitably gather. Ask around at the churches and missions for permission to camp in their grounds or at the local police station.

Eating

Food

Every village will have a small shop selling basic tinned and dried foods. The larger villages have basic supermarkets, though more luxury items and fresh food like cheese or vegetables and fruit (other than those grown locally) can only be found in supermarkets in major towns, or should be purchased in South Africa prior to coming to Lesotho. Maize is the staple food of most Basotho. It is usually made into a stiff porridge, *pap*, and eaten with stew twice or even three times a day. It is fairly tasteless but if properly cooked and accompanied by a flavoursome stew it is enjoyable and very filling. Poorer households, however, generally eat plain *pap*.

In the mountain areas where wheat is grown, bread forms an important part of the staple diet. The bread is baked in huge saucepans greased with mutton fat over fires – delicious.

In most towns, a profusion of street vendors can be found selling a wide variety of goods from homemade fried cakes called *makoenya* to pap and barbecued meat. Outside Maseru most restaurants serve boring but filling meals. Vegetarians will have a very limited choice. After experiencing excellent high levels of service in restaurants in South Africa, you may find the pace somewhat slower in Lesotho. Rather than complaining, try to enjoy the laid-back atmosphere.

Drinking

All the major South African beers are available throughout the country and there is also a decent commercial local variety, **Maluti Beer**. Maize beer is brewed by many women as an additional source of income: a white flag (usually made from a faded maize bag) is hung outside the house when this beer is for sale. The beer has a thick, almost porridge-like, head and is usually not enjoyed by visitors, though it is well worth the experience. South African wine can be purchased in Maseru and some of the larger towns but is not widely drunk by Basotho. Whisky is popular and sold at many bars.

Festivals and events

Public holidays

New Year's Day 1 January; **Moshoeshoe's Day** 11 March; **Hero's Day** 4 April; **Good Friday**; **Easter Monday**; **Workers' Day** 1 May; **King's Birthday** 17 July; **National Independence Day** 4 October; **Christmas Day** 25 December; **Boxing Day** 26 December.

Festivals

Morja Arts and Cultural Festival 1 October.

Sport and activities

Hiking

As all land in Lesotho is owned 'by the nation' there are very few fences and certainly none outside the densely inhabited lowland towns and villages. This makes walking in Lesotho a unique experience – you can effectively walk anywhere you choose.

The mountains are criss-crossed by numerous footpaths and bridle tracks, but by no means all of them are shown on even the best maps. The physical geography of the country means that most routes consist of long level stretches on either the plateaux tops or valley bottoms interspersed by very steep ascents and descents – this should obviously be borne in mind when planning routes. Maps (1:50,000 and

Herd boys

Hiking in the remote mountains you will come across almost no-one except for occasional herd boys that shepherd their goats or cattle to the highest pastures on the mountains. These boys are sometimes as young as 11-12 and spend much of their young lives roaming the countryside. If a hiker suddenly appears over the horizon, they get very excited and are likely to badger you over quite some distance. While it is true that some of the herd boys are a fairly lawless bunch and some are involved in crime – usually either stock theft or *dagga* (marijuana) growing and dealing – many herd boys are actually very lonely and only too pleased for any company, though as they very rarely ever go to school they do not speak any English. Care should be taken, however, when approaching the cattle post where herd boys live; they often have dogs that are trained to go for any unknown passers-by as a guard against stock theft.

1:25,000) can be bought from the **Department of Lands, Surveys and Physical Planning** ⓘ *Lerotholi Rd, Maseru, T22322376*. For more practical hints on hiking in Southern Africa's mountain areas, see page 444.

For much of the year the mountain skies are clear and the air crisp. Rain, snow and low cloud can close in very rapidly, however, and you should go equipped for these eventualities. Heavy snowfalls have, in the past, resulted in hikers being trapped in remote areas and having to be rescued by South African military helicopters. People planning adventurous hikes should bring equipment with them as it is not readily available in Lesotho.

Lesotho offers some of the most challenging and remote hiking terrains in Southern Africa.

Some hikers entering Lesotho from South Africa stick to the highest and uninhabited peaks along the Drakensberg escarpment. While these routes cover some of the most beautiful scenery in southern Africa they exclude one of the major joys of hiking in Lesotho – meeting local people. Plan routes that include sections in the mountain valleys as well as the high peaks. People in the mountain villages are usually very pleased to see outsiders and will often offer them places to sleep and food: indeed, the hospitality is sometimes overwhelming. **Semonkong Lodge, Trading Post Adventures** and **Malealea Lodge** (see below, and pages 774 and 786), organize hikes.

Mountain pony trekking

The Basotho are renowned as a nation of horsemen, and for generations the strong Basotho pony has been bred as the ideal form of transport in the rugged mountains. A cross between a European full mount and short Javanese horses, the first ponies were captured from the invading Griqua people in the early 1800s. Gentle and extremely sure-footed, they are ideal for people who have not sat on a horse before. Pony trekking centres have a number of tours that take you through the magnificent scenery, ranging from one hour to six days with overnight stops in local villages, mountain lodges and campsites. Don't expect mad gallops across open spaces; much of the trekking goes up and down steep and rocky mountainsides, where the ponies pick out a route, often sidestepping or following the course of a mountain stream. It is quite extraordinary how these strong little ponies cope with the terrain. Ponies can be organized from a number of establishments but the two main pony trekking centres are: **Malealea Lodge,** T051-4473200 (South Africa), www.malealea.co.ls (see page 774); **Trading Post Adventures,** T22340202, www.tradingpost.co.za (see page 773), and **Semonkong Lodge,** T051-9333106 (South Africa), www.placeofsmoke.co.ls (see page 774).

Removing the stigma

Lesotho has the third highest infection rate of HIV/AIDS in the world – an estimated 30,000 people died of the disease in 2003 alone. In late 2005, the government introduced a US$12 million programme to offer free AIDS tests for everyone – the first country in the world to offer tests to its entire population. The first person to take a public test at the launch of the programme was King Letsie III, who did so at a clinic in Maseru. Authorities hope that this gesture will go some way towards removing the stigma associated with HIV/AIDS, thus encouraging those that test positive to get the treatment they need.

Trout fishing

A popular sport with visitors to Lesotho is fishing, and there are good accessible sites including: the **Malibamat'so River** near Oxbow Lodge, the **Khubelu** in Mokhotlong district and the upstream sections of **Mokhotlong River** itself; the **Tsoelikane River** in and around Sehlabathebe National Park; and the **Makhalaneng River** near Molimo-Nthuse Lodge. There are also two well-stocked dams near **Thaba Tseka.** There are many other excellent sites, though these are often only accessible via long treks on foot or horseback. During the rainy season (summer) rivers tend to be very silty and fishing is badly affected. The trout fishing season is from 1 September to 31 May, when there is a daily limit of 12 trout over 30 cm imposed on fishermen. Permits and further information about good sites and regulations can be obtained from the **Ministry of Agriculture** ⓘ *Parliament St, Maseru, T266316407*.

Other sports

Other outdoor sports such as **hang gliding** and **kayaking** are possible for the experienced, but no organized facilities exist within Lesotho, although there are plans for a kayaking facility at Mohale Dam. Gentle **river rafting** trips are available at Malealea Lodge in the summer months only.

Health

Its high altitude makes Lesotho a healthier place than many African countries. Malaria is non-existent and other tropical diseases are rare. There are, nevertheless, many health risks that visitors need to consider. Water-borne microbes often cause **diarrhoea** and care should be taken to boil or purify drinking water. As livestock and herd boys are often found in even the highest areas great care should be taken in using water from mountain streams. In rural areas, milk is often unpasteurized so tea and coffee is served with boiled milk – if it isn't boiled, take it black.

HIV/AIDS is perhaps the country's biggest challenge today (see box, above). Blood products and medical equipment in the main hospital should be safe, but in smaller clinics there are no guarantees. If you plan to travel to remote areas, take a sterilized medical pack but make sure it is clearly marked with an official hospital stamp to avoid suspicion of intravenous drug use.

Some visitors to the highest mountain areas may feel short of breath, tired and dizzy, especially if they arrive via Sani Pass from the coast. It's best to acclimatize and gradually work your way into the mountains over a couple of days. People with fair skin should be aware of sunburn; it might feel cool, but the sun can be strong in the rarefied air of the mountains; always wear sunscreen and a hat.

Keeping in touch

Communications

Internet facilities are only available in Maseru, in offices next to the **Basotho Hat** craft shop, and at the Maseru Sun Hotel. The main **post office** is on central Kingsway in Maseru, where you will spend a very long time in a queue to purchase a stamp. The international postal service is fairly quick and reliable. The local **telephone** system is reasonable in the lowlands but there is poor coverage in the mountain areas. There are no area codes. The international code for Lesotho is +266. International calls are very expensive and only possible to make from the larger centres. It is possible to send telegrams from all post offices. Note that some accommodation options In Lesotho have reservation telephone numbers in South Africa; if you are calling these in Lesotho, you must dial the country's access code (00) followed by the international code for South Africa (27). Mobile phone reception is improving steadily and you'll be surprised to find you can pick up reception in the most remote places. This is largely due to the fact that a number of mobile phone towers have been put in place in outlying areas during the Lesotho Highlands Water Project.

Media

Lesotho TV has news and current affairs programmes that are broadcast (in Sesotho) every evening at 1800, and South African TV channels are available at the larger hotels that have satellite dishes. The BBC World Service has a relay station near Maseru, and there are five local radio stations, three of which broadcast primarily in English.

Maseru

→ *Colour map 4, grid B4.*

Maseru must be one of the world's sleepiest capital cities – though in comparison to the rest of the country life here seems almost frantic. The city centre straggles along the Clarendon River, with most of the shops, offices, hotels and restaurants strung along one long central street, called Kingsway. Even this main road is surprisingly quiet, however, with the languid pace of life broken only by beeping minibus taxis. Although largely modern and unremarkable with very sights, it is a pleasant enough place for a wander and a good spot to soak up the vibrant feel of an African town. The Basotho people are outstandingly friendly, and it's not uncommon for people to approach you in the street simply to ask how you are and where you come from. During the day, moreover, safety isn't an issue (although it's best to avoid wandering around after dark, particularly around the eastern end of Kingsway). Approaching from the rural farmland on the South African side, the city centre appears unexpectedly and even the newer tower blocks look pretty behind the numerous trees of the more affluent suburbs above the river. In the other direction, the city sprawls for miles of poorer, often unplanned, suburbs. » *For Sleeping, Eating and other listings, see pages 767-770.*

Ins and outs

Getting there

Moshoeshoe I International Airport is 27 km south of Maseru along the Main South Road. There are buses or taxis to most centres in Lesotho. Long distance buses depart from the **bus station** about 500 m along the Main South Road from Cathedral Circle. The main bus and taxi station is on and around Market Street one block from Cathedral

1998 riots and the torching of the Basotho Hut

The only blip in Maseru's history happened in 1998, when the results of the general election sparked a dispute. The election was won by the Lesotho Congress of Democrats party who claimed almost all of the seats. This led to calls of vote rigging by the opposition who called for fresh elections. The government refused and the opposition began a long-running protest. The Southern African Development Community (SADC) became involved in mediation, but with the military becoming restive, Prime Minister Mosisili appealed to SADC to send in troops to prevent a military coup. South African troops entered Lesotho in September 1998 and confusion spread throughout the country as most people did not know exactly what was going on and were under the mistaken impression that South Africa was invading Lesotho. In response, there were widespread riots and the South African shops in Maseru and some of the other larger towns were looted and a large number of commercial buildings burnt down. In Maseru, one of these included the landmark Basotho Hat, a craft shop built to resemble Lesotho's famous straw hat. Its large conical thatched roof must have made quite a bonfire. The South African troops quickly restored order and promptly left the country.

Circle where buses for the towns in the Lowveld depart, and from where taxis depart randomly to all centres in the country. » *For further details, see Transport, page 769.*

Getting around

Despite recent growth, the city is easily navigated on foot. If you're in a car, there is parking outside the shopping centres, in a guarded carpark behind the Besotho Hat building, and in front of the tourist office. A fairly constant stream of minibus taxis moves up and down Kingsway from Cathedral Circle down to the border post.

Tourist information

The **Lesotho Tourist Board Office** ⓘ *Basotho Shield building, central Kingsway (opposite the Basotho Hat building; both are hard to miss thanks to their huge thatched roofs), T22312427, www.ltdc.org.ls*, is extremely helpful and welcoming, with a wide range of leaflets on accommodation, national parks and tour operators. They also produce a useful official brochure, with info and addresses on sights and accommodation. The staff can assist with advice on road conditions, and the best routes around the country. If you are crossing into the country through Maseru Bridge, drop in at the **Moloti Tourist Office** in Ladybrand which also covers Lesotho in its jurisdiction. (See Free State chapter, page 657, for details.)

Background

Maseru was founded in 1869 when Lesotho's second colonial leader, Commandant JH Bowker, sited his headquarters at this strategically important site overlooking a good fording point on the Clarendon. Shortly afterwards the first traders were also established, on the site now occupied by the Lancer's Inn. In the early years the city grew only very slowly and up to independence in 1966 the city centre underwent few changes. The main street was only tarred when King George VI visited in 1947 (when it was also renamed Kingsway) and by the mid-1960s there were still no buildings over two storeys.

Since the 1960s the city has grown rapidly, both in terms of population and urban development. Along central Kingsway there are modern office and shopping buildings holding the same high street shops as you'll find in urban South Africa.

Sights

There are very few sights worth visiting. There is nothing of architectural significance, though a couple of buildings are interesting for historical reasons. In front of **Lancer's Inn**, on Central Kingsway, is **St John's Church**. Built in 1912 the small church's interior has a number of inscriptions to some of Maseru's more important past residents.

Behind the Lesotho **National Bank Tower** is a park, which houses a statue of **Moshoeshoe I**, the founder of the Basotho nation. It was unveiled in 1976 to mark 10 years of independence. To the north of Kingsway and along Constitution and Parliament roads there are many of the main government departments, mostly in colonial sandstone one-storey buildings.

The newer **parliament** building is at the far end of Parliament Road and is a fairly impressive modern structure in well-maintained grounds.

Sleeping

Maseru *p765, map p768*

For a capital city, Maseru has very few hotels, or indeed eating and drinking venues.

AL Lesotho Sun, off Nightingale Rd, behind Queen Elizabeth Hospital, T22313111, www.suninternational.com. The most luxurious hotel in Lesotho, on a hilltop setting overlooking town. Large, modern, with 194 a/c rooms with satellite TV, great city views, simple bathrooms and comfortable brown and faux-African decor. There are 2 popular bars, a smoky attached casino, 2 good restaurants, gym, massage room, outdoor swimming pool with a pleasant terrace, a shopping arcade with internet café, and a cinema showing nightly films. Transfers to and from the airport available.

A Maseru Sun, 12 Orpen Rd, T22312434, www.suninternational.com. The other luxury choice in town, also part of the Sun International Chain, smaller than the **Lesotho Sun**, but modern with 115 a/c rooms, all with South African TV and good standard decor. Restaurant, 2 bars, gym, sauna, swimming pool, tennis courts, internet facilities at the office next to the front gate. Small casino with slot machines attached.

B Hotel Victoria, central Kingsway, T22313687, hotelvictoria@leo.co.ls. Recently refurbished, housed in a modern multi-storey in the centre of town. Comfortable, contemporary rooms with a/c, TV. Popular, if slightly dreary, restaurant serving international dishes, bar. Good central location, popular with business travellers.

B Lancer's Inn, central Kingsway, T22312114. Historical hotel bang in the centre of town, with 21 rooms, some self-catering, and a few cosy en suite rondavels in the garden. 2 popular bars, gym, decent restaurant, bakery, bottle store, swimming pool, relaxed atmosphere. It was upgraded fairly recently, as it was totally looted during the 1998 riots.

B Mpilo Lodge, Maluti Rd, off Kingsway, T58859499, mpilo@ilesotho.com. Family-run guesthouse on the western outskirts of town, a low-key alternative. 15 spacious en suite rooms, with satellite TV and telephones, simple tiled floors and vaguely African theme. Restaurant and bar with views over the golf course and mountains.

F Anglican Mission Training Centre, Assissi Rd, T22322046. One of the few places in town offering backpacker accommodation, with rather bare twin rooms with shared bathrooms. Usually used by church groups.

Eating

Maseru *p765, map p768*

Various international chains are springing up around town, including a **Steers**, opposite the post office, and a **KFC**, just north of Cathedral Circle. There are street vendors all along Kingsway and around the taxi station selling the staple Basotho meal of stiff maize porridge (pap) and stew, or roasted maize.

Lehaha Grill, Lesotho Sun Hotel, Nightingale Rd, T22313111. The main à la carte restaurant in the basement of the hotel, popular with Maseru's richer residents. Rather grand, if slightly faded decor, but very friendly service and decent meals, including Lesotho trout and traditional stewed oxtail. Reservations necessary at weekends and public holidays. Recommended.

The Regal, next door to the Basotho Hat craft shop, T22313730. Vaguely oriental décor in this international restaurant, serving good value lunches (chicken with chips or pap, plus toasted sandwiches) and steaks or grills in the evenings. Very friendly service, and excellent coffee served all day.

Rendezvous, Lancer's Inn, Kingsway, T22312114. Popular restaurant, with a vaguely African theme, serving standard international dishes. Some outside seating in the garden.

China Garden, LNDC shopping centre, closed Sun, T22313915. Reasonable Chinese food, catering in part for the city's burgeoning Chinese populations. Central location, service is notoriously slow but the food isn't bad. Popular early evening bar attached.

Bars and clubs

Maseru *p765, map p768*

The few bars are either attached to the big hotels or to restaurants. The small public bar at **Lancer's Inn** is often referred to as the alternative Parliament; it is frequented by a regular clientele of (male) civil servants, teachers and lecturers from the National University and newcomers will often be quizzed about their political opinions. The lounge bar has a more relaxed atmosphere, especially for women, and there are a couple of pool tables; ignore the sign that says the bar is for hotel residents only – everybody

Maseru

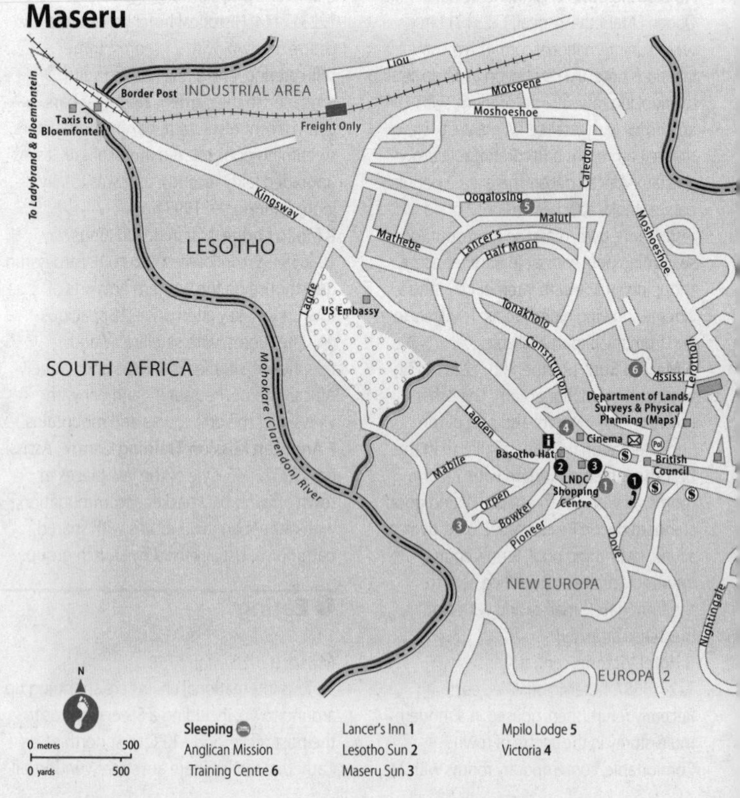

else does. The casino at the **Lesotho Sun Hotel** is popular with guests, and the basement bar is a busy meeting spot for well-heeled locals.

Entertainment

Maseru *p765, map p768*

Cinemas

Kingsway Cinema, opposite the tourist office on Kingsway, was closed at time of writing, but due to re-open soon. In the meantime, fairly up-to-date films are shown at the cinema in the **Lesotho Sun Hotel**.

Shopping

Maseru *p765, map p768*

Central Maseru has various outlets of South African chain stores and supermarkets, including upmarket shops like **Woolworths**, most of which can be found in the shopping centres on Kingsway. The main hotels all have craft or curio shops but these tend to be overpriced. The best craft shop is the **Basotho Hat**, opposite the tourist office, although even here the selection of local crafts is basic. The best buys include mohair blankets and woven baskets. Mohair, woollen, sheepskin and leather products (all important local craft industries) can be bought from a handful of workshops around Maseru – look out for signs by the road as you drive out of town. You can also ask at the tourist office, and have a look at the traditional wicker Basotho hats being sold by women just outside.

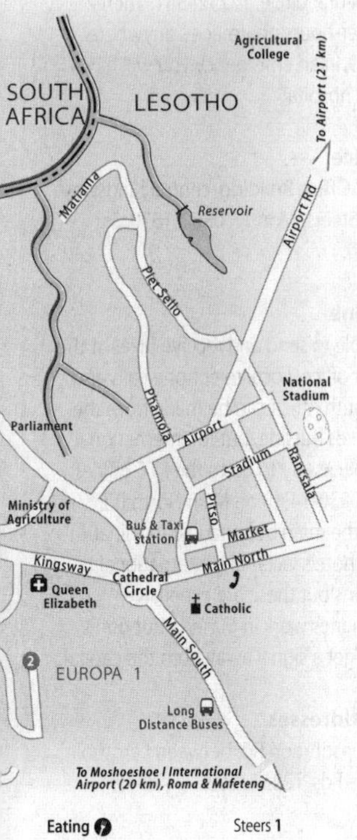

Eating
China Garden 3
Regal 2
Steers 1

Activities and tours

Maseru *p765, map p768*

The **Lesotho Tourist Board** can recommend local guides to take you to areas of scenic, historic or artistic interest within easy reach of Maseru, although most of these areas are easily explored alone. The big Sun hotels also organize tours. **Harvey World Wide Travel**, next to the Hotel Victoria on Kingsway, T22323706 is a branch of a quality South African travel agency, and useful for international travel and flight confirmations.

Transport

Maseru *p765, map p768*

Air

There is an airport departure tax of M20 for all international flights. **South African Airways, (SAA)**, central reservations T011-9781111,www.flysaa.com, operates the route between Moshoeshoe I International Airport and Johannesburg International Airport. There are 3 flights per day. Flying time is 1hr 10 mins. Expect to pay around R900 one way.

Bus

Long-distance buses, run by **Lesotho Freight**, running to **Thaba Tseka** or **Semonkong** depart from the main bus terminal about 500 m along the Main South Rd from Cathedral Circle. Buses to the **Mokhotlong** depart from next to the Feida Supermarket (also known as Chen Si).

Car hire

Avis, Lesotho Sun Hotel, T22314325, and at Moshoeshoe I International Airport, T22350328. **Budget**, Maseru Sun Hotel, T22316344, can arrange pick up and drop off at the airport. **Imperial Fleet**, T58323116, info@impfleet.co.ls, rents 4WDs for reasonable rates, with drop-offs at the airport.

Taxis

Note that there have been reports of muggings in the area around the Cathedral Circle and bus and taxi terminal. Avoid the area after dark.

Local Minibus taxis depart from the maze of streets around Market St just north of the Cathedral Circle. There is a regular stream of minibus taxis up and down Kingsway from Cathedral Circle down to the Border Post. Minibus taxis will take you off their set route for a negotiable price as long as they do not have other passengers. For conventional taxis try **Moonlight Telephone Taxis**, T22312695, or **Luxury Telephone Taxis**, T22326211.

Long distance Taxis heading north tend to leave from the northern end of the maze of streets around Market St, just north of the Cathedral Circle, near the KFC; taxis to the suburbs and surrounding villages leave from the central area; taxis heading towards **Roma** leave from near the small post office; and taxis and buses heading south leave from the Cathedral end of the area. Taxis heading towards **Bloemfontein** and **Ficksburg** in South Africa leave from the South African side of Maseru Bridge border post.

Directory

Maseru *p765, map p768*

Banks

The **Central Bank of Lesotho**, **Lesotho Bank 1999**, **Nedbank** and **Standard Bank** are all on central Kingsway, Mon-Fri 0830-1530, Sat 0830-1200. The Central Bank of Lesotho charges no commission on foreign exchange transactions, but the process takes much longer than at the 2 international banks. Credit card withdrawals are possible at the South African ATM of the Standard Bank.

Embassies and consulates

Most countries have closed their Maseru missions in recent years as they deal with Lesotho from their embassies in South Africa. Exceptions are: **South Africa** (High Commission), 10th floor, Lesotho Bank Centre, Kingsway, T22315758, (visa section) T22314700. sahcls@lesoff.co.za. **USA**, 254 Kingsway, T22312666.

Internet

Leo Internet Services, T22322772, next to the Basotho Hat, offers reasonable internet connections during normal office hours. There is also an internet café in the Lesotho Sun hotel. Both charge around R15 for half an hour.

Medical services

Maseru Private Hospital, T22313260. **Queen Elizabeth Hospital**, Kingsway, T22312501. Reasonably well equipped and staffed, but patients with serious illness or injuries will be transported to a South African hospital.

Cathedral Pharmacy, Main North Rd, near Cathedral Circle, T22324351. There are no after-hours pharmacies anywhere in Lesotho, in an emergency you will have to go to a hospital.

Post office

New Post Office Building, central Kingsway opposite Steers, Mon-Fri 0800-1630, Sat 0800-1200.

Telephone

It is possible to send and receive faxes at the main post office. Local telephone calls and calls to South Africa can be made from the phone boxes outside, but for international calls it is necessary to go to the **LTC** offices (Mon-Fri 0830-1430) on Main North Rd, opposite the main bus and taxi terminal. The main hotels will make international connections but these are expensive. Mobile phones work in Maseru, but don't expect to get a signal away from the capital.

Useful addresses

Police Constitution Rd, between Lerotholi and Palace Rds, T22317262.

Maseru to Semonkong

There are three main routes out of Maseru: the well maintained Main North Road that runs along Lesotho's narrow lowland strip; the Main South Road through the farming towns of the wider lowland strip; and the road from Maseru branching off to Semonkong in the central mountains or Thaba Tseka in the east (see page 780). Beyond Roma, the road climbs into the eastern side of the Thabo Pusoa Mountains, part of the Lesotho Highlands, and ends at Semonkong. This dramatic drive passes through beautiful mountain scenery and a string of traditional Lesotho villages, with very different lifestyles from those of Maseru's city streets. ▸▸ *For Sleeping, Eating and other listings, see pages 773-774.*

Thaba Bosiu → *Colour map 4, grid B4*

Thaba Bosiu, 20 km outside Maseru, was the mountain stronghold of the founder of the Basotho nation, Chief Moshoeshoe. It is an isolated and steep-sided mountain with a large flat plateau at the top. From this secure defensive position Moshoeshoe was able to launch raids against his neighbours before retreating to safety. He, and many other important Basotho (including King Moshoeshoe II who died in 1996 in a car accident), are buried at the mountain's summit. There are remnants of Moshoeshoe's village and his restored two-roomed house. Also here on a protruding rock is a chiselled out footprint left by Maleleka, one of Moshoeshoe's sons. The story goes that he was forbidden to marry the girl he loved because she was below his rank, so lamenting the loss of his loved one, he carved the footprint as an epitaph before throwing himself off the mountain to his death. Thaba Bosiu means 'mountain at night' and legend has it that what is a hill during the day becomes a mountain at night. Today regarded as a national monument, it has recently earned recognition as a UNESCO World heritage Site for its importance to the Lesotho people.

There are a number of pathways up the mountain but visitors usually use the steep Rafutho's Pass. The defensive wall built by Moshoeshoe's men when they first arrived at the mountain can still be seen. The views are lovely, and nearby is **Qiloane**, a strangely nipple-shaped mountain, the shape of which is supposed to have inspired the Basotho Hat.

Tour guides can be found at the car park and small visitors' centre between 0800-1700 at the base of the mountain; most are fairly knowledgeable and will give visitors a fascinating (if not always completely accurate) account of the role of the Thaba Bosiu stronghold and much of Lesotho's early history. The tours usually take about two hours in total and the price will depend on your skills of negotiation.

Roma → *Colour map 4, grid B5.*

Roma is 31 km east of Maseru along the road to Semonkong. It is the site of the National University of Lesotho and a large number of churches, presbyteries and schools. The town itself is little more than a few houses scattered around these institutions in a pretty, wooded valley at the foothills of the Maluti. The University was founded in 1945 by the Catholic Church. It became part of the combined university of Botswana, Lesotho and Swaziland in the 1960s until that institution collapsed and it was brought under the sole control of the Lesotho Ministry of Education. The entrance to the University is on the left as you enter the town from Maseru. Few of the University buildings are of any historical interest but the campus is green and well maintained and visitors are welcome to wander around.

Chief Moshoeshoe and Thaba Bosiu

Chief Moshoeshoe, often regarded as the founder of the Basotho nation, was born in about 1786 at Menkhoaneng in the north of present day Lesotho. Though he was later to become one of the most powerful chiefs in southern Africa, he was by birth no more than a village headman. According to oral tradition, however, even as a young man he had dreams of becoming a great chief. Fearing that his short temper and overweening ambition would lead him into trouble, Moshoeshoe's father sent him for instruction from the famous chief Mohlomi. Mohlomi impressed on the young Moshoeshoe the need for a ruler to gain loyalty from his followers not just through violence but by ensuring they were materially reliant upon his protection.

Moshoeshoe learnt his lessons well and realized that control of large numbers of cattle was the key to political power. With many cattle he could afford the brideprice needed to marry many wives (eventually over 40) and therefore bind other lineages and clans to his own, and by lending some of his cattle to his supporters he was able to make them materially reliant upon his power. So Moshoeshoe set about building up his herds by both careful management and raiding his neighbours. His reputation soon grew and with his followers he broke away from his previous clan to establish a new chieftainship on Butha-Buthe.

Through a careful strategic balance of making alliances with stronger chiefs and attacking weaker ones (and raiding their cattle), Moshoeshoe soon built up his power base. He never went into any battle he could risk losing and often managed to buy off enemies with gifts of cattle – sometimes raiding the same herds back if his rival fell upon hard times. Nevertheless the interior of South Africa in the early 19th century was a violent and complex political world and Moshoeshoe came under increasing military pressure from nearby chiefs. Realizing Butha-Buthe was not easy to defend Moshoeshoe sent out his brother to find a new stronghold. He returned with news of a larger flat-topped mountain with plenty of water resources two days' journey to the south.

In June 1824 Moshoeshoe and his followers set off on the dangerous trek to their new headquarters. Despite coming under attack during the move and losing Moshoeshoe's grandfather to a band of cannibals, he and his followers managed to secure themselves in their new stronghold. From this new position Moshoeshoe was able to extend his power and controlled the whole of the Clarendon Valley and a large number of followers.

Later in his reign he came under intense pressure from the new Boer republics and lost much of his kingdom, eventually turning to the British for protection. Nevertheless this remarkable leader had managed to build a powerful and unified kingdom during a time of intense strife and continual conflict out of an initial handful of followers. He died at Thaba Bosiu in 1870.

Semonkong and around » pp773-774.

Colour map 4, grid B5.

From Roma to Semonkong (85 km) the road climbs into the central mountains and the scenery becomes more dramatic, passing through tiny villages and past Lesotho horsemen in their gum boots and blankets. The tar road turns to gravel at **Moitsupeli,** 19 km beyond Roma, after which it continues to climb through **Ramabanta** (access point for the excellent **Trading Post Adventures** lodge) and into the Thabo Putsoa Mountains, peaking at 2000 m. Under normal conditions, the journey from Maseru to Semonkong (120 km) is about four hours – a 4WD is vital in winter or if it's wet. Alternatively there is a daily bus (two at the weekends) that takes about six hours and leaves Maseru at 1100 or 1400. **Semonkong** is at the end of the road and is a small town that historically had a reputation for being a secret hideout of outlaws.

Maletsunyane Falls

Semonkong is of interest mainly because of the nearby **Maletsunyane Falls** which are the highest single drop falls in southern Africa. They are also referred to as the **Semonkong Falls**, Semonkong means 'place of smoke', or the **Lebinhan Falls** after Father Francois Le Binhan, the first European to see them in 1881. They can be visited on a hike or pony trek from **Semonkong Lodge** or on a pony trek from **Malealea Lodge.** Though the volume of water is usually small, the falls are very impressive and drop 192 m (twice the drop of the Victoria Falls, though a fraction of the width) into a huge gorge that winds through the mountains for many kilometres. Part of the attraction is that there are absolutely no tourist facilities around the falls. They are about 4 km south of Semonkong; it is possible to drive part of the way but the walk from Semonkong is easy. They are best seen during the late rainy season when they are full. At the end of very dry periods they are often reduced to little more than a trickle and occasionally in winter they freeze, forming spectacular ice pinnacles.

Ketane Falls

Very few people have seen the pristine Ketane Falls which drop 122 m as they are in one of the highest and most remote regions of Lesotho, midway between Semonkong and Malealea (see page 783). From Semonkong it's possible to reach them in a day's hike or to drive (by 4WD only) to the tiny village of Ha Bati, 5 km from the falls, and hike the rest of the way. From both Semonkong and Malealea lodges the option is to get to the falls by horseback, overnight from Semonkong and four days from Malealea. This is stunning mountain scenery and you are unlikely to see other people, except for the occasional herd boy.

Sleeping

Thaba Bosiu *p771*

C **Mmelesi Lodge**, near the bottom of the main path, T52500007, has a restaurant and bar selling cold drinks, snacks, and reasonable meals to day visitors, and has a few comfortable en suite rondavels out back.

Roma *p771*

B-D **Trading Post Guest House**, T2234020, www.tradingpost.co.za, signposted off the main street in Roma. Offers a mix of luxury rondavels and more basic backpackers accommodation in an original sandstone trading post building built in 1903. Self-catering or meals by prior arrangement, small swimming pool. Also owns the excellent Trading Post in Ramabanta. Ashley and Jennifer Thorn are experts on the area and can organize short pony treks to the surrounding hills above Roma. Recommended.

F **Roma Roman Catholic Mission**, T22340224, has dorms, doubles and singles in basic accommodation. The mission is behind the large Catholic Church on the right about 1 km further on from the University entrance.

Semonkong and around *p772*

B-D **Trading Post Adventures**, T22340202, www.tradingpost.co.za, signposted from the centre of the village of Ramabanta. Stunning location in a trading post dating from 1939, with wide-reaching mountain views. Luxurious and stylishly decorated rondavles, looking straight onto the mountains, or more basic en suite rooms in the old stables. Delicious meals served in the candle lit dining room. Huge range of activities on offer, from short walks, to pony treks, 4WD routes, dirt-bike tracks and overnight stays in a nearby village. Run by the affable and hugely knowledgeable Rosemary. Highly recommended.

C-F Semonkong Lodge, T27006037, T62021021 (mob), www.placeof smoke.co.ls. This popular lodge offers a handful of thatched en suite huts, with African decor and log fires, plus simpler rooms in the house, a dorm and camping space. Excellent meals served in the restaurant, bar, well-equipped communal kitchen, braai fire pits and gas braai, plenty of hot water (unless pipes freeze in which case boiling water is provided from the kitchen), pool table. There is broad range of outdoor activities on offer.

Eating

Roma *p771*

Speak Easy, restaurant and bar, opposite University entrance, has a limited but fairly cheap menu, the bar with a wide variety of alcoholic drinks is popular in the evening and a good place to meet students or staff of the University. It is also possible to eat lunch at the **University dining room** which serves one, usually tasty, dish a day.

Semonkong and around *p772*

There is a restaurant in Semonkong Lodge, and a couple of bars near the main bus stop that serve up alcohol and basic meals.

Activities and tours

Semonkong and around *p772*

Semonkong Lodge, reservations T/F051-9333106 (South Africa), www.placeof smoke.co.ls. Offers pony trekking packages from 1-5 days. Overnight rides are quite strenuous and involve 6-7 hrs riding each day but they can be attempted by novices. Accommodation is in Basotho huts with cooking equipment. Pack horses are also available for hire to hikers. A recent initiative is the world's highest commercial abseil, a 206 m drop down Maletsunyane Falls.

Trading Post Adventures, T2234020, www.tradingpost.co.za. Offers a wide range of activities from short self-guided walks, crossing the valley and passing through villages, to longer pony treks with a local Basotho guide. 4WD trails are opening up in the wilder reaches of the mountains. Overnight stays in villages can be arranged, as well as singing performances from local children. Recommended.

Transport

Thaba Bosiu *p771*

Taxi

There are frequent taxis to and from Thaba Bosiu directly from **Maseru** along a good tarred road. If you are arriving from **Roma** or the Semonkong road, taxis and the twice-daily bus from **Semonkong** will drop you off at the junction with the Thaba Bosiu road, from where it is fairly easy to pick up a connecting taxi. The main hotels in Maseru organize frequent half-day trips to the mountain, though it is just as easy and cheaper to go under your own steam.

Roma *p771*

Bus

The bus between **Maseru** and **Semonkong** passes through Roma in the afternoons.

Taxi

Taxis to and from **Maseru** leave throughout the day, but stop at sunset. This is the last place to buy fuel if you are driving to **Semonkong**, a further 85 km away.

Semonkong and around *p772*

Bus

The gravel road to Semonkong is fairly good except for the last 10 km or so. There are two daily buses to and from **Maseru** leaving at 1100 and 1400, and the journey takes about 6 hrs. If you just miss the bus in Maseru, it is worth catching a taxi to Roma, which will inevitably overtake the slow-moving buses. If you miss the daily bus at the Semonkong end, ask about lifts at the bar next to the bus stop.

Directory

Roma *p771*

Banks Lesotho National Bank, opposite the main University entrance. Will make foreign transactions, open 0900-1300.

North from Maseru

The main route north out of Maseru is along the well-maintained Main North Road that runs along Lesotho's narrow lowland strip. The countryside on either side of the route is fairly heavily populated, dotted with affluent villages and banded by terraced fields, with good views across to the mountains. Commonly referred to as the 'Roof of Africa', these northern mountains are the highest and harshest in southern Africa. The high mountain peaks have a stark beauty, desolate and empty bar the odd herd boy during summer, and cloaked in snow every winter. There is one main road that runs across the area, from Butha-Buthe to Sani Pass, known for being the highest road in all of Africa. Recently upgraded to tar, the 200 km stretch between Butha-Buthe and Mokhotlong has opened up the entire region to visitors.

▶▶ *For Sleeping, Eating and other listings, see pages 777-780.*

Teya-Tayaneng → *Colour map 4, grid B5.*

The ramshackle town of Teya-Tayaneng, 'TY' as it is referred to, was founded as an administrative centre by the British colonial authorities in 1886. Teya-Tayaneng, meaning 'the place of quick sands', takes its name from the quicksand in the river that runs past the town occasionally sucking in hapless cattle. TY is well-known as a handicraft centre and this is the primary reason most people visit the town. Traditional Sesotho goods tend to be cheaper here than in Maseru and there are well-established centres that are run to ensure that profits return to the artists and not middlemen (see details under Shopping). Having said that, don't expect slick shops or smart complexes; here, goods are sold in run-down cement blocks by the roadside.

Leribe (Hlotse) → *Colour map 4, grid B5.*

Hlotse is the administrative centre of Leribe district (and is often also known simply as Leribe). Founded in 1876, it was an important town in the 1880 Gun War. Still to be seen today are the remains of a British fort and a primitive statue of a kneeling British soldier. The Anglican Church dates from 1877 and is the oldest building in town. About 8 km north on the old Butha-Buthe road, in the Subeng stream about 400 m downstream from the bridge, are three- and five-toed dinosaur tracks estimated to be 108-200 million years old. Ask for directions in the village.

Butha-Buthe ▶▶ *pp777-780. Colour map 4, grid A5.*

Butha-Buthe is the northernmost town in the lowlands, and not too far from the Caledonspoort border post. From here you can either continue north into South Africa or turn east onto the mountain road. Butha-Buthe gets its name from the mountain that dominates the town; the name means 'place of lying down' or 'place of security' and it is here that Moshoeshoe had his first mountain stronghold. Towering above the town, this is the main attraction. The walk to the top is fairly strenuous but is worth it for the fine views across the town and surrounding countryside. The town itself is a busy centre with a number of supermarkets where people from the highlands come every few weeks to stock up on provisions. Recently, a large suburb known as Likileng was constructed to provide accommodation for the workforce engaged on the tunnelling and hydropower components of the Lesotho Highlands Water Project.

About 30 km from Butha-Buthe is the **Liphofung Cave Cultural and Historical Site**, an initiative of the Lesotho Highlands Water Project to promote tourism in the region. This cultural centre includes three traditional Basotho huts, and a pathway and boardwalk leading to some San rock paintings, dotted under and around a large

Lesotho Highlands Water Project

The massive Lesotho Highlands Water Project, one of the biggest of its kind in the world, is currently under construction with final completion expected in the 2020s. The project has been largely funded by South Africa, which maintains a large degree of control over the project's administration, though the project will eventually provide the whole of Lesotho with electricity.

The first phase of the project, the construction of a huge dams at Katse, was completed in 1997, which pumps water into the South African river system to help meet the demand of thirsty mines and industry in Gauteng. The second phase, the construction of the Mohole Dam further upstream, was completed in 2003, and in early 2006 had finally filled up, which should double the water supply to South Africa through an interconnecting tunnel into Katse reservoir.

The **Lesotho Highlands Development Authority** (LHDA) has stressed tourism development as a major part of the project and has promised the development of water-based recreational facilities, campsites and new lodges and hotels. More importantly, it has established new national reserves, including Ts'ehlanyane National Park and the Bokong Nature Reserve, both north of the Katse Dam. For more information and updates, visit www.lhwp.org.ls.

overhang of rock. Local guides accompany visitors and explain the significance of the art. The curio **shop** ① *daily 0900-1630*, sells high standard local handicrafts.

Oxbow → *Colour map 4, grid A5*

This is the centre of the Lesotho ski industry – as you'd expect, the industry isn't exactly booming, so don't expect much. There are actually no facilities other than some skis for hire at the **New Oxbow Lodge** (see page 778), although there have been murmurings of a new ski lift being built at some point in the future. For the time being, hardy skiers pitch up here occasionally but it's mostly a spot for hikers. This is the last petrol stop until Mokhotlong (114 km).

Leiseng Le Trai

The road between Oxbow and Mokhotlong (114 km) snakes and twists higher until almost at the halfway point it reaches the **Tlaeeng Pass**. The summit of the highest road in Africa is 3275 m above sea level. As you can imagine, the views here are truly outstanding, and the drive offers undulating mountain scenery and clean crisp air. The only significant stop is **Leiseng Le Trai** about 10 km after the pass, a small cluster of huts housing a community of people who make a living from mining for diamonds in the waste tips of a now abandoned **Anglo-American diamond mine**. It is a wild lawless place high in the mountains and conjures up images of the Wild West. Prospectors will try to sell diamonds to visitors; these are cheap but also highly illegal, so don't be tempted.

Mokhotlong → *Colour map 4, grid B6. Population: 75,000.*

Mokhotlong Town or Camp is one of Lesotho's remotest towns and is the administrative and economic centre of the northern mountain area. The town's name means 'the place of the bald ibis', and these birds can still be seen along the river and in the surrounding valleys. The town was established as a police post in 1905 and grew as a trading centre supplied by pack ponies coming over the Drakensberg from KwaZulu Natal. Until 1947 when radio contact was established with Maseru, it had no connections with the rest of the country and until the 1950s it had no road connection with the outside world. In winter, Mokhotlong can be cut off for many weeks by snow

There is little of great interest in the town itself, but it retains something of an isolated outpost atmosphere. Sheep and goats are still shorn by hand in the surrounding sheds. An interesting sight is the Basotho in their striking blankets, hitching their horses outside and entering the modern computerized bank to do their banking. This is also the logical place from which to start exploring the remote valleys and high mountains of this area. The main supply stores are either near the bank or next to the airfield. There is a petrol station opposite the bank.

Sani Pass → *Colour map 4, grid B6.*

This torturously steep, cork-screwing road is the only road pass from the northern mountains into South Africa and is only open to 4WDs. The views across the mountains of KwaZulu Natal are awe inspiring. The Sani Pass was originally a bridle track for pack horses and was opened to vehicular transport in the 1950s. About 12 km from Sani Pass is the highest mountain in southern Africa, Thabana-Ntlenyana (3482 m). The name means 'pretty little mountain', hardly a fitting name for what is the 2nd tallest mountain in Africa after Kilimanjaro. There are some beautiful walks in this rugged area; for details of hikes see page 458.

Moteng Pass

Between Butha-Buthe and Oxbow (68 km) is the scenic **Moteng Pass** (2840 m). Travelling northeast, spending much of the journey over 2500 m, this tightly twisting road climbs up gradients of over 35% and the summit offers excellent views of the authentic Basotho homesteads in the valley below. This is the original 'Roof of Africa' motor rally route that takes place annually at the beginning of summer.

Sleeping

Teya-Tayaneng *p775*

C **Blue Mountain Inn**, signposted from Main North Rd, T22500362. The only hotel in town is in an ugly red-brick block just outside the centre, with a simple bar and restaurant (serving, oddly, pizza) with cane furniture, and 43 fairly basic but comfortable rooms with TV. Pleasant gardens and friendly staff, secure parking.

C **Palace Hotel**, 15 km south of TY and 25 km north of Maseru on Main North Rd, T58864905. A modern motel popular as a conference location for businesses from Maseru, but in a pleasant rural setting. Rooms have big beds, decent bathrooms, TV, phone and communal balconies (ensure doors are locked at all times). The restaurant and bar serves the usual meat and chicken with chips, rice or pap, and there's a nightclub next door that gets very noisy at the weekends.

Leribe (Hlotse) *p775*

D **Leribe**, town centre, T22400559. 33 en suite rooms with TV, in either a motel style terrace or rondavels in the pretty garden, 2 bars. Restaurant serves standard grills, steak and trout. Dilapidated exterior but pleasant enough inside.

F **Anglican Mission**, will sometimes allow visitors to camp in their grounds, no charge but leave a donation.

Butha-Buthe *p775*

D **Crocodile Inn**, in the southern suburbs of town, signposted from main road, T22460223. Local hangout (more for its heaving bar than its rooms), with 29 basic rooms with en suite bathrooms and TV. Restaurant serves good quality Basotho food if requested. 2 bars, pool table, secure parking, camping allowed.

F **Butha-Buthe Youth Hostel**, about 3 km outside town past St Paul's Roman Catholic

Mission, turn off Main Rd at the **Guys and Girls Fashion Store**, then ask directions, T22460223. Also known as Mr Ramakatane's Home Hostel, the owner has turned part of his house into a YHA affiliated hostel that provides accommodation for the nearby World Vision Vocational School. The female dorm sleeps 6, the male dorm sleeps 10, campsite, basic facilities, communal kitchen, borehole water, gas cookers, lights, and heaters are used. Friendly set up but is only accessible by 4WD or on foot and you need to bring your own food. Staying here gives one a good insight into village life in the Lowlands.

Oxbow *p776*

C New Oxbow Lodge, T051-9332247 (South Africa), www.oxbow.co.za. 32 cosy en suite chalets, either in doubles or family rooms, set in a mix of Alpine and thatched Lesotho buildings. Licensed restaurant, great bar overlooking the river, log fires in the lounge. Camping allowed in grounds, natural rock pool for swimming, skiing equipment, pony trekking, 4WD routes, guides and trout fishing arranged, popular especially when there is snow which attracts curious South Africans, so make reservations in advance.

Mokhotlong *p776*

D Senqu Hotel, on left hand side of road as you enter town from west, T22920330. Standard small-town hotel with 10 poky but clean en suite rooms. Restaurant with the usual standard meat and chicken. Bar and public lounge with TV. Not a great option, but probably the best bet in town.

D-F Molumong Guest House, 15km from Mokhotlong on the Thaba Tseka Rd, T832543323. An old colonial trading post homestead, high on the mountainside affording great views. Dorms, doubles with bedding, and fully equipped kitchen. Basic supplies are available, and a bottle store is close by. There is no signpost to the lodge from the road, but 'Molumong' is painted on the roof. Confusingly, it is not in Molumong village, but in upper Rafalotsane village. Ask for Derek

Sani Pass *p777*

A-B Sani Pass Hotel, Sani Pass Rd, T033-7021320 (South Africa), www.sanipasshotel.co.za. Large resort hotel offering accommodation either in the hotel building or in luxury cottages in the gardens. Sporting facilities include squash, fly fishing, tennis, bowls, riding and swimming. Large restaurant with a reasonably priced set menu. Beautiful location, but overpriced.

C-D Sani Top Chalet, top of the pass, next to the Lesotho border post on the South African side, T033-7021158 or T082-7151131 (mob; both numbers South African), www.sanitopchalet.co.za. A combination of double rooms in the main building or backpacker bunks in rondavels out back. You can camp but you'll need thermals. The hotel has a licensed pub (the highest in Africa) and diningroom warmed with roaring wood fires, overlooking the dramatic road below. Fantastic hikes and pony trekking to awesome viewpoints along the escarpment. When it does snow it is possible to hire skis from the hotel. They are currently building more up-market accommodation on site.

D-E Sani Lodge, 19 km from Underberg on the Sani Pass rd, T033-7020330 (South Africa), www.sanilodge.co.za. Great backpackers with small dorms, 5 large double rooms with pine ceilings and good insulation, 2 private rondavels, a 22-bed dorm. Large kitchen, comfortable lounge with open fire for the winter months when it can get very cold, and a veranda with a superb uninterrupted view of the Drakensberg escarpment. Great meals served. Run by Russell and Simone who are experts on hiking in Lesotho.

Eating

Teya-Tayaneng *p775*

The Blue Mountain Inn has a decent standard restaurant and bar, and there are numerous (very) basic cafés and bars around the main road junction of the Main North Rd.

Leribe (Hlotse) *p775*

There is little to be found in town other than a handful of basic cafés scattered around town serving pap and stew.

Butha-Buthe *p775*

There are a number of small, cheap eateries on the main road near the bus stop.

Mokhotlong *p776*

The **Senqu Hotel** has a reasonable restaurant with a fairly varied menu. There are a large number of small eating and drinking houses and street vendors along the main street, selling mutton stew and *pap* or the delicious local brown bread with a hot sauce. The **Sunshine Bar**, is the busiest in town thanks to its satellite television, which draws in highland horsemen in droves.

Shopping

Teya-Tayaneng *p775*

Helang Basali Handicrafts, on Main North Rd to the south of town centre, is run by a local mission and sells reasonably priced rugs, blankets, tapestries and other handicrafts from a rundown shop next to the road. Visitors can watch women weaving at the excellent **Setsoto Design** (opposite Blue Mountain Inn), Lesotho's oldest and finest weaving company. A great selection of wall hangings and carpets, all hand-woven with homespun mohair, are for sale in the showroom. Be wary of paying with credit cards, however, as we've had reports of card fraud here. On the right coming into town, look out for the **Hatooa Mose Moasali** showroom, meaning 'a woman must stand up and work hard', a women's weaving cooperative that produces wall hangings.

Leribe (Hlotse) *p775*

Leribe Craft Centre, T22400323, on the northern outskirts of the town, sells mohair blankets, ponchos, scarves, baskets, hats and beadwork.

Transport

Teya-Tayaneng *p775*

There are frequent taxis, leaving from near the main junction, in both directions along the Main North Rd. If you are going to **Leribe (Hlotse)** it is usually necessary to change taxis at the junction for Maputsoe where most turn off the Main North Rd for the Ficksburg border crossing. There are plenty of fuel stations in the centre of town.

Leribe (Hlotse) *p775*

Taxi

Taxis to **Butha-Buthe** leave throughout the day from the south end of the main street. Taxis towards **Teya-Tayaneng** and **Maseru** leave from the same area, though passengers usually have to change at **Maputsoe** (where the approach road to the Ficksburg border crossing turns off from the Main North Rd).

Butha-Buthe *p775*

Bus

The bus towards **Oxbow** and **Mokhotlong** leaves from the far side of the petrol station near the main junction. This is a steep road so your nerves need to be up to it.

Taxi

Taxis heading towards **Leribe Maseru**and the South African towns of **Ficksburg**, and **Fouriesburg** leave from the other end of the main street. This is the last place to get fuel before Oxbow, 68 km away.

Oxbow *p776*

Bus and Taxi

The 2 daily buses and occasionally a taxi service between **Butha-Buthe** and **Mokhotlong**, stop at Oxbow; timetables are flexible so ask at the lodge.

Mokhotlong *p776*

Car

The road from Mokhotlong to **Sani Pass** (60 km) is very poor and should only be attempted by 4WDs. It is a spectacular road that winds over the Black Mountain pass (3240 m) then down to the Sani Flats and Sani Top village. There are no buses so travellers without their own transport will have to hitch a lift over the Sani Pass.

Bus

There is a twice daily bus to and from **Butha-Buthe**, departing about 0800 and a few hours later, but the timetable is very flexible. Buses depart from outside the **Pep** store on the main street. There is also a slightly more expensive, but much faster, taxi service, that sometimes does the route.

Directory

Teya-Tayaneng *p775*
Banks The main banks have branches in the town centre, near the Blue Mountain Inn.

Mokhotlong *p776*
Banks The Central Bank of Lesotho on the north side of the main street, slow foreign exchange transactions. **Post office** Next to the police station and LTC Office. **Telephone** Local and international calls can be made from the LTC Office. **Useful addresses** The Lesotho Mounted Police is at the east end of the main street, near the large radio mast.

Central mountains

The central mountain areas are the most accessible highland regions from Maseru. The new dams built here as part of the Lesotho Highlands Water Project have created excellent tar roads, opening up the region to tourists. This is the best area to visit for a glimpse of mountain life if you lack the time to travel in the more challenging areas to the north and the less accessible areas to the south. ▸▸ *For Sleeping, Eating and other listings, see page 782.*

Mohale Dam

The recently-completed Mohale Dam, part of the Lesotho Highlands Water Project (see box, page 776), is accessed along the A3, at the junction by the little town of St Michael's. There is a small **information centre** ⓘ *0800-1700*, which can help organize activities, although at time of writing visitors had to bring their own equipment, such as canoes. While there's little to see at the dam itself, the drive is beautiful, passing through untouched swathes of mountains east of the usual tourist route.

The road passes through the small town of Nazareth and dips down before climbing up to Bushmen's Pass at 2263 m, offering beautiful views towards the highlands. From here, you dip down into a series of winding valleys, dotted with homesteads, to a police check point. Do not under any circumstances pass the 'Stop' sign here without permission: the bored officers have been known to root for bribes for the tiniest breach of the rules. Also look out for the rather aggressive herd boys, who run into the road to try and sell lumps of quartz and cutting from rare aloes (it is illegal to buy the latter). The road then continues up to the wonderfully-named **God Help Me Pass**, at 2281 m and past the **Basotho Pony Trekking Centre** (T22312318), which offers a range of treks in the area. Continue on over **Blue Mountain Pass**, and you'll catch your first glimpse of the impressive dam, mirroring the peaks around it. From here, the road turns to gravel and continues over the mountains to Thaba-Tseka.

Thaba Tseka → *Colour map 4, grid B5.*

This new town was established in 1980 as the administrative centre for a new mountain district. There have been a large number of aid projects established in and around Thaba Tseka and there are, therefore, a disproportionate number of government and aid organization offices in the town. There is little of interest in the town itself, although it is a place through which most visitors to the central mountains will pass. The advent of the Lesotho Highlands Water Project has had considerable impact on Thaba Tseka. Apart form a good gravel road linkage, the project sponsored a skills training centre to enable inhabitants to acquire expertise that would help them find jobs with project contractors.

National dress of Lesotho

As the Basotho are one of the few African ethnic groups living in a mountainous environment, they have had to make adaptations to their living conditions. The Basotho blanket is one example. Most people in the rural areas wear colourful blankets attached at the shoulder with giant pins to form a sort of coat to provide warmth and keep the rain off. These are usually worn with well-patched gumboots, essential in the cool mountain climate. However neither garment is produced locally and both the gumboots and blankets are imported from South Africa. Moshoshoe was presented with a blanket by European traders in the 1860s; before then people wore clothing made from animal hides. A decade later there was insatiable demand for these blankets that were once imported from the textile regions of England around Leicester and Coventry. Many of the trading stores and centres in today's Lesotho were built on the selling of blankets. Lesotho's national dress has developed simply out of necessity rather than tradition; they are worn to keep one warm.

Katse Dam » *p782. Colour map 4, grid B5.*

The new road from Leribe (Hlotse) to the Katse Dam (121 km) is an impressive feat of engineering. The drive from Hlotse to the visitors' centre at Katse Dam takes about 1½ hours but allow more time for stops at the top of the mountain passes to take in the sweeping views. What used to be the roughest track in the country is now smooth tar, though there are some very steep ascents and sheer drops to the side of the road. Bearded vultures and other unusual montane birds can often be seen from the pass summits and this region is also home to the ice rat, a rodent that is endemic to Lesotho and only lives above 2000 m. The highest point is the **Matika-Lisiu Pass** (3000 m), where there is a carpark and viewpoint and the visitors' centre for the **Bokong Nature Reserve** (see below).

From the pass, the road drops down to the northern end of the Katse Dam and passes the **Intake Tower** which marks the beginning of the tunnel that takes water through to Gauteng. It then crosses the impressive **Malibamatso Bridge** at the northern end of the dam before climbing again to 2600 m over the **Laitsoka Pass** and 2500 m over the **Nkaobee Pass** before dropping to below the dam wall where the growing settlement of Katse is located. The dam itself is an impressive structure and worth seeing for its own sake and its views. The dam wall is 185 m high and 60 m thick and curves inward to such an extent that when looking down from the top, the bottom of the dam wall is invisible – an odd experience. As you enter Katse you will see the modern yellow building with a blue roof of the Lesotho Highlands Development Authority **visitor centre** ⓘ *Mon-Fri 0800-1200, 1300-1600, Sat-Sun 0800-1200*, where popular tours into the dam wall can be organized. The centre also has displays on the dam's construction, with a video and models of how water will be moved around when all five dams are completed in the 2020s.

Bekong Nature Reserve

ⓘ *T22913206, www.lhwp.org.es. Daily sunrise to sunset, M5.*

Bekong Nature Reserve covers 1970 ha and straddles the main road from Hlotse to Katse Dam at the 3000 m high Mafika Lisiu Pass. It claims to be one of the highest nature reserves in Africa and there are some outstanding views across the highlands. There is an **information centre** ⓘ *daily 0800-1700*, perched on the edge of a 100-m cliff, which features exhibits on the ecology of the highlands, information on the overnight hiking trail and the network of shorter trails, and pony trekking. At this alpine altitude the reserve is of course not exactly full of animals, other than colonies of the ice rat, the occasional hardy rhebuck and a number of raptors including the bearded vulture. However, the scenery is tremendous, with extensive wetlands at the source of the Bokong River and vast heath covered plateaus. In winter the Lepaqoa Waterfall freezes into a column of ice.

Ts'ehlanyane National Park

ⓘ *T22444207, www.lhwp.org.es. 24 hrs. M15.*

Ts'ehlanyane National Park covers some 5600 ha, and lies at the junction of the Ts'ehlanyane and the Holomo rivers on the western range of the Maluti mountains. To get there take the gravel road which leaves the main north road 3 km south of Butha-Buthe. The 32-km road parallels the Hlotse River along a very picturesque valley until it reaches the park entrance. In the park are extensive tracts of woodlands and it's full of rivers and streams bordered by bamboo and montane fynbos. Again there are very few animals but it's a haven for butterflies and birds. Developments in the park include picnic areas, overnight trails with accommodation huts, and a series of walks and trails of varying length, as well as pony rides.

Sleeping

Thaba Tseka *p780*

C **Mountain Star Hotel**, T22900415. Relatively new hotel with simple en suite rooms, popular with local business men, friendly service, simple restaurant and bar.

F **Agricultural Training Centre**, T22090304, behind the police station in the south of town. Has 12 basic rooms, communal showers and kitchen, often full with students during the week but empty at weekends.

Katse Dam *p781*

D **Katse Lodge**, Katse village, T22910202. A sprawling ex-construction worker settlement that has been transformed into tourist accommodation. Basic rooms with stunning views over the dam and a decent restaurant.

Eating

Thaba Tseka *p780*

There are a couple of basic options in town. There are numerous small, cheap eating and drinking places in the older section of town on the north side of the stream running through the town.

Transport

Thaba Tseka *p780*

There are 3 roads into Thaba Tseka: from Leribe (Hlotse) via the Katse Dam (tarred as far as the dam followed by good gravel); a gravel road from Mokhotlong; and a decent gravel road from Maseru, tarred for about the first 50 km out of Maseru. The latter is a beautiful route through the mountains, crossing the lowlands before ascending the first range of the Maluti Mountains via Bushman's Pass (2268 m). It is commonly known as the Mountain Rd simply because it was the first road into the mountains that could be negotiated by a saloon car.

There are 3 daily buses to and from **Maseru** leaving at 0900, 0930 and 1000 from the main bus terminal. Minibus taxis run to and from **Katse Dam**, from where there are buses and taxis to **Leribe (Hlotse)**. There is a daily bus to **Mokhotlong** leaving at 0630 from the Feida supermarket in Maseru. There are no roads from Thaba Tseka to Semonkong, but a basic gravel road (4WDs only) runs south to or the Selabathebe National Park.

Katse Dam *p781*

The tar stops at Katse but the road that continues to Thaba Tseka (45 km) is good gravel. From Katse there are taxis to and from **Thaba Tseka**, from where there are buses and taxis to **Maseru** that follow the mountain road. There are also buses and taxis to **Leribe (Hlotse)** where again you can hook up with a bus to **Maseru** via Main North Rd.

South from Maseru

The main route south from Maseru runs along the southern lowland strip. This is one of the main farming regions, but it tends to be a drier area than further north. There are a number of important urban centres along the route connected by tar roads, so it's easy to get around, although none of them could be considered tourist attractions.

The southern mountain area is dominated by the Senqu River Valley that winds through the area. The majestic river meanders through rugged mountain scenery and past steep cliffs. In a few years time the water level will be reduced considerably when all the dams of the Lesotho Highlands Water Project are completed. The mountain road from Moyeni (Quthing) in the Lowveld is tarred until just past Mphaki, passing through beautiful highland terrain. From here the road is gravel until Whitehill, where it become tarred again as far as Qacha's Nek. This stretch can, in fine weather, be managed in an ordinary vehicle, but you'll need a 4WD to get to the Sehlabathebe National Park. ▸▸ *For Sleeping, Eating and other listings, see pages 786-788.*

Morija/ Matsieng → *Colour map 4, grid B4.*

Morija is the site of Lesotho's oldest church and a well-run museum. The French Protestant missionaries who established the church named the town after Mount Moriah in Palestine. Lesotho's first printing press was established here and the village is still an important centre for culture, theology and printing. Books in more than 50 languages have been printed here for export to other African countries. The **Morija Museum** ⓘ *T22360308, Mon-Fri 0800-1700, Sun 1200-1700, entry M6*, is the only museum in Lesotho, and has a number of important historic and prehistoric exhibits and a well organized archive of personal and church papers. There is a large fossil collection and a good display on the dinosaur relics found throughout the country, and there are some of Moshoeshoe's personal belongings on display, including his china tea set. It's all a bit jumbled but the staff are very helpful. There is a delightful tea shop in the grounds serving tea, cold drinks, and snacks. The annual **Morija Arts and Cultural Festival** (contact the museum or visit www.morijafest.com for information) takes place here in the first two week of October, and includes concerts, traditional dance, choirs, food and craft fairs. This is the only event of its kind in Lesotho's so it's worth making an effort to get here if you are in the country at the time.

About 7 km from Morija is the royal family's country home, **Matsieng**. The royal court met at Matsieng more or less throughout the colonial period and, in theory, all decisions taken by the colonial authorities in Maseru had to be agreed to by the monarch. Though the village is of great historical interest there is unfortunately not a great deal to see or anywhere to stay.

Malealea → *Colour map 4, grid B4*

South from Morija the road continues to Mafeteng. About 10 km south of Morija the B40 turns off the Main South Road to the left and follows through to Malealea about 32 km away. This popular pony trekking and hiking centre is in the foothills of the Thaba Putsoa range, 85 km south of Maseru. Here there are San rock paintings, isolated waterfalls, rock pools and peaceful hikes in the surrounding mountains.

Mafeteng → *Colour map 4, grid B4.*

Mafeteng is 36 km south on the Main South Road from Morija. It is the main commercial and administrative centre for the southern lowlands. The town is a 15- minute drive from Van Rooyens border post so this will be the first place you get to if crossing from Wepner in South Africa's Free State. There are pleasant views from the town across the lowlands towards the Thaba- Putsoa range of mountains. The town suffered considerably during

Lesotho's 1998 riots. The **British War Memorial**, erected in memory of members of the Cape Mounted Rifles who died during the Gun War of 1880, is located near St John's Primary School on the road from Mafeteng towards the Van Rooyens border post.

Mohales Hoek → *Colour map 4, grid B4.*

This is a pleasant town named after King Moeshoeshoe's younger half-brother. There are San cave paintings in the cliffs beside the Main South Road as you enter town from the north, but they are difficult to get to. There are also paintings in various caves about 10 km from the Main South Road up the Maphutseng Valley. Although there is nothing to see in town, the most interesting story behind this region are the **Cannibal Caves**, 2 km south near the Agricultural Training Farm. Found throughout Lesotho, they are a reminder of *lifaqane*, 'the terrible time', when in the 1820s roving bands of warriors fleeing the Zulu attackers prevented farmers from growing crops, and people resorted to cannibalism to survive.

Moyeni (Quthing) » *pp786-788. Colour map 4, grid B5.*

Moyeni ('place of the wind') is the administrative centre of Quthing district (the town itself is often also called Quthing – 'Qu' means river in San). It was established as an administrative centre by the British in 1877 but was abandoned three years later during the Gun War, and later rebuilt. It straddles one main street running uphill from the Main South Road. The town is in the far south of the lowlands at the point where the Senqu (Orange) River leaves the mountains and winds out across the flatter central South African plateau.

Sights

There are a couple of good sets of **dinosaur footprints** on the riverbank on the northern outskirts of Moyeni. There are also some dinosaur footprints further up the **Qomoqomong Valley** though they are hard to find without a guide. The Qomoqomong Valley is also the home to some of the best preserved **San cave paintings** in Lesotho; follow the small road east out of Moyeni towards the village of Qomoqomong (where the road ends), the caves are in the hills to the southwest. **Masitise Cave House**, T89794167, about 5 km to the west of Moyeni near Masitise Primary School. The cave house, which was recently renovated and turned into a small museum, has five rooms and was home to the Reverand DF Ellenberger and his family who established a mission in the area in the late 19th century. This is now a national monument, and there are displays of objects from that time in the house.

Southern mountains » *pp786-788.*

Mount Moorosi → *Colour map 4, grid B5.*

About 40 km beyond Moyeni (Quthing) towards Qacha's Nek is Mount Moorosi and the village of the same name. This is an important historical site. In the mid-19th century it was the home of the Chief of the Baphuthi clan (Moorosi), who carried out numerous raids against white settlers in nearby areas. After the British made Moyeni the district capital in 1877, they tried to subdue Moorosi by taking his son captive, but Moorosi resisted and managed to free his son. The British then spent over two years trying to eliminate the threat of Moorosi, eventually succeeding in capturing his mountain stronghold and massacring him and about 500 of his followers, including many children. Near to the village is **Letsie Lake**, a reeded wetlands area that attracts waterbirds. A wildlife conservation project has recently been set up here involving the local people in the protection of the bearded vulture.

Qacha's Nek → *Colour map 4, grid B5.*

This border town at the southeastern corner of Lesotho is on the only road pass from the southern mountain area into South Africa's Eastern Cape. Its location means that, unlike most of the country, there are residents from a number of southern African ethnic groups and visitors are as likely to hear Xhosa being spoken in the street as Sesotho. Until 1970, Qacha's Nek had no direct road communication with the rest of Lesotho, and depended on the town of Matatiele in the Eastern Cape for supplies. This linkage was particularly important, given that Matatiele had a rail link by which migrant workers could travel to the South African mines. Qacha, meaning hideaway, was the name of a local 19th-century chief who was apparently able to disappear into the mountains for months at a time. The British established an administrative centre at the location in 1888 in an attempt to maintain control of this region which had a reputation for lawlessness. This is one of the few regions of Lesotho that is heavily forested and of particular interest are the giant California redwood trees, which exceed 25 m and are over 60 years old. Interestingly, the government hospital here is used exclusively to treat tuberculosis patients.

Sehlabathebe National Park » *pp786-788.*

Colour map 4, grid B6.

This national park is isolated, inaccessible and rugged – but these are the main reasons for coming here. The park is situated in the far east of Lesotho on the border with South Africa and has more than 6500 ha of sub-alpine grasslands, with an average elevation of 2400 m. At time of writing, the Maloti Drakensberg Transfrontier Project, a joint environmental management initiative between Lesotho and South Africa, announced that they plan on bringing down the boundaries between Sehlabathebe and the uKhahlamba-Drakensberg National Parks. This will effectively create a transfrontier park, and is likely to improve the park's infrastructure. For now, facilities are limited and the park is only really popular with South Africa 4WD owners and trout fishermen.

There is little large game within the park, except for the occasional hardy eland or baboon but there is plenty of birdlife, including the rare bearded vulture and black eagle. There is excellent trout fishing and the park is also home to the water lily of the Sehlabathebe and the tiny Maluti minnow, a flower and fish both thought to be extinct for many years. The park was gazetted in 1970; the prime minister of the time, Leabua Jonathan, loved trout fishing, which may explain the park's existence. The park lodge used to be called Jonathan's Lodge, and when he stayed all the other guests had to leave.

Ins and outs

Getting there There are two routes into the park: one via Sehlabathebe village and one across the border from South Africa. Access to Sehlabathebe village is either from **Qacha's Nek** about 100 km to the southwest, or from **Thaba Tseka** about 120 km to the northwest. Both roads are difficult and a 4WD is essential, but the route from Thaba Tseka is especially challenging. The route from South Africa is possible on foot or horse only; the path crosses the border at **Nkonkoana Gate** and then heads down to the South African border post at **Bushman's Nek**. Sehlabathebe Lodge is a 10 km walk or ride from Bushman's Nek. There are no border facilities here on the Lesotho side but there is a small office on the South African side, next to which is a basic campsite and a hikers hut run by KZN Wildlife.

Sleeping

Morija *p783*
C-D **Morija Guesthouse**, perched on a hill right at the top of the village behind the museum, ,T58845432/22316555, gugesthouse@morijafest.com. An attractive sandstone and thatch house with outstanding views of the Maluti Mountains (on a clear day you can see for 45 km), and a veranda and pretty gardens. The main house sleeps 7 in 3 bedrooms with shared bathroom, kitchen and lounge, while 3 smaller, ethnic-themed rondavels in the garden sleep 2. Meal on request. The lodge has introduced pony trekking to the region, and can organize 4WD trips in to the mountains. Several easy walks start here, too. Stunning spot, recommended.

Malealea *p783*
B-E **Malealea Lodge**, reservations South Africa, T051-4366766, T082-5524215 (mob) or at the lodge, www.malealea.co.ls. A collection of en suite rooms, and comfortable thatched Basotho huts, plus dorms in the old farmhouse, built around old trading post, established in 1905. Communal kitchens for self-catering, or great meals served on request. Camping allowed in grounds, honesty bar, general store, beautiful setting. Owners Mick, Di and Glenn are active in supporting community projects in the area, and introduced pony trekking for tourists here. They also offer walking, and visits to villages. Recommended.

Mafeteng *p783*
C **Mafeteng Hotel**, town centre, T58855555. 27 en suite rooms or cottages with satellite TV, swimming pool set around the odd looking main building, which looks not unlike an air traffic control tower. Restaurant, and 3 bars. The whole set-up is slightly shabby and can get noisy at weekends when the bars and the Las Vegas disco in the hotel grounds fill up.

Mohales Hoek *p784*
C **Hotel Mount Maluti**, north of the town centre, T22785224, mmh@leo.co.ls. One of the oldest hotels in Lesotho, 34 en suite rooms with TV and heating and colourful, if rather dark, decor. Restaurant has a good vegetarian choice (rare in Lesotho), bars, tennis courts, swimming pool, nice gardens, one of the country's better small town hotels, run by Danny and Anne who are very helpful in organizing activities. Reservations recommended.

Moyeni *p784*
There are a couple of run-down hotels in town, but you're better off staying in Mohales Hoek and visiting here on a day trip.

Mount Moorosi *p784*
There is no official accommodation in Mount Moorosi, but, as elsewhere in Lesotho, it should be possible to find somewhere to stay by simply asking around. Camping is possible throughout the valley, but always ask permission before pitching a tent.

Qacha's Nek *p785*
B-D **Nthatuoa Hotel**, near the airfield, T22950260. Variety of tidy en suite rooms set in a series of blocks of varying size and price. Good restaurant with high ceilings and ancient chandeliers, bar, rates include an excellent breakfast, can arrange pony treks or trout fishing, camping in grounds, reservations necessary.
F **St Joseph's Mission**, in a wooded valley to the north of the town centre. Visitors may camp in the grounds or stay in one of the outbuildings.

Sehlabathebe National Park *p785*
E **Sehlabathebe Lodge**, c/o Lesotho National Park, Ministry of Agriculture, PO Box 92, Maseru 100, T22323600. Note that the park will be undergoing changes as part of the Maloti Drakensberg Transfrontier Project. For now, accommodation is for 12 people in 5 very basic rooms, communal showers, toilets and kitchen, a little faded but clean, bedding, eating and cooking equipment provided, horse riding available. Camping is allowed but you have to buy a permit from the park office. There is no food available and very little in Sehlabathebe village, so bring your own supplies. Payment can only be made in cash.

Eating

Mafeteng *p783*
Other than the restaurants in the **Mafetung** and **Golden** hotels, there are a large number of street vendors in the town centre and some cafés in the area just to the south. There is a popular open-air restaurant and a KFC near the taxi terminal.

Mohales Hoek *p784*
There are few places to eat other than the **Hotel Mount Maluti** restaurant. There are a couple of cafés and street vendors on Mafoso Rd.

Moyeni *p784*
The **Orange River Hotel** has the town's only restaurant though there are numerous street vendors and cafés around the taxi terminal in lower Moyeni. There are a number of popular and noisy bars in lower Moyeni.

Mount Moroosi *p784*
There is a good café next to the Mitchell Brothers' Trading Store which serves as the village's main petrol station and general store.

Qacha's Nek *p785*
The **Nthatuoa Hotel** dining room has a varied menu and a good reputation, reservations often needed. There are a number of smaller cafés selling cheap and filling meals near the bus and taxi terminal.

Activities and tours

Malealea *p783*
Malealea Lodge, T082-5524215.
Mike and Di Jones who were born in Lesotho, can organize pony treks (no experience necessary), hikes or 4WD tours to all the local sites from 1 hr to 6 days. These include day treks to the Botsoela Waterfalls and Pitseng Gorge and rock pools plus overnight treks to the Ribaneng (2 days), Ketane (4 days) and Maletsunyane waterfalls (4 days), the 3 highest in Lesotho. This is one of the best places to visit if to try pony trekking. Treks are priced on a daily basis, expect to pay in the region of M120-200 per person for day treks, and M185 per person for small groups on overnight treks. The horses and huts are hired from local Basotho, who also act as guides. If riding's not your thing, there are plenty of walks in the area, taking you through beautiful natural features and remote mountain villages. Ask at Malealea Lodge for advice on routes and sights; overnight guided treks cost from M260. Mike and Di can also arrange informal performances by the village youth choir, accompanied by homemade instruments, plus visits to local villages. Other activities include a 40-m abseil between the twin Botsoela Waterfalls and gentle river rafting during the summer months. All activities can be arranged as soon as you get to the lodge.

Transport

Morija *p783*
There are frequent buses and taxis to and from **Maseru**, **Mafeteng** and **Mohale's Hoek**.

Malealea *p783*
Road
Malealea Lodge is about 7 km down a tarred road to the east of the B40. The road goes over the spectacular and aptly named Gate of Paradise Pass, an escarpment that opens out to a broad panorama over the plains below, dotted with Basotho villages. In the spring the sides of the road are covered in flowering mountain plants.

Bus
There is a daily bus between **Malealea** and **Mafeteng**. If travelling from **Maseru**, you can intercept the bus at Motsekuoa where the B40 turns off from the Main South Rd (about 10 km south of Morja). If travelling from **Mohales Hoek** or if you miss the bus at Motsekuoa you can catch one of the taxis going along the road marked B40 on most maps (though not on signposts).

Taxi
Some taxis go all the way to **Malealea Lodge**. If none of these are running get dropped off at the Malealea turning (about 25 km from the Main South Rd) and walk or hitchhike the last 7 km.

Mafeteng *p783*
There are buses and taxis to and from **Maseru** via **Morija**, and to and from **Mohales Hoek** and **Moyeni**. This is also the place to pick up public transport to **Malealea Lodge**, and there is a daily bus that leaves very early in the morning and the occasional taxi.

Mohales Hoek *p784*
Taxis leave from either side of Mafoso Rd. People hitchhiking south may find it easier to get a lift if they first get a taxi about 4 km out of town to the turn off to the **Makhaleen Bridge** border post. The road to Zastron in South Africa is a good gravel road.

Moyeni *p784*
Frequent buses and taxis towards **Maseru** via **Mohales Hoek** leave from near the petrol station in lower Moyeni. There is 1 bus a day to **Qacha's Nek** that leaves at around 0630 and takes about 8 hrs, and frequent taxis to the nearby border post **Tele Bridge** 21 km away.

Mount Moorosi *p784*
Road
This is the last place to get fuel before Qacha's Nek, 130 km. The road towards Qacha's Nek is now mostly tarred; the gravel has been improved in recent years and is passable in a saloon car (but check locally in wet weather).

There are fairly frequent taxis running the route between **Moyeni** and **Mount Moorosi** and the daily bus between **Moyeni** and **Qacha's Nek** passes through the town.

Qacha's Nek *p785*
Air
Given Qacha's Nek's distance from the main towns, air travel is a popular form of transport and the airfield has a tarred runway and is relatively busy. There are no scheduled flights but it is possible to pay for a seat on one of the many charter flights that operate between here and **Maseru**, weather permitting. Ask at the airfield for information.

Car
The drive to Qacha's Nek border post is steep and winding, but can be accessed in a saloon car (but check locally if the weather is wet). Visitors without their own transport wanting to cross into **South Africa** will have to walk across the border and then hitchhike.

Taxi
There are daily taxis between Qacha's Nek and **Moyeni** that depart from outside the Shell petrol station.

Directory

Mafeteng *p783*
Banks Standard Bank and the Central Bank of Lesotho have branches in the town centre.

Mohales Hoek *p784*
Banks Standard Bank is on Mafoso Rd and the Central Bank of Lesotho is on Maluti Ring Rd near the post office.

Moyeni *p784*
Banks There is a branch of the Central Bank of Lesotho in upper Moyeni.

Qacha's Nek *p785*
Banks There is a branch of the Central Bank of Lesotho on the western outskirts of town.

Background

History

This brief section is not a history of all Basotho, but rather of the separate Basotho state. As the history of Lesotho is so tied up in that of South Africa, you should also refer to that section (see page 733).

The rise of the Basotho state

The roots of modern day Lesotho were in an era of intense political upheaval known to the Basotho as the *difaqane* (and the Zulu and Xhosa as the *mfecane*). The exact causes of the *difaqane* are a subject of considerable debate (see page 717) but what is clear is that out of this intense upheaval a new and powerful Basotho state was forged under the influential ruler Moshoeshoe. Before this time there had not been such a thing as a Basotho state, but simply a set of clans speaking similar dialects and with similar cultural practices. These clans formed constantly shifting sets of loose alliances and rivalries and their fortunes tended to wax and wane over time.

During the early 19th century these clans came under attack from highly organized and militarily ruthless Zulu and Ndebele armies (*impis*). Instead of uniting against these new enemies most clans ended up attacking their neighbours in an attempt to raid back cattle and grain lost to the *impis*. Moshoeshoe, chief of the insignificant Koena clan, however, had a more sophisticated approach. He carefully sued for peace with all the more powerful clans or marauding *impis* with whom he came into contact and would send them tribute gifts of cattle. At the same time he attacked and stole the cattle of weaker clans and then invited them to join with him in a new alliance. Using this strategy, Moshoeshoe was able to build up the power and influence of the Koena clan, especially after moving his headquarters to the strong defensive position at Thaba Boisiu. Soon his influence spread over the whole of the southern highveld with his chiefdom centred on the fertile Clarendon Valley. Unlike Shaka and Dingane, kings of the Zulu, Moshoeshoe did not insist that all his followers give up their previous clan identity and indeed his new Basotho state was more an alliance of a number of different clans than a united and centralized kingdom.

Wars with the Free State

During the 1830s, two new forces entered into the Basotho sphere from the south and west: Voortrekkers leaving the Cape Colony in search of new territory (see page 717); and missionaries looking for converts. These groups offered both threats and opportunities for the new Basotho state. The first missionaries to arrive in Lesotho were French Protestants. Moshoeshoe was keen to have them in Lesotho, partially because he wanted to learn more about the powerful Europeans impinging more and more on his state and partially to help him gain access to European guns. Their presence also presented a threat, however, as the converts' loyalty could sometimes be divided.

A more obvious threat came from the Voortrekkers. They wanted land and, unlike other new African arrivals, were unwilling to show allegiance to a Basotho state. With their guns and wagons they were a powerful military force and over the next 30 years slowly gained more and more control over areas formerly belonging to the Basotho. By the end of the 1860s the Basotho had lost half of their best arable land in the Clarendon Valley to the new Voortrekker Free State republic. But despite this major setback the Voortrekkers also provided the Basotho with an opportunity. Most were unable or unwilling to survive by farming, instead relying on hunting, trading and land speculating as their economic mainstay. They, therefore, had to buy food, especially grain, and the Basotho were able to provide them with it. Using new techniques, often learnt from the missionaries, and the new grain crop maize, brought by Europeans from the Americas, the Basotho developed a thriving agricultural economy. They soon began to trade not just with the Voortrekkers but also further afield, especially with the eastern districts of the Cape Colony. In exchange for grain the Basotho bought new European goods, especially guns.

Moshoeshoe realized, however, that their booming economy did not make them immune to attack from the Free State and he decided to turn to the British for help. At first the British refused to become involved but over time they began to realize that it was in their interests to have peace between the Boers and Basotho. In 1868, with Voortrekker commandos laying siege to Thaba Bosiu and burning acres of the Basotho's maize, the British declared Lesotho a British Protectorate. At a peace convention the following year the boundaries of Lesotho, or 'Basutoland' as the British named the area, were firmly established. The Basotho had lost huge swathes of their territory to the Free State but British protection did allow them to maintain a degree of political independence. This was more or less the last big political manoeuvre by Moshoeshoe, who died just two years later.

British Protection and the Gun War

At first the sole concern of the British was to maintain peace along the new boundaries, but that changed when administration was handed over from direct British rule to rule by the Cape Colony. The Cape Colony began to intervene in a more direct way in the government of the country. Chiefs found their powers reduced and everybody found themselves subject to a new hut tax. Not surprisingly, many Basotho were unhappy about these new arrangements. There were also tensions between the new Paramount Chief Letsie and his two brothers and also between the main Koena lineage and other clans who had been integrated into the Basotho state. One of these clans, the Phuti in southern Lesotho, refused to recognize the authority of the local Cape magistrate. When the magistrate tried to arrest the son of the Phuti's chief, Moorosi, open conflict broke out. To the disgust of many Basotho, Letsie sided with the Cape Colony and assisted in putting down the rebellion. In November 1879 after months of fighting the Cape forces finally stormed Moorosi's stronghold, slaughtering him and many of his people.

The following year there was another, more serious, outbreak of fighting. The immediate cause was the attempts by the Cape Colony to enforce a general policy of disarming all Basotho. For most Basotho, already unhappy about the way they were being administered and worried about rumours that the south of the country would be opened to white settlement, this was too much. The so-called Gun War of 1880-1881 saw the Cape forces verging on the brink of outright defeat and there were numerous bloody battles. Not all chiefs agreed with the war, however, and Letsie himself never publicly supported the attacks on the Cape authorities. Fighting broke out, especially in the north, between elements in favour of the war and those against it. Peace only returned when the British agreed to suspend the policy of enforced disarmament and agree that administration should be taken away from the Cape Colony and returned to rule from London.

Colonial era

The return to British rule also saw a return to the much less interventionist policy, and the country was basically administered through the chiefs, not white magistrates. The British continued with the policy right through until the 1930s and there were few significant political developments. Economically and socially, however, the country changed drastically. The early years of British rule saw the agricultural economy continue to thrive, especially as the new diamond mines at Kimberley gave the Basotho a new and profitable market to serve. Over time, however, these markets became less and less lucrative. The arrival of railways meant that Basotho farmers had to compete with cheap imported grain from places like the USA and Canada. And as time went on, white farmers were also providing more and more competition, especially after they began to receive vast quantities of state subsidies and other assistance. The agricultural economy began to falter and during the first decades of the 20th century the country no longer managed to produce enough food for export and indeed became a major importer. Part of the problem was also the migrant labour system that the Basotho found themselves tied into. Basotho men began to travel to the mines to earn wages to buy European goods and to pay taxes, but as the agricultural economy faltered it became more important for simple survival. This created a vicious cycle, as more Basotho men went to the mines there were fewer of them to help their wives with agriculture which, as a consequence, became less productive.

The early decades of the 20th century also saw the growth of a small but important educated class within Lesotho. They resented the continued political power of the chiefs and, through their Progressive Association, lobbied the British to introduce a more democratic system of administration. Another more radical political organization also began to make a mark. Known as *Lekhotla la Bafo* (Council of Commoners) this group was highly critical of both the British and of the chiefs, who they claimed were corrupt, and conniving with the British to impoverish the Basotho nation. While criticizing the chiefs for their individual actions they strongly supported the institution of chieftainship and advocated a return to pre-colonial systems of government.

One of the key reasons the British never bothered to intervene (and certainly not invest any money) in Lesotho was their belief that the country would at some stage be incorporated into the rest of South Africa. Over time, however, this eventuality became less and less likely, especially with the enactment of increasingly racist segregation legislation in South Africa. The British colonial authorities realized that transferring the country's administration to South Africa would not only encounter stiff opposition in Lesotho but also from the increasing number of people in Britain criticizing the South African government. From the mid-1930s and especially after 1945 the British colonial authorities, therefore, began to take a more active interest in the internal affairs of Lesotho, and even began to invest some capital into development schemes for the country.

The Progressive Association lobbied the British hard for the introduction of a more democratic government, believing that they, the educated élite, should be the country's natural leaders not the chiefs. Starting in the late 1930s, the British started to reform the system of government. These reforms at first had the effect of increasing the power of a few of the most important chiefs, to the detriment of some of the less important ones. This was one of the major causes of an outbreak of 'medicine murders' in which people were killed in order to use parts of their bodies in 'medicines' believed to bring power or protection. A number of the most important chiefs were implicated in these murders, which were seen by many as further proof that the chiefs were incapable of running the country. From the mid-1950s onwards new reforms led to a decrease in all chiefs' political powers and the gradual handing over of the national administration to the developing political parties.

The first of these new political parties was the Basutoland Congress Party (BCP). The BCP had many of its roots in the *Lekhotla la Bafo* organization and strong links with the ANC in South Africa, especially with the 'Africanist' wing of the ANC who later split to form the PAC (see pages 726-733). Not unlike *Lekhotla la Bafo*, which withered away as the BCP grew, the BCP did not call for a return to 'traditional' Basotho political systems but for a new democratic and independent nation. One of the key elements of its platform was strong criticism of the racist South African regime. This stance was opposed by some more conservative elements within the organization and they split to form a rival Basutoland National Party (BNP). The BNP was more traditional in outlook and received substantial support from the Catholic Church. The first elections in the country were held in 1960 to elect members to District Councils who then sent representatives to the National Council. These elections returned BCP candidates around the country, but the turnout was extremely low and women had still not been granted suffrage.

The British colonial authorities entered into wide-ranging discussions with the members of the National Council about writing a new national constitution under which the country would be granted its independence. After numerous wranglings a new constitution, based on the Westminster model, was produced. There would be a directly elected lower house from which the prime minister and cabinet would be chosen and an appointed upper house (Senate) consisting of the most important chiefs. The Senate's powers were limited to delaying legislation. Much to the dismay of the new and young incumbent, Moshoeshoe II, the monarch was to be no more than a ceremonial Head of State. Under this new constitutional framework elections were held in 1965 to form the government to take Lesotho to independence. To the surprise of many these were won by a tiny majority by the BNP. Their leader, Leabua Jonathan, therefore became the country's first Prime Minister and on 4 October 1966 Lesotho became an independent country.

Independence

Most Basotho had high expectations for this new system of government; expectation which the BNP proved incapable of fulfilling. The civil service was dominated by BCP members and the BNP was unwilling to work with them and instead relied on many expatriate workers, including a number from South Africa. The BNP's inability to deliver once in power helped the BCP regroup and in the 1970 elections they won a clear majority, maintaining their urban powerbase and managing to gain widespread support in the mountains as well. To the surprise of just about everyone Leabua Jonathan refused to hand over power, declared a state of emergency and arrested hundreds of BCP supporters. At first it looked as if he would have to come to an agreement with the BCP especially when Britain suspended all aid to Lesotho but as the crisis dragged on and Britain and other countries resumed their aid programmes the BNP's position became stronger.

Under pressure from Britain the BCP split, with some moderates entering into a new national assembly appointed by Jonathan to write a new constitution and others turning to more radical methods. An attempted counter-coup by elements of the BCP in January 1974 was a fiasco and the BNP tightened their grip on power. BCP civil servants were purged and activists arrested or sent into exile. Jonathan concentrated more and more power into his hands and developed many of the state security policies of other dictators. His attitude towards South Africa, however, shifted somewhat unexpectedly. From having been an advocate of close and cordial relations with the Apartheid regime he began to be more and more outspoken in his opposition. He developed close links with the ANC, who were offered support within Lesotho. This stance in turn brought him into confrontation with South Africa and led to attempts by South Africa to destabilize his regime. On the other hand the changed stance gave him increased legitimacy in the eyes of the international community and the government benefited from a generous influx of development aid.

The BCP, meanwhile, tried to build on its links with the PAC and some of their members received guerrilla training at camps in Libya. Elements within the South African security apparatus actively courted members of the BCP and offered them assistance in their attempts to wage a guerrilla war against Jonathan's regime. Some BCP members seemed willing to drink from this poison chalice and during much of the 1980s the country suffered a very low-level guerrilla war. Some members of the military were very unhappy with the situation and in 1986 the South Africans managed to toppled Jonathan's government.

At first the new government was a coalition between the military and Moshoeshoe II. Though they promised to hold new elections under a new constitution in the near future things moved very slowly and if anything the new regime was more corrupt than the previous one. Relations soon broke down between the military and Moshoeshoe II, who went into exile. In the early 1990s the military government began to make arrangements for new elections, with the process being spurred on by outbreaks of rioting and by the negotiation process across the border in South Africa. These long awaited elections finally took place in March 1993 and the BCP won a huge majority and every single seat in the national Parliament. Twenty three years after being denied his position the leader of the BCP, Ntsu Mokhehle, at last became Prime Minister.

Modern Lesotho

Politics

With the March 1993 election Lesotho returned to a system of parliamentary democracy, suspended in 1970 after Chief Jonathan refused to hand over power to the Basotho Congress Party. The current Prime Minister is Pakalitha Mosisili, who chairs a Cabinet made up of members of Parliament. In addition to the main elected legislative lower house there is an upper house, with the power to delay and comment upon legislation, made up of the most senior chiefs and a number of appointed members. The monarch again fulfils the largely ceremonial role of Head-of-State, with a limited political role.

Despite sweeping the board in the 1993 election the Basotho Congress Party (BCP) failed to build on its strong political position. Many people in the country felt that after so many years in the wilderness the BCP came to power with surprisingly few new policies in the pipeline. Periodic political unrest has continued despite the advent of democratic elections. The first of these turmoils was in August 1994 when King Letsie III (who had succeeded his father, Moshoeshoe II, when he was exiled in November 1990) dismissed the BCP government. Though the exact links between this royal coup and the military and the opposition BNP are a little hazy it is clear that Letsie III was not acting on his own. His excuse for declaring the suspension of the government was the allegation that the leader of the BCP, Ntsu Mokhehle, had entered into talks with neighbouring heads of government to deploy a peace-keeping force because of his fears about political interference from the military. In the ensuing political unrest a number of people were shot dead and many more injured when the police and the military broke up demonstrations against Letsie's actions. Mokhehle and the BCP refused to acknowledge that the head-of-state had dismissed their government and, after direct involvement from regional heads-of-government, Letsie III eventually backed down and re-instated the elected government.

Another element in this confused political situation was that Letsie III wanted to abdicate in favour of his father, Moshoeshoe II. Moshoeshoe II had returned to Lesotho shortly before the return to democracy, but had not taken over the throne. Moshoeshoe had fairly wide domestic support and was respected by many individuals in the international development community because of his pronouncements on human rights while in exile in the early 1990s (although some of his actions while in coalition with the first military government painted a slightly different picture). This popularity explained the reason why the BCP were not altogether keen on seeing him reinstated as King, despite Letsie's actions in August 1994. Nevertheless, in February 1995, after another bout of intense political activity, Letsie did abdicate in favour of his father. Moshoeshoe II's reign on the throne proved to be short-lived, on the 16 January 1996 he was killed in a car accident.

The BCP itself has been plagued by internal political wranglings, which came to a surprising climax in June 1997. Soon after the BCP came to power two tendencies emerged within the party: one became known as the Pressure Group and the other as Majelathoko. The Pressure Group, who saw themselves as more progressive, were led by Molapo Qhobela, whilst the more conservative faction organized itself around Prime Minister Mokhehle. The division became wider when Mokhehle sidelined Qhobela in both government and the party.

In retaliation, the Pressure Group attempted to remove Mokhehle from his position as leader of the BCP, a move that under the 'Westminster system' of government would have also forced him to stand down as Prime Minister. In mid-1997 the Pressure Group seemed to be on the verge of winning this political battle when Mokhehle totally outflanked them with a cunning political move. While Mokhehle knew there was a good chance that the party as a whole would vote against him he also calculated that he had the support of the majority of BCP members of Parliament. He therefore resigned from the BCP, registered a new political party (the Lesotho Congress of Democrats) – with him as leader, and managed to persuade 40 of the 63 elected BCP parliamentarians to join him in the new party. After a vote of confidence, his position as Prime Minister and a Lesotho Congress of Democrats (LDC) government were both confirmed, and the BCP became the official opposition party. While this move was unprecedented, it did not appear to be unconstitutional.

The opposition parties tried to restructure and reposition themselves to contend the 1998 general elections, which were won by the LDC under new leader Pakalitha Mosisili. Although the elections were deemed free and fair by international observers, opposition parties rejected the results, and protests intensified. This culminated in a violent demonstration outside the royal palace in August 1998. In September, junior members of the armed services mutinied, and, to prevent a full military coup, Prime Minister Mosisili appealed to the Southern African Development Community (SADC) to intervene and restore stability. A military group, comprising South African and Botswana troops, entered the country in September and encountered stiff resistance from the Lesotho Defence Force. Confusion spread throughout the country and there followed a period of intense unrest, with widespread looting and destruction of property. The South African shops in Maseru were looted and a large number of commercial buildings burnt down. Eventually South African and Botswana forces restored order and quelled the mutiny, and a long process of mediation began.

An interim council was established to prepare a new electoral system, under which elections are now processed. SADC troops left Lesotho in May 2000. Given Apartheid-era tensions, South Africa was uneasy about deploying troops in Lesotho, but the SADC intervention was ultimately successful in helping to maintain political stability. South Africa has set about improving relations with its neighbour, and is keen to emphasize Lesotho's sovereign equality. In 2001 the foreign ministers of Lesotho and South Africa met to begin mapping out a new relationship for the two countries. Elections in Lesotho in 2002 passed peacefully. The ruling LDC swept to victory and there were no signs of the instability that had followed the elections four years earlier.

Culture

Lesotho's population, of just under two million, is made up almost exclusively of Basotho people, and Sesotho is the language spoken by the vast majority. There are a few Xhosa speakers in Qacha's Nek district and a handful of Asian and European settlers in the lowland towns. One of the key reasons why there are few non-Basotho settlers in Lesotho is that (officially) all land is owned communally 'by the nation'. Unofficially there is a market in land but it is very difficult for a non-Basotho to own or even lease land.

Sotho: what's in a name?

Lesotho is one of the few countries in Africa in which the vast majority of people belong to the same ethnic ('tribal') group: the Basotho. Many people in South Africa will talk about 'the Sotho' but in Lesotho you will rarely hear the phrase: rather people will use the word Basotho, meaning 'the Sotho people'. The singular of Basotho is Mosotho, Sesotho is the language spoken by the Basotho and Lesotho means the place, or home, of the Basotho. Today there are as many Basotho living in South Africa as in Lesotho.

Population density in the lowlands is very high and the urban sprawl around Maseru merges into neighbouring towns and villages. In contrast the population in the mountain regions is very low and concentrated into the valleys. The high mountain tops are more or less uninhabited with the exception of the occasional herd boy. Over 80% of the population is rural, though the high density of population sometimes makes the rural/urban distinction a little hazy.

The vast majority of **Basotho**, over 80%, would classify themselves as Christians. The Catholic church is the largest and richest church in the country. In the past it received generous external funding, especially from Quebec, and indeed many of its priests were French Canadian. This has, however, dried up in recent years and efforts have been made to localize all the clergy. The Catholic Church was strongly associated with the establishment of the BNP and, though many priests were uneasy with the stance, it rarely voiced opposition to the autocratic regime of Chief Jonathan. The largest Protestant church, the Lesotho Evangelical Church (LEC), has received far less external funding and is much poorer, though its position as the first major autonomous church in Lesotho has given it prestige and strong local support. It was the first major church to ordain women and a growing number of its trainee clergy are female. The LEC frequently criticized the actions of Chief Jonathan and in return its leaders were persecuted by the government and many forced into exile. The Anglican church is also well represented in Lesotho and, as it is a diocese of the South African Anglican structure, it has good external contacts. There are also a large number of smaller churches and spiritualist movements which are receiving growing support, such as the Methodists, Pentacostalists, Zionists and Seventh Day Adventists. Whatever the specific church, Christianity plays an important part in the lives of most Basotho and the church is a focal point of many communal activities.

As in all societies, however, Christianity in Lesotho co-exists with other (sometimes contrary) beliefs and rituals. Many Basotho continue to include some elements of 'ancestor worship' in their religious practice and there is a strong belief in the power of witchcraft. Initiation ceremonies, including circumcision lodges for young men, still exist in many areas of Lesotho, indeed there is some evidence they have made something of a comeback in recent years.

One of Lesotho's biggest modern-day challenges is HIV/AIDS. The country has the third highest infection rate of HIV/AIDS in the world, with a prevalence rate of around 29%. The UN estimates that this rate is likely to increase to 36%, with a dramatic drop in national life expectancy. As in South Africa, the Lesotho government has been slow to recognise the scale of the crisis, although it now has a programme of education, counselling and treatment. In late 2005, it introduced the world's first HIV/AIDS testing project for the entire population (see page 764), which it hopes will reduce the stigma associated the HIV/AIDS and its treatment.

Land and environment

Geography

Lesotho is a small country of 30,350 square km totally surrounded by South Africa. The country is made up of a thin lowland strip along the Clarendon River valley in the west and a high mountain plateau cut into by numerous deep valleys. The lowland strip is in reality part of the great central plateau of southern Africa and hence the lowest altitude in Lesotho is over 300 m above sea level – the highest 'low point' in the world.

The vast majority of the country's rivers drain south and east. The headwaters of the famous Orange River (known as the Senqu in Lesotho) are in the far northwest of the country and its deeply incised valley runs diagonally across the mountain area, eventually flowing into South Africa across the southeastern border. Water is one of the few resources Lesotho has in abundance and, given the growing constraints of water shortages on South Africa's economy, it is a resource that is becoming increasingly valuable. The headwaters of a number of tributaries of the Senqu River are currently being developed in the massive Highlands Water Project to allow water to be transferred to economically important South African river systems. Phase one of the scheme was successfully completed in 1996. The huge weight generated by filling up the dam triggered a number of minor local earth tremors, but these problems now seem to have been overcome. The Mohole dam was operational by 2004. Lesotho has few other natural resources. Some diamonds have been discovered but not in profitable quantities and there is little hope of any lucrative mineral deposits.

With the exception of a few willows and fruit trees in sheltered kloofs and government sponsored woodlots, Lesotho is treeless. The lowlands and mountain valleys are planted with maize and, in the higher areas, wheat. The vast majority of the country is given over to communal grazing: the mountain grasses are considered to be some of the best sheep pasture in southern Africa.

Wildlife

Lesotho's large mammalian fauna has been decimated by hunting and displaced by agriculture. If you are very lucky you may see an eland in Sehlabathebe National Park or perhaps the occasional baboon or jackal, but there is none of the large game generally associated with southern Africa. There are, however, a number of interesting and unusual bird species, such as the bald ibis, found particularly in Mokhotlong district. The natural flora is dominated by grasses.

Swaziland

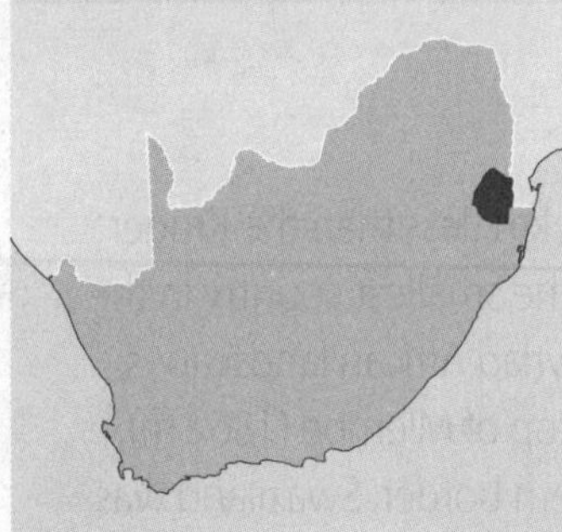

Footprint features

Introduction

With an area of just over 17,000 sq km (less than the Kruger National Park), Swaziland may be the smallest country in the southern hemisphere but it has myriad African landscapes, all of which can be seen from the top of Mlembe (1862 m), a mountain on the country's western border. Swaziland was plundered by European gold prospectors in the 19th century but, unlike South Africa, huge fortunes were never really made here and even throughout the colonial period, the government was more or less left in the hands of the royal family. Following independence in 1968, Swaziland has remained one of only three monarchies left in Africa, and is the only absolute monarchy on the continent.

On the whole, Swaziland is an accessible country to visit; it has moderate temperatures all year round, you can travel between the highveld and the lowveld in a day, and none of the major sights are more than a two-hour drive away. The tourist industry developed during the Apartheid years, when South African tourists left their puritanical regime to visit Swaziland's casinos and nightclubs. Unfortunately, as a consequence, the country developed a reputation for seedy sex and gambling holidays, but since the change of government in South Africa, this market has, thankfully, plummeted. Thanks to a handful of pioneering conservationists, effective anti-poaching initiatives and substantial animal restocking, Swaziland's game parks have improved dramatically in recent years. It's also a good destination for adventurers, with a good backpackers' set-up and a number of adventure activities on offer. The Swazi people are friendly and expert craft makers, producing a wealth of high-quality African curios. Compared to South Africa, Swaziland is a country where tribal values, craftsmanship and royal loyalty have withstood the test of encroaching modernization.

★ Don't miss...

1 **Swazi Trails** Get your adrenaline pumping on a white-water rafting or caving trip, in the safe hands of an excellent tour operator, page 800.
2 **Mlilwane Wildlife Sanctuary** Sleep in a traditional Swazi beehive hut and share the landscape with zebra, giraffe, warthog and wildebeest, page 805.
3 **Swazi Cultural Village** Watch traditional dancing and singing and, if you are very lucky, an authentic marriage ceremony, page 806.
4 **Royal Swazi Spa** Try out the intriguingly named Cuddle Puddle at this good-value pampering centre, page 811.
5 **Nisela Safaris** Frolic with some lion cubs at this informative private game reserve; kids will love it, page 815.

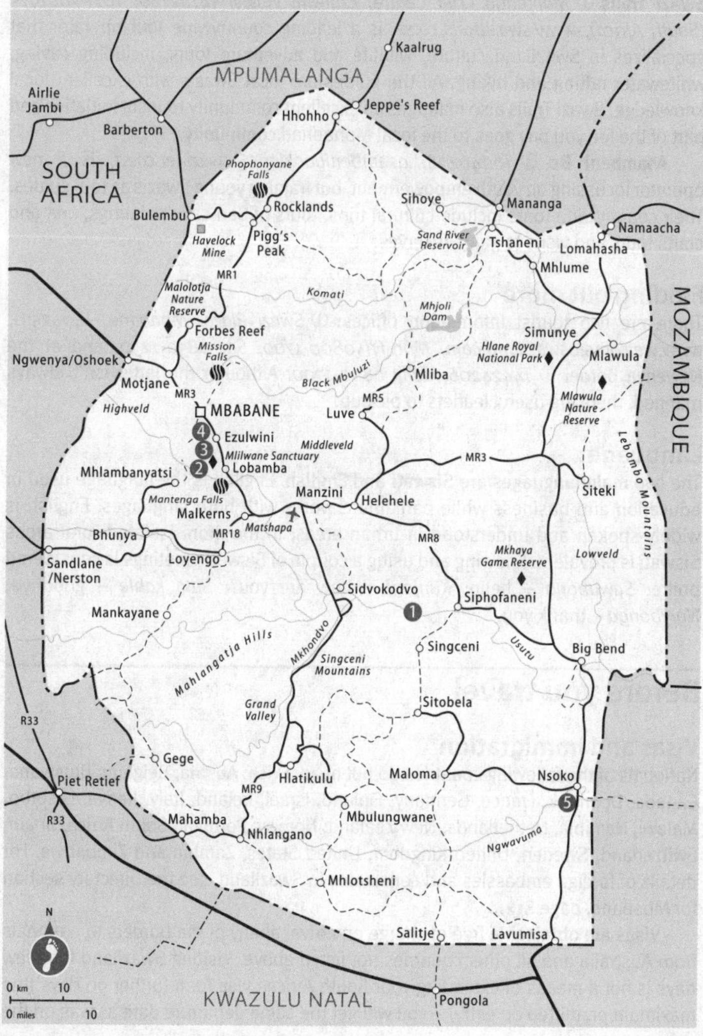

Essentials

Planning your trip

When to go
The climate varies between the different geographical regions but all the areas are affected by high summer rainfall. The mountains in the northwest are cooler than the southeast lowveld where temperatures can become swelteringly hot. The coolest time of year is April to September; the high summer temperatures and the rainy season are from October to March.

Tour operators
Swazi Trails ⓘ *Mantenga Craft Centre, Ezulwini Valley, T4162180; T011-7041975 (South Africa), www.swazitrails.co.sz*, is a leading countrywide tour operator that specializes in Swaziland culture, wildlife and adventure tours, including caving, whitewater rafting and hiking. All the guides are local Swazis with excellent local knowledge. Swazi Trails also manages an excellent community tourism initiative and part of the fee you pay goes to the local Mphaphati community.

Asambeni Bo ⓘ *T6046238, asambenibookings@swazinet.co.sz*, is a new operator focussing on youth empowerment, but training young Swazis as tour guides. Their countrywide tours include cultural trips, tours of San cave paintings, arts and crafts tours and visits to game reserves.

Finding out more
There are two tourist information offices: ⓘ *Swazi Plaza, Mbabane, T4042531, www.welcometoswaziland.com, Mon-Fri 0800-1700, Sat 0830-1230*, and at the Ngwenya border ⓘ *T4424206, daily 0800-1700*. Although the latter isn't always manned, there are useful leaflets to pick up.

Language
The two main languages are **Siswati** and **English**. English is the language used in education and business while parliament works with both languages. English is widely spoken and understood in urban areas; in the more isolated rural areas Siswati is prevalent. Knowing and using a couple of Siswati greetings is considered polite: *Sawubona* – hello; *Kunjani* – how are you?; *Sala kahle* – goodbye; *Ngiybonga* – thank you.

Before you travel

Visas and immigration
Nationals of the following countries do not need a visa: Austria, Belgium, Botswana, Canada, Denmark, France, Germany, Finland, Israel, Ireland, Italy, Kenya, Lesotho, Malawi, Namibia, Netherlands, New Zealand, Norway, Portugal, South Africa, Spain, Switzerland, Sweden, United Kingdom, United States, Zambia and Zimbabwe. For details of foreign embassies and consulates in Swaziland, see the Directory section for Mbabane, page 812.

Visas are obtainable free of charge on arrival at any of the borders to nationals from Australia and all other countries not listed above. Visiting Swaziland for a few days is not a means of extending your South African visa for a further 90 days (the maximum permitted on entry) – you will get the same departure date as was on the

Touching down

- → **Police** T42221
- → **Business hours** **Banks** Mon-Fri 0830-1400, Sat 0830-1100. **Post offices** Mon-Fri 0800-1600, Sat 0800-1100. **Shops** Mon-Fri 0830-1700, Sat 0830-1300. Some larger supermarkets are open on Sunday mornings.
- → **IDD code** +268
- → **Time** GMT +5
- → **Voltage** 220-240v
- → **Weights and measures** The metric system is more common than imperial.

original South African visa. If your South Africa visa expires while you are in Swaziland, South African immigration on re-entry to South Africa will give you another one- to two-week stamp allowing you enough time to get to a Department of Home Affairs office and extend in the proper way. See www.home-affairs.gov.za, to find out the nearest office.

Money

Swaziland's currency is the **Lilangeni** (plural *Emalangeni*, E) and is equivalent to the South African Rand. Traveller's cheques can be changed in Mbabane but the process is slow. You are better off bringing in cash in the form of South African Rand. Both the Rand and the Emalangeni are accepted currencies just about everywhere.

Make sure you change any Emalangeni back into Rand or other currencies before leaving the country – Emalangeni is not a convertible currency. There are no restrictions on the import/export of local and foreign currency, and it is not worth changing your Rand into Emalangeni for just a short visit. Travellers' cheques can be changed at the following banks: **First National Bank, Nedbank, Standard Bank, Swazi Bank** and **Central Bank of Swaziland.**

Major credit cards such as **Visa, Mastercard** and **American Express** are accepted in hotels, large town chainstores, some restaurants, and the national parks and game reserves for accommodation, though you are advised to use cash for smaller items and services. ATMs are available in Mbabane and Manzini; credit cards can be used to withdraw cash, either through the machine or from a teller.

Getting there

There are 13 border posts in total, 11 with South Africa and two with Mozambique. Visas for Mozambique are now issued at the border. The border posts are open every day of the year, including public holidays, and immigration and customs formalities take about 30 minutes. The four principal entry points from South Africa are **Ngwenya/Oshoek** (to Ermelo and the most convenient for Gauteng), the largest and busiest border, daily 0700-2200; **Mahamba** (to Piet Retief in Mpumalanga), daily 0700-2200; **Lavumisa** (KwaZulu Natal and most convenient for Durban), daily 0700-2200; and **Lomahasha/Namaacha**, (Mozambique) daily 0700-2200. Minor entry points tend to have shorter opening hours (eg Bulumbu, daily 0800-1600). There is an E5 road tax on all vehicles entering Swaziland and cars hired in South Africa are usually permitted into Swaziland. » *For further details, see Ins and outs, page 803, and Transport, page 811.*

Getting around

The easiest way of getting around is by car and, in such a little country, everything of interest is within a couple of hours' drive. Roads are well signposted and tarred, though beware of drunk driving in the evenings and weekends (the laws are far less stringent here than in South Africa). Note the law requires that all vehicles move to the side of the road and stop when approached by an official (usually royal) motorcade led by police escorts. The **Baz Bus** offers an efficient and frequent service through Swaziland. Frequent minibus taxis ply the road through the Ezulwini Valley between Mbabane and Manzini.

Festivals and events

New Year's Day 1 January; **Good Friday; Easter Monday; King Mswati III's Birthday** 19 April; **National Flag Day** 25 April; **Ascension Day; King Sobhuza II's Birthday** 24 May; **Public Holiday** 22 July; **Umhlanga Dance** August/September; **Independence Day** 6 September; **Christmas Day** 25 December; **Incwala Day** December/January.

Shopping

There is a concentration of craft outlets and farm shops along the Ezulwini Valley road, and at the **Mantenga Craft Centre**, see page 807, which has a varied selection of high-quality handcrafted clothes, screen prints, leather goods, ceramics, rugs and carvings.

Sport and activities

Caving

Guided adventure caving excursions are available to the largely unexplored Gobholo cave system near Mbabane. This is the only known major cave system in granite rock in southern Africa and thus presents a unique experience. The deepest distance travelled is 90 m below the surface and the total distance travelled underground is about 800 m. See Swazi Trails, page 800, for further details.

Golf

In addition to the major hotel development that was designed to attract South Africans to Swaziland, some superb golf courses were built. The course at the **Royal Swazi Sun** (see page 808) holds an annual championship, while smaller country club courses present a challenge to most players.

Hiking

Some of Southern Africa's finest hiking can be found in **Malolotja Nature Reserve**, a wild a rugged reserve peppered with waterfalls and broken up by streams (see page 818). **Sibebe Rock**, just outside of Mbabane, is arguably one of the steepest walks in southern Africa. The rock is a 300-m high granite dome and there are some great views of rural Swaziland from the top, which is littered with massive boulders and caves once inhabited by the San. A new initiative is the **Ngwempisi Hiking Trail**, T6256004, situated in the Ngwempisi Gorge in the south, a 33-km trail following the river and passing through indigenous forest, with overnight stays in huts. Other hikes include guided and self-guided trails in the nature reserves, such as the two-hour rhino walk in **Hlane Royal National Park** (see page 813), and the walk to the falls in Malolotja Nature Reserve.

National parks

There are seven reserves which are all worth a visit for different reasons. Three of the reserves are privately run, the other four are managed by the Swaziland government. The **National Trust Commission** ① *National Museum, PO Box 100, Lobamba, T4161481, www.sntc.org.sz*, manages Malolotja, Mantenga, Hawane and Mlawula. **Big Game Parks** ① *T5283944/3, www.biggameparks.org*, manages Hlane Royal National Park, Mlilwane Wildlife Sanctuary and Mkhaya Game Reserve.

Whitewater rafting

Operated by **Swazi Trails** (see page 800), whitewater rafting is offered year-round on the Great Usutu River. A new stretch of river has opened in the remote Bulunga Gorge with a couple of adrenaline-pumping grade IV and V rapids. Two-man rafts are used, shepherded by guides in kayaks. The average full-day trip is 13 km; a longer trip of 23 km and a shorter half-day trip of 7 km are undertaken on occasions.

Health

Swaziland has malaria risk in all lowland areas. Follow the health advice for South Africa on page 58.

Keeping in touch

Telephone

When making a call within the country there are no area codes to remember. If you are calling Swaziland from abroad, the IDD code is +268. So, when calling from South Africa, dial the international access code 09, followed by Swaziland's IDD code (+268), then the telephone number. Direct dialling for international calls is possible in Mbabane but in rural areas you will need to book such a call. All the luxury hotels have an efficient telephone system but they charge very high rates for international calls. If your mobile phone has international roaming it will work throughout Swaziland.

Mbabane and around

➔ *Colour map 2, grid C5. Altitude: 1,250 m.*

Mbabane is a small modern town built on the site of a trading station on the busy route between Mozambique and the Transvaal. After the Boer War the British established their administrative headquarters here and the town grew up around them. The main street is named after Allister Miller, a journalist who moved from Barberton. He founded the Times of Swaziland *and helped to deal with the fiasco caused by the concessions (see Background, page 821). But Mbabane never benefited architecturally from these eras. Over the last few decades, development has been in the form of a disorganized collection of unattractive concrete blocks and a snarled traffic system, broken up by modern shopping malls. It remains a small town, however, and the main business district is spread over a small grid of busy streets in the centre of town.* ▸▸ *For Sleeping, Eating and other listings, see pages 808-812.*

Ins and outs

Getting there and around Matsapha Airport is Swaziland's main airport where all international passenger flights arrive. The airport is 8 km from Manzini and 25 km from Mbabane. A departure tax of E50 is payable on departure.

There are buses from Mbabane to all major centres in Swaziland, though they may only run a couple of times per day on each route – arrive early at the bus station. Minibus taxis run regular short routes, but the vehicles are generally of poor standard, making them dangerous. Do not use them. The **Baz Bus** (see page 39) includes Swaziland on its route between Durban and Johannesburg and Pretoria and drops off and picks up at the backpacker hostels. ➤ *For further details, see Transport page 811.*

Tourist information The **Swaziland Information Office** ⓘ *Swazi Plaza, T4042531, www.welcometoswaziland.com, Mon-Fri 0800-1700, Sat 0830-1230*, is an extremely helpful office with a wide range information on hotels, nature reserves and tour operators. It also produces a useful annual brochure, covering the whole country.

Sights

Mbabane is a cluster of concrete shopping malls at the bottom of a hill, surrounded by ring roads and the highway that leads to the nearby Ezulwini Valley. There isn't much to do here and it's the valley itself that holds the best of the Swazi attractions, but the **Swazi market** near the central roundabout is worth a quick look for its excellent display of fresh produce. Piled in high pyramids on wooden stalls are mangoes, tomatoes, cabbages, pineapples and avocados. You can engage in some good- humoured bartering with the Swazi women. There are also a few curios, although you'll get better value in the rural areas where these items are made. Mbabane also has a selection of South African chain stores, which are useful for stocking up.

Ezulwini Valley

➤ *pp808-812. Colour map 2, grid C5.*

Clearly signposted from Mbabane, the Ezulwini Valley (the Valley of Heaven) is the centre of Swaziland's tourist industry. The tourist route follows the old main road through Ezulwini. Take the fly-off at the bottom of Malagwane Hill. In the daytime there are superb views as you leave the highveld and drop into the middleveld. The valley itself has no real centre, but every few hundred metres you will pass a smart hotel, craft shop or restaurant. The 30 km long valley ends at Lobamba, the Royal Village of the King.

Ezulwini Valley to Manzini

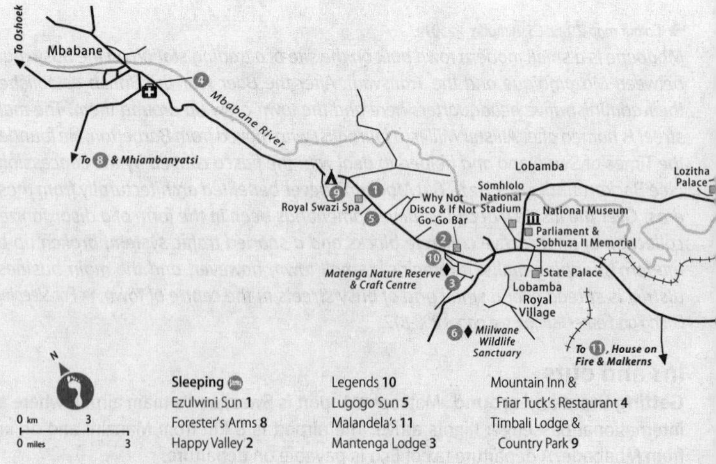

Lobamba

At the eastern end of the Ezulwini Valley before the airport is the royal village of Lobamba, set amongst typical open bush countryside. This is where the present king, King Mswati III, lives and from where he rules Swaziland with his Queen Mother or Ndlovukazi, meaning 'she-elephant'. Every August the king gets to add to his growing stable of wives at the **Umhlanga (Reed) Dance** when virgins perform in front of the 'she-elephant' and the King picks out his next wife – an honour she cannot refuse. The custom has attracted increasing criticism over the years, notably in 2003 when the King's choice was not supported by the bride's family. Nevertheless, it is an astounding event, where hundreds of young women from across the country congregate and dance bare-breasted in front of a congregation of royalty, subjects and curious tourists.

All of the royal buildings are closed to the public, but the **Somhlolo National Stadium** is the venue for major celebrations, including sports events, musical shows and royal events such as the annual independence celebrations and the Reed Dance. On no account try to take any photographs of the Lozitha Palace or the Embo State Palace. The parliament buildings are open to visitors but the effort to gain admittance is not worth the tour.

Of much greater interest is the **National Museum** ① *T4161178, Mon-Fri 0800-1300, 1400-1545, Sat and Sun 1000-1300, 1400-1545, E10*, which has some excellent displays relating to Swazi life throughout history, with old photographs, traditional dress and Stone Age implements. If you wish to find out more ask for a guided tour, well worth it for an insight into local life and customs. The offices of the National Trust Commission are in the museum;l they are responsible for the management of Malolotja, Mantenga and Mlawula Nature Reserves. Opposite the museum is a memorial to King Sobhuza II and a small museum depicting his life. His statue stands under a domed cover with open arches and an immaculate white tiled floor.

Mlilwane Wildlife Sanctuary » pp808-812.

Mlilwane is one of the most popular of Swaziland's nature reserves and covers a varied landscape of highveld and lowveld along a section of the Ezulwini Valley. It is a peaceful and beautiful reserve, allowing a wide range of activities, from self- guided walking to mountain biking, with a good chance of getting very close to wildlife. The land which now makes up the sanctuary was originally used as farm-land and for tin mining. The hydraulic sluicing used to mine the tin with high pressure water jets had caused massive damage to the landscape leaving it scarred with ravines. The mine operators had simply abandoned the land after the mine closed, leaving a wasteland of slag heaps and open excavations behind.

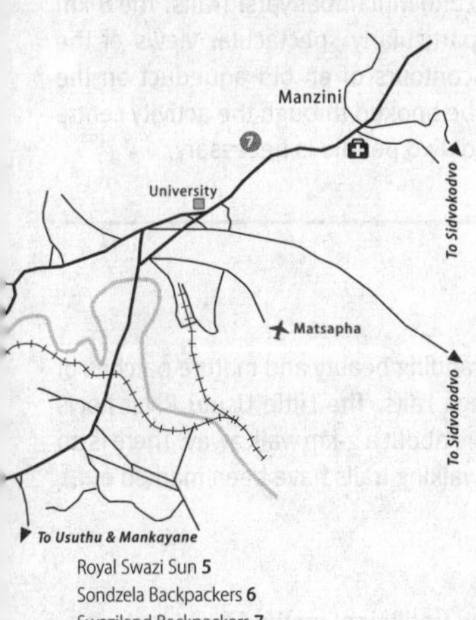

The land has been extensively regenerated into a wildlife sanctuary, and it is now possible to see a wide variety of bird and animal species, including: hippo, giraffe, crocodile, eland, zebra, blue wildebeest, kudu, nyala, klipspringer, waterbuck, impala, steenbuck, duiker, warthog, suni antelope, oribi, many species of waterfowl and purple-crested

The world's most dangerous road?

The road to Manzini and the Ezulwini Valley from Mbabane has to be one of the world's most dramatic roads. It is very straight and alarmingly steep. Before the recent completion of a double-lane highway, which involved whole sides of the mountain being blasted away, this road was little more than a narrow track going straight down a cliff face. All other traffic had to get out of the way if the royal family's motorcade was going up or down between Mbabane and the Royal Palace in the Ezulwini Valley. It once made a listing in the Guinness Book of World Records as having the highest car accident rate in the world. The father of Ted Reilly (the man who was instrumental in reintroducing wildlife into Swaziland's parks), owned the first car in Swaziland, a Model T Ford. This road was so steep for the rudimentary car that the only way he could get back up to the top was in reverse.

lourie, the brilliantly coloured national bird of Swaziland. For more information visit www.biggameparks.org.

Ins and outs

Getting there The reserve is signposted just past the Caltex service station at Lobamba. Turn right and travel 4 km to Sangweni Gate at eSitjeni. Gates are open 24 hours allowing guests staying in the reserve to visit the nightlife, casinos and restaurants in the Ezulwini Valley. Entry is R25 per person, which covers the whole length of your stay within the sanctuary. The Interpretorium in the rest camp and the Sangweni Gate complex offer interesting information on nature conservation in Swaziland, including anti-poaching efforts.

Sights

There are over 100 km of dirt roads, with some marked for 4WD vehicles only. As there are no predators in the park, the wildlife is quite relaxed, enabling close viewing. Alternatives for exploring the sanctuary include guided horse rides, open 4WD game drives, guided mountain-bike rides, and an extensive system of self-guided walking trails including the Macobane, Sondzela, Hippo and Mhlambanyatsi Trails. The 8-km **Macobane Trail** offers an easy gradient and particularly spectacular views of the Ezulwini Valley as it winds its way along the contours of an old aqueduct on the Nyonyane Mountain (1136 m). All activities can be booked through the activity centre at the main camp. For all activities a minimum of two people is necessary.

Mantenga Nature Reserve

ⓘ *T4161151, www.sntc.org.sz. E25.*

Close to the Mantenga Lodge is an area of outstanding beauty and mature patches of forest between the main road and the Mantenga Falls. The Little Usutu River flows through the area and the well-known waterfalls are about a 2-km walk away. There is an authentic cultural village, and picnic spots and walking trails have been marked out.

Swazi Cultural Village

ⓘ *Daily 0830-1800.*

Every aspect of this 'show' village is based upon traditional methods and materials. This is exactly how a medium-sized Swazi homestead would have looked 100 years ago. There are 16 beehive-shaped huts built from local materials, laid out in a plan that can be seen throughout rural Swaziland. The huts form a semicircle partly surrounded by a cattle kraal. The focal point is a larger hut, the 'great hut', and the kraal. This is a polygamous homestead – each wife has her own circle of huts for cooking, making beer and sleeping in. Slightly separate are the huts for unmarried mature boys and girls and for married sons.

The whole complex is brought to life by traditional dance performances and songs as the guides show visitors around. You will also see food being prepared, clothes and household objects being made. The **Swazi River Café** is a great place for a sundowner (see Eating, page 811).

Mantenga Craft Centre

ⓘ *T4161136, www.mantengacrafts.com. Daily 0830-1700.*

The Mantenga Foundation was formed in 1974 to retail the finished works of local artists in the Mantenga Craft Centre. From the outset, the project has been managed on the basis of long term self-sufficiency. The centre stocks an excellent range of jewellery, crafts, clothes, gold and silver, screen prints, leather goods, ceramics, rugs and carvings. There is also a coffee shop and snack bar and a small tourist information desk with a selection of brochures. **Swazi Trails** are also based here. See Tour operators, page 800.

Swaziland is an excellent place to buy curios, with a wider selection and lower prices than in South Africa.

Malkerns Valley

About 5 km beyond the National Museum is a right turning for Malkerns, M18. This makes for an enjoyable circuit from Mbabane which can easily be covered on a day trip, although most people choose to stay overnight in Mlilwane Wildlife Sanctuary (see page 809). This is the ideal place to discover a more typical Swazi lifestyle than you encounter along the Ezulwini Valley. One kilometre from the junction towards Malkerns is a cluster of roadside shops and farmstalls. **Swazi Candles** ⓘ *T5283219, www.swazicandles.com*, is one of the best known shops in the country, producing interesting candles in a variety of designs and colours. A newer addition is the **House on Fire**, a stylish complex which includes the **Malandela** restaurant, an internet café, a live music venue and a B&B (see page 809). Also here is **Baobab Batik** and **Gone Rural**, which sells stylish, contemporary woven goods in bright colours.

The spiky, dark-green plants growing in the fields along the Malkerns Valley are pineapple plants.

Bhunya and around

The road south from Malkerns towards Bhunya (26km) is tarred, and for part of the route it follows the Great Usutu River, passing rolling farmlands; be careful of groups of schoolchildren and cattle straying into the road. As the road climbs up into the highlands, the forest closes in and it can get quite cool out of the sunlight. The factory town of Bhunya is the centre of the local timber industry – the local pulp mill is responsible for much of the local pollution. From Bhunya there is a choice of two routes. The road to the South African border (34 km) at **Sandlane/ Nerston** (daily 0800-1800) crosses the Lusutfu River and then climbs steeply for 2 km into the coniferous plantations. This is the **Usutu Forest** a man-made plantation which extends for over 65,000 ha. All along this road are numerous lookout towers protecting Swaziland's forests. The second road out of Bhunya heads north towards **Mhlambanyatsi** and Mbabane.

Sleeping

Mbabane *p, map p808*

A **Mountain Inn**, 4 km out of town on the road to Ezulwini Valley, T4042781, www.mountaininn.sz. 60 smart, comfortable rooms, en suite bathrooms, telephone, TV, swimming pool and need lawns, **Friar Tuck** à la carte restaurant, balconies have commanding views over the mountains and valley. Offers a range of excursions and rents out mountain bikes.

B **City Inn**, Allister Miller St, city centre, T4042406, cityinn@realnet.co.sz. 28 rooms, en suite bathroom, some a/c, TV, laundry service, **Pablo's** restaurant and **Caribbean Coffee Shop**. Big difference between the new rooms and the originals in the old part of the hotel. Advisable to look at the room on offer before making your mind up.

C **Kapola Guest House**, T4048266, kapolaeden@swazi.com, phone Annette for directions, 6 km in a suburb to the west of town. 5 en suite rooms, comfortable decor, TV lounge, breakfast buffet, secure parking.

C **Khula Golden Guest House**, Moba St, well signposted from Allister Miller St, 3 km from town in an upmarket suburb, T4045095, khula@africaonline.co.sz. B&B rooms or self-catering units, swimming pool, braai areas, secure parking in lock-up garages, nice views over the city.

E **All Ways**, 18 Mabandla St, T4050741, all-ways@mailfly.com. Double-storey thatched house, long-standing backpacker's but recently refurbished. Dorms, double rooms, secure off-street parking, large garden with space for tents, good meals prepared, shared kitchen. Baz Bus stop.

Ezulwini Valley *p804, map p804*

AL **Royal Swazi Sun**, T4165000, www.suninternational.com. 149 a/c rooms, TV, bar, restaurant, gym, sauna, spa, swimming pool, bowls, squash, tennis, horse riding, 18-hole golf course, **Gigi's** French restaurant, casino, every room has magnificent views of the valley and mountains, probably the most luxurious hotel in Swaziland, an amazing contrast to life in the rest of the country.

A **Ezulwini Sun**, T411550, www.suninternational.com. 60 a/c rooms, TV, **Valley Blues** restaurant, coffee shop, swimming pool, sauna, tennis, horse riding, volleyball, casino next door, ghastly Caribbean decor.

B **Lugogo Sun**, in the grounds of the **Royal Swazi**, T4164000, www.suninternational.com. 202 a/c rooms, Ilanga restaurant, bar, a large establishment aimed at families, caters for conferences and large tour groups, 'pub night' on Wed has a live band – popular with ex-pats and locals from all over the country.

C **Happy Valley Hotel**, T4161061, www.happyvalley.co.sz. Good value and lots going on, next door to the **Why Not Disco**, and **If Not Go-Go Bar**. There are several restaurants, bars, and nightclubs in and around the hotel so it's the place to go if you want to live it up, probably not suitable for children though. 57 a/c rooms with fridge,

Mbabane

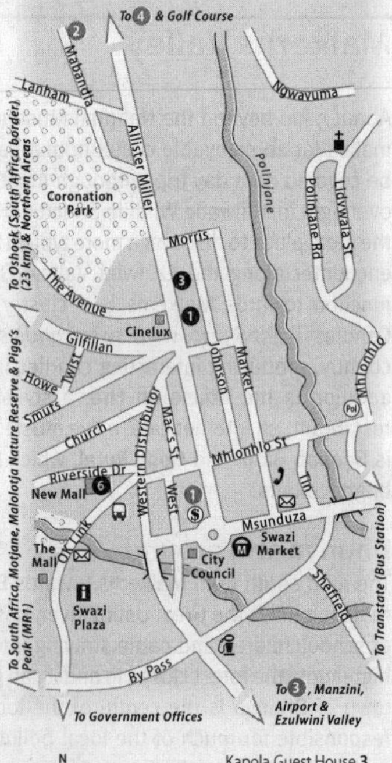

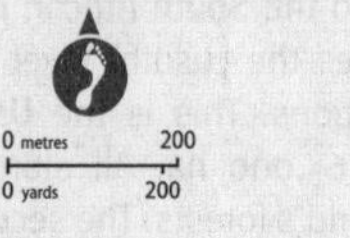

Sleeping
All Ways 2
City Inn 1
Kapola Guest House 3
Khula Golden Guest House 4

Eating
Finesse 6
La Casserole 3
Mediterranean 1

TV, in a simple concrete block around a pool, rates include breakfast and entry to the disco and the Royal Swazi Casino, ask for special 3-day weekend specials.

C **Mantenga Lodge**, T4161049, www.mantengalodge.com. 38 en suite double rooms with satellite TV, à la carte restaurant with wide outdoor terrace, lively bar, swimming pool, sauna, hidden amongst the trees this is a pleasant country hotel next to the **Mantenga Craft Centre** and in the Mantenga Nature Reserve, with easy access to the Mlilwane Wildlife Sanctuary.

C-E **Timbali Lodge & Country Park**, T4161156, www.timbali.co.sz. 24 nicely decorated en suite rooms, fridge, TV, and 3 self-catering family cottages, popular for conferences. Also has campsite covering 1½ ha with 30 terraced sites and is well grassed and shady. Pool, dinner is served in a boma, braais or a variety of potjies. **Joy's Coffee Shop** serves breakfasts and light lunches.

E **Legends** , opposite the **Matenga Craft Centre**, T4161870, www.legends.co.sz. Rather run-down hostel with doubles, dorms, camping, internet access, bar and meals on request. Friendly staff and a good setting, but needs an overhaul.

Mlilwane Wildlife Sanctuary

p805, map p804

Reservations for all through **Big Game Parks**, T5283944/3, www.biggameparks.org.

A **Reilly's Rock Hilltop Lodge**, or 'kaGogo', 3 km from the Main Camp, www.reillys rock.com. This is an exclusive 6-room period guesthouse and 4-bed family cottage, brimming with antiques and local history, en suite facilities, set in a lush tract of botanical gardens with fabulous views of the game sanctuary. Rates include entry, dinner, bed and breakfast. This is the original home of Ted Reilly's father and the main house dates back 100 years. Recommended.

D **Nyonyane Camp**, on the park's eastern periphery, 3 self-catering and en suite wooden cottages with communal braai area.

D-F **Main Camp**, traditional Swazi thatched huts known as the Beehive Village, 15 twin en suite, 17 twin and 3 triple with ablution block, camping ground under the shade of eucalyptus trees, self-catering facilities, bedding provided. NB If you are self catering, watch your food – the local warthogs don't think twice about foraging in tents or kitchen huts. Hippo Haunt restaurant with a lovely deck overlooking a hippo pool. Warthogs, ostriches and impalas frequently wander through the grounds. Swimming pool. Traditional dancing team, made up of park staff, performs on a nightly basis in The iNkhundla, a boma in the Main Camp.

E-F **Sondzela Backpackers**, 15 mins' walk from the main camp, T5283117, www.sondzela.com. Excellent backpackers in a stunning setting overlooking the Nyonyane Mountains, in the centre of the reserve. Spotless dorms, twins and doubles in the large main house, plus very comfortable and spacious thatched rondavels sleeping up to 4, with shared ablutions. Camping, tents and bedding can be hired, pool, volleyball court, bar with pool table. Great meals served around a roaring fire, shop selling basic food, ATM machine. Travel desk can arrange a wide choice of tours in the area, making this a great choice for people without their own transport. Baz Bus stop. Excellent value, good fun and in a beautiful setting – the best budget option in the country. Highly recommended.

Malkerns Valley *p807*

B **Forester's Arms**, 12 km out of Bhunya, T4674177, www.forestersarms.co.za. Delightful hotel set in the cool Great Usuthu highlands with a number of pretty waterfalls and surrounded by forest in its own colourful garden. 30 en suite rooms, colourful decor, restaurant which serves excellent meals and caters for vegetarians, cosy pub with log fire, it's less than 40 km away from the Nerston/ Sandlane border so people from South Africa come here for the famous Sunday lunch, and occasional Swazi dancing performed in the evenings. Swimming pool, sauna, trout and bass fishing in the local dams, tennis and squash courts, hiking, horse riding from their own stables, mountain bikes for hire. Rates include dinner, bed and breakfast.

B **Malandela's**, Malkerns road, T5283448, malandelas@africaonline.co.sz. New set-up, attached to an excellent restaurant and the House on Fire venue. Set in quiet gardens, pool, 5 stylish en suite double rooms, Afro-chic decor, family-run, friendly staff, great addition to the area. Recommended.

Ted Reilly and wildlife conservation in Swaziland

Like the rest of Africa, Swaziland used to team with game before the Europeans arrived in the mid-1800s with guns, modern farming methods and medical knowledge. Morality went downhill, the human population flourished and the need for space meant that the wildlife was doomed. This was followed by other problems. The cattle plague, *rinderpest*, reached Swaziland by 1896, wiping out not only cattle but many antelope which led to the death by starvation of many predators. During the 1930s the so-called 'wildebeest scourge' led to one of the most shocking episodes in the history of wildlife conservation. A great number of wildebeest entered Swaziland following a migratory route, as they had for centuries. Their invasion of farmland led to them being declared vermin and they were exterminated by any possible means. Whole herds were wiped out by machine guns and drinking water was poisoned, the latter undoubtedly causing the deaths of many other animals and birds. By 1960, most of Swaziland's remaining game had been decimated by uncontrolled hunting, poaching and by rapid commercial and agricultural development. That something was done to preserve the few wild animals that survived, and to reintroduce species that had become extinct, is largely due to the efforts of two men – the late King Sobhuza II and Ted Reilly, founder of Mlilwane Wildlife Sanctuary. In 1963, Reilly turned the family farm in the Ezulwini Valley into a game reserve, planted indigenous trees, created wetland habitat, and began a game restocking programme. Meanwhile the king asked Reilly to help stamp out poaching in the royal reserve of Hlane and for three decades Reilly embarked on a near-military campaign to eradicate poaching in Swaziland. In 1967, Sobhuza declared Hlane a protected national park and it was restocked with wildlife from neighbouring countries. The Reilly family then donated Mlilwane to a non-profit making trust in 1969 and it has since grown to 10 times it original size. All of Swazi's parks are now home to substantial numbers of game and at least some of the country again looks like it did 150 years ago. Without Ted Reilly and King Sobhuza II, the Swaziland game reserves would simply not exist. Today the Reilly family still live at Mlilwane where they manage Big Game Parks. Ted's daughter, Anne, contributed information to this book.

Eating

Mbabane *p803, map p808*

La Casserole, Omni Centre, Allister Miller St, T4046426. Smart restaurant serving German and international cuisine, fully licenced, pizza oven, outside patio, relaxed, charming atmosphere.

Friar Tuck's, Mountain Inn, T4042781. Good quality hotel restaurant in a somewhat dark vaulted cellar, also has pleasant outside tables with great views, filling buffet lunches, and à la carte evening menu.

Finesse, New Mall, T4045936. French-owned à la carte restaurant with a seasonal menu, excellent seafood such as lobster with vanilla sauce or oriental prawns and Mozambique chicken.

The Mediterranean, Allister Miller St, T4043212. Despite the name, this serves Indian cuisine, excellent and cheap curries, seafood, snacks, fully licenced, good South African and Portuguese wines, takeaway service, all food is halal, good for vegetarians. Also has a bar.

Ezulwini Valley *p804, map p804*

Calabash, T4161187, close to **Timbali Lodge**. Delicious German and Austrian meals and seafood, Austrian beers on draught, a very popular venue, one of Swaziland's top à la carte restaurants, booking advised.

First Horse, close to **Timbali Lodge**, T4161137. An excellent restaurant serving a mix of continental dishes and some Chinese and Indian meals, enjoy a cool beer at the bar before your meal, run by a Swiss chef.

Malandela's, T5283115. Excellent restaurant in a stylish setting, surrounded by gardens, pleasant shady deck, great menu, fusion food mixing African and European dishes. Also has a popular pub and is attached to the House on Fire live music venue.

Village Café, Mantenga Nature Reserve, open all day for breakfast, lunch and dinner, plus teas and coffees. Specializing in African dishes with a twist such as stroganoff made from game meat and peri peri chicken livers, there's late bar, and it's great place for a sundowner on the wooden deck. Also has weekly braais at the waterfalls.

Woodlands, between **Royal Swazi Sun** and **The Gables** mall, T4163466. Smart addition to the valley, airy dining room serving good international cuisine, open 1100-late, popular Sun buffets.

Sirloin Steakhouse and **Bella Vista Pizzeria**, in the **Happy Valley Motel**, T4161061, open until 0200, closed Sun. Both serve hearty, good-value portions, good atmosphere, booth seating.

Entertainment

Ezulwini Valley *p804, map p804*

House on Fire, Malkerns Rd, T5282100, www.house-on-fire.com. Excellent new venue which has quickly become the country's leading spot for live music. Open air, extravagant, funky decor including colourful, mirrored mosaics, surreal statues, moulded seating area around circular stage. Rock music and live jazz on most nights.

Why Not Disco & Night Club and **If Not Go-Go Bar** (adult cabaret), T4161061. Swaziland institution that has been going for decades, at the weekends bands perform here, all very tacky but fun. Open nightly except Sun at 2200, live bands/cabaret acts at 2345 and 0100.

Shopping

Mbabane *p803, map p808*

Crafts and curios

African Fantasy, The Mall, T4161877. A wide selection of curios. Look out for Swazi candles, made in the Malkerns Valley.

Swazi Market, Msunduza Rd, at the end of Allister Miller St. A full range of curios from all over the country, although you will have to haggle for the best bargains. The fruit and vegetable market is here too and is an excellent place to buy fresh guavas, mangoes, lychees and other tropical fruits.

Shopping malls

Swazi Plaza, The Mall and New Mall, are all within walking distance of each other on OK Link Rd. They are large, covered, modern malls with department stores, banks, pharmacies, travel agents, cafés and restaurants.

Ezulwini Valley *p804, map p804*

The main road passing through the valley is lined with craft stalls selling a good range of handmade curios. See also page 807 for details of the **Mantenga Craft Centre** and page 807 for craft shops in the Malkerns Valley. **The Gables** is a modern shopping mall.

Activities and tours

Ezulwini Valley *p804, map p804*

Royal Swazi Spa, T4161164, hugely popular resort, mainly for the intriguingly named 'cuddle puddle', a swimming pool fed by a hot natural mineral spring. Housed in dome-shaped buildings modelled on a Swazi village, there are 2 large saunas, 2 indoor hot mineral pools, cold plunge pools, whirl and bubble bath, an aromatherapy steam-tube. Also has a gym.

Tour operators

Swazi Trails and **Asambeni Bo** run a range of tours in the area (see Tour operators, page 800, for full details).

Transport

Mbabane *p803, map p808*

Air

There is an airport departure tax, E20. Swazi Express, Matsapha Airport,

T5186840, www.swaziexpress.com, has daily flights between Swaziland and **Durban,** and twice-weekly to **Maputo** (Mozambique). **South African Airways** (SAA), reservations South Africa, T011-9781111, www.sa airlink.co.za. Flies 4 times a day to **Johannesburg** .

Bus
The South African **Baz Bus**, T021-4392323, www.bazbus.com, includes Swaziland on its route 3 times a week.

Car hire
Affordable Car Hire, Mbabane Plaza, T4049136, affordable@posix.co.za. **Avis**, Matsapha airport office, T5186222, www.avis.co.za. **Imperial Car Rental**, Matsapha airport office, T5184396, Mbabane Office (Engen Garage, Main Rd), T4041384, www.imperialcarrental.co.za. It is also possible to drive South African hire cars as long as you have a covering letter from the company you hired the car from, so remember to mention this when you hire it.

Directory

Mbabane *p803, map p808*
Embassies and consulates It may be easier to contact embassies in South Africa; see the Pretoria Directory, page 536, for a full list of offices in the region. **Germany**, Dhlan'ubeka House, Tin and Mhlonhlo Sts, T4043174. **Mozambique**, Alister Miller St, T4043700. **Portuguese Consulate**, Portuguese Club, OK Rd, T4046780. **South Africa**, New Mall, OK Rd, T4044651. **USA**, Central Bank Building, Warner St, T4046441. **Hospitals** Mbabane Clinic (private), St Michael St, T4042423. **Mbabane Government Hospital**, Usutu Rd, T4042111. **Useful telephone numbers** Police, T4042221, emergency T999.

Central and southern Swaziland

Manzini

» pp816-818. Colour map 2, grid C5.

This town is an industrial centre with a brewery, a meat-processing plant and electronics factories that attract commuter labourers from outlying areas. The industrial atmosphere is not particularly pleasant and there is little of interest for the visitor. The **market** ⓘ *corner of Mhlakuvane St and Mancishane Rd, Thu*, brings the local farming communities into town once a week and is worth a browse. This is one of the busiest local markets in Swaziland, selling fresh fruit and vegetables, clothes, a good selection of curios and freshly cooked snacks. The **Bhunu Mall** on Ngwane Street and **The Hub** on Mhlakuzane Street are Manzini's newest shopping centres. **Tiger-City** on Villiers Street is a small complex where the cinema and a couple of restaurants are located.

Background

The first trading station was opened here in 1885 and was originally run from a tent. The plot was later sold on to Alfred Bremer who built a hotel and a shop. Manzini was originally known as Bremersdorp after Alfred Bremer, but it was renamed Manzini after the Boers burnt the settlement to the ground during the Anglo-Boer War. The administrative centre then moved to Mbabane. In 1894, while Swaziland was being administrated by a temporary government composed of representatives of the Transvaal, the British government and the king, the headquarters were in the local hotel.

Hlane Royal National Park

» pp816-818. Colour map 2, grid C5.

ⓘ T5283943, www.biggameparks.org. Park gates close at sunset, notify in advance if you think your arrival will be after dark. E25 per person.

Formerly a royal hunting ground, Hlane was declared a protected area in 1967 by King Sobhuza II. Covering 30,000 ha, this is the kingdom's largest protected area. Following heavy poaching in the 1960s, the park has been restocked by **Big Game Parks,** with wildlife from neighbouring countries as well as species propagated at Mkhaya Game Reserve. A number of predators have been reintroduced and the park now has healthy numbers of lion, cheetah and leopard. Other game includes elephant, white rhino, herds of wildebeest, and zebra, kudu, steenbuck, bushbuck, giraffe, impala, hyena and jackal. In the past, poaching was such a serious problem that the rhino had to have their horns removed for their own protection. Hlane supports the densest population of raptors in the kingdom, with vultures in particular being very visible at kills and waterholes. The nesting density for the white-backed vulture is the highest in the whole of Africa, and the most southerly nesting colony of marabou stork is found here. Birdlife in and around the two camps is prolific.

Ins and outs

Getting there The park is 67 km from Manzini towards Simunye, where the main road bisects the park. Turn left into the Ngongoni Gate, where all arrivals must report.

Sights

The western area of the park is linked with a network of roads which the visitor can use for game viewing. The area around the **Black Mbuluzi River** attracts animals during the dry winter season. Close to Ndlovu camp is an **Endangered Species area,** where elephant and rhino have been concentrated for security reasons. The **Mahlindza waterhole**, with its hippo, crocodile and waterbird population, is one of the most peaceful picnic sites in the country. A wide range of activities are offer in the park include guided walks, guided mountain biking, horse riding trails, full-day Land Rover tours with lunch, and two-hour game drives (day or night). These can all be booked at the park office, where you can also pick up a guide to accompany you in your own car to a nearby Swazi village 20 km from the park gates.

Simunye

» pp816-818. Colour map 2, grid C5.

Simunye is a small town that is quite unusual in that the centre lies behind the boom gate of the Royal Swazi Sugar Corporation that owns the surrounding sugar plantations. There is nothing much here but it is a stop-off en route to Hlane, Mlawula and the border with Mozambique at Lomahasha/Namaacha. The main road to Simunye coming north skirts Hlane Game Sanctuary and there are amusing if sobering signposts warning cyclists and pedestrians to beware of lion and elephant.

Mlawula Nature Reserve

» pp816-818. Colour map 2, grid C5.

ⓘ Reservations: National Trust Commission, T4161179, www.sntc.org.sz. Daily entrance charge E25.

Mlawula is signposted after Simunye and Hlane. The nature reserve covers an area extending from the Lebombo Mountains down to the lowveld and is part of the greater Lubombo Conservancy. The Siphiso Valley and the Mbuluzi Gorge are good areas for game viewing on hiking trails or game drives.

Ins and outs

Best time to visit Summers are hot and humid with high rainfall, the winters are warm and dry although they can be cold at night with the occasional frost. The best time for birdwatching is between September and October.

Sights

This is a region of amazing and varied scenery ranging from Lebombo Mountain forest to dry thorn savanna and coastal thickets. The reserve is criss-crossed with 33 m of rough roads for self-guided tours. Over 1000 species of plant have been identified here although this region is best known for its birdlife: 350 species have been recorded including African fin foot, crested guinea fowl and yellow spotted nicator, and facilities include the vulture feeding area and the bird hide. The **Mbuluzi Gorge** is an excellent area for birdwatching but the road is not always in good condition. The game likely to be seen in the reserve includes kudu, oribi, mountain reedbuck, samango monkeys, and Sharpe's grysbok, but sadly there are no longer any rhino. Early traces of *homo sapiens* dating back 100,000 years have been found in the riverbeds of the Mbuluzi and Mlawula rivers, good places to spot crocodiles. Many of the animals which are protected here are particularly difficult to spot and include rare species of reptile and amphibian. The interesting plantlife includes the rare Lebombo ironwood and the *encephalartos umeluziensis*, a cycad that only grows in the deep mountain valleys of the reserve. Visitors to the reserve are encouraged to hike on the network of trails, which pass through beautiful gorges, pools, waterfalls and rapids with views over Mozambique from the top of the escarpment. There is a leaflet on the trails and the reserve available from the camp shop where you can also pick up a guide to go with you.

Shewula Nature Reserve » *pp816-818. Colour map 2, grid C6.*

ⓘ *T6051160, www.shewulacamp.com.*

The community-owned Shewula Nature Reserve just north of Mlawula is also part of the Lebombo Conservancy, straddling the 500-m high Lebombo Mountains on the border with Mozambique and covering an escarpment of ancient ironwood mountain forest stretching down the Mbuluzi River. The views from the **Shewula Mountain Camp**, which is literally perched on top of a mountain, are incredible – on a clear day the high-rise blocks of Maputo can be seen to the east, and there is an uninterrupted 100-km view across Swaziland.

Ins and outs

The Shewula turning is 10 km south of the Lomahasha/Namaacha border with Mozambique. The camp is a further 30-minute drive from here. Apart from during heavy rains (December to Febraury) it is accessible by ordinary saloon cars. When the road is too muddy, it is possible to leave your vehicle at the chief's office in the village, and be transported in a 4WD.

Manzini to Mahamba » *pp816-818.*

Grand Valley

The drive down through Grand Valley passes through beautiful mountain scenery with cliff faces rising above the Mkhondvo River and forests on either side of the road. The MR9 passes through the village of **Hlatikulu** before reaching Nhlangano. The weather here is often misty with drizzle, which for many is a welcome relief after the hot and humid plains.

Nhlangano → *Colour map 2, grid C5*

Nhlangano means 'meeting place' and was named to commemorate when King Sobhuza II met King George VI here in 1947. This used to be a popular resort with South African tourists who crossed the border to gamble and watch films which were banned at home. Since the end of Apartheid, the number of South African visitors has fallen sharply. There is a small shopping centre in town and a market. Buses depart from the station next to the mall to Manzini, Mahamba and Lavumisa.

Mahamba border post

The MR9 continues south to the border at Mahamba, daily 0700-2200. The routes into South Africa from here lead to Piet Retief in Mpumalanga.

Manzini to Lavumisa » pp816-818.

Mkhaya Game Reserve → *Colour map 2, grid C5*

ⓘ *Access by prior reservation only, T5283943, www.biggameparks.org.*

This small reserve is now one of the best places in southern Africa to see black rhino. It is Swaziland's most exclusive reserve, set in an area of acacia lowveld southeast of Manzini. Mkhaya was established as a game reserve in 1979 to protect the Nguni breed of long-horned cattle from extinction that today graze among the zebra and wildebeest, but it has expanded over the years to include other endangered species such as black rhino, roan and sable antelope, tsessebe, white rhino, and elephant. In 1995 the park received six black rhino from South Africa, a project funded, rather oddly, by the Taiwanese Government, and during 1997 the first two baby elephant to be born in Swaziland in 100 years were born at Mkhaya. At present the only large cat you might see is the leopard. The birdlife here is interesting and there are chances of seeing a good number of raptors including bateleur, booted, martial and tawny eagles. The summers here are very hot and humid with potentially heavy thunderstorms, while in winter the climate is warm during the day and cool at night.

Ins and outs Travelling from Mbabane and Ezulwini Valley go through Manzini. 8 km after Manzini take a right turn and continue towards Big Bend. The reserve is signposted to the left after about 44 km. If you are approaching from Durban via the Lavumisa border follow the road to Big Bend and then Siphofaneni. The turning is on the right, 22 km after Big Bend. All visitors are met at the locked gates by a ranger. This is a private reserve and guests must arrange to arrive at either 1000 and 1600 when the rangers will pick you up. Because Mkhaya is a private reserve it can only be visited by prior reservation as an overnight visitor staying at the tented safari camp. Open-top Land Rover game drives are the main activity, with the opportunity to take guided bush walks, all promising close contact with a variety of big game. Rates include all activities.

Big Bend → *Colour map 2, grid C5*

Big Bend is named after the loop of the Lusutfu River that passes by the town. The land around Big Bend is covered in sugar plantations and the Ubombo Ranches sugarmill in town is the area's main processing centre. The terrain here is very similar to South Africa's northern KwaZulu Natal, which is only 50 km to the south. The town is a quiet, neatly laid out settlement with a small shopping centre and craft centre, **Emoya Crafts,** which sells crafts from all over Swaziland – ethnic clothing, glassware, candles, cotton rugs, place mats, tablecloths, batiks, baskets and ethnic jewellery.

Nisela Safaris

ⓘ *T3030247, www.niselasafaris.co.za. Day visitors E10, for game drives and walks there needs to be a minimum of 6 people.*

Nisela Safaris is a fairly new private game lodge development nestled at the foot of the Lebombo Mountains, near the village of Nsoko, 30 km south from Big Bend on the road to the Lavumisa border, which is a further 20 km. This is a small private reserve where game including lion, wilderbeest, giraffe, and zebra have been introduced; existing populations of nyala, red and grey duiker, jackal, bushbuck, reedbuck and steenbok are also present. There are also a number of hand-reared lion cubs to visit near the entrance gate. At the entrance to the reserve is a coffee shop and curio stall.

Lavumisa Border Post → *Colour map 2, grid C5*

Lavumisa is a busy border post which most travellers pass through on their way to Big Bend or into KwaZulu Natal. There is one main street lined with snack bars and petrol stations. The border is open 0700-2200. The bus station is on the main street and buses regularly depart for Big Bend, Manzini and Mbabane. The road that runs the entire length of Swaziland from Lavumisa border to Lomahasha border with Mozambique is in the process of being upgraded to a highway. It is intended that this will be the main truck route from the port in Durban all the way through to Maputo in Mozambique, and traffic is already increasing along this route.

Sleeping

Manzini *p812*
There are a couple of excellent backpackers in the Manzini region, both are Baz Bus stops.
E **Myxo's Backpackers**, 6 km from town off the Siteki Big Bend Rd, turn left at the Big Surprise Bottle Store, T5058363, www.earthfoot.org. Locally-managed hostel, pick-ups/drop-offs from Big Surprise Bottle Store where the Baz Bus stops. Dorms, double rooms in a 2-storey house, camping on lawn. Bar, Swazi meals on request, shared kitchen. Overnight trips to Myxo's home village in the mountains can be arranged.
E **Swaziland Backpackers**, T5187225, swazilandbackpackers@realnet.co.sz. Located 12 km out of Manzini on the road to Mbabane, go past the **Salt & Pepper Club** for 1½ km, on the right opposite the Chinese Agricultural Centre. Farm location, dorms, doubles, camping, internet and laundry facilities. The main house has a comfy lounge, pretty gardens with pool, communal kitchen for self-catering or meals provided with advance notice. Range of tours on offer, including free hikes in the area.

Hlane Royal National Park *p813*
Reservations: T5283943, www.biggameparks.org. Traditional dance performances, open-air bar and restaurant at Ndlovu but in Bhubesi visitors must be fully self-sufficient.
C-E **Ndlovu Camp**, 6 en suite thatched rondavels, sleeping up to 8, bedding, towels, cutlery, crockery provided, hot outside showers. Ndlovu Camp has no electricity, paraffin lanterns provide light, the fridges are gas powered and cooking is carried out over an open fire, a camp assistant will help with this and he keeps the fire going all day, you just need to bring food, or eat at the camp restaurant. Next to a waterhole. A small shop sells some provisions and curios; game activities can be organized. There are few simple camping sites nearby, with an ablution block at Ndlovu Camp.
D **Bhubesi Camp**, 6 self-catering stone cottages, 2 bedrooms, bathroom, kitchenette, bedding and towels, electricity, a beautiful setting overlooking the Umbuluzana River.

Simunye *p813*
C-D **Simunye Country Club**, once through the boom gate turn right, T3134000, dlischka@rssc.co.sz. Owned by the Royal Swazi Sugar Corporation, accommodation is in a variety of rooms, self-catering houses and flats. Pool, nice restaurant, 3 bars, TV lounge. Tennis, squash and gym available for a nominal fee. Nothing special but conveniently located, 15-min drive to Mozambique, and 30 mins to South African borders.

Mlawula Nature Reserve *p813*
Reservations: T4161179, www.sntc.org.sz
C **Tented camp**, 4 tents sleeping 2, each with braai area, communal lounge and kitchen, bring all your own food. The highlight here is the position of the

tents, perched on the edge of a sheer cliff with outstanding views and the outside bathrooms have a boiler heated by fire and a galvanized bath tub hidden in a cleft of rock on the cliff edge.

D **Mapelepele**, self-catering cottage sleeping 4. Nearby campsite on the banks of the usually dry Sipisi stream with an ablution block and cooking facilities, firewood is available.

Shewula Nature Reserve *p814*

E **Shewula Mountain Camp**, T6051160, shewula@realnet.co.sz. Beautiful hilltop setting, community-owned, 4 huts sleeping up to 6, camping ground, shared ablution block and kitchen, no electricity, but there are gas stoves and fridge, paraffin lamps, hot showers. Bedding is not supplied so you will need a sleeping bag. Traditional meals can be ordered, prepared by local families. Activities include guided nature walks, swimming in the river, cultural tours around the villages.

Manzini to Mahamba *p814*

A **Nhlangano Sun** , 4 km out of Nhlangano, T2078211, www.suninternational.com. 47 chalet-style rooms with private terrace, TV, restaurant, bar, swimming pool, horse riding, disco, casino, tennis, all set in 18 ha of lush grounds.

Mkhaya Game Reserve *p815*

Reservations: T4161179, www.sntc.org.sz. Overnight rates include entry, 3 meals and 3 guided game-viewing trips.

AL **Stone Camp**, 12 semi-open self-contained stone and thatched cottages sleeping 3-5 shaded by hardwood forest, thatched summerhouse, meals are prepared by the camp staff and are served with South African wines. One of the most comfortable game viewing experience in Swaziland.

Big Bend *p815*

C-D **The New Bend Inn**, on a hill to the south of town, T3636855. 24 a/c plain but adequate rooms, some with en suite bathroom, restaurant, indoor and outdoor bars, TV lounge, swimming pool, snooker, gets very lively at the weekends.

Nisela Safaris *p815*

Reservations: T3030247, www.niselasafaris.co.za.

B-C **Game Lodge**, 5 luxury rooms sleeping 2-4. The pool, bar, and restaurant here is used by guests in all the facilities.

C **Guest House**, 10 rooms in a very pleasant colonial house, B&B, en suite, a/c and ceiling fans, attractive lawns surrounding the house.

D-E **Overland Camp**, 2 4-bed rustic self-catering chalets, 22 km into the bush on a dirt road, only accessible by 4WD.

E **Beehive Village**, traditional Swazi grass huts with 4 beds, shared ablution block and kitchen. There's also a campsite. Card-carrying backpackers (ISAC, YHA) qualify for a discount and get the 4th night free.

Eating

Manzini *p812*

¥ **Fontana di Trevi Pizzeria**, The Hub, corner of Villiers and Mhlakuvane Sts, T5053608. Standard coffee shop and good value pizzas and some pasta dishes throughout the day.

¥ **Gil Vicente**, Martin St, T5053874, Ilanga Centre, closed Mon. Portuguese dishes, and good peri peri chicken in the boring environs of a shopping centre.

Simunye *p815*

¥¥ **Simunye Club Restaurant**, Simunye Country Club, T3134000, dlischka@rssc.co.sz. Has a popular family restaurant, a la carte menu and buffet meals, pizzas, braais every Fri, seating on terrace.

Big Bend *p815*

¥¥ **Lismore**, Lismore Lodge, T6366920. Small restaurant specializing in seafood from Mozambique. Also has good mountain trout, and range of Portuguese dishes.

Transport

Manzini *p812*

Air

Swaziland's main airport, Matsapha Airport, is 8 km west of Manzini. There are buses and minibus taxis going to Manzini and Mbabane. See page 803 for details of flights.

Bus
Buses and minbus taxis leave from the bus station on Louw St to **Mbabane**, **Big Bend**, **Lavumisa**, **Nhlangano** and **Mahamba**.

Car hire
There are offices at the airport for **Avis**, T5186266, and **Imperial**, T5184396.

Big Bend *p815*
Buses to **Manzini**, **Mbabane** and **Lavumisa**.

Northern districts

The only settlement of note between Mbabane and South Africa is Motjane, where the MR1 branches north to Malolotja Nature Reserve and Pigg's Peak. There are two good places to stay in this region. » *For Sleeping, Eating and other listings, see page 819.*

Mbabane to South Africa » *p819.*

Motjana and around

Motjane is a good centre for curio items. **Ngwenya Glass** ⓘ *5 km before the border, T4424053, www.ngwenyaglass.co.sz*, and attached coffee shop is a popular stop-off for coach parties. All the items for sale are made from 100% recycled glass, and you can watch glass blowers do their thing. A kilometre or so on the road behind the glass factory is **Endlotane Studios** ⓘ *T4424196*, which sells a varied collection of crafts from mohair tapestries to rugs, wall hangings, paintings, woodcrafts and pottery.

The border with South Africa is west of Motjane at **Ngwenya/Oshoek** ⓘ *23 km from Mbabane, daily 0700-2200*. Tourist information is available here. Close to the border post are numerous curio stalls, worth a glance if you are leaving Swaziland. Buses to the capital and the rest of the country depart from Ngwenya.

The road north from Motjane is the MR1; 9 km along this road is the small **Hawane Nature Reserve** and dam. As the surfaced road heads north it passes through the small settlement of **Forbes Reef**. A general store is the centre of activity here, hidden close by are the remains of a long abandoned gold mine.

Hawane Nature Reserve Reserve → *Colour map 2, grid C5.*

ⓘ *T4161151, www.sntc.org.sz.*

Established in 1978, this small nature reserve protects an area of wetlands along the Mbuluzi river. When the Hawane Dam was built in 1988, the reserve was extended to protect the area's water supply. The main reason for coming here is for the excellent birdwatching, with many rare species being attracted by the river and dam. Look out for the endangered red hot poker plant, which can be found here. There is a good birdwatching trail set out in the park. Other activities include horseback trails, available from the **Hawane Resort** (see page 819).

Malolotja Nature Reserve » *p819. Colour map 2, grid C5.*

Malolotja is a wild region of mountains and forest along the northwestern border with Mpumalanga, offering the country's finest hiking. Mgwayiza, Ngwenya (1829 m) and Silotfwane (1680 m) are three of Swaziland's highest peaks and local hikes cross deep forested ravines, high plateaux and grasslands dotted with waterfalls. Archaeological remains show that this region has been inhabited for thousands of years and the site of the world's oldest mine, thought to be 43,000 years old, is within the park. The diggings were used to excavate red and black earth, possibly for use as pigments.

Ins and outs

Getting there From the MR3 there is a turning at Motjane on to the MR1 heading north to Pigg's Peak. The turning into the reserve, easily identified by the collection of curio sellers (look out for the fine soapstone sculptures), is 7 km from the junction of the two roads and the park gates are a further 18 km from the MR1. Be wary of traffic along this road; there are a few precipitous drops and the buses tend to drive down in the middle of the road.

Best time to visit The weather can change suddenly with rain and fog closing in without warning. The summers here are hot and humid with heavy rains. Winter is warm and dry but the nights can be bitterly cold with occasional frost.

Wildlife

There is a chance of seeing blesbok, klipspringer, oribi, zebra and both blue and black wildebeest, and surplus game from other reserves is gradually being introduced. Rare plants here include aloes, Barberton and Kaapasche Hoop cycads, proteas, orchids and fever trees. The small herbarium at the main camp has a good collection of unusual plants. Malolotja is an excellent area for birdwatching, and over 280 species have been recorded here. There is a breeding colony of the rare bald ibis at the **Malolotja Falls** which drop an impressive 90 m into the Nkomati River. This is also a site for breeding blue swallows and the blue crane. There is a 25-km network of gravel roads for self-guided game drives but the best way to see the park is on foot by going on one of the many hiking trails. The longest is 7 km and leads up to the 95-m Malolotja Falls. Maps for the overnight hiking trails, information brochures and wildlife lists are all available from the Malolotja camp office.

This is a challenging landscape for hikers with altitudes rising from 615 m to 1800 m.

Further north » p819.

Phophonyane Nature Reserve

On leaving Malolotja Reserve, instead of rushing north to the South African border, look out for a signpost for Phophonyane Lodge and Reserve about 15 km after the mountain community of Pigg's Peak. This is one of the most beautiful and relatively unspoilt patches of Swazi countryside, including dense riverine forest, home to small mammals such as duiker, bushbuck and the clawless otter. A number of 4WD and walking trails have been set out, including to the **Phophonyane Falls** – some of the best known falls in Swaziland. An artificial swimming pool has been created in the rocks just below the lower Phophonyane Falls.

Pigg's Peak → *Colour map 2, grid C5.*

This small, straggling town was named after William Pigg, a French gold prospector who came here in 1884. There was a working gold mine here until 1954, although no great fortunes were ever recovered. There's nothing here to warrant a stop, other than to stock up on cool drinks and petrol.

Bulembu and Jeppe's Reef border posts

From Pigg's Peak, the MR20 dirt road, heads west to the border post at **Bulembu** (daily 0800-1600). There is another scenic route north on a tarred road through Rocklands and Hhohho to the border post at **Jeppe's Reef** to Barberton in South Africa (daily 0800-1800).

Sleeping

Mbabane to South Africa *p818*

A-E Hawane Resort, 9 km from Ngwenya/ Oshoek border post and 2 km south of Malolotja, T4424744, www.hawane.co.sz. 16 luxury chalets, intriguing mix of traditional Swazi and contemporary architecture, stylish décor with splashes of bright colour. Excellent restaurant serving fusion cuisine in a stylish open-plan dining room. Also has a bright lounge area and bar. The whole set-up is on the banks of the Hawana Dam which is good for birdwatching and safe for swimming and the **Hawane Stables** can organize horse and pony treks in the surrounding countryside.

E Sobantu Guest Farm, 26 km north of Motjane look out for the turning to Maguga Dam, the farm is 6 km on this dirt road, T083-4919989, sobantu@swaziplace.com. A backpackers with basic doubles, dormitories and camping space, nice farmland views, bar, kitchen (you can buy organic vegetables), or meals provided, short hikes through the farm or borrow the mountain bike, swimming in the dam or nearby rock pools.

Malotja Nature Reserve *p818*

Reservations: T4161179, www.sntc.org.sz.

C Log cabins, 5 self-catering cabins, sleeping up to 6, fully equipped, set in a beautiful mountain location.

Campsite

The main site has room for 15 tents or caravans, an ablution block and a communal cooking area, firewood available. There are very basic campsites along the hiking trails but you will need to be totally self-sufficient, and as no fires are allowed outside the main campsite, a portable cooker is essential.

Phophonyane Nature Reserve *p819*

B Phophonyane Lodge, 3km off the MR1, T4371429, www.phophonyane.co.sz. Designed for peace and privacy, 23 guests sleep in luxury cottages and tented camps, perched on stilts with fabulous private balconies. Some units are self-catering. Good à la carte restaurant, **Driftwood** bar has a prime location on a balcony overlooking the river. Recommended.

Pigg's Peak *p819*

B Orion Pigg's Peak, 10 km northeast of Pigg's Peak, T4371104, www.orion group.co.za. 102 upmarket rooms set in a vast unattractive block but in a beautiful setting, en suite bathrooms, TV, telephone, great views of the deeply forested Phophonyane Valley from every balcony, 2 restaurants, 4 bars, nightclub, swimming pool with pool bar, tennis courts, squash courts, bowls, horse stables, gym, sauna, casino, live entertainment most nights, set in beautiful highlands.

Background

History

The precolonial history of Swaziland started with the Dlamini clan in the late 16th century when they migrated south settling in the region around what is now Delagoa Bay. Around two centuries later, in 1750, Ngwane III migrated to what is now Swaziland. The land was a well-watered mountain area with fertile soils and good pastures for raising cattle. The mountainous territory also offered good protection from Zulu raids.

By the 19th century, Swaziland had become a major power in the region controlling a much larger area than it does today. Europeans arrived in 1836, and called the place Swaziland after the leader at the time Mswasi II. After gold was discovered at Pigg's Peak and Forbes' Reef, large numbers of foreigners were attracted to the area and pressure for land concessions increased. The 'concession rush' occurred during the reign of Mbandeni when speculators believed there was about to be a great boom in Swaziland. Five hundred concessions were eventually granted on which the king received a payment. When the gold rush ended without any great results most of the concessionaires left the country.

The Transvaal administered Swaziland from 1894-1903. After the Anglo Boer War the British took control of the country leaving the traditional forms of government in the hands of the royal family. One of the country's major problems was that most of the land had been granted to foreigners in concessions. The Swazis believed that the concessions were only temporary but a government commission recognized the concessions as valid as long as the rents continued to be paid. In 1907 a third of the land under concession was expropriated to give the Swazis somewhere to live. Sobhuza II, the grandson of Mbandeni, became king in 1921 and spent his resources on regaining the land for the Swazi nation. Over 60% of the land has now been bought back from the concession holders.

Political activity in modern Swaziland began in the 1960s with the formation of the Swaziland Progressive Party by younger educated Swazis. The party later split into three factions of which the Ngwane National Liberatory Congress (NNLC), became the most influential. Swazi royalists formed the Imbokodvo National Movement in 1964. They formed an alliance with the European Advisory Council which had been established to look after the interests of European farmers and miners. The elections held before independence in 1964 were won by Imbokodvo who controlled all the seats.

Modern Swaziland

Swaziland became independent in 1968, and although the constitution guaranteed a parliamentary system when the NNLC won three seats in the 1972 election, the Swazi royal family dissolved parliament and banned all political parties. Since then political opponents have regularly been imprisoned and until 1993 attempts to reintroduce a parliamentary constitution failed. The government is now headed by the king, who is assisted by the prime minister; there are two legislative houses, the Senate and the House of Assembly. Non-party elections were held in September and October 1993, and the power of the king has been slightly reduced.

A Constitutional Review Commission was appointed by King Mswati in 1996 and while Swazis were promised that the new constitution would contain a bill of rights, it was assumed that power would remain in the hands of the king. Labour unions, banned political parties and human rights organisations boycotted the commission's work, arguing that it was un-democratic and open to manipulation by the authorities. In the absence of formal political opposition, the labour movement and the media have led the call for democratization.

The Swaziland Federation of Trade Unions represents 83,000 people out of a total population of 1 million. Tensions between the government and the pro-democracy movement reached boiling point in 2000/2001. Protest meetings were moved to neighbouring South Africa after they were banned by Prime Minister Sibusiso Dlamini. Leaders of the trade union movement were put on trial for organizing a strike, restrictions were placed on the media, and the independence of the judiciary was effectively ended. Internal opposition and a threat by the US to take away Swaziland's trade privileges however pressured Mswati into lifting these restrictions in July 2001. The king has been heavily criticized in recent years for his excessive spending, notably in 2002 when he spent US$45 million on a luxury jet, during a period of terrible drought and famine in the country. Tensions between Royalists and pro-democracy campaigners continue to fluctuated considerably; at time of writing, the king was once again under international fire for imprisoning dozens of his opponents, and Swaziland remains Africa's last absolute monarchy.

As with the rest of southern Africa, Swaziland has one of the world's highest rates of HIV/AIDS infection – thought to be second only to that of Botswana. Infection rates now stand at an estimated 38%. Anti-retrovirals were introduced in 2003, but the disease is still surrounded by taboo, which is both hindering effective education about transmission, and preventing people from seeking treatment. Life expectancy in the country has now dropped from 51 (mid-1990s) to 39 (2006).

Economy

Swaziland is virtually surrounded by South Africa and is dependent on this market for much of its external trade. It is a prosperous country with iron, coal and asbestos mines. Much of the higher western mountainous regions have been planted with timber plantations, whilst the central and eastern lowveld regions are dedicated to cotton, tobacco, citrus fruits, sugar cane and cattle ranching. Subsistence farming is the main occupation for the majority of Swazis and much of the landscape is devoted to small scale agricultural plots and cattle pastures. One of the largest foreign direct investments in Swaziland in years came in 2000 when a Taiwanese firm opened a textile factory which employed thousands of workers. Swaziland is one of the few countries that has diplomatic relations with Taiwan.

Culture

This is a traditional African society preserving many long-standing ceremonies and customs. The *Umhlanga* dance, for example, is celebrated every two years at Loamba where the nation's young girls dance and sing in homage to the Queen Mother.

Land and environment

Landscape

The **Highlands** in the northwest are Swaziland's most important economic region with extensive forestry plantations and mining development. This is the coolest region of the country where the mountains, forests and streams of Malolotja and Pigg's Peak attract many visitors. The road descending through the Ezulwini Valley from Mbabane to Manzini is Swaziland's most popular region for tourists. The **Middleveld** runs through the centre of the country and is the major agricultural region covered in rolling grasslands. The **Lowveld** is a hot dry region of typical African savanna where pineapples and sugarcane are cultivated. Hlane National Park is a good example of this landscape. The **Lebombo** region is part of the escarpment rising up to 600 m which runs from Maputaland through the eastern boundaries of Swaziland and on into Mpumalanga. This is the least populated area with only two notable settlements at Big Bend and Siteki.

Game and nature reserves

The game reserves in Swaziland are rather overwhelmed by Kruger which is only a short drive away. However, the private game reserve at **Mkhaya** is one of the best places in Africa to see black rhino and **Malolotja** offers some challenging opportunities for hikers. Malolotja is a wilderness area developed for hikers with only the most basic facilities. The amazing mountain scenery is a relatively undiscovered, top hiking area, where a good network of trails has been developed in recent years. The Mbuluzi Gorge in **Mlawula Nature Reserve** is a little visited region with over 300 recorded species of birds and a new network of hiking trails.

Footnotes

Index

D

E

F

G

M

N

O

P

Q

R

S

Map index

Advertisers' index

Footnotes Map index

Glossary

Braai outside barbeque, usually a metal grill where you light your own fire underneath with wood or coals
Dorp literally meaning 'town', though usually refers to a small urban centre with just a collection of houses and a few farmers wandering around.
Lapa thatched outside shelter, usually without walls, for entertaining, especially when braaiing.
Kraal traditional African hut for living in, usually thatched with mud or stone walls.
Kopjie a hill or outcrop of rocks, which are usually balanced on top of each other and a common feature on wide open plains.
Potjiekos three-legged cast iron pot used for cooking over coals.
Bakkie a pick up car.
Biltong dried meat to chew on as a snack, similar to beef jerky, often spiced.
Boerwors spicy beef or game sausage popular for braaiing.
Robot South African term for traffic lights.
Shebeen township pub.

Acknowledgements

Francisca Kellett My biggest thanks, as always, go to the members of South Africa's tourist industry – from museum guides to guest house owners – who made the process of updating this guidebook so much easier. In a similar vein, thanks also to Sheryl Ozinsky and her brilliant team at Cape Town Tourism, as well as the boundlessly enthusiastic and well-informed tourist offices in KwaZulu-Natal, Limpopo, Mpumalanga, North West Province, Lesotho and Swaziland. For their crucial help with logistics, thanks to Debbie Wylde at Footprint, Nadine Jeoffreys at National Alamo Car hire and Hazel Smith at Kenya Air. Thanks also to Valeri Senekal at CC Africa, Marianda Brits at Three Cities and Claire Roadley at Ethos Marketing. Thank you also to everyone at Footprint including Alan Murphy, Nicola Jones and Sarah Sorenson. Finally, a big thank you to the following readers who took the time to write in with their valuable feedback, comments and recommendations: Sven Bauer, Uli Kress, Paolo Bonesso, Nicole Maroscheck, Ralf Figi, Alistair Park, David Robinson, Inge van der Valk, Sandra Ziegler, Julian and Mary Ashby, Christine Duxbury, Colette Sweers, Mary M, Claire Ferguson, Dennis and Karen Nicholson, Donald D. Barrett, Ashley Taylor, Ran Jan, Chris and Muriel Parsons, Thomas Hunter, Brian Delaney, Peter Duby, Hayley Harvey, Wayne Olson, Tricia Stanton, Emma Dixon, John Lahey, Grant and Marie, Val and Ian Stanley, Eddie Joseph, Sandra Ziegler, Karen Davies, Caroline Jacobs, Noam Schimmel, Caroline Rogers, Russell Norton, Wynand and Christel Breytenbach, Gordon Smith, Tim Parker, Albert and Mennielene Botha.

Lizzie Williams Lizzie would like to thank the various tourism bureaus, offices, and associations throughout South Africa for their continued support for this book, and their compelling enthusiasm for tourism in this varied country. Thanks to Mark & Astrid from the Beach Lodge in Durban, Steve and Mignon, and Peter from the Backpackers Ritz in Jo'burg, the Bam family from the Lions Head Lodge in Cape Town, and Leanne and all the staff at Africa Travel Co. also in Cape Town. Thanks to all my friends and colleagues in the tourism industry for their great company and updates. Thanks for the readers that found time to write in with suggestions and updates. These include Linda Benn, Trevor and Margarita Arnold, Nils Johansen, Colette Sweers, Katie Quinn, Tricia Stanton, Wayne Olson, Frank Breckenridge, Brian Delaney, Chis and Murial Parsons.

Credits

Footprint credits
Editor: Nicola Jones
Map editor: Sarah Sorensen
Picture editor: Robert Lunn
Proofreaders: Sarah Sorensen, Stephanie Lambe
Publisher: Patrick Dawson
Editorial: Alan Murphy, Sophie Blacksell, Felicity Laughton,
Cartography: Robert Lunn, Claire Benison, Kevin Feeney, Angus Dawson
Series development: Rachel Fielding
Cover design: Robert Lunn
Design: Mytton Williams and Rosemary Dawson (brand)
Sales and Marketing: Andy Riddle, Daniella Cambouroglou
Advertising: Debbie Wylde
Administration: Elizabeth Taylor

Photography credits
Front cover: Superstock (Cape sugarbird)
Back cover: Images of Africa
Inside colour section: Images of Africa

Print
Manufactured in Italy by LegoPrint
Pulp from sustainable forests

Footprint feedback
We try as hard as we can to make each Footprint guide as up to date as possible but, of course, things always change. If you want to let us know about your experiences – good, bad or ugly – then don't delay, go to www.footprintbooks.com and send in your comments.

Information for the health section was provided by Professor Larry Goodyer Head of the Leicester School of Pharmacy and director of Nomad Medical, and the Department of Health, www.dh.gov.uk.

Publishing information
Footprint South Africa
8th edition

ISBN 1 904777 67 8
CIP DATA: A catalogue record for this book is available from the British Library

Published by Footprint
6 Riverside Court
Lower Bristol Road
Bath BA2 3DZ, UK
T +44 (0)1225 469141
F +44 (0)1225 469461
discover@footprintbooks.com
www.footprintbooks.com

Distributed in the USA by
Publishers Group West

Map symbols

Administration

- Capital city
- Other city, town
- International border
- Regional border
- Disputed border

Roads and travel

- Main road (National highway)
- Minor road (including unsealed)
- 4WD Track
- Footpath
- Railway with station
- Airport
- Bus station
- Metro station
- Cable car
- Funicular
- Ferry

Water features

- River, canal
- Lake, ocean
- Seasonal marshland
- Beach, sandbank
- Waterfall

Topographical features

- Contours (approx)
- Mountain, volcano
- Mountain pass
- Escarpment
- Gorge
- Glacier
- Salt flat
- Rocks

Cities and towns

- Main through route
- Main street
- Minor street
- Pedestrianized street
- Tunnel
- One way-street
- Steps
- Bridge
- Fortified wall
- Park, garden, stadium
- Sleeping
- Eating
- Bars & clubs
- Building
- Sight
- Cathedral, church
- Chinese temple
- Hindu temple
- Meru
- Mosque
- Stupa
- Synagogue
- Tourist office
- Museum
- Post office
- Police
- Bank
- Internet
- Telephone
- Market
- Medical services
- Parking
- Petrol
- Golf
- A Detail map
- A Related map

Other symbols

- Archaeological site
- National park, wildlife reserve
- Viewing point
- Campsite
- Refuge, lodge
- Castle
- Diving
- Deciduous, coniferous, palm trees
- Hide
- Vineyard
- Distillery
- Shipwreck
- Historic battlefield

South Africa

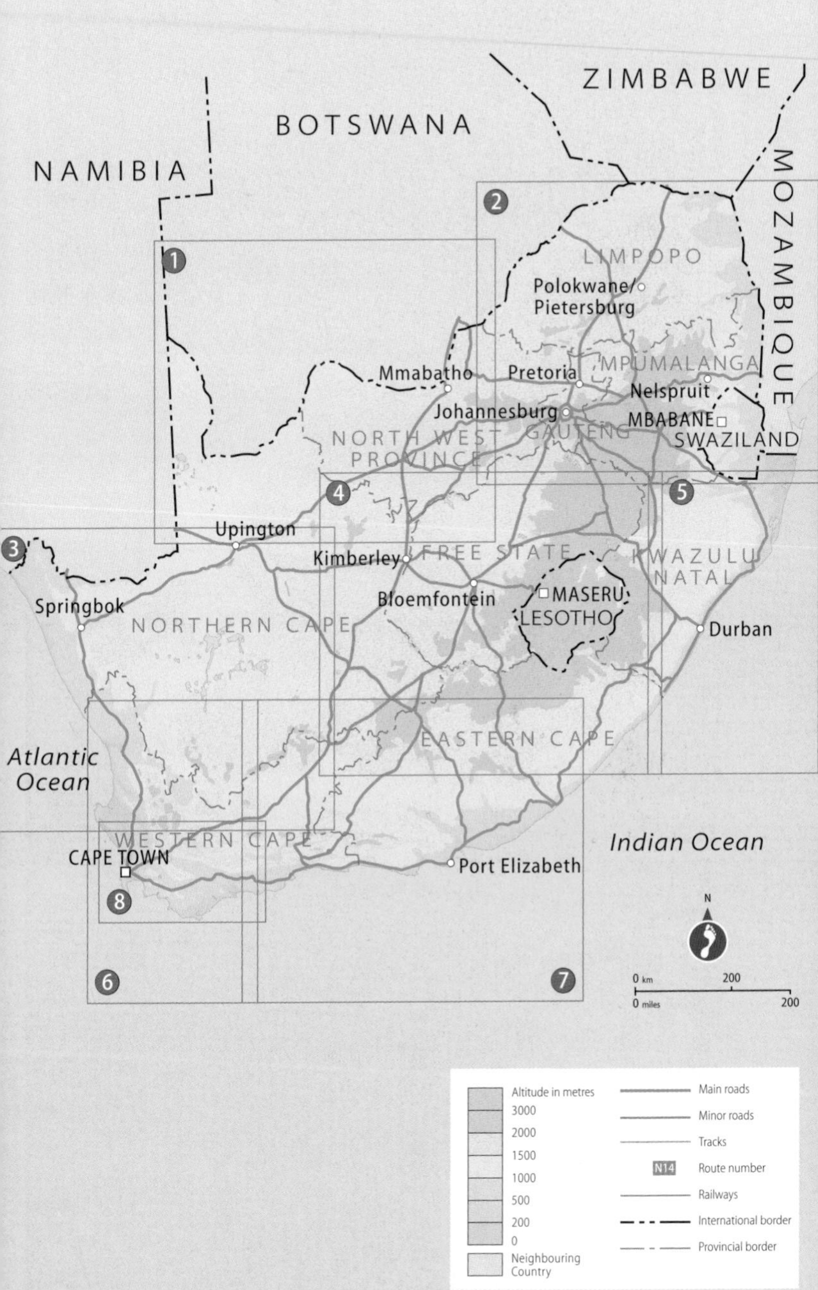

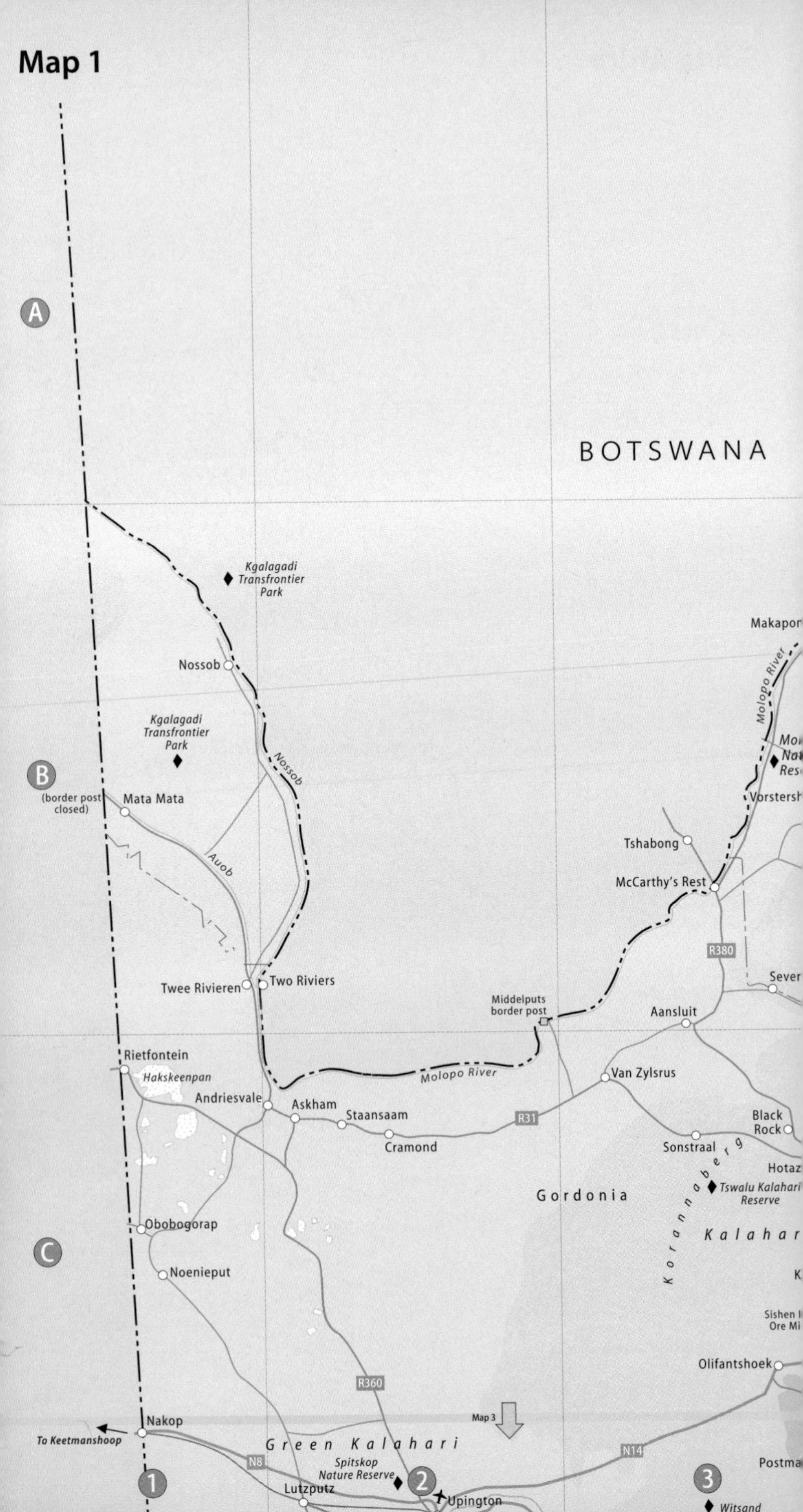
Map 1
BOTSWANA
A
B
C
Kgalagadi Transfrontier Park
Nossob
Kgalagadi Transfrontier Park
Nossob
(border post closed)
Mata Mata
Auob
Twee Rivieren
Two Riviers
Rietfontein
Hakskeenpan
Andriesvale
Askham
Staansaam
Cramond
R31
Molopo River
Middelputs border post
Makapor
Molopo River
Vorstersh
Tshabong
McCarthy's Rest
R380
Sever
Aansluit
Van Zylsrus
Black Rock
Sonstraal
Hotaz
Tswalu Kalahari Reserve
Korannaberg
Gordonia
Kalahar
Obobogorap
Noenieput
Sishen Ore Mi
Olifantshoek
R360
Nakop
To Keetmanshoop
Map 3
Green Kalahari
N8
Spitskop Nature Reserve
N14
Postma
Lutzputz
Upington
Witsand
1
2
3

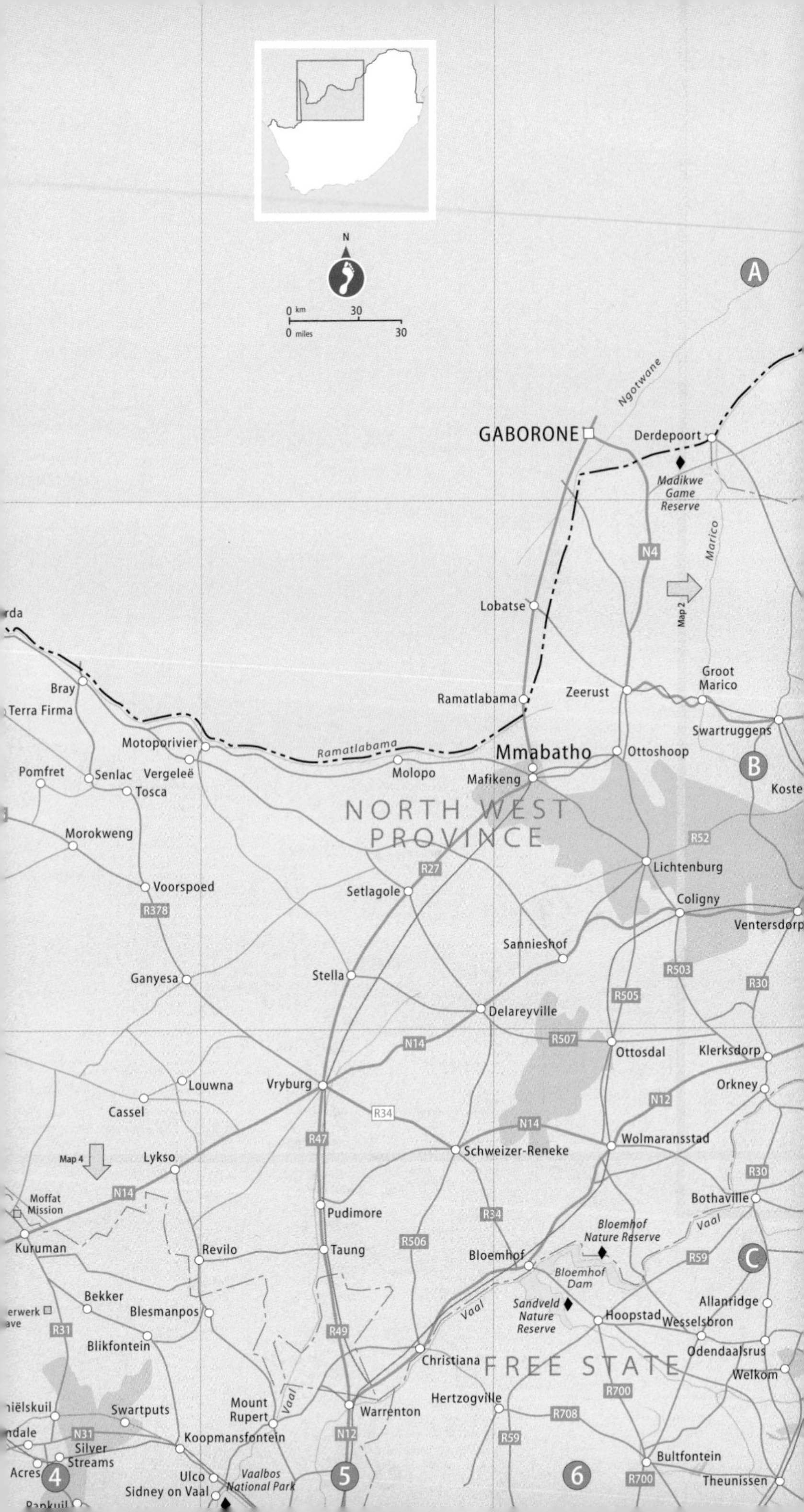

N
0 km 30
0 miles 30
A
B
C
GABORONE
Derdepoort
Ngotwane
Madikwe Game Reserve
Marico
N4
Map 2
Lobatse
Groot Marico
Zeerust
Ramatlabama
Bray
Terra Firma
Swartruggens
Motoporivier
Ramatlabama
Mmabatho
Ottoshoop
Molopo
Mafikeng
Pomfret
Senlac
Vergeleë
Tosca
Koste
NORTH WEST PROVINCE
Morokweng
R52
Lichtenburg
R27
Voorspoed
Setlagole
Coligny
R378
Ventersdorp
Sannieshof
R503
Ganyesa
Stella
R30
R505
Delareyville
R507
N14
Ottosdal
Klerksdorp
Louwna
Vryburg
Orkney
Cassel
N12
R34
N14
Wolmaransstad
R47
Schweizer-Reneke
Map 4
Lykso
R30
Moffat Mission
N14
Bothaville
Pudimore
R34
Bloemhof Nature Reserve
Vaal
Kuruman
Revilo
Taung
R506
Bloemhof
R59
Bloemhof Dam
Bekker
Allanridge
Blesmanpos
Sandveld Nature Reserve
Hoopstad
Wesselsbron
Vaal
R31
R49
Blikfontein
Odendaalsrus
Christiana
FREE STATE
Welkom
R700
Hertzogville
Swartputs
Mount Rupert
Vaal
Warrenton
R708
N31
Koopmansfontein
N12
R59
Silver Streams
Bultfontein
Acres
Ulco
Vaalbos National Park
Sidney on Vaal
R700
Theunissen
4
5
6

Map 2
BOTSWANA
LIMPOPO
MPUMALANGA
GAUTENG
A
B
C
1
2
3
Pontdrif
Shashe
Bridgewater
Gregory
Alldays
N572
Limpopo River
Carlow
Zout
Vivo
Tom Burke
N11
Baltimore
Dendron
Palala
R572
Stockpoort
Setateng
N518
Ellisras
Marken
Gilead
N521
Mogalakwena
Buffelsdrifthek
Lapalala Wilderness Area
Polokwane/ Pietersburg
Percy Fyfe National Reserve
Ngotwane
Spanwerk
Mokolo Dam
Melkrivier
Mahwelereng
Mogol
Sentrum
Vaalwater
Mokopane/ Potgietersrus
Matlabas
Marakele National Park
Strydpoort Berge
Waterberge
Derdepoort
Thabazimbi
Roedtan
Madikwe Game Reserve
Modimolle/ Nylstroom
Springbok
N1
R510
Mabula
Leeupoort
R516
R33
Holme Park
Bela-Bela/ Warmbaths
Marico
Map 1
Marble Hall
Radium
Borakalalo Game Reserve
Klovoor Dam
Groblersdal
Pilanesberg National Park
Rust de Winter Nature Reserve
N573
Mogwase
Temba
Sun City
Groot Marico
Loskop Dam Game Reserve
Mabopane
Pandsdrif
Zeerust
Swartruggens
Brits
Roodeplaat Nature Reserve
Lammerskop
Rustenburg
Cullinan
Hartbeespoort
N4
Magaliesberg
Hartbeespoort Dam
PRETORIA
Middelburg
Koster
Maanhaarrand
Hekpoort
N12
Bapsfontein
Witbank
R52
Krugersdorp
Tembisa
Arbor
Lichtenburg
Rodeport
Boksburg
Johannesburg
Kriel
Coligny
N14
Soweto
Springs
R35
Ventersdorp
Germiston
Leandra
Nigel
Svikerbosrand Reserve
Kinros
Bethal
Ennerdale
Heidelberg
Fochville
R30
Secunda
Sharpeville
Meyerton
R503
Vanderbijlpark
Vereeniging
Balfour
Potchefstroom
R50
Morgenzon
Klerksdorp
Sasolburg
N3
N12
N1
Deneysville
R23
Grootdraai Dam
Orkney
Parys
Orenjeville
Standerton
Rhenoster
Vredefort
Vaal Dam Reserve
Villiers
Viljoenskroon
Koppies Dam Nature Reserve
Perdekop
Koppies
Map 4
R30
R59
Heilbron
Cornelia
Frankfort
Bothaville
R34
Vaal
R57
N26
Vrede

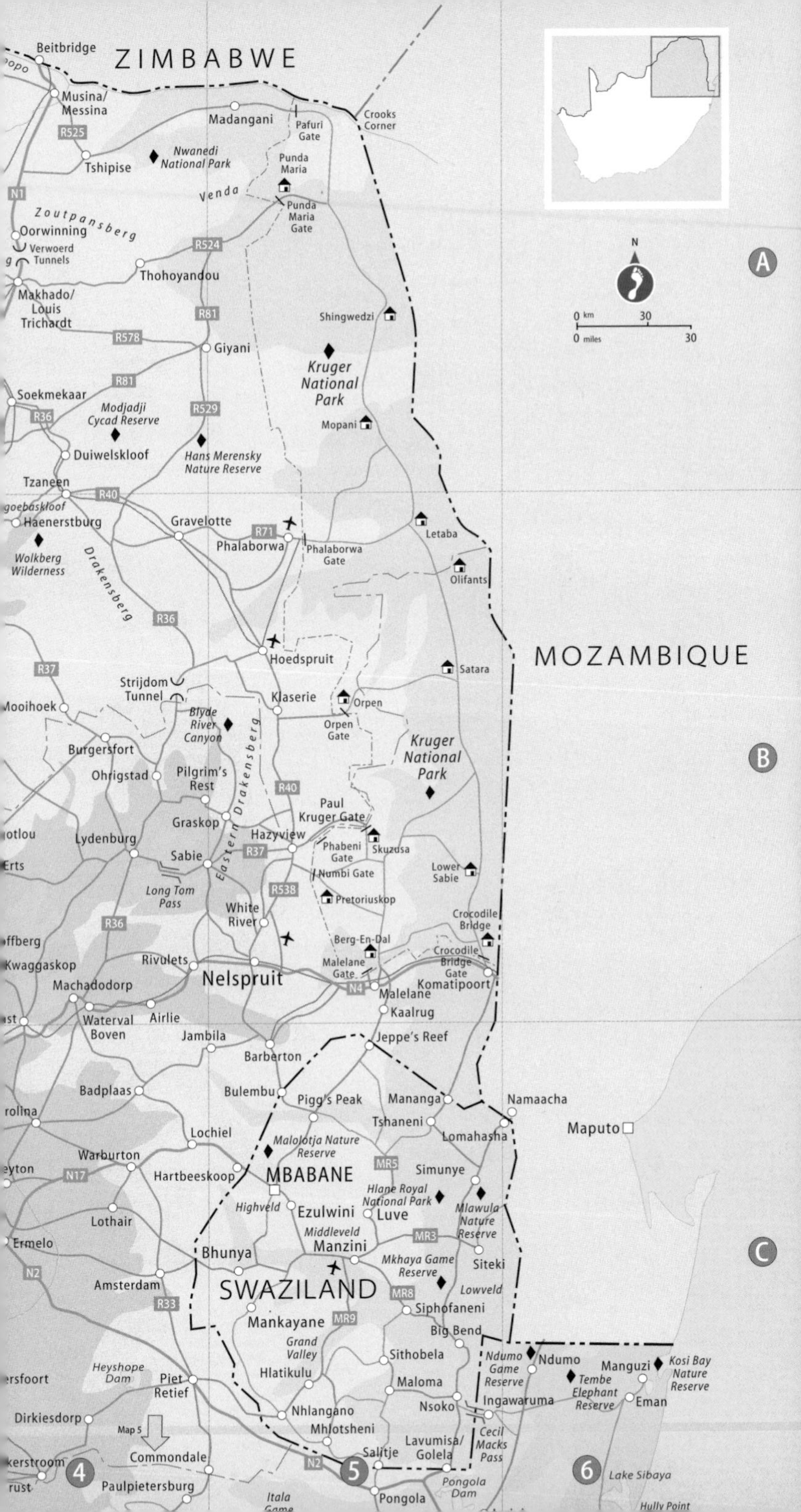

ZIMBABWE
MOZAMBIQUE
SWAZILAND
MBABANE
Beitbridge
Musina/ Messina
Madangani
Pafuri Gate
Crooks Corner
Tshipise
Nwanedi National Park
Punda Maria
Venda
Punda Maria Gate
Zoutpansberg
Oorwinning
Verwoerd Tunnels
Thohoyandou
Makhado/ Louis Trichardt
Shingwedzi
Giyani
Kruger National Park
Soekmekaar
Modjadji Cycad Reserve
Mopani
Duiwelskloof
Hans Merensky Nature Reserve
Tzaneen
Haenerstburg
Gravelotte
Phalaborwa
Phalaborwa Gate
Letaba
Wolkberg Wilderness
Drakensberg
Olifants
Hoedspruit
Satara
Strijdom Tunnel
Klaserie
Orpen
Orpen Gate
Mooihoek
Blyde River Canyon
Burgersfort
Ohrigstad
Pilgrim's Rest
Eastern Drakensberg
Graskop
Paul Kruger Gate
Lydenburg
Hazyview
Phabeni Gate
Skukuza
Sabie
Numbi Gate
Lower Sabie
Long Tom Pass
Pretoriuskop
White River
Crocodile Bridge
Berg-En-Dal
Rivulets
Kwaggaskop
Nelspruit
Malelane Gate
Crocodile Bridge Gate
Komatipoort
Machadodorp
Malelane
Waterval Boven
Airlie
Kaalrug
Jambila
Jeppe's Reef
Barberton
Badplaas
Bulembu
Pigg's Peak
Mananga
Namaacha
Tshaneni
Maputo
Lochiel
Malolotja Nature Reserve
Lomahasha
Warburton
Simunye
Hartbeeskoop
Highveld
Ezulwini
Hlane Royal National Park
Luve
Mlawula Nature Reserve
Lothair
Middleveld
Ermelo
Bhunya
Manzini
Mkhaya Game Reserve
Siteki
Amsterdam
Lowveld
Siphofaneni
Mankayane
Big Bend
Grand Valley
Sithobela
Ndumo Game Reserve
Ndumo
Manguzi
Kosi Bay Nature Reserve
Heyshope Dam
Piet Retief
Hlatikulu
Maloma
Tembe Elephant Reserve
Nsoko
Ingawaruma
Eman
Dirkiesdorp
Nhlangano
Mhlotsheni
Cecil Macks Pass
Map 5
Lavumisa/ Golela
Salitje
Commondale
Paulpietersburg
Lake Sibaya
Pongola Dam
Itala
Pongola
Hully Point
N1
R525
R524
R81
R578
R529
R36
R40
R71
R37
R538
N4
N17
N2
R33
MR5
MR3
MR8
MR9
N
0 km 30
0 miles 30
A
B
C
4
5
6

Map 3

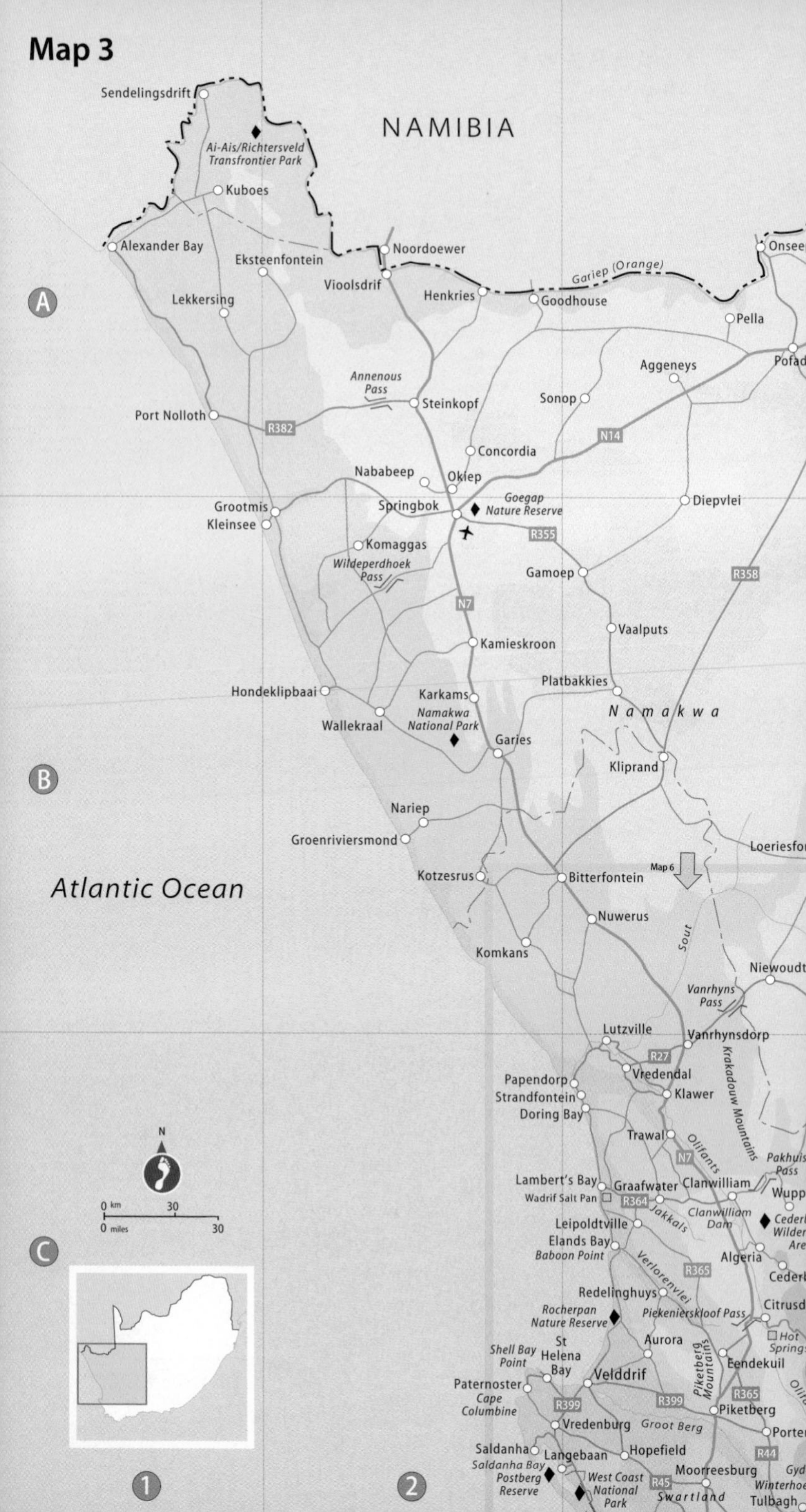

NAMIBIA
Sendelingsdrift
Ai-Ais/Richtersveld Transfrontier Park
Kuboes
Alexander Bay
Eksteenfontein
Noordoewer
Vioolsdrif
Henkries
Gariep (Orange)
Goodhouse
Onseep
Pella
Pofad
Lekkersing
Aggeneys
Annenous Pass
Steinkopf
Sonop
Port Nolloth
R382
N14
Concordia
Nababeep
Okiep
Grootmis
Kleinsee
Springbok
Goegap Nature Reserve
Diepvlei
R355
Komaggas
Wildeperdhoek Pass
Gamoep
R358
N7
Vaalputs
Kamieskroon
Platbakkies
Hondeklipbaai
Karkams
Namakwa
Wallekraal
Namakwa National Park
Garies
Kliprand
Nariep
Groenriviersmond
Loeriesfor
Atlantic Ocean
Kotzesrus
Bitterfontein
Map 6
Nuwerus
Sout
Komkans
Niewoudt
Vanrhyns Pass
Lutzville
Vanrhynsdorp
R27
Krakadouw Mountains
Papendorp
Vredendal
Strandfontein
Klawer
Doring Bay
Trawal
Olifants
N7
Pakhuis Pass
Lambert's Bay
Graafwater
Clanwilliam
Wadrif Salt Pan
R364
Jakkals
Clanwilliam Dam
Wupp
Cedert Wilder Are
Leipoldtville
Elands Bay
Baboon Point
Verlorenvlei
Algeria
R365
Cedert
Redelinghuys
Rocherpan Nature Reserve
Piekenierskloof Pass
Citrusd
Hot Springs
Aurora
Shell Bay Point
St Helena Bay
Piketberg Mountains
Eendekuil
Velddrif
Paternoster
Cape Columbine
R399
R399
R365
Piketberg
Vredenburg
Groot Berg
Porter
Saldanha
Langebaan
Hopefield
R44
Saldanha Bay
Postberg Reserve
West Coast National Park
R45
Moorreesburg
Swartland
Gyd
Winterhoe
Tulbagh
A
B
C
1
2
N
0 km 30
0 miles 30

Green Kalahari
Nakop
Spitskop Nature Reserve
Lutzputz
Upington
Louisvale
Grootdrink
Witsand Nature Reserve
Map 1
Owendale
Postmasburg
Augrabies
Keimoes
Cannon Island (Kanoneiland)
Kakamas
Volop
Groblershoop
Griekwastad
A
Westerberg
Draghoender
Marydale
Niekerkshoop
Higg's Hope
Kenhardt
Kraandraai
Gariep (Orange)
Prieska
Copperton
Omdraaisvlei
Sodium
Houtwaterdam
Grootvloer
Verneuk Pan
Van Wyksuki
Brandvlei
Riet se Vloer
Vosburg
Smartt Syndicate Dam
B
Map 4
Sakrivier
Carnarvon
Pampoenpoort
Map 7
Sterling
Williston
Victoria West
Loxton
Hutchinson
Remhoogte
Calvinia
Saaifontein
Three Sisters
Fraserburg
Middlepos
Bloukrans Pass
Great Karoo
Tankwa Karoo National Park
Roggeveldberge
Teekloof Pass
Nuweveldberge
Molteno Pass
Karoo National Park
Beaufort West
Sutherland
Tweefontein
Letjiesbos
C
Dwyka
Komsberg
Merweville
Leeu-Gamka
Rietbron
Zwarts
WESTERN CAPE
Prince Albert Road
Dwyka
Gamka
Laingsburg
Matjiesfontein
Prince Albert
Gamkapoort Dam
Swartberg Pass (1,577m)
Die Hel
Klaarstroom
4
Map 8
Rooinek
5
6
Anysberg Nature Reserve
Seven Weeks Poort
N8
N14
R360
N8
R27
R361
R357
R386
R357
R357
N10
R357
R384
N12
R27
R63
R63
R353
N1
R354
R356
R353
R61
N1
N12
R332
R356
R354
R328
R353
R323

Map 4
Lykso
Moffat Mission
Kuruman
Kathu
Sishen Iron Ore Mine
Wonderwerk Cave
Bekker
Blesmanpos
Revilo
Pudimore
Taung
Schweizer-Reneke
Wolmaransstа
Bloemhof Nature Reserve
Bloemhof
Bloemhof Dam
Sandveld Nature Reserve
Hoopstad
Wesselsbron
Vaal
Blikfontein
Christiana
Hertzogville
Warrenton
Mount Rupert
Daniëlskuil
Swartputs
Owendale
Koopmansfontein
Silver Streams
Lime Acres
Postmasburg
Ulco
Sidney on Vaal
Vaalbos National Park
Papkuil
Barkly West
Bultfontein
Map 1
FREE STATE
Boshof
Griqualand West
Schmidtsdrif
Campbell
Griekwastad
Kimberley
Dealsville
Soutpan
Bran
Soetdoring Reserve
Modder
Diamantveld
Magersfontein
Ritchie
Douglas
Bucklands
Jacobsdal
Petrusburg
Bloemfontein
Gariep (Orange)
Higg's Hope
Niekerkshoop
Riet
Koffiefontein
Kalkfontein Dam Nature Reserve
Hopetown
Prieska
Luckhoff
Fauresmith
Jagersfontein
Edenburg
Reddersb
Orania
Map 3
Krankuil
Strydenburg
Poupan
Petrusville
Vanderloof Dam
Trompsberg
Omdraaisvlei
Sodium
Philippolis
Smith
Houtwaterdam
Springfontein
Houtkraal
Philipstown
Gariep/Orange
Bethulie
Tussen Riviere Re
Gariep Dam & Reserve
Goede
Vosburg
Britstown
Smartt Syndicate Dam
De Aar
Bletterman
Norvalspont
Colesberg
Vaalskrantz
Burgersdorp
npoenpoort
Hanover
Noupoort
Map 7
Suurberg
Steynsburg
Victoria West
Richmond
Hutchinson
Remhoogte
Middelburg
Rosmead
Molte
Sterks
Bamboesb
Tafelberg
Hofmeyr
Conway
EASTER
Nieu Bethesda
Sneeuberg Pass
N
0 km 30
0 miles 30
Visriver
Tark
Blanco Nature Reserve
Oudeberg
Karoo Nature Reserve
Graaff-Reinet
Karoo Mountain Zebra Park
Cradock
Winterb
eaufort West
Aberdeen
Kendrew
Amat
A
B
C
1
2
3
N14
R47
R34
R506
R31
R49
R700
R708
R59
N31
N12
R64
N8
R357
R705
R48
R706
R704
N10
N1
R369
R389
N9
R58
R398
R63
R56
R61
R337

Villiers
Viljoenskroon
Koppies
Koppies Dam Nature Reserve
Frankfort
Cornelia
Perdekop
R59
R34
Heilbron
Rhenoster
Volksrust
Charlestown
Vrede
Map 2
N26
Edenville
R57
Tweeling
R34
Botha Pass
Westleigh
Kroonstad
(Petrus Steyn)
Memel
Utre
Drakensberg
Newcastle
R707
Reitz
Vals
R34
Lindley
Warden
A
N1
Steinsrus
R76
R57
R722
Welkom
Danielsrus
Dannhauser
Virginia
Ventersburg
Kransfontein
Vals
Wilge
Glencoe
William Pretorius Game Reserve
Bethlehem
N5
Harrismith
N11
Map 5
Senekal
Sterkfontein Dam
Van Reenen Pass
Wasbank
N5
R70
Golden Gate National Park
Phuthaditjhaba
Elandslaagte
Winburg
Clarens
Woodstock Dam
Spioenkop Dam Nature Reserve
Ladysmith
Fouriesburg
Rustler's Valley
Caledonspoort
Royal Natal National Park
Marquard
Oxbow
Bergville
Colenso
Ficksburg
R26
Botha Bothe
Mt Aux Sources (3,299m)
Drakensberg
Winterton
R74
Clocolan
Leribe (Hlotse)
Cathedral Peak (3,004m)
Frere
Excelsior
R703
Malibamatso
Bokong Nature Reserve
Estcourt
Pitseng
Champagne Castle (3,248m)
Monk's Cowl
Thaba Nchu
Ladybrand
N8
Teyateyaneng
LESOTHO
Giant's Castle
Thaba 'Nchu
MASERU
Mokhotlong
Mooi River
Katse
Sinqua
Thabu Bosiu
Nottingham Road
R26
uKhahlamba-Drakensberg National Park
Thabana Ntlenyana (3,482m)
Katse Reservoir
Roma
Senqunyana
Thaba Tseka
Howick
Matsieng
Marakabei
Mkhomazi Wilderness Area
Sani Pass
Wepener
Morija
Thaba Putsoa (3,096m)
Himeville Nature Reserve
Pietermaritzb
Himeville
Underberg
Mafeteng
Malealea
Semonkong
Bulwer
B
Caledon Nature Reserve
Makhakhe
Maletsunyane Falls (192m)
Sehlabethebe National Park
Coleford Nature Reserve
Richmond
Makhaleng
Donnybrook
Pedlars Peak (2,906m)
Sekake
Qacha's Nek
Kingscote
Umzimkulu
Sinqua
Ixopo
Mohales Hoek
R26
Zastron
R56
Mount Moorosi
Highflats
Matatiele
R26
Franklin
R626
Mount Curie National Park
Moyeni (Quthing)
Rouxville
Kinirapoort
Gariep (Orange)
Tsatsana (2,950m)
Kokstad
N2
Oribi Gorge Nature Reserve
Harding
Mzimhlava
Aliwal North
Mount Fletcher
Witteberge
Tina
Umtamvuna
Lady Grey
Rhodes
Elands Height
Bizana
Izingolweni
Mt Aycliff
Katcop
Magusheni
R58
Prentilesberg (1,989m)
Redoubt
Mount Frere
R61
N6
Barkly East
R56
Tsitsa
Jamestown
Ben Dearg (2,770m)
Maclear
Banner Rest
Roussow
Map 7
Drakensberg
Qumbu
Flagstaff
Mkambati Nature Reserve
Ugie
R61
Barclay Pass
Mt Ararat (1,896m)
Inxu
R396
Msimvubu
Msikaba
Elliot
Tsolo
Lusikisiki
Port Grosvenor
Dordrecht
R56
Qiba
Grosvenor 1782
Mtata Dam
Libode
Indwe
Cala
Embotyi
R61
C
Xuka
R393
Lady Frere
Coghlan
Umtata
R61
Silaka Nature Reserve
Port St Johns
Engcobo
APE
Ncora Dam
Viedgesville
Umngazi River Bungalows
Mtata
Hluleka Nature Reserve
Queenstown
Ngqungqu
Dick King Memorial
Cofimvaba
Ocean View Hotel
Elliotdale
Anchorage Hotel
Hole in the Wall
Coffee Bay
Tsomo
Mbashe
St Marks
R67
N2
Alderley
Santo Alberto 1593
Idutywa
Haven Hotel
Tsomo
Wild Coast
R352
The Haven
Willowvale
Sada
Cweba Nature Reserve
Kob Inn Hotel
Cathcart
Butterworth
Bolo
Frontier III 1939
4
5
R364
6
Qora Mouth
Stola Mountains
Seymour
Mazeppa Bay

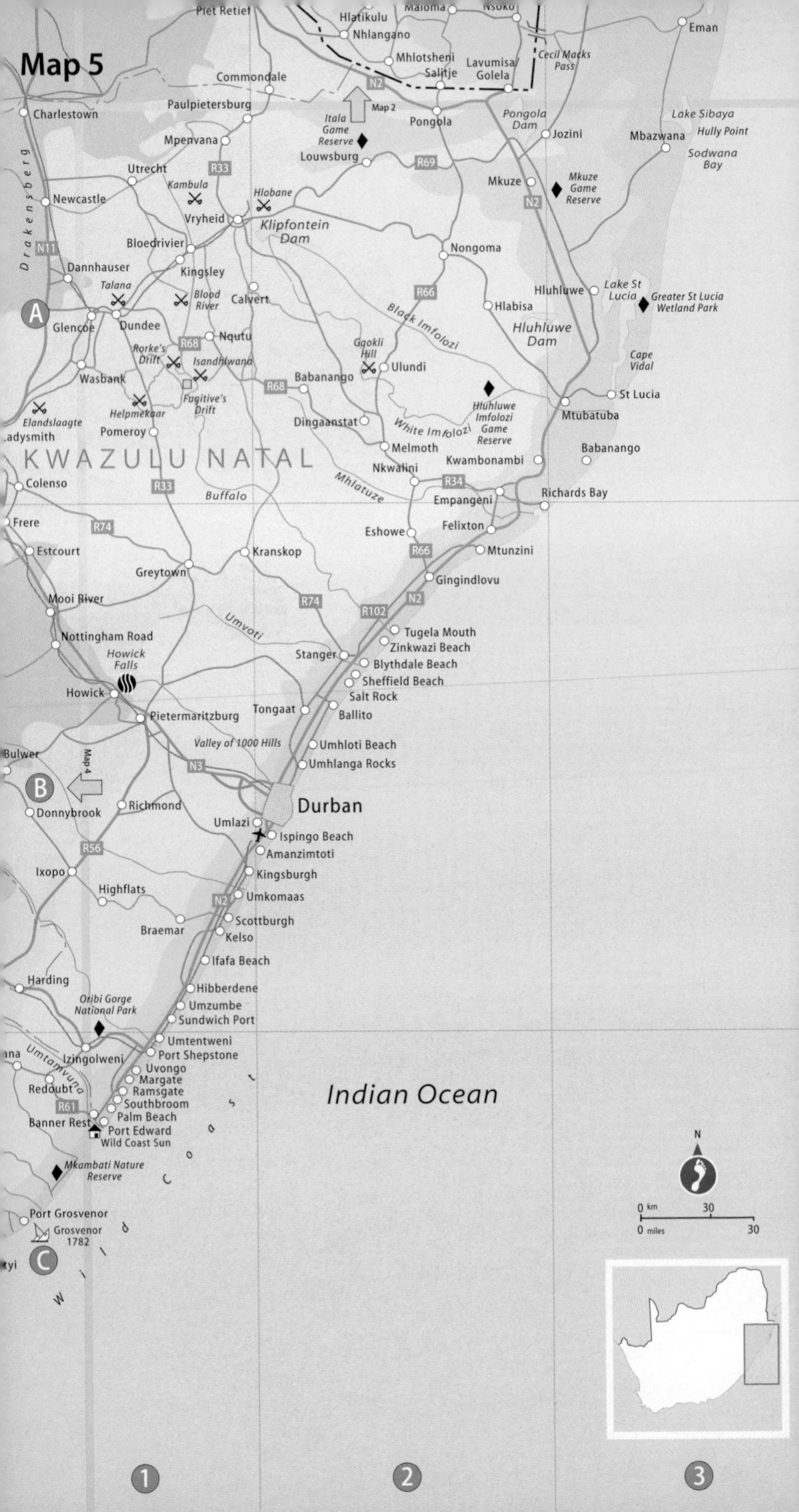

Map 5
KWAZULU NATAL
Indian Ocean
Durban
Pietermaritzburg
Richards Bay
Charlestown
Newcastle
Ladysmith
Dundee
Vryheid
Ulundi
Eshowe
Stanger
Howick
Port Shepstone
Margate
Port Edward
Port Grosvenor
St Lucia
Greater St Lucia Wetland Park
Hluhluwe Imfolozi Game Reserve
Mkuze Game Reserve
Itala Game Reserve
Oribi Gorge National Park
Mkambati Nature Reserve
Drakensberg
Map 2
Map 4
A
B
C
1
2
3
N
0 km 30
0 miles 30

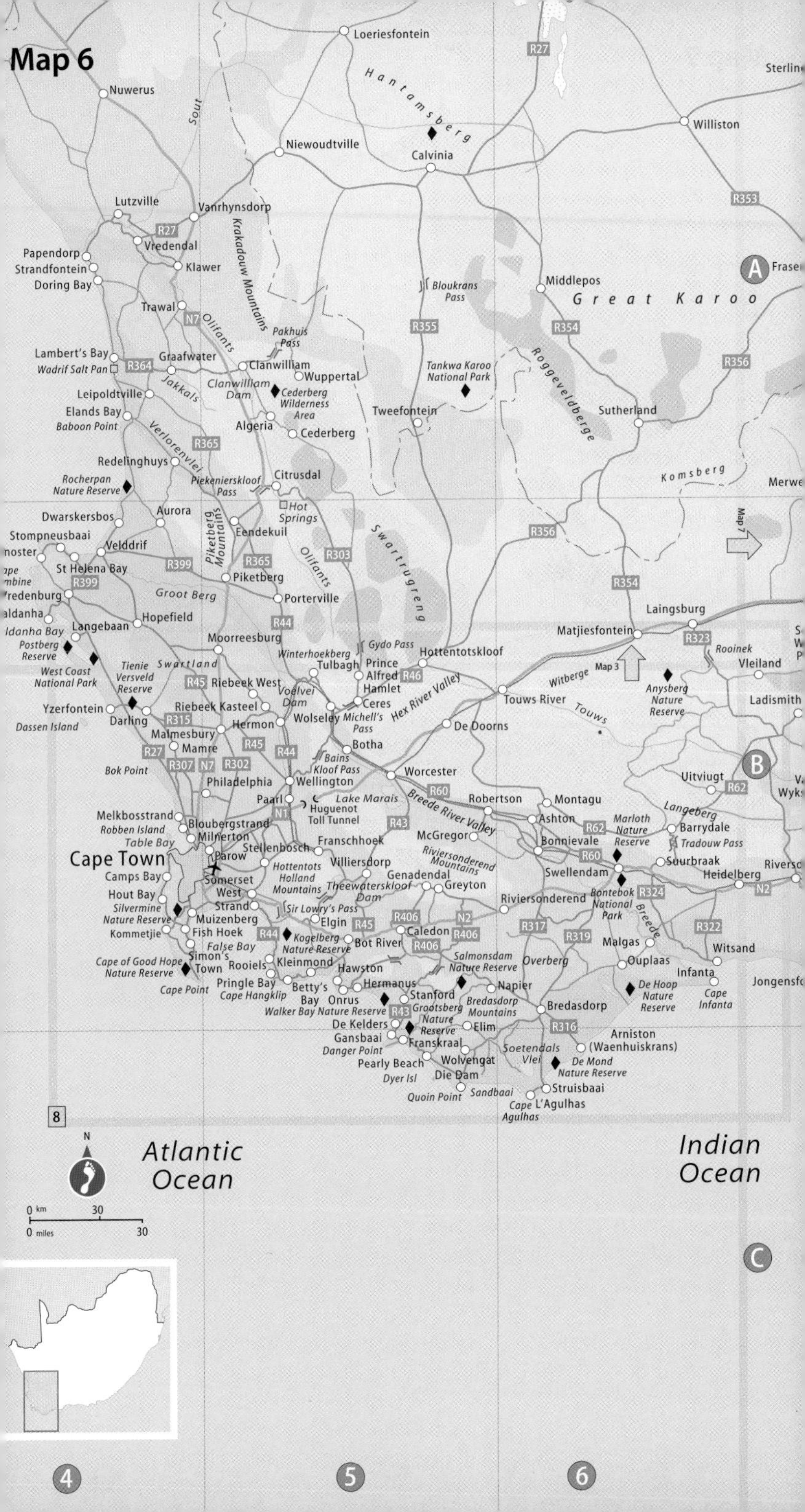
Map 6
Loeriesfontein
Nuwerus
Hantamsberg
Niewoudtville
Calvinia
Williston
Lutzville
Vanrhynsdorp
Vredendal
Papendorp
Strandfontein
Doring Bay
Klawer
Trawal
Krakadouw Mountains
Bloukrans Pass
Middlepos
Great Karoo
Pakhuis Pass
Lambert's Bay
Wadrif Salt Pan
Graafwater
Clanwilliam
Wuppertal
Tankwa Karoo National Park
Roggeveldberge
Leipoldtville
Clanwilliam Dam
Cederberg Wilderness Area
Elands Bay
Baboon Point
Algeria
Cederberg
Tweefontein
Sutherland
Redelinghuys
Verlorenvlei
Rocherpan Nature Reserve
Piekenierskloof Pass
Citrusdal
Komsberg
Hot Springs
Dwarskersbos
Aurora
Stompneusbaai
Velddrif
Eendekuil
Piketberg Mountains
St Helena Bay
Piketberg
Swartrugeng
Groot Berg
Porterville
Langebaan
Hopefield
Laingsburg
Matjiesfontein
Moorreesburg
Gydo Pass
Postberg Reserve
West Coast National Park
Tienie Versveld Reserve
Swartland
Winterhoekberg
Hottentotskloof
Tulbagh
Prince Alfred Hamlet
Rooinek
Vleiland
Riebeek West
Voëlvlei Dam
Witberge
Anysberg Nature Reserve
Yzerfontein
Riebeek Kasteel
Ceres
Hex River Valley
Touws River
Ladismith
Dassen Island
Darling
Wolseley
Michell's Pass
Touws
Malmesbury
Hermon
De Doorns
Mamre
Botha
Bok Point
Bains Kloof Pass
Worcester
Uitviugt
Philadelphia
Wellington
Paarl
Lake Marais
Huguenot Toll Tunnel
Robertson
Montagu
Breede River Valley
Langeberg
Melkbosstrand
Bloubergstrand
Robben Island
Milnerton
Table Bay
Ashton
Marloth Nature Reserve
Barrydale
Tradouw Pass
McGregor
Franschhoek
Stellenbosch
Bonnievale
Cape Town
Parow
Riviersonderend Mountains
Swellendam
Sourbraak
Heidelberg
Villiersdorp
Hottentots Holland Mountains
Camps Bay
Somerset West
Genadendal
Greyton
Hout Bay
Theewaterskloof Dam
Riviersonderend
Bontebok National Park
Silvermine Nature Reserve
Strand
Sir Lowry's Pass
Breede
Muizenberg
Elgin
Kommetjie
Fish Hoek
Caledon
Kogelberg Nature Reserve
Bot River
Malgas
Witsand
False Bay
Salmonsdam Nature Reserve
Overberg
Cape of Good Hope Nature Reserve
Simon's Town
Rooiels
Kleinmond
Ouplaas
Infanta
Hawston
Napier
De Hoop Nature Reserve
Cape Infanta
Cape Point
Pringle Bay
Cape Hangklip
Betty's Bay
Onrus
Hermanus
Stanford
Grootsberg Nature Reserve
Bredasdorp Mountains
Bredasdorp
Walker Bay Nature Reserve
De Kelders
Elim
Gansbaai
Danger Point
Franskraal
Soetendals Vlei
Arniston (Waenhuiskrans)
De Mond Nature Reserve
Pearly Beach
Wolvengat
Dyer Isl
Die Dam
Quoin Point
Sandbaai
Struisbaai
Cape Agulhas
L'Agulhas
Map 3
Map 7
Atlantic Ocean
Indian Ocean
0 km 30
0 miles 30
A
B
C
4
5
6
8

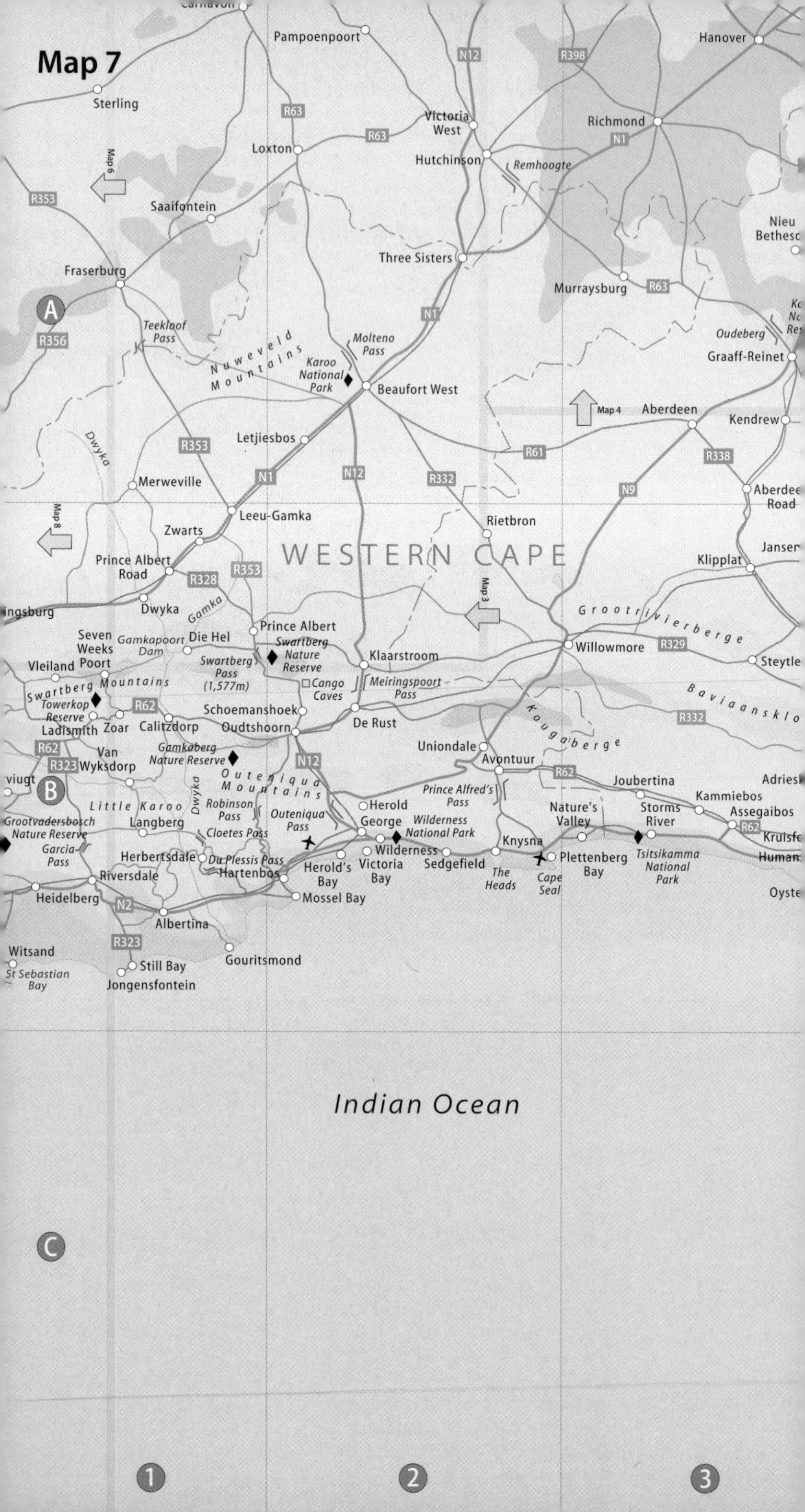
Map 7
Pampoenpoort
Hanover
Sterling
Victoria West
Richmond
Loxton
Hutchinson
Remhoogte
Map 6
Saaifontein
Nieu Bethesda
Three Sisters
Fraserburg
Murraysburg
A
Teekloof Pass
Molteno Pass
Oudeberg
Graaff-Reinet
Nuweveld Mountains
Karoo National Park
Beaufort West
Map 4
Aberdeen
Kendrew
Letjiesbos
Dwyka
Merweville
Aberdeen Road
Map 8
Leeu-Gamka
Rietbron
Zwarts
WESTERN CAPE
Jansen
Prince Albert Road
Klipplat
Map 3
Dwyka
Gamka
Prince Albert
Grootrivierberge
Seven Weeks Poort
Gamkapoort Dam
Die Hel
Swartberg Nature Reserve
Willowmore
Vleiland
Swartberg Pass (1,577m)
Klaarstroom
Steytle
Swartberg Mountains
Cango Caves
Meiringspoort Pass
Baviaanskloof
Towerkop Reserve
Schoemanshoek
Ladismith
Zoar
Calitzdorp
Oudtshoorn
De Rust
Kouga Berge
Van Wyksdorp
Gamkaberg Nature Reserve
Uniondale
Avontuur
Outeniqua Mountains
Joubertina
B
Little Karoo
Dwyka
Robinson Pass
Prince Alfred's Pass
Herold
Kammiebos
Storms River
Assegaibos
Grootvadersbosch Nature Reserve
Langberg
Outeniqua Pass
George
Wilderness National Park
Nature's Valley
Cloetes Pass
Knysna
Tsitsikamma National Park
Garcia Pass
Herbertsdale
Du Plessis Pass
Wilderness
Sedgefield
Plettenberg Bay
Riversdale
Hartenbos
Herold's Bay
Victoria Bay
The Heads
Cape Seal
Heidelberg
Mossel Bay
Albertina
Witsand
Still Bay
Gouritsmond
St Sebastian Bay
Jongensfontein
Indian Ocean
C
1
2
3

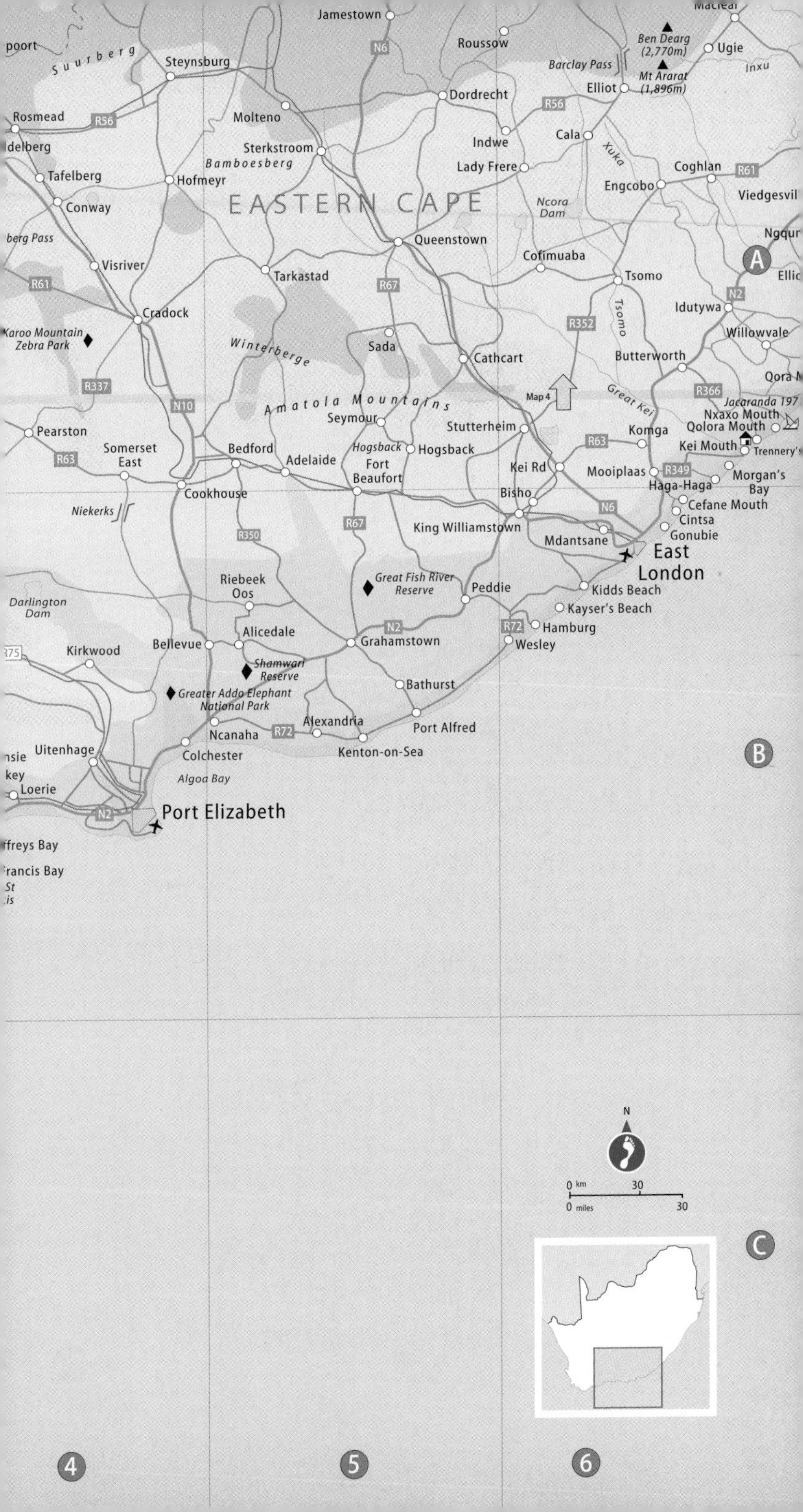
EASTERN CAPE
Jamestown
Roussow
Ben Dearg (2,770m)
Mt Ararat (1,896m)
Barclay Pass
Elliot
Ugie
Inxu
Maclear
poort
Suurberg
Steynsburg
Rosmead
Molteno
Dordrecht
Indwe
Cala
Xuka
delberg
Sterkstroom
Bamboesberg
Lady Frere
Coghlan
Engcobo
Viedgesvil
Tafelberg
Hofmeyr
Conway
Ncora Dam
berg Pass
Queenstown
Nqqur
Cofimuaba
Visriver
Tarkastad
Tsomo
Ellic
Idutywa
Cradock
Karoo Mountain Zebra Park
Winterberge
Sada
Willowvale
Cathcart
Butterworth
Qora M
Great Kei
Jacaranda 197
Amatola Mountains
Map 4
Nxaxo Mouth
Qolora Mouth
Seymour
Stutterheim
Komga
Pearston
Kei Mouth
Trennery's
Somerset East
Bedford
Hogsback
Adelaide
Kei Rd
Mooiplaas
Morgan's Bay
Haga-Haga
Fort Beaufort
Cookhouse
Bisho
Cefane Mouth
Niekerks
Cintsa
King Williamstown
Gonubie
Mdantsane
East London
Great Fish River Reserve
Riebeek Oos
Peddie
Kidds Beach
Darlington Dam
Kayser's Beach
Alicedale
Hamburg
Bellevue
Grahamstown
Wesley
Kirkwood
Shamwari Reserve
Bathurst
Greater Addo Elephant National Park
Alexandria
Port Alfred
Ncanaha
Kenton-on-Sea
Colchester
Uitenhage
Algoa Bay
Loerie
Port Elizabeth
ffreys Bay
Francis Bay
N6
R56
R61
R67
R352
N2
R337
N10
R366
R63
R349
R350
R72
N
0 km 30
0 miles 30
A
B
C
4
5
6

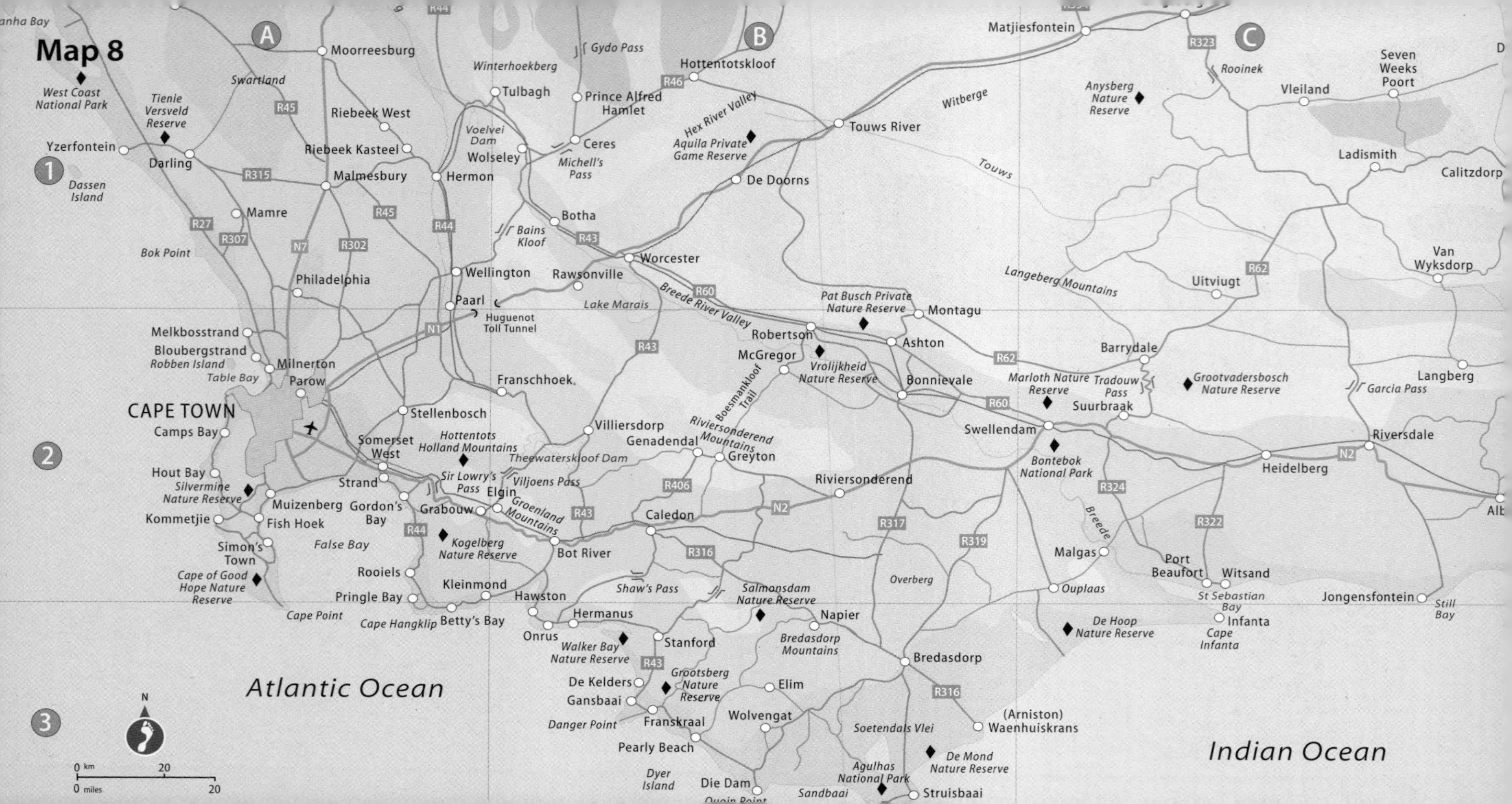
Map 8
A
B
C
1
2
3
West Coast National Park
Yzerfontein
Dassen Island
Tienie Versveld Reserve
Darling
Swartland
Moorreesburg
Riebeek West
Riebeek Kasteel
Malmesbury
Mamre
Bok Point
Philadelphia
Melkbosstrand
Bloubergstrand
Robben Island
Table Bay
Milnerton
Parow
CAPE TOWN
Camps Bay
Hout Bay
Silvermine Nature Reserve
Kommetjie
Muizenberg
Fish Hoek
Simon's Town
Cape of Good Hope Nature Reserve
Cape Point
False Bay
Strand
Gordon's Bay
Somerset West
Stellenbosch
Franschhoek
Paarl
Huguenot Toll Tunnel
Wellington
Hermon
Wolseley
Voelvei Dam
Tulbagh
Winterhoekberg
Gydo Pass
Prince Alfred Hamlet
Ceres
Michell's Pass
Bains Kloof
Botha
Rawsonville
Lake Marais
Worcester
Hottentotskloof
Hex River Valley
Aquila Private Game Reserve
De Doorns
Touws River
Witberge
Touws
Matjiesfontein
Rooinek
Anysberg Nature Reserve
Vleiland
Seven Weeks Poort
Ladismith
Calitzdorp
Van Wyksdorp
Uitviugt
Langeberg Mountains
Breede River Valley
Pat Busch Private Nature Reserve
Montagu
Robertson
Ashton
McGregor
Vrolijkheid Nature Reserve
Boesmankloof Trail
Bonnievale
Barrydale
Marloth Nature Reserve
Tradouw Pass
Grootvadersbosch Nature Reserve
Garcia Pass
Langberg
Suurbraak
Swellendam
Bontebok National Park
Riversdale
Heidelberg
Alb
Hottentots Holland Mountains
Theewaterskloof Dam
Villiersdorp
Genadendal
Riviersonderend Mountains
Greyton
Riviersonderend
Sir Lowry's Pass
Viljoens Pass
Elgin
Grabouw
Groenland Mountains
Kogelberg Nature Reserve
Bot River
Caledon
Rooiels
Pringle Bay
Kleinmond
Cape Hangklip
Betty's Bay
Hawston
Onrus
Hermanus
Shaw's Pass
Salmonsdam Nature Reserve
Walker Bay Nature Reserve
Stanford
Napier
Bredasdorp Mountains
Overberg
Bredasdorp
De Kelders
Gansbaai
Grootsberg Nature Reserve
Elim
Danger Point
Franskraal
Wolvengat
Pearly Beach
Dyer Island
Die Dam
Soetendals Vlei
Agulhas National Park
Sandbaai
De Mond Nature Reserve
Struisbaai
(Arniston) Waenhuiskrans
Malgas
Ouplaas
Breede
De Hoop Nature Reserve
Port Beaufort
Witsand
St Sebastian Bay
Infanta
Cape Infanta
Jongensfontein
Still Bay
Atlantic Ocean
Indian Ocean
N1
N2
N7
R27
R43
R44
R45
R46
R60
R62
R302
R307
R315
R316
R317
R319
R322
R323
R324
R406
N
0 km
20
0 miles
20